THE TRIAL:
Principles, Process and Evidence

THE TRIAL: Principles, Process and Evidence

Second Edition

Jill Hunter
BA, LLB (UNSW), PhD (London)
Professor, Faculty of Law & Justice, University of New South Wales

James Metzger
BA (magna cum laude, Tufts University), JD (Northwestern University), LLM (UNSW), PhD (UNSW)
Lecturer, Faculty of Law & Justice, University of New South Wales

Terese Henning
BA (UTas), LLB (Hons 1) (UTas), MPhil Crim (Cambridge)
Adjunct Associate Professor, Faculty of Law, University of Tasmania

Gary Edmond
BA (Hons) (Medal) (Wollongong), LLB (Hons) (Sydney), PhD (Cambridge)
Professor, Faculty of Law & Justice, University of New South Wales
Research Professor (Fractional), School of Law, Northumbria University

Rebecca McMahon
BA, LLB, LLM (Crim) (UNSW)
Senior Visiting Fellow, Faculty of Law & Justice, University of New South Wales
Barrister

Mehera San Roque
BA, LLB (Hons) (Syd), LLM (UBC)
Associate Professor, Faculty of Law & Justice, University of New South Wales

Helen Cockburn
BA (UTas), LLB (Hons) (UTas), PhD (UTas)
Lecturer, Faculty of Law, University of Tasmania

Foreword

Nicholas Cowdery AO, QC, FAAL
Director of Public Prosecutions, New South Wales (1994-2011)

THE FEDERATION PRESS
2021

Published in Sydney by
The Federation Press
PO Box 6178, Alexandria, NSW, 2015.
8 Birmingham Street, Alexandria, NSW, 2015.
Ph (02) 9552 2200. Fax (02) 9552 1681
E-mail: info@federationpress.com.au
Website: http://www.federationpress.com.au

First edition 2015
Second edition 2021

NATIONAL LIBRARY OF AUSTRALIA
A catalogue record for this book is available from the National Library of Australia

ISBN 978 176002 293 8 (pbk)

Typeset by The Federation Press, Alexandria, NSW.
Printed by OPUS Group in Australia.

Foreword

Nicholas Cowdery AO, QC, FAAL

This Second Edition of *The Trial: Principles, Process and Evidence* improves upon the first (as it might be expected to). 'How is that possible?' the reader asks, remembering my Foreword to the First Edition in 2015.

It is made possible by the thorough attention the authors have paid to the developments in the law that have occurred since and by their substantial revisiting of the contents of this book, distilling analysis and discussion in the context of new issues and legal changes. The authors update legislation to the end of 2020 and, as one might expect, include consideration of appellate interpretations and other recent developments with new analyses and explanations.

Much has happened in the past six years. As the authors explain, the responses to the important Royal Commission into Institutional Responses to Child Sexual Abuse have led to profound tangible and intangible changes in evidence and procedure. Some events, such as the findings of the McMurdo Royal Commission into Ms Nicola Gobbo and the Victoria Police, highlight *The Trial's* appreciation that understanding the workings of an Australian criminal trial cannot be limited to events following arraignment. Events such as those disclosed by these Royal Commissions highlight the need for law-makers to equip the criminal trial to expose and respond to such egregious distortions of accusatorial justice.

In 2015 I said:

> This is a book that goes beyond theory, crammed as it is with practical description, legal references and ideas for dealing with the stages and aspects of the criminal trial that criminal practitioners (for whom this should be an ever-present handbook) encounter every day. Even to experienced practitioners there will be something new or something tacitly recognised for which a thorough explanation is now given.

This remains the case in and for 2021.

I commended the First Edition, as I do the second, to law students, law teachers, lawyers, judges, the public, and especially to the media and politicians if they really want to understand what the trial is about and why.

The authors revisit in this Second Edition the epic journey of the evolution of accusatorial, adversarial criminal trial processes over the centuries. They use the criminal trial, as we know it in Australia in 2021, as the lens through which relevant procedural and evidentiary law under the uniform Evidence Acts is examined and assessed. This is particularly effective, because the separation in most criminal trials between the legal and procedural regulator (the judge) and the tribunal of fact (the jury) enables a sharp focus to be drawn on the role and legal requirements of each, the lawyers' roles, and their interaction in practice.

This Second Edition of an already exceptionally valuable work, discussing what is and synthesising what might be, extends analysis of theory in its practical context with legal references. It discusses ideas for dealing with the aspects of the criminal trial at its various stages in a manner relevant to all criminal practitioners. It includes the impacts on procedure of SARS-CoV-2, recognising that the 2020 court responses to the pandemic will leave indelible marks on criminal trial processes. The authors note that the nature and extent to which reforms inspired by courts' pandemic responses enhance or diminish the administration of justice remain unclear, raising the question of the extent to which 'a day in court' – compared to an electronic communication or 'Zoom justice' – has meaning beyond transactional convenience.

This work continues as an invaluable practical reference and theoretical analysis. It shows the right way to proceed – and what can go wrong – and how the criminal justice system can prepare for and deal with that.

Nicholas Cowdery AO, QC, FAAL
Former Director of Public Prosecutions, NSW
Former President, International Association of Prosecutors
Inaugural Co-Chair, Human Rights Institute, International Bar Association
Former President, NSW Council for Civil Liberties
Visiting Professorial Fellow, Faculty of Law, University of NSW & Justice
Adjunct Professor, Sydney Institute of Criminology

List of Chapters

For detailed Table of Contents, *see over*

Contents

Preface

In this edition we continue the practice from the First Edition of *The Trial: Principles, Process and Evidence* of weaving threads that contextualise the uniform *Evidence Act* (*UEA*). In particular, we seek to inject the human element into the examination and analysis of rules of evidence and procedure. To this end, we draw on the social and behavioural sciences to challenge some of the Law's assumptions and impact, and to offer guidance on how the Law might better achieve its goals. We also continue to acknowledge the role of history on the trial. This includes *structures*, such as the historical and continuing reliance of the criminal trial on orality and on adversarialism; *processes*, focusing on history's role in developing the common law rules of evidence and procedure; and most profoundly history's *erasure of First Nations identities*. We acknowledge that *The Trial* describes Australian structures and processes that are based on a colonial past and that operate on stolen Country.

This book continues the First Edition's identification of the inadequate consideration given Aboriginal and Torres Strait Islander culture and heritage in the Australian trial, the small steps taken to attempt to reduce the injustices so caused, and the ongoing systemic failure to deliver appropriate justice to First Nations Australians. History's lessons in other respects also speak to dysfunctionality. For example, the law of competence and of corroboration is built on histories of racism and misogyny. And Wigmore's naïve appreciation of cross-examination's truth-seeking powers further reveal the gulf in cultural values between the past and this century's embrace of accusatorial justice and dignitarian rights for vulnerable witnesses and (not quite so prominently) defendants. This evolutionary dimension of the trial, and of the law of evidence and procedure, makes this field important, fascinating – and frustrating.

The powerful Brett Whiteley cover to the two editions of *The Trial: Principles, Process and Evidence*, with its tacit link to lost liberty, evokes a criminal justice setting. It assists to remind us why criminal trials are hard-fought – even if that fight is now a more limited one due to the continuing intrusion of case management practices into the traditional adversarial trial. Those readers who seek to apply the rules of evidence to civil matters will also find this book informative. It addresses the doctrinal principles and rules relevant to that context (albeit without specific reference to the 'level playing field' of civil litigation). The major evidentiary rules (the hearsay rule, the credibility rule, the opinion rule, the tendency and coincidence rules) operate in both spheres. Similarly, the procedural rules and obligations for witness questioning, refreshing memory, determining client legal privilege, seeking directions or leave of the court, assessing competence and compellability and so forth, vary across civil and criminal domains largely by virtue of context. The key differences that exist, typically in the *exceptions* to evidentiary rules, differ in ways that are rarely complex.

In this edition, we have retained an introduction to the language and concepts of human rights, which provides a gateway into the international language of trial-based rights. Although Australia is unusual for its very modest embrace of human rights legislation, we believe human rights jurisprudence offers an important lens for understanding the intrinsic expectations of what constitutes a fair trial. However, at the end of the day, the focus of this book remains the imperfectly uniform law and jurisprudence of the (so-called) uniform *Evidence Acts* (*UEA*), with particular reference to New South Wales.

Some (small) uniformity has taken place in the interpretation of the *UEA* since the First Edition. This was done through the quartet of High Court decisions in *IMM*,[1] *Hughes*,[2] *Bauer*[3] and *McPhillamy*.[4] These important cases resolve the divergence of interpretations of the tendency rule that existed between the apex courts of Victoria and New South Wales. The judgments in those cases also put to rest the continuing application of the common law principle expressed in *Hoch*[5] – well and truly displaced by the terms of the Act. However, the swings and roundabouts of uniformity took a step back in 2020 when New South Wales responded to the Royal Commission into Institutional Responses to Child Sexual Abuse with changes to prosecution tendency and coincidence evidence,[6] and with the inclusion of a specific application of the tendency rule for child sexual assault proceedings.[7] These amendments have come after the significant step away from uniformity that Victoria had taken before (and as recounted in) the First Edition with its jury directions legislation. Variations amongst the versions of the *UEA* operating in the different Australian jurisdictions add further challenges to providing comprehensive, detailed coverage of all *UEA* jurisdictions within a manageable book of this type.

Outside of the *UEA*, but inextricably linked to it, this book continues to document research on the jury. The major content of this book – the law of evidence – owes much to the enormous actual and symbolic presence of the jury. Trusting the jury with evidence, or not trusting the jury with it, is a theme that runs thickly through the discourse of evidence law. It remains hotly contested. The jury, and the explicit adversarial dynamic of parties calling and testing witnesses for evaluation by it, created our rules of evidence and procedure. These influences continue to shape it. Finally, no book written in 2020 and 2021 can ignore the COVID-19 pandemic's test of many traditional understandings of the conduct of jury trials.

The Second Edition restructures the First Edition in the following way:

- Chapters 1, 2 and 4 from the First Edition (accusatorial principles, prosecutors, proof and pleadings) are now located in Chapters 1 and 2. These two chapters might be typed broadly as an accused-rights focused (Chapter 1) and a prosecution- and a proof-focused chapter (Chapter 2).
- Chapters 10-13 from the First Edition, addressing the accused's right to silence at trial, profiling the accused, and the uses of evidence of the accused's character, now sit in Chapters 1, 7 (rights to silence, trial and pre-trial), 10 and 11 (character evidence, including tendency and coincidence evidence) in this edition.

---

1 [2016] HCA 14; 257 CLR 300.
2 [2017] HCA 20; 263 CLR 338.
3 [2018] HCA 40; 266 CLR 56.
4 [2018] HCA 52; 361 ALR 13.
5 [1988] HCA 50; 165 CLR 292. With the 2020 amendment to the *UEA* (NSW), s 94(5), adding a belt to the courts' braces on the rejection of the *Hoch* principle.
6 *Evidence Act 1995* (NSW), s 101. These changes are partnered by restrictions on NSW courts ordering offences be heard in separate trials in cases where tendency or coincidence evidence is relied upon by the prosecution that relates to two or more offences: *Criminal Procedure Act 1986* (NSW), ss 21, 29A.
7 *Evidence Act 1995* (NSW), s 97A.

In all other respects,[8] the book follows its previous format. There have been some changes in authorships. We welcome Helen Cockburn.

- Jill Hunter, as well as her role with Chapters 5 and 6, revised Chapters 1, 2 (*Accusatorial Justice*; *Prosecutors, Pleadings and Proof*), 4 (*Introducing the Law of Evidence*), 10, 11 (*Character Evidence*; *Tendency and Coincidence Evidence*), 14 and 15 (*Judicial Warnings*; *Epilogue*);
- James Metzger, the original author of Chapter 3 (*Client Legal Privilege*), revised it, and also reviewed and revised Chapters 8 and 9 – *The Hearsay Rule* and *Hearsay – The Exceptions to the Rule* (originally researched and written by Terese Henning);
- Helen Cockburn and Terese Henning contributed substantially, with Jill Hunter, to revising and updating the two witness chapters (Chapter 5, *The Witness in the Box*, and Chapter 6, *Cross-examination, Witness Credibility and Related Challenges*). These chapters were originally researched and written by Jill Hunter;
- Rebecca McMahon, Gary Edmond and Mehera San Roque are each authors of one chapter, which they have each revised: Chapters 7, 12 and 13 (*Police Questioning and The Accused: Silence and Admissions*; *Opinion Evidence*; and *Identification Evidence*), respectively.

We again offer special thanks to Wendy Whiteley and the NSW Art Gallery for permitting us to enrich this book with a most evocative artwork by Brett Whiteley. We are grateful to Nicholas Cowdery AO QC FAAL, Visiting Professorial Fellow at UNSW, former Director of Public Prosecutions for the State of New South Wales, and champion of due process and fair trial principles, for his generous Foreword.

Finally, it is a pleasure to be published by The Federation Press. We acknowledge the Press's continuing spirit of generosity, writ large by Chris Holt in his original commissioning of this book. To Trisha Valliappan, Jason Monaghan and Belinda Rimmer, thank you for your support of, and patience with, this Second Edition. To Kathy Fitzhenry – a special thanks for your scrupulous care, patience and eagle eye in preparing the manuscript for publication.

The authors acknowledge the enduring role of Elders for caring for this Country.

1 May 2021
University of New South Wales,
on the land of the Bedegal people,
Sydney, Australia

8 Other than moving Chapter 14 (Police Questioning/Admissions) earlier, to Chapter 7.

Abbreviations

UEA is the abbreviation used for the uniform evidence statutes throughout the book. These are the *Evidence Act 1995* (Cth); *Evidence Act 2011* (ACT); *Evidence Act 1995* (NSW); *Evidence (National Uniform Legislation) Act 2011* (NT); *Evidence Act 2001* (Tas); *Evidence Act 2008* (Vic).

ACC	Australian Crime Commission
AFP	Australian Federal Police
AIC	Australian Institute of Criminology
AIJA	Australian Institute of Judicial Administration
ALRC	Australian Law Reform Commission
ATSI	Aboriginal and Torres Strait Islander
AVO	Apprehended Violence Order
BOCSAR	Bureau of Crime Statistics and Research (NSW)
CAN	Court Attendance Notice
CARA (NSW)	*Crimes (Appeal and Review) Act 2001* (NSW)
CCRC	Criminal Cases Review Commission (England and Wales)
CDPP	Commonwealth Director of Public Prosecutions
CPA (NSW)	*Criminal Procedure Act 1986* (NSW)
DPP	Director of Public Prosecutions
EAGP	Early Appropriate Guilty Plea
ERISP	Electronically Recorded Interview with a Suspected Person
HREOC	Human Rights and Equal Opportunities Commission (now Australian Human Rights Commission)
ICCPR	*International Covenant on Civil and Political Rights*
JCCD	Judicial Council on Cultural Diversity
JDA 2015 (Vic)	*Jury Directions Act 2015* (Vic)
LEPRA (NSW)	*Law Enforcement (Powers and Responsibilities) Act 2002* (NSW)
LEPRR (NSW)	*Law Enforcement (Powers and Responsibilities) Regulation 2016* (NSW)
NAS	US National Academy of Sciences
NSWCC	New South Wales Crime Commission
NSWLRC	New South Wales Law Reform Commission
NZLC	New Zealand Law Commission
ODPP	Office of the Director of Public Prosecutions
RCIRCSA	Royal Commission into Institutional Responses to Child Sexual Assault

Table of Cases

(References in **bold** type are to extracts of cases)

Table of Statutes

Northern Territory

Queensland

Chapter 1

Accusatorial Justice

Introduction

> [T]he whole of the process for the investigation, prosecution and trial of an indictable Commonwealth offence is accusatorial. It is accusatorial in the sense that an accused person is not called on to make any answer to an allegation of wrong-doing, or to any charge that is laid, until the prosecuting authorities have made available to the accused particulars of the evidence on which it is proposed to rely in proof of the accusation that is made. And even after that information has been provided, the accused person need say or do nothing more than enter a plea of guilty or not guilty to the charge. If the accused person chooses to plead not guilty at trial, he or she is entitled to put the prosecution to proof of the charge and, as part of that process, to test the strength of the evidence which the prosecution adduces at trial. The only relevant limit on the accused person's testing of the strength of the prosecution's case is provided by the accused person's instructions to his or her lawyer. The lawyer cannot test the prosecution case in a manner inconsistent with the accused person's instructions.[1]

The most obvious influence of our justice system's English heritage is the jury of 12 citizens, randomly selected to adjudicate on indictable offences.[2] In both the literal and metaphorical senses, the trial is the public face of criminal justice. Twelve members of the public participate as jurors taking on the dual role of having the final word[3] and of also bearing witness to the proceedings. Jurors' central role in the trial ensures that lawyers strive to make the process comprehensible to lay people. While the jury trial gives the public significant agency in the contest between the individual and the state, its role is much circumscribed. No longer are juries the decision-makers for most offences and even the most serious offences can now be determined by judge-alone trials in most States of Australia.[4]

---

1 See *X7 v Australian Crime Commission* [2013] HCA 29; 248 CLR 92, [101] (Hayne and Bell JJ).

2 Subject to options for a judge-only trial.

3 Outside appeal courts, that is.

4 The major difference between jury and non-jury (and especially non-criminal) trials is not in the content of rules but in the enhanced potential to relax the rules of evidence in non-jury environments. See, eg, *UEA*, s 190 (waiver of rules of evidence). This section does not expressly refer to non-jury trials, but the court-ordered power to dispense with rules of evidence in s 190(3) operates in civil proceedings which are overwhelmingly dominated by judge-alone determinations. Otherwise particular rules of evidence may be waived only if the parties consent. Further, even in instances where the rules of evidence do not apply, such as in many tribunals, the principles underpinning those rules remain an important guide in decision-making.

In NSW courts from July 2018-June 2019 the courtrooms, sometimes revered as mansions[5] or temples[6] of justice, played host to contested criminal trials with just under 18,500 defendants. The vast majority of these – over 16,000 – were heard in the Local Court. With respect to charges against slightly over 13,500 defendants the prosecution shifted the presumption of innocence to establish guilt beyond reasonable doubt for at least one charge. Only just over 3500 were found not guilty on all charges.[7] Even more striking is the fact that of the just under 140,000 defendants before the NSW courts in this 2018-19 period, nearly 88,000 of them pleaded guilty and proceeded directly to a sentencing hearing without a trial.[8] That only a fraction of criminal charges are finalised by a contested trial (and a much smaller fraction by a contested *jury* trial) speaks to the diminished direct practical impact of the trial (and to the jury) in the Australian justice system. However, the *indirect* impact of the jury is profound. In particular, the jury has defined both the need for and the shape of our law of evidence. The law of evidence is obviously material to the resolution of criminal charges (and civil disputes), and further this law is central to determining the *choice* of criminal charges brought against a defendant, as well as to pre-trial charge and plea negotiations. This is because in all these situations the strength of the prosecution is defined by the presence or otherwise of *admissible* evidence supporting its allegations.

This book treats the trial as criminal justice's 'main event' and this chapter sets the stage for *The Trial*'s detailed consideration of concepts and issues under Australia's uniform evidence law and procedures.[9] Its focus is on the theory, significance and practice of the legal rules and processes that primarily take place in a courtroom, or as described by the 1960's US criminologist Kamisar, the 'mansion'[10] of justice. Kamisar's thesis at that time was grounded in the poverty of justice in the police station, which he likened to the 'gatehouse'. For Kamisar the trial gave defendants the presence and protection of a judge tasked to ensure fairness, and a structured process which embeds rights,[11] including, for serious offences at least, legal representation for defendants.[12] This book's final chapter (Epilogue) examines structural and institutional issues relevant to understanding how miscarriages of justice occur. This book does not have the capacity to speak

5 See below Y Kamisar, 'Equal Justice in the Gatehouses and Mansions of American Criminal Procedure' in *Criminal Justice in Our Time* (University Press of Virginia, 1965).

6 *Nudd* [2006] HCA 9; 225 ALR 161 (Kirby J).

7 Ten defendants were found not guilty by reason of mental illness in the Supreme Court; 18 in the District Court and 2247 had charges dismissed by the lower courts due to mental illness (and 230 in the Children's Court dismissed on this basis): <https://www.bocsar.nsw.gov.au>. The 2020 statistics show a drop in numbers in all categories due to COVID-19 and, as such, are not representative. 2020 aside, since July 2015 in approximately 6500 cases annually the prosecution has withdrawn all charges.

8 See <https://www.bocsar.nsw.gov.au>.

9 Its focus tends to be on procedural legislation as applied in New South Wales.

10 Kamisar, above n 5.

11 For example, the right to have the prosecution case presented fully and finally before opening the defence case; the right to cross-examine prosecution and co-accused witnesses; an asymmetry in the rules of evidence embedding restraint in prosecution evidence and permitting greater leeway for defence evidence, and the right to silence – to insist that the prosecution case be tested without an obligation to present defence evidence.

12 In the 1960s, without innovations like mandatory electronic recording of police interviews of suspected persons or open recognition of the high potential for police to act corruptly, anything could happen in the gatehouse. Nowadays suspects have some improved protections but not all changes have been protective of suspects' rights, who still remain vulnerable to police pressure: <https://www.piac.asn.au/project-highlight /the-suspect-targeting-management-plan/>.

to Australia's biggest justice challenge, that is the 'imposition of the "white man's vision" of justice', as described by Aboriginal human rights and social justice campaigner Tom Calma. Calma makes clear that it 'is misconceived to believe that justice can be delivered without due consideration being given to cultural factors', a view supported by confronting statistics revealing the shortfall of equality of justice in Australia.[13] Calma advocates that courts' day-to-day operation must understand and respect Indigenous cultures, heritage and histories, 'constructed in a way that is capable of providing justice for our people and communities'.[14] Generally speaking there is some recognition of the major contemporary challenge in the delivery of justice, with steps taken to support Indigenous defendants – there are Koori Courts in Victoria,[15] Aboriginal Community Courts (WA), Circle Sentencing (NSW), Murri Courts (Qld) and Nunga Courts (SA). These initiatives aim to reduce the harm created by a justice system embedded into a history of Indigenous dispossession. However, they do not implement de-colonising strategies that integrate Indigenous culture into the justice system.[16]

Right to a Fair Trial

The common law trial is not an inquiry into 'the truth'. It is a process by which the prosecution seeks to prove guilt beyond reasonable doubt, and in various ways the presumption of innocence manifests. For the defence, gaps in the prosecution case are typically its focal point. They have no ultimate burden of proof, but their focus will be on raising reasonable doubt regarding the prosecution's case. This focus on procedural truth, in contrast to objective truth, acknowledges that truth-seeking is an objective, but not the sole objective. To quote from the well-known observations of Vice-Chancellor Knight Bruce in the 1846 English case of *Pearse v Pearse*[17] – '[t]he discovery and vindication and establishment of truth are main purposes ... of the existence of Courts of Justice'. However, truth-seeking is not without boundaries. And, from the same judgment, as the banner head quotation at the commencement of Chapter 3 indicates, truth is to be pursued with moderation, fairness and by fair means. The former Chief Justice of New South Wales, the Hon JJ Spigelman AC,[18] after quoting from *Pearse v Pearse*, noted that 'prevailing community standards' set the standards of fairness and of what constitutes fair means.[19] Spigelman noted that '[r]estraints on the processes for determining the truth are multi-faceted', emerging in various

13 Percentage of the remand and sentenced prison population that is Aboriginal in NSW tends to be steady around 25%, a severe over-representation compared to their ratio of the Australian population. This percentage almost doubles when young Aboriginal people are considered: <https://www.bocsar.nsw.gov.au>.

14 T Calma, 'The Integration of Customary Law into the Australian Legal System', <https://www.humanrights.gov.au/news/speeches/integration-customary-law-australian-legal-system-calma>.

15 See <https://www.countycourt.vic.gov.au/ news-and-media/news-listing/2018-11-29-county-koori-court-reflects-10-years>; and see also <http://rightnow.org.au/ opinion-3/accessing-koori-court-human-right/>.

16 See also <https://www.publicdefenders.nsw.gov.au/barbook>. Regarding doubts with respect to the effectiveness of Circle Sentencing: <https://www.bocsar.nsw.gov.au/Documents/CJB/cjb115.pdf>.

17 (1846) 1 De G & Sm 12; 63 ER 950.

18 JJ Spigelman AC, 'The Truth Can Cost Too Much: The Principle of a Fair Trial' (4th Gerard Brennan Lecture, 2003).

19 Quoting from *Swaffield* [1998] HCA 1; 192 CLR 159 (Toohey, Gaudron and Gummow JJ).

contexts. Spigelman suggests this jurisprudence of the fair trial is 'entitled to constitutional significance'.[20]

The underlying logic of the adversarial ideal is explained by Lord Devlin in *The Judge*:

> The English say that the best way of getting at the truth is to have each party dig for the facts that help it; between them they will bring all to light. The inquisitor works on his own but has in the end to say who wins and who loses. …
>
> [I]t can also be argued that two prejudiced searchers starting from opposite ends of the field will between them be less likely to miss anything than the impartial searcher starting at the middle.[21]

With adversarialism, parties' self-interest creates the checks and balances of testing and challenging opposing evidence. It works well if power imbalances are appropriately moderated. The biggest threat with adversarialism is the beguiling attraction for one (or both) of the 'two prejudiced searchers' being drawn into a battle vortex of win-at-all-costs. The logic of harnessing self-interest in opposing advocates also applies to testing and responding rigorously and energetically to damaging evidence. Judges are expected to ensure rules of process and of evidence are adhered to, and they can seek clarification of a witness's testimony through questions, but they cannot raise new issues or cross-examine witnesses. This is quite different from the inquisitorial/civilian model that dominates in Europe. There, the judge is the dominant inquisitor. Adversarialism exists but it is muted. In Australia, civil litigation is often 'managed' by a judicial officer from early on, issues are more likely to be isolated and narrowed, and hearings are likely to be akin to the episodic classic inquisitorial process than the 'main event' common law tradition.

Human rights norms play a growing role in 21st century criminal jurisprudence. It is unfortunate that 21st century Australia has been very slow in embracing comprehensive legislated human rights – see the *Charter of Human Rights and Responsibilities Act 2006* (Vic),[22] the *Human Rights Act 2004* (ACT)[23] and the *Human Rights Act 2019* (Qld).[24] There is a certain amount of overlap in the common law appreciation of rights and those expressed in human rights instruments. The **presumption of innocence**, expressed also in the *International Covenant on Civil and Political Rights* (*ICCPR*) below (at Article 14.2), applies unless and until a person is convicted.[25] In addition, the most obvious pre-trial rights are:

- **rights to privacy** – no one can just march into a suspect's house to search for evidence;
- **rights to silence** – no one can demand a suspect explain his or her whereabouts, motivations or feelings; and
- **rights to liberty** – no one can detain or lock up a suspect because that is more convenient than allowing them to remain at large.

These rights are not absolute rights and, despite having long common law heritages, are particularly prone to challenge in recent decades. The evolved common

20 Spigelman, above n 18.
21 P Devlin, *The Judge* (Oxford University Press, 1979), 60-1.
22 Section 25(2)(k).
23 Section 22(2)(i).
24 Sections 31, 32, 33, 34.
25 *Betts* [2016] HCA 25; 258 CLR 420.

law jurisprudence of the right to a fair trial differs in shape and lacks the clarity of Article 14 of the *ICCPR*.[26]

International Covenant on Civil and Political Rights[27]

14.1. *All persons shall be equal before the courts and tribunals. In the determination of any criminal charge against him, or of his rights and obligations in a suit at law, everyone shall be entitled to a fair and public hearing by a competent, independent and impartial tribunal established by law.* The press and the public may be excluded from all or part of a trial for reasons of morals, public order (*ordre public*) or national security in a democratic society, or when the interest of the private lives of the parties so requires, or to the extent strictly necessary in the opinion of the court in special circumstances where publicity would prejudice the interests of justice; but any judgement rendered in a criminal case or in a suit at law shall be made public except where the interest of juvenile persons otherwise requires or the proceedings concern matrimonial disputes or the guardianship of children.

2. Everyone charged with a criminal offence shall have the right to be presumed innocent until proved guilty according to law.

3. In the determination of any criminal charge against him, everyone shall be entitled to the following minimum guarantees, in full equality:

- *(a) To be informed promptly and in detail in a language which he understands of the nature and cause of the charge against him;*
- (b) To have adequate time and facilities for the preparation of his defence and to communicate with counsel of his own choosing;
- *(c) To be tried without undue delay;*
- (d) To be tried in his presence, and to defend himself in person or through legal assistance of his own choosing; to be informed, if he does not have legal assistance, of this right; and to have legal assistance assigned to him, in any case where the interests of justice so require, and without payment by him in any such case if he does not have sufficient means to pay for it;
- *(e) To examine, or have examined, the witnesses against him and to obtain the attendance and* examination of witnesses on his behalf under the same conditions as witnesses against him;
- (f) To have the free assistance of an interpreter if he cannot understand or speak the language used in court;
- *(g) Not to be compelled to testify against himself or to confess guilt.*

4. In the case of juvenile persons, the procedure shall be such as will take account of their age and the desirability of promoting their rehabilitation.

5. Everyone convicted of a crime shall have the right to his conviction and sentence being reviewed by a higher tribunal according to law.

6. When a person has by a final decision been convicted of a criminal offence and when subsequently his conviction has been reversed or he has been pardoned on the ground that a new or newly discovered fact shows conclusively that there has been a miscarriage of justice, the person who has suffered punishment as a result of such conviction shall be compensated according to law, unless it is proved that the non-disclosure of the unknown fact in time is wholly or partly attributable to him.

---

26 See J Gans, T Henning, J Hunter and K Warner, *Criminal Process and Human Rights* (Federation Press, 2011), chs 9, 10 and 11.

27 Adopted and opened for signature, ratification and accession by General Assembly resolution 2200A (XXI) of 16 December 1966, entry into force 23 March 1976, in accordance with Article 49. Emphasis added. See also *Charter of Human Rights and Responsibilities Act 2006* (Vic), s 25; *Human Rights Act 2004* (ACT), s 22; *Human Rights Act 2019* (Qld), ss 31, 32.

> *7. No one shall be liable to be tried or punished again for an offence for which he has already been finally convicted or acquitted in accordance with the law and penal procedure of each country.*

Article 14 illustrates that the right to a fair trial is a bundle of rights. This is the case whatever the tradition. For example, the common law fair trial obligations applying under Australian law include the following:

- With respect to the criminal pleadings, an accused has the right to know the charges with sufficient particularity to meet those charges.
- Courts have an obligation to ensure that a fair trial is not impeded by the charging practices of the prosecution (for example, with inappropriate multiple or repetitive charges).[28]
- The common law[29] provides defendants with disclosure rights of the prosecution case (now supplemented in many jurisdictions by statute).
- There is no common law right to a speedy trial but, if delay prevents a fair trial, it will be stayed.[30]
- The accused has a right for the trial to be conducted in the presence of a judge who acts impartially, with detachment[31] and appropriately;[32] and who assists unrepresented litigants (who are not otherwise entitled to legal representation); and who directs the jury appropriately, including with respect to assessing certain evidence, particularly unreliable evidence.[33]
- The prosecutor must act fairly in court,[34] including putting the prosecution case fully.[35]
- Where an accused is to be tried on a serious offence, a court will stay proceedings unless there is legal representation.[36]
- The accused has the right to an interpreter, if one is needed.[37]
- In addition, in exceptional circumstances, a court will quash a conviction if defence counsel is flagrantly incompetent.[38]

Article 14 illustrates another feature shared by the common law, which is the fact that the right to a fair trial pivots upon the obligation to be fair to *the accused*. This raises questions regarding the rights of witnesses and, in particular, of victims of crime? Their role in the trial is discussed in later chapters but suffice to say that traditionally they have not been the beneficiary of procedural

---

28 *Connelly v DPP* [1964] AC 1254; *Sutton* [1984] HCA 5; 152 CLR 528; *De Jesus* [1986] HCA 65; 61 ALJR 1.

29 *Grey* [2001] HCA 65; 75 ALJR 1708; *Brown (Winston)* [1998] AC 367.

30 *Jago v District Court (NSW)* [1989] HCA 46; 168 CLR 23; *Edwards* [2009] HCA 20; 255 ALR 399.

31 *Antoun* [2006] HCA 2; 224 ALR 5.

32 And who does not fall asleep and distract proceedings: *Cesan* [2008] HCA 52; 236 CLR 358; or bully: M Kirby, 'Judicial Stress and Judicial Bullying' (2014) 14 *Queensland University of Technology Law Review* 1.

33 See Chapter 14; *Bromley* [1986] HCA 49; 161 CLR 315; *McKinney* [1991] HCA 6; 171 CLR 468; *Domican* [1992] HCA 13; 173 CLR 555; *Pollitt* [1992] HCA 35; 174 CLR 558.

34 See Chapter 2 and *Evans* [2007] HCA 59; 235 CLR 521.

35 *Nguyen* [2020] HCA 23; *Soma* [2003] HCA 13; 212 CLR 299; *Apostilides* [1984] HCA 38; 154 CLR 563; *Richardson* [1974] HCA 19; 131 CLR 116; *Whitehorn* [1983] HCA 42; 152 CLR 657.

36 *Dietrich* [1992] HCA 57; 177 CLR 292. See also *Gassy* [2008] HCA 18; 236 CLR 293; *Gidley* [1984] 3 NSWLR 168.

37 *Hakimi* [2011] ACTSC 55; *Rostom* [2007] SASC 210; 98 SASR 528; *Saraya* (1993) 70 A Crim R 515.

38 *Nudd* [2006] HCA 9; 225 ALR 161; *TKWJ* [2002] HCA 46; 212 CLR 124; *Birks* (1990) 19 NSWLR 677.

protections. Instead, any loss of privacy or dignity they might suffer through the way they were questioned in court was seen as collateral damage, intrinsic to the adversarial accusatorial process and its key goals of securing a fair trial for the accused and enhancing the integrity of the verdict through the application of rules of evidence. However, this has changed. Since the 1980s there has been a growing movement recognising that community standards require greater respect be afforded to witnesses' treatment in court.[39] Psychological research has assisted greatly in this and other respects. It has also revealed that some people:

- particularly those who are emotionally or mentally vulnerable, will admit to crimes that they have not committed;[40]
- particularly children and others who are vulnerable, will become overwhelmed under cross-examination in court such that this questioning impedes a witness giving full and accurate testimony;
- perhaps all people sub-consciously, form a negative view of a criminal defendant who has a criminal past, such that it influences their verdict irrationally; and/or
- far more than the lay person typically appreciates, some people will wrongly (but honestly and confidently) identify a person they saw, or heard, as the thief, murderer or fraudster.

The public face of justice (and its non-public dimensions)

The public nature of the trial is akin to a parade of justice consisting of oral legal argument, legal representation, witness questioning and a judge guiding 12 randomly chosen citizens. Arguably the trial parades an idealised version of the administration of justice. The open court with a gallery for the public to view proceedings and for media to report them is also a traditional feature of open justice. However, nowadays it is recognised that witnesses have interests that should be protected and the impact of pervasive and unfettered media on an accused's rights have created a new dynamic for courts, creating a notable trend in recent years in the use of suppression orders. These orders typically aim to protect the dignity of witnesses during trials relating to sexual assault offences, to protect national security or to remove the risk of prejudicial publicity.[41] However, access to day-to-day court rulings, the taking of evidence, the delivery of verdicts and the sentencing of offenders are important aspects of transparency and accountability. The 2020 court responses[42] to the COVID-19 pandemic have shown the need for high quality technology, and the potential to use that technology for efficiency gains such that it is probable that certain aspects of Australian court process will change in the long term as a result of the 2020 COVID-19 period. In particular, for portions of 2020 (and in some respects, beyond 2020) the

---

39 See, eg, *UEA*, ss 41 and 192(2)(b).

40 See, eg, SM Kassin and GH Gudjonsson, 'The Psychology of Confessions: A Review of the Literature and Issues' (2004) 5 *Psychological Science in the Public Interest* 33; D Starr, 'The Confession' (2019) 364 *Science* 1022.

41 See generally J Bosland, 'Two Years of Suppression under the Open Courts Act 2013 (Vic)' (2017) 39 *Sydney Law Review* 25. For a novel application of suppression orders, see *Lacey (a Pseudonym) v Attorney General (NSW)* [2021] NSWCA 27, [31] (Basten JA).

42 See, eg, *COVID-19 Legislation Amendment (Emergency Measures) Act 2020* (NSW) and C Akthar 'Pre-recorded Evidence Hearings in Response to Covid-19: Issues to Consider', <https://www.publicdefenders.nsw.gov.au/Documents/covid-19-pre-recorded-evidence-hearings-15-4-20.pdf>.

virtual courtroom replaced dimensions of the physical one (including extending pre-recorded evidence). Trials were put on hold. In short, the public nature of trials was significantly revised.

However, with every efficiency gain, there are risks that erosions of accused rights and lost transparency will take away vital checks and balances. For example, does a virtual courtroom fulfil both the need to do justice and for justice to be seen to be done? Does zoom justice equate with the accused *confronting* their accusers? Further, it is easy to take for granted courts' solemnity and formality in the uniquely spacially-configured physical courtroom. However, solemn and formal processes create cultural legitimacy, including demonstrating the Law's authority. These less tangible features of court process are not readily achievable in an online environment. Nor does zoom justice lend itself to the potential human connectedness acquired by being in the same room as the accused, as witnesses and as family and others in the public gallery. There are other perspectives as well – what do jurors lose (or gain) by evidence obtained virtually? Does the remoteness of witnesses blunt their emotional connection (and, if so, does that matter)? Further, does zoom justice remove important informal interactions – the casual conversations that lawyers have with clients, with witnesses, with opposing counsel? These and other issues may be on the reform agenda for future decades.

On the topic of transparency, consider the Victoria Police's reliance on Melbourne criminal barrister Nicola Gobbo as a registered police informer. This corrosive relationship exposes a dimension of justice delivery that has undermined the fundamentals of accusatorial justice and severely threatened the integrity of the Victorian criminal justice system.[43] On her own admission, Ms Gobbo prioritised her police informant role over acting in the best interests of those who had retained her. She also operated as a double agent feeding information back to the Melbourne criminal underworld. Gobbo's conduct and that of Victoria police officers were investigated in 2014 by the Independent Broad-based Anti-corruption Commission (IBAC) with Victoria Police resisting disclosure of the ensuing report on the ground of public interest immunity, later joined by Ms Gobbo relying on the equitable obligation of confidence. Resisting disclosure was based on the virtual certainty that revelations would endanger the life of Ms Gobbo. All avenues of appeal finally resolved the matter in favour of disclosure in *AB (a Pseudonym) v CD (a Pseudonym)*.[44] The police force's scandalous reliance on Gobbo as a police informant shows the damage of secret dirty deals:

> EF's actions in purporting to act as counsel for the Convicted Persons while covertly informing against them *were fundamental and appalling breaches of EF's obligations as counsel to her clients and of EF's duties to the court*. Likewise, *Victoria Police were guilty of reprehensible conduct in knowingly encouraging EF to do as she did and were involved in sanctioning atrocious breaches of the sworn duty of every police officer to discharge all duties imposed on them faithfully and according to law* without favour or affection, malice or ill-will. As a result, *the prosecution of each Convicted Person was corrupted in a manner which debased fundamental premises of the criminal justice system*. It follows … that the public interest favouring disclosure is compelling: the maintenance of the integrity of the criminal justice system demands that the information be disclosed and that the propriety of each Convicted Person's conviction be re-examined in light of the

43 Also known as Informer 3838 and Lawyer X, and as EF in *AB (a Pseudonym) v CD (a Pseudonym)* [2018] HCA 58; 93 ALJR 59, 62, revealed through the Victorian Independent Broad-based Anti-Corruption Commission (IBAC) report in 2015. See also Chapter 15.

44 [2018] HCA 58; 93 ALJR 59.

> information. The public interest in preserving EF's anonymity must be subordinated to the integrity of the criminal justice system.[45]

The McMurdo Royal Commission[46] into Ms Gobbo and Victoria Police completed its hearings in early 2020 revealing that this informant relationship has impacted on just under 1300 matters in the Victorian criminal justice system. There will be years of hearing a steady trail of appeal cases.[47] One would expect (and hope) that this scenario is exceptional. However, as we see in the in-court scenarios briefly discussed in the following pages, and the *X7* and *Lee* line of cases also discussed below, assaults on the fundamentals of adversarial and accusatorial justice manifest in numerous ways. Indeed, New South Wales has its own example of police misconduct seeking to subvert an accused person's right to independent legal representation. The Operation Monza Report to NSW Parliament in March 2021[48] describes police targeting for two days a solicitor representing a motor cycle club member. Police engaged in 'deliberate, deceitful and malicious harassment', apparently a response to the solicitor's insistence that police witnesses be required to attend court to give evidence in person rather than remotely. The police pressure forced the solicitor to withdraw.

These incidents draw attention to the scope of the criminal trial to redress pre-trial police illegalities and unchecked pre-trial disempowerment of the suspect. Gaudron J in *Dietrich*[49] highlighted the criminal trial's potential as 'the stage for a retrospective check on evidence-gathering, investigation and prosecution decision-making'. She spoke with significant optimism at the trial's capacity to 'retrospectively, within boundaries, make good lost rights ... [and] investigative illegality and impropriety ... through the judicial discretion to exclude evidence so obtained'.[50] However, these sentiments need to be understood in light of the fact that major power imbalance is not readily repaired after individual rights have been lost and that the scope of the trial to review police behaviour tends to be incidental.

We review in the final chapter some of the notorious locations for weakness in this parade of justice as well as their consequences in generating miscarriages of justice. The ways in which a determination of guilt through the trial process can be flawed include frailties in the generation, reception and understanding of forensic science evidence[51] and in interpreting non-English-speaking witness testimony,[52] as well as flawed jury processes,[53] flawed judicial processes and

---

45 *AB (a Pseudonym) v CD (a Pseudonym)* [2018] HCA 58; 93 ALJR 59, [10] (Kiefel CJ, Bell, Gageler, Keane, Nettle, Gordon and Edelman JJ) (emphasis added).

46 See <https://www.rcmpi.vic.gov.au/>.

47 K Sweeney, 'Lawyer X: 1297 people might be affected', AAP General News Wire, Sydney, 21 February 2020. See also <https://www.podcastoneaustralia.com.au/podcasts/understate-lawyer-x/>.

48 *Report to Parliament Pursuant to s 132, Law Enforcement Conduct Commission Act 2016*, 'Operation Monza', March 2021, <www. lecc.nsw.gov.au>.

49 [1992] HCA 57; 177 CLR 292, [25].

50 Gans, Henning, Hunter and Warner, above n 26, 405, referring to s 138. And consider also the importance of ensuring police engage in full disclosure to the prosecution (and the prosecution to the defence), see *Visser v DPP (Cth)* [2020] VSCA 327 and *Mokbel v DPP (Cth)* [2020] VSCA 325, and Chapter 2.

51 See Chapter 12.

52 See Chapter 5.

53 Including engaging in their own research and investigation: JB Hunter, 'Jurors' Notions of Justice: An Empirical Study of Motivations to Investigate & Obedience to Judicial Directions' (Law and Justice Foundation of NSW, 2014), <http://www.lawfoundation.net.au/>.

distortions created by lawyers' advocacy.[54] To a certain extent justice also depends on luck – luck to not be misidentified as the thief, rapist or murderer; luck that DNA exonerates; luck that an alibi can be proven by objective evidence (and not that the defendant was at home watching TV with his mum). Luck is not socially or economically neutral. One only needs to examine documented miscarriages of justice to recognise that a trial is captive of the larger social, political, human and resource challenges.

Presuming innocence, the right to silence and accusatorial trials

At first glance the rights highlighted above in the *ICCPR*, Article 14, seem straightforward. In fact, the presumption of innocence and the right to silence operating in Australia sit on heavily contested ground. To gain a better understanding of their enforceability and of their intersection with prosecutors' obligations and the law of evidence it is important to canvass some of the case law describing accusatorial justice. Two broad lines of cases (discussed below) illustrate 21st century contexts in which the rights under discussion – and accusatorial justice principles – have been under siege. In both contexts the High Court has demanded that the accusatorial features of the criminal trial not be undermined. In these cases the High Court has articulated what is termed *the fundamental principle* of the common law, namely 'that the accusatorial nature of a criminal trial means that, under the common law, *the onus of proof is upon the prosecution to prove its case*' (emphasis added).[55] The principle that *an accused person cannot be required to testify* has been termed a '*companion rule*' (that is, as a 'companion' of criminal trials). They are both aspects of the accusatorial trial.[56] It is clear that these principles are not formulations plucked out of a vacuum. They are said to be defined by the individual's relationship to the state, or as described in 2014 in *Lee*[57] by virtue of the 'balance struck between the power of the State to prosecute and the position of an individual who stands accused'. A major domain where accusatorial justice principles have been analysed involves criminal trials where the jury hear from a presiding judge or a prosecutor that an accused has an obligation that is in fact in breach of accusatorial principles. Instances include comments about:

- *the fact that the accused, in the police station, acted on legal advice and refused to answer police questions*: In *Hogg*[58] White JA held no adverse inference could be drawn from the appellant's refusal to answer police questions as the Crown did not cross-examine Hogg on his explanation (legal advice) for not answering police questions.

---

54 Whilst the criminal trial might seem a minefield, so can be avoiding trials by encouraging pleas of guilty.

55 *Construction, Forestry, Mining and Energy Union v Boral Resources (Vic) Pty Ltd* (*CFMEU* case) [2015] HCA 21, [36].

56 Ibid [3], [37] (French CJ, Kiefel, Bell, Gageler and Keane JJ), citing *Caltex* [1993] HCA 74; 178 CLR 477, 528 and *Lee v New South Wales Crime Commission* [2013] HCA 39; 251 CLR 196, [313], [318]. The uniform *Evidence Act* provides that the prosecution cannot compel a person charged with a crime to assist in the discharge of its onus of proof: s 17.

57 [2014] HCA 20; 253 CLR 455, [32] (*Lee No 2*).

58 [2019] NSWCCA 323 (Wright and Wilson JJ agreeing) considering *UEA*, s 89A: 'In a criminal proceeding for a serious indictable offence, such unfavourable inferences may be drawn as appear proper from evidence that, during official questioning in relation to the offence, the defendant failed or refused to mention a fact …'.

- *the fact that the accused person failed to testify*: In *Azzopardi*[59] and *GBF*[60] the trial judges were held to have crossed the line into inappropriate comment that failed to acknowledge the accused's right to remain silent and to be presumed innocent when they told the jury that they might consider (in *Azzopardi*) 'the fact that the accused did not deny or contradict evidence about matters which were within his personal knowledge'.[61] Such a judicial observation 'invited members of the jury to engage in the false process of reasoning that was contrary to the directions of law earlier given'.[62] When the circumstances are apt, it is desirable to give an *Azzopardi* direction.[63]
- *suggesting to the jury to scrutinise the accused's testimony closely:* In *Robinson*[64] the trial judge was ruled to have breached the presumption of innocence when he suggested to jurors that they 'might think that the greater the interest the more carefully you should scrutinise a witness's evidence', followed up by a direct reference to examine closely Robinson's evidence:

  > You might think – it is a matter solely for you – that the accused had the greatest interest of all the witnesses you saw and heard and that, therefore, you should scrutinise his evidence closely.

- *suggesting the accused would do anything to avoid conviction:* Consider also *Wise*[65] where the defendant's explanation for what motivated his statement to police (fear of the Rebels Motorcycle Gang – 'what would happen if I did speak') and his inconsistent evidence in court where he was 'on trial fighting – fighting for my life, really' was relied upon by the prosecutor in closing to the jury,

  > He tells a story which demonstrates his innocence. But unfortunately, you could have no confidence whatsoever in the evidence he gave to you from that witness box … He said "I am fighting for my life" and he is fighting for his life. He does not want to go to gaol. There is no doubt about it. … When you do fight for your life you do anything you have to save yourself. He was determined, I would suggest, to provide an account to you that would convince you of his innocence.

  The court applied *Robinson*, and allowed the appeal.

---

59 [2001] HCA 25; 205 CLR 50. In *Hargraves* [2011] HCA 44; 282 ALR 214 the trial judge managed to stay on the right side of the requirements of accusatorial justice in his comment that suggested close scrutiny of whether witnesses have lied. It was held to have been clearly a reference to witnesses that did not include the accused.

60 [2020] HCA 40.

61 And in very similar terms also in *GBF*.

62 *Azzopardi* [2001] HCA 25; 205 CLR 50, 75 [68] (Gaudron, Gummow, Kirby and Hayne JJ) (and relied on by the court in *GBF*).

63 Namely: '[I]f an accused does not give evidence at trial it will almost always be desirable for the judge to warn the jury that the accused's silence in court is not evidence against the accused, does not constitute an admission by the accused, may not be used to fill gaps in the evidence tendered by the prosecution, and may not be used as a make-weight in assessing whether the prosecution has proved its case beyond reasonable doubt': *Azzopardi* [2001] HCA 25; 205 CLR 50, [51]. See *Martinez and Tortell* [2019] NSWCCA 153; and, on the role of counsel in requesting the direction, see *JPM* [2019] NSWCCA 301. In Victoria, the common law is replaced by *Jury Directions Act 2015* (Vic), ss 41, 42 and s 12.

64 [1991] HCA 38; 180 CLR 531, [3]. See also *Beavis* [2018] NSWCCA 248.

65 [2019] NTCCA 10.

- *suggesting the accused failed to offer an explanation for the prosecution allegations*: In *Palmer*[66] the High Court held that the following cross-examination by the prosecution distracted from the jury's fundamental task of deciding whether the prosecution proved the elements of the charged offence beyond reasonable doubt. It shifted the process from the prosecution bearing the burden of proof to a focus on the accused.

  Q: Mr Palmer, as I understand it, from the questions that were put to [L] yesterday, you would really, it seems, be at an absolute loss to think as to why she should make up the allegations?
  A: … I have no idea why she has said what she has. …
  Q: So far as you are concerned there is absolutely nothing about your behaviour towards [L] in the past prior to the 4th July, or at all, that would account for her making such an allegation against you?
  A: I have, as I said before, … no, I have done nothing.
  Q: So even with the benefit of hindsight, or as in the time that has elapsed from the time you were questioned by police … you are still at a loss?
  A: Yes. …
  Q: At this stage, as you sit there today, you can't think of any reason, or anything you have done to her —?
  A: No, I haven't.
  Q: As to why she would make this up?
  A: I am saying that to you, that is correct. (emphasis added)

- *suggesting the accused failed to call a witness*: For example, in *Dyers*[67] where the prosecutor said to the jury, 'My friends haven't called Wendy Tinkler … You may think that whoever Wendy is, that person cannot assist the defence case'. The High Court held this breached accusatorial justice principles because (Gaudron and Hayne JJ, with Kirby J and Callinan J agreeing) '[n]ot only is the accused not bound to give evidence, it is for the prosecution to prove its case beyond reasonable doubt'.

The second broad line of cases arise because the ideology of a commission of inquiry, an inquisitorial-style process,[68] is an investigative fact-finding body and as such clashes with the accusatorial ideology because a criminal defendant is forced to answer questions that traverse criminal charges awaiting trial.[69] A number of cases have required the High Court to rule on whether commission of inquiry processes (which abrogates the privilege against self-incrimination) risk subverting a pending criminal trial on the same matter. A string of cases since 2013 has informed our understanding of accusatorial justice. First, in *X7 v Australian Crime Commission*,[70] X7, who had been charged and was awaiting

66 [1998] HCA 2; 193 CLR 1, [6].

67 [2002] HCA 45; 210 CLR 285.

68 See, eg, the Australian Crime Commission (ACC), <http://www.crimecommission.gov.au/>. The ACC was established under the *Australian Crime Commission Act 2002* (Cth).

69 For example, the ACC can order people to submit to compulsory examination for the purpose of investigating serious and organised crime (irrespective of whether charges have been laid). Information given to statutory bodies through compulsory examination is usually limited in how it can be used. The ACC Act, for example, requires an examiner to make directions safeguarding the fair trial of a person compulsorily examined, to insulate a criminal accused from any accusatorial compromises in its processes. A commission of inquiry may create an immunity (known as a 'direct use immunity') meaning that compelled answers are not admissible in criminal proceedings. A 'derivative use immunity' may also exist, meaning that compelled answers cannot be used to find other incriminating evidence, a protection that can be difficult to enforce.

70 [2013] HCA 29; 248 CLR 92.

trial on drug-related conspiracy offences, sought a declaration and injunctive relief claiming that the exercise of the Commission's compulsory examination powers created an impermissible interference with his constitutional right to a fair trial under Chapter III, including s 80, of the Constitution. The High Court accepted the core of X7's claims. Hayne and Bell JJ (at [124]) explained why.

> [It] would fundamentally alter the accusatorial judicial process that begins with the laying of a charge and culminates in the accusatorial (and adversarial) trial in the courtroom. [This is because] [n]o longer could the accused person decide the course which he or she should adopt at trial, in answer to the charge, according *only* to the strength of the prosecution's case as revealed by the material provided by the prosecution before trial, or to the strength of the evidence led by the prosecution at the trial. The accused person would have to decide the course to be followed in light of that material and in light of any self-incriminatory answers which he or she had been compelled to give at an examination conducted after the charge was laid. That is, the accused person would have to decide what plea to enter, what evidence to challenge and what evidence to give or lead at trial according to what answers he or she had given at the examination.

Two cases that were before the High Court after *X7* are *Lee (No 1)* and *Lee (No 2)*[71] concerned Jason and Seong Won Lee who were facing firearm and drug-related criminal conspiracy charges. The Lees resisted orders under the *Criminal Assets Recovery Act 1990* (NSW) made on behalf of the New South Wales Crime Commission (NSWCC). These orders, issued from the NSW Supreme Court, required the Lees to be compulsorily examined on their financial affairs on oath before a Supreme Court Registrar. The Lees unsuccessfully relied on *X7 v Australian Crime Commission* in their appeal to the High Court: *Lee (No 1).*[72] The court considered different legislation from the *X7* context – State, rather than federal, and personal examinations that were to be undertaken in the Supreme Court of New South Wales. By a slender majority,[73] the court appeared to draw back from the breadth of their *X7* judgments. It held the Supreme Court powers to prevent unfairness were sufficient to protect the Lees' accusatorial rights with Crennan J noting (at [151]) that the Supreme Court's powers to control the examination could 'prevent the prosecution from obtaining an unfair forensic advantage'. Gageler and Keane JJ added (at [323]) that the impact of the compulsory examination should be assessed as a matter of 'practical reality' and so while the 'legal representatives would, of course, be prevented from setting up an affirmative case inconsistent with the evidence ... they would not be prevented from ensuring that the prosecution is put to proof or from arguing that the evidence as a whole does not prove guilt'.

The minority view (Hayne, Kiefel and Bell JJ) found that the legislature authorising the Lee's compulsory examination had failed to express by words of clear intendment the abrogation or restriction of a fundamental right. Kiefel J added (at [212]) that to describe the effects of an examination as the loss of some forensic advantage in an accused person 'tends to trivialise both them and the fundamental principle'. This was not the last of the Lees in appellate case law. In *Lee v The Queen (Lee (No 2))*[74] they successfully appealed their convictions, producing evidence revealing that the Commission had given to the prosecution

71 *Lee v New South Wales Crime Commission* [2013] HCA 39; 251 CLR 196 (*Lee (No 1)*) and *Lee (No 2)* [2014] HCA 20; 253 CLR 455.

72 [2013] HCA 39; 251 CLR 196.

73 French CJ, Crennan, Gageler and Keane JJ, with Hayne, Kiefel and Bell JJ dissenting.

74 [2014] HCA 20; 253 CLR 455.

team preparing to run the Lees' criminal trial the transcript (and associated compulsorily produced documents) from the compulsory NSWCC examination – a disclosure that assisted the prosecution case to counter elements of the defence.[75] The High Court (French CJ, Crennan, Kiefel, Bell and Keane JJ) unanimously held that the disclosure amounted to a removal of the privilege against self-incrimination and it 'affected this criminal trial in a fundamental respect, because it altered the position of the prosecution vis-à-vis the accused' (at [51]).[76] Kiefel J had been a minority voice in *Lee (No 1)* but her Honour's articulation of what the High Court calls '*the fundamental principle*'[77] has become the court's settled view. For this reason, some of her Honour's additional observations from *Lee (No 1)* bear restating as they show how so many procedural elements of the investigation, charging and trial process have evolved around the fundamental principle or have built upon the generalised and individuated principle of a fair trial.

> 186. Other inter-related rights and immunities have grown out of the system of justice which is founded upon the fundamental principle. Substantive and procedural matters have become woven into the law. For example, persons suspected of having committed a crime are immune from having to answer, under compulsion, questions of the police. This in turn led to rules about confessions that are involuntary and those obtained unfairly. …
>
> 187. … Reference was … made [in *Tofilau*[78]] to what Frankfurter J had said in *Rogers v Richmond*:[79]
>
> > "[O]urs is an accusatorial and not an inquisitorial system – a system in which the State must establish guilt by evidence independently and freely secured and may not by coercion prove its charge against an accused out of his own mouth."
>
> 188. … *It is the duty and function of the court in which the trial is pending to ensure that the trial will be in accordance with law. This requires, at a minimum, that it be conducted in accordance with the fundamental principle and the requirements that flow from it.* ...
>
> 190. To ensure a "fair trial", it has been said, by way of example, that: sufficient particulars of an alleged offence should be provided; the prosecution should make available material evidence; and a judge should give such directions to the jury as are necessary to ensure a fair trial of the accused. Although regarded as a concept which is fundamental to the system of criminal justice in Australia and "so elementary as to need no authority to support it", it is understandable that there has been no judicial attempt to list, exhaustively, the attributes of a fair trial. It may, however, be said that the concept is not entirely one-sided. The public interest in the administration of justice also requires that the process be fair to the prosecution. Thus, an accused is required to give notice of alibi and other evidence of particular kinds. …
>
> 193. … [I]t cannot be doubted that the fundamental principle remains essential to the system of criminal justice administered by our courts, as does the accusatorial nature of the process. … The requirement of proof is recognised in various statutes relating to criminal evidence and procedure.[80]

---

75 Ibid [10].

76 This action also breached the intent of the governing NSWCC legislation, but the court considered it inappropriate to merely treat the breach akin to improperly obtained evidence (that is, subject only to a court's discretionary power to exclude evidence).

77 That is, 'that the accusatorial nature of a criminal trial means that, under the common law, *the onus of proof is upon the prosecution to prove its case*' (emphasis added).

78 [2007] HCA 39; 231 CLR 396, 485 (Callinan, Heydon and Crennan JJ).

79 [[1961] USSC 38; 365 US 534, 541.]

80 Some citations omitted and emphasis added. Cases cited by Kiefel J include a list of pivotal decisions of the past century: *Woolmington v DPP* [1935] UKHL 1; [1935] AC 462, 481; *X7 v Australian Crime Commission* [2013] HCA 29; 248 CLR 92; *James v Robinson* [1963] HCA 32; 109 CLR 593; *Packer v Peacock* [1912] HCA 8; 13 CLR 577; *RPS* [2000] HCA 3; 199 CLR 620;

In *Strickland (a pseudonym) v CDPP*[81] the High Court restored the primary judge's order which had permanently stayed proceedings on the basis that they constituted an abuse of process where, after refusing to answer police questions, the three appellants had been compelled to divulge information during ACC examinations. It was held that the special investigation of the appellants' conduct by the ACC had been driven by the Australian Federal Police (AFP) for the purposes of its own criminal investigations. On this basis the court held unanimously that the ACC had acted unlawfully. Prosecution evidence against the appellants came directly from information obtained from the examinations. The majority of the court based the stay order on the view that allowing the prosecution to proceed would bring the administration of justice into disrepute. A plurality of the court added further support for the stay on the basis that the prosecution had gained an unfair forensic advantage and had also constrained the appellants' legitimate forensic choices in conducting their trials. The wide dissemination of the product of the examination within the AFP and the OCDPP created incurable prejudice to the appellants receiving fair trials. The next section of this chapter emphasises the asymmetry in the criminal trial whereby the accused has *rights*[82] and the prosecution has *obligations*. This asymmetry is displayed throughout the rules of evidence and procedure. Prosecutors' obligations are discussed more extensively in Chapter 2.

The presumption of innocence: social media vs legal principles

> *Man charged with toddler's murder – North Coast*
>
> 1 August 2011 at 4:16pm
>
> Homicide Squad detectives have charged a man with the murder of a toddler [JP] on the state's north coast four months ago. The two-year-old girl was admitted to Coffs Harbour Base Hospital on Wednesday 30 March 2011, suffering severe head injuries. She was airlifted to The Children's Hospital at Westmead, where she died two days later (Friday 1 April 2011).
>
> A post mortem examination revealed the toddler had suffered significant head trauma, including a fractured skull. Detectives from State Crime Command's Homicide Squad formed Strike Force Embley to investigate the circumstances surrounding her death. About 2pm yesterday (Monday 1 August 2011), a 44-year-old man was arrested by police at a Coffs Harbour residence.
>
> The man was taken to Coffs Harbour Police Station and charged with murder. He was refused bail to appear in Coffs Harbour Local Court today.
>
> *Facebook*

Azzopardi [2001] HCA 25; 205 CLR 50, 65 [38]; *Johnson v Miller* [1937] HCA 77; 59 CLR 467; *S* [1989] HCA 66; 168 CLR 266; *Walsh v Tattersall* [1996] HCA 26; 188 CLR 77; *Kirk v Industrial Court (NSW)* [2010] HCA 1; 239 CLR 531; *Grey* [2001] HCA 65; 184 ALR 593; *Jago v District Court (NSW)* [1989] HCA 46; 168 CLR 23; *R v Macfarlane; Ex parte O'Flanagan and O'Kelly* [1923] HCA 39; 32 CLR 518; *Dietrich* [1992] HCA 57; 177 CLR 292; *McKinney* [1991] HCA 6; 171 CLR 468.

81 [2018] HCA 53; 266 CLR 325.

82 Note however, that a prosecutorial obligation does not necessarily convert to a defence right directly enforceable considering the obligation. An accused's right may be limited to their entitlement to a fair trial, which can be protected by courts – if necessary by a stay order (see below) – to enable provision of whatever is needed to ensure their trial is fair. For example, see *Marwan v DPP* [2019] NSWCCA 161, [29]-[30] (Leeming JA, with RA Hulme J agreeing) with respect to prosecutors' duty of disclosure, citing also *Dietrich* [1992] HCA 57; 177 CLR 292, 299.

FEW was the anonymised name of the man arrested and tried for the murder of the toddler.[83] At 10.21am on Wednesday, 30 March 2011, FEW woke BJP with a phone call, saying '[JP] has had a stack ... come as quick as possible'. BJP (JP's mother) arrived with LB, her de facto partner, to find FEW at the front door. Inside, JP's pram was on its side. JP was lying on the lounge in what was described in the judgment as a 'severely compromised state of orientation and consciousness'. FEW thought JP had fallen from her pram. An ambulance was called at 11:31am, over an hour after the call to BJP, and JP died in hospital within two days. FEW told police that beforehand, at 9.46 am, he had taken JP to the chemist to collect some medication. JP was described as 'sad and perhaps unwell' but upright in her pram and capable of responsive movement – a presentation that was inconsistent with the fractured skull, associated intracranial bleeding, bilateral subdural haemorrhages, brain swelling and bilateral multi-layered retinal haemorrhages diagnosed at hospital. If FEW was telling the truth then JP died as a result of a tragic accident.

FEW was JP's former *de facto* grandfather (that is, he had had a relationship, no longer on foot, with JP's biological grandmother, RW). He was maintained on a methadone regime. Just under a month before JP's death, BJP had travelled to Brisbane with LB. JP was left with FEW as her sole carer. JP called FEW 'Poppy'. He would call her 'Peanut'. It was uncontested that the two of them had a reciprocating close and warm relationship and, aside from the contested facts regarding how JP died, there was no evidence that FEW had ever hurt JP. BJP's evidence was that when she returned from Brisbane JP's 'locution had improved, and her ability to form sentences had also improved. She said that she believed the child was happy, had been well fed, and generally well looked after'. In police interviews after JP had died, BJP said of FEW, 'I just can't see him doing anything like this to her. Like when I saw them playing it puts a smile on, they were so happy together'.

FEW told police that he was not in the same room (and no one was present) when JP's injuries occurred. Applying what Dawson J observed in *Shepherd*,[84] that 'it may be possible for a jury to conclude that the accused was guilty as a matter of inference beyond reasonable doubt from evidence of *opportunity*, *capacity* and *motive* without expressly identifying the intermediate fact that the accused was present when the crime was committed'. However, the challenge for the prosecution in *FEW (No 2)* was motive.

Facebook comments were overwhelmingly of the following ilk:

> There'll be judgement say here and in heaven when this murderer comes knocking on heavens door!! He's on a one way ticket to hell! RIP lil angel girl ~ heavenly hugs n kisses to you xxx ...; As for the scum bag charged (innocent until proved guilty remember) ... but how would you like to dance with a man?! This makes me sick! What has our 'developed' society turned into?! ...; r.i.p. baby girl ... good work new south wales police ...; I guess we're not allowed to have an opinion when it suggests capital punishment? My post was deleted ...; bring in capital punishment our law is 2 soft wen it come to these child bashers or let the public do to him wot he did 2 that poor little girl r.i.p ...; what a coward! ... he had to pick on a poor defensless little 2yr old! ... hope he rots! ...; This has been going for quite awhile n dont u worry there has been enough evidence to prove

83 *FEW (No 2)* [2013] NSWSC 1771 (subject to a non-publication order on the names of the victim, the victim's mother and the accused). See also *Director General Dept of Family and Community Services v FEW* [2013] NSWSC 1448; *FEW* [2013] NSWSC 1486.

84 [1990] HCA 56; 170 CLR 573 (Dawson J, with Toohey and Gaudron JJ concurring, and Mason CJ expressing general agreement) (emphasis added).

> this man done this HORRIBLE Abuse to our baby J ... just so you know the Mongrel was a 'so called' family friend n Im So Happy now her mum can put this to rest n the rest of OUR Family!!!

The only comment from the community that referred to the presumption of innocence expressed it in the following terms.

> I meen no disrespect to this child's family but what happened to inecent until proven guilty?? The police make horrible mistakes everyday and it has the potential to destroy peoples lives ... Mabey keep and open mind until they acutely have some evidence against this man. RIP little angel!
>
> Anon, *Facebook*

The trial followed two and a half years after JP's death. It took 13 days. It was necessary for the prosecution to establish that the accused intentionally caused JP's fatal injuries. The post-mortem showed that, as well as the fatal head injuries, JP had suffered so-called secondary non-fatal injuries at some time. She had extensive bruising to her forehead, bruising to the right area of her scalp, to both ears, to both buttocks and extensive bruising to her left thigh. While some secondary bruising could be explained as accidental, some quite extensive bruising lacked an innocent explanation, and it was accepted as being the result of inflicted injury. These inflicted injuries, while not the cause of JP's death, raised interesting burden of proof issues.[85]

When BJP and LB returned from Brisbane, JP continued to live with FEW. BJP and LB visited at least daily but lived with RW nearby. JP stayed with FEW while relocation arrangements were put in place – BJP's car needed repairs before it could be registered, money was tight, she needed to visit friends and plan the trip. There is no doubt that the arrangements for caring for JP and the lifestyle of those involved were unconventional and there was evidence – ultimately quite crucial evidence – that BJP had been reported to the Department of Family and Community Services at one time. Irrespective of whether judges *might* have a direct appreciation of these circumstances a jury of 12 randomly selected people from all walks of life might be seen to serve the justice process well where the factual context features an extended family at the lowest socio-economic end of society, surviving on Centrelink payments, crisis housing, methadone programs and financial struggles – features referred to in the evidence. However, in *FEW*, Fullerton J sat without a jury. New South Wales[86] permits trial by judge alone if both the prosecutor and the accused agree. As we see in the extract below, Fullerton J's reasoning to her verdict is framed by the law. It uses measured language. The full judgment details consideration of evidence, weighing testimonial and other evidence to determine whether the prosecution has proven its case to the criminal standard. The presumption of innocence is prominent. The judgment is in a form and tone that is strikingly distant from the emotion and disinhibition generated by social media.

FEW's case shows the operationalising of the presumption of innocence in a circumstantial evidence case with the following paragraphs (emphasis added) from Fullerton J's judgment explaining how and why the prosecution fell short of proving its case beyond reasonable doubt.

---

85 Taking into account the different obligations on the prosecution to prove dispensable compared to indispensable facts: *Shepherd* [1990] HCA 56; 170 CLR 573.

86 *Criminal Procedure Act 1986* (NSW), ss 132 and 132A. Without special legislation a murder trial like *FEW (No 2)* must be before a jury. See also Chapter 2.

> 297. Were I left in no doubt as to the credibility of the evidence of the child's mother and her boyfriend, and in particular, were I left in no doubt that it was the accused, and only the accused who had the opportunity to inflict the injuries on the child, thereby excluding any reasonable possibility that BJP or LB or both might have assaulted the child, and were I also able to accept their evidence that when they left at 5pm on 29 March the child was well in all observable respects, then logic would dictate that I would find that it was the accused who inflicted the secondary injuries given their frank presentation on her admission to hospital and that he was the only person who had access to her in the preceding 24 hours. Were I able to reason in that way, it would also allow me to afford preponderant weight to the Crown's submission that the secondary injuries were inflicted by the accused at some time after 5pm on 29 March and before 9.45am the following morning after he lost control, perhaps only momentarily, and repeatedly struck the child (or threw or dropped her) perhaps as a consequence of the interplay of environmental, physical and emotional stressors the Crown submitted were in play,[87] and that in a state of abject remorse he telephoned his doctor for assistance and made a telling admission in the process. …
>
> 304. Accepting as I do for the purposes of this analysis that the accused called the child's mother at 10.21am and told her that the child had harmed herself in a fall, and that it was within minutes that she arrived to find the child unconscious, if the accused deliberately inflicted the head injury there was a very narrow time frame, measured in minutes, after he left the chemist and returned home to do so. …
>
> 306. *Because the combined weight of the medical and biomechanical evidence cannot exclude the possibility that the child sustained the fatal head injury from the postulated fall from the pram, in the absence of other evidence available to the Crown to discount that as a reasonable possibility, I am compelled to the conclusion that the Crown has not disproved beyond reasonable doubt that the child's fatal injury was the result of an accident.* [emphasis added]
>
> 307. … I direct myself that it is for the Crown to prove guilt beyond reasonable doubt and in this case the Crown has failed to discharge that heavy onus. …

Reaching this conclusion required Fullerton J to evaluate witness testimony and other evidence (such as the timing of phone calls). The contrast of social media commentary expressing intuitive notions of guilt is a sobering reminder that fundamental legal principles and legal reasoning are not necessarily the public's reasoning or its perception of justice. Hence the challenge of fixing legal principles when jurors determine the verdict in criminal cases.

Right to Silence in Court

Because of the hold of the testimonial oath in the common law trial, and the religious significance of a breach of the oath,[88] it was not until the end of the 19th century[89] that the accused was able to give sworn testimony. The right to testify was optional and until the early 1990s an accused had the additional choice of making an unsworn (or dock) statement, preventing cross-examination. The abolition of dock statements means now the accused must choose between silence or giving sworn evidence (and the likelihood of cross-examination). Even

87 The prosecution asserted that FEW was 'a man under financial, physical and emotional pressure, such as to render him capable of explosive and episodic violence', but described by Ms Yehia SC, defence counsel, as 'without any evidentiary foundation and … nothing more than a strained attempt by the Crown to explain the inexplicable'.

88 It was based on the logic that the temptation to perjure him or herself and the hellish consequences of perjury meant no defendant should be placed in such jeopardy.

89 In New South Wales, *Evidence Act 1898* (NSW), s 5.

accused who remain silent are not immune from discrediting evidence where their own prior representation is admitted into evidence.[90] However, given the profile of disadvantage that is common in those before the criminal courts, it is not surprising that for many the prospect of cross-examination makes not testifying very attractive (especially for those fearful of meeting adversaries such as the Crown prosecutor in *Libke*[91]). As noted by Kirby J in *Dyers*,[92] it is concerning that the loss of the dock statement appears to have facilitated a reversion to the imbalance found in 19th century trials where the accused was not *permitted* to give sworn evidence. Nowadays, it is fear that might keep the poorly equipped (mentally, intellectually, socially and educationally) from the witness box, creating the danger, described by Kirby J, as unduly stacking the cards against the accused – referring to the potential for the accusatorial elements of the criminal trial to be lost by the 'distraction' of the accused's silence of failure to defend him or herself in a particular way – in *Dyers*, as we saw above, it was in not calling the potential witness, 'Wendy'.

An accused is entitled to maintain their right to silence in court.[93] This right is subject to the confusing influence of the 1993 High Court case of *Weissensteiner*.[94] Fortunately, the cases of *Azzopardi*[95] and *Dyers*[96] mark the dramatic decline in reliance on the *Weissensteiner* principle. The principle is expressly described as applying only in 'rare and exceptional' contexts.[97] Before 2001, case statistics show that *Weissensteiner* was more likely to be applied in State courts than be distinguished, but since then the reverse is the case. A mere handful of courts have sought to apply or follow *Weissensteiner* since 2002. In light of the more recent High Court case law repeatedly describing and protecting the fundamental principle and its companion rule, even though *Weissensteiner* has not been expressly overruled by the High Court, it seems to be only in semantics that there could be room to permit the inference suggested by the trial judge in Weissensteiner's trial.

---

90 See *UEA*, ss 108A and 108B.

91 [2007] HCA 30; 230 CLR 559, discussed in Chapter 2.

92 [2002] HCA 45; 210 CLR 285.

93 Note that *UEA*, s 89, preserves the right to silence during the investigation period by ensuring juries do not draw unfavourable inferences from a failure to answer or respond to police questions. Of course, before the trial they, as suspects or under charge, may have had to submit to fingerprinting, DNA testing and other non-testimonial processes but (subject to the impact of *UEA*, s 89A, in New South Wales) there remains no *compulsion* to speak to police.

94 [1993] HCA 65; 178 CLR 217. This case has been a confusing influence on understanding the accused's lack of obligations in an accusatorial framework. It permitted a judge to indicate to a jury where an accused had not given 'evidence from the accused to add to, or explain, or to vary, or contradict the evidence put before [the court] ... by the prosecution' and there were matters within the accused person's 'peculiar knowledge' that '[t]he consequence of that failure is ... this is a case in which the truth is not easily, you might think, ascertainable by the prosecution. *It asks you to infer guilt from a whole collection of circumstances. It asks you to draw inferences from such facts as it is able to prove. Such an inference may be more safely drawn from the proven facts when an accused person elects not to give evidence of relevant facts which it can easily be perceived must be within his knowledge.* You might, for example, think in this case it requires no great perception *that the accused would have direct knowledge of events which can be canvassed only obliquely from the point of view of seeking to have you draw an inference from the evidence which has been led by the Crown. The use that you make of the fact that there is no evidence given or called by the defendant in these proceedings is that*' (emphasis added).

95 [2001] HCA 25; 205 CLR 50.

96 [2002] HCA 45; 210 CLR 285.

97 *GBF* [2020] HCA 40.

Failure to testify and impermissible comment

Section 17 of the *UEA* provides that an accused is not even *competent* to testify as a witness for the prosecution. Nor can an 'associate defendant' (essentially a defendant charged in connection with facts giving rise to the offences charged, but not yet finalised)[98] be compelled to testify for or against a defendant, unless tried separately. As the majority of the High Court noted in *Kirk v Industrial Court (NSW)*[99] any breach of s 17 – in *Kirk*, by requiring a defendant to testify for the prosecution – is a substantial departure from the rules of evidence. Heydon J developed the analysis of the majority. His Honour observed that the error that occurred in the prosecutor calling Mr Kirk as its own witness was an error by oversight, not intent. Nevertheless, a jurisdictional error occurred.

As well as noting the importance of s 17 to the maintenance and extension of the traditional accusatorial protections enjoyed by the accused, there is the companion provision, s 20, which seeks to prevent comment that suggests the accused's failure to testify was because the accused was guilty, or believed that they were.

All UEA jurisdictions, excepting Victoria

Section 20 of the *UEA* limits the comments that can be made during the trial with respect to an accused who exercises their right to silence. It broadly reflects pre-existing common law principles, except that it expressly applies only to indictable offences. In its terms, the section distinguishes between three quite different perspectives – comments on an accused's silence by a *co-accused*, a *judge* and a *prosecutor*:

- the co-accused has no fetters on their comments about another accused's silence in court;
- the judge can comment on an accused's failure to give evidence, but cannot suggest that such failure implies guilt, or belief of guilt, on the accused's part (*UEA*, s 20(2)); and
- the prosecutor cannot comment at all on an accused's silence.

Parallel provision is made with respect to comment regarding the lack of testimony from a near relative (spouse, de facto partner, parent or child) of the accused: *UEA*, s 20(3). As noted with respect to *UEA*, s 18,[100] the limitation on near relatives is disappointingly unsympathetic to Aboriginal and Torres Strait Islander (ATSI) family relationships where very close familial relationships to the accused may not be necessarily limited to a partner, parent or child. Very often an aunt, uncle and/or grandparents will be the people with whom the ATSI accused has close family ties.

Wherever there is a stark contrast between on accused testifying, and a co-accused remaining silent, a so-called *Azzopardi* direction[101] will invariably be required, more so where a cut-throat defence is employed:

---

98 See *UEA* Dictionary (or *Evidence Act 2001* (Tas), s 3).

99 [2010] HCA 1; 239 CLR 531, [53] (French CJ, Gummow, Hayne, Crennan, Kiefel and Bell JJ).

100 See Chapter 5.

101 That is, that silence: is not evidence against the accused, does not constitute an admission by the accused, may not be used to fill gaps in the evidence tendered by the prosecution, and may not be used as a make-weight in assessing whether the prosecution has proved its case beyond reasonable doubt, see *Martinez and Tortell* [2019] NSWCCA 153, [114]-[118] and *UEA*, s 20(5). See below for *JDA 2015* (Vic).

> 54. … That a co-accused may [wish to suggest silence is suggestive of guilt] … is hardly surprising. If only one of two accused persons gives evidence at their joint trial, it is inevitable that the accused who has given evidence will want to urge the jury to contrast that with the course taken by the other accused. It is well-nigh inevitable that in urging that the evidence given by the accused demonstrates innocence, the suggestion will be made, explicitly or implicitly, that the co-accused stayed silent because, unlike the accused who did give evidence, he or she was guilty.[102]

Victoria

Victoria has abolished the *Azzopardi* and *Weissensteiner* directions[103] and repealed *UEA*, s 20. The *Jury Directions Act 2015* (Vic) (*JDA 2015* (Vic)), ss 41 and 42, has replaced this caselaw. Under this Act the requirements expressed in *Azzopardi* are for counsel's own forensic determination, that is, it is for counsel to request directions from the judge.

> The request process imposes a greater obligation on all lawyers involved in a criminal proceeding to give thought to the content of the judge's charge and to indicate what directions are necessary and what matters are in issue. The Act emphasises that the parties must take a proactive role in shaping the judge's charge, rather than a reactive role of merely taking exceptions to a charge which has been given. This is consistent with recent judicial practice, and gives the parties a greater opportunity to influence the content of the judge's charge and focus the attention of the jury on the matters in issue. The Act should be seen as evolutionary of existing practices …[104]

JDA 2015 (Vic), s 41, summarises the essence of the *Azzopardi* direction by providing that if the accused does not give evidence (or call a witness) and a request is made:

> 41.[105] (2) … the trial judge must explain –
> (a) the prosecution's obligation to prove that the accused is guilty; and
> (b) that the accused is not required to give evidence or call a witness (as the case requires); and
> (c) that the jury should not guess or speculate about what might have been contained in –
> (i) the evidence that was not given by the accused; or
> (ii) the evidence that might have been given by a witness who was not called –
> as the case requires; and
> (d) that the fact that the accused did not give evidence or call a witness (as the case requires) –
> (i) is not evidence against the accused; and
> (ii) is not an admission by the accused; and
> (iii) must not be used to fill gaps in the evidence adduced by the prosecution; and
> (iv) does not strengthen the prosecution case.

102 *Azzopardi* [2001] HCA 25; 205 CLR 50 (Gaudron, Gummow, Kirby and Hayne JJ).

103 *JDA 2015* (Vic), s 44.

104 M Weatherson, 'New Jury Directions Act' (2014) 1 *Judicial College of Victoria Online Journal* 34, 44-5.

105 The note to s 41 states: 'Note: Section 14 requires the trial judge to give this direction, if requested, unless there are good reasons for not doing so. Section 16 requires the trial judge to give a direction if the trial judge considers that there are substantial and compelling reasons for doing so'.

Section 42 prevents the trial judge, the prosecution and defence counsel (or, if the accused is unrepresented, the accused) saying or suggesting in any way (even from a co-accused) that because an accused did not give evidence (or call a particular witness) the jury may:

(a) conclude that the accused is guilty from that fact; or
(b) use the failure of the accused to provide an explanation of facts, which must be within the knowledge of the accused, to more safely draw an adverse inference based on those facts which, if drawn, would prove the guilt of the accused; or
(c) draw an inference that the accused did not give evidence or call a witness (as the case requires) because that would not have assisted their case.

Section 7 of this 2015 Act provides for a correction where such a comment is made. Unlike *UEA*, s 20, this statutory modification does not prohibit comment with respect to the accused's family members, nor does it specifically separate the co-accused's rights to comment. This legislation is part of larger law reform where Victoria has taken the lead in Australia in exploring the simplification of common law judicial directions such as those linked to the right to silence. This Act seeks to 'raise the bar' on the common law requirements for judicial directions by placing greater responsibility on counsel to seek from the trial judge directions to be given to the jury. According to the Act's guiding principles (s 5) directions to the jury should:

- reflect only so much of the law as the jury needs to know to determine the issues in the trial; and
- avoid using technical legal language wherever possible; and
- be as clear, brief, simple and comprehensible as possible.

To some extent this aspiration matches the approach in *UEA*, s 165(2), with respect to evidence of a kind that may be unreliable.[106] This attempt to create a cultural shift to party responsibility for initiating direction requests is still backed up by the formal obligation of the trial judge to determine directions to the jury[107] and 'a residual obligation ... to give any direction necessary to avoid a substantial miscarriage of justice even if it is not sought or a party has indicated that the matter is not in issue'.[108]

The accused's post-offence conduct – flight, threats and lies

> Lies, or suggested lies, are no strangers to criminal trials. The very nature of such proceedings makes it common, particularly where the accused gives evidence, that claims and counterclaims about lies will arise for the jury's consideration. This has long been so.[109]

A lie told by an accused either to bystanders, to police, to family, or even while testifying can be used as an inference of guilt,[110] directly supporting a guilty verdict (and not just limited to a matter relevant to the accused person's credibility), but only when it fits the following requirements.

106 Notably, under *JDA 2015* (Vic) there is also substantial change to *UEA*, s 165. See Chapter 14.

107 *JDA 2015* (Vic), s 5(2)(b); for the unrepresented accused, see s 13 for trial judges' obligations.

108 Weatherson, above n 104, 41. This obligation 'is intended to be confined to rare cases, such as where the failure to request a direction raises a concern about the competence of counsel' (ibid 43), citing the second reading speech, the explanatory memorandum and the report from the Department of Justice.

109 *Zoneff* [2000] HCA 28; 200 CLR 234, [29] (citations omitted). Kirby J was in dissent that the judge had erred. He considered infelicities had occurred, but not errors.

110 Perhaps more accurately, self-belief of guilt: see, eg, *SW* [2013] NSWCCA 103.

> A lie can constitute an admission against interest only if it is concerned with some circumstance or event connected with the offence (ie it relates to a material issue) and if it was told by the accused in circumstances in which the explanation for the lie is that he knew that the truth would implicate him in the offence. Thus, in any case where a lie is relied upon to prove guilt, the lie should be precisely identified, as should the circumstances and events that are said to indicate that it constitutes an admission against interest. And the jury should be instructed that they may take the lie into account only if they are satisfied, having regard to those circumstances and events, that it reveals a knowledge of the offence or some aspect of it and that it was told because the accused knew that the truth of the matter about which he lied would implicate him in the offence, or, as was said in *Lucas* (*Ruth*), because of 'a realization of guilt and a fear of the truth'.[111]

However, '[a] lie may be told out of panic, to escape an unjust accusation, to protect some other person or to avoid a consequence extraneous to the offence'.[112] Where a jury considers one of these 'innocent' explanations applies, or that the accused's departure from the truth was the result of confusion, poor memory, or just a misunderstanding (and so not deliberate), the 'lie' cannot be regarded at law as arising from a consciousness of guilt. Case law encourages a cautious approach to using an accused's lie as evidence of their consciousness of guilt. The majority in *Zoneff*[113] established that there should be a direction to the jury in these terms:

> You have heard a lot of questions, which attribute lies to the accused. You will make up your own mind about whether he was telling lies and if he was, whether he was doing so deliberately. It is for you to decide what significance those suggested lies have in relation to the issues in the case but I give you this warning: *do not follow a process of reasoning to the effect that just because a person is shown to have told a lie about something, that is evidence of guilt.*

In addition, the above 'innocent' explanations for a misstatement by the accused should be clearly described to the jury both whenever the prosecution seeks to rely on an accused person's lie as exhibiting consciousness of guilt' and whenever there is a risk that a jury may treat what the accused as said as a deliberate lie relating to a material issue.[114] An example which illustrates the potentially mixed motivations an accused has to lie arose in *Lane*[115] where the accused was on trial for the murder of her baby, Tegan, whose whereabouts were unknown. The accused lied on various occasions when seeking to explain the absence of the baby whom she had secretly given birth to in 1996. She had also given birth, also secretly, to two babies in 1995 and 1999. In settling the arrangements for the adoption of the last-born baby, adoption agency personnel became aware of the 1996 birth, that is, Tegan. After denying this birth on a number of occasions to agency personnel Lane stated by fax:

> There were 3 children obviously I can't lie anymore as the paperwork is there. The middle child lives with a family in Perth although I have not had contact with them for a long time. They befriended me just before I had her and supported us. I am not able to give you many details as I am not sure of them myself. If my story isn't unusual enough as it already is! I know you probably can't believe it but I know that somehow that you know I am now being honest with you.[116]

111 *Edwards* [1993] HCA 63; 178 CLR 193, [14] (Deane, Dawson and Gaudron JJ).
112 Ibid [15] (Deane, Dawson and Gaudron JJ).
113 [2000] HCA 28; 200 CLR 234, [23] (emphasis added).
114 Ibid [16]. See, eg, *Abdirahman-Khalif* [2020] HCA 36, [72].
115 [2011] NSWCCA 157.
116 Ibid [27].

The relevant lies in issue were the various accounts given by Lane concerning the various adoption arrangements regarding Tegan (that is, that Andrew Norris, Andrew Morris or the Perth couple adopted the baby).[117] The Court of Criminal Appeal accepted that there may be an innocent explanation for Lane's statements, even if they were lies. For example, with the 'Perth couple lie', it may be that Lane was seeking to discourage any delay in the adoption of her newborn third child. The court concluded that there was evidence to enable the jury to conclude beyond reasonable doubt that these lies were potentially evidence of consciousness of guilt.[118] Thus, the *Zoneff* direction should be given by the trial judge. Whilst an accused's silence is not a basis for incrimination of an accused, and a lie must meet the *Edwards* test, what about if an accused flees the scene of the crime (or the jurisdiction), if they threaten[119] a witness, or attempt to conceal potentially inculpatory evidence?

Essentially, the same legal principles apply, requiring a judicial direction that cautions the jury in finding a consciousness of guilt: namely that '[t]he flight (or lie) may only be used as evidence of a consciousness of guilt of the offence charged where the jury is satisfied that it points unequivocally to consciousness of guilt of that offence and not some other offence or discreditable conduct'.[120] This means that a judge should direct the jury to appreciate that this conduct might be motivated by panic, to protect someone else, or from fear of unjust accusation, or of a shameful revelation (but not the crime charged). In *Baden-Clay*[121] the prosecution claimed Baden-Clay murdered his wife in a domestic violence scenario. The jury returned a guilty verdict. The Court of Appeal upheld Baden-Clay's appeal that there was insufficient evidence of intent and substituted a verdict of manslaughter. On appeal to the High Court, evidence of Baden-Clay's post-offence concealment and lies played a significant role in the court returning the verdict to murder. Baden-Clay had falsely denied his ongoing affair, had checked with his girlfriend as to whether she had revealed their affair to police, and warned her to 'lie low'. According to the High Court, these acts

> were all capable of being regarded by the jury as evidencing a strong anxiety to conceal from police the existence and true nature of his affair … . This anxiety could reasonably be seen as indicative that, in his mind, the affair and the killing were inter-related, and that the killing was not an unintended, tragic death of his wife, but an intentional killing.

The court pointed out that there

> may be cases where an accused goes to such lengths to conceal the death or to distance himself or herself from it as to provide a basis on which the jury might conclude that the

117 'The Perth couple lie': was stated in the fax, but during ERISP interviews Lane 'prevaricated in relation to that explanation'; the 'Andrew Morris lie': Lane in her first ERISP interviews in 2001 said she gave Tegan to her natural father, Andrew Morris; the 'Andrew Norris lie': in later ERISPs in 2002, Lane maintained that she handed Tegan to Andrew Norris, who was her natural father.

118 There was no issue regarding the admissibility of the evidence of lies. The issue related to whether there should be a limitation on the use that might be made of them: *UEA*, s 136: *Lane* [2011] NSWCCA 157, [76] (Simpson J).

119 *Martinez and Tortell* [2019] NSWCCA 153, alleging that Martinez told the eyewitness to '[m]ake sure you keep your mouth shut, I'm watching'. The same principle may apply to offering a false name, silence include *McKey* [2012] NSWCCA 1; 219 A Crim R 227, [26] (Latham J, with Whealey JA and Hislop J agreeing) (cited in *Martinez and Tortell*).

120 *Cook* [2004] NSWCCA 52, [50] (Simpson J).

121 [2016] HCA 35; 258 CLR 308, [74] (French CJ, Kiefel, Bell, Keane and Gordon JJ). For an excellent discussion of the case, see <https://sociallitigator.com /2016/09/02/ high-courts-take-down-of-court-of-appeal-inbaden-clay-too-much-or-just-right/>.

> accused had committed an extremely serious crime and so warrant a conclusion beyond reasonable doubt as to the responsibility of the accused for the death and the concurrent existence in the accused of the intent necessary for murder ... [leading to the conclusion that it] was open to the jury ... to regard the lengths to which the respondent went to conceal his wife's body and to conceal his part in her demise as beyond what was likely, as a matter of human experience, to have been engendered by a consciousness of having unintentionally killed his wife.[122]

Victoria

Part 4, Div 1 (ss 18-24) of the *JDA 2015* (Vic) governs the situation where a prosecution seeks to rely on the accused's incriminating conduct (such as lies). First, the prosecution must give notice of its intentions pre-trial: s 19. In addition, the trial judge must determine that, 'on the basis of the evidence as a whole, the evidence of conduct is reasonably capable of being viewed by the jury as evidence of incriminating conduct' and, if so, provide mandatory directions to the jury based on, but with some modification, the common law direction: ss 20, 21. This Act provides for the defence to request that the judge explain to the jury that 'there are all sorts of reasons why a person might behave in a way that makes the person look guilty' and 'the accused may have engaged in the conduct even though the accused is not guilty of the offence charged' and 'even if the jury thinks that the conduct makes the accused look guilty, that does not necessarily mean that the accused is guilty': s 22 (and see also s 23). The Act abolishes the common law requirements expressed in *Edwards* and *Zoneff*, and the application of *Shepherd*[123] to post-offence conduct.[124]

Conclusion

This chapter has surveyed the philosophical fundamentals shaping the Australian criminal trial. While the criminal trial is structured in an adversarial contest, its 'accusatorial' dimensions defining rights and obligations are inserted into the processes of witness questioning, adducing evidence and lawyers' speeches. Adversarialism and accusatorialism often operate in tension. We saw examples of this in in cases such as *Strickland*, *Azzopardi* and *Dyers* where adversarial combat was moderated to ensure breathing space for accusatorial rights.

In the next chapter our focus shifts first to pre-trial processes, pleadings and the legal and ethical obligations of counsel, particularly those of the prosecutor. The moderation of prosecutorial and police excesses in Kamisar's gatehouse of justice tends to be by regulation, ethical obligations and indirect court control – that is, by soft management. Cases such as *Mallard*,[125] *Wood*,[126] *Libke*[127] and *Kirk*,[128] and the shocking deceptions by Victoria Police and Lawyer X (discussed above), illustrate the frailties of such regulation where an adversarial process

---

122 [2016] HCA 35; 258 CLR 308, [74], [76] (French CJ, Kiefel, Bell, Keane and Gordon JJ).

123 [1990] HCA 56; 170 CLR 573.

124 For the removal of common law obligations, see *JDA 2015* (Vic), s 24 (and accompanying notes regarding the repeal of these common law rules by the *Jury Directions Act 2013* (Vic)).

125 *Mallard* [2005] HCA 68; 224 CLR 125, and see Chapters 2 and 7.

126 *Wood* [2012] NSWCCA 21; 84 NSWLR 581, and see Chapter 2.

127 *Libke* [2007] HCA 30; 230 CLR 559, and see Chapter 2.

128 *Kirk v Industrial Court (NSW)* [2010] HCA 1; 239 CLR 531, and see Chapter 2.

has embedded asymmetrical rights, powers and resources. In particular, they show the challenge of managing an unequal contest where, despite accusatorial values, the might of the state can still distort the contest. The remainder of the next chapter examines a number of topics linking proof, persuasion and jury decision-making. It concludes with a trial judge's verdict in a judge-alone trial, *Mumbulla*.[129] This reasoning to a final verdict is presented for the reader to witness the application of the principles of adversarialism, accusatorialism and the presumption of innocence carefully articulated in the context of evidence presented at trial.

First, however, the next chapter begins with the pre-trial period, revealing the pressures of modernity at play, with court resources under the pump and law reform initiatives amplifying the practice of parties negotiating outcomes, combined with a trend towards symmetrical disclosure.

129 [2020] NSWDC 207.

Chapter 2

Prosecutors, Pleadings and Proof

Ours for the most part is a system of pleas, not a system of trials

Kennedy J in *Lafler v Cooper*
132 S Ct 1376, 1388 (2012)

Introduction

This chapter examines some of the complexities associated with the prosecution charge document for indictable offences, the indictment as well as associated issues. It begins by examining plea negotiation – a process that assumes charges have been laid. This topic is placed first because of its function in by-passing the whole trial process. Then we examine some of the issues associated with drafting prosecution charges. While these are often relevant to plea negotiation, they are examined in the context of this book's focus – the trial. Central to this pre-trial phase are the ethical obligations placed on prosecutors and parties' obligations of disclosure. However, while this chapter is about trial preparation, it also exhibits the tension that is ripe in practice, namely, the finalisation of criminal accusations by way of a guilty plea.

Plea Negotiations

To the extent that Kennedy J's 'system of pleas' characterisation is correct, his observation provokes the question of whether Yale Kamisar[1] might have included prosecution offices with police stations in his category of 'gatehouses'. This is not necessarily because of a history of prosecutors being notoriously destructive of defence rights but because whatever takes place in prosecutors' offices, including any plea negotiations, is less transparent than the trial, and is less likely to be structured with protections for an accused's legal rights. Kamisar in fact acknowledged in 2015 – 50 years after his famous 'mansion' and 'gatehouse' metaphors – that with 'criminal trials ... on the verge of extinction' the fixing of flaws outside the police 'gatehouse' may be more urgent than policing reforms because, as he explained:

1 See Chapter 1.

> We cannot continue to move in this direction. We must execute a turnaround. To quote Professor Pizzi, "we need to ask some very hard questions about charging, about plea bargaining, and about our trial system and the avoidance of that system".[2]

Both Kamisar and Kennedy J in *Lafler v Cooper* are describing the US environment where plea bargaining is controversially dominant because of prosecutors' coercive plea practices.[3] This is an interesting backdrop for considering contemporary steps taken in Australia (and also in England and Wales) to address the cost and delay of criminal trials. Prosecutors' charging a multiplicity of offences may enhance wriggle room in plea negotiations, but too many charges can encourage the defence to delay, hoping the prosecution will reduce charges close to the trial. If the number of charges is not reduced, the trial on multiple counts that follows can be unwieldy and unduly complex.

While a plea of guilty[4] achieves reduced court congestion and delay, care is required to ensure incentives to plead do not inadvertently create perverse incentives that marginalise fair process principles and remove mechanisms directed to creating equality of arms. Even *if* the parties are equally resourced and informed, studies show that people accused of crimes may confess or plead guilty despite being innocent.[5] They may be tempted to plead guilty to avoid charges becoming broadly known (and so to avoid embarrassment, stress or loss of employment). Some may perceive the guilty plea as a lesser evil than defending charges because defending charges will be costly or because they believe that the system is pitched against them.[6] A change of the accused's legal representation can produce late consideration to pleading guilty, especially where an accused holds out a hope that the prosecution case will be weak (for example, a key prosecution witness

---

2 Y Kamisar, 'A Look Bar at the "Gatehouses and Mansions" of American Criminal Procedure' (2015) 12 *Ohio State Journal of Criminal Law* 645, 658, quoting W Pizzi, 'Revisiting the Mansions and Gatehouses of Criminal Procedure: Reflections on Yale Kamisar's Famous Essay' (2015) 12 *Ohio State Journal of Criminal Law* 633, 643.

3 See, eg, NL Reimer and MA Sabelli, 'The Tyranny of the Trial Penalty: The Consensus that Coercive Plea Practices Must End' (2019) 31 *Federal Sentencing Reporter* 215.

4 Note that a plea of guilty must be entered 'in open court by a person who is of full age and apparently of sound mind and understanding, provided the plea is entered in exercise of a free choice in the interests of the person entering the plea. There is no miscarriage of justice if a court does act on such a plea, even if the person entering it is not in truth guilty of the offence': *Meissner* [1995] HCA 41; 184 CLR 132, 141-2 (Brennan, Toohey and McHugh JJ).

5 On the ethical obligations associated with these so-called 'convenience pleas', see *Legal Profession Uniform Conduct (Barristers) Rules 2015*, r 41, requiring a barrister who is informed that the client denies committing the offence, but insists on pleading guilty to it, the barrister has obligations to explain the consequences, as detailed in the Rule; *Allison* [2003] QCA 125; 138 A Crim R 378, 384 under the heading: 'I am not guilty but I'll plead guilty' – referred to by Howie J in *Wong v DPP (NSW)* [2005] NSWSC 129; 155 A Crim R 37, [38]. See also B Bickford, 'Convenience Pleas', <https://www.hunterstreetchambers.com.au/wp-content/uploads/2014/01/Convenience-Pleas.pdf>. Also see the Innocence Project accounts: <https://www.innocenceproject.org/false-confessions-recording-interrogations/>. An extreme example is David Hicks's plea of guilty to enable him to leave Guantanamo Bay, see <http://www.smh.com.au/national/david-hicks-terrorism-charges-us-admits-he-is-innocent-20150122-12vzke.html>. If an accused pleads guilty and then wishes to change their plea afterwards, courts will permit a change to a not guilty plea but only where it is shown that the guilty plea arose because the actual plea lacks integrity. Classically, the 'plea of guilty must however be unequivocal and not made in circumstances suggesting that it is not a true admission of guilt' (that is, not a 'guilty, but ...' plea). See *Kanakaradnam* [2018] NSWCCA 282.

6 Either because of the perceived or actual power imbalance in relation to the prosecution; mandatory sentencing discounting encouraging pleading guilty for a lesser sentence, and the impact of standard non-parole periods in New South Wales (see <https://www.judcom.nsw.gov.au/publications/benchbks/sentencing/appendix_a.html>).

refuses to testify). Some accused may wish to postpone the inevitable as long as possible – or they may in fact be not guilty as charged. Or they may wish to rely on the state proving its case beyond reasonable doubt. Not all offences have the same dynamics. In New South Wales, a 2014 study[7] found that those facing domestic violence and child sexual assault offences tended to plead not guilty and, where they pleaded guilty, they did so later than those facing other types of charges.

In a Victorian 2018 study, the Negotiating Guilty Pleas Project, Flynn and Freiberg examined 50 Victoria Legal Aid (VLA) files from 2012-14 that had been finalised by a guilty plea and interviewed solicitors from the Office of Director of Public Prosecutions (ODPP), Crown prosecutors, defence practitioners (legal aid and private practice) and judicial officers. They observed that plea negotiation is 'part of everyday legal life in a semi-adversarial criminal justice system', that the majority (81%) of guilty pleas were entered before the committal hearing and, while between 87-100% of guilty pleas across all court levels were by negotiated agreement, interviewees suggested an even higher base line:

> 'Every case is negotiated.' (Judge02MR)
>
> 'I don't think there's a file that you wouldn't negotiate on.' (Defence02F)
>
> 'There's always room for a discussion in any case.' (Defence15M)
>
> 'Every case.' (Defence18M) 'Occurs in every single case—9.5 out of 10.' (Defence11M)
>
> 'I can't think of any situation where you can't really engage in negotiations.' (Defence12FR).[8]

Of the negotiation process Flynn and Freiberg found that it was typically quite extensive, often with multiple interactions (face to face, or by phone, letter or most commonly, by email), and that the defence initiated over 90% of negotiations. The files showed that, where defence submissions were not accepted initially, the prosecution generally responded in a reasoned response manner, and most commonly the Victorian ODPP proposed a counter-offer. As a striking hallmark of the unsystematic nature of the process, Flynn and Freiberg's study identified the personality of the opposing party as a significant consideration in the process, sitting with the strength of the evidence and (for prosecutors) the public interest and (for defence practitioners) their clients' interests. The authors identified that, typically, active negotiations took place early. They suggest this arises from ODPP and Victoria Police soft management mechanisms encouraging guilty pleas to lesser charges which in turn has promoted a strong early resolution culture in courts and the VLA as well. While this infers a breaking down of the battle-hardened culture of adversarialism, it also raises the question of the extent to which an accused's guilty plea arising from agreed facts reducing culpability, despite inconsistency with the victim's account, means that the victim's voice is closed out of these processes – that is, for expedience sake, her role is ignored in the attainment of justice.[9]

7 C Ringland and L Snowball, 'Predictors of Guilty Pleas in the NSW District Court' *Crime and Justice Statistics* (Issues Paper 96, BOCSAR, 2014), 8, analysing 9094 matters (3078 of which were finalised in 2011, 2848 in 2012 and 3168 in 2013).

8 A Flynn and A Freiberg, 'Plea Negotiations: An empirical analysis', *Trends and Issues in Crime and Criminal Justice* (No 544, AIC, 2018).

9 See, eg, the Coomber negotiation, described in A Flynn and A Freiberg, *Plea Negotiations: Pragmatic Justice in an Imperfect World* (Palgrave Socio-Legal Studies, 2018) and see also <https://www.theage.com.au/national/victoria/let-s-make-a-deal-20180830-p500oz.html>.

In most Australian States, plea negotiations between defendants and police or defendants and prosecutors[10] typically include a legislated sentencing reduction in return for a guilty plea. Twenty-five per cent is a not-uncommon discount for an early plea of guilty,[11] reflecting the fact that maximum resource savings are achieved where a guilty plea is made early, that is, before a case is listed for trial, before the jury is empanelled, before a judge is allocated and before lawyers have fully prepared for trial. However, no guilty plea can be expected until the prosecution has fulfilled its obligations to disclose its case and, whatever takes place during plea negotiations, one thing is clear – the process lacks the trial's transparency and its checks and balances. Instead, a series of invisible dynamics are at play.

New South Wales, like England and Wales, has pressed ahead with initiatives strongly focused on efficiency and delay reduction.[12] The New South Wales Early Appropriate Guilty Plea (EAGP) system replaces the old committal proceedings for indictable offences. These Local Court proceedings are significant. The EAGP system timetables disclosure and compulsory conferencing between parties,

> with a new procedure overseen by a Magistrate that requires the prosecutor to disclose a brief of evidence to the accused person and to certify the charges to be proceeded with. The new committal proceedings ... also provide for a formal conferencing procedure to enable opportunities for appropriate early guilty pleas to be considered during committal proceedings [and] ... to provide for specified sentencing discounts for the utilitarian value of guilty pleas to indictable offences.[13]

The EAGP process sets a sliding scale of mandatory sentence discounting that is on a sliding scale reducing as the time before trial shortens. This EAGP system was instituted after a Rolling List Court (RLC) study[14] evaluated by BOCSAR. The

---

10 On negotiated pleas (or charges, depending on one's perspective), see generally CDPP, *Charge Negotiation* (February 2014), <https://www.cdpp.gov.au/publications/charge-negotiation-gd-manual>.

11 See, eg, *Sentencing Act 1995* (WA), s 9AA; *Matthews* [2015] NSWSC 49; *Amital* [2015] NTCCA 1. The New Zealand Supreme Court in *Hessell* [2010] NZSC 135, [47] set the value of the expedience to the justice system of a guilty plea at a maximum of 25% sentence reduction which is identical to the South Australian discount: D Field, 'Plead Guilty Early and Convincingly to Avoid Disappointment' (2002) 14 *Bond Law Review* 250, 255. See also Sentencing Advisory Council (Tasmania), *Statutory Sentencing Reductions for Pleas of Guilty* (Final Report, No 10, October 2018).

12 Compare the approach in the *Leveson* Inquiry where its focus was on finding soft management mechanisms assisted by improvements in utilising IT (email, video-links etc) that streamline the disposal of criminal cases and consequently reduce costs across the board. Rather than pressuring the tensions between efficiency and the accused's rights, the Inquiry established, as its first over-arching principle, 'Getting it Right First Time': B Leveson (President, Queen's Bench Division), *Review of Efficiency in Criminal Proceedings* (Judiciary of England and Wales, January 2015) (Leveson Report). See particularly [21]-[39], [47].

13 *Justice Legislation Amendment (Committals and Guilty Pleas) Bill 2017* (NSW), Explanatory Note. See *Criminal Procedure Act 1986* (NSW) (*CPA* (NSW)), ss 55-81, and *Crimes (Sentencing Procedure) Act 1999* (NSW), s 25D (providing sentencing discounts from 5%-25%, depending on timing of guilty plea). See also *Cameron* (2002) 209 CLR 339, 362 (Kirby J): 'If the prisoner and the prisoner's legal advisers do not know the measure of the discount, it cannot be expected that pleas of guilty will be encouraged in proper cases'. For a flowchart of the process, see <https://psa.asn.au/wp-content/uploads/2018/04/Attach.-5-Lifecycle-of-an-EAGP-Matter.pdf>.

14 S Rahman, S Poynton and D Weatherburn, 'The NSW Rolling List Court Evaluation: Final Report', *Crime and Justice Bulletin* (No 208, BOCSAR, 2017). For other efficiency reforms, see H Thorburn and D Weatherburn, 'An evaluation of measures taken to increase finalisations in the NSW District Criminal Court', *Crime and Justice Bulletin* (No 217, BOCSAR, 2018). See pp 7-8 for the different forms of negotiation. The most common forms were withdrawing and substituting charges, rolled up and representative counts, fact bargaining, and agreement on facts regarding sentencing submissions.

study's findings support early briefing of practitioners and pre-trial negotiations creating a 20% increase in cases resolved by a guilty plea before the trial date. The BOCSAR report observed:

> *The mechanism identified by most interviewees was that guilty pleas were obtained earlier because counsel and clients could negotiate and make decisions before the trial with the certainty that nothing would change closer to the trial date.* Defence practitioners said that this was aided by having certainty of which judge would preside over sentencing. *Practicing lawyers on both sides found the build-up of trust within teams* important for bringing about disclosure and the subsequent resolution of matters.[15] (emphasis added)

It is unlikely the EAGP system can replicate the RLC conditions (of selected cases, fixed teams of legal aid and ODPP lawyers, and a single judge). This study, like the Flynn and Freiberg study, did not seek to evaluate the 'appropriateness' of the pleas obtained in the RLC.

Prosecutors, Prosecutors' Pleadings and Fairness Obligations

In Australia, the Offices of the Director of Public Prosecutions (ODPP) institute prosecutions for indictable offences on behalf of the Crown.[16] It is for the prosecution, in its sole discretion, to shape its charges and, as a result, to influence what may follow on.[17] Today's prosecutorial 'minister of justice' has a number of obligations. They must adhere to obligations of fairness before they reach the bar table as well as in court. A 'prosecution should not be instituted or continued unless there is admissible, substantial and reliable evidence that a criminal offence known to the law has been committed by the alleged offender'. The decision whether or not to proceed with charges requires consideration of 'the interests of the victim, the suspected offender and the community at large ... fairness and consistency ... are of particular importance'.[18] A 'prosecution should not be instituted or continued unless there is admissible, substantial and reliable evidence that a criminal offence known to the law has been committed by the alleged offender'.[19] The prosecutor's application of 'the public interest' considerations is governed by the criteria articulated in the *Prosecution Policy of the Commonwealth, Guidelines for the Making of Decisions in the Prosecution Process*.[20] Too much intervention and a judge may appear aligned in some way with the prosecution camp, but too little control where a prosecutor misjudges or engages in misconduct (however that might be defined) and courts risk giving tacit judicial approval to either the conduct or the subsequent consequences. The breadth of prosecutorial discretion is not doubted,[21] but the scope of judicial review is much more complex. Courts

15 Rahman, Poynton and Weatherburn, above n 14, 13.

16 See also *Director of Public Prosecutions Act 1983* (Cth), ss 6(1)(d), 9(5)(b).

17 *Magaming* [2013] HCA 40; 302 ALR 461.

18 24 February 2021, [2.2]-[2.3] (*CDPP Policy*). See <https://www.cdpp.gov.au/sites/default/files/CDPPProsecutionPolicy_0.pdf.>. These include the seriousness (or not) of the offence (including whether it relates to an obsolete, or obscure law), mitigating or aggravating circumstances, whether the alleged offender has special vulnerabilities, their antecedents, the circumstances of the alleged offence, the degree of alleged culpability, the attitude of the victim, the harm caused, degree of cooperation in relation to other prosecutions, and alternatives to prosecution.

19 Ibid [2.4]. The *NSW Prosecution Guidelines*, 29 March 2021, [1.1]-[1.4] list specific criteria linked to prospects of conviction and public interest. Paragraph [1.8] provides guidance regarding retrial determinations.

20 *CDPP Policy*, [2.10].

21 *Maxwell* [1996] HCA 46; 184 CLR 501; *Likiardopoulos* [2012] HCA 37; 247 CLR 265.

cannot afford to compromise their independence and impartiality by dipping into the business of deciding how a prosecution frames its case, or what evidence it tenders.[22] Considerations relevant to the general unavailability of judicial review include:

> the importance of maintaining the reality and perception of the impartiality of the judicial process. A related consideration is the importance of maintaining the separation of the executive power in relation to prosecutorial decisions and the judicial power to hear and determine criminal proceedings. A further consideration is the width of prosecutorial discretions generally and, related to that width, the variety of factors which may legitimately inform the exercise of those discretions. Those factors include policy and public interest considerations which are not susceptible to judicial review, as it is neither within the constitutional function nor the practical competence of the courts to assess their merits. Moreover, ... trial judges have available to them sanctions to enforce well-established standards of prosecutorial fairness and to prevent abuses of process.[23]

In *Likiardopoulos* the prosecutor alone was acknowledged as the one to determine prosecution decisions such as whether:

- to prosecute;
- the charge includes aggravated elements, or is just the offence *simpliciter*;[24]
- to withdraw charges;[25]
- to proceed irrespective (or without) a committal hearing (by entering a no bill or *nolle prosequi*);
- to accept a plea of guilty to a lesser offence, or to have a change of the prosecutorial mind and withdraw acceptance of a plea.[26]

Indictments and other prosecutors' pleadings

The traditional division between summary and indictable offences – those determined summarily (by a magistrate), and those determined (usually) by a jury in a higher court – has faded somewhat due to statute redefining and refining both the nature of offences and how they can be finalised. Indictable offences, the most serious end of the criminal calendar,[27] follow the archetypal criminal profile. Unless (as is increasingly common) there is a reverse burden of proof, the prosecution must prove each physical and legal element to a beyond reasonable doubt standard. Indictable offences commence with an indictment that is filed in a higher court charging the accused with an offence triable before a jury. Where the defendant contests charges for indictable offences, in some jurisdictions, committal proceedings, held before a magistrate, determine the adequacy of the prosecution case, to establish whether the prosecution case had sufficient

---

22 *Richardson* [1974] HCA 19; 131 CLR 116, 119; *Whitehorn* [1983] HCA 42; 152 CLR 657, 674; *Nguyen* [2020] HCA 23, [33]-[35].

23 *Likiardopoulos* [2012] HCA 37; 247 CLR 265, [2] (French CJ), endorsing *Maxwell* [1996] HCA 46; 184 CLR 501.

24 *De Simoni* [1981] HCA 31; 147 CLR 383 (Gibbs CJ, with Mason J and Murphy J agreeing at 395). The offence was under the *Criminal Code* (WA), s 393.

25 By entering a no bill or *nolle prosequi*. See, eg, *Director of Public Prosecutions Act 1986* (NSW), s 7(2).

26 *Maxwell* [1996] HCA 46; 184 CLR 501.

27 See, eg, *CPA* (NSW), s 3, which provides that an indictable offence is one that may be commenced by indictment (and to the same effect, see *Interpretation Act 1987* (NSW), s 21); *Crimes Act 1914* (Cth), s 4G, which states that an offence that provides for more than 12 months' imprisonment is an indictable offence, unless the contrary intention appears.

evidence to justify putting the accused to answer the charges. It is also not uncommon for the prosecution to determine not to proceed with a case 'if there is no reasonable prospect of a conviction being secured'.[28] In New South Wales, while the magistrate no longer determines the sufficiency of evidence for a committal for trial, the Local Court 'committal stage' proceedings are now particularly significant in managing the pre-trial process regarding the prosecutor's service to the defence of a brief of evidence and charge certificate, and (where the accused is represented) case conferencing.[29]

Drafting pleadings[30] is a highly technical exercise and slip-ups and egregious errors in drafting prosecutors' pleadings can occur easily. Despite the undoubtedly broad scope to amend pleadings and to waive minor errors, there is a continuous run of cases in appellate courts where cases fail because of their pleadings.[31] For example, in *Attorney General (NSW) v Built NSW Pty Ltd*[32] the person authorised to commence proceedings mistakenly thought they could delegate this role to their legal representative. This was not permitted under the legislation and so the judge was obliged to dismiss the charges because without a valid charge there was no jurisdiction for the court. Pleadings, often known as the charge document (the indictment, information or Court Attendance Notice (CAN)) remain a constant reference point for court proceedings. They are vital because charges:

- define a court's jurisdiction;
- establish the legal and factual elements the prosecution must prove[33] and put the defence on notice of what to meet;[34] and
- are the touchstone for determining questions of admissibility of evidence.[35]

---

28 See CDPP Prosecution Policy (24 February 2021), <https://www.cdpp.gov.au/sites/default/files/CDPPProsecutionPolicy_0.pdf.>, para [2.5] for example: 'A prosecution should not proceed if there is no reasonable prospect of a conviction being secured'.

29 There are often numerous potential charges that might apply to a piece of conduct. As a result, prosecutors face choices, moderated by their obligations of fairness, about the level of offences and the number of counts or charges. These operate to discourage over-loading an indictment, particularly where the function of a multiplicity of charges is to put pressure on an accused to negotiate charges in return for pleas of guilty. See, for an extreme example (and extensive judicial discussion), the Canadian case of *Auclair* [2013] QCCA 671 (Doyon JA) (*Auclair* [2014] SCC 6 (McLachlin CJ agreeing)).

30 The difference between pleadings in criminal cases and their civil counterparts is most accentuated with the accused's pleadings. They are rarely more than a couple of words: guilty, not guilty and, less commonly, *autrefois acquit*, *autrefois convict*. See discussion in *Gilham* [2007] NSWCCA 323; 73 NSWLR 308, pardon or demurrer (see *Levy v Victoria* [1997] HCA 31; 189 CLR 579 (*Duck Shooting* case)).

31 That is, the CAN, or whatever the initiating process document is called. The word 'information' is most commonly used to mean the document by which criminal proceedings are instituted before a magistrate. The function of such an information is to provide sufficient information for the issue of a summons directing the accused to appear to answer the charge. Depending on the context, however, the word may have a wider meaning. For an instance of charges not being sufficient to create a charge in any way, see *McGregor v Jenkins* [2018] NTSC 84.

32 [2013] NSWCCA 299 (*Built NSW*).

33 *Goldsmith v Sandilands* [2002] HCA 31; 190 ALR 370; 76 ALJR 1024 (Gleeson CJ); *John Holland Pty Ltd v Industrial Court (NSW)* [2010] NSWCA 338; 202 IR 82, [47] (Spigelman CJ); and, in terms of the fairness to accused aspect, see *Built NSW* [2013] NSWCCA 299, [46] (Bathurst CJ).

34 *Johnson v Miller* [1937] HCA 77; 59 CLR 467.

35 Modern procedural law allows certain defects in these pleadings to be waived, see, eg, *CPA* (NSW), s 16(1): 'An indictment is not bad, insufficient, void, erroneous or defective on any of the following grounds: ... (g) except where time is an essential ingredient, for omitting to state the time at which an offence was committed, for stating the time wrongly or for stating the time imperfectly ...'.

The crucial function of these criminal pleadings goes hand in hand with some key requirements. Pleadings must have *sufficiency*. This means they must describe the essential legal *and factual* elements of the offence (*the time, the place, and the manner* in which the alleged offence took place).[36] Insufficiency of pleadings caused the prosecution to fail in *Kirk v Industrial Court (NSW)*[37] where the accused was charged with failing in its occupational health and safety obligations to an employee who died driving an all-terrain vehicle on Kirk's farm. The High Court ruled that the pleadings lacked sufficient detail of the manner in which the offence allegedly occurred. This meant Kirk was unable to determine what he should (or should not) have done in the management of the farm to prevent the accident that occurred.

Pleadings must have *clarity*. This legal obligation – not merely a matter of professional pride – is often enforced through the requirement of certainty[38] and the rule against duplicity. The roots of the rule against duplicity go back to 17th century English case law.[39] The rule requires that each charge be for a single offence, irrespective of the initiating document. Pleading rules are important because the elements of the offence expressed or implied by common law delimit the evidence that is admissible in court, and when the charge is finalised as an acquittal or a conviction exactly the same charge (ie, the same combination of elements of an offence) cannot be re-prosecuted. A useful summary of the rule against duplicity through one of the seminal Australian cases is provided by Leeming JA in *EPA v Truegrain*, showing not only the single-charge limitation but also the way in which the pleadings then limit the evidence that can be led at trial:[40]

> 41. … An influential example of a duplicitous information which went to the merits was *Johnson v Miller* [1937] HCA 77; 59 CLR 467. It was an offence in South Australia to be a licensee of premises which a person was found on or seen coming out from on a Sunday morning. A complainant proposed to lead evidence that there had been some thirty men seen coming out from the premises, but laid a complaint before a special magistrate charging a single offence on the basis that "certain persons" had been seen. That was amended to "a certain person". The complainant refused to provide particulars of the men. A majority of the Court overturned the decisions of the South Australian Supreme Court and upheld the special magistrate's dismissal of the complaint.

---

36 The factual elements are defined in *Johnson v Miller* [1937] HCA 77; 59 CLR 467; *John L Pty Ltd v Attorney-General (NSW)* [1987] HCA 42; 163 CLR 508. See also *CPA* (NSW), s 175(3), regarding the requirements for a CAN. It must 'do the following: (a) describe the offence, (b) identify the essential factual elements of the alleged offence, (c) contain the name of the prosecutor, (d) require the accused person to appear before the court at a specified date, time and place, unless a warrant is issued for the arrest of the person or the person is refused bail …'.

37 [2010] HCA 1; 239 CLR 531.

38 For the classic dilemma of uncertainty, see *S* [1989] HCA 66; 168 CLR 266, dealing with the challenge of specifying dates of alleged sexual assaults occurring over a course of years when the complainant was a child. The High Court quashed the convictions. As Dawson J put it (at [7]), there was 'obvious embarrassment to the applicant in having to defend himself in relation to an indeterminate number of occasions, unspecified in all but two instances, any one of which might, if it occurred in one of the relevant years, constitute one of the offences charged'. To resolve the difficulty of proceeding with child sexual assault prosecutions in light of this ruling, State legislatures legislated new offences of maintaining a sexual relationship with a young person or child (or persistent sexual abuse of a child), see M Powell, K Roberts, B Guadagno, 'Particularisation of Child Abuse Offences: Common Problems when Questioning Child Witnesses' (2007) 19 *Current Issues in Criminal Justice* 64.

39 J Hunter, 'Prosecutors' Pleadings and the Rule against Duplicity' (1980) 3 *UNSW Law Journal* 248; *Walsh v Tattersall* [1996] HCA 26; 188 CLR 77.

40 [2013] NSWCCA 204.

> 42. As initially formulated, the complaint was duplicitous. As amended, duplicity was cured, because it only charged a single offence, but it continued to be bad because it was no longer possible for the accused to know the particular offence he was called upon to answer.

The duplicity in charging will be latent if the evidence reveals multiple offences in a charge. For example, on the *Johnson v Miller* facts, where the charge referred to a 'certain person' drinking after hours, if the prosecution called more than one person to testify that they were on the premises after hours it would expose a latent duplicity in the charge. If a prosecutor elects to amend a duplicitous charge, or with latent duplicity limit the evidence appropriately, the problem is cured. If not, the charge is bad.

Because statute defines the legal elements of an offence it is tempting to assume that it is sufficient to frame the charge in pleadings by following the terms of the statutory provision creating the offence,[41] but this needs to be undertaken with care. For example, an additional error in the *Built NSW* case was that the summons used the language of one subsection of the legislation but charged an offence in another subsection. This meant the summons did not charge an offence known to law. This was another defect that could not be corrected by amendment or further particulars,[42] nor could it be treated as 'some slip or clumsiness' that could be ignored.[43] These examples highlight the significance of pleadings – without them no trial can proceed.[44] Re-charging following the realisation of the defect may be possible, but not always. If the pleadings relate to summary offences (that is, they are CANs) they may be time-barred[45] and no prosecution can recommence.

Multiple accused – single trial: Where persons are charged with committing an offence jointly, multiple trials can mean a duplication of prosecution witness accounts and a potentially unnecessary expenditure on judicial, curial and juror resources. In the South Australian Court of Appeal in *Webb and Hay*,[46] on the question of separate trials, King CJ observed that there are 'strong reasons of principle and policy why persons charged with committing an offence jointly ought to be tried together. That is particularly so where each seeks to cast the blame on the other'.[47]

---

41 Certainly, *CPA* (NSW), s 11, creates this impression: 'The description of any offence in the words of an Act or statutory rule or other document creating the offence, or in similar words, is *sufficient* in law' (emphasis added).

42 Particulars, that is factual detail, are also important to ensure the defence is sufficiently on notice of the prosecution allegations. See, eg, *Dacre* [2018] VSCA 150, considering *Johnson v Miller* [1937] HCA 77; 59 CLR 467 and *S* [1989] HCA 66; 168 CLR 266, the latter case acknowledging that the Crown cannot be compelled to give particulars which it is impossible to give, though a failure to particularise may make a trial unfair.

43 *Built NSW* [2013] NSWCCA 299, [142] (Bathurst CJ); see also *Shields* [2011] EWCA Crim 2343; [2012] 1 Cr App R 9.

44 *Kirk v Industrial Court (NSW)* [2010] HCA 1; 239 CLR 531.

45 For example, *CPA* (NSW), s 179, provides the default and general position that the time limit for the commencement of summary proceedings is six months from when the offence was alleged to have been committed. That period can be varied in other legislation.

46 (1992) 59 SASR 563, 585.

47 Such blame is known as the cut-throat defence, It may be facilitated by the *UEA* in two ways: by provisions that specifically permit an accused to defend criminal charges at the expense of a co-accused: *UEA*, ss 20 (excepting Victoria), 104(6), 111; and provisions that enable a co-accused to avoid onerous limitations and obligations that in the same trial curtail the prosecutor: *UEA*, ss 101, 137; and see also s 65(8). See D Ross, 'One Accused's Evidence of Another's Criminal Disposition' (2006) 11(1) *Deakin Law Review* 179.

Toohey J in the High Court appeal[48] quoted King CJ approvingly, adding that 'consideration by the same jury at the same trial is likely to avoid inconsistent verdicts, particularly when each accused tries to cast the blame on the other or others'.[49] However, a consideration that is addressed in later chapters, but useful to state here to illustrate the role of pleadings in the practicalities of the trial, was raised by Toohey J who noted that '[t]here are of course dangers for an accused in a joint trial by reason of the admission of evidence which would not be admitted at the trial of one accused. That risk must be obviated by express and careful directions to the jury as to the use they may make of the evidence so far as it concerns each accused'.[50] Ultimately the question is whether a joint trial will cause (or has caused) a substantial miscarriage of justice, described by Toohey J, 'or ... whether improper prejudice has been created against an accused'.

The guiding principles in *Middis*[51] are influential in determining whether co-accused charged with committing an offence jointly should have a separate trial based on concerns about 'improper prejudice).[52] These require the accused seeking a separate trial to show a positive injustice (that cannot be cured by even clear emphatic judicial direction) arising from a joint trial. Briefly, the *Middis* principles are that:

> 1. where the evidence against an applicant for a separate trial is significantly weaker than and different to that admissible against another or the other accused to be jointly tried with him, *and*
> 2. where the evidence against those other accused contains material highly prejudicial to the applicant although not admissible against him, *and*
> 3. where there is a real risk that the weaker Crown case against the applicant will be made *immeasurably* stronger by reason of the prejudicial material,
>
> a separate trial will usually be ordered in relation to the charges against the applicant. (emphasis added)

These principles were teased out further by Adams J in *Pham*[53] who questioned the persuasiveness of 1.,[54] stating 'the crucial issue is the potential effect of the

48 *Webb and Hay* [1994] HCA 30; 181 CLR 41, 88-9 (Mason CJ and McHugh J agreeing). Toohey J noted that King CJ fleshed out these strong reasons of principle in *Collie* [1991] SASC 2996; 56 SASR 302, 307-11.

49 Citing *Demirok* [1976] VicRp 19; [1976] VR 244, 254.

50 Citing *Harbach* (1973) 6 SASR 427, 433. See also *Amos* [2014] NSWCCA 302.

51 Unreported, NSWSC, 17 March 1991.

52 See, eg, *Friend* [2007] NSWCCA 41, [147]; *Madubuko* [2011] NSWCCA 135; *Destanovic* [2015] VSCA 113.

53 In *Pham* [2004] NSWCCA 190 the evidence tipped in favour of separating the defendants' trials. There were significant credibility issues with two eye witnesses who implicated all accused plus a record of interview that was admissible against one accused only. As the record of interview corroborated the eyewitness testimony the judge's task of directing the jury would have required an impossibly complex task for jurors – namely, to consider the record of interview (and its support of the eye witness testimony) in relation to only one accused, but not the others. Thus separate trials were justified. In *Madubuko* [2011] NSWCCA 135, [29] the ruling went the other way due to the way in which cross-examination took place, making evidence of admissions admissible, but only against one accused. See also *Jenkin* [2018] NSWSC 547; *Afu and Caleo (No 8)* [2018] NSWSC 187.

54 *Pham* [2004] NSWCCA 190, [40]: 'I am doubtful that the weakness of the applicant's case as compared with that of the co-accused against whom it is proposed to tender the prejudicial evidence can be a relevant consideration. Assume that the case against the co-accused was much weaker than the applicant, even with the prejudicial evidence. If there was a significant risk that the prejudicial evidence could be used by the jury adversely to the applicant and that evidence was itself significantly prejudicial, I am unable to see why the mere fact that it was adduced in a weaker co-offender's case is material. Indeed, the opposite would seem to be the

inadmissible evidence on the jury's consideration of the applicant's case'[55] and with reference to 3., suggesting:

> The starting point is that the inadmissible, prejudicial material is completely irrelevant. If, when placed on the scales, it would be likely to turn a potential acquittal to a conviction then this would, I think, amount to "positive injustice". Of course, the likelihood cannot be measured: if it is real, as distinct from inconsequential, having regard both to its inherent character and the context of the Crown case, then the trial must necessarily embarrass the affected accused. The question then arises whether the risk that the material might be placed by the jury on the scales is such that the trial miscarried.[56]

Multiple charges – single accused: A judge cannot determine how many charges an accused should face, but 'judges have been unwilling to surrender entirely to the conscience of a prosecutor the fairness of subjecting an accused to the peril of prosecution and punishment'.[57] This observation reflects that courts can act where there is a tangible risk that the trial would be unfair,[58] and they can do so before a trial has commenced, for example, by ordering a stay of proceedings that are an abuse of process, discussed further below.

Note, however, that there is growing pressure to facilitate joint trials, particularly in New South Wales.[59] Where, in a trial involving more than one accused a jury is required to separate evidence against particular co-accused, or where a single accused faces a multi-count indictment in a single trial, limiting instructions need to meet the 'spill-over' from contamination of evidence in one charge impacting on another charge, especially in complex trials with numerous counts. The conventional view from psychological research is that the story model of decision-making prevents jurors from isolating pieces of information to limit or disregard their role in deliberation in a particular respect – and so it will be difficult to separate the influence of evidence relating to one charge impacting on another charge, especially in complex trials. This is because (so it is said) jurors assess evidence holistically, informed by pre-existing frames of reference – the ones that

---

case since, if the co-accused's case was weak, or weaker than the applicant's, the prejudicial evidence might well assume even more importance than otherwise.'

55 Ibid [40]. In turn, these observations by Adams J have been quoted approvingly in *Madubuko* [2011] NSWCCA 135, [28] (Hodgson JA, with Hoeben J and Grove AJ agreeing) and in *Lockett* [2013] NSWSC 859 (Price J).

56 [2004] NSWCCA 190, [39].

57 *Pearce* [1998] HCA 57; 194 CLR 610; 156 ALR 684, 705-6 (Kirby J). See also *Achurch* [2014] HCA 10.

58 Or, perhaps, a higher threshold for the accused to establish, namely, 'the trial is likely to be unfair': *Gould v DPP (Cth)* [2018] NSWCCA 109, [63]-[64] (Basten JA, with Johnson and Adamson JJ agreeing), relying on the language of *Dietrich* [1992] HCA 57; 177 CLR 292, 311. See discussion by Leeming JA in *Marwan v DPP* [2019] NSWCCA 161, [23]-[26]. In particular, see *CPA* (NSW), s 21(2), regarding the ordering of separate trials on counts where the accused 'may be prejudiced or embarrassed in his or her defence by reason of being charged with more than one offence in the same indictment'. See also *CPA* (NSW), s 29(1), regarding hearing offences in a single trial against an accused where the offences arise out of the same set of circumstances or the offences form or are part of a series of offences of the same or a similar character.

59 In particular, see *CPA* (NSW), s 29A, which operates subject to s 21(2). Section 29A provides that, where the prosecution has given notice that it intends to rely on tendency or coincidence evidence that relates to two or more offences, the court must hear and determine counts against the same person where the offences are charged in the same indictment or where they are listed for hearing on the same day, and at the same place. This mandatory joining of offences in such broad terms arises from legislative changes in NSW following the Royal Commission on Institutional Responses to Child Sexual Assault (RCIRCSA) that recommended reducing the occasions on which a complainant is required to testify. See the discussion of these 2020 legislative changes in Chapter 11.

also guide their day-to-day interactions and decision-making as well how they reach a verdict. However, as Sklansky points out,[60] the story model of decision-making acknowledges that jurors in fact are constantly required to review the connections they make with evidence to refit the story to new evidence. Sklansky, while generally critical of blind faith in limiting instructions, is not completely pessimistic of jurors' capacities to follow judicial directions. He suggests:

> All of this is consistent with jurors combining coherence-based story construction with some amount of conscious, atomistic reasoning. In fact, jurors must do something along these lines. In order to assimilate an item of evidence into a story, jurors must have some sense of what the evidence is and what it tends to show.
>
> Exculpatory testimony from an alibi witness cannot be treated the same as expert testimony that the defendant's fingerprints were found at the crime scene. And much of this atomistic processing could be subject to conscious control. When comparing how well rival stories fit with a body of evidence, a juror might plausibly constrain the analysis by limiting the kinds of inferences that could be drawn from a particular piece of evidence. For example, a juror might deliberately put to one side the fact that a particular story is contradicted by a hearsay statement that was admitted only for other purposes.
>
> No doubt some jurors will find it difficult to constrain their reasoning in this way. Still, there is no reason to assume, a priori, that the difficulties they encounter will be so large that the limiting instructions will do little real work.[61]

The rule against double jeopardy

The rule against double jeopardy (the *autrefois* pleas) is a complex area of law. It functions to prevent the state having more than one attempt to prosecute a person for the same crime, often referred to as 'one bite at the cherry'. A useful description surveying this topic is given by Gummow and Hayne JJ in *Island Maritime Ltd v Filipowski*.[62] Their Honours refer to three maxims that are embodied by the rule against double jeopardy:

- it is in society's interest that there be an end to litigation (*interest reipublicae ut sit finis litium*);
- what is adjudicated is taken as the truth (*res judicata pro veritate accipitur*);[63] and
- no one should twice be vexed for one and the same cause (*nemo debet bis vexari pro una et eadem causa*).[64]

60 DA Sklansky, 'Evidentiary Instructions and the Jury as Other' (2013) 65 *Stanford Law Review* 407, referring in particular to LJ Demaine, 'In Search of an Anti-Elephant: Confronting the Human Inability to Forget Inadmissible Evidence' (2008) 16 *George Mason Law Review* 99; D Simon, 'A Third View of the Black Box: Cognitive Coherence in Legal Decision Making' (2004) 71 *University of Chicago Law Review* 511.

61 Sklansky, above n 60, 423 (footnotes omitted). See further Chapter 10.

62 [2006] HCA 30; 226 CLR 328.

63 On this particular point the complexity and fine-grained analysis that this 'truth' is between the state and the convicted or acquitted person only, see *Likiardopoulos* [2012] HCA 37; 247 CLR 265, [35]-[36]: 'the conviction and sentence of John Likiardopoulos and Aydin for the manslaughter of the deceased was conclusive in proceedings between each man and the Crown. The Crown could not controvert the conviction for manslaughter by leading evidence in subsequent proceedings against either man to establish that he had murdered the deceased. However, John Likiardopoulos and Aydin were strangers to the proceedings brought against the appellant. Their convictions for manslaughter were not conclusive against the world of the facts on which they were based. The Crown was not precluded from adducing evidence to establish the fact that John Likiardopoulos and Aydin murdered the deceased'.

64 On the incontrovertibility of acquittals, see *Garrett* [1977] HCA 67; 139 CLR 437, [21] (Barwick CJ, with Stephen, Mason and Jacobs JJ agreeing): 'the acquittal may not be questioned or

> 41. … It is these values that underpin the rule that evidence is inadmissible where, if accepted, it would overturn or tend to overturn an acquittal.[65] It is these values that inform the rules governing successive prosecutions – rules which find their origins in the pleas in bar of autrefois convict and autrefois acquit but now have wider application than those pleas in bar. …
>
> 43. The plea of *autrefois acquit* 'is the species of estoppel by which the Crown is precluded from reasserting the guilt of the accused when that question has previously been determined against it'.[66] It is a plea that prevents the re-litigation of matters already determined in favour of the accused. Like the plea of *autrefois convict*, the plea of *autrefois acquit* prevents inconsistent decisions, serves to maintain the acceptance of orders and other solemn acts of the courts as incontrovertibly correct, and avoids the injustice occasioned by the re-litigation of what has already been determined. But until more recent times, the pleas of *autrefois acquit* and *autrefois convict* 'remained the only manifestations of the rule against double jeopardy'.[67] As the criminal law has become more complex, and as the number of offences that may be dealt with summarily has increased, questions of double jeopardy have taken on greater significance. When criminal offences were relatively few and distinct, a single course of conduct would constitute but one offence. With the proliferation of overlapping and related statutory offences, a single allegedly criminal transaction will often yield numerous offences.[68]

The *International Covenant on Civil and Political Rights* (ICCPR) Article 14(7) confirms the rule against double jeopardy. While appeals from a guilty verdict are justified as a check against an unsafe conviction, an acquittal verdict[69] is traditionally treated at common law as final.[70] Perhaps the most significant feature of the rule against double jeopardy in the 21st century is the extent to which jurisdictions[71] have introduced exceptions to it. In New South Wales this step takes place through *Crimes (Appeal and Review) Act 2001* (NSW) (*CARA* (NSW)), s 100, requiring an order from the Court of Criminal Appeal based on the presence of 'fresh and compelling evidence' and a finding that it is in the interests of justice for a retrial after an acquittal to proceed.[72] The impetus for this legislation arose from advocacy in relation to the tragic murders of three Indigenous children between September 1990-February 1991 in Bowraville, a small town

---

called into question by any evidence which, if accepted, would overturn or tend to overturn the verdict'. The width of that proposition, so far as it related to evidence calling the acquittal into question or tending to overturn the verdict, was questioned in *Carroll* [2002] HCA 55; 213 CLR 635, [37], [45]-[47], [93], cited and quoted in *Koloamatangi and Popovic* [2020] NSWCCA 52, [300] (Bathurst CJ).

65 [*Garrett* [1977] HCA 67; 139 CLR 437, 445; *Rogers* (1994) 181 CLR 251, 277-8; *Carroll* (2002) 213 CLR 635.]

66 [Spencer Bower, Turner and Handley, *The Doctrine of Res Judicata* (3rd ed, 1996), 311.]

67 [J Hunter, 'The Development of the Rule Against Double Jeopardy' (1984) 5 *Journal of Legal History* 3, 14.]

68 [*Ashe v Swenson* [1970] USSC 78; 397 US 436, 445 (1970).]

69 For a very useful consideration of the double jeopardy and abuse of process issues in challenging acquittals in various contexts, see *Koloamatangi and Popovic* [2020] NSWCCA 52, [294]-[317] (Bathurst CJ, with Bell P and Price J agreeing).

70 Cf Tasmania (see *Vallance* [1961] HCA 42; 108 CLR 56; *Williams* [1986] HCA 88; 161 CLR 278); Canada (see *Morin* [1988] 2 SCR 345; *Morgentaler* [1988] 1 SCR 30); New Zealand (see *Gwaze* [2009] NZCA 430; [2010] 1 NZLR 646, [37], [60]-[78] and [228]-[232]). The right of a Crown appeal on acquittal is treated as meaning that the verdict is not final until the appeal is determined.

71 See, eg, *Criminal Justice Act 2003* (UK), ss 77, 78 ('new and compelling evidence' test) and also *A* [2009] 2 All ER 898; *Double Jeopardy (Scotland) Act 2011* ('new evidence'); and *Criminal Procedure Act 2011* (NZ), s 154 ('new and compelling evidence', on a Court of Appeal order).

72 For definitions and limitations, see *CARA* (NSW), ss 100-102.

on the mid north coast of New South Wales. Racism and indifference hampered thorough and timely police investigations. XX was charged with the murders of Clinton Speedy and Evelyn Greenup. In 1993 Justice Badgery-Parker applied the similar fact rule to reject the prosecution proceeding against XX in a single trial for these murders. XX was ultimately acquitted of each of these murders in two separate trials, one in 1994 (Clinton Speedy) and the other (Evelyn Greenup) following a coronial inquiry in 2006. By the time of the second trial the *UEA* had replaced the similar fact rule with the less demanding uniform Evidence Acts' tendency and coincidence rules,[73] but it was not possible for the prosecution to overcome the rule against double jeopardy. This rule prevented any challenge, even an indirect one, to XX's earlier acquittal in the second trial. This meant the prosecution could not lead as 'coincidence evidence' any evidence incriminating XX for Clinton Speedy's murder. No charges were laid with respect to Colleen Walker's disappearance and her body was never recovered.

In 2018 the Attorney General brought proceedings[74] for an order under *CARA*, s 100(1), to permit the retrial of XX for the two murders where he had been tried and acquitted (and in the same re-trial, for Colleen Walker's murder). The Attorney General argued that *CARA*'s 'fresh evidence' requirement was satisfied by new evidence concerning the disappearance and presumed death of Colleen Walker, but the court found that this evidence was not fresh in relation to Clinton Speedy and Evelyn Greenup's murders and so ruled against the application, finding the evidence failed the 'fresh' test (s 102(2)).[75]

Disclosure

> 46. The accusatorial system in criminal proceedings imposes a duty on a prosecutor to disclose material which, first, is or might be relevant to an issue in the case; secondly, raises a new issue, the existence of which is not apparent from the prosecution case; or, thirdly, holds out a real prospect of providing a lead on evidence in the first two categories.[76]
>
> 47. The obligation requires the prosecutor to take a "broad view of relevance". Hodgson JA said in *Reardon* at [58]:
>
>> "It was accepted for the Crown that there is no onus on the defence to demonstrate a forensic purpose in relation to material said to be subject to the Crown's duty of disclosure. This is clearly correct: the defence is simply not in a position to know what this material is. It seems to me that *the correct view is that a decision by the Crown concerning what to disclose should take a broad view of relevance and of what are the issues in the case*. The Crown has all the material available to it, and one basis of the rule about disclosure is that it is to ameliorate the inequality of resources as between the Crown and the accused. In those circumstances, it would seem inappropriate for the prosecution authorities to take a narrow view as to what

73 See Chapter 11 below.

74 *Attorney General (NSW) v XX* [2018] NSWCCA 198; 98 NSWLR 1012 (Bathurst CJ, Hoeben CJ at CL and McCallum J). See also D Box, *Bowraville* (Viking, 2019). It was submitted to the court that if the evidence of the deaths and disappearances of all three children had been considered by a jury in a single trial the evidence would have established the guilt of XX for each murder through 'coincidence reasoning' based on the alleged similarities of circumstances between each of the murders.

75 An alleged 'implied admissions of guilt' made by XX to a journalist failed the 'compelling' test (*CARA* (NSW), s 102(3)). The High Court refused special leave to appeal: *Attorney General (NSW) v XX* [2019] HCATrans 52

76 Citing *Reardon (No 2)* [2004] NSWCCA 197; 60 NSWLR 454, [46]-[54] (Hodgson JA), which was approved in *Spiteri* [2004] NSWCCA 321; 61 NSWLR 369.

the defence might be or as to what might prove useful to the defence, as to what might open up useful lines of enquiry to the defence ...". [Emphasis added.]

48. In *Gould v Director of Public Prosecutions (Cth)*,[77] which followed *Reardon*, Basten JA (Johnson and Adamson JJ agreeing) said at [65]:

> "[T]he duty of disclosure extends to material which might open up useful lines of inquiry to the defence, without any narrow view being taken of what might be relevant".[78]

Modern obligations for prosecutors to play fair and to give disclosure evolved in the latter part of the 20th century and now tend to go hand-in-hand with defining the circumstances for a negotiated early guilty plea. As the statements made by Adamson J as well as those quoted by her Honour suggest, the most significant disclosure obligations are upon the prosecutor. They reveal that no longer is there the 18th century notion that ambushing the accused with an in-court confrontation of the prosecution case assists to reveal 'the truth'.[79] Today, the principle of equality of arms, a dimension of ensuring a trial is fair, requires equipping the accused to be able to meet and challenge the prosecution case effectively, including ensuring prosecutors fulfil their obligations of disclosure. This reflects the view that a fair process requires equipping an accused to meet the might of the state and, for this reason, the duty of disclosure is a duty to the court, not merely to a party.[80]

Consistent with this cards-on-the-table[81] approach, the prosecution is now obliged to disclose all evidence in its possession (or material it should obtain) that is relevant to the case before and throughout the trial. Relevance is assessed in terms of the totality of the case – not just the prosecution's take on the evidence. The breadth of this disclosure can be quite challenging. It includes material:

- gathered during investigation but not intended to be used by the prosecution,
- that assists the defence case, or
- that relates to the credibility of prosecution witnesses.[82]

Disclosure and charging decisions are internal prosecutorial determinations (that is, outside Kamisar's 'mansion' of justice). Self-evidently, ethical practice obligations are crucial. Experience indicates that prosecutorial zealotry can be the under-belly of adversarial competition causing information to be suppressed, evidence fabricated[83] and inappropriately aggressive or manipulative behaviour.[84]

77 [[2018] NSWCCA 109; 359 ALR 142.]

78 *Bradley v Chilby* [2020] NSWSC 145 (Adamson J).

79 Based on the view that the 'simplicity and innocence, artless and ingenuous behaviour' of the defendant that allowed innocence to shine through: W Hawkins, *A Treatise of the Pleas of the Crown*, vol 2 (1716-21), 400, quoted in JH Langbein, *The Origins of the Adversary Criminal Trial* (Oxford University Press, 2003), 35-6.

80 *Marwan v DPP* [2019] NSWCCA 161, [29] (Leeming JA, with RA Hulme and Adamson JJ agreeing).

81 In contrast to holding cards close to the prosecutorial chest, P Roberts and A Zuckerman, *Criminal Evidence* (Oxford University Press, 2010), 61.

82 *Anile* [2018] VSCA 235.

83 See, eg *Roberts* [2020] VSCA 277, [259]-[260] (T Forrest and Osborn JJA and Taylor AJA) (arising from the Victorian Lawyer X affair). This case involved police manipulating evidence, perjury and (perhaps unsurprising in light of the misconduct) police non-disclosure, amounting to 'a gross and fundamental corruption of the trial process ... impropriety and unfairness permeated and affected the trial to an extent that it ceased to be a fair trial according to law'.

84 See, eg, *Gregg* [2020] NSWCCA 245; *Wood* [2012] NSWCCA 21; 84 NSWLR 581 (use of rhetorical questions in prosecutor's closing address). Sometimes, as we see in Chapter 15, flaws in evidence just pass unnoticed.

In Australia, the prosecution guidelines of each ODPP reflect these principles.[85] Disclosure obligations in New South Wales find their place in legislation through the *Criminal Procedure Act 1986* (NSW) (*CPA* (NSW)) and the *Legal Profession Uniform Conduct (Barristers) Rules 2015*, rr 87 and 88.[86] The *CPA* (NSW), s 142, requires that *the prosecution provide the defence* with:

- the notice of the case for the prosecution, including a copy of the indictment, a statement of facts, each document and each witness statement to be adduced at trial, a copy of exhibits, charts, summaries, copies of all items provided by the police,[87] or in the prosecutor's possession, 'that would reasonably be regarded as relevant to the prosecution case or the defence case', and that has not otherwise been disclosed to the accused person; and
- a list of items also reasonably regarded as relevant, but not in the prosecutor's possession, together with a copy of items informing on prosecution witnesses' and the accused person's reliability or credibility.[88]

With the goal of enhancing efficiency both pre-trial and during the trial in New South Wales *the defence must respond to the s 142 prosecution 'disclosure' notice*, providing:[89]

---

85 Simpson J in *Grey* [2000] NSWCCA 46; 111 A Crim R 314 (dissenting but upheld by the High Court) referred to the ODPP prosecution guidelines and Bar Rules rather than the English cases. Hodgson JA in *Reardon (No 2)* [2004] NSWCCA 197; 60 NSWLR 454 (as quoted by McColl JA in *Lipton* [2011] NSWCCA 247) observed that the first paragraph of the Disclosure Guidelines (as at 2004) was modelled on *Keane* [1994] 2 All ER 478; [1994] 1 WLR 746. For NSW, see *NSW Prosecution Guidelines*, 29 March 2021, <https://www.odpp.nsw.gov.au/prosecution-guidelines>.

86 Should the prosecution wish to resist disclosure, presumably because they claim an exception applies, they are obliged to consider the alternatives of withdrawing or reducing the charge. For disclosure-related cases, see *Marwan v DPP* [2019] NSWCCA 161 (discussion of duty of disclosure extending to making further inquiries); *Edwards* [2020] NSWCCA 57 (issue of late production, nature and extent of prosecutors' disclosure obligations); *Spiteri* [2004] NSWCCA 321; 61 NSWLR 369, [20]; *Reardon (No 2)* [2004] NSWCCA 197; 60 NSWLR 454, [46]-[54] (Hodgson JA); *Cornwell* [2010] NSWCCA 59, [210] (McClellan CJ at CL, with Johnson J agreeing); *Lipton* [2011] NSWCCA 247 (McColl JA). Importantly, *Lipton* placed an obligation on the DPP to assess whether police have appropriately disclosed information, documents or other things that are the subject of a bona fide claim of privilege, public interest immunity or statutory immunity. For a useful discussion of public interest immunity, in the context of a defence subpoena seeking information argued as relevant to the credibility of a prosecution witness, see *Atashi and Katakouzinos* [2021] NSWDC 91. In response, s 15A(6) of the *Director of Public Prosecutions Act 1986* (NSW) was added, imposing a duty on police officers investigating alleged offences to disclose to the DPP all relevant information, documents or other things obtained during the investigation that might reasonably be expected to assist the case for the prosecution or the case for the accused person (but not any information etc the subject of a bona fide claim of privilege, publication restriction or immunity, such as public interest immunity in relation to an under-cover officer or a police informant). This removed the DPP's legal obligation to oversee police claims of immunity or privilege. The sunset clause on the amendment has not stopped the provision continuing. See also discussion in *Hamilton v New South Wales* [2020] NSWSC 700, [971]-[1000] (Walton J). In Victoria, the Lawyer X situation has given police disclosure significant focus: see *Visser v DPP (Cth)* [2020] VSCA 327 and *Mokbel v DPP (Cth)* [2020] VSCA 325.

87 See *Director of Public Prosecutions Act 1986* (NSW), s 15A; *Director of Public Prosecutions Regulation 2020* (NSW); and see *Hamilton v New South Wales* [2020] NSWSC 700, [971]-[1000] (Walton J) and *Lipton* [2011] NSWCCA 247 for comprehensive discussions of police disclosure issues.

88 See also Guideline 13.3, *NSW Prosecution Guidelines*, 29 March 2021, <https://www.odpp.nsw.gov.au/prosecution-guidelines>. For timetables regarding disclosure, currently for District Court cases, the prosecution must provide disclosure within three weeks of the date set for trial, with the follow up prosecution response to the defence response being given before the date set for trial.

89 *CPA* (NSW), s 143. See also L Line, C Wyld and D Plater, 'Pre-Trial Defence Disclosure in South Australian Criminal Proceedings: Time for Change?' (2016) 37 *Adelaide Law Review* 101.

- the name of the relevant legal representative appearing on behalf of the accused;
- the nature of the defence, including particular defences;
- any factual matters or circumstances in the prosecution case that the defence intends to take issue;
- any points of law to be raised by the defence, notices of alibi or claims of substantial mental impairment; and
- notice of waiver of rules of evidence under *UEA*, s 190.

After the defence has responded to the notice of the case for the prosecution, a second wave of prosecution disclosure may be required.[90] This puts the defence on notice of any prosecution intention to raise issues, or dispute accuracy or admissibility regarding any aspects of the disclosed defence case. All disclosure obligations under the *CPA* (NSW) are ongoing.[91] Sanctions[92] for non-compliance by a party include a court order that:

- evidence not disclosed be excluded from the trial;
- expert evidence be excluded from the trial where a copy was not provided in accordance with pre-trial disclosure requirements; and/or
- grants an adjournment;[93] and
- where the defence fails to comply with pre-trial disclosure obligations (and the prosecution has complied), s 146A(2) provides that a:

> (a) … court, or any other party with the leave of the court, may make such comment at the trial as appears proper, and
> (b) … court or jury may then draw such unfavourable inferences as appear proper.

Section 146A(3) expresses what surely needs no articulation, namely that a direct inference of the accused's guilt arising from the defence failure to comply with disclosure obligations cannot be the sole basis for finding them guilty.[94] Arguably, any inference of guilt from non-compliance will be difficult to achieve. For the prosecution of indictable offences, the *CPA* (NSW) has removed many grey areas with respect to disclosure. It also provides for pre-trial conferences[95] (to establish parties' agreement on disclosure and the admissibility of evidence) and pre-trial hearings[96] (to enable parties' submissions and court orders resolving outstanding matters in advance of trial) in an attempt to streamline parties' case preparation and trial processes. They are important in reducing trial interruptions where jurors might be required to wait in the jury room while legal issues are resolved.

An accused may request the court issue a subpoena to obtain documents within the ambit of the prosecution's duty of disclosure.[97] While an accused will

90 *CPA* (NSW), s 144.
91 *CPA* (NSW), s 147.
92 *CPA* (NSW), s 146. See also s 145.
93 Sanctions preventing the defence adducing evidence can only be ordered if the prosecutor has complied with its disclosure requirements.
94 *CPA* (NSW), s 145(3).
95 See *CPA* (NSW), s 140(4).
96 See *CPA* (NSW), s 139.
97 See, eg , *Mokbel (Ruling No 1)* [2005] VSC 410, [74] (Gillard J), ruling in favour of the defence seeking documents relating to the credibility of former members of the Drug Squad charged with offences committed while they were police officers, and ruling '[a]n accused man must have the opportunity to inspect any document which may provide an opportunity to cross-examine'; and see *Jenkin (No 2)* [2018] NSWSC 697, [21] (Hamill J) applying these principles.

not be able to seek an order from the court to require prosecution disclosure, it can seek a stay of the proceedings to prevent an unfair trial or if there is a tangible risk it would be unfair.[98] A breach of the duty to disclosure may be a basis for quashing a conviction, should it be found the ensuing trial was unfair.[99] A major contributor to miscarriages of justice in Australia, England and the United States is the non-disclosure of prosecution evidence.[100] Andrew Mallard's case[101] is a classic and tragic example of the failure of disclosure resulting in an appalling miscarriage of justice. Mallard appealed his 1994 conviction for the murder of a Perth jewellery shop proprietor twice to the High Court. He had previously also unsuccessfully petitioned for clemency. He was successful in his second High Court appeal, in 2005. This appeal revealed multiple instances of non-disclosure with both police and prosecutorial failures: 'Of particular concern are the items in which evidentiary material, consistent with innocence and presenting difficulties for the prosecutor's hypothesis of guilt, were actually suppressed or removed from the material supplied to the defence'.[102]

Abuse of court process – staying proceedings

A stay may be temporary (and typically, conditional) or, as a last resort, it can be permanent. Courts' pervasive powers and obligations to prevent abuse of their processes is linked to their obligation to ensure an accused has a fair trial. The situations where a stay may be available involves complex terrain.[103]

> There is a powerful social imperative for those who are charged with criminal offences to be brought to trial and, for that reason, it has been said that a permanent stay of prosecution should only ever be granted where there is such a fundamental defect in the process leading to trial that nothing by way of reconstitution of the prosecutorial team or trial directions or other such arrangements can sufficiently relieve against the consequences of the defect as to afford those charged with a fair trial. … [T]here is, too, a fundamental social concern to ensure that the end of a criminal prosecution does not justify the adoption of any and every means for securing a conviction and, therefore, a recognition that in rare and exceptional cases where a defect in process is so profound as to offend the integrity and functions of the court as such, it is necessary that proceedings be stayed in order to prevent the administration of justice falling into disrepute.[104]

Precedents offer guidance on the shape and scope of stays:

---

98 *Bradley v Chilby* [2020] NSWSC 145.

99 See *Grey* [2001] HCA 65; 75 ALJR 1708, discussed in Chapter 14.

100 See also Chapter 15.

101 *Mallard* [2005] HCA 68; 224 CLR 125. See also Chapters 2 and 7 and <http://netk.net.au/MallardHome.asp>; 27 September 2010 – ABC Australian Story, 'The Wronged Man' Part One – Transcript; 4 October 2010 – ABC Australian Story, 'The Wronged Man' Part Two – Transcript; 26 July 2012 – *The Australian*, 'Mallard case prosecutor fined'; 25 July 2012 – *Perth Now*, 'Mallard prosecutor Ken Bates fined $10,000, reprimanded'.

102 [2005] HCA 68; 224 CLR 125, [58]. Andrew Mallard died in 2019: <https://www.abc.net.au/news/2019-04-24/teenager-charged-over-andrew-mallard-hit-and-run-death-in-us/11044648>.

103 See *UBS AG v Tyne* [2018] HCA 45 (a civil litigation context) and generally J Gans, 'The Integrity of Charging' in J Hunter, P Roberts, SNM Young and D Dixon (eds), *The Integrity of Criminal Process: From Theory into Practice* (Hart Publishing, 2015), which has contributed substantially to the following discussion.

104 *Strickland (a pseudonym) v CDPP* [2018] HCA 53; 266 CLR 325, [106]. See also *Jago v District Court (NSW)* [1989] HCA 46; 168 CLR 23, 31, 34 (Mason CJ), 60 (Deane J), 76 (Gaudron J); *Glennon* [1992] HCA 16; 173 CLR 592, 605 (Mason CJ and Toohey J); *Dupas* [2010] HCA 20; 241 CLR 237, 250 [33]-[35].

- where the initiation of process by police is severely compromised (eg, unlawful extradition; entrapment);[105]
- when the committal process is marred in some way;[106]
- when it seems a *nolle prosequi* is being utilised to stop a trial where the prosecution is going badly, and the prosecution then commences on the same charges again;[107]
- where delay[108] or pre-trial publicity[109] has made a fair trial not possible;
- where there is a breach of the spirit of double jeopardy *principles* that limit over-charging;[110]
- where a prosecution is brought for an improper purpose, that is, for some sort of collateral advantage;[111] and
- where an accused is unrepresented and is facing charges for serious indictable offences;[112]
- where the fair and proper administration of justice will be fatally compromised by conducting a hearing before a male magistrate, a conditional permanent stay will be justified;[113]
- where if to proceed without disclosure would create a tangible risk that the trial would be unfair.[114]

Prosecutors' In-court Fair Trial Obligations

A prosecutor acting in accordance with the responsibilities of their office is not to be expected to be detached or disinterested in the trial process.[115] A prosecutor is to be expected to act to high professional standards and therefore to be concerned about the presentation of evidence to the jury. It is to be expected that some forensic decisions may

105 *R v Horseferry Road Magistrates' Court; Ex parte Bennett* [1994] 1 AC 42; *Levinge v Director of Custodial Services* (1987) 9 NSWLR 547; *Steffan* (1993) 30 NSWLR 633 (CCA); *Taouk (*1992) 65 A Crim R 387 (NSWCCA); *Lavelle* (1994) 72 A Crim R 402 (WASC).

106 The trial has been preceded by unfair committal proceedings: *Basha* (1989) 39 A Crim R 337 (NSWCCA). The prosecution has used an *ex officio* indictment to avoid committal proceedings: *Barton* [1980] HCA 48; 147 CLR 75.

107 See, eg, *CPA* (NSW), s 208, and extensive discussions in *TR v DPP* [2020] NSWSC 255 (Davies J) and *YL* [2004] ACTSC 115 (Crispin J); *DPP v 'A' (A Child)* [2001] WASC 2; *Jemielita* (1995) 12 WAR 362; 78 A Crim R 91; *Lorkin* (1995) 15 WAR 499; 82 A Crim R 196; *Leece* (1996) 65 FCR 544; 86 A Crim R 494 (Burchett J); *H* (1995) 83 A Crim R 402 (SACCA).

108 *Jago v District Court (NSW)* [1989] HCA 46; 168 CLR 23; *Adler v District Court (NSW)* (1990) 19 NSWLR 317; *Davis* (1995) 57 FCR 512 (delay meant medical records destroyed); *Edwards* [2009] HCA 20; 225 ALR 399.

109 *Connell (No 3)* (1993) 8 WAR 542.

110 See *Connelly v DPP* [1964] AC 1254; *Walton v Gardiner* [1993] HCA 77; 177 CLR 378; *Peters* (1995) 83 A Crim R 142 (NSWCCA). Note that over-charging is complex to define.

111 *Williams v Spautz* [1992] HCA 34; 174 CLR 509; and see *Victoria International Container Terminal Ltd v Lunt* [2021] HCA 11.

112 *Dietrich* [1992] HCA 57; 177 CLR 292.

113 *Lacey (a Pseudonym) v Attorney General (NSW)* [2021] NSWCA 27, [20] (Basten JA). In this case the applicant, a 15-year-old Indigenous girl had been filmed by CCTV during a strip search. The footage revealed her exposed chest and buttocks. Evidence from an ALS Field Officer indicated that in Aboriginal cultures showing this footage was women's business, not to be revealed to men, and 'the division of men's and women's business is lore to Aboriginal people that has been practiced for thousands of years' and showing the footage would cause 'cultural shame' and be 'extremely distressing' (McCallum JA at [52], [59], and see [117]-[118]).

114 *Marwan v DPP* [2019] NSWCCA 161, and see E Johnston, 'The adversarial defence lawyer: Myths, disclosure and efficiency – A contemporary analysis of the role in the era of the Criminal Procedure Rules' (2020) 24 *International Journal of Evidence & Proof* 35.

115 [*Whitehorn* [1983] HCA 42; 152 CLR 657, 675.]

> need to be made. It is not to be expected that they will be tactical decisions which advance the Crown case and disadvantage the accused.[116]

Case law and statute join prosecutors' guidelines and professional rules to set ethical obligations for prosecutor's in-court conduct. Breach of these obligations may not always, however, have serious repercussions in appeal courts' assessment of the trial process. Ultimately, the question for the court is whether any breach of these obligations has created a miscarriage of justice. The Australian Bar Rules[117] set base-line standards drawing on case law. These include the requirements of:

- *impartiality* (that the 'prosecutor must fairly assist the court to arrive at the truth, must seek impartially to have the whole of the relevant evidence placed intelligibly before the court' (r 83), correct any misleading statement (r 25) and 'must not press the prosecution's case for a conviction' (r 84));[118]
- *fairness* (not engaging in inflammatory language or conduct that biases the court against the accused (r 85)); and
- *professionalism* (not putting propositions the prosecution does not believe on reasonable grounds to be probative (r 86)). This includes also the obligation to present all available, cogent and admissible evidence, including all credible witnesses relevant to the unfolding of the narrative who can give testimony that is 'admissible and necessary for the presentation of all of the relevant circumstances'.[119] These obligations require ensuring 'a proper presentation of the Crown case conformably with the dictates of fairness to the accused'.[120]

To these obligations comes the following (rare) consideration:

> What has been said about the obligations which attach to the power or discretion of a prosecutor with respect to the tender of evidence does not detract from the need for a prosecutor to consider factors about particular evidence which may properly influence the decision whether to call that evidence. There may be valid reasons not to do so. In *Richardson* the prosecutor had grounds for believing that the witness in question was not credible or truthful. The prosecution could not be expected to tender the evidence of a witness whose account has been carefully prepared or is otherwise contrived.[121] It would not be necessary for the full presentation of the prosecution case to adduce evidence which is no more than a scurrilous attack on the character of a witness or when it is clear to demonstration that it is false, as where it is contradicted by other, objective evidence. *It should only be where the reliability or credibility of the evidence is demonstrably lacking that the circumstances may be said to warrant a refusal, on the part of a prosecutor, to call such evidence.*[122]

There is, unfortunately, an ever-replenished array of examples of prosecutors in court overstepping the mark showing that an adversarial culture, set in an

---

116 *Nguyen* [2020] HCA 23, [45] (Kiefel CJ, Bell, Gageler, Keane and Gordon JJ). See also *Soma* [2003] HCA 13; 212 CLR 299.

117 *Legal Profession Uniform Conduct (Barristers) Rules 2015*.

118 *Nguyen* [2020] HCA 23; *Soma* [2003] HCA 13; 212 CLR 299.

119 *Whitehorn* [1983] HCA 42; 152 CLR 657, 676; *Apostilides* [1984] HCA 38; 154 CLR 563, 573. See *Legal Profession Uniform Conduct (Barristers) Rules 2015*, r 89. Note that the traditional emphasis on 'credible' witnesses is loosened as a limitation on the prosecutor's obligation where *UEA*, s 38, applies.

120 *Richardson* [1974] HCA 19; 131 CLR 116, 119; *Nguyen* [2020] HCA 23.

121 [*Pearce* (1979) 69 Cr App R 365, 370.]

122 *Nguyen* [2020] HCA 23, [44] (Kiefel CJ, Bell, Gageler, Keane and Gordon JJ), citing *Apostilides* [1984] HCA 38; 154 CLR 563, 575-6 (emphasis added).

adversarial setting, overwhelms the 'minister of justice' philosophy of constraint – the cornerstone of prosecutor's ethical obligations. The following observation is from the judgment of Hayne J in *Libke*:[123]

> *An unfair trial?*
>
> 71. A criminal trial in Australia is an accusatorial and adversarial process. In that process, prosecuting counsel has a role that is bounded by long-established duties and responsibilities. Those duties and responsibilities are summarised when it is said that '[t]he duty of prosecuting counsel is not to obtain a conviction at all costs but to act as a minister of justice'. In [*Boucher* [1955] SCR 16 in] the Supreme Court of Canada, Rand J described the role of the prosecutor as being:
>
> > 'not to obtain a conviction, it is to lay before a jury what the Crown considers to be credible evidence relevant to what is alleged to be a crime. Counsel have a duty to see that all available legal proof of the facts is presented: it should be done firmly and pressed to its legitimate strength but it must also be done fairly. The role of prosecutor excludes any notion of winning or losing; his function is a matter of public duty than which in civil life there can be none charged with greater personal responsibility. It is to be efficiently performed *with an ingrained sense of the dignity, the seriousness and the justness of judicial proceedings*.' (emphasis added)
>
> A central, even the central, element in that role is 'ensuring that the Crown case is presented *with fairness to the accused*'.

Libke involved the prosecutor questioning an accused, seeking to undermine his credibility and to gain concessions that he, the accused, knew or suspected the complainant was intellectually impaired. The accused had responded, conceding nothing, but the prosecutor's comments, such as 'Look, I've heard all of that. I'm trying to convey to you I'm not buying it' and 'Hopeless asking a question', at times intruded the prosecutor's personal view, but no objection was made at trial.

These comments were not fatal to Libke's appeal, '[n]ot least ... because it must be recognised that counsel for an accused person may well hesitate before objecting to a line of questioning put in cross-examination of the accused, lest it appear to the jury that counsel feels a need to protect the witness'.[124] Aside from the comments, Hayne J observed that:

> Some questions might have been framed better than they were. Some carried imputations critical of the appellant's evidence. Some questions were founded on assertions that were not established or admitted. But the appellant was able to and did give the account he wished to give of the events about which he was asked.[125]

Though the court held the prosecutor should not have made the comments (because his opinion of the accused's veracity was not relevant), it concluded that the comments did not distract the jury from their task of assessing whether the evidence established the appellant's guilt beyond reasonable doubt. Nevertheless, intervention by the judge would have been preferable.

The trial of Gordon Wood[126] reveals the ways beyond cross-examination in which the battle to win the minds (and hearts) of jurors can, as the NSW Court of Criminal Appeal found, step beyond the mark of ethical practice. McClellan CJ at CL upheld the appeal and entered a verdict of acquittal. His Honour observed (at [19]) that the prosecutor advanced a motive for Wood's murder of Ms Byrne

123 [2007] HCA 30; 230 CLR 559.
124 Ibid [76] (Hayne J).
125 Ibid [78] (Hayne J).
126 *Wood* [2012] NSWCCA 21; 84 NSWLR 581.

that 'was entirely speculative and internally inconsistent'. A number of the bases for the trial miscarrying were upheld by the court. Many related to the prosecutor's advocacy in submitting conclusions that were not sustainable on the evidence before the court. For example, McClellan CJ at CL referred to an incident described by witnesses where Caroline Byrne was crying, and Wood was standing beside her:

> 294. Having raised this [argument] with the jury, the prosecutor … used it in an entirely impermissible manner. He told the jury that the Crown submission was that:
>
> > 'This argument must have been something very serious, and it must have had something to do with the accused's employment with Rene Rivkin. That's why Gary Redding was standing next to him. I mean, would you have a rip roaring row with your spouse or partner with one of your fellow employees from your work standing next to you? … It must have had something to do with Rene Rivkin for Gary Redding to be there.'
>
> 295. This submission was entirely speculative. If an argument did occur it could have been as a consequence of trouble in the relationship, which had nothing to do with the applicant's employment with Rivkin. Redding was a friend of the applicant's. The fact that he was present (if he was) may have had nothing to do with Rivkin. It is plain that the prosecutor introduced the prospect that the event was related to Rivkin in order to support his theory as to the applicant's motive. It was a speculative smear.

His Honour also referred[127] to the fact that there was no evidence to support other submissions made by the prosecutor, including that Wood had

> 'a very negative side … very dark and unwanted and verging on being stalking … absolutely controlling and possessive behaviour'; or that Wood 'had confidential information about powerful people, including people in government. He had told people things, including Caroline … that you might think would have horrified Rene Rivkin if he knew. So Rene Rivkin had every reason to be paranoid about Caroline …'.

An additional successful appeal ground focused on the prosecutor's closing address where he listed 50 questions for the jury to consider which, it was ruled, invited speculation, were unreasonably prejudicial, reversed the burden of proof and 'unfairly invited the jury to be suspicious of the applicant's dealings with Rivkin in a manner which was clearly intended to smear his character' (at [605], [615]).

The Function and the Art of Proof

Proof is at the heart of a trial. It is its rationale and also its end game. Proof also arises during the trial. Aside from the *evidential* burden of proof[128] (which refers merely to a party bearing the obligation to *raise* an issue), proof arises:

- with respect to the ultimate proof of the charge which is, of course, a matter to be proven by the *prosecution* to a beyond reasonable doubt standard (*UEA*, s 141(1)); and
- when the *defence* bears a legal burden of proof, for example, due to a statutory reversal of the burden of proof or to establish insanity, the balance of probabilities standard also applies (*UEA*, s 141(2));

127 Ibid [304], [312].

128 That is, the burden of 'adducing or pointing to evidence that suggests a reasonable possibility that the matter exists or does not exist'. The legal burden of proof of a matter 'means the burden of proving the existence of the matter': see *Criminal Code* (Cth), ss 13.1 and 13.3.

- where the court is required to establish what is described in *UEA*, s 189(1), as a '*preliminary question*', that is, finding whether a particular fact exists for a court's determination of whether evidence should be admitted (whether in the exercise of a discretion or not), or evidence can be used against a person or a witness is competent or compellable,[129] those facts must be established on a balance of probabilities (*UEA*, s 142);
- where a judge takes *judicial notice* of facts or law (where parties need not meet any burden) (*UEA*, s 144);
- on *the drawing of inferences, as distinct from speculating*, in the context of jury and judicial fact-finders' decision-making; and
- in the context of directed acquittals.

Advocacy

It is important to appreciate the context in which evidence law is applied in a criminal trial. First, counsel does not just dump information before the jury. They recognise that jurors, like all people, need to understand how information fits into the context of a party's case. It is at this point that counsel has the opportunity to 'shape' their case. Second, court process does not follow typical discourse as to how a person learns of events. Instead, there is a rigid ordering of the trial. It begins with the judge giving some short instructions ('initial remarks') to the jurors when they have been empanelled. The prosecutor then makes an opening address, summarising the case that the prosecution intends to prove before the jury. At this stage defence counsel may (or may not) make an opening address.[130] Then each prosecution witness enters the witness box serially. Each may be examined by the prosecutor, cross-examined by defence counsel, and perhaps re-examined by the prosecutor. Typically witnesses give direct evidence of an event they have witnessed. They are limited to testifying to their personal knowledge (to what they saw, heard or otherwise perceived). Witness questioning is highly regulated, and each witness's account contains information that, like tiles in a mosaic, will, counsel hopes, form the desired picture. It is rare that every fact in a story can be proved (because not all tiles will be available). The trial is generally set in an austere courtroom, with large spaces between protagonists, with a public gallery, court officers, papers, microphones and sundry background activities taking place and the judge acts as a referee applying legal rules that can at any moment halt questions and answers. This process means that, aside from the undoubted complexity of rules of evidence and procedure, the context of evidence presentation and testing brings its own challenges to jurors and witnesses. This brings us to the third and final dominant element of the criminal trial context, namely, that it

129 See *UEA*, ss 13-19. Or any other procedural occasion under the *UEA* where a factual finding is required, eg, granting a party leave or permission or making a direction (s 192), providing a judicial warning (eg, such as whether the facts support the evidence being categorised as 'evidence of a kind that may be unreliable': s 165). Preliminary questions must be determined on a *voir dire*, that is, a trial within the trial proper: see *UEA*, s 189. On a *voir dire* parties can call witnesses, cross-examine opponent's witnesses and make submissions – as they might in the trial proper. The *voir dire* will typically involve the jury leaving the courtroom so that should evidence be ruled inadmissible or disputed questioning not permitted the jurors' minds are not tainted by prior exposure.

130 It may be subject to limitations, see *MM* (2004) 145 A Crim R 148 and *CARA* (NSW), s 159(2): 'Any such opening address is to be limited generally to an address on: (a) the matters disclosed in the prosecutor's opening address, including those that are in dispute and those that are not in dispute, and (b) the matters to be raised by the accused person'.

takes place in an environment where the regular players, the judge and lawyers, know the ropes and understand the process. However, the accused, the witnesses and the jurors are (most often) lay people, whose knowledge of legal process is through popular culture or learnt 'on the job'. For most, their experiences in the courtroom are once or twice in a lifetime. They are the equivalent of tourists in a legal land. Their official tour guide is the presiding judge. The law of evidence and procedure controls the information that is placed before the jury, and to a certain extent how that information is presented. As we saw above in relation to trials involving co-accused, judicial direction is seen as a key moderator where issues of unfair prejudice may arise.[131] Notably, the following well-known observation by McHugh J from *Gilbert*[132] infers judges possess powerful skills when it comes to directing juries:

> 31. The criminal trial on indictment proceeds on the assumption that jurors are true to their oath, that, in the quaint words of the ancient oath, they hearken to the evidence and that they obey the trial judge's directions. On that assumption, which I regard as fundamental to the criminal jury trial, the common law countries have staked a great deal. If it was rejected or disregarded, no one – accused, trial judge or member of the public – could have any confidence in any verdict of a criminal jury or in the criminal justice system whenever it involves a jury trial. If it was rejected or disregarded, the pursuit of justice through the jury system would be as much a charade as the show trial of any totalitarian state. Put bluntly, unless we act on the assumption that criminal juries act on the evidence and in accordance with the directions of the trial judge, there is no point in having criminal jury trials. It is of course true that, if a jury persists in returning a verdict that is contrary to law, the trial judge must accept it.[133] But that only means in Lord Mansfield's words that, although "[i]t is the duty of the Judge ... to tell the jury how to do right ... they have it in their power to do wrong".[134]
>
> 32. In my respectful opinion, the fundamental assumption of the criminal jury trial requires us to proceed on the basis that the jury acted in this case on the evidence and in accordance with the trial judge's directions and that they would have done so even if manslaughter had been left as an issue, as it should have been left. In *Spratt*,[135] Pidgeon J said, correctly in my opinion, "that an appellate court must proceed on the basis that the jury have understood and applied the law in reaching a true verdict."

Counsel's audience may be judges, magistrates or jurors. The first two, the professional audiences, are familiar with advocates' strategies as they were probably advocating before their judicial appointments. Jurors, of course, are novices in court. As the rulings in the Court of Criminal Appeal in the case of *Wood* indicate, counsel cannot make submissions based on speculation. To do so offends the rationalist tradition at its heart. As we see in Chapter 4, the rationalist tradition is at the foundation of the law of evidence. But the boundaries of advocacy, whether they are wielded by the prosecutor or defence counsel, require making qualitative judgments that are built on professional standards of propriety and a good appreciation of the philosophies that drive trials. As a rule of thumb, unless a breach trips a prescribed fundamental principle or rule, such as the burden of proof or the presumption of innocence and so creating a miscarriage of justice, it tends to be seen as incidental to adversarialism.

---

131 See also *Symss* [2003] NSWCCA 77, [76] (Sheller JA, with James J and Smart AJ agreeing); *Ignjatic* (1993) 68 A Crim R 333, 339.

132 [2000] HCA 15; 201 CLR 414.

133 [*Gammage* [1969] HCA 68; 122 CLR 444, 451.]

134 [*Shipley* (1784) 4 Doug 73, 170; 99 ER 774, 824.]

135 [(1982) 8 A Crim R 361, 372.]

Advocacy as the art of persuasion seeks to ensure a party's quantum of evidence is given maximum impact. Advocates cannot change many things (the evidence, their own personal qualities, the personal qualities of their witnesses or of the jurors) but they can seek to make their interpretation of evidence connect optimally with jurors. In this task prosecutors cannot appeal to 'prejudice or passion'.[136] However, as psychological research indicates, human emotion cannot be disengaged in the absorption and evaluation of information. Barristers are natural psychologists. Consider the observations of David Bennett AO QC, former Commonwealth Solicitor-General.

> You must never forget that you are not mechanically putting the argument you have so carefully prepared. It's not like that. You're persuading a human being to come to a particular viewpoint, and that's terribly important. That's basic to everything ...[137]

Bennett gives the following examples of advocacy stratagems to advance an argument to the preferred conclusion:

> Suppose you have a case where a solicitor has been convicted of driving at a speed dangerous, and there is then a disciplinary proceeding based on that conviction. Now suppose you argue for the solicitor that *a traffic offence can never justify disciplinary proceedings*. What's the first question you're going to be asked? '*What about drunken driving causing death?*' Suppose you're for the Law Society and you argue that any infraction of the law leading to a criminal sanction is capable of justifying disciplinary action. What is the first question you're going to get? '*What about a parking ticket?*'. ... The second question could be answered in two ways. You could answer by saying, '*even a parking ticket justifies disciplinary action*'; or you could answer by saying, '*driving at a speed dangerous is different from a parking offence. You could take either approach.*'

An element of lawyers' gamesmanship is revealed in the Crown prosecutor's opening sequence of questions cross-examining Ivan Milat (the 'backpacker murderer case').[138] These questions painstakingly took Milat through his activities the day before his arrest; for example: 'By 12.10 had you driven to the intersection at Campbelltown Road and the freeway? ... At about 1.27 did you drive the service vehicle away from the CSR depot on Rosehill? ... Did you stop off somewhere shortly after ...'. The questioning revealed (only to Milat) that he had been under police surveillance and served the purpose of making the accused aware of the prosecutor's breadth and depth of knowledge of his movements and, perhaps, wondering what didn't the prosecution know?[139] The questioning proceeded to the point where Milat responds to a question by identifying that he had visited a shop (Lombardo's) where he had previously met Paul Onions, an English backpacker who had escaped from Milat, and thus Milat's own answer linked in to support an important aspect of the prosecution case.

Of course, human beings are complex creatures. As the following brief introduction into the realm of emotion and psychology indicates, decision-making in a trial (like all decision-making) is influenced by numerous variables, including how information resonates with our senses. Human emotion impacts on judgment, often without conscious advertence to this impact. Emotion is pervasive. It 'helps

136 *Libke* [2007] HCA 30; 230 CLR 559, [83] (Hayne J, using these terms to indicate that the prosecutor in *Libke* had conducted himself inappropriately in various respects, but not with respect to appealing to prejudice or passion).

137 D Bennett, 'The Art of Persuasion through Oral Advocacy' (2007) 28 *Adelaide Law Review* 145, 148-9.

138 D Howard, *R v Milat: A Case Study in Cross-Examination* (LexisNexis, 2014).

139 Ibid 35-8.

sort, evaluate, highlight, and prioritize information and provides an impetus to act upon it. It is "like an unseen lens that colors all our thoughts, actions, perceptions, and judgments".'[140] Bandes and Blumenthal[141] identify from the literature four ways emotion influences legal judgments. These relate to 'people's strategies for processing information'; by 'biasing the perception, recall, or evaluation of facts in a particular direction'; 'by providing informational cues to proper attribution of blame'; and 'by anticipating future emotions that might follow from a judgment'. How evidence is depicted in a trial, whether it be written or audio-visually recorded impacts on judgment. These emotions are not ones that can be erased on judicial instruction.[142] As Bandes and Blumenthal observe:

> If empathy is the capacity to understand the thoughts and feelings of another, it becomes clear that it is not an occasionally employed sentiment or a sentiment directed solely at those less fortunate, but a tool that is in constant (albeit not always accurate) use in legal decision making. Once empathy is understood in this light, it becomes possible – and essential – to investigate how empathy is employed in a variety of legal contexts. For example, studies suggest not only that juries have difficulty empathizing with defendants from other racial and demographic backgrounds but also that juries in homicide cases tend to feel more empathetic toward some homicide victims than others and that this selective empathy influences their verdicts. The science and social science of empathy also point the way toward the possibility of addressing empathy deficits or selective empathy; empathy appears to be a capacity that is eminently trainable.[143]

As we know the claimed strength of adversarial fact-finding is in persuading the jury by a battle of stories. Subject to the prosecutor's obligation to call all material witnesses, parties determine the witnesses they call, the evidence that is before the court, the questions to be asked of witnesses and the issues to be contested. In other words, parties and parties' advocacy dominate the trial process. The presiding judge must defer to the parties on the substance of the 'contest'.

The Mechanics of Proof

There was a time in Australia when a trial judge had a power to invite the jury to consider its verdict at the conclusion of the prosecution case (and therefore without hearing the defence case): *Prasad*.[144] The so-called *Prasad* Direction typically required the defence to make a request of the judge, and for the jury to then accept the invitation from the judge to hear no further evidence. The *Prasad* Direction was based on the judge forming the view that, although there was evidence *capable* in law of supporting a conviction, it may be 'insufficiently cogent' to support a verdict of guilty.[145] This option no longer exists. In *DPP Reference No 1 of 2017*[146] the High Court ruled that the Direction was inconsistent with the division of

140 S Bandes and J Blumenthal, 'Emotion and the Law' (2012) 8 *Annual Review of Law and Social Science* 161, 166, citing J Goodwin et al (eds), *Passionate Politics: Emotions and Social Movements* (University of Chicago Press, 2001), 10.

141 Bandes and Blumenthal, ibid, 166, drawing on N Feigenson, 'Emotional Influences on Judgments of Legal Blame: How They Happen, Whether They Should and What to do About It' in B Bornstein and B Wiener (eds), *Emotion and the Law: Psychological Perspectives* (Springer, 2010).

142 Bandes and Blumenthal, above n 140, 166-7.

143 Ibid 170 (citations omitted).

144 (1979) 23 SASR 161.

145 *Pahuga* (1987) 49 SASR 191, 201 (King CJ).

146 [2019] HCA 9; 364 ALR 407 (Kiefel CJ, Bell, Gageler, Keane, Nettle, Gordon and Edelman JJ).

functions between judge and jury and that it had the potential for jurors to perceive the judge's direction to them as an authoritative pronouncement that the prosecution evidence is so unsatisfactory as to warrant an acquittal. The High Court also added (at [57] and [86]) that jurors would be called upon to consider their verdict in potentially profound ignorance if they were invited 'to stop a trial without having heard all of the evidence, without having heard counsel's final addresses, and without the understanding of the law and its application to the facts'.

> If evidence taken at its highest is capable of sustaining a conviction, it is for the jury as the constitutional tribunal of fact to decide whether the evidence establishes guilt beyond reasonable doubt. A jury is not fully equipped to make that decision until and unless they have heard all of the evidence, counsel's addresses and the judge's summing-up. Anything less falls short of the trial according to law to which both the accused and the Crown are entitled.[147]

However, if at the close of the prosecution case there is not sufficient evidence capable of supporting a guilty verdict, the defence may seek a directed acquittal. The test of sufficiency is long-standing and requires the trial judge to determine,

> if there is evidence (even if tenuous or inherently weak or vague) which can be taken into account by the jury in its deliberations and that evidence is capable of supporting a verdict of guilty, the matter must be left to the jury for its decision. Or, to put the matter in more usual terms, a verdict of not guilty may be directed only if there is a defect in the evidence such that, taken at its highest, it will not sustain a verdict of guilty.[148]

Standard of Proof

Beyond reasonable doubt

The ultimate proof requirement in a criminal prosecution, referred to since the case of *Woolmington v DPP* as 'the golden thread',[149] is the obligation on the prosecution to satisfy each legal element of the charge to the criminal standard of proof beyond reasonable doubt. The *UEA*, s 141(1), confirms this.

Australian common law treats any judicial explanation of beyond reasonable doubt to a jury as unacceptable, a matter on which the High Court has remained firm. As the NSW Law Reform Commission (NSWLRC) noted, the High Court's 'view has been that further explanation is unnecessary and dangerous'; because it is a phrase that is 'in ordinary and common use and is a 'well understood expression'; and 'because it is for the jury to say whether or not a doubt is reasonable, and to set for themselves the parameters of what is reasonable in the context of the case'.[150] The High Court case of *Green* articulated the philosophical indivis-

---

147 Ibid [57] (Kiefel CJ, Bell, Gageler, Keane, Nettle, Gordon and Edelman JJ). See also *Warwick (No 80)* [2020] NSWSC 115.

148 *Doney* [1990] HCA 51; 171 CLR 207, 214-15 (Deane, Dawson, Toohey, Gaudron and McHugh JJ), reaffirmed in *A2, Magennis and Vaziri* [2019] HCA 35; 93 ALJR 1106, [88] (Kiefel CJ and Keane J).

149 *Woolmington v DPP* [1935] UKHL 1; [1935] AC 462, 481-2. *Woolmington* overturned 18th century authority, *Foster's Crown Law* (1762), that stated that for murder 'the law presumeth the fact to have been founded in malice, unless the contrary appeareth' (and so shifting the burden to the accused to prove accident where the prosecution case showed that Woolmington had shot his wife).

150 NSWLRC, *Jury Directions in Criminal Trials* (Report No 136, 2012), Directing the Jury on the Criminal Standard of Proof, [4.3], citing *Brown* [1913] HCA 70; 17 CLR 570, 584 (Barton ACJ); *Dawson* [1961] HCA 74; 106 CLR 1, 18 (Dixon CJ); *Thomas* [1960] HCA 2; 102 CLR 584, 595 (Kitto J); *La Fontaine* [1976] HCA 51; 136 CLR 62, 71-2 (Barwick CJ), and see 80-1 (Gibbs J).

ibility between the essence of a jury's role and 'objective community standards'.[151] A determination of a reasonable doubt is one 'which the particular jury entertain in the circumstances', by the standards set, 'bring[ing] to bear their experience and judgment'.[152] A number of instances where judges have forgotten themselves suggest the High Court's view is soundly based. One of the more spectacular judicial trivialisations of this criminal standard of proof occurred in the trial on appeal in *Condo*[153] when the trial judge suggested the jury take guidance from cricket, saying:

> You would have seen an endless number of times in the course of the World Cup Cricket where the[re] is an appeal for an LBW decision ... and you hear the commentators, 'There must have been a reasonable doubt; the batsman has been given the benefit of that'.[154]

This description was unacceptable. A strikingly similar inspiration from cricket was drawn in the 2014 case of *CBK*[155] where the trial judge included intricacies on the LBW 'rule' in directing the jury such as:

> [Y]ou can look at where the front foot is, you can look at the height of the ball, you can look at the snicker and any other replays that are available, where the ball pitched, whether it was in line with the stumps. And if you're satisfied of all of those things, the batsman's out. But if you're not sure that that ball is really going to hit the stumps or whether there's some element of doubt about whether the ball pitched in line or not, you have to give the benefit – the umpires have to give the benefit of the doubt to the batsman. And that's the thing about criminal trials; the benefit of the doubt goes to the defendant.

It too was held to be inappropriate to 'trivialise the solemn role the community demands of jurors' (in a case involving sexual abuse of a child), of no assistance to those who do not follow cricket, or to those who do follow cricket because 'beyond reasonable doubt' does not apply to the rules of cricket, and it ran the risk that jury deliberations would digress to focus on the analogy rather than the evidence in the case. The dangers inherent in judges attempting to explain 'beyond reasonable doubt' to the jury are not just of the *Condo* or *CBK* cricket-inspired ilk – that is, just plainly getting it wrong. Judges can over-complicate the direction with an inappropriately demanding test on the jury. In *Green* it was suggested that jurors 'are both unaccustomed and not required to submit their processes of mind to objective analysis' of the kind suggested to them by the trial judge.[156] However, for each of these cases, there are others which show that jurors seek assistance and become frustrated when it is not forthcoming. For example, in support of its recommendation to remove the High Court requirement that judges maintain a vow of silence, the NSWLRC cites an example of the absurdity that can be created:

> [I]n the Victorian case of *R v Chatzidimitriou* ... the jury asked the trial judge to provide a definition of 'doubt', 'reasonable doubt' and 'beyond reasonable doubt'. The judge

151 See, eg, *CPA* (NSW), s 132 ('Orders for trial by Judge alone'), articulating that a court may refuse an application for a judge-alone trial 'if it considers that the trial will involve a factual issue that requires the application of objective community standards, including (but not limited to) an issue of reasonableness, negligence, indecency, obscenity or dangerousness'.

152 *Green* [1971] HCA 55; 126 CLR 28, 32-3, relying on *Brown* [1913] HCA 70; 17 CLR 570; *Thomas* [1960] HCA 2; 102 CLR 584; *Dawson* [1961] HCA 74; 106 CLR 1.

153 (1992) 62 A Crim R 11.

154 Taken from JB Hunter and K Cronin, *Evidence, Advocacy and Ethical Practice: A Criminal Trial Commentary* (Butterworths, 1995), 138.

155 [2014] QCA 35.

156 *Green* [1971] HCA 55; 126 CLR 28, 32-3.

declined to do so beyond repeating the standard direction, in the course of which he observed that 'the law has always taken the view that those are very plain English words and ought to be interpreted by the jury to mean exactly what they say, namely beyond reasonable doubt. It is impossible to put another definition on them'. Shortly after retiring, the jury sent out a request for a dictionary, which was then provided. It was accepted by the parties that the jury had requested the dictionary in an attempt to obtain further content in relation to the various words. The Court of Appeal dismissed the challenge to the way in which this aspect of the direction had been managed. Justice Cummins accepted that the jury could define for itself the meaning of the expression 'beyond reasonable doubt', and for that purpose to have access to a dictionary. Justice Phillips thought that while it had been undesirable for the trial judge to have acceded to the jury's request nevertheless concluded that it did not give rise to error.[157]

Even more compelling evidence of the need to review the blanket ban on judicial explanation is the empirical research cited by the NSWLRC.[158] For example, a NSW Bureau of Crime Statistics and Research study[159] of over 1200 jurors from over 100 NSW Supreme Court and District Court criminal trials in 2007-08 revealed that from four options only 55% of the jurors equated 'beyond reasonable doubt' (BRD) with meaning '*sure*'[160] that the defendant is guilty. The remainder were content with '*almost sure*' that the defendant is guilty (23%); '*very likely*' (12%) and '*pretty likely*' (10%) that the defendant is guilty. In response to cases like *Chatzidimitriou*, the *Jury Directions Act 2015* (Vic), s 63, permits a trial judge to respond to a direct or an indirect jury request for guidance. Section 64 lifts the ban on judicial explanations of the meaning of beyond reasonable doubt if the jury has asked a direct question about its meaning, or has raised the question indirectly. Such a judge's response should answer the jury question and may:

(a) refer to –
  (i) the presumption of innocence; and
  (ii) the prosecution's obligation to prove that the accused is guilty; or
(b) indicate that it is not enough for the prosecution to persuade the jury that the accused is probably guilty or very likely to be guilty; or
(c) indicate that –
  (i) it is almost impossible to prove anything with absolute certainty when reconstructing past events; and
  (ii) the prosecution does not have to do so; or
(d) indicate that the jury cannot be satisfied that the accused is guilty if the jury has a reasonable doubt about whether the accused is guilty; or
(e) indicate that a reasonable doubt is not an imaginary or fanciful doubt or an unrealistic possibility.

---

157 NSWLRC, above n 150, [4.34] (citations omitted), citing *Chatzidimitriou* [2000] VSCA 91; 1 VR 493.

158 NSWLRC, above n 150, [4.36].

159 L Trimboli, 'Juror Understanding of Judicial Instructions in Criminal Trials', *Crime and Justice Bulletin* (No 119, BOCSAR, 2008), 4.

160 This test has been adopted in England and Wales. For a useful summary of the cases, see NSWLRC, above n 150, [4.20]-[4.22]. In New Zealand, in *Wanhalla* [2006] NZCA 229; [2007] 2 NZLR 573 the Court of Appeal also encourages trial judges to explain beyond reasonable doubt in terms of 'if, after careful and impartial consideration of the evidence, you are sure that the accused is guilty you must find him or her guilty' but it also encouraged elements of the Canadian *Lifchus* [1997] 3 SCR 320 formulation, discussed below. United States authority is similarly committed to an explanation centred on a 'firmly convinced' belief of guilt: see NSWLRC, above n 150, [4.23]-[4.29].

These considerations pick up elements from the Canadian approach in *Lifchus*[161] where Cory J observed that the presumption of innocence obligation that infuses the whole trial process is also embodied in the ultimate standard of proof.

The NSWLRC report, *Jury Directions*,[162] notes that '[o]n any view, the standard of proof is pivotal to the criminal justice system' and prefers a single Australian approach that has been subjected to empirical testing to ensure that the chosen formulation is more easily understood, consistently applied and does not result in a change in the standard required'.[163] As it notes, a High Court resolution to the problem is unlikely and so suggests legislation should be considered that draws on the experiences in England and Wales, Canada or New Zealand.

Balance of probabilities and the *Briginshaw* principles

The balance of probability standard applies to proof determinations in a number of situations, that is, where the judge must establish facts relevant to determining the admissibility of evidence and where the defence bears the burden of proof: see *UEA*, ss 141, 142, 189.[164] In relation to the judge's task of establishing preliminary questions the *Briginshaw v Briginshaw*[165] principles articulate that satisfying the balance of probabilities standard depends on its context. These principles are imported into the *UEA* through ss 140(2) and 142(2), requiring the court to consider, among other matters, 'the importance of the evidence in the proceeding, and ... the gravity of the matters alleged in relation to the question'. In other words, assessing balance of probabilities 'does not involve a mechanical weighing of probabilities – satisfaction as to whether the civil onus had been discharged [depends] ... upon *the gravity of the allegation and its consequences*'.[166]

> The strength of the evidence necessary to establish a fact or facts on the balance of probabilities may vary according to the nature of what is sought be proved. Clear or cogent or strict proof is necessary where so serious a matter as fraud is to be found. These statements should be understood as reflecting a conventional perception that members of our society do not ordinarily engage in fraudulent or criminal conduct, and a judicial approach that a court should not lightly make a finding that, on the balance of probabilities, a person has been guilty of such conduct.[167]

Taking into account 'the gravity of the matters alleged in relation to a question' (s 142(2)(b)) impacts on situations where, for instance, a preliminary fact relating to the admissibility of evidence relies on allegations that someone has made a fraudulent statement or has acted illegally or inappropriately. For example, in relation to admissions (or confessions) the defence may raise the issue of duress.[168] The court will then need to establish to a balance of probabilities standard as

161 [1997] 3 SCR 320, [36], [37] (Cory J, delivering the judgment of the court).

162 NSWLRC, above n 150, [4.3], [4.69].

163 Ibid [4.74].

164 *UEA*, s 140.

165 [1938] HCA 34; 60 CLR 336. See also *Re Day* [2017] HCA 2, [15]-[18] (Gordon J).

166 *R (Cth) v Petroulias (No 8)* [2007] NSWSC 82, [16] (emphasis added) (Johnson J), citing *B v Medical Superintendent of Macquarie Hospital* (1987) 10 NSWLR 440, 460-1 (McHugh JA); *Neat Holdings Pty Limited v Karajan Holdings Pty Limited* [1992] HCA 66; 67 ALJR 170, 170-1 (Mason CJ, Brennan, Deane and Gaudron JJ). See also *Granada Tavern v Smith* [2008] FCA 646; *Amalgamated Television Services Pty Ltd v Marsden* [2002] NSWCA 419, [61]; *Palmer v Dorman* [2005] NSWCA 361, [40]-[47].

167 *R (Cth) v Petroulias (No 8)* [2007] NSWSC 82, [16].

168 See *UEA*, s 84 (discussed in Chapter 7).

to whether 'violent, oppressive, inhuman or degrading conduct' influenced the making of the admission (with the burden on the party wishing to have the admission admitted to satisfy the court that it was not so influenced). The court must also consider the importance of the evidence as well: *UEA*, s 142(2)(a).

Judges and Sources of Proof – 'Matters of Common Knowledge'

When a judge is a trier-of-fact he or she, like jurors, must rely on evidence properly admitted. If there is evidence of a matter, then no judge can go beyond the evidence before the court.[169] However, courts have some limited scope to take 'judicial notice' of matters of common knowledge. This form of a proof 'short cut' exists because it would be disproportionate to the required use of time, effort and resources for parties to prove some matters which are in fact readily established. This is the logic of *UEA*, s 144, namely the practicality of accepting that parties should not be obliged to formally prove the obvious.

For example, it 'is a matter of common knowledge that a bullet piercing the brain of a human being will in all likelihood prove fatal'.[170] As s 144(1)(a) indicates, they might include a locality, public building or monument (eg, Sydney Harbour Bridge), the date of Christmas Day or that New Year's Eve is celebrated with fireworks on Sydney Harbour (even during a pandemic). Facts such as these need no proof if they are '*not reasonably open to question*' and are

> (a) common knowledge in the locality in which the proceeding is being held or generally, or
> (b) capable of verification by reference to a document the authority of which cannot reasonably be questioned.[171]

Even politics is not beyond judicial notice as common knowledge at least when it is 'capable of verification by reference to a document the authority of which cannot reasonably be questioned'. Similarly, appropriately researched studies explaining the impact of disadvantage on offenders, relevant in sentencing, comes within s 144.[172] The following observation from McHugh J in 2002 reveals the broad potential in s 144, referring to facts that have been judicially noticed without inquiry as including:

> that cancer is a major health problem in the community and, despite research, little progress has been made in controlling it; ... that a child victim of sexual assault may be reluctant to resist, protest or complain about the sexual assault, due to fear of punishment or rejection; and that many lawyers now charge hundreds of dollars an hour for their services, that legal aid is often unavailable to litigants in tort cases and that the cost of those services is substantially increased when lawyers cannot give advice to their clients because the law is unpredictable.[173]

---

169 *Amante* [2020] NSWCCA 34, [70] (N Adams J, with Payne JA agreeing).

170 *Cross on Evidence Australian Edition* (Online Service – LexisNexis), [3220], citing *Rostad v Portland Ry, Light and Power Co* 201 P 184, 187 (SC Or, 1921) (Burnett CJ).

171 See *UEA*, s 144(1). *UEA*, s 143 (Matters of law), provides judicial knowledge (that is, proof is not required) for legislation, proclamations or orders of the 'Governor-General, the Governor of a State or the Administrator or Executive of a Territory made, or purporting to be made, under such an Act or Ordinance'. A judge is at liberty to inform him or herself as the judge thinks fit: sub-s (2).

172 N Cowdery, J Hunter and R McMahon, 'Sentencing and disadvantage: the use of research to inform the court' (2020) 32 *Judicial Officers Bulletin* 43.

173 *Woods v Multi-Sport Holdings* [2002] HCA 9; 208 CLR 460, 479 (McHugh J) (footnotes omitted).

Cross on Evidence[174] extensively summarises cases in which various phenomena have been considered common knowledge. This includes that triers of fact are familiar with an understanding of the ordinary use of English and basic arithmetic (and without it they could not grasp the evidence presented to them).

> Common knowledge and experience of physical phenomena may be taken into account. An example is the behaviour of fires – the tendency of brush, stubble or grass fires to flare up and die down, but then to remain smouldering for days before flaring up again;[175] the likelihood of a fire being started by a man lighting his pipe and lying down on straw to smoke it.[176] Another is that depending on the position of the moon, on whether it is waxing or waning, and on the depth of cloud, some nights are darker than others.[177]

Other examples in past cases include:

- The capacities of people to engage in physical activities, such as walking, running and bathing. Dixon CJ in the well-known case of *Plomp* referred to taking judicial notice of the capacity of the deceased, a 'good swimmer', such that 'it was not likely that [she] would have been lost unless ... her efforts at recovery were in some way obstructed'.[178]
- The same is true of the 'basic psychology' of door-to-door selling, 'taught by life experience and common sense'.[179] Also in the realm of psychology, judicial notice has been taken of the eating habits of shoppers in country shopping centres.[180] In *Rogic v Samaan*[181] Kunc J took judicial notice of the fact that 'document retention requirements mean that it would be highly unlikely that any financial or similar institutions would have retained loan, tax or other records going back nearly 30 years'.
- In *Farkas*[182] the NSW Court of Criminal Appeal relied on published research from a research Centre at the University of New South Wales to establish the median 'street' purity of drugs regarding a sentencing appeal (where the sentencing judge had provided no basis for relying on a purity level inconsistent with the published research).

Section 144(2) permits a judge to 'acquire knowledge ... in any way the judge thinks fit'. This qualification clearly has limits. For example, it would not extend to overriding s 144(1)(b) and extending a judge's reliance to facts established from mass media. A clear example beyond s 144's scope arose for consideration in *DPP v Gramelis*[183] where the magistrate at first instance had responded to Gramelis's speeding defence that the defendant stated that he put the truck into second gear and knew that the loaded truck '[did] not do more than 40 km/h in second gear' with the retort that 'I take judicial notice of the fact that in second gear in

174 *Cross on Evidence Australian Edition* (Online Service – LexisNexis).
175 [Ibid [3215], citing *Miller v Sabinske* 322 SW 2d 941, 947-8 (1959).
176 [Ibid [3220], citing *Lillibridge v McCann* 75 NW 288, 289 (1898).]
177 [Ibid [3220], citing *Alexander* [1979] VR 615, 629.]
178 Ibid [3235], citing *Plomp* [1963] HCA 44; 110 CLR 234, 241.
179 Ibid [3240), citing *Australian Competition and Consumer Commission v Lux Distributors Pty Ltd* [2013] FCAFC 90; [2013] ATPR ¶42-447.
180 Ibid [3240], citing *Strong v Woolworths Ltd* [2012] HCA 5; 246 CLR 182, [69]-[70].
181 [2018] NSWSC 1464, [132].
182 [2014] NSWCCA 141.
183 [2010] NSWSC 787.

the average car as I drive a manual one myself one cannot generally get to the limit of sixty kilometres per hour'.[184] Nor would it be apt for a judge to rely on facts established in another case, for example whether a location was within the Australian Fishing Zone.[185] The location of the AFZ boundary and the distance between Australia and Timor Leste are not matters of 'common knowledge' nor ones to be ascertained by a judge relying on another court's decision. The limits on what is sufficiently established as 'not reasonably open to question' (*UEA*, s 144(1)) are inevitably hazy but s 144(4) protects parties by requiring the judge 'give a party such opportunity to make submissions, and to refer to relevant information, relating to the acquiring or taking into account of knowledge of that kind as is necessary to ensure that the party is not unfairly prejudiced': *UEA*, s 144(2) and (3).

The High Court in the case of *Aytugrul*[186] considered the possibility of relying on psychological research which it argued should be considered by the court as evidence of 'legislative facts' to aid applying the phrase 'unfair prejudice to the defendant', relevant to the exclusion of prosecution evidence under *UEA*, s 137.[187] The evidence was to support the argument that the DNA analysis should have been expressed by reference to a frequency ratio, namely, that one in 1600 people in the general population would be expected to share the recovered DNA profile rather than, as the prosecution expert did, by an exclusion ratio (that 99.9% of the population did not share the DNA profile). However, the research was not adduced in the trial. It was before the appeal courts. French CJ, Hayne, Crennan and Bell JJ concluded that the research findings could not be treated as within s 144,[188] because:

> [T]he level of technical sophistication involved in the material on which the appellant relied is so great that it would not be satisfactory for this Court to take it into account without the assistance of expert witnesses who had been cross-examined. It would be very difficult for this Court, without that aid, to resolve any controversies which may arise. To borrow the words of Judge Frank speaking about psychiatry, it would be dangerous for the Court 'to embark – without a pilot, rudder, compass or radar – on an amateur's voyage on [this] fog-enshrouded sea.' The appellant submitted that the respondent had not made 'any significant challenge to the research' relied on. Even if this is so – and the respondent disagreed – if the expert material were to be taken into account, it was highly preferable that it be presented through expert witnesses, preferably during a pre-trial hearing to determine admissibility. The admissibility and weight of the expert material could then be considered publicly and critically.[189]

184 Appeal upheld due to non-compliance with s 144(4). Price J added that the magistrate did not take into account the context of Gramelis's loaded Isuzu truck under prevailing conditions, adding that an adjournment might have been sought to enable consideration of whether to call expert evidence on the point.

185 *Aregar v Cox* [2018] NTCA 3.

186 [2012] HCA 15; 247 CLR 170 (citations omitted).

187 See Chapter 4.

188 One issue related to the evidence as legislative facts, and this also engaged the question whether the common law position of judicial notice might apply, rather than s 144, in which case the majority concluded at [73] that 'it is unlikely that the material was sufficiently uncontroversial for judicial notice to be taken of it'.

189 *Aytugrul* [2012] HCA 15, [74], citing *United States v Flores-Rodriguez* [1956] USCA2 348; 237 F 2d 405, 412 (2nd Cir 1956).

The Jury, Decision-making and Avoiding Speculation

A jury of 12 citizens remains central to the zeitgeist of the criminal justice system. It is 'the constitutional tribunal for deciding issues of fact'.[190] They are prescribed under s 80 of the Constitution for all Commonwealth offences tried on indictment and they are the default for trials on indictment in the States and Territories.[191] Jurors' anonymity, randomness and transient status in the criminal justice system mean that they are a check against state power. As Lord Devlin poetically put it, although '[p]ower lies beneath their feet ... they tread on it so swiftly that they are not burnt'.[192] The jury, in effect, infuses democratic engagement in adjudication, enabling its verdict to be promoted as a community decision.[193] As Basten JA observed in *Brown v DPP (NSW)* they are 'a mechanism for preserving confidence in the criminal justice system', preventing the trial becoming the 'closed shop of the legal expert'.[194] In terms of the role of challenges to a prospective juror, and particularly the role of the peremptory challenge, in essence the accused must have

> a reasonable opportunity to see the prospective juror's face, before they enter the jury box. There is no prescribed practice. The opportunity may be provided by employing the traditional practice of a 'parade' by the prospective jurors past the dock or by directing prospective jurors, whose name or number is called, to stand up and turn to face the accused in the dock before proceeding to enter the jury box, or by some other procedure which satisfies the objective of enabling a visual inspection of the potential jurors.

As is apparent from this description by Redlich and McLeish JJA in *Theodoropoulos*,[195] an accused has a brief visual inspection as the basis on which to challenge a prospective juror's participation. States vary from those, like New South Wales and Western Australia that reveal no information about prospective jurors, to Tasmania, Victoria and Queensland where a name or a number can be used to identify prospective jurors, and finally where in Victoria in addition the occupation is revealed. Peremptory challenges have been removed in England and Wales and in Canada. In Canada they were removed because of their potential to racially skew the jury if used in a discriminatory fashion.[196] Former High Court

---

190 *Hocking v Bell* [1945] HCA 16; 71 CLR 430, 440, quoted by *Baden-Clay* [2016] HCA 35; 258 CLR 308, 329 [65] (French CJ, Kiefel, Bell, Keane and Gordon JJ).

191 *CPA* (NSW), s 131.

192 P Devlin, 'The Conscience of the Jury' (1991) 107 *Law Quarterly Review* 398, 404.

193 *Belghar* [2012] NSWCCA 86; 217 A Crim R 1 (McClellan CJ at CL). This stands in contrast to the inquisitorial ideal where the compilation of a dossier-style document forms the backbone of the hearing, with information 'confirmed' during the trial. A number of countries, despite having a long history within the civilian inquisitorial tradition, in recent decades have opted to move to the communitarian benefits of jury trials: see, for example, Italy, Spain, Japan, South Korea and Russia. These late adoptions of the jury system tend to involve hybrid professional/lay judge mixed jury: see F Pakes, *Comparative Criminal Justice* (Willan Publishing, 3rd ed, 2015).

194 [2018] NSWCCA 94, [31]. See also Z Bankowski, 'The Jury and Reality' in M Findlay and P Duff (eds), *The Jury Under Attack* (Butterworths, 1988), 20.

195 [2015] VSCA 364, [93] and see also a variation of the timing of the empanelment in *Beqiri and Hajko* [2017] VSCA 112 (appeal dismissed), and *Johns* [1979] HCA 33; 141 CLR 409 on the common law, and *Beqiri and Hajko* at [153] where Beale AJA lists the Victorian statutory requirements, which are broadly illustrative of the Australian position. For a comprehensive summary of empanelment processes across Australia, see [166]-[178] (Beale AJA dissenting on this ground).

196 See also *Chouhan* 2020 CanLII 75817 and *Josipovic* 2020 ONSC 6300; and *First Nations Representation on Ontario Juries*, Report of the Independent Review Conducted by The Honourable

Justice Dyson Heydon described a number of strengths and weaknesses juries bring to the trial process:

> First, the procedure is cumbersome. It can be slow. It can therefore be expensive for all who take part in it and for the state. Trial by jury is likely to take longer than trial by judge alone. Hence it can increase delays in all types of litigation.
>
> Some elements of jury trial can generate brevity. One is its orality. Evidence given orally is usually less voluminous than evidence given through statements prepared by lawyers. Witnesses testifying orally tend to forget some of what actually happened. They resist carefully crafted material being foisted on them by lawyers.
>
> Jury trial is also shortened by the jury's inability to reserve judgment. In contrast, a trial judge sitting alone can reserve judgment for – though this is uncommon – unconscionably long periods of months or years.
>
> But there are pressures the other way. Trials conducted by judges and legal practitioners alone will tend to proceed with fewer interruptions. The need to assemble 12 people at a particular time creates the risk that day to day accidents will cause late starts. Even Australia's mild and brief winters can cause occasional absences through minor illness. Unpredicted serious illness can play havoc with a jury trial. Advocacy to juries tends to proceed more slowly than advocacy to judges sitting alone – judges can indicate quickly when they need no further elaboration.[197]

There are numerous theories of decision-making. No single theory, or even cluster of theories explains all decision-making. None pretends to offer any universal truth on this score, but psychological research indicates that it is human nature to cast information we receive into stories and that we are all prone to embrace stories that resonate with cultural norms and with stereotypes. As Devine observes:

> Extensive research in social cognition shows that humans comprehend their surroundings by using various cognitive structures that represent categories of people, objects, and events – *schemas*. ... In trial contexts, jurors acquire information relevant to their decisions from a variety of sources – both internal and external – and use this information to form a mental representation of the events that precipitated the trial.[198]

The story model assumes jurors sift through the evidence, making sense of it with the influences mentioned above operating upon them. There are other cognitive structures that assist to help all of us understand the world around us, to fill in gaps and to organise new information, and promote its retention and retrieval. Two particular structures are the use of *scripts* and *stereotypes*.

> *Scripts* are event-centered cognitive structures that involve a series of actions occurring in a causal sequence. *Stereotypes* are person-centered cognitive structures consisting of a category label and a set of associated characteristics. ... At trial, jurors' scripts and stereotypes may be activated by learning the nature of the case and seeing the parties involved ...[199]

Scripts and stereotypes are shaped by life experiences and, as Devine points out, for jurors scripts can be activated from the moment the jury views the parties

---

Frank Iacobucci (February 2013), <https://www.attorneygeneral. jus.gov.on.ca/english/ about/ pubs/iacobucci/First_Nations_Representation_ Ontario_Juries.html>.

197 JD Heydon, 'Juries on Trial', *Australian Financial Review*, 2 August 2013.

198 DJ Devine, *Jury Decision Making: The State of the Science* (NY University Press, 2012), 189-90. N Pennington and R Hastie, 'Cognitive Theory of Juror Decision Making: The Story Model' (1991) 13 *Cardozo Law Review* 519, has been the most influential research on the story model approach. See N Steblay et al, 'The Impact on Juror Verdicts of Judicial Instruction to Dis-regard Inadmissible Evidence: A Meta-Analysis' (2006) 30 *Law and Human Behavior* 469.

199 Devine, ibid, 190.

and the nature of the case is known. No doubt societies vary. Devine isolates race, gender, socio-economic status and trust in the legal system[200] as, according to the psychological literature, factors that can be particularly important.

There are likely to be competing stories before the jury. These competing stories create choices. Psychologists identify three key considerations that will come into play in making choices about which story to accept:

- *coverage* (the extent to which the facts in the story are accounted for by the evidence);
- *coherence* (the logical robustness and believability of the story);[201] and
- *uniqueness* of a story as being the extent to which it alone satisfies the evidence.

Where only one party presents an account that satisfies all the evidence it will be immensely persuasive because the choice is essentially one-sided. If both parties present accounts that satisfy all the evidence neither has a unique story and the other criteria come into play.[202]

Of course, jurors decide as a group, not in isolation from each other. The deliberation process is likely to be influential, as is the prosecution's prime position in being the party who first opens its case (and explains and then leads evidence of its 'story'). Personal characteristics and the dynamics of a particular style of group dynamics will also add a layer of influence to this process. For example, Pennington and Hastie suggest that:

> [T]here is limited evidence suggesting that once a juror has committed to a decision, it becomes more difficult for that juror to change stories. This suggests that deliberation strategies which combine maximal sharing of information and minimal early commitment to decisions will ensure the broadest coverage of evidence and relevant background knowledge.[203]

Some witnesses will appear more compelling than others. Witness credibility depends on a multitude of considerations. Confidence and consistency are said to promote a witness's believability.[204] And other considerations can come into play, depending on the role of the witness. For example, Devine points to characterisations that jurors might apply to an expert witness: a *benevolent educator*, a *hired gun* or a *superfluous pontificator*. Of course, if a juror does not understand technical aspects of a witness's evidence then their impressions of the evidence may be shaped by other qualities (qualifications, age and gender). Further, research also suggests that the form of expert evidence can affect its attractiveness to jurors, for example, that specific evidence applied to the case at hand is more persuasive than general evidence; clinical support rather than actuarial support for conclusions is similarly more compelling.[205]

Judges will often direct juries not to speculate but, unlike the judge-alone verdict, Australian juries do not deliver a reasoned verdict. Their deliberation

---

200 Ibid 191.

201 Consistency, completeness and plausibility are key criteria here.

202 These theories can be applied to *Mumbulla* [2020] NSWDC 207, extracted below.

203 Pennington and Hastie, above n 198, 556.

204 See Loretta Re, 'Oral v Written Evidence: The Myth of the "Impressive Witness"' (1983) 57 *Australian Law Journal* 679; Devine, above n 198, 125-9 (focusing on identification evidence).

205 Devine, above n 198, 131-2. On assessing expert witnesses, see DW Shuman et al, 'Juror Assessments of the Believability of Expert Witnesses: A Literature Review' (1996) 36 *Jurimetrics Journal* 371; RH Underwood, 'Truth Verifiers: From the Hot Iron to the Lie Detector' (1996) 84 *Kentucky Law Review* 597.

processes remain secret,[206] and judicial instruction, direction and warnings to juries run the danger of being elevated to art forms without the capacity to truly communicate to their audience in the jury room, particularly if they are focused on communicating to an audience in the appeal court. The NSWLRC Report on *Jury Directions in Criminal Trials* observed the 'growing awareness that jury directions are not always working well in guiding jurors in their task ... that [they] ... are becoming too complex and uncertain to meet their intended purposes, and that they rely on outmoded communication methods that may confuse rather than assist the jury ... and that lengthy and complex directions unnecessarily prolong already lengthy trials'.[207] These sentiments have been repeated elsewhere, and in Victoria acted on with statutory formulations of many directions replacing common law ones: see the *Jury Directions Act 2015* (Vic).

In *Gui v Weston*,[208] the Victorian Court of Appeal discussed the trial judge's direction to the jury where she presented three hypothetical fact situations to assist the jury to distinguish between inference and speculation. The situations were:

1. *The 'rain example'* – where an inference can be drawn that it had rained during the night because the ground and trees were wet in the morning. In other words, it is possible to draw an inference about the night-time rain without actually seeing the rain.
2. *The 'plane example'* – where an inference is drawn by jurors at the Melbourne trial who then took a 5pm flight to Sydney where they went to a restaurant at 8pm and saw the two barristers who were at the trial at 4pm also in the Sydney restaurant. It would be safe to infer that counsel flew to Sydney. 'However, it would not be open to infer that they had flown with Qantas, or that they had travelled together'. This would be 'merely guesswork or speculation'.[209]

There are logical limitations of drawing inferences from a collection of information that may, to use the terms employed by Dawson J in *Shepherd*,[210] form a chain of reasoning (with the facts inter-dependent) or strands of reasoning (where the strands act independently). The source of these metaphors seems to be Lord Pollock's judgment in the 1866 case of *Exall, Edwards and Skelton* where Lord Pollock in directing the jury to weigh explanations from the accused said:

> It has been said that circumstantial evidence is to be considered as a chain, and each piece of evidence as a link in the chain, but that is not so, for then, if any one link broke, the

206 *Smith v Western Australia* [2014] HCA 3; 250 CLR 473 (revealing voting patterns of jurors); *Smith* [2015] HCA 27; 255 CLR 161; *WG and KG* [2020] NSWCCA 155 (sheriff investigations into allegations of misconduct by jurors); JB Hunter, 'Jury Deliberations and the Secrecy Rule: The Tail that Wags the Dog?' (2013) 35 *Sydney Law Review* 809.

207 NSWLRC, above n 150.

208 [2013] VSCA 364 (Tate JA, with Whelan and Santamaria JJA agreeing).

209 The third example relied on by the trial judge was controversial because it was an amusing hypothetical story about 'Jennifer and Brian' concluding with a punchline suggesting Brian's mother had played a trick to establish whether Jennifer and Brian slept in the same bed). This example was found by the appeal court to be potentially distracting to jurors: [2013] VSCA 364, [41], [43], [55] (Tate JA, with Whelan and Santamaria JJA agreeing).

210 [1990] HCA 56; 170 CLR 573 (Dawson J, with Toohey and Gaudron JJ concurring, and Mason CJ expressing general agreement). Note that in Victoria the *Jury Directions Act 2015* (Vic) (*JDA 2015* (Vic)), s 62, removes the common law obligation on a trial judge in a criminal trial to direct a jury regarding an indispensable intermediate fact in accordance with *Shepherd*. The only obligation on a trial judge to direct a jury with respect to being satisfied beyond reasonable doubt is listed in s 61 of this Act (that is, regarding the elements of the offence charged or an alternative offence and the absence of any relevant defence).

> chain would fall. It is more like the case of a rope composed of several cords. One strand of the cord might be insufficient to sustain the weight, but three strands together may be quite of sufficient strength.[211]

Anatomy of a Criminal Trial

Most Australian States and Territories have legislated to permit judge-alone trials and to permit majority verdicts.[212] Typically, a majority verdict requires the jury to have deliberated for a significant time first and that the judge has given a *Black* Direction,[213] a shortened version of which states:

> Members of the jury, I have been told that you have not been able to reach a verdict so far. I have the power to discharge you from giving a verdict but I should only do so if I am satisfied that there is no likelihood of genuine agreement being reached after further deliberation. …
>
> Each of you has sworn or affirmed that you will give a true verdict according to the evidence. That is an important responsibility. … Each of you takes into the jury room your individual experience and wisdom and you are expected to judge the evidence fairly and impartially in that light. You also have a duty to listen carefully and objectively to the views of every one of your fellow jurors. … Calm and objective discussion of the evidence often leads to a better understanding of the differences of opinion which you may have and may convince you that your original opinion was wrong. That is not, of course, to suggest that you can, consistently with your oath or affirmation as a juror, join in a verdict if you do not honestly and genuinely think that it is the correct one.
>
> Experience has shown that often juries are able to agree in the end, if they are given more time to consider and discuss the evidence. … So, in the light of what I have already said, I ask you to retire again and see whether you can reach a verdict.

Even where there are no juries, in judge-alone trials the judge's verdict must 'give reasons sufficient to identify the principles of law applied by the judge and the main factual findings on which the judge relied'.[214] The adequacy of a judge's reasons depends essentially upon addressing the issues in the case according to three respects:

- the relationship of these issues to the elements of the offence;
- their significance during the trial; and
- the extent to which the prosecution and the defence relied on them.

Despite the increasing provision for judge-alone trials they are not to 'be had for the asking'[215] because 'trial on indictment before a judge without a jury is

211 [1866] EngR 22; 4 F & F 922, 929.

212 *Black* [1993] HCA 71; 179 CLR 44. On majority verdicts, see, eg, *Jury Act 1977* (NSW), s 55F(2), permitting a court to take a verdict with 11 jurors out of 12 agreeing (or 10, out of 11) after not less than eight hours of deliberation and where the court is satisfied the jury is unlikely to reach a unanimous verdict. Cf in the United States: 'if the Sixth Amendment's right to a jury trial requires a unanimous verdict to support a conviction in federal court, it requires no less in state court': *Ramos v Louisiana* 140 S Ct 1390 (2020).

213 There can be complications with meeting the requirements of *Jury Act 1977* (NSW), s 55F(2), see *Joyce (a pseudonym)* [2019] NSWCCA 187, and in giving the *Black* Direction: *Hunt* [2011] NSWCCA 152; 81 NSWLR 181.

214 Though it is not necessary to explain every item of evidence of every step in the reasoning process: *DL* [2018] HCA 26, [32]-[34], quoting from *Douglass* [2012] HCA 34. For a case discussing inadequate reasons and counsel's role in seeking further reasons, see *Makeham v Sheppard* [2020] VSCA 242.

215 See *Simmons; Moore (No 4)* [2015] NSWSC 259 (for a detailed consideration of factors relevant to making an order for a trial by judge-alone under *CPA (NSW)*, s 132, in the context of a large

exceptional. … [and available only where it] is in the interests of justice that that be the mode of trial'.[216] In considering the interests of justice, a refusal may be justified if the trial requires 'the application of objective community standards, including (but not limited to) an issue of reasonableness, negligence, indecency, obscenity or dangerousness': *CPA* (NSW), s 132(5). However, the impact of unfettered globalised media has raised new issues.

> Times, however, have changed. Lack of restraint by traditional news media, and the ubiquity of incensed, overwrought and uncontrolled comment in social media, pose significant challenges to the integrity of trial by jury in sex offences, drugs and other cases. In some cases, judicial direction simply will not be adequate to nullify the prejudice engendered by pretrial publicity (or ongoing prejudicial publication on social media). The proliferation of social media has made it virtually impossible for a trial judge to monitor potential sources of prejudicial material to which a jury may have been exposed. And since a jury does not have to give reasons, and what occurred in the jury room can rarely be explored, it is impossible to determine whether in any given case a jury's verdict has been influenced by improper considerations.[217]

There is much to be learnt from a methodical evaluation of evidence through judge-alone reasons for verdict. Clearly, this evaluation is unlikely to replicate jury room deliberations. However, it does closely reflect law's adjudicative expectations, and so provides a useful blueprint for seeing how the *UEA* provisions and related case law interact with the evaluation of a prosecution case, particularly where the prosecution case relies on circumstantial evidence and where there are a number of bases to reasonably doubt witnesses' accounts.[218]

The entirety of Mumbulla's trial was conducted by audio-visual link due to the COVID-19 pandemic. The courts' responses in early 2020 to the COVID-19 pandemic were ground-breaking. The removal of crowding, the obligation to maintain social distance and the threat to people's well-being created by this highly contagious coronavirus led to the lengthy postponement of trial by jury.[219]

---

volume of prejudicial character evidence being before the court to contextualise events (and not as direct proof of guilt), and for which jury directions would be insufficient to alleviate the prejudice that would be aroused); *Fardon* [2010] QCA 317 (Chesterman JA), quoted by McClellan CJ at CL in *Belghar* [2012] NSWCCA 86; 217 A Crim R 1, [64], and Hidden J, [118]. On the ACT reliance on judge-alone trials and the exclusion of jury trials, see *UD (No 2)* [2020] ACTSC 90. See also *CPA* (NSW), s 132A. The legislation builds in protections for ensuring an accused is legally represented before he or she accepts (or rejects) a trial by judge order. It also permits trial by judge orders where there is a substantial risk of threat or interference to jurors that may not reasonably be mitigated by other means. See also *Juries Act 1927* (SA), s 7; *Criminal Procedure Act 2004* (WA), s 188; *Supreme Court Act 1933* (ACT), s 68B; J O'Leary, 'Twelve Angry Peers or One Angry Judge: An Analysis of Judge Alone Trials in Australia' (2011) 35 *Criminal Law Journal* 154.

216 *Fardon* [2010] QCA 317, [81] (Chesterman JA). On the application of 'interests of justice' in the extraordinary times of the COVID 19 pandemic (*COVID-19 Legislation Amendment (Emergency Measures) Act 2020* (NSW)), see *BD (No 1) (Judge alone application)* [2020] NSWDC 150 and *Johnson* [2020] NSWDC 153 ('The Covid-19 pandemic has turned the world upside down … Jury trials in this state have ceased and it is unclear when they will resume').

217 *UD (No 2)* [2020] ACTSC 90, [39] (Elkaim J), quoting from P Priest, 'Crime and Evidence' (2020) 94 *Australian Law Journal* 110.

218 Including engaging prior inconsistent statements, motives to lie and health issues such that the witness is 'unable to be aware of matters to which his or her evidence relates' (s 106(2)(d)). See generally *UEA*, *ss* 43, 44, 45, 48, 101A, 102, 103, 106. With respect to the hospital records, see *UEA*, ss 59, 65, 66, 69.

219 See, eg, in the ACT, the *COVID-19 Emergency Response Act 2020* (ACT) amended ss 68B and 68BA of the *Supreme Court Act 1933* (ACT) to provide for judge-alone trials instead of jury trials during the 'COVID-19 emergency period' where the court is satisfied that a judge-alone

Courts at all levels and across all of Australia were similarly impacted. Instead of open court, the courtroom was for the judge and audio-visual screens – rarely any other participants. Audio-visual links replaced parties, lawyers and witnesses attending court.[220] Email replaced court mentions. The impact on people awaiting trial, particularly while on remand, was immense, as was the potential for a humanitarian disaster in Australian gaols.

Mumbulla

[2020] NSWDC 207

Mumbulla was charged with three counts: 1. Assault occasioning actual bodily harm; 2. Break and enter with intention to commit a serious indictable offence; and (in the alternative to 2) 3. Intentionally destroying property by fire. The prosecution case consisted of the complainant's (Ashley Ellington) evidence, and that of Skye Brennan (a house mate of Ellington's), Bernard Daly (forensic expert) and documents, including records of text messages. Gillian Wright was also called as a prosecution witness. She had phones and/or SIM cards that she lent to others. They were relevant to the alleged communications between Ellington and Mumbulla. She is Mumbulla's cousin, and Ellington's friend. It was not disputed that a bruise is sufficient to constitute actual bodily harm or that intentional destruction of property is a serious indictable offence. The following summarises the prosecution case:

> 4. The Crown case is that the accused and Ms Ellington were in a relationship during the months leading up to 3 August 2018. On 1 August 2018 after leaving hospital, it is alleged that the complainant returned home, and got into an altercation with the accused. On the stairs it turned physical, and Ms Ellington was struck by the accused two to three times with a curtain rod to her arm. It caused her pain. It subsequently caused her swelling and a large bruise. That is the allegation that forms Count 1 on the indictment.
>
> 5. The Crown case in relation to Counts 2 and 3 is that in the days leading up to 3 August 2018, the accused spoke to the complainant over the phone and threatened to burn her house down. That threat was repeated in the early hours of the morning on 3 August 2018. Later the accused presented at Ms Ellington's back door. The accused managed to open that door, and as a result Ms Ellington and Ms Brennan ran out of the house. Some short time later Ms Ellington's home was ablaze. The accused called Ms Ellington to inform her, to look at her house which was on fire, and was laughing as he did so. Fire fighters and police attended the house a short time later, the fire was extinguished, but not before the house was totally destroyed. …

---

trial 'will ensure the orderly and expeditious discharge of the business of the court … and … is otherwise in the interests of justice'. In *UD (No 2)* [2020] ACTSC 90, UD resisted a judge-alone trial preferring to wait for a jury trial after the lifting of the courts' pandemic responses. Elkaim J rejected the arguments of both the prosecution and the accused. It was argued that, as UD was resisting a judge-alone trial and the evidence was not vulnerable to delay, there was no harm in UD waiting even a year for a jury trial. Elkaim J rejected the submission: 'The business of the court must proceed and is constrained only by the interests of justice. If there is no reason why a judge alone trial is not fair to the accused, then the trial should proceed'. His Honour also stated that '[i]t is not in the interests of justice or the administration of justice (the business of the court) that persons, especially those in custody, wait for excessively long periods to come to trial. The criminal justice system is always at pains to avoid backlogs in criminal trials. A backlog is almost synonymous with a failure of the system. … This is for good reason. Innocent persons languishing in prison, and even on bail, awaiting trial are being denied justice'.

220 And for a flavour of the chaos, see *Macdonald, Obeid (Edward) and Obeid (Moses) (No 11)* [2020] NSWSC 382.

Weinstein DCJ summarised his obligations in a judge-alone trial.

> 8. In *Fleming* [1998] HCA 68; 197 CLR 250 the High Court stated that it is necessary for the judge to expose the reasoning process linking the principles of law with the findings of fact and justify the process and ultimately the verdict that it has reached.
>
> 9. I am required, as the trial judge, to take into account any warning, direction or comment in considering my verdict that any law would require to be given or made to a jury in such circumstances. There are general directions that I must take into account. These are fundamental rules designed to ensure that an accused person receives a fair trial, according to law.
>
> 10. Having brought the charges, it is the Crown who bears the onus of proving the charges. The accused is presumed by law to be innocent of the charges brought against him unless, and until the evidence satisfies the tribunal of fact that each and every element of the relevant offence has been proved beyond reasonable doubt. If the evidence fails to satisfy the court beyond reasonable doubt of any or all of the elements of a particular offence charged, then the presumption of innocence continues and a verdict of not guilty on that count must be returned. The evidence before the court must be approached with an open and unbiased mind. The court must proceed logically and rationally without acting capriciously. It is necessary to bring into account when assessing the evidence, the common sense of the court and to deliver any verdict according to the evidence. The abovementioned principles of law must be applied to the facts as I find them to be.

The following judgment includes analyses of lay and expert evidence, the drawing of inferences (and not speculation) to direct and circumstantial evidence,[221] the framing of credibility issues and reliance on the fundamentals of accusatorial justice discussed in Chapter 1. The following articulates core principles that are applied to evaluating the evidence before the court. These include:

- the accused's right to silence;
- that in assessing a witness's account, their honesty is relevant, but a witness may be honest but still give an account that is wholly or in part unreliable or inaccurate, and that evaluating a witness's account on the basis of demeanour is complex. Consider the following observations by Weinstein DCJ, relating it to the nature of witness questioning, to how accurately one can evaluate the considerations listed by his Honour, and compare with the discussion of credibility evaluation below at Chapter 6:
  (1) 'In considering the question of honesty, I might consider the impression the witness made upon me. Demeanour and impression are important and valid factors to take into account. Did a particular witness impress me as someone doing their best to be truthful or did the witness impress me as someone deliberately trying to deceive me? Did the witness appear evasive or prone to exaggeration or embellishment? Did the witness demonstrate an ability to listen to the question and answer what was asked? Did the witness strike me as being objective and impartial or did the witness strike me as appearing to be colouring his or her evidence in some way?'[222]
  (2) 'To determine how accurate a particular witness's evidence is, I may look to a number of factors. How carefully did the witness observe the event or the matter about which they were giving evidence? Was the

221 That is, 'evidence of a basic fact or facts from which the jury is asked to infer a further fact or facts': *Shepherd* [1990] HCA 56; 170 CLR 573, [4] (Dawson J, with Toohey and Gaudron JJ concurring, and Mason CJ expressing general agreement).

222 [2020] NSWDC 207, [16].

witness calm and composed at the time of the event, or affected by any emotion such as stress, panic or fear that might have impacted their powers of observation and/or the laying down of an accurate memory? Are there issues relating to drug dependency or mental illness? How important to the witness were surrounding details of an incident or event such that the witness focused on committing to his or her memory all aspects of the event, as opposed to what the witness perceived to be significant parts of the event? Has the witness provided a consistent account of the incident or event?'[223]

(3) What is the significance of:
- evidence of motive and of inconsistencies in accounts (comparing peripheral matters – such as Ellington's hospital admission and departure with those central to the facts);
- the potential significance of the objective evidence (photographs, text messaging, medical records); and
- the danger of unreliability in identification evidence, in hearsay evidence and on testimony arising from witnesses' health issues.

Perhaps the most profound message from this carefully crafted set of reasons is in its application of the prosecutor's burden and standard of proof where his Honour's circumspection on 'what in fact transpired between 1 August and 3 August 2018' drives home the gulf between possible or maybe probable, and beyond reasonable doubt.

Weinstein DCJ: 11. The accused did not give evidence in this case. Although an accused person is entitled to give or call evidence in a criminal trial, there is no obligation upon him to do so. He does not have to disprove the Crown case. I direct myself that as a matter of law, his decision not to give evidence cannot be used against him in any way. That decision cannot be used as amounting to an admission of guilt. I must not draw any inference or reach any conclusion based upon the fact that he decided not to give evidence. I cannot use that fact to fill any gaps that I might think exist in the evidence tendered by the Crown. It cannot be used in any way as strengthening the Crown case or in assisting the Crown to prove its case beyond reasonable doubt. I must not speculate about what the accused might have said, had he given evidence. …

13. … What I have to decide in relation to the evidence of a particular witness is whether I consider their evidence to be sufficiently reliable such that I can act upon it.

14. My function in deciding what evidence I accept as proved and what is not, involves making an assessment of the witnesses. In making an assessment of whether I accept evidence is established by a particular witness's account, I need to bear in mind that what I am concerned with is not just the honesty of the witness, but the reliability of the witness. Of course, I may well decide not to rely on the evidence of a particular witness if it appeared to me that the witness was not giving evidence honestly. However, I must also bear in mind that the evidence of a completely honest witness may not be reliable because of errors in observation, errors in the witness's recall of events or a witness's inability to accurately describe what it is he or she saw or heard. I bear in mind that I do not have to accept everything that a witness said or reject everything that that witness said. It is open to me to conclude that I would not accept a particular witness at all as to anything that witness said to me, but equally, it is open to accept certain parts of what the witness said as reliable evidence that I can act on, but I am not prepared to accept that witness about other parts of the evidence that he or she gave.

223 Ibid [18].

15. In making my assessment of witnesses I am not obliged to confine myself to looking at the evidence of a given witness in isolation. I am entitled to weigh all the evidence together in arriving at the factual determinations that I make.

16. I acknowledge that reliability depends upon two quite different but overlapping factors. One factor is the witness's honesty and the other is the witness's accuracy. There are many factors which can have a bearing upon a witness's honesty. …

17. Although demeanour and impression are matters that I am entitled to take into account, I must bear in mind that witnesses can be affected by the stress and anxiety of giving evidence in legal proceedings. A witness might be anxious, worried or embarrassed. Demeanour and impression alone do not determine the honesty or accuracy of the witness's evidence.

18. If I conclude that a particular witness has been doing his or her best to be honest, I would need to move to the second aspect of reliability which relates to a witness's accuracy. A witness can be perfectly honest and accurate or perfectly honest, but completely or partly inaccurate. …

19. Judges do not have the ability to discern if a witness is telling the truth by only observing their demeanour. It is for that reason that the courts are required to scrutinise evidence by comparison with other evidence in the way I have set out above.

Inferences/Circumstantial Case

20. I come now to the question of inferences. If inferences are to drawn from any part of the evidence, I should examine any possible inference to ensure that it is a justifiable inference, and I should not draw such an inference unless it is the only rational inference in the circumstances.

21. Part of my role involves drawing inferences from direct evidence. They are conclusions rationally drawn from a combination of proved facts. It is possible to draw inferences too quickly and to speculate. It is important that I do not rush to an inference too quickly and I must not speculate about matters. I must approach the evidence calmly, rationally and logically, applying my reasoning to it and considering the various possibilities as to the inferences that may properly be drawn from the evidence that I am satisfied has been established. I need to look carefully at the facts that I find established, and to consider cautiously the inference or inferences that I might draw from the particular facts with which I am concerned.

22. In some cases, a person's acts may themselves provide the most convincing evidence of their intention. Where a specific result is the obvious and inevitable consequence of a person's act, and he deliberately does that act, I may readily conclude that he did that act with the intention of achieving that specific result.

23. In this case, the Crown relies on circumstantial evidence with respect to Counts 2 and 3. In relying upon circumstantial evidence, the Crown asks me to find certain basic facts and then from those facts to draw a conclusion as to the existence of a further fact or facts.

24. Circumstantial evidence can be contrasted with direct evidence. Direct evidence is what a witness says that he or she saw or heard or did. In a direct evidence case, if the evidence is accepted beyond reasonable doubt, it is capable of proving the guilt of the accused. However, that is not to say that all direct evidence is accepted.

25. In a circumstantial case, the Crown lacks direct evidence of that kind. A case that relies, either wholly or in part upon the drawing of inferences, may be just as convincing and reliable as a case based upon direct evidence. In a circumstantial case, no individual fact can prove the guilt of the accused. Instead the Crown will attempt to establish basic facts from the evidence. I am then asked to infer or conclude from a combination of those established facts that a further fact or facts existed. The ultimate fact the Crown asks me to find based upon the basic facts, is that an accused person is guilty of the offence charged.

26. The correct approach is first to determine what facts I find established by the evidence. I then consider all of those facts together as a whole and ask myself whether I

can conclude from those facts that the accused is guilty of the offence charged. If such a conclusion does not reasonably arise, then the Crown's circumstantial case fails because I am not satisfied of guilt beyond reasonable doubt. Of course, it follows that I must then find the accused not guilty.

27. However, if I find that such a conclusion is a reasonable one to draw based upon a combination of those established facts then before I can convict the accused, I must determine whether there is any other reasonable conclusion arising from those facts that is inconsistent with the conclusion the Crown says is established. If there is any other reasonable conclusion arising from those facts that is inconsistent with the guilt of the accused, the circumstantial case fails because I am not satisfied beyond reasonable doubt of the accused's guilt. …

Evidence of Ms Ellington

30. Ms Ellington told the court that she had been dating the accused for about four months at the time of the fire on 3 August 2018. She said that the relationship ended a couple of days before the house burnt down and that she and the accused had been fighting in the lead-up. She said that on Wednesday 1 August 2018, the accused had threatened to burn her house down. She told the court that Ms Brennan owed the accused $50 for heroin and that he was hounding her over the money. She said that she put the money in the letterbox but then took it out and decided to keep it. Ms Ellington stated that the "threats" had been continuing from Wednesday 1 August 2018. On the morning of Friday 3 August 2018 the accused called her and apparently said "you're a dead dog" and told her that he was going to burn her house down. She then sent him a message in response to his threats to burn the house down saying "fucking do whatever the fuck you want to the house" but asking to remove all of Jonah's (her son's) things first. Her responses are contained in messages numbered 29, 30 and 31 in exhibit 12.

31. Ms Ellington said that she was taken to hospital for a drug overdose at night-time on 1 August 2018. She checked herself out of hospital in the morning and was picked up by her neighbour Shontelle. When she got home, she said that Mr Mumbulla … [was] in her front yard. Ms Ellington and the accused started to argue as she didn't want him in her house or near her. The accused came into her house and they had a fight upstairs. She said that he grabbed a curtain rod and struck her two or three times on the left forearm and it then snapped. She said that she believed that he was going to stab her. She stated that he was looking for drugs he thought that he had left there, but she said that he had smoked them earlier. She then apparently tried to leave the house, but the accused was standing in the door and pushed her into the lounge room. He came through the door with a knife he had found on the coffee table. She then left then house. Ms Ellington said that she told Ms Brennan what happened as she was trying to go out the door, and that Ms Brennan was in the house when this all occurred.

32. The day before the fire (2 August 2018), Ms Ellington said that she was coming back from Newcastle. On the night of the fire, Ms Ellington said that someone came up the back steps and that there was someone creeping around her house all night. She did not call the police. At about 6 am, she was sitting with Ms Brennan in the lounge room in the dark and could hear footsteps. She said that she could see an outline of someone coming towards the door. She believed that it was the accused because of all the threats he had made, so she and Ms Brennan ran away towards her sister's home which was not far away. She stated that it was not even five minutes later that her house was on fire. She then called 000. Just after the fire occurred, Ms Ellington said that the accused rang her laughing and said "I told you it was going to happen" and "your house is on fire, have a look." She said that she replied with abuse. Ms Ellington told the court how much the house meant to her and how hard she had worked to secure it.

33. In cross-examination, Ms Ellington revealed that a week after her house burnt down, she contacted the accused. She said that she did so because she wanted to find out

why the accused had burnt her house down. She also said that the accused later bought her a pair of shoes because her brother (who was a friend of the accused) was in gaol.

34. Ms Ellington admitted that there was a text of the accused breaking up with her and that after he broke up with her, she continued to text him things such as "luv you". However, she stated that they both knew the breakup was going to happen as they were arguing so much, but that he "didn't like that I was agreeing with him".

35. Ms Ellington confirmed that she consumed a "point" of methamphetamine (by injection) every second day. She also smoked marijuana and consumed Valium. She stated that Ms Brennan smoked cigarettes, but that no one was allowed to smoke inside the house. She also stated that she had been taken to hospital due to a drug overdose. Issues were also raised about her ability to afford her drug habit on her unemployment benefits and limited work as an event cleaner.

36. When describing the assault, Ms Ellington said that the accused slammed the front door and pushed her into the lounge. He went to the kitchen, slammed a steak knife on the coffee table and threatened her. She stated that Ms Brennan was there during this incident, laying back on the recliner.

37. The evidence of when she returned from the hospital, on what day that occurred, at what time of day that occurred, the timing of the assault, and when she went to Newcastle (if at all), varied throughout her evidence in chief and cross-examination. She conceded at several points that she was not sure on what dates those events occurred. She said that she lied to Mr Mumbulla when she texted him saying she was on the way to Newcastle as she had organised a lift for the next day. She conceded too that her memory of events between 1 and 3 August 2018 was affected in part by her drug taking. It is fair to say that the date of particular incidents and their timelines remain unclear with respect to 1, 2 and 3 August 2018.

38. On the day of the fire she sent the accused a text message at 5:27am saying she was going to babysit at her sister's house and had left money for the accused in the mailbox. Ms Ellington was unable to explain why she did not go to babysit at that time.

Evidence of Ms Brennan

39. Ms Brennan lived with the complainant, and she resided in the lounge room of the house. She said that she did not know the accused but had talked to him once or twice. She had met him a few years back through Ms Ellington. … She said that they would often fight, and on occasion these fights were physical. … On a date leading up to 3 August 2018, Ms Brennan remembered that the accused hit Ms Ellington with a curtain rod. She stated that she did not see it occur, but she could "hear all the commotion upstairs" and she could hear arguing and an aggressive tone. The accused then came down the stairs and left. Ms Ellington then came down holding her arm in pain and said the accused had hit her with a curtain rod. Ms Brennan said that Ms Ellington was crying and said "he was a fucking dog. He just hit me with a curtain rod".

40. Ms Brennan said that she owed the accused $50 for methamphetamine purchased on 2 August 2018 (not heroin), and that she gave the money to Ms Ellington to give to the accused because they were in a relationship. Ms Ellington told Ms Brennan that she wasn't going to give him the money. Ms Brennan told the court that she smokes but was not allowed to smoke inside. She said that Ms Ellington smokes sometimes.

41. Sometime before the fire (in the early hours of 3 August 2018), and after Ms Brennan believed that Ms Ellington had a phone conversation with the accused, they both caught a taxi because Ms Ellington told Ms Brennan she was scared of the accused. They sat in the dark whilst the taxi was called. I note that exhibit 12 records a taxi arriving at 5.39 am. They drove up the road in the taxi, and then apparently returned back to the house.

42. Ms Brennan was then sitting in the lounge. She said that she saw a man standing outside in a hooded jumper trying to open the back door. She said that she assumed that it was the accused, but she could not see his face. She assumed it was the accused because

he had apparently telephoned Ms Ellington and said he was coming. Ms Ellington told her to run, so they grabbed a bag and ran out the front door as the person was coming in the back door. After they ran 7-8 houses away, or for 3-5 minutes, they saw an orange light and Ms Ellington said it was her house. She then called the fire brigade who came approximately 15 minutes later. While they were watching the house, Ms Ellington was screaming, "Bill you dog".

43. Ms Brennan said that the accused kept ringing her phone, asking her to put Ms Ellington on. She said that at one point he was on speaker, and Ms Brennan said that a male police officer was there who could hear the conversation. The accused apparently told Ms Ellington and Ms Brennan to tell the police that it was a cigarette that caused the house to alight.

44. In cross-examination Ms Brennan said that she had never spoken to the accused on the phone before 3 August 2018, but she knew what his voice sounded like. She then said she did not know what his voice sounded like on that day (3 August 2018).

45. Ms Brennan stated that she was an ice user (not a heroin user), that she injected ice and that she was unemployed on job seeker benefits. She bought ice on her pay days. She bought half a gram every fortnight which she rationed until her next pay day, but on 2 August 2018 she bought $50 worth of ice "on tick" from the accused. She and Ms Ellington were looking to purchase ice in the early morning hours of 3 August 2018. They were awake all night because they were "stimulated" from the ice they had consumed the previous day.

46. When the taxi arrived (at about 5.40am on 3 August 2018), she believed that Ms Ellington wanted to go to the early opening of the pub to gamble.

47. Ms Brennan stated that when Ms Ellington was holding her arm it was in the morning or midday – definitely day time – but she never saw the accused strike her. She said that she was unaware of Ms Ellington's overdose, her being taken to hospital or her going to Newcastle between 31 July 2018 – 3 August 2018.

48. Ms Brennan said that she had a disability. She said that she has a very bad memory as her Multiple Personality Disorder leads to a loss of concentration. Ms Brennan stated that she has Schizophrenia, Multiple Personality Disorder and Bipolar Disorder. She said that she is on medication and is currently taking Zyprexa, anti-psychotic medications by depot injection and anti-depressant medications. Her symptoms include delusional thoughts, hallucinations, hearing voices, bad concentration, bad memory and poor energy. She said that some of her memories and perceptions could be affected by her mental health, and that sometimes she does not know what is happening because another personality comes out.

49. When asked about the hooded figure, Ms Brennan said that to be "totally honest" she may have been hallucinating. She could not say whether the figure was male or female but said the person was tall like the accused. She conceded that she assumed that it was the accused because of what Ms Ellington had said to her.

50. Ms Brennan insisted that a police officer had overheard a telephone conversation with the accused on the phone after the fire. She agreed that there was no like comment in her statement to police. There were other inconsistencies in her police statement, which she frankly admitted.

51. Ms Brennan said that she took methamphetamine to counter the effect of drowsiness caused by her other medications, and that she loses track of what she is doing and of time. She conceded that she did not have a clear and uncluttered memory of the events of 3 August 2018.

Evidence of Ms Wright

52. Ms Wright, age 46, is the cousin of the accused, and a long-time friend of the complainant, Ms Ellington. She also knows Ms Brennan as they live in the same area. Ms Wright stated that at the material time she had a couple of phones and phone numbers. From about May 2018, one of her numbers ended in 796. She stated that she lost that

phone, but she could not remember when. She was asked by the Crown whether she sent a text on 22 July 2018 at 12.31 am, containing the words, "it's Mumbulla, call me". She denied sending it, stating that she would have been asleep at the time because she has sciatic nerve damage. She denied ever sending anyone a message pretending to be the accused.

53. In cross-examination by Mr Todd, Ms Wright accepted that when speaking to the police, she told them that she lost the phone in mid-September 2018. She confirmed that it may have been around this time, but could not remember precisely when. She further confirmed that she had previously spoken to Ms Ellington on that number.

54. Ms Wright told the court that she would loan her phone out to others and was "generous with allowing people to use that phone." She clarified that they would use the phone in the house, but would not leave the house with it, and she agreed that it was possible for someone to take the SIM card out and use it with other devices.

55. I am satisfied that from about 22 July 2018 to 3 August 2018, the accused had the use, if not exclusive use of the phone number ending in 796. It is clear from the documents containing the text messages, being exhibits 8 and 12, that he used that number to contact Ms Ellington and Ms Brennan (and others) during that period.

Expert evidence of Mr Daly

56. Mr Daly was called as an expert witness. The expert evidence of Mr Daly was only challenged in limited ways by Mr Todd, and not with respect to his expertise. An expert witness is a person who has specialised knowledge based on their training, study or experience. Unlike other witnesses, a witness with such specialised knowledge may express an opinion on relevant matters within his or her particular area of expertise. Other witnesses may speak only as to facts, that is, what they saw or heard, and are not permitted to express their opinions.

57. The value of any expert opinion is very much dependent on the reliability and accuracy of the material which the expert used to reach his or her opinion. It is also dependent upon the degree to which the expert analysed the material upon which the opinion was based and the skill and experience brought to bear in formulating the opinion given. Experts can differ in the level and degree of their experience, training and study, yet each can still be an expert qualified to give an opinion where that opinion is based on that witness's specialised knowledge.

58. Expert evidence was admitted to provide me, in the case of Mr Daly, with information and an opinion within his expertise as a Fire Investigator with the rank of Senior Firefighter. The evidence was admitted to provide me with an understanding of the possible causes of the fires, how it might have been lit, and the origin and direction of the fire. Accordingly, if it is not unbelievable, I would need to have a good reason to reject it – for example, that it does not fit with other facts which I have found proved.

59. Mr Daly gave evidence to the court about the fire … An accelerant detection canine was deployed around all the external extremities and no accelerant was found. The canine was trained to detect 5 accelerants: petrol, thinners, kerosene, turpentine and methylated spirits. Mr Daly said that although no accelerant was found, it was possible that it had all been burned.

60. Mr Daly … stated that there was no evidence of any electrical event, and all the switches were found in the off position. Accidental fires tend to have a slow, steady ignition. Here, there was an immediate flame observable from several houses away.

61. … Mr Daly confirmed that it was very unlikely that a cigarette on the back deck would have caused this fire, as the deck is a fuel load that does not readily ignite. He was asked whether it would be different had there been a lot of detritus in the vicinity of the balcony, for example cans and papers. Mr Daly confirmed that it was still very unlikely as it would be insufficient to sustain the burning. He was then asked whether the existence of paper blinds on the back deck could have ultimately led to a fire that engulfed the house. Mr Daly said that if the blinds were paper, they would ignite but that it was still

very unlikely that would spread to the house. He concluded that the cases where fires are attributed to cigarettes are "very specific circumstances and they're quite rare".

62. In his report dated 4 November 2018 (Exhibit 6), Mr Daly concludes that the cause of the fire was undetermined, meaning that the cause could not be proved to an acceptable level of certainty. This was because, inter alia, a thorough investigation of the area of origin was not able to be conducted. Therefore neither an accidental, nor an incendiary fire cause classification could be ruled out given the limited data collected at the scene. An incendiary fire is a fire that is deliberately set.

63. In his supplementary report, dated 6 April 2020 (Exhibit 7), Mr Daly stated that an incendiary fire cause classification was merely a possibility. …

Evidence of Detective Senior Constable Cavan

64. Detective Senior Constable Cavan confirmed … that Ms Ellington used the phone number ending in 674 and that Ms Brennan used the number ending in 124. He was informed that the number the accused was using ended in 796. After receiving this information, Detective Cavan applied for a stored communications search warrant for those three numbers. He then received a stored communications document containing the text messages sent and received by the number ending in 796, which is exhibit 8.

65. Detective Cavan told that court that … between 19.42 to 19.49 on 3 August 2018 there were text messages from the number ending in 796 received by Ms Ellington's phone.

66. Detective Cavan was the officer who placed the accused under arrest for the fire and advised him that he didn't have to say or do anything unless he wanted to, and that anything he did or said would be recorded and may be used in court. In response to that, the accused said "What fire? This is bullshit." He declined to be interviewed.

67. Detective Cavan also gave evidence about Ms Ellington's admission to hospital due to a drug overdose. … He confirmed that Ms Ellington advised police that she broke up with Mr Mumbulla and that he was upset about it. …

Objective Evidence

68. Several items of evidence are objective and relevant. Exhibit 4 consists of 3 photographs taken on 3 August 2018 showing bruising to Ms Ellington's left arm.

69. Exhibit 8 details all the text messages to and from the telephone number ending in 796. Of particular note are the following:

(1) On 1 August 2018 there is a text message from Ms Ellington's number to the number ending in 796 at about 16.44 pm, the content of which includes, "Thanks for the fractured arm";

(2) On 3 August 2018 the number ending in 796 sent a message to Ms Brennan's phone at about 6.25 am saying "U are a dog u call the police cunt";

(3) On 3 August 2018 the number ending in 796 sent numerous messages between 6.25 am and 6.38 am to an unidentified number saying, inter alia, "say it was a smoke";

(4) On 3 August 2018 the number ending in 796 at about 6.42 am, sent a message to Ms Brennan's phone saying "say it was a smoke fuck";

(5) On 3 August 2018, there are 16 messages from an unidentified number, between 8.03am to 10.33am, to the number ending in 796 saying "niggs ash house on fire"; and

(6) On 3 August 2018 at about 23.55, there are messages from the number ending in 796 to Ms Ellington's phone saying, "Are you OK Ware are you" and "Do you need anything".

70. Exhibit 10 contains the records of Liverpool Hospital where Ms Ellington was admitted, brought in by ambulance with an overdose at 12.08 am on 1 August 2018. She had apparently taken an unknown quantity of alcohol, ice and Valium after a recent break-up with her partner. The notes record that a syringe was found at Ms Ellington's home. On assessment, she was found to be unable to open her eyes wide enough for

an assessment. At about 2am, Ms Ellington absconded [from] the hospital taking her belonging[s] with her.

The Crown's submissions

71. The Crown submitted that if I accept the evidence of Ms Ellington, in relation to the assault on 1 August 2018, that each essential element related to Count 1 on the indictment is made out. Ms Ellington described an assault, and injuries that resulted from it.

72. The Crown says that there was a large degree of consistency to the account she provided in relation to Count 1 and that her description remained consistent through cross-examination. … No other explanation of the injury as photographed by police was provided. As previously stated, in Exhibit 12 there is a text message containing the message "thanks for the fractured arm". There was no response from that number.

73. The Crown submitted that if I accepted the evidence of Ms Ellington and Ms Brennan with respect to events that occurred in the early hours of the morning on 3 August 2018, each essential element in relation to count 2 has been made out. There is a break, being the opening of the glass sliding door, there is an entry on to the property, being on the rear porch or patio, and a brief entry into the home. …

74. The Crown noted that Ms Ellington described seeing a person at the rear glass door of her house, in circumstances where she said she had received threats from the accused to burn her house down on this night. Ms Ellington said she had seen the accused fleetingly, and recognised him instantly. She knew the accused intimately, and she knew what he looked like.

75. The Crown pointed to the overall tenor of Ms Ellington's evidence. He said that she presented as someone with a steadfast and unwavering belief that the accused burnt her house down. She received calls from the accused moments after her house was on fire, when the accused laughed, and told her to have a look. She also saw the message saying "say it was a smoke." Further, there is evidence of the complainant sending messages which related to threats to burn her house down. …

77. The Crown submitted that there are three conclusions to draw in relation to the speed of the fire. First, that an accidental fire went unnoticed for a substantial period of time by Ms Ellington and Ms Brennan who were inside the house. Second, Ms Ellington and Ms Brennan noted the fire, but deliberately delayed calling 000. The third possibility is the speed of the fire was assisted by accelerant. The Crown says that I would have no difficulty excluding the first two. Further, for the accused to know that the house was on fire before the call was made to 000, the Crown says discloses intimate knowledge that could only arise from someone who was there at the scene of the fire.

78. The accused sent a message to Ms Ellington at 6.42am, which read, "Say it was a smoke, fuck". The Crown says that Ms Ellington immediately understood what the accused was trying to tell her – tell the police a cigarette caused the fire. He was upset that she called the police. He was concerned about what she would tell them, and he asked her to lie for him. At 6.38 am, two text messages were sent (to another number), "Say it was a smoke" and "Pick up". Four minutes later that message, "Say it was a smoke, fuck" was sent to Ms Ellington. The Crown says that I would draw an inference that those first two messages were inadvertently sent to that number, before it was sent to the correct recipient, which was Ms Brennan's phone.

79. In relation to Counts 2 and 3, the Crown says that I have consistent and believable evidence of the two witnesses who were in the house on the morning of the fire, and the phone evidence proving there was contact between the accused and the complainant before and after the fire. There was a fire moving at speed through the house which is inconsistent with one accidentally lit. There was a fire originating from the spot that two witnesses saw a person in the early hours of the morning before they ran out of the house. Further, I have text messages disclosing knowledge of things that the Crown submits could only be known if the accused was in the area.

80. … The Crown concedes that Ms Ellington had difficulty with certain dates and times with respect to her hospital admission. Nevertheless, the Crown said that there were aspects of her evidence, and the way in which she gave her evidence, which would enable me to accept most of what she said, and, in particular, that I would accept what she said to me with respect to the elements of the offences on the indictment. On many occasions she was unable to remember the dates, or times, some things happened. The Crown also pointed to concessions Ms Ellington made about things which did not portray her in a particularly favourable light. These included her longstanding issues with drugs, and making threats to the accused. She also conceded that she met up with the accused because she was stupid enough to still love him, after the incident.

81. Ms Brennan freely disclosed a constellation of mental health issues, including issues with her memory. However, the Crown submitted that there is objective evidence which corroborates Ms Brennan. In particular, the Crown points to the attendance of the taxi. The Crown says that combined with the other corroborating evidence, I should find that Ms Brennan was ultimately a reliable witness.

82. The Crown also submitted that Ms Brennan presented as a remarkably frank witness. He said that there were really only two inconsistencies between her statement and her evidence-in-chief upon which she was cross-examined. Those were in relation to the phone call, which she said took place in the presence of the police, and the phone contact with the accused.

The Accused's submissions

83. Mr Todd submits that the Crown does not go far enough in conceding the lack of reliability and accuracy of Ms Ellington and Ms Brennan. He cavils with the suggestion that there can be some value placed upon the concessions that those witnesses made. Mr Todd submits that they did not volunteer those concessions about their lack of memory, their reliability, or their drug or mental health issues, but rather they had to be extracted in cross-examination.

84. With respect to Ms Ellington and Ms Brennan, he says that the lack of cogency and coherence about their versions of events are significant. It is not in respect to forgetting minor details. Rather, Ms Brennan did not observe Ms Ellington being taken to hospital, and Ms Ellington completely omitted to tell the police that she went to Newcastle, if in fact she did. The state of evidence from Ms Ellington, he says, is such that it is unclear whether she actually did in fact go to Newcastle.

85. The position of the accused is that there is a fundamental basis why I would reject the Crown case, and that is because if one looks at Ms Ellington and Ms Brennan, and if I undertake a critical analysis of their evidence, it is quite clear that the hallmarks of a good witness are lacking. The hallmarks of a good witness are ones where their accuracy, reliability and honesty are established.

86. With respect to Count 1, … Mr Todd noted that there is no evidence of the age of the bruises.

87. Ms Brennan did not see the incident. When Ms Ellington informed Ms Brennan of the incident, Ms Brennan says this occurred "midday or morning", "definitely daytime", contrary to Ms Ellington's various versions. For the court to accept Ms Ellington's version, there would need to be an established basis for concluding Ms Ellington's evidence had the hallmarks of accuracy, reliability and honesty. In Mr Todd's submission, her evidence had none of those qualities.

88. Mr Todd submitted that each version of Ms Ellington's story is markedly different. The first version Ms Ellington gave was to police on 3 August 2018, 2 days after the alleged incident in Count 1. In her evidence-in-chief, she told the court she was taken to hospital on the night of 1 August 2018 or the early hours but that she could not recall other than it was night time. When she allegedly returned home, she was attacked by the accused. Ms Ellington alleges that after this fight the accused threatened her with a knife in the lounge area. Ms Brennan gave no corroborative evidence that she saw the

accused present with a knife in the lounge room and threaten Ms Ellington despite being present in the lounge at that time. The next sequential issue was Ms Ellington travelling to Newcastle, apparently on the day before the fire when she was allegedly receiving threatening calls from the accused including in relation to the house. In Mr Todd's submission, it is clear that even from 3 August 2018 when she gave her first version to police, there were glaring errors and oversights in her version and patent falsehoods.

89. The medical records and the Ambulance Service documents clearly show that late on 31 July 2018/ early 1 August 2018 Ms Ellington was taken to hospital having overdosed on methamphetamine, alcohol and Valium. The notes record that she had "had a recent break-up with her partner" and that she absconded from her bed at around 2.09am. This is directly contradictory to her version to police and in chief. Mr Todd says that the evidence of when she returned from the hospital, what day that occurred, what time of day that occurred, when she went to Newcastle (if at all) are left in such a state of confusion that it is unclear what final version the witness wished to state.

90. Mr Todd submitted that Ms Ellington had a significant drug habit at the time of the alleged incident. Even when she spoke to police she believed she was "probably" affected by drugs. She conceded she consumed a "point" of methamphetamine (by injection) every second day. She also smoked marijuana and consumed Valium. The drug injection habit was long-standing, at about 10 years.

91. In Mr Todd's submission, the purported motive does not bear up to scrutiny. It appears from a reading of the initial complaint to police, that Ms Ellington allegedly broke off the relationship and that caused the accused to be angered. Mr Todd submitted that is a lie, given the nature and extent of the text messages in Exhibit 12. The other purported basis for anger leading to a motivation to destroy the property by fire is a drug debt. At its height this appears to have been $50 owed by Ms Brennan that the accused was allegedly "hounding" Ms Ellington to repay. However, the evidence from the text messages in Exhibit 12 is that Ms Ellington initiated contact with the accused in an attempt to buy further drugs off him, offered him the $50 debt by placing it in a letterbox and otherwise was seeking drugs from the accused and others in the early hours of 3 August 2018.

92. Mr Todd says that it was open to the Crown, if they wished to do so, or the police in their investigations if they wished to do so, given the wealth of cell tower and other information they could have obtained from telephones, to find where the operator of each and every one of those phones was using it by reference to cell towers. There is no such evidence. There is nothing that would establish that the accused, or the operator of the phone ending 796, was in the Macquarie Fields area as at 3 August 2018. There is also an absence of evidence that would show forensic material to link the accused being present at the time of the fire at that house. There are no fingerprints on anything that shows a link to the property. There is no DNA showing a link to the property. There is nothing found on the accused or in any dwelling that shows clothing that was fire affected, or that was soaked in some accelerant. There are no accelerants found in or around his property. There are no forensic pieces of evidence that link the accused to that place at that time, such that he could have been said to have set the fire.

93. Mr Todd submits that there is difficulty in accepting Ms Ellington's version that she was somehow continually being threatened that her house was going to be burned down. In his submission, it is illogical that she would continue to invite the accused back to her home, entice him to her home, keep contact with him, including offering money for drugs, while remaining in her home. It is illogical, he says, that Ms Ellington would be initiating contact and meeting with a man who had physically beaten her, burnt down her family home, laughing as he did so, and left her in a parlous state. She stated that she still then and apparently now loves the accused. Mr Todd says that this is inconsistent with her evidence that she sought to end the relationship days before the fire.

94. With respect to Counts 2 and 3, Mr Todd submitted that there is no evidence that identifies the accused as being present when the fire commenced or shortly before. The evidence of Ms Brennan on this point was clarified after an initial version that she

saw the accused, to an acknowledgement that she assumed it was the accused because of what Ms Ellington had told her, not because of what she saw. Mr Todd says that Ms Brennan's evidence must be approached with significant circumspection. She suffers from serious, multiple mental health issues which clearly affect her capacity to reason, recall and differentiate truth from fiction. Some of her evidence, including that a police officer overheard the accused speak on a telephone was patently wrong.

95. The Crown placed significant weight on a text message said to be sent from the number ending in 796 at 6.42 am on 3 August 2018. Mr Todd said that while there is no doubt the accused had access to that phone, that access was not exclusive. Exhibit 8 also shows that the communication "Say it was a smoke" was sent to a number ending in 185. This was not Ms Ellington's number. The Crown cannot explain whether this communication was meant for the initial recipient or Ms Ellington. In any event, if the text was from the accused, it is not an admission that he had set the fire. There are in fact no admissions in any text used by the accused. It is noted that when arrested for setting the fire the accused told Detective Cavan "What fire? This is bullshit".

96. The Crown must prove beyond reasonable doubt that the accused was not only present but set the fire and intended to burn down the property. In Mr Todd's submission, there is no compelling evidence that an intentional fire was set when one considers the evidence of Mr Daly. At its highest he raises this as a possibility in his second report. Furthermore, Mr Daly's second opinion proceeded on assumptions not borne out by evidence from Ms Ellington of three loud bangs or Ms Brennan seeing "a bright flash". He submitted that the absence of this evidence in the trial from the witnesses further significantly undermines the reliability of those witnesses, and also undermines the opinion of Mr Daly in his second report.

97. Despite Mr Daly's uncertainty over the possibility of a cause of the fire being accidental from other circumstances as arose from the evidence, Mr Todd submitted that there is evidence that a fire could have started from another source. Smoking was conducted outside, near the table on the back porch on which there were blinds. Given the lack of detection by the trained dog of any accelerant, the absence of any vessel remains that carried an accelerant, or identification by any witness of such an accelerant, Mr Todd submitted that the Crown case fails to establish there was an intentional act of destruction by the accused of the house by fire.

98. As there is no definitive identification of the accused as being present at the house at the time, and no definitive proof of how the fire was set or started, Mr Todd submits that the Crown case fails on these counts.

Identification

99. I direct myself with respect to the evidence of the identification of the accused given by Ms Brennan pursuant to section 116 of the *Evidence Act*, and pursuant to section 165(1) of the *Evidence Act* with respect to Ms Ellington's evidence of the recognition of the accused. These are important directions.

100. Evidence that the accused has been identified by a witness must be approached with special caution before I accept it is reliable. …

101. Special caution is necessary before accepting identification evidence because of the possibility that a witness may be mistaken in their identification of a person accused of a crime. The experience of the criminal courts over the years, both here in Australia and overseas, has demonstrated that identification evidence may turn out to be unreliable. There have been some notorious cases over the years in which evidence of identification has been demonstrated to be wrong after innocent people have been convicted.

102. I must carefully consider the circumstances in which Ms Brennan made her observation of the accused. The circumstances in which the witness made her observation of the person can affect the reliability of identification evidence, there are number of matters that have been specifically raised in this case that require consideration. First, Ms Brennan hardly knew the accused. It is obviously harder to identify strangers than it is to identify the people who are well known to us. Ms Brennan gave evidence that

she relied on the description of the accused made by Ms Ellington. Second, Ms Brennan had a very limited opportunity to make her observation of the accused. It was fleeting, it was dark outside … Third, both Ms Brennan and Ms Ellington had been up all night and were likely drug affected by methamphetamine at the time the alleged identification was made. Fourth, Ms Brennan has significant mental illnesses, and she conceded in cross-examination that she may well have hallucinated the event of the identification. Fifth, Ms Brennan may not have made the identification at all, but rather it could have been suggested to her by Ms Ellington.

103. In the case of the evidence of Ms Ellington, whilst she knew the accused, her evidence of recognition occurred in the same circumstances, that is it was dark outside and she and Ms Brennan were sitting in the dark in the lounge room. She too had been up all night and was likely drug affected by methamphetamine at the time of the alleged recognition. Further, she could only describe an outline or a shadow of someone whom she believed was the accused.

104. … Mistakes have been known to be made by friends and even by relatives of a person who thought it was their friend or relative they had seen. Just because the witness claims to have known the person, there remains a possibility of mistake.

105. In my opinion, given the concession by Ms Brennan that she may have hallucinated the identification of the accused, her evidence is entirely unreliable on this point. As to the evidence of Ms Ellington, it is so vague as to have virtually no probative value whatsoever. …

Section 165 warning – Ms Ellington

106. With respect to the evidence of Ms Ellington, Mr Todd requested a direction pursuant to section 165(1)(c) of the Evidence Act on the basis that her evidence is of a kind that may be unreliable because of her use of drugs, and in particular her use of methamphetamines. Her evidence was that she was drug affected throughout the period 31 July 2018 to 3 August 2018. Furthermore she was an intravenous user of methamphetamine. I agree with Mr Todd that such a direction ought to be given. I direct myself that her use of methamphetamine during the time period in question (and over a period of about 10 years), may indicate that the entirety of her evidence was unreliable and I warn myself of the need for caution in determining whether to accept her evidence and the weight to be given to it. There are many examples in this case of Ms Ellington being unable to recall events with any precision, including the timing and content of telephone calls, that may be attributable to her significant drug use, notwithstanding the fact that the events the subject of the proceedings took place less than two years ago. I note too that she was constantly drug seeking during the relevant period. I note also that contrary to her evidence and apparently her statement to police, it was not Ms Ellington who ended the relationship with the accused. The texts in exhibit 12 demonstrate that it was the accused who had ended the relationship with Ms Ellington, and that she was angry.

107. In addition, there were at least three items of evidence that cause me concern. First there is the unexplained evidence that at about 5.30am on 3 August 2018, Ms Ellington was going to go babysit her sister's children. Then there is evidence that a taxi was called a short while later to either go to the pub, or to escape the house because she was in fear, but that she returned home. This evidence is irreconcilable with the fear she was apparently feeling through the early hours of 3 August 2018. Finally, there is evidence that after the assault, the accused threatened Ms Ellington with a knife in front of Ms Brennan. Ms Brennan denies seeing such an incident and there is no evidence of this in their reports to police. In my opinion, the entirety of Ms Ellington's evidence is unreliable.

Section 165 warning – Ms Brennan

108. The same can be said for the evidence of Ms Brennan, who also was an intravenous user of methamphetamine at the relevant time and was likely affected by methamphetamine in the early hours of 3 August 2018. Likewise her evidence is unreliable for the same reasons.

> 109. In addition, Mr Todd asked for a direction pursuant to section 165(1)(c) of the Evidence Act, because of Ms Brennan's significant mental illnesses which include Multiple Personality Disorder, Bipolar Disorder and Schizophrenia. She was on antipsychotic and antidepressant medication (as well as methamphetamine) at the time of these events. Her symptoms include hallucinations, hearing voices, lack of energy and poor concentration. She gave evidence that her other personalities took over without notice, and as noted above, she may have hallucinated critical events ...
>
> 110. Mr Todd also asked for a direction pursuant to section 165(1)(a) of the Evidence Act with respect to the hearsay evidence given by Ms Brennan in the proceedings. The most significant piece of hearsay evidence given in the proceedings by Ms Brennan, was her statement that Ms Ellington told her that the accused had assaulted her with a curtain rod, although she attributed many other statements to Ms Ellington. ... I direct myself that the reliability of Ms Brennan's evidence, both generally and for hearsay purposes requires me to exercise caution in determining whether to accept her evidence and the weight to be given to it. ...
>
> 111. There were several other oddities about the evidence of both Ms Ellington and Ms Brennan that deserve mention and are matters that I take into account when considering their reliability.

[His Honour then discussed irreconcilable details between Ellington and Brennan's evidence.]

> 115. As I have said, I find both Ms Ellington's and Ms Brennan's evidence to be unreliable. The objective evidence alone does not discharge the onus which the Crown bears.

[His Honour indicated that, in relation to Counts 1, 2 and 3, the evidence of Ms Ellington and Ms Brennan was entirely unreliable. With Count 1, with only the objective evidence, his Honour held a reasonable doubt that the accused had assaulted Ms Ellington. With Counts 2 and 3, the lack of evidence linking the accused to the house and Mr Daly's conclusion that an incendiary fire was not even probable, there remained also reasonable doubt.]

> **Conclusion**
>
> 119. ... I entertain a reasonable doubt about the essential elements of each offence in dispute. I find the accused not guilty of all 3 Counts.

If there are no positively proved facts from which an inference can be made, what is left is mere speculation or conjecture,[224] and, as *Mumbulla's* case illustrates, an inference is only as strong as the primary facts upon which it is drawn.[225] Weinstein DCJ also shows that not all logical inferences are legally permissible ones.[226] The court in the Victorian Court of Appeal case of *Wannouch and Lee*[227] (discussed in Chapter 4) illustrates the distinction between inferences and impermissible speculation, and the application of the cornerstone admissibility provision, *UEA*, s 55[228] (that is, the rational *capacity* of evidence to permit inferences to be drawn).

224 *Sullivan* [2014] NZHC 2501, [403]. The difficulty of applying these principles is illustrated by the High Court's criticism of the Queensland Court of Appeal in *Baden-Clay* [2016] HCA 35; 258 CLR 308, [55], [79].

225 See the discussion in *Kinghorn* [2014] NZCA 168, [19]-[22] (Hammond J).

226 For example, drawing of an adverse inference from the accused not testifying breaches the accused's right to silence. No (adverse) inference is permitted: *UEA*, s 20, and discussion in Chapter 1.

227 [2019] VSCA 97.

228 Providing the definition of base line relevance for evidence to be admissible in terms of whether it 'could rationally affect (directly or indirectly) the assessment of the probability of the existence of a fact in issue in the proceeding'.

Conclusion

Looking at the broader criminal justice landscape, one can see a tension between the image of the Atticus Finch typology of the lawyer from *To Kill a Mockingbird*, zealously protecting the accused against an almighty (and potentially oppressive) state and the cooperative lawyer whose personal qualities draw out the best negotiated arrangements for an accused structured through conferencing, disclosure and admissions. This erosion of a battle mentality is not necessarily retrograde, but it only advances justice where embedded and enforceable system-based protections ensure that power and knowledge imbalances do not drive the finalisation of charges. Without such protections, woolly ethical obligations, often in tension with adversarialism, form a potentially inadequate basis for enforcing accusatorial fundamentals.

This chapter has also introduced some of the devil-in-the-legal-detail relevant to prosecutors' pleadings and to proof, between which the topics of the jury and advocacy have taken us further into the trial and connected to end-game – jury deliberations and proof beyond reasonable doubt. Chapter 3 begins the long excursion through the major principles and rules governing the law of evidence and procedure in the *UEA* (and occasionally beyond it). Subsequent chapters examine foundational principles and structures of the law of evidence – how relevance is defined, the scope and roles of discretions, the presentation of evidence and the various exclusionary rules of evidence.

Chapter 3

Client Legal Privilege

> The discovery and vindication and establishment of truth are main purposes certainly of the existence of Courts of Justice; still, for the obtaining of these objects, which, however valuable and important, cannot be usefully pursued without moderation, cannot be either usefully or creditably pursued unfairly or gained by unfair means, not every channel is to be open to them. ... Truth, like all other good things, may be loved unwisely – may be pursued too keenly – may cost too much. *And surely the meanness and the mischief of prying into a man's confidential consultations with his legal adviser ... are too great a price to pay for truth itself.*[1]

The preceding chapters address the adversarial nature of the trial and the mechanics by which proof of a party's case may be gathered and presented in court. Privileged communications are an additional aspect of these mechanics because in certain circumstances the common law or the legislature (or both) have determined that the public interest in maintaining confidential communications between parties outweighs the public interest in allowing parties to adduce all relevant and otherwise admissible evidence in court.[2] This chapter addresses the most important and most fundamental of these privileges that limit a court's ability to receive information – client legal privilege. In the most general of terms, this privilege protects confidential communications between clients and their lawyers. In essence, client legal privilege is:

> the shorthand description for the doctrine that prevents the disclosure of confidential communications between a lawyer and a client, confidential communications between a lawyer and third parties when they are made for the benefit of a client, and confidential material that records the work of a lawyer carried out for the benefit of a client unless the client has consented to the disclosure.[3]

As we see towards the end of this chapter, communications between clients and lawyers are not the only confidential communications that the public interest justifies protecting from disclosure. But client legal privilege is pre-eminent because it is more than a mere evidentiary privilege and it possesses a long pedigree at common law.

---

1 *Pearse v Pearse* (1846) 63 ER 950, 957 (Knight Bruce V-C) (emphasis added).

2 The privilege against self-incrimination is discussed briefly below, p 99. It is not a communication privilege per se.

3 *Commissioner Australian Federal Police v Propend Finance Pty Ltd* [1997] HCA 3; 188 CLR 501, 550 (McHugh J).

Historical Background and Rationale of Client Legal Privilege

Client legal privilege is 'an ancient doctrine'.[4] It 'emerged in the sixteenth century as a natural exception to the then novel right of testimonial compulsion',[5] during the reign of Elizabeth I. At the time of the emergence of client legal privilege, the focus and location of the privilege were with the lawyer, as the privilege arose from the oath, honour and duty of the lawyer based on his professional relationship with his client.[6] Thus, in its original conception, it was the lawyer who had the power to waive privilege.[7] This circumstance likely led to the privilege being termed 'legal professional privilege',[8] a term that lingers even in modern cases under both the common law[9] and the *Evidence Act* (referred to as *UEA*).[10]

It was not until the late 18th century that the modern doctrine of client legal privilege began to develop, beginning with the key distinction that the privilege belonged to the client, rather than the lawyer.[11] With that change came the basic recognition in the common law that 'the privilege extends to protect the client, as well as the legal adviser, from being compelled to disclose confidential communications about legal matters'.[12] Centring the privilege around the rights and protections owed to the client also created the ongoing confusion caused by the name 'legal professional privilege', leading Murphy J to comment in *Baker v Campbell* that use of this name was 'unfortunate, because it suggests that the privilege is that of the members of the legal profession, which it is not. It is the client's privilege, so that it may be waived by the client, but not by the lawyer'.[13] As will be discussed below, the *Evidence Act* has attempted to eliminate this confusion by using the term 'client legal privilege'.[14]

Rationale for client legal privilege

Although the focus and location – as well as the name – of the privilege have changed over time, the rationale for having client legal privilege, and the tensions that accompany that rationale, have remained fairly consistent. The central tension inherent in maintaining client legal privilege is the possibility, or even the likelihood, that relevant material that could assist the parties, the court or the jury in discovering the truth about a matter will be kept confidential – and therefore hidden – because of the operation of the privilege. The rationale for the privilege is sufficiently important, however, that the case law leaves little doubt that a proper exercise of client legal privilege will trump the desire of a party to obtain a particular piece of evidence.

---

4 See, eg, *Attorney General (NT) v Maurice* [1986] HCA 80; 161 CLR 475, 487 (Mason and Brennan JJ).

5 *Baker v Campbell* [1983] HCA 39; 153 CLR 52, 127 (Dawson J).

6 See RJ Desiatnik, *Legal Professional Privilege in Australia* (LexisNexis Butterworths, 3rd ed, 2017) 11; *Baker v Campbell* [1983] HCA 39; 153 CLR 52, 127.

7 Desiatnik, above n 6, 13 (citing *Bishop of Winchester v Fournier* (1752) 28 ER 284).

8 See ibid.

9 See, eg, *Baker v Campbell* [1983] HCA 39; 153 CLR 52.

10 See, eg, *DPP (Cth) v Galloway (a Pseudonym)* [2014] VSCA 272.

11 See Desiatnik, above n 6, 14; *Carter v Managing Partner Northmore Hale Davy and Leake* [1995] HCA 33; 183 CLR 121, 132 (Deane J).

12 *Carter v Managing Partner Northmore Hale Davy and Leake*, ibid.

13 [1983] HCA 39; 153 CLR 52, 85.

14 See *UEA*, Part 3.10, Div 1.

The essential rationale for the existence of client legal privilege is that it promotes full and frank communications between lawyers and clients, and that such communications, whether oral or in writing, can be made without fear that they will be used as evidence in an ongoing or future proceeding.[15] One of the classic statements of the rationale for client legal privilege was made by the High Court in *Grant v Downs*. There, it was stated:

> The rationale of this head of privilege, according to traditional doctrine, is that it promotes the public interest because it assists and enhances the administration of justice by facilitating the representation of clients by legal advisers, the law being a complex and complicated discipline. This it does by keeping secret their communications thereby inducing the client to retain the solicitor and seek his advice, and encouraging the client to make a fair and frank disclosure of the relevant circumstances to the solicitor. The existence of the privilege reflects, to the extent to which it is accorded, the paramountcy of this public interest over a more general public interest, that which requires that in the interests of a fair trial litigation should be conducted on the footing that all relevant documentary evidence is available. As a head of privilege legal professional privilege is so firmly entrenched in the law that it is not to be exorcised by judicial decision.[16]

In the High Court judgment in *Baker v Campbell*, Wilson J described the historical basis for the privilege, stating:

> It may be accepted that the basic reason why the law has come to respect professional confidences between lawyer and client is the belief that in so doing the client will be encouraged to be entirely open and candid in telling his story to the lawyer … Conversely, the cloak of secrecy may encourage the lawyer to be completely frank in the expression of his advice. But confidentiality alone cannot supply the reason for the privilege. Originally it may have done so, in common with the protection which the law at the time afforded to other confidential relationships. In the sixteenth and seventeenth centuries the privilege was based in the duty of the solicitor to respect professional confidences. It was a matter of honour and consequently the privilege belonged to him rather than the client. However, in the eighteenth century, the law moved decisively away from this approach … The public interest, not merely the protection of confidentiality, became the reason for the rule. Thereafter, the only profession to have the privilege of non-disclosure was the legal profession …[17]
>
> The public interest which led the common law to favour the relationship between solicitor and client over other confidential relationships was the recognition that the involvement of representatives skilled in the law who had been fully instructed was indispensible to the proper functioning of the legal system, the law being a "complex and complicated discipline": *Grant v Downs* …
>
> The multiplicity and complexity of the demands which the modern state makes upon its citizens underlines the continued relevance of the privilege to the public interest. The adequate protection according to law of the privacy and liberty of the individual is an essential mark of a free society and unless abrogated or abridged by statute the common law privilege attaching to the relationship of solicitor and client is an important element in that protection.
>
> It is not only a matter of protection of the client. The freedom to consult one's legal adviser in the knowledge that confidential communications will be safeguarded will often make its own contribution to the general level of respect for and observance of the law within the community.[18]

---

15 See, eg, *Esso Australia Resources v Commissioner of Taxation* [1999] HCA 67; 201 CLR 49, [35].

16 [1976] HCA 63; 135 CLR 674, 685 (Stephen, Mason, Murphy JJ).

17 See below for a short discussion regarding the jurisdictions under the *UEA* that have extended privilege to other communications.

18 [1983] HCA 39; 153 CLR 52, 93-5 (some citations omitted).

Similarly, in his judgment in *Baker*, Dawson J observed:

> Whilst legal professional privilege was originally confined to the maintenance of confidence pursuant to a contractual duty which arises out of a professional relationship, it is now established that its justification is to be found in the fact that the proper functioning of our legal system depends upon a freedom of communication between legal advisers and their clients which would not exist if either could be compelled to disclose what passed between them for the purpose of giving or receiving advice … The restriction of the privilege to the legal profession serves to emphasize that the relationship between a client and his legal adviser has a special significance because it is part of the functioning of the law itself …
>
> *The conflict between the principle that all relevant evidence should be disclosed and the principle that communications between lawyer and client should be confidential has been resolved in favour of the confidentiality of those communications.* It has been determined that in this way the public interest is better served because the operation of the adversary system, upon which we depend for the attainment of justice in our society, would otherwise be impaired.[19]

The importance of client legal privilege to the most basic workings of the justice system has led the High Court to describe the privilege variously as: 'a fundamental and general principle of the common law';[20] more than a 'mere rule of evidence';[21] 'a substantive general principle of the common law';[22] 'play[ing] an essential role in protecting and preserving the rights, dignity and freedom of the ordinary citizen … under the law';[23] 'a practical guarantee of fundamental constitutional or human rights';[24] 'a natural … corollary of the rule of law and a potent force for ensuring that equal protection of the law is a reality';[25] and 'an important common law right or, perhaps, more accurately, an important common law immunity'.[26]

These statements are not, however, absolutes or to be taken completely literally. As the High Court clarified in its judgment in *Glencore*, extracted below, a separate right of action does not exist with respect to client legal privilege, even in circumstances where privileged documents have been stolen, for example through the hacking of law firm servers as occurred in *Glencore*, and the documents provided to third parties. Instead, the privilege only extends to circumstances in which disclosure might be compulsory, such as on subpoena or subject to statutory disclosure. In other circumstances where privileged material has ended up in the hands of an interested party, privilege holders will have to rely on remedies found in breaches of confidence or, if no such breach exists, may be left without a remedy.

Glencore International AG v Commissioner of Taxation

[2019] HCA 26 (citations omitted)

Glencore brought proceedings in the High Court's original jurisdiction seeking to enjoin any officer of the Australian Taxation Office (ATO) from making use of

19 Ibid 128-9 (emphasis supplied).

20 Ibid 117 (Deane J).

21 Ibid 129 (Dawson J).

22 *Attorney-General (NT) v Maurice* [1986] HCA 80; 161 CLR 475, 491.

23 *Carter v Managing Partner Northmore Hale Davy and Leake* [1995] HCA 33; 183 CLR 121, 133 (Deane J).

24 Ibid 161 (McHugh J).

25 Ibid.

26 *Daniels Corporation International Pty Ltd v Australian Competition and Consumer Commission* [2002] HCA 49; 213 CLR 543, [11] (Gleeson CJ, Gaudron, Gummow and Hayne JJ).

documents that had been acquired by the ATO as a result of the theft of those documents in the Paradise Papers leak. The documents had allegedly been stolen in a hack of the electronic file management system of Appleby, a law practice incorporated in Bermuda, which had been advising Glencore on corporate restructuring matters. The documents had been distributed to journalists worldwide and many had been made publicly available. Glencore claimed, the High Court accepted, that the documents were subject to client legal privilege. Glencore argued in the High Court that the doctrine of privilege gave rise to an actionable legal right and the consequent remedy of an injunction preventing any use of privileged material. The ATO filed a demurrer seeking dismissal of Glencore's claims, arguing that Glencore had not stated a justiciable cause of action.

The High Court unanimously upheld the demurrer and dismissed the claims on the grounds that client legal privilege does not provide an independent cause of action or remedy.

Kiefel CJ, Bell, Gageler, Keane, Nettle, Gordon and Edelman JJ:

The demurrer must be upheld

12. The plaintiffs' argument cannot be accepted. Fundamentally it rests upon an incorrect premise, namely that legal professional privilege is a legal right which is capable of being enforced, which is to say that it may found a cause of action. The privilege is only an immunity from the exercise of powers which would otherwise compel the disclosure of privileged communications, as *Daniels Corporation* holds.

13. It is not sufficient to warrant a new remedy to say that the public interest which supports the privilege is furthered because communications between client and lawyer will be perceived to be even more secure. The development of the law can only proceed from settled principles and be conformable with them. The plaintiffs' case seeks to do more than that. It seeks to transform the nature of the privilege from an immunity into an ill-defined cause of action which may be brought against anyone with respect to documents which may be in the public domain. …

The privilege and admissibility

19. The cases [cited in the full judgment] do not suggest as possible any further relief beyond that which ensured that privileged documents need not be produced. Nor do they suggest that effect was being given to an enforceable legal right. Where documents were withheld from disclosure no question of restraining persons from accessing them could arise. If they had come into the possession of another person in circumstances which raised an equity, an injunction could be granted in order to protect their confidential nature. …

An immunity

21. Legal professional privilege has been described as a right which is fundamental to persons and to our legal system. It has also been described as "a practical guarantee of fundamental, constitutional or human rights". Such descriptions point up the importance of the privilege. They serve to show that it is not merely an aspect of curial procedure or a mere rule of evidence but a substantive right founded upon a matter of public interest. The same distinction has been drawn in New Zealand and the United Kingdom.

22. What cannot be discerned from these cases is that the "right" spoken of in connection with the privilege is an actionable right. If one asks what this "right" gives to a person, the answer could be stated as "a right to resist the compulsory disclosure of information" or "the right to decline to disclose or to allow to be disclosed the confidential communication or document in question", as the Privy Council and the House of Lords respectively have held. So understood it is a freedom from the exercise of legal power or control, which is to say an immunity, and that is what *Daniels Corporation* held its true character to be.

23. In *Daniels Corporation* Gleeson CJ, Gaudron, Gummow and Hayne JJ, having observed that it is now settled that legal professional privilege is a rule of substantive law and not merely a rule of evidence, made the statement referred to earlier in these reasons that:

> "It is an important common law right or, perhaps more accurately, an important common law immunity."

24. McHugh J likewise described it as "a person's immunity from compulsion to produce documents that evidence confidential communications about legal matters" between lawyers and clients.

25. Contrary to the plaintiffs' submissions, there is nothing tentative in their Honours' characterisation of the privilege as an immunity provided by the common law. In the manner stated it is a considered correction of a possible misunderstanding arising from the description of it as a common law right. There can be little doubt that the joint judgment was drawing a clear distinction, for the context of the statement was the application of the principle of legality to the construction of statutes which may have the effect of abrogating "important common law rights, privileges and immunities". Their Honours' characterisation of the privilege as an immunity is consistent with its history.

26. The statements in *Daniels Corporation* accord with what Gummow J had said in *Propend*. His Honour described legal professional privilege as "a bar to compulsory process for the obtaining of evidence". In his Honour's view, the privilege is "not to be characterised as a rule of law conferring individual rights, breach of which gives rise to an action on the case for damages, or an apprehended or continued breach of which may be restrained by injunction". And they accord with the view expressed by Brennan J in *Carter*, that the justification for the privilege is not to be found in the enforcement of some private right, but rather in the public interest.

The policy of privilege – the public interest

27. The rationale for the rule was stated in *Grant v Downs*. It is that the rule promotes the public interest because it "assists and enhances the administration of justice by facilitating the representation of clients by legal advisers". By keeping secret their communications, the client is encouraged to retain a lawyer and to make full and frank disclosure of all relevant circumstances to the lawyer. This would appear to accord with the explanation given by Blackstone and, later, in the nineteenth century. A similar rationale for the privilege has been accepted by the Privy Council and the House of Lords where the descriptor "the rule of law rationale" was accepted. …

29. It was recognised in *Grant v Downs* that there was another, more general, public interest which legal professional privilege did not promote. That public interest lies in the fair conduct of litigation, which requires that all relevant documentary evidence be available. But the public interest which supports the privilege is paramount to the more general public interest. In the provision of the privilege the law has struck the balance between two competing public interests. Consequently, once the privilege is found to exist, no more is required for effect to be given to it. In that sense it may be described as absolute.

30. The paramountcy afforded to the public interest which the privilege supports can have serious consequences. By way of example, an accused person can be denied access to documents which might assist his or her defence. Because of the significance of the effect of the privilege on the conduct of litigation, and the other considerations identified in *Grant v Downs*, it was there said that the privilege "should be confined within strict limits". That note of caution was to be repeated in subsequent cases.

Other relief?

31. In striking the balance between the two competing public interests, the law was not concerned to further a client's personal interest in preventing the use which might be made by others of the client's communications if they obtained them. In providing an immunity, the law's purpose was to enhance the administration of justice. And in settling

the conditions which must be present for the privilege to operate, it defined the boundaries of the privilege.

32. It is the policy of the law that the public interest in the administration of justice is sufficiently secured by the grant of an immunity from disclosure. That has been the policy of the law for a very long time. *Grant v Downs* gave examples of difficulties which would arise in litigation if the balance struck by the privilege was not maintained as such. What was said in *Grant v Downs* and in later cases strongly implies that there is unlikely to be a warrant for providing anything more than an immunity from disclosure.

33. The relief sought by the plaintiffs points to further difficulties. Some were mentioned earlier in these reasons: the nature of the cause of action which is to found, the relief, and the fact that the information the subject of the claimed privilege is now in the public domain. In the latter respect the circumstances of this case identify a particular problem were an injunction to be granted. It is that the defendants would be required to assess Australian entities within the Glencore group to income tax on a basis which may be known to bear no real relationship to the true facts.

34. On the present state of the law, once privileged communications have been disclosed, resort must be had to equity for protection respecting the use of that material. Although the policy upon which legal professional privilege is founded is not irrelevant to the exercise of that jurisdiction, the juridical basis for relief in equity is confidentiality. …

40. The plaintiffs' case for the grant of relief on a basis other than confidentiality is simply this: that any furtherance of the public interest which supports the privilege is sufficient to warrant the creation of a new, actionable right respecting privileged documents. This is not how the common law develops. The law develops by applying settled principles to new circumstances, by reasoning from settled principles to new conclusions, or determining that a category is not closed. Even then the law as developed must cohere with the body of law to which it relates.

41. Policy considerations may influence the development of the law but only where that development is available having regard to the state of settled principles. Policy considerations cannot justify an abrupt change which abrogates principle in favour of a result seen to be desirable in a particular case.

42. In the absence of further facts it is not possible to say whether the plaintiffs are without any possibility of a remedy. But if there is a gap in the law, legal professional privilege is not the area which might be developed in order to provide the remedy sought.

Applying the Law of Client Legal Privilege

Part 3.10 of the *UEA* establishes circumstances in which the *Evidence Act*, rather than the common law, will apply to determine objections to evidence on the grounds of client legal privilege.[27] In all circumstances not covered by the *Evidence Act*, the common law will continue to apply. Importantly, by their terms, the *Evidence Act* provisions addressing client legal privilege apply only to the *adducing* of evidence.[28] Therefore, none of ss 118, 119 or 120 will have any application where evidence is not 'being adduced'.[29] Nonetheless, the courts are obliged to determine which law to apply in order to utilise the appropriate privilege analysis.

Because the *Evidence Act* provisions establishing client legal privilege are restricted to the adducing of evidence, they do not automatically apply to any

27 *UEA*, ss 118-120.

28 *UEA*, ss 118, 119.

29 Often, the answer to whether privilege attaches or has been lost or waived will be the same whether the *Evidence Act* or the common law applies. See *El-Zayet* [2014] NSWCCA 298, [86], [88].

situation where evidence may be produced, but is not being adduced in a proceeding. This means that ss 118-120 of the *UEA* do not reach evidence produced with respect to discovery, subpoenas and inspection of documents.[30] In *Esso Australia Resources v Commissioner of Taxation*,[31] the High Court overturned the decision of the Full Federal Court in *Adelaide Steamship Co Ltd v Spalvins*[32] and held that the *Evidence Acts* had no derivative application to the common law and had to be confined to their own terms. The common law, following the High Court decisions in *Baker v Campbell* and *Mann v Carnell*,[33] was not restricted to the adducing of evidence. It did extend to pre-trial and administrative procedures, so privilege could be addressed by reference to the common law rather than by derivative application of the *Evidence Act*.[34]

Subsequent to the decision in *Esso*, and following the recommendation by the Australian Law Reform Commission (ALRC) in its 2005 review of the *UEA*,[35] the *Evidence Acts* in New South Wales, Victoria, Tasmania, the Australian Capital Territory and the Northern Territory were amended to add s 131A.[36] This section, in slightly different forms in each of the jurisdictions, extends the reach of the privilege protections to certain specified pre-trial procedures in which there is a '*disclosure requirement*'.[37] These disclosure requirements include summonses or subpoenas to produce documents or give evidence,[38] pre-trial or non-party discovery,[39] interrogatories,[40] and notices to produce.[41] These extensions of the *Evidence Act* privilege to pre-trial procedures specifically do not apply where defendants are adducing evidence pursuant to s 123,[42] such that defendants have no further right under the *UEA* to obtain privileged material in criminal proceedings than they would have under common law.[43] Consequent to the addition of s 131A, courts have had to determine whether the *UEA* or the common law applies with reference to ss 118 and 119 as well as s 131A, as the following case extract demonstrates.

El-Zayet

[2014] NSWCCA 298

El-Zayet and a co-accused had been charged with murder. Before the trial commenced, the Director of Public Prosecutions made a direction that no further proceedings were to be brought against either accused and the charges were dismissed. At the directions hearing, the Crown Prosecutor handed the court a

30 See *Esso Australia Resources v Commissioner of Taxation* [1999] HCA 67; 201 CLR 49, [35].
31 Ibid.
32 [1998] FCA 144; 81 FCR 360.
33 [1999] HCA 66; 201 CLR 1.
34 *Esso Australia Resources v Commissioner of Taxation* [1999] HCA 67; 201 CLR 49, [16].
35 ALRC, *Uniform Evidence Law* (Report No 102, 2006), [14.42].
36 To date, the Commonwealth has not enacted a parallel version of s 131A, and the Commonwealth Act extends the scope of the privilege provisions only to journalists' privilege: *Evidence Act 1995* (Cth), s 131A.
37 *UEA*, s 131A(2).
38 *UEA*, s 131A(2)(a).
39 *UEA*, s 131A(2)(b), (c).
40 *UEA*, s 131A(2)(d).
41 *UEA*, s 131A(2)(e).
42 *UEA*, s 131A(1).
43 See *DPP (Cth) v Galloway (a Pseudonym)* [2014] VSCA 272, extracted below.

document purporting to be the last page of the legal advising report on which the Director had signed the direction for the court's inspection and to be placed in the court file. Following the directions hearing, a costs hearing was scheduled. At that hearing, the judge asked the Crown whether reasons would be given for the termination of proceedings and the Crown Prosecutor stated that privilege would not be waived. The judge then informed the parties that a copy of the brief report, revealing the reasons for terminating proceedings, as well as the Director's direction were in the court file. El-Zayet made notice of motion to have access to the full document for use in the costs hearing on the grounds that the Crown Prosecutor had waived privilege when the document was handed to the court and placed in the court file. Price J had found that questions of privilege and waiver should be determined with reference to the provisions of the *UEA* (ss 118, 119 and 122). The complexity of determining the source of privilege, and therefore its precise contours, is revealed in the following NSW Court of Criminal Appeal ruling.

Beazley P and Emmett JA (McColl JA agreeing):

Did his Honour err in relying on the Evidence Act provisions?

84. The applicant's argument on the appeal, that his Honour erred in his reliance on the *Evidence Act* provisions governing privilege and its waiver, was advanced on the basis that the *Evidence Act* provisions are premised upon evidence being adduced. The applicant contended that this was not the position here, as in his notice of motion he was seeking access to a document that was on the court file. The applicant further contended that the provisions of s 131A did not apply as the document was not produced pursuant to a "disclosure requirement" within the meaning of that section, or pursuant to any obligatory court process. It followed that the question whether privilege had been waived had to be determined on the basis of common law principles …

86. For reasons which are explained below, the question whether the *Evidence Act* applies will not affect the outcome in this case. However, as the issue was raised by the applicant, it is appropriate to deal with it briefly.

87. There is no dispute that the contents of the last page of the legal advising report were privileged. Pursuant to s 118, if a client objects, evidence is not to be adduced if the court finds that adducing the evidence would result in the disclosure of a confidential communication between a lawyer and a client for the dominant purpose of the lawyer providing legal advice to the client: s 118(a). Section 119 provides, relevantly, that evidence is not to be adduced if, on objection by the client, the court finds that adducing the evidence would result in the disclosure of the contents of a confidential document prepared for the dominant purpose of the client being provided with professional legal services relating to an Australian proceeding: s 119(b).

88. There was no requirement for formal proof of the Director's decision in order for the court to act upon a direction made under the *Director of Public Prosecutions Act*, s 7(2)(b). Barr AJ could have discharged the applicant upon being informed orally of the Director's decision by a representative of the Director. At the time that the document was handed to the court, Barr AJ was not engaged in a hearing, nor was any evidence required or adduced. The document was not marked as an Exhibit, nor was it provided to the applicant. At the point where it is alleged that privilege was waived, ss 118 and 119 of the Evidence Act were therefore not engaged. Accordingly, subject to the application of s 131A, no question of waiver or privilege arose under the Evidence Act. We should add that ss 118 and 119 were also not engaged in the application before Price J as the last page of the legal advising report was not sought to be adduced in evidence on that application.

89. The Crown submitted, however, that s 131A applied. In particular, the Crown contended that:

"... the terms of the amended order seeking production of the document pursuant to s 133 of the *Evidence Act* ... compelled the application of Part 3.10 (Client Legal Privilege) due to the provision of s 131A ..."

90. Section 133 provides that if a question arises under the privilege provisions in Pt 3.10 relating to a document, the court may order that the document be produced to it and may inspect the document for the purpose of determining the question. In the present case, Price J considered that it was not necessary that he see the document and he made no order for its production. Section 131A was not, therefore, engaged.

91. Nor, in our opinion, did s 131A otherwise have application. That section governs claims for client legal privilege pursuant to a disclosure requirement, as identified in the section, to give information or to produce a document. Disclosure requirements include the requirement to produce documents pursuant to subpoena, pre-trial discovery, interrogatories, notices to produce and the like. In his amended application, the applicant sought an order that he have immediate access to the document handed to the court on 1 June 2012 or have leave to file a notice to produce returnable immediately seeking the production of the document. However, an application to the court for access to the document in the terms sought by the applicant, including his application for leave to serve a notice to produce, does not fall with the meaning of a disclosure requirement. The position may be contrasted with a subpoena, which operates as an order of the court to produce documents or to attend to give evidence. Likewise with a notice to produce, which requires, of its own force, the production of documents to the court. In the present case, the applicant was seeking an order that the document be produced or, alternatively, that leave be granted to serve a notice to produce. The Crown was not, at the point of the court's hearing the applicant's notice of motion, subject to any disclosure requirement.

The Scope of Client Legal Privilege

In general, and under both common law and the *Evidence Act*, the scope of client legal privilege protects the client from the disclosure of communications, oral or written, made between the client and her solicitor or barrister, where those communications are made for the dominant purpose of seeking or giving legal advice or for use in existing or anticipated litigation.[44] So long as this dominant purpose test can be satisfied, the communication will attract the privilege. Thus, a communication that satisfies the dominant purpose test will be privileged no matter what form that communication takes.[45] It is for this reason that the High Court has held that copies of documents that were not privileged when originally created may attract the privilege if the purpose of creating the copies was a part of providing confidential legal services to a client.[46]

Definitions and scope of client legal privilege under the *UEA*

The *UEA* largely reflects the common law of the '*legal advice privilege*',[47] covering confidential communications made for the purpose of seeking or obtaining legal advice, and the '*litigation privilege*',[48] covering communications or materials prepared for the purpose of providing a client with legal services for litigation

44 See, eg, *Esso Australia Resources v Commissioner of Taxation* [1999] HCA 67; 201 CLR 49, [35].

45 See *Commissioner Australian Federal Police v Propend Finance Pty Ltd* [1997] HCA 3; 188 CLR 501, 553 (Gaudron J).

46 Ibid.

47 See *UEA*, s 118.

48 See *UEA*, s 119.

that is current, pending or anticipated.[49] However, rather than merely codifying the common law, the *UEA* made some important modifications, which have in turn influenced the common law (in addition to applying the name client legal privilege to replace 'legal professional privilege').[50]

The *UEA* provides a broad definition of '*client*'[51] that includes 'a person or body who engages a lawyer to provide legal services or who employs a lawyer (including under a contract of service); an employee or agent of a client; and an employer of a lawyer if the employer is the Commonwealth or a State or Territory or a body established by a law of the Commonwealth or a State or Territory'.[52] Similarly, the *UEA* defines the terms '*lawyer*' and '*party*' broadly.[53] Section 117 also defines '*confidential communication*' and '*confidential document*' to cover a communication made (or a document prepared) 'in such circumstances that when it was made [or prepared] (a) the person who made [or prepared] it, or (b) the person to whom it was made [or for whom it was prepared], was under an express or implied obligation not to disclose its contents, whether or not the obligation arises under law'.

Sections 118 and 119[54] (along with s 131A) define the scope of client legal privilege, subject to the circumstances listed in ss 121-126 that indicate when the privilege is lost. The final role of the *UEA* provisions relate to the procedures for assessing a claim of client legal privilege.

The dominant purpose test

An important alteration to the common law made by the *Evidence Act* was the decision to apply a dominant purpose test, as set forth in ss 118 and 119 of the *UEA*, rather than the sole purpose test that was required by the common law.[55] Subsequently, the High Court brought the common law into accord with the *UEA* and the dominant purpose test is now applied under both common law and the *Evidence Act*.[56] To apply the dominant purpose test, the NSW Court of Appeal, in *Westpac Banking Corporation v 789TEN Pty Ltd*,[57] endorsed the formulation of the test stated by Branson J in the Federal Court decision in *Sparnon v Apand Pty Ltd*.[58] According to these courts:

> It will be a question of objective fact whether in any case any one purpose 'dominated' the decision to bring the document into existence. Such objective fact is not necessarily to be ascertained by reference solely to the intention of the author of the document, or solely to the intention of the individual upon whose instructions the document was brought into existence …
>
> Plainly if two purposes were of equal weight, one would not dominate the other. *If the decision to bring the document into existence would have been made irrespective of any intention to obtain professional legal services, I am inclined to doubt that the purpose of*

49 See, eg, Desiatnik, above n 6, 28; see also ALRC, *Uniform Evidence Law*, above n 35, [14.50]-[14.52].

50 See ALRC, *Evidence* (Interim) (Report No 26, 1985) [438].

51 *UEA*, s 117.

52 Ibid.

53 See Ibid.

54 *UEA*, s 120, which specifically applies client legal privilege to unrepresented parties, reflects the scope of ss 118-119.

55 *Grant v Downs* [1976] HCA 63; 135 CLR 674.

56 *Esso Australia Resources v Commissioner of Taxation* [1999] HCA 67; 201 CLR 49.

57 [2005] NSWCA 321.

58 (1996) 68 FCR 322, 324-5.

> *obtaining professional legal services could be regarded as the dominant purpose for the making of the document.* It seems to me that ... the choice of the expression 'dominant purpose' rather than 'sole purpose' in ... the Act is intended to bring within the scope of client legal privilege, a document brought into existence for the purpose of a client being provided with professional legal services notwithstanding that some ancillary use of the document was contemplated at that time.[59]

The onus of establishing that a communication was made for the requisite dominant purpose will fall to the party claiming the privilege.[60]

The legal advice privilege

> **118. Legal advice**
> Evidence is not to be adduced if, on objection by a client, the court finds that adducing the evidence would result in disclosure of:
> (a) a confidential communication made between the client and a lawyer, or
> (b) a confidential communication made between 2 or more lawyers acting for the client, or
> (c) the contents of a confidential document (whether delivered or not) prepared by the client, lawyer or another person,
>
> for the dominant purpose of the lawyer, or one or more of the lawyers, providing legal advice to the client.

Section 118 of the *UEA* codifies the common law legal advice privilege as applied to evidence to be adduced in a proceeding. 'Legal advice' has been construed broadly, such that it is not limited to merely advising a client on the law, but extends to include advice as to what should prudently and sensibly be done in the relevant legal context.[61] The s 118 privilege will attach both to confidential communications, whether made between a client and a lawyer or between lawyers acting for the client, and to confidential documents, regardless of whether the document was prepared by the client, a lawyer or a third party. Section 118 was amended specifically to include the privilege for confidential documents prepared by third parties following the ALRC's 2005 review of the *Evidence Act*.[62] The recommended amendment was largely a response to the development of the common law in *Pratt Holdings Pty Ltd v Federal Commissioner of Taxation*,[63] in which the Full Court of the Federal Court held that the legal advice privilege should not be limited to documents prepared by an agent of the client or solicitor, but should be applied more broadly to any confidential document that satisfies the dominant purpose test. As explained by Stone J:

> 86. ... Extending legal professional privilege to protect communications made for the dominant purpose of obtaining legal advice does not require all communications between legal adviser and client to be protected. If, however, the policy implicit in the rationale for legal professional privilege is not to be subverted, the dominant purpose criterion must be applied recognising that the situations in which people need legal advice are increasingly complex and that the client may need the assistance of third party experts if he or she is to be able to instruct the legal adviser appropriately ...

---

59 [2005] NSWCA 321, [57] (emphasis and omissions in original).

60 See, eg, *Perish* [2015] NSWCCA 98, [39], [42]; *AusNet Electricity Services Pty Ltd v Liesfield* [2014] VSC 474, [115].

61 *WorkCover Authority of NSW v Law Society of NSW* [2006] NSWCA 84, [77].

62 See ALRC, *Uniform Evidence Law*, above n 35, [14.118], [14.121]-[14.122].

63 [2004] FCAFC 122; 207 ALR 217.

105. The coherent rationale for legal professional privilege developed by the High Court does not lend itself to artificial distinction between situations where that expert assistance is provided by an agent or alter ego of the client and where it is provided by a third party. Nor, in my view, should the availability of privilege depend on whether the expert opinion is delivered to the lawyer directly by the expert or by the client. Provided that the dominant purpose requirement is met I see no reason why privilege should not extend to the communication by the expert to the client.

106. I do not accept that this approach would lead to uncontrollable extension of the privilege. The difficulties in proving the relevant purpose should not be underestimated. Advice as to commercially advantageous ways to structure a transaction are extremely unlikely to attract privilege because the purpose in putting the advice together will, in most cases, be quite independent of the need for legal advice. Even if the parties have in mind that the advice will be submitted to a lawyer for comment, the purpose is unlikely to be the *dominant* purpose. Determining the dominant purpose underlying a communication may be difficult but no more so than many questions that come before courts. Courts would need to take into account exactly what function was served by the expert advice and whether it was really required in order to instruct the legal advisers fully. Obviously if the third party is an agent of the client and the client has the requisite purpose the determination is comparatively simple. Similarly if the material sought by the lawyer is required for litigation it is not difficult to determine the chain of authority and to find the requisite purpose … Ultimately the question is one of fact and the onus is on the person seeking privilege protection to establish the case.[64]

The litigation privilege

119. Litigation

Evidence is not to be adduced if, on objection by a client, the court finds that adducing the evidence would result in disclosure of:

(a) a confidential communication between the client and another person, or between a lawyer acting for the client and another person, that was made, or

(b) the contents of a confidential document (whether delivered or not) that was prepared,

for the dominant purpose of the client being provided with professional legal services relating to an Australian or overseas proceeding (including the proceeding before the court), or an anticipated or pending Australian or overseas proceeding, in which the client is or may be, or was or might have been, a party.

The s 119 privilege will attach to communications for the provision of professional legal services made in relation to ongoing, pending or anticipated proceedings. Where there is a question regarding whether proceedings were anticipated at the time of the making of the communication, the general rule is that ‘there must be a real prospect of litigation, as distinct from a mere possibility, but it does not have to be more likely than not’.[65] The party claiming privilege must demonstrate that litigation was anticipated at the time of the making of the communication. A demonstration that litigation actually eventuated will not suffice to justify privilege attaching to a communication where no litigation was anticipated at the time of its making.[66]

64 Emphasis in original; see also *Asahi Holdings (Australia) Pty Ltd v Pacific Equity Partners Pty Ltd (No 4)* [2014] FCA 796, [27]-[44].

65 *New South Wales v Jackson* [2007] NSWCA 279, [67] (citing *Mitsubishi Electric Australia Pty Ltd v Victorian WorkCover Authority* [2002] VSCA 59, [19]).

66 See ibid [69].

Unrepresented parties

Section 120 of the *UEA* specifically grants the privileges contained in ss 118 and 119 to unrepresented parties. The section is framed in broader terms than those used in either s 118 or 119, as the privilege will apply to communications made or documents prepared 'for the dominant purpose of preparing for or conducting the proceeding' in which the party is unrepresented.[67]

Procedural aspects of client legal privilege

The *UEA* also includes several provisions addressed to the procedures of privilege determinations. Section 132 provides that the court is under an obligation to satisfy itself that a witness or party, who may be able to make an objection or application on grounds that evidence is privileged, is aware of the privilege protections. Section 133 gives the court the power to order production of a document over which privilege is claimed to the court to allow the court to inspect the document and make a determination on privilege. Finally, s 134 provides that a document that may not be adduced due to the attachment of privilege is not admissible in the proceeding.

Waiver and Loss of Privilege

Waiver and loss of privilege: common law

Under the common law, the protection afforded by client legal privilege is not absolute and may be lost if the client waives it, either intentionally or impliedly, or if the communication is made for an ulterior or illegal purpose. As explained by Deane J in *Baker v Campbell*:

> It is the privilege of the client and protects him from being compelled to make disclosure of such communications either in testimony or by the production of documents for inspection. It also protects him from such disclosure, in the absence of his consent by his legal adviser. The privilege does not extend to protect communications which are in themselves part of a criminal or fraudulent proceeding or course of conduct or which constitute the whole or part of an actual dealing or transaction. Nor does it extend to protect things lodged with a legal adviser for the purpose of obtaining immunity from production. The privilege may be lost by waiver and, arguably, by the content of the communication ceasing to be confidential.[68]

The scope of the common law of client legal privilege, including whether and when privilege may be lost, has been the subject of some refinement in the High Court. For example, in *Baker*, the High Court considered the question of whether a search warrant, issued pursuant to the *Crimes Act 1914* (Cth), could be used to seize documents from a solicitor's office which would be privileged if adduced at trial. There was no question raised concerning whether client legal privilege attached to the documents. The only question to be answered was: 'In the event that legal professional privilege attaches to and is maintained in respect of the documents held by the firm can those documents be properly made the subject of a search warrant issued under … the *Crimes Act*?'[69]

---

67 *UEA*, s 120(1).

68 [1983] HCA 39; 153 CLR 52, 112 (citation omitted).

69 Ibid 58.

The High Court was being asked to determine whether the scope of the privilege, which until then had been confined to legal proceedings, should be extended to cover administrative proceedings and pre-trial procedures as well. By a 4-3 majority, the High Court held that the privilege should be extended, due to the principles underlying the existence of the privilege, namely the facilitation of unfettered communication between lawyers and clients. As Deane J explained:

> Once one recognizes that the principle underlying legal professional privilege is that a person should be entitled to seek and obtain legal advice without the apprehension of being prejudiced by subsequent disclosure of confidential communications and that the privilege is not confined to such communications as are made in the course of or in anticipation of litigation but extends generally to confidential communications of a professional nature between a person and his lawyer made for the purpose of obtaining or giving legal advice, common sense points to a conclusion that the principle should not be seen as restricted to compulsory disclosure in the course of such proceedings. Indeed, the doctrine of legal professional privilege would represent an aberration of the common law if it withheld from the courts information or documents which were material in the search for truth in circumstances where the disclosure thereof could be compelled as a matter of course by any administrative officer with a relevant and general statutory mandate to require the provision of information or the production of documents ...
>
> [T]he underlying principle that a person should be entitled to preserve the confidentiality of certain communications between himself and his attorney is regarded as of such importance by the common law that the courts themselves do not require disclosure of the content of such communications even if it appears that such disclosure would be conducive to justice in a particular case and even if the proceedings be between parties neither of whom is entitled to claim the protection of the privilege as regards the relevant documents or information. Both logic and authority support the present-day acceptance of the preservation of that confidentiality as a fundamental and general principle of the common law. It is to be presumed that if the Parliament intended to authorize the impairment of that confidentiality by administrative action it would frame the relevant statutory mandate in express and unambiguous terms.[70]

Similarly, as stated by Dawson J:

> The privilege extends beyond communications made for the purpose of litigation to all communications made for the purpose of giving or receiving advice and this extension of the principle makes it inappropriate to regard the doctrine as a mere rule of evidence. It is a doctrine which is based upon the view that confidentiality is necessary for proper functioning of the legal system and not merely the conduct of particular litigation. It is inconsistent with that view to conclude that the compulsory disclosure of communications between legal adviser and client is in the public interest merely because the compulsion is for administrative rather than judicial purpose.[71]

The outer scope of client legal privilege has also been considered with regard to when and how the privilege may be lost. As this extract from the High Court decision in *Carter v Managing Partner Northmore Hale Davy and Leake*[72] demonstrates, as far as the common law is concerned there are no exceptions to client legal privilege. Rather, where privilege is held not to attach, it is because the communication in question was never privileged in the first place.

> **Deane J**: ... The point that legal professional privilege is itself the outcome of a balancing process and is conclusive when it attaches has also been made in a number of recent

70 Ibid 115-17.

71 Ibid 129.

72 [1995] HCA 33; 183 CLR 121, 134 (some citations and internal quotation marks omitted).

judgments in this Court. Thus in *Waterford v The Commonwealth*, Mason and Wilson JJ said:[73]

> "If the conditions giving rise to legal professional privilege are satisfied, and the privilege is not waived, then the document is not disclosed ... Legal professional privilege is itself the product of a balancing exercise between competing public interests whereby, subject to the well-recognized crime or fraud exception the public interest in the perfect administration of justice is accorded paramountcy over the public interest that requires, in the interests of a fair trial, the admission in evidence of all relevant documentary evidence. Given its application, no further balancing exercise is required."

To the same effect is the following extract from the judgment of Dawson J in *Attorney-General (NT) v Kearney*:[74]

> "More importantly, once it (*ie*) legal professional privilege is claimed it is conclusive, provided that the relevant communication does not fall within the recognized exceptions. It is not for the court to enter upon a balancing exercise as in the case of Crown privilege in order to determine where the public interest lies in the individual case. It is established that as a matter of principle the public interest lies in preserving the confidentiality of those communications falling within the ambit of the doctrine."

As Dawson J's reference in the above passage to "the recognized exceptions" suggests, legal professional privilege is subject to a number of established and settled "exceptions". In particular, the privilege does not extend to communications or documents made or brought into existence for the purpose of, or as part of the process of, crime, fraud, abuse of statutory powers or, in some circumstances, defeating or frustrating the administration of justice by the courts. For present purposes, a critical characteristic of those "exceptions" is that they are exclusions from the reach of legal professional privilege rather than exceptions to the scope of the protection which it affords. They are directed to circumstances in which the privilege does not attach with the result that the particular communication or document is not protected by legal professional privilege at all. They are not directed to circumstances in which, notwithstanding that legal professional privilege does attach, the courts will override the privilege and order that the privileged document be produced for inspection or that the privileged communication be disclosed. Nor, in accordance with what has been said above, are they directed to identifying circumstances in which the courts will embark upon a balancing process to determine whether the considerations favouring disclosure outweigh the considerations favouring confidentiality. In that regard, the established position in this country is that, in the absence of waiver or loss of confidentiality ... the protection which legal professional privilege accords to the communications or documents to which it actually attaches is, for so long as that attachment persists, unqualified. And there is a powerful reason why that is so. I turn to identify it.

As has been seen, the focus of the modern theory of legal professional privilege is upon the removal of "apprehension" of compelled disclosure: the necessity of *providing subjectively for the client's freedom of apprehension* in consulting his legal adviser. The achievement of that "necessity" is not frustrated by the established exclusions in the form of particular identified circumstances in which legal professional privilege will not attach. Those circumstances can be identified in advance and the client can be advised that, provided they do not exist at the time when the relevant communication or document is made or comes into existence, legal professional privilege will attach to it and will, in the absence of waiver or loss of confidentiality, provide conclusive protection in the future ... In contrast, if the privilege could be overridden by the courts by reason of the outcome of some subsequent balancing process or whenever particular circumstances arise in subsequent litigation, an assurance of confidentiality could never be given and the "necessity" for "the client's freedom of apprehension" could never be fully achieved.

73 [(1987) 163 CLR 54, 64-5 (internal quotations marks omitted).]

74 [(1985) 158 CLR 500, 532. And see also *Baker v Campbell* (1983) 153 CLR 52, 95-6; *Waterford v Commonwealth* (1987) 163 CLR 54, 74, 98-9.]

At issue in *Carter* were privileged documents subpoenaed by the accused, which might have materially assisted in his defence or proved his innocence. There was no question that the documents were privileged; the only question was whether privilege should be defeated in circumstances where privileged material may assist an accused. It is clear from *Carter* that courts do not consider themselves in a position to engage in a balancing process to determine whether or not privilege should attach in a particular case or in particular circumstances. This principle applies even where it is claimed that protected communications will assist in an accused's defence or even to prove the innocence of an accused.

In reaching this conclusion, the High Court in *Carter* rejected an argument advanced by the accused that the judgment in the English case of *Barton*[75] should be adopted in Australia. In that case, Caulfield J held:

> If there are documents in the possession or control of a solicitor which, on production, help to further the defence of an accused man, then in my judgment no privilege attaches. I cannot conceive that our law would permit a solicitor or other person to screen from a jury information which, if disclosed to the jury, would perhaps enable a man either to establish his innocence or to resist an allegation made by the Crown. I think that is the principle that should be followed.[76]

The High Court found that the common law of Australia allowed for no such ability for judges to create exceptions to the 'fundamental principle' of privilege. As explained by Deane J:

> [T]he statement that no privilege 'attaches' to documents which 'help to further the defence of an accused man' cannot properly be seen as equating the suggested qualification with one or other of the recognised exclusions which preclude communications or documents made or brought into existence in certain circumstances from ever coming within the ambit of legal professional privilege. As has been said, those recognised exclusions do not defeat the rationale of legal professional privilege or undermine the protection of the confidentiality of communications or documents to which the privilege attaches. They operate only if the relevant circumstances exist at the time the relevant communication or document is made or comes into existence. If those circumstances exist at that time, there will simply be no privilege. If they do not exist at that time, the relevant exclusion is spent. Obviously, it would ordinarily be impossible to say at that time whether a particular communication or document might 'help to further the defence of an accused man' on some subsequent criminal trial. That being so, it would seem that Caulfield J's statement that no privilege 'attaches' must be understood as meaning not that legal professional privilege does not attach at all to the relevant communications or documents but that, notwithstanding that it has attached, it will be unavailing if and wherever the designated circumstances might subsequently arise. That means that the qualification would, if accepted, conflict with the rationale and undermine the efficacy of legal professional privilege by creating a necessarily unpredictable gap in the general protection which it accords to documents to which it has attached. It would convert an unqualified and conclusive privilege into a qualified and provisional one.[77]

The High Court thus determined that there could never be any 'compelling legal considerations which would justify this Court in curtailing the protection afforded by legal professional privilege' by allowing accused people to gain access

75 [1973] All ER 1192, 1194; [1973] 1 WLR 115.

76 The decision in *Barton* has since been overruled by a decision of the House of Lords, such that the common law of privilege in the UK is in accord with *Carter*: see *R v Derby Magistrates' Court; Ex parte B* [1995] 4 All ER 526 and see *DPP (Cth) v Galloway (a Pseudonym)* [2014] VSCA 272, [48], extracted below.

77 (1995) 183 CLR 121, 137.

to privileged communications.[78] Central to this determination was the notion that any such curtailment could undermine the basic rationale for the privilege itself – the facilitation of open communication between a client and her lawyers without fear that those communications will later be used in evidence. If a criminally accused client did not have the absolute protection of privilege, a danger would be created that accused persons would withhold information from their lawyers for fear that any admissions made in the seeking of legal advice would later be used against them:

> A person in need of legal advice in respect of an apprehended criminal charge will commonly, even if innocent, be implicated to some extent in the circumstances surrounding the alleged offence. If the professional advice is to be informed, it will often be inevitable that some damaging admissions will either deliberately or inadvertently be made. If the position were that any documents prepared by such a person for the information of his or her lawyer were susceptible to compulsory disclosure on the trial of another person, the competent lawyer would warn the client of that danger. A possible result of such a warning would be that no uninhibited written statement was made. If the lawyer's own note of any oral communication was susceptible to such compulsory disclosure, the lawyer would be conscious of the danger to the client involved in the making or retaining of an uninhibited record. Even if communication between lawyer and client were confined to the completely oral, the danger would persist that the client and the lawyer could, if called to give evidence and subject to the limits of admissibility, be cross-examined about the content of the communication to the disadvantage of the client. Nor could reliance be placed upon the privilege against self-incrimination for protection in such circumstances since that privilege would offer no protection in respect of damaging admissions which, however injurious to standing, reputation and civil liability, did not tend to incriminate or in respect of incriminating documents or information in the possession of the legal adviser. In that regard, the suggested curtailment of legal professional privilege would inevitably, to some extent, also reduce the efficacy of the privilege against self-incrimination.
>
> In these circumstances, the task of balancing the considerations favouring disclosure to an accused person in the postulated circumstances against the more general considerations favouring the "perfect security" of the protection afforded by legal professional privilege is a difficult one. There is not, however, any compelling legal consideration requiring rejection of the common law's entrenched conclusion that the outcome of that balancing process should be the complete protection of the privileged communication or document. It follows that I am not persuaded that this Court would be justified in curtailing the protection afforded by legal professional privilege in the manner sought by the appellant.[79]

The *UEA*, in s 123, appears to provide a statutory exception to client legal privilege for evidence adduced by a defendant that the common law would not have recognised. However, as discussed below, the practical effect of s 123 is often likely to accord with the common law position described in *Carter*.[80]

Waiver and loss of privilege: *UEA*

The waiver and loss provisions of the *UEA* are structured as exceptions to the privileges established by ss 118-120. This is in contrast to the common law, which treats the privilege as absolute and identifies only circumstances in which the privilege will be found not to have attached, such as where a communication

78 Ibid 138-9.

79 Ibid 139-40 (Deane J).

80 See below discussion of s 123 and *DPP (Cth) v Galloway (a Pseudonym)* [2014] VSCA 272.

is made in furtherance of a fraud or other crime or offence.[81] Because the *UEA* considers the waiver and loss provisions to be exceptions to the rules establishing client legal privilege, the burden will be on the applicant opposing privilege protection to demonstrate that the privilege has been lost or waived.[82]

Section 122 of the *UEA* establishes the circumstances under which client legal privilege that would ordinarily attach may be deemed waived due to the actions of the privilege holder. Circumstances that would result in waiver of privilege include consent of the privilege holder,[83] actions by the privilege holder that are inconsistent with the maintenance of the privilege,[84] and disclosure of the substance of the privileged material to a third party.[85]

122. Loss of client legal privilege: consent and related matters

(1) This Division does not prevent the adducing of evidence given with the consent of the client or party concerned.

(2) Subject to subsection (5), this Division does not prevent the adducing of evidence if the client or party concerned has acted in a way that is inconsistent with the client or party objecting to the adducing of the evidence because it would result in a disclosure of a kind referred to in section 118, 119 or 120.

(3) Without limiting subsection (2), a client or party is taken to have so acted if:

(a) the client or party knowingly and voluntarily disclosed the substance of the evidence to another person, or

(b) the substance of the evidence has been disclosed with the express or implied consent of the client or party.

(4) The reference in subsection (3)(a) to a knowing and voluntary disclosure does not include a reference to a disclosure by a person who was, at the time of the disclosure, an employee or agent of the client or party, or of a lawyer of the client or party, unless the employee or agent was authorised by the client, party or lawyer to make the disclosure.

(5) A client or party is not taken to have acted in a manner inconsistent with the client or party objecting to the adducing of the evidence merely because:

(a) the substance of the evidence has been disclosed:

(i) in the course of making a confidential communication or preparing a confidential document, or

(ii) as a result of duress or deception, or

(iii) under compulsion of law, or

(iv) if the client or party is a body established by, or a person holding an office under, an Australian law – to the Minister, or the Minister of the Commonwealth, the State or Territory, administering the law, or part of the law, under which the body is established or the office is held, or

(b) of a disclosure by a client to another person if the disclosure concerns a matter in relation to which the same lawyer is providing, or is to provide, professional legal services to both the client and the other person, or

(c) of a disclosure to a person with whom the client or party had, at the time of the disclosure, a common interest relating to the proceeding or an anticipated or pending proceeding in an Australian court or a foreign court.

(6) This Division does not prevent the adducing of evidence of a document that a witness has used to try to revive the witness's memory about a fact or opinion or has used as mentioned in section 32 (Attempts to revive memory in court) or 33 (Evidence given by police officers).

81 See *Carter v Managing Partner Northmore Hale Davy & Leake* [1995] HCA 33; 183 CLR 121, 134.

82 See *El-Zayet* [2014] NSWCCA 298, [112].

83 *UEA*, s 122(1).

84 *UEA*, s 122(2).

85 *UEA*, s 122(3).

In its 2005 review of the *UEA*, the ALRC recommended that the waiver provisions of s 122 be amended to ensure conformity with developments in the common law and to clarify that waiver should be based on an objective view of the behaviour of the party who it was alleged had waived privilege, rather than focusing on extrinsic notions such as fairness, which the original version of s 122 did not adequately restrict.[86] The following extract from the joint judgment in *Mann v Carnell*[87] sets out the test for waiver under the common law, which is now reflected in the current version of s 122 of the *UEA*. In *Mann*, the question was whether privilege had been waived with respect to documents that the plaintiff in the action alleged contained defamatory statements about him. He claimed that privilege in the documents – advices of counsel and a report from the ACT Government Solicitor concerning separate litigation in which the plaintiff was involved – had been waived because they had been provided by the defendant, the ACT Chief Minister, to Mr Moore, a member of the ACT Legislative Assembly, in a purportedly confidential communication. The High Court considered the issue of waiver and concluded:

> 28. … Legal professional privilege exists to protect the confidentiality of communications between lawyer and client. It is the client who is entitled to the benefit of such confidentiality, and who may relinquish that entitlement. It is inconsistency between the conduct of the client and maintenance of the confidentiality which effects a waiver of the privilege. Examples include disclosure by a client of the client's version of a communication with a lawyer, which entitles the lawyer to give his or her account of the communication, or the institution of proceedings for professional negligence against a lawyer, in which the lawyer's evidence as to advice given to the client will be received.
>
> 29. Waiver may be express or implied. Disputes as to implied waiver usually arise from the need to decide whether particular conduct is inconsistent with the maintenance of the confidentiality which the privilege is intended to protect. When an affirmative answer is given to such a question, it is sometimes said that waiver is "imputed by operation of law". This means that the law recognises the inconsistency and determines its consequences, even though such consequences may not reflect the subjective intention of the party who has lost the privilege. Thus, in *Benecke v National Australia Bank*,[88] the client was held to have waived privilege by giving evidence, in legal proceedings, concerning her instructions to a barrister in related proceedings, even though she apparently believed she could prevent the barrister from giving the barrister's version of those instructions. She did not subjectively intend to abandon the privilege. She may not even have turned her mind to the question. However, her intentional act was inconsistent with the maintenance of the confidentiality of the communication. What brings about the waiver is the inconsistency, which the courts, where necessary informed by considerations of fairness, perceive, between the conduct of the client and maintenance of the confidentiality; not some overriding principle of fairness operating at large. …
>
> 33. It does less than justice to the respondent's position to describe what occurred in the present case as disclosure to a third party. The privilege was that of the body politic, the Australian Capital Territory. The head of the Territory's Executive, the Chief Minister, in response to a question raised by a member of the Territory's Legislative Assembly as to the reasonableness of the conduct of the Territory in relation to certain litigation, gave the member, confidentially, access to legal advice that had been given to the Territory, and on the basis of which it had acted. Although "disclosure to a third party" may be a convenient rubric under which to discuss many problems of this nature, it represents, at the least, an over-simplification of the circumstances of the present case.

86 ALRC, *Uniform Evidence Law*, above n 35, [14.145]-[14.147] (citations omitted).

87 [1999] HCA 66; 201 CLR 1.

88 [(1993) 35 NSWLR 110.]

34. The purpose of the privilege was to enable the Australian Capital Territory to seek and obtain legal advice, in relation to the litigation which [the appellant] had instituted, without the apprehension of being prejudiced by subsequent disclosure of that advice. That included, and perhaps included above all, subsequent disclosure to [the appellant]. If Mr Moore had been given copies of the legal report and advice given to the Territory in relation to the proceedings brought by the appellant upon the basis that he was at liberty to show them to the appellant (even if to nobody else), that would have waived the privilege, because it would have been inconsistent with the confidentiality protected by the privilege. It is not difficult to imagine other circumstances in which the basis on which the communications were made available to Mr Moore, even though limited, would have been inconsistent with the purpose of the privilege and thus would have resulted in waiver. Disclosure by a client of confidential legal advice received by the client, which may be for the purpose of explaining or justifying the client's actions, or for some other purpose, will waive privilege if such disclosure is inconsistent with the confidentiality which the privilege serves to protect. Depending upon the circumstances of the case, considerations of fairness may be relevant to a determination of whether there is such inconsistency …

35. The purpose of the privilege being to protect the Territory from subsequent disclosure of the legal advice it received concerning the litigation instituted by the appellant, there was nothing inconsistent with that purpose in the Chief Minister conveying the terms of that advice, on a confidential basis, to a member of the Legislative Assembly who wished to consider the reasonableness of the conduct of the Territory in relation to the litigation.

36. The conclusion of the Full Court of the Federal Court, that privilege was not lost, was correct.

37. The appeal should be dismissed with costs.

Questions of client legal privilege, and waiver or loss of the privilege, may arise in criminal proceedings where communications are made to and with witnesses, and witness statements are subsequently prepared. The following case extract demonstrates how the courts have applied both the common law and *UEA* principles of client legal privilege to the Crown in criminal prosecutions, including the matter of who is the client in a criminal prosecution.

R (Cth) v Petroulias (No 22)
[2007] NSWSC 692

Petroulias faced charges under the *Crimes Act 1914* (Cth), including defrauding the Commonwealth. Petroulias issued a subpoena seeking production of '[a]ll notes of conferences held between counsel and/or Commonwealth Director of Public Prosecutions (CDPP) solicitors for the Crown for conferences held with or without any participating officers, agents or lawyers from the ATO or Australian Federal Police and the following [14] witnesses in this case'. The CDPP claimed that the conference notes recorded communications that were for the dominant purpose of a pending Australian proceeding within the meaning of *UEA*, s 119. Petroulias was unsuccessful due to Johnson J upholding the CDPP's claim for client legal privilege.

Johnson J: *Who is the Client?*

55. The term "*client*" is defined in s 117(1) *Evidence Act 1995* in the following terms: [s 17 extracted]

56. I accept the CDPP's submission that the CDPP is the client and lawyers working within the office of the CDPP are persons providing legal services to the CDPP as the

client: *R v Bunting* [(2002) 84 SASR 378] at [44]-[45]. There is nothing in the *Director of Public Prosecutions Act 1986 (Cth)* which is inconsistent with this conclusion …

Are the Communications During Conferences Between Prosecution Lawyers and Witnesses Caught by Privilege?

57. The present case involves a claim of litigation privilege under s 119 *Evidence Act 1995* which is in the following terms: [s 119 extracted]

58. I have examined the documents contained within MFI11 for the purpose of determining whether they are notes of conferences held this year between prosecution counsel and solicitors and Crown witnesses. I have had regard to the evidence of Ms Wildermoth in her affidavit sworn 20 June 2007 concerning the conferences and their purpose [for use in the conduct of the prosecution]. I am satisfied that the conference notes record confidential communications for the dominant purpose of a pending Australian proceeding, being the trial of the Accused, and thus fall within s 119 *Evidence Act 1995*.

59. If the common law principles were applicable, I would likewise be satisfied that the documents record communications passing between the CDPP's legal representatives and third persons, namely witnesses, for the purposes of pending litigation: *Trade Practices Commission v Sterling* (1978) 36 FLR 244 at 246. I am satisfied that the communications contained in the documents were made for the dominant purpose of a lawyer providing legal services so as to attract client legal privilege at common law: *Esso Australia Resources Limited v Commissioner of Taxation* [[1999] HCA 67] at 73, 107 …

62. In my view, documents recording communications between prosecution lawyers and prosecution witnesses for the dominant purpose of pending criminal proceedings against the Accused are clearly subject to privilege, whether the statutory test or common law principles are applied …

Has Privilege Been Waived in the Circumstances of this Case?

66. Section 122 *Evidence Act 1995* is relevant to the question of waiver: [s 122 extracted] …

68. Mr Walsh submits that privilege has been waived in this case by the Crown calling in the committal proceedings, the 2005 trial and/or the 2007 aborted trial the witnesses identified in the schedule to the subpoena. He submits that, applying common law principles of waiver, relevant inconsistency and unfairness arises in these circumstances where the CDPP seeks to maintain a claim of privilege with respect to the conference notes caught by the subpoena. He relies upon *Attorney-General (NT) v Maurice* (1986) 161 CLR 475 at 481, 487-488, 497; *Goldberg v Ng* at 84, 95-98 and *Mann v Carnell* at [28]-[29], [34] …

70. I do not consider that the calling of a prosecution witness at committal proceedings or at trial constituted an implied or imputed waiver for the purpose of a further trial. If this view was correct, than the mere act of the prosecution serving witness statements under the *Criminal Procedure Act 1986*, in advance of committal proceedings, would constitute waiver. The calling of a witness or witnesses at committal proceedings would have the same effect. The calling of the witnesses at trial would, likewise, have the same effect. Indeed, from the moment that the witness was sworn or affirmed, any privilege would be waived. With respect, this cannot be correct. I do not consider that the bare fact that a witness or witnesses have been called at committal proceedings or at an earlier trial satisfies the test for waiver at common law …

71. I do not accept the defence submission that the calling of witnesses by the Crown, per se, constitutes waiver at common law (if that test was applicable). The authorities point to an additional requirement. For example, in *Mann v Carnell* at [29], Gleeson CJ, Gaudron, Gummow and Callinan JJ said: [*Mann v Carnell* quoted].

72. In this passage, their Honours referred to the decision of the New South Wales Court of Appeal in *Benecke v National Australia Bank* (1993) 35 NSWLR 110 where waiver of privilege arose from the giving of evidence in legal proceedings *concerning instructions to a barrister in related proceedings whilst the client attempted, at the same*

> *time, to prevent the barrister from giving the barrister's version of those instructions.* For privilege to be waived at common law, an inconsistent stance must have been taken. That has not been demonstrated in the present case. Accordingly, even if the common law principles of waiver were applicable as the Accused submits, the privilege has not been waived in this case.
>
> 73. I do not accept that the calling of witnesses at committal proceedings or at earlier trials of the Accused gives rise to waiver applying the statutory test in s 122 *Evidence Act 1995* …
>
> 75. Whether the common law or the *Evidence Act 1995* applies, I am satisfied that the privilege has not been waived in this case.

Just as the Crown calling witnesses in committal proceedings will not constitute waiver of Crown privilege, so also will the principles of client legal privilege protect communications with witnesses for an accused sought by the Crown, as shown in the decision of the NSW Supreme Court in *Gittany (No 3).*

Gittany (No 3)
[2013] NSWSC 1670

Simon Gittany was being tried before a judge, without jury, on the charge of murdering his fiancée, Lisa Harnum. The Crown case was that Gittany had deliberately lifted Harnum over the balcony railing of their 15th floor apartment and caused her to fall to her death. The defence case was that Harnum had climbed over the railing herself and had either slipped or committed suicide. In support of this defence claim, the defence delivered a tendency notice pursuant to *UEA*, s 97,[89] indicating its intention to call witnesses of Harnum's tendency to place herself in a position of danger, to self-harm and to attempt suicide. The prosecution made a formal call[90] 'for any witness statements, conference notes or other notes relating to the potential witnesses identified in the tendency notice', but not statements by the accused.[91] The defence resisted the call, claiming that the documents were protected by client legal privilege. The prosecution claimed that privilege could not be sustained because:

> [E]ither by serving the tendency notice or upon the calling of each tendency witness, the accused has or will have knowingly and voluntarily disclosed the substance of the evidence and so acted in a way that is inconsistent with the objection to production, resulting in the loss of the privilege in accordance with s 122 of the Act …[92]

McCallum J held that merely serving a tendency notice will not constitute behaviour inconsistent with the maintenance of the privilege.

> **McCallum J**: 6. The privilege arises by operation of s 119 in part 3.10 of the *Evidence Act* …
>
> 10. As noted by Mr Strickland on behalf of the accused, it is necessary to read [s 122] in the context of s 119. The protection attaches to the communication with or confidential document prepared by the lawyer. The test is whether the party concerned has acted inconsistently with maintaining that confidence, such as by knowingly and voluntarily disclosing the substance of the confidential communication (as distinct from the substance of the anticipated evidence concerning the underlying event). An example is where a former client sues a lawyer and deploys, in that action, evidence as to what advice the

89 See Chapter 11.
90 Cf *UEA*, s 167.
91 [2013] NSWSC 1670, [4] (McCallum J).
92 Ibid [8].

lawyer gave. The open reliance upon the words said by the lawyer is inconsistent with an objection that the words were said in confidence.

11. The Crown acknowledged that, if the proposition for which he contends is correct, the corollary is that client legal privilege is lost over witness statements and notes of conferences with witnesses in every legal proceeding at the point when the witness is called and perhaps upon service of an outline of the evidence a party anticipates the witness will give (depending on whether the statement or outline was served pursuant to an order of the court: see s 122(5) of the Act) …

13. Mr Strickland's submissions have persuaded me that I should follow the decision in *Petroulias (No 22)*. In my respectful opinion, Johnson J was right to hold in that case (at [70]) that the calling of a prosecution witness at committal proceedings or at an earlier trial does not constitute an implied or imputed waiver of client legal privilege in respect of communications with those witnesses for the purpose of a further trial …

22. I am not persuaded that the privilege (which it is accepted exists) has been lost … The determinative consideration is the fact that neither the service of [a s 97 tendency] notice nor the calling of a witness discloses the substance of confidential communications with the lawyer. It may be anticipated that in most cases the content of the notice and of the evidence will coincide with such confidential communications but that is not the test.

23. For those reasons, I ruled that the accused was not obliged to answer the Crown's call.

The *UEA* provides for other circumstances in which client legal privilege will be lost. For example, privilege is lost with respect to evidence relevant to the question of the intentions or legal competence of a client or party who has died, to evidence that, if not adduced, would prevent the court from enforcing an order of an Australian court, or to evidence of a communication or document that affects a right of a person.[93] Privilege will also be lost where a communication or document was made in furtherance of the commission of a fraud, offence or other act that renders a person liable for a civil penalty, or where the communication or document was made in furtherance of a deliberate abuse of power.[94] Where privilege is deemed to have been lost, privilege may also be lost with respect to other communications or documents that are reasonably necessary to enable a proper understanding of the original communication or document.[95]

Exception to client legal privilege for accused persons

123. Loss of client legal privilege: defendants [Cth & NSW Acts Only]/Loss of client legal privilege – accused [Vic Act Only]

In a criminal proceeding, this Division does not prevent [a defendant/an accused] from adducing evidence unless it is evidence of:

(a) a confidential communication made between an associated [defendant/accused] and a lawyer acting for that person in connection with the prosecution of that person, or

(b) the contents of a confidential document prepared by an associated [defendant/accused] or by a lawyer acting for that person in connection with the prosecution of that person.

Note: ***Associated defendant*** is defined in the Dictionary.

As mentioned above, s 123 of the *UEA* diverts from the common law to create an exception to client legal privilege that applies only to accused persons in criminal

93 *UEA*, s 121.

94 *UEA*, s 125.

95 *UEA*, s 126.

prosecutions. Section 123 provides that the privileges established in ss 118-120 of the *UEA* will be lost with respect to communications that are adduced by an accused in a criminal proceeding, except where the communications involve an '*associated accused*'. This loss of privilege is not absolute and unqualified in every aspect of a criminal matter, as s 123 will only apply where evidence is actually being adduced in a proceeding. This means that s 123 does not reach and will not lift client legal privilege with respect to any pre-trial or administrative matter, such as subpoenas or notices to produce, to which privilege would ordinarily attach pursuant to s 131A (in the jurisdictions other than the Commonwealth).[96] In such circumstances, the common law, rather than s 123, will apply. Thus, where a question of privilege arises with respect to an accused person's evidence, the courts must determine whether the *Evidence Act* applies to the evidence in question and, if so, whether evidence is being adduced in the proceeding, such that s 123 might apply, or whether the evidence is being produced pursuant to one of the procedures listed in s 131A, such that the common law applies. Moreover, the court may have to consider whether the evidence is in the accused's possession at the time that the privilege question arises, as the s 123 exception will apply only where the accused already has possession of the privileged material.

These restrictions on the applicability of s 123 are likely to have the practical effect of negating the apparent diversions from the common law. In *DPP (Cth) v Galloway*, extracted below, the Victorian Court of Appeal held that s 123 was not meant to abrogate any common law rights to privilege and only codified the common law that allowed an accused to adduce evidence of privileged documents already in their possession.

DPP (Cth) v Galloway (a Pseudonym)

[2014] VSCA 272 (citations omitted)

At a preliminary hearing, a solicitor for the CDPP was asked in cross-examination to disclose the content of legal advices given by the CDPP to the Australian Federal Police (AFP). The trial judge ruled that the cross-examination was permitted because it fell within s 123 of the *UEA* (s 131A not operating to prevent the application of s 123). As the Victorian Court of Appeal summarised (at [26]), '[t]he judge expressed her conclusion in these terms:

> 'I agree with the ACC accused [the present respondents] that, on the proper construction of ss 123 and 131A, legal privilege does not apply to evidence sought to be adduced by the accused at any stage in a criminal proceeding, unless it is a co-accused's legal privilege. It follows that legal privilege would not be a valid basis for objecting to CDPP and AFP witnesses being asked questions in cross-examination in the ACC applications.'

The Court of Appeal confirmed that s 131A is not applicable.

> 24. The cross-examination of a witness falls squarely within the scope of the legal professional privilege provisions as originally enacted. It is part of the process of adducing evidence in court proceedings. Accordingly, the eliciting of evidence about the content of legal advice is prohibited by ss 118 and 119 unless s 123 applies. For completeness, we should record our view that neither a direction to a witness to attend for cross-examination, nor a direction to answer a question in cross-examination over objection, falls within the scope of "disclosure requirement" within the meaning of s 131A(2).

96 *UEA*, s 131A(1).

25. … We respectfully agree with her Honour that the issue has arisen "in a criminal proceeding", as those words are used in s 123. The question is whether the eliciting of evidence in cross-examination on behalf of an accused falls within the scope of the phrase "adducing evidence" as used in s 123.

However, it overturned the trial judge's ruling, stating:

70. … It cannot seriously be supposed that the Victorian Parliament effected a wholesale abrogation of legal professional privilege in criminal proceedings without intending to do so or realising that it was doing so. Common law rights cannot be removed inadvertently or accidentally. As we have already pointed out, such a change in the law can only be effected by the clearest statutory language, expressing unambiguously the Parliament's intention to make the change …

Maxwell P, Neave and Coghlan JJA: 6. The common law recognised an exception to legal professional privilege in favour of an accused who had come into possession – even by unlawful means – of a document or information to which legal professional privilege would otherwise attach. In those circumstances, the accused person could introduce the privileged information into evidence. The present case is not of that kind, however. Those representing the accused are not in possession of the legal advice sought, and do not know its contents. If the argument which they advance is correct, then the enactment of s 123 effected a very substantial abrogation of legal professional privilege, going far beyond the limits of the common law exception.

7. For reasons which follow, we have concluded that the Victorian Parliament intended no such abrogation of the privilege when it enacted s 123 …

8. In our view, s 123 of the Act was intended to do no more than create a statutory exception (from the privilege created by ss 118 and 119) corresponding to the exception recognised by the common law. Without s 123, the holder of the privilege would have been entitled under ss 118 and 119 to object to the accused adducing evidence of a privileged communication already in his/her possession.

9. Plainly enough, if defence counsel could investigate without restriction the contents of any relevant privileged communication of which any prosecution witness had knowledge, legal professional privilege in the context of criminal proceedings would be virtually destroyed. As already mentioned, the Court would not conclude that such a step had been taken unless the legislature had declared in the clearest terms its intention to do so. The legislative record contains no such indication. As will appear, the only express reference to legal professional privilege is to the opposite effect …

Does s 123 Apply? …

27. In this Court, the respondents advanced two principal submissions in support of [the trial judge's] conclusion. The first directed attention to the phrase "adducing evidence", as it appears in ss 118 and 119 and again in s 123. As can be seen above, ss 118 and 119 prohibit the adducing of evidence if to do so would result in the disclosure of a confidential communication, or the contents of a confidential document, to which legal professional privilege attaches. Section 123 exempts from that prohibition evidence adduced by an accused in a criminal proceeding (except where that would result in disclosure of information to which a co-accused's legal professional privilege attaches).

28. According to the submission, the use of the same phrase – "adducing evidence" – in both the prohibition and the exception demonstrates that the scope of the exception in s 123 was intended to be coterminous with the scope of the prohibition to which it relates. Accordingly, s 123 was intended to abolish legal professional privilege in connection with the adducing of evidence by an accused by any means, including by eliciting answers in cross-examination.

29. The second submission was that, although s 123 thus created a significant exception to legal professional privilege, it did not take away common law rights. According to the respondents' written outline, s 123 "was purporting to codify the common law as set

out in *R v Barton* and *R v Ataou*". Far from "contradict[ing] or overturn[ing]" the common law, it was submitted, s 123 amounted to a "statutory re-enactment" of the common law. That being so, there was no occasion to invoke the principle of legality.

30. We deal first with the textual argument.

Textual Analysis …

36. … The intended meaning of "adducing evidence" in any particular provision falls to be determined by reference to the purpose of that provision and its context. (Even where the presumption applies, it readily gives way where context indicates that a different meaning was intended.)

37. It is highly relevant, therefore, that ss 118 and 119 serve a quite different purpose from that of s 123. The former sections were enacted to give statutory force and protection to legal professional privilege, a "fundamental and general principle of the common law". The sections protect the two recognised forms of legal professional privilege – advice privilege and litigation privilege. That being so, and in the absence of any indication to the contrary, Parliament is to be taken to have intended the broadest scope for the phrase "adducing evidence" in ss 118 and 119, in order to provide legal professional privilege protection for evidence in whatever form it is brought before a court.

38. Quite different considerations apply to provisions – like s 123 – which remove the privilege. For obvious reasons, the consideration which favours a broad reading of the phrase "adducing evidence" in ss 118 and 119 – that it preserves a fundamental common law right – does not apply in relation to a provision which abrogates that right. Applying the principle of legality, the contrary must be true. That is, a section which abrogates the right must be interpreted as having no broader scope than Parliament can be seen clearly to have intended …

41. To give the phrase "adducing evidence" in s 123 the construction contended for by the respondents would likewise "virtually eliminate the legal professional privilege as a ground for non-admission of evidence" in criminal proceedings. It would mean, quite simply, that no prosecution witness could decline to answer a question in cross-examination on the ground that to do so would result in the disclosure of a privileged communication or the contents of a privileged document.

42. Plainly, that would represent a profound change in the way criminal trials are conducted. (If s 123 did indeed effect such a change when first enacted in 1995, it seems remarkable that defence counsel in trials have not until now exploited the forensic opportunity opened up by the change). It is therefore necessary to consider the respondents' second submission, to the effect that on its first enactment in 1995 s 123 reflected, rather than changing, the common law of Australia as it stood at that time. Before doing so, however, we should point out that the existence of s 131A is itself a serious obstacle to the broader interpretation of s 123.

43. As can be seen from the text of s 131A … its manifest purpose is to preserve legal professional privilege as a ground of objection when a person is required to produce documents or provide information under a coercive process of a court ("disclosure requirement"). Section 131A(2)(a) gives, as an example of a "disclosure requirement", a subpoena to produce documents or to give evidence. Counsel for the respondents accepted, as they were bound to, that if the CDPP solicitor presently under cross-examination had been subpoenaed to produce copies of the relevant legal advices or to give evidence about their content, and had objected on the grounds of legal professional privilege, the judge would have been bound by s 131A to uphold the objection (absent any argument about waiver or illegality).

44. It follows that, if the respondents' construction of s 123 were correct, a wholly anomalous position would have been created. Disclosure of legal advice in answer to a subpoena could be resisted on the grounds of legal professional privilege but disclosure of the content of the same advice, in answer to a question in cross-examination, could

not. When it is appreciated that s 131A would also apply where a subpoena was made returnable at the trial of the proceeding, the anomaly becomes even more striking …

Did s 123 change the common law?

47. As noted earlier, the submission for the respondents was that, in effectively removing legal professional privilege as a ground of objection in criminal trials, s 123 was a codification of the common law of Australia as it stood in 1995. The decisions in *Barton* and *Ataou* were said to express the common law "principle" thus given expression in s 123. Both were decisions of English courts, however, and counsel were unable to identify any Australian authority which supported the proposition. The only reference to an Australian decision was to the dissenting judgment of Gibbs CJ in *Baker*.

48. This submission must be rejected. First, as will appear, the English authorities established no such broad "principle". Secondly, and in any event, such modification of legal professional privilege as those decisions may have temporarily effected in English law (until they were both overruled by the House of Lords in 1995) was never part of the common law of Australia …

57. As the High Court's decision in *Carter* makes clear, Australian law has never viewed the determination of a claim for legal professional privilege as involving any "balancing" exercise … As Deane J explained, the privilege itself "represents the outcome of a such a balancing process and reflects the common law's verdict that the considerations favouring the 'perfect security' of communications and documents provided by the privilege must prevail". The position is the same under English law, as the House of Lords made clear in overruling *Barton* and *Ataou*.

58. What matters for present purposes is that the authorities relied on by the respondents did not establish any "principle" that legal professional privilege in criminal trials was overridden whenever the accused could show that access to the privileged information was required for his/her defence …

Not part of Australian common law

59. Whatever might have been the exact scope of the short-lived *Barton*/*Ataou* "principle", no such principle ever formed part of the common law of Australia. So much was made clear by the majority judgments in the High Court in *Carter* …

66. It follows that, if s 123 as originally enacted in 1995 had been intended to operate as the respondents contend, it would have fundamentally altered the common law of Australia. There is, however, nothing in the language of s 123, or in the extrinsic materials of the time, to suggest that such a change was ever contemplated …

86. … As Grove J held in *R v Wilkie*:

> "[T]he effect of the section is to enable an accused to use what would otherwise be privileged information if he has possession of it, but it does not in its own terms provide a vehicle for enforced production of such material."

87. The intended operation of s 123 is, in our view, helpfully illustrated by the following example set out in the submission for the Commissioner. (We have made one modification, as marked):

> "To illustrate, a company director may be charged with a criminal offence in circumstances where that director, in the course of his or her duties, had come into possession of legal advice provided to the company. The director may wish to give evidence about that advice in order to explain his or her state of mind (because, for example, it may assist to meet an allegation of dishonesty or recklessness). In the absence of s 123, s 118 would allow the company (the client) to claim legal professional privilege, with the result that evidence of the advice could not be adduced, and therefore would be inadmissible pursuant to s 134. Properly construed, s 123 reverses that situation so that the advice is admissible.
>
> Critically, however, in a case where the director did not already have the advice, s 123 would have no work to do. If any attempt was made to require the company to produce the advice, s 131A would prevent any reliance on s 123. Further, if a

> witness was asked about the advice during cross-examination, the witness could claim legal professional privilege [under s 118] to avoid answering the question because legal professional privilege operates at the point of compulsion, rather than at the subsequent point of determining the admissibility of the answer."

The Victorian Court of Appeal referred to the decision of Grove J in *Wilkie*.[97] In that case, defence counsel sought to subpoena the CDPP's notes of a conference between prosecuting counsel and an intended witness, Spratt. The defence had Spratt's witness statements made on three earlier occasions and Grove J accepted that there were observable inconsistencies in the content of these statements. Wilkie's counsel sought the conference notes, claiming that there was a legitimate forensic purpose in having access to the notes 'in order to be informed as to how these changes [resulting in the inconsistencies] came about'. Grove J rejected the defence submission. His Honour observed:

> 3. I should however first note an argument that the effect of s 123 of the *Evidence Act 1995*, particularly in the context of rule changes following the decisions of the High Court in *Esso Resources v Commissioner of Taxation* (1999) 201 CLR 49 and *Mann v Carnell* (1999) 201 CLR 1, should be interpreted so that effectively there has been an abolition of the right of a prosecutor to claim privilege against disclosure of material of the nature which I have mentioned. In my view the statute in s 123, whilst it does not prevent an accused from adducing evidence about matters which would be the subject of privilege in the hands of a prosecutor, it is to be observed that it says nothing in its terms about enforced production of such material. A wholesale change in such a fundamental legal concept of privilege would in my view require much clearer statutory expression than appears in s 123.
>
> 4. My attention was drawn to the decision in *R v Petroulias (No 22)* [2007] NSWSC 692 where the proposition was not advanced in the terms that it is now brought forward. I consider that the Crown's submission is correct, that the effect of the section is to enable an accused to use what would otherwise be privileged information if he has possession of it, but it does not in its own terms provide a vehicle for enforced production of such material.[98]

Other Protected Communications

As stated in the Introduction, client legal privilege is not the only privilege recognised by the *UEA*. Other privileges conferred by the *UEA* include a general privilege for religious confessions;[99] specific privileges related to self-incrimination of a witness;[100] a privilege for matters of state, including matters of national security;[101] and a privilege for evidence related to settlement negotiations.[102] These other privileges, like client legal privilege, are justified by the public interest – for example, to facilitate open communication among the protected parties or, in the case of the privilege against self-incrimination, to ensure that witnesses are not unfairly forced to provide evidence for use in their own conviction[103] – and

97 [2008] NSWSC 885.

98 Under the analysis in *Wilkie*, the prosecution would be able to resist any disclosure requirement that would otherwise require the disclosure of a document or communication on grounds of client legal privilege. See Chapter 2 for discussion of prosecution disclosure requirements.

99 *UEA*, s 127.

100 *UEA*, s 128.

101 *UEA*, s 130.

102 *UEA*, s 131.

103 See Chapters 1 and 2 for discussion of the right to silence and the burden of proof, respectively.

so provide a mechanism by which the communications may be kept confidential.[104] However, unlike client legal privilege, the privilege that attaches to these communications is likely to be less stringent and may involve the court specifically balancing the public interest in the confidentiality of communications with the competing public interest in the 'efficient and informed disposal of litigation'.[105]

Protected confidences: For example, the NSW, ACT and Tasmanian *Evidence Acts* each include a Div 1A in Part 3.10 that provides a privilege for '*protected confidences*' made within a professional confidential relationship.[106] The provisions provide a limited privilege for communications made by a '*protected confider*' to a '*confidant*', who, for purposes of the privilege, was acting in a professional capacity in the course of the relationship and who was under an express or implied obligation not to disclose the contents of the communication.[107] Relationships that may be covered by the professional relationship privilege may include those between doctor and patient, nurse and patient, psychotherapist and patient, social worker and client, accountant and client, or journalist and source.[108] The privilege is intended to be 'sufficiently flexible to allow the court to protect information in a range of relationships where confidentiality is particularly important'.[109]

The professional confidential relationship privilege is a limited one because it is not a 'true privilege',[110] as it does not automatically provide privilege protection whenever a 'protected confidence' is made, but rather establishes a balancing test for the court to determine whether it will apply the privilege on a case-by-case basis.[111] Section 126B of the NSW, ACT and Tasmanian Acts provides that the court is to give a direction that evidence of a protected confidence or the contents of a document recording a protected confidence or protected identity information is not to be adduced if the court is satisfied that '(a) it is likely that harm would or might be caused (whether directly or indirectly) to a protected confider if the evidence is adduced, and (b) the nature and extent of the harm outweighs the desirability of the evidence being given'.[112] '*Harm*' is defined to include 'actual physical bodily harm, financial loss, stress or shock, damage to reputation or emotional or psychological harm (such as shame, humiliation and fear)'.[113] The court is directed to take certain matters into account when performing the balancing test, such as the probative value and importance of the evidence in the proceeding; the nature and gravity of the relevant offence, cause of action or defence; and the likely effect of adducing the evidence, including the likelihood and nature of harm that would be caused to the protected confider.[114] The court is also directed to consider the public interest in preserving the confidentiality of the evidence.[115]

---

104 See ALRC, *Uniform Evidence Law*, above n 35, [15.4].
105 Ibid [15.4].
106 See *Evidence Act 1995* (NSW), *Evidence Act 2011* (ACT), *Evidence Act 2001* (Tas), ss 126A, 126B.
107 Ibid s 126A.
108 See ALRC, *Uniform Evidence Law*, above n 35, [15.4]; S Odgers, *Uniform Evidence Law* (Thomson Reuters, 15th ed, 2020) [EA.126A.30].
109 ALRC, *Uniform Evidence Law*, above n 35, [15.12].
110 See ibid [15.10].
111 See *Styles v Clayton Utz* [2011] NSWSC 1314, [11].
112 *UEA* (NSW, Tas and ACT), s 126B(1), (3).
113 Ibid s 126A(1).
114 Ibid s 126B(4).
115 Ibid s 126B(4)(i), (j).

Journalists' privilege: The Commonwealth, NSW, Victorian, ACT and NT Acts also include a specific privilege protecting the identity of journalists' sources.[116] As with the confidential professional privilege, on application of a party, the court may order that the privilege is not to apply if the public interest in disclosure of the source's identity outweighs any adverse effect of the disclosure on the source or other person and also outweighs the public interest in the communication of facts and opinion to the public by the news media and in the ability of the news media to access sources of facts.[117]

Sexual assault communications privilege: NSW, Victoria, Tasmania, the ACT and the NT all include provisions protecting communications with counsellors by, to or about victims of sexual assaults.[118] The privilege applies to protected communications made before or after the commission of the assault. In NSW, Vic, the ACT and NT production of protected communications may not be compelled in preliminary criminal proceedings.[119] However, in the criminal proceedings themselves, protected communications may not be compelled except with leave of the court. In NSW, Victoria, and the NT, leave may be granted if the communication will have substantive probative value; if other documents or evidence about the matters to which the protected confidence relates are not available; and the public interest in maintaining the confidential nature of the communication and protecting the confider from harm are outweighed by the public interest in admitting evidence that has substantial probative value. The ACT contains a similar formulation – however, the fundamental leave inquiry in criminal proceedings is whether the public interest in ensuring the accused is given a fair trial outweighs the public interest in preserving the confidentiality of the protected confidence.[120] Whether the evidence has substantial probative value is one of the considerations that may affect the leave considerations.[121] In all jurisdictions, the victim can consent to the disclosure of the communication. In Tasmania, consent is the only circumstance in which a protected communication can be disclosed.[122]

Conclusion

As these various privileges, confidential communications protections and balancing tests indicate, determining whether and when to grant or apply a privilege comes with many challenges. The main question to be considered is when the public interest is strong enough that a privilege should be granted, even though it will deprive parties and the court of a piece of relevant or possibly determinative evidence. For client legal privilege, the answer is that there has been a consistent determination over the past 400 years that the public interest requires that communications between clients and lawyers be protected. Even though it is clear that any balancing test to determine whether client legal privilege

116 *Evidence Act 1995* (Cth), s 126H; *UEA* (NSW, Vic and ACT), ss 126J, 126K; *UEA* (NT), s 127A.

117 Ibid.

118 *UEA* (NSW), Ch 3, Pt 3.10, Div 1B (referencing *Criminal Procedure Act 1986* (NSW), ss 295-306); *Evidence (Miscellaneous Provisions) Act 1958* (Vic), Pt 2, Div 2A; *UEA* (Tas), s 127B; *Evidence (Miscellaneous Provisions) Act 1991* (ACT), Ch 4, Pt 4.4, Div 4.4.3; *Evidence Act 1939* (NT), Pt 7.

119 *Criminal Procedure Act 1986* (NSW), s 299D; *Evidence (Miscellaneous Provisions) Act 1958* (Vic), s 32D(1); *Evidence Act 1939* (NT), s 56E.

120 *Evidence (Miscellaneous Provisions) Act 1991* (ACT), s 79H(1)(b).

121 Ibid s 79H(3)(d).

122 *UEA* (Tas), s 127B(3), (4).

should be applied in a particular case is inappropriate, there are still disputes among the jurisdictions in Australia regarding the outer scope of the privilege, with New South Wales, Victoria, Tasmania, the Australian Capital Territory and the Northern Territory extending client legal privilege protection to preliminary proceedings and the Commonwealth so far deciding not to do the same.

Debate over whether evidence should be withheld and the truth potentially obscured will almost certainly continue so long as any communication is deemed worthy of receiving the status of a privileged communication. It is equally likely, however, that client legal privilege will continue its more than four century run as a fundamental principle of substantive law that transcends other rules confined to the law of evidence alone.

Chapter 4

Introducing the Law of Evidence: Relevance, Discretionary and Mandatory Exclusions

Over a century ago the United States treatise writer Thayer noted famously that the common law rules for excluding relevant evidence from a trial are 'the characteristic thing ... stamping [the common law of evidence] ... as the child of the jury system'.[1] He was referring to the fact that the common law filters, through evidentiary rules and discretions, the information jurors may receive. The principles for excluding or otherwise regulating evidence[2] in this way fall into three broad categories, namely, evidence that is:

- '*too conjectural and remote a connection*'. For example, the evidence might add something (such as indicating a witness has a sense of humour) but it does not add significantly in assisting to prove or disprove the case before the jury (especially if one takes into account time, inconvenience, cost concerns[3]); or
- *the evidence may be 'dangerous' to the fairness of the trial* in that it may be 'likely to be misused or overestimated' by jurors. For example, second hand hearsay evidence may be given too much weight, or evidence of a previous conviction for an unrelated offence to that charged shows the defendant in a bad light and might with no logic (and so irrationally) encourage the jury to pre-judge the defendant as a bad person;[4] or
- *evidence that is 'unsafe on public grounds'*, for example, where it relates to public interest immunity (because governance of the state justifies withholding information), or where the police have acted illegally gathering evidence.

---

1 J Thayer, *Preliminary Treatise on Evidence* (1898), 266.

2 For example, by limiting the use of evidence by judicial direction: see, eg, *UEA*, ss 95, 136.

3 For example, *UEA*, s 136.

4 See ALRC, *Uniform Evidence Law* (Report No 102, 2006), 16.45: 'In the Interim Report for the previous Evidence inquiry, the ALRC referred not only to unfair prejudice arising from evidence which might inflame emotions, but also to unfair prejudice resulting from mis-estimation by the fact-finder of the weight to be given to particular evidence' (citations omitted); see also *Candir* 2009 ONCA 915, [59]: 'evidence may mislead [the tribunal of fact] because its impact on a trier of fact, especially a jury, may be disproportionate to its reliability' (citations omitted).

Thayer's observations hint at the high level of control that the law places on trials – and especially criminal trials. The second of Thayer's three limbs introduces an important trial dynamic – that is, the well-known maxim that it is better that 10 guilty people go free, rather than one innocent person is convicted.[5] Australian[6] evidence law was transformed over 25 years ago from being primarily common law and rooted in 19th century concepts and values to today's uniform evidence law.

The Uniform Evidence Acts

This law, known collectively as the uniform Evidence Acts is the product of an extensive Australian Law Reform Commission (ALRC) review in the 1980s. It drew on multi-disciplinary research for its national blueprint, a draft Bill. The Commonwealth and New South Wales were first adopters: *Evidence Act 1995* (Cth) and (NSW).[7] A 10-year review of the *Evidence Act 1995* led to some revisions to the Acts. Now the uniform *Evidence Act* (*UEA*, *UEL*, or 'the Acts') dominate the Australian evidence law and court process landscape. Uniformity, the goal of the ALRC and the Commonwealth government, has been achieved imperfectly. While the differences in each UEA jurisdiction are relatively small, history indicates that they are prone to enlargement.[8]

The pre-*UEA* common law of evidence and procedure was supplemented in New South Wales by a rather thin *Evidence Act 1898* (NSW). Other Australian jurisdictions that have shifted to the *UEA* have also left similar hybrid models of statute and common law. The *UEA* modernised evidence law in ways that initially challenged the legal profession, such that even three years into its operation, in *Graham*[9] (one of the first *UEA* cases before the High Court), it was clear that neither counsel nor judge during the trial realised that they should be applying the Act. Even by 2007, at least one court decision[10] showed that the bench and the bar table had been caught out by a well-established common law principle that now informed the Act: '*EVIDENCE – proper application of Briginshaw principle – isn't there something in the Evidence Act about this?*'.[11] These are just two illustrations of the massive shift created by the uniform Acts. The Acts are

---

5 Attributed to W Blackstone, *Commentaries on the Law of England* (1765), and typically referred to as the Blackstone ratio. See Alexander Volokh, '*n* Guilty Men', 146 *University of Pennsylvania Law Review* 173 (1997), <www2.law.ucla.edu/volokh/guilty.htm>.

6 Excepting Queensland, South Australia and Western Australia.

7 Until 2001, federal courts, ACT courts (through the Commonwealth Act) and NSW courts were the only locations where the uniform Acts applied. Tasmania followed in 2001; Norfolk Island in 2004; Victoria in 2008; and in 2011 the ACT and the Northern Territory (*Evidence (National Uniform Legislation) Act 2011* (NT)). Surprisingly, there are other adoptions outside Australia: the *Evidence Act* (Barbados), *Evidence Act 2006* (St Lucia) and *Evidence Act 2011* (St Christopher and Nevis) reflect a growth export industry in the legislation as well. See <http://www.easterncaribbeanlaw.com/> (and thanks to Professor Jeremy Gans, Melbourne Law School, for his indefatigable scanning of the globe for observations on the law of evidence).

8 See, eg, for Victoria, *Evidence Act 2008*, s 41 (which is specifically directed at vulnerable witnesses), s 165B (delayed proceedings and disadvantage), and *Jury Directions Act 2015* (Vic). For Tasmania, *Evidence Act 2001*, see ss 113-115, 194A-194M, 196A-196C.

9 [1998] HCA 61; 195 CLR 606.

10 *Smith v Granada Tavern (No 2)* [2007] FMCA 904.

11 Catchwords to *Granada Tavern v Smith* [2008] FCA 646; 173 IR 328 (Heerey J) regarding *Briginshaw v Briginshaw* [1938] HCA 34; 60 CLR 336. See *UEA*, ss 140(2) and 142(2) (and Chapter 2).

not a codification of the law in that they are not a full comprehensive statement of the law of evidence and procedure, but they are code-like[12] in many areas. Which areas are code-like and which are not is not well-signposted, requiring lawyers to begin by going first to the Act's provisions[13] (and then to any case law interpretations) and recognising that certain entrenched common law principles may need to be inserted into an application of the Act in particular situation. Consider, for example, the rule in *Browne v Dunn*.[14]

The Acts may not have simplified the law of evidence but much of their content is more accessible, more ordered and with an expanded repertoire of forensic aids compared to its hybrid common law/statute predecessor. Its novel dimensions include:

- A comprehensive **Dictionary** defining words, such as 'probative value',[15] 'the hearsay rule',[16] the opinion rule,[17] admissions,[18] credibility evidence,[19] and also phrases such as 'unavailability of persons'.[20] These definitions sweep aside a significant amount of uncertainty concerning the scope of particular rules of evidence.

- **Additional checks and balances** to facilitate the effective use of the adversarial trial as a forum for testing evidence. So, for example, there is provision for parties to put other parties on *notice*, with respect to evidence a party seeks to bring within certain exceptions to the hearsay rule[21] or when seeking to tender admissible tendency or coincidence evidence.[22] These notices aim to prevent ambushing an opposing party with the evidence that might benefit by a party's opportunity to assess its weaknesses.

- **Requests** can be made of a party by another of evidence of a previous representation, a criminal conviction or in relation to the authenticity, identity or admissibility of a document or thing. These requests allow parties to investigate and assess the qualities of documentary or hearsay evidence (or evidence of convictions) to be adduced by another party. At common law the evidence would either have been excluded (and so reducing a trial's information base) or admitted (and potentially left with its testing compromised by a party caught unawares). Requests can be potentially backed up by court order and can be made for numerous matters, including that a party:

12 See, eg, the clarification in *Ellis* [2003] NSWCCA 319; 58 NSWLR 700 by Spigelman CJ (with Sully, O'Keefe, Hidden and Buddin JJ agreeing), regarding whether s 101(2) of the *UEA* should be applied independently of the High Court's pronouncement in the field in *Pfennig* [1995] HCA 7; 182 CLR 461. This judgment concluded that the Act indicates 'an overall intention to cover the relevant field [tendency and coincidence evidence, known at common law as similar fact evidence] in a comprehensive manner'.

13 A rule from the English case of *Browne v Dunn* (1893) 6 R (HL) 67 (which is also informed in its application by *UEA*, s 46).

14 (1893) 6 R (HL) 67.

15 This is used in many provisions, including the discretions (*UEA*, ss 135-138) and with respect to tendency and coincidence evidence (*UEA*, ss 97, 98 and 101).

16 *UEA*, s 59.

17 *UEA*, s 76.

18 *UEA*, Dictionary (except for Tasmania, for which see *Evidence Act 2001*, s 3).

19 *UEA*, s 101A.

20 *UEA*, Dictionary (except for Tasmania, for which see *Evidence Act 2001*, s 3).

21 *UEA*, ss 67-68.

22 *UEA*, ss 99, 100.

- call the witness who made the previous representation;
- call a particular witness regarding the production or maintenance of a specified document (or call the person who has possession or control of a specified document); or
- produce some or all of a specified document (or thing) to permit the requesting party to examine, test or copy the whole or part of the document.[23]

- **Documents** are broadly defined[24] to mean '*any record of information*'. This includes 'anything on which there is writing, marks, figures, symbols, perforations having a meaning for people qualified to interpret them'. It also includes anything from which sounds, images or writings can be reproduced with or without the aid of anything else. Any reference to a document includes a reference to a part, copy, duplicate of the document or of any part of the document, and any part of such a copy, reproduction or duplicate.[25] Unlike in the past, there is no need to prove that the 'original' document is unavailable when wanting to rely on a copy.
- Further, the requirements regarding **copies of documents** have been radically relaxed. They need not be identical copies for the purposes of Part 2.2 (Documents), which in practical terms means that for proving contents of documents (s 48) and proving voluminous or complex documents (s 50), a copy need only be 'identical to the document in question in all *relevant* respects': s 47.
- Through disclosure and perhaps aided by the **formal agreement processes** in the *UEA*,[26] the defence may agree not to dispute certain matters. Limiting the facts in issue (that is, in dispute) arguably creates efficiencies (which is, in fact, the role of 'agreements as to facts' process). Section 191 of the *UEA* has created clear processes. In New South Wales increased case management with the Early Appropriate Guilty Plea (EAGP) reforms, discussed in Chapter 2, means there is a formal place in pre-trial processes to enhance pre-trial fact agreement.
- **There are other numerous novel approaches** with no common law heritage.[27] See, for example,
  - modernised rules regarding the **competency of witnesses**;
  - giving evidence in **narrative form**;[28]
  - using **charts, summaries** or other explanatory material;[29]
  - **recalling** witnesses;[30]
  - allowing **responsive prosecution tendency and coincidence evidence** that by-passes the demanding test set by s 101(2);[31]

---

23 See generally *UEA*, ss 166, 167, 168 (time limits), 169 (non-compliance).
24 See *UEA* Dictionary (except for Tasmania, for which see *Evidence Act 2001*, s 3).
25 *UEA* Dictionary, Pt 2, cl 8.
26 *UEA*, s 191 (agreement as to facts).
27 *Ellis* [2003] NSWCCA 319; 58 NSWLR 700.
28 *UEA*, s 29(2).
29 *UEA*, s 29(4).
30 *UEA*, s 46.
31 *UEA*, s 101(3) and (4).

- special provision for **picture/photo identification** and **identification parades**;[32] and
- **the abolition of corroboration** requirements for children and for sexual assault complainants.

There is no doubt that the Acts could have used a stiffer broom, particularly with respect to lingering technicalities that appear tenacious rather than useful. Undoubtedly 21st century advances remain a work in progress.

The architecture of the Acts

The Acts are divided into five chapters. The major working provisions are contained in Chapters 2 (Procedure) and 3 (Admissibility). The structure of the Acts is nicely summarised in its notes:

> Chapter 2 is about how evidence is adduced in proceedings.
> Chapter 3 is about admissibility of evidence in proceedings.
> Chapter 4 is about proof of matters in proceedings.
> Chapter 5 deals with miscellaneous matters.[33]
>
> ... Chapter [2] is about ways in which evidence is adduced.
> Part 2.1 is about adducing evidence from witnesses.
> Part 2.2 is about adducing documentary evidence.
> Part 2.3 is about adducing other forms of evidence.[34]
>
> ... Chapter [3] is about whether evidence adduced in a proceeding is admissible.
> Part 3.1 sets out the general inclusionary rule that relevant evidence is admissible.
> Part 3.2 is about the exclusion of hearsay evidence, and exceptions to the hearsay rule.
> Part 3.3 is about exclusion of opinion evidence, and exceptions to the opinion rule.
> Part 3.4 is about admissions and the extent to which they are admissible as exceptions to the hearsay rule and the opinion rule.
> Part 3.5 is about exclusion of certain evidence of judgments and convictions.
> Part 3.6 is about exclusion of evidence of tendency or coincidence, and exceptions to the tendency rule and the coincidence rule.
> Part 3.7 is about exclusion of evidence relevant only to credibility, and exceptions to the credibility rule.
> Part 3.8 is about character evidence and the extent to which it is admissible as exceptions to the hearsay rule, the opinion rule, the tendency rule and the credibility rule.
> Part 3.9 is about the requirements that must be satisfied before identification evidence is admissible.
> Part 3.10 is about the various categories of privilege that may prevent evidence being adduced.
> Part 3.11 provides for the discretionary and mandatory exclusion of evidence even if it would otherwise be admissible.[35]

Note that in the above extracts Chapters 4 and 5 are omitted, as are Schs 1 (oaths and affirmations) and 2 (which contains the Dictionary).[36]

---

32 See *UEA*, ss 114, 115, which establish special provision for picture/photo identification and identification parades (excepting *Evidence Act 2001* (Tas)).

33 *UEA*, Note to Chapter 1.

34 *UEA*, Note to Chapter 2.

35 *UEA*, Note to Chapter 3.

36 For all jurisdictions (except for Tasmania, for which see *Evidence Act 2001*, s 3).

Starting with Relevance

> [T]he scheme of Chapter 3 of the Act, which deals with admissibility of evidence, begins with the proposition, stated in s 56, that, subject to the other provisions of the Act, evidence that is relevant in a proceeding is admissible, and evidence that is not relevant is not admissible. Section 55 states that evidence that is relevant in a proceeding is evidence that, if it were accepted, could rationally affect (directly or indirectly) the assessment of the probability of the existence of a fact in issue in the proceeding. ... Having established those fundamental propositions, the Act goes on to deal, amongst other things, with various exclusionary rules, and exceptions to those exclusionary rules.[37]

The 'fundamental propositions' quoted above are central to applying evidence law under the Act. As Gleeson CJ and Hayne J state in *Papakosmas*, evidence must be relevant to be admissible. It must then navigate exclusionary rules and discretions. The exclusionary rules and discretions conform to a rationalist tradition of evidence law and combine with adversarial principles to promote the reception of evidence that assists to strengthen or weaken parties' cases with its flaws exposed through cross-examination and opposing evidence. This was described by Gleeson CJ in *Goldsmith v Sandilands* in terms of the adversarial criminal trial proceeding by the 'advance, or cut down, [of] the case of a party in accordance with the rules of statute or common law that determine the nature of the information a court will receive' and with the trial judge having the obligation 'to control the proceedings, to exclude irrelevancy'.[38]

Whilst it is not the topic of this chapter, it is important to appreciate that adversarial assumptions should not be accepted uncritically. Cross-examination can be ineffective in exposing weaknesses in certain contexts.[39] It can also create the false impression of weak credibility in a vulnerable witness.

The admissibility framework of the *UEA* is structured according to the Acts' Chapter 3 chart (*see next page*).

This chart reveals the pre-eminent role of the relevance of evidence as a threshold issue.[40] There can be reasons for not receiving relevant evidence. These may relate to the content, the form or the circumstances in which it is tendered.[41] Although *Stephenson*'s case, discussed below, and the common law terminology (logical and legal relevance) might suggest that ss 55 and 135 are a close-stepped two-stage process, this is not the case. The Acts' chart shows that Chapter 3 admissibility is a three-stage approach:

---

37 *Papakosmas* [1999] HCA 37; 196 CLR 297, [23], [24] (Gleeson CJ and Hayne J).

38 *Goldsmith v Sandilands* [2002] HCA 31; 190 ALR 370; 76 ALJR 1024, [1] (Gleeson CJ).

39 See, eg, G Edmond, E Cunliffe, K Martire and M San Roque, 'Forensic Science Evidence and the Limits of Cross-Examination' (2019) 42(3) *Melbourne University Law Review* 858, quoting from D McQuiston-Surrett and MJ Saks, 'The Testimony of Forensic Identification Science: What Expert Witnesses Say and What Factfinders Hear' (2009) 33(5) *Law and Human Behavior* 436, 439 (citations omitted); and also quoting from the Law Commission of England and Wales, where similar doubts were raised: Law Commission, *Expert Evidence in Criminal Proceedings in England and Wales* (Report No 325, 21 March 2011), 5 [1.20].

40 'Relevance' under the Act operates in (at least) two ways. First, as we see in ss 55 and 56, it establishes threshold admissibility. It also applies in many of the exclusionary rules in another sense. For example, in s 59 evidence is only excluded by the hearsay rule if it is relevant and admissible for that purpose. It may be relevant to a non-hearsay purpose. Another example is tendency evidence: see s 97 and its definition in the *UEA*. These are discussed later, but it is useful to be alert to the conceptual challenge ahead of time.

41 *HML* [2008] HCA 16; 235 CLR 334, [5] (Gleeson CJ).

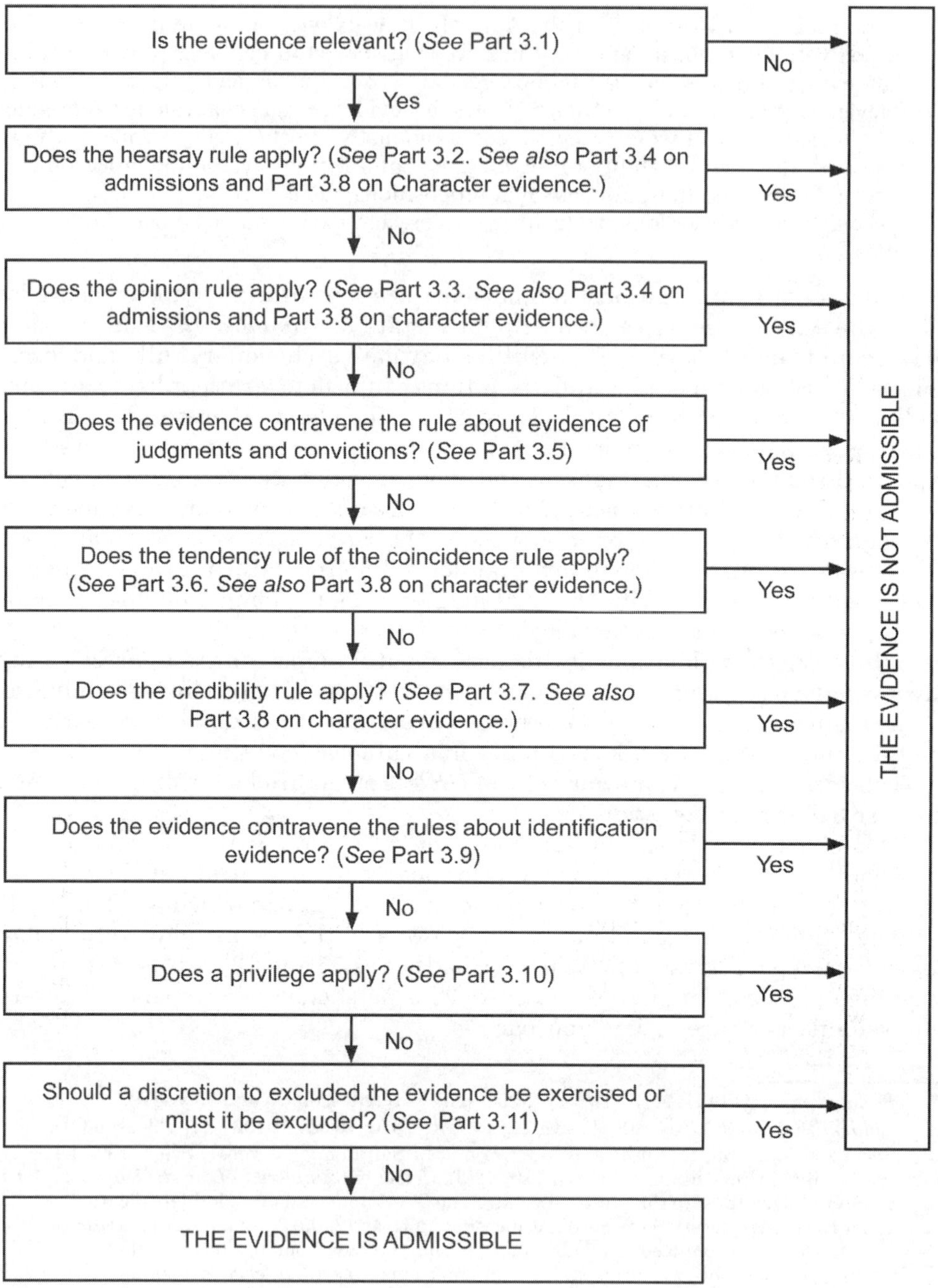
Is the evidence relevant? (*See* Part 3.1)
No
Yes
Does the hearsay rule apply? (*See* Part 3.2. *See also* Part 3.4 on admissions and Part 3.8 on Character evidence.)
Yes
No
Does the opinion rule apply? (*See* Part 3.3. *See also* Part 3.4 on admissions and Part 3.8 on character evidence.)
Yes
No
Does the evidence contravene the rule about evidence of judgments and convictions? (*See* Part 3.5)
Yes
No
Does the tendency rule of the coincidence rule apply? (*See* Part 3.6. *See also* Part 3.8 on character evidence.)
Yes
No
Does the credibility rule apply? (*See* Part 3.7. *See also* Part 3.8 on character evidence.)
Yes
No
Does the evidence contravene the rules about identification evidence? (*See* Part 3.9)
Yes
No
Does a privilege apply? (*See* Part 3.10)
Yes
No
Should a discretion to excluded the evidence be exercised or must it be excluded? (*See* Part 3.11)
Yes
No
THE EVIDENCE IS ADMISSIBLE
THE EVIDENCE IS NOT ADMISSIBLE

First stage:	establishing relevance, which includes establishing use (or purpose) of evidence (ss 55, 56)
Second stage:	applying the exclusionary rules and if a rule applies, any exceptions (Pts 3.2-3.9)
Third stage:	applying the mandatory and discretionary exclusions (Pt 3.10). The Part 3.10 provisions also require consideration of the role of possible judicial warnings to stem the danger of unfair prejudice (Pt 4.5).[42]

Where the 'evidence [is] of a kind that may be unreliable' the *UEA* anticipates under s 165 whether a judicial warning to the jury (upon the request of a party) will remedy the danger of evidence misleading the jury.[43] These are modernised formulations from the common law's corroboration law.

To begin, to satisfy the first line in the chart: *'Is the evidence relevant?' ss* 55 and 56 must be considered.

55. Relevant evidence

(1) The evidence that is relevant in a proceeding is evidence that, if it were accepted, could rationally affect (directly or indirectly) the assessment of the probability of the existence of a fact in issue in the proceeding.

(2) In particular, evidence is not taken to be irrelevant only because it relates only to:

(a) the credibility of a witness, or
(b) the admissibility of other evidence, or
(c) a failure to adduce evidence.

56. Relevant evidence to be admissible

(1) Except as otherwise provided by this Act, evidence that is relevant in a proceeding is admissible in the proceeding.

(2) Evidence that is not relevant in the proceeding is not admissible.

One should not lose sight of the 'basic distinction between the relevancy of evidence and its sufficiency'.[44] Sufficiency is ultimately determined at the conclusion of a trial while relevance is a consideration when a party wishes to adduce an item of evidence. Information may be relevant and therefore admissible if in applying s 55(1) '[i]t may explain a statement or an event that would otherwise appear curious or unlikely. It may cut down, or reinforce, the plausibility of something that a witness has said. It may provide a context helpful, or even necessary, for an understanding of a narrative'.[45] The binary position expressed in s 56 makes its application straightforward. Section 55, the equivalent of the common law 'logical relevance',[46] is more complex. The term 'probative value', central to s 55,

---

42 See *UEA*, s 165, and various authorities such as *Lock* (1997) 91 A Crim R 356; *Symss* [2003] NSWCCA 77; *BD* (1997) 94 A Crim R 131; *Papakosmas* [1999] HCA 37; 196 CLR 297, [94]. Of course, the efficacy of warnings may raise other issues.

43 For Victoria, see *Jury Directions Act 2015* (Vic).

44 *BBH* [2012] HCA 9; 245 CLR 499, [51] (French CJ) (citations omitted), quoting from Wigmore, *Evidence in Trials at Common Law* (Tillers rev, 1983) Vol 1A, 1032, which includes the quote: 'In the immortal words of Professor McCormick, "A brick is not a wall".' Evidence law concerns itself largely with assessing the quality of the bricks that make up the wall.

45 *HML* [2008] HCA 16; 235 CLR 334, [6] (Gleeson CJ) (citations omitted).

46 With the common law term 'legal relevance' applied being the equivalent of s 135. It operates to permit the exclusion of evidence that has the capacity to logically assist the decision-maker, but it has disadvantages (listed in s 135) that indicate on balance it is more desirable that it be excluded than admitted: see below.

is also found in numerous provisions within the Act, typically with respect to the admissibility (or exclusion) of evidence (either in an exclusionary rule[47] or a discretionary or mandatory[48] exclusion).[49]

Facts in Issue

The term 'facts in issue' is a central feature of establishing relevance. Facts in issue emerge from the pleadings[50] and in criminal prosecutions they are initially defined by the prosecutor's pleadings which contain the legal and factual matters that are in dispute. The following statement from Gleeson CJ in *HML*[51] articulates step-by-step the role of evidence law and its relation to the indictment, proof and the rules of admissibility. Importantly, it also shows the low threshold that applies to the test of relevance.

> 4. Evidence is information which, according to certain governing general principles and more detailed rules, will be received by a court for the purpose of deciding issues of fact that arise for its decision. ... In a criminal trial of an indictable offence, the indictment identifies the alleged offence. The prosecution sets out to prove the elements of the offence, that is to say, the specific offence alleged to have been committed by the accused. The jury will be directed, as a matter of law, that for a verdict of guilty it is necessary to be satisfied beyond reasonable doubt of those elements. ... Depending upon the way in which the prosecution seeks to prove its case, or the way in which the defence is conducted, it may appear, as a matter of fact, that an element of the offence charged will not be established beyond reasonable doubt unless some subsidiary fact, relevant to a fact in issue, is proved to that standard. However, the legal requirement as to onus and standard of proof is related to the elements of the offence charged. In some cases, there may be only one available path to a conclusion of guilt, but often that is not so. Jurors are commonly instructed that they may be selective in their approach to the evidence, and even in their approach to different parts of the evidence of the one witness.
>
> 5. ... [The language of s 55(1)] directs attention, in a criminal case, to the elements of the offence charged, the particulars of those elements, and any circumstances which bear upon the assessment of probability. The prosecution may set out to establish that an accused had a motive to commit an offence charged. Motive may rationally affect the assessment of the probability of the existence of one or more of the elements of an offence. Evidence that tends to establish motive, therefore, may rationally affect such assessment. If so, it is relevant. When the prosecution sets out to establish motive that is often a step in the prosecution case that is not indispensable. If it is established, motive may support (sometimes powerfully) the prosecution case, but juries are often told that failure to establish motive does not mean the case must fail. The legal necessity is to establish beyond reasonable doubt the elements of the offence. ...

As these observations indicate, layers of relevance may come into play. Once the elements of the offence charged are identified, then the framework for

---

47 For example, *UEA*, ss 97, 98, 101, 137.

48 Note that the language of s 137 is not a true discretion: see *GK* [2001] NSWCCA 413; 53 NSWLR 317; *Clark* [2001] NSWCCA 494; 123 A Crim R 506, [228] (Heydon JA and Dowd J); *Cook* [2004] NSWCCA 52, [27] (Simpson J)).

49 *UEA*, ss 135-136, 138.

50 See *HML* [2008] HCA 16; 235 CLR 334 (Gleeson CJ); *Goldsmith v Sandilands* [2002] HCA 31; 190 ALR 370; 76 ALJR 102 (Gleeson CJ).

51 [2008] HCA 16; 235 CLR 334 (citations omitted), citing *Chamberlain (No 2)* [1984] HCA 7; 153 CLR 521; and *Shepherd* [1990] HCA 56; 170 CLR 573.

establishing the facts in issue is created. Each element must be proved beyond reasonable doubt (by proving the existence of facts that constitute the elements of the offence). As Gleeson CJ, Gaudron, Gummow and Hayne JJ observed in Mundarra Smith's case the next layer lies

> [b]ehind those ultimate issues [where] there will often be many issues about facts relevant to facts in issue ... Thus, the question is whether the evidence, if it were accepted, could rationally affect (directly or indirectly) the assessment by the tribunal of fact ... of the probability of the existence of a fact in issue in the proceeding.[52]

This passage was also quoted by their Honours in *Cornwell*[53] who were responding (and rejecting) defence submissions to narrow the facts in issue. To drive home their concerns their Honours offered a hypothetical example showing the impact of narrowly confining s 55:

> 79. Assume that a man's body is found in a locked room. The cause of death is a single bullet fired into his head. One 'fact in issue' on a defendant's trial for murder is whether the defendant shot the deceased. Evidence that the defendant was outside the room just before the time of death in possession of a fully loaded revolver is, *on the accused's construction*, not evidence of a "fact in issue". Nor is evidence that the defendant was outside the room just after the time of death in possession of a revolver fully loaded save that one shot had been fired. Nor is evidence that the defendant was the only person possessing a key to the room. Nor is evidence that the defendant had a motive for killing the deceased. [But, and rejecting the defence submissions], *all of these matters of fact other than the actual shooting are matters of fact relevant to the material 'fact in issue', being the shooting by the defendant, but are not themselves 'facts in issue'. They are items of circumstantial evidence tending to establish that the defendant had the opportunity, the means and the motive to shoot the deceased.* (emphasis added)

Unlike its common law precursor, s 55 has been the subject of numerous appeals to the High Court. One consideration in particular that occupied some State appellate courts[54] intensively in the decade to 2016 relates to admissibility decisions where evidence is tainted by features of unreliability – such as where a witness's account has (or will have) internal inconsistencies, patent confusion or other flaws; or where identification evidence has hallmarks of unreliability – perhaps the identifying witness is colour blind, or was not wearing her prescription glasses when she identified the accused and his clothing. Potential unreliability is typically a foundation for exclusionary rules (for example, the rule against hearsay) but if an exclusionary rule has an exception that makes the evidence admissible, there is no further basis for exclusion outside *UEA*, ss 135-139, discussed below. The presence of the judicial warning provision, *UEA*, s 165 (*Unreliable evidence*) a provision that applies only to evidence that is before the tribunal of fact, points to a conclusion reached by the High Court in *IMM* (below), namely that the question of reliability is a 'jury question'. *IMM* resolved the disagreement between New South Wales and Victorian courts centred on consideration of the *UEA* definition of 'probative value' (extracted in the introduction to *IMM*).

---

52 *Smith (Mundarra)* [2001] HCA 50; 206 CLR 650, 654 [7] (Gleeson CJ, Gaudron, Gummow and Hayne JJ) (citations omitted).

53 [2007] HCA 12; 231 CLR 260, [76].

54 See debates and case law stemming from *Dupas* (2012) 40 VR 182 and *Shamouil* (2006) 66 NSWLR 228.

Probative value and unreliability

IMM

[2016] HCA 14; 257 CLR 300[55]

This Northern Territory appeal arose from a trial following allegations of child sexual assault, allegedly occurring in 2002, 2004 and late 2004/early 2005 and 2011 when the complainant (C), IMM's step-granddaughter, was aged approximately 4 years, 5 years, 6 years and 11 years of age. C complained to family members in August 2011. The police were informed. They conducted interviews in late August 2011, early September 2011 and January 2012. C's complaint evidence was admitted to prove the allegations. The complainant's testimony was the only direct evidence of the offences.[56] Her evidence of a separate incident to those charged (the so-called 'massage incident' (that is, that IMM 'ran his hand up my leg')) was admitted under *UEA*, ss 97 and 101, to prove IMM's tendency to have a sexual interest in C.

IMM was found guilty of three counts. The main focus of the judgment is on the admissibility of tendency evidence and on this basis IMM's appeal was successful.[57] Importantly, the court supported the New South Wales' line of authorities variously holding (French CJ, Kiefel, Bell and Keane JJ) that in assessing the probative value of evidence to determine its admissibility, a trial judge must assume that the jury will accept the evidence and that questions relating to credibility or reliability are matters for the tribunal of fact (that is, the jury). They are not relevant to admissibility. The majority stated:

> 36. … Questions that arise in connection with admissibility arise at the point when a piece of evidence is tendered, which is normally before all of the evidence is admitted and the witnesses examined, and therefore before the full picture has emerged. In a practical sense, a trial judge's ability to assess the place and weight of the evidence in question when a ruling on its admissibility is made will usually be limited. For the reasons which follow, it is to be inferred that the tests in question with respect to the admissibility of evidence under the Evidence Act acknowledge these limitations.

It is in the context of this timing of when admissibility is determined by a trial judge that the court considered 'probative value', a term central to both s 55 and s 97 (the tendency rule):

> ***probative value*** of evidence means the extent to which the evidence could rationally affect the assessment of the probability of the existence of a fact in issue.[58]

The court unanimously allowed the appeal from the NT Court of Criminal Appeal, quashing the convictions and ordering a new trial.

---

55 Some citations omitted, emphasis added. For applications of *IMM*, see *Volpe* [2020] VSCA 268 and *Taylor* [2020] NSWCCA 355, and see Chapter 11.

56 'The complainant's evidence of that history of sexual abuse was admitted, without objection, as "context evidence" and the jury were directed as to the limited way that context evidence might be used': [2016] HCA 14; 257 CLR 300, [118] (Nettle and Gordon JJ).

57 The trial judge was held to have correctly applied s 55 but the majority ruled that her Honour's application of s 97 (the tendency rule) was flawed. The High Court held that the complainant's evidence did not qualify as having significant probative value to satisfy *UEA*, s 97.

58 See *UEA*, Dictionary (or for Tasmania, s 3).

French CJ, Kiefel, Bell and Keane JJ:

The "probative value" of evidence under the Evidence Act

... 37. The first question, posed by Pt 3.1, is a threshold one for all evidence – whether it is relevant. Before that question may be answered, *it is necessary to identify the purpose or purposes* for which the evidence is tendered. The identification of its purpose may have important consequences, especially in areas such as opinion evidence and tendency evidence.

38. By s 55, evidence is relevant if it "could rationally affect (directly or indirectly) the assessment of the probability of the existence of a fact in issue in the proceeding." There can be no doubt that the reference to the effect that the evidence "could" have on proof of a fact is a reference to the capability of the evidence to do so. *The reference to its "rational" effect does not invite consideration of its veracity or the weight which might be accorded to it when findings come to be made by the ultimate finder of fact.*

39. The question as to the capability of the evidence to rationally affect the assessment of the probability of the existence of a fact in issue is to be determined by a trial judge on the assumption that the jury will accept the evidence. This follows from the words "if it were accepted", which are expressed to qualify the assessment of the relevance of the evidence. This assumption necessarily denies to the trial judge any consideration as to whether the evidence is credible. Nor will it be necessary for a trial judge to determine whether the evidence is reliable, because the only question is whether it has the capability, rationally, to affect findings of fact. There may of course be a limiting case in which the evidence is so inherently incredible, fanciful or preposterous that it could not be accepted by a rational jury. In such a case its effect on the probability of the existence of a fact in issue would be nil and it would not meet the criterion of relevance.

40. Because evidence which is relevant has the capability to affect the assessment of the probability of the existence of a fact in issue, it is "probative". Therefore, evidence which is relevant according to s 55 and admissible under s 56 is, by definition, "probative". But neither s 55 nor s 56 requires that evidence be probative to a particular degree for it to be admissible. Evidence that is of only some, even slight, probative value will be prima facie admissible, just as it is at common law.

41. Relevant evidence is admissible under s 56 unless an exclusionary rule operates, the court is required to exclude evidence by a provision such as s 137, or a discretion provided by the Evidence Act to exclude evidence is exercised. The exceptions provided with respect to the exclusionary rules of the Evidence Act have the effect that if relevant evidence liable to be excluded comes within an exception, it may nevertheless retain its character as admissible. ...

42. ... As mentioned, the Dictionary definition of the "probative value" of evidence describes evidence which is probative in the same terms as how relevant evidence is described in s 55, namely evidence which "could rationally affect [...] the assessment of the probability of the existence of a fact in issue".

43. The enquiry for the purposes of s 55 is whether the evidence is capable of the effect described at all. The enquiry for the purposes of determining the probative value of evidence is as to the extent of that possible effect. But the point is that in both cases the enquiry is essentially the same; it is as to how the evidence might affect findings of fact. An assessment of the extent of the probative value of the evidence takes that enquiry further, but it remains an enquiry as to the probative nature of the evidence.

44. *The assessment of "the extent to which the evidence could rationally affect the assessment of the probability of the existence of a fact in issue" requires that the possible use to which the evidence might be put, which is to say how it might be used, be taken at its highest.* The definition must be read in the context of the provision to which it is applied. ...

45. The use of the term "probative value" and the word "extent" in its definition rest upon the premise that relevant evidence can rationally affect the assessment of the

probability of the existence of a fact in issue to different degrees. Taken by itself, the evidence may, if accepted, support an inference to a high degree of probability that the fact in issue exists. On the other hand, it may only, as in the case of circumstantial evidence, strengthen that inference, when considered in conjunction with other evidence. The evidence, if accepted, may establish a sufficient condition for the existence of the fact in issue or only a necessary condition. The ways in which evidence, if accepted, could affect the assessment of the probability of the existence of a fact in issue are various. *Within the framework imposed by the statute and, in particular, the assumption that the evidence is accepted, the determination of probative value is a matter for the judge. …*

50. At a level of logic it is difficult to see how a trial judge could approach the question as to what the probative value of the evidence could be in any other way, for the reasons alluded to by Gaudron J in *Adam v The Queen*.[59] It must also be understood that the basis upon which a trial judge proceeds, that the jury will accept the evidence taken at its highest, does not distort a finding as to the real probative value of the evidence. The circumstances surrounding the evidence may indicate that its highest level is not very high at all. The example given by JD Heydon QC[60] was of an identification made very briefly in foggy conditions and in bad light by a witness who did not know the person identified. As he points out, on one approach it is possible to say that taken at its highest it is as high as any other identification, and then look for particular weaknesses in the evidence (which would include reliability). On another approach, it is an identification, but a weak one because it is simply unconvincing. The former is the approach undertaken by the Victorian Court of Appeal; the latter by the New South Wales Court of Criminal Appeal. The point presently to be made is that it is the latter approach which the statute requires. This is the assessment undertaken by the trial judge of the probative value of the evidence.

51. At a practical level, it could not be intended that a trial judge undertake an assessment of the actual probative value of the evidence at the point of admissibility. As Simpson J pointed out in *R v XY*,[61] the evidence will usually be tendered before the full picture can be seen. A determination of the weight to be given to the evidence, such as by reference to its credibility or reliability, will depend not only on its place in the evidence as a whole, but on an assessment of witnesses after examination and cross-examination and after weighing the account of each witness against each other.

52. Once it is understood that an assumption as to the jury's acceptance of the evidence must be made, it follows that no question as to credibility of the evidence, or the witness giving it, can arise. For the same reason, no question as to the reliability of the evidence can arise. If the jury are to be taken to accept the evidence, they will be taken to accept it completely in proof of the facts stated. There can be no disaggregation of the two – reliability and credibility – as *Dupas v The Queen*[62] may imply. They are both subsumed in the jury's acceptance of the evidence.

With respect to a trial judge's assessment of evidence for the purposes of s 56, applying s 55, note the crucial guidance outlined in [44] above is that 'the possible use to which the evidence might be put, which is to say how it might be used', requires the judge in determining the relevance of evidence to be adduced in court to give the evidence 'its highest' capacity 'to rationally affect the assessment of the probability of the existence of a fact in issue'. It will be up to the tribunal of fact to determine what actual use – and weight – it gives the evidence.

---

59 [(2001) 207 CLR 96, 115 [60].]

60 [Heydon, 'Is the Weight of Evidence Material to Its Admissibility?' (2014) 26 *Current Issues in Criminal Justice* 219, 234.]

61 [[2013] NSWCCA 121; 84 NSWLR 363, 400 [167], [170].]

62 [[2012] VSCA 328; 40 VR 182, 242.]

Logic and relevance

Trial judges are obliged to exclude irrelevancies 'to maintain proper limits upon the extent to which the parties and their lawyers will be permitted to raise and investigate matters that are of only marginal significance'.[63]

The plethora of s 55 judicial analyses[64] in Australia's apex court marks the contestability of the concept of relevance and its centrality in hard-fought, strategically driven litigation.[65] *Graham*,[66] the first case under the NSW Act, is considered below. *Papakosmas*[67] followed a year later. Like *Graham* it considered sexual complaint evidence, although in *Papakosmas* the complaint was made without delay and the complainant repeated it publicly. Despite this timing, the appellant sought to have the complaint admitted on a limited basis, that is, only to support the complainant's credibility, and not directly to proof of the absence of consent. These two cases underscore the importance of asking the 'relevance' questions raised by the plurality judgment in *IMM*. These can be reduced to:

- first, for what purpose is the evidence relevant?
- and, second, how is relevance impacted if rules of evidence limit the actual use in court of evidence that is relevant in a number of respects?

In both *Graham* and *Papakosmas* a complainant in a sexual assault case 'complained' (that is, told) someone that she had been assaulted by the defendant. These 'complaints' had two potential purposes in court:

- to assist with enhancing the *complainants' credibility* by revealing to the jury that the complainants' in-court account was consistent with what they had told witnesses just after the alleged assault (or in the case of the complainant in *Graham*, some six years later); and
- second, as direct evidence to support the major fact in issue, namely, did the defendant sexually assault the complainant?

In *Papakosmas*, Gaudron and Kirby JJ illustrated that common law principles (in this instance, the *res gestae* doctrine) remain relevant to explain the potential application of s 55. *Res Gestae* at common law enabled events, including statements that were close in time to the subject incident, to be admitted into evidence, irrespective of any exclusionary rule. The logic with respect to statements is that, if they are made in the midst of the subject incident, they are likely to be unfiltered by self-interest, and so it is likely to be a true statement. The common law was described by Gaudron and Kirby JJ thus:

> 53. … A broader application was acknowledged in *Ratten v R*, it being said in that case that if "the drama, leading up to the climax, has commenced and assumed such intensity and pressure that the utterance can safely be regarded as a true reflection of what was

---

63 *Goldsmith v Sandilands* [2002] HCA 31; 190 ALR 370; 76 ALJR 1024.

64 *Graham* [1998] HCA 61; 195 CLR 606; *Papakosmas* [1999] HCA 37; 196 CLR 297; *Smith (Mundarra)* [2001] HCA 50; 206 CLR 650; *Festa* [2001] HCA 72; 208 CLR 593; *Goldsmith v Sandilands* [2002] HCA 31; 190 ALR 370; 76 ALJR 1024; *Evans* [2007] HCA 59; 235 CLR 521; *IMM* [2016] HCA 14; 257 CLR 300.

65 Gleeson CJ in *Goldsmith v Sandilands* [2002] HCA 31; 190 ALR 370; 76 ALJR 1024, [1] alludes to the 'sport' of advocacy where gaining advantage over opposing parties is strategic to success – like counsel 'start[ing] a hare' – a greyhound racing analogy – and opposing counsel then 'pursu[ing] it'.

66 [1998] HCA 61; 195 CLR 606.

67 [1999] HCA 37; 196 CLR 297 (citations omitted).

unrolling or actually happening, it ought to be received." The approach taken in *Ratten* was expressly accepted as correct by Mason CJ in *Walton v R* and impliedly so in the joint majority judgment of Wilson, Dawson and Toohey JJ.

54. The more general statement of the principle in *Ratten* is in these terms:

'[H]earsay evidence may be admitted if the statement providing it is made in such conditions (always being those of approximate but not exact contemporaneity) of involvement or pressure as to exclude the possibility of concoction or distortion to the advantage of the maker or the disadvantage of the accused.'

Their Honours resisted the appellant's contention that the common law relating to complaint should apply, noting that the hearsay rules under the *UEA* had changed the situation significantly. They added, however:

52. What does emerge from the common law as a reflection of elementary logic is that, without more, evidence that a particular statement was made is probative only of its making and its contents and those inferences which, in the circumstances, may be drawn. On the other hand, it also emerges from the common law, and, again, as a matter of logic, that the circumstances in which a statement is made may sometimes render it probative of the facts asserted. …

56. The nature and degree of the connection necessary before a statement is probative of the fact asserted in it will, of course, depend on the nature of that fact and, if it be different, the fact ultimately to be proved. Even so, the connection will ordinarily be found in the close contemporaneity of the statement with the fact in issue and the consideration that the statement is a statement of the kind that might ordinarily be expected from the maker if the fact were true. Similarly, a statement that is closely contemporaneous with the fact in issue and is contrary to what would ordinarily be expected if that fact were true rationally bears on the improbability of its having occurred.

57. The question whether, in the particular circumstances, a statement that is not closely contemporaneous (for example, a subsequent statement to police) is probative of the facts asserted in it can logically only be answered in a case in which those circumstances arise. However, there must be some connecting circumstances because, otherwise, evidence that a particular statement was made is probative only of its making and its contents and such inferences as, in the circumstances, may be properly drawn.

58. As a matter of logic, the statement is not, as such, proof of the facts asserted. People do make false statements of fact and false accusations. Nothing in the Act requires the admission of a statement unless, in the terms of s 55, it could rationally affect, directly or indirectly, the assessment of the probability of the facts asserted. There has to be more than the fact that the statement is made to produce the conclusion required by s 55 as the price of admissibility. Rationality connotes logical reasoning.

59. In the present case, the statements to Ms Ovadia, Ms Stephens and Ms Fahey were closely contemporaneous with the events alleged by the complainant and were of a kind that might ordinarily be expected if those events occurred. That being so, they rationally bear on the probability of the occurrence of those events and, thus, were admissible as evidence of the facts asserted in them.

In *Graham*,[68] the complainant (K), aged nine at the time of the alleged incident, delayed for six years making her 'complaint'. Graham was her father. The High Court was asked to consider the admissibility of *the fact* of K making a delayed complaint.[69] The majority (Gaudron, Gummow and Hayne JJ) observed:

68 [1998] HCA 61; 195 CLR 606.

69 That is, not what she said, but the fact she said it. This was an important distinction because the court held that K's complaint was not admissible under *UEA*, s 66 (a ruling that led to a statutory amendment to overcome the limitations expressed by the court regarding this exception).

> 9. How does the making of a complaint six years after the events bear upon that question [of K fabricating her evidence]? Unless the making of the complaint can be said to assist the resolution of that question, the evidence of complaint is not important and would do nothing except add to the length of the hearing. And in this case, it is by no means clear that the making of a complaint six years after the event does assist in deciding whether the complainant had fabricated her evidence. Although trial counsel for the appellant suggested to the complainant, by his last question in cross-examination, that she was 'making it all up' the allegation of fabrication of evidence did not loom large in the trial. No question was put, and no answer was given, from which the time of alleged fabrication could be identified. The complaint having been made in 1994, and it having led at once to the start of police investigations, it may be doubted that a jury could gain assistance from its making in deciding whether the complainant had fabricated her story. (citations omitted)

The decisions in *Papakosmas* and *Graham* illustrate the dynamics of the hearsay exclusionary rule on a complaint that is potentially relevant for two purposes (to prove the facts in issue and to support the complainant's credibility). The first purpose (or use) of the complaint evidence was not available in *Graham*'s case due to the court's narrow interpretation of the hearsay exception (s 66), meaning a six-year delay prevented K's complaint being on matters 'fresh' in her memory. Thus, unlike the immediately expressed complaint in *Papakosmas*, the prosecution could not rely on the 'truth' value of the complaint. The prosecution could only press to admit evidence of K's complaint to support her credibility. The High Court held the complaint lacked relevance for that purpose – it was too delayed.[70] It is worth reflecting on the logic and experience that supports this view that the jury would gain no (logical) assistance from hearing evidence that K, when she reached the age of 15 years, spoke to her friend N and then to her mother about the events she accused Graham of committing when she was nine years old. Arguably, there are psycho-social reasons that might impact on the willingness of a nine-year-old describing such events. Clearly, whereas logic is fixed, factual assumptions are based on experience and personal values. This means that the trumpeted 'rationality' of evidence law can mask the rulings on the relevance of evidence due to embedded and unarticulated assumptions.

Another example is found in the Tasmanian case of *Neal*,[71] where Crawford J's observations that '[e]vidence is either relevant or it is not' belies the interpretative challenges in that case. Neal was convicted of child sexual assault. The question on appeal was whether prosecution evidence that Neal had said 'things about his wife's frigidity or lack of enthusiasm for sex' was relevant (and therefore admissible under ss 55 and 56 of the *UEA*) to whether he had sexually assaulted a child. Tennent J held the evidence to be relevant but all three judges (Crawford and Tennent JJ and Hill AJ) agreed that the prejudicial effect of the evidence outweighed its probative value (applying s 137, discussed further below). Crawford J articulated his interpretation of the logical connection with the evidence as being relevant to motive:

> 10. … Sexual acts with a very young child are of a very different character than those performed between adults. The question that may be posed is this, will men who suffer an unhappy and sexless marriage have more reason to want to commit sexual acts against young children than men who enjoy a happy and sexually satisfying marriage. With some

70 See *UEA*, s 66(2A), inserted as a response to the decision of the High Court in *Graham* (1998) 195 CLR 606.

71 [2005] TASSC 70, [10].

> hesitation, I have concluded that the answer is in the affirmative and for that reason, the minor fact, concerning the appellant's marriage, could rationally affect the assessment of the major fact in issue. It was evidence akin to evidence establishing motive. The probative value of it was weak and it added little of value to the Crown's case, but that is insufficient to prevent it from being relevant.

A number of High Court cases have developed the notion of the capacity of evidence to assist the decision-maker by throwing light on already admitted evidence. These cases are *Smith* (*Mundarra*)[72] and *Evans*.[73] In *Smith*, where the charges related to a bank robbery, the key question before the jury was whether Mundarra Smith was the person depicted at the right-hand side in CCTV photographs taken in the bank. The prosecution had called two police officers who testified that they recognised the accused in the CCTV photographs. The question before the High Court was whether the evidence given by two police officers was relevant – that is, 'could [their evidence, if accepted by the jury] rationally affect (directly or indirectly) the assessment of the probability' that Mundarra Smith was present in the bank during the robbery? The majority of the High Court concluded the police officers' evidence could not pass s 55 because jurors were in a position to make their own comparisons and the police officers had no greater advantage in drawing their conclusions than the jurors (who were able to look at Smith in the dock during the trial). Gleeson CJ, Gaudron, Gummow and Hayne JJ summed up the logical lack of connection between the police officer's evidence and the jury's task:

> 11. ... The fact that someone else has reached a conclusion about the identity of the accused and the person in the picture does not provide any logical basis for affecting the jury's assessment of the probability of the existence of that fact when the conclusion is based only on material that is not different in any substantial way from what is available to the jury. The process of reasoning from one fact (the depiction of a man in the security photographs) taken with another fact (the observed appearance of the accused) to the conclusion (that one is the depiction of the other) is neither assisted, nor hindered, by knowing that some other person has, or has not, arrived at that conclusion. Indeed, if the assessment of probability is affected by that knowledge, it is not by any process of reasoning, but by the decision-maker permitting substitution of the view of another, for the decision-maker's own conclusion.[74]

However, the police evidence would have been relevant if the police had an advantage over the jurors – for example, if Smith's physical appearance had significantly changed since the robbery, or if there was an identifying feature not apparent to the jury (for example, special clothing, a particular way of moving, perhaps a limp).[75]

---

72 [2001] HCA 50; 206 CLR 650.

73 [2007] HCA 59; 235 CLR 521.

74 [2001] HCA 50; 206 CLR 650, [11]. Kirby J dissented on the relevance test because in his view the police witnesses had advantages over jurors who had only seen Smith sitting immobile in the courtroom, not, as the police had, from different angles, in daylight and moving. Kirby J indicated that as a matter of policy the hurdle of relevance should not be too high. His Honour would have excluded the police evidence under the opinion evidence rule: *UEA*, s 76.

75 *TA* [2003] NSWCCA 191; 57 NSWLR 444 shares similarities with *Smith* (and, on Gummow and Hayne JJ's analysis, the *Evans* case). *TA* concerned an appeal from convictions for sexual assault offences occurring after the appellant had, on the prosecution case, administered a stupefying drug. Defence counsel wished to cross-examine the complainant regarding her perception of her conduct during the alleged results and captured in the recording played to the jury. Spigelman CJ relied on *Smith* as 'indistinguishable' to conclude that as the complainant had no independent recollection of the incident, due to the drugs, she was in no better position than the jury to assess her conduct on the electronic recording.

In *Evans*,[76] also a case concerning the identity of a bank robber, the prosecution case included evidence from eye witnesses to the robbery and evidence from police that they had seized items from Evans's premises, including red balaclavas and blue overalls that were consistent with the eye witness descriptions of the robber's disguise. The robber also wore sunglasses. The s 55 relevance question before the High Court required assessing the relevance of the accused in court, at the request of the prosecution (and over defence objection) dressing in the exhibits (the recovered balaclava and overalls) and wearing the prosecutor's sunglasses and then parading in front of the jury saying words attributed to the robber. The appeal was allowed. Kirby J described the issue in the following terms.

> 101. … [W]hen one reflects on whether the evidence that the prosecutor was seeking to adduce could 'rationally affect (directly or indirectly) the assessment of the probability of the existence of a fact in issue in the proceeding', one such fact was clearly whether the appellant was the offender who had committed the crimes alleged. Relevant to that question was (to put it broadly) whether, when dressed in overalls and a balaclava; when walking in front of the jury; and when saying words ascribed to the offender at the scene, there were apparent similarities, in the jury's view, between the appearance and conduct of the appellant and the earlier evidence and descriptions given (or viewed on videotape) concerning the offender.

His Honour added that the prosecutor did not act improperly, but exercised 'an error of judgment'. Heydon J (Crennan J and Kirby J agreeing)[77] held the demonstration to be relevant. A different majority found it to be inadmissible.[78]

> **Heydon J**: 183. *The relevance of walking in overalls.* Counsel for the accused submitted that a "demonstration" of what the accused looked like in overalls not asserted to have been worn by the offender was not relevant. That submission must be rejected. There was evidence of similarity as well as dissimilarity between what the offender wore and Ex O. There was evidence of many physical similarities between the offender and the accused. According to prosecution counsel's submission to the jury, there was a similarity between the way the accused walked in the overalls before the jury (and indeed in the way he walked between the dock and the witness box) and the gait which Mrs Gleeson observed. The evidence was that the offender was wearing a shirt or t-shirt under the overalls, and that the overalls looked baggy. According to prosecution counsel's final address, so did the overalls worn by the accused. And defence counsel said that the accused looked like "a Michelin man" in them. Prosecution counsel was careful to ensure, after the accused had expressed willingness to put the overalls on over what he was already wearing, that the accused remove his outer garments first. She was thus attempting to bring the conditions before the jury as close to the conditions described by the witnesses as possible.
>
> 184. The appearance of the accused walking in overalls in front of the jury was capable of making an impression on the jury which was favourable to the accused (as his counsel submitted in final address) as much as it was capable of causing an impression adverse to him (as prosecution counsel submitted). Either way the evidence was relevant.

---

76 [2007] HCA 59; 235 CLR 521.

77 Overall, Heydon and Crennan JJ dissented.

78 Gummow, Hayne and Kirby JJ formed the majority. Gummow and Hayne JJ were in the minority holding that the demonstration by Evans was *irrelevant*, but they were in the majority, joining Kirby in finding the demonstration to be inadmissible. Kirby J was in the minority in finding the demonstration to be inadmissible on the basis of its overwhelming unfair prejudice (applying s 137). However, his Honour refused to rule on relevance because it had not been argued before the court.

The majority held that the proviso should not have been applied by the NSW Court of Criminal Appeal.[79] For another clothing scenario case raising relevance challenges, see *Volpe*[80] where opinion evidence indicated that a shoe found in the hallway of the accused's home *could* have made the footprint that was found close to where the body was found. The shoe was seized a year after the investigation and was similar to shoes photographed during a search of the premises a year earlier. The shoe contained a mixed, partial DNA profile, with three contributors – 'it was 100 billion times more likely ... the applicant was one of the contributors'. There was evidence that 257 units of this size and brand of shoe had been sold in Australia but no there was evidence whether the seized shoe was owned by Volpe or by someone else living in the same house. At issue before the Victorian Court of Appeal was could the 'shoe evidence', if accepted, rationally affect the assessment of the probability of the existence of a fact in issue? That is, 'taken at its highest', was the evidence rationally capable of 'affecting the issue of whether the prosecution could establish the applicant's presence at the location where the deceased's body was found' (at [39]). Priest, T Forrest and Weinberg JJA held:

> 42. ... [T]he evidence permitted the inference that the applicant had possessed and worn the shoe seized by police. The shoe was found in the hallway of his home, where, presumably, he had easy access to it. Further, although other possible inferences were pressed by the defence, it could reasonably be inferred, first, that the applicant's DNA was located in the shoe's innersole toe region – the DNA evidence was 100 billion times more likely if the applicant was one of the contributors – and, secondly, that his DNA was deposited in the toe region of the shoe in the course of wearing it.

They added (at 44]), citing Heydon J in *Evans* (at [177]), '[o]ne must also have regard to the other evidence in the case. Relevance does not depend on the capacity of a particular piece of evidence by itself to prove the prosecution case on a particular issue. ... [O]ne must look to the effect of the contested evidence taken in conjunction with the other evidence in the case'. However, the shoe evidence was of slight probative value, insufficient to overwhelm the danger of unfair prejudice raised in the 'palpable risk that it might assume an undeserved mantle of potency and legitimacy in the eyes of the jury',[81] and in *Volpe* this undeserved mantle was unfortunately prominent in the trial judge's directions to the jury.

---

79 *Criminal Appeal Act 1912* (NSW), s 6(1): 'The court on any appeal under section 5(1) against conviction shall allow the appeal if it is of opinion that the verdict of the jury should be set aside on the ground that it is unreasonable, or cannot be supported, having regard to the evidence, or that the judgment of the court of trial should be set aside on the ground of the wrong decision of any question of law, or that on any other ground whatsoever there was a miscarriage of justice, and in any other case shall dismiss the appeal; *provided that the court may, notwithstanding that it is of opinion that the point or points raised by the appeal might be decided in favour of the appellant, dismiss the appeal if it considers that no substantial miscarriage of justice has actually occurred*'. The proviso is the portion of s 6(1) that is *emphasised*.

80 [2020] VSCA 268.

81 Quoting from *DPP v Paulino* [2017] VSCA 38; 54 VR 109, 132 [103] (Priest JA). In *Volpe* the court held the shoe evidence should have been excluded under *UEA*, s 137. *DPP v Paulino* provides illuminating discussions of logical and marginal relevance/irrelevance regarding DNA evidence on the accused's clothing and on his shoes and boots (Priest JA, [77]-[78], applying ss 55, and Weinberg JA, [14]-[21], applying s 55, and in terms of the CSI effect, s 137).

Wannouch and Lee
[2019] VSCA 97

Wannouch and Lee were charged in separate counts with importing a marketable quantity of heroin in two suitcases, described as 'bag 670' and 'bag 667' on the same Kuala Lumpur to Melbourne flights. Lee's charges related only to bag 667, and Wannouch's charges related to both bags. Bag 670 was checked in by Wannouch in Kuala Lumpur. It was seized at Melbourne Airport containing just over 15 kilograms of heroin. Bag 667 was checked in by Lee on departure but was never recovered. Lee said he checked it in for a friend and did not intend to collect it on arrival. There was evidence Wannouch had spent a number of hours at the airport, apparently looking for a lost bag. The prosecution sought to rely on the evidence relating to bag 670's contents to prove that bag 667 contained a comparable amount of heroin. Priest, Kyrou and Emerton JJA held that the judge was correct to rule that regarding the contents of bag 670 was irrelevant (applying s 55) to the issue of whether bag 667 contained heroin. (Some citations omitted.)

> **Priest, Kyrou and Emerton JJA**: 54. In ruling that the impugned evidence was not relevant, the trial judge held that to show that there was heroin in one suitcase, bag 670, does not establish the presence of heroin (or any border controlled drug) in the other suitcase, bag 667. His Honour said that this 'does not change, whether the evidence is considered alone, or in conjunction with the other pieces of circumstantial evidence', since there is 'a gap in the direct evidence and all of the circumstantial evidence cannot fill the gap'. Ultimately, the judge said that from this 'it flows that it is not an inference reached by deductive reasoning to conclude that bag 667 contained heroin', but rather 'a guess' or 'speculation'. …
>
> 56. The difference between permissible inference and conjecture or speculation was discussed by Spigelman CJ in *Seltsam Pty Ltd v McGuiness*:[82]
>
> > It is often difficult to distinguish between permissible inference and conjecture. Characterisation of a reasoning process as one or the other occurs on a continuum in which there is no bright line division. Nevertheless, the distinction exists.
> >
> > Lord Macmillan in *Jones v Great Western Railway Co* (1930) 144 LT 194, in the context of stating that a possibility that a negligent act caused injury was not enough, said (at 202):
> >
> > > The dividing line between conjecture and inference is often a very difficult one to draw. A conjecture may be plausible, but is of no legal value, for its essence is that it is a mere guess. An inference in the legal sense, on the other hand, is a deduction from the evidence, and if it is a reasonable deduction it may have the validity of legal proof. The attribution of an occurrence to a cause is, I take it, always a matter of inference. …
> >
> > As Lord Wright put it in a frequently cited passage in *Caswell v Powell Duffryn Associated Collieries Ltd* [1940] AC 152 at 169-170:
> >
> > > Inference must be carefully distinguished from conjecture or speculation. There can be no inference unless there are objective facts from which to infer the other facts which it is sought to establish. In some case the other facts can be inferred with as much practical certainty as if they had been actually observed. In other cases the inference does not go beyond reasonable probability. But if there are no positive proved facts from which the inference can be made, the method of inference fails and what is left is mere speculation or conjecture.
> >
> > The test is whether, on the basis of the primary facts, it is reasonable to draw the inference: see, eg, *Luxton v Vines* [1952] HCA 19; (1952) 85 CLR 352 at 358.

82 [(2000) 49 NSWLR 262, 275-6 [84]-[88].]

57. At the risk of repetition, in order for it to be relevant, the evidence concerning bag 670 must be capable of rationally affecting the assessment of the probability of the existence of the critical fact in issue. In other words, the evidence that bag 670 contained heroin – taken with other evidence – must be capable of rationally founding the inference that bag 667 contained heroin. Inference is the product of logical deduction rather than the product of speculation. It is a process of reasoning by which, as a matter of logic, a fact in issue may be deduced from other facts established by the evidence. As was said in another context, for an inference to be reasonable, it 'must rest upon something more than mere conjecture'.[83] For the prosecution to establish relevance, therefore, it is necessary that the prosecution be able to point to a process of reasoning by which the evidence in question could affect the jury's assessment of the probability of the existence of the relevant fact in issue.

58. Quite obviously, given the evidence concerning bag 670, a high level of suspicion attaches to bag 667 and its contents. Indeed, the suggestion that bag 667 probably contained heroin is seductively credible, even if only superficially so. Taken alone or in combination with the other evidence, however, we consider that the impugned evidence is incapable of rationally founding an inference that bag 667 contained heroin. The assertion that the contents of bag 667 were heroin is a very plausible conjecture, but we consider that in its essence it amounts to no more than mere guesswork or surmise.[84]

59. As we have endeavoured to convey, drawing an inference involves a process of reasoning by which a factual conclusion is deduced logically from facts established by the evidence. It is to be contrasted with speculation, guesswork or conjecture, which involves reaching a conclusion despite there being a gap or deficiency in the evidence. Unlike inferential reasoning, speculation involves reaching a conclusion without sufficient evidence. For the evidence surrounding bag 670 to be relevant (and therefore admissible), it must be capable of rationally founding an inference that bag 667 contained heroin. Taking the evidence as a whole, we consider that it is incapable of doing so.

Discretionary Exclusions and the Mandatory 'Discretion'

'Discretion' is a notion that 'signifies a number of different legal concepts'. In general terms, it refers to a decision-making process in which 'no one [consideration] and no combination of [considerations] is necessarily determinative of the result'. Rather, the decision-maker is allowed some latitude as to the choice of the decision to be made. The latitude may be considerable as, for example, where the relevant considerations are confined only by the subject matter and object of the legislation which confers the discretion. On the other hand, it may be quite narrow where, for example, the decision-maker is required to make a particular decision if he or she forms a particular opinion or value judgment.[85] (footnotes omitted)

In this section we consider s 137 (which demands an 'evaluative judgment mandating exclusion'),[86] ss 135 and 138 (discretions that exclude evidence), as well

83 [*Peacock* [1911] HCA 66; 13 CLR 619, 661; *Barca* [1975] HCA 42; 133 CLR 82, 104.]

84 [See *Jones v Great Western Railway Co* (1931) 144 LT 194, 202; [1930] All ER Ext 830, 842 (Lord Macmillan) and [56] above.]

85 *Coal and Allied Operations Pty Ltd v Australian Industrial Relations Commission* [2000] HCA 47; 203 CLR 194, [19] (Gleeson CJ, Gaudron and Hayne JJ), quoted in *Riley* [2020] NSWCCA 283, [94] (Bathurst CJ) (in relation to *UEA*, s 138(1)). Note also his Honour's observation (in the context of determining the requirement to demonstrate a *House* [1936] HCA 40; 55 CLR 499 error) at [98] of the distinction between a 'judgment' and a 'discretion' risking 'the danger of applying a label, rather than conducting an analysis of the applicable statutory regime' (citing *DAO* [2011] NSWCCA 63; 81 NSWLR 568, [51] (Spigelman CJ)).

86 *IMM* [2016] HCA 14; 257 CLR 300, 312 [16] (French CJ, Kiefel, Bell and Keane JJ), noting also that s 138 also mandates exclusion upon determination of a balancing of considerations.

as the discretion to limit evidence (*UEA*, s 136). The discretions we examine in this part are distinguishable from exclusionary rules because these discretions do not operate within discrete domains the way the rules do (be they rules relating to opinion evidence, admissions, character etc). Sections 135, 136 and 138 are generalist and permissive in their operation. With respect to ss 135 and 137, self-evidently the former's equation with legal relevance explains its broad and (for the party seeking to exclude the evidence) demanding test to persuade a court to exclude otherwise probative and admissible evidence. The court is not *obliged* (though it *may*) exclude evidence, but it must satisfy the test of having its probative value *substantially* outweighed *by the danger* that the evidence *might* be unfairly prejudicial[87] to a party. This exclusionary discretion applies to either party and in both civil and criminal trials.

Section 137 applies only to prosecution evidence and, as indicated above, it is non-permissive (that is, mandatory) in its application.[88] Further (as the chart above confirms), the operation of these provisions is considered once evidentiary rules of exclusion, such as the hearsay rule or the opinion rule, have been held to be inapplicable. A trial judge will also consider whether a judicial warning to the jury could correct the concerns that otherwise attract a particular discretion.[89] Before exploring the three provisions' reference to the danger of unfair prejudice,[90] it is important to recall the impact of *IMM*[91] in the judge's appraisal of the probative value of evidence when determining admissibility. As indicated earlier, French CJ, Kiefel, Bell and Keane JJ observed (at [52]) in *IMM* that the assumption that the jury accepts the evidence means 'that no question as to credibility of the evidence, or the witness giving it, [or] ... the reliability of the evidence can arise'.

Their Honours at [82] drew on the fact that the Act's definition of credibility ('ability to observe or remember facts and events' relevant to a witness's evidence) overlaps with notions of reliability of evidence. Neither reliability nor credibility is considered in relation to s 137, concluding that a trial judge should only consider the reliability of evidence in relation to admissibility decisions where it is expressly provided by the Act (see s 65(2)(c) and (d), and s 85). Otherwise, consistent with the court's consideration of s 55, it concluded that it 'is the evident policy of the Act that, generally speaking, questions as to the reliability or otherwise of evidence are matters for a jury, albeit that a jury would need to be warned by the trial judge about evidence which may be unreliable pursuant to s 165'. Their Honours also added, apparently by way of further clarification (at [58]):

---

87 Of course, similarly broad discretions apply with respect to the other two limbs of s 135 (misleading or confusing and causing or resulting in undue waste of time).

88 Note also the body of opinion that, despite the mandatory nature of s 137, objection must still be taken for s 137 to apply (subject to the judge's overriding obligation to ensure a fair trial according to law): see *Kapanadze* [2017] NSWCCA 69, [57] (Hoeben CJ at CL, with Walton J and Hulme JA agreeing). A number of authorities in this debate are discussed by Basten JA in *Tieu* [2016] NSWCCA 111, [38]-[39] (see *FDP* [2008] NSWCCA 317; 74 NSWLR 645, [16]ff (McClellan CJ at CL, Grove and Howie JJ); *Steve* [2008] NSWCCA 231; 189 A Crim R 68, [60]; *Le* [2002] NSWCCA 186; 54 NSWLR 474, [90] (Heydon JA); *Penza and Di Maria* [2013] NSWCCA 21, [194] (arising from *Chand* [2011] NSWCCA 53); *Poniris* [2014] NSWCCA 100, [46]).

89 Discussed below.

90 See also *UEA*, s 101(2). At the time of *IMM* and *Bauer*, it stated: 'Tendency evidence about a defendant, or coincidence evidence about a defendant, that is adduced by the prosecution cannot be used against the defendant *unless the probative value of the evidence substantially outweighs any prejudicial effect it may have on the defendant*' (emphasis added). See Chapter 11 for the amended NSW provision.

91 [2016] HCA 14; 257 CLR 300.

> It would not seem to be necessary to resort to an assessment of the reliability of evidence of this quality for it to be excluded under s 137. For the reasons already given, evidence which is inherently incredible or fanciful or preposterous would not appear to meet the threshold requirement of relevance. If it were necessary, the court could also resort to the general discretion under which evidence which would cause or result in an undue waste of time may be rejected.

The conclusions in *IMM* are far-reaching. They are also contentious. One long-standing issue that has been put to rest by *IMM* (as confirmed in *Bauer*[92]) relates to whether the risk of a witness's evidence being unreliable due to concoction, collusion (or otherwise affected by contamination) is a matter for admissibility, or for the tribunal of fact.[93] This has been a major issue where multiple sexual assault complainants make allegations against an accused, particularly if the complainants know each other. The court in *Bauer* ruled that a judge's obligation to take evidence at its highest when determining admissibility meant,

> [a]ccordingly [that], unless the risk of contamination, concoction or collusion is so great that it would not be open to the jury rationally to accept the evidence, the determination of probative value excludes consideration of credibility and reliability. Subject to that exception, the risk of contamination, concoction or collusion goes only to the credibility and reliability of evidence and, therefore, is an assessment which must be left to the jury.[94]

IMM (at [57]) left open the possibility that an assessment of the 'reliability' of evidence may be permissible as part of an inquiry into the 'danger of unfair prejudice' that would arise from its admission for the purposes of applying s 137.[95] The extent to which this possibility exists, *Bauer*[96] makes it clear that there is limited scope for a trial judge to consider the weak reliability of evidence in the context of 'unfair prejudice' in s 137 (and 'prejudicial effect' in s 101, 'unfairly prejudicial' in s 135). These different expressions of unfair prejudice each convey 'essentially the same idea of harm to the interests of the accused by reason of a risk that the jury will use the evidence improperly in some unfair way'.[97] This is further fleshed out below and later in the context of particular categories of evidence.

The danger of unfair prejudice

A focal point (but not the sole operation) of the danger of unfair prejudice relates to the danger of evidence being misused by the tribunal of fact in some unfair way. For example, because the evidence has created strongly negative emotions against the accused, such as to arouse horror, provoke a desire to punish, or triggering other reactions that distract in a way unfair to the accused from the logical import of the evidence.[98] The following extract from the High Court case of

---

92 [2018] HCA 40; 266 CLR 56, allowing the Crown appeal from the Victorian Court of Appeal where the convictions had been quashed.

93 The common law considered these matters relevant to admissibility, at least under the similar fact rule: *Hoch* [1988] HCA 50; 165 CLR 292.

94 *Bauer* [2018] HCA 40; 266 CLR 56, [69].

95 *Xie* [2021] NSWCCA 1, [301] (Bathurst CJ, RA Hulme and Beech-Jones JJ).

96 [2018] HCA 40; 266 CLR 56.

97 Ibid [73], citing various authorities, including *BD* (1997) 94 A Crim R 131,139 (Hunt CJ at CL). To like effect, see *Dickman* [2017] HCA 24; 261 CLR 60. A useful example of lack of reliability fitting within the required framework is the application by Weinberg JA in *Paulino* regarding the danger of the CSI effect on the jury (discussed above at n 81).

98 ALRC, *Uniform Evidence Law*, above n 4, 16.24.

Aytugrul considers the 'danger of unfair prejudice' in the context of DNA evidence of a hair found under the deceased's thumbnail, expressed in court in what was argued as an unfairly prejudicial manner when it was described as an exclusion percentage – that is, that 99.9% of people would not be expected to have the DNA profile matching that recovered from the deceased.[99]

Aytugrul

[2012] HCA 15; 247 CLR 170[100]

The appellant argued (unsuccessfully)[101] that the prosecution should have only expressed the results of the testing by reference to a frequency ratio, namely, that one in 1600 people in the general population would be expected to share the recovered DNA profile. The case shows the benefit of parties bringing expert evidence to support a claim under s 137 at trial.

> **French CJ, Hayne, Crennan and Bell JJ: Unfair prejudice: the appellant's case**
> 66. The appellant submitted that the evidence that 99.9% of the population could not be the offender created prejudice of the following kinds. It encouraged mathematical rather than deductive reasoning. It carried a risk of fallacious reasoning, including encouraging the jury to give undue attention to the seeming precision of figures. And it distracted attention from what should have been the central focus – the possibility that the hair found on the deceased was not the appellant's but someone else's. The appellant relied on *R v GK*, which held that DNA evidence giving a relative chance of paternity of 99.9995% and 99.9993% was rightly excluded under s 137. The basis for exclusion was "the residual risk of unfairness deriving from the subliminal impact of the raw percentage figures". ... The appellant submitted ... it had become common practice in Australian courts for evidence of the statistical probability of a DNA match to be expressed as a "random occurrence ratio" or a "frequency estimate", rather than as an "exclusion percentage". The appellant relied on *R v Doheny*, in which the latter practice was disfavoured. The appellant relied on writings by experts, including analysis of experimental research, on juror comprehension, or incomprehension, of DNA evidence. ...[102]
> 69. The teachings of the expert material could have been employed in two ways. They could have been employed before the jury as a warning against the dangers of uncritically accepting the statistical evidence. So used, the material would have been similar to evidence admitted in the United States about the fallibility of eyewitness identification, the low rate of recidivism among those convicted of murder on a hearing to determine sentence, the relevance of "battered woman syndrome" to self-defence and the characteristics of abused children. And, so used, it would have been similar to evidence admitted in Australia about "infantile amnesia", the effect of mental impairment on a witness's powers of observation, recollection or expression, the language or communications difficulties bearing on the ability of Aboriginal witnesses to give reliable or complete evidence, the relevance of "battered woman syndrome" to duress, the incidence of recovered memory syndrome and the effects on children of separation from their parents.

99 Such that s 137 applied because the probative value of the evidence was outweighed by the danger of unfair prejudice to the defendant.

100 Citations omitted.

101 The court also rejected an argument based on common knowledge (s 144) – see Chapter 2.

102 Their Honours noted that these writings were raised in submissions to the High Court, but (although referred to by McClellan CJ at CL in his dissenting judgment) they were not 'relied on by either party in the Court of Criminal Appeal and [were] not raised in argument for their consideration. The second problem is that no evidence supporting the reasoning in the expert writings had been tendered to the trial judge or to the Court of Criminal Appeal' (at [66]).

70. … [T]he material just referred to establishes general principles against which the court can assess particular evidence, or the conduct of a party or witness. That is, it helps the court to assess adjudicative facts. When material of this kind is so used, it must be established by evidence. The appellant's reliance on the material was rather directed to establishing that 'exclusion percentage' evidence was always or almost always so prejudicial, and so little lacking in probative value once 'frequency estimate' evidence had been admitted, that s 137 should invariably be employed to exclude it. Section 137 is not expressed in the language of discretion, but it does depend on a weighing process. The inquiry is whether the probative value of a specific piece of evidence is 'outweighed' by the danger of unfair prejudice flowing from that specific piece of evidence. An inquiry of that kind is not lightly to be trammelled by universal or general rules. …

Unfair prejudice

75. There was no unfair prejudice for the following reasons. No doubt both the "frequency estimate" and the "exclusion percentage" evidence, like many other aspects of the expert evidence, were difficult for the jury to deal with. The field is arcane. But any criminal jury of 12 is likely to contain at least one juror capable of realising, and demonstrating to the other jurors, that the frequency estimate was the same as the exclusion percentage. Further, detailed evidence was given about how the "exclusion percentage" evidence was derived from the concededly admissible "frequency estimate" evidence, and how their significance was identical. [Referring to the case of *GK*,[103] the 'trial judge made it plain while argument was proceeding about the reception of the "exclusion percentage" that no-one participating in the trial would express that percentage as being "somewhat like the 'prosecutor's fallacy', that is it's 99 percent sure that it is the accused". No-one did.'] In addition the reception of evidence which might sometimes create unfair prejudice can be lawful if the conduct of the trial, including the possibility of a curative influence from other evidence, from counsel's handling of the impugned evidence and from the trial judge's directions, is likely to nullify or water down the prejudice. Whether this was foreseeable or not at the time of tender, counsel here treated the exclusion percentage as a minor aspect of the case. It was mentioned only rarely. After its initial reception, it was mentioned once by Gina Pineda, once by a defence witness and not at all by counsel in address. The trial judge's summing up pointed out that the exclusion percentage was "another way" or "the reverse way" of putting the frequency estimate. The trial judge warned against treating the mitochondrial haplotype evidence as "definitely" or "necessarily" establishing that the hair came from the appellant. There was no request from the appellant for the trial judge to withdraw any part of his summing up, or to give a curative direction or warning. There is no ground of appeal in this Court that the summing up was wrong. Even if not all these post-tender events were foreseeable, they amounted, as Wigmore might have said, to a restrospectant demonstration that there was no unfairness.

76. Once it was accepted that the "frequency estimate" evidence was admissible, the reception of the "exclusion percentage" evidence did not create a danger of unfair prejudice within the meaning of s 137.[104]

The 'danger of unfair prejudice' or 'unfairly prejudicial' evidence can potentially arise in numerous contexts. Some common ones include:

---

103 [2001] NSWCCA 413; 53 NSWLR 317, [100] where it was held that 'the residual risk of unfairness deriving from the subliminal impact of the raw percentage figures would have been, to me, both real and unacceptable' (Sully J, with Mason P and Dowd J agreeing). Mr Goetz, forensic biologist, in evidence described the issue: '[T]he problem is it was easy when you had a 99 per cent probability paternity. That was 100 to 1. As DNA testing has increased the nines have increased and therefore it becomes more complicated to explain what this 99 with all these nines after it mean. Whereas a number like 200,000 or 50,000 or 500,000,000 are quite easy to explain. People can understand that'.

104 Their Honours added that the evidence was not misleading or confusing within s 135(b). Nor, in the specific circumstances of this trial, was the 'exclusion percentage' evidence attended by a danger that it might be misleading or confusing.

- identification evidence;[105]
- opinion evidence;
- 'scenario evidence': that is, evidence demonstrating the accused's preparedness to participate in crime including, as already noted, 'illegal prostitution, money laundering, illegal firearms, police corruption, trafficking in ecstasy and hashish, illicit diamond sales and armoured truck robbery';[106]
- evidence of admissions;[107]
- evidence of downloaded terrorist-related audio-visual recordings and documents;[108]
- DNA evidence giving a relative chance of paternity of 99.9995% and 99.9993%.[109]

In terms of court process, the danger of unfair prejudice may operate:

- as a consideration of whether the judge should order **a demonstration, experiment or inspection** under s 53(3)(c);[110]
- as a consideration in determining the extent to which a party may make submissions and 'refer to relevant information' where a trial judge takes **judicial notice** of matters of common knowledge: s 144(4);[111] and
- where a party is unfairly disadvantaged in not being able to investigate evidence or cross-examine a maker of a representation.[112]

Fairness to a party or witness is also a consideration for a trial judge in the context of a decision to give a party **leave, permission or direction** to proceed in a particular way: s 192(2)(b).The notion of fairness (or more specifically unfairness) when it relates to criminal defendants operates in the context of a very specific kind of disadvantage.[113] Whether a general unfairness discretion exists is unclear.

---

105 *Dickman* [2017] HCA 24; 261 CLR 601. See Chapter 13.

106 *Standage v Tasmania* [2017] TASCCA 23 (evidence not excluded). At issue was four hours of audio-visual recordings taken during an undercover police operation where in a police 'sting' they befriended the accused and persuaded him that he could join a lucrative organised crime gang if he proved himself by committing some less serious simulated crimes. This was a ploy by the police to gain the accused's trust and to encourage him to make admissions to murder.

107 *SG* [2017] NSWCCA 202.

108 *Abbas, Chaarani and Mohamed (Rulings 1-40)* [2019] VSC 855, discussed below.

109 *GK* [2001] NSWCCA 413; 53 NSWLR 317.

110 That is, 'the danger that the demonstration, experiment or inspection might be unfairly prejudicial, might be misleading or confusing or might cause or result in undue waste of time'.

111 *UEA*, s 144(4): 'The judge is to give a party such opportunity to make submissions, and to refer to relevant information, relating to the acquiring or taking into account of knowledge of that kind as is necessary to ensure that the party is not unfairly prejudiced'.

112 ALRC, *Uniform Evidence Law*, above n 4, 16.25-16.32, which cites ALRC, *Evidence* (Interim Report No 26, 1985) Vol 1, [644]; *Papakosmas* [1999] HCA 37; 196 CLR 297, [91]; *BD* (1997) 94 A Crim R 131, 139; and *Lockyer* (1996) 89 A Crim R 457, 460: '16.32 In *Roach v Page (No 11)*, [2003] NSWSC 907 at [97] per Sperling J considered that the inability to test the truth of a representation is a legitimate ground for excluding or limiting the use of evidence. However, whether this fact will result in limitation or exclusion in a particular case depends on the basis upon which the hearsay rule did not apply. Where hearsay evidence has been admitted pursuant to an exception to the hearsay rule because of the unavailability of the maker, there are 'special reasons' for not excluding or limiting the use of the evidence on that ground. Conversely, where the maker of the hearsay representation is available to give evidence and has not been called, this is a legitimate consideration in favour of finding that there has been unfair prejudice.' For example, *Dyldam Developments Pty Ltd v Jones* [2008] NSWCA 56, discussed below.

113 In relation to criminal defendants, see s 90 with respect to the admissibility of **admissions**, and see Chapter 7 and with respect to holding **an identification parade** (s 114(4)) (note, not applying under the *UEA* (Tas)).

The High Court in *Police v Dunstall*[114] left the matter open when it concluded that admitting a breath analysis reading in a DUI case where it had not been possible to obtain a blood alcohol reading did not make Dunstall's trial unfair. As the parties did not contest the existence of a general fairness discretion[115] (that is, beyond *UEA*, ss 90 and 137):

> 47. … [I]t [was] inappropriate to determine the scope, if any, of a residual discretion to exclude lawfully obtained, probative, non-confessional evidence that is unaffected by impropriety or risk of prejudice on the ground that admission of the evidence would render the trial of the defendant an unfair trial.
>
> 48. It remains to observe that the power of the court to prevent unfairness arising from the continuation of criminal proceedings that are oppressive or unjust involves a test of fairness that requires the court to balance the interests of the defendant and those of the community. Where the evidence that is sought to be excluded is critical to the prosecution case and the basis of exclusion is said to be that admission of the evidence would render the trial unfair, the remedy lies in determining whether the circumstances justify a permanent stay and not in circumventing that inquiry by the exclusion of the evidence in the exercise of a "general unfairness discretion".

Legal relevance: section 135

> **135. General discretion to exclude evidence**
>
> The court may refuse to admit evidence if its probative value is substantially outweighed by the danger that the evidence might:
>
> (a) be unfairly prejudicial to a party,[116] or
>
> (b) be misleading or confusing, or
>
> (c) cause or result in undue waste of time.[117]

The first discretion is, in common law parlance, known as *legal relevance*. It is distinguishable from *logical relevance* by virtue of the fact that, first, it assumes logical relevance (s 55) has been satisfied; and, second, because it is driven by public policy considerations, not by logic. The points of distinction are obvious if one compares s 55 and s 135.

Legal relevance requires the court to weigh the probative value of evidence, that is, 'the extent to which the evidence could rationally affect the assessment of the probability of the existence of a fact in issue' against three broad public policy concerns – the danger that evidence might be unfairly prejudicial to a party,

114 [2015] HCA 26; 256 CLR 403, citing *Jago v District Court (NSW)* [1989] HCA 46; 168 CLR 23, 33 (Mason CJ); *Williams v Spautz* [1992] HCA 34; 174 CLR 509, 518-19 (Mason CJ, Dawson, Toohey and McHugh JJ); *Subramaniam* [2004] HCA 51; 79 ALJR 116, 122-3; 211 ALR 1, 9 [27]; *Moti* [2011] HCA 50; 245 CLR 456, 463-4 [10]-[11] (French CJ, Gummow, Hayne, Crennan, Kiefel and Bell JJ).

115 As found in *Haddara* [2014] VSCA 100, [12], [16], [50] (Redlich and Weinberg JJA); *Edelsten* (1990) 21 NSWLR 542, 554; *R v McLean; Ex parte Attorney-General* [1991] 1 Qd R 231, 239-40 (Kelly SPJ), 241, 246 (Derrington J).

116 Consider the observation with respect to the prosecution relying on s 135(a) by Refshauge J in *BI (No 3)* [2016] ACTSC 356, [56]-[58]: 'It was difficult to comprehend precisely the unfair prejudice to the Crown, save that the jury might reject TM's evidence by reasoning that as the conviction showed TM to have a criminal history, he should therefore not be believed. Arguably to have TM's evidence rejected because of false reasoning is unfair to the party which has relied on his evidence. … If that is the unfair prejudice, I am satisfied that the giving of appropriate directions to the jury would likely remove any unfair prejudice, but I view it as non-existent'.

117 The Victorian Act has added s 135(d) 'unnecessarily demean the deceased in a criminal proceeding for a homicide offence' and contains a note indicating the section 'does not limit evidence of family violence that may be adduced under Part IC of the *Crimes Act 1958*'.

misleading or confusing, or cause or result in an undue waste of time: s 135(a), (b) and (c). The relationship between logical and legal relevance was summed up nearly 40 years ago in the 1976 Victorian common law classic case of *Stephenson*:

> Although logic is the test of relevance, not all evidence which is logically relevant is legally admissible. The logical connection between a fact and the issue to be determined may be so slight that the fact is treated as too remote and evidence of it as inadmissible. In some cases, such evidence is described as being irrelevant, an expression which must be taken to indicate that its weight is so minimal that it does not serve to add to or detract from the probability of the principle issue being established. Such evidence may be more correctly described as insufficiently relevant or too remotely relevant.[118]

The case of *Stephenson* also provides a useful illustration of measures of remoteness testing the logical link, the capacity of evidence to 'rationally affect (directly or indirectly) the assessment of the probability' that the accident was not caused by Stephenson (that is, the fact in issue). It concerns a negligent driving prosecution arising from a two-car accident where the accident was caused by one of the drivers running a red traffic light. It was the prosecution case that Stephenson was in the wrong. Stephenson's defence was that he had had a green light and the driver of the other car – a red Fiat – was at fault. He wished to support his defence with reference to the likelihood that the Fiat driver had an excessive blood alcohol reading but Stephenson could not identify the driver of the Fiat. All three possible drivers had been killed. Each had a blood alcohol reading of varying levels. Was evidence of these three blood alcohol readings relevant logically? Legally? The court answered both questions in the negative:

> The connection of the condition of the driver of the Fiat with the question of whether the applicant was guilty of the charge was extremely tenuous, and the logical relevance of the former to the latter in this case may well have been regarded as so slight that evidence of the former became inadmissible on the ground of remoteness. When to that fact is added the fact that the driver could not be identified and that any evidence elicited as to the condition of one or more of the men in the car could not be linked with the driver, the examination which counsel sought to undertake lost even the colour of relevance and was properly excluded.

Consider how this case would be applied under the *UEA*?[119] In light of this conclusion where the remoteness of the relevance of the evidence means the defence has been unable to rely on evidence to display a potential reasonable doubt, perhaps one might consider whether the principles expressed in the extract from the Canadian Supreme Court case of *Grant*[120] at the end of this chapter offer an alternative and persuasive approach – namely, that accusatorial principles should be harnessed to inform upon the measure of probative value relative to the 'burden' (or, to be precise, non-burden) placed on the criminal accused. Even then, cases will still arise where a bright line is hard to find, and a multitude of arguments can be brought to bear.

Another example of *UEA*, s 135(c), 'cause or result in undue waste of time', shows the diversity of applications. It is the civil case of *Dyldam Developments Pty Ltd v Jones*[121] where the defendant's delayed production of a building site journal

---

118 [1976] VicRp 34; [1976] VR 376, 380-1 (Young CJ, Nelson and Harris JJ) in Victoria's Supreme Court (Full Court).

119 See *UEA*, ss 55 and 135.

120 [2015] SCC 9.

121 [2008] NSWCA 56, [30].

potentially ambushed the plaintiff, Jones. Jones either needed to accept Dyldam's claim that the names in the journal did not support the plaintiff or he needed to gain an adjournment to investigate the names properly. The plaintiff's medical position meant he was in constant pain, agitated and not coping with the stress of the litigation. Because of the delay, and the pressures on the plaintiff's health, the NSW Court of Appeal excluded the journal on the basis its late production created unfair prejudice to the plaintiff. Basten JA noted (at [91]) precedent[122] for failing to provide evidence in a timely manner for it 'to be properly considered and responded to by the applicants'.

As Basten JA explained, the potential waste of time arose from the need to grant an adjournment to avoid the delayed production disadvantaging the plaintiff. His Honour noted (at [93]) that '[o]nce it is accepted that the probative value of the proffered evidence is significant or substantial, there may be limited scope for exclusion on the basis of a danger of "undue waste of time".' His Honour concluded that para (c) of s 135

> may properly be invoked despite the potential significance of the proffered evidence ... where the real probative value of the evidence is not able to be adequately addressed without further investigation. These circumstances, which existed in the present case, suggest that both paragraphs (a) and (c) were available as a basis for engaging the discretionary power.

Probative value outweighed by danger of unfair prejudice: section 137

The contrast between s 135 with s 137 is noteworthy. Section 137 mandates a judge exclude prosecution evidence if its probative value is (merely) outweighed by the danger of unfair prejudice. Section 137 applies solely to the criminal accused.

> **137. Exclusion of prejudicial evidence in criminal proceedings**
> In a criminal proceeding, the court must refuse to admit evidence adduced by the prosecutor if its probative value is outweighed by the danger of unfair prejudice to the defendant.

In *Aytugrul*,[123] extracted above, the High Court considered – and rejected – submissions relying on s 137, claiming the danger of unfair prejudice to the accused arose from the psychological impact of how DNA profile matching was expressed. In assessing the danger of unfair prejudice, a trial judge is expected to consider the extent to which the danger of unfairness can be neutralised by judicial warnings to the jury. The High Court case of *Dickman*, extracted in Chapter 13,[124] reinforces courts' embedded reliance on judicial warnings to address the danger of unfair prejudice in preference to exclusion under s 137. The following ruling by Beale J in *Abbas, Chaarani and Mohamed (Rulings 1-40)*,[125] responding to submissions to exclude under *UEA*, s 137, graphic images in nine pro-Islamic State videos, illustrating courts' 'confidence' in the capacity of jurors to control their emotional responses to confronting images:

---

122 *Barrett Property Group Pty Ltd v Metricon Homes Pty Ltd* [2007] FCA 1509, [161] (Gilmour J).

123 [2012] HCA 15; 247 CLR 170. See also the discussion above of *Volpe* [2020] VSCA 268 (evidence excluded under s 137), and reference to *DPP v Paulino* [2017] VSCA 38; 54 VR 109 (evidence excluded under ss 55 and/or 137).

124 At pp 600-603. Intrinsic in reliance on judicial warnings is that they be effective, cf *Gilbert* [2000] HCA 15; 201 CLR 414, extracted at p 50 above, and the discussions on the psychological research questioning blind reliance on judicial warnings in Chapter 10, pp 426-428, and Chapter 14, pp 620-622.

125 [2019] VSC 855.

> 61. … [T]he videos give one a more vivid and fulsome appreciation of the extremism of IS ideology. Although the logic of that ideology is twisted and depraved – particularly in its failure to recognise the intrinsic worth of every human being regardless of creed – the videos also help one to understand how supporters of IS justify in their own minds the barbarity of terrorist attacks. Accordingly, I considered that the videos had significant probative value, even though P [the prosecution] did not allege that D1 accessed these videos and P alleged that the co-conspirators only accessed some of these videos.
>
> 62. In relation to the danger of unfair prejudice, intermediate appeal courts in *Elomar* and *Benbrika* were of the view that if properly directed and cautioned against emotive responses, juries are robust enough to receive such material and use it for a proper purpose. Whilst I acknowledge that these videos were very confronting, I shared the confidence of these higher courts in the capacity of jurors to cope with this kind of material, especially if the most brutal parts of the videos are redacted. To that end I ruled that P's permission to play the videos to the jury was conditional on P redacting, inter alia, images and audio of actual executions and their aftermath. …

In another pre-trial ruling Beale J excluded the video 'Address by Musa Cerantonio', described as a 'sermon'[126] and found on devices belong to the accused. His Honour excluded evidence of the recording entirely, in part because of the potentially complex turn of events in managing the danger of unfair prejudice if Cerantonio pleaded guilty during the trial of the three accused, leading to significant media publicity.

> 173. … Given the fact that P [the prosecution] could rely on less problematic evidence to make the same points it wished to make from this video, I considered that the probative value of the evidence was outweighed by the danger of unfair prejudice.

The discretion in s 137 is derived from the well-known statement by Lord Moulton in the 1914 English case of *Christie*:

> The law is so much on its guard against the accused being prejudiced by evidence which, though admissible, would probably have a prejudicial influence on the minds of the jury which would be out of proportion to its true evidential value, that there has grown up a practice of a very salutary nature, under which the judge intimates to the counsel for the *prosecution* that he should not press for the admission of evidence which would be open to this objection, and such an intimation from the tribunal trying the case is usually sufficient to prevent the evidence being pressed in all cases where the scruples of the tribunal in this respect are reasonable. Under the influence of this practice, which is based on an anxiety to secure for every one a fair trial, *there has grown up a custom of not admitting certain kinds of evidence which is so constantly followed that it almost amounts to a rule of procedure*.[127]

These fair trial principles have evolved and strengthened since 1914 through a line of Australian late 20th and early 21st century cases, though exclusion under *UEA*, 137, is relatively uncommon. In a different context, and in an Australian common law setting, McHugh J in *Pfennig*[128] considered what the balancing or weighing process actually meant. As McHugh J observed, at its heart this process is a value judgment, not a balance of mathematics, and it requires consideration of the fairness and potentially the integrity of the trial.

> 39. … [T]he proposition that the probative value of the evidence must outweigh its prejudicial effect is one that can be easily misunderstood. The use of the term 'outweigh'

---

126 Musa Cerantonio at the time was facing a 'foreign incursion' offence in a separate trial.

127 [1914] AC 545, 559 (HL) (emphasis added).

128 [1995] HCA 7; 182 CLR 461, considering the equivalent of *UEA*, s 101.

suggests an almost arithmetical computation. But prejudicial effect and probative value are incommensurables. They have no standard of comparison. The probative value of the evidence goes to proof of an issue, the prejudicial effect to the fairness of the trial. In criminal trials, the prejudicial effect of evidence is not concerned with the cogency of its proof but with the risk that the jury will use the evidence or be affected by it in a way that the law does not permit. …

40. If there is a real risk that the admission of such [similar fact] evidence may prejudice the fair trial of the criminal charge before the court, the interests of justice require the trial judge to make a value judgment, not a mathematical calculation. The judge must compare the probative strength of the evidence with the degree of risk of an unfair trial if the evidence is admitted. Admitting the evidence will serve the interests of justice only if the judge concludes that the probative force of the evidence compared to the degree of risk of an unfair trial is such that fair minded people would think that the public interest in adducing all relevant evidence of guilt must have priority over the risk of an unfair trial.

Finally – and as food for thought – consider the 2015 Canadian Supreme Court decision in *Grant*[129] and its determination that, where the accused offers evidence that is logically relevant, scrutiny of its admissibility is additionally infused with the accusatorial principles discussed earlier in the book. In *Grant* the evidence was 'similar fact' evidence implicating a third party (and thus exonerating the accused). *Grant* is not a precedent in Australia. We return later to the *UEA* equivalent of 'similar fact' evidence (known as tendency and coincidence evidence (*UEA*, ss 97, 98, 101)), but for the present our concern is with the extent to which this infusion of accusatorial principles that lighten the admissibility load for the accused might apply as an interpretive guidepost more broadly under the *UEA*. These issues are not without expression in Australia. A similar scenario occurred in *Lockyer*,[130] where Hunt CJ at CL ruled that defence evidence (suggesting that another person was responsible for the crime) would satisfy the *UEA* threshold hurdle applying to both prosecution and defence evidence,[131] even though the evidence was vague, because its probative value was to be measured relative to the lack of burden placed on the accused. Had such evidence been tendered by the prosecution it is unlikely to have satisfied the threshold (or the ultimate) admissibility requirements. *Grant* raises the question whether evidence under the *UEA* tendered by the defence should generally be given more latitude. Grant was charged with the first-degree murder of Candace Derksen. This was a notorious cold-case murder that occurred in Winnipeg, Manitoba, almost 23 years earlier. Grant's prosecution stemmed from newly tested and potentially flawed DNA evidence. Grant sought to adduce evidence to suggest that, based on the modus operandi and other physical evidence, the victim's abductor was in fact a person who had also abducted another victim (PW) while Grant was in custody. Karakatsanis J (delivering the judgment of the court) agreed with the Manitoba Court of Appeal that Grant should have been permitted to lead the evidence. His Honour examined whether defence-led evidence required particular consideration.

7. … [F]irst principles governing the admissibility of evidence properly balance the competing interests that arise when the defence seeks to lead evidence of an unknown

---

129 [2015] SCC 9. Grant was acquitted in 2017 in his second trial, <https://www.cbc.ca/news /canada/manitoba/mark-grant-retrial-derksen-decision-1.4360436>.

130 (1996) 89 A Crim R 457 and see also *Symss* [2003] NSWCCA 77.

131 *UEA*, s 97, sets a threshold hurdle for such evidence (namely, that the evidence be of 'significant probative value') irrespective of the party adducing it, but provides an additional and demanding hurdle for prosecution evidence about a defendant.

third party suspect. In such cases, the defence must first establish the logical relevance of the evidence. This may be done by demonstrating a sufficient connection – or similarity – between the crime charged and another crime the accused could not possibly have committed to support the logical inference that the same person committed both crimes. Once this threshold is met, the evidence will be admissible unless its prejudicial effects substantially outweigh its probative value (*R v Seaboyer*, [1991] 2 SCR 577). …

20. In order for the judge to put a defence to the jury, the accused must point to evidence on the record that gives the defence an air of reality (*R v Cinous*, 2002 SCC 29, [2002] 2 SCR 3). The trial judge must determine whether there is some evidence that is "reasonably capable of supporting the inferences required for the defence to succeed" (ibid, at para 83). The air of reality test applies to all defences, and acts as a threshold to ensure that "fanciful or far-fetched" defences are not put before the trier of fact … . When applying this test, the trial judge must take the evidence to be true and must not assess credibility or make other findings of fact (*Cinous*).

21. These principles are distinct, but may be interrelated. In most cases, where the defence evidence relates to the facts underlying the offence charged, the logical relevance and the admissibility of the evidence will be obvious. However, where the evidence refers to a factual matrix beyond the offence charged, its relevance to a fact in issue or an available defence may be less clear. In such circumstances, the gate-keeping role of the trial judge may require her to determine whether the evidence is logically relevant and connected to a defence that has an air of reality. For example, while the degree of similarity may be logically relevant to whether the same person committed the offence, it will not relate to a fact in issue at trial unless the defence has an air of reality. In this case, the unknown third party suspect defence will not have an air of reality unless there is evidence that the accused could not have committed the other offence. Thus, logical relevance will sometimes be assessed with reference to whether the defence for which the evidence is tendered is available. …

The discretion to limit the use of evidence: section 136

136. General discretion to limit use of evidence

The court may limit the use to be made of evidence if there is a danger that a particular use of the evidence might:

(a) be unfairly prejudicial to a party, or

(b) be misleading or confusing.

Section 136 does not operate to *exclude* evidence. It operates to limit the use that can be made of evidence where that evidence has multiple bases for admission. To appreciate the role of s 136, and a number of other provisions[132] in the *UEA*, it is important to be mindful of the distinction between the 'admissibility' and the 'use' of evidence – a distinction explained by Leeming JA in *BH Australia Constructions Pty Ltd v Kapeller*:

58. … Very regularly, the authorities – especially the older authorities – refer to these rules in terms of "admissibility". Those references reflect usage which is poorly adapted to proceedings to which the *Evidence Act 1995* (NSW) applies. That Act distinguishes between admissibility and use. An example is sufficient to illustrate the point. Suppose there be a dispute whether a contract was formed, and also, if a contract was formed, as to its terms. Evidence as to the post-contractual conduct of the parties is relevant, within the meaning of s 55 of the *Evidence Act*. It follows that it is *admissible*. However, that evidence may only be *used* for the purpose of determining whether or not a contract exists. Post-contractual conduct may not be *used* for the purpose of construing the terms of the

132 For example, *UEA*, ss 60, 77, 95 and 101A.

> contract, if one exists. *The distinction in the Evidence Act between admissibility and use is perhaps made plainest in provisions such as s 95 (which refers to both concepts) and s 136 (which empowers the court to limits the use which may be made of evidence which is admitted).*[133]

In other words, it provides for admitted evidence to have permissible and impermissible uses. Section 136 typically operates where an exception to an exclusionary rule permits evidence to be used for more than one use (or purpose) – for example, a ruling in the judge-alone trial of Leonard Warwick, who faced 24 charges relating to the 1980 murder of Family Court judge, Justice Opas, the 1984 bombings of the Family Court building, two Family Court judges' houses and the Casula Jehovah's Witness Kingdom Hall.[134] In response to defence claims of police incompetence in their investigations the prosecution wished to tender police running sheets in relation to one bombing as evidence of the comprehensive nature of the police investigation. Under *UEA*, ss 60 and 77, the documents making up the police running sheet were admissible to prove the truth of their contents. Garling J (at [12]) applied s 136 to limit the running sheets so that they 'would not be used as the truth of the representations contained in it but, rather, as evidence of the investigations undertaken and the results of those investigations by the Police at that time'. This limitation meant that the inability to cross-examine the police officers who made the running sheets was significantly diminished, dismissing the obligation to apply s 137. His Honour was 'not persuaded that the evidence would be misleading or confusing or would cause or result in undue waste of time' (at [15]).

Warwick illustrates the not uncommon use of s 136 with respect to admissible hearsay evidence. It has the potential to operate where a representation, for example the representations in the running sheet, has relevance (or purpose) justifying admissibility in different ways. Other examples include evidence that a medical expert witness relied on (say) statements from a patient (for example, 'I felt nauseous after I drank the coffee'). This evidence is relevant to the weight the jury might give to the medical evidence. The patient's statements may be *also* relevant to the facts in issue independently of their role in founding the medical opinion – for example, to show that the coffee contained a drug. Section 136 may justify a limitation if the patient's statement might be unfairly prejudicial to a party, or misleading and confusing. In a jury trial the limitation operates by way of the judge directing the jury, that if it accepts the evidence it must limit its use of the patient's statement only to weighing the expert opinion and not to supporting any other inferences. The section was central to the unsuccessful arguments of the appellant in *Papakosmas* that the evidence of complaint be admitted only for its credibility purpose – to show that the complainant's evidence in court was consistent with what she told eyewitnesses shortly after the alleged rape (and not for its hearsay or 'truth' purpose to support directly the prosecution case of rape). The High Court rightly rejected this limited use as it would have put the *UEA* law in conformity with the common law (which was drenched in misogynist assumptions about rape victims' 'proper' responses to sexual violation).[135]

---

133 [2019] NSWSC 1086, citing *AH* (1997) 42 NSWLR 702, 708; *El-Haddad* [2015] NSWCCA 10; 88 NSWLR 93, [38]-[45]; and *Cherry v Steele-Park* [2017] NSWCA 295; 96 NSWLR 548, [50] and [55] (emphasis added).

134 *Warwick (No 60)* [2018] NSWSC 1875.

135 See *Lillyman* [1896] 2 QB 167; *Kilby* [1973] HCA 30; 129 CLR 460. Both cases are referred to extensively in the judgments.

We move now to examine two quite different discretions. The first responds to illegally or improperly obtained evidence. The second is a less certain discretion, a residual common law fairness discretion.

Discretion[136] to exclude evidence due to impropriety or illegality: section 138

The Australian High Court has been, in the common law world, a trail blazer in its recognition that investigative misconduct in the acquisition of prosecution evidence is something courts can and should review. This was a matter of some controversy in the 1970s. Stephen and Aickin JJ, in the pivotal 1978 case of *Bunning v Cross*,[137] quoted from Barwick CJ who in 1970 in *Ireland*[138] sowed the seeds for the establishment of this wide-ranging discretion when his Honour observed:

> [W]henever such unlawfulness or unfairness appears, the judge has a discretion to reject the evidence. He must consider its exercise. In the exercise of it, the competing public requirements must be considered and weighed against each other. On the one hand there is the public need to bring to conviction those who commit criminal offences. On the other hand is the public interest in the protection of the individual from unlawful and unfair treatment. Convictions obtained by the aid of unlawful or unfair acts may be obtained at too high a price. Hence the judicial discretion.

That statement represents the law in Australia; it was concurred in by all other members of the High Court in *Ireland* and has since been applied in a number of Australian cases. Its concluding words, '[c]onvictions obtained by the aid of unlawful or unfair acts may be obtained at too high a price', echo the sentiments expressed long ago by Knight Bruce VC, in a different yet relevant context.[139] In *Bunning v Cross*[140] Stephen and Aickin JJ observed:

> What *Ireland* involves is no simple question of ensuring fairness to an accused but instead the weighting against each other of two competing requirements of public policy, thereby seeking to resolve the apparent conflict between the desirable goal of bringing to conviction the wrongdoer and the undesirable effect of curial approval, or even encouragement, being given to the unlawful conduct of those whose task it is to enforce the law. This being the aim of the discretionary process called for by *Ireland* it follows that it by no means takes as its central point the question of unfairness to the accused. It is, on the contrary, concerned with broader questions of high public policy, unfairness to the accused being only one factor which, if present, will play its part in the whole process of consideration. ...
>
> The relevance of the competing policy considerations to which we have referred becomes of especial importance in an age of sophisticated crime and crime detection when law enforcement increasingly depends upon electronic surveillance and eavesdropping, the unannounced search of premises or of the person and upon scientific methods, whether of identification, by fingerprints or voiceprints, or of ascertainment of bodily states, as by blood alcohol tests and the like. In many such cases the question of fairness does not play any part. "Fair" or "unfair" is largely meaningless when considering fingerprint evidence obtained by force or a trick or even the evidence of possession of, say, explosives or weapons obtained by an unlawful search of body or baggage, aided by electronic scanners. There is no initial presumption that the State by its law enforcement

136 Note the mandated exclusionary language 'is not to be admitted': *UEA*, s 138(1).

137 [1978] HCA 22; 141 CLR 54, 72, 75.

138 [1970] HCA 21; 126 CLR 321.

139 *Pearse v Pearse* [1846] EngR 1195; 1 De G & Sm 12; 63 ER 950, 957 (and quoted in the banner head quote at the beginning of Chapter 3).

140 [1978] HCA 22; 141 CLR 54, [27], [29].

> agencies, will in the use of such measures of crime detection observe some given code of good sportsmanship or of chivalry. It is not fair play that is called in question in such cases but rather society's right to insist that those who enforce the law themselves respect it, so that a citizen's precious right to immunity from arbitrary and unlawful intrusion into the daily affairs of private life may remain unimpaired. A discretion exercisable according to the principles in *Ireland's Case* serves this end whereas one concerned with fairness may often have little relevance to the question.

It is within this common law background that the *UEA*, through s 138, strengthened, broadened and clarified the application of what had been called the *Bunning v Cross*, or public policy, discretion. Whilst the discretion undoubtedly serves an important function consistent with the accusatorial framework of justice and the maintenance of the integrity of the curial and broader justice process,[141] an early empirical study by Bram Presser, when only the NSW South Wales and Commonwealth legislation was in place, concluded with respect to the change from the common law onus of proof in s 138(1) that it

> appears to be a legislative 'helping hand' in this regard, and it can be seen that judges in the ACT have seized the opportunity to utilise it. Unfortunately, the same cannot be said of their colleagues in NSW. Nevertheless, legislatures still searching for an effective way to ensure integrity and competence in their police services would do well to enact similar legislation. By doing so, they will provide judges with a better opportunity to fulfil their prescribed role as the guardians' guardians.[142]

Unlike its common law predecessor, it applies also in non-criminal contexts.

> **138. Exclusion of improperly or illegally obtained evidence**
>
> (1) Evidence that was obtained:
>
> (a) improperly or in contravention of an Australian law, or
>
> (b) in consequence of an impropriety or of a contravention of an Australian law,
>
> is not to be admitted unless the desirability of admitting the evidence outweighs the undesirability of admitting evidence that has been obtained in the way in which the evidence was obtained.
>
> (2) ...[143]
>
> (3) Without limiting the matters that the court may take into account under subsection (1), it is to take into account:
>
> (a) the probative value of the evidence, and
>
> (b) the importance of the evidence in the proceeding, and
>
> (c) the nature of the relevant offence, cause of action or defence and the nature of the subject-matter of the proceeding, and
>
> (d) the gravity of the impropriety or contravention, and
>
> (e) whether the impropriety or contravention was deliberate or reckless, and
>
> (f) whether the impropriety or contravention was contrary to or inconsistent with a right of a person recognised by the *International Covenant on Civil and Political Rights*,[144] and

141 Bell J has provided a detailed and comprehensive analysis of this law in the context of civil rights and the *Charter of Human Rights and Responsibilities Act 2006* (Vic): *DPP v Kaba* [2014] VSC 52.

142 B Presser, 'Public Policy, Police Interest: A Re-Evaluation of the Judicial Discretion to Exclude Improperly or Illegally Obtained Evidence' (2001) 25(3) *Melbourne University Law Review* 757 (citations omitted).

143 Section 138(2) applies solely to admissions.

144 The section also contains the following: '**Note**: The *International Covenant on Civil and Political Rights* is set out in Schedule 2 to the *Human Rights and Equal Opportunity Commission Act 1986* of the Commonwealth'.

(g) whether any other proceeding (whether or not in a court) has been or is likely to be taken in relation to the impropriety or contravention, and
(h) the difficulty (if any) of obtaining the evidence without impropriety or contravention of an Australian law.

French CJ in the High Court in *Parker v Comptroller-General of Customs*[145] considered the scope and meaning of some key terms in s 138, namely, 'improperly', 'impropriety' and 'contravention'. Quoting from *The Oxford English Dictionary*[146] his Honour observed that the relevant ordinary meanings of 'improper' include 'not in accordance with truth, fact, reason or rule; abnormal, irregular; incorrect, inaccurate, erroneous, wrong', and 'contravention' refers to '[t]he action of contravening or going counter to; violation, infringement, transgression'. He noted that 'the core meaning of "contravention"' involves:

> disobedience of a command expressed in a rule of law which may be statutory or non-statutory. It involves doing that which is forbidden by law or failing to do that which is required by law to be done. Mere failure to satisfy a condition necessary for the exercise of a statutory power is not a contravention. Nor would such a failure readily be characterised as "impropriety" although that word does cover a wider range of conduct than the word "contravention".[147]

Basten JA in *Robinson v Woolworths Ltd*[148] helpfully added some shape to these definitions.

> 23. … [T]he identification of impropriety requires attention to the following propositions. First, it is necessary to identify what, in a particular context, may be viewed as "the minimum standards which a society such as ours should expect and require of those entrusted with powers of law enforcement". Secondly, the conduct in question must not merely blur or contravene those standards in some minor respect; it must be "quite inconsistent with" or "clearly inconsistent with" those standards. Thirdly, the concepts of "harassment" and "manipulation" suggest some level of encouragement, persuasion or importunity in relation to the commission of an offence: thus, in describing the first category of cases (at 39) the joint judgment in *Ridgeway* referred to offences being procured or induced.

Finally, s 138(3) makes clear that the discretion is guided by at least eight considerations. The gravity of the impropriety or contravention (s 138(3)(d)) was discussed in *Marijancevic*,[149] where it was held by Warren CJ, Buchanan and Redlich JJA that impugned conduct may be characterised by reference to a spectrum of least to most serious:

> 67. At the least serious end of spectrum of improper conduct would be that which did not involve any knowledge or realisation that the conduct was illegal and where no advantage or benefit was gained as a consequence of that impropriety. In the middle of the range would be conduct which was known to be improper but which was not undertaken for the purpose of gaining any advantage or benefit that would not have been obtained had the conduct been legal. At the most serious end of the range would be conduct which was known to be illegal and which was pursued for the purpose of obtaining a benefit or advantage that could not be obtained by lawful conduct. Cases such as *Ridgeway* exemplify this category of impropriety. There are of course other factors which will bear

145 [2009] HCA 7; 252 ALR 619.
146 2nd ed (1989), Vols III and VII.
147 [2009] HCA 7; 252 ALR 619, [29], [30] (French CJ).
148 [2005] NSWCCA 426.
149 [2011] VSCA 355; 33 VR 440, 458 (Warren CJ) (and quoted by Bell J in *DPP v Kaba* [2014] VSC 52, [348]).

upon how seriously the impropriety should be characterised such as the nature of the illegality and the extent to which it is widespread.

Examples of points in the investigation process where impropriety commonly arises include at all phases where an individual's rights are potentially seriously compromised – namely, police search,[150] detention,[151] questioning[152] and arrest.[153] The most significant difference between *UEA*, s 138, and the common law is the location of the burden of proof.

It is on the party seeking to adduce illegally or improperly obtained evidence. There is thus a two-stage process. The party seeking admission of the evidence has the burden of proof of facts relevant to matters weighing in favour of admission. It also has the burden of persuading the court that the desirability of admitting the evidence outweighs the undesirability of admitting evidence obtained in the way in which it was obtained.[154] Bathurst CJ in the NSW Court of Criminal Appeal case of *Gedeon*[155] referred to the modifications that s 138 of the *UEA* had made to the law developed by *Ireland*,[156] *Bunning v Cross*[157] and *Ridgeway*.[158] His Honour referred to the important aspect of burden of proof, provided in s 138(1), confirmed[159] the continuing importance of the sentiments expressed in the Australian High Court cases that shaped the common law version of this discretion, and emphasised that the discretion 'depends on considerations of "high public policy" relating to the question of whether the effect of the illegality or impropriety on the administration of justice outweighs the legitimate public interest in the conviction of the guilty'.[160]

A five-judge bench High Court considered comprehensively the application of s 138 to an animal rights agency commissioning a documentary photographer to illegally film footage of 'live bait' training of greyhounds for racing where this surveillance footage then provided a basis for the RSPCA to obtain evidence by way of search warrant. Admissions were also obtained.

Kadir and Grech

[2020] HCA 1[161]

Grech and Kadir where jointly charged with a number of offences in relation to the alleged use of rabbits as 'live bait' in training racing greyhounds at Mr Kadir's property. Seven audio-visual recordings of this baiting were made by a documentary photographer, Ms Lynch, on behalf of Animals Australia. They

150 See, eg, *Kotynia-English* [2014] TASSC 63; *Tasmania v Seabourne* [2010] TASSC 35.

151 See, eg, *Campbell v DPP* [2008] NSWSC 1284 (Hidden J) regarding the failure to call the Aboriginal Legal Service officer.

152 *FE* [2013] NSWSC 1692 (failure to caution a young person and continuing to question a suspect who had initially refused to answer questions).

153 *DPP v Carr* [2002] NSWSC 194; 127 A Crim R 151.

154 *Parker v Comptroller-General of Customs* [2009] HCA 7; 252 ALR 619, [28] (French CJ), citing *Employment Advocate v Williamson* [2001] FCA 1164; 111 FCR 20, 43-4 [78] (Branson J).

155 [2013] NSWCCA 257.

156 [1970] HCA 21; 126 CLR 321.

157 [1978] HCA 22; 141 CLR 54.

158 [1995] HCA 66; 184 CLR 19.

159 To the same effect, see *Robinson v Woolworths Ltd* [2005] NSWCCA 426 (Basten JA; Barr J agreeing).

160 [2013] NSWCCA 257, [177].

161 Citations relating to the appeal court judgment omitted.

were in breach of the *Surveillance Devices Act 2007* (NSW) (the SDA). From this information the RSPCA obtained further material supporting the prosecution. In addition, Ms Lynch twice attended the property and obtained admissions from Mr Kadir. The trial judge applied s 138 to reject all of the above evidence in light of the way the evidence had been obtained, holding that the desirability of admitting the evidence was outweighed by the undesirability of admitting the evidence. This ruling was reversed in the NSW Court of Criminal Appeal. The High Court upheld the State appeal court's ruling that the evidence of Mr Kadir's admissions and the evidence obtained when executing the search warrant were admissible but found that the trial judge had correctly excluded the surveillance evidence. In particular the High Court rejected the reasoning of the State appeal court in relation to s 138(3)(h), observing at [9] that 'demonstration of the difficulty of obtaining evidence of the commission of acts of animal cruelty lawfully at the Londonderry property *did not* weigh in *favour* of admitting evidence obtained in deliberate defiance of the law' (emphasis added). This rejected the appeal court position (quoted at [36]) 'that the difficulty of lawfully obtaining evidence of live baiting "tip[ped] the balance" in favour of admitting the first video-recording ... [because] there were "real concerns as to the unlikelihood of an anonymous complaint being able to be properly and effectively investigated" and the suspected criminal activities were of a "high degree of seriousness"').

> **Kiefel CJ, Bell, Keane, Nettle and Edelman JJ**: 37. The gravity of the contravention (factor (d)) and the difficulty of obtaining evidence lawfully (factor (h)), along with whether the impropriety or contravention was deliberate or reckless (factor (e)), are overlapping factors. In the circumstances of this case, the trial judge did not err in failing to weigh the s 138(3) factors separately in relation to the first video-recording. His Honour was right to find that each video-recording was the product of a serious contravention of Australian law. The seriousness of the contravention was in each case the greater because the recording was made in deliberate contravention of the law with a view to assembling evidence which it was believed the proper authorities would be unable to lawfully obtain. To the extent that it was more difficult to lawfully obtain evidence of live baiting before the first video-recording was made, this was a factor which weighed against admitting it. ... His Honour's determination that none of the surveillance evidence is admissible is correct.
>
> 38. ... The undesirability of receiving the search warrant evidence and the admissions, in the way each was obtained, materially differed from the undesirability of receiving the surveillance evidence in the way it was obtained. In the case of the search warrant evidence, while there was a serious breach of the SDA by Animals Australia which led to obtaining the search warrant, the RSPCA acted lawfully in the performance of its regulatory functions. In the case of the admissions, the causal connection between obtaining them, and the contravention of the SDA, was "tenuous".
>
> 39. Mr Kadir submits that the Court of Criminal Appeal misapprehended the trial judge's reasons, and that the trial judge did not say that the surveillance evidence and search warrant evidence were obtained in the same way. Rather, the findings made with respect to the s 138(3) factors in relation to the surveillance evidence were, in fact, directly applicable to the admissibility of the search warrant evidence and the admissions. Ms Grech submits that the Court of Criminal Appeal's error was to read the reference in s 138(1) to "the *way* in which the evidence was obtained" narrowly, with the result that the legislative policy of excluding evidence obtained in consequence of impropriety or illegality is undermined. The "way" evidence is obtained, in Ms Grech's submission, is to be understood as referring to the entire chain of causation and not merely the final link in the chain.

40. As the Court of Criminal Appeal observed, s 138 does not enact the doctrine that prevailed in the United States, requiring the exclusion of the "fruit" of official illegality unless the impugned evidence was derived "by means sufficiently distinguishable to be purged of the primary taint".[162] Section 138 provides for the exclusion of evidence obtained by, or in consequence of, impropriety or illegality, unless the product of balancing the competing public interests favours admitting the evidence. The trial judge's analysis of the admissibility of the search warrant evidence and the admissions did not go beyond satisfaction of the causal link between the evidence and the contravention of the SDA. The causal link engages s 138, but the weighing of the competing public interests under s 138(1) involved considerations which are not the same as those applying to the admissibility of the surveillance evidence.

41. As the Court of Criminal Appeal also observed, where the misconduct involves the same investigative body, the considerations relevant to weighing the public interests will commonly be the same in respect of evidence obtained under s 138(1)(a) or (b). Here, the surveillance evidence was obtained in contravention of the law by a private body (or persons engaged by it), whereas the search warrant evidence was obtained by a regulator acting lawfully and without prior knowledge of the contravention, albeit that it was procured on the strength of the surveillance evidence. The causal link between the contravention and the admissions was tenuous, a consideration which the Court of Criminal Appeal was right to find was capable of affecting the weighing of the public interest in not giving curial approval or encouragement to the unlawful conduct.

42. Self-evidently, factor (a), the probative value of the evidence, and factor (b), the importance of the evidence in the proceeding, cannot be picked up from findings made with respect to the surveillance evidence and applied to the search warrant evidence or the admissions. None of the s 138(3) factors can be considered in isolation. Evidence may possess high probative value but not be important in the proceeding in a case in which other equally probative evidence is available to the prosecution. In this case, the importance of the search warrant evidence, and, in Mr Kadir's case, the admissions, is greater by reason of the exclusion of the surveillance evidence. Moreover, the weighting of the factors that are concerned with the impropriety or illegality to the balancing of the public interests may differ as between the surveillance evidence, the search warrant evidence and the admissions.

43. The appellants challenge the Court of Criminal Appeal's re-determination of the admissibility of the search warrant evidence and Mr Kadir challenges the re-determination of the admissibility of the admissions. It is unnecessary to address these grounds of complaint. The Court of Criminal Appeal's re-determination of the admissibility of each of these categories of evidence was based upon the assumption that the difficulty of obtaining the evidence lawfully mitigated the gravity of the contravention and that the first video-recording is admissible. Neither assumption is correct.

44. The respondent submits that in the event error is found in the Court of Criminal Appeal's re-determination of the admissibility of any of the evidence, this Court should determine the matter itself or remit the proceeding to the Court of Criminal Appeal. The appellants submit that, in this event, the matter should be remitted to the trial judge for reconsideration. Mr Kadir submits that the trial judge is best placed to determine the admissibility of evidence and to take into account any matters which have occurred (or will occur) subsequent to the voir dire. Mr Kadir submits that new material may arise requiring the trial judge to revisit the issues that are the subject of the appeals and that the trial judge will "almost certainly need to evaluate the nature and extent of the RSPCA's knowledge of and involvement in criminal activity (a matter so far not fully or adequately explored)".

45. … Taking into account the history of the proceedings, the appropriate course is for this Court to determine the admissibility of the search warrant evidence and the

162 [*Grech and Kadir* [2017] NSWCCA 288, [120], citing *Wong Sun v United States* (1963) 371 US 471, 484, 488; and see ALRC, *Evidence*, Report No 26 (Interim) (1985), Vol 1, 532-533 [961].]

admissions. While there is the possibility of events occurring which may require the trial judge to revisit any evidentiary ruling, the suggestion that the admissibility of the search warrant evidence should be determined on remitter to enable the trial judge to evaluate matters which were not fully or adequately explored at the voir dire hearing is distinctly unpersuasive. Mr Kadir's opportunity to adduce such evidence, and put such submissions, respecting the conduct of the RSPCA was at the voir dire hearing.

46. The Court of Criminal Appeal rejected Mr Kadir's submission that the search warrant evidence was obtained by contravention of Australian law within s 138(1)(a) because, in receiving the surveillance evidence, officers of the RSPCA were themselves in breach of the SDA. Section 12 makes it an offence to possess a record of the carrying on of an activity knowing that it has been obtained by the use of an optical surveillance device in contravention of the SDA. Mr Kadir submits that it is apparent from the surveillance evidence that it is (or is likely to have been) the product of a breach of the SDA. On the hearing in this Court, senior counsel for Mr Kadir maintained the submission that there is no warrant for finding that the RSPCA was not itself involved in the contravention of Australian law. Such a proposition was not put to Mr O'Shannessy, and, as the Court of Criminal Appeal rightly held, in these circumstances it was not open to the trial judge to find that any breach of the SDA was deliberate, reckless or possibly even negligent.

47. The onus is upon the respondent to establish that the desirability of admitting the search warrant evidence outweighs the undesirability of admitting evidence obtained in the way it was obtained. The capacity of the search warrant evidence to rationally affect the assessment of the probability that the appellants committed acts of serious animal cruelty is high. The fact that the prosecution case does not include the surveillance evidence increases the importance of the search warrant evidence in the proceeding. Its importance is high. The nature of the offence is, as the trial judge found, serious. The gravity of the contravention is, as his Honour found, "very high". The contravention was repeated and deliberate. It interfered with Mr Kadir's privacy, a breach of Art 17 of the ICCPR. In circumstances in which the recording was confined to activity in the bullring and did not extend to Mr Kadir's home, and in light of the nature of the activity conducted in the area that was the subject of the recording, his Honour was right to accord this factor no particular weight. The circumstance that neither Ms White nor Ms Lynch is likely to be subject to any proceeding arising out of the contravention is a neutral consideration. In circumstances in which the RSPCA was not complicit in the contravention, factor (h) is also neutral.

48. The admissibility of the search warrant evidence arises in criminal proceedings in which the desirability of admitting the evidence reflects the public interest in the conviction of wrongdoers. The undesirability of admitting evidence obtained in consequence of the deliberate unlawful conduct of a private "activist" entity is the effect of curial approval, or even encouragement, of vigilantism. The RSPCA had no advance knowledge of Animals Australia's plan to illegally record activities at the Londonderry property. There is nothing to suggest a pattern of conduct by which Animals Australia or other activist groups illegally collect material upon which the RSPCA takes action. The desirability of admitting evidence that is important to the prosecution of these serious offences outweighs the undesirability of not admitting evidence obtained in the way the search warrant evidence was obtained.

49. Before turning, in Mr Kadir's appeal, to the factors bearing on the admissibility of the admissions, it is necessary to deal with one matter which appears to have been raised for the first time in Mr Kadir's submissions in reply. Mr Kadir invokes s 138(2)(b) of the Act, which deems evidence to have been obtained "improperly" if an admission is made during questioning, if the person conducting the questioning knowingly makes a false statement, knowing that making the false statement was likely to cause the person to make an admission. The submission is that Ms Lynch's "questioning" was conducted upon a knowingly false basis that was likely to elicit an admission about the use of live baiting in training greyhounds at the Londonderry property, and that this is a consideration

> to which substantial weight should be given in determining whether the prosecution has discharged its onus under s 138.
>
> 50. Section 138(2) deems admissions made during or in consequence of questioning of the kind in para (a) or (b) to have been obtained improperly, thereby engaging conditional exclusion under s 138(1). These proceedings have been conducted on the basis that the admissions engage conditional exclusion under s 138(1)(b) because they were obtained in consequence of the illegality in obtaining the surveillance evidence. No attention was directed to the applicability of s 138(2) to circumstances in which the "person conducting the questioning" is not a police officer or other official.[163] On the hearing, senior counsel for Mr Kadir disavowed any suggestion that the provision applies to admissions obtained in "sting operations", or "pretext" telephone calls. Senior counsel submitted that the obtaining of the admissions by subterfuge was to be taken into account "as part of the panoply of factors". It is not apparent that the fact that the admissions were obtained by subterfuge has any relevant bearing on the competing public interests with which s 138 is concerned. The trial judge separately considered, and rejected, that the circumstances in which the admissions were made were unfair within s 90 of the Act or gave rise to the danger of unfair prejudice within s 137 of the Act.
>
> 51. Since the evidence of the admissions is capable of rational acceptance,[164] consideration of the probative value of the admissions is to be assessed upon the assumption that the evidence will be accepted.[165] Their probative value is high and they are important evidence in the case against Mr Kadir. The remaining factors under s 138(3) have the same weight in relation to the admissions as to the search warrant evidence. The undesirability of admitting the admissions does not raise the same concerns with respect to condoning vigilantism as does the search warrant evidence. As the Court of Criminal Appeal rightly observed, the obtaining and viewing of the surveillance evidence was a step in the investigation by Animals Australia that led to Ms Lynch speaking with Mr Kadir, but that was all. And as their Honours also observed, Ms Lynch did not make use of any knowledge that she gained from the surveillance evidence in her conversation with Mr Kadir. Their Honours' conclusion, that the bare connection between the contravention of Australian law and obtaining the admissions is unlikely to convey curial approval or encouragement of the contravention, is apt. The undesirability of admitting evidence obtained in the way the admissions were is outweighed by the desirability of the evidence being admitted in support of the prosecution case.

In *Riley*,[166] in a trial on the charge of dangerous driving causing death, a s 5[167] appeal arose around the trial judge's application of s 138 excluding blood test results because one (of two) caps was removed from the vial containing blood sent for testing. No impropriety was alleged. The remaining cap ensured the contents were safe, but (and contrary to the evidence of the nurse who took the blood), the DPP conceded contravention of the statutory requirement of fixing the vial's seal. Bathurst CJ (with Button and Wilson JJ agreeing) determined the court was obliged to take the evidence at its highest because ultimately it was for the jury to assess whether they accepted the blood sample results, and overturned the trial judge's exclusion. His Honour noted the seriousness of the charge and that the jury could rationally conclude the blood sample had not been interfered with – even though the integrity of the sample could not be guaranteed.

---

163 [ALRC, *Evidence*, Report No 38 (1987), xxxix [66].]

164 [*IMM* (2016) 257 CLR 300, 312 [39], 317 [58] (French CJ, Kiefel, Bell and Keane JJ); *Bauer* [2018] HCA 40; 92 ALJR 846, 865 [69] (Kiefel CJ, Bell, Gageler, Keane, Nettle, Gordon and Edelman JJ).]

165 [*IMM* (2016) 257 CLR 300, 315 [52] (French CJ, Kiefel, Bell and Keane JJ).]

166 [2020] NSWCCA 283.

167 *Criminal Appeal Act 1912* (NSW), s 5F.

Conclusion

The centrality of relevance is hardly controversial, nor is the need to moderate the exclusion of evidence by discretionary or mandated considerations. Despite the centrality and apparent disarming simplicity of these features of evidence law, difficult questions arise in the context of applying the relevance provisions. This is illustrated by the extent to which *UEA*, s 55, has attracted hard-fought battles in the High Court on threshold admissibility issues. Before 1995 this issue was rarely a battleground. Now, the scope to interpret s 55 draws on the language in the Act as well as broader procedural and structural contexts linked to the jury's role in the trial.[168] One might speculate that, with a code-like statement of relevance replacing the common law, the legal profession has been attracted (like moths to a light) to testing the boundaries of the legislative language where shades of interpretation, meaning and distinctions in words and phrases compete to give ascendancy to one party in the forensic battle.

168 See, eg, *Pell* [2020] HCA 12; *Baden-Clay* [2016] HCA 35; 258 CLR 308; *Fennell* [2019] HCA 37.

Chapter 5

The Witness in the Box

Introduction

Together with Chapter 6, this chapter details the major regulation of court processes relevant to testimonial evidence and credibility evidence. There are six broad themes across these two chapters.

First, we begin with an examination of the requirements for witness competence and compellability. The *UEA*, s 12, provides that everyone is competent and compellable to be a witness, meaning that everyone is both able to and can be required to testify. The provisions that follow, however, set exceptions to this general rule by establishing who lacks capacity to be a witness and who cannot be compelled to testify.

The next two themes in this and the next chapter are procedural in nature. Their dominant function is to promote independent testimony from witnesses. Typically, the parties who call witnesses know what evidence they can give to assist their case. For this reason, procedural rules attempt to prevent parties from putting words into 'friendly' witnesses' mouths. Thus, the rules seek to prevent questioning that might introduce the questioner's influence into a witness's account in court. The first of the two themes in this category arises where a party calls a witness. Accordingly, it deals with rules that apply to examination-in-chief and re-examination. Additionally, these rules address concerns that witnesses might be inclined to please parties who call them, and so assent to questions that hint at preferred answers.

Cross-examination is discussed in Chapter 6. Where a witness is questioned by another party (and so the questioning is cross-examination) the rules focus on the need to control questions that excessively or inappropriately battle or berate 'unfriendly' or 'unhelpful' witnesses. Here, procedural law is predominantly concerned with placing boundaries on cross-examiners' attacks on other parties' witnesses. The focus is on preventing 'improper'[1] questioning and ensuring witnesses are given an opportunity to explain themselves in various contexts.

The fourth broad theme in Chapters 5 and 6 regulates and limits parties' inclination to concentrate on witnesses' credibility, either by attempting to bolster it or erode it. Clearly, a witness's credibility may be crucial to weighing their evidence, but the rules seek to ensure the witness's testimony about the facts in

1 *UEA*, s 41.

issue is not over-shadowed by a questioner hijacking a trial through unnecessary duels that are not about the facts in issue and only remotely address the believability of witnesses. For this reason, where discrediting evidence is concerned, the rules seek to ensure that only evidence that is sufficiently robust is admitted in a trial. The rules also set limits on evidence, the sole purpose of which is to enhance the credibility of a witness.[2] Under the *UEA*, the focus is on 'credibility evidence' – that is, evidence that is adduced because it is relevant and admissible *solely* for the purpose of 'assessing the credibility[3] of the witness or person'.[4] That is, it is not directly relevant and admissible to facts in issue.

It may come before the court either through witness questioning or by other means (such as through the contents of a document or by calling another witness). The major complexities of credibility evidence are discussed in the first half of the next chapter because cross-examination is where the key credibility pressure points arise. Cross-examination of the accused is a particularly sensitive issue, and our fifth theme addresses the special rules that relate to cross-examination of the accused on matters pertaining solely to credibility. This is in Chapter 6.

Finally, there are two procedural issues not discussed previously that relate to fairness of process. At the end of this chapter we look briefly at the first of these, which is the prosecution's obligation to put its case fully at the commencement of the trial; that is, not to re-open its case with evidence that – as a matter of fairness to the defence – should have been part of its case in chief and not introduced after the defence case has closed: *Chin*'s case.[5] The second procedural issue, known as the rule in *Browne v Dunn*,[6] concludes Chapter 6. This rule requires all parties to 'put' (that is, question) witnesses on all matters that the party ultimately wishes to rely on in its case. Witnesses (and parties) should be given the opportunity, through such questions being asked in court, to answer any allegations against them that are part of an opposing case: for example, that the witness has lied, is mistaken, is biased, etc. The rule in *Browne v Dunn* sets this requirement. This rule is a principle of fair play to witnesses as well as to parties.

Getting the Witness in the Box

Competency and the witness

It is a fundamental rule of contemporary Australian trials that witnesses must be 'competent' to give *sworn* evidence.[7] Competency to testify is established by assessing witnesses' *capacity* to testify. In New Zealand it is referred to as 'eligibility' and there are *no* preconditions to eligibility.[8] Australia has, however,

---

2 By way of the credibility rule, see *UEA*, s 102.

3 Credibility 'includes the witness's ability to observe or remember facts and events about which the witness has given, is giving or is to give evidence': *UEA*, Dictionary (or for Tasmania, *Evidence Act 2001*, s 3, the definition section).

4 Defined by *UEA*, s 101A.

5 [1985] HCA 35; 157 CLR 671.

6 (1893) 6 R (HL) 67.

7 By oath or affirmation.

8 *Evidence Act 2006* (NZ), s 71(1): 'In a civil or criminal proceeding, ... (a) any person is eligible to give evidence ...'. Section 72 provides eligibility limitations for the presiding judge, jurors and counsel in proceedings.

hung onto competency requirements. They are relatively undemanding and, if a witness is not competent to give sworn evidence, they may nevertheless be able to give unsworn evidence. There appear to be no evidentiary implications where evidence is unsworn rather than sworn. For example, the High Court in *GW*[9] considered whether the jury should be directed in relation to the difference between sworn and unsworn evidence and the need to take that difference into account in assessing the reliability of unsworn evidence. The court concluded that neither the *UEA* nor the common law requires such a direction. This being the case, it is arguable that it is time to reconsider the whole notion of competency and whether the New Zealand model might not set a sensible precedent for Australia, particularly because compliance with competency regimes can, on occasion, trip courts up on technicalities.[10]

The most likely category of prospective witnesses to have their competency challenged are young children or those with cognitive or severe communication incapacities. The capacity requirements can create a significant access-to-justice dilemma because these witnesses are often seeking to give evidence as prosecution witnesses regarding allegations they have made of sexual or other abuse. If they are unable to give evidence the prosecution case is substantially weakened – and may well fail altogether. Protecting such people, often the most vulnerable in the community to predatory violence, is a challenge for their family, for institutions, for policing and also for the criminal courts. There are levels of complexity that are sometimes beyond the strict rules of evidence and procedure. Consider the following account by Terese Henning:

> In July 2011, the South Australian Director of Public Prosecutions discontinued the prosecution of a bus driver alleged to have sexually abused a child with an intellectual disability. The prosecution formed the view that the child could not give reliable evidence and would not be able to withstand cross-examination. The accused was released. The complainant's parents were shocked and dismayed. So too were the wider community and parents of other children allegedly abused by the accused.
>
> Here we see as a primary driver of the decision not to prosecute, a negative assessment of the complainant's capacity to perform under cross-examination. He had apparently limited comprehension levels, which had clear implications for his ability to understand questions about the events in issue and, importantly, to deal with cross-examination and adhere to a credible account of those events. To the public the decision not to prosecute appeared to demonstrate that the criminal justice system was incapable of protecting children with mental impairments from sexual predation. Adapting the words of the Canadian Supreme Court in *R v Dai* [2012] SCC 5, [67] the decision suggests that the law permits violators to sexually abuse children with mental disabilities with near impunity. The apparent inability to prosecute jeopardizes one of the fundamental desiderata of the rule of law: that the law be enforceable. It also effectively immunizes an entire category of offenders from criminal responsibility for their acts and further marginalizes the already vulnerable victims of sexual predators. Without a realistic prospect of prosecution, they become fair game for those inclined to abuse.[11]

In earlier times competency was assessed through a person's ability to understand and swear to a Christian oath before they testified. For centuries people were required to take a Christian oath – and therefore they had to be Christians. It was not until the 17th century that the issue of oath-taking and non-Christians

9 [2016] HCA 6, 258 CLR 108.

10 See, eg, *SH* [2012] NSWCCA 7 and *Brooks* (1998) 44 NSWLR 121, and further below.

11 T Henning, 'Obtaining the Best Evidence from Children and Witnesses with Cognitive Impairments – "Plus ça Change" or Prospects New?' (2013) 37 *Criminal Law Journal* 155.

arose. As Weinberg[12] details, in *Robeley v Langston*[13] the courts first held that Jews were competent to take an oath and in 1744 *Omychund v Barker*[14] extended this competence

> to infidels[15] who believed in a God as the creator of the world and in future rewards and punishments based on present conduct. Thus persons of the Gentoo religion who gave evidence on commission in India, the form of oath consisting of the witness touching the feet and hands of the Brahmin or priests of the Gentoo sect, were accepted as capable of taking the oath. In addition, Quakers, who regarded all forms of oath as repugnant, were permitted to testify by means of a statutory affirmation as early as 1696.[16]

Weinberg's 1976 account of the law and practice relating to oaths and competency reveals the chaos that existed outside the mainstream in determining who could testify and what needed to be proved. He lists numerous instances showing the pretence and disarray often attaching in such circumstances. Weinberg's examples include an English case where Chinese witnesses were sworn by a ceremony involving breaking a saucer and reciting: 'You shall tell the truth and the whole truth; the saucer is cracked and if you do not tell the truth your soul will be cracked like the saucer'. The trial reportedly ended up with the last witness standing 'ankle deep in smashed crockery'.

> Other trials involving Chinese have required witnesses to write sacred characters on paper which was burnt, the witness stating that his soul would be similarly burnt if he swore falsely. An even more spectacular oath was said to occur when a Chinese witness cut the head off a rooster with a similar invocation. Snuffing out a candle is another variant.[17]

The significance of these 'oaths' is not their variety or strangeness, but, as Weinberg observed, that they bore 'no relationship at all to Chinese court procedure either before or after 1948, where no oath is used. They are merely rituals attaching to certain secret societies which have been adapted to the judicial procedure of Her Majesty's Courts of Justice'.[18] Further examples of indignities forced upon witnesses are listed by Weinberg. Nevertheless, religious conviction remained the defining element of competency right up until the late 20th century. One early exception, legislated in the colony of New South Wales in 1839 for Indigenous witnesses, reveals the hold of religion, albeit in this instance giving way to the perceived needs of the time. The *Aboriginals Competent Witnesses Act 1839* (NSW) provided for 'the more effectual prosecution of crimes and misdemeanours that the evidence of the Aboriginal Natives of the Colony of New South Wales should be receivable in all Courts of Criminal Jurisdiction', stating:

> [W]hereas they have not at present any distinct idea of religion or fixed belief in a future state of rewards and punishments and therefore cannot be admitted as competent witnesses in any Court of Law without the authority of the Legislature of the said Colony Be it enacted by the Governor of said Colony … [that they] shall be permitted to make an affirmation or declaration to tell the truth the whole truth and nothing but the truth or in such other form as may be approved of by the Court instead of taking an oath in

---

12 M Weinberg, 'The Law of Testimonial Oaths and Affirmations' (1976) 3 *Monash University Law Review* 25, 28.

13 (1668) 2 Keb 314; 84 ER 196.

14 (1744) 1 Atk 22; 26 ER 15.

15 [The term 'infidel' is used in this article in its secondary sense as referring to non-Christians. In *Omychund v Barker* the term was used in this manner.]

16 [7 & 8 Will c 34 s 1.]

17 Weinberg, above n 12, 31.

18 Ibid.

> any criminal proceedings that shall be instituted in said Colony and that the evidence so given shall be of so much weight only as corroborating circumstances may entitle it to.

Aside from such exceptional situations, witnesses whose competency was challenged before the reforms instituted by the *UEA* (and in some Australian jurisdictions, by other legislation) had to prove their competency by displaying an understanding of the consequences of breaching the testimonial oath (that is, showing 'a belief in God and an accompanying acknowledgment that an oath taken in the name of God had a binding effect on the witness's conscience').[19] The *UEA* changed this, though not radically.[20] The drafters of the Act resisted the strong dissent by the Chair of the Australian Law Reform Commission (ALRC) (and later High Court Justice, Michael Kirby) in its 1985 Interim Report *Evidence*.[21] This dissent had recommended the abolition of the oath with instead:

> [A] simple requirement that witnesses promise to tell the truth, coupled with a warning against false evidence:
>
> 'Question: Do you declare that the evidence you shall give to this Court shall be the truth'?
>
> Answer: I so declare.
>
> Question: Do you understand that, if you do not tell the truth, you may commit an offence and be punished?
>
> Answer: I do'.

Over a decade earlier, the English law reform body had also recommended the abolition of the oath,[22] indicating that it is 'a primitive verbal formula akin to a curse',[23] that adds nothing either for non-believers or for those with genuine religious conviction who are thus likely to tell the truth irrespective of the oath. These recommendations have fallen on deaf ears. As *UEA*, s 21, indicates unless a witness is merely producing a document or other object, an oath or an affirmation remains a prerequisite for testifying.[24] At least now religious conviction is an optional extra. The text for these forms of acknowledgement[25] is contained in the *UEA*:

> I swear (or the person taking the oath may promise) by Almighty God (or the person may name a god recognised by his or her religion) that the evidence I shall give will be the truth, the whole truth and nothing but the truth. …
>
> I solemnly and sincerely declare and affirm that the evidence I shall give will be the truth, the whole truth and nothing but the truth.[26]

In addition (except for the Commonwealth Act), *UEA*, s 24A, provides an alternative oath:

> **24A. Alternative oath**
>
> (1) A person may take an oath even if the person's religious or spiritual beliefs do not include a belief in the existence of a god.

19 Applying *Brasier* [1730] EngR 38; 168 ER 202; 1 Leach 199 (as described by the court in *WG* [2010] VSCA 34, [34] (citations omitted)).

20 *UEA*, s 16, excludes judges and jurors from being competent to testify in current proceedings (though a juror is competent to give evidence in the proceeding about matters affecting conduct of the proceeding). See Chapter 1 regarding competence of the criminal defendant.

21 ALRC, *Evidence (Interim)* (Report No 26, 1985), [576] (citations omitted).

22 Eleventh Report of the Criminal Law Revision Committee, *Evidence (General)* (Cmnd 4991, 1972), 163ff.

23 Weinberg, above n 12, 39.

24 That is, not for unsworn evidence (see *UEA*, s 13).

25 And regarding the relationship between these texts and the *Oaths Act 1900* (NSW), see *Micar Group Pty Ltd v Insul-Trade LLC* [2010] NSWSC 1391.

26 *UEA*, Sch 1.

(2) Despite anything to the contrary in this Act, the form of oath taken by a person:
(a) need not include a reference to a god, and
(b) may instead refer to the basis of the person's beliefs in accordance with a form prescribed by the regulations.

All forms of swearing are of equal value in the eyes of the law, and issues of competency no longer rely on understanding the language of the oath (or affirmation) *per se*. One can accept that the expression of a formal statement may focus a witness's attention on the importance of the occasion (as will court ritual, architecture and the garb of counsel and judge). The old law detailed above remains significant in explaining the continued reliance on the terminology of 'sworn' and 'unsworn' evidence, and the continuing references to bibles when assessing competency. However, if there was doubt, *GW*[27] indicates that archaic assumptions about the power of the oath are dead:

> 51. … [T]he jury observed witnesses giving evidence on oath or affirmation as the case may be and may be taken to have heard those witnesses undertake to tell the truth, the whole truth and nothing but the truth. By contrast, the jury did not see R take an oath or make an affirmation before giving her evidence. It strains credulity to suggest that in order to avoid the risk of a miscarriage of justice it was necessary to instruct the jury that R's evidence had been received without the solemnity of an oath or affirmation or the possibility of sanction should it be intentionally false. It might be thought unlikely that it would occur to jurors to think a six-year-old child was at risk of prosecution for perjury regardless of whether the child's evidence was taken on oath or otherwise. …
>
> 56. The Evidence Act does not treat unsworn evidence as of a kind that may be unreliable. Had a direction been requested under s 165(2), there was no requirement to warn the jury that R's evidence may be unreliable because it was unsworn. Nor was there a requirement under the common law to warn the jury of the need for caution in accepting R's evidence and in assessing the weight to be given to it because it was unsworn. Nor was there a requirement under common law, falling short of a warning of that kind, to direct the jury to take into account the differences between sworn and unsworn evidence in assessing the reliability of R's evidence.

Earlier in the judgment, observations were made about the requirements of competency under the *UEA*.

> 43. Section 12 provides that every person is competent to give evidence subject to any other provision of the Evidence Act. Section 13 makes other provision in sub-ss (1) and (2). Section 13 distinguishes competence to give sworn evidence from competence to give unsworn evidence (sub-ss (3) and (4)). Competence to give sworn evidence is presumed, subject to the contrary being proved (sub-s (6)). This presumption is the only respect in which the Evidence Act may be said to give "primacy" to sworn evidence; the evidence of a competent witness will be given sworn unless the presumption is displaced. Where the presumption applies, s 21(1) requires a witness in a proceeding to take an oath or make an affirmation before giving evidence. The form of the oath and the affirmation are set out in Sched 1 to the Evidence Act. In each case, the person undertakes that the evidence to be given "will be the truth, the whole truth and nothing but the truth". An oath requires the person to give that undertaking by swearing to do so by Almighty God or the god recognised by the person's religion. An affirmation requires the person to give that undertaking by a solemn and sincere declaration to do so. Section 21(5) provides that an affirmation has the same effect for all purposes as an oath. Where the presumption of competence to give sworn evidence is displaced, s 21(2) relieves the witness of the requirement to take an oath or make an affirmation. In either case, the evidence of the witness is before the court. The assessment of the reliability of the evidence is for the

27 [2016] HCA 6; 258 CLR 108 (French CJ, Bell, Gageler, Keane and Nettle JJ).

> trier of fact. Sections 12, 13(3), (4) and (6) and 21 do not support a conclusion that the Evidence Act accords primacy to sworn evidence as a bolster to the reliability of evidence.

As the above observation from *GW* makes clear, *UEA*, s 12 makes competency of all witnesses the default position, unless challenged. In a nutshell, and as described by the High Court in *GW*, a case concerning six-year-old R's competence to give sworn evidence:

> [C]ompetence to give evidence about a fact is confined to the person's capacity to understand a question about the fact and to give an intelligible answer to the question. It is only competence to give sworn evidence that requires the person to have the capacity to understand that, in giving evidence, he or she is under an obligation to give truthful evidence.[28]

Witnesses challenged for their competency must meet the relatively undemanding standards set by *UEA*, s 13.[29] In *UEA* jurisdictions a witness who is to give sworn evidence must satisfy s 13(1) and (3) relating to their capacity to understand and communicate answers to questions and, in this context, understand the obligation to give truthful evidence. As the language of this section is crucial, it bears close examination.

> **13 Competence: lack of capacity**
>
> (1) A person is not competent to give evidence about a fact if, for any reason (including a mental, intellectual or physical disability):
>
> (a) the person does not have the *capacity to understand a question about the fact*, or
>
> (b) the person does not have the *capacity to give an answer that can be understood to a question about the fact* –
>
> *and that incapacity cannot be overcome.*
>
> (2) A person who, because of subsection (1), is not competent to give evidence about a fact may be competent to give evidence about other facts.
>
> (3) A person who is competent to give evidence about a fact is not competent to give sworn evidence about the fact *if the person does not have the capacity to understand that, in giving evidence, he or she is under an obligation to give truthful evidence.*
>
> (4) A person who is not competent to give sworn evidence about a fact *may*, subject to subsection (5), be competent to give unsworn evidence about the fact.
>
> (5) A person who, because of subsection (3), is not competent to give sworn evidence *is* competent to give unsworn evidence if the court has told the person:
>
> (a) that it is important to tell the truth, and
>
> (b) that he or she may be asked questions that he or she does not know, or cannot remember, the answer to, and that he or she should tell the court if this occurs, and
>
> (c) that he or she may be asked questions that suggest certain statements are true or untrue and that he or she should agree with the statements that he or she believes are true and should feel no pressure to agree with statements that he or she believes are untrue.[30]
>
> (6) It is presumed, unless the contrary is proved, that a person is not incompetent because of this section.

It is important to appreciate that a prospective witness will only lack competency if he or she 'does not have the *capacity to understand a question* about the fact'

28 Ibid [13] (French CJ, Bell, Gageler, Keane and Nettle JJ).

29 The current version is a revision of the cognitive competency requirements introduced in the original Act.

30 Emphasis added. See also the note to this section: 'See sections 30 and 31 for examples of assistance that may be provided to enable witnesses to overcome disabilities'.

or he or she 'does not have the *capacity to give an answer* that can be understood to a question about the fact' and that incapacity cannot be overcome. As sub-s (2) indicates, competency might be fact-specific. A prospective witness might be able to speak about *a* fact, even though not other facts. To give **sworn evidence** the person must satisfy sub-s (1) and, additionally, must '*have the capacity to understand that, in giving evidence, he or she is under an obligation to give truthful evidence*': sub-s (3). Even if a witness is capable of giving sworn evidence, s 14 indicates that the obligation to give evidence can be dispensed with by a court where practical considerations impact on achieving the requirements of s 13(1) and the witness is not indispensable because there are other sources of evidence.

By virtue of sub-s (4) it is possible for a witness to give **unsworn evidence** if they satisfy sub-s (1) requirements, but not the sub-s (3) requirements for sworn evidence, and the judge explains the expectations as listed in sub-s (5).[31] Despite the use of the word 'may' in sub-s (4), the judge has no discretionary power to refuse to allow a child to give unsworn evidence if the court is satisfied about the child's capacity to understand a question and give a comprehensible answer under sub-s (1).[32]

With regard to sub-s (5), as Dowsett J put it in *Muller*:[33]

> 41. … Section 13(5) requires only that the directions be given, and not that they be understood or even acknowledged. …
>
> 43. Competence to give unsworn evidence depends upon:
>
> - the potential witness not being incompetent pursuant to s 13(1);
> - the witness being incompetent to give sworn evidence pursuant to s 13(3); and
> - the judge having performed the functions prescribed by s 13(5).
>
> 44. Although it may be appropriate to ask questions in order to determine whether any further explanation is necessary, testing of the potential witness's understanding of the judge's directions is not part of the process prescribed by s 13(5). No particular level of understanding is required as a condition of admissibility, always assuming that ss 13(1) and 13(3) have been satisfied.

In other words, as long as the baseline standard in sub-s (1) is satisfied, the light demands of sub-s (5) need only be met for the witness to give unsworn evidence. It may be good judicial practice 'for a judge to try to ensure that the proposed witness has understood the directions given under s 13(5)' as long as questioning is appropriate to the capacity of the prospective witness[34] *and* it is recognised that the answer is not decisive of compliance with sub-s (5) in any way. In other words, an '*I don't know*' reply to the question, '*What do you understand by me telling you that it is important to tell the truth?*', is irrelevant to satisfying sub-s (5).[35]

In all, s 13 demands very little of a witness. For example, in *ABR (a Pseudonym)*[36] the complainant, aged approximately eight or nine years old, gave

31 He or she does not need to establish that the explanation is understood.

32 *SH* [2012] NSWCCA 79; 83 NSWLR 258, [8], [9] (Basten JA); *Muller* [2013] ACTCA 15, [41] (Dowsett J).

33 [2013] ACTCA 15. His Honour also made observations regarding the sensitivities of complying with *UEA*, ss 165 and 165A, and the danger that these provisions might be compromised (or might themselves truncate) a trial judge explaining the concepts in s 13 in a jury's presence (or this is occurring by way of a pre-recorded conversation).

34 *Muller* [2013] ACTCA 15, [3].

35 Ibid [45]-[46].

36 [2020] NSWCCA 33.

sworn evidence after the trial judge questioned her and was satisfied that she had a 'clear understanding' of the difference between the truth and a lie and her obligation to give truthful evidence. The Court of Criminal Appeal held at [103] that 'for the complainant to give sworn evidence, his Honour needed to be satisfied on the balance of probabilities that the presumption under *Evidence Act*, s 13(6), that she was competent to give sworn evidence was not displaced by her answers to his questions'. Further, 'the totality of the lengthy exchange between the trial judge and the complainant indicates that she understood that a lie means saying something that "did not happen". The complainant also clearly understood that she was under an obligation to tell the truth when giving evidence. Thus, it was open to the trial judge to be satisfied ...'. The questioning included the following exchange between the trial judge and the complainant:

> Q. What I want to ask you is do you know what telling a lie is?
> A. Being bad. ...
> Q. If I said that I was wearing a top with a red sash, would that be true?
> A. Yes.
> Q. Can you see a red sash on me? The red—
> A. I don't know what a sash is.[37]

The court in *ABR* applied the High Court decision in *GW*,[38] rejecting an insistence on a formulistic approach to applying s 13,[39] holding that whilst the trial judge's conclusion as to the child's competency to give sworn evidence was not expressed 'in the terms of the statute' it did not follow that his Honour had not complied with the *substance* of the provision.[40] As the Act provides through s 13(8)[41] for a court determining competency to 'inform itself as it thinks fit', there is a strong case for reliance on an expert[42] (such as a psychologist) or someone with special understanding of the witness (such as a parent or carer), particularly where gaining a rapport with a child is challenging.

In other cases, the problem for trial judges lies in a simple mis-reading of s 13, an assumption that some part of the previous law (typically the common law) remains, or just misunderstanding what competency assessment actually means.[43]

A mis-conceived competency test may be fatal to proceedings because child sexual assault prosecutions rely on the complainant to testify.[44] Their evidence

---

37 Ibid [104] (Meagher JA, with Bellew and Lonergan JJ agreeing).

38 [2016] HCA 6; 258 CLR 108.

39 Though presumably not if there is a failure to apply a requirement of s 13; see, eg, *SH* [2012] NSWCCA 79; 83 NSWLR 258 where the conviction was set aside because the trial judge failed to inform the witness she 'should feel no pressure to agree' (sub s (5)(c)). But see also *MK* [2014] NSWCCA 274; *RAG* [2006] NSWCCA 343; *RJ* [2010] NSWCCA 263; *Muller* [2013] ACTCA 15 (where the trial judge (wrongly) asked the child complainant, in consideration of sub-s (3)); *Brooks* (1998) 44 NSWLR 121; *J and AP* [2012] SASCFC 95; *Cooper* [2007] ACTSC 74.

40 *GW* [2016] HCA 6; 258 CLR 108, 123.

41 *UEA*, s 13(8): 'For the purpose of determining a question arising under this section, the court may inform itself as it thinks fit, including by obtaining information from a person who has relevant specialised knowledge based on the person's training, study or experience'.

42 That is, a 'person who has relevant specialised knowledge based on the person's training, study or experience'.

43 *RAG* [2006] NSWCCA 343.

44 This no doubt explains why legislative provision for a competence test to give unsworn evidence first arose in cases of child rape. See M Harris and G Urbas, 'Children's Unsworn Evidence: Historical Developments and Contemporary Issues' (2017) 40 *UNSW Law Journal* 1392.

is central to the prosecution case. Latham J in *RAG*,[45] quoting Parkinson,[46] noted that the administration of competency testing is a particular challenge:

> Young children do not understand abstract concepts, and questions need to be asked which avoid ambiguities and abstractions. Even the word "truth" is ambiguous. Its double meaning is revealed by examining its opposites – a falsehood and a lie. One may make a false statement without intending to deceive. Thus, for a young child, the notion of a lie is more concrete than the notion of truth, and the child's declaration … is consequently framed in the negative: "I will not tell lies".
>
> The manner in which a competency test is administered may thus affect the way in which a child's ability to distinguish between the truth and a lie is perceived. Furthermore, if a child responds in the affirmative to the question, "do you understand the difference between the truth and a lie?", it does not necessarily mean that the child does understand it. The child need only answer "yes" and the court will be little the wiser. On the other hand, if the child is asked, "what is the truth?" or "what is a lie?" a competent child witness may still not be able to give a satisfactory answer. Such a question asks for a definition. A young child's ability to distinguish between the truth and a lie may be much greater than his or her ability to define that distinction. A young child cannot be expected to explain an abstract concept.

There is growing recognition of the need to reconsider accepted judicial practice for testing the competency of child witnesses. The Royal Commission into Institutional Responses to Child Sexual Abuse (RCIRCSA) has recommended that 'where there is any doubt about a child's competence to give evidence, a judge should establish the child's ability to understand basic questions asked of them by asking simple, non-theoretical questions'.[47] This recommendation echoes Latham J's comments in *RAG* above, that abstract concepts, multi-faceted questions, legal jargon, double-negatives and passive speech should all be avoided when assessing competency.[48]

Given the centrality of cross-examination to testing the unreliability of witness testimony in the modern criminal trial, the dubious benefits of competency-testing of children based on truth/lie understandings (such as required in s 13(3)),[49] and the price of quashed convictions for non-compliance with s 13, the

45 [2006] NSWCCA 343, [44].

46 P Parkinson, 'The Future of Competency Testing for Child Witnesses' (1991) 15 *Criminal Law Journal* 186.

47 RCIRCSA, *Criminal Justice Report* (Executive Summary and Parts I-II, August 2017), recommendation 62. This recommendation draws on research commissioned by the Royal Commission citing academic literature suggesting that 'testing whether a child knows the difference between a truth and a lie (the difference type) is not a good indicator of whether a child will tell the truth in their evidence': RCIRCSA, *Criminal Justice Consultation Paper* (September 2016), 364.

48 [2006] NSWCCA 343, [26], citing J Cashmore, 'Problems and Solutions in Lawyer-Child Communication' (1991) 15 *Criminal Law Journal* 193. See also *Gray* [2020] NSWCCA 240 (Lonergan J, with Hoeben CJ at CL and Johnson J agreeing), concerning the witness Jane, a six-year-old girl who had been diagnosed with autism spectrum disorder and a hearing impairment. The judgment details (i) the danger of conflating competency requirements and a witness's needs under s 41 (regarding a witness finding some questions confusing); (ii) the extensive questioning to assess Jane's competence to give sworn evidence (at [43]-[51]) and the ruling that Jane was competent to give unsworn evidence (at [64]); (iii) in relation to the issue of Jane's competence and the associated s 13 inquiry, the benefits of the Witness Intermediary Assessment Report (at [52]-[59]); and (iv) the failure to proceed without a witness intermediary created an unfairness (to 'Jane') but the extent to which Jane's evidence was unreliable was an issue for the jury, not a competence one.

49 See AD Evans and TD Lyon, 'Assessing Children's Competency to take the Oath in Court: The Influence of Question Type on Children's Accuracy' (2012) 36 *Law & Human Behavior* 195.

New Zealand approach of abolishing competency requirements for witnesses[50] has much merit.[51]

Compellability and the witness

Section 12 of the *UEA* deals with the compellability of competent witnesses and creates a presumption that they are compellable. As mentioned, s 14 allows for a relaxation of compellability stipulations for witnesses of 'reduced capacity' who need assistance to meet the standards of s 13 and where the *cost or delay* in meeting with a witness's requirements is substantial and adequate evidence from another source is available.

A complex situation can arise where the spouse, de facto partner, parent or child of an accused does not wish to give evidence as a witness for the prosecution. Family relationships may be destroyed by compelling such a witness and a judicial discretion exists in certain circumstances[52] to permit a witness to decline to testify. Where a potential witness has one of the above familial relationships with the accused, s 18 permits a court to weigh up the desirability of hearing the witness's evidence over his or her objection to testifying against the likelihood of harm to the relationship with the accused or personal harm (for example, caused by distress). The reason for this exemption relates to the clear public benefit of maintaining family relationships and recognition that the accused is presumed innocent.

> **18. Compellability of spouses and others in criminal proceedings generally**
> (1) This section applies only in a criminal proceeding.
> (2) A person who, when required to give evidence, is the spouse, de facto partner, parent or child of a defendant may object to being required:
> (a) to give evidence, or
> (b) to give evidence of a communication between the person and the defendant,
> as a witness for the prosecution.
> (3) The objection is to be made before the person gives the evidence or as soon as practicable after the person becomes aware of the right so to object, whichever is the later.
> (4) If it appears to the court that a person may have a right to make an objection under this section, the court is to satisfy itself that the person is aware of the effect of this section as it may apply to the person.
> (5) If there is a jury, the court is to hear and determine any objection under this section in the absence of the jury.
> (6) A person who makes an objection under this section to giving evidence or giving evidence of a communication must not be required to give the evidence if the court finds that:
> (a) there is a likelihood that harm would or might be caused (whether directly or indirectly) to the person, or to the relationship between the person and the defendant, if the person gives the evidence, and
> (b) the nature and extent of that harm outweighs the desirability of having the evidence given.

50 That is, subject to *Evidence Act 2006* (NZ), s 72 (judges, jurors and counsel in current proceedings).
51 With respect to children's evidence, trial judges can, at the request of a party, inform the jury that the evidence of the particular child may be unreliable and the reasons why it may be unreliable. See, generally, Chapter 14. Importantly, a reliability warning must be justified with regard to factors relating to the particular child and must not suggest that children as a class are unreliable witnesses, or require increased scrutiny, or that corroborative evidence is needed to support their evidence.
52 That is, excepting offences within *UEA*, s 19.

(7) Without limiting the matters that may be taken into account by the court for the purposes of subsection (6), it must take into account the following:

(a) the nature and gravity of the offence for which the defendant is being prosecuted,

(b) the substance and importance of any evidence that the person might give and the weight that is likely to be attached to it,

(c) whether any other evidence concerning the matters to which the evidence of the person would relate is reasonably available to the prosecutor,

(d) the nature of the relationship between the defendant and the person,

(e) whether, in giving the evidence, the person would have to disclose matter that was received by the person in confidence from the defendant.

(8) If an objection under this section has been determined, the prosecutor may not comment on:

(a) the objection, or

(b) the decision of the court in relation to the objection, or

(c) the failure of the person to give evidence.

The NSW District Court case of *BO*[53] illustrates the challenging situations that exist, even allowing for the exemptions created by s 19, discussed below. In that case BO was charged with the manslaughter of his partner's baby. The prosecution wanted to call BO's sons who had left the house on the morning of the baby's death and could give evidence that the child was unharmed. The prosecution wanted to call the boys to establish a clear rebuttal of any defence suggestion that one of them was responsible for the baby's injuries. This possibility, it was indicated, had arisen in intercepts of BO's telephone conversations. Haesler DCJ ruled that the potential for harm to the children outweighed the desirability of having the boys' evidence before the court.[54]

In contrast, in *A2, KM and Vaziri (No 4)*[55] concerning a prosecution for female genital mutilation offences, Johnson J declined an application under s 18 by the two complainants, daughters of one of the accused. In ruling that the girls were compellable as witnesses for the prosecution his Honour noted the importance of their evidence in the case, the fact that their physical integrity had been compromised by the criminal acts of their mother and that the manner in which their evidence would be given would limit substantially the risk of harm to their relationship with her.[56]

A particular deficiency in s 18, noted in the ALRC report, *Recognition of Aboriginal Customary Laws*, is that Aboriginal communities typically embrace a broader sense of family than the list of relationships in s 18 and (for example) 'it

53 [2012] NSWDC 195.

54 The extent to which the loss of prosecution evidence might be addressed through reliance on witness statements (in *BO*, the boys' statements to police) is a determination that involves the rule against hearsay exception (*UEA*, s 65). In *DPP v Nicholls* [2010] VSC 397, Beach J held in favour of applying the exception. In *BO*, Haesler DCJ considered the requirements of s 18(6) would continue to apply to such statements.

55 [2015] NSWSC 1306.

56 In *Jurd* [2020] NSWCCA 91, Ms Best, the de facto partner of the accused, was not informed of her rights under s 18 until the day after she commenced giving evidence when the error was revealed. The judge took evidence on a voir dire, ruling that any harm to the relationship was more likely to flow from Ms Best's police statement as her testimony threw doubt on that statement; and, while she was clearly stressed testifying, there was no evidence of such stress having long term impact. In considering the appeal against conviction, Price J noted that defence counsel's failure to bring the s 18 issue to the trial judge's attention might have been a forensic choice based on the view that her police statement (admissible under *UEA*, s 65, should she be unavailable) might have been more damaging than her testimony. Held, no procedural unfairness to the accused.

may be more important not to compel a mother-in-law to give evidence about her son-in-law' than some of the relationships now privileged in s 18.[57]

It is important to note that s 19 of the *UEA* overrides the discretion in s 18 for the offences listed there and that all *UEA* jurisdictions other than Victoria include a list of offences in s 19 for which the s 18 discretion cannot apply. The terms of s 19 vary in each jurisdiction. They essentially relate to offences of a sexual or non-sexual violent nature against family members and their impact is to compel family members to testify. In New South Wales, s 19 avoids the application of s 18 for specified domestic violence, child abuse or child endangerment prosecutions, referring to *Children and Young Persons (Care and Protection) Act 1998* (NSW), ss 222, 223, 227, 228, and to *Criminal Procedure Act 1986* (NSW) (*CPA* (NSW)), s 279. In the case of *LS v DPP (NSW)*,[58] s 19 of the *UEA* applied to override s 18. The defendant was the 15-year-old son of the witness who objected to testifying in relation to an offence of property damage (relating to the witness's house). Victoria determined to not include exceptions to s 18.[59]

The Witness in the Box

There is a lot that can be (and should be) considered in relation to the witness who is required to give evidence. Self-evidently, it is likely to be a stressful experience for many people. Some witnesses, such as very young children or adults with cognitive impairment, may find the process tests their capacities to the limit.

Witness support: children and the cognitively impaired

For children, as Henning notes: 'Article 12 of the UN Convention on the Rights of the Child (1989) places an obligation on courts to create the optimum circumstances in which a child as witness is free to give his or her account of events'.[60] This is achieved by 'special measures'[61] for children and other vulnerable witnesses.[62] Before we study the procedural limitations placed on examination-in-chief, it is useful to consider the special situation pertaining to children's evidence.

57 ALRC, *Recognition of Aboriginal Customary Laws* (Report No 31, 1986), [134], Submission 491 (16 September 1985), 4-5.

58 [2011] NSWSC 1016; 81 NSWLR 551.

59 See Victorian Law Reform Commission (VLRC), *Implementing the Uniform Evidence Act* (Report, 2006), [2.27]-[2.38].

60 Henning, above n 11, quoting from the Bar of England and Wales, Submission to the European Commission, *Consultation on the European Commission Communication on the Rights of the Child 2011-2014*, <http://ec.europa.eu/justice/news/consulting_public/0009/contributions/unregistered_organisations/127_bar_council_england_wales_sept10.pdf>, 2. See to the same effect Article 13 of the United Nations *Convention on the Rights of Persons with Disabilities*.

61 Special measures most commonly enable children to give their evidence via closed circuit television (CCTV) and/or by pre-recorded video statements, to be screened in court from the defendant and to have support persons with them while they are testifying: Henning, above n 11.

62 All States in Australia provide protection for vulnerable witnesses. In New South Wales child witnesses' examination-in-chief can be by way of pre-recorded interview to police; they can respond to cross-examination by CCTV connection to a remote room; they can have a support person with them; and if, for any reason, the trial is aborted after they have given evidence, the transcript (or recording) of their original evidence given in cross-examination can be used in a subsequent trial rather than requiring them to submit to the process again. See, eg, *Crimes Act 1914* (Cth), Pt 1AD; *CPA* (NSW), Pt 6, Div 1; *Evidence Act 1977* (Qld), ss 21A-21AZC; *Evidence Act 1929* (SA), ss 13A-13D; *Evidence (Children and Special Witnesses) Act 2001* (Tas), s 5; *Criminal Procedure Act 2009* (Vic), ss 366 and 369; *Evidence Act 1906* (WA), s 106H. In

Processes relating to child witnesses was a topic of significant reflection in the ALRC review of the *UEA* in 2005. The common law view that children are unreliable witnesses prone to fantasy and fabrication has been discredited, with research indicating that children's cognitive and recall skills are not inherently less reliable than that of adults.[63] The *Seen and Heard: Priority for Children in the Legal Process* Report, as quoted by the ALRC Report on *Uniform Evidence Law*,[64] observed that research

> into children's memory and the sociology and psychology of disclosing remembered events has established that children's cognitive and recall skills have been undervalued ... The presumed gulf between the reliability of evidence from children and that from adults appears to have been exaggerated ... Children, including very young children, are able to remember and retrieve from memory large amounts of information, especially when the events are personally experienced and highly meaningful.[65]

The ALRC *Uniform Evidence Law* Report added in light of this observation:

> 18.57 The Report emphasised that the reliability of an individual child's memories and perceptions, both at the time of initial questioning and at a later date, is likely to be influenced by factors such as the manner and context in which the child is questioned. It noted that the use of misleading and suggestive questioning techniques adversely affects the ability of young children to recall events accurately, and that the most effective way of eliciting accurate and more detailed information is through the use of non-leading cues. The Report also found that younger children may have difficulties when questioned about particular times and dates, and hence may be unable to recount events in chronological order, but that this has no bearing on the accuracy of the description of the events reported. ...

Children have special vulnerabilities. Some of these issues were mentioned in relation to competence-testing above. Compared to adults, children are more likely to recant an allegation or to deny allegations falsely where they are fearful or placed under pressure. '[T]o avoid punishment, to keep promises not to tell or to avoid revealing embarrassing information, most children will deny knowing information about an event that they know occurred.'[66] All jurisdictions in Australia have enacted 'special measures' which enable children and other vulnerable witnesses to give their evidence via closed circuit television (CCTV), to be screened in court from the defendant and to have support persons with them while they are testifying.[67] For example, in New South Wales, when testifying in criminal proceedings children and witnesses (including complainants and defendants) with cognitive impairments[68] are entitled to have a support person with

---

New South Wales (and some other jurisdictions) there are also restrictions on unrepresented defendants personally cross-examining specified witnesses: Henning, above n 11.

63 ALRC, *Uniform Evidence Law* (Report No 102, 2006), [18.55], and see *Seen and Heard: Priority for Children in the Legal Process* (ALRC No 84, 1997), [14.19]-[14.20].

64 ALRC, *Uniform Evidence Law*, ibid, [18.56] (some citations omitted).

65 [See ALRC, *Seen and Heard*, above n 63, [14.19]-[14.20].]

66 Ibid [14.23].

67 See Henning, above n 11, and *Evidence (Children and Special Witnesses) Act 2001* (Tas), s 5; *Evidence Act 1906* (WA), s 106H; *CPA* (NSW), Pt 6, Div 1; *Criminal Procedure Act 2009* (Vic), ss 360-365, 366-368A; *Evidence Act 1929* (SA), ss 13A-13D; *Crimes Act 1914* (Cth), Pt 1AD; *Evidence Act 1977* (Qld), ss 21A-21AZC. In some jurisdictions, there are also restrictions on unrepresented defendants personally cross-examining specified witnesses.

68 That is, 'vulnerable persons' (a child or a cognitively impaired person (*CPA* (NSW), s 306M(1)), and includes for criminal proceedings and AVO proceedings a person 16 years or over but under the age of 18 years: see *CPA* (NSW), s 306ZK(2) and (6), (7). For complainants, see *CPA* (NSW), s 294C(7).

them who may act as an interpreter and assist them to give evidence. Further, in any criminal proceedings, any witness who has difficulty communicating[69] may use a person who may assist him or her to do so, but only if the witness *ordinarily receives such assistance on a daily basis*. While this is a significant restriction on the operation of this provision, it does mean that the assistance could potentially be provided by a family member. Additionally, there does not appear to be any reason why this provision should not apply to defendants.

In all Australian jurisdictions there is the potential for courts to give advance direction at pre-trial directions hearings in relation to the style and nature of questioning during cross-examination of witnesses. This power might reside in the inherent jurisdiction of the court or be supplemented by statutory rules and provisions.[70] Western Australia, Tasmania, Victoria, New South Wales, South Australia, Queensland, the Northern Territory and the ACT have also enacted legislation that enables the totality of *particular* witnesses' testimony to be pre-recorded in the absence of the jury and replayed at trial.[71]

The difficulties facing children and people with cognitive impairments when giving evidence was the focus of a number of recommendations made by the RCIRCSA.[72] The Commissioners recommended the establishment of intermediary schemes in each State and Territory, based on the model in England and Wales.[73] Intermediaries provide assistance at trial and may also be involved in the investigative and pre-trial stages of the criminal justice process. Intermediary schemes are currently in the forefront in trying to ameliorate the problems faced by people with communication needs when involved in the criminal justice system both in Australia and overseas.[74] Progress in this respect is discussed below. In broad terms, legislated special measures for vulnerable witnesses target comprehension and communication difficulties faced by children and witnesses with cognitive and mental impairments. They include:

- preventing the use of inappropriate language and forms of communication in cross-examination;
- structured pre-trial assistance for counsel preparing topics and questions for cross-examination including advice and/or 'ground rules' for cross-examination;

69 *CPA* (NSW), s 275B.

70 See, eg, *UEA*, s 192A: *Criminal Procedure Act 2009* (Vic), ss 179, 181 and 199; *Evidence Act 1977* (Qld), s 21AX; *Criminal Code* (Qld), s 590AA; *Justices Act 1886* (Qld), s 83A; *Justices Act* (NT), s 201A; *Supreme Court Rules* (NT), r 81A.18; *CPA* (NSW), ss 130, 136, 139, 140, 247D, 247G and 247H; *District Court Rules 1973* (NSW), rr 53.10 and 53.11; *Criminal Procedure Act 2004* (WA), ss 64 and 98; *Criminal Law Consolidation Act 1935* (SA), s 285A; *Criminal Code* (Tas), s 361A; *Criminal Rules 2006* (Tas), Pt 1A.

71 *Evidence Act 1929* (SA), ss 12AB and 13A; *Evidence Act 1977* (Qld), ss 21A, 21AI-21AO; *Criminal Procedure Act 2009* (Vic), Pt 8.2, Div 6; *Evidence Act 1906* (WA), s 106HB; *Evidence (Miscellaneous Provisions) Act 1991* (ACT), Div 4.2B; *Evidence Act 1939* (NT), s 21E; *Evidence (Children and Special Witnesses) Act 2001* (Tas), ss 6 and 6A; *CPA* (NSW), Sch 2, Pt 29, cls 84-87. This was recommended by RCIRCSA, *Criminal Justice Report*, above n 47, recommendation 53.

72 See RCIRCSA, *Criminal Justice Report*, above n 47, recommendations 52-3.

73 Ibid recommendation 59.

74 See Henning, above n 11; P Bowden, D Plater and T Henning, 'Balancing Fairness to Victims, Society and Defendants; Cross-Examination of Vulnerable Witnesses: an Impossible Triangulation?' (2014) 37 *Melbourne University Law Review* 539 for detailed discussion of and further references relating to this proposition. England and Wales have an established 'Registered Intermediary Scheme' which is influential in Australia. For example, the VLRC recommended the introduction of an intermediary scheme modelled on the UK scheme: VLRC, *The Role of Victims of Crime in the Criminal Trial Process* (Final Report, 2016), recommendations 30 and 31.

- pre-recording of witnesses' entire testimony in the absence of the jury to enable early capture of their evidence and to advance judicial control of questioning;
- obtaining the assistance, including advice from intermediaries, expert in communication to facilitate these witnesses' communication with the court.

Most Australian jurisdictions have legislated specifically for intermediary schemes[75] – the ACT, Western Australia,[76] Tasmania,[77] South Australia,[78] Queensland,[79] New South Wales and Victoria. The ACT scheme was introduced and commenced operation in January 2020. There are material differences in the scope of the different schemes (to whom they apply, at what point in the criminal justice process and in which cases) and in the roles assigned to intermediaries and in who can perform the role of an intermediary.

At the very least intermediaries/communication assistants should perform a pre-trial *advisory function* to judges, counsel and investigative agencies about the comprehension and communication capacities and the types and styles of

75 New South Wales and Victoria's schemes are discussed below. The Northern Territory Government has not yet responded to the RCIRCSA recommendation.

76 Applying to children and to witnesses with physical or mental impairments: *Evidence Act 1906* (WA), s 106F and s 106R respectively. Section 106F of the WA Act makes communication assistance available to *children in any proceedings*. Arguably, it applies to child witnesses and child defendants but the definitions in s 106A and the reference to 'affected child' in s 106R, which in turn relates back to s 106F, suggest that child defendants *may* be ineligible. Under s 106R(4)(b), those declared by courts to be 'special witnesses' *may* also be assisted by communicators when testifying. It is unclear whether this program extends to defendants – see Tasmania Law Reform Institute (TLRI), *Facilitating Equal Access to Justice: An Intermediary / Communication Assistant Scheme for Tasmania* (Final Report, No 23, 2018), see <https://nla.gov.au/nla.obj-591287678/view>, [4.2.37], discussing ss 106R(4b), 106F and 106A. See *WKS v Western Australia (No 4)* [2020] WASCA 178 where the court discusses this complex legislation. Note also that the existing scheme sits alongside a ground rules hearings initiative in the District Court for very young children, a precursor to an intermediary scheme as recommended by the RCIRCSA.

77 See *Evidence (Children and Special Witnesses) Act 2001* (Tas) Pt 2A, as inserted by *Evidence (Children and Special Witnesses) Amendment Act 2020*, s 9: Pt 2A commenced in March 2021. It applies to all children under the age of 18 and all adults with a communication need who are victims or witnesses in sexual offence matters and homicide matters. It does not apply to defendants. Intermediaries are allocated from an expert panel. The role of the intermediary is to prepare an assessment report and provide advice to the court in specified proceedings (including preliminary proceedings) about ways to facilitate the taking of evidence from the witness.

78 South Australia has the broadest application (people with 'complex communication needs' and 'vulnerable witnesses'), including defendants entitling them to communication assistance at investigative and trial stages and applies in all proceedings, to interactions with counsel and other criminal justice agencies. This State has a legislated scheme of 'communication partners', trained volunteers who assist at trial and pre-trial investigative stages: see *Statutes Amendment (Vulnerable Witnesses) Act 2015* (SA) ss 5, 9, 12. Intermediaries can give advice to police (*Summary Offences Regulations 2016* (SA) (regs 19 and 23 made under *Summary Offences Act 1953* (SA), s 74H); to courts (*Evidence Act 1929* (SA), s 13A(9)), providing for expert evidence to assist the court to determine the special arrangements that should be made for taking the evidence of the vulnerable witness; and to legal counsel (RCIRCSA Public Hearing – Case Study 46, Transcript Day 234, 23903). It is apparent that many agencies (partners including Child Protection Services, solicitors, the Legal Services Commission and members of legal teams) are able to request and use the assistance of communication, see RCIRCSA, above n 47, 23903. However, the breadth of its operation may be effectively curtailed due to funding cuts. The scheme moved to a fee-for-service model from early 2020.

79 The Queensland Government, in response to the RCIRCSA recommendation, has legislated to implement an intermediary scheme with features similar to the Tasmanian format: *Criminal Code (Child Sexual Offences Reform) and Other Legislation Amendment Act 2020* (Qld). For the ACT, see *Evidence (Miscellaneous Provisions) Amendment Act 2019* and *Victims Rights Legislation Amendment Act 2020*.

questioning that will optimise or detract from the ability of people with communication needs to give coherent accounts of events.[80] Such advice should address the level of sophistication and style of questioning appropriate for these witnesses. Where courts are concerned, expert intermediary advice may be provided at preliminary hearings to set the ground rules for the type and style of permissible questioning. In the absence of explicit provision, legislation dealing with directions hearings generally provides a potential basis for courts to obtain such advice pre-trial.[81]

The second primary function that intermediaries/communication assistants may serve is as *translators or quasi-interpreters*, explaining questions to those with communication needs and their answers to courts, counsel and the police.[82] Thirdly, intermediaries may be empowered to *intervene during questioning*. For example, in Victoria '[w]hen necessary and as directed by the Court, [intermediaries may] ... actively assist and intervene during questioning. The extent to which they do so (if at all) depends on factors such as the communication needs of the witness, and the skill of counsel in adapting their language and questioning style to meet those needs'[83] to alert courts and the police to questioning that does not match the communication capacities of witnesses with communication needs. This support is facilitated during trial questioning by pre-recording of witnesses' testimony (because it is possible to edit the recording before it is played to the jury).

Intermediary schemes: New South Wales and Victoria

The schemes in New South Wales and Victoria both began as pilot schemes. The Victorian pilot was planned to operate from mid-2018 to mid-2020, now extended beyond this date. The New South Wales pilot commenced operation in early 2016

---

80 *Multi-Jurisdictional Court Guide for the Intermediary Pilot Program: Intermediaries and Ground Rules Hearings* (Victorian Supreme Court, 2018), <https://www.countycourt.vic.gov.au/files/documents/2018-08/multi-jurisdictional-court-guide-intermediary-pilot-program-2806180.pdf>, 11-12.

81 See, eg, *Criminal Procedure Act 2009* (Vic), ss 179, 181, 199; *Evidence Act 2008* (Vic), s 192A; *Evidence Act 1977* (Qld), s 21AX; *Criminal Code* (Qld); s 590AA; *Justices Act 1886* (Qld), s 83A; *Justices Act* (NT), s 201A; *Supreme Court Rules* (NT), r 81A.18; *Evidence (National Uniform Legislation) Act 2011* (NT), s 192A; *CPA* (NSW), ss 136, 139, 247D, 247G; Sch 2, Pt 29, cl 89(3), (6); *Evidence Act 1995* (NSW), s 192A; *District Court Rules 1973* (NSW), rr 53.10-53.11; *Criminal Procedure Act 2004* (WA), ss 64, 98; *Criminal Law Consolidation Act 1935* (SA), s 285A; *Evidence Act 2001* (Tas), s 192A; *Criminal Code* (Tas), s 361A; *Criminal Rules 2006* (Tas), Pt 1A. Additionally, statutory provisions relating to the competence of witnesses that focus on their comprehension and communication capacities (for example, s 13 of the uniform *Evidence Acts*) provide a vehicle for obtaining this advice.

82 Similarly, the designated role of intermediaries during questioning under the Western Australian, Victorian and the different New South Wales regimes is to communicate and explain to people with communication needs the questions put to them to enable them to be understood, and to explain to the court the answers given: *Evidence Act 1906* (WA), s 106F(2); *CPA* (NSW), s 306ZK(3)(b) (children and witnesses with cognitive impairments may have a support person with them when they testify, who may act as an interpreter and assist them to give evidence); *CPA* (NSW), s 275B (any witness who has difficulty communicating may use a person who may assist him or her to do so if the witness ordinarily receives such assistance in everyday life) and *CPA* (NSW), Sch 2, Pt 29, cls 88-90 (the intermediary is to communicate: (a) to the witness, questions put to the witness, and (b) to any person asking such a question, the answers given by the witness in replying to them, and to explain such questions or answers so far as necessary to enable them to be understood by the witness or person in question).

83 Though this is not explicitly provided for in the governing legislation: *Multi-Jurisdictional Court Guide for the Intermediary Pilot Program*, above n 80, 10.

and was originally scheduled to run for three years, but is now a permanent program in existing District Court and Child Abuse Unit locations.[84] The intermediary scheme in New South Wales operates on a *mandatory* basis in respect of child witnesses[85] under 16 years of age (but not for child defendants).[86] Under the *CPA* (NSW) an intermediary is an officer of the court who has a duty to impartially facilitate the communication of, and with, the witness so the witness can provide the witness's best evidence.[87] An intermediary is mandatorily assigned to any child witness for the prosecution and to any complainant who is under 16 years of age,[88] but only in prescribed sexual offences cases.[89] Intermediaries are able to give advice to the police[90] and courts.[91]

The Victorian scheme is based on the English model.[92] The intermediary must have specialist skills in communication. He or she is an officer of the court with a duty to act impartially when providing communication assistance for a witness who has communication needs.[93] The Victorian scheme applies to witnesses including complainants who are children or who have cognitive impairments. It applies in courts declared to be participating venues[94] and only to criminal proceedings for prescribed criminal offences.[95] Like the NSW model, the Victorian pilot scheme does not apply to defendants.[96] In Victoria, directions that can be given at the ground rules hearings[97] include directions about the manner and

---

84 *CPA* (NSW), Sch 2, cl 81; <https://www.victimsservices.justice.nsw.gov.au/Pages/vss/vs_victims/vs_childrens-champion.aspx>, with a funding commitment to 2022.

85 *CPA* (NSW), Sch 2, Pt 29 (Provisions relating to child sexual offence evidence pilot scheme), cl 88. See also ss 275B and 306ZK.

86 *CPA* (NSW), Sch 2, Pt 29, cls 82, 83, 88(1). Its first evaluation was highly positive, see J Cashmore, I Katz, R Shake and K Valentine, *Evaluation of the Child Sexual Offence Evidence Pilot: Process Evaluation* (Social Policy Research Centre, Sydney, 2017).

87 *CPA* (NSW), Sch 2, Pt 29, cl 88. An intermediary must have a tertiary qualification in Psychology, Social Work, Speech Pathology, Teaching or Occupational Therapy or such other qualifications, training, experience or skills as prescribed (cl 89).

88 For minors over the age of 16, the court may, of its own motion or on the application of a party to the proceedings, appoint an intermediary if satisfied that the witness has difficulty communicating: *CPA* (NSW), Sch 2, Pt 29, cls 82 and 89(3)(b).

89 *CPA* (NSW), Sch 2, Pt 29, cl 89(3). It commenced operation in early 2016 and has been extended to run until mid-2022, and see *Criminal Procedure Regulation 2017* (NSW), cl 108A. Initially it operated only in two locations (Newcastle District Court and Sydney Downing Centre, District Court).

90 RCIRCSA, Public Hearing – Case Study 46, Transcript Day 234, 23913, 23915, 23919-23.

91 *CPA* (NSW), Sch 2, Pt 29, cl 89(3) and (6); arguably, s 106S of the *Evidence Act 1906* (WA) might likewise be deployed by courts to obtain this kind of advice.

92 The introduction of an intermediary scheme was recommended (recommendation 30) in the 2016 VLRC, above n 74.

93 *Criminal Procedure Act 2009* (Vic), s 389I.

94 Ibid s 389F(1).

95 This includes sexual offences, family violence offences within the meaning of the *Family Violence Protection Act 2008* (Vic), homicide matters, indictable offences which involve an assault on, or injury or a threat of injury to, a person and offences against s 23 or 24 of the *Summary Offences Act 1966* (Vic) if the offences are related to the other offences specified, see *Criminal Procedure Act 2009* (Vic), s 389A(1).

96 *Criminal Procedure Act 2009* (Vic), ss 389A(3) and 389F(1). See discussion of the exclusion of defendants in the TLRI, above n 76.

97 See *Criminal Procedure Act 2009* (Vic), ss 389E and 389B(3) (requiring a ground rules hearing be held if an intermediary is appointed). 'A ground rules hearing is a pre-hearing process used to discuss and establish how vulnerable witnesses will be enabled to give their best evidence, by the Court setting ground rules for the questioning of the witness. The ground rules take the form of Court directions': *Multi-Jurisdictional Court Guide for the Intermediary Pilot Program*, above n 80, 2.

duration of questioning a witness, about the use of models, plans, body maps or similar aids, about the questions that may or may not be put to a witness, and about allocating topics for questioning if there is more than one accused. A direction can also be given that a party is not obliged to put the entirety of evidence in cross-examination that contradicts or challenges the evidence of a witness. The Victorian *Multi-Jurisdictional Court Guide for the Intermediary Pilot Program: Intermediaries and Ground Rules Hearings* also suggests that the court may direct counsel (at a directions hearing) to identify witnesses' needs, advise on the need to assess or appoint an intermediary and/or arrangement to facilitate communication and even direct counsel to prepare for the court before the ground rules hearing written proposed questions or topics to be asked of the witness for discussion[98] at the ground rules hearing. Although not in the legislative scheme, Victoria Police are included in the program.[99]

The Commonwealth Government response to the RCIRCSA recommendation is that, while the RCIRCSA recommendation is directed to States and Territories, the government supports victims of comparable Commonwealth offences being afforded the same protections, but because some jurisdictions are already piloting intermediary schemes these should be fully assessed before settling a position at the Commonwealth level on this recommendation. Consideration will be given to how and whether a Commonwealth scheme could supplement or stand alongside other schemes so as not to complicate processes or overburden court resources.[100]

Before we consider cultural or language issues, it is useful first to explore the challenges associated with assessing how much trust should be placed in the evidence given by a witness.

Evaluating Witnesses

The common law trial is built on an assumption that trials are public and witnesses give oral evidence. This remains the norm for criminal charges that are contested and are determined in court. This preference relates not only to giving the public access to observing court processes but is also founded on the view that *oral* rather than *written* testimony is the gold standard for evaluating a person's words. As Heydon J observed (in a civil action context), '[i]n our system of oral trial, it is not customary to disbelieve witnesses whom the court has not had the opportunity of seeing and hearing'.[101] However, this gold standard has been subjected to close scrutiny in recent years as psychological research has revealed the complexity of reading witnesses' demeanour to assess accuracy and honesty. As a result, appellate courts as well as psychologists and others have recognised many of the fraught issues associated with evaluating witnesses. A summary of the findings of psychological research on witness credibility is found in KA Peace et al who observe that:

98 *Multi-Jurisdictional Court Guide*, above n 80, 6 (or shared confidentially with an appointed intermediary for suggestions on the appropriate form of questioning).

99 Ibid 3 (fn 3). Four police sexual offence and child abuse investigative team sites (SOCIT) are included in the pilot.

100 See <https://www.ag.gov.au/RightsAndProtections/Australian-Government-Response-to-the-Royal-Commission-into-Institutional-Responses-to-Child-Sexual-Abuse/Pages/default.aspx>, 39.

101 *Hadid v Redpath* [2001] NSWCA 416; 35 MVR 152, [58].

> Statements perceived as rich in detail are often believed to be more credible than statements with poor details.[102] Concurrently, inconsistencies often raise concerns about the accuracy of the eyewitness' overall accounts and lead the jurors to view them as less reliable.[103] … [R]esearch also suggests that perceptions of credibility may be influenced by factors that are unrelated to the quality and accuracy of eyewitness testimony.
>
> In general, unusual details affected credibility, with statements became [sic] less plausible with increased bizarreness. [But] … mild bizarreness in a statement enhances perceived credibility, and … the number of bizarre details mentioned is important. In a court system, it may be the case that jurors are looking for a few bizarre details to anchor the story as something concrete and credible.[104]

For some time, psychologists have considered whether a distorting effect on a listener's impression of reliability (in terms of accuracy) arises where a speaker is confident when relating their account of an event. It is certainly the case that witnesses can have misplaced confidence in identifying offenders. This is a major source of miscarriages of justice.[105] But research on the relationship between accuracy and confidence suggests that the picture is particularly complex. First, some people are in general prone to speak confidently. Some are characteristically under-confident when they speak. Hence, to measure a witness's confidence levels on particular aspects of their evidence, one needs to know where they fit on this spectrum. Time in the witness box may be too short, and questioning too focused, to achieve this measure. Second, there is in fact a correlation between confidence and accuracy. Chabris and Simons observe that 'all other things being equal, a confident witness is more likely – much more likely – to be accurate than an unconfident one'.[106] In support of their conclusion, Chabris and Simons cite the well-known 1995 study of Sporer, Penrod, Read and Cutler[107] who found on average that highly confident witnesses are accurate 70% of the time and under-confident witnesses are accurate only 30% of the time. More recently, Odinot et al

---

102 Citing a number of authorities, including BE Bell and EF Loftus, 'Trivial Persuasion in the Courtroom: The Power of (a Few) Minor Details' (1989) 56 *Journal of Personality and Social Psychology* 669; K Colwell, C, Hiscock-Anisman, ARA Memon and L Colwel, 'Vividness and Spontaneity of Statement Detail Characteristics as Predictors of Witness Credibility' (2007) 25 *American Journal of Forensic Psychology* 4.

103 Citing N Brewer, R Potter, RP Fisher, N Bond and MA Luszcz, 'Beliefs and Data on the Relationship between Consistency and Accuracy of Eyewitness Testimony' (1999) 13 *Applied Cognitive Psychology* 297; and RP Fisher, A Vrij and DA Leins, 'Does Testimonial Inconsistency Indicate Memory Inaccuracy and Deception? Beliefs, empirical research, and theory' in BS Cooper, D Griesel and M Ternes (eds), *Applied Issues in Investigative Interviewing, Eyewitness Memory, and Credibility Assessment* (Springer, 2013), 173-90, and see the discussion regarding inconsistent statements in Chapter 6.

104 KA Peace, KL Brower and A Rocchio, 'Is Truth Stranger Than Fiction? Bizarre Details and Credibility Assessment' (2015) 30 *Journal of Police and Criminal Psychology* 38, 48 (some citations omitted).

105 See Chapter 15 and consider the case of Ronald Cotton (see <http://www.innocenceproject.org/cases-false-imprisonment/ronald-cotton>) where the misplaced confidence of the rape victim, Jennifer Thompson, that she had correctly identified Cotton was a significant factor in his wrongful conviction: see C Chabris and D Simons, *The Invisible Gorilla: How our Intuitions Deceive Us* (Broadway Paperbacks, 2010), 114; G Odinot, G Wolters and A van Giezen, 'Accuracy, Confidence and Consistency in Repeated Recall of Events' (2013) 19 *Psychology, Crime and Law* 629, citing EF Loftus, *Memory* (Addison-Wesley, 1980); EF Loftus, 'Planting Misinformation in the Human Mind: A 30-year Investigation of the Malleability of Memory' (2005) 12 *Learning & Memory* 361.

106 Chabris and Simons, above n 105, 113.

107 SL Sporer, S Penrod, D Read and B Cutler, 'Choosing, Confidence, and Accuracy: A Meta-Analysis of the Confidence-Accuracy Relation in Eyewitness Identification Studies' (1995) 118 *Psychological Bulletin* 315.

also found, in their 2011 study, 'a clear positive and linear relationship between accuracy and confidence'.[108] Further, 'repeatedly asking the same question did not [in the study participants] inflate the confidence expressed in the answers provided. Even when identical information was repeatedly and consistently retrieved from memory, confidence was not enhanced'.[109]

Psychological research shows that people become less confident over time regarding their memory of everyday events. This correlates with their memory of such events becoming worse. But where the recollection is of a 'flashbulb memory' – an emotionally charged 'crisis' event (such as witnessing or being a victim of certain crimes) – the accuracy of our memories is more prone to unconscious distortion. In other words, our confidence in our recollection is more likely to be misplaced.[110] Research does not support treating confidence as a predictor of accuracy, but it does suggest that any distortion arising from witness confidence is not straightforward merely because of the existence of a history of eyewitness miscarriages of justice.

Finally, psychological research also suggests that a witness's relationship to the subject event can impact on how others assess their credibility. For example, studies of mock jurors have found victim accounts to be less plausible than bystander accounts. This may be explicable in various ways. One suggestion by researchers is that bystander witnesses are less impacted by distress and this enhances their attention and recall of detail.[111] Does being a judge (or a lawyer) make a difference? In an analysis of what is described as intuitive and deliberative reasoning Guthrie, Rachlinski and Wistrich in 'Blinking on the Bench: How Judges Decide Cases' made the following observations:

> We believe that most judges attempt to 'reach their decisions utilizing facts, evidence, and highly constrained legal criteria, while putting aside personal biases, attitudes, emotions, and other individual factors.' ... Despite their best efforts, however, judges, like everyone else, have two cognitive systems for making judgments – the intuitive and the deliberative – and the intuitive system appears to have a powerful effect on judges' decision making. The intuitive approach might work well in some cases, but it can lead to erroneous and unjust outcomes in others. The justice system should take what steps it can to increase the likelihood that judges will decide cases in a predominantly deliberative, rather than a predominantly intuitive, way.
>
> In his recent book, *How Doctors Think*, Dr Jerome Groopman observes that '[m]uch has been made of the power of intuition, and certainly initial impressions formed in a flash can be correct. But as we hear from a range of physicians, relying too heavily on intuition has its perils. Cogent medical judgments meld first impressions – gestalt – with deliberate analysis' ... Like cogent medical judgments, cogent legal judgments call for deliberation. Justice depends on it.[112]

Case law supports a preference for fact-finders to focus on evidence that provides objective proof of events over making intuitive assessments of witnesses' credibility.

---

108 Odinot et al, above n 105, 640.

109 Ibid 639, stating that this finding is inconsistent with the findings by JS Shaw, 'Increases in Eyewitness Confidence Resulting from Postevent Questioning' (1996) 2 *Journal of Experimental Psychology: Applied* 126; and JS Shaw and KA McClure, 'Repeated Postevent Questioning can lead to Elevated Levels of Eyewitness Confidence' (1996) 20 *Law and Human Behavior* 629.

110 Chabris and Simons, above n 105, 76.

111 Peace, Brower and Rocchio, above n 104, 42, 48; MJ Holcomb and KM Jacquin, 'Juror Perceptions of Child Eyewitness Testimony in a Sexual Abuse Trial' (2007) 16 *Journal of Childhood Sexual Abuse* 79.

112 C Guthrie, J Rachlinski and AJ Wistrich, 'Blinking on the Bench: How Judges Decide Cases' (2007) 93 *Cornell Law Review* 101, 141, quoted by Forgie DP in *Zheng v Minister for Immigration and Citizenship* [2011] AATA 304, n 106.

State Rail Authority of New South Wales v Earthline Constructions Pty Ltd (in liq)
[1999] HCA 3; 160 ALR 588[113]

The question before the court was whether the NSW Court of Appeal had erred in finding that the trial judge was entitled to reject the evidence of the appellant's principal witnesses in circumstances where their evidence was inherently probable, had not been denied or answered in evidence by the respondents, and had been substantially corroborated by the respondents' own documents. The court needed to consider the extent to which appeal courts are constrained in revisiting factual issues determined by a trial judge largely on an assessment of witnesses' credibility. The case raises for consideration the extent to which trial judges are advantaged by seeing and hearing witnesses give evidence when it comes to assessing their evidence. The High Court unanimously concluded that the Court of Appeal was in fact obliged, by the proof of objective documentary evidence, to give attention to all of the evidence of the case.

> **Kirby J**: 88. There have been many changes in the appellate function since the rules outlined above were first stated. The changes have included the following: …
>
> 4. There is a growing understanding, both by trial judges and appellate courts, of the fallibility of judicial evaluation of credibility from the appearance and demeanour of witnesses in the somewhat artificial and sometimes stressful circumstances of the courtroom. Scepticism about the supposed judicial capacity in deciding credibility from the appearance and demeanour of a witness is not new. In *Societe D'Avances Commerciales (Societe Anonyme Egyptienne) v Merchants' Marine Insurance Co* (*The 'Palitana'*),[114] Atkin LJ remarked that 'an ounce of intrinsic merit or demerit in the evidence, that is to say, the value of the comparison of evidence with known facts, is worth pounds of demeanour'. To some extent, the faith in the judicial power to discern credibility from appearances was probably, at first, a consideration which the judiciary assumed that it inherited from juries. It was natural enough that trial judges, accustomed to presiding over jury trials, would claim, and appellate judges would accord, the same 'infallible' capacity to tell truth from falsehood as had historically been attributed to the jury. Nowadays, most judges are aware of the scientific studies which cast doubt on the correctness of this assumption.[115] Lord Devlin in *The Judge* ((1979), 63) quoted with approval a remark of MacKenna J: 'I question whether the respect given to our findings of fact based on the demeanour of the witnesses is always deserved. I doubt my own ability … to discern from a witness's demeanour, or the tone of his voice, whether he is telling the truth.' It was a becoming but entirely accurate modesty.
>
> Apart from all else, demeanour is, in part, driven by culture. Studies suggest that evaluation of the evidence of women may sometimes be affected by stereotypes held by the decision-maker. This is doubtless also true in the case of evidence given by members of minority groups, whether racial, sexual or otherwise. Distaste or prejudice can cloud evaluation. Further, in a society such as Australia's, the capacity of the judiciary to respond to every cultural variety of communication is limited. Fifty years ago, the Supreme Court of Canada[116] wisely declined to offer guidelines about the kinds of demeanour that would afford reliable indicators of the trustworthiness of witnesses. The studies of experimental

---

113 Footnotes have been omitted in large part. See also *Fox v Percy* [2003] HCA 22; 214 CLR 118, a similar case, with a similar result.

114 [(1924) 20 LI L Rep 140, 152.]

115 [*Trawl Industries v Effem Foods Pty Ltd* (1992) 27 NSWLR 326, 348 (Samuels JA).]

116 [*White* (1947) 89 CCC 148, 151.]

psychologists since that time have confirmed the danger of placing undue reliance upon appearances in evaluating credibility. Such studies were not available to the appellate courts when the rules of deference to the assessments of trial judges on questions of credibility were first written. They are available to us today. Although they have not yet resulted in a re-expression of the appellate approach (and by no means expel impressions about witnesses from the process of decision-making) the studies have two consequences. Trial judges should strive, so far as they can, to decide cases without undue reliance on such fallible considerations as their assessment of witness credibility. And appellate courts should refrain from needlessly expanding the categories of trial conclusions about the facts which are effectively unreviewable because of presumed or inferred credibility considerations.

5. In the future, technology may be developed which will assist courts in the conclusive determination of issues of witness credibility where these are disputed. ... [But until then our] courts must therefore continue to struggle with the aid of human estimation. Until the courts are afforded technological relief, they do well to realise the imperfections of the currently available tools of decision-making. They need to minimise, and not exaggerate, the role of the judicial assessment of credibility from appearances.

Witness credibility: the trial judge's real advantages

89. None of the foregoing considerations requires the abandonment of the respect which appellate courts, by present legal authority, must pay to the advantages enjoyed by the trial judge. Instead, they require renewed attention to precisely what the advantages are which the trial judge has over those enjoyed by the appellate court, conducting a second look at the facts, usually with more opportunity to evaluate particular facts than is possible in the midst of a trial and with the appellate advantage of viewing such facts in the context of the record of the complete trial hearing.

90. The true advantages in fact-finding which the trial judge enjoys include the fact that the judge hears the evidence in its entirety whereas the appellate court is typically taken to selected passages, chosen by the parties so as to advance their respective arguments.[117] The trial judge hears and sees all of the evidence. The evidence is generally presented in a reasonably logical context. It unfolds, usually with a measure of chronological order, as it is given in testimony or tendered in documentary or electronic form. During the trial and adjournments, the judge has the opportunity to reflect on the evidence and to weigh particular elements against the rest of the evidence whilst the latter is still fresh in mind. A busy appellate court may not have the time or opportunity to read the entire transcript and all of the exhibits. As it seems to me, these are the real reasons for caution on the part of an appellate court where it inclines to conclusions on factual matters different from those reached by the trial judge.[118] These considerations acquire added force where, as in the present case, the trial was a very long one, the exhibits are most numerous, the issues are multiple and the oral and written submissions were detailed and protracted. In such cases, the reasons given by the trial judge, however conscientious he or she may be, may omit attention to peripheral issues. They are designed to explain conclusions to which the judge has been driven by the overall impressions and considerations, some of which may, quite properly, not be expressly specified.[119]

In the Canadian Supreme Court case of *NS*,[120] discussed below in relation to witnesses wearing burqas, Abella J (dissenting in her reasons and conclusion)

---

117 [*Lend Lease Development Pty Ltd v Zemlicka* (1985) 3 NSWLR 207, 209-10; *Jones* (1997) 191 CLR 439, 467.]

118 [*Galea v Galea* (1990) 19 NSWLR 263, 265-6; *Devries v Australian National Railways Commission* (1993) 177 CLR 472, 483.]

119 [*Housing Commission of New South Wales v Tatmar Pastoral Co Pty Ltd* [1983] 3 NSWLR 378, 385-6; *Soulemezis v Dudley (Holdings) Pty Ltd* (1987) 10 NSWLR 247, 260-1, 269-71, 280-1.]

120 [2012] SCC 72; [2012] 3 SCR 726.

reviewed Canadian jurisprudence and research on demeanour, beginning first with the definition of 'demeanour' offered by Morrison, Porter and Fraser,[121] namely that demeanour encompasses 'every visible or audible form of self-expression manifested by a witness whether fixed or variable, voluntary or involuntary, simple or complex'. Her Honour added that '[t]rial judges often rely on many indicators *other than* facial cues in finding a witness credible, including:

> certitude in speaking, dignity while on the stand, exhibition of disability, exhibition of anger, exhibition of frustration, articulate speaking, thoughtful presentation, enthusiastic language, direct non-evasive answering, non-glib answering, exhibition of modesty, exhibition of flexibility, normal (as in as expected) body movement, cheerful attitude, kind manner, normal exhalation, normal inhalation.[122]

Her Honour added 'that relying on the "appearance of sincerity [would lead to] a purely arbitrary finding and justice would then depend upon the best actors in the witness box".'[123] According to the court, demeanour 'is but one of the elements that enter into the credibility ... of a witness', with other factors including the witness's opportunity for knowledge, powers of observation, judgment, memory and ability to describe clearly what he or she has seen and heard. Abella J[124] also confirmed the conclusions reached by Kirby J above, noting that caution with respect to demeanour assessment was also urged in *Pelletier*:

> I question whether the respect given to our findings of fact based on the demeanour of the witnesses is always deserved. I doubt my own ability, and sometimes that of other judges, to discern from a witness's demeanour, or the tone of his voice, whether he is telling the truth. He speaks hesitantly. Is it the mark of a cautious man, whose statements are for that reason to be respected, or is he taking time to fabricate? Is the emphatic witness putting on an act to deceive me, or is he speaking from the fullness of his heart, knowing that he is right? Is he likely to be more truthful if he looks me straight in the face than if he casts his eyes on the ground, perhaps from shyness or a natural timidity? For my part I rely on these considerations as little as I can help.
>
> ... I judge a witness to be unreliable if his evidence is, in any serious respect, inconsistent with these undisputed or indisputable facts, or of course if he contradicts himself on important points. I rely as little as possible on such deceptive matters as his demeanour.[125]

As Abella J noted,[126] the inherent limitations in relying on demeanour are formalised in the Canadian Judicial Council's Model Jury Instructions effectively cautioning jurors not to rely on their intuition, assumptions and values without knowing a lot about the people testifying (which is invariably unlikely).

> What was the witness's manner when he or she testified? Do not jump to conclusions, however, based entirely on the witness's manner. Looks can be deceiving. Giving evidence in a trial is not a common experience for many witnesses. People react and appear differently. Witnesses come from different backgrounds. They have different intellects, abilities, values, and life experiences. There are simply too many variables to make the manner in which a witness testifies the only or the most important factor in your decision.[127]

121 Ibid [98]; see BR Morrison, LL Porter and IH Fraser, 'The Role of Demeanour in Assessing the Credibility of Witnesses' (2007) 33 *Advocates' Quarterly* 170, 179.

122 Quoting from Morrison et al, ibid, 189.

123 [2012] SCC 72; [2012] 3 SCR 726, [99], quoting *Faryna v Chorny* [1952] 2 DLR 354, 356, 356-7.

124 [2012] SCC 72; [2012] 3 SCR 726, [100].

125 (1995) 1995 ABCA 128 (CanLII); 165 AR 138, [18] (citing a 1973 paper by Justice MacKenna and approvingly quoted in P Devlin, *The Judge* (Oxford University Press, 1979), 63). Abella J also referred to *Levert* [2001] CanLII 8606 (ON CA); 159 CCC (3d) 71, 81.

126 [2012] SCC 72; [2012] 3 SCR 726, [101].

127 Model Jury Instructions, Part I, Preliminary Instructions, 4.11 Assessing Testimony (online).

While it may be 'more difficult not to tell the truth about a person when looking at that person eye to eye ... it is difficult to dogmatize about this – and in some cases ... eye to eye contact may frustrate the obtaining of as true an account from the witness as is possible'.[128] All these observations are relevant to the consideration of how witnesses are treated in court, how they are questioned and the opportunities afforded to the accused to test prosecution witnesses' accounts.

Language, culture and interpretation in court

An interpreter *may* resolve some language problems. An interpreter can assist 'unless the witness can understand and speak the English language sufficiently to enable the witness to understand, and to make an adequate reply to, questions that may be put about the fact'.[129] While s 30 appears to create a prima facie right to an interpreter, the use of an interpreter essentially lies within the discretion of the court, based on genuine need. However, the witness, the lawyers or the judge may fail to appreciate that the witness's grasp of English is inadequate.[130] The Council of Chief Justices of Australia and New Zealand has approved the Judicial Council on Cultural Diversity's (JCCD) *Recommended National Standards for Working with Interpreters in Courts and Tribunals*. The standards contain sections on 'Plain English Strategies', 'Four-part test for determining need for an interpreter', 'Recommended Standards for Interpreters', and 'What judicial officers can do to assist the interpreter'.[131] Information on working with interpreters can also be found in the *Equality before the Law Bench Book*. Concerns about courts' ability to monitor the accuracy of interpreters' work and their independence and impartiality have been addressed by the creation of model rules for interpreters. The JCCD's Model Rules are set out in the *Recommended National Standards for Working with Interpreters in Courts and Tribunals*. In South Australia, Western Australia, New South Wales, and Queensland, court guidelines have been developed for working with interpreters.[132] The JCCD Model Rules provided the basis for the amendments to the *Uniform Civil Procedure Rules 2005* (NSW) (UCPR) contained in Part 31, Div 3 (rr 31.55-31.64), which apply in civil proceedings, but may, nevertheless, provide a touchstone for criminal proceedings. The application of the *Evidence Act 1995* is unaffected by these amendments. The amended UCPR also provide for a Court Interpreters' Code of Conduct at Sch 7A to the UCPR. The main purposes of the amendments are:

(a) to ensure that the court has control over the giving of evidence that is interpreted or translated into English;

---

128 *Levogiannis* [1990] CanLII 6873 (ON CA); 1 OR (3d) 351 (CA) (Morden ACJO), quoted by Abella J at [107].

129 See *UEA*, s 30 (and see also ss 22, 23 and Sch 1 regarding the oath or affirmation obligations of interpreters).

130 See <https://www.judcom.nsw.gov.au/publications/benchbks/local/interpreters.html>.

131 See <https://jccd.org.au/publications/>.

132 *Guideline: Working with Interpreters in Queensland Courts and Tribunals* (28 June 2019), <https://qldbar.asn.au/baq/v1/viewDocument?documentId=844>; *Interpreter Protocols SA – Courts Administration Authority*, <http://www.courts.sa.gov.au/Translation/Lists/Translation%20Document%20List/Attachments/1/Interpreter%20Protocols%20SA.pdf>; *Local Court Bench Book (NSW)*, <https://www.judcom.nsw.gov.au/publications/benchbks/local/interpreters.html>; District Court of Western Australia, *Consolidated Practice Directions & Circulars to Practitioners, Criminal Jurisdiction*, <https://www.districtcourt.wa.gov.au/_files/DC_Consolidated_Criminal_Procedure.pdf>.

(b) to recognise the special status of an interpreter in the administration of justice by declaring the duties of an interpreter in relation to the court and the parties to proceedings;
(c) to provide for rules based on the Model Rules set out in the *Recommended National Standards for Working with Interpreters in Courts and Tribunals* prepared by the JCCD.

As well as providing a Code of Conduct, the amended UCPR now give key guidance on when interpreters may be engaged, who may perform the role of an interpreter (certified interpreters), the functions of interpreters, their duties of competence and confidentiality, and the court's power to issue directions concerning interpreters. Sometimes interpretation raises new complexities or leaves untouched matters that can create a miscommunication or a false impression.[133] This can occur because the interpretation of behaviour can be culturally shaped – for example, a witness may express politeness or deference differently from those on the jury and from counsel questioning them. Their reactions may therefore seem counter-intuitive to the projection of honesty, accuracy, integrity and confidence – all important attributes for the acceptance of witnesses' evidence. Speaking of her research from parts of Queensland, Eades observes that Aboriginal cultural assumptions that may run counter to the legal system's 'norms' include that:

> People who use silence should be respected for their thoughtfulness and their recognition of the value of time … [and that it is] rude to make direct eye contact with a person you should respect, especially an older person … [that establishing whether a person is honest and trustworthy means] you need to take time to get to know them, don't rush them, and don't talk all the time when you are with them … [that] [i]interrupting a person's story with questions makes it harder for them to be accurate and consistent … [and that] [a]sking lots of questions is rude, and it's a very ineffective way of finding things out.

Finally:

> If a White person in authority asks you lots of questions, especially in a pressured situation, the best thing is to say *yes*, and keep them happy. (If it's a negative question, say *no.*) [and] … [a]nswering *I don't know* is one way of handling excessive questioning from White people.

As implied by Abella J in the Canadian case of *NS*[134] (discussed below) and illustrated by Anthony Parker from the defence bar,[135] sometimes distortion can advantage the witness. Aside from the processes of interpretation providing the partly bilingual witness with additional time to consider their answer, Parker notes in the context of an interpreter assisting an accused in the witness box:

> In addition to the obvious reasons, many interpreters are experienced and presentable people, and the accused gains in presentation as a result; in South Australia, one of the accredited interpreters of the Pitjantjatjara language is a woman so presentable, so obviously decent, so Christian and so just plain likeable that it is said that no jury has ever convicted her.

---

133 See, eg, S Hale, 'Interpreting Culture. Dealing with Cross-Cultural Issues in Court Interpreting' (2013) *Studies in Translatology* 1; D Eades, *Aboriginal Ways of Using English* (Aboriginal Studies Press, 2013), 159-60.

134 [2012] SCC 72; [2012] 3 SCR 726.

135 A Parker, 'Preparing a Client for Cross-Examination' (c 1996), <http://www.publicdefenders.justice.nsw.gov.au/pdo/public_defenders_research/public_defenders_papers_pd.html>.

Interpreters are treated by the court as conduits for a witness's words, but if a party wishes to place before the court an explanation of features of a witness's behaviour in court or manner of testifying based on their cultural background, they must call the appropriate expert witness.[136] If the evidence of this expert is relevant solely to a witness's credibility, additional complications may arise. The expert evidence will need to find an exception to the credibility rule.[137] This rule (discussed below) is a major and complex dynamic in the law of evidence.

It is important to keep at the forefront of one's consideration that trial judges have the power to control the questioning of witnesses, including the way witnesses are questioned, the production and use of items connected with that questioning, the order of witnesses, the order of questioning and whether any person should leave the courtroom.[138] In light of Diana Eades's research there is a strong case for trial judges and/or parties in appropriate cases to relax witness questioning to a process that is within the witness's comfort zone and apply s 29(2) to '*direct that the witness give evidence wholly or partly in narrative form*'.[139] The challenge to utilising s 29(2) is professional cultural resistance to an approach that empowers the witness to give their account in their own way. This runs counter to the control ethos of witness questioning in adversarial philosophy.

Finally, an issue that has arisen in a number of countries, including Australia, has been with women of Islamic faith wearing the traditional head attire (that is, the burqa or the niqab) when they testify. This has arisen for consideration by criminal courts in New South Wales, Western Australia, Canada and New Zealand,[140] raising thorny and complex dilemmas associated with individual rights and communication norms regarding the extent to which a witness can be permitted to interfere with the traditional legal assumption that a witness's 'demeanour' – that is, their facial expressions and how they present themselves in the witness box – is important to measuring their reliability and honesty.[141] In *Elzahed v New South Wales*, the NSW Court of Appeal found no error in the trial judge's refusal to allow the appellant, a party in the case and not merely a witness, to give evidence with her face covered by a niqab. The court stated:

> The resolution of the case would require the primary judge to make findings about whether to accept the appellant's evidence or the conflicting evidence of the NSW police officers. Viewing the appellant's face while she was giving her evidence was capable of affecting the resolution of that conflict.[142]

---

136 See Chapter 11.

137 *UEA*, s 102. See also ss 101A and 108C.

138 *UEA*, s 26.

139 In *Isherwood v Tasmania* (2010) 20 Tas R 375, [78], the Tasmanian Court of Appeal observed that '[t]he direction will be required in every case of an unrepresented litigant giving evidence, otherwise he or she will be unable to give it'. See also *UEA*, s 29(4): 'Evidence may be given in the form of charts, summaries or other explanatory material if it appears to the court that the material would be likely to aid its comprehension of other evidence that has been given or is to be given'.

140 See also *SAS v France* (1 July 2014, Application No 43835/11), where the Grand Chamber of the European Court of Human Rights upheld the French ban on the burqa being worn in public; R Barker, 'Of burqas (and niqabs) in courtrooms: the neglected women's voice' in R Ahdar (ed), *Research Handbook on Law and Religion* (Edward Elgar Publishing, 2018), 397; R Barker, 'Burqas and Niqabs in the Courtroom: Finding Practical Solutions' (2017) 91 *Australian Law Journal* 225.

141 Discussed below, Chapter 6, pp 212-215.

142 [2018] NSWCA 103; 97 NSWLR 898, [64]; and see *Chaarani (Ruling 1)* [2018] VSC 387 (judge refusing to permit a member of the public to sit in the gallery wearing a niqab).

In the New Zealand case of *Police v Razamjoo*,[143] the judge allowed the two Afghani witnesses who wished to wear burqas to testify behind a screen. This preserved their modesty while allowing the judge and counsel (there was no jury) to view their faces.[144] As Griffiths[145] relates, the judge accepted social science research that facial demeanour does not assist evaluating lie detection but concluded that significant departure from the principle of public justice would damage public confidence. In the Canadian case of *NS*[146] a clash of rights under the *Canadian Charter of Rights and Freedoms* – to a fair trial and to religious freedom – arose for consideration. NS was the complainant in relation to sexual assault charges against her cousin and uncle. At the preliminary hearing she sought to testify while she wore a niqab (described as only permitting NS's eyes to be seen). The court held by a majority (McLachlin CJ, Deschamps, Fish and Cromwell JJ) that even where a witness had a sincere religious commitment requiring her to wear a niqab while testifying, where reasonably available alternative measures could not prevent the serious risk to the fairness of the trial, she would be required to remove her veil where the salutary effects of requiring its removal, including on trial fairness, 'outweigh the deleterious effects of doing so, including the effects on freedom of religion'.[147] LeBel and Rothstein JJ concurred with the majority conclusion but would have required the niqab to be removed as a matter of course because:

> 74. A system of open and independent courts has become a core component of a democratic state, ruled by law … [and this] system is part of the complex web of institutions, rules and values embraced by the notion of the rule of law, of a state and a society living under and within the law. …
>
> 76. From this broader constitutional perspective, the trial becomes an act of communication with the public at large. … The principle of openness ensures that the courts and the trial process belong to all regardless of religion, gender or origin.
>
> 77. … Wearing a niqab … does not facilitate acts of communication. Rather, it restricts them. It removes the witness from the scope of certain elements of those acts on the basis of the assertion of a religious belief in circumstances in which the sincerity and strength of the belief are difficult to assess or even to question. The niqab shields the witness from interacting fully with the parties, their counsel, the judge and, where applicable, the jurors.

However, Abella J provided a compelling dissent, concluding that one needed to weigh 'the impact of not having full access to the usual "demeanour assessment package"' in terms of its actual material harm to trial fairness justifying NS yielding her religious rights. Her Honour cast the issue similarly to the other judges, that is, in weighing competing harms, but concluded that 'with very limited exceptions, the harm to a complainant of requiring her to remove her niqab while testifying will generally outweigh any harm to trial fairness'.[148] Her Honour conceded 'without reservation that seeing more of a witness' facial expressions is better than seeing less'.[149] However, unless an accused 'can demonstrate that the

143 *Police v Razamjoo* [2005] DCR 408 (DC).

144 The *New Zealand Bill of Rights Act 1990*, s 15, guarantees freedom of religion; and s 25(a) and (f) guarantee the right to a fair and public hearing and the right to examine witnesses for the prosecution.

145 D Griffiths, 'Defining the Secular in the New Zealand Bill of Rights Era: Some Cases and Controversies' (2011) 12 *Otago Law Review* 497. See also D Griffiths, 'Pluralism and the Law: New Zealand Accommodates the Burqa' [2006] *Otago Law Review* 8.

146 [2012] SCC 72; [2012] 3 SCR 726.

147 Ibid [3].

148 Ibid [91], [86].

149 Ibid [82].

witness's face is directly relevant to the case, such as where the witness's identity is in issue' making her face 'central to the issues at trial, rather than merely being a part of the assessment of demeanour',[150] the veil should remain. Her Honour pointed out that a complainant would have to choose between removing their niqab in public and bearing witness against an alleged aggressor, but the requirement to remove her veil also had implications for the rights of an accused who would face a choice between her religious rights and the ability to give evidence in her own defence. Her Honour cited examples of compromises to the ideal of viewing witnesses with uncovered faces in open court including where statements or transcripts from prior proceedings are admitted as exceptions to the rule against hearsay and where screens are provided to allow children to give evidence. Abella J also noted that physical limitations such as a speech impairment or a stroke may remove demeanour cues and are departures from the 'demeanour ideal', but they do not disqualify a witness from testifying. Finally, her Honour surveyed the research on demeanour assessment (discussed and quoted above), pointing out that a niqab still permits a witness to express herself through her eyes, body language, gestures, verbal account, including tone, inflection and cadence of her speech, and, of course, through the substance of her evidence. She remains available for cross-examination. Abella J stated that partial interference with what is 'only one part of an imprecise measuring tool of credibility, [leaves us] to wonder why we demand full "demeanour access" where religious belief prevents it',[151] and concluded that the more harmful consequence of forcing such witnesses to remove their niqab outweighs the consequences of not being able to see their whole face.

Examination-in-chief

The *UEA* expressly provides the right to question witnesses and that, unless ruled otherwise, examination-in-chief, cross-examination and re-examination are the default order for the questioning of each witness.[152] The *UEA* permits parties to question as they 'think fit',[153] subject to directions from the trial judge and compliance with *UEA*, Chapter 2 (ss 12-54).[154]

As indicated above, the party who has called a witness, questions first 'in chief'. Procedural law seeks to eliminate the danger that the questioner, succumbing to adversarial culture, may attempt to 'lead' the witness – that is, suggest 'helpful' responses – with the result the court will not have the benefit of the witness's own unvarnished account. Further, a questioner will want a witness to present as well as possible in the witness box. To that end, there is a temptation to question in a manner that brings forth a witness's impressive credibility attributes, whatever they may be. However, one of the assumptions embedded into procedural law is that questioning that is solely to enhance a witness's credibility is deeply unattractive. It is likely to be a time-waster because *what* a witness has to say and how they respond under questioning are considered more important than evidence that merely accredits a witness as good, honest or honourable. Thus, it has been a traditional assumption of the law that if a party chooses to call a witness they are doing so because they are a 'witness for the truth'. Consequently, parties are not

150 Ibid [83].
151 Ibid [108], [109].
152 *UEA*, ss 27, 28.
153 *UEA*, s 29(1).
154 *UEA*, s 29(2) and (3).

at liberty, without more, to aggrandise[155] their witnesses' credibility (also known as 'accrediting' witnesses) in front of the jury.[156] There are some exceptions. A witness's occupation may be elicited under questioning. Second, with expert witnesses it is a requirement for the admissibility of their opinion evidence that the credentials of their expertise be given. Jurors will be at liberty to take the length of their curriculum vitae into account when assessing an expert witness's evidence. Thirdly, a form of witness accreditation may be permitted through *UEA*, s 108(3)(b).[157] This permits questioning on a witness's prior statement that is relevant and admissible solely because it shows the witness's evidence in the witness box is consistent with this earlier statement. It only applies where 'it is or *will be suggested* [that is, in cross-examination] ... that evidence given by the witness has been fabricated or re-constructed (whether deliberately or otherwise) or is the result of a suggestion' (emphasis added). After we have discussed procedural rules associated with examination-in-chief we return below to explore the scope of the credibility rule (*UEA*, s 102).

Procedural rules

There are three categories of questioning that remain to be considered in relation to examination-in-chief:

- the first relates to the obligation *not to lead witnesses* (s 37);
- the second to the circumstances and the procedure associated with a witness being permitted to *refresh* their *memory* from a document; and, finally,
- the more complex situation where a *witness* called to give evidence by a party disappoints in a way that permits them to be declared *unfavourable* within the meaning of s 38(1). Where this occurs, the witness may be subject to cross-examination by the party who called them.

Leading questions

The concern that a witness may be vulnerable to suggestion is the foundation for the rule against leading questions in examination-in-chief: *UEA*, s 37. This section reflects common law practice.

> ***leading question*** means a question asked of a witness that:
> (a) directly or indirectly suggests a particular answer to the question, or
> (b) assumes the existence of a fact the existence of which is in dispute in the proceeding and as to the existence of which the witness has not given evidence before the question is asked.[158]
>
> **37. Leading questions**
> (1) A leading question must not be put to a witness in examination in chief or in re-examination unless:
> (a) the court gives leave, or
> (b) the question relates to a matter introductory to the witness's evidence, or
> (c) no objection is made to the question and (leaving aside the party conducting the examination in chief or re-examination) each other party to the proceeding

155 On the question of whether a party can discredit their own witness, see the discussion of *UEA*, s 38, below.
156 *UEA*, s 102 (the credibility rule). See also s 101A.
157 Section 108 is an exception to the credibility rule (*UEA*, s 102).
158 Definition from *UEA*, Dictionary (except in Tasmania, *Evidence Act 2001*, s 3).

is represented by an Australian legal practitioner, legal counsel or prosecutor, or

(d) the question relates to a matter that is not in dispute, or
(e) if the witness has specialised knowledge based on the witness's training, study or experience – the question is asked for the purpose of obtaining the witness's opinion about a hypothetical statement of facts, being facts in respect of which evidence has been, or is intended to be, given.[159]

A useful summation of the principles that inform the common law and relevant to the application of s 37 is found in Canadian case law. Charron JA in *Rose*[160] described the essence of common law practice:

> 9. A leading question is one that suggests the answer. It is trite law that the party who calls a witness is generally not permitted to ask the witness leading questions. The reason for the rule arises from a concern that the witness, who in many instances favours the party who calls him or her, will readily agree to the suggestions put in the form of a question rather than give his or her own answers to the questions. Of course, the degree of concern that may arise from the use of leading questions will depend on the particular circumstances, and the rule is applied with some flexibility. For example, leading questions are routinely asked to elicit a witness' evidence on preliminary and non-contentious matters. This practice is adopted for the sake of expediency and generally gives rise to no concern. Leading questions are also permitted to the extent that they are necessary to direct the witness to a particular matter or field of inquiry. Apart from these specific examples, the trial judge has a general discretion to allow leading questions whenever it is considered necessary in the interests of justice: *Reference Re R v Coffin* (1956), 114 CCC 1, 22 (SCC).

The courts' sensitivity to leading questions with an interviewee or witness who is vulnerable to suggestibility is vividly illustrated in the High Court's quashing of the judge-alone determination in *Douglass*.[161] This case arose following the complainant, CD aged four, telling her parents that her grandfather had asked her a week earlier to hold his penis. The circumstances of the complaint were described in the High Court judgment:

> 24. CD's parents were separated at the time of these events. On 27 October 2008, CD and her older brother, MD, were staying with their father, TD. It was about a week before CD's fourth birthday. Both the children were in TD's bedroom when CD asked "Do you have a beautiful penis, daddy?". TD had never heard CD use the word "penis" before and he was shocked by her question. The following day a further incident occurred. TD had taken CD with him to visit the home of a friend. During the course of the visit, TD urinated in the backyard of his friend's house. CD asked, "Did you just do wees, daddy?", TD said that he had, and CD volunteered "I had to hold grandpa's willy while he did wees". She said that this had happened on the weekend. CD did not understand the distinction between weekends and week days at the time. She had not stayed with the appellant on the weekend; however she had stayed with him overnight on the previous Wednesday.

Under South Australian law, CD's statements in interview were admissible as her examination-in-chief.[162] She was interviewed a few weeks after her complaint to

---

159 Subsection (2) provides an exception in civil proceedings 'to a question that relates to an investigation, inspection or report that the witness made in the course of carrying out public or official duties'. Subsection (3) acknowledges that rules of court may allow a written statement or report to be tendered or treated as evidence in chief of its maker.

160 (2001) 153 CCC (3d) 225 (Ont CA).

161 [2012] HCA 34; 290 ALR 699.

162 *Evidence Act 1929* (SA), s 34CA, as repealed by *Statutes Amendment (Vulnerable Witnesses) Act 2015* (SA), s 15. The amending legislation inserted s 13BA into the principal Act, expanding the circumstances in which pre-recorded evidence is admissible as examination-in-chief.

her parents. It was this interview that caused the High Court to have heightened concerns about the safety of the verdict. Its salient portions were extracted in the High Court judgment:[163]

> L Has someone ever asked you to touch their willy?
> [CD] … I touched [m]y brother's.
> L You touched your brother's did you. And what happened?
> [CD] … I told to MD to pee in the bucket.
> L Did you? And he did. Oh Okay. And what about anybody else. Did someone ask you to touch their willy?
> [CD] No.
> L Or do anything to their willy?
> [CD] No.
> L Or. Some people call this a penis. Did you know that? That's the proper word for it isn't it.
> [CD] Yes.
> L Has anyone asked you to touch their penis?
> [CD] No.
> L Are you sure?
> [CD] No.
> L Yeah? Okay. I was just was talking with mum about all that sort of stuff before.
> [CD] …
> L If somebody did ask you to hold or touch their penis.
> [CD] I touched on my grandpa's.
> L O did you? You touched your grandpa's? Oh, tell me about that. What happened?
> [CD] I don't know.
> L Oh, okay. Well do you know what. I wasn't there and you were there. So what if I try and figure out what happened and you help me. Okay?
> [CD] Yes.
> L Alright. So where were you when that happened?
> [CD] In the shed.
> L You were at the shed, were you? At whose house?
> [CD] His shed.
> L His shed, yeah, and what were you do[i]ng in the shed?
> [CD] Holding his willy.
> L Holding his willy. Ohm, and how did that happen, like?
> [CD] He told me.
> L Yeah, and then what, he said, what did he say to you?
> [CD] He just said I said to him I didn't want to.
> L Oh did you? Good. That was good. And then what happened?
> [CD] Mmm, I holded his willy again.
> L Did you? Even though you said you didn't want to?
> [CD] Yes,
> L Yeah. That was a bit rough wasn't it.
> [CD] Yeah.

The High Court quashed the conviction on three bases: the interviewer's reliance on leading questions when questioning such a young complainant, CD's inconsistent account of the location of the incident in evidence and the trial judge's inadequate reasons for the verdict. The court observed that '[i]n the circumstances of this trial, it was an error for the Court of Criminal Appeal to hold that it had been open to the trial judge to be satisfied of the *reliability* of CD's statements in the interview and to reason from that, despite the appellant's denials, to a

163 [2012] HCA 34; 290 ALR 699, [29].

conclusion that his guilt had been proved beyond reasonable doubt'.[164] The High Court explained its position thus:

> 45. … [S]ince it was at least possible that CD could not recall the day of the alleged offence when she gave evidence 22 months later, her firmness in cross-examination, while capable of bearing on her truthfulness, was an uncertain foundation for accepting that her account in the interview was reliable.
>
> 46. … How was the judge to arrive at a state of satisfaction beyond reasonable doubt of the reliability of CD's statements in the interview given that the limited detail of the allegation was supplied in response to leading questions and only after initial denials? Those statements were the only evidence of the commission of the offence.
>
> 47. In later statements, CD gave inconsistent accounts of the scene of the offence. It is understandable that CD may have been confused when she was shown the plan of her great-grandmother's property and asked to identify the shed. Nonetheless, the fact that CD gave three different accounts of the scene of the offence cannot be dismissed in any assessment of her reliability as an historian.

The dangers of relying on leading questions were recognised also in the 2011 English Court of Appeal case of *Edwards*,[165] where the court upheld as appropriate the trial judge's repeated attempts to prevent a six-year-old witness being led, even though the questioning was cross-examination (the occasion where leading questions are generally considered appropriate: *UEA*, s 42). The English Court of Appeal has also provided guidance on some of the consequences that may flow where cross-examination breaches acceptable practice.

The *UEA* recognises that for some categories of witness and in some circumstances, the restrictions on leading questions should be lifted. Section 37(1) lists some situations where leading questions are permissible and also provides for relaxation of the rule in other cases with the leave of the court. Generally speaking, the s 37(1) exceptions involve questions about matters that are not in dispute, where considerations of trial efficiency warrant lifting the rule and where the witness may not be vulnerable to suggestion. Examples of circumstances that may warrant a grant of leave include where a leading question is necessary to direct the witness to the point of their evidence and where it might be necessary to prompt a witness who does not understand what information is being sought by non-leading questions, no matter how couched or arranged. Some witnesses, like police officers, valuers and inspectors testify frequently and in cases with very similar circumstances. The leading questions rule may unnecessarily impede obtaining accurate evidence from them. Section 37(3) provides for one way of dealing with this. Section 33 deals with this problem specifically for police officers – that they are in court regularly testifying to events where detail can become blurred, especially with respect to timing and what was done and said, by whom and when. As a result, police are accorded greater freedom than other witnesses with respect to being led through (or reading) a previously made written statement. The only limitations that apply to police in this respect are contained in s 33(2), namely:

> (a) the statement was made by the police officer *at the time of or soon after the occurrence of the events* to which it refers, and
> (b) the police officer signed the statement when it was made, and

---

164 Ibid [48], emphasis in the original text. It is suggested that in cases where the prohibition has been breached there is scope for the operation of ss 138 and 137 of the uniform *Evidence Acts*.

165 [2011] EWCA Crim 3028. See Chapter 6 which also includes an extract from Bowden, Plater and Henning, above n 74.

(c) a copy of the statement had been given to the person charged or to his or her Australian legal practitioner or legal counsel a reasonable time before the hearing of the evidence for the prosecution. (emphasis added)

There is some guidance in the cases on the contemporaneity of the police statement relative to the events it describes. In *Orchard v Spooner*[166] Newman J considered an earlier version of the current s 33 to hold that a statement made six weeks after the events fell outside the provision. In *Steve*[167] it seems to have been accepted that a statement made approximately eight days after the events came within s 33, and in *Chisari (No 2)*[168] the same time delay created no error. In *Chisari* the NSW Court of Criminal Appeal noted that the discretionary nature of the judgment meant that it may in some instances be preferable for a police witness, rather than merely reading a statement, to be led through the statement by question and answer. Button J in *Briggs (No 4)*[169] reviewed these authorities and concluded that just under three days brought the statement clearly within s 33 (particularly bearing in mind that 18 months had passed since the events in question had taken place). Button J ruled it was a matter for the prosecutor whether the evidence was adduced from the witness reading the statement or by being led through it.

Answers to impermissible leading questions are admissible. However, the weight that is accorded to them will be affected.[170]

Testifying after time

Delay is a major enemy of precise recall. A witness's testimony may change its significance depending on small details and there are a number of situations where detail can be a real challenge for witnesses to recall, especially because it is highly likely that a period of time will have transpired between the events under scrutiny and the trial. Some events will involve complexity in terms of what happened, who did it, when and in what order. When the recollection of these events slips due to the passage of months or years this detail also slips. Of course, different people have different capacities to grasp and recall detail. The very old, the infirm, the very young, those who have found the events stressful, those who find testifying in court stressful – all these variables can come into play. Stress and infirmity aside, regular witnesses to similar events that come before the court, such as police, security guards and nightclub bouncers, may also find it even more difficult to remember each brawl, stabbing, incident and altercation in appropriate detail. Further, fact-finders are more likely to return a robust verdict if courts can maximise the quantum of available reliable and accurate information. For this reason, courts have long accepted that witnesses should be able to refresh their memory from certain documents made contemporaneously to events. Section 32 of the *UEA* provides that before a witness can refresh their memory:

- the court must first give leave to the witness – this requires consideration of the matters listed in s 192(2); and
- for the granting of leave, two additional discretionary considerations apply:

166 (1992) 28 NSWLR 114.
167 [2008] NSWCCA 231; 189 A Crim R 68.
168 [2006] NSWCCA 325.
169 [2014] NSWSC 853.
170 *Ireland v Taylor* [1949] 1 KB 300, 313; *Moor v Moor* [1954] 1 WLR 927; [1954] 2 All ER 458 (CA).

- first, whether the witness has exhausted his or her memory, that is, 'whether the witness will be able to recall the fact or opinion adequately without using the document' (s 32(2)(a)); and
- second, whether the document to be used for refreshing memory is one that the witness wrote of the events in question when they were fresh in her memory (or whether, if written by someone else, it was found at that time by the witness to be accurate) (s 32(2)(b)(i)).

With respect to the witness's freshness of memory at the time the document was written or found by the witness to be accurate, the temptation to rely on precedents applying *UEA*, s 66, particularly the case of *Graham*,[171] needs to be tempered by the quite different context in which freshness is under consideration in s 32. In the current refreshing memory context, 'freshness of memory' is merely a consideration relevant to the grant of leave, not a statutory prerequisite for the admission of otherwise inadmissible evidence.

Section 32 also permits, subject to leave of the court, a witness to read portions of a document aloud in court and, if a party requests, it provides for a court to direct that the portions in a document used to refresh memory are produced to that party.[172]

We saw above that leading questions may reduce the persuasiveness of witness evidence. Refreshing memory from a document may have a similar taint because, in essence, the jury is required to determine the strength of the evidence from the circumstances relating to the making of the document relied on by the witness. When one reflects on the Act's heavy regulation of hearsay evidence through s 59 and its exceptions, the liberality of memory refreshment can seem out of synchrony. However, at least with s 32 (and with leading questions) the jury can see these prompts. This is not the case where jurors are not privy to a witness getting help with their memory which can occur where witnesses read statements that they (or someone else) wrote after events. These might have been written by other witnesses or even by journalists relying on third party observations at the time of the incident (and accessed by witnesses online). Witnesses might undergo hypnosis after an incident. In all these circumstances a witness may present quite differently (and potentially falsely) compared to their completely unaided recollection in the witness box. Prosecutorial disclosure obligations and *UEA*, s 34, can provide some potential transparency with respect to witnesses who refresh their memory out of court – but only if a party knows that the witness has acted in this way.

The unfavourable witness

Witnesses *can* disappoint the party that calls them – but it must be remembered that the law is alert to the fact that witnesses are obliged by their oath or affirmation to tell the truth, not keep to a party's script. We are all prone to memory loss, suggestibility, and perception flaws to some extent. And sometimes

---

171 [1998] HCA 61; 195 CLR 606, which considered 'freshness' as 'very likely be measured in hours or days' (Gaudron, Gummow and Hayne JJ) in the hearsay exception context, without the presence of s 66(2A) which now considerably expands considerations relevant to assessing freshness. See also *Roth (a Pseudonym)* [2014] VSCA 242.

172 The common law required that a document called (to be produced) by a party could be forced into evidence. *UEA*, s 35, gets rid of this rule which had turned reliance on documents in the hands of counsel or witnesses into a major source of game play.

witnesses deliberately do not tell the truth. As Andrewartha observes, '[d]espite popular misconception, people's lies are not telegraphed via cues as blatant as Pinocchio's telltale nose'.[173] This poses particular problems for the assessment of witness credibility in situations where the party's own witness is giving unhelpful, unfavourable or damaging evidence. The general rule, contained in s 102, is that parties may not cross-examine or impeach the credit of their own witnesses. At common law, cross-examination or discrediting of a party's own witnesses is only permitted where they are 'hostile' or 'adverse' to the party's case in the sense that they are adverse to the truth or unwilling to tell the truth, thus essentially ambushing the party who called them. Evidence contradicting a witness may be adduced from another source, provided that the evidence is not directed solely at discrediting the witness. But that presents its own tactical drawbacks. The *UEA* response, embodied in s 38, has seen a considerable liberalisation of the common law approach. Where a party[174] calls a witness who is then unfavourable to the party's case within the terms of *UEA*, s 38, then subject to fulfilling the requirements of s 38 and the granting of leave from the court, the witness becomes vulnerable to cross-examination by the party that called them, including facing discrediting questions and the admission of any prior inconsistent statements. As we see below, s 38(1) recognises that witnesses are not simplistically liars or truthful. They may be somewhere in between.

Nowadays, it is recognised that cross-examination of one's own witness may be beneficial to the goal of reaching an accurate verdict. The ALRC in its 1985 Interim Report discussed the dynamics associated with shifting from the common law approach:

> It is argued that where a party knows that a witness will not swear up to his proof of evidence, but calls such a witness intending to attack his evidence, it is a misuse of evidence – the witness is not being put forward as a witness of truth. Thus, this argument is based on the 'vouching the witness' theory which has been discredited. As to the prosecution, it is argued that it will receive a tactical advantage because, where a prior statement is used, it will go into evidence as an exhibit and go to the jury room. The prosecution, however, has suffered the tactical disadvantage of having to call a witness to prove its case and that witness has supported the defence. The argument also wrongly assumes that the defence will never have the need to call an unfavourable witness. A grave danger in imposing the requirement that the unfavourable evidence is unexpected is that it would enable criminals to defeat prosecutions by suborning key witnesses. The prosecution will normally find out before the hearing, particularly where there is a committal, that a witness is unfavourable.[175]

Importantly, s 38's liberalisation of cross-examination in this context has effectively transformed the calling and examination of prosecution witnesses.[176] Before the *UEA*, prosecutors could be faced with a difficult situation created by their obligation to call all material and credible witnesses whose evidence is necessary to give a complete picture of events, even where they know that some or all of those witnesses may not give evidence supportive of the Crown case. The common law restrictions on challenging these witnesses' testimony and credibility could

---

173 In D Andrewartha, 'Lie Detection in Litigation: Science or Prejudice?' (2008) 15 *Psychiatry, Psychology and Law* 88, 88-9.

174 On the scope given to the notion of 'party', see also *UEA*, s 38(7).

175 ALRC, *Evidence (Interim)*, above n 21, [626], quoted by McClellan CJ at CL in *Burrell* [2007] NSWCCA 65; 190 A Crim R 148, [238] (Sully and James JJ agreeing).

176 See *Doyle* [2014] NSWCCA 4 (Bathurst CJ); *Kanaan* [2006] NSWCCA 109 (Hunt AJA, Buddin and Hoeben JJ).

run counter to the desired outcome of presenting a complete and accurate account of events. Instances where the Act has changed this position for prosecutors are discussed below.

Section 38, combined with the Act's more liberal exceptions to the rule against hearsay, adds another important facet to the legislation's broad practical shift to expanding the information base for modern curial fact-finding. Nevertheless, the law still prevents a party cross-examining their own witness unless there is good reason – or a *good enough* reason. This is where the terms of s 38 come into play. First, when a witness gives evidence that fails to assist a party's case – or worse, damages it – techniques such as limited leading questions or memory refreshment by document may assist to resolve a witness's confusion or mistake. Where these techniques leave a witness's account potentially 'unfavourable', s 38 may permit a party to obtain court leave to expose the weaknesses in the witness's account through cross-examination (that is, questioning designed to test and challenge a witness's account).

To cross-examine one's own witness under s 38, a party needs leave of the court[177] and to establish that the witness:

- is 'unfavourable' (s 38(1)(a)); and/or
- is not 'making a genuine attempt to give evidence' in examination-in-chief on 'a matter of which the witness may reasonably be supposed to have knowledge' (s 38(1)(b)); and/or
- has *at any time* 'made a prior inconsistent statement' (s 38(1)(c)).

Section 38(1) does not permit the party to cross-examine the unfavourable witness at large. The party is limited to cross-examining in relation to those matters that established the particular ground(s) in sub-s (1) that supported the grant of leave. Where parties wish to cross-examine their own witnesses on matters relevant only to their credibility, separate and specific leave to do so must be obtained under s 38(3).[178] Cross-examination on credibility is also subject to the requirements of *UEA*, ss 103 and 106. To be clear, questioning under s 38(3) cannot occur unless the requirements of Part 3.7 are satisfied *and*, in addition, the court grants leave. If a court grants leave to cross-examine under any part of s 38, the cross-examination must comply with rules relating to cross-examination, including *UEA*, ss 41 and 42, and the common law rule in *Browne v Dunn*.[179] Subject to these rules, the party may question the witness using leading questions.

As noted, the limbs in s 38(1) limit the matters on which cross-examination may be permitted. As Bathurst CJ observed in *Doyle*[180] 'the use of the word "about" in the chapeau to s 38(1) makes it clear that leave may be granted to not only conduct cross-examination specifically directed to one of the subjects referred to in s 38(1), but also to the probability of establishing a factual state of affairs in relation to the matters contended for by the party conducting the cross-examination'. This does not mean that a general cross-examination can be undertaken. Initially, such questioning must be limited to the ground on which leave is granted, though in conformity with s 38(1)'s reliance on the term 'about'

177 See discussed below and see *UEA*, ss 38(6) and 192. Section 192 is discussed in greater detail also at Chapter 10, pp 428-429.

178 The rules about admissibility of evidence relevant only to credibility are set out in *UEA*, Pt 3.7.

179 (1893) 6 R 67.

180 [2014] NSWCCA 4, [293] (Price and Campbell JJ agreeing), citing Heydon JA in *Le* [2002] NSWCCA 186; 54 NSWLR 474, [67] and [73].

as Bathurst CJ indicated, this permits questions on a topic 'touching it, concerning it, in the matter of it, in reference to it, or in regard to it'.[181] Thus, as well as proving a witness's prior inconsistent statement the cross-examination could extend, for example, to questioning the witness on their bias (to support the truth of the prior statement over their testimony).

With regard to the meaning of the term, 'unfavourable' there seems to be little doubt that the 'broad meaning' given by Smart J in *Souleyman*[182] in the early days of the operation of the *UEA* has been accepted generally.[183] Smart J stated:

> The word "unfavourable" in s 38(1)(a) does not mean "adverse". It means "not favourable." That construction could have wide ranging ramifications but the Court is given a discretion and would carefully examine the circumstances to see how the discretion should be exercised. A far fetched example would be if a witness said he could not remember something that happened three years ago. The discretion is important and designed to prevent any form of abuse in the administration of the more liberal test of "unfavourable."

Evidence that is not favourable to a party's case includes anything that goes against their case. It could also include an omission to give evidence that helps the party's case and may include an omission due to a genuine lack of memory (though in this situation the leave of the court might first be sought to lead the witness under s 37 or for the witness to refresh their memory under s 32). Clearly, the term 'unfavourable' is not without limitations. It would not apply merely because a witness fails to accord with a prosecutor's wished-for version of facts. However, despite some earlier contradictory authority,[184] Victorian the Court of Appeal in *DPP v Garrett*[185] confirmed that '[i]f the evidence of the witness called by that party is inconsistent with, or "likely to be contradictory" of, that identified case, it will ordinarily satisfy the description of "unfavourable".'[186]

The extensive case law considering s 38 reveals its liberal application. One of the earliest appellate determinations of s 38 is the High Court case of *Adam*,[187] where Gleeson CJ, McHugh, Kirby and Hayne JJ gave a generous interpretation to the section. It effectively permitted Sako, an early-in-investigation suspect in the killing of police officer David Carty, to be called as a prosecution witness. Sako had been interviewed by police a number of weeks after the killing and had made a statement implicating the accused, but once in the witness box he refused to give evidence in accordance with his statement or indeed even to acknowledge

181 Heydon JA in *Le* [2002] NSWCCA 186; 54 NSWLR 474, [59], relying on the *Oxford English Dictionary* (2nd ed) definition of 'about', cited in *Kanaan* [2006] NSWCCA 109, [83] and in *Doyle* [2014] NSWCCA 4, [294] (Bathurst CJ).

182 (1996) 40 NSWLR 712, 715.

183 See the detailed discussion in *SH, MV and KC* [2011] ACTSC 198, [29]-[35] by Refshauge J, indicating it has been followed in *Lozano* (unreported, NSWCCA, 10 June 1997). It has also been followed by the Full Court of the Federal Court in *Colonial Mutual Life Assurance Society Ltd v Donnelly* (1998) 82 FCR 418, 430. See also *Velevski (No 2)* (1997) 93 A Crim R 420, 422; *Cakovski* [2002] NSWSC 632; 133 A Crim R 18, 22 [13]; *White* [2003] NSWCCA 64; 140 A Crim R 63, 72 [56]; *Fowler* [2000] NSWCCA 142, [12]; *Taylor* [2003] NSWCCA 194, [14]; *Radisich v Molina* [2009] FMCA 1121, [34]; *DPP v McRae* [2010] VSC 114, [24]; *Anyang (Ruling No 1)* [2011] VSC 31, [10]; *Ronen* [2004] NSWSC 1298, [49]; *Lee* [2009] NSWCCA 259, [30]. See also *Doyle* [2014] NSWCCA 4; *Kanaan* [2006] NSWCCA 109, [83].

184 *Kneebone* [1999] NSWCCA 279; 47 NSWLR 450, 461 [54] (Greg James J); *Doyle* [2014] NSWCCA 4.

185 [2016] VSCA 31.

186 Ibid [68] (citations omitted).

187 [2001] HCA 57; 207 CLR 96. Cf the strong dissent by Gaudron J.

that he had witnessed the stabbing. Sako's unwillingness to assist the prosecution and implicate the accused was not unexpected (a matter that would have been significant at common law). However, *UEA*, s 38(1)(b) and (c), and sub-s (3), enabled Sako's early statement to police to be put before the jury as a prior inconsistent statement and, even though it was otherwise inadmissible hearsay evidence, it became admissible to establish the facts via *UEA*, s 60.[188] In response to the challenge that it was bizarre for the law to allow (and thus encourage) the prosecution to call an unreliable witness, discredit him and then rely on his out-of-court inadmissible hearsay statement to be before the jury because it conflicted with his testimony, the majority on the court observed:

> 37. … No longer were tribunals of fact to be asked to treat evidence of prior inconsistent statements as evidence that showed no more than that the witness may not be reliable. The prior inconsistent statements were to be taken as evidence of their truth. Thus far from the result being, as the appellant asserted, bizarre or unintended, it is the intended operation of the Act.[189]

Cross-examination on what Sako had seen of Carty's killing was complicated because Sako told the court his statement to police was merely repeating what others had told him. As was pointed out by the High Court, the only effective cross-examination of Sako open to the defence, aside from suggesting his observations were affected by drink and/or his own injuries on the night, was to expose Sako's self-interest in telling the police what was recorded in the statement (namely, that the accused committed the stabbing) to move suspicion from himself and his brother. Thus, and importantly for explaining the scope of s 38(1)(a), the High Court has recognised that 'to give evidence which, at best, is unhelpful to the party calling it, and to do so without "making a genuine attempt to give evidence", is to give evidence "unfavourable" to that party'.[190] *Adam*'s case illustrates the significance of the greater availability of cross-examination to a prosecutor of its own witness. It seems clear that s 38 now places more emphasis on the prosecution's obligation to call witnesses, irrespective of their credibility. This was noted by the NSW Court of Criminal Appeal in *Kanaan*,[191] which also added:

> 84. … Section 38 is living up to its potential for transforming the traditional procedure in criminal trials: *R v Parkes* [2003] NSWCCA 12; 147 A Crim R 450 at [81], [141]. In *R v Ronen* [2004] NSWSC 1298 at [32], Whealy J observed that the increasingly common use of s 38 has often demonstrated its value in getting to the truth of the matter, although great care must be taken to ensure that the trial does not become side-tracked by a collateral issue carrying with it the real possibility of prejudice to the accused. That observation was correct, but attention is drawn to the accepted interpretation of "unfairly prejudicial" in ss 135-136 and of "unfair prejudice" in s 137, that prejudice to the accused is not unfair merely because the evidence tends to establish the Crown case: *R v BD* (1997) 94 A Crim R 131 at 139; *Papakosmas v R* [1999] HCA 37; 196 CLR 297 at [29], [91], [98].

---

188 Since *Adam*'s case the Act was amended, though the result in *Adam* would be the same. Sako's police statement would now be admissible via s 66 (which was amended by the addition of sub-s (2A) in 2009). For applications under the current legislative regime, see Chapter 9 and *Col* [2013] NSWCCA 302, [29]-[32], and *Ryan (No 7)* [2012] NSWSC 1160; 218 A Crim R 384, [16]ff.

189 Citing ALRC, *Evidence* (Report No 38, 1987), [144]; ALRC, *Evidence (Interim)*, above n 21, [334], [685].

190 *Adam* [2001] HCA 57; 207 CLR 96, [27].

191 [2006] NSWCCA 109 (Hunt AJA, Buddin and Hoeben JJ), and quoted approvingly in *Doyle* [2014] NSWCCA 4 (Bathurst CJ).

Some light is shed on the broader issues concerning prosecutorial behaviour in the NSW criminal appeal case of *Gilham*.[192] In 1995 Jeffrey Gilham, the appellant, pleaded guilty to the manslaughter of his brother (Christopher) whom, he said, he had discovered in the act of setting fire to the family home after stabbing their parents. Gilham claimed that he had killed Christopher following the discovery of his brother's actions in killing their parents. Jeffrey was sentenced to three years' imprisonment, deferred by placing him on a five-year good behaviour bond. A coronial inquiry concluded consistently with Jeffrey's account. A renewed police investigation in 1999 led to a second inquest that terminated in April 2000 with a finding that there was evidence capable of satisfying a jury that Jeffrey had murdered his parents. In July 2000 the Director of Public Prosecutions determined that there was no reasonable prospect of a conviction and decided not to prosecute Jeffrey for his parents' murders but, when a year later a private prosecution of Jeffrey for murder was launched by Jeffrey's uncle, the proceedings were taken over by the DPP[193] and no evidence was offered. Jeffrey was discharged. Yet another police investigation took place and in 2005 a further brief of evidence was sent to the DPP. An *ex officio* indictment was filed in the Supreme Court in 2006, charging Jeffrey with the murder of his parents. He was found guilty on both counts in late 2008 and sentenced to life imprisonment. He successfully appealed to the NSW Court of Criminal Appeal in 2012. One of the appeal grounds related to the prosecutor's failure to call Professor Cordner. It was claimed that he was not called solely because his evidence conflicted with the prosecution case theory. An aspect of this 'conflict' was discussed by the Court of Criminal Appeal:

> 410. Professor Cordner was expressly invited to offer his views about a wide range of issues that had been the subject of comment by Dr Oettle, including the relatively small amount of blood transferred to the applicant, which might have been explained by the applicant washing. To this Professor Cordner raised the question, which we note was then the subject of considerable focus at the trial, whether the applicant could have stabbed Christopher 17 times without being spattered with blood. He said:
>
> > "Assuming that Jeffrey was spattered with blood, why wash – and if he washed where and how did he do this? The inference is that he washed because he had some of his mother's and father's blood on him too. He had no need to wash (assuming he is acting rationally, which may be a significant assumption) if it was only his brother's blood because he is going to concede that he killed his brother. But why wash the knife too? Blood from all the victims would be on it however the murders happened. (Incidentally, I can see no report of a formal examination of the knife to confirm the absence of blood, although as far as one can see from the photographs, there is no obvious blood on it. In the absence of any blood, an additional question would need to be asked – was it indeed the weapon?)."
>
> 411. We regard these questions and those set out in paragraph 10 of his report as sensible questions posed interrogatively for the attention of the investigators. They were questions that Professor Cordner thought might have been overlooked. He recommended submitting Christopher's shave coat and the applicant's shorts to analysis for hydrocarbons and accelerants if they were still available (they were not) and reviewing the formal report of the examination of the knife (there was none). He also suggested that the applicant's clothes and shoes found upstairs be submitted for examination, particularly for hydrocarbons or blood (they were no longer available, having been disposed of by police in 1995).

192 [2012] NSWCCA 131.

193 See *Director of Public Prosecutions Act 1986* (NSW), s 9.

The court accepted this ground of appeal and allowed the appeal. It quoted from the judgments of Smart AJ and Greg James J in *Kneebone*:

> 49. Since both experience and logic confirm that merely because a witness' evidence is inconsistent with or contradicts other evidence, it need not be untrue, it is necessary that a prosecutor whose decision is under examination be able to point to identifiable factors which can justify a decision not to call a material witness on the ground of unreliability: see *R v Apostilides* (at 576); Director of Public Prosecutions Guidelines, at least if the suggestion of attempting to obtain an improper tactical advantage is to be avoided. It is therefore necessary for the prosecutor to take appropriate steps, including, where necessary interviewing witnesses to be able to form the opinion.
>
> 50. In reaching a view as to reliability, it is clear that it is not an adequate basis to conclude that the witness is unreliable, merely because the witness' account does not accord with some case theory which is attractive to the prosecutor. An approach, whereby the witness is not called at all or is left to the defence to call because the witness' evidence is seen as not fitting the prosecution's view of the case is likely to lead to a miscarriage of justice. *R v Apostilides* deals with the consequence of such an approach. A case theory should accord with the evidence. The prosecutor should not espouse a theory and tailor a case accordingly: *R v Anderson* [*Hilton Bombing* case] (1991) 53 A Crim R 421.[194]

The prosecution had stated that '[u]nlike civilian witnesses, the Crown does not believe that it is appropriate to call an expert whom it intends to discredit by obtaining leave to cross-examine under s 38 of the *Evidence Act*. Based upon the decision of the High Court in *Apostilides*,[195] the Crown will make Professor Cordner available for you to call'. The Court of Criminal Appeal considered the prosecution stance inadequate and noted that:

- It was not suggested that Professor Cordner lacked academic or professional esteem nor was any other expert witness asked to comment on any weaknesses (or otherwise) in Professor Cordner's approach.
- The prosecution relied on its decision not to call Professor Cordner in 2008 on statements in the Professor's report dated July 1999 and also asserted that Professor Cordner's views were based on 'a complete acceptance of the accused's account', '[did] not withstand scrutiny' and 'after Professor Cordner gave evidence on the voir dire in March 2008 concerning his approach to the preparation of his report, an objective and detached prosecutor would have rejected any suggestion of bias in his methodology or his conclusions'.[196]

The court also noted that, should the prosecutor perceive 'a persisting bias or imbalance' in Professor Cordner's approach after leading evidence from him concerning the pattern of injuries 'and after giving his views the careful consideration they deserved', s 38 cross-examination would have been available.

> 404. … The Crown is simply not entitled to discriminate between experts, in particular between those whose views they have sought, calling only those that advance the Crown case, any more than it is entitled to call some lay witnesses and not others for some perceived tactical advantage. The fact that there is disagreement between the experts from whom the Crown have sought an opinion provides no basis for the Crown to elect to call only those experts who will give evidence that supports the Crown case, or whose views are consistent with the Crown case theory, and to refuse to call those witnesses whose views do not support the Crown case. This is particularly so where the subject

194 [1999] NSWCCA 279; 47 NSWLR 450 (Spigelman CJ agreeing).
195 [1984] HCA 38; 154 CLR 563.
196 [2012] NSWCCA 131, [370].

> matter about which the opinions are expressed is controversial. The Crown Prosecutor's obligation is to call all relevant evidence at his or her disposal. That obligation is a continuing obligation which persists until the Crown case is closed. The *Apostilides* principles are not the rules of a game. They are rules designed as a protection against unfairness or the abuse of prosecutorial power (see *R v Gibson* [2002] NSWCCA 401 (Sully J at [49], Wood CJ and Howie J agreeing)), quoting *Randall v The Queen* [2002] UKPC 19; [2002] 1 WLR 2237 at 2243).

The court then elaborated on the Crown's ability to resort to s 38, observing:

> 405. … Where the views of the experts differ, the extent and basis for disagreement can then be tested, if necessary, with the Crown seeking leave to cross-examine where the evidence might prove to be unfavourable under s 38 of the *Evidence Act* (as occurred in *Velevski*). It is in that process that the interests of justice are preserved and advanced. The assertion by the Solicitor for Public Prosecutions that it is not appropriate to utilise s 38 for the purpose of calling an expert witness who the Crown intends to discredit by obtaining leave to cross-examine is not soundly based, whether in the context of this case or generally. On the appeal it was only faintly suggested that this approach to the construction of s 38 provided justification for the Crown's decision not to call Professor Cordner. …
>
> 412. We are satisfied that Professor Cordner's report fairly reflects the opinion he held at the time of the trial in October 2008 and that the Crown's failure to call him as a witness cannot be justified.

Lane[197] reveals the application of s 38 with respect to a prosecution witness whose account potentially assists the defence, but who had made inconsistent statements on prior occasions. The case concerned Keli Lane who was arraigned in 2010 on three counts of perjury and one count relating to the murder of her newborn baby on or about 14 September 1996. Lane claimed that she had given birth to the baby, that its father was Andrew Norris (or Morris) who had lived at the relevant time in units in Wisbeach Road, Balmain, and who had been given the child. Peter Clark also lived in these units at the same time. At trial, leave was granted under s 38(1)(a) and (c) for the prosecution to cross-examine Clark on statements he made in 2008 and 2010 relating to the presence or not of mail addressed to Andrew Norris or Andrew Morris at the units at times relevant to the defence case. On the *voir dire* held on 22 September 2010 Clark repeated the substance of one of his statements:

> 52. … I saw some mail for Andrew Morris I'd say on more than one occasion. Andrew Norris was just the once. I think for one of those occasions for Andrew Morris, it may even have been in the foyer of the building, but I'd be prepared to say that Andrew Norris once, Andrew Morris more than once.

The trial judge granted leave to the prosecutor to undertake limited cross-examination of Clark (regarding the mail) and ruled that the defence could cross-examine afterwards. In essence, the defence case was that Clark's statements failed to disclose 'a clear inconsistency within the meaning of s 38 of the *Evidence Act*' and the trial judge should have exercised his discretion under s 192 to reject the prosecutor's application to cross-examine Clark. The appellate court held that there was no unfairness or inconsistency with the prosecutor's obligation to act fairly. Bathurst CJ, Simpson and Adamson JJ observed:

> 165. In our view, s 38 does not create an inconsistency with … the duties of prosecutors. It provides a mechanism whereby the party calling a witness is, with leave, permitted

197 [2013] NSWCCA 317. Special leave to the High Court refused, [2014] HCATrans 171.

> to cross-examine its own witness, in circumstances that include where the witness is unfavourable or has made a prior inconsistent statement. A grant of leave does not remove the right of the other party, in this case the appellant, to cross-examine the witness.
>
> 166. Section 192 provides added protection to the opposing party in that, by s 192(2), it obliges the trial judge to take certain matters into account in deciding whether leave ought be granted. Such matters include the extent to which to do so would be unfair to a party or to a witness: s 192(2)(b).
>
> 167. The effect of the prosecutor's decision to call Mr Clark in the Crown case was to provide an opportunity for the defence to cross-examine him. Had the discretion been exercised not to call Mr Clark, the appellant would have had no choice but to call Mr Clark if she wished to have the benefit of his evidence. The prosecutor sought leave under s 38 to cross-examine Mr Clark. For the reasons given, the conditions for a grant of leave were met in two respects: his evidence was unfavourable and he had made at least one if not two prior inconsistent statements.

Finally, reference should be made to the diversity of situations where s 38 may arise. There are cases like *Velevski (No 2)*[198] where the family members of the accused are material witnesses whom the prosecution are obliged to call. As Dunford J observed:

> The fact that a most important witness, who was in the house at the relevant time, who is the father of the accused and a person whom the Crown must exclude as a possible suspect (unless acting in conjunction with the accused) has departed substantially in giving evidence from his statement is obviously of great significance. What that significance is can, in my view, only be ascertained, if at all, if he is cross-examined.
>
> A number of possible explanations [regarding inconsistencies between his testimony and a prior statement] are that he is lying in his evidence to protect his son, or himself, or both of them or that he was lying when he made his statement. There may be other explanations but, if there are, such other possible explanations should be explored. ... Defence counsel may not wish to challenge in cross-examination the version he has given in his evidence in chief.[199]

Similarly, in *Pell*,[200] in accordance with its obligation to call all witnesses who could throw light on the events, the prosecution called 23 witnesses some of whom it was expected would give evidence of church practices that were inconsistent with the Crown case. In order to confront this difficulty, the prosecutor applied for an advance ruling from the trial judge under *UEA*, s 192A, for leave to cross-examine the witnesses with respect to the evidence that was expected to be unfavourable (s 38(1)(a)) and with respect to a prior inconsistent statement made by one witness (s 38(1)(c)). The trial judge held that evidence adduced by the prosecution that was 'inconsistent with, or likely to contradict [the complainant's] account of events was relevantly "unfavourable"'[201] and granted the leave sought. This ruling was not contested on appeal. However, the prosecution's apparent non-compliance with the rule in *Browne v Dunn* in conducting the cross-examination was a factor in the High Court's quashing of Pell's conviction (see further in Chapter 6 at p 219). The prosecution's pre-trial application, in this case, for a ruling under s 38 is an example of parties' ability to seek leave under s 38 on an anticipatory basis. They do not have to wait until trials are underway and witnesses give 'unfavourable' evidence. Provided they can establish that the evidence will be 'unfavourable', s 38 leave to cross-examine may be granted.

---

198 (1997) 93 A Crim R 420. A similar situation occurred in *DPP v Bourbaud* [2011] VSC 103.

199 (1997) 93 A Crim R 420, 427.

200 [2020] HCA 12.

201 Ibid [28].

Leave considerations

The phrase, 'without limiting the matters that the court may take into account in determining whether to give leave or a direction' under s 38(6), requires a court to consider whether the party seeking leave gave notice of their intentions 'at the earliest opportunity'[202] and whether the witness has been, or is likely to be, relevantly questioned by another party, and the extent of that cross-examination. In addition, s 192(2) of the Act provides general considerations for the granting of leave (or permission or direction). These considerations are whether granting leave (or not) will impact on the length of the hearing, create unfairness to a party or to a witness, the importance of the evidence, the nature of the proceedings, and (where relevant) the power a court has to adjourn or make any other order (or give direction) in relation to the evidence. Refshauge J illustrates the application of leave criteria in a s 38 context in the following case.

SH, MV and KC

[2011] ACTSC 198

This was a ruling on a *voir dire* by Refshauge J. The defendants were charged with sexual intercourse without consent. Their defence was that the complainant consented. The complainant (C) had given evidence that she was very distressed when she returned to college after the alleged assaults. Four prosecution witnesses had made statements to this effect but it became clear that they intended to give evidence to the contrary, stating that C was happy and not distressed. These four witnesses were all material and credible witnesses. Refshauge J considered an application by the prosecutor for an advance ruling (under *UEA*, s 192A) declaring these witnesses unfavourable under s 38(1)(a) and seeking leave to cross-examine them on the issue of C's demeanour when she returned to college. Defence counsel opposed the application. As no evidence had been given by the witnesses, his Honour was required to rely on their police statements. He accepted that for a court to grant leave to cross-examine in this context there was strong authority (including *Adam*'s case) for not maintaining the traditional common law requirement that a party be unexpectedly confronted by a witness's change of heart.

> **Refshauge J**: 36. It seems to me that the state of the complainant's demeanour after returning to the college is a very relevant matter to assist the jury to determine whether the sexual intercourse was consensual or not. It also goes directly to the credibility of the complainant who, notoriously in cases of sexual offences, is often the only direct witness for the prosecution to the offences, especially where consent is an issue.
>
> 37. For these reasons, I am satisfied that the evidence of the four young women as to the state of the complainant when she returned to college is unfavourable to the Crown within the meaning of section 38(1)(a) of the *Evidence Act*.
>
> 38. Counsel for the accused submitted that because there was only one witness, the complainant, asserting that she was distressed and four other witnesses to be called by the Crown who assert to the contrary, the evidence cannot be unfavourable.
>
> 39. I do not accept that. In the first place, I do not consider that this is a matter of numbers. In that, I am supported by the decision in *DPP v McRae* where, similarly, four witnesses were in the same relative position.

---

202 In *Meyer* [2018] VSCA 140, [173], counsel for the respondent conceded that the trial judge erred in granting leave to the prosecutor pursuant to s 38 to cross-examine the prosecution witness after defence counsel had concluded his cross-examination. The majority stated that, in the circumstances of the case, 'there was no reason why the prosecutor could not have sought leave to cross-examine ... at the conclusion of ... evidence in chief': at [187].

40. In the second place, it seems to me that the Crown case depends upon an absence of consent. The Crown is entitled to prosecute its case and I am not prepared to accept that it has not been professionally considered so that the test provided for in the Prosecution Policy has not been properly applied, namely that, "there is reliable evidence, duly admissible in a court of law, that a criminal offence has been committed by the person accused … [and that] … [t]he evidence [provides] reasonable prospects of a conviction": ACT Director of Public Prosecutions, *Prosecution Policy*, at http://www.dpp.act.gov.au/publications/prosecutions_policy, at [2.3].

41. The question, then, is whether leave should be granted. That depends on the application of ss 38(6), 135, 137 and 192(2) of the *Evidence Act*. I shall deal with these in sequence:

(a) Section 38(6)(a). I was first informed of such notice yesterday, before the evidence of the complainant had been completed and some time before the first of the young women was to be called. It was, in fact, raised by Mr Pappas from which I infer that notice had been earlier given to counsel for the accused. No point was taken by any counsel for the accused as to any delay in giving notice. There is nothing in that ground to justify a refusal of grant of leave.

(b) Section 38(6)(b). No party other than the Crown submitted that they would be questioning any of the women. No doubt the accused would wish to ask such questions as would strengthen the defence to the charges. They are entitled, of course, to do so. I have found no authority on this point, but it would seem to me that the use of "question" in this paragraph really means, as in s 38(1) "question… as though the party were cross-examining the witness," for the point is that if another party is likely to be testing the evidence, as cross-examination does, then the need for leave to permit the party calling the witness to do so is much diluted. Here, no suggestion was made that any other party would wish to test the evidence in this sense. There is nothing in this ground that would suggest grant of leave should be refused.

(c) Section 135. No submission was made as to what unfair prejudice would be visited on any of the accused, how any cross-examination would be misleading or confusing or what time would be unduly wasted. Given the nature of the likely ambit of any leave, I cannot conceive of any undue waste of time that would be occasioned, especially as I have some power under s 41 of the *Evidence Act* to restrict, for example, repetitive questioning, under s 55 of the Act to reject irrelevant evidence and generally under s 11 to ensure that time is not unduly wasted.

I cannot see that the cross examination would be misleading or confusing.

As to unfair prejudice, I do not see that the cross-examination would be likely to result in the jury using the evidence, thereby elicited, on an improper, perhaps emotional, basis or one that is logically unconnected with the issues in the case. For example, it is unlikely to lead the jury to adopt an illegitimate form of reasoning: *R v Yates* [2002] NSWCCA 520 (at [252]). Indeed, it seems to me that the cross-examination would be of assistance to the jury in determining whether to accept the evidence of the young women, or not.

Given that none of these grounds are made out there is, perhaps, no need for me to consider the probative value of the evidence. That is difficult for the cross-examination has not taken place. Again, no submissions were made to me about the weakness or strength of the likely evidence to be elicited by the cross-examination. That the evidence would be reliable or credible is, perhaps, not of importance: *R v Shamouil* [2006] NSWCCA 112 (at [60] to [64]).

It seems to me that there is no basis for limiting the evidence or rejecting leave under this section.

(d) Section 137. This section provides a mandatory exclusion of evidence, where the probative value is outweighed by the danger or unfair prejudice to the accused. Again, no such unfair prejudice was identified. I am not satisfied that there is any.

(e) Section 192(2)(a). As noted above I do not consider the cross-examination on this limited issue will unduly add to the length of the trial.
(f) Section 192(2)(b). Again, for the reasons noted above, I do not consider that the grant of leave to the Crown to cross-examine the proposed witnesses on this issue would be unfair to the accused. Further, I do not consider that it would be unfair to any of the proposed witnesses.
(g) Section 192(2)(c). The evidence is very important, both because it goes to the heart of the counts of sexual intercourse without consent and it goes to the credibility of the complainant, who is the primary and, in some senses, only Crown witness to the central issues of the counts.
(h) Section 192(2)(d). I do not consider the nature of the proceedings, a criminal trial, as determinative. That they are the trial of counts on the indictment means that the fairness of the trial to both parties, especially the accused, is important. The fairness to the Crown favours the grant of leave. There is, in my view, no unfair prejudice to the accused.
(i) Section 192(2)(e). The capacity to adjourn a jury trial is very limited. In this case, this consideration seems to me to be irrelevant.
(j) Section 192 generally. It is clear that the matters to be taken into account set out in s 192(2) are not exhaustive and do not limit what else the court can take into account. Nothing further, however, was put to me that I could take into account, either for or against the grant of leave. I do take into account, however, insofar as I consider it is relevant in this issue, the approach indicated by Adams J in *R v Pantoja* and Greg James J in *Kneebone*. Leave should not be readily granted to the Crown, particularly where it is simply a matter of a forensic tactic and, unlike this case, not related to a central and critical issue in the case.

42. In all the circumstances I am prepared to grant leave to the Crown to cross-examine the four witnesses, as to the demeanour of the complainant when she returned to the college in the afternoon of 19 June 2009 and, to that extent, the circumstances in which they say they saw her and any issues of credibility relating to these specific matters.

43. I was also asked to grant leave for the Crown to cross-examine one of the young women, in respect of the terms of a conversation she says she had with the complainant by telephone while the complainant was at the house. The terms of that conversation were denied by the complainant.

44. I do not, however, consider that, as an exercise of my discretion, that passage should be the subject of such leave. It is not, in my view, the case that every difference in evidence between witnesses for the Crown should be the subject of such cross-examination. In any event, I am not at all convinced that, so far as the Crown case is concerned, the difference between the statements amounts to evidence that is unfavourable, in the sense in which I have indicated above that it should be construed.

Strictly speaking, following obiter statements in *DPP v Garrett*, 'ss 135 and 137 of the Act do not themselves provide a basis for rejecting an application made under s 38 of the Act',[203] rather, leave considerations are governed by ss 38 and 192. Where leave is granted, in an appropriate case, the discretionary and mandatory exclusions may be engaged in relation to evidence subsequently given in response to questions posed in cross-examination.

The application of leave criteria was also considered in *Kaddour*.[204] Ground 3 of the appeal submitted that the judge erred in granting leave to cross-examine the primary prosecution witness in a murder trial, in accordance with s 38 of the *Evidence Act*, in relation to so-called admissions made to him by the appellant, which were recorded in an earlier statement to police. A related ground of appeal

203 [2016] VSCA 31, [79].
204 [2019] NSWCCA 90.

was that the witness statement could not, in light of s 60(3) of the *Evidence Act*, be used as proof of the truth of the admissions and that its use was limited to the credit of the witness (see further in Chapter 9).

Kaddour

[2019] NSWCCA 90

'Biggie' Kaddour, Mohamed El-Chami and Daniel Azar were charged with the murder of Bassem Salameh on 14 August 2013. Kaddour was found guilty of murder, Azar pleaded guilty to manslaughter and El-Chami pleaded guilty to concealing a serious offence. El-Chami received a discounted sentence for assisting in the prosecution of Kaddour and Azar. The events arose in the deceased's unit in Sydney.

Around 4.00 am on Tuesday 13 August 2013, police had attended the deceased's unit regarding an allegation of malicious damage relating to a broken window. The deceased alleged that a man by the name of Ray had smashed his window. The deceased was heavily intoxicated and drug affected when the police spoke to him. They also spoke to El-Chami, who was present at the deceased's unit. El-Chami identified the alleged offender who was later found bleeding. He told police he had been assaulted by the deceased and three other men whom he did not know. The alleged murder occurred later in the morning. How it is alleged to have occurred is set out below. The body was discovered by the maintenance supervisor checking broken windows, one of which was at Bassem's unit. It transpired that Kaddour threw a lawn bowl through the window to cause the police to attend. The forensic pathologist report indicated that Bassem had died as a result of a number of injuries, with the major injuries being brain damage and skull fractures. He had multiple rib fractures as well.

The prosecution case was a circumstantial one relying on joint criminal enterprise between Biggie Kaddour and Daniel Azar. It included fingerprints (on a pole and a table) implicating Kaddour and lies told by Kaddour to police (as evidence of consciousness of guilt), but El-Chami's testimony was key. The prosecution submitted that El-Chami's first statement to police (MFI 5) on 20 August 2013 demonstrated a joint criminal enterprise between Kaddour and Azar to inflict grievous bodily harm on the deceased. It included the following:

> 8. During the second interview I explained how Daniel AZAR and I were at Bassem's house on Tuesday 13th August and at some point Bassem grabbed Daniel on the arse. This lead to Daniel throwing a punch at Bassem, which then lead [sic] to Daniel and I leaving Bassem's unit though the window. We met up with Biggie, also known as Ahmad K as we had previously been in contact with him over the phone. When we met up with him we told him how Bassem had grabbed Daniel on the arse. A short time later the three of us went back to Bassem's unit where the three of us hung out with Bassem. At one point, *Biggie just got up and started laying punches into Bassem. Daniel then joined in with him and then they were both bashing him. I decided to leave, I wasn't involved in the bashing of Bassem.* I walked out of the unit and waited down the street for about twenty minutes thinking they would just come down. … (emphasis added)

Paragraph [11] of MFI 5 included admissions that El-Chami claimed Kaddour had made to him.

> 11. After we had left, Biggie and Daniel told me what had happened. *They both said Biggie smashed a table of [on] Bassem's head. Biggie also said something about stabbing*

> *him with a screwdriver. At some point Biggie rang his mum, and he said she was going to buy him a ticket to Lebanon so he wouldn't get caught.* Biggie then left Daniel and I. … (emphasis added)

In a second statement (MFI 4), made shortly before he was sentenced, El-Chami stated:

> 17. I don't have a recollection myself of the actual time but I understand that police attended at about 3:45am in the early hours of Tuesday morning. After the police and ambulance had gone Daniel and I stayed at Bassem's. …
>
> 23. We were all there for some time having a smoke. I remember that Daniel, Biggie and Bassem were smoking ice as well as cones. I was mostly smoking cones although I might have had a few puffs of ice. I also had a number of Xanax tablets which I describe as having some 'zanies'. …
>
> 24. At some time later in the night while we were all sitting around (Bassem, me, Biggie and Daniel) the subject of being 'gay' and Bassem having pinched Daniel's arse came up again. I can't remember the exact conversation but the conversation got heated. …
>
> 25. At some stage it got physical although I can't remember precisely how that occurred. *As far as I remember Daniel threw the first punch and then Biggie went over to Bassem. Bassem had stood up as Daniel approached him and Daniel hit him. I remember after Daniel hit him, Bassem fell on the bed. After Daniel hit Bassem, Biggie launched himself onto Bassem.* (emphasis added)

El-Chami gave the principal account of events in his evidence at trial. He acknowledged in court that what he had told police in MFI 4 was the truth.

After being questioned by the prosecutor in chief as to the time when the murder occurred, in response to the question, 'Did you at any stage see the accused Biggie punch Bassem?' El-Chami responded, '[N]o, I didn't. I seen him launch himself on to him so I don't know what he was doing. I was already leaving at that time.'

The prosecutor then made the first of two applications to cross-examine El-Chami pursuant to s 38, on the basis of the prior inconsistent statement in the italicised portion of MFI 5, para 8. Her Honour granted leave, agreeing that it was inconsistent and noting that the evidence involved a crucial matter. Defence counsel did not oppose the granting of leave. This first grant of leave (regarding things that El-Chami told police he actually saw) was not subject to appeal. However, a subsequent s 38 application made in relation to evidence of the 'so-called admissions' (things that El-Chami said he heard from Kaddour) contained in para 11 of MFI 5 was the subject of grounds 2 and 3 of the appeal to the Court of Criminal Appeal.

The second application became necessary because the prosecutor neglected to lead evidence of Kaddour's admissions. Defence counsel opposed a second grant of leave, arguing it would be unfair. Counsel had made a forensic decision in light of the way that evidence was adduced by the Crown in cross-examination of El-Chami not to air matters relating to the alleged admissions. There was thus a risk the jury would speculate as to why El-Chami was not cross-examined on these matters in the first place. Her Honour granted leave over objection on the basis that it was an important piece of evidence, describing it as a 'damning piece of evidence' and 'highly relevant',[205] and any prejudice to the accused would be ameliorated by telling the jury that the irregularity was a result of an omission by the Crown.

205 Ibid [84].

This decision gave rise to two of the grounds of appeal. At issue was whether El-Chami could be cross-examined under s 38 in relation to the 'so-called admissions' recorded in MFI 5. Counsel for the appellant submitted that, since El-Chami could not recall making the statement in para 11 of MFI 5, the admissions contained therein were impermissible second-hand hearsay. They could only be admitted as going to credit. Where evidence is only relevant to credibility, there are stronger reasons to refuse leave under s 192 since the witness cannot be cross-examined on the evidence. The court agreed that, where the only purpose of leading evidence under s 38 is to discredit the witness, there are powerful reasons to reject the application. But that was not the basis on which the second application was made. The application was made for the purpose of leading the admissions, described by Her Honour at trial as 'a matter of "fundamental importance".'[206] The court also noted that, in fact, El-Chami affirmed the truth of MFI 5 in the following exchange:

> Q. If you look at paragraph 11 and I'm just going to read part of it?
> A. Yep.
> Q. Because we're only concerned in this Court with what Biggie said to you?
> A. Okay.
> Q: 'After we had left, Biggie told me what had happened. He said "Biggie smashed a table on Bassem's head". Biggie also said something about stabbing him with a screwdriver.' True?
> A. True.[207]

Moreover, this exchange occurred during cross-examination following the second grant of leave under s 38. When the question of leave was considered, her Honour was not then in a position to know whether El-Chami would affirm or deny the truth of MFI 5.

Re-Examination of One's Own Witness

Re-examination provides an opportunity for the party that called a witness to attempt to repair any damage or ambiguity created by opposing counsel's cross-examination. Re-examination is, however, limited to 'matters arising out of evidence given by the witness in cross-examination' (unless the court gives leave): *UEA*, s 39. This section's terms, *'arising out of evidence'* given in cross-examination, are particularly wide. However, the original ALRC intention appears to have been to permit questioning where cross-examination left something unexplained or incomplete and, as a result, failed to reveal 'the whole truth'.[208] This would give re-examination a more limited role than the terms of s 39. This limited role was adopted[209] by courts early in the life of the *UEA* but, since then, re-examination appears to have been generally without controversy. Probably the most important limitation on re-examination is one self-imposed by the opposing advocate. It arises where a cross-examiner decides not to extend cross-examination to a particular topic because to do so will enable opposing counsel to revisit the topic in re-examination to repair inadequacies from the witness's evidence given in chief.

---

206 Ibid [77].
207 Ibid [55].
208 ALRC, *Evidence (Interim)*, above n 21, [628].
209 See *Hadid v Australis Media Ltd (No 14)* (unreported, NSWSC, 5 November 1996, Sperling J).

Section 108(1)[210] of the *UEA* provides a broad and unconditional exception to the credibility rule for any evidence adduced in re-examination. This makes sense because the topic will already have had to find a basis for admission in cross-examination.

Prior consistent statements and rehabilitating credibility

Where, in cross-examination, a witness has been accused of fabricating or reconstructing her evidence (a form of attack that not uncommonly involves adducing a prior inconsistent statement) the party calling the witness, subject to the grant of leave,[211] gains an opportunity to rehabilitate the witness's credibility in re-examination by adducing evidence of a prior consistent statement,[212] even where it is relevant and/or admissible solely to credibility[213] (s 108(3)). This, with some variations, reflects the common law which also permitted credibility to be re-established in such circumstances. Subsection (3)(b) is broad enough to encompass adducing evidence of the witness's prior consistent statement in examination-in-chief because it refers to the future tense as well as to the present tense (it '*will be suggested* ...'). In *Doyle*[214] Bathurst CJ noted:

> 176. [Section 108(3)(b) is] narrower than the general law insofar as it requires the leave of the court prior to the introduction of the evidence. However, the references to non-deliberate reconstruction and suggestion widen it, as does the omission of any requirement that the statement be made sufficiently early to be inconsistent with the evidence at the trial being a recent invention: JD Heydon, *Cross on Evidence*, (9th Aust ed 2013) at [17315].

Case law has considered what is sufficient to bring a suggestion of fabrication within s 108(3). It is clear that cross-examination which provides 'the only possible import' that the witness has fabricated her evidence is sufficient (subject to leave considerations). It is clear that mere denial of allegations that are the subject of witness testimony is not sufficient. The case of *Doyle* provides some guidance on how the courts apply s 108(3). The appeal concerned the prosecution of 38 charges of sexual assault related offences from various dates in the 1980s, in 1990 and 2003 concerning five young male complainants. Doyle denied all charges. In the first trial in 2011, there was a hung jury on all but one count (which was the subject of a directed verdict). In a second trial, presided over by District Court Judge Woods in 2012 (from which the Court of Criminal Appeal judgments arise), Doyle was found guilty on all charges. One appeal ground related to the ruling by Woods DCJ that complaint evidence of DL (a complainant in relation to charges from 1986 and 1987) and KL was admissible under s 108(3). This ruling had relied on the cross-examination of DL from the first trial regarding incidents occurring one evening. Doyle's alibi evidence was also relied on in the first trial and anticipated in the second trial – namely, that Doyle had been at a birthday celebration at a Chinese restaurant and returned close to midnight. A portion of DL's cross-examination (referred to below by Bathurst CJ[215]) was:

210 'The credibility rule does not apply to evidence adduced in re-examination of a witness.'

211 *UEA*, s 192(2), therefore requires consideration.

212 '*prior consistent statement*' of a witness means a previous representation that is consistent with evidence given by the witness: *UEA*, Dictionary (or for Tasmania, *Evidence Act 2001*, s 3).

213 That is, it is within *UEA*, s 101A, and thus also within the credibility rule, s 102.

214 [2014] NSWCCA 4.

215 Ibid [177].

> 173. …
> Q. This storm that apparently – this incredible storm that took place that you told us about, are you absolutely certain that that occurred on the evening when you were taken to the accused's place of residence and there was this kind of mutual masturbation? A. Yes I'm sure.
> Q. No, are you absolutely sure? A. Yes, I am.
> Q. There can't be any doubt in your mind that this was the night that this storm took place because the bridge was knocked out, was that correct? A. That's correct.
> …
> Q. Then the next paragraph if we can start there. You talk about moving his hips up and down and his penis rubbed against my hand, then you say after about an hour of Doyle masturbating and fondling my penis, you see that? A. Yes.
> Q. Do we take that seriously, he's grabbing hold of your penis, masturbating for about an hour, is that right? A. Yes.

The trial judge had ruled the evidence was admissible because the alibi evidence would, by implication, suggest DL had fabricated his evidence of sexual assault on the night of the storm. Bathurst CJ noted that Woods DCJ appeared to accept that mere denial of the allegations by Doyle did not constitute a suggestion of fabrication. His Honour concluded that the pre-condition to the grant of leave under s 108(3)(b) was made out by the strong inference of fabrication. His Honour continued:

> 177. It has been stated that a mere denial of evidence does not suggest that the evidence was fabricated: *R v Whitmore* [1999] NSWCCA 247; 109 A Crim R 51 at [39]; cf *Graham v R* [1998] HCA 61; 195 CLR 606 at [7]. However the appellant's case went well beyond that. The complaint related to an event on a specific identifiable date. The appellant not only denied the event but also gave notice that he proposed to lead evidence that he was not in the vicinity of where the event took place. When this is considered in conjunction with the cross-examination of DL at the first trial referred to in par [173] above, it seems to me that it was being at least suggested by implication that DL was fabricating his evidence. In *Pavitt v The Queen* [2007] NSWCCA 88; 169 A Crim R 452 at [105], McColl JA and Latham J stated that there was no warrant for reading into s 108(3) a requirement that fabrication be explicitly raised or strongly inferred before the credibility rule is waived. Adams J who dissented in the result did not deal with this issue. In my opinion, in the present case, fabrication was in fact strongly inferred.

One aspect of the appeal regarding reliance on s 108(3) was whether what DL told KL was 'evidence of complaint'. DL's testimony of his conversation with KL 'in the 1990s' about the night of the storm was that he was working at the theatre and that he 'stayed in his [the appellant's] bed that night'. KL's account was that in 1991 DL told her that when the river flooded his parents let him stay at the appellant's home, they shared a bed and that 'Phil would touch [DL]'s penis and [DL] would touch Phil's penis'. KL said the conversation only occurred once, although in cross-examination she said they discussed obtaining counselling and that DL told her that it did happen again (which was inconsistent with DL's account). Bathurst CJ concluded that Woods DCJ's ruling was appropriate.

> 180. The appellant submitted that the evidence of DL was not evidence of complaint. That may be so, but the evidence that he told KL "I stayed in his bed that night", referring to the night of the storm, was consistent with the version he gave at the trial, albeit not going as far as that version.
>
> 181. The fact that the evidence of KL went further … and thus was not entirely consistent with the evidence of DL did not provide a basis for declining to admit the

evidence. Counsel for the appellant at trial was able, if he so desired, to cross-examine on such inconsistency.

His Honour also provided guidance regarding the implication of the five-year delay in DL's complaint to KL, concluding that it was a matter relevant to the grant of leave, but not a pre-condition to coming within the terms of s 108(3) – which is clear from the language of the provision.

182. Whilst, in my opinion, the fact that the consistent statements were not fresh was relevant to the exercise of the discretion, it is not a precondition for leave being granted under s 108(3) of the *Evidence Act*. Although the statements were said to have been made some five years after the alleged incident, they were made well prior to the trial. Although the trial judge did not refer to this matter, he was expressly referred to the complaints being late in the argument that took place on the day of his ruling and in those circumstances there is no reason to doubt that he took this into account.

Re-opening the Prosecution Case

It is a fundamental principle of fairness to the accused that the prosecution must present its case fully (and fairly) before the accused is called on to consider its own course.[216] There are occasions where the unfolding of the defence case may enable the prosecution to re-open its case to rebut defence evidence. On these occasions the prosecution is rebutting an aspect of the defence case, not splitting its own case. For example, the accused in the witness box may raise character as an issue for the first time and in a manner that justifies the prosecution both cross-examining the accused and calling additional evidence. The key issue is whether or not the matter on which the prosecution seeks to re-open is one that could and should have been included in the prosecution's case in chief.[217] If it is, the prosecution is splitting its case by seeking to raise the matter after it has closed its case. As noted by the Victorian Court of Appeal in *SLS* (where neither trial counsel nor judge had appreciated the prosecution's intended breach of this requirement) '[t]he rule is venerable'.[218]

Chin's[219] case is the leading Australian High Court authority. It illustrates the relevant principles and also reveals the strictness with which prosecutors must adhere to the rule. Chin and Choo both lived in Malaysia and it was the prosecution case that Chin acted in concert with Choo delivering a suitcase containing heroin to Chin in Sydney. Chin arrived in Australia approximately a week before Choo. When Choo arrived, he was arrested when Customs officers found he had heroin in his suitcase. Both Chin and Choo claimed that they did not know each other. Choo also claimed to be ignorant of the fact that the suitcase he had brought into Australia contained heroin. One of Choo's explanations was that a Singaporean friend had asked him to deliver the suitcase to a Sydney hotel where it would be collected.

Chin was convicted of being knowingly concerned in the importation of heroin. Choo was found not guilty. Chin appealed his conviction on the basis of procedural unfairness arising from the prosecution splitting its case to prove Choo's visa application form (against Choo alone) after it had questioned Choo

216 *Chin* [1985] HCA 35; 157 CLR 671.
217 *Kane* (1977) 65 Cr App R 270, 274 (and quoted by Gibbs CJ and Wilson J in *Chin*).
218 [2014] VSCA 31, [262] (Ashley, Redlich and Priest JJA).
219 [1985] HCA 35; 157 CLR 671.

on the fact that he had relied on the same Penang telephone contact numbers in his Visa application as Chin. The inference from this telephone connection was that they were in reality drug-importation associates. The trial judge refused to permit the prosecution to adduce Chin's visa application form at this late stage. It was, however, marked for identification. Chin's counsel unsuccessfully applied for a discharge of the jury on the basis of his application that the revelation of the telephone number connection was the only prosecution evidence linking the two. It should have formed part of the prosecution case and Chin had had no opportunity to explain the evidence. After the prosecution had completed its re-opened case, Chin's counsel recalled Chin to the witness box. Chin explained that the relevant telephone number was to a coin-operated telephone on the bar counter of his father's escort agency in Penang. It was open to any member of the public who was a customer.

The NSW Court of Criminal Appeal quashed Chin's conviction on the basis that the prosecution had split its case. The prosecution appealed to the High Court. The High Court agreed with the State appeal court. It concluded that both Chin and Choo's visa forms could have been proved in the prosecution case – and that is what should have happened, with notice so as not to ambush the accused. 'The effect of permitting the prosecution to tender the document by way of reply was to allow it to split its case in circumstances which, on the material before us, were unexceptional and did not warrant any departure from the rule that the prosecution must offer all its proofs during the progress of the prosecution case.'[220]

The court's conclusion was summarised by Dawson J:

> 25. … The trial judge apparently thought that the document was only an admission by Choo and directed the jury accordingly. But his direction could hardly have overcome the prejudice caused to Chin by allowing the prosecution to tender the document in reply. The tendency of the evidence was to establish a connexion between Choo and Chin and was thought sufficient to require Chin to be recalled in order to provide an explanation of how Choo came to be in possession of the telephone number. This inevitably highlighted in an unfair way evidence which would not have received undue emphasis had it been led during the course of the prosecution case. The prosecution should not have been allowed to tender Choo's visa application form after the close of the cases for the defence. The trial of Chin miscarried, in my view, as a result of the document being admitted by way of reply.

Dawson J also added the following statements of principle:

> 14. … The prosecution may be permitted to adduce evidence after the close of the defence case in the discretion of the trial judge. The discretion is, however, to be exercised in favour of the prosecution only in exceptional circumstances and the guiding principle is that the prosecution ought not to be permitted to split its case. That is to say, the prosecution must call all the evidence available to it in support of its case during the presentation of that case. If it fails to do so, it ought not to be allowed to remedy the situation by calling evidence in reply except in exceptional circumstances. Beyond saying that exceptional circumstances do not embrace a situation which ought reasonably to have been foreseen by the prosecution or which would have been covered if the prosecution case had been fully and strictly proved, this Court has declined, having regard to the multifarious directions which a criminal trial may take, to lay down any rigid formula. In *Shaw v R*[221] Dixon, McTiernan, Webb and Kitto JJ expressed the view that:

220 Ibid [24].

221 [(1952) 85 CLR 365, 380.]

> It is probably enough to say that the occasion must be very special or exceptional to warrant a departure from the principle that the prosecution must offer all its proofs during the progress of the Crown case and before the prisoner is called upon for his defence.
>
> The prosecution will not, of course, be seeking to split its case when the evidence which it wishes to call by way of reply is to rebut evidence which forms no part of its proofs as, for example, where the defence of insanity is raised or evidence of good character is called by the accused. Even then, if the nature of the evidence which the accused intends to call should have been known to the prosecution so that it would have been possible to deal with it by calling evidence in the prosecution case, the proper course may be to refuse the prosecution permission to reopen its case in order to call rebutting evidence. …
>
> 15. The relevant principle is essentially one of fairness. The accused is entitled to know the case which he has to meet so that he may have adequate opportunity to determine what questions he may wish to ask in cross-examination, what evidence, if any, he may wish to call and what objections, if any, he may wish to raise in the case against him. Ordinarily the depositions upon which he is committed for trial will provide him with this information in advance and if the prosecution intends to call additional evidence it is required to give notice of its intention to do so. The whole procedure would be undermined if the prosecution were permitted, save in exceptional circumstances, to call evidence in support of its case after the close of the case for the defence.
>
> 16. The principle of fairness which underlies the general rule that the prosecution must lead the evidence, upon which it relies to establish its case, in the course of presenting that case, has an application beyond the exercise of the discretion to allow the reopening of the prosecution case. If in the course of cross-examination of an accused person or his witnesses, the prosecution asks questions with a view to eliciting evidence for the first time which could and should have formed part of its evidence in chief, then that evidence may be excluded in the discretion of the trial judge if its admission for the first time during cross-examination would unduly prejudice the accused, having regard to the obligation resting upon the prosecution to make its case known before the presentation of the defence case.[222]

Conclusion

This chapter has detailed a number of legal and non-legal issues that reveal the numerous layers of complexity that can arise in making decisions regarding the calling, questioning and evaluating of witnesses in a party's own case. The chapter has shown that, while courts cannot necessarily control influences on witnesses outside the court and before trial, procedural law attempts to create a fair (though not necessarily level)[223] playing field for both parties and also for witnesses. While procedural law attempts to structure questioning of a party's own witnesses in a fair way, it is clear from psychological research (and also acknowledged by the High Court) that it is a particularly difficult exercise for human beings to evaluate the credibility of others. Spotting liars is not easy, nor is accounting for minor inconsistencies in accounts, or even evaluating someone who, unbeknown to the fact-finder, has a stutter.

Except by way of brief discussion regarding prior consistent statements relevant and/or admissible solely to a witness's credibility under s 108(3), this chapter has not addressed the complex law associated with credibility evidence. This task is central to the next chapter.

---

222 [See *Kane* (1977) 65 Cr App R 270.]

223 Due to the application of accusatorial justice principles, see Chapter 1.

Chapter 6

Cross-examination, Witness Credibility and Related Challenges

Introduction

The task of cross-examination is to test witnesses' accounts through questioning. It is premised on a mistrust of witness testimony[1] and is the quintessential adversarial element of the common law tradition.[2]

This chapter explores cross-examination by reference to the trial context and through the repertoire of evidence and procedural law. This law creates a mixture of obligations and constraints. However, constraint is dominant. An advocate's excessive zeal in testing the witness is a significant threat to the optimal functioning and management of the trial as well as to an accused person's rights to a fair trial and to witnesses' dignitarian rights. Law's controls include the following limitations:

- on questioning that seeks solely to discredit a witness;
- in pursuing challenging a witness's credibility beyond such questioning;
- in establishing baseline propriety requirements on questioning;
- on questioning the accused.

These issues occupy most of this chapter, but the chapter concludes with a discussion of the complex issues surrounding the obligations on a cross-examiner to question a witness on matters that are subsequently to be relied on in the party's case (the rule in *Browne v Dunn*).

Cross-examination

Common law courts have long recognised the crucial role of cross-examination in testing the veracity of a witness and the accuracy and completeness of their

1 J Hunter, 'Battling a Good Story: Cross-examining the Failure of the Law of Evidence' in P Roberts and M Redmayne (eds), *Innovations in Evidence and Proof: Integrating Theory, Research and Teaching* (Hart Publishing, 2007), 261.

2 See, eg, *Lee* (1998) 195 CLR 594, 602 [32] (Gleeson CJ and Gummow, Kirby, Hayne and Callinan JJ); *Whitehorn* [1983] HCA 42; 152 CLR 657, 661 (Murphy J) ('one of the fundamental guarantees of life and liberty ... long deemed to be essential for the due protection of life and liberty'). For an extensive survey of these and other authorities on the importance of cross-examination, see *Stack v Western Australia* [2004] WASCA 300, [76]-[129] (Steytler J).

account. However, it was not until towards the middle of the 18th century that English courts recognised the right of the defence to cross-examine prosecution witnesses. Before that, judges dominated the questioning process. A particularly well-known description is John Henry Wigmore's[3] aphorism that cross-examination is 'the greatest legal engine ever invented for the discovery of truth'. Wigmore published in 1904, when adversarial cross-examination was only 150 years old and lawyers' role in the criminal trial was in its relative infancy.[4] However, his sentiments are often repeated in different ways. In England, also in the first half of the 20th century, Lord Hanworth in *Mechanical and General Invention Co Ltd v Austin*[5] observed that '[c]ross-examination is a powerful and valuable weapon for the purpose of testing the veracity of a witness and the accuracy and completeness of his story'.

Further, the same principles are expressed in United States constitutional law where the Sixth Amendment,[6] the right to confrontation, has shaped a particularly robust rule against hearsay evidence[7] and created a vibrant cultural respect for effective cross-examination within the legal profession. The common law's commitment to cross-examination is repeated in its centrality in numerous human rights instruments. The ACT *Human Rights Act 2004* is a useful exemplar of how this right is typically expressed. It provides:

> Anyone charged with a criminal offence is entitled to the following minimum guarantees, equally with everyone else [including] ... to examine prosecution witnesses, or have them examined, and to obtain the attendance and examination of witnesses on his or her behalf under the same conditions as prosecution witnesses.[8]

In a jurisdiction not dissimilar to Australian legal practice (albeit with its own *Canadian Charter of Rights and Freedoms*, 1982), Cory J in *Osolin*[9] linked an accused's right to cross-examine to the presumption of innocence and a fair trial, stating that cross-examination enables 'an accused ... [to] make full answer and defence ... [and] is fundamental to providing a fair trial to an accused'. Cory J added that cross-examination is 'the ultimate means of demonstrating truth and of testing veracity' and 'of essential importance in determining whether a witness is credible. Even with the most honest witness, cross-examination can provide the means to explore the frailties of the testimony'. These themes are regularly repeated in case law and beyond, with Lord Hanworth and Wigmore often quoted

---

3 JH Wigmore, *A Treatise on the Anglo-American System of Evidence in Trials at Common Law* (Little, Brown & Co, 1940) Vol 5, [1367], 29.

4 See below, pp 261-262.

5 [1935] AC 346, 359.

6 'In all criminal prosecutions, the accused shall enjoy the right ... to be confronted with the witnesses against him.'

7 Undoubtedly, the ability to test a witness's account through cross-examination influenced the development and the presence of exceptions to the rule against hearsay. This rule, if no exception exists, prevents evidence of (oral and written) representations made outside the witness box being communicated to the jury as proof of the facts that the maker intended to assert. On the inability to test (or confront) the original narrator in cross-examination, see *Al-Khawaja and Tahery v United Kingdom* (2009) 49 EHRR 1; *Horncastle* [2009] UKSC 14; [2010] 2 AC 373; *Crawford v Washington* 541 US 36 (2004); M Redmayne, 'Confronting Confrontation' in P Roberts and J Hunter (eds), *Criminal Evidence & Human Rights: Reimagining Common Law Procedural Traditions* (Hart Publishing, 2013), 283; and see Chapters 8 and 9.

8 *Human Rights Act 2004* (ACT), s 22(2)(g). Similarly, *Charter of Human Rights and Responsibilities Act 2006* (Vic), s 25(2)(g), 'to examine, or have examined, witnesses against him or her, unless otherwise provided for by law'; *Human Rights Act 2019* (Qld), s 32(g).

9 (1993) 86 CCC (3d) 481,516-17 (SCC) (Cory J, with Sopinka, Iacobucci and Major JJ agreeing).

in support of the importance of cross-examination. No one can doubt the continuing centrality of cross-examination in modern common law trials.

This positioning of cross-examination as an accused's fair trial right explains observations like those made by Sydney counsel, John Stratton SC:

> For the criminal defence lawyer, there are few things more important than cross-examination. In my experience, if a case is going to be won, it is usually during the prosecution case. As Phil Boulten SC once said, "a case rarely looks better for the defence than the moment that the Crown says 'That's the case for the Crown'."[10]

Psychological research supports these sentiments – that is, that for the accused cross-examination serves a particularly important function in drawing the listener away from complacent acceptance of prosecution witness testimony.[11] Research shows that our default position is to take the world as we see it and we are more intellectually tempted to seek confirmatory information than to seek disabusing information. This is elucidated upon by the US academic Craig Callen[12] drawing on the work of the psychologist, Gilbert.[13] Callen explains that human cognitive processes, strained by information overload (as is often the case for jurors in criminal trials), incline to *accept* rather than *reject* information. As Callen states, Gilbert's theory extrapolates to legal contexts. It can helpfully illuminate 'how cross-examination might prevent ... confirmatory tendencies in human cognition that might otherwise cause jurors to be prejudiced and to under-invest cognitive resources in finding facts'.[14]

As Callen adds, this understanding 'reinforces the importance of cross-examining prosecution witnesses in criminal trials in order to expose jurors to alternative hypotheses and counter-possibilities'.[15] This is because the very fact that a question is put to a witness can function implicitly to prioritise a topic or fact that a listener (or juror) may know but may have forgotten. By being placed on notice that the topic is pertinent the listener is more likely to locate facts in the narrative according to the cross-examiner's case theory. In this way cross-examination and advocacy address the dangers of juror cognitive overload.[16]

Assessing witness credibility

The inherent fallibility of human observation, retention and recollection of events necessarily makes witness testimony imperfect – we are all prone to memory loss, suggestibility, and perception flaws to some extent. Disputes that end up in court, especially those involving a criminal sanction, inevitably have points of disagreement. Some witnesses lie. They deliberately 'attempt, without forewarning, to create in another a belief which the communicator considers to be untrue'.[17]

---

10 J Stratton SC (as Deputy Senior Public Defender), 'Cross-Examination', 1 August 2007, <http://www.Publicdefenders.justice.nsw.gov.au/pdo/public_defenders_crossexamination_stratton.html>.

11 C Callen, 'Human Deliberation in Fact-Finding' in Roberts and Hunter, above n 7, 321-3.

12 Ibid.

13 DT Gilbert, 'How Mental Systems Believe' (1991) 46 *American Psychologist* 107.

14 Callen, above n 11, 322.

15 Ibid 322.

16 As Callen notes, above n 11, 322-3, relying on D Wilson and D Sperber, 'Truthfulness and Relevance' (2002) 111 *Mind* 583, 604.

17 A Vrij, *Detecting Lies and Deceit: The Psychology of Lying and the Implications for Professional Practice* (Wiley, 2000), quoted in D Andrewartha, 'Lie Detection in Litigation: Science or Prejudice?' (2008) 15 *Psychiatry, Psychology and Law* 88, 89.

Psychological research indicates that we are lied to successfully at least one to two times a day and confirms what (perhaps) we already know – that is, that lying is 'a normal, natural, indispensable facet of daily life'.[18] In the courtroom this raises questions about the extent to which a person's propensity to lie is diminished by the oath (or affirmation) and the consequential criminal implications flowing from perjury, the formality of the process and the austere surroundings of the courtroom. In daily life, lies are not all of the same significance.

Andrewartha[19] describes lies as sitting within a hierarchical order in terms of their relationship to the truth and to social motivators for lying. At the most egregious end of the spectrum are '*outright lies*', which are complete fabrications where 'truth is wholly disregarded and new information generated and presented as the truth'; to '*exaggeration*', that is, lies that 'overstate or downplay the truth'; and then '*subtle lying*', which deploys 'intentional misuse of literal truths or the omission of pertinent facts to create a false impression'.[20] At the other end of the spectrum are possibly the most common and the most socially acceptable lies, the so-called '*white lie*', which is told to diminish the sense of shame or impropriety associated with deceit[21] and, at least by the speaker, justified as a way of facilitating social interaction rather than personal gain. In court, witnesses must always tell the truth. Strictly speaking, there is no room even for the white lie.

As Andrewartha identifies, we are all also socialised to stretch the truth. Indeed, it is the willingness of the witness who wishes to please, socialised to reading cues and conforming to others' wishes in social settings that is one of the reasons for condemning leading questions in examination-in-chief. However, what is particularly concerning is that lies and deceit are very difficult to pick. Andrewartha summarises the literature, observing that:

> Despite popular misconception, people's lies are not telegraphed via cues as blatant as Pinocchio's telltale nose. In fact, a growing body of research demonstrates that the verbal and non-verbal features associated with deception are contrary to expectation and are typically undetectable or misinterpreted. In daily social interactions, this need not provoke concern. … Just as alcohol is a social lubricant, deception is a social prophylactic; it shields people from unpalatable and potentially damaging truths and interpersonal confrontations.
>
> Although a degree of undetected duplicity is beneficial in everyday interactions, when it comes to the investigation and prosecution of criminal transgressions, all but the guilty yearn for something as conspicuous and incriminating as a nose that grows when an untruth is uttered by its bearer.[22]

The case of *Whisprun Pty Ltd v Dixon*[23] and the observations made by Kirby J reveal the complexity of witness questioning and assessing the significance of

18 Andrewartha, ibid, citing BM DePaulo, DA Kashy, SE Kirkendol, MM Wyer and JA Epstein, 'Lying in Everyday Life' (1996) 70 *Journal of Personality and Social Psychology* 979; Vrij, ibid; DA Kashy and BM DePaulo, 'Who lies?' (1996) 70 *Journal of Personality and Social Psychology* 1037; J Campbell, *The Liar's Table: A History of Falsehood* (WW Norton & Company Ltd, 2001); BM DePaulo, JJ Lindsay, BE Malone, L Muhlenbruck, K Charlton and H Cooper, 'Cues to Deception' (2003) 129 *Psychological Bulletin* 74; CV Ford, *Lies! Lies! Lies! The Psychology of Deceit* (American Psychiatric Press Inc, 1996).

19 Andrewartha, above n 17.

20 Ibid, citing, DePaulo et al, above n 18; Vrij, above n 17.

21 Andrewartha, above n 17, 96, suggests '[t]he use of "white", a colour historically associated with purity, chastity, and goodness, is a shining example of this phenomenon'.

22 Ibid 88-9.

23 [2003] HCA 48; 200 ALR 447.

witnesses who 'stretch' the truth. Dixon suffered from Q fever, contracted as a result of her work at the appellant's abattoir. She claimed to have suffered chronic fatigue syndrome. The trial judge dismissed her action for damages because he was not satisfied that she suffered from chronic fatigue syndrome. The trial judge relied on video footage and photographs revealing that Dixon rode horses and attended a wedding during the period she claimed to be suffering extreme fatigue. This was reversed by the NSW Court of Appeal. The majority of the High Court (Gleeson CJ, McHugh and Gummow JJ) restored the trial judge's determination, indicating that the trial judge was entitled to take the view of the case that he did. Kirby and Callinan JJ dissented. The majority of the High Court saw the issue in terms of Dixon's credibility also but in a more limited manner ('whether Ms Dixon was credible when she claimed to be suffering from symptoms that were consistent with that syndrome [Q fever]').[24] The following observation by Kirby J relates to the challenge of assessing a witness's demeanour:

> 119. Some judges in the past regarded untruthful evidence – even about peripheral or irrelevant matters – as fatal to a litigant. Most judges today understand that the evaluation of evidence involves a more complex function, requiring a more sophisticated analysis. Courts, after all, are not venues for the trial of the parties' morality or credibility, as such. As judges often explain to juries in criminal trials, people sometimes tell lies in court and elsewhere for extraneous and irrelevant reasons, having nothing to do with the legal issues in the trial. If this is true in criminal trials, it is equally true in civil trials. What is important is not the proof of untruthfulness, as such, but the significance (if any) of any demonstrated falsehoods for the issues at trial. That significance can only be judged when measured against the entirety of the relevant testimony. By its logical force, that testimony may well require that falsehoods be ignored as irrelevant or immaterial to the decision-maker's ultimate conclusion. In particular cases, it may require the decision-maker, within the pleadings, to consider and decide a case different from – or even contrary to – that advanced by the party, because such is the legal entitlement of the person concerned. ...
>
> 121. ... [In this instance] I am left with a reminder of the features of jury trials in days gone by. The advocate tackled the respondent with a view to damaging her credibility. She was a soft target – a former abattoir worker, of limited education, inarticulate, living in a country town, with an alleged medical condition one feature of which was its possible impact upon her powers of concentration and memory. In the old days of civil jury trials, parties would fight such cases with as much bluster and prejudice as they could respectively get away with. In this trial, considerable latitude was allowed. But, in the end, objectively at least, what did the attack prove? That the respondent, on isolated occasions, when cameras were present, was able to partake in some recreational activities? That she was able to walk briskly over three kilometres on a kind of outing while in Sydney attending a medical appointment? That she was not entirely truthful or clear about her property holdings or about her relationship with a de facto partner who was the father of her child? That she had horses which she rode more often than she admitted? And that she joined one night in the exuberance of a country wedding and drank alcohol there like most of the other guests?

Kirby J then made comments that restated the conclusions reached by the High Court in *Fox v Percy*[25] and *State Rail Authority of New South Wales v Earthline Constructions Pty Ltd (in liq)*,[26] regarding the need to draw on all evidence, especially that evidence that does not rely on the frailties of demeanour assessment and witnesses' in-court prowess under questioning.

---

24 Ibid [18].
25 [2003] HCA 22; 214 CLR 118.
26 [1999] HCA 3; 160 ALR 588.

> 122. *Consideration of all the evidence:* A rational approach to the respondent's entitlements would make full allowance for such evidence – and the dents that it made in her assertions of general fatigue. But it would also make sure that it had taken into full account the objective and consistent evidence in the case. These included the respondent's clear initial infection with Q fever, her protracted weight loss and other consistent recorded signs and the extensive evidence about the well documented features of this particular infection (including extended fatigue during the phase following acute infection and ups and downs of symptoms of exhaustion thereafter). To reduce the case to a simple contest of credibility was to fall into the trap of irrationality and the risk of prejudice – turning the court's process into one of punishing the respondent for her forensic performance instead of evaluating the objective testimony in the context of all of the evidence called at the trial.

The High Court case of *Fox v Percy* has been prominent in galvanising appellate courts to revisit first instance determinations based on an assessment of witness credibility. As Gleeson CJ, Gummow and Kirby JJ observed, 'in recent years, judges have become more aware of scientific research that has cast doubt on the ability of judges (or anyone else) to tell truth from falsehood accurately on the basis of such appearances'.[27] Where it is clear – and it can be difficult to draw such a conclusion in jury trials compared to judicial fact-finding – that decisions as to credibility have been based merely 'upon matters of impression' and on 'an otherwise minor issue',[28] and more objective evidence points otherwise, appeal courts will intervene. In *Fox v Percy* Gleeson CJ, Gummow and Kirby JJ described the tension between the appellate obligation to properly review a trial and the need for appellate restraint out of deference to the advantages of fact-finders who have viewed and heard the case unfolding and the first-hand accounts of witness testimony. However:

> 25. ... Appellate courts are not excused from the task of 'weighing conflicting evidence and drawing [their] own inferences and conclusions, though [they] should always bear in mind that [they have] neither seen nor heard the witnesses, and should make due allowance in this respect'.[29] ...
>
> 28. Over more than a century, this court, and courts like it, have given instruction on how to resolve the dichotomy between the foregoing appellate obligations and appellate restraint. ... In particular cases incontrovertible facts or uncontested testimony will demonstrate that the trial judge's conclusions are erroneous, even when they appear to be, or are stated to be, based on credibility findings.
>
> 29. That this is so is demonstrated in several recent decisions of this court. In some, quite rare, cases, although the facts fall short of being 'incontrovertible', an appellate conclusion may be reached that the decision at trial is 'glaringly improbable'[30] or 'contrary to compelling inferences'[31] in the case. ... In such a case, making all due allowances for the advantages available to the trial judge, the appellate court must 'not shrink from giving effect to' its own conclusion.

---

27 [2003] HCA 22; 214 CLR 118, [31], referring to resources cited by Samuels JA in *Trawl Industries of Australia Pty Ltd v Effem Foods Pty Ltd* (1992) 27 NSWLR 326, 348 and noted in *State Rail Authority of New South Wales v Earthline Constructions Pty Ltd (in liq)* [1999] HCA 3; 160 ALR 588, 617-18 [88].

28 *Re Refugee Review Tribunal; Ex parte Aala* [2000] HCA 57; 204 CLR 82, [4] (Gleeson CJ).

29 [*Dearman v Dearman* [1908] HCA 84; 7 CLR 549, 564 citing *The Glannibanta* (1876) 1 PD 283, 287.]

30 [*Brunskill v Sovereign Marine & General Insurance Co Ltd* [1985] HCA 61; 59 ALJR 842, 844; 62 ALR 53, 57.]

31 [*Chambers v Jobling* (1986) 7 NSWLR 1, 10.]

The cross-examiner

> 'The way to find out whether a witness is lying is to basically confront that witness,' Mr [S] said. 'Does the witness squirm, does the witness sweat, does the witness not have a ready answer? It's that moment that's at the heart of the trial.[32]

Cross-examination includes:

> [T]he asking of direct, leading and pressing questions which may be put to the witness with a view to breaking down his testimony. It includes also examination by direct and leading and pressing questions to elicit facts which may tend to make the facts he has deposed to improbable. He may be cross-examined as to prior inconsistent statements, questioned as to bias or interest or memory or misconduct or any other such matter which might be useful to the cross-examining party as suggesting that the witness's testimony should not be accepted.[33]

The pervasive respect with which the role of cross-examination in the trial is viewed translates in legal practice to a strong admiration for those who are highly accomplished in its art. There is much professional pride in a good 'performance', in being able deftly and patiently to lay groundwork to develop a case theory through a witness who is, by definition, prone to damage it. Cross-examination must minimise damage to one's own case[34] and maximise gain to one's case theory. This art is accomplished through propositional, singular and simple questions that are structured, ordered and sequenced to optimal effect, deployed with exhibits that maximise the witness's 'useful' answers (that is, the ones that support the cross-examiner's case theory) to underscore links, to probe and press, to take control and to manage artfully the 'unhelpful' response. If it is effective, cross-examination will provide 'the ammunition for a persuasive closing address'[35] to the jury. In other words, skilled counsel operate to a carefully calibrated and exacting game plan.

Further, effective barristers are intuitive psychologists. Those well practised in technique have a portfolio of stratagems to meet every occasion and every witness type.[36] For this reason they can be a formidable force in their natural habitat, the courtroom. This is a place that is rarely a comfortable location for the witness under cross-examination. To appreciate the potential imbalance between the questioner and questioned one need only reflect on Kirby J's observations in *Whisprun Pty Ltd v Dixon*[37] describing Dixon as a 'soft target' for attack by the cross-examiner; or compare the intellectual and experiential stock-in-trade of counsel with the attributes of most witnesses, particularly the vulnerable ones. For all these reasons, there is cause to reflect on the significant trend to protect witnesses in various ways from some manifestations of 'the greatest legal engine ever invented for the discovery of truth' because, in truth, cross-examination's marketing has overrated its functionality at least for *all* purposes and *all* witnesses. Consider, for example, the observations of Bowden et al:

---

32 P Belluck, 'Court Ruling May Remove Some of the Drama from Massachusetts Criminal Trials', *New York Times*, 2 April 2006.

33 *Hunter* [1956] VicLawRp 5; [1956] VLR 31, 36 (Martin, O'Bryan and Deane JJ).

34 As Anthony Parker from the defence bar observed, '[w]e all know … through bitter experience the spectacle of the witness who is unimpressive in chief being transformed by an unwise cross-examination; logically we must be able to rely on the prosecutors to achieve this from time to time': A Parker, 'Preparing a Client for Cross-Examination', 1996, <https://www.publicdefenders.nsw.gov.au/Documents/preparingclientcrossexamination.pdf>.

35 Stratton, above n 10.

36 Ibid.

37 [2003] HCA 48; 200 ALR 447.

> The cross-examination of children and intellectually disabled witnesses can result in inconsistent and inaccurate evidence,[38] as well as cause further trauma to victims.[39] This is due to the nature of cross-examination, the tactics often used by counsel, the language and phrasing of questions, and the delay between the initial complaint and trial. Despite the traditional preference for, and reliance on, witnesses to give evidence through live oral testimony in an adversarial system,[40] this does not necessarily result in the 'best' evidence being received when the witness is a child or has an intellectual disability.[41]

This is not to say that cross-examination never matches its acclaim. Clearly it will often do so.[42] But it is important to appreciate two matters. First, as we saw in Chapter 2, advocacy (the art of persuasion) is an important aspect of the criminal trial (as are the adversarial and accusatorial dynamics) and, unless adequately controlled, cross-examination runs the risk of creating wanton destruction of a witness. Second, even for witnesses who withstand cross-examination, it can be a gruelling experience. In fact, early recognition of the tension between cross-examination's testing function and witnesses' dignitarian rights was expressed by Lord Hanworth in *Mechanical and General Invention Co Ltd v Austin*[43] when he observed that a 'measure of courtesy to the witness' is required in light of a witness's 'burden' facing 'a skilful, yet powerful, cross-examination'.

The principle that vulnerable witnesses need measures of protection from adversarial excesses is now widely recognised in Australian courts. It is a signature element of the *UEA* and it is reinforced in other legislation across Australia. As detailed in Chapter 5, in response to recommendations by the Royal Commission into Institutional Responses to Child Sexual Abuse (RCIRCSA)[44] a number of Australian jurisdictions have legislated to allow suitably qualified intermediaries to assist particular witnesses (most usually children and witnesses with cognitive impairments).[45] The principle is also generally backed up through professional

---

38 [In relation to children, see A Cossins, 'Cross-Examination in Child Sexual Assault Trials: Evidentiary Safeguard or an Opportunity to Confuse?' (2009) 33 *Melbourne University Law Review* 68, 71, 90-1; E Davies, E Henderson and K Hanna, 'Facilitating Children to Give Best Evidence: Are There Better Ways to Challenge Children's Testimony?' (2010) 34 *Criminal Law Journal* 347, 352; R Zajac, J Gross and H Hayne, 'Asked and Answered: Questioning Children in the Courtroom' (2003) 10 *Psychiatry, Psychology and Law* 199, 201. In relation to persons with an intellectual disability, J Benedet and I Grant, 'Taking the Stand: Access to Justice for Witnesses with Mental Disabilities in Sexual Assault Cases' (2012) 50 *Osgoode Hall Law Journal* 1, 14-15, 18-26; MR Kebbell, C Hatton and SD Johnson, 'Witnesses with Intellectual Disability in Court: What Questions Are Asked and What Influence Do They Have?' (2004) 9 *Legal and Criminological Psychology* 23, 25-6.]

39 [In relation to children, see C Eastwood and W Patton, 'The Experiences of Child Complainants of Sexual Abuse in the Criminal Justice System' (Research Report, Queensland University of Technology, 2002), 30; Cossins, 'Cross-Examination in Child Sexual Assault Trials', above n 38, 69. In relation to persons with an intellectual disability, see A Gray, S Forell and S Clarke, 'Cognitive Impairment, Legal Need and Access to Justice' (Paper No 10, Law and Justice Foundation of New South Wales, March 2009), 8.]

40 [*Butera v DPP (Vic)* [1987] HCA 58; 164 CLR 180, 189 (Mason CJ, Brennan and Deane JJ); L Ellison, 'The Protection of Vulnerable Witnesses in Court: An Anglo-Dutch Comparison' (1999) 3 *International Journal of Evidence & Proof* 29, 34.]

41 P Bowden, T Henning, D Plater, 'Balancing Fairness to Victims, Society and Defendants in the Cross-examination of Vulnerable Witnesses: An Impossible Triangulation?' (2014) 37(3) *Melbourne University Law Review* 539, 550. The authors' arguments that develop this observation are extracted below, pp 268-271.

42 See, eg, D Howard, *R v Milat: A Case Study in Cross-Examination* (LexisNexis, 2014).

43 [1935] AC 346, 359 (Lord Hanworth).

44 RCIRCSA, *Criminal Justice Report – Executive Summary and Parts I–II* (2017).

45 *Criminal Procedure Act 2009* (Vic), Pt 8.2A, as amended by *Justice Legislation Amendment (Victims) Act 2018* (Vic), s 25.

rules. For example, principles of propriety in witness questioning are addressed in rr 61 and 62 of the *Legal Profession Uniform Conduct (Barristers) Rules 2015* which operate in both New South Wales and Victoria. These rules reflect a more limited version[46] of that provided in the *UEA*, s 41, but they are *soft* requirements, particularly given the woolly language in which they are expressed.

Further, unless the Bar self-regulates through embedding its own culture of restraint, the broader context of the trial means that formal restrictions are not easy to implement.[47] Fortunately, skilled advocates may recognise that they should not alienate fact-finders by tormenting vulnerable witnesses; however, adversarialism, fuelled by accusatorial justice principles, also sends strong messages. Not only does it enable advocates to press their client's case but professional ethics also *oblige* (using strong language) counsel to do so. For example, in New South Wales, r 35 requires a barrister to 'promote and protect fearlessly and by all proper and lawful means the client's best interests to the best of the barrister's skill and diligence, and do so without regard to his or her own interest or to any consequences to the barrister or to any other person'. There are, of course, baseline obligations: barristers 'must exercise the forensic judgments called for during the case independently'[48] and they bear 'an overriding duty to the Court to act ... in the interests of the administration of justice'[49] including 'not deceiv[ing] or knowingly or recklessly mislead[ing] the Court'.[50] They must act 'to correct any misleading statement made by the barrister to a court'.[51] Parallel obligations exist to opponents.[52] There are constraints that have developed through case law as well. For example, as a general principle, a witness should not be questioned on whether another witness is (or is not) telling the truth.[53]

Returning to more general concerns arising from cross-examination, it is clear from the High Court's observations in the 1990 case of *Wakeley* that the imposition of constraint on cross-examination is a sensitive matter. Their Honours observed that '[t]he limits of cross-examination ... [are] not susceptible of precise definition, for a connection between a fact elicited by cross-examination and a fact in issue may appear, if at all, only after other pieces of evidence are forthcoming'. Their Honours continued, acknowledging the need for professional restraint and the obligations and limitations of judicial control. They moved on to discuss the elasticity of the application of the concept of relevance to cross-examination, pointing out that:

> Nor is there any general test of relevance which a trial judge is able to apply in deciding, at the start of a cross-examination, whether a particular question should be allowed. Some of the most effective cross-examinations have begun by securing a witness' assent to a proposition of seeming irrelevance. Although it is important in the interests of the administration of justice that cross-examination be contained within reasonable limits, a judge should allow counsel some leeway in cross-examination in order that counsel may

---

46 Cf *Evidence Act 2008* (Vic), discussed below in relation to s 41.

47 This point is made in the English Court of Criminal Appeal cases of *Kalia* (1974) 60 Cr App R 200 and *Maynard* (1979) 69 Cr App R 309 (cited and supported by Mason CJ, Brennan, Deane, Toohey and McHugh JJ in *Wakeley* [1990] HCA 23; 93 ALR 79, [20]).

48 *Legal Profession Uniform Conduct (Barristers) Rules 2015*, r 42.

49 Ibid r 23.

50 Ibid r 24. See also r 64 (belief on reasonable grounds of proper basis for facts).

51 Ibid r 25.

52 Ibid rr 49-51.

53 See *JG* [2014] NSWCCA 138, citing *Gonzales* [2007] NSWCCA 321; 178 A Crim R 232; *Foley* (1998) 105 A Crim R 1.

> perform the duty, where counsel's instructions warrant it, of testing the evidence given by an opposing witness.[54]

However, as we saw above, subject to controlling abuse, psychological research provides support for granting breadth to the cross-examiner. However, just as over-zealous cross-examination can be problematic, so too, on occasion can constrained cross-examination. The rule in *Browne v Dunn* discussed below, deals with one aspect of such problems. The decision of the High Court in *Pell*[55] demonstrates another. In this case, the Crown, in fulfilment of its obligation to call all material witnesses (even witnesses unsupportive of the Crown case) who might throw light on the events in issue, called 23 witnesses who testified about Catholic Church customs and Pell's practices at the time of the alleged offences and the rigidity to which they were adhered. Essentially, this was evidence that, if accepted, denied any realistic opportunity for the defendant to have committed the offences charged. The Crown was granted leave under s 38 of the *UEA* to cross-examine these witnesses with respect to this evidence, specifically about whether Pell was always with another person when robed and whether he always greeted congregants on the cathedral steps following Sunday mass for a length of time that would have precluded his commission of the offences. If these practices were always observed, then the offences could not have occurred as the complainant described them. The Crown cross-examination canvassed the strictness with which these practices were observed and whether it was possible that on occasion they were not. The Crown did obtain concessions from a number of witnesses that there might be times when departures from these practices occurred.

One witness, the master of ceremonies Monsignor Portelli, testified that, on the dates in question, he was with Pell while he met and greeted congregants and thereafter accompanied him to the priests' sacristy, where the offences were alleged to have been committed, and assisted him to remove his vestments. The High Court found that this evidence was not challenged. The sacristan, Max Potter, testified that he had an actual recollection of being with Pell on the cathedral steps and the length of time he spent there, and rejected the contention that Pell might have on occasion returned to the sacristy alone. He did concede that there might have been occasions when Pell's meet and greet practice might be shorter than usual, but could not recall it being 'just a short time' unless the weather was inclement. In reaching its determination that the Crown evidence did not establish guilt to the requisite standard, the High Court placed particular emphasis (at [91]-[101]) on the fact that Portelli's evidence was unchallenged. This finding means that, in excluding a reasonable doubt, the Crown must be specific and detailed in its cross-examination of witnesses whose evidence offers any support to the defence. They cannot rely on generalised propositions or possibilities to undermine that evidence, but must dig into the precise details relating to the alleged defences and displace them.

Leading questions

Leading questions[56] are pivotal to cross-examination. This is reflected in *UEA*, s 42(1), which permits leading questions in cross-examination 'unless the court disallows the question or directs the witness not to answer it'. Leading questions

---

54 *Wakeley* [1990] HCA 23; 93 ALR 79, [20] (Mason CJ, Brennan, Deane, Toohey and McHugh JJ).

55 [2020] HCA 12.

56 Defined in the *UEA*.

in cross-examination are to be disallowed or rejected by a court 'if the court is satisfied that the facts concerned would be better ascertained if leading questions were not used': s 42(3). Aside from the sorts of situations listed in *UEA*, s 42(2), cross-examiners enjoy broad ambit in leading the witness. Considerations relevant to disallowing a question or giving a direction that it not be answered include:

> (a) evidence that has been given by the witness in examination in chief is unfavourable to the party who called the witness, and
> (b) the witness has an interest consistent with an interest of the cross-examiner, and
> (c) the witness is sympathetic to the party conducting the cross-examination, either generally or about a particular matter, and
> (d) the witness's age, or any mental, intellectual or physical disability to which the witness is subject, may affect the witness's answers. (*UEA*, s 42(2))

This list reflects scenarios that are, each in their own way, instances where cross-examination no longer appropriately tests a witness's account. A further example from the English Court of Appeal case of *Edwards*, discussed in relation to the rule in *Browne v Dunn* later in this chapter, shows an instance where the trial judge required cross-examining counsel to limit his cross-examination of a six-year-old complainant witness regarding events occurring 18 months earlier. These limitations were explained to the jury. During cross-examination the judge made it clear he was concerned that leading the witness had turned into 'suggestions to the witness, and ordinarily that would be absolutely appropriate, but making suggestions to a six-year-old about matters so long ago, I wonder whether we're sure we're getting accurate information. Could you make the questions a little bit open so we can test whether she does remember?' and 'I'm only saying that if you can make the question more open so that she's demonstrating what she can remember rather than agreeing with you I think it will be more help to demonstrate her memory rather than an ability to agree or disagree'.[57] An appeal based on the limitations placed on defence counsel exploring inconsistencies, credibility and reliability was unsuccessful. The trial judge's ruling disallowing certain leading questions was unsuccessfully appealed in circumstances giving rise to a risk that the child complainant would adopt the leading questions in an effort to assist her mother who was also a defendant in the case.

Conversely, in *Stack v Western Australia*[58] Steytler J ruled that the trial judge erred in preventing leading questions during the cross-examination of an 18-year-old Aboriginal eye witness to a stabbing murder who had been called by the prosecution. With respect to that ruling, Steytler J noted:

> There is nothing in any of this evidence which would indicate that any generalised phenomenon, such as that of gratuitous concurrence, or any other failure to give appropriately responsive answers, was applicable to him. … [and] a reading of the transcript of the witness's evidence reveals very little to indicate that the phenomenon of gratuitous concurrence was applicable to him (or, as the trial Judge put it, that he was largely agreeing with whatever was being put to him by way of leading questions) or that he lacked the ability to understand and answer the questions asked of him. … the transcript discloses that, on those occasions in which Vernon Lawrence Junior was not clear as to the purport of a question, he asked for it to be repeated. On very many occasions he disagreed with propositions which were put to him, sometimes vigorously so.[59]

57 *Edwards* [2011] EWCA Crim 3028, [25] (Rafferty LJ). See below, p 274.
58 [2004] WASCA 300.
59 Ibid [118]-[119].

Mention was made above of the blurry distinction between lying and exaggeration. For the cross-examiner, both exaggeration and lying are excellent bases to discredit a witness. In addition, as we see below, exposing a witness's bias is considered acutely relevant to credibility impeachment. Further, inaccuracy in testimony can be unconscious as well as conscious. Witnesses can make mistakes without realising it.

Discrediting Witnesses

In this section we address the law relating to credibility evidence and the application of the credibility rule and its exceptions. It is a most intricate area. In the previous chapter, we examined the complexity of assessing a witness's credibility. It is interesting, in fact, to reflect on the relative recency of the legal limitations on parties relying on credibility evidence in a trial. This is for a number of reasons. First, in the early period of the modern common law trial the focus was on excluding the long list of potential witnesses who were considered *incompetent* to testify. Second, partly as a result of the reach of incompetency rules and partly through the nature of the evolution of trial process,[60] until the early 19th century there was no rule excluding evidence because its only role was to impeach a witness's credibility.[61] Before then, the witness privilege, a forerunner of the privilege against self-incrimination, protected witnesses' reputational interests.[62] It prevented questioning that incriminated a witness (and for which there was no proof by way of conviction), but up until the mid-19th century it also gained some unusual extensions protecting witnesses against shameful disclosures and even, according to Langbein, preventing a cross-examiner from accusing a witness of lying (that is, perjury).[63] The common law gradually narrowed its limitation on evidence going solely to the 'credit' of a witness to mean a witness's truthfulness (rather than general reliability or accuracy per se). The *UEA* has now shifted to a broader understanding of credibility. The Act defines credibility:

> ***credibility*** of a witness means the credibility of any part or all of the evidence of the witness, and includes the witness's ability to observe or remember facts and events about which the witness has given, is giving or is to give evidence.
>
> ***credibility evidence***, in relation to a witness or other person, is evidence relevant to the credibility of the witness or person that:
>
> (a) is relevant[64] only because it affects the assessment of the credibility of the witness or person; or
>
> (b) is relevant:
>
> (i) because it affects the assessment of the credibility of the witness or person; and

60 J Langbein, *The Origins of Adversary Criminal Trials* (Oxford University Press, 2003), in particular 332-4.

61 *J and SM* [2013] SASCFC 96, [50]-[52] (Blue J). We see below, in the context of proving bias, the early but still cited statement of Pollock CB in *Attorney-General v Hitchcock* [1847] EngR 616; 1 Exch 91, 100; 154 ER 38, 42.

62 Langbein, above n 60, 281-4.

63 Ibid 283-4.

64 'Evidence is not irrelevant "only because it relates only to... the credibility of a witness". However, it will not be relevant unless it could, at least indirectly, affect the assessment of a fact in issue. While credibility evidence may be relevant in this sense, that is not the sense in which "relevant" is used in s 101A': *Tieu* [2016] NSWCCA 111; 92 NSWLR 94, [28]-[29] (Basten JA).

(ii) for some other purpose for which it is not admissible, or cannot be used, because of a provision of Parts 3.2 to 3.6.[65]

The credibility rule – introduction and its rationale

> It sometimes happens, in the course of litigation, that counsel will start a hare. The response of the opposing counsel may be to pursue it. One of the duties of a trial judge is to control the proceedings, to exclude irrelevancy, and to maintain proper limits upon the extent to which the parties and their lawyers will be permitted to raise and investigate matters that are of only marginal significance.[66]

In this section we examine how to identify a 'hare', as referred to by Gleeson CJ (presumably drawing an analogy to greyhound racing). The challenge for evidence lawyers lies in determining whether evidence is 'relevant [and/or admissible] *only* because it affects the assessment of the credibility of the witness': *UEA*, s 101A. The credibility rule (s 102) limits such evidence, as detailed below. It is a rule driven by policy and its application relies on judgment calls based on logic applied within a complex legal and factual matrix.

McHugh J described the policy driving the rule in *Nicholls*,[67] stating that it 'is important to the efficient conduct of litigation' that the principal issues in a trial are not 'overwhelmed by charge and counter-charge remote from the cause of action being litigated' and (quoting from Lord Pearce in *Toohey v Metropolitan Police Commissioner*[68]), while many controversies between parties or concerning their witnesses may 'obliquely throw some light on the issues [they must] in practice be discarded because there is not an infinity of time, money or mental comprehension available to use them'. For McHugh J, the rule's primary rationale is to 'confine the trial process', but it also provides 'fairness to the witness'[69] because it 'protects witnesses from having to defend themselves against discreditable allegations that are peripheral to the issues'.[70] And, as we know from the banner quotation above from Gleeson CJ in *Goldsmith v Sandilands*,[71] the rule is one of pragmatism. It helps to avoid a multiplicity of issues and to confine cases in a manageable manner.

Part 3.7 of the *UEA* reflects this cautious approach to credibility evidence about a witness[72] and seeks to create the right balance. No one wants a case to be distracted or hijacked by a party's foray into attacking opposing witnesses'

65 *UEA*, Dictionary (and *Evidence Act 2001* (Tas), s 3). The breadth of this definition has been the subject of debate, see *Peacock* [2008] NSWCCA 264; 190 A Crim R 454 and *Dupas* [2012] VSCA 328; 218 A Crim R 507. Arguably the court's point of disagreement reflects a misunderstanding of the point being made by Simpson J in *Peacock*. See also '*credibility* of a person who has made a representation that has been admitted in evidence means the credibility of the representation, and includes the person's ability to observe or remember facts and events about which the person made the representation': ibid.

66 *Goldsmith v Sandilands* [2002] HCA 31; 190 ALR 370, [1] (Gleeson CJ).

67 [2005] HCA 1; 219 CLR 196, [55] (McHugh J).

68 [1965] AC 595, 607.

69 *Goldsmith v Sandilands* [2002] HCA 31; 190 ALR 370, [37], quoting from *Natta v Canham* (1991) 32 FCR 282, 298, and citing also *Palmer* [1998] HCA 2; 193 CLR 1, 22.

70 *Nicholls* [2005] HCA 1; 219 CLR 196, [55].

71 [2002] HCA 31; 190 ALR 370 (in relation to the common law finality rule – broadly expressed in *UEA*, s 102). See also *Nicholls* [2005] HCA 1; 219 CLR 196; *Stanoevski* [2001] HCA 4; 202 CLR 115, 130-2 (Hayne J); and *Funderburk* [1990] 2 All ER 482, 485.

72 Credibility evidence will also apply to a non-witness, for example, a person whose non-testimonial statement ('representation') is before the court (by-passing the rule against hearsay) but he or she is not called as a witness: see ss 108A and 108B.

personal qualities.[73] However, there is a tension. As we know, witnesses can be economical with the truth, exaggerate, confuse facts, obfuscate and make mistakes, and the robustness of a verdict can depend on fact-finders being alert to witnesses' potential lack of credibility. Parties can have legitimate (but sometimes not legitimate) desires to present to fact-finders enlarged views of witnesses' credibility, be it by impeachment or by aggrandisement. Further, parties will seek the most liberal pathway for the admission of evidence. Under the *UEA* this will often mean seeking to establish that evidence falls outside the s 101A 'credibility evidence' definition and thus outside the credibility rule (s 102).

As well as acknowledging the utility of the rule, in *Nicholls* McHugh J advocated that:

> 56. The collateral evidence rule[74] should ... be seen as a case management rule that is not confined by categories. Because that is so, evidence disproving a witness's denials concerning matters of credibility should be regarded as generally admissible if the witness's credit is inextricably involved with a fact in issue. Consistently with the case management rationale of the finality rule, however, a judge may still reject rebutting evidence where, although inextricably connected with a fact in issue, the time, convenience or expense of admitting the evidence would be unduly disproportionate to its probative force. In such cases, the interests of justice do not require relaxation of the general rule that answers given to collateral matters such as credit are final.

Part 3.7 achieves the policy goals (and some measure of flexibility) by a relatively common *modus operandi* of the Act. It creates a broad rule and then numerous, quite targeted, exceptions. Generally speaking, the Part follows the broad contours of the modern common law. Section 102 ('the credibility rule') prevents parties from discrediting (or accrediting) witnesses. Exceptions follow. Thus, the credibility rule can best be appreciated as containing a gateway provision (s 102) that excludes precisely defined 'credibility evidence' (s 101A) unless one of the relatively liberal, though typically conditional, exceptions apply.

> **102. The credibility rule**
> Credibility evidence about a witness is not admissible.
>
> **101A. Credibility evidence**
> Credibility evidence, in relation to a witness or other person, is evidence relevant to the credibility of the witness or person that:
> (a) is relevant only because it affects the assessment of the credibility of the witness or person, or
> (b) is relevant:
> (i) because it affects the assessment of the credibility of the witness or person, and
> (ii) for some other purpose for which it is not admissible, or cannot be used, because of a provision of Parts 3.2 to 3.6.[75]

73 *UEA*, Part 3.7, contains the credibility rule (s 102), the definition of 'credibility evidence' (s 101A) and the main exceptions to the rule (ss 103-108C).

74 This is a common law expression. Collateral evidence is evidence that is not relevant to a fact in issue.

75 Parts 3.2 to 3.6 of the *UEA* regulate the admissibility of evidence of hearsay, opinion, admissions, judgments and convictions tendency, coincidence. Section 101A contains the following important notes: '1 Sections 60 and 77 will not affect the application of paragraph (b), because they cannot apply to evidence that is yet to be admitted. 2 Section 101A was inserted as a response to the decision of the High Court of Australia in *Adam v The Queen* (2001) 207 CLR 96.'

The application of ss 101A and 102 is typically quite complex. Interpreting the scope of the credibility rule requires interpreting the scope of the definition of credibility evidence. This, in turn, requires a sharp appreciation of the application of principles of relevance and, in particular (with respect to the operation of s 101A(b)), an appreciation that evidence may be relevant for more than one purpose. Credibility evidence is inadmissible (subject to an exception) if it:

- is *only* relevant to a witness (or other person's) credibility (s 101A(a)); **or**
- it has relevance beyond such credibility *but* the operation of one or more of the provisions within the Parts of the *UEA* addressing hearsay, opinion, admissions, judgments and convictions, tendency and coincidence evidence exclude reliance on the non-credibility purpose of the evidence, meaning that the evidence is admissible solely for its credibility purpose: s 101A(b).

As we see in the case law below, complexity is increased by the fact that at times it is difficult to draw a clear line between the credibility relevance (or purpose) of evidence and its relevance (or purpose) to facts in issue. The following examples vary in their complexity and their engagement with provisions beyond Part 3.7.

Credibility evidence examples

The first limb of s 101A – that is, para (a), is quite straightforward. If the evidence is relevant to credibility (as described above) but has no (direct) relevance to a fact in issue, it is credibility evidence.

Example 1: A simple example of s 101A(a) can be illustrated in the following way. Witness (W), testifying in the trial of A, who is charged with assault occasioning grievous bodily harm upon B, has a recent *conviction for perjury*. W's conviction is only relevant to W's credibility. It is credibility evidence (excluded under s 102, and admissible only if an exception applies). Of course, this conviction may be important information for the jury to consider in determining whether to accept W's evidence and, if accepted, how much weight to give to it. The most likely exception will be s 103 (the credibility rule exception for cross-examination) and, subject to what W says in cross-examination and what follows, possibly s 106(2)(b) and/or (e) will permit proof of the conviction (facilitated by *UEA*, s 178).[76]

Example 2: A more complex application of s 101A(a) involves engaging parts of the *UEA* beyond Part 3.7. For example, consider the same scenario as above except that W emails another person (P) a day or so before she (W) is to testify in A's trial. The email states, '*I intend to tell a pack of lies when I give evidence against A. I hate A. I will do anything to see him put away*'. Each of the three prior representations in this email is credibility evidence. If we wish to use them to establish that W actually does hate A and that she will do anything to see him put away, rather than simply to prove that she *said* this, then they are also hearsay representations, made inadmissible by *UEA*, s 59. They are in addition credibility evidence within s 101A, and so excluded by the credibility rule (s 102). Are there exceptions to these two rules that might apply? First, perhaps ss 66 and 66A (and perhaps also s 71) may apply to make each email representation

76 *Peacock* [2008] NSWCCA 264; 190 A Crim R 454, [58]: 'Subject to the restrictions imposed by s 103, and, in a criminal case, s 104, cross-examination of that witness on that subject is permissible; but what used to be called the collateral evidence rule, now s 102, precludes the adducing of such evidence from another source'.

an exception to the rule against hearsay. Even if the representations fit within an exception to the hearsay rule, the representations remain relevant solely to W's credibility. They show that she intends to lie under oath and she is highly motivated to use her lies to punish A. Like the perjury conviction (and we now understand a little more about W and her perjury conviction, it seems), W's email contains important information for the jury and for any cross-examiner. The most likely exception will be (as with the perjury conviction) s 103 and, subject to what follows, possibly s 106(2)(a) will permit the email to be admitted into evidence and put before the jury.

The second limb to s 101A – that is, para (b), is slightly more complicated because one must assess evidence that possesses multiple relevance. The evidence must be at least relevant for a credibility purpose and also for a non-credibility purpose.

Example 3: Consider a variation of Example 2. W emails P in the same circumstances as above except (i) that the email was sent 10 years after the assault and (ii) in the email W states, '*I think I saw A attack B with a cricket bat*'. What W intended to assert in the email is relevant solely to a fact in issue, that is, that A attacked B. It is not credibility evidence.

However, in court W gives evidence in chief that is inconsistent with her email representation. She testifies, '*I did not see A attack B at all*'. Now W's email is a prior inconsistent statement. This inconsistency between W's representation in her email and her evidence in chief is relevant to her credibility. Either W needs to explain the inconsistency – for example, do her email and her testimony relate to the same or different incidents? Has someone hacked W's email and she did not make the prior representation? – or, if there is no explanation, at least one of W's statements is intentionally or unintentionally false.[77]

Thus, the email is relevant in two different ways – one is as proof of the facts in issue (the assault) and, secondly, as indicating that W may not be a credible witness. To prove the fact in issue element (that is, what W intended to assert), a party must find an exception to the rule against hearsay. Section 66 is unlikely to be satisfied – the representation is unlikely to be 'fresh in the memory' of W if it was made 10 years after the assault. The email is therefore likely to be inadmissible to prove the facts in issue. Thus, evidence of the email is relevant to a fact in issue, but inadmissible for that purpose. But proof of the fact that W *made* the inconsistent assertions, which is relevant to her credibility, does not require consideration of exceptions to the rule against hearsay.[78] Thus, the email in these circumstances is credibility evidence within s 101A(b) and is excluded by s 102. However, subject to ss 43 and 103 a cross-examiner may be permitted to question W on the differences between her testimony and what she has stated in her email as shedding light on W's credibility. Her credibility will ultimately have an impact (indirectly) on the facts in issue: see s 55(1) and (2)(a). If cross-examination is permitted, s 106(1) and (2)(c) may also be satisfied and, as well as cross-examination, evidence of the email may be proved. Finally, if this occurs, the contents of the email may be admissible as evidence of what A intended to assert by virtue of s 60.[79]

77 W has also behaved in a manner within *UEA*, s 38(1), making her vulnerable to being declared an unfavourable witness, see Chapter 5.

78 Chapter 8, p 350.

79 As Note 1 to *UEA*, s 101A, indicates, once evidence is established to be credibility evidence because it is within s 101A(b) and it can be admitted through an exception to the credibility rule,

Example 4: The facts in Example 3 are identical, but the email was sent two days after the alleged assault (that is, the fact in issue). The email is relevant in the same two ways as discussed above, but evidence of what W intended to assert in the email will now be *admissible* (ss 66 and 71 are likely to apply). Even though the evidence is potentially relevant also to W's credibility by virtue of the inconsistency there is no need to seek an exception to the credibility rule (s 102) because the evidence is already admissible to prove the facts in issue. It is *therefore* not credibility evidence. A cross-examiner can question W on the apparent inconsistency and the only issue for the cross-examiner is compliance with the *UEA*'s procedural requirements.[80]

Determining whether evidence is relevant solely to credibility

In *Peacock*,[81] Simpson J distinguished the credibility of the *witness* from the credibility of *evidence* (the latter generally referred to as 'reliability'). As Simpson J observed with reference to the limitations created by the credibility rule (*UEA*, s 102), '[t]he reliability of *evidence* given by a witness might be challenged by evidence *contradicting* all, or part, of that witness's evidence'.[82] Where evidence is relevant and admissible solely to go to the credibility of a witness, it can be contradicted only if there is an applicable exception to the credibility rule. The situation in *Peacock* illustrates her Honour's point. The relevant charges Adam and Brendan Peacock faced were wounding Shane Baker with intent to murder, detaining Baker for advantage and occasioning him actual bodily harm. It was the prosecution case that the motivation for these crimes was because Baker had burgled their house.

Baker testified for the prosecution and admitted to the burglary (that is, confirming the motive). Baker indicated that the burglary was committed with Dale Biddle. Biddle was not called to testify but, after the trial, Biddle made a statement that he (Biddle) was not involved in the burglary. On appeal the appellants argued that the prosecution should have (and could have) called Biddle. The burglary was an earlier and quite separate incident to the attempted murder, but it gained its connection to the charges through its role, on the prosecution case, as a motivation for the alleged criminal conduct. Simpson J (with McClellan CJ at CL agreeing)[83] considered Biddle's evidence as outside the credibility rule because it merely contradicted Baker's evidence of facts (that is, a motive) relevant to

---

then (and only then) ss 60 and/or 77 may permit this credibility evidence to be used for additional purposes (bypassing the hearsay and/or opinion rules through s 60 or 77). A cautionary note, s 66A will not be applicable in this example.

80 *UEA*, s 43 is the most likely concern.

81 [2008] NSWCCA 264; 190 A Crim R 454.

82 Ibid [57]. Her Honour observed that only the former notion comes within the Act's definition of credibility (and so is caught by the credibility rule in s 102).

83 Nettle AJA dissented, saying that, if Biddle had testified that he was not a burglar with Baker, his evidence 'would have gone only to a collateral issue calculated to impeach the credit of the complainant and thus would not have been admissible (*Evidence Act 1995*, s 102)' ([2008] NSWCCA 264; 190 A Crim R 454, [16]). It would not have gone to a fact in issue (nor would it come within s 106). His Honour concluded: 'In the result, as it seems to me, Baker's evidence that Biddle was with him at the burglary could no more have been contradicted by Biddle's evidence that Biddle was not present at the burglary than the witness's evidence in *Piddington v Bennett & Wood* [1940] HCA 2; 63 CLR 533 that the witness was present because he had been banking could be contradicted by the evidence of the bank manager that the witness had not done any banking' (at [20]).

facts in issue. As a result, it may also have reflected on Baker's credibility but did not solely do so.

> 53. Motive was certainly relevant to the identification of the appellants as the perpetrators. Baker's evidence went directly to that question.
>
> 54. Could, then, the evidence that Biddle would have given also go to that issue? In my opinion it could, although less directly.
>
> 55. The answer depends upon an analysis of the content of the evidence given by Baker. It was not merely an assertion that he had entered the Peacock home and stolen property. It went further than that, and gave colour to that evidence by the addition of supporting detail: one detail was that he was in company with Biddle, others were what each of them did, and stole, whilst in the premises. …
>
> 59. I make no comment on the weight that might be attributed to Biddle's evidence. Biddle's evidence, if accepted, would have been capable of casting doubt on Baker's account of the thefts in respect of the surrounding detail, and therefore upon the central fact that he alleged. It is true, as Nettle AJA says, that Biddle's evidence could not have *established* that Baker was not involved in the burglary. But that is not the question posed by s 102. That question is whether Biddle's evidence was *relevant* to some issue other than Baker's credibility. In my opinion it was. True it is that Biddle's evidence is more remote than that of Baker, and, therefore, has less probative value. But that does not mean that it was not relevant to a fact in issue.
>
> 60. The issue might be tested this way: could the appellants have called Biddle to deny that he was involved in the entry and theft? I find it difficult to imagine that any trial judge would reject, as evidence going only to the credibility of a Crown witness, evidence of a defence witness directly contradicting one significant aspect of the evidence of that Crown witness. This neatly illustrates the slipperiness of the distinction between fact in issue evidence and credibility evidence.
>
> 61. If the appellants could have called him, the Crown could have called Biddle. I have come to the conclusion that Biddle's evidence, had he been called, would not have been inadmissible by reason of s 102.

In Australia there are a number of occasions where the High Court has considered whether evidence is relevant solely to credibility or not. Undoubtedly, the signature case is the 1940 appeal, *Piddington v Bennett and Wood Pty Ltd*.[84] Its pre-eminence stems from the fact that it involved (i) an ordinary event – a pedestrian being struck by a motorcycle as he crossed Phillip Street in Sydney, and (ii) an ordinary issue – how far a party can explore whether an eyewitness is authentic. It was in another respect quite unusual. The pedestrian was Albert Piddington who 25 years before the accident – almost to the day – had been appointed as a High Court Justice. His appointment lasted for one month[85] because controversy surrounding his appointment led to his standing down before he ever sat on a case.[86] As a result of the 1938 motor accident:

> [Piddington] sustained injuries of some severity … [and] he was unable to give an account of the accident himself, and in order to make out his case he depended upon the evidence of such bystanders as he was able to call as witnesses. His chief witness, a man called Donellan, gave evidence which, if believed, would establish that the accident arose from the excessive speed of the motor cycle, which prevented it from pulling up or avoiding the plaintiff as he crossed the street in an ordinary manner.[87]

---

84 [1940] HCA 2; 63 CLR 533.

85 From March-April 1913.

86 See M Roe, *Australian Dictionary of Biography* (Melbourne University Press, 1988) Vol 11.

87 [1940] HCA 2; 63 CLR 533, 553 (Dixon J).

Donellan was an occupant/caretaker of a building close by in Phillip Street. He testified in the plaintiff's case that he was on the opposite side of the road from the accident and had a good view of it and 'he stood there pretty often in order to get a bit of sun when it comes out'. As Dixon J observed, '[t]here was nothing surprising or unnatural in his standing there'. However in cross-examination the defendant suggested that Donellan had not in fact witnessed the accident. In this context the cross-examiner asked what the witness had been doing at the relevant time. Donellan's reply was that:

> [He] was on a message for one Major Jarvie, who had business in the building of which the witness was caretaker; he was going to or coming from a bank in Hunter Street where he cashed a cheque or paid one in for Major Jarvie. He said that he stood waiting to speak to an acquaintance whom he saw conversing with another man two yards away.

The contentious evidence admitted by the trial judge (which the Full Court of the NSW Supreme Court and Latham CJ and Starke J – both dissenting – also considered admissible) came from the manager of Major Jarvie's bank, Mr Sheridan, called by the defendant. His evidence was to the effect that 'Major Jarvie's account at the bank disclosed neither a payment in nor a payment out nor any other transaction on the day of the accident'.

Piddington was unsuccessful in his action for damages at trial. He appealed. The issue on appeal was whether evidence from Sheridan should have been excluded by the trial judge because it was *only* relevant to discredit Donellan – and so offended the common law finality rule (which is, for present purposes, expressed in the credibility rule). Piddington was unsuccessful in the NSW Full Court. The dissenting view of Latham CJ in the High Court was that a witness's description of his presence and capacity to observe the events in dispute are facts relevant to the facts in issue because it would be implausible that an eye witness could testify to events 'without saying that he was then and there present, and observed the events' and hence evidence casting doubt on a witness's presence and capacity to observe the accident *was* relevant to a fact in issue. The majority (Dixon, Evatt and McTiernan JJ) allowed Piddington's appeal, agreeing that Sheridan's evidence was relevant solely (and at best) to Donellan's credibility and that Sheridan should not have been permitted to testify. The greyness of the dividing line in the circumstances of the case make it a classic illustration. To have gained sufficient relevance to be admissible, Evatt J (in majority) observed the situation would have had to have been different in key respects:

> There may be cases where, by reason of some closely related incident of a somewhat special character, a witness of an accident volunteers a positive explanation of his presence at the scene of the accident, and where direct contradiction of such alleged incident and such alleged explanation is permissible despite the inevitable delay caused by such an extension of the ordinary scope of the investigation. Such evidence may be admissible upon the ground that the fact of the presence of the witness at the scene of the accident is deemed to be a fact relevant to the issue, and that it cannot reasonably be dissociated from the incident, event or circumstance by which he has explained his being an eye-witness.
>
> Under special conditions such as the above, it may possibly be said that the particular witness has garnished his account of the relevant facts with associated details designed to give verisimilitude – to quote from one of the judgments in the Supreme Court.
>
> In my opinion, this present case belongs to no such special category. The witness Donellan did not explain his presence at the scene of the accident by reference to any special event, incident or circumstance. It was fully established that the place of Donellan's residence and occupation was close by the scene of the accident. It was almost fanciful to

> say that the witness attempted to garnish his story by attaching special significance to his message to the bank. On the contrary, his recollection as to the bank visit was obviously not very clear, and he never suggested that the visit formed any integral or even relevant portion of his narrative of the accident. We are then left with a chain of reasoning which seeks to infer the fact that A was not present at one place at a certain time by proving that A was not present at a different place at a somewhat earlier point of time. The reasoning is fallacious. It would be very different if it could be proved that A was at a different place at the very time of the accident.
>
> ... A subordinate obstacle to the reception of the evidence of the bank manager was correctly emphasised by Bavin J and counsel for the defendant now seems to agree with the suggestion. The point made by Bavin J is that the bank manager's evidence does not even establish the fact that Donellan had not been on a visit to the bank on the day of the accident; for it is quite possible that the purpose of the message was to change one form of cash for another, in which case no record would have appeared in the bank's books relating to Jarvie. This subordinate point reinforces the objection to the evidence.[88]

With reference to the evidence in question his Honour observed:

> [T]here is no logical relevance between the fact permitted to be proved, viz the *absence* of Donellan from the scene of the accident, and the fact sought to be proved, viz his *absence* from a different place at a different time of the day. Even the logical relevance of a particular circumstance to a matter relevant to a matter in issue is not necessarily a ground for the admissibility of such particular circumstance. But logical irrelevance is always a reason for exclusion.[89]

One can apply the facts in *Piddington's* case to Australian uniform evidence law. The result would be the same, but by a different route. It entails considering *UEA*, ss 101A-106. The cross-examination of Donellan as to whether he had truly been at the vantage point of the accident as claimed in his examination-in-chief satisfies s 55. It is relevant to facts relevant to the fact in issue. However, it does not appear a question was asked of Donellan concerning his presence at the *bank*. That information appears to have been volunteered by the witness. *If* the question was asked and Donellan's answer was given in a way that made it 'integral or even [a] relevant portion of his narrative of the accident', cross-examination on it *may* come within the standard required by s 103. If this was the case and if having been asked in cross-examination Donellan had insisted he had banked on Mr Jarvie's behalf, s 106(2)(d)[90] *may* have applied as an exception to the finality rule. In both instances, the key issue would be the reasons of logical irrelevance expressed by Evatt J above. Thus, there would be little likelihood of a court applying the *UEA* granting leave to admit Sheridan's evidence because, even assuming it satisfied s 55 (and was not excluded by s 135),[91] it would be 'credibility evidence' within s 101A(a) and by virtue of the way evidence was elicited it would be unlikely to satisfy the standard of probative value required under s 103 (and thus satisfy s 106(1)).

Mr Goldsmith should have considered *Piddington's* case more closely before his appeal in the 2002 High Court case of *Goldsmith v Sandilands*.[92] Both Goldsmith and Sandilands were police officers. Goldsmith unsuccessfully brought an action for damages arising from injuries to his back in a high-speed police

88 Ibid 558-9.

89 Ibid 559.

90 See also *UEA*, ss 106(1) and 192(2).

91 *UEA*, s 135: 'The court may refuse to admit evidence if its probative value is substantially outweighed by the danger that the evidence might: ... (b) be misleading or confusing, or (c) cause or result in undue waste of time'.

92 [2002] HCA 31; 190 ALR 370.

car chase. Sandilands and others denied liability, claiming that Goldsmith's back injury had actually occurred playing indoor cricket three nights before the car chase. The defendants claimed Goldsmith admitted this to Sandilands when the latter collected him from the cricket venue. Goldsmith denied the admission in cross-examination but he agreed that he had played indoor cricket and that he may have played indoor cricket at the time claimed. Counsel for Goldsmith cross-examined Sandilands on the location of the cricket venue and elicited only vagueness and uncertainty. The issue before the High Court was whether Goldsmith (the appellant) should have been permitted to re-open his case to recall Goldsmith to prove the location of the cricket centre and to establish differences between its actual location and the location described by Sandilands. Not surprisingly, the court held against Goldsmith. The reasoning varied but that of Gleeson CJ, McHugh and Hayne JJ was that the evidence was only remotely relevant to Sandiland's credibility.

> 10. The name and description of the street in which the indoor cricket arena was located was a collateral fact.[93] It was a circumstantial detail relating to the evidence of the alleged admission. And, having regard to what the appellant conceded in his evidence, it was of negligible significance. It is possible that, if there had been a dispute about whether the appellant had ever played indoor cricket, then the details about the location of the arena, if seriously in contest, might have had some real bearing on the credit of the first respondent. Even in that circumstance, it would have been collateral. ... Presumably counsel for the first respondent was trying to make the first respondent's evidence as to the admission more credible by pressing for as much circumstantial detail as possible. And counsel for the appellant's cross-examination of the first respondent's evidence on the issue was aimed at attacking his credibility. Even if the evidence could reasonably have been regarded as bearing on the credit of the first respondent, the matter was collateral. Furthermore, having regard to the first respondent's disclaimers as to his recollection, the proposed further evidence did not even bear significantly on his credit.

Credibility rule exceptions

Section 102's credibility rule is, of course, not the final word in the Act regarding credibility evidence. If it were, parties would be sorely circumscribed in exposing witnesses who lie or who are economical with the truth. This would be unfair and defeat the imperatives of justice. In fact, there are a number of provisions in the *UEA* that address different categories of situations where 'credibility evidence' that would be excluded by s 102 is, or may be, admissible: ss 103-108C, 110, 112. Note that in the majority of these situations[94] the threshold issue is constant: in considering any exception to the credibility rule one must first establish that the evidence in question (i) is relevant (s 55) and (ii) is actually 'credibility evidence' as defined in s 101A:

- *in cross-examination* as long as the evidence is of sufficient relevance that it 'could substantially affect the assessment of the credibility of the witness' (ss 103, 104)[95] (additional considerations apply for an accused person/witness);

---

93 It is not uncommon for the term 'collateral fact', or a similar term to be used to refer to evidence that lacks relevance to a fact in issue (or a fact relevant to a fact in issue).

94 That is, not in *UEA*, s 110 or 112.

95 Note also the application of the considerations listed in s 192 with respect to leave provisions and the potential to obtain an advanced ruling from the trial judge. Regarding the role of ss 135 and

- *beyond cross-examination*, where in cross-examination when put to a witness, the witness has denied or has not admitted or agreed to the substance of the evidence, the credibility rule does not apply to evidence within the categories listed in s 106(2) (or with leave of the court, beyond those categories) (s 106(1));
- as evidence that rehabilitates or assists a witness's credibility, *in re-examination* (s 108(1));
- where, as we saw in the previous chapter, a witness's *prior consistent statement* can logically respond to and/or explain a cross-examiner's allegations of fabrication and the like (s 108(3)). This can apply in *examination-in-chief* or in *re-examination*;
- where a hearsay exception permits admission of a *non-witness*'s representation and credibility evidence could substantially affect the assessment of that person's credibility (s 108B, accused person),[96] (s 108A, other non-witness);
- credibility evidence from *an expert* (s 108C);[97]
- where evidence of the *character of the accused person* is admissible: s 110 (and see s 112).

Cross-examination and credibility evidence

Goldsmith v Sandilands and *Piddington v Bennett* show two quite different contexts in which the relevance of evidence to a witness's credibility (and to no fact in issue) arose. Both involved whether extra evidence could be called. In both cases the evidence was held to be too remote. However, the most significant exception to the credibility rule (and a prerequisite to calling extra evidence (such as Mr Sheridan in *Piddington v Bennett*)) is where a cross-examiner seeks from a witness an answer which is 'credibility evidence'.[98] As we saw in the examples applying ss 101A and 102, this questioning might seek to elicit from a witness that he or she has a conviction for perjury, or has a motive to lie, or a bias,[99] or has made a prior inconsistent statement. Section 103 of the Act requires credibility evidence elicited from a witness in cross-examination to have the capacity

---

137 in a credibility context, there is a school of thought suggesting that this mandatory discretion does not apply to evidence relevant solely to credibility. This is based on the definition of the key dimension of ss 135 and 137, namely 'probative value' ('the extent to which the evidence could rationally affect the assessment of the probability of *the existence of a fact in issue*') – emphasis added. Probative value does not interact with 'credibility evidence' (defined in s 101A(a) and (b)(i)) as 'is relevant only because it affects the assessment of the credibility of the witness') or with s 103 which requires consideration of whether the evidence 'could substantially affect the assessment of the credibility of the witness'). '[T]here are two different exercises (weighing the probative value of the evidence [with respect to ss 135, 137] and weighing the credibility of the witness [with respect to the requisite standard required by s 103]), thus ... [cast] doubt upon the application of ss 135 and 137 in the exercise of the discretionary power granted by s 104(2). The point was not, however, addressed in argument and it is not necessary to reach a final view as to the operation of these provisions': *Tieu* [2016] NSWCCA 111; 92 NSWLR 94, [26]-[28], [47] (Basten JA).

96 See *Jacobs (a Pseudonym)* [2019] VSCA 285 (where leave had not been sought – and the evidence failed the 'substantially affect' requirement).

97 See, eg, *Jacobs (a Pseudonym)* [2019] VSCA 285 where close analysis of the evidence showed that the expert evidence of sexual assault complainants' counter-intuitive behaviour was not raised in the case (and so did not even satisfy s 55, let alone s 103).

98 *UEA*, s 101A.

99 And these are not relevant to a fact in issue in the trial.

to '*substantially affect the assessment of the credibility of the witness*' – that is, it is far more compelling than merely logically assisting an assessment of the witness's credibility.

103. Exception: cross-examination as to credibility[100]

(1) The credibility rule does not apply to evidence adduced in cross-examination of a witness if the evidence could substantially affect the assessment of the credibility of the witness.

(2) Without limiting the matters to which the court may have regard for the purposes of subsection (1), it is to have regard to:

(a) whether the evidence tends to prove that the witness knowingly or recklessly made a false representation when the witness was under an obligation to tell the truth, and

(b) the period that has elapsed since the acts or events to which the evidence relates were done or occurred.

According to *IW*[101] 'the word "substantially" (in s 103(1)) must be given effect. It requires establishing that the line of questioning in cross-examination was capable of having a real bearing,[102] or a real and persuasive significance,[103] on the overall credibility of the appellant'.[104] In that case the evidence was potentially a prior inconsistent statement (but it arose in a chaotic set of questioning in the trial and the prosecution conceded s 103 was not satisfied). A good example of the application of s 103 (in combination with s 104) is found below in the case of *El-Azzi*.[105] In addition, the considerations in s 103(2)(a) and (2)(b) must be considered. Whealy J provides guidance on making relevant distinctions in a s 103 context in *Lodhi*.[106] His Honour observes that evidence 'must have such potential to affect the jury's assessment of the credit of the witness in respect of the evidence he or she has given that the credit of the witness cannot be determined adequately without regard to it'.[107] The evidence in *Lodhi* was not a criminal conviction, but the assessment by Whealy J shows deceit in providing a resume for a job application on an occasion where a person relies on the truth 'passes that hurdle, by a relatively small margin'. *Lodhi's* case also illustrates an

---

100 The scope of this section (and also of *UEA*, s 108(1)) has been interpreted as accommodating the tender of documents during ('*in*') cross-examination: see *Aslett* [2006] NSWCCA 49 and *McMahon v John Fairfax Publications Pty Ltd (No 5)* [2012] NSWSC 218, [21]-[39] (with respect to s 103) and *Commonwealth v McLean* (1996) 41 NSWLR 389 (with respect to s 108(1), and apparently consistent with the common law: *Col* [2013] NSWCCA 302, [31] (Latham J, with Rothman and Davies JJ agreeing). In *Ryan (No 7)* [2012] NSWSC 1160, SG Campbell J suggested s 106 was an appropriate vehicle for admitting documents within its terms. The Act's definition of cross-examination suggests it is limited to questioning: '(2) A reference in this Act to cross-examination of a witness is a reference *to the questioning of a witness by a party* other than the party who called the witness to give evidence' (emphasis added). The definition of 're-examination of a witness' illustrates the same point with respect to s 108.

101 [2019] NSWCCA 311, [181].

102 *El-Azzi* [2004] NSWCCA 455, [183].

103 *Castaneda (No 2)* [2015] NSWSC 979, [17] (Wilson J).

104 [2019] NSWCCA 311. This language has been applied previously when s 103 included the term, 'substantial probative value' (replaced by the current s 103 phraseology in 2009): *RPS* (unreported, NSWCCA, 13 August 1997); *Fowler* (unreported, NSWSC, 6 May 1997); *Ronen (No 4)* [2004] NSWSC 1290; 211 FLR 297, [48]; *Lodhi* [2006] NSWSC 670; *W* [2006] TASSC 52; 162 A Crim R 264, 279 [46].

105 [2004] NSWCCA 455, [179]-[190]. See also *Rogerson (No 28)* [2016] NSWSC 160, [32] (a passage of time of 22 years too long since the prior offence and conviction to constitute substantial probative value).

106 [2006] NSWSC 670.

107 Ibid [18].

application of s 103(2)(a), namely, 'evidence [that] tends to prove that the witness knowingly or recklessly made a false representation when the witness was under an obligation to tell the truth'.[108] Whealy J stated:

> 27. The starting point in my reasoning is the assumption, which I think is proper to make for the purposes of the section, that a lie was involved in the format of the material in Exhibit VV. It is true, as Mr Boulten argued, that there may be an explanation for the lie which will rob the credit issue of its sting. But for the purposes of the ruling, I think it is appropriate to assume, as I have said, that the material was an untrue representation. Secondly, I agree with the Crown that a potential employer would consider it important that a potential employee should provide truthful information about his or her past working experience. Thirdly, this is particularly so in the case of a qualified and registered architect whose professional standards should be beyond reproach. Fourthly, the accused has put himself forward as a person of high religious standards and a person who struggles for inner perfection and moral virtue.
>
> 28. I think that credibility is very much in issue in this trial and the question which arises is: Does the fact that the accused has told a lie, if that be the fact, about his work experience in the written document I have identified carry with it the type of probative value that I have identified as being necessary under s 103? For the reasons I have given, I conclude that it does, although I should say that it perhaps passes that hurdle, by a relatively small margin. I am prepared to allow the Crown to ask the question.

Criminal convictions

A witness's prior convictions are more likely to have the capacity to 'substantially affect the assessment of [his or her] ... credibility' where they relate to offences associated with the administration of justice, such as subornation of witnesses and perjury,[109] subject to *when* the offences in question took place (s 103(2)(b)). Similarly, prior convictions relating to dishonesty will have the potential capacity to achieve this standard of probative value[110] – although the seriousness and the timing of criminal conduct will be always an important consideration. Thus, a 16 year old forging a parent's signature on an absentee note for school a year earlier does not meet the standard required by s 103.[111] In terms of timing, in *Montgomery*[112] the NSW Court of Criminal Appeal considered the propriety of cross-examination of a defence alibi witness on his criminal record which was a minimum of 50 years old and concluded that the evidence could not have 'substantial probative value'.[113] As well as being very old convictions, most were minor and with respect to the most serious charge (rape) the witness was acquitted on appeal.[114] Further, Simpson

108 And see in *Jacobs (a Pseudonym)* [2019] VSCA 285 where an attempt to prove by tendering a lease that Jacobs had lied to the complainant that he had just moved into a studio failed to meet the 'substantially affect the assessment of [that] person's credibility' (as expressed in s 108A) in relation to his denials of non-consensual sexual intercourse.

109 *Fowler* (unreported, NSWSC, 15 May 1997).

110 See *Jones (No 7)* [2007] NSWSC 1158 (Buddin J) (conviction for obtaining money with false or misleading statements in the circumstances of the case). See also *Smith* [2014] NSWSC 768.

111 *ATM* [2000] NSWCCA 475. Note professional rules, such as r 64 of the *New South Wales Bar Rules*, require a barrister not to allege 'any matter of fact amounting to criminality, fraud or other serious misconduct against any person' without belief on reasonable grounds that the allegation can be supported on a proper basis.

112 [2013] NSWCCA 73.

113 Ibid [6]. Fullerton J doubted that it would logically bear on the witness's veracity at all.

114 It appears the prosecutor was unaware that the rape conviction had been overturned on appeal, see ibid [136]. Fullerton J would have upheld this ground of appeal. Simpson J (with McClellan CJ at CL) held that the quick intervention of Zahra DCJ and the re-examination effectively and shortly directed the jury to the age of the conviction.

J (with McClellan CJ at CL agreeing) was critical of the prosecutor's failure to obtain a ruling in advance of the cross-examination regarding whether s 103 was satisfied. Her Honour referred to this as 'a serious departure from proper standards of conduct required of a Crown prosecutor'.[115]

Would a witness's convictions for other types of offences be capable of substantially affecting the assessment of a witness's credibility? It depends. Obviously, they must have a 'substantial' bearing on his or her credibility. In *Fowler*,[116] Dowd J rejected cross-examination on a witness's prior convictions involving assault, observing that convictions for larceny, assault and murder are typically irrelevant to credibility, and '[e]ven a murderer can be truthful'. In *El-Azzi*,[117] a case discussed below, the NSW Court of Criminal Appeal considered that a criminal conviction relating to serious dishonesty (corruption) satisfied s 103 but evidence of disciplinary misconduct did not.

Witness bias

An example of cross-examination regarding a witness's bias was permitted in *Kamm*.[118] This trial related to child sexual offence allegations of events from approximately 10 years earlier. Kamm was the leader in a religious community in rural New South Wales where he was considered by the community to be the prophet of God. The prosecution sought to prove that Kamm had taken the complainant (C) to a particular hotel for sexual intimacy at a date that coincided with C being underage. It had no proof of payments. The defence called a member of the community, Ms Candace Hepi, who testified that she merely worked as the defendant's assistant and that she had thoroughly disclosed to the prosecution all credit card documentation (none of which revealed relevant payments). The cross-examiner sought to challenge the completeness of Ms Hepi's disclosure suggesting that Ms Hepi had a more intimate relationship with Kamm, as one of his queens,[119] not merely an office assistant, and that her bias explained the lack of disclosed payments (rather than the fact that none existed). Considering s 103 and s 137, Giles JA, Latham J and Mathews AJ observed:

> 57. … Questioning the completeness of the disclosure made by Ms Hepi was legitimate and met the test of substantial probative value, and there was no outweighing danger of unfairness to the appellant; it was not a case of no more than a dark cloud of suspicion …

With respect to considering the role of s 137 in the context of the admissibility evidence Basten JA in *Tieu*[120] observed that a balancing between the 'probative value' of evidence and the danger of unfair prejudice draws in the definition of 'probative value' ('the extent to which the evidence could rationally affect the

---

115 [2013] NSWCCA 73, [6].

116 Unreported, NSWSC, 15 May 1997.

117 [2004] NSWCCA 455. See below, pp 237-241.

118 [2008] NSWCCA 290, special leave to the HCA refused, S124/2010: [2010] HCATrans 258.

119 Kamm claimed to communicate with the Virgin Mary and his teachings included that '12 queens would be chosen by the Virgin Mary to bear his children and 72 princesses would be chosen able to marry others but to bear his children if they wished'. All would become his wives: [2008] NSWCCA 290, [3].

120 [2016] NSWCCA 111; 92 NSWLR 94, [44] and [47]: 'The specific amendment gives support for the proposition that there are two different exercises (weighing the probative value of the evidence and weighing the credibility of the witness), thus casting doubt upon the application of ss 135 and 137 in the exercise of the discretionary power granted by s 104(2). The point was not, however, addressed in argument and it is not necessary to reach a final view as to the operation of these provisions'.

assessment of the probability of the existence of a fact in issue',[121] using the language of s 55 ('without expressly adverting to the effect being either direct or indirect'). His Honour continued:

> While, in a literal sense, these provisions can apply to credibility evidence, s 101A draws a clear distinction between credibility evidence which is relevant "only because it affects the assessment of the credibility of the witness" and evidence which is otherwise relevant to a fact in issue, such as a recounting of the perceptions of the witness of a particular event. *The reason for thinking that s 137 may not operate with respect to credibility evidence is that it raises a different issue, namely the "probative value" of the evidence, rather than an assessment of the credibility of the witness. The credibility of the witness is not a fact in issue*; the witness may have low credibility, but there may be reasons for thinking that the evidence adduced from the witness as to facts in issue is entirely credible. This distinction is implicit in the exception to the credibility rule (namely that credibility evidence is not admissible) in s 103(1) which asks, not whether the evidence has probative value, but whether the evidence 'could substantially affect the assessment of the credibility of the witness'.[122]

Prosecution Cross-examination of Accused on Credibility Evidence

Chapter 10 examines the relevance of evidence of an accused's character to facts in issue. In this section we explore cross-examining the accused on matters relevant solely to his or her credibility. It may be a bias or a motive to be untruthful,[123] or his or her inability to be aware of or recall matters to which his or her evidence relates. Subject to s 101A, the rules governing a challenge to an accused's credibility by way of a prior inconsistent statement[124] will also be within Part 3.7 (Credibility). The concern to avoid unfair prejudice requires in many instances that a party seek leave before cross-examining an accused on a matter solely relevant to his or her credibility.

As well as satisfying s 103, unless a prosecutor is cross-examining the accused on bias or a motive to be untruthful, on his or her inability to be aware of or recall matters to which his or her evidence relates, or on a prior inconsistent statement, a court must apply the leave requirements expressed in s 192 before permitting a prosecutor to cross-examine an accused solely on matters relevant to credibility: s 104(2), (3). In all other instances, a cross-examiner must seek leave: see s 104(2). Leave requires compliance with the terms of s 192 and specifically regard for the considerations listed in s 192(2) below. As leave considerations are relevant also to s 106 (discussed below), it is useful to extract them at this point.

> (2) Without limiting the matters that the court may take into account in deciding whether to give the leave, permission or direction, it is to take into account:

---

121 [2016] NSWCCA 111; 92 NSWLR 94, [44].

122 Ibid [45] (emphasis added).

123 Note the observation by Basten JA in *Tieu* [2016] NSWCCA 111; 92 NSWLR 94, [33]: 'A person accused of a serious crime of which he or she is guilty, will always have a motive to be untruthful. However, the prosecution is entitled to put its case to an accused in order to establish that the accused is guilty and thus has a motive to be untruthful: such questions would go to the ultimate issue and would not be relevant only to the assessment of the accused's credibility. Arguably, they would therefore be relevant to an issue, not inadmissible and, accordingly, not within the definition of "credibility evidence" in s 101A' (or s 104). Note the limitations on this line of cross-examination, *Robinson* [1991] HCA 38; 180 CLR 531, [3]. See also *Ramey* (1994) 68 ALJR 510 – a special leave application; *Beavis* [2018] NSWCCA 248 (and see Chapter 1).

124 *UEA*, s 104(3).

(a) the extent to which to do so would be likely to add unduly to, or to shorten, the length of the hearing, and
(b) the extent to which to do so would be unfair to a party or to a witness, and
(c) the importance of the evidence in relation to which the leave, permission or direction is sought, and
(d) the nature of the proceeding, and
(e) the power (if any) of the court to adjourn the hearing or to make another order or to give a direction in relation to the evidence.

Generally speaking, it is a relatively rare case where bad character evidence will be relevant solely to the defendant's credibility, that is, not also raise implications of guilt.[125] *El Azzi*[126] and *Tieu*[127] extracted below are two of those relatively rare cases. Both are NSW Court of Criminal Appeal cases raising the application of the *UEA* provision in the context of the credibility rule and prosecution cross-examination. As the judgments show, both raised procedural complexity in determining relevance, applying ss 103 and 104, and also considering ss 137 and 192.

Prosecution cross-examination of accused: attack on prosecution witnesses

A prominent feature of traditional common law was that an accused in a trial who discredited a prosecution witness automatically exposed himself to having evidence of prior convictions brought into evidence. Its purpose was to prevent gratuitous attacks on prosecution witnesses in cross-examination (though it potentially stifled bona fide challenges to witnesses with high potential to perjure themselves in their evidence as part of the prosecution case). The automatic loss of the accused's 'character shield'[128] is no longer part of the law governed by the *UEA*.

All UEA jurisdictions, excepting Tasmania

In addition to the leave requirement in *UEA*, s 104(2), s 104(4) and (5) state:

(4) Leave must not be given for cross-examination by the prosecutor under subsection (2) unless evidence adduced by the defendant has been admitted that:
(a) tends to prove that a witness called by the prosecutor has a tendency to be untruthful, and
(b) is relevant solely or mainly to the witness's credibility.

---

125 *Campbell* [2007] 2 Cr App Rep 28, [30], [39], Lord Phillips CJ stating 'a defendant who has committed a criminal offence may well be prepared to lie about it, even if he has not shown a propensity for lying whereas a defendant who has not committed the offence charged will be likely to tell the truth, even if he has shown a propensity for telling lies'. Psychological literature is RJC Munday, 'Reflections on the Criminal Evidence Act 1898' (1985) 44(1) *Cambridge Law Journal* 62, 66-7, pointing to psychological research literature on the context-driven nature of honesty and deceit, though to date there is no research in courtroom contexts. It may be fair to say that psychology is still finding its way in this field (LM Hough, FL Oswald and J Ock, 'Beyond the Big Five: New directions for personality research and practice in organizations' (2015) 2 *Annual Review of Organizational Psychology* 183).

126 [2004] NSWCCA 455. See also *IW* [2019] NSWCCA 311.

127 [2016] NSWCCA 111; 92 NSWLR 94.

128 The common law position used to be that where an accused discredited a prosecution witness the accused's 'character', typically in the form of prior convictions, was opened up for counter-attack under cross-examination. The rationale lay in the fact that where the jury hears discrediting evidence about a prosecution witness it should be entitled to weigh up the credibility (and character) of the person (the accused) who has levelled the accusations. This situation is referred to as *lifting (or raising) the accused's character shield*.

(5) A reference in subsection (4) to evidence does not include a reference to evidence of conduct in relation to:

(a) the events in relation to which the defendant is being prosecuted, or
(b) the investigation of the offence for which the defendant is being prosecuted.

Section 104(4) and (5) set the boundaries of the possibility that the defence may lose his or her 'character shield' through cross-examining prosecution witnesses on their credibility. These provisions reveal that the *UEA* does not seek to 'penalise' a defence attack on a prosecution witness where it involves the adducing of evidence that tends to prove that the witness has a 'tendency to be untruthful' and that 'is relevant solely or mainly to the witness's credibility': s 104(4). Further, even if such evidence is adduced, the attack on prosecution witnesses must have extended *beyond*:

- incidents or events other than those giving rise to the charges against the defendant (s 104(5)(a)); or
- incidents or events other than those related to the investigation of the offences the subject of the charges before the court (s 104(5)(b)).

In other words, if the accused limits discrediting of a prosecution witness to adducing evidence within the factual confines of s 104(5) no leave can be given to cross-examine the accused under s 104. This means, subject to other legislation and other admissibility requirements in the *UEA*, that an accused is at liberty to cross-examine a victim about their conduct at the time of the alleged crime (for example, whether they have fabricated their evidence identifying the accused or describing the incident in question); or cross-examine a police officer regarding their conduct during the investigation (for example, that his or her evidence regarding the making an admission is fabricated). These topics in sub-s (5) are considered well within the bounds of appropriate defence testing of the key aspects of the prosecution case. *Even* if the defence cross-examines beyond these areas, the prosecution will still need to meet the s 192(2) leave considerations and also overcome ss 135 and 137. Unlike the common law, where defence cross-examination of prosecution witnesses goes beyond ss 104(4) and (5), so permitting discrediting of the accused, *UEA*, ss 108A and 108B enable discrediting evidence (that could have been the basis of cross-examination of the accused) to be admitted even if the accused does not testify.[129]

Below we consider these issues in relation to the cross-examination of an accused on credibility through the NSW Court of Criminal Appeal case of *El-Azzi*, the *UEA*'s protection of the accused in the context of the credibility rule and prosecution cross-examination. The successful appeal in *Tieu*[130] confirms that the trial judge must afford proper attention to the separate requirements of ss 103, 104 and 192.

El-Azzi

[2004] NSWCCA 455[131]

El-Azzi, a police officer, was convicted of conspiracy to produce large commercial quantities of methylamphetamine. Prosecution witnesses had been cross-examined

129 If evidence of a previous representation made by the accused has been admitted and the equivalent test to s 103 is satisfied: see *UEA*, s 108B (and leave is granted on the bases expressed in s 108A). This mirrors the scope and content of s 104, placing it in the context of admission of evidence about an accused who is not a witness.

130 [2016] NSWCCA 111; 92 NSWLR 94.

131 Special leave refused: *El-Azzi* [2005] HCATrans 781.

by the defence. Simpson and Sperling JJ found the defence had 'thrown wide open'[132] the gate in s 104(4) by the extensive cross-examination of prosecution witnesses. Simpson J found in favour of the judge's ruling 'after considerable hesitation'. Her Honour observed:

- the cross-examination on matters of credibility of Simpson (the prosecution witness in *El-Azzi*) extended over 194 pages of transcript. It involved a wide range of matters, including bribery (of police officers), tax evasion, assaults and domestic violence, involvement in illicit drugs and drug use and perjury (in courts and tribunals); and
- other witnesses were cross-examined on matters such as forging documents, asserting one witness was a 'career fraudster' and then proceeding to detail his extensive criminal history.

Relying on s 104(4), the trial judge granted leave to the prosecution to cross-examine El-Azzi on:

- two police departmental charges of misconduct (failure to make an occurrence pad entry regarding travel);
- alleged threats made by the accused to two witnesses, Simpson and Ingall;
- a criminal corruption conviction in 1994 under s 186 of the *Crimes Act 1900* (NSW) (corruptly taking $4500 for helping to recover stolen property – and not using due diligence to bring those involved in the theft to trial).

Importantly, Simpson J described the exercise of the judicial discretion to grant leave as one involving 'a fine balancing of competing considerations' with fairness considerations taken into account, adding that 'a different judicial mind may have reached a different result' but, without an error in the exercise of the trial judge's discretion, there was no basis to substitute the trial judge's discretion for that of the appeal court. Her Honour added:

> 200. … Legal representatives of persons charged with serious criminal offences must have substantial flexibility in their approach to cross-examining prosecution witnesses, without fear that attacks on those witnesses, if made within proper limits, will expose their clients to the potential disclosure of their criminal histories, or alternatively, operate as a disincentive to their exercising the option to give evidence.

Sperling J noted that because of the danger of unfair prejudice to the accused, it is an 'exceptional circumstance' that permits evidence that an accused has a criminal history to go before a jury. His Honour observed that the defence cross-examination brought out the serious criminal histories of the prosecution witnesses, important evidence tending to establish that the relevant witnesses had a motive to lie in support of the Crown's case. In addition, like Simpson J, his Honour observed that the evidence to be adduced through s 104 was not 'especially prejudicial' due to the different nature of the subject charge (drug crime) and the prior conviction being for corruption. His Honour found that there was an absence of special features 'which ought to have tipped the balance one way rather than the other',[133] noting that the trial judge considered relevant matters, including those in s 192 as well as ss 135 and 137. In conclusion, the court dismissed the appeal, but held that:

---

132 [2016] NSWCCA 111; 92 NSWLR 94, [191] (Simpson J).
133 Ibid [269] (Sperling J).

- the trial judge had not erred in permitting cross-examination on El Azzi's conviction for corruption. The conviction was of substantial probative value (s 103)[134] to El Azzi's credibility because it was an offence of serious dishonesty; and
- El Azzi's threats to witnesses were innocuous and evidence of them caused no harm; but
- El Azzi's professional misconduct matters did not involve dishonesty – they were not relevant to credit and did not satisfy s 103. They should not have been the subject of cross-examination but the proviso in *Criminal Appeal Act 1912* (NSW), s 6(1), applied.

The judgment of Simpson J articulates the importance of ss 103, 135 and 137 (as well as s 104) and the grant of leave under s 192.

> **Simpson J**: 174. I should note that I agree with Sperling J that the cross-examination of the appellant concerning the two departmental disciplinary matters ought not to have been permitted. It had no probative value whatsoever, and was, as Sperling J has characterised it, "utterly irrelevant" to the applicant's credibility. I also agree with Sperling J that no harm was done by the permitted cross-examination in relation to threats alleged to have been made by the appellant to Simpson and Ingalls. I agree that, in relation to the evidence concerning the disciplinary matters, no substantial miscarriage of justice could have been caused by the admission of the evidence, and that the proviso to s 6 of the *Criminal Appeal Act 1912* should be applied.
>
> 175. I take a different approach, but leading to the same result, to Sperling J, however, in relation to the cross-examination that elicited from the appellant an admission of a previous conviction for a corruption offence. My analysis is as follows.
>
> 176. At the conclusion of the Crown case the Crown Prosecutor sought leave, pursuant to s 104(2) of the *Evidence Act* to cross-examine the appellant about a series of matters that were acknowledged to be relevant only because they were relevant to his credibility. On 6 December 2002 Armitage DCJ gave leave in relation to the four matters identified in ground 5, and set out in the judgment of Sperling J. …
>
> 177. As is evident from the fact that the application was made under s 104(2), the evidence was, and could have been (and it was so acknowledged) relevant in respect of no issue other than the appellant's credibility. It was therefore made inadmissible by s 102, unless, in accordance with s 103(1), it was held to have substantial probative value, and, under s 104(2), leave was given to the prosecution to cross-examine the appellant on that subject matter, such leave to be given in the light of the s 192 considerations. I emphasise the conjunction in the previous sentence: for the Crown to be entitled to cross-examine the appellant on this subject matter, it was necessary that it get over two hurdles, the first that created by s 103(1) and the second that created by s 104(2). In my opinion, rather than being the subject of separate determination, ss 135(a) and 137, on which reliance was also placed, raised considerations relevant to the grant of leave: that is, if, in terms of s 135(a), the trial judge were of the view that the evidence would be unfairly prejudicial to such an extent as to outweigh its probative value, then leave under s 104(2) ought to have been refused; similarly, if, in terms of s 137, he came to the view that the probative value of the evidence was outweighed by the danger of unfair prejudice to the appellant, then he was obliged to refuse leave.
>
> 178. A common theme, expressed in slightly different ways and prescribing slightly different tests, runs through s 135(a), s 137, and s 192(2)(b). That theme is unfairness.
>
> 179. The first question for determination was the question raised by s 103(1): did the evidence have substantial probative value? That raises a further question: substantial probative value of what?

---

134 This refers to the language of s 103 before the 2009 amendment. The change is not significant to the *El Azzi* judgments.

180. "Probative value" is defined in the Dictionary to the Evidence Act as:

... the extent to which the evidence could rationally affect the assessment of the probability of the existence of a fact in issue. ...

183. In my opinion, for this evidence to have had substantial probative value within the meaning of s 103(1), it must have had the potential to have a real bearing upon the assessment of the appellant's credibility – and, particularly, to the appellant's credibility in relation to the evidence he had given, or would give, at the trial. It cannot have had substantial probative value for the purposes of s 103(1) unless it was capable, in a significant way, of bearing upon that assessment. ...

187. The appellant's submissions on appeal focused, as they did at trial, upon the prejudicial effect of the evidence relative to its probative value.

188. In relation to the conviction evidence, only one substantial question was put to the appellant in cross-examination. ...

189. I have come to the view that evidence of a conviction for corruption as a police officer (that is, a conviction for serious dishonesty) had substantial probative value in relation to the appellant's credibility and/or reliability, and specifically so in relation to the jury's assessment of the evidence he gave in the trial.

190. Thus, although the trial judge did not specifically address the correct question under s 103(1), no error in this respect is disclosed in the outcome.

191. The next question is whether cross-examination of Crown witnesses on behalf of the appellant had opened the gateway to s 104(2) provided by s 104(4)(b). Again, no issue is raised in this respect in the written submissions. On this question I agree with Sperling J. The gate was thrown wide open. ...

Sperling J: ... 270. In exercising his discretion pursuant to s 104(2), his Honour was bound to take into account the considerations mentioned in s 192. His Honour did not mention, in that connection, two of the matters he was required to take into account pursuant to the section, namely, prospective unfairness and the nature of the proceedings. However, it is apparent that his Honour was alert to those considerations.

271. The question for this court is not how it would have exercised the discretion to grant leave but whether the trial judge erred in the exercise of the discretion. I am not satisfied that he did err.

272. Although stated as a separate question, the considerations which arose in relation to s 135 and s 137 were not materially different from those which applied in relation to the grant of leave pursuant to s 104(2). Again, minds may differ as to the appropriate course, but I am satisfied that his Honour did not err in declining to exclude the evidence of the prior conviction pursuant to either of those sections in the exercise of his discretion.

273. In summary, of the four matters as to which cross-examination was allowed, cross-examination in relation to the two instances of misconduct in the police service should not have been allowed, cross-examination on the alleged threats was innocuous and allowing cross-examination in relation to the prior criminal conviction did not involve an error in the exercise of the judge's discretion.

274. In view of the error in granting leave to cross-examine in relation to the two instances of misconduct, the appeal against conviction should be allowed subject to the application of the proviso to s 6 of the Criminal Appeal Act 1912.

275. I am satisfied that there was no miscarriage of justice as a result of the error in allowing evidence of the two instances of misconduct to be brought out in cross-examination. These were not matters involving dishonesty. They involved no serious moral culpability. The trial judge instructed the jury immediately after the evidence was led and again in the summing-up that these and the other matters brought out in cross-examination were relevant only if the jury thought they were relevant to the appellant's credibility. The two matters were not relevant to the appellant's credibility, and so obviously not that I do not believe the jury would have accorded them any significance in that regard. Nor do I think there was any serious risk that the jury might have seen these

episodes of misconduct as being of significance in any other impermissible way. In the broad view of the case, they were far too unimportant to be seen as significant in any way.

276. I would, for these reasons, apply the proviso to s 6.

277. In the result, the appeal should not be allowed on this ground of appeal.

Tieu involves a similarly extensive cross-examination of a prosecution witness. The extracted judgments are important because they reinforce the importance of applying s 55 and of adhering to the leave requirements in s 104. Basten JA dissented with respect to the significance of some aspects of the way the judge and the defence counsel proceeded in *Tieu*. He refused leave to appeal on this ground, relying on *Criminal Appeal Rules* (NSW), r 4. Nevertheless, his discussion of s 104(5) is informative.

Tieu

[2016] NSWCCA 111; 92 NSWLR 94[135]

Andrew Tieu appealed five convictions for armed robbery related offences. It was the prosecution's case that Tieu was the getaway driver for Christopher Hibbard who robbed a number of premises armed with a shotgun. Hibbard testified for the prosecution. His evidence was that he and Tieu knew each other through their ice habit and Tieu had offered a car and to drive Hibbard to and from robberies. Tieu also testified. He said he lent a 'community' car to Hibbard on the dates that coincided with two of the robberies. For the third robbery Tieu admitted he drove Hibbard, but denied he knew Hibbard was engaged in armed robbery. He believed he was driving Hibbard for debt collection purposes. Tieu testified that while driving from the final premises he panicked and crashed the car when a police car appeared. Hibbard had put a gun to his head and told him to 'drive'. Tieu then ran because he had drugs in the car. Defence counsel cross-examined Hibbard extensively on the following:

- Hibbard's significant sentencing discount for pleading guilty and giving evidence against Tieu (and another, Singh);
- Hibbard's convictions for 14 armed robberies, including discharging a shotgun on one occasion;
- Hibbard and Singh smoking ice together and Hibbard purchasing drugs from a dealer (not Tieu);
- Extensive cross-examination of details of Hibbard's robberies with Singh (showing CCTV footage of these robberies) and on Hibbard recruiting others to commit armed robberies;
- Hibbard's various other charges and/or convictions for larceny and break and enter (2002, 2003, 2008);
- Hibbard's 2010 'assault occasioning' against his wife in response to Hibbard's claim that he had never hurt anybody in any of his crimes; and
- Hibbard's internet browsing for pornography (revealed from phone records).

On the basis of this cross-examination the prosecutor applied 'for leave to cross-examine the accused about matters that might be seen as going to his credit' (at [62]). The jury already knew of Tieu's involvement in dealing in drugs. No explicit reference was made to s 104(4). The prosecutor indicated the cross-examination on credibility would build on the proposition that people involved in drug use

135 Citations referring to trial transcripts omitted.

and supply become practised at deceiving so that deception becomes an essential part of their life. Trial judge and counsel discussions in the absence of the jury concluded with the trial judge saying, 'If that's as far as it goes I will give you leave but you might like to think about that further and see how much further you want to go? ... I just want to review this. You wouldn't be getting to that until lunchtime anyway, ... I just want to have a look at – ... I just want to double check ... [attacks on credit]'. The prosecutor noted that he had leave and the judge specifically confirmed that the prosecutor was 'not proposing to go into any prior record' at that stage (at [112]-[115], McCallum J). In addition to drugs, Tieu had a background linked to crimes of dishonestly obtaining property by deception (involving false identification documents) and proceeds of crime offences (and had been found guilty of supplying drugs while on a good behaviour bond for these last offences).[136] The prosecutor indicated he wished to draw links between Tieu's criminal history for obtaining by deception to cast doubt on 'the believability of why he [Tieu] left his wallet at home'.[137] Basten JA describes with quotes from the trial transcript the breach of s 104(2) before the lunch break (with no objection raised by defence counsel).

> 68. ... [T]he prosecutor commenced his cross-examination. The applicant agreed that he was selling ice to support his habit (drug use) and also to support his gambling habit. He said he considered the drug trade "as a business" and it was "a flow of income." He agreed that it was necessary to take steps to avoid telephone intercepts and to take steps to avoid being caught. He was asked whether people who used drugs are "deceptive" and said that, "some people are, yes." He agreed in similar terms that some people who use drugs are dishonest. However he did not agree with the suggestion that through his experience with using and selling drugs he was experienced in deception and with being dishonest. ...
>
> 71. ... "Mr Crown I didn't know you were going on to deal with those matters of his convictions before lunchtime, we had that exchange before. ...

After discussion, the trial judge addressed this confusion with a direction to the jury not to apply tendency reasoning because the accused's prior convictions were to be considered only for the purpose of assessing Tieu's credibility. McCallum J combined with Davies J to form the majority view based on the trial judge's failure to apply the *UEA* provisions (albeit pre-empted by the prosecutor's breach of *UEA*, s 104(2), requiring leave).[138] They granted leave to appeal, allowed the appeal and ordered a new trial.

---

136 McCallum J referred to these as not relevant to Tieu's credibility as a witness, '[t]he submission equated disobedience with dishonesty; in my view, they are quite different' (at [115]).

137 He did not have a valid licence, and so did not want to have ID on him. This was challenged on the basis that Tieu was practised in using fake licences. The prosecutor's stance was that offences of dishonesty (unrelated to fake licences) were relevant generally to Tieu's credibility.

138 The court split over the application of *Criminal Appeal Rules*, r 4, because of the defence counsel's lack of objection: 'No direction, omission to direct, or decision as to the admission or rejection of evidence, given by the Judge presiding at the trial, shall, without the leave of the Court, be allowed as a ground for appeal or an application for leave to appeal unless objection was taken at the trial to the direction, omission, or decision by the party appealing or applying for leave to appeal'. For consideration of the application of r 4, see *Tieu* [2016] NSWCCA 111; 92 NSWLR 94, [80]-[88]. McCallum J (in majority) agreed r 4 did not exclude the appeal, such that failing to object did not trigger r 4, noting that it was the prosecution's responsibility to seek a ruling and also that '[t]he trial judge bears ultimate responsibility to ensure that the trial is fair and is conducted according to law' (at [119]). The contravention of the *UEA* warranted granting leave to appeal under *Criminal Appeal Act 1912* (NSW), s 5(1)(b). Davies J followed a slightly different path, also linked to the lack of application of s 104(4), to consideration of matters of fairness (s 192), or the balancing exercise required by s 137 justified granting leave, notwithstanding r 4, adding that '[w]hen those matters are combined with the Crown Prosecutor's having embarked

McCallum J: 125. Further, I would respectfully not share Basten JA's confidence (at [76]) that the trial judge did address the question whether the gateway to cross-examination, with leave, had been opened. The judge said:

> "Prior convictions may be relevant to credit it was said as was said (sic) in *R v Hanson* [2005] 1 WLR at 169. Here the cross-examination was going essentially to the capacity to show a propensity to be untruthful."

126. The reference to the decision of the English Court of Appeal in *Hanson* is obscure; that decision was concerned with an application by the prosecution to rely upon prior convictions to establish a propensity on the part of the accused to commit offences of the kind charged. In my view, it is clear that the judge was referring to the cross-examination of *the applicant*, whereas s 104(4)(a) is concerned with cross-examination by a defendant tending to prove that *a witness called by the prosecutor* has a tendency to be untruthful (the establishment of which is one of the requirements in the absence of which leave to cross-examine a defendant about matters relevant to the assessment of his credibility "must not be given"). …

129. Had the provisions of the Act been considered in the present case, it is difficult to imagine that the cross-examination as to prior convictions would have been allowed. The applicant concedes, correctly in my view, that his prior convictions for offences of dishonesty were capable of substantially affecting the assessment of his credibility so as to fall within the exception to the credibility rule provided for in s 103 of the Act. The applicant submits, however, that the further protection provided by s 104 should have applied in his favour. Specifically, it was submitted that Ms Orman-Hales' cross-examination of Mr Hibbard did not tend to prove "a tendency to be untruthful" but rather was directed more narrowly to rebutting specific assertions he had made in his evidence. On that basis, it was submitted that the requirements of s 104(4) were not met, with the result that leave to cross-examine as to the record could not be granted.

130. It was further submitted that, even if that is wrong, the probative value of the evidence was outweighed by the danger of unfair prejudice to the defendant, such that the evidence was inadmissible under s 137 of the Act.

131. In my view, there is force in those submissions. The connection between the prior convictions for possessing fake licences and the believability of the applicant's explanation for leaving his wallet behind was tenuous at best. The point was not made good in any specific way during the cross-examination. There was evidence in the trial as to the contents of the wallet, which apparently included a fake licence. The applicant readily admitted that it was a fake licence and that he had had dealings with fake licences … Those concessions were enough to sustain the proposition put to the applicant … that he did not leave his wallet at home because he didn't want to have his expired licence on him, but because he knew he was "going out to do armed robberies". The further cross-examination as to prior convictions for similar matters and other, unrelated dishonesty offences was extremely prejudicial, in my view.

132. … As noted by Basten JA, [defence counsel] … appears to have perceived and been resigned to a risk that the prosecutor would take the course he did and to have assessed the prejudicial effect to be limited in the context of the "robust defence" she was conducting on the applicant's behalf. Ultimately, however, my analysis of the record of the trial has led me to a less sanguine assessment of the degree of unfair prejudice to the applicant. The fact that he was an admitted drug user and drug supplier did not of itself equate to his having convictions for offences of dishonesty.

Davies J (substantially agreeing with McCallum J):

---

upon the cross-examination as to previous convictions without leave and the failure of the primary judge to prevent that course, I consider that the trial miscarried and that the ground of appeal is made out' (at [149]). Basten JA agreed the breaches had occurred but dissented on upholding the appeal.

135. Section 103 provides the test for the credibility rule not to apply. Section 104 sets out a clear pathway which must be followed in criminal matters before an accused can be cross-examined about a matter relevant to the assessment of his or her credibility. Section 104(4) is a gateway provision and is concerned with evidence adduced by the accused that tends to prove a prosecution witness has a tendency to be untruthful and is relevant solely or mainly to the witness's credibility. Section 192 requires the court giving the leave under s 104(2) to take into account the matters in s 192(2). It may be that s 137 is required to be considered: In *R v El-Azzi*,[139] but I note [44]-[47] in Basten JA's judgment.[140] In the present case the issue of prejudice to the applicant was raised by his counsel in response to the course the prosecutor asked to take. …

141. None of the Crown Prosecutor's submissions concerned the gateway provision in s 104(4). There was no reference to evidence that tended to prove that Mr Hibbard had a tendency to be untruthful and that the evidence that was adduced was relevant solely or mainly to Mr Hibbard's credibility. Nor does the primary judge make any reference to Mr Hibbard's evidence in that regard. …

142. Nor, as McCallum J points out, is there any indication that the provisions of s 103 were considered (although, in the event, the test in s 103 was probably satisfied) …

143. Although counsel for the applicant made a passing reference to prejudice to the applicant, the primary judge does not deal specifically with prejudice nor with the question of unfairness as s 192(2) requires. To the extent that the primary judge was to engage in the balancing exercise required by s 137, I do not consider what he said ... shows that this exercise was undertaken. …

148. In *R v El-Azzi* Simpson J said at [200] that it would not be every case where an attack is made upon the credibility of the Crown witnesses that would warrant the exercise of the 104(2) discretion to grant leave to cross-examine. Her Honour stressed the need to assess the matter for overall fairness and for the balancing exercise required by s 137. Her Honour said at [201] that this Court would not substitute its own discretion for that of the trial judge unless error in the exercise has been shown.

Basten JA was the only judge to consider s 104(5):[141]

59. As counsel made clear in her opening to the jury, the primary (if not sole) purpose of the cross-examination of Hibbard was to persuade the jury that he should not be believed on his oath in his account of the applicant's involvement in the five offences with which the applicant had been charged. In so far as the cross-examination related to those offences, it did not form evidence which could lift the prohibition in s 104(4). Counsel for the applicant submitted that the extensive cross-examination in relation to other armed robbery offences in which the applicant was not involved also fell within the exclusion in s 104(5) because those offences were dealt with as part of one investigation which included, but was not limited to, the offences for which the applicant was prosecuted. That submission should not be accepted. No part of the investigation of the offences committed by the applicant related to those other offences: there was a chronological connection only. There was, no doubt, one investigation so far as Hibbard was concerned, but a separate investigation in relation to the applicant. To the extent that Hibbard was cross-examined at length about those matters, it was undoubtedly to seek to persuade the jury that this was a man who could not be trusted on his oath because of his willingness to do whatever was necessary in order to satisfy his own needs and interests. It was evidence that he had a tendency (or more) to be untruthful and it was evidence which went mainly (if not solely) to his credibility.

139 [[2004] NSWCCA 455.]

140 See extracts, above n 95.

141 For the majority, s 104(5) did not arise for consideration by them. McCallum J considered (at [129]) that there was force in defence counsel's submissions that defence 'cross-examination of Mr Hibbard did not tend to prove "a tendency to be untruthful" but rather was directed more narrowly to rebutting specific assertions he had made in his evidence', and, if not, s 137 would make the matters referred to in cross-examination by the prosecution inadmissible within s 137. Davies J focused on the lack of reference to s 104.

> 60. Although the evidence was less extensive, the same analysis must apply to evidence of his drug use with Daljit Singh, including at their common workplace, his recruitment of another person for involvement in armed robberies and the otherwise irrelevant questioning as to what he was viewing on the internet, which turned out to be pornography.
>
> 61. The evidence as to his convictions for larceny and break and enter were designed to demonstrate that he was lying when he said he did not steal from people [just clubs and corporations]. The cross-examination about his conviction for assault occasioning actual bodily harm on his wife was designed to establish that he was lying when he professed an unwillingness to harm people and asserted that he carried the gun only to keep people at a distance.

Tasmania

Amongst *UEA* jurisdictions, Tasmania has adopted the least dramatic modifications of the common law. The *Evidence Act 2001* (Tas) retains the situation described above, namely the need to satisfy s 103 and the lack of need to obtain leave where a prosecutor cross-examines an accused on whether they are biased or have a motive to be untruthful, on their inability to be aware of or recall matters to which their evidence relates, or on a prior inconsistent statement.[142] In addition, as with the other *UEA* jurisdictions, a court must apply the leave requirements expressed in s 192 before granting a prosecutor leave to cross-examine an accused solely on matters relevant to credibility. In Tasmania, a prosecutor can only obtain leave to cross-examine in these circumstances if the accused relies on his or her good character when questioning a prosecution witness or the defence involves imputations on the character of a prosecution witness (or the prosecutor):

> (4) Leave must not be given for cross-examination by the prosecutor under subsection (2) unless –
>
> (a) the defendant or the person representing the defendant has questioned the witnesses for the prosecution to prove that the defendant is, either generally or in a particular respect, a person of good character; or
>
> (b) the nature or conduct of the defence involves imputations on the character of the prosecutor or any witness for the prosecution.

In *Phillips*[143] the High Court considered the equivalent Queensland provision.[144] Mason, Wilson, Brennan and Dawson JJ observed:

> 5. … [I]t has long been established that not every assertion by an accused person which reflects injuriously upon the prosecutor or witnesses for the prosecution will have the effect of bringing into play the discretion of the trial judge to allow cross-examination of him with respect to other offences or to his bad character. A mere denial, even an emphatic denial, of the existence of facts alleged against him will not be sufficient, notwithstanding that imputations on the character of the prosecutor or of a prosecution witness may necessarily be implied;[145] nor will a defence of consent to a charge of rape involve an imputation on the character of the complainant within the meaning of the section.[146]

142 *UEA*, s 104(3).

143 [1985] HCA 79; 159 CLR 45.

144 This follows in large part the terms of *Evidence Act 1977* (Qld), s 15(2)(c).

145 *Rouse* [1904] 1 KB 184.

146 Citing *Turner* [1944] KB 463. See also *Curwood* [1944] HCA 40; 69 CLR 561, 569-78 (Latham CJ), 587-9 (Dixon J); *Brown* [1960] VicRp 62; [1960] VR 382, 396-7 (Smith J); *Selvey v DPP* [1970] AC 304, 339.

6. On the other hand, it is also well established that the foregoing instances are of limited operation. The debate that has taken place from time to time during the past century (and which found its expression in the division of opinion in this Court in *Curwood*) as to whether the reference in the section to imputations on the character of the prosecutor or the prosecution witnesses should be confined to material "advanced for the purpose of destroying or impairing confidence in them as persons who would tell the truth" (per Dixon J in *Curwood* at p 584) as distinct from material relevant to the issues pertaining to the indictment would seem to have been put finally to rest. The issue was determined first by an enlarged Court of Criminal Appeal in *R v Hudson* [1912] 2 KB 464 when in the judgment of the Court at p 470-471 it was said:

> We think that the words of the section, 'unless the nature or conduct of the defence is such as to involve imputations,' &c, must receive their ordinary and natural interpretation, and that it is not legitimate to qualify them by adding or inserting the words 'unnecessarily', or 'unjustifiably', or 'for purposes other than that of developing the defence', or other similar words.

... Although in *Dawson* Dixon CJ was in dissent on the question whether the discretion to admit the cross-examination arose at all on the facts of the case, his Honour's elaboration of the reasoning underlying the first of the two exceptions we have mentioned is, in our view, entirely consistent with the trend of authority. His Honour said, at pp 9-10:

> ... what is referred to (by 'the nature or conduct of the defence' etc) is not a denial of the case for the Crown, not a denial of evidence by which it is supported, but the use of matter which will have a particular or specific tendency to destroy, impair or reflect upon the character of the prosecutor or witnesses called for the prosecution, quite independently of the possibility that such matter, were it true, would in itself provide a defence. The phrase assumes that a denial of the case for the prosecution, although the evidence of the prosecution is necessarily contradicted, does not carry with it an imputation of the kind to which the provision refers. Further the word 'involves' refers to what is a part of the defence or, at all events, an element or ingredient in the defence or what arises from the manner in which the defence is conducted. It is not meant to cover inferences, logical implications or consequential deductions which may spell imputations against the character of witnesses. ...

15. It is right to stress the exceptional character of a case in which the credibility of an accused person is open to be attacked by reference to his bad character or previous convictions and it is undoubtedly right that the discretion of a trial judge to permit such an attack be sparingly and cautiously exercised. ... [As] there will always be a keen appreciation that the admission of the evidence may in the absence of countervailing considerations operate unfairly to his prejudice. ...

17. It remains now to consider the manner in which the trial judge exercised his discretion. It is accepted that the nature or conduct of the defence was such as to involve imputations on the character of the principal witness for the prosecution, namely, the woman who testified that she had been raped. The imputations were that the woman had smoked marihuana with the applicant at his home and that she had requested the applicant to obtain a substantial quantity of marihuana for her to supply to some friends of hers. The trial judge gave detailed reasons for exercising his discretion to allow the prosecutor to cross-examine the applicant on his previous convictions. He described the circumstances of the alleged rape with particular reference to the absence of any resistance on the part of the woman, noting that they exhibited

> "some unusual features or, at least, might be thought by some jurors, at least, to present an unusual set of circumstances in a case of rape". ...

18. In our opinion, the applicant has failed to show that the discretion was exercised wrongly.

The discussion in both *El-Azzi*[147] and *DPP v Kocoglu*[148] (below) – regarding applications of the equivalent to *Evidence Act 2001* (Tas), s 104(4)(b), the application of leave and the ss 135 and 137 discretions – applies also in the Tasmanian context.

DPP v Kocoglu

[2012] VSC 185

The accused was charged with murder. Apart from one eye witness to the alleged murder who gave evidence under the pseudonym of XYZ there were no other eyewitness accounts, fingerprints or DNA evidence implicating the accused. It was the defence case that XYZ alone (or with another) committed the murder and that drugs were potentially a motivating factor. XYZ had over 50 criminal convictions relating to drugs, motor traffic offences, breach of bail offences, crimes of violence (actual and threatened), property offences (obtaining by deception, handling/receiving/disposing of stolen goods), dishonesty, weapons offences. They ranged from late 2005 to 2010. The accused had prior convictions that were also extensive – including drug use and other drug offences, motor traffic offences, breach of bail, dishonesty, weapons, assault, proceeds of crime offences. They ranged from 1997 to 2008. Kyrou J provided an advance ruling on ss 103 and 104 and the consequence to the defence of a far-ranging cross-examination of XYZ.

> **Kyrou J**: 32. Evidence of XYZ's dishonesty offences satisfies the requirements of s 104(4) of the Act. Accordingly, such evidence would enliven the Court's discretion under s 104(2) to grant leave for the Accused to be cross-examined about matters that are relevant to the assessment of his credibility, provided that the evidence is capable of substantially affecting that assessment as required by s 103(1).
>
> 33. The Accused's dishonesty offences are, when considered collectively, capable of substantially affecting the assessment of the Accused's credibility. Those offences tend to prove that the Accused knowingly or recklessly made a false representation when he was under an obligation to tell the truth and that he is not an honest person. All of the convictions for the dishonesty offences occurred within the last 11 years and are sufficiently recent to reflect upon the Accused's current tendency to lie. …

[But:]

> 35. Evidence of XYZ's drug offences does not tend to prove that he has a tendency to be untruthful. Accordingly, such evidence does not fall within s 104(4)(a). Even if the evidence does so, it is not relevant solely or mainly to XYZ's credit. That evidence goes to facts that are relevant to the facts in issue and it therefore does not fall within s 104(4)(b) of the Act.[149] …
>
> 38. To a certain extent, the evidence of drug dealings and drug use is also … relevant to the defence case that XYZ has a strong motive to lie and to shift the blame to the Accused.
>
> 39. It follows from the above that if defence counsel confines the cross-examination of XYZ to his drug offences, the Court would not have the power to grant leave to the prosecution to cross-examine the Accused on any part of his criminal record.

---

147 [2004] NSWCCA 455.

148 [2012] VSC 185. See also *Rogerson (No 28)* [2016] NSWSC 160, [32] and *BI (No 3)* [2016] ACTSC 356.

149 His Honour then detailed that XYZ's drug offences were relevant to explain various relationships, 'the unusual nocturnal meetings between relative strangers' and the significance of key evidence going to the facts in issue. The evidence of drug dealings and drug use were also relevant to explaining who (other than the accused) may have a motive to murder the deceased) and to assist the jury to understand XYZ's discussions and dealings with police after his arrest.

Discretionary considerations

40. In the event that defence counsel cross-examines XYZ on his dishonesty offences and other prior offences, rather than confining the cross-examination to XYZ's drug offences, the question whether an order should be made granting leave to the prosecution to cross-examine the Accused on his criminal record will depend on the matters set out in s 192 of the Act and any other matters that may be relevant to the particular evidence that is in fact adduced.

Considerations in s 192 of the Act

41. Cross-examination of the Accused on his criminal record is unlikely to unduly add to the length of the hearing.

42. The extent to which cross-examination of the Accused on his criminal record would be unfair to the Accused and the importance of that cross-examination to the prosecution case are discussed below.

43. As this is a criminal proceeding, I have taken into account the primary exclusionary rule in ss 102 and 104(2) and the principles set out in *Phillips* in relation to the exercise of discretion to permit cross-examination of the Accused on his criminal record.

44. The power of the Court to adjourn the hearing or to make another order is not relevant. However, as appears below, I have taken into account the Court's power to give a direction to the jury in relation to the use to which evidence of the Accused's criminal record may be put.

Other considerations

45. … [T]he Accused can only be convicted if the jury accepts the evidence of XYZ that the Accused stabbed the Deceased. If the jury does not accept that evidence, the Accused must be acquitted. It is therefore fundamentally important that the jury knows the character and qualities of the person who is alleging that the Accused murdered the Deceased. This is particularly so in the light of the defence case that XYZ murdered the Deceased and the fact that the Crown's case allows for the possibility that XYZ had an involvement in the death of the Deceased. The attack on XYZ's credit is central to the defence case that he, rather than the Accused, killed the Deceased. It is neither incidental nor gratuitous.

46. For these reasons, defence counsel requires considerable latitude in cross-examining XYZ on his criminal record and character. Of course, the jury will need to be given a clear direction that it can only use XYZ's criminal record in relation to his credit and cannot rely on it for the purposes of tendency reasoning in relation to his possible involvement in the death of the Deceased, particularly as regards the offence of making a threat to kill. The circumstances of that offence will need to be explained, including the fact that XYZ was discharged in relation to that offence.

47. While it is clear that it would be legitimate for defence counsel to extensively cross-examine XYZ on his criminal record, it is also clear that fairness and the interests of justice require that the Accused not be cross-examined on all of his prior convictions. This is because there is an unacceptable risk that, if he is, the jury will reason that the Accused and XYZ are as bad as each other and that they were both equally involved in the murder of the Deceased.

48. The evidence adduced thus far does not indicate that there was any link at any time between the Accused and an associate of the Deceased and XYZ, namely, Shane Gaby. The only link between the Accused and the Deceased is XYZ's evidence that he introduced them to each other in the early hours of Sunday 17 February 2008. If the Accused is cross-examined on his drug-use offences, there is a risk that the jury will blur the relationships between the individuals and treat XYZ's associates as the Accused's associates. The jury might consider them all to be drug dealers and speculate that the Deceased was killed by the Accused, XYZ and possibly Shane Gaby in the course of a drug deal that had gone wrong, in circumstances where there is no evidence implicating the Accused in any drug deal involving the Deceased.

49. Notwithstanding a strong warning by me that the evidence is only relevant to the Accused's credit and that the jury must not engage in such reasoning, I am not confident that such a warning will completely eradicate the risk that the jury will be influenced, at least subconsciously, by such reasoning. Accordingly, I am of the view that the prejudicial effect of the admission of all aspects of the Accused's criminal record would dwarf any assistance that that record would provide to the jury in assessing the credibility of the Accused.

50. If the Accused gives evidence, the key evidentiary contest will be between the Accused and XYZ. In these circumstances, at first blush, it may seem only fair that the jury should know the character and qualities of both men. However, if that approach were adopted, the benefit to the jury of knowing about the Accused's credit would be swamped by the overwhelming prejudice that the Accused would suffer by the jury succumbing to the impermissible reasoning that the Accused and XYZ are as bad as each other and therefore they both killed the Deceased.

51. This risk is magnified by the existence of the text message.[150] That message is ambiguous and, from the Accused's perspective, is capable of both innocuous and incriminating meanings. However, any prospect that the jury might give the Accused the benefit of the doubt in relation to the text message would be lost if the Accused's extensive criminal record is admitted. There is a clear risk that if the jury became aware of the Accused's extensive criminal record, the jury would use the text message as confirmation of its suspicions that the Accused and XYZ both killed the Deceased.

52. The above considerations provide an overwhelming case against the exercise of the discretion under s 104(2) of the Act to grant leave to the prosecution to cross-examine the Accused on all aspects of his criminal record.

53. The question remains as to whether the above discussion would be applicable if cross-examination on the Accused's criminal record were confined to the dishonesty offences. In my opinion, the risks to which reference is made at [47] to [52] above would not arise if cross-examination on the Accused's criminal record were confined to his dishonesty offences. The jury will readily understand a direction that those offences are relevant only the Accused's credit and are not probative on the question of guilt. There is no risk of the jury adopting tendency reasoning. The jury would not reason that a person who lies is the type of person who also kills.

54. In my opinion, if XYZ is extensively cross-examined on all aspects of his criminal record and cross-examination of the Accused is not permitted in relation to his dishonesty offences, the trial will be unfair to the Crown because the jury will treat the Accused as having led an unblemished lifestyle. In circumstances where the credit of the indispensable Crown witness is all but destroyed by reference to his criminal record, it would be artificial and unfair to withhold from the jury evidence that casts doubt on the Accused's honesty.

55. The same considerations do not apply to the Accused's drug-use offences. Evidence of those offences – whether the offences are considered individually or collectively – is not capable of substantially affecting the jury's assessment of the Accused's credibility for the purposes of s 103(1) of the Act. This is because the drug-use offences, considered in the light of XYZ's evidence that on 16 and 17 February 2008, the Accused only consumed Xanax tablets, would not be sufficient to indicate that the Accused's prior drug use impaired his ability to perceive and remember the events of that weekend.

56. Even if the evidence of the Accused's prior drug-use offences falls within s 103(1) of the Act, it is appropriate in the circumstances of this case not to exercise the discretion in s 104(2) to grant leave to the prosecution to cross-examine the Accused on those offences.

150 Sent from Kocoglu to XYZ on the day the body was discovered: 'What the hell!! Is going on. Why are you avoiding me and avoiding my fucking money. I'll tell you why because you don't need me anymore since I have helped you kill a Serb that may be the reason. Also, I want my cash back in cash! ASAP thank you. One difference between you and me, I haven't got anything to lose my dear friend'.

> 57. This is because, for the reasons that I have already discussed, the granting of leave to the prosecution to cross-examine the Accused on his drug-use offences would result in an unacceptable risk that the jury would reason that the Accused and XYZ are as bad as each other, that they are both involved in drugs and that they both killed the Deceased.
>
> 58. In my opinion, the benefit to the jury of receiving evidence about the Accused's drug-use in assessing the Accused's credit would be very limited. …
>
> 59. The limited benefit to the jury of evidence about the Accused's drug-use in assessing his credit, would be significantly exceeded by the prejudice to the Accused from the jury engaging in the impermissible reasoning to which I have referred.
>
> 60. For the reasons set out at [36] to [38] above, the evidence of XYZ's drug offences is an important part of the defence case. Cross-examination of XYZ on his drug offences would be for a legitimate forensic purpose and would not be either gratuitous or incidental.
>
> 61. Accordingly, on the basis of the current evidence and submissions of the parties, if defence counsel extensively cross-examines XYZ on all aspects of his criminal record and the Accused subsequently gives evidence, I would grant leave to the prosecution to cross-examine the Accused only on his dishonesty offences.

Kyrou J also addressed an additional issue that arose during XYZ's cross-examination, namely, that 'XYZ said that he had limited knowledge and experience of the criminal justice system and that he had previously been cautioned in relation to road traffic offences and an assault'.[151] The defence claimed that these assertions conveyed a misleading impression to the jury and thus created an additional justification for defence counsel to extensively cross-examine XYZ. Kyrou J rejected the submission, pointing out that XYZ's broad and diverse experience with the criminal justice system was already before the jury and so the defence could already overcome any misleading impression XYZ may have created 'without the need to expose his entire criminal record'.

Credibility Evidence and Cross-examination of Accused by Co-accused

We saw in Chapter 2 the tension that can exist in seeking to ensure all accused receive a fair trial where multiple accused are tried together but where the danger of improper prejudice may arise from, for example, the admissibility of prosecution evidence against one, but not the other, accused. In these situations separate trials will be ordered if steps, such as a judicial direction, are considered insufficient to address the danger of improper prejudice.[152]

Sometimes for an accused the prosecution is not the only adversary. It is an acknowledged dynamic that an accused may seek to cast the blame on another accused, that is, they run a 'cut-throat' defence.[153] This form of defence may be inhibited in *UEA*, s 104, if the accused testifies. However, it is also facilitated by the Act in other ways. First, the Act contains provisions that specifically permit an accused to defend criminal charges at the expense of a co-accused.[154] Second, a co-accused can avoid onerous limitations and obligations that in the same

151 *Webb and Hay* [1994] HCA 30; 181 CLR 41. See also *Madubuko* [2011] NSWCCA 135; *Pham* [2004] NSWCCA 190. On judicial directions to the jury, see *Gilbert* [2000] HCA 15; 201 CLR 414, quoted in Chapter 2.

152 *Webb and Hay* (1992) 59 SASR 563, 585.

153 See D Ross, 'One Accused's Evidence of Another's Criminal Disposition' (2006) 11(1) *Deakin Law Review* 179.

154 See, eg, *UEA*, ss 20 (excepting Victoria), 104(6), 111.

trial curtail the prosecutor.[155] Where a defence case involves adducing evidence adverse to a co-accused, that co-accused can seek leave to cross-examine solely on the credibility of the accused who adduced the adverse evidence.[156] The NSW Court of Criminal Appeal case of *Fernando*[157] provides authority on how 'adverse' is interpreted in this context. The case concerned the Fernando brothers, Vester and Brendan. In their joint trial Brendan attributed major responsibility for the murder to Vester. Vester gave a version of events that was inconsistent with that of Brendan, opening himself up to cross-examination by Brendan's counsel. The Court of Criminal Appeal drew upon the House of Lords decision in *Murdoch v Taylor*[158] (despite the different language used in the relevant statutory provision) to conclude that inconsistent evidence, in this context, was 'adverse' to the co-accused.

Exceptions to the Finality Rule

With respect to credibility impeachment, s 106 is a most important provision. As sub-s (1) indicates it operates *after* cross-examination and permits credibility evidence to be proved in five relatively limited instances or, on other occasions, subject to leave of the court. Unless the situation falls within the terms of s 106 the cross-examiner must rest content with the answers received to his or her questions. They are final (and thus the common law expression 'the finality rule'). The context in *Piddington v Bennett and Wood Pty Ltd*, discussed above in relation to s 101A issues,[159] illustrates this rule. The witness, Donellan, explained his presence at the vantage point to the accident. Under the *UEA*, evidence to contradict his assertion, as credibility evidence, would have to come within the terms of s 106. In addition, the cross-examiner would have had to have first gained a denial (or a non-admission or non-agreement) of the substance of the evidence put to him or her by the questioner.

Section 106 is in two parts. Section 106(1) requires the above questioning protocol to be put to the witness and the witness's non-acceptance of the questioner's position. Section 106(2) allows a party to lead credibility evidence that is within any of five categories. Section 106(1)(b) was added in 2009. It adds flexibility where credibility evidence is not within one of these sub-s (2) categories but is sufficiently important (and meets the s 192(2) considerations) that the court will grant leave for it to be adduced. The flexibility introduced by s 106(1)(b) reduces the need to precisely define the enumerated categories in s 106(2)(a)-(e).

106. Exception: rebutting denials by other evidence

(1) The credibility rule does not apply to evidence that is relevant to a witness's credibility and that is adduced otherwise than from the witness if:

(a) in cross-examination of the witness:

(i) the substance of the evidence was put to the witness, and

(ii) the witness denied, or did not admit or agree to, the substance of the evidence, and

(b) the court gives leave to adduce the evidence.

155 Such as *UEA*, ss 101, 137; and see also s 65(8).
156 See *UEA*, ss 104(6), 192.
157 [1999] NSWCCA 66.
158 [1965] AC 574.
159 See above, pp 227-229.

(2) Leave under subsection (1)(b) is not required if the evidence tends to prove that the witness:

(a) is biased or has a motive for being untruthful, or
(b) has been convicted of an offence, including an offence against the law of a foreign country, or
(c) has made a prior inconsistent statement, or
(d) is, or was, unable to be aware of matters to which his or her evidence relates, or
(e) has knowingly or recklessly made a false representation while under an obligation, imposed by or under an Australian law or a law of a foreign country, to tell the truth.

The s 106 requirement that the witness be cross-examined on the substance of the evidence (and that the witness deny or not admit or agree with the questioner) reflects the fundamental principle of procedural fairness that parties must give witnesses an opportunity to refute or explain allegations that pertain to them or their evidence. The case of *Copmanhurst Shire Council v Watt*[160] provides an example of this dynamic within a s 106(1) context. It also demonstrates the role of a prior inconsistent statement relevant solely to credibility and principles arising from the rule in *Browne v Dunn*[161] (discussed in the next section). Watt was the driver of a car involved in a crash on 24 March 1998 on one of the appellant Council's roads in an area that was subject to road works. Watt brought an action for damages arising from the accident, claiming the crash arose from the Council's failure to maintain safe road conditions, namely it had allowed loose gravel to remain on the road. The Council denied liability, responding that driver negligence caused the crash.

The defendant called Constable Carroll who had attended the scene on the day of the accident. The constable testified that he had inspected the road by driving along it within the speed limit and replicated braking the car heavily at the relevant location, which he testified was achieved without skidding and 'that there was no loose material on the road surface other than the rubber from the tyres of the car'. Carroll's evidence of the lack of loose material was from unaided recollection seven years after the event and his evidence significantly contradicted other witnesses. Neither Constable Carroll's notebook nor the official police record made within a few days of the accident recorded gravel on the road. Section 106(1) was engaged following an exchange in cross-examination regarding Constable Carroll's interview with Mr McNabb, a private investigator, some 2-3 months after the crash. In cross-examination Carroll was asked whether he remembered being interviewed by Mr McNabb. He said that he could not recall.

As detailed in the judgment of Giles JA, the cross-examination continued

32. …

Q. Do you remember saying to Mr McNabb that the road was bitumen; that you had no specific recollection of whether or not there was gravel or sand on the road?
OBJECTION
MCCULLOCH: Unless my friend intends to call Mr McNabb as a witness.
HIS HONOUR: You can put the matter to him surely.
MCCULLOCH: Your Honour has heard my objection. The question is being put in a positive way with respect.
HIS HONOUR: I will allow it.

160 [2005] NSWCA 245; 140 LGERA 333.
161 (1893) 6 R (HL) 67.

TOOMEY: Q. Do you remember saying that to Mr McNabb, Mr Carroll?
A. No, I do not.
Q. Was it the truth?
OBJECTION. QUESTION REJECTED
Q. Was it the truth that as at 26 June 1998 you had no memory of whether or not it was gravel or sand on the road?
A. I don't recall saying that to Mr McNabb.
HIS HONOUR: You are not being asked that now.
TOOMEY: Q. I am asking you was it the truth that as at 26 June 1998 you couldn't remember whether or not there was dirt or gravel on the road?
A. I can't answer that.

33. … Mr McNabb gave evidence that he interviewed Constable Carroll and prepared a detailed file note. When he was asked to "have a look at this document", plainly enough with a view to evidence that Constable Carroll told Mr McNabb that he could not remember whether or not there was gravel or sand on the road, the appellant objected. After argument, the judge ruled that evidence to that effect would be admissible because, contrary to the appellant's submission, what Constable Carroll said to Mr McNabb would be a prior inconsistent statement and in the judge's view Constable Carroll had denied its substance.

34. Mr McNabb gave the evidence. In cross-examination it was suggested to him that Constable Carroll had said that he could not remember there being any gravel on the bitumen at the scene of the accident (it is not easy to see how this would have assisted the appellant). Mr McNabb did not agree. The file note was tendered in re-examination, but was rejected.

35. … In the course of making his findings, [the judge] after saying that he thought Constable Carroll was mistaken in his recollection of the state of the roadway, he said that he accepted Mr McNabb's "account of his conversation with Constable Carroll". He did not more specifically relate that acceptance to the view he took of Constable Carroll's evidence, but it must have played a part. …

38. The appellant … submitted that there had not been a denial of the substance of the evidence to be given by Mr McNabb. The judge said –

> On my reading and overall impression of the police officer's evidence, I come to a contrary view. It seems to me that the provisions of s 43 have been enlivened.[162] Mr McCulloch submitted that under s 106 of the Evidence Act what was required as a foundation for the evidence now sought to be elicited is that the witness has denied the substance of the evidence which Mr McNabb is expected to be about to give. In my opinion, he has denied that substance.

39. This part of the ruling should be understood in the light of the judge's observation, made in the course of final submissions that his impression of Constable Carroll's response of non-remembrance was that it amounted to "I didn't say that". The judge said in the ruling that, in his opinion, Constable Carroll denied the substance of the evidence Mr McNabb was expected to give. Material to the opinion was the way Constable Carroll gave his evidence. The judge was in an advantageous position in so concluding, and in my opinion no error has been shown in the ruling.

The remainder of the judgment addresses the application of s 106(2)(c), admitting a prior inconsistent statement, and the precondition created by *UEA*, s 43. Tobias and Brownie JJ agreed with Giles JA.

Before examining ss 43 and 106(2)(c), brief mention should be given to the role of s 106(1)(b) and s 192(2).[163] Section 106(1)(b) provides flexibility to the credibility rule as applied post-cross-examination of a witness. Concern with

---

162 There had also been a submission, rejected by the trial judge and on appeal, that the circumstances of making the statement were not sufficiently stated.

163 Sections extracted above at pp 251-252 and Chapter 10, p 428.

the common law's inflexibility in this respect – expressed by both Kirby J in *Goldsmith v Sandilands*[164] and McHugh J in *Palmer*[165] and in *Nicholls*[166] – has been to a large extent rectified by the insertion of this leave provision. It permits the calling of credibility evidence of sufficient merit – that is, on consideration to the importance of the evidence, the nature of the proceedings and the fairness to parties and witnesses: s 192(2). It means that the efficiency and fairness goals of the credibility rule are protected, but without rigidity. It also avoids situations such as in *Piddington v Bennett*, with its sharply conflicting judgments resting on hair-splitting distinctions that give rise to uncertainty, and risk costly and elongated processes. Further, as McHugh J noted in *Nicholls* with respect to the advantage of flexibility in this context:

> 55. ... Avoiding miscarriages of justice is more important than protecting the efficiency of trials. And in cases where the rule needs to be relaxed, it is unlikely that any question of potential unfairness to a witness will arise. That is because the allegations will be inextricably connected with the issues. If unfairness to a witness is likely to arise – for example, because the witness is not in a position to meet the allegation – the trial judge can take steps to ensure that no unfairness arises.

Notably, as we see in Chapter 10, the High Court has made it crystal clear that the requirements expressed in s 192 are not to be sidelined or ignored by courts.[167]

Bias, motive for being untruthful

The common law recognises the bias exception to the finality rule. The classic statement of the common law precursor to s 106(2)(a) is from Pollock CB in *Attorney-General v Hitchcock*:

> It is certainly allowable to ask a witness in what manner he stands affected towards the opposite party in the cause, and whether he does not stand in such a relation to that person as is likely to affect him, and prevent him from having an unprejudiced state of mind, and whether he has not used expressions importing that he would be revenged on some one, or that he would give such evidence as might dispose of the cause in one way or the other. *If he denies that, you may give evidence as to what he has said.*[168]

The equivalent situation under the *UEA* means that, for example, cross-examination of a witness alleging that he or she has been bribed to give false evidence can be followed up, after cross-examination and subject to s 106(1), with proof of evidence of a motive for being untruthful.[169] Similarly, evidence of an intention to lie (for example, proof that a witness has threatened the opposing party) can be adduced as evidence within s 106(2)(a).

In *Nicholls*, a murder case, the High Court held that evidence from a witness (Ross) came within the common law exception where it had the capacity to expose that a key prosecution witness (Davis) intended to maintain a false allegation in the witness box because it would assist him to secure a reduced sentence for his own involvement in the crime. Ross's evidence revealed that:

164 [2002] HCA 31; 190 ALR 370; 76 ALJR 1024.
165 [1998] HCA 2; 193 CLR 1.
166 [2005] HCA 1; 219 CLR 196. See also *BDX* [2009] VSCA 28.
167 See *Stanoevski* [2001] HCA 4; 202 CLR 115. See too *Tieu* [2016] NSWCCA 111; 92 NSWLR 94.
168 [1847] EngR 616; 1 Exch 91, 100; 154 ER 38, 42 (emphasis added). See also *Umanski* [1961] VR 242; *De Angelis* (1979) 20 SASR 288. Under the *UEA* there is no need to show hostility to the party: *Nicholls* [2005] HCA 1; 219 CLR 196, [263].
169 *Marsden v Amalgamated Television Services Pty Limited* [2000] NSWSC 659.

> [P]olice were not offering [Davis] a bribe in the form of money, but something even more valuable – a measure of liberty. That offer could have been seen by the jury as a means of stimulating in Davis a willingness to obstruct the discovery of the truth by manufacturing false testimony.[170]

In a joint judgment, Hayne and Heydon JJ, with whom Gleeson CJ, Gummow, Callinan and Kirby JJ agreed in relevant respects, described the exception:

> 261. *Did the bias exception apply?* Potential bias on the part of witnesses is frequently pointed to in litigation, whether it is said to derive from a relationship of family or blood or business or employment or friendship, or from self-interest (as where a witness is a party or likely to be affected by the success or failure of a party). Often the source of potential bias is obvious or is revealed by the party calling the witness. Often, even though it is not obvious, it is conceded at once in answer to a single question in cross-examination, partly because it is honest to do so and partly because it is foolish not to. The present problem arises only where it is not obvious, not revealed by the party calling the witness, and not conceded by the witness in cross-examination.
>
> 262. Wigmore explained that the exception related to three different "*kinds of emotion* constituting untrustworthy partiality", that is, bias, interest, and corruption. He drew a useful distinction between "bias", in the sense of all varieties of hostility or prejudice against the opponent *personally* or of favor to the proponent personally"; "interest" in the sense of "the specific inclination which is apt to be produced by the relation between the witness and the *cause at issue* in the litigation"; and "corruption", in the sense of "the *conscious false intent* which is inferrible [sic] from giving or taking a bribe or from expressions of a general unscrupulousness for the case in hand". These three categories are related, and will often overlap. As Wigmore explained, in relation to evidence showing corruption, "the essential discrediting element is a willingness to obstruct the discovery of the truth by manufacturing or suppressing testimony". Below they will be described as "bias" unless the context makes another course desirable.
>
> 263. Ross's evidence revealed that Davis was prepared to lie on oath in order to ingratiate himself with the police, in the hope that they might influence his sentence. …
>
> 266. [The exception] … extends to all "matters which affect the motives, temper, and character of the witness … with reference to his feelings towards one party or the other". Thus, bias may be found in a wife's willingness falsely to accuse her husband of incest unless he gave her property. Bias was found in a child complainant's motive to level a false charge against an accused, who was concerned about the influence of the complainant on his daughter. Bias may be found in a reluctance to give evidence against an accused due to a fear of reprisals: "a statement to the effect that a person if required to give evidence will give false evidence out of a desire not to offend certain of the parties is a statement indicating partiality in relation to the parties or the cause, whether that partiality stems from friendship or fear". Bias was inferred from the attempt by a person claiming to be a victim of an abduction to procure a witness to give false evidence, because the brother of the supposed victim wanted to ensure that the accused was falsely convicted. Bias may also be established where a witness has been coached by a person who is hostile to the party against whom the witness's evidence has been tendered. …
>
> 268. … The exception may operate where a witness is willing to withdraw allegations against persons being prosecuted if disciplinary proceedings against him are dropped. A threat to make a false complaint against a person one dislikes is admissible. Evidence of a witness's having solicited a bribe is admissible. An offer by a witness for the prosecution to give favourable testimony for the defendant if the defendant's friends arrange for the dropping of a charge is admissible. Where the defendant is sued for slanderously saying that the plaintiff had knowingly received stolen cattle from a witness for the defendant, who was convicted of stealing the cattle, an offer by that witness to swear that the plaintiff "was

170 [2005] HCA 1; 219 CLR 196, [270].

> in with him in stealing the cattle" in order to obtain a pardon is admissible. These last three instances, in particular, are very close to the present circumstances. (footnotes omitted)

Another example of proof of a lie and of bias, also under common law, arose in *Abebe and Mulugeta*[171] where Owen J (with Wallwork J agreeing) described the scenario under consideration and its relationship to this exception to the rule.

> At trial, evidence was given of a money dispute between Mulugeta and Ms Seifu following the breakdown of their relationship. Ms Seifu acknowledged that she was attempting to recover some items of property and an amount of $700 which she said was owing to her. She also acknowledged that she had prepared a letter dated 20 January 1993 addressed to the Immigration Department containing certain allegations that might be thought to be adverse to Mulugeta's attempts to remain in Australia. A copy of the letter had been given to a third party, Mr Ahmed. During cross-examination of Ms Seifu by counsel for Mulugeta, this exchange occurred:
>
> Q–Isn't it the case that you told Mr Mulugeta that you wanted to make trouble for him?
>
> A–No.
>
> Q–And that's why you wrote that letter? A–No, I didn't say that.
>
> Q–What date did you give … [the letter dated 20 January 1993] to Mahadi Ahmed?
>
> A–On 18 January 1993.
>
> Q–Two days before the date on the letter? A–Yeah.
>
> Q–Didn't you say, 'I'll give him until the 20th to sign the property over and give me the money, otherwise I'll make trouble?' A–No, I said, I want my money, you know.
>
> Judge: Mr O'Brien, I think you have gone far enough. It's only going to credit. We are not going to have a family law case here.
>
> Counsel: No sir, but I really think it goes to the issue.
>
> Judge: How can it go to the issue? The issue is whether he was the driver of a motor car.
>
> Counsel: That's right.
>
> Judge: What has that got to do with whether he has some personal problems with this lady? …
>
> … The challenge to the trial Judge's ruling was advanced on alternative bases. First, that it was relevant to a fact in issue. Alternatively, that Ms Seifu had denied an allegation that clearly went to bias and, accordingly, it was open to the accused to bring forward evidence to rebut her denial. On the hearing of the appeal counsel for Mulugeta conceded [he would not press] … the primary challenge that the evidence was relevant to an issue … I think the concession was properly made. In my view the trial Judge correctly identified 'the issue', namely, whether Mulugeta was driving a motor car. Whether or not Ms Seifu might have told a third party some time after the event that unless Mulugeta paid her the money that she thought was due to her she would make trouble for him does not, in my opinion, have the required nexus with the identified fact in issue to make it directly relevant to that fact.
>
> In my view it is more appropriate to focus attention on the alternative challenge, namely, the question of bias. The allegation was that the witness had threatened to disclose to the Immigration authorities information adverse to the accused as a means of 'making trouble for him' unless he acceded to her demands. I think this is an allegation which could, if established, indicate a motive to give false evidence against the accused. It therefore has the character of bias and the materiality to justify a departure from the general rule. In my opinion counsel for Mulugeta should have been permitted to pursue the line in cross-examination and should have been afforded the opportunity to call evidence in rebuttal.

171 Unreported, WACCA, 3 February 1994.

Criminal convictions

Subject to satisfying s 103 and s 106(1) (cross-examining the witness whether he or she has convictions and eliciting a denial or non-admission or non-agreement), evidence that the witness has prior criminal convictions will be admissible under s 106(2)(b): see the discussion in relation to s 103, at pp 233-234.

Prior inconsistent statements

Inconsistency is often perceived by lawyers as emblematic of error. Consistency of account is conversely a proxy for accuracy. Within the law of evidence a prior inconsistent statement (defined by the *UEA* as 'a previous representation[172] that is inconsistent with evidence given by the witness') has been traditionally considered in this light. Thus, it is not surprising that where a witness fails to admit inconsistency, proof of the inconsistency can be given, even where the statement is not relevant (or admissible) to a fact in issue (and thus is 'credibility evidence').[173]

However, not every consistency and inconsistency in fact merits equal levels of trust and distrust. For example, consistency may be explicable because the witness has been coached to rote learn facts and consistency between witnesses can be the result of collaboration. Further, the nature and context of any inconsistency are vital to evaluating its true worth as an indicator of a witness's credibility. This is particularly so in relation to children and other vulnerable witnesses. In *Ward*[174] the majority judgment noted, '[t]here are numerous reported decisions in which apparent inconsistencies in the evidence have been attributed to the inherent difficulties in cross-examining children, rather than to any specific deficiencies in the evidence itself'.[175] Psychological researchers Odinot et al[176] caution when assessing the significance of inconsistencies that it is important to distinguish various forms of inconsistency:

> Information remembered the first time may not be remembered later (forgotten), or vice versa (reminiscence).[177] Information remembered the first time can also be remembered differently a second time (contradiction), in this case it is obvious that at least one of the recall results is inaccurate.

Odinot et al observed that 'inconsistent information (at least forgetting and reminiscence) can be accurate, and consistent reports can be inaccurate'. Their own study confirmed what has been reported in other studies, namely that inconsistencies caused by forgetting and reminiscence were recalled almost as accurately as consistently recalled information.[178] However, as well as finding that

172 'Previous representation' means a representation made otherwise than in the course of giving evidence in the proceeding in which evidence of the representation is sought to be adduced: *UEA*, Dictionary (and *Evidence Act 2001* (Tas), s 3).

173 A prior statement that shows a clear recall of events in the context of a witness who testifies to an extinct memory of the same events is a prior inconsistent statement: *Rees* [2001] NSWCCA 23, [20].

174 [2017] VSCA 37.

175 Ibid [109], citations omitted.

176 G Odinot et al, 'Accuracy, confidence and consistency in repeated recall of events' (2013) 19 *Psychology, Crime and Law* 629, 631.

177 That is, recalling information that was not recalled previously.

178 Citing a number of studies, including T Smeets, I Candel and H Merckelbach, 'Accuracy, Completeness and Consistency of Emotional Memories' (2004) 117 *American Journal of Psychology* 595; and JEA Gilbert and RP Fisher, 'The Effect of Varied Retrieval Cues on Reminiscence in Eyewitness Memory' (2006) 20 *Applied Cognitive Psychology* 723.

inconsistently recalled information can be quite accurate the researchers also found that, *overall*, inconsistently recalled information is less accurate than consistently recalled information.[179]

To some extent lawyers and courts appreciate that consistency-related challenges require a nuanced assessment. For example, in the High Court case of *MWJ*,[180] a case discussed at the end of the chapter, only the majority judgment referred to the potential differences between two prosecution witnesses as inconsistencies. Gleeson CJ and Heydon J said:

> 7. ... The complainant was not asked, and she did not say, that nothing like that ever happened again at Sutcliffe Street. In cases of alleged child sexual abuse, where the events allegedly happened many years previously, it may be quite wrong to treat a complainant, who is only asked about a single incident which is the subject of one charge, and who is not asked about other uncharged incidents of a like kind, as intending to imply that the incident about which evidence is given was an isolated incident. Here, the complainant was invited to give evidence, and gave evidence, about uncharged incidents at Jeffries Street. The prosecutor told the judge that the complainant thought that only one incident occurred at Sutcliffe Street. Whether the prosecutor was right or wrong about what the complainant thought is unknown. The complainant did not give evidence, one way or the other, on that topic. To say that the mother's evidence of complaint was inconsistent with the complainant's evidence is incorrect.

Similarly, in the NSW Court of Criminal Appeal in *JG*,[181] an appeal ground related to whether a complainant witness (GB) was so discredited due to the inconsistencies exposed by cross-examination that JG's convictions were unsafe and unsatisfactory. The court rejected these submissions. Hall J noted that the inconsistencies centred on the accuracy of recollection many years after the alleged events and on matters that were essentially peripheral in nature. His Honour added:

> 579. ... The reliability or otherwise of [GB's] ... recollection and evidence on such matters required the jurors to assess the *significance* of his recollection upon them and the extent to which they found his account of the events concerning the offences alleged and his evidence on the peripheral matters to be persuasive and reliable.

In rejecting the submissions Hall J also drew on the following statement from Spigelman CJ in *Reed*:[182]

> 64. Cross-examination of sexual assault complainants often proceeds as if the reliability of their evidence about the assault can in some way be shaken by a failure to be precise about surrounding tangential detail. This approach is, in my opinion, rarely appropriate. Memory of surrounding detail has few if any implications, in my opinion, for a person's reliability about the central details of a traumatic event. The psychological assumptions that appear to underlie much cross-examination have no scientific basis and, indeed, are contrary to what we do know about human memory.[183]

The same observations were made by the RCIRCSA. 'The strategies used to cross-examine witnesses implement two key misconceptions about memory by focusing on disparities in recall for peripheral details and memory inconsistencies over

179 Odinot et al, above n 176, 639. This finding regarding overall relative accuracy contrasts with earlier findings by Gilbert and Fisher, ibid.

180 [2005] HCA 74; 222 ALR 436.

181 [2014] NSWCCA 138.

182 [2006] NSWCCA 314.

183 Citing RJ McNally, *Remembering Trauma* (Harvard University Press, 2003), 48-62.

time to suggest that core memory is unreliable'.[184] If a prior inconsistent statement is credibility evidence (because s 101A applies) the cross-examiner must, of course, satisfy the requirements of s 103 before the witness can be questioned on the prior statement. Typically, prior inconsistent statements are likely to relate to facts in issue because classically they are a description of an event that is the subject matter of the trial. It is not uncommon for a prior inconsistent statement scenario to arise where a witness recants from a statement inculpating the accused. Where this is the case, the statement will only be credibility evidence within the terms of s 101A where it is *inadmissible* to prove facts in issue. Further, it is not uncommon for this to arise in the context of the prosecution calling the witness, and then (after leave is granted under s 38 of the *UEA*) denial, non-admission or non-agreement by the witness of the substance of the prior inconsistent statement permitting its proof under s 106(2)(c). This was the situation in the High Court case of *Adam*.[185] Here Sako had been interviewed by police as a suspect (in a stabbing murder). Six weeks after the murder he made a statement to police indicating Adam was guilty. In court Sako said his statement was merely a product of what others had told him. His statement was relevant to a fact in issue, but because of the delay (and the limitations that existed at that time regarding the hearsay exception in s 66) it was inadmissible hearsay.[186] With Sako no longer a willing prosecution witness and his police statement inadmissible hearsay, the s 106(2)(c) route became the only option for the prosecution to benefit from his evidence. Once the police statement was admitted to show the inconsistency of Sako's evidence with what he had said to police, the prior statement became admissible to prove the facts in issue.[187]

To prove the prior inconsistent statement other than from the witness, the cross-examiner must then meet the requirements of s 106(1)(a) (that in cross-examination 'the substance of the evidence was put to the witness'). This is likely to be achieved through compliance with s 43(2) which, out of fairness (and in particular to enable a witness to offer an explanation and/or acknowledge any inconsistencies), requires that the witness be informed of enough of the circumstances of the making of the statement to identify the statement and to be drawn to the portions of the statement that are inconsistent with his or her evidence. If a witness concedes the inconsistency the process with respect to the prior statement will not proceed beyond cross-examination. However, if the witness denies, or does not admit or agree to the substance of the evidence, the prior inconsistent statement (written, oral or even a representation by conduct)[188] can be proved from another witness, from a document or other source. This occurred in *Copmanhurst Shire Council v Watt*[189] (above) where the constable was cross-examined about (i) his lack of reference in notes made contemporaneous to the accident to loose

184 RCIRCSA, *Research Report – Empirical Guidance on the Effects of Child Sexual Abuse on Memory and Complainants' Evidence* (July 2017), 22.

185 [2001] HCA 57; 207 CLR 96. See Chapter 5, pp 193-194.

186 Where, unlike the present *UEA*, s 66, freshness of memory was subject to an interpretation permitting only a delay of hours or days in making a representation for the exception to the hearsay rule to apply: *Graham* [1998] HCA 61; 195 CLR 606.

187 *UEA*, s 60. This is discussed below. Nowadays a six-week delay in making a statement about a murder is likely in this sort of scenario to be an admissible hearsay representation and so the statement would be admitted without recourse to *UEA*, s 106(2)(c) or 103. Section 43 would still apply, however.

188 For an example in a *UEA*, s 108(3), context, see *KNP* [2006] NSWCCA 213 (McClellan CJ at CL).

189 [2005] NSWCA 245; 140 LGERA 333.

material on the road and (ii) whether he had said less than three months after the accident to Mr McNabb that he had no specific recollection of the presence of dirt or gravel. Following what was, effectively, a denial by the constable, Mr McNabb was permitted to give evidence contradicting the constable's in-chief version of the conversation under s 106(c).

Finally, it should be noted that the *UEA* places limitations on cross-examination of a witness where it relates to prior statements made by someone other than the witness and those statements will not be admitted into evidence.[190] The limitations enforce that one cannot use cross-examination to by-pass rules that have made a document otherwise inadmissible. For this reason *UEA*, s 44, requires that the witness is made familiar with the representations in any document in a manner that ensures that neither the contents nor information identifying the document are put before the jury – for example, by reading it to themselves or, if it is an electronic recording, listening to it through headphones. Then, 'the witness must be asked whether, having examined (or heard) the contents of the document, the witness stands by the evidence that he or she has given'.[191]

'Inability to be aware of matters to which his or her evidence relates'

Section 106(2)(d) originates from a much narrower common law position than that described by the terms of this subsection. The common law permitted a psychiatrist to testify regarding a witness's psychiatric condition that caused the witness to be detached from reality and thus potentially an unreliable witness. *Toohey v Metropolitan Police Commissioner*[192] is typically referenced as creating the foundation for the modern common law position. Nowadays psychology has advanced understanding of the complexities of memory and, as a consequence, matters such as unconscious transference and post-event information contamination come within the terms of para (d), as would evidence of visual face recognition[193] and post-event/pre-testimonial hypnosis.[194] With respect to the last example, s 106(2)(d) would enable evidence from an expert in the impact of hypnosis to be led to inform the jury of its impact on a witness who has been subjected to hypnosis pre-trial. Such impact can include heightening suggestibility and/or creating and reinforcing 'memory' of events that have not actually occurred. Establishing the impact of hypnosis may require clarification of the actual hypnosis process undertaken by the witness (typically by it being electronically recorded).[195] The degree of leading questions, command and suggestibility during hypnosis will all be relevant to establishing its impact on a witness's evidence.

---

190 *UEA*, s 44(2), (3).

191 *UEA*, s 44(3)(c). The document used in this way may be marked for identification (MFI). See also s 45.

192 [1965] AC 595.

193 This has arisen in a number of evidentiary contexts with the door having been firmly shut by the common law, but opened under the *UEA*: see *Smith* (1990) 64 ALJR 588; *Smith* (2000) 116 A Crim R 1; *Forbes* [2009] ACTSC 1; *Dupas* [2012] VSCA 328; 218 A Crim R 507, [257]-[275]; and also s 108C.

194 Hypnosis-affected testimony arose as an issue in *DPP (NSW) v JG* [2010] NSWCCA 222. See also *BJS* [2013] NSWCCA 123.

195 *McFelin* [1985] NZCA 63; [1985] 2 NZLR 75 contains a useful discussion of issues relating to hypnosis and witness testifying (outside a *UEA* context).

'Knowingly or recklessly making a false representation'

Before the introduction of s 106(1)(b) this limb of s 106 was the only element in the *UEA* that created scope to enhance flexibility to the finality exception of the credibility rule. On a literal reading the scope of s 106(2)(e) appears to permit any intentional or reckless *perjury* from a witness but this exception does not, and was not intended to apply to lies alleged to have been made while testifying in the proceeding at hand.[196] The subsection is limited to legal obligations to tell the truth (unlike s 103 which includes moral obligations to tell the truth). Section 106(2)(e) may provide a mechanism for adducing evidence where a witness denies in cross-examination that he or she had been coached,[197] though such a scenario may also give rise to the bias exception.

Improper Questioning

Some historical background informs the current rather tentative regulation of improper questioning. The following description sums up the spirit of witness questioning in Tudor and Stuart England when no trial took more than 20 minutes. It reveals the low standards in questioning etiquette set by judges. Landsman, quoting in part from historian Cockburn, states that trials were

> "nasty, brutish, and essentially short." Counsel seldom participated, few, if any, rules of evidence constrained enquiry, judges routinely examined witnesses and defendants in the most vigorous, and at times ruthless, manner, [and] only prosecution witnesses were allowed to swear testimonial oaths and thereby enhance the credibility of their statements, ..., judges frequently introduced their political views into proceedings ...[198]

Further, '[b]iting sarcasm and a free interpretation of what Chief Justice Dyer bluntly called his power of "lawful menace" were commonplace'.[199] When defence counsel eventually took over questioning it is not surprising that they were similarly attached to sarcasm, taunts and sneering jibes.[200] The centrality of cross-examination in the common law trial was not fully cemented until the beginning to the middle of the 19th century. To develop rules around witness questioning lawyers needed to be embedded into the cut and thrust of the trial and it is now an often-neglected fact that the right of the accused to have a lawyer to make speeches and submissions as well as test prosecution witnesses only gained legal status in England in 1836.[201] The Australian colonies immediately followed and adopted the terms of the 1836 Act.[202]

---

196 See ALRC, *Uniform Evidence Law* (Report No 102, 2006), [12.80].

197 *Australian Automotive Repairers' Association (Political Action Committee) Inc (in liq) v Insurance Australia Ltd* [2006] FCAFC 33; [2006] ATPR ¶42-111.

198 S Landsman, 'The Rise of the Contentious Spirit: Adversary Procedure in Eighteenth Century England' (1990) 75 *Cornell Law Review* 496, 515, quoting from the historian JS Cockburn, *A History of the English Assizes 1558-1714* (Cambridge University Press, 1972), 109. Some footnotes omitted.

199 Landsman, ibid.

200 See also JM Beattie, 'Scales of Justice: Defense Counsel and the English Criminal Trial in the Eighteenth and Nineteenth Centuries' (1991) 9 *Law and History Review* 221, 239-47 regarding these questioning techniques.

201 By way of the *Prisoners Counsel Act 1836* (6&7 Will IV, c 114).

202 JM Bennett, *Sir James Dowling: Second Chief Justice of New South Wales, 1837-1844* (Federation Press, 2001), 141-3.

Landsman suggests that, because before 1836 the law had limited lawyers *only* to cross-examination, they had given it all their energies. Prosecution reliance on dubious witnesses[203] helped fuel reliance on testing witnesses through questioning and thus placed further reliance on counsel. Before this time there were few rules. Landsman quotes from Twining (who in turn cites Wigmore) that '[a]t the trial of Warren Hastings in 1794, Edmund Burke is reported to have said that he knew a parrot who could learn the rules of evidence in a half-hour and repeat them in five minutes'.[204] As lawyers became embedded, combat over rules of procedure and evidence began and so the late 18th and early 19th centuries saw what Wigmore described as the 'spring-tide of the [evidence] system',[205] a view also adopted by contemporary legal commentators. In other words, cross-examination confirmed the centrality of lawyers (and the rule against hearsay).

The pivotal role of cross-examination has made control of excessive and improper cross-examination a contentious and much overdue law reform. The now repealed *Evidence Act 1898* (NSW), ss 56-58, replicated the English model (and has parallels in legislation across Australia). These provisions were introduced in 1922 and gave courts discretion to disallow questions relevant solely to credibility but lacking materiality – a forerunner to the far stricter requirements in *UEA*, s 103. Courts could also forbid questions solely relevant to credibility that the court regarded as 'indecent or scandalous' or it considered were 'intended to insult or annoy', or were 'needlessly offensive in form' – the forerunner to *UEA*, s 41 (extracted below). However, even by the 1980s these controls on witness questioning tended to be perceived as rules of professional courtesy and best practice, rather than legal obligation.

The NSW case of *Albrighton v Royal Prince Alfred Hospital*[206] is a striking example for two reasons. First, the witness was a distinguished medical specialist called by the plaintiff. Second, and indicative of the disinclination to censure counsel, the court's criticism of cross-examining counsel was omitted from the New South Wales Law Reports. Yet counsel cross-examined in a manner that would undoubtedly have breached current professional Bar Rules and would also have activated the s 41 judicial requirement to intervene. In *Albrighton* the witness doctor was accused of dishonest answers, lying and tailoring his responses to the plaintiff's case (apparently because they were unhelpful to the cross-examiner's case). He was shouted at and accused, without basis, of ignorance. The NSW Court of Appeal criticised the cross-examination, pointing out that it achieved nothing forensically useful. Reynolds JA drew attention to the significant power counsel possessed, adding that '[c]ases can be conducted with the greatest vigour without discourtesy and insult to witnesses and no room should be left for any uneasy feeling to be created that counsel reflecting the attitude of their clients act on the basis that "where proof is impossible prejudice may suffice".'[207] Hope JA expressed similar sentiments, stating '[t]he privilege of counsel to use in court language which would not be tolerated out of court is only justified when the ends

203 Landsman, above n 198, 572-80.

204 W Twining, *Theories of Evidence: Bentham and Wigmore* (Weidenfeld and Nicolson, 1985), citing JH Wigmore, *A Treatise on the Anglo-American System of Evidence in Trials at Common Law* (2d ed, 1923) Vol 1, 237.

205 JH Wigmore, 'A General Survey of the History of the Rules of Evidence' in *Selected Essays in Anglo-American Legal History*, Vol 2, 695, quoted by Landsman, above n 198, 596.

206 [1980] 2 NSWLR 542.

207 *Albrighton v Royal Prince Alfred Hospital* – Supreme Court, NSWCA, 29 September 1980 (CA No 297/79 CL No 5034/77).

of justice require it. The cases when it is justified are not common'.[208] His Honour also left the primary obligation to ensure that the required restraint is observed upon the cross-examiner, but 'counsel should not regard himself as entitled to harass a witness until he is pulled up'.[209]

In *Albrighton*, counsel's conduct, the court's soft censure and the Law Reports' non-publication of the gentle criticism of counsel show that standards of propriety in witness questioning were still to approach their modern shape, as evidenced in cases such as *Libke*.[210] However, arguably, *Albrighton* reveals the tip of an iceberg. There is no doubt that, for example, sexual assault complainants fared worse than most witnesses. Henning and Hunter, with reference to the 1960's Kamisar[211] metaphor of the courtroom as a 'mansion' (where the accused person's rights were far better protected than in the 'gatehouse' of justice (the police station)), describe the historical treatment of witnesses, especially sexual assault witnesses, before the reforms of the late 20th century. They note that by the end of the 20th century:

> The courtroom, however, was by comparison *relatively* rich in its protections for defendants. It was a mansion of rights.
>
> However, for vulnerable witnesses in Kamisar's time, no part of the criminal justice system was a mansion. During the investigation of sexual assault and domestic violence crimes complainants were as suspicious to investigators as the accused. In the name of eliminating false complaints they were (in the words of Kamisar describing police treatment of suspects) 'sized up' and subjected to 'interrogation tactics and techniques most appropriate for the occasion', the objects of curiosity, suspicion and humiliating investigative practices. They fared no better at trial. Here they were 'game to be stalked and cornered', harried, bullied and hemmed in, their credibility, integrity and morality attacked. It is hardly a matter of surprise that for such witnesses the trial process was 'ritualised degradation dressed up as court process' and their treatment, 'state sanctioned victimisation'. For vulnerable witnesses the criminal justice process resembled the Roman Circus.[212]

What some might consider hyperbole is in fact recognised on the bench and from empirical studies. See, for example, the observations of Spigelman CJ from *TA*,[213] a case discussed below:

---

208 Ibid.

209 Ibid. His Honour referred to the above-mentioned 1922 provisions of the now repealed *Evidence Act 1898* (NSW). See also *R v Noud; Ex parte McNamara* [1991] 2 Qd R 86, 94-6 (McPherson J); *Alister* [1984] HCA 85; 154 CLR 404; *Clyne v NSW Bar Association* [1960] HCA 40; 104 CLR 186, 200, referred to by Malcolm CJ in *Campbell* (unreported, WACCA, 25 August 1993).

210 [2007] HCA 30; 230 CLR 559. See Chapter 2, p 47.

211 Y Kamisar, 'Equal Justice in the Gatehouse and the Mansions of American Criminal Procedure' in A Howard (ed), *Criminal Justice in Our Time* (Virginia University Press, 1965).

212 T Henning and J Hunter, 'Finessing the Fair Trial: Complainants and the Accused: Mansions of Justice or Castles in the Air?' in P Roberts and J Hunter (eds), *Criminal Evidence and Human Rights: Reimagining Common Law Procedural Traditions* (Hart Publishing, paperback ed, 2013), 364-5 (quoting from Kamisar, ibid). See also T Henning, 'Sexual Reputation and Sexual Experience Evidence in Tasmanian Proceedings Relating to Sexual Offences' (University of Tasmania Press, Occasional Paper No 4, 1996); T Henning and S Bronitt, 'Rape Victims on Trial: Regulating the Use and Abuse of Sexual History Evidence' in P Easteal (ed), *Balancing the Scales: Rape, Law Reform and Australian Culture* (Federation Press, 1998); *Heroines of Fortitude: The Experiences of Women in Court as Victims of Sexual Assault* (Gender Bias and the Law Project, Department of Women, New South Wales Government, November 1996); M Heenan and H McKelvie, *The Crimes Rape Act 1991: An Evaluation Report* (Report No 2, Rape Law Reform Evaluation Project, Department of Justice of Victoria, 1997); S Bronitt and P Easteal, *Rape Law in Context* (Federation Press, 2018), ch 5.

213 [2003] NSWCCA 191; 57 NSWLR 444 (Spigelman CJ, with Dowd J agreeing).

> 8. The difficulties encountered by complainants in sexual assault cases in the criminal justice system has been a focus of concern for several decades. Judges play an important role in protecting complainants from unnecessary, inappropriate and irrelevant questioning by or on behalf of an accused. That role is perfectly consistent with the requirements of a fair trial, which requirements do not involve treating the criminal justice system as if it were a forensic game in which every accused is entitled to some kind of sporting chance.

Section 41, as well as representing a legislative lineage dating back to the early 20th century, has also evolved from earlier versions enacted in New South Wales.[214] Section 41 was amended from a discretion to create a judicial *duty* to intervene to protect a witness from improper questioning. In the Northern Territory the obligation of the judge to intervene is limited to 'a vulnerable witness'.[215]

> **41. Improper questions**[216]
>
> (1) The court must disallow a question put to a witness in cross-examination, or inform the witness that it need not be answered, if the court is of the opinion that the question (referred to as a ***disallowable question***):
>
> (a) is misleading or confusing, or
>
> (b) is unduly annoying, harassing, intimidating, offensive, oppressive, humiliating or repetitive, or
>
> (c) is put to the witness in a manner or tone that is belittling, insulting or otherwise inappropriate, or
>
> (d) has no basis other than a stereotype (for example, a stereotype based on the witness's sex, race, culture, ethnicity, age or mental, intellectual or physical disability).
>
> (2) Without limiting the matters the court may take into account for the purposes of subsection (1), it is to take into account:
>
> (a) any relevant condition or characteristic of the witness of which the court is, or is made, aware, including age, education, ethnic and cultural background, gender, language background and skills, level of maturity and understanding and personality, and
>
> (b) any mental, intellectual or physical disability of which the court is, or is made, aware and to which the witness is, or appears to be, subject, and
>
> (c) the context in which the question is put, including:
>
> (i) the nature of the proceeding, and
>
> (ii) in a criminal proceeding – the nature of the offence to which the proceeding relates, and
>
> (iii) the relationship (if any) between the witness and any other party to the proceeding.
>
> (3) A question is not a disallowable question merely because:
>
> (a) the question challenges the truthfulness of the witness or the consistency or accuracy of any statement made by the witness, or
>
> (b) the question requires the witness to discuss a subject that could be considered distasteful to, or private by, the witness.
>
> (4) A party may object to a question put to a witness on the ground that it is a disallowable question.
>
> (5) However, the duty imposed on the court by this section applies whether or not an objection is raised to a particular question.

214 *Criminal Procedure Act 1986* (NSW), s 275A, was the precursor to the current *UEA* (NSW), s 41.

215 *Evidence (National Uniform Legislation) Act 2011* (NT), s 41(2). 'Vulnerable witness' is defined in s 41(4) of the Act. The Victorian Act was amended in 2018 to bring it substantially into line with the other jurisdictions. See *Justice Legislation Miscellaneous Amendment Act 2018* (Vic) s 57(1). The Victorian provision continues to refer to 'improper questioning' rather than a 'disallowable question'. By definition, s 41(3), this includes a sequence of questions.

216 *Evidence (National Uniform Legislation) Act 2011* (NT), s 41, is drafted differently.

(6) A failure by the court to disallow a question under this section, or to inform the witness that it need not be answered, does not affect the admissibility in evidence of any answer given by the witness in response to the question.

Note. A person must not, without the express permission of a court, print or publish any question that the court has disallowed under this section – see section 195.

Some jurisdictions also back up the obligations in s 41 through professional Bar rules. In New South Wales, r 62[217] limits witness questioning that is intended 'to mislead or confuse the witness' or is intended 'to be unduly annoying, harassing, intimidating, offensive, oppressive, humiliating or repetitive' to 'proceedings in which an allegation of sexual assault, indecent assault or the commission of an act of indecency is made and in which the alleged victim gives evidence'. It also obligates the questioner to take into account 'any particular vulnerability of the witness in the manner and tone of the questions that the barrister asks'.

What is considered offensive?

There is not a lot of judicial commentary interpreting s 41.[218] The case of *TA*[219] was an appeal from sexual assault convictions relating to conduct where the complainant was also drugged, resulting in her having no independent recollection of events. The incident had been also electronically recorded. Spigelman CJ rejected cross-examination of the complainant on her opinion of her state of mind at the time of the incident as revealed from watching an electronic recording of the alleged assault. The Chief Justice indicated that the complainant's answer was irrelevant (relying on *Smith (Mundarra)*[220]) and his Honour also ruled that the questions were offensive and oppressive and excluded under s 41(1)(b). Spigelman CJ (with whom Dowd J agreed) delivered the leading judgment on this aspect:

> 12. Section 41, of course, operates on the assumption that there is an element of relevance in the line of questioning. Even assuming, contrary to the opinion I have expressed, that there was some relevance, its probative force was so slight that even a small element of harassment, offence or oppression, would be enough for the Court to exercise its discretion under s 41(1)(b). However, in the present case, the line of cross-examination inviting the complainant to interpret the transcript of the videotape in which she was depicted, but of which she had no material recollection was, on any objective analysis, highly distressing.
>
> 13. The words of s 41 direct attention to the effect of questioning upon the witness. In a sexual assault matter, it is appropriate for the Court to consider the effect of cross-examination and of the trial experience upon a complainant when deciding whether cross-examination is unduly harassing, offensive or oppressive. In the present case, that standard was clearly exceeded.

In *Kamm*[221] the following questioning was unsuccessfully challenged under s 55 and the equivalent to s 41 'as having no basis other than a stereotype of how the bible should be held and suggestive that the bible was being held away from the witness so that she could lie on oath'. The court reported that the question was not

217 *Legal Profession Uniform Conduct (Barristers) Rules 2015* (NSW).

218 As an example, see comments of Adamson J in *Let's Go Adventures Pty Ltd v Barrett* [2017] NSWCA 243. Her Honour stated: 'The latitude commonly afforded to cross-examiners does not amount to a licence to offend, ridicule or vilify' (at [123]).

219 [2003] NSWCCA 191; 57 NSWLR 444.

220 [2001] HCA 50; 206 CLR 650.

221 [2008] NSWCCA 290; special leave to the High Court refused: [2010] HCATrans 258. The facts of this case are described above.

asked offensively, 'nor as it was left was it suggestive of lying on oath'. Further, no more was made of the point than is extracted below.

> *Q. Mrs [name of witness] when you entered the witness box you took an oath to tell the truth didn't you?*
> *A. Yeah.*
> *Q. I noticed when you took hold of the bible you held it far away from your body arm outstretched, does that have any particular significance in your religion?*
> *A. No.*
> *Q. None at all?*
> *A. No.*

Giles JA (with Latham J and Mathews AJ agreeing) observed:

> 35. No objection was taken by the appellant's counsel at the time.
>
> 36. I do not agree that the cross-examination was impermissible in this respect. We have only the question's description of the manner in which the witness held the bible, but if it was an unusual manner it was open to the Crown Prosecutor, in a case in which religious beliefs played a relevant and prominent part, to make the enquiry, and an answer in the affirmative may have led on – '[s]ome of the most effective cross-examinations have begun by securing a witness' assent to a proposition of seeming irrelevance'. (*Wakeley v R*).[222]
>
> 37. The Crown referred to *R v VN* [2006] VSCA 111, in which the witness was directly cross-examined to suggest that he took an affirmation rather than an oath because he was telling lies, rather than (as he said) because a Baptist never swore on the bible. A complaint of miscarriage of justice which included that this was 'unfair' was rejected, and it was said that the statutory availability of an affirmation did not preclude cross-examination to suggest that the witness was not giving truthful evidence (at [104]-[106]).

These examples from *TA* and *Kamm* are particularly situation-specific. But there is a large amount of academic commentary and research concerning the issues that arise regarding the inequality of counsel and certain witnesses, particularly children, those who are cognitively impaired, and indeed anyone with vulnerability.

A number of commentators have noted the replacement of the judicial discretion to stop improper questioning with the current mandatory judicial intervention, raising doubts about whether the obligation will make a great deal of difference,[223] especially given the judge's requirements to appraise the witness's degree of vulnerability within the terms of s 41(2). This is not easily achieved unless the witness's vulnerabilities are sufficiently pronounced to have become prominent either in examination-in-chief or earlier in cross-examination. The use of CCTV to replace examination-in-chief makes such observations even more challenging. Further, prosecution counsel may be loath to interrupt and object for fear of creating an impression in front of the jury that the witness is not credible. However, of even more concern is the language of the statutory provision. For example, the notion of '*unduly* annoying, harassing, intimidating, offensive, oppressive, humiliating or repetitive' assumes a base-line tolerance in cross-examination for annoying, harassing, intimidating, offensive, oppressive, humiliating and repetitive questions. Why? Perhaps some of these qualities

---

222 [1990] HCA 23; 93 ALR 79, 86.

223 See Cossins, 'Cross-Examination in Child Sexual Assault Trials', above n 38; A Cossins, 'Alternative Models for Prosecuting Child Sex Offences in Australia' (Report, National Child Sexual Assault Reform Committee, March 2010), 270 [4.106]; T Henning, 'Control of Cross-Examination – A Snowflake's Chance in Hell?' (2006) 30 *Criminal Law Journal* 133, 137.

– 'humiliating' for example – are difficult to isolate where the subject matter of a hearing has intrinsically humiliating elements, but this does not explain the full string of descriptors that are modified by the term 'unduly'. Thus, the presence of 'unduly' merely gives licence to create a large blur of uncertainty over the kind of questioning that is truly improper.[224] This blur is highly problematic because of the challenge that already exists of enforcing appropriate standards of civility in the broader accusatorial and adversarial trial dynamic. As Hunter observed:

> Can we realistically expect judges to step in to protect witnesses? Common law judges by their very appointment are wise to the courtroom clash of case-constructed stories; indeed they utilize similar devices in their own professional narrative, the judgment. If they step into the fray in front of the jury they risk compromising judicial impartiality, and in any case the advocate's creativity is part of the taken-for-granted scenery of the common law trial. Cultural attachment to adversarialism is psycho-politically embedded in the symbolism of the accused's right (through his agent) to conduct his own defence in answer to criminal charges. Culturally-embedded practice does not vanish overnight. Legal culture is tenacious ...
>
> Any even remotely plausible attempt to ameliorate the current plight of witnesses testifying in criminal trials must recognise that adversarialism will remain our dominant paradigm for the foreseeable future. The challenge for reformers is to accommodate the values of respect, humanity and dignity within an appropriately modified adversarial framework.[225]

It is clear that s 41 is not, without more, the answer to the problem of questions that annoy, harass, intimidate, offend, oppress, humiliate and badger a witness within a repertoire of adversarial gamesmanship. A particularly concerning area is cross-examination of child witnesses and of witnesses with cognitive impairment. As mentioned in the previous chapter,[226] the English Court of Appeal has made a number of rulings in this area. For example, in *RT and Stuchfield*,[227] a conspiracy to rob trial, the 16-year-old witness, Ms F, refused to continue with defence cross-examination on behalf of Stuchfield after a series of unacceptable repetitious questions, and then an inappropriate question ['are you going to continue to lie?']. Other questioning had included (at [24], emphasis added):

> *"Okay. Did you send him any messages which might be interpreted or misinterpreted as being romantic messages?"* was too long and required the witness to process whether the messages were being interpreted or misinterpreted. It is not particularly surprising that the answer began *"I don't know"*. Another question which would be difficult for any witness, let alone a vulnerable 16 year old witness was *"Is that something that you would not just remember?"* because the question required processing of what someone would remember, rather than a simple question about whether the witness remembered something.

An undertaking to Ms F by the trial judge that questions would be limited to 20 minutes, and the questions 'closely monitored', did not change Ms F's mind. RT's defence counsel was unable to cross-examine at all. The defence applied to

224 ALRC 102 seems to have intended that 'unduly' qualify only the word 'annoying': 'The ALRC and the NSWLRC hold the view that there are no circumstances in which misleading, harassing, offensive or confusing questions are appropriate for any witness' (at [5.110]).

225 Hunter, above n 1, 287.

226 See Chapter 5, p 188.

227 [2020] EWCA Crim 155. See also *(S)G* [2017] EWCA Crim 617; [2017] 2 Cr App R 20 and *Wyatt* [1990] Crim LR 343, and *YGM* [2018] EWCA Crim 2458; [2019] 2 Cr App R 5 (Hallett LJ) (sorting out limitations on cross-examination of vulnerable witnesses before cross-examination started).

stop the trial and discharge the jury, which was refused. Dismissing the appeal against the convictions, Dingemans LJ noted that there were a number of occasions where the hearsay rule permitted the admission of representations despite the impossibility of cross-examination. His Lordship also noted the questioning was not deliberately carried out to provoke the witness as a matter of principle – '[i]t would be entirely inappropriate if counsel were permitted to fail to observe the proper approach to questioning a vulnerable witness, cause them to refuse to continue giving evidence, and then argue that the trial should stop' (at [36]).

Some issues that would have arisen in cross-examination were addressed by agreed facts (for example, through a selection of screenshots of Facebook messages between Ms F and Stuchfield). These enabled the jury to make 'a fair assessment of the credibility and reliability of Ms F's evidence' (at [42]). Dingemans LJ held that there was no abuse of process in continuing the trial, noting also that the jury had seen Ms F under some cross-examination and that the trial judge identified to it the limitations in Ms F's evidence.

This topic, and the important insights that can be learnt from psychological research, is discussed by Phoebe Bowden, Terese Henning, and David Plater in 'Balancing Fairness to Victims, Society and Defendants in the Cross-Examination of Vulnerable Witnesses: An Impossible Triangulation?'.[228] Their article arises in the context of the South Australian child sexual assault prosecution that was discontinued by the State DPP in 2011 due to communication difficulties perceived to create overwhelming obstacles to successful prosecutions. A short description by Henning of the circumstances surrounding the discontinuance is extracted in Chapter 5.[229]

The extract from Bowden et al below contains a quote from former South Australian Director of Public Prosecutions Stephen Pallaras QC, whose comments are referable to this discontinued prosecution. It is pertinent to keep in mind that South Australia possesses a provision equivalent to *UEA*, s 41 (obligating judicial intervention). Although the *Evidence Act* has since been amended in that jurisdiction to allow for the prerecording of the entirety of the evidence of certain vulnerable witnesses and for the use of communication partners to advise courts as to the appropriate nature and style of questioning for these witnesses, particularly during cross-examination,[230] the comments remain apposite. They reveal that an experienced prosecutor considers the current tinkering with criminal trial protocols inadequate to accommodate these vulnerable people. As Pallaras observes (quoted by Bowden et al):

> 'A problem that cries out for inventive solutions is how better to facilitate the complaints of sexual abuse made by children and, in particular, children with disabilities. … [A] prosecutor looks to the witnesses to provide a coherent account of the allegations, for unless that can be done no court can properly convict an accused. In the absence of a coherent account the prospects of obtaining a conviction could never be adjudged to be reasonable. However the very thing that a child complainant, disabled or not struggles to do is to give a coherent account.'[231]

228 Bowden, Henning, Plater, above n 41 (some citations omitted).

229 See Chapter 5, p 158.

230 *Evidence Act 1929* (SA), s 13BA, and ss 13A, 14A and 12AB; and see the detailed discussion of the witness special measures including the use of intermediaries in Chapter 5.

231 [Office of the Director of Public Prosecutions (SA), *Annual Report 2010–11* (2011), 2.]

... Pallaras subsequently argued that the only solution to the problems in the cross-examination of complainants generally in sexual assault trials is a fundamental shift away from the common law adversarial system. He asserted that the adversarial model 'is ill-equipped to deal with cases involving allegations of sexual assault particularly for children'. Pallaras claimed that '[s]o long as we look at the adversarial trial model as the only method by which we can deal with these cases, [he does not] see a solution'.[232]

... Further, research suggests that, despite their mandatory nature, these provisions will not be adequate to displace courts' traditional reluctance to intervene in the cross-examination of vulnerable witnesses.[233] Justice Sleight provides insight into this reluctance. His Honour suggests:

> If a Judge frequently interrupts cross-examination then the process can become disjointed, confrontational between the Judge and counsel and often add to the trauma of the complainant giving evidence.[234]

Henderson additionally suggests that despite judges having the power to control and limit cross-examination, albeit restricted by the requirements of fairness, they may not recognise problems when they arise.[235] Judges may also be reluctant to intervene in defence cross-examination for fear of jeopardising the defendant's right to a fair trial and because they are conscious of the risks of an appeal if the accused is convicted.[236] The discretionary elements of the current regime limit the ability of the implemented measures to systematically improve outcomes for child witnesses and those with an intellectual disability. Any proposed reforms must operate to negate this difficulty inherent in the adversarial system.

III COMPLICATIONS ARISING FROM CROSS-EXAMINATION

... [However,] Eastwood and Patton argue that the true purpose of cross-examination has very little, if anything, to do with accuracy or truth. Rather, they contend the purpose of cross-examination 'is more a process of manipulating the witness through suggestive questioning, avoiding unfavourable disclosures, and obtaining jury sympathy'.[237] They conclude that '[c]ross-examination techniques are specifically designed to damage the effectiveness of the testimony and mute the voice of the complainant'.[238] Birch similarly doubts the value of cross-examination and argues that a skilled cross-examiner merely serves 'to make an honest witness appear at best confused and at worst a liar'.[239]

---

232 [ABC News, 'Charges Against Alleged Sex Abuser Likely to be Dropped', ABC Radio, *PM*, 7 December 2011 (Nance Haxton).]

233 [In relation to children, see R Boyd and A Hopkins, 'Cross-Examination of Child Sexual Assault Complainants: Concerns About the Application of s 41 of the *Evidence Act*' (2010) 34 *Criminal Law Journal* 149; J Cashmore and L Trimboli, 'An Evaluation of the NSW Child Sexual Assault Specialist Jurisdiction Pilot' (Research Report, NSW BOCSAR, 2005), 51-6; Judge Roy Ellis, 'Judicial Activism in Child Sexual Assault Cases' (Paper presented at National Judicial College of Australia Children and Courts Conference, Sydney, 5 November 2005), [35]; Justice James Wood, 'Child Witnesses: The New South Wales Experience' (Paper presented at Child Witnesses – Best Practice for Courts Conference, Australian Institute of Judicial Administration (AIJA), NSW District Court, Parramatta, 30 July 2004), 4. In relation to persons with an intellectual disability, see CME O'Kelly et al, 'Judicial Intervention in Court Cases Involving Witnesses with and Without Learning Difficulties' (2003) 8 *Legal and Criminological Psychology* 229, 237-8.]

234 [Judge Kevin Sleight, 'Managing Trials for Sexual Offences – A Western Australian Perspective' (Paper presented at AIJA Criminal Justice in Australia and New Zealand – Issues and Challenges for Judicial Administration Conference, Sydney, 7-9 September 2011), 20.]

235 [E Henderson, 'Alternative Routes: Other Accusatorial Jurisdictions on the Slow Road to Best Evidence' in JR Spencer and ME Lamb (eds), *Children and Cross-Examination: Time to Change the Rules*? (Hart Publishing, 2012), 43, 59.]

236 [ALRC, *Uniform Evidence Law*, above n 197, 149 [5.97].]

237 [Eastwood and Patton, above n 39, 4-5.]

238 [Ibid 5.]

239 [DJ Birch, 'The *Criminal Justice Act 1988* – Documentary Evidence' (Pt 2) [1989] *Criminal Law Review* 15, 17.]

This criticism has proved especially applicable in respect of children[240] and complainants with an intellectual disability.[241] Assessments about the credibility of a witness's statement are central in an adversarial trial. In trials for alleged offences of sexual or physical abuse, where the principal evidence is usually the complainant's account of events weighed against that of the accused, assessments regarding credibility are often the deciding factor. In the case of a vulnerable complainant, an acquittal may well not be based on disbelieving the complainant's account, but rather finding that the high standard of proof in a criminal case has not been satisfied.[242]

The testimony of children is often discredited for factors relating to their development, confidence or intellect, as opposed to the reliability of their account.[243] This allows cross-examiners to easily characterise a child witness as 'the aggressor', 'unchildlike', 'less than innocent', confused or unreliable.[244] The discrediting of complainants' testimony because of unavoidable developmental or cognitive factors undermines the values and concepts that underpin the criminal justice system.

Further, when cross-examining, a defence lawyer is in a position of control and power and can readily confuse, intimidate, manipulate and even bully children and witnesses with intellectual disabilities.[245] Cross-examining a child has been likened to 'shooting rats in a barrel ... it's easy to confuse them and make out they're telling lies'.[246] ... In addition, Spencer has observed the consequences of intimidation in numerous trials; for example, he notes that sometimes [children] cannot be cross-examined because they are scared out of their wits and unable to communicate at all: like a little girl in a case I once watched at Snaresbrook Crown Court, who got up from her chair as soon as cross-examination started and just ran away.[247]

When children become anxious, the accuracy of their testimony typically diminishes due to difficulties in recalling memories.[248] Even when questioned by professional and non-aggressive defence and prosecution lawyers, children often do not understand the questions posed to them.[249] This is exacerbated by such witnesses being unlikely to seek

240 [ALRC, *Seen and Heard: Priority for Children in the Legal Process* (Report No 84, 1997), [14.110]-[14.111]; 'Alternative Models for Prosecuting Child Sex Offences in Australia' (Report, National Child Sexual Assault Reform Committee, March 2010), Cossins, 'Alternative Models for Prosecuting Child Sex Offences, above n 224, 255 [4.42], 266; L Ellison, 'The Mosaic Art?: Cross-Examination and the Vulnerable Witness' (2001) 21 *Legal Studies* 353, 353-4.]

241 [See, eg, Ellison, ibid, 353-4, 361-2; Benedet and Grant, above n 38, 15-16.]

242 [See, eg, *Douglass* [2012] HCA 34; 290 ALR 699, 711-12 [48] (French CJ, Hayne, Crennan, Kiefel and Bell JJ).]

243 [In relation to children, see HL Westcott and M Page, 'Cross-Examination, Sexual Abuse and Child Witness Identity' (2002) 11 *Child Abuse Review* 137, 140-3. Given the similarities in vulnerability found in witnesses with an intellectual disability, it is likely that similar problems will arise: see Ellison, above n 240, 353-4.]

244 [Westcott and Page, ibid, 143-6.]

245 [See generally Ellison, above n 240, 360-2; A Keane, 'Cross-Examination of Vulnerable Witnesses: Towards a Blueprint for Re-Professionalism' (2012) 16 *International Journal of Evidence and Proof* 175, 176-9.]

246 [M Brennan and RE Brennan, *Strange Language – Child Victims under Cross Examination* (Riverina Murray Institute of Higher Education, 2nd ed, 1988), 3.]

247 [JR Spencer, 'Introduction' in JR Spencer and ME Lamb (eds), *Children and Cross-Examination: Time to Change the Rules*? (Hart Publishing, 2012), 1.]

248 [L Henry et al, 'Perceived Credibility and Eyewitness Testimony of Children with Intellectual Disabilities' (2011) 55 *Journal of Intellectual Disability Research* 385, 386.]

249 [See M Brennan, 'The Discourse of Denial: Cross-Examining Child Victim Witnesses' (1995) 23 *Journal of Pragmatics* 71, 73; Brennan and Brennan, above n 246. Cf GH Murphy and ICH Clare, 'The Effect of Learning Disabilities on Witness Testimony' in A Heaton-Armstrong et al (eds), *Witness Testimony: Psychological, Investigative and Evidential Perspectives* (Oxford University Press, 2006), 43, 51 [3.28], who suggest that adjusting the style of questions during cross-examination can minimise these problems in relation to persons with an intellectual disability.]

> clarification when they do not understand questions.[250] Further, children and persons with intellectual disabilities may acquiesce to statements they do not actually agree with.[251]
>
> … [A]ny discussion of proposed measures to adduce improved evidence from children and people with intellectual disabilities must also include consideration of defence lawyers' professional duties to represent their client's case vigorously and to put all relevant propositions to a witness. …
>
> *C Language and Phrasing of Questions*
>
> Unnecessarily complex cross-examination questions may also impede vulnerable witnesses' comprehension. Closed questions, which elicit a simple 'yes' or 'no' answer from witnesses, have been shown to be the most frequently used but to elicit the least reliable evidence. One study found that children aged from five to eight years attempted to answer 75 per cent of nonsensical closed questions (eg, 'Is a box louder than a knee?') but only a small proportion of nonsensical open questions (eg, 'What do bricks eat?').[252] Closed questions can be rephrased as non-leading or open questions, which are less confusing and obtain more accurate responses.[253]
>
> Similarly, leading questions, which are questions that 'directly or indirectly sugges[t] a particular answer to a question' also obtain inaccurate responses.[254] Confusing questions, such as questions containing double negatives,[255] are also regularly used in the cross-examination of children and complainants with intellectual disabilities.
>
> When questioned in a supportive and non-intimidating manner, children have been shown to make fewer mistakes due to reduced anxiety. Further, Kebbell, Hatton and Johnson state that the 'accuracy and completeness' of testimony from witnesses with an intellectual disability 'can be significantly improved if suitable questioning strategies are adopted.'[256] The persistence of questioning techniques known to be unreliable supports the contention that traditional cross-examination is not a reliable mechanism for testing the evidence of either children or persons with an intellectual disability. The problem is exacerbated by judicial failure to intervene in inappropriate cross-examination.

Bowden et al[257] observe that the great Wigmore, such an admirer of cross-examination, also noted '[a] lawyer can do anything with a cross-examination … He may, it is true, do more than he ought to do … [he] may make the truth appear like falsehood'.[258] The authors then add:

---

250 [In relation to children, see Zajac, Gross and Hayne, above n 38, 199-200. In relation to persons with an intellectual disability, see Benedet and Grant, above n 38, 15.]

251 [In relation to children, see Zajac, Gross and Hayne, above n 38, 200; R Zajac, S O'Neill and H Hayne, 'Disorder in the Courtroom? Child Witnesses under Cross-Examination' (2012) 32 *Development Review* 181, 186. In relation to persons with an intellectual disability, see Murphy and Clare, above n 249, 50-1 [3.25]-[3.26]; Kebbell et al, above n 38, 29, 32; Benedet and Grant, above n 38, 15.]

252 [AH Waterman, M Blades and C Spencer, 'Do Children Try to Answer Nonsensical Questions?' (2000) 18 *British Journal of Developmental Psychology* 211, 222.]

253 [D Caruso, 'I Don't Want to Play Follow the Leader – Part 2' (Paper presented at the AIJA Criminal Justice in Australia and New Zealand — Issues and Challenges for Judicial Administration Conference, Sydney, 9 September 2011), 8; A Keane, 'Towards a Principled Approach to the Cross-Examination of Vulnerable Witnesses' [2012] *Criminal Law Review* 407, 417.]

254 [In relation to children, see Caruso, ibid, 2. In relation to persons with an intellectual disability, see Benedet and Grant, above n 38, 15; Kebbell et al, above n 38, 24. See also N Perry et al, 'When Lawyers Question Children: Is Justice Served?' (1995) 19 *Law and Human Behavior* 609.]

255 [For example, 'Now, when you did that you did not say that it was something that you did not like?': Kebbell et al, above n 38, 27.]

256 [Ibid 24.]

257 Bowden, Henning, Plater, above n 41, 56.

258 See also FE Vandervort, 'A Search for the Truth or Trial by Ordeal: When Prosecutors Cross-Examine Adolescents How Should Courts Respond?' (2010) 16 *Widener Law Review* 335, 335.

> This is particularly true for children and witnesses with intellectual disabilities. … [F]or vulnerable witnesses, traditional cross-examination may not expose unreliability so much as produce it. A defendant's 'right' to cross-examination should not justify using methods and techniques known to confuse or mislead vulnerable witnesses, especially where this may lead to inaccurate evidence being adduced at trial.
>
> This proposition finds support in the *Convention on the Rights of the Child*[259] and the *Convention on the Rights of Persons with Disabilities*.[260] The former provides that the child's best interests must be a primary consideration of courts during legal proceedings.[261] The latter stipulates that a person with a disability who is a witness in legal proceedings must be appropriately accommodated in order to facilitate effective and equal participation.[262] Further, the United Nations' *Guidelines on Justice Matters Involving Child Victims and Witnesses of Crime* aims to ensure that measures are developed and implemented to make it easier for children to testify.[263]

The concerns of Bowden et al are echoed in the findings and recommendations of the RCIRCSA. The Commission made 12 recommendations relating to pre-recording, the use of intermediaries as communication assistants, ground rules hearings and other special measures in a bid to assist vulnerable witnesses to provide more reliable evidence.[264]

The 'Rule' in *Browne v Dunn*

In this final section we examine a major obligation on cross-examiners. This is the rule in *Browne v Dunn*,[265] a 'principle of fair conduct on the part of an advocate'.[266] Its requirements were stated by Gummow, Kirby, Callinan JJ in *MWJ*[267] as obligating a party 'to give appropriate notice to the other party, and any of that person's witnesses, of any imputation that the former intends to make against either of the latter about his or her conduct relevant to the case, or a party's or a witness's credit'. This obligation can even extend to a party's own witnesses (obviously under *UEA*, s 38 circumstances).[268] Typically, this notice is satisfied by cross-examining the relevant witness on their credibility or the matters on which

259 [Opened for signature 20 November 1989, 1577 UNTS 3 (entered into force 2 September 1990).]

260 [Opened for signature 13 December 2006, 2515 UNTS 3 (entered into force 3 May 2008).]

261 [*Convention on the Rights of the Child*, Article 3(1). See also Articles 12, 39.]

262 [*Convention on the Rights of Persons with Disabilities*, Article 13(1).]

263 [*Guidelines on Justice Matters Involving Child Victims and Witnesses of Crime*, ESC Res 2005/20 (22 July 2005), [30]-[31], [40]-[42].]

264 RCIRCSA, above n 44, *Criminal Justice Report*, recommendations 52-63. And see detailed discussion in Chapter 5, pp 170-174, about the implementation of these measures. Also adding weight to the concerns are the findings of Zajac et al in a study which compared cross-examination questioning of child complainants in the 1950s with that used in contemporary cases. The authors suggested little change in 60 years except that contemporary questions were more likely to be complex and contemporary complainants were asked 'far more questions overall': R Zajac et al, 'The "Good Old Days" of Courtroom Questioning: Changes in the Format of Child Cross-Examination Questions over 60 Years' (2018) 23 *Child Maltreatment* 186, 191.

265 (1893) 6 R (HL) 67.

266 *MWJ* [2005] HCA 74; 222 ALR 436, [18] (Gleeson CJ and Heydon J).

267 Ibid [38]. In terms of giving notice, in *Parsons (a Pseudonym)* [2016] VSCA 17, [42], Maxwell P, Redlich and Priest JJA observed that '[i]n limited circumstances, pre-trial notice – where the substance of the evidence proposed to be given by each side is notified in advance by affidavit or statement – has been regarded as sufficient notice to a witness of the submission ultimately intended to be put to the court. But the rule in *Browne v Dunn* will require more extensive cross-examination in criminal trials and in cases where all the evidence is given orally', citing *West v Mead* [2003] NSWSC 161.

268 *Kanaan* [2006] NSWCCA 109.

the opposing party seeks to rely because this enables the witness (and the party calling him or her) to respond.[269]

Numerous judicial expositions of the rule indicate that its obligations are reflective of principles of fairness. As Lord Halsbury stated in *Browne v Dunn*:

> To my mind nothing would be more absolutely unjust than not to cross-examine witnesses upon evidence which they have given, so as to give them notice, and to give them an opportunity of explanation, and an opportunity very often to defend their own character, and, not having given them such an opportunity, to ask the jury afterwards to disbelieve what they have said, although not one question has been directed either to their credit or to the accuracy of the facts they have deposed to.[270]

Gleeson CJ and Heydon J usefully describe the pervasiveness, rationale and sensitivity of consequences in *MWJ*:

> 18. The principle of fair conduct on the part of an advocate, stated in *Browne v Dunn*, is an important aspect of the adversarial system of justice. It has been held in England,[271] New South Wales,[272] South Australia,[273] Queensland,[274] and New Zealand,[275] to apply in the administration of criminal justice, which, as well as being accusatorial, is adversarial. Murphy J, in this Court, even applied it to the conduct of an unrepresented accused.[276] However, for reasons explained, for example, in *R v Birks*,[277] and *R v Manunta*,[278] it is a principle that may need to be applied with some care when considering the conduct of the defence at criminal trial. Fairness ordinarily requires that if a challenge is to be made to the evidence of a witness, the ground of the challenge be put to the witness in cross-examination. This requirement is accepted, and applied day by day, in criminal trials. However, the consequences of a failure to cross-examine on a certain issue may need to be considered in the light of the nature and course of the proceedings.

The prosecution's burden of proof and the core accusatorial principles that guide the structure, process and function of the criminal trial mean that defence obligations under *Browne v Dunn* are not as exacting as those on the prosecution. This was classically illustrated and expressed in the High Court case of *MWJ*,[279] an appeal from a judge-alone trial that had taken place a year or so after the complainant alleged a series of sexual assaults upon her by her mother's de facto partner. The complainant was between 8 and 13 years of age at the time of these alleged assaults. She made the complaint 11 years after the last alleged incident and she was 25 years old at the time of the trial. Her evidence differed from that of her mother with respect to the number of assaults alleged to have taken place at the first of two relevant locations. At issue on appeal was whether defence counsel should have cross-examined the complainant on the apparent inconsistencies between the two prosecution witnesses. The majority (Gummow, Kirby, Callinan JJ) observed:

---

269 See, generally, *MWJ* [2005] HCA 74; 222 ALR 436; *Kuhl v Zurich Financial Services Australia Ltd* [2011] HCA 11; 243 CLR 361.

270 (1893) 6 R (HL) 67, 76, see also at 76-7.

271 [*Fenlon* (1980) 71 Cr App R 307; *Lovelock* noted in [1997] *Criminal Law Review* 821.]

272 [*Birks* (1990) 19 NSWLR 677.]

273 [*Manunta* (1989) 54 SASR 17.]

274 [*Foley* [2000] 1 Qd R 290.]

275 [*Gutierrez* [1997] 1 NZLR 192.]

276 [*McInnis* [1979] HCA 65; 143 CLR 575, 590-1.]

277 [(1990) 19 NSWLR 677, 686-91.]

278 [(1989) 54 SASR 17, 23.]

279 [2005] HCA 74; 222 ALR 436.

> 39. … In this case, the appellant was confronted with a forensic dilemma: whether to seek to have the mother's evidence of her daughter's assertions of repeated misconduct at Sutcliffe Street excluded by reason of its prejudicial effect, or deliberately to leave it untouched to provide a basis for a submission that a fundamental inconsistency tainted the whole case. In the event the appellant chose the former. In that endeavour he failed, but was still able, albeit unsuccessfully, to rely on it as setting up a significant inconsistency. *On no view was the appellant obliged however to seek to have the complainant recalled as a condition of his reliance upon the inconsistency which had emerged in the case for the prosecution.* (emphasis added)

Their Honours added an observation regarding an important limitation of the *Browne v Dunn* obligations with respect to the running of a criminal defence case.

> 41. The obligation of the prosecution to present its whole case in chief and the existence of the unavoidable burden of proof carried by the prosecution are of particular relevance here. … It is not for the defence to clear up, or resolve inconsistencies in the case for the prosecution. As soon as the inconsistency emerged, and the trial judge rejected the appellant's objection to the evidence intended to be adduced from the complainant's mother, it was open for the prosecution to offer to tender the complainant for further cross-examination. Had that happened it would then, and only then have been for the appellant, to decide whether to embrace the offer or not. If he had not, then and only then would the criticism that the Court of Criminal Appeal made of his conduct have been valid. The position of an accused who bears no burden of proof in a criminal trial cannot be equated with the position of a defendant in civil proceedings. *The rule in Browne v Dunn can no more be applied, or applied without serious qualification, to an accused in a criminal trial than can the not dissimilar rule in Jones v Dunkel.*[280] *In each case it is necessary to consider the applicability of the rule (if any) having regard to the essential accusatory character of the criminal trial in this country.* (emphasis added)

Bowden et al[281] pose the question whether *Browne v Dunn* obligations need more flexibility. They reason that, as modern evidence law accepts that the rule against hearsay will permit statements to be admitted into evidence despite the makers of the statement not being available to testify,[282] the fairness of the trial process if broadly conceived[283] justifies acceptance that the rule in *Browne v Dunn* can (and should) be relaxed in relation to the cross-examination of vulnerable prosecution witnesses. This occurred in the English Court of Appeal case of *Edwards*[284] (discussed above)[285] where the court supported the trial judge's management of the cross-examination of the six-year-old complainant, including the ruling that 'the defence did not need to put its case on the incident itself, and the result of such questioning would be to cause confusion in one so young, unhelpful to a jury trying to conclude, at the end of the day, whether the Crown had made it sure of guilt'. As long as the jury is not misled by the reduced testing of a prosecution witness's account this approach is consistent with treating the prosecution as bearing the burden of proof. In *Ward*[286] the court acknowledged that the task of

280 [[1959] HCA 8; 101 CLR 298]

281 Bowden et al, above n 41, 562.

282 The authors indicate that, in England, courts have altered their views on the centrality of cross-examination to the accused person's right to a fair trial, citing *Barker* [2010] EWCA Crim 4, [42] (Lord Judge CJ for the court); *Edwards* [2011] EWCA Crim 3028; *Watts* [2010] EWCA Crim 1824, [17] (Mackay J for the court).

283 Bowden et al, above n 41, 562.

284 [2011] EWCA Crim 3028, [28] (Rafferty LJ for the court).

285 Above p 220.

286 *Ward* [2017] VSCA 37.

cross-examining a child complainant was one of 'considerable complexity' involving 'two related forensic challenges'.[287]

> 11. The first challenge is to formulate questions which are age-appropriate. This is necessary as a matter of basic fairness to the child witness, so that he or she can understand the questions and respond. But it is equally important in the interests of the accused. Unless the questions are age appropriate, answers which appear to create inconsistencies in the evidence are unlikely to serve the desired purpose of creating a doubt in the minds of the jury or – on appeal – of persuading this Court that the jury 'must have had a doubt' about the evidence.
>
> 12. The second challenge is that, so far as practicable in the circumstances, the child witness must be given the opportunity to say whether something they have said, and which the accused disputes, is true. This is the obligation of fairness to which expression is given in the rule in *Browne v Dunn*. The content of this obligation is, of necessity, different in the case of young children, who will not generally respond with understanding or accuracy to a formal challenge to their evidence, or 'puttage' as to the accused's case. As a result, there is a significant risk that they will accept suggestions made to them by cross-examining counsel without understanding their implications.[288]

The issue was also the focus of discussion in the RCIRCSA. Whilst not the subject of a formal recommendation, the Commissioners proposed that 'in any guidance prepared to assist courts and practitioners in conducting ground rules hearings ... the issue of whether, or the extent to which, it is necessary for the defence to comply with the rule in *Browne v Dunn* should be considered'.[289]

Broad principles of fairness interact with *Browne v Dunn* requirements. These principles manifest in various ways. For instance, in the Australian High Court case of *Kuhl v Zurich Financial Services Australia Ltd*[290] a question of fairness to the witness (also the plaintiff) arose with respect to inferences that could be drawn from his economical (and arguably merely inarticulate) description of the accident that gave rise to his claim for damages. The factual circumstances giving rise to the hearing were that Mr Kuhl worked as a 'reactor rat'. His job, in Port Hedland, Western Australia, was to enter the employer's iron ore reactors, break up and remove small pieces of iron ore (called 'fines') using a large vacuum hose. A 'hole watcher' would monitor this work and assist with the handling of the hose. The *Browne v Dunn* question arose in the context of the judge, as fact-finder, drawing negative inferences from the way in which the plaintiff (Kuhl) responded to questions in examination-in-chief concerning the incident where an industrial suction hose took off Kuhl's arm. French CJ and Gummow extracted the relevant evidence:

> What happened when the hose was handed back towards you? – *My arm was caught in it, in the end, opening of it, whatever you want to call it.*
>
> If you could just describe in your own words to the court, how was the hose passed back towards you? – *Passed direct –*
>
> What was the physical action? – *Just passed directly back to me. I moved it a bit to the side to grab it as it was the only way to do it and the next thing my arm was gone.*
>
> Which arm? – *Left, sucked in.*
>
> And how far was your left arm sucked into the hose? – *Up to my shoulder.*

The trial judge stated:

287 Ibid [10].

288 Ibid [11]-[12] (citations omitted).

289 RCIRCSA, above n 44.

290 [2011] HCA 11; 243 CLR 361, [74] (emphasis added).

> The plaintiff was less than expansive when describing how his arm was drawn into the vacuum hose, *and I formed the view that for whatever reason he was reluctant to say precisely what happened.* I accept the essentially unchallenged evidence of Mr Kelleher that the suction inlet was directed away from the plaintiff as the hose was passed to him, and I am left to infer that some subsequent action by the plaintiff caused his arm to be drawn in by the suction force.
>
> I am satisfied that the plaintiff was acutely aware of the necessity not to allow any part of the body to come into contact with the suction inlet. Not only does the plaintiff accept that, but the associated risks were obvious.[291]

However, there was no cross-examination as to how Kuhl's arm came to be caught in the hose. This absence was described by Heydon, Crennan and Bell JJ as arising from 'the cross-examiner's gamble', that is, the cross-examiner making a choice between asking questions of the opposing party's witness in an attempt to strengthen his or her own case on a matter or leaving the matter alone, resting on what the witness has said (badly) in examination-in-chief. The tension arises from the desire to avoid inviting an unwanted answer but the need to meet *Browne v Dunn* obligations. The joint judgment of Heydon, Crennan and Bell JJ formed the majority determination in favour of Kuhl. Regarding whether Kuhl should have been put on notice by cross-examination of the inferences that the judge intended to draw, their Honours added some explanation of the tactical dilemma – the gamble – facing the defendant's counsel in this case,

> 74. … Normally cross-examining counsel will prefigure and lay the ground work for any criticism a judge may feel minded to make of a witness's evidence in chief. But here there was no cross-examination on the plaintiff's evidence in chief about what happened in the moments before he sustained his injuries. This created a difficulty for the trial judge. The tactical decision of defence counsel not to cross-examine on that topic may well have been shrewd. When Wigmore enunciated his celebrated but controversial proposition [regarding cross-examination] … he immediately stated another much less controversial proposition by way of caveat: *A lawyer can do anything with a cross-examination – if he is skillful enough not to impale his own cause upon it.*[292] The truth of the second proposition lies in the fact that when a cross-examiner seeks to extract from a witness testimony which is more favourable to the cross-examiner's client than that which the witness gave in chief, the new testimony often turns out to be adverse to the client. If evidence in chief is thought to be too feeble to serve its purpose, cross-examiners often think it best to leave it alone, for to cross-examine will do no more than strengthen it: the repeated questions may cause the witness to think harder, may cause the witness to become more determined, may trigger better recollection and may result in the witness giving the more detailed evidence which was not given in chief. But decisions by cross-examiners of that kind are gambles, and the gambles can be lost. …

The majority concluded that the cross-examiner's 'gamble' did not pay off.

> 62. *The significance of the trial judge's finding.* The conclusion of the trial judge that the plaintiff was 'reluctant to say precisely what happened' is an important one. If that conclusion were soundly arrived at, it would be a significant factor against the plaintiff's success. So, at least, the trial judge, the Court of Appeal majority and the first respondent thought. It would be significant because of the following considerations. Witnesses are supposed to answer questions put by counsel responsively: they are supposed to give a full answer, but no more. It is one thing to say that a witness was not asked the right questions. It is another thing to say that a witness did not answer the questions that were asked. And it is an even more serious thing to say that a witness was 'reluctant' to answer.

291 Ibid [60] (emphasis added).

292 [Wigmore, *Evidence in Trials at Common Law* (Chadbourn rev, 1974) Vol 5, 32 [1367].]

The duty of a witness is to tell the truth, the whole truth, and nothing but the truth so far as the questions asked seek it. The duty of a witness to answer questions responsively involves not only a negative duty (not to volunteer material for which the question does not call), but also a positive duty (to proffer all material within the witness's knowledge for which the question does call). To conclude that a party-witness is reluctant to say what happened is to conclude that the party-witness is deliberately failing to comply with the duty to tell the whole truth. That is a serious conclusion to reach, for the following reasons. …

65. The trial judge certainly appears to have perceived the plaintiff's answers to have operated as a kind of admission. … The trial judge plainly assumed that the plaintiff had not exercised proper care, and had deliberately or carelessly placed his arm too near the hose. In the trial judge's apparent view, it was this which he was reluctant' to reveal in his 'less than expansive' description of what happened.

66. It is true that at the end of his reasons for judgment the trial judge took a different stand. He said (*Kuhl v Zurich Financial Services Australia Ltd* [2009] WADC 4, [40]):

> the plaintiff having failed to satisfy me as to how and why his arm was drawn into the suction inlet, it is not … possible to identify a relevant breach, and causally relate the incident to it.

Whether the plaintiff has demonstrated that the trial judge was right or wrong about that will be examined below. But it is one thing to say that a plaintiff's evidence is inadequate to make out a claim; it is another thing to say that a plaintiff's evidence is not only inadequate, but that it has been tailored by deliberate non-responsive suppression.

67. It is not sound judicial technique to criticise a party-witness for deliberately withholding the truth in a fashion crucial to a dismissal of that party's claim unless two conditions are satisfied. First, reasons must be given for concluding that the truth has been deliberately withheld. Secondly, the party-witness must have been given an opportunity to deal with the criticism. …

71. An allegation in final address that the plaintiff suppressed evidence would be in substance a suggestion that he was not speaking the truth and ought not to be believed: for he had been asked in effect to describe the whole of what he observed and remembered about what happened when the hose was handed back towards him, and the allegation would be that he had failed to speak the truth by deliberately not describing the whole of what he remembered, but suppressing unfavourable parts of it. So to allege would have been to 'impeach' the plaintiff as a witness. The remedies might have included a refusal by the judge to accept or entertain the submission, and a recall of the plaintiff to the witness box to deal with the allegation.

72. Now if it was not open to counsel for the first respondent to make the postulated allegation, how can it have been open to the trial judge, without warning, to incorporate into his reasons for judgment a finding to the same effect as the allegation? …

75. … In the absence of any challenge from the cross-examiner to the frankness and completeness of the plaintiff's evidence, it was incumbent on the trial judge, if his conclusion that the plaintiff had not been frank and complete was to play a role in his decision adverse to the plaintiff, to make the challenge himself. Perhaps the criticism in the judgment did not occur to the trial judge until after the plaintiff had left the box, or until after the hearing had concluded and before the judge's reserved judgment was given. It remained necessary either to recall the plaintiff or to have no regard to that aspect of the plaintiff's evidence.

In the NSW Court of Criminal Appeal case of *Birks*[293] the *Browne v Dunn* issue arose not in the failed execution of strategic nuances designed to maximise a party's case, but through inexperience and lack of competence. Counsel failed to

293 *Birks* (1990) 19 NSWLR 677. See also *Drash* [2012] VSCA 33 and *Orchard* [2013] NSWCCA 342, [43] (Rothman, Fullerton and Beech-Jones JJ) regarding the need for circumspection from the trial judge in this context.

challenge the sexual assault complainant on two disputed aspects of her account regarding how the rape and a related assault took place. When Birks testified he denied these elements that should have been raised in the complainant's cross-examination. This led to extensive cross-examination by the prosecutor suggesting that Birks was lying and that he had concocted these parts of his account. The prosecutor included this point in his closing address and the judge referred to the cross-examination in his summing up. Only when the jury retired did defence counsel inform the judge that his failure to cross-examine the complainant on the disputed matters was due to his own inadvertence. Birks was convicted. The court allowed the appeal. It also adopted the views expressed by King CJ in *Manunta*[294] of the need for caution in drawing adverse inferences from the accused's counsel's failure to cross-examine certain matters, indicating that there may be an 'innocent' explanation (suggesting '[f]orensic pressures may have resulted in looseness or inexactitude in the framing of questions. The matter might simply have been overlooked'). This case for caution was reinforced by Heydon, Crennan and Bell JJ in *MWJ*.[295] Their Honours stated that 'judges should in general abstain from making adverse findings about parties and witnesses in respect of whom there has been non-compliance' with the rule. In addition their Honours also pointed to the benefits of remedying a breach by recalling a witness.

> 40. Reliance on the rule in *Browne v Dunn* can be both misplaced and overstated. If the evidence in the case has not been completed, a party genuinely taken by surprise by reason of a failure on the part of the other to put a relevant matter in cross-examination, can almost always, especially in ordinary civil litigation, mitigate or cure any difficulties so arising by seeking or offering the recall of the witness to enable the matter to be put. In criminal cases, in many jurisdictions, the salutary practice of excusing witnesses temporarily only, and on the understanding that they must make themselves available to be recalled if necessary at any time before a verdict is given, is adopted. There may be some circumstances in which it could be unfair to permit the recalling of a witness, but in general, subject to the obligation of the prosecution not to split its case, and to present or make available all of the relevant evidence to an accused, the course that we have suggested is one that should be able to be adopted on most occasions without injustice.

The *UEA* does not restate the rule in *Browne v Dunn*. Remediation of a breach by recall of the witness is the sole footprint of *Browne v Dunn* that is expressed in the *UEA* (in s 46). The presence of s 46 reaffirms the rule's existence to the extent that it provides a response to address the potential unfairness of its breach where a witness could have given, but did not give, evidence about a matter in examination-in-chief. It is clear that s 46 does not by implication limit the power to recall a witness to its terms.[296] Obviously it can only repair damage while the trial remains on foot.

> **46. Leave to recall witnesses**
>
> (1) The court may give leave to a party to recall a witness to give evidence about a matter raised by evidence adduced by another party, being a matter on which the witness was not cross-examined, if the evidence concerned has been admitted and:

294 (1989) 54 SASR 17.

295 [2005] HCA 74; 222 ALR 436, [39].

296 *Doyle* [2014] NSWCCA 4, [311]-[312].

(a) it contradicts evidence about the matter given by the witness in examination in chief, or

(b) the witness could have given evidence about the matter in examination in chief.

(2) A reference in this section to a matter raised by evidence adduced by another party includes a reference to an inference drawn from, or that the party intends to draw from, that evidence.

Unlike in some portions of the *UEA* where evidence or procedural law has been given extensive legislative treatment – such as hearsay evidence – the light touch given in the *UEA* to the rule in *Browne v Dunn* raises the possibility that the rule's continued relevance in *UEA* jurisdictions could be interpreted with less vigour than at common law. Apart from the flow of case law since 1995 suggesting otherwise, the presence of *UEA*, s 11, preserving courts' inherent powers to control the conduct of proceedings (other than where the Act indicates expressly or 'by necessary intendment'), makes clear that a principle of fairness to witnesses and parties remains of continuing importance. The lack of formal expression of the rule is immaterial to the continuing relevance of *Browne v Dunn* principles but, and in light of the lead taken by the English in cases such as *Edwards*,[297] it also supports flexibility to waive the rule where it is in the interests of justice to do so.

Conclusion

Despite the problems linked to cross-examination, it will remain a central part of the common law trial. This is because adversarialism is a developing trend globally and the trend is unlikely to halt. However, gamesmanship defeating the goals of justice is increasingly recognised as an intolerable intrusion into the workings and purpose of the criminal justice system. There is much to commend the suggestions by Bowden et al that more control is needed of witness questioning of vulnerable witnesses. Preserving the accused's rights is, however, crucial. To think creatively outside the current conventional courtroom trial paradigm may be the answer. A suggestion from Bowden et al[298] seeks to 'triangulate' the interests of defendants, victims and society by entrusting examination-in-chief and cross-examination to a 'suitably qualified third-party in advance of trial'. The goal of this new third party would be to enable 'higher quality evidence, improve the trial process for victims and preserve the defendant's right to a fair trial'. This proposal implicitly recognises the inadequacy of statutory modifications such as *UEA*, s 41. However, as Chapter 5 indicates, since the Bowden et al article was published in 2014 there has been a rapid uptake in most Australian jurisdictions of witness intermediary schemes (including witness intermediary assistance reports and ground rules hearings). The schemes vary in their breadth and potential efficacy but reliance on witness intermediaries appears to offer scope to bridge accusatorial goals and witnesses' psychological needs. However, it is particularly unfortunate that the provision of intermediaries is often limited to prosecution witnesses (typically the child complainant). As we see in Chapter 2 in cases such as *Libke*,[299] prosecutors' combative witness questioning no doubt

297 [2011] EWCA Crim 3028, discussed above.

298 Bowden et al, above n 41, 545.

299 See *Libke* [2007] HCA 30; 230 CLR 559, Chapter 2, p 47.

discourages many defendants from testifying, and an intermediary scheme for all potentially vulnerable witnesses (as well as for vulnerable suspects facing police questioning) would recognise the non-partisan nature of communication needs and psychological well-being wherever a power imbalance might cause injustice.

The next decade will reveal the extent to which accusatorial fair trial principles can co-exist with witness intermediaries finding a place in the justice system.[300]

300 For an example of the potential effectiveness of guidance and support of a witness intermediary, see *Gray* [2020] NSWCCA 240, discussed in Chapter 5, p 165, fn 48.

Chapter 7

Police Questioning and The Accused: Silence and Admissions

Introduction

The right to silence is one of the most fundamental tenets of our criminal justice system. While its origins lie in the common law, where it remains embedded, it has also been given legislative effect in the *UEA*. In particular, s 89 of the *UEA* prevents unfavourable inferences from being drawn by a jury from an accused's silence during the investigation period.[1]

Given the historical value placed on the right to silence, how then does the law deal with evidence where an accused breaks their silence, and said or done something, out of court, which has the potential to be incriminating in relation to the offence for which they are charged? The *UEA* defines admissions as out-of-court representations by accused persons which are adverse to their interests in the proceedings. The breadth of the meaning of what constitutes an 'admission' is considered, as is the pathway for evidence of admissions, ordinarily caught by the hearsay rule, to be admissible in the prosecution case.[2]

This chapter commences with a reminder of some of the important reasons underpinning the need for preserving the right to silence, in particular, the vulnerability of a suspect in custody. The operation of the provisions which govern the admissibility of admissions is examined with a focus on the ever-present tension between admitting persuasive evidence to secure convictions on the one hand and, on the other, preserving the right to silence and ensuring fairness by excluding admissions which may be unreliable or which have been unfairly, illegally or improperly obtained.[3] The importance of adequately resolving this tension is no more apparent than in the context of wrongful convictions based on false confessions.

In this chapter, attention is paid to the history of widespread misconduct by police in fabricating and unfairly inducing admissions. These practices led to the

1 *UEA*, s 89. In New South Wales, s 89A allows for unfavourable inferences to be drawn if the conditions set out in that provision are met.

2 *UEA*, ss 81, 82 and 60.

3 Relevant exclusionary provisions: *UEA*, ss 84, 85, 90, 138. Note, general exclusionary provisions and provisions limiting the use of admissions may also be relevant: *UEA*, ss 135, 137, 136.

introduction of the ERISP[4] and provisions mandating that certain admissions be electronically recorded as a prerequisite to admission into evidence.[5]

Given the profound impact that evidence of admissions can have in determining the outcome of criminal proceedings,[6] ensuring that any admissions which are admitted into evidence are reliable and obtained fairly is paramount. Consequently, mandatory and discretionary exclusion provisions which apply specifically to evidence of admissions have been included in the *UEA*.[7]

The cases discussed in this chapter encourage reflection on the impact of police conduct and questioning and the vulnerabilities particular to accused persons which may affect the reliability of admissions or unfairly influence them to make admissions, thus compromising their right to silence.

The Right to Silence When Questioned by Police

It is fundamental to our system of criminal justice that the prosecution prove its case beyond a reasonable doubt before a verdict of guilty may be returned. It 'is never for the accused person to prove its innocence'.[8] This principle infuses numerous aspects of the criminal trial.[9] At the heart of the measures which give effect to this principle is the right to silence, which encompasses the privilege against self-incrimination.[10] The right may also be understood as a 'collection of immunities'[11] which are afforded to a person suspected of having committed a criminal offence:

> immunity from adverse consequences for lack of cooperation in the investigation process (including questioning), protection from self-incrimination, torture and mistreatment directed to obtaining confessions, and from being required to testify in proceedings against themselves.[12]

In general terms, the right to silence before trial[13] refers to a suspect or accused's entitlement not to respond to police when being questioned or spoken to in relation to an alleged offence and, traditionally, for the exercise of this right not to be held against an accused at trial.[14] The right to silence is fundamental to the criminal justice system, as expressed by the High Court in *Petty and Maiden*:[15]

> 2. A person who believes on reasonable grounds that he or she is suspected of having been a party to an offence is entitled to remain silent when questioned or asked to supply

4 Electronically Recorded Interview with a Suspected Person.

5 The provision which governs the recording of admissions, s 281 of the *Criminal Procedure Act 1986* (NSW) (*CPA* (NSW)).

6 *Nicholls and Coates* [2005] HCA 1; 219 CLR 196, [196] (Gummow and Callinan JJ, with McHugh J agreeing).

7 *UEA*, ss 84, 85, 90. These are in addition to ss 137 and 138.

8 *Petty and Maiden* [1991] HCA 34; 173 CLR 95, [16] (Gaudron J).

9 See, in particular, Chapter 1 and *UEA*, s 20.

10 [1991] HCA 34; 173 CLR 95, [16] (Gaudron J).

11 D Dixon and N Cowdery, 'Silence Rights' (2013) 17 *Australia Indigenous Law Review* 23.

12 Ibid.

13 The right to silence also refers to a person's right not to give evidence at trial, see Chapter 1.

14 See also *Carr v Western Australia* [2007] HCA 47; 232 CLR 138, [136] (Kirby J): 'There is no doctrine of the common law that explains precisely what the observance of the right to silence entails in the context of the questioning of a suspect by police officers. However, this Court has indicated that the observance of the right might require more from police officers in circumstances where a suspect is uneducated or otherwise disadvantaged, than is necessary where a suspect is intelligent or educated'.

15 [1991] HCA 34; 173 CLR 95 (Mason CJ, Deane, Toohey and McHugh JJ).

> information by any person in authority about the occurrence of an offence, the identity of the participants and the roles which they played. That is a fundamental rule of the common law which, subject to some specific statutory modifications, is applied in the administration of the criminal law in this country.

The value of the right to silence is given further weight when considering factors which explain how a suspect's silence may be consistent with innocence:

> An innocent person may not answer a question for any number of reasons such as mental capacity, intoxication, age, stress, loss of recall, professional advice, misunderstanding of the question, ignorance of rights and duties, and fear of consequences.[16]

A suspect's ability to communicate with police may also be compromised for a number of reasons, including language skills and level of education.[17] Aboriginal and Torres Strait Islander people may experience specific vulnerabilities when being questioned by police. For example, a suspect may be reluctant to engage in questioning because, culturally, they are not allowed to talk about the matter.[18] Issues relating to language and culture are well documented[19] as are the limited availability of interpreters.[20] Significantly, the relationship between Aboriginal and Torres Strait Islander people and police has been characterised in many circumstances by power imbalances and distrust.[21] Such issues create obvious disincentives for engaging in police questioning and thus explain silence on the part of an innocent suspect.

It is not only the matters particular to the accused that explain a suspect's silence and provide reasons for protecting suspects. The impact of arrest and the custodial context in which suspects are invariably questioned may be confronting and intimidating. Arrest and detention invariably involve a significant power imbalance in favour of the police:[22]

> For a suspect a police station is a very scary place. Police, often young and energetic, have the power to: interrogate or not, initiate criminal proceedings or not and to deprive or curtail a person's liberty or not – according to the exercise of their own judgment.
>
> Police interviewers can be extremely foreboding – even when they are acting entirely within the law. It is not just the questioning that is difficult for a suspect; it is the context in which it takes place. Usually, the suspect is questioned after an arrest. Being arrested

16 R Ratnapala, 'Our Right to Silence is too important to lose', *The Conversation*, 1 October 2012, <http://theconversation.com/our-right-to-silence-is-too-important-to-lose-9830>.

17 Ibid.

18 D Yehia, 'Admissibility of Admissions, Aboriginal and Torres Strait Islander Suspects' (Public Defenders Office, 2012), <http://www.publicdefenders.justice.nsw.gov.au/agdbasev7wr/pdo/documents/pdf/admissibilityofadmissionsatsisuspects.pdf>, 2.

19 For example, see A Bowen, 'You Don't Have to Say Anything': Modality and Consequences in Conversations About the Right to Silence in the Northern Territory' (2019) 39 *Australian Journal of Linguistics* 347; L Bartels, 'Police Interviews with Vulnerable Adult Suspects', *Research in Practice* (Report No 21, AIC, 2011), 3; D Eades, 'Aboriginal Ways of Using English' (Aboriginal Studies Press, 2013); NSWLRC, *The Right to Silence* (Report No 95, 2000), [2.118]; F Sharifian, 'Cultural Conceptualisations in Intercultural Communication: A Study of Aboriginal and Non-Aboriginal Australians' (2010) 42 *Journal of Pragmatics* 3367.

20 Yehia, above n 18; and Human Rights and Equal Opportunity Commission (amicus curiae), 'Submission of the Aboriginal and Torres Strait Islander Social Justice Commissioner on Common Difficulties Facing Aboriginal Witnesses', in *Giblet v Queensland* [2006] FCA 537 (HREOC Submission), see <https://www.humanrights.gov.au/commission-submission-1>.

21 H Douglas, 'The Cultural Specificity of Evidence: The Current Scope and Relevance of the *Anunga* Guidelines' (1998) 21(1) *UNSW Law Journal* 27, 29.

22 P Boulton SC, 'The Attack on the Right to Silence' (11 February 2013), <http://www.criminalcle.net.au/attachments/Right_to_SilenceFebruary_2013_Boulten_SC.pdf>, 4.

> is a shocking experience. It is often meant to be a shock. Arrests are timed for police convenience – often late at night or early in the morning.
>
> Sometimes an arrest is at gunpoint. Always an arrest is accompanied by actions that make it clear that the suspect is no longer a free agent. People who are arrested, handcuffed and locked in a cell are not in a good condition to be able to make important decisions about what to say in their defence.
>
> Not everybody who is arrested is a "hardened criminal".[23]

This context can be intimidating even in circumstances where police are acting within their powers. Illegal or improper conduct (reckless or deliberate) can only exacerbate the power imbalance and provide further justification for preserving the right to silence.

The NSW Law Reform Commission (NSWLRC) recognised the intensity of the early stages of an investigation and the unreasonable conclusion that silence equates to guilt:

> It is reasonable that innocent persons faced with a serious accusation might wish to consider their situations carefully before making any disclosure, especially where the circumstances appear suspicious but it cannot be assumed that they are rational and articulate. In many cases, suspects may be emotional, perhaps panicked, inarticulate, unintelligent, easily influenced, confused or frightened or a combination of these. They may be unable to do themselves justice. Such persons may be well advised to hold their peace, at least at an early stage. They may, of course, have something to hide, but that something may simply be shameful and not a crime, or it may implicate others for whom they feel responsible. The supposition that only a guilty person has a reason for not speaking freely to investigating police is an unreasonable assumption.[24]

The High Court has also acknowledged the special vulnerability of suspects in police custody to fabrication,[25] and that the observance of the right to silence may 'require more from police officers in circumstances where a suspect is uneducated or otherwise disadvantaged'.[26] It has also acknowledged that being in custody robs a suspect of the opportunity to obtain corroborative evidence to challenge police allegations of admissions which they deny making,[27] such that warnings may be given to juries in relation to the reliability of evidence of admissions which are in dispute.[28] The crucial importance of the common law and statutory protections of the right to silence is abundantly clear when the practical reasons underpinning the vulnerability of suspects are considered. This is particularly so when some of the reasons for remaining silent, discussed above, are complex and there is a risk that they may not be readily understood by some jurors.[29]

The right to silence is supported by common law and statute in a number of ways, directly and indirectly, at different stages of an investigation and criminal proceedings. These include the requirement that suspects be cautioned when arrested and questioned by police[30] and detained,[31] the denial of the power to arrest for the purpose of questioning,[32] and the protections and rights afforded

---

23 Ibid.

24 NSWLRC, *The Right to Silence*, above n 19, [2.116].

25 *McKinney* [1991] HCA 6; 171 CLR 468, [23] (Mason CJ, Deane, Gaudron and McHugh JJ).

26 *Carr v Western Australia* [2007] HCA 47; 232 CLR 138, [136] (Kirby J).

27 *McKinney* [1991] HCA 6; 171 CLR 468, [23] (Mason CJ, Deane, Gaudron and McHugh JJ).

28 Ibid; and see warnings below, p 331. See also Chapter 14.

29 NSWLRC, *The Right to Silence*, above n 19, [2.128].

30 *UEA*, s 139.

31 *LEPRA* (NSW), s 122.

32 *Zaravinos v New South Wales* [2004] NSWCA 320.

to suspects detained for the purpose of investigation.[33] The *UEA* exclusionary provisions have a role to play in excluding evidence of admissions which may have been obtained in ways which have the potential to compromise the right to silence, such as where obtained unfairly, illegally or influenced by oppressive or threatening conduct.[34] In the course of a trial, the right to silence is traditionally supported by directions to the jury that adverse or unfavourable inferences cannot be drawn where an accused fails or refuses to respond to police questioning,[35] or fails to give evidence in their trial.[36]

Section 89 of the *UEA* provides protection for an accused at trial who does not respond to police questioning.

> **89. Evidence of silence generally**
>
> (1) [Subject to s 89A,][37] in a criminal proceeding, an inference unfavourable to a party must not be drawn from evidence that the party or another person failed or refused:
>
> (a) to answer one or more questions, or
>
> (b) to respond to a representation,
>
> put or made to the party or other person by an investigating official who at that time was performing functions in connection with the investigation of the commission, or possible commission, of an offence.
>
> (2) Evidence of that kind is not admissible if it can only be used to draw such an inference. …

Section 89 (subject to s 89A in New South Wales) preserves and enshrines in legislation the common law right to silence. It does so by requiring judges to exclude evidence relevant only to show such silence and to ensure juries do not draw unfavourable inferences (for example, an inference as to the accused's credibility or to prove consciousness of guilt[38]) in relation to an accused's failure to answer police questions (or representations) during the investigation period:[39]

> An incident of that right of silence is that no adverse inference can be drawn against an accused person by reason of his or her failure to answer such questions or to provide such information. To draw such an adverse inference would be to erode the right of silence or to render it valueless.[40]

Section 89(3) permits the use of evidence of silence 'to prove that the party or other person failed or refused to answer the question or to respond to the representation', but only if the failure or refusal is a fact in issue in the proceeding. It would apply where, for example, a person is required to provide police with information, such as in s 12 of the *Law Enforcement (Powers and Responsibilities) Act 2002* (NSW) (*LEPRA* (NSW)), which makes it an offence not to disclose identity where police suspect on reasonable grounds that a person may be able to assist the police with the investigation of an alleged offence.

---

33 See *Law Enforcement (Powers and Responsibilities) Act 2002* (NSW) (*LEPRA* (NSW), Pt 9.

34 See exclusionary provisions below, pp 318-322.

35 *Petty and Maiden* [1991] HCA 34; 173 CLR 95, [2] (Mason CJ, Deane, Toohey and McHugh JJ).

36 See Chapter 1.

37 Only in New South Wales as it is the only State which has enacted s 89A.

38 The term 'unfavourable inference' is defined in s 89(4): '*inference* includes: (a) an inference of consciousness of guilt, or (b) an inference relevant to a party's credibility'.

39 *UEA*, s 89(1), limits the relevant investigation period.

40 *Petty and Maiden* [1991] HCA 34; 173 CLR 95, [16] (Gaudron J).

Drawing an unfavourable inference from silence in New South Wales

In 2013 New South Wales legislated to provide that a judge may direct the jury that it is permissible to draw an unfavourable inference where the accused person failed to provide the police with information under questioning.

> **89A. Evidence of silence in criminal proceedings for serious indictable offences**
> (1) In a criminal proceeding for a serious indictable offence, such unfavourable inferences may be drawn as appear proper from evidence that, during official questioning in relation to the offence, the defendant failed or refused to mention a fact:
> (a) that the defendant could reasonably have been expected to mention in the circumstances existing at the time, and
> (b) that is relied on in his or her defence in that proceeding. ...

The rationale for this dilution of an accused's right to silence was described during its passage through Parliament as enhancing the early detection of issues and defences which 'will later assist in the efficient management of the trial process' should a suspect be charged with a serious indictable offence and contest those charges. The Attorney-General made assurances that the legislation would remove 'none of the protections afforded to vulnerable people' and cited 'efficient management of the trial processes' and 'common sense'[41] as the key reasons for proposing s 89A:

> I say it is simply a matter of *common sense that a jury should be allowed to consider drawing an unfavourable inference against such a defendant who relies on something at trial the defendant could have mentioned during questioning*, subject to certain safeguards. This bill represents a targeted and balanced response to community concerns and has been the subject of considerable community, police and Government concern ...[42]

However commentators at the time disputed these claims, saying the provision does not promise efficiency gains but rather 'diminish[es] human rights, add[s] to the complexity of criminal justice, and increase[s] the risk of wrongful conviction'.[43]

There are a number of restrictions on the application of s 89A. The provision only applies:

- where the investigating official had reasonable cause to suspect that the defendant had committed the serious indictable offence;[44] and
- the defendant was given a special caution[45] before the defendant's refusal or failure to mention the fact[46] in respect of which the unfavourable inference is sought to be drawn.

The caution must have been given in the presence of a lawyer and the accused must have had the opportunity to consult with the lawyer about the effect and nature of the caution.[47]

---

41 G Smith, New South Wales, Legislative Assembly (*Hansard*), 13 March 2013, 18578.

42 Ibid (emphasis added).

43 D Hamer and G Edmond, 'When You Say Nothing at All: NSW and the Right to Silence', *The Conversation*, 22 March 2013, <http://theconversation.com/when-you-say-nothing-at-all-nsw-and-the-right-to-silence-12962>. See also Dixon and Cowdery, above n 11.

44 *UEA*, s 89A(2)(a).

45 *UEA*, s 89A(9): '*special caution* means a caution given to a person that is to the effect that: (a) the person does not have to say or do anything, but it may harm the person's defence if the person does not mention when questioned something the person later relies on in court, and (b) anything the person does say or do may be used in evidence'.

46 *UEA*, s 89A(2)(b).

47 *UEA*, s 89A(2)(c) and (d).

The provision does not apply to:

- an accused who, at the time of the official questioning, is under 18 years of age; or
- an accused who is incapable of understanding the general nature and effect of a special caution.[48]

And, for all suspects, no unfavourable inference can be drawn:

- if 'evidence of the failure or refusal to mention the fact is the only evidence that the defendant is guilty of the serious indictable offence'.[49]

The provision does not prescribe or limit the nature of the inference which may be drawn. There is limited case law relating to s 89A. In *Hogg*[50] the appellant was charged with sexual assault of a 16-year-old girl. His lawyer was present at the police station and he exercised his right to silence when questioned by police. In evidence at his trial, the appellant denied that he was at the location of the alleged offence at any point on the date the complaint said the offence occurred. He gave further evidence that he maintained his silence at the time of the investigation on legal advice. The trial judge permitted the jury to consider drawing an adverse inference:

> As part of his defence Mr Hogg relies upon his assertion that he was never at The Rocks at any time on 29 July 1988. This was a matter that he did not mention when the allegation was put to him by Detective Huisman and this may, in the words of the caution 'harm his defence'. This is because you may decide that his assertion is untrue and he has since invented this assertion to support his defence. But you may only draw that conclusion if you are satisfied of four things:
>
> i. firstly that the prosecution case being presented at the time he was cautioned was such that it called for an answer; and
> ii. secondly he could have reasonably been expected to mention the matter he now relies on at the time he was cautioned; and
> iii. thirdly that the only sensible reason for not raising the assertion that he was never at The Rocks on 29 July 1988 was that he had not yet thought of it; and
> iv. fourthly, that it is fair and proper to draw such a conclusion …
>
> … You should also take into account that the allegation that was put to Mr Hogg is said to have occurred nearly 28 years prior at the time the police spoke to him. Having considered that matter, you should consider whether Mr Hogg could reasonably have been expected to mention the assertion that he was never at The Rocks on that date; an assertion upon which he now seeks to rely.
>
> If, for example, you think that he had or may have had an answer but he generally relied on legal advice which was given to remain silent (whether or not you think it was reasonable for him to do so) you should not draw any conclusion against him. But if, on the other hand, you are sure that Mr Hogg had no answer and merely decided to hide behind the legal advice that he had been given, you would be entitled to draw a conclusion against him, subject to the directions I have given you.
>
> So, if you are sure there is no good reason for not putting forward in the interview the assertion he now relies upon to the effect that he was never at The Rocks on that date, you are entitled to consider that failure as providing some support for the prosecution case, but you must not convict him wholly or mainly on the strength of it.

48 *UEA*, s 89A(5)(a).
49 *UEA*, s 89A(5)(b).
50 [2019] NSWCCA 323.

The NSW Court of Criminal Appeal held (White JA, with Wright J and Wilson J agreeing) that it was an error for a direction pursuant to s 89A to have been given, consistent with the principles in *Browne v Dunn*.

> 113. The appellant gave as his reason for maintaining silence that he had been advised to do so. There was no issue that he had been so advised. It was therefore for the Crown to establish that his true reason for maintaining silence was not because he had been advised to do so, but because he had no satisfactory explanation to give consistent with innocence. The Crown did not assay that task. No issue should have been left to the jury as to whether an adverse inference could be drawn against the appellant for his refusal to answer questions. The jury should have been directed that because the Crown did not challenge the appellant's explanation that his reason for not responding to questions from the police was that he had been advised not to do so, no adverse inference should be drawn against him.

Fundamentally, counsel for the appellant argued that the s 89A direction:

> was impermissible and should not have been given because it was contrary to the accusatorial process where the appellant was "merely silent". The appellant's submission was that s 89A had no work to do where the accused exercised his or her right of silence. No unfavourable inference could be drawn from an accused's exercising his or her right of silence because that was a fundamental common law right of an accused that could not be displaced, except by express words or necessary intendment.[51]

The court disagreed, and affirmed that the section intended to affect the accused's right to silence.[52]

Section 89A and vulnerable suspects

It is true, as was stated in the second reading speech, that s 89A did not amend 'protections afforded to vulnerable people'[53] in that direct changes were not made to protections to 'vulnerable persons' in custody under Part 9 of *LEPRA* (NSW) and the *Law Enforcement (Powers and Responsibilities) Regulation 2016* (NSW) (*LEPRR* (NSW)).[54] However, this provision may operate to reduce protections afforded to vulnerable persons because it does not import the full definition of 'vulnerable persons' under *LEPRR* (NSW) or provide any special protections for the categories of suspects within this definition.[55] Therefore, suspects from a non-English speaking background, those with impaired intellectual functioning and Aboriginal suspects will all be subject to the provision unless they are 'incapable' of understanding the 'general' nature and effect of the special caution. The only restrictions (in terms of vulnerability) directly relevant to this section are whether the defendant is under the age of 18 or is incapable of understanding the general nature and effect of a special caution.[56] This is significant in the context of the impact that cultural and language differences can have in relation to Aboriginal suspects' understanding and responses to cautions.[57]

51 Ibid [96].

52 Ibid [97].

53 Smith, above n 41, 18578.

54 The protections to 'vulnerable persons' in custody under Part 9 of *LEPRA* (NSW), and Part 3 of *LEPRR* (NSW), in particular, Div 3.

55 Clause 28 of *LEPRR* (NSW) defines vulnerable persons to include children, persons who have impaired intellectual functioning, impaired physical functioning, Aboriginal and Torres Strait Islander people and people who are of non-English speaking background.

56 *UEA*, s 89A(5)(a).

57 Dixon and Cowdery, above n 11, 30-1; and Yehia, above n 18, 2.

An unintended side-effect of the introduction of s 89A is that the section may discourage lawyers' attendance at police stations, given 89A(1) does not apply unless the special caution was given in the presence of an Australian legal practitioner acting for the accused at the time.[58] Whilst non-attendance may ensure that unfavourable inferences cannot drawn against an accused at trial, the unfairness which may arise is that suspects may no longer have available the support and protection which a lawyer can provide at the station or during questioning,[59] particularly for a vulnerable suspect or a suspect facing allegations in relation to a serious or complex matter.

Admissions

> [A]n admission is usually evidence of a very powerful and persuasive kind, well capable of tilting the balance in practically any case.[60]

What is an admission?

An admission is defined in the *UEA* as a 'previous representation' that is:

(a) made by a person who is or becomes a party to a proceeding (including a defendant in a criminal proceeding), and
(b) adverse to the person's interest in the outcome of the proceeding.

The definition thus imports the definition of 'previous representation' and so includes express or implied representations (oral or in writing) and conduct.[61]

The 'classic' confession[62] constitutes an admission. Such an admission was made by Jason Naa, whose case is discussed below, in the context of a police siege in which he said:

> ... come on shoot me. I've already stabbed her.[63]

In *Kadir*,[64] the appellant was charged with acts of serious animal cruelty, allegedly using rabbits as 'live bait' in training racing greyhounds at his property. Animals Australia arranged for someone to pose as a greyhound owner, recording a conversation with the appellant who allegedly made the following admissions:[65]

> [S]he asked about Mr Kadir's training methods. Mr Kadir is alleged to have responded, *"I get 30 live rabbits a week from a guy and I put them in the bullring with the dogs"*. Ms Lynch returned to the Londonderry property on 18 January 2015 where she again spoke with Mr Kadir. On this occasion it is alleged that Mr Kadir stated, *"[y]ou know,*

---

58 *UEA*, s 89A(2)(c).

59 A right provided by s 123 of *LEPRA* (NSW).

60 *Nicholls and Coates* [2005] HCA 1; 219 CLR 196, [196] (Gummow and Callinan JJ, with McHugh J agreeing).

61 See Chapter 8, p 341. While a representation can be inferred from conduct, 'conduct' is not of itself included within the ambit of the definition of 'representation' in the *UEA*. It is clear that, where a representation can be inferred from conduct, it will be considered an 'implied representation', and thus fall within the definition.

62 The terms admission and confession are at times used interchangeably. A confession is an 'admission' and therefore subject to the *UEA* provisions.

63 *Naa* [2009] NSWSC 851; 76 NSWLR 271, [13].

64 [2020] HCA 1.

65 The admissions were ultimately excluded at trial pursuant to *UEA*, s 138. The High Court upheld the decisions of the lower courts to exclude the admissions but held that the approach to s 138(3)(h) was misconceived. For further discussion of s 138, see Chapter 4.

> *this is a coursing sport"*. "Coursing" is the pursuit of game or other animals by dogs.[66] (emphasis added)

The words allegedly said by the appellant were clearly adverse to his interests if admitted at trial.

Admissions may be representations contained in documents, for example, the diary entries made by Kathleen Folbigg's diary.[67] Less inherently inculpatory representations (and in some instances representations which were doubtless intended by their makers to be exculpatory) have also been held to be admissions. This is because the definition of admission is very broad, capturing representations made by an accused[68] which assist the prosecution case by, for example, supporting a prosecution witness's testimony.[69] In *JGW*,[70] the appellant appealed his convictions in relation to child sexual assault offences, the complainant being his son, NW. The appellant's answers in his ERISP to the effect that he resided with NW at the time the offences allegedly took place; that he owned a pornographic movie of the kind mentioned by NW; that the family holidayed at Dunleigh Caravan Park at the end of 1993; and that it had a shower block with cubicles of the kind NW described, were all characterised as admissions by Wood CJ at CL. The basis for so finding was that they 'were relevant, and of advantage to the Crown in presenting its case'[71] and were 'capable of rationally affecting the assessment of the probability of the existence of the facts asserted by [the complainant], in relation to the offences charged'.[72] Therefore, evidence of an accused which corroborates a complainant's account may be considered admissions.

Exculpatory representations

Suspects often make statements in an attempt to exonerate themselves, such as in the case of *Horton*,[73] where the appellant had been convicted of murdering her partner by stabbing him. The Crown led evidence that the police attended the scene a short time after the stabbing and the following exchange took place:

> Constable Evans attended the scene within minutes of the stabbing. After making arrangements for an ambulance, he spoke to Mr O'Hara-Fitzgerald and asked him what had happened. He received the reply: 'She stabbed me.'
>
> Constable Evans asked: 'Who stabbed you?', to which Mr O'Hara-Fitzgerald said: 'Anne did', nodding in the direction of the appellant.
>
> Constable Evans then asked the appellant: 'What happened, Anne?' She replied: '*He fell on the knife*.' He asked: 'Where is the knife now?', to which he received the reply: 'I haven't got it.' Constable Evans pronounced words of arrest and gave her a formal caution.[74]

The court was concerned with whether the answer to police, 'he fell on the knife', was an admission.[75] Horton's statement was not adverse to her interest (and

66 [2020] HCA 1, [30].
67 *Folbigg* [2005] NSWCCA 23, [131]. See Chapter 11.
68 'otherwise than in the course of giving evidence in the proceeding'.
69 *JGW* [1999] NSWCCA 116, [41].
70 [1999] NSWCCA 116.
71 Ibid [41].
72 Ibid [41].
73 (1998) 45 NSWLR 426. See also *Esposito* (1998) 45 NSWLR 442.
74 (1998) 45 NSWLR 426, 427 (emphasis added).
75 Note the court was considering admissibility in the context of the now repealed s 424 of the *Crimes Act 1900* (NSW) which operated to exclude admissions not electronically recorded unless

therefore not an admission) at the time it was made, but, rather, became so in the course of the trial in light of the defence case. Once the appellant raised as her defence at trial that she did not have the requisite intent to murder due to her level of intoxication, the answer became adverse to her interests. It was held that the jury could draw an inference from the answer that 'the appellant had been functioning cognitively within a time proximate to the stabbing, and hence formed the intention required for murder'.[76] *Esposito*[77] involved a similar legal scenario in that Esposito had denied to police being in the location of the crime, but at trial her defence was that she had no recollection of the events on the day of the offence.

In *Esposito*, Wood CJ at CL considered whether denials could be 'admissions', and applied *Horton* to hold that:

> [A] statement that qualifies as an "admission" under the *Evidence Act* is not confined to one that is inculpatory. The statements here were adverse so far as they were relied upon as constituting an implied admission of guilt, even when they were on their face exculpatory.[78]

This approach has been the subject of some controversy.[79] Ultimately, the breadth of the meaning of 'admission' is significant as, once a representation falls within the definition, requirements for its admissibility into evidence (linked to fairness and reliability considerations), such as electronic recording of admissions and exclusionary provisions, are triggered.

ERISPs containing 'mixed statements'

'Mixed statements' refer to statements by accused persons in a record of interview which include both inculpatory and exculpatory statements. In *Nguyen*[80] the accused made admissions to assault charges but also exculpatory statements that were the basis of a claim of self-defence. The High Court explained the admissibility pathway for mixed statements. If the statements are relevant:

> It is through the combined operation of s 81(1) and (2) that the exculpatory aspects of a mixed statement may be admissible under the Uniform Evidence Act. Once admitted they are evidence of the truth of what is there stated, subject to questions of weight.[81]

---

the prosecution could establish that there was a reasonable excuse for not doing so. Section 281 of the *CPA* (NSW) replaced s 424. See below, pp 297-298.

76 (1998) 45 NSWLR 426, 434 (Wood CJ at CL).

77 (1998) 45 NSWLR 442.

78 Ibid 458.

79 In *GH* (2000) 105 FCR 419, [16], Spender J held that a statement which is 'exculpatory on its face is not a representation which is adverse to the interests of the accused', regardless of whether surrounding circumstances provide context which imbue the statement with that quality (for example, demonstrated falsity). The majority in *GH*, while agreeing as to the disposition of the appeal, decided on an alternative basis and stated that they were not calling *Horton* into question: at [90]. The validity of *Horton* was also raised in submissions by the Crown in *Spathis* [2001] NSWCCA 476 but left unresolved by Carruthers AJ at [416]. The High Court refused special leave in relation to this issue: *Spathis* [2002] HCATrans 566. The decision in *Beckett* [2014] NSWCCA 305, [179]-[184] (Beazley P, with RA Hulme and Bellew JJ agreeing) shows *Horton* and *Esposito* continue to be applied in New South Wales. Similarly, in Victoria, see *Nabole* [2014] VSCA 297, [19], Redlich JA citing and quoting *Bertrand* [2008] VSCA 182; 20 VR 222, 229 n 1.

80 [2020] HCA 23.

81 Ibid [21].

Section 81 provides an exception to the hearsay rule to evidence of a previous statement:

> (a) that was made in relation to an admission at the time the admission was made, or shortly before or after that time, and
> (b) to which it is reasonably necessary to refer in order to understand the admission

The court noted that there may be other ways that the statements in an interview may be relevant; however, exculpatory statements in an interview with admissions, will usually satisfy the requirements of s 81(2)(a) and (b).[82]

Whilst mixed statements may be relevant and admissible via this pathway, the *UEA* does not provide an obligation for the prosecution to tender mixed statements.[83] After reviewing the differences in prosecution practice across the jurisdictions the court affirmed that the prosecutor's duty of fairness 'encompasses the presentation of all available, cogent and admissible evidence'.[84] The court went on to conclude that unless it was unfair to the accused to tender a record of interview:

> [W]here an accused provides both inculpatory and exculpatory statements to investigating police officers, it is to be expected that the prosecutor will tender that evidence in the Crown case, unless there is good reason not to do so, if the prosecutorial duty is to be met.[85]

Denials and refusals

The words constituting a refusal to participate in a police investigative procedure remain safe from being considered admissions. It has been held that refusing to participate in an identification parade[86] or a search[87] does not amount to an admission. This is because it has been held in *DPP v Leonard*[88] that the refusal (or consent) does not fall within the meaning of a representation:

> The uttering of words by a person giving or refusing consent is not a representation about something else, it is a fact or event in itself; it is not a representation that the person is consenting or refusing to consent, it itself constitutes the giving or refusing of consent. In the present case, the defendant, by uttering the words "*Go for it. There is nothing in here, mate*" and the word "*Fine*" was not representing that he was consenting to a search of his vehicle; by uttering those words he was actually consenting to a search of his vehicle … the making of such an utterance should not be characterised as a representation about the maker's then state of mind.

Admissions: hearsay exception and restrictions on admission for non-hearsay purpose

Hearsay rule: UEA, ss 81 and 82

Characterisation of a representation as an admission can, depending on the circumstances of the case, also be helpful to the prosecution given that, once it has been established that a representation falls within the definition of an admission,

82 Ibid [22].
83 Ibid [25].
84 Ibid [36].
85 Ibid [41].
86 *Ah-See v Heilpern* [2000] NSWSC 627; 115 A Crim R 1, [44] (Bryson J).
87 *DPP v Leonard* [2001] NSWSC 797.
88 [2001] NSWSC 797, [94] (James J) (emphasis added).

s 81 of the *UEA* operates to provide exceptions to the operation of the hearsay (s 59) and opinion (s 76) rules. As set out above, these exceptions also apply to evidence to which it is reasonably necessary to refer in order to understand the admission made close in time to the admission.[89]

Admissions are only admissible as exceptions to the rules against hearsay and opinion evidence if they are first hand hearsay. That is, the evidence must be 'given by a person who saw, heard or otherwise perceived the admission being made or it is a document in which the admission is made'.[90] Thus where, for instance, an accused said to a police officer on presenting themselves to a police station for questioning 'I did it', the prosecution would be able to lead evidence from the police officer of that admission for the hearsay purpose of proving that the accused committed the crime. On the other hand, if an accused presented to the police station in the company of a friend, and the friend said to the police officer 'She told me she did it', the police officer would not be able to give evidence of the accused's alleged admission for the hearsay purpose of proving the guilt of the accused, because the officer did not see, hear or otherwise perceive the admission being made. Rather, that evidence would need to be given by the friend to whom the admission was allegedly made.

Non-hearsay purpose: UEA, s 60

Section 60(3)[91] expressly excludes s 60(1) and (2), which create an exception to the hearsay rule for hearsay evidence that is relevant for a 'non-hearsay purpose', from applying to evidence of an admission. The effect of s 60(3) is that, if evidence of an admission is admissible for a non-hearsay purpose (but inadmissible for a hearsay purpose), the prosecution cannot, as would be permitted by s 60(1) for non-admission evidence, use the admission as proof of the truth of the admission. Further, it prevents evidence of an admission which is second hand or more remote hearsay from being admitted for a non-hearsay purpose (as pursuant to s 60(2) would otherwise be the case), consistent with s 82.

An example of the operation of the section would be where, for instance, the friend who accompanied the accused to the police station, when called as a witness by the prosecution in the trial of the accused, denied ever having stated to police: 'She told me she did it'. In those circumstances, the prosecution may be entitled to lead evidence from the police officer to whom the friend spoke that the friend made that representation, but only for the purpose of leading it as a prior inconsistent statement going to the credibility of the friend (and thus for the hearsay purpose of proving that the friend did in fact make the representation to police). If, when in the witness box, the friend recanted her statement to police, evidence of her prior and inconsistent statement regarding the accused's confession could not be led from the police officer and then, through s 60, used as evidence of the truth of the confession allegedly made by the accused.[92] If the representation were to be admitted on the basis that it went to the credibility of the friend, it would need to satisfy s 137 of the *UEA* (no easy task, as the High Court noted in *Lee*) and then clear directions would be required under s 136 as to the limited use able to be made of the evidence (that is, restricting it to its non-hearsay purpose).

89 *UEA*, s 81(2)(a).

90 *UEA*, s 82.

91 See Chapter 9, p 401.

92 *Lee* [1998] HCA 60; 195 CLR 594; *Klein* [2007] NSWCCA 206.

Common purpose: UEA, s 87

Section 87 provides for circumstances where a previous representation is taken to be an admission when the representation is made by a third party, for example, representations made on authority or by employees.[93] The provision which is most relevant in a criminal law context is s 87(3)(c), which provides that a previous representation is taken to be an admission by a party, and the court is to admit the representation, if 'the representation was made by the person in furtherance of a common purpose (whether lawful or not) that the person had with the party or one or more persons including the party'.

This provision was considered by the NSW Court of Criminal Appeal in *Higgins*.[94] In that case, the applicant for leave to appeal was convicted of three sexual offences relating to a student at a school where he taught. One of the offences alleged that the applicant anally penetrated the complainant and that this act stopped when Brother Downey entered the room and screamed at the applicant. The complainant gave evidence that Brother Downey drove him home and said to tell his parents 'I was late, I missed the bus, and I fell over and hurt my backside'. The mother also gave evidence, that she recalled Brother Downey saying to her that the complainant 'fell over, hurt his bottom, and I drove him home'. The Crown contended that the two statements by Brother Downey constituted admissions pursuant to s 87. The 'common purpose' identified between the applicant and Brother Downey (to engage the section) was to 'cover up' the commission of the offence. There was no allegation that there was a common purpose in relation to the commission of the sexual offence. The court made it clear that a representation made by a person who shares a common purpose with the party to the litigation is confined to representations made 'in furtherance of' the common purpose alleged – that is, *the* common purpose alleged in those proceedings.[95] It was accepted by the prosecution that there was no common purpose alleged between the applicant and Brother Downey in relation to the offences before the court. The court held that relying on 'a' common purpose to cover up the offence was not a sufficient basis to admit the statements by Brother Downey.[96]

Proof of admissions: UEA, s 88

The standard of proof in determining whether evidence of an admission is admissible[97] is provided in s 88 of the *UEA*, namely, an admission is admissible 'if it is reasonably open [for the court] to find that [an accused] made the admission'. The obvious application of the provision will be where there is some dispute as to who made the alleged admission. An example of where this issue arose is the case of *Hall*[98] where a conversation was recorded by police and the defence disputed that it was reasonably open to find that the alleged admissions were made by the accused. Greg James J ruled that s 88 would exclude the evidence because, among other things, it was difficult to distinguish between the voices participating in the

93 *UEA*, s 87(1)(a) and (b).
94 [2020] NSWCCA 149.
95 Ibid [37].
96 Ibid [39].
97 That is, not as the ultimate standard of proof for the trier of fact.
98 [2001] NSWSC 827.

conversation. The judge rejected an argument propounded by the Crown that the jury might be better able than him to do so.[99]

Exclusion of evidence of admissions against 'third parties': UEA, s 83

Section 83(1) states that s 81 does not prevent the application of the hearsay rule or the opinion rule to evidence of an admission in respect of the case of a third party[100] (that is, a co-accused). This means where two or more co-accused are being tried jointly, the evidence of an admission by an accused is generally not admissible in the case against the co-accused. However, the evidence of an admission by an accused may be admitted in the case against the co-accused, if the co-accused consents.[101]

Consider a scenario in which the accused and the co-accused are both charged with armed robbery. Assume, further, that the accused participated in an ERISP, admitting that he committed the robbery and advancing a defence of claim of right, but also saying that he did the robbery on his own. The starting position is that s 83(1) excludes the accused's admissions in the co-accused's case. Therefore, if the co-accused does not consent, this evidence (which in this example exculpates the co-accused) would not be admissible in his case. However, if the co-accused consents to the evidence of the accused's admissions being used in his case, then the evidence may be admissible pursuant to s 83(2).[102] Consent cannot be given in respect of only part of the evidence (of the admission),[103] thus precluding the possibility of an accused only consenting to the admission of favourable portions of a co-accused's admissions.

Electronically Recording Admissions

Background and importance of recording admissions

The *Fitzgerald Inquiry* in Queensland (1989)[104] and the *Wood Royal Commission* in New South Wales (1997)[105] identified extensive police corruption and misconduct, and found 'verballing'[106] to be common practice. The Fitzgerald Inquiry reported the evidence of former police Inspector Jack Reginald Herbert, who cooperated under an indemnity and frankly exposed the practice:

> Herbert said that although some police would not verbal, there was usually no need to sound out an unknown police officer to see whether he would give false evidence. It was

99 Ibid [29].

100 *UEA*, s 83(4).

101 *UEA*, s 83(2).

102 Where an accused makes admissions which also inculpate the co-accused, this may form the basis of an application for a separate trial. See Chapter 2, where some issues associated with the grounds for separate trials are discussed.

103 *UEA*, s 83(3).

104 *Commission of Inquiry into Possible Illegal Activities and Associated Police Misconduct* (Report, Chair GE Fitzgerald, Queensland, 1989), <http://www.ccc.qld.gov.au/about-the-ccc/the-fitzgerald-inquiry> (Fitzgerald Royal Commission Report).

105 *Royal Commission into the NSW Police Service* (Final Report, Chair J Wood, New South Wales, 1997), <https://www.pic.nsw.gov.au/OtherReportsAndPublications.aspx> (Wood Royal Commission Report).

106 A '*verbal*' refers to 'false evidence given by police that a suspect had confessed or made inculpatory remarks at the time of arrest or during an interview': Wood Royal Commission Report, ibid, Vol 1, xiii.

> just accepted. When a person was arrested police would sit down at the typewriter and "You would make the story up as you went along".[107]

Key issues identified by the Fitzgerald Inquiry which allowed verballing to flourish included a police culture which accepted the practice and the unlikelihood of a police officer being held to account for fabricating admissions:

> There is virtually no risk involved for police in misconduct such as verballing and the chances of success are excellent. Ordinarily, any issue relating to disputed evidence involves a contest between an accused, whose credibility will usually be questionable and who most often will prefer not to enter the witness box, and police officers who support and corroborate each other. Even in blatant cases where lies have been exposed action has seldom been taken against the police concerned.[108]

The Wood Royal Commission reported that the evidence from the inquiry was 'replete' with examples of verballing.[109] The High Court in *Driscoll*[110] acknowledged the temptation of police to fabricate evidence:

> It is very common for an accused person to deny that he made an oral confession which police witnesses swear that he made. The accused has an obvious motive to claim that police testimony of this kind is false. On the other hand it would be unreal to imagine that every police officer in every case is too scrupulous to succumb to the temptation to attempt to secure the conviction of a person whom he believes to be guilty by saying that he has confessed to the crime with which he is charged when in fact he has not done so.[111]

Gleeson CJ, Hayne and Heydon JJ in *Kelly*[112] remarked that disputes in trials relating to unrecorded admissions were not only in relation to fabrication but included 'misunderstanding, misrecollection, coercion, or oppression in a broad sense'. Dixon notes that controversies relating to police interrogation relate not only to police fabricating confessions but also to the inducement of false confessions.[113] Misconduct in grave or even more subtle forms has the potential to affect whether or not proceedings are initiated and continued. If admitted, that evidence has the very real capacity to prejudice the fairness of an accused's trial and, at worst, may lead to a miscarriage of justice.[114]

As noted by the majority in *Kelly*, there are also efficiency concerns in relation to alleged admissions, given that disputes about confessions required a considerable amount of court time to resolve.[115] Further, disputes about confessions were, whether ultimately held to be well founded or not, 'damaging to public confidence in the criminal justice system'.[116] The majority in *McKinney*[117] expressed the desirability for recording admissions to be standard police procedure.

---

107 Fitzgerald Royal Commission Report, above, n 104, 206.
108 Ibid 207.
109 Wood Royal Commission Report, above n 105, Vol 1, 70.
110 [1977] HCA 43; 137 CLR 517.
111 Ibid [25] (Gibbs J).
112 [2004] HCA 12; 218 CLR 216, [25] (Gleeson CJ, Hayne and Heydon JJ).
113 D Dixon, 'Videotaping Police Interrogation' [2008] *UNSWLRS* 28, [1].
114 For example, the conviction of the Mickelberg brothers in Western Australia in 2002 in which police later admitted to fabrication: see R Dioso-Villa, 'Without Legal Obligation: Compensating the Wrongfully Convicted in Australia (Revealing the Impact & Aftermath of Miscarriages of Justice)' (2012) 75 *Albany Law Review* 1329, 1346.
115 [2004] HCA 12; 218 CLR 216, [25]; and Dixon, above n 113, [10].
116 [2004] HCA 12; 218 CLR 216, [25].
117 [1991] HCA 6; 171 CLR 468, 473-4 (Mason CJ, Deane, Gaudron and McHugh JJ), 497 (Toohey J).

In a number of jurisdictions in Australia police began routinely electronically recording interviews, as a matter of practice, in relation to serious offences in the early 1990s.[118] This was followed by a shift towards introducing legislation requiring admissions in more serious cases to be recorded as a prerequisite to being admitted into evidence at trial. In New South Wales, the first such provision was enacted in 1995.[119] The second reading speech, introducing the Bill to Parliament, clearly acknowledged the history of misconduct and made clear that the reasons underpinning the legislation included deterring unfair and improper police behaviour and deterring the making of unfair and false allegations.[120]

Judicial criticism of police conduct echoed these legislative responses. Further, as Kirby J (dissenting) acknowledged in *Kelly*,[121] courts have a major role to play in protecting societal values and the integrity of the justice system in this context:

> 145. … [I]n Australia and elsewhere, to the problem of contested confessions and admissions to officials and "police verbals" must be given due weight. But so must the generic problem to which, in their differing ways, the legislative texts respond. …
>
> 146. As Slicer J points out in his dissenting opinion below, the problem presented by such confessions and admissions was not only that of protecting the innocent accused against wrongful conviction. … "*the protection of the system* itself by ensuring that the repression of crime through the conviction of the guilty is done in a way which reflects our fundamental values as a society". Because, in Australia, such protection lies substantially in the hands of the judiciary, in ascertaining the meaning of legislative prescriptions such as those in the Act, it is essential that real weight should be given to the serious problem for the administration of criminal justice that such legislation addresses.

Statutory requirements for electronically recording admissions

The statutory provisions in Australian jurisdictions mandating electronic recording of admissions made to police are not within the *UEA*. They are spread across different legislation and they lack uniformity in relation to the circumstances in which admissions must be recorded.[122] In New South Wales, the law is governed by s 281 of the *CPA* (NSW), and in particular by s 281(2).

> **281. Admissions by suspects**
>
> (1) This section applies to an admission:
>
> (a) that was made by an accused person who, at the time when the admission was made, was or could reasonably have been suspected by an investigating official[123] of having committed an offence, and

118 D Dixon and G Travis, 'Interrogating Images, Audio-visually Recorded Police Questioning of Suspects' (Institute of Criminology Series No 23, 2007), 2.

119 *Crimes Act 1900* (NSW), s 424A (replaced by *CPA* (NSW), s 281).

120 New South Wales, Legislative Council (*Hansard*), 24 May 1995, 117, referring to the reasons underpinning the Criminal Law Review's report recommendation that police interviews be electronically recorded: '1. To provide the courts with a reliable account of statements made by persons accused of crime whilst in police custody; 2. To provide an objective means of resolving disputes about the conduct and substance of police interviews; 3. To deter and/or prevent the use of unfair practices by the police prior to, during, and after interviews; 4. To deter the making of unfair and false allegations of improper behaviour by police'.

121 [2004] HCA 12; 218 CLR 216.

122 See *Crimes Act 1914* (Cth), s 23V (applies also in the ACT: s 23A(6)); *Evidence Act 2001* (Tas), s 85A; *Crimes Act 1958* (Vic), s 464H; *Police Administration Act 1978* (NT), ss 142, 143.

123 Defined in *CPA* (NSW), s 281(4): '*investigating official* means: (a) a police officer (other than a police officer who is engaged in covert investigations under the orders of a superior), or (b) a person appointed by or under an Act (other than a person who is engaged in covert investigations

(b) that was made in the course of official questioning,[124] and
(c) that relates to an indictable offence, other than an indictable offence[125] that can be dealt with summarily without the consent of the accused person.

(2) Evidence of an admission to which this section applies is not admissible unless:
(a) there is available to the court:
(i) a tape recording[126] made by an investigating official of the interview in the course of which the admission was made, or
(ii) if the prosecution establishes that there was a reasonable excuse[127] as to why a tape recording referred to in subparagraph (i) could not be made, a tape recording of an interview with the person who made the admission, being an interview about the making and terms of the admission in the course of which the person states that he or she made an admission in those terms, or
(b) the prosecution establishes that there was a reasonable excuse as to why a tape recording referred to in paragraph (a) could not be made. …

If the three requirements set out at s 281(1)(a) are not satisfied and the interview was not recorded then, generally, the admission will not be admissible. One exception, provided for in s 281(2), applies where the prosecution can establish that there was a *reasonable excuse* for not having recorded the original admission but the police conduct a 'second interview' with the accused in relation to the making and terms of the admission. This might occur where a suspect refuses to have the questioning electronically recorded or where a police officer is taken by surprise by admissions made by a person.[128] Even if police do not conduct a second interview, the legislation provides a final *reasonable excuse*[129] option that might permit admitted evidence of an unrecorded admission.

Who is a suspect?

There may be rare occasions in which a person volunteers a confession to a crime without any evidence to suggest they are a suspect. In such circumstances, an investigating officer could not have reasonably suspected the person had committed the offence and there is no legal obligation to electronically record the admission. Such spontaneous confessions occurred in *Taouk*[130] where the appellant

under the orders of a superior) whose functions include functions in respect of the prevention or investigation of offences prescribed by the regulations'.

124 Defined in *CPA* (NSW), s 281(4): '*official questioning* means questioning by an investigating official in connection with the investigation of the commission or possible commission of an offence'.

125 *CPA* (NSW), s 281(1)(c), means that admissions that relate to summary offences and 'Table 1' offences need not be recorded to be admissible unless they *relate to* an indictable offence. See *DPP v Farr* [2001] NSWSC 3; 118 A Crim R 399, [35] (Smart AJ) for an example of admissions made to goods in custody and possession of cannabis charges (summary offences) that would 'relate to' a charge of supply (indictable offence) as they would have significant probative value in relation to the trial of the supply offence.

126 *CPA* (NSW), s 281(4): '*tape recording* includes: (a) audio recording, or (b) video recording, or (c) a video recording accompanied by a separately but contemporaneously recorded audio recording'.

127 *CPA* (NSW), s 281(4): '*reasonable excuse* includes: (a) a mechanical failure, or (b) the refusal of a person being questioned to have the questioning electronically recorded, or (c) the lack of availability of recording equipment within a period in which it would be reasonable to detain the person being questioned'.

128 *LMW* [1999] NSWSC 1128.

129 *CPA* (NSW), s 281(2)(b).

130 [2005] NSWCCA 155; 154 A Crim R 69.

attended Burwood police station in the early hours of the morning on the day of the deaths of his wife and brother-in-law. According to the constable on duty:

> I approached the counter and the defendant (that is, the accused) said to me 'I want to report a disturbance at my house.'
> I said: 'What's happened?'
> He said: 'I have just shot someone at my house. I had an argument with my brother and he had a gun. I took it off him and I fired a few shots'.[131]

Taouk was subsequently charged with, and convicted at trial of, their murders. On appeal the NSW Court of Criminal Appeal held that there was no basis for reasonably suspecting the appellant had committed an offence and so no requirement to electronically record his admissions.[132]

In an earlier case of *LMW*,[133] the accused, a young person,[134] made admissions to police when they attended his house following the drowning death of a child. Consequently, the admissions were unrecorded and made without caution:

> Sergeant Foster [introduced himself] to the accused's mother as officers from the Macquarie Fields Detectives' Office, he asked the child's mother: *"Do you have a son named [LMW]?"* He received an affirmative reply and the accused then came to the front door where the police officer had introduced himself. This conversation then occurred, according to Constable French (and for the purposes of this judgment I include the various paragraph numbers to be found in the relevant statement made by Constable French):
>
> *"(Paragraph 13) '[LMW] do you know Corey from across the street?' He said, 'No.' The young child's mother said, 'Little Corey?' [Constable French] said, 'Yes.' She said 'You know Corey.' The young child said, 'Yes.' [Constable French] said 'When was the last time you saw Corey?' He said, 'Yesterday.' [Constable French] said 'Where were you when you saw Corey?' He said, 'I was riding my skateboard.'*
>
> *(Paragraph 14) [Constable French] then said to the young child, 'Did you see him any other time yesterday?' He said, 'No.' [Constable French] said 'Do you know [GW2] from next door to Corey?' He said, 'Yes.' [Constable French] said 'Did you tell her that you saw Corey at the creek?' He said, 'No.' [Constable French] said 'She has told me you told her that.' He said 'I didn't tell her, I told [GW1].' [Constable French] said 'Her sister?' He said, 'No, she's Corey's sister.' [Constable French] said 'Did you tell her that you saw Corey at the creek?' He said 'No. Ah, I saw Corey with two boys in the bush, that's what I told her.'*
>
> *(Paragraph 15) [Constable French] then said to the young child 'The girls told me that you said he was at the creek.' He said 'The boys told me they were going to the creek.' [Constable French] said 'Are you fibbing?' He said, 'Sure, I pushed him. What do you think' and the young child became upset and walked away. [Constable French] said to the young person's mother, 'Corey drowned in the river yesterday afternoon.' She said, 'Oh no'. [Constable French] said 'The only person that we have been told that knew he was there is [LMW].'*
>
> *(Paragraph 16) The young child's mother said 'Corey (sic), come back here' and the young child returned to the front door and said, 'Yeah, I pushed him in the creek. So what.' The young child's mother said '[LMW], don't be cheeky.'*
>
> *(Paragraph 17) [Constable French] then said to the young child, 'What happened?' He said, 'Well, the two boys kicked and punched him and I told them to stop, and he followed me down to the creek. He wouldn't go away and kicked me like he did last year so I pushed him in the creek. When I pushed him in I ran and*

---

131 Ibid [39].

132 Ibid [73] (James J, with whom Hislop J agreed).

133 [1999] NSWSC 1128.

134 A young person is a person under the age of 18 years.

> *got help.' [Constable French] said 'Why didn't you tell me that at first?' He said 'I don't want to get in trouble.'*[135]

Police gave evidence that the officer went to the young person's home 'in effect to track the deceased's movements and to find out who was the last to see the young child'.[136] On appeal, the Crown contended that s 281 did not apply because at the time the accused was not suspected, nor could he reasonably have been suspected, of having committed an offence. Studdert J agreed.[137] LMW subsequently refused to participate in a record of interview at the police station and the court held this refusal constituted a reasonable excuse for not taping an interview recording the terms and making of the admission.[138]

In the course of 'official questioning'

'Official questioning' is defined in s 281(4) of the *CPA* (NSW), essentially linking investigative interviews to the commission of a possible offence. The High Court decision in *Kelly*[139] illustrates the importance of the way in which the term is interpreted with respect to the requirement that police electronically record admissions.

In *Kelly*, the appellant allegedly told police in November 1999 that he (with his co-accused, Marlow) was involved in the murder of a man who went missing in 1990, and asked police about an indemnity in return for his assistance. After the body was found in March 2000, the appellant, in an electronically recorded interview, accepted that he had made a confession, but said the original confession was false and explained to police why he made the original confession. This second interview, retracting the confession, ended at 9.17pm. After the interview, the appellant made some phone calls, and was charged, fingerprinted and photographed. It was then proposed that the appellant go to the Launceston Hospital for various forensic procedures to be carried out. Moments before getting into the police car, the appellant allegedly said the vital statement which constituted the admission which was the subject of the appeal:

> Sorry about the interview – no hard feelings, I was just playing the game. I suppose I shouldn't have said that, I suppose you will make notes of that as well.[140]

Police did not make notes of the statement, nor did they record a further interview putting to the appellant what he had allegedly just said. Police reports of the time lapse between the conclusion of the interview at 9.17pm and the alleged admission ranged between 30 minutes to an hour. The majority of the High Court (Gleeson CJ, Hayne and Heydon JJ) noted:

> 45. A person may make admissions during a period in which police officers are conducting official questioning without those admissions being responsive to any particular question. This can arise in two ways. First, an answer proffered may simply be quite unresponsive or unrelated to the particular question. Secondly, deliberately or fortuitously, the persons asking the questions may fall silent, and the person who is with them may, whether because of a desire to fill the silence or for some other reason, confess. The legislation does not in terms require that the statement be made 'in response to a question put' …

135 [1999] NSWSC 1128, [3].
136 Ibid [11].
137 Ibid [13].
138 Ibid [13].
139 [2004] HCA 12; 218 CLR 216.
140 Ibid [14].

> [T]he words "in the course of" do not require that there be any causal connection between the admission and the official questioning. Thus "a monologue in response to a general enquiry about what happened" [*Donnelly* (1997) 96 A Crim R 432, 437 (Hidden J)] has been held to be in the course of official questioning for the purposes of s 85 of the *Evidence Act 1995* (NSW) and an answer volunteered by the person being questioned is in the course of questioning even though it is not directly responsive to any question [*Julin* [2000] TASSC 50, [12] (Evans J)].

The majority also considered when official questioning is deemed to have come to an end. Counsel for the appellant, in urging the court to find that the statement was made 'in the course of official questioning', proposed a number of broad interpretations of the phrase. One of the more conservative interpretations proposed by counsel for the appellant was that 'in the course of' official questioning meant 'arising out of' or 'as a result of' official questioning.[141] The majority of the court rejected this interpretation:

> 52. *The expression 'in the course of official questioning" ... marks out a period of time running from when questioning commenced to when it ceased ...*
>
> 53. *In this matter "the course of official questioning" ended when Detective Sergeant Lopes ceased to ask questions and said at 9.17pm: "[W]e'll conclude the interview".* Other activities of the appellant not related to official questioning and other police procedures not involving questioning then took place. *No further question was asked which triggered the impugned statement. To treat the impugned statement as having been made in the course of official questioning would be to ignore the statutory language.* The impugned statement in this case is in the same position as the statement made by the accused in *R v Julin* where, after questioning had ceased, the accused had been arrested and cautioned, and driven half a kilometre to the scene of the crime during which time no conversation took place between him and the police officer: "[t]he official questioning of the accused concluded prior to the car trip when he was arrested and cautioned ...".[142] (emphasis added)

The majority held that the statement was not made 'in the course of official questioning', and thus held that the mandatory recording provision did not apply.[143] As a result, a narrow and literal statutory interpretation was adopted, limiting the obligation to record admissions to the period between when the interview formally commenced and when it formally ceased. This narrow interpretation was arrived at despite the majority acknowledging that the object of the provision was to address police misconduct, including the fabrication of admissions.[144]

In dissent, McHugh J and Kirby J each held that the section should have applied and the evidence should have been rejected. However, both agreed with the majority that the appeal should be dismissed, applying the proviso. McHugh J and Kirby J both preferred a broader interpretation of the phrase 'in the course of official questioning'. McHugh J adopted a purposive approach, holding that the section should be interpreted in light of the mischief it was aimed to address, including 'protect[ing] the rights of accused persons during a period when their rights are vulnerable by reason of the mistaken recollection or lies of police officers':[145]

141 Ibid [44].

142 Gleeson CJ, Hayne and Heydon JJ.

143 The High Court was considering the term 'in the course of official questioning' in the context of the Tasmanian mandatory recording provision: *Criminal Law (Detention and Interrogation) Act 1995* (Tas), s 8.

144 [2004] HCA 12; 218 CLR 216, [22]-[27].

145 Ibid [96].

> 106. Given the purpose of the section, there is no difficulty in construing the words "confession or an admission … made in the course of official questioning" as referring to a confession or admission *made in connection with* police questioning. Nor do I think there is any difficulty in holding that the section applies to any confession or admission that is made in response to an intimation that the officer intends to question the suspect. (emphasis added)

Kirby J, also preferring a purposive approach, adopted the broadest interpretation of all:

> 170. … I would conclude that the "course of official questioning" *begins, in the case of an accused person who is or ought reasonably have been suspected of an offence* and who is later tried for a serious offence, when that reasonable suspicion arose, or ought reasonably to have arisen, in the minds of the police officers detaining that person. It is not terminated or interrupted by silence on the part of the police officer. It includes responsive or unresponsive statements made whilst the accused is detained by the police officer in connection with the investigation of the commission, or the possible commission, of an offence. The official questioning is not concluded at the termination of any formal interview, the termination by police of video recording or other decisions wholly within the power of police officers. The termination only occurs when the investigation of the offence whilst the accused person is in police detention *is terminated either by the release of that person or by the action of police in bringing the accused to a judicial officer* upon a charge laid by the police officer concerning an offence. (citations omitted, emphasis added)

The phrase 'in the course of official questioning' was further considered in the context of two very different circumstances of police conversations with suspects in *Sharp*[146] and *Naa.*[147]

In *Sharp*, the accused was on trial on a charge of accessory before the fact to murder. Police were aware before talking to the accused that the deceased had been staying with her and her co-accused shortly before his remains were found. Police were also aware that the accused had given an account of the disappearance of the deceased to her employer.[148] Police spoke to the accused at her place of employment and she denied knowledge of the offence. They took the accused to her unit so that she could be present at the search. At trial, the prosecution sought to lead evidence, under objection, that while in the police car just before the search the following conversation, not electronically recorded, took place:

> 7. … Bennett: How are you doing?
> Accused: Okay, I just don't understand why all the guns.
> Bennett: This is a dangerous situation, we're investigating a very violent murder, we're not going to take any risks and you can't tell us whether he is in there or not.
> Accused: I know it's a serious matter.
> Bennett: We're about to do a search warrant here, before we get in there is there anything at all you want to tell me about before we go in.
>
> The accused, without replying put her head in her hands and commenced to cry. The conversation continued:
>
> Bennett: Are you okay, what is scaring you?
> Accused: No, I'm not.
> Bennett: Whatever is scaring you, whatever is scaring you, we can help.
> Accused: No you can't, you don't know him, he's going to kill me, he's going to kill my family.

146 [2003] NSWSC 1117, 143 A Crim R 344.
147 [2009] NSWSC 851; 76 NSWLR 271.
148 [2003] NSWSC 1117, 143 A Crim R 344, [4].

> Bennett: We can give you protection.
> Accused: You don't understand.
> *Bennett: I think I do, but I'd rather you tell me what did happen.*
> *Accused: Brad and him had a fight and Brad hit him with a hammer.*
> Bennett: *Where?*
> *Accused: Over the head.*
> *Bennett: Yes, but whereabouts?*
> *Accused: In the flat, in there.* (emphasis added)

Howie J admitted the evidence and held that the conversation did not occur in the 'course of official questioning'. In doing so, it was held that the court is to make an objective assessment of the circumstances in determining whether a conversation is 'in the course of official questioning':

> 17. The policy behind the legislation is, as I have stated, obvious. It is an attempt to limit the opportunities both for a police officer to fabricate the making of an admission by a suspect …
>
> 19. But it seems to me that, because the legislation does not require that all admissions be electronically recorded, police should be able to determine with some degree of certainty what is and what is not "official questioning" for the purposes of the section and thus know when it is that they should takes steps to have a conversation electronically recorded to preserve any admission made by the suspect. However, where a police officer engages a suspect in conversation on any matter touching the investigation of an offence without recording the conversation, the officer takes a real risk that a court will find it to be official questioning regardless of the belief of the officer on that subject …
>
> 20. I hesitate to attempt to give any more meaning to the words of the section that arise from the definitions contained in it and the policy behind the legislation. *But the word used is "questioning" and it seems to me that it at least implies that the police officer is attempting to elicit from the person a response that the officer foresaw might provide information relevant to the investigation of the commission of an offence or possible offence, or be to the person's prejudice in that regard.* I would be prepared to find in an appropriate case that statements made by the officer to the suspect might amount to "questioning" even though there may be no question asked. However, the mere fact that an admission occurs in response to a question or statement made by a police officer cannot retroactively convert the conversation into "official questioning" if it did not fall within the definition at the time the admission was made.
>
> 21. I wish to emphasise that, in my opinion, *the court is required to make an objective assessment of the circumstances surrounding the making of the alleged admission in determining both whether it was made during official questioning and whether there is a reasonable excuse in failing to electronically record it. If my view of official questioning is correct, it would follow that, if the police officer did not foresee that a response might be given to the statement or question made to the suspect but ought to have done so, the conversation would amount to "official questioning".* To that extent the conduct of the police officer is subject to the court's review so far as the admissibility of any admission allegedly made by the accused is concerned.
>
> 22. Nothing that I have said in this judgment should be taken as a green light for police to ignore the provision or return to the type of practices that caused Parliament to enact it. The legislature might find that a point in time has been reached when it is opportune to reconsider the provision and further limit the opportunities for disputes to arise about admissions, as occurred before me. This is particularly so given the advance of technology for recording the human voice since the section was enacted.
>
> 23. … It was not inappropriate, in my opinion, for Detective Bennett to speak to the accused at the scene in order to see how she was and to attempt to alleviate her concerns when she expressed her fears. I do not believe that he intended by anything he said, to elicit an admission from her or to obtain information beneficial to their investigation of

> the murder. Nor should the officer have reasonably foreseen that an admission might be made as a result of what he said to the accused.
>
> 24. I acknowledge that the intention of the police officer cannot take a conversation outside the scope of the provision if otherwise it falls within the meaning of "official questioning". But in this case, I am satisfied that the intention of the officer was not to question the accused at all but rather to allay her fears. I accept his evidence that the admission made by the accused was, so far as he was concerned, unresponsive to the statement made by him that occasioned it.
>
> 26. … For these reasons I admitted the evidence of the conversation between the accused and Detective Bennett. However, I should note that, in my view, the facts of this case were at the very margin of the circumstances in which the provision would not operate to exclude the evidence. (emphasis added)

Naa[149] involved admissions allegedly made during a police siege. The accused was charged with the murder of his former partner and there was no dispute that the accused caused her death by stabbing. The accused, having armed himself with a knife and a piece of wood, entered the unit in which he had been living with the deceased. Police were called and a siege resulted which lasted for approximately three hours. The issues at trial were whether the accused had the necessary intent to establish his guilt for murder and, if so, whether substantial impairment was available as a partial defence to murder. Counsel for the accused argued unsuccessfully that the admissions were inadmissible under s 281.[150] In his judgment in relation to the admissibility of the admissions, Howie J described the admissions made during the siege:

> 12. The first police officers on the scene were Constables McCarthy and Knight. They were in a patrol car at about 12.07am when they received two messages. … When they arrived at the scene, they saw the accused waving two knives, one in each hand. This was at about 12.08am.
>
> 13. Both police officers exited their vehicle and drew their pistols pointing them toward the accused. Both called on him to throw down the knives. The accused said, *"Shoot me. Come on shoot me. I've already stabbed her. Its not gonna matter. Just shoot me"*. Similar exchanges continued for a short time, the police calling upon the accused to drop the knives, and he stating that he had killed the deceased and he wanted to be shot …
>
> 17. A conversation ensued between the two during which they exchanged first names. McCarthy said, "Put down the knives Jason, I want to help you." The accused said, "No you don't. You're lying. You've got on the blue uniform and you lie. *You're here because I stabbed her, you're here because I stabbed her.*" McCarthy said, "Yes, you are right that is why we were called here. But now I want to talk with you and find out what is happening with you." The accused said, "She deserved it, I am sick of this shit. Six years". (emphasis added)

Further admissions to stabbing the victim were made in the context of Constable McCarthy and the accused talking about the deceased and his children while the constable tried to encourage him to disarm.

Howie J ruled that Naa's comments were not made in the 'course of official questioning'; rather, they were made in the context of the negotiations designed to end the siege. Thus, s 281 did not apply to the statements:

> 78. … [A]s soon as they [McCarthy and her partner] arrived at the scene they were confronted with the accused armed with two knives and acting in an aggressive manner towards

149 [2009] NSWSC 851; 76 NSWLR 271.

150 It was also argued that the admissions were inadmissible as they were made without caution (s 138) and pursuant to s 90.

them. It is clear that from this point they had no intention or purpose other than to try to get the accused to disarm and in the meantime to protect themselves and others from him.

79. The conversation between McCarthy and the accused could not be further from an interrogation of a suspect by a police officer, even an informal one at the scene of a crime. First the accused was armed and committing a serious offence at the time by his threatening conduct to the two officers. Secondly the accused was at time attempting to have the police shoot him. Thirdly both officers were armed with weapons trained on the accused. Fourthly McCarthy was seriously considering whether she would need to shoot the accused and at one stage had her finger squeezing the trigger. Fifthly McCarthy was not seeking to find out information from the accused but to build some rapport with him so that she could gain his trust with the ultimate purpose of having him drop his weapons. *This was negotiation not interrogation. I accept that the subjective purpose of the officer engaging with a suspect might not be decisive as to whether the officer is involved in "official questioning" but I believe it is relevant.* Sixthly this was a "police operation" in response to a "critical situation" as Chief Inspector Winmill described it. The concern was to keep the accused talking in order to secure the safety of himself, police and others.

80. In my opinion s 281 does not apply to the admissions allegedly made by the accused at the scene of the stabbing. (emphasis added)

Reasonable excuse

Section 281(4) provides a non-exhaustive definition of 'reasonable excuse' which includes mechanical failure and lack of availability of recording equipment within the time which is reasonable to detain a person. If the accused refuses to be interviewed,[151] or to be recorded while being interviewed, there is no doubt that this is a 'reasonable excuse'. In *LMW*, discussed above, it was held that there was a reasonable excuse for not recording the admissions because the officer did not go to LMW's home suspecting that he would make any admissions and he was taken by surprise by the admissions.[152] In relation to the unavailability of a second interview by police regarding the making and terms of the admission by LMW, the fact that the young person refused to be interviewed further was considered a reasonable excuse.[153] Counsel for the accused made the argument, seeking compliance with s 424A,[154] that:

> [T]he section required, even where there was a refusal to be interviewed generally, that an attempt to make a more limited interview remained necessary under the section. That is to say, where a person refuses to be interviewed at large the police should persist in seeking a tape recorded interview for the limited purpose of having recorded only the admissions previously made orally.[155]

151 See, eg, *Doklu* [2010] NSWCCA 309, with Macfarlan JA (with whom Hall and Simpson JJ agreed) affirming the position that a general refusal to be interviewed following the making of unrecorded admissions is sufficient to constitute a reasonable excuse for not making a recording about the making and terms of the admission. In *Schiavini* [1999] NSWCCA 165, Studdert J considered whether options should be put to an accused in relation to the manner of the recording and questioned whether a refusal to be interviewed by 'audio and visual recording' constituted a reasonable excuse in circumstances where an 'audio-only' recording was not offered. His Honour held that, 'h[a]ving regard to the object intended to be served by s 424A, prudence requires that any interviewing officer explain to a person being interviewed in relation to an indictable offence the alternative forms of "*tape recording*" available. It is conceivable that a person being interviewed may be prepared to be interviewed by way of audio recording but not by way of video recording'.

152 [1999] NSWSC 1128, [18].

153 For example, *Walsh* [2003] NSWSC 1115.

154 *Crimes Act 1900* (NSW) s 424A. This section preceded *CPA* (NSW), s 281(2)(b).

155 [1999] NSWSC 1128, [21].

Studdert J gave the submission 'anxious consideration' but rejected the approach, holding that 'the submission reads into the section more than it requires'.[156]

In finding a reasonable excuse not to have recorded the admissions in *Sharp*,[157] Howie J stated:

> 25. … [I]t was unrealistic and unreasonable to expect that the police officer would, in the course of the conversation, realise that it was official questioning. … It has to be accepted as a matter of common sense, that not all conversations with suspected persons will amount to "official questioning" and it is impracticable to require that police officers be in a position to record any statement made to them by a suspect howsoever it might occur.

Howie J indicated in *Naa* that, even if s 281 was ruled to apply to negotiations, he would have found that a reasonable excuse nevertheless existed for not electronically recording the admissions, given the police were preoccupied with protecting themselves and others involved with the siege.[158] His Honour further held that had s 281 applied he would also have found that there was a reasonable excuse for the failure of the police to have a recording of the accused adopting the admissions said to have been made by him at the scene: *CPA* (NSW), s 281(2)(b). Howie J held that there was a reasonable excuse for not so doing because it was 'obvious that the accused determined not to answer questions about anything that occurred'.[159]

The validity of this reasoning is questioned, for two reasons. One, particular to the case of *Naa*, is that the interview stretched over some 396 questions. It was not until question 350 that the interviewing officer even started to approach the topic of why it was that police attended the residence of the accused on the night of the siege. Howie J stated:

> 93. … [I]t was in my opinion a matter for the police officer as to how he structured the interview. He said that it was his practice to ask about admissions late in the interview after having the accused give his account of the incident. That was an approach that was reasonably open to him.

Another case dealing with 'reasonable excuse' was *Nicholls and Coates*[160] where the High Court held, by a 4:3 majority, that there was no reasonable excuse for failing to record admissions made during a toilet break in a recorded interview. It is important to note that the decision in *Nicholls and Coates* did not overturn the decision in *Kelly* as it related to the meaning of 'in the course of official questioning'.[161] However, it is interesting to note that the majority of the High Court in this case adopted a purposive interpretation of the relevant definition. McHugh J held on this issue as follows:

> 103. The natural meaning of "interview" in s 570D is the entirety of a discussion between a police officer and a suspect carried out on a particular day for the purpose of eliciting statements from the suspect concerning the commission of a "serious offence". It is

156 Ibid [22].

157 [2003] NSWSC 1117; 143 A Crim R 344.

158 *Naa* [2009] NSWSC 851; 76 NSWLR 271, [84].

159 When the allegations of the offence were put to the appellant, he repeated a number of times 'I don't wish to discuss it': ibid [34].

160 [2005] HCA 1; 219 CLR 196. This was an appeal from the WA Court of Criminal Appeal and was concerned with the *Criminal Code* (WA), s 570D.

161 On the impact of *Nicholls and Coates* on *Kelly*, see *Bryant* [2011] NSWCCA 26, [147] (Howie AJ): 'The terms of s 281 are similar to those that were considered by the High Court in *Kelly* and this Court should follow the majority in that decision. There is nothing in *Nichols* to overturn the interpretation of "in the course of official questioning" as defined in *Kelly*, being the formalised interview that had occurred before the appellant was delivered to the Sergeant in her role as custody manager'.

unlikely that the Legislature in using the term intended it to mean each separate question and answer or statement made on a particular occasion, so that each such question and answer or statement constituted an "interview". It seems absurd to think that the Legislature intended the occasion of Coates' interrogation to constitute at least four separate interviews, consisting of two videotaped interviews and two unrecorded interviews during the toilet breaks.

104. A purposive construction also supports interpreting "interview" to mean the entirety of a discussion between a police officer and a suspect carried out on a particular day for the purpose of eliciting statements from the suspect concerning the commission of a "serious offence". Such a construction assists in having a record of the entire discussion between the police officer and the accused on a particular day at a particular place instead of records of parts of the discussion. In accordance with the policy of the section, it also reduces – although it cannot eliminate – the occasions for disputes between accused persons and police officers as to what was said in "interviews", particularly interviews at police stations. A purposive construction also provides an incentive to police officers to have off-camera admissions recorded or at all events referred to when recording resumes.

105. Hence, by interpreting "interview" to cover all exchanges between Coates and the police while he was under caution, s 570D applies to the times when filming was suspended. Because Coates did not withhold consent to the entire series of exchanges being videotaped, his refusal to consent to some of the exchanges being videotaped (if he did) did not fall within the meaning of "reasonable excuse" as defined in s 570D(4)(c).

Gummow and Callinan JJ,[162] in paying steadfast regard to the policy behind the provision, noted that the purpose of the legislation could easily be frustrated by claims of reasonable excuse based on police not *initiating* the unrecorded interview. Kirby J reiterated the importance of contemporaneously putting unrecorded admissions to the accused in a recorded form:[163]

220. The fact that, in some circumstances, the accused might be upset by the police immediately repeating an inculpating statement made off-camera as soon as possible thereafter (and certain risks associated with that course) is less significant than the desirability of laying to rest, as far as possible, disputes such as have now arisen in *Kelly* and in this case. The accused will be more than upset if the alleged conversation is raised years later at a trial, without contemporaneous notes and in circumstances (as here) of sharp contest. Parliament has now spoken on the matter. And the general purpose of Parliament in these provisions of the Code is to put an end to contested police "verbals". The construction preferred by McHugh J and Gummow and Callinan JJ has that effect. With respect, the construction preferred by Hayne and Heydon JJ perpetuates the very mischief that the provisions of the Code were intended to prevent.

Could the legislation be amended to better achieve its intended purpose?

The policy behind the electronic recording of official questioning is to reduce the incidence of fabrication and the frequency of disputes in relation to the admis-

162 [2005] HCA 1; 219 CLR 196, [152].

163 Note ibid [219] where Kirby J stated: 'The alleged admissions were not put on the record immediately after the break in the recording. As a matter of law, they did not have to be, under the Code, in order to be admissible at trial. But could there have been a safer and fairer way to ensure transparency of the process that ensued and to demonstrate the integrity of the police conduct than to take that course?'. The construction of the WA provision did not require the admissions to be read back to the accused and recorded, but there is a clear desirability in doing so, as so expressed. Section 281(2)(a) of the *CPA* (NSW) requires a 'second interview' to be recorded with the accused in relation to the making and terms of the admission unless there is a reasonable excuse for not doing so, as outlined above.

sibility of alleged admissions. For a number of reasons, however, it may be questioned as to whether the section is adequately achieving its intended purpose.

It is evident that the narrow interpretation of 'official questioning' adopted in *Kelly* has required the courts to determine the purpose of the conversation or questioning by police when determining whether or not it constitutes official questioning, as required by *CPA* (NSW), s 281(1) (that is, to allay the fears of the suspect in *Sharp* or a negotiation in the case of *Naa*). Perhaps the policy behind the provision, being to curb misconduct and reduce disputes, may be better achieved if recording were required not according to whether it related to official questioning, but rather whether the person being questioned was a suspect.[164] Such an approach would be consistent with the broad definition given to detention during investigation that permits questioning. The definition obligates the provision of strict custodial rights in a wider range of situations than just arrest. The same breadth applied to police questioning would operate similarly to enhance the legislative purposes of mandatory electronic recording. This approach is consistent with the recommendations of the Australian Law Reform Commission (ALRC). In 2006 the ALRC[165] suggested the basis of a uniform approach between all jurisdictions within Australia would be to follow the Victorian provision. This avoids reliance on 'in the course of official questioning' to define the obligation to record, as set out by the ALRC in its report:

> 10.44 … [Section] 464H of the *Crimes Act 1958* (Vic), requires exclusion of all admissions made to investigating officials and police officers by persons who 'were or ought reasonably to have been suspected of having committed an offence', unless the admission was tape- or video-recorded. There is an exception to this requirement if the party seeking to adduce the evidence shows that the circumstances which gave rise to the admission not being recorded were 'exceptional' and 'justify the reception of the evidence'.

Some support has been expressed for a broader approach. For example, in *Reid*,[166] Spigelman CJ suggested that a 'strongly preferable course is that, in cases of serious crime, interviews with questions asked and answers given at crime scenes be recorded by an audio tape recorder, albeit that it is a pocket one and only one recording can be made'. If the law required recording of conversations in broader circumstances, with the focus being on whether or not the person was a suspect, police may be more inclined either to refrain from conversations which may run the risk of eliciting admissions (even if they were not designed to do so at the outset) or otherwise simply record them for fear of cogent evidence being inadmissible if unrecorded. This would not mean that, in unusual cases such as *Naa*, the admissions would necessarily need to be recorded as the dangerous circumstances of that case would provide a basis for the reasonable excuse exception. However, for cases analogous to *Sharp* and cases in which police engage in less formal conversations with suspects[167] where recording equipment is available, the incidence of misconduct and disputes must surely reduce if recording requirements were broader.

164 In line with the purposive approach expressed above by Kirby J in *Kelly* [2004] HCA 12; 218 CLR 216, [170].

165 ALRC, *Uniform Evidence Law* (Report No 102, 2006).

166 [1999] NSWCCA 258, [66].

167 It was noted in *Kelly* [2004] HCA 12; 218 CLR 216, [52] that recording of admissions is required wherever they are made, so long as they are in the course of official questioning, whether that be 'in police stations, in police cars, at the scene of a crime, or during informal encounters'.

Exclusion of written records of oral questioning

Finally, although most alleged admissions are electronically recorded, reasonable excuse situations and limitations on the scope of *CPA* (NSW), s 281, will mean sometimes there will be no recording. These include where a suspect is charged with an offence that falls outside the scope of s 281(1)(c))[168] or where a reasonable excuse exists for not electronically recording the questioning in which the admission was made.

In circumstances where an accused makes an admission to police in response to a question put or a representation made by an investigating official, s 86 of the *UEA* excludes documents (typically police notebooks) from being tendered into evidence unless the suspect has acknowledged on the document, for example by a signature or mark, that its contents are true. Section 86 of the *UEA* only relates to the contents of the document. An officer may still be able to give oral evidence of an alleged admission that otherwise satisfies *CPA* (NSW), s 281,[169] and the *UEA* exclusionary provisions discussed below.

False and Unreliable Confessions

Wrongful convictions involving false confessions are a sobering reminder of how vulnerable suspects can be and the importance of judicial review of police conduct and issues particular to the accused which may render their admissions unreliable. The Innocence Project in the United States identified that, of the 367 cases in which people were convicted of crimes and later exonerated by DNA evidence, 28% of the cases involved evidence of false confessions.[170] Adam and van Golde's[171] summary of particular 'categories' of false confessions is a helpful starting point when considering why an innocent person might admit to a crime they did not commit. First, they identify that some people knowingly make 'voluntary false confessions', for reasons including protecting the true offender or for notoriety. They note that some people voluntarily confess because of psychological issues, where the person is confused about reality.[172] Secondly, 'coerced-compliant false confessions' are those where the circumstances influence a person who knows they are innocent to make a confession to avoid punishment or to escape the investigation or to gain some sort of reward.[173] The third category identified is the 'coerced-internalised false confession' which arises from problematic styles of investigation where, because of the nature of the questioning, the person comes to believe they did commit the crime alleged.[174] Sullivan also explores the reasons for false confessions:

> While being questioned by police, a suspect may make a false confession while exhausted, intoxicated or withdrawing from drugs or alcohol; they may not understand the purpose

168 Section 281(1)(c) applies to an indictable offence. It does not apply to summary offences or an indictable offence that can be dealt with summarily without the consent of an accused.

169 A document containing a signed record of interview is not admissible if it is an admission that should be recorded in accordance with *CPA* (NSW), s 281: *Schiavini* (1999) 108 A Crim R 161, [16].

170 Innocence Project, see <https://www.innocenceproject.org/dna-exonerations-in-the-united-states/>.

171 L Adam and C van Golde, 'Police Practice and false confessions: A search for the implementation of investigative interviewing in Australia' (2020) 45 *Alternative Law Journal* 52.

172 Ibid 54.

173 Ibid 55.

174 Ibid 55.

> of the interview or how their confession will be used in court; or their confession may be influenced by mental illness or intellectual disability … given the prevalence of mental disorders, cognitive impairment and language disorders in the criminal justice system, the caution and language used may be too complex for a significant number of suspects … Researchers who have investigated the basis of false confessions highlight interrogation techniques and tactics that may increase untrue confessions, as well as characteristics of the person being questioned. In particular, they propose some people are suggestible, will acquiesce, or are unduly compliant. In the context of an emotionally charged interview, they may be prone to confessing to offences they didn't commit. Even when subsequently retracted, the confession evidence may be sufficient to result in conviction.[175]

The following false confession cases echo this research and reinforce the importance of Part 3.4 of the *UEA* exclusionary provisions and the Part 3.11 'discretions' in attempting to achieve a fair trial for the accused. Lord Kerr in the Privy Council decision in *Pora (New Zealand)*[176] noted, quoting from Elias CJ in *Television New Zealand Ltd v Rogers*,[177] that 'apparently reliable confessional evidence has led to significant miscarriages of justice'. Lord Kerr continued:

> 57. … Any court must therefore be astute to examine the reliability of seemingly straightforward confession of guilt where that comes under later challenge. In the present case it is clear that none of the police officers exerted pressure on Pora. Indeed, they were, if anything, fastidiously correct in their treatment of him. The natural inclination therefore is to assume that his confession (which was certainly not the product of any form of coercion) must be true. But it is precisely because of the experience that people confess to crimes that they did not commit that one should be vigilant to examine possible reasons that confessions may be false.

Lord Kerr quoted Canadian prosecutor, Bruce MacFarlane, who observed that 'judges and juries … are usually unwilling to accept that someone who has confessed did not actually commit the crime' and then observed that this 'entirely natural and to-be-expected reaction' means that careful attention should be given 'to reasons given [by the defence] that it was in fact untrue'. His Lordship concluded that 'such is the potential potency of confession evidence that particular care is required in examining whether it reflects the true state of affairs'.[178] These observations address the tension between the traditional view that the truth of a confession is a jury matter, not one related to admissibility. The *UEA* reflects some shift from that traditional stance, for example, s 85 which requires a baseline reliability, typically to the circumstances in which it was made, as a precondition to admissibility.

The case of *Pora (New Zealand)* is also instructive regarding the dangers of a false confession, even where police act entirely properly. Seventeen-year-old New Zealand Maori, Pora, was arrested regarding a stolen car. He told investigators that 'mobsters' were looking for him. He then asked police if they had arrested anyone for the Burdett murder. After a discussion of possible rewards and indemnities, police questioning continued. Lord Kerr, who delivered the Privy Council opinion quashing Pora's conviction for murder, described what followed:

175 D Sullivan, 'Justice for All: How Should the Law Deal with False Confessions?', *The Conversation*, 18 November 2014, <http://theconversation.com/justice-for-all-how-should-the-law-deal-with-false-confessions-32625>. See also <http://thepsychreport.com/conversations/coerced-to-confess-the-psychology-of-false-confessions/>.

176 [2015] UKPC 9.

177 [2007] NZSC 7; [2008] 2 NZLR 277, [14], quoted by Lord Kerr in *Pora* [2015] UKPC 9, [57].

178 [2015] UKPC 9, [57].

7. There then followed a series of interviews which continued over four days during which Pora gave various accounts of his knowledge of and later his involvement in the invasion of Ms Burdett's home, the attack on her, the rape that was perpetrated on her and, eventually, the circumstances in which she was murdered. It is unnecessary to rehearse the content of those interviews at length. Pora's accounts are strewn with inconsistencies, contradictions, implausibility and vagueness. At various times his replies to questions are halting, hesitant, incoherent and bizarre. A few examples will be sufficient to illustrate the nature of his responses.

8. … Soon after he gave this account [of going to the deceased's home to commit a burglary with two men named 'dog' and 'hound'], Pora accompanied police to a house where he said that Dog and Hound lived. On his return to the police station he said that he had lied about his involvement in the murder. He said that he had gone to Ms Burdett's home but only as a lookout. He did not enter the house. Within a short time of giving this version, however, he said that he did indeed go into the house and there observed Dog and Hound raping Ms Burdett.

9. … When he was taken by police on a drive designed to show his route to Ms Burdett's house, he appeared disorientated, unable without assistance to indicate the way to her house and had great difficulty in identifying the house even when he was standing directly outside it.

10. It was on the issue of how entry to the house was obtained, however, that Pora was at his most vague and inconsistent, not only when he accompanied police to the property but also in the accounts given during interview. At first he claimed that he had climbed through a window; then he said that he had waited outside the back door and was admitted to the house by Dog. This complete volte-face occurred within the space of three transcribed lines and two successive questions on the interview record. Later during interview … he said that all three had climbed through a window. But within moments he said that Hound had gone in through the door. Then he reverted … to the account that all three had climbed through the window.

There were many other inconsistencies and pointers to Pora's account being untrue. Rewa, a man unassociated with Pora, was convicted of raping Mrs Burdett. He had an extensive track record of similarly committed rapes. There were, however, elements in Pora's accounts that were consistent with police investigations. Pora was charged. At trial, his confessions were unsuccessfully disputed, not on mental impairment grounds, but arising from the reward and indemnity conversation. The confessions were the sole basis for Pora being found guilty. His appeal was successful, but he was convicted on a retrial and his second appeal was unsuccessful. His confession does not appear to have featured significantly on the appeal. As 'new evidence' before the Privy Council, an assessment by Dr Valerie McGinn, a clinical neuropsychologist, was admitted. It was based on information that Pora's mother had an extensive drinking history during pregnancy. Dr McGinn administered tests that revealed that he suffered from foetal alcohol spectrum disorder (FASD) and concluded that Pora fulfilled the diagnostic criteria of an alcohol-related neurodevelopmental disorder (ARNO). Included in her report were the following 'highly important conclusions' Some extracts explain Dr McGinn's findings:[179]

37. … "… In everyday life … [the] results indicate that Mr Pora has deficits of regulatory control and this is a common feature in those with FASD who struggle to regulate their moods and actions. When placed in a complex situation Mr Pora is likely to show a tendency to act impulsively with reduced capacity to think through to consequences.

179 Ibid [37].

In terms of his FASD diagnosis, Mr Pora has significant impairments of executive function including impaired reasoning, literal and limited thinking, cognitive rigidity and deficits of regulatory control." …

… "FASD is often described as 'Swiss cheese brain damage', with some processes remaining intact while others are in deficit. It is the variability of function that is typical but can be deceptive with those affected often seeming more capable on the surface than they actually are. Intellect is lowered but not always in the retarded range, even with full FASD. Many adults with FASD function in the Borderline to Low Average range intellectually as Mr Pora does. However, adaptive function is known to be more affected and they are functionally disabled in their everyday life and tend to lack common sense. Mr Pora shows impairment of his daily living skills in the areas of functional academics, community use, self-care, leisure and social function. Conceptual and social domains were impaired while practical skills were strong when living in a well-structured and supported environment."

… "Most notable on testing was Mr Pora's impairments of executive functioning. He showed no capacity for abstract thought, interpreted sayings entirely literally and could not appreciate deeper or implied meaning. He was cognitively rigid, sticking to one way of responding and was unable to appreciate a range of differing options. This indicates that he will get something in his mind and stick to it even when the evidence is contrary to it. He will not be well able to match his thinking to the circumstances and adapt with changes of situational demands. Mr Pora also showed deficits of regulatory control suggesting that he will tend to respond without due consideration especially in complex situations. As well as behavioural dysregulation those with FASD tend to be emotionally dysregulated and cannot tolerate or manage stress well …".

The Privy Council concluded that:

55. [The neuropsychological and psychiatric evidence] … unquestionably establishes the risk of a miscarriage of justice. It provides an explanation as to why Pora's confessions may have been false. This is of central and critical importance to one's approach to the question whether his convictions can be regarded as safe.

56. The impact that evidence of a confession will have, especially a confession to heinous crime, is difficult to overstate. The natural reaction to such an admission is that it is bound to be true. Why would someone confess to a dreadful crime if they were not guilty of it? But experience has shown that false confessions, even to the most serious of offences, are often made. The intuitive response to the fact of confession to crime is, inevitably, that it must be right but that intuitive reaction may be very dangerous. In *R v Oickle* [2000] SCR 3 the Supreme Court of Canada confronted the phenomenon of false confessions. Iacobucci J, [34] and [35] said:

> '… it may seem counterintuitive that people would confess to a crime that they did not commit. And indeed, research with mock juries indicates that people find it difficult to believe that someone would confess falsely. See *SM Kassin and LS Wrightsman, "Coerced Confessions, Judicial Instructions, and Mock Juror Verdicts"* (1981), 11 J Applied Soc Psychol 489. However, this intuition is not always correct. A large body of literature has developed documenting hundreds of cases where confessions have been proven false by DNA evidence, subsequent confessions by the true perpetrator, and other such independent sources of evidence. See, eg, *RA Leo and RJ Ofshe, 'The Consequences of False Confessions: Deprivations of Liberty and Miscarriages of Justice in the Age of Psychological Interrogation'* (1998), 88 J Crim L & Criminology Justice …'.

Australia has its own cases of accused persons being convicted on unreliable confessions. In *Mallard*[180] the appellant made 'some highly fanciful, indeed incredible assertions and claims, as well as apparently inculpatory, confessional state-

180 [2005] HCA 68; 224 CLR 125.

ments'[181] that were plainly at odds with established facts.[182] The circumstances of the interviews were concerning. Police first interviewed the appellant on the day he was discharged from a psychiatric hospital. The interview went for eight hours and 20 minutes, and he was not cautioned immediately before the interview. At trial, the appellant gave evidence in relation to this interview, saying he 'was in total confusion to the point where anything that he [Detective Sergeant Caporn] suggested to me I would adopt'.[183]

The second, unrecorded, interview, lasted three hours. Police conducted the interview, knowing that the appellant had spent the previous night at a nightclub, had been beaten and had little sleep.[184] After this unrecorded interview, there was a 30-minute recorded interview which the Court of Criminal Appeal described as of a 'very unusual nature':[185]

> 30. … At the beginning of the interview, the appellant said: 'I want to be video recorded so that I can be cleared.' His closing words were that his account was 'my version, my conjecture, of the scene of the crime.' In this interview, he often spoke of himself in the third person (for example, 'initially I entered into the room, or this person entered the room … thinking that he was on his own'). He also spoke about Mrs Lawrence as if he were speculating about her conduct rather than reporting his observations of it (for example, "I would say she would have done …"). Several times he was interrupted by the interviewers (for example, when he said, "Judging by the damage that was shown to me in photographs …"). During it he offered further suggestions about the murder, such as:
>
> "DET SGT BRANDON [sic]: … You said that you approached her from the rear of the shop and she asked you 'What are you doing here?'
>
> MR MALLARD: Yeah.
>
> DET SGT BRANDON: Is that right?
>
> MR MALLARD: That's right.
>
> DET SGT BRANDON: Okay. And that you said to her that you were going to rob her. This is what you told us. Okay?
>
> MR MALLARD: This is what I imagine this person would say. …
>
> DET SGT BRANDON: … Now, you also said that she gave you a purse?
>
> MR MALLARD: A purse.
>
> DET SGT BRANDON: All right.
>
> MR MALLARD: I would say it would have to be a matching purse. Being a woman of taste, she would have had a matching handbag and a matching purse. At a last resort, I would have gone for a Glomesh bag.
>
> DET SGT BRANDON: Okay. All right. You told us that she was dressed in what?
>
> MR MALLARD: A skirt of some sort. Again, being a woman of taste and sophistication, she would have had to be --- worn a nice skirt like this, but one that joins up. …
>
> DET SGT BRANDON: Right, and I think you said that you virtually ran there [the Stirling Bridge] from the scene?
>
> MR MALLARD: Would have had to.
>
> DET SGT BRANDON: Yeah.
>
> MR MALLARD: Or caught a train much --- probably at North Fremantle, but I don't think so because the tapes --- there's no videotapes of that day.

---

181 Ibid [14].

182 See also Chapter 2, p 44, regarding background information and failure to disclose issues. Kirby J (ibid [86]) notes that the suppression of the evidence also had the capacity to cast doubt upon the reliability of 'confessions' made by the appellant which were foundational to the prosecution case.

183 [2005] HCA 68; 224 CLR 125, [28].

184 Ibid [29].

185 Ibid [30].

DET SGT BRANDON: No problems.
MR MALLARD: So he was either very fit or he had a push-bike."

The court held:

> 39. Enough appears to indicate that there was substance in the appellant's contention in this Court that the Court of Criminal Appeal wrongly declined to entertain a submission that most or all of the matters said by the respondent to be uniquely within the murderer's knowledge, were not objectively true, or were contradicted by other matters, or were equivocal, or were patently false: and, in consequence, for those and other reasons, including the appellant's denial that he had said what was attributed to him about them, the so-called confessions were unreliable.

The High Court allowed psychiatric evidence of the appellant's mental health to be considered in the appeal, concluding that 'it provided a basis for further argument in favour of an inference that it [the confessional evidence] should be treated as being of no or little reliability'.[186] The High Court allowed the appeal, quashed the conviction and ordered a retrial. The prosecution eventually discontinued proceedings. Mr Mallard spent 12 years in prison in relation to this offence.

In *Gibson v Western Australia*,[187] the Western Australian Court of Appeal quashed Mr Gibson's conviction in relation to the charge of manslaughter (also allowing the plea of guilty entered in relation to this charge to be set aside). The allegations related to the death of a 21-year-old man who was hit by a car in the early hours of the morning in Broome in 2010. Initially, Mr Gibson, who was 18 years old at the time of the alleged offence, was not a person of interest. Two years later, Mr Gibson was taken into custody by police and questioned (as a witness). This questioning was recorded and the interview lasted three hours, with no interpreter present. English was not Mr Gibson's spoken language, as he spoke Pintupi, a local Aboriginal language. He made an admission in relation to being involved in the death of the deceased[188] and was charged with murder. Shortly before his trial commenced, the interview with police was ruled inadmissible by the WA Supreme Court on the basis that various police procedures were breached and the confessional statements were not voluntary (he did not understand his right to silence).[189] He nevertheless pleaded guilty to manslaughter and was sentenced to seven years and six months in prison. The WA Court of Appeal permitted Mr Gibson to withdraw his plea of guilty on the basis that a miscarriage of justice had occurred for reasons including:

> (a) the likelihood that the appellant did not understand adequately:
> (i) the legal process;
> (ii) the State's case against him;
> (iii) the advice that his legal advisers gave him about his plea; or
> (iv) the options that were available to him, at the time he entered his plea, as well as the consequences of a plea of not guilty; and
> (b) the real (as distinct from fanciful) risk that the plea was not attributable to a genuine consciousness of guilt.[190]

186 Ibid [41] (Gummow, Hayne, Callinan and Heydon JJ).
187 [2017] WASCA 141.
188 *Western Australia v Gibson* [2014] WASC 240, [8]-[10].
189 *Gibson v Western Australia* [2017] WASCA 141.
190 Ibid [157].

On appeal, it was found that Mr Gibson suffered 'significant and pervasive' cognitive impairments, he was unable to communicate or understand oral English in the context of the issues raised in the record of interview, give instructions or receive advice in the course of the legal proceedings.[191] It was held that he had a 'tendency for gratuitous concurrence'.[192] For these reasons (and the circumstances of the meetings with his legal advisers), it was held that the integrity of Mr Gibson's plea had been impugned.[193] In quashing the conviction, the court held that 'the admissible evidence against the appellant is not sufficiently cogent to support a conviction of murder or manslaughter. Indeed, the admissible evidence does not establish a case for the appellant to answer'.[194]

Mental Illness and Impairment

People with mental conditions are overrepresented in the criminal justice system.

In terms of intellectual disability, as the table below shows (*see over page*), over one-third of accused persons present with an IQ score no greater than 70. Indeed, the prevalence of people with **mental health disorders and cognitive impairment** caught in the web of the criminal justice system is particularly concerning. The summary snapshot of the NSW position, taken from a paper by R McCausland, S Johnson, E Baldry and A Cohen,[195] presents striking figures. A number of sources are relied on in compiling the figures (and for this reason they do not form a direct controlled comparison) but they permit broad comparisons with the rate per general population and the rates within the criminal justice system being particularly prominent.

---

191 Ibid [163].

192 Dr Eades gave expert evidence at the Supreme Court, including explaining the effect of gratuitous concurrence: 'Many of the accused's answers to questions regarding his rights were a simple yes or a head nod. Dr Eades states that the possibility that such responses were gratuitous concurrence and did not indicate agreement or understanding cannot be discounted. She describes gratuitous concurrence as a strategy used when people do not fully understand the language they are being questioned in or when people are in an oppressive situation. She says that it is a widely recognised response by Aboriginal people. Some factors increase the likelihood of gratuitous concurrence, including repeated questioning, a power imbalance between the person asking the questions and the person answering them and any difficulty by the interviewee in understanding the questions. In Dr Eades' view, all of these factors were involved in the police interview with the accused': *Western Australia v Gibson* [2014] WASC 240, [118].

193 *Gibson v Western Australia* [2017] WASCA 141, [200].

194 Ibid [210].

195 R McCausland, S Johnson, E Baldry, A Cohen, 'People with Mental Health Disorders and Cognitive Impairment in the Criminal Justice System: Cost-Benefit Analysis of Early Support and Diversion' (Report, UNSW, PWC, 2013), 3. These figures are taken from various sources: the NSWLRC, *People with Cognitive and Mental Health Impairments in the Criminal Justice System: Criminal Responsibility and Consequences* (Report No 138, 2013), 9; S Begg, T Vos, B Barker, C Stevenson, L Stanley and A Lopez, 'The Burden of Disease and Injury in Australia 2003' (Cat No PHE 82, AIHW, 2007); figures regarding lifetime prevalence of head injury where loss of consciousness is greater than 15 minutes is taken from D Indig, L Topp, B Ross, H Mamoon, B Border, S Kumar and M McNamara, *2009 NSW Inmate Health Survey: Key Findings Report* (Justice Health, 2010). The authors cite <http://www.corrections.vic.gov.au/utility/publications+manuals+and+statistics/>, regarding similarly high rates of mental disorders and cognitive impairment amongst Victorian prisoners.

Mental Health Conditions, Psychotic Disorders, Intellectual Disability, Brain Injury in the NSW Criminal Justice System and General NSW Population

	Mental health condition	Psychotic disorder	Intellectual disability (IQ <70)	Brain injury
General population	22%	1%	2%	6%
Court defendants	*45%*	*9%*	*36%*	
Prison inmates	77%	9%	8%	49%
Young people in custody	87%	9%	48%	

As these figures show, for the accused in court, inmates in prison and young people in custody in New South Wales, their incidence of mental ill health and intellectual disability is many times – from double to nine times – that in the general population in New South Wales. As Baldry et al note, these disadvantages are criminogenic factors only to the extent that they dispose someone to being caught in the criminal justice system. They are not indicators of a propensity to commit crime. According to Baldry et al:

> [T]he majority of research finds no inherent link between psychiatric disability or intellectual disability and *crime*, but a strong causal link between psychiatric disability and *incarceration* highlighting the impacts that social disadvantages such as homelessness, visibility, prejudice, fear, lack of support and services, and lack of family ability, capacity or will to assist may well be having on these people's life courses. It has been suggested 'offending by intellectually disabled persons is directly related to the levels of community care and support and the availability of specialist services'.[196]

In terms of alcohol and other drugs, the Australian Institute of Health and Welfare (2020) has reported the higher prevalence of alcohol and other drugs within the criminal justice system, noting:

- Prison entrants in 2018 were more likely than the general population to be non-drinkers – however, those who did drink were more likely to drink at high risk levels than people in the general community.
- In 2018, more than two-thirds (67%) of prison entrants smoked tobacco daily.
- In 2018, almost one in three (30%) police detainees indicated that illicit drug use contributed to their offending.
- Two-thirds (65%) of prison entrants in 2018 reported using illicit drugs in the 12 months before incarceration.
- Over three-quarters (79%) of police detainees who provided a urine sample in 2018 tested positive for a least one drug type.[197]

Additionally, compared to non-Indigenous defendants with the same problems, Aboriginal and Torres Strait Islander people with mental health and cognitive impairment problems have a significantly greater over-representation in the

196 E Baldry, L Dowse, M Clarence, *People with Mental and Cognitive Disabilities: Pathways into Prison* (Background Paper for the National Legal Aid Conference, Darwin, 2011), 5-6 (citations omitted), quoting I Byrnes, 'People with an Intellectual Disability in the Criminal Justice System' in M Jones and L Basser Marks (eds), *Disability, Divers-Ability and Legal Change* (Martinus Nijhoff, 1999), 315.

197 Australian Institute of Health and Welfare, *Alcohol, Tobacco and other drugs in Australia* (2020), <https://www.aihw.gov.au/reports/alcohol/alcohol-tobacco-other-drugs-australia/contents/priority-populations/people-in-contact-with-the-criminal-justice-system>.

criminal justice system (and particularly in prisons).[198] Thus, for this cohort, the observations of Baldry et al regarding the impact of social disadvantages (homelessness, visibility, prejudice, fear, lack of support and services, and lack of family ability, capacity or will to assist) apply with additional force, stemming from two bases of disadvantage.

Sullivan, in the context of discussing unreliable admissions, makes the important point that recognition of mental disorders, impairments or language issues relies on recognition of these issues by police.[199] In Australia lessons have been learnt from these experiences. Police are obliged to provide a higher degree of support and assistance for people detained for the purpose of investigation (including questioning) who fall into one of the categories set out in the clause which defined 'vulnerable persons'.[200] Additional support includes assistance in understanding their rights while detained,[201] and also allow for a support person to be present during investigative procedures, including any interview which is made.[202]

Despite the existence of the provisions aimed at protecting vulnerable suspects, legal and practical issues operate inadequately to protect suspects with mental illness and impairments because such suspects are not within the 'vulnerable persons' definition. The only category related to mental functioning is 'impaired intellectual functioning'.[203] Secondly, a vulnerable person 'does not include a person whom the custody manager reasonably believes is not a person falling within any of those categories',[204] thus relying on the lay judgment of a custody manager, whose 'reasonable' error in not recognising impaired intellectual functioning does not affect the unlawfulness or impropriety of failing to provide proper support to a vulnerable suspect. Further, without the assistance of mental health professionals, it is unrealistic to expect police to consistently make reliable assessments, as they are simply not qualified. This is an area in need of law reform to avoid mentally ill and cognitively impaired suspects being put at risk of providing unreliable admissions (or otherwise compromising their right to silence) due to inadequate safeguards.

A significant proportion of Magistrates Courts in Australian States and Territories are assisted by court liaison officers (such as those employed by NSW Justice Health) who screen and assess people for mental health conditions detained in custody.[205] It is on these assessments that the court may take appropriate action in relation to diversion or otherwise make recommendations with regard

198 Baldry et al, above n 196, 2. Shepherd et al note that the higher proportion of Indigenous cognitively impaired persons calls for culturally appropriate disability assistance networks at every stage of the justice system: S Shepherd, J Ogloff, Y Paradies and J Pfeifer, 'Aboriginal prisoners with cognitive impairment: Is this the highest risk group?, *Trends and Issues in Crime and Criminal Justice* (No 536, AIC, 2017), 9.

199 Sullivan, above n 175. See also Bartels, above n 19, 2.

200 Defined at cl 28 of *LEPRR* (NSW) *to include* children, persons who have impaired intellectual functioning, impaired physical functioning, ATSI people and people who are of non-English speaking background.

201 *LEPRR* (NSW), cl 29.

202 *LEPRR* (NSW), cl 30.

203 For a discussion of the meaning of the terms mental illness and cognitive impairment, see NSWLRC, *People with cognitive and mental health impairments in the criminal justice system: an overview* (Consultation Paper No 5, 2010), 1.26-1.33.

204 *LEPRR* (NSW), cl 28(1).

205 See D Bradford and N Smith, 'An Evaluation of the NSW Court Liaison Services' (BOCSAR, 2009).

to the future care for the person in custody or in the community. Investing in a similar, independent, service would certainly assist police and provide protection to suspects in relation to a wide range of circumstances,[206] including assessments before any questioning and making bail determinations. Such a service would also provide an evidentiary basis for a person's mental health close in time to the questioning, useful in determining admissibility matters as well.[207]

The Exclusion of Admissions under the *UEA*

The exclusionary provisions in Part 3.4 of the *UEA* apply to all admissions. There are no limitations on the application of those provisions depending on whether the offence to which the admission relates is an indictable offence, or whether the admissions are electronically recorded. Sections 84 and 85 of the *UEA*, respectively, operate to create a mandatory exclusion to evidence of admissions:

- if the court is not satisfied that the admissions were not made under influence of duress or oppressive conduct;[208] and
- unless the circumstances in which the admission was made were such as to make it unlikely that the truth of the admission was adversely affected.[209]

Section 90 provides the court with discretion to exclude admissions in which it would be unfair in the circumstances to admit the evidence. Section 138 provides for the exclusion of admissions where they were obtained as a result of illegal or improper conduct and the desirability of admitting the evidence does not outweigh the undesirability of admitting evidence in the way in which the evidence was obtained. The general exclusionary provisions discussed in Chapter 4, and set out in Part 3.11 of the *UEA*, may also be relied on to exclude evidence of admissions.

Admissions influenced by violence, oppression and other conduct: *UEA*, s 84

If the court is not satisfied that the admissions (and the making of the admissions) were not influenced by violent, oppressive, inhuman or degrading conduct (whether towards the person who made the admission or towards another person),[210] or a threat of conduct of that kind,[211] then the admissions must be excluded: *UEA*, s 84.

---

206 See J Ogloff, M Davis, G Rivers, S Ross, 'The Identification of Mental Disorders in the Criminal Justice System', *Trends and Issues in Crime and Criminal Justice* (No 334, AIC, 2007), 3: 'No jurisdictions have structured screening devices for identifying individuals likely to have a mental disorder at the time of initial contact'. Recommendation 4: 'All accused being taken into police custody following arrest should undergo a mental health screen. Where possible and feasible such screening should be conducted by a nurse or mental health professional using a structured and standardised approach, such as the Jail Screening Assessment Tool. Where it is not possible for practical reasons to routinely screen all people in these circumstances, alternative mechanisms should be put in place. Such mechanisms could include screening by police, using measures that do not require administration by a health professional, or it may be possible to have mental health staff from agencies such as forensic mental health services conduct screenings on an as-needs basis'.

207 This may lead to exclusion pursuant to *UEA*, s 85. Consider also exclusions under ss 90 and 138 if vulnerable and the person is not afforded vulnerable protections under *LEPRA* (NSW).

208 *UEA*, s 84.

209 *UEA*, s 85.

210 *UEA*, s 84(1)(a).

211 *UEA*, s 84(1)(b).

The terms 'violent', 'oppressive', 'inhuman' and 'degrading' are not defined in the *UEA*. To raise an objection under s 84 there must be 'some evidence that indicates through legitimate reasoning that there is a reasonable possibility an admission or its making were influenced by proscribed conduct, however it is not necessary that that evidence prove as a fact that an admission or its making were so influenced'.[212] Section 84(2) places an evidentiary onus on the party (usually the accused) who raises an issue about whether the admission or its making was influenced by violent, oppressive, inhuman or degrading conduct (or threat of conduct of that kind). Once the issue is raised, the party tendering the evidence (generally the prosecution) then has to satisfy the court that the conduct did not so influence the making of the admission,[213] on the balance of probabilities: *UEA*, s 142.

In *Zhang*[214] the accused made admissions during an interview with police, during the course of which an offer was made for police protection when he was offered the options of cooperating with police or being charged with murder. Further, in the course of being afforded this 'choice', he was offered a reduction in his sentence for assisting authorities, threatened with violence and was told that, after police left the room, there would be no further opportunities to assist police.[215] It was held, unsurprisingly, 'that the conduct of the police as a whole was designed to and did in fact oppress the accused',[216] and the evidence was held to be inadmissible.

It was held in *Higgins*[217] that s 84 'does not require the isolation of a single reason or a single incident of conduct provoking the confession. There may be a number of factors working together'. It was further held that 'mental and psychological pressure' was capable of constituting oppressive conduct and that this term was not limited to physical or threatened physical conduct. As to the meaning of 'influence', which connects the terms set out in s 84(1)(a) to the admission, it was held in *Habib* that 'the test to determine the causal relationship between the conduct and the admission is not a stringent test'.[218]

The case of *Sumpton*[219] is a good example of how a 'number of factors working together' may amount to oppressive conduct. The accused confessed to the stabbing murder of a woman in South Grafton. He gave a number of exculpatory accounts to police before an extensive interview. On that day, the accused was interviewed by police at the Grafton police station over a long period of time, which went into the early hours of the next day, when he made admissions, after 20 hours in police custody. Hamill J, in considering the application of s 84 to the admissions, found that the accused was treated in an oppressive manner, applying the Dictionary definition of 'oppression' which was referred to in *Fulling*: '[The] exercise of authority or power in a burdensome, harsh or wrongful manner; unjust or cruel treatment of subjects, inferiors etc; the imposition of unreasonable or unjust burdens'.[220]

---

212 *Habib v Nationwide News Pty Ltd* [2010] NSWCA 34; 76 NSWLR 299, [234] (Hodgson, Tobias and McColl JJA).

213 Ibid [228]-[235].

214 [2000] NSWSC 1099.

215 Ibid [40].

216 Ibid [41].

217 [2007] NSWCCA 56, [26] (Hoeben J, with whom Sully and Bell JJ agreed).

218 *Habib v Nationwide News Pty Ltd* [2010] NSWCA 34; 76 NSWLR 299, [239]-[240] (Hodgson, Tobias and McColl JJA), citing, with approval, Simpson J's statement in *Zhang* [2000] NSWSC 1099, [44].

219 [2014] NSWSC 1432.

220 Ibid [128], citing *Fulling* [1987] 2 All ER 65.

The accused's treatment included unlawful and lengthy detention (23 hours in total), significant periods of sleeplessness, ignored requests for a lawyer, badgering questioning and a situation where the custody manager 'was not involved in any meaningful way before, during or after the interview'.[221] In addition, the accused was subjected to psychological and emotional pressure to change his version of events and he was left uninformed regarding the timing of his being taken before a magistrate for questions of bail to be determined. Hamill J in *Sumpton* summarised the aspects of the police questioning which led to the exclusion of the admissions under s 84 as follows:

> 135. … Aspects of the questioning of the accused at the time of his arrest ("I want to know why you did it") and towards the end of the ERISP was unfair and improper in that it assumed his guilt and ridiculed and belittled his answers.
>
> When he terminated the interview after a period of many hours, the detectives continued to question him for a short period and put to him that he was doing so because he was guilty of murder.
>
> The implicit suggestion that his termination of the interview was capable of giving rise to an inference that he was guilty was never withdrawn. …
>
> He was told that the offence with which he was charged 'effectively carried life', that his account didn't add up and that the detectives were giving him an "opportunity" to talk before he was taken to Coffs Harbour. Thereafter, he was told that he could "ring [the detectives] from gaol."
>
> He was approached to provide further information after he had clearly, and repeatedly, indicated that he sought to exercise his right to silence after more than 2,000 questions in the ERISP.

This case, and the multiplicity of reasons that led to the exclusion of the admissions pursuant to s 84, demonstrates that it is necessary to examine the police conduct and the circumstances as a whole to determine whether the accused was influenced by oppressive conduct.

Circumstances affecting reliability of admissions: *UEA*, s 85

Section 85 requires the court to make a determination as to whether 'the circumstances in which the admissions were made were such as to make it unlikely that their truth was adversely affected'.[222] Unless the court is able so to find, the admission is excluded. It is for the defence to raise an 'arguable point' in regards to whether the truth of the admission was adversely affected.[223] If, on the evidence, 'a question legitimately arises as to whether the circumstances were such that the truth (or untruth) of the admission might have been adversely affected, then it falls to the Crown to establish on the balance of probabilities (*UEA*, s 142) that it was unlikely that this was the case'.[224] The purpose of s 85(2) was set out in the ALRC 2006 report:

> 10.87 The purpose of s 85(2) is to enhance the truth of admissions. Accordingly, as a general rule the question is not whether the circumstances did *in fact* adversely affect the truth of the admission (resulting in an admission that is in fact untrue), but whether

221 Ibid [135].

222 *UEA*, s 85(2).

223 *Esposito* (1998) 45 NSWLR 442, 459.

224 Ibid 460. Wood CJ at CL also stated at 460: 'The inquiry undertaken by the judge is not concerned with the question as to whether the admission was in fact made, or whether it was true (or untrue); each is for the jury'.

> they were *likely* to do so. As such, the court should not consider evidence as to the actual truth of the admission when determining its admissibility under s 85(2). Rather, the focus should be on the likelihood that the reliability of an admission made in such circumstances would be adversely affected by those circumstances.[225]

The 'circumstances' may relate to issues particular to the accused, such as 'any relevant condition or characteristic of the person who made the admission, including age, personality and education and any mental, intellectual or physical disability to which the person is or appears to be subject',[226] as well as issues external to the accused such as the nature and manner of questioning and the nature of any threats, promises or inducements.[227]

Section 85(1) sets out the context in which the section applies. Unlike ss 84 and 138, the section applies only in criminal proceedings and only where an admission is:

> (a) to, or in the presence of, an investigating official who at that time was performing functions in connection with the investigation of the commission, or possible commission, of an offence, or
> (b) as a result of an act of another person who was, and who the defendant knew or reasonably believed to be, capable of influencing the decision whether a prosecution of the defendant should be brought or should be continued.

Before the High Court decision in *Kelly*, s 85(1)(a) had encompassed the phrase 'in the course of official questioning'. Section 85(1)(a) was amended in response to *Kelly*. The ALRC expressed the view that limiting the application of the 'official questioning' period was unsatisfactory and could allow police to circumvent s 85 simply by nominating times for the beginning and end of questioning.[228] Further, s 85(1)(a) in its current form does not place any limits on whether the person is arrested or a suspect and the wording does not require a link between the conduct of police and the making of the admission.[229]

An example of questioning within the scope of s 85 and ruled inadmissible may be found in the case of *Ul-Haque*.[230] There the accused, who was charged with receiving training with respect to combat and the use of arms from a terrorist organisation, had been subjected to unlawful detention (among other forms of improper conduct) by ASIO on the evening of 6 November 2003 and into the early morning of the following day. The questioning was not electronically recorded in any way. During the course of this questioning an Australian Federal Police (AFP) officer by the name of Gordge was present, though not participating in the questioning. The accused then participated in interviews with the AFP on that following day, 7 November 2013, and again on 12 November 2003 and 9 January 2004. Federal Agent Gordge was present at each of the November interviews.

Adams J said of the nature of the questioning the accused was subjected to by ASIO:

> 102. … Questioning of that kind is calculated to extract what the person being questioned believes the questioner wants to hear. It is inevitable that the truth of what is said is likely – if not certainly – to be adversely affected. The prosecution's ability to establish, as

225 ALRC, *Uniform Evidence Law*, above n 165.
226 *UEA*, s 85(3)(a).
227 *UEA*, s 85(3)(b).
228 ALRC, *Uniform Evidence Law*, above n 165, [10.56]-[10.58].
229 S Odgers, *Uniform Evidence Law* (Thomson Reuters, 15th ed, 2020), [85.150].
230 [2007] NSWSC 1251; 177 A Crim R 348.

> it must, that this is not the case is made doubly difficult by the fact that there is no record made by ASIO of the course of questioning, though there is a narrative of the results.

Section 85 applied to the admissions made during the course of the AFP interviews on the basis that even though those interviews, considered alone, did not raise the problem of truthfulness, they needed to be considered in the context of the questioning of the accused as a whole, by both ASIO and the AFP, particularly in light of the connection between the two afforded by Federal Agent Gordge. Accordingly, the interviews were held inadmissible by virtue of s 85 (and further and separately, s 84 and s 138).

Condition and characteristics of the accused

There are many factors particular to an accused that may render their admissions unreliable. The overrepresentation of people with mental illness and cognitive impairment in the criminal justice system renders it unsurprising that these conditions commonly form the basis of an application to exclude evidence of alleged admissions under s 85.

Suspects who are taken into custody are also frequently still under the influence, or perhaps withdrawing from, drugs or alcohol. If admissions were made at a time when the person was intoxicated or ill from withdrawal, this may be a circumstance in which an admission becomes unreliable. In *Ray*,[231] while not making a determination on the admissibility of evidence in that case pursuant to s 85, Wood CJ at CL provided general guidance on the issue:

> 106. The adage "in vino veritas" is of dubious validity, particularly as a general proposition, a matter reflected by the circumstance that intoxication commonly needs to be taken into account, pursuant to s 85 of the Evidence Act, when considering whether evidence of an admission, which had been made in the course of official questioning, in circumstances affecting its reliability, should be excluded.

This is not to say that the admissions made by an intoxicated person, even when the police knew the person to be intoxicated, will necessarily be excluded. In *Moffat*,[232] an appeal against a murder conviction, the appellant confessed to hitting the deceased with a hammer and putting his hands around the deceased's throat until he stopped breathing. The appellant gave evidence that he was a heavy drinker '8 to 12 litres a day, you know, and that's including about two litres of metho on top of that, that's a lot of drinking, a big day'.[233] It was estimated by a forensic pharmacologist that his blood alcohol reading would have been between 0.20 and 0.245 grams per 100 ml at the time of the ERISP. It was held that the trial judge was not in error in finding that, despite the appellant's intoxication, it was unlikely that the truth of the admission was adversely affected, paying particular regard to his high level of tolerance for alcohol (based on expert opinion), his manner of responding in the ERISP and his actions at the time of the offence, including checking the deceased's pulse and breathing shortly after the attack. The NSW Court of Criminal Appeal found no error in the application of s 85.[234]

231 [2003] NSWCCA 227; 57 NSWLR 616.
232 [2000] NSWCCA 174; 112 A Crim R 201.
233 Ibid [16].
234 Ibid [59]-[60].

The unfairness discretion: *UEA*, s 90

> Doubtless, deep-lying values inform judicial responses to the question presented. Amongst such values are those concerned with the right to a fair trial conducted within a criminal justice system that adheres to the accusatorial principle. That principle dictates that it is for the prosecution to prove a criminal accusation against an accused. In gathering evidence, police and prosecutors cannot ordinarily oblige a suspect to make admissions, and thus to furnish otherwise missing proof of guilt. Furthermore, even where a reliable admission is made, a court of trial may refuse to admit it if its use would, having regard to the circumstances in which it was made, be unfair to the accused.[235]

In a criminal proceeding, the court may refuse to admit evidence of an admission (or refuse to admit the evidence to prove a particular fact) if the evidence is adduced by the prosecution and, having regard to the circumstances in which the admission was made, it would be unfair to a defendant to use the evidence.[236] The onus of demonstrating that it would be unfair to accused persons to use the evidence under s 90 rests on the defence.[237] The meaning of 'unfairness' is not defined in the *UEA* and thus its meaning is derived from the common law. The High Court in *Swaffield*[238] acknowledged that the term 'unfairness' necessarily lacks precision and requires an evaluation of circumstances, but was direct on the point that unfairness relates to an accused's right to a fair trial.[239] *Swaffield* interpreted 'unfairness' in the broadest of terms:

> 89. The Australian decisions … in terms of voluntariness, they have tended to approach the matter in terms of an immunity from compulsion. The emphasis has been on whether duress has been brought to bear on the suspect, that is whether the will has been overborne in some way. That emphasis is well placed when voluntariness is at issue but it is too narrow when the exercise of discretion is involved. …
>
> 91. However, the notion of compulsion is not an integral part of the fairness discretion and it plays no part in the policy discretion. In the light of recent decisions of this Court, it is no great step to recognize … an approach which looks to *the accused's freedom to choose to speak to the police and the extent to which that freedom has been impugned. Where the freedom has been impugned the court has a discretion to reject the evidence. In deciding whether to exercise that discretion, which is a discretion to exclude not to admit, the court will look at all the circumstances. Those circumstances may point to unfairness to the accused if the confession is admitted. There may be no unfairness involved but the court may consider that, having regard to the means by which the confession was elicited, the evidence has been obtained at a price which is unacceptable having regard to prevailing community standards.* This invests a broad discretion in the court but it does not prevent the development of rules to meet particular situations.[240]

While *Swaffield* was not concerned with s 90 of the *UEA*, authorities considering the application of s 90 nevertheless frequently refer to the principles set out in that case. It may be said that, although it does not provide complete guidance on how s 90 should be applied, some important aspects of *Swaffield* were adopted by the High Court in *Em*.[241] For example, in relation to the relevance of reliability,

---

235 *Em* [2007] HCA 46; 232 CLR 67, [127] (Kirby J).

236 *UEA*, s 90. See also *Police v Dunstall* [2015] HCA 26; 256 CLR 403 which discusses the relevance of the common law unfairness discretion in a *UEA* context outside s 90.

237 *Em* [2007] HCA 46; 232 CLR 67, [63] (Gleeson CJ and Heydon J). The proof of any facts in meeting this burden will be on the balance of probabilities pursuant to s 142.

238 [1998] HCA 1; 192 CLR 159.

239 Ibid [53]-[54] (Brennan CJ).

240 Toohey, Gaudron, Gummow JJ (emphasis added).

241 [2007] HCA 46; 232 CLR 67.

Gleeson CJ and Heydon JJ cited Toohey, Gaudron and Gummow JJ in *Swaffield* in holding that unreliability is an important aspect of the unfairness discretion but it is not exclusive.[242] The majority of the court was split on this issue.[243] Gummow and Hayne JJ departed from this view, stating that s 90 operated as a 'safety net' to be applied after the other discretionary provisions had been exhausted (including those dealing with questions of reliability (for example s 85), and illegal and improper conduct (for example, s 138)) and therefore questions relating to reliability and illegal or improper conduct are not relevant to s 90.[244] Kirby J, in his dissenting judgment, was critical of this approach: 'In a statute of general application, the existence of differently expressed powers of exclusion that may, in a given case, have more particular application to the circumstances of a trial, is not a reason for reading down the alternative grounds for exclusion provided by the Act, including s 90' (footnoting the judgment of Gummow and Hayne JJ on this point).[245]

The result of *Em* is that some aspects of the interpretation of s 90 remain unclear.

Subsequent cases applying *Em* have provided some, but not authoritative, guidance on its application. Howie J in *Gilham*[246] interpreted *Em* as authority that the reliability of the evidence is a relevant factor to be taken into account in relation to s 90, and the focus of the unfairness relates to the admission of the evidence at trial not the unfairness in relation to how it was obtained.[247]

Until more comprehensive guidance is provided, the interpretation and breadth of 'unfairness' in the context of s 90 may be better understood by looking to individual cases and their circumstances:

> The language in s 90 is so general that it would not be possible in any particular case to mark out the full extent of its meaning ... the application of s 90 is likely to be highly fact specific.[248]

Some of the salient factual issues in *Em* and the High Court's findings as to whether or not the appellant's right to silence was impugned are discussed below.

Covertly recorded admissions

Section 90 is often applied to determine the admissibility of covertly recorded conversations with accused persons. Covert recordings are justified on the basis that there is an 'undoubted desirability of bringing wrongdoers to justice. Modern surveillance technology and covert police operations are potentially effective means for achieving that end'.[249] Covert recordings take place in a wide range

242 Ibid [73].

243 The majority being Gleeson, CJ and Heydon, Gummow and Hayne JJ.

244 [2007] HCA 46; 232 CLR 67, [109]-[113].

245 Ibid [179].

246 (2008) 190 A Crim R 341, [46].

247 Ibid [46]. Note, this was contrary to earlier authority in which Grove J stated that *Swaffield* provided useful guidance to the notion of 'unfairness' in s 90, relying on the joint judgment of Toohey, Gaudron and Gummow JJ: '[T]he unfairness discretion would achieve nothing beyond what is already required by the general law if it were concerned solely to ensure a fair trial' (*Swaffield* [1998] HCA 1; 192 CLR 159, 193-4), quoted by Grove J in *Nelson* [2004] NSWCCA 231, [19].

248 *Em* [2007] HCA 46; 232 CLR 67, [56] (Gleeson CJ and Heydon J).

249 *Swaffield* [1998] HCA 1; 192 CLR 159, [147] (Kirby J).

of scenarios.[250] In the NSW Court of Criminal Appeal in *Em*[251] the issue was the admissibility of conversations (arguably containing admissions) which were secretly recorded by police officers who were speaking to the appellant after he had refused to participate in an electronically recorded interview. The appellant agreed to be questioned without being taped. The police, wearing recording devices, asked him to go with them to a park, assuring him that he was not under arrest. Police reminded him of a caution given previously and said 'Mate, you don't have to talk to us if you don't want to', but failed to then, or at any other time, say that what was said may be used against him in criminal proceedings.[252] Therefore only half of the caution was administered.[253] Police also said: '[W]e haven't tried to trick you once, have we? We've brought you to a God damn park. We're not, we haven't got you in the police station'.[254] The appellant was assured he was not under arrest. On appeal to the High Court, a key question in this case was whether the appellant's freedom to speak or stay silent had been impugned.

Gleeson CJ and Heydon JJ found the admissions to be reliable[255] and that the appellant was not under any pressure to speak.[256] The mere fact that the conversation took place in a park did not amount to unfairness and noted that admissible confessions are made in places other than police stations.[257] Their Honours found that, when all circumstances were analysed, 'it is impossible to conclude that that freedom was impugned':[258]

> 78. … The appellant knew he was speaking to police officers. He knew they were investigating two home invasions, one involving a murder. He knew, having been cautioned several times on 22 February and 24 April 2002,[259] that he was not obliged to speak to the police officers. He spoke to those officers knowingly and willingly … He gave a version of events. In his evidence before the jury he claimed that he planned to give that version – according to him, a non-incriminating mixture of denials, admissions, lies, evasions, jokes and questions. Apart from the admissions he made, that account of the version of events lacked credibility, but he certainly wanted his version of events to be accepted by the detectives. He had an awareness of his rights and a capacity to act on them. While s 281 compelled the detectives to record what was said if they wanted to tender it, the appellant possessed no right not to be recorded once the listening device warrants had been obtained from O'Keefe J. The appellant was free to leave. The questioning was not overbearing … [there was no] obligation on the detectives to caution him. The appellant did not know the conversation was being recorded, but he accepted that that did not make it unfair to receive the evidence. The appellant did not contend that he spoke because of any threat of violence, or any illegality, or any impropriety. He did not contend that the circumstances were likely to affect the truth of the admissions. *He thought that the conversation could not be used against him in criminal proceedings, but that cannot of itself make it unfair for*

250 For example, in *Swaffield* [1998] HCA 1; 192 CLR 159, a close friend of the accused secretly recorded conversations on behalf of police in an attempt to gain admissions in relation to a murder investigation. In *Burton* [2013] NSWCCA 335, police recorded conversations between a sexual assault complainant and their suspect. Criminal associates or informants may agree to secretly record conversations with suspects in the hope of gaining benefits (for example, reduced sentences).

251 [2006] NSWCCA 336.

252 Ibid [16].

253 The contents of the caution are set out in s 139, below, p 329.

254 [2006] NSWCCA 336, [20].

255 [2007] HCA 46; 232 CLR 67, [72]-[23].

256 Ibid [62].

257 Ibid [75].

258 Ibid [78].

259 Note, the conversation which was the subject of these proceedings took place on 15 May 2002.

> *the conversation to be received in evidence.* The detectives kept secret from him the fact that the conversation was being recorded, and hence his freedom to speak was affected in the sense that a factor that was important to him was kept secret from him. But that is true of virtually all cases of lawfully authorised secret surveillance. Virtually all persons who are the subject of that type of surveillance have been deprived of the opportunity to make an informed choice about whether or not to exercise their right of silence ...
>
> 79. ... [The] use of the first part of the 15 May 2002 conversation was not unfair to the appellant.[260] (emphasis added)

With regard to the assertion that the police failed to correct the appellant's incorrect assumptions that the conversations were not recorded and that the evidence could not be used against him, it was said:

> The difficulty is that every day police officers take advantage of the ignorance or stupidity of persons whom they eventually prosecute, and a mistake of the kind the appellant was operating under was simply a species of ignorance or stupidity.[261]

Kirby J's dissenting judgment was highly critical of police conduct, holding that their conduct had the effect of depriving the appellant of his right to a fair trial.[262] The failure of the police to administer the second half of the caution[263] (relating to the *use of the evidence in criminal proceedings* against him) was unfair to the appellant. This unfairness was compounded by police assurances that he was not being 'tricked' and that he was not under arrest, which, along with the selection of the park venue, deceived the appellant into believing that he was talking to police 'off-the-record'.[264]

In *DRF*,[265] the NSW Court of Criminal Appeal upheld a Crown appeal in relation to the exclusion of evidence of admissions by the trial judge that were covertly recorded (wearing a lawful surveillance device) by the complainant of a child sexual assault allegations, holding that there was no basis under s 90 to hold that the circumstances in which the evidence was obtained rendered the admission of the evidence unfair.[266] The recordings took place after the accused had refused to speak to police. Leeming JA made the following general remarks in relation to the dangers which may be associated with complainants' covert recordings:

> 3. ... [I]n every case involving a surveillance device, the complainant will be aware of the fact that a recording is being made, while the accused will not. There is inevitably an element of deception taking place. It is established that those facts alone do not render the

260 Note, the 'first part of the interview' was admitted by James J at trial. It is this 'first part of the interview' which was the subject of the appeal. The 'second part of the interview', which was excluded at trial under s 90, related to detailed admissions relating to the home invasion and shooting, following one of the officers saying: 'Maybe you might feel better if you tell us. It's not as though we're going to slap the handcuffs on you and take you away otherwise we'd be at the police station if we were gunna do that, wouldn't we?' (at [21]-[26]).

261 [2007] HCA 46; 232 CLR 67, [70]. Note that Kirby J was highly critical of this remark: 'This approach implies that the educated and the clever enjoy a special position under the law which the ignorant and stupid do not. I could never agree with such a view ... The law is not silent for vulnerable people who are "ignorant" about their rights and who are regarded as "stupid". This point was made by this Court in 1950 in a powerful passage in *Lee* [[1950] HCA 25; 82 CLR 133, 159] ... As far as I am concerned, nothing has changed in this respect since 1950. The expansion of covert police operations and techniques only heightens the continuing force of what the Court then said': at [228], [230].

262 [2007] HCA 46; 232 CLR 67, [206]-[207].

263 Ibid [208].

264 Ibid [219], [225]-[226].

265 [2015] NSWCCA 181.

266 Simpson JA (Leeming JA and Schmidt J agreeing).

> use of the recording unfair: see for example *Em v The Queen* [2007] HCA 46; 232 CLR 67 at [78] and [116]. However, in most if not all cases where a complainant is equipped with a lawfully authorised surveillance device to record a conversation, the complainant will be motivated in part by animosity to the accused; this distinguishes the position from that of an undercover police operative. I would not lightly conclude that in no circumstances can there be s 90 unfairness.
>
> 4. I can readily imagine a spectrum of more or less deceptive conduct by the complainant which may at least arguably lead to the use of the recording being unfair (I am not to be taken to be implying that any of what follows applies to the particular complainant in this appeal). The complainant may choose a time at which the accused is particularly vulnerable (for example, because under the influence of legal or illegal drugs) which may not be apparent on the recording. More subtly, the complainant may use words with a special meaning, or which are deliberately ambiguous. The complainant's words may be accompanied by unrecorded gestures or facial expressions so as to enhance the ambiguity of what is conveyed with a view to controlling the subject matter and content and apparent meaning of the conversation. I do not regard the ambiguities to which I have referred as academic. It is sufficient to consider a case where a complainant believes correctly that he or she was indecently assaulted by the accused, but further believes incorrectly that he or she was much more seriously violated as well. To my mind, it is easy to see how a complainant motivated by animosity and with the knowledge and desire to obtain as damaging an admission as is possible may in any particular case engage in conduct which could render the recording unfair.

What is the likely messaging and practical impact on police practices created by courts treating admissions obtained in circumstances akin to those in *Em* and *DRF* to be outside s 90? Would a stricter approach discourage police from engaging such tactics? Would discouragement be consistent with the importance given to the right against self-incrimination in Australia's accusatorial justice system and so justifiable in offering some protection to suspects, particularly vulnerable suspects, from the forms of deception suggested by Leeming JA?

The public policy discretion: *UEA*, s 138

Where admissions are obtained illegally or improperly, s 138 of the *UEA* applies and the court is not to admit the admission unless the desirability of admitting the evidence outweighs the undesirability of admitting evidence.[267] This provision and the principles relating to the exercise of this discretion are discussed in Chapter 4. In relation to admissions specifically, s 138(2) provides that evidence of an admission that was made during or in consequence of questioning[268] is taken to have been obtained *improperly* if the person conducting the questioning:

- did, or omitted to do, an act in the course of the questioning even though he or she knew or ought reasonably to have known that the act or omission was likely to impair substantially the ability of the person being questioned to respond rationally to the questioning; or[269]
- made a false statement in the course of the questioning even though he or she knew or ought reasonably to have known that the statement was false and that making the false statement was likely to cause the person who was being questioned to make an admission.[270]

267 *UEA*, s 138.
268 And evidence obtained in consequence of the admission.
269 *UEA*, s 138(2)(a).
270 *UEA*, s 138(2)(b).

An admission may also be excluded if it was gained as a consequence of an improper exercise or breach of a police power or responsibility.[271] For example, if an admission was obtained as a consequence of an illegal or improper arrest,[272] illegal detention[273] or in the context of a search warrant improperly executed, the admissibility of the admission may be sought to be excluded pursuant to s 138.

Police are required to comply with a broad range of responsibilities relating to the rights of suspects who are in custody for the purpose of questioning.[274] These include the right to communicate with a friend, relative or a lawyer,[275] and provision of an interpreter or medical attention. Suspects considered 'vulnerable persons' are afforded additional rights as discussed above.[276]

Campbell v DPP[277] is an example of the capacity of admissions to be excluded on the basis of non-compliance with police responsibilities relating to vulnerable persons. The evidence was found to be illegally obtained on the basis that former cl 33 of *LEPRR* (NSW) (now cl 37) was not complied with. This clause made special provision relating to Aboriginal and Torres Strait Islander people, requiring the police to notify the Aboriginal Legal Service (ALS) that an Aboriginal or Torres Strait Islander person was detained and to inform the person detained that this notification would be made. In this case, the ALS not only was not notified but, further, Hidden J found that the failure to comply with the notification requirements under cl 33 was deliberate.[278] The police knew the accused persons were Aboriginal and, despite that, arrangements had been made for them to attend the station outside normal business hours, when lawyers would not be at the ALS office. Hidden J found that the magistrate, in undertaking the balancing exercise required by s 138, failed to take into account the gravity of the contravention in this case and so the exercise of his discretion miscarried.[279] Hidden J noted:

> 22. … [T]he obligation under cl 33 is twofold: not only to notify the ALS that an Aboriginal person is in detention, but also to inform that person that the ALS will be notified. That additional requirement is itself an important safeguard, ensuring that the suspect is aware of the availability of legal assistance through that organization.

The significance of cl 33 cannot be understated. The Royal Commission into Aboriginal Deaths in Custody made the recommendation for a requirement that there be 'notification of the Aboriginal Legal Service when Aboriginal people are arrested or detained'.[280] The clause ensures that the person has an opportunity to seek legal advice from the ALS but also provides the opportunity for the ALS to check on the person's mental and physical wellbeing and communicate with family members as appropriate.

---

271 Each State and Territory has its own legislative and regulatory requirements relating to police powers and responsibilities, as well as police codes of conduct and handbooks which also set standards of conduct.

272 For example, *LEPRA* (NSW), s 99.

273 *LEPRA* (NSW), Pt 9 and s 99.

274 *LEPRA* (NSW), Pt 9.

275 *LEPRA* (NSW), s 123.

276 See above, p 317.

277 [2008] NSWSC 1284 (Hidden J).

278 Ibid [20].

279 Ibid [21].

280 Royal Commission into Aboriginal Deaths in Custody (1987-1991) Vol 5, Recommendation 223(a), <http://www.austlii.edu.au/au/other/IndigLRes/rciadic/national/vol5/>.

The caution

Cautioning of suspects so that they are made aware of their right to silence is a key provision supporting that right. Failure to caution in accordance with s 139(1)-(3) of the *UEA* amounts to an impropriety, pursuant to s 139, thus potentially rendering any admissions subsequently made inadmissible by virtue of s 138. Section 139 provides:

> **139. Cautioning of persons**
>
> (1) For the purposes of section 138(1)(a), evidence of a statement made or an act done by a person during questioning is taken to have been obtained improperly if:
>
> (a) the person was under arrest for an offence at the time, and
>
> (b) the questioning was conducted by an investigating official who was at the time empowered, because of the office that he or she held, to arrest the person, and
>
> (c) before starting the questioning the investigating official did not caution the person that the person does not have to say or do anything but that anything the person does say or do may be used in evidence.
>
> (2) For the purposes of section 138(1)(a), evidence of a statement made or an act done by a person during questioning is taken to have been obtained improperly if:
>
> (a) the questioning was conducted by an investigating official who did not have the power to arrest the person, and
>
> (b) the statement was made, or the act was done, after the investigating official formed a belief that there was sufficient evidence to establish that the person has committed an offence, and
>
> (c) the investigating official did not, before the statement was made or the act was done, caution the person that the person does not have to say or do anything but that anything the person does say or do may be used in evidence.
>
> (3) The caution must be given in, or translated into, a language in which the person is able to communicate with reasonable fluency, but need not be given in writing unless the person cannot hear adequately.
>
> (4) Subsections (1), (2) and (3) do not apply so far as any Australian law requires the person to answer questions put by, or do things required by, the investigating official.
>
> (5) A reference in subsection (1) to a person who is under arrest includes a reference to a person who is in the company of an investigating official for the purpose of being questioned, if:
>
> (a) the official believes that there is sufficient evidence to establish that the person has committed an offence that is to be the subject of the questioning, or
>
> (b) the official would not allow the person to leave if the person wished to do so, or
>
> (c) the official has given the person reasonable grounds for believing that the person would not be allowed to leave if he or she wished to do so. …

The purpose of the section is to protect the suspect. The breadth of the circumstances which constitute a person being 'under arrest', as set out in s 139(5), is a feature of the section which helps to achieve this aim.

In *FE*,[281] there was a failure by police to caution. In addition, persistent questions were asked in the face of a refusal to answer questions. FE was 15 years old and interviewed in relation to a stabbing homicide on 12 July 2012 and again on 2 August 2012, and subsequently charged with murder. During the course of those interviews, she made admissions, the admissibility of which was challenged at her trial. The circumstances in which her admissions were obtained in her first interview were described by Adamson J, in her Honour's judgment on the *voir dire*, as follows:

281 [2013] NSWSC 1692 (Adamson J).

> 112. The accused was not cautioned prior to, or during, questioning. She did not know that she did not have to say anything or take part in the interview. She was not taken to the custody manager who was obliged, since she was a vulnerable person, to assist her to exercise her legal rights. Her rights under Part 9 of LEPRA were neither read out, nor explained to her. She was not advised of the free Legal Aid Youth Hotline service. Her mother, although regarded by police as a "support person", did not appreciate what her role was and was not taken through the "Role of a Support Person" document. She was, in any event, not capable of fulfilling the role in any substantial way because of the limitations of her English vocabulary.

In relation to the second interview, her Honour described the manner of the accused's participation in it in the following terms:

> 134. The accused declined, through Ms Hopgood, to participate in an interview and also declined to have her refusal to answer questions filmed. The unequivocal communication of her intention was disregarded. She was led to the interviewing room in utter derogation of her right to silence.

Adamson J regarded the contravention of the accused's rights by interviewing police in relation to each interview as being 'very grave' improprieties.[282] It was held that the admissions obtained in each of the two interviews were improperly obtained and, pursuant to s 138, excluded.[283] Adamson J also found that had s 138 not applied she would also have separately excluded the admissions pursuant to s 90 for 'substantially the same reasons'.[284]

In *Taleb*[285] the accused was charged with a Commonwealth offence relating to doing acts preparatory to engaging in hostile activity in a foreign country. The defence raised an objection to admissions in a record of interview based on the impropriety that police continued interviewing the suspect after he said that he wanted to exercise his right to silence. Police went on to caution the accused (without asking whether or not he wanted to exercise his right to silence) and then question the accused in relation to a range of matters, with admissions being made. The interview went for about three and a half hours. Hamill J summarised the impropriety as follows:

> 127. The "rule of practice" referred in *Ireland* in 1970[286] remains part of the law in NSW. Legislative enactments have emphasised the right to silence. Section 139 of the *Evidence Act* provides that a failure to advise an arrested person of their right to silence will result in a finding that the evidence was obtained improperly. While no automatic consequence flows from a failure to issue a caution, or from a failure to respect a suspect's clear statement that they wish to remain silent, there seems little point in requiring police to ensure the person knows their right, if their decision to exercise that right is ignored or side-stepped.
>
> 128. The questioning in the present case was impermissibly persistent. Mr Taleb indicated he wished to remain silent from the outset of the interview. He repeated this desire on at least six occasions over the following 17 pages of transcript. It is true that he gave answers to some questions while saying "no comment" to others as the interview went on. It is also true that he was asking the police why they were charging him and what evidence they had. However, until Mr Taleb spoke with his solicitor three hours later, there was no occasion where the officers appeared to be prepared to stop questioning him

282 Ibid [113], [135].
283 Ibid [137].
284 Ibid [137].
285 [2019] NSWSC 241.
286 *Ireland* (1970) 126 CLR 321. See also Chapter 4 and the discussion on the policy behind s 138.

> when he said he wished to remain silent. On each occasion, the police told him they would complete the "process" or simply stated their intention to do certain things – to read the allegations, to ask him questions, to play him recordings. Mr Taleb must have been given the impression that there was a "process" involved that had to be recorded by video. This is not correct. The obvious alternative, and one not referred to or contemplated until the solicitor became involved, was to terminate the interview. There was no legal requirement to put the allegations to the accused while on tape and no established "process" that had to be completed. Nothing in the interview suggests that Mr Taleb would have known that one option was that the interview could simply be terminated.

Hamill J excluded the admissions having regard to the factors in s 138(3),[287] and also 'taking into account the importance of the maintenance of the right against self-incrimination and the desirability that interviews such as this be terminated once it is clear that a suspect has expressed a clear desire not to answer questions'.[288] These cases demonstrate how vulnerable suspects can be to self-incrimination in the face of persistent questioning. As frustrating as it may be for investigating officers, *FE* and *Taleb* make it clear that proper regard to the right to silence requires police to demonstrate restraint by terminating interviews and cease asking questions.

Warnings to the Jury

Where disputed admissions make their way to the jury, the majority of the High Court in *McKinney*[289] held that warnings should be given where the alleged confessions were made in circumstances where the accused is held in custody by police, police evidence of the alleged confession is disputed, and its making is not reliably corroborated.[290] Section 165 provides for warnings to be given to juries in a wider scope of circumstances, highlighting the reasons which may cause the evidence to be unreliable[291] and the need for caution in determining whether to accept the evidence.[292] Section 165(a) identifies admissions as a general category of evidence which may be unreliable as well as oral admissions, recorded in writing, which have not been acknowledged by the defendant.[293] Section 165 is discussed in Chapter 14.

Conclusion

This chapter has sought to demonstrate how the right to silence is supported by the *UEA* and case law. Historically, the right to silence suffered widespread abuse through police misconduct. The cases discussed in the context of the exclusionary provisions such as *Sumpton*, *Ul-Haque* and *FE* demonstrate that suspects remain at serious risk of police conduct which, in effect, derogates the suspect's right to silence. The *UEA* exclusionary provisions are an important source of power for the

---

287 See Chapter 4; *UEA*, s 138(3).

288 [2019] NSWSC 241, [132].

289 [1991] HCA 6; 171 CLR 468.

290 Ibid [16] (Mason CJ, Deane, Gaudron and McHugh JJ).

291 *UEA*, s 165(2)(b).

292 *UEA*, s 165(2)(c).

293 *UEA*, s 165(1)(f); s 32 of the *Jury Directions Act 2015* (Vic) provides that directions may be given in relation to unreliable evidence and s 31(a) and (e) of that Act define 'evidence of a kind that may be unreliable' in equivalent terms to s 165(a) and (f) of the *UEA*.

court to replace 'spoken words with legal silence'.[294] It is no easy task to resolve the tension between admitting persuasive evidence of admissions and excluding evidence obtained without due regard to vulnerabilities, or that is obtained unfairly, illegally or by the influence of oppressive or threatening conduct.

The introduction of mandatory recording provisions as a prerequisite to the admissibility of admissions was a positive step towards addressing issues of police misconduct. However, the false confession cases discussed above are a stark reminder of the need to continue to reform law and police practices to avoid failures to appropriately account for the vulnerabilities of many suspects who are questioned by police and consequently exposed to the severe consequences of the criminal justice system.

294 J Gans, 'Silence in the High Court' (2008) 19(1) *Public Law Review* 5, 5.

Chapter 8

Hearsay – The Rule

Han said, "He shot first."
"Han said he shot first."
"Han said, 'he shot first.'"

Introduction

The three sentences above may appear at first glance to be identical, but look at them more closely and they begin to reveal important differences. One difference is grammatical, as each potentially tells you something different about who committed the act of shooting. The other difference will matter most where one or more of those statements is offered as evidence at trial. Depending on the timing, context and manner of delivery by which each statement is offered, the difference may be very important or not important at all. The difference is what is known as hearsay, and it will be the subject of this and the next chapter.

Dean John Wigmore described hearsay as 'that most characteristic rule of the Anglo-American law of evidence, – a rule which may be esteemed, next to jury-trial, the greatest contribution of that eminently practical legal system to the world's jurisprudence of procedure'.[1] Whatever one's view of the hearsay rule's contribution to the jurisprudence of procedure, it is undoubtedly one of the most challenging and contentious of the exclusionary rules of evidence. Its challenge lies partly in the fact that it is difficult to convey all essential elements of the rule with simplicity and clarity, so that its true meaning, effect and scope can be understood. In essence, at common law, the rule precludes the admission of assertions made outside of the current, ongoing proceedings where those assertions are adduced to prove the existence of any fact asserted. Distilled slightly, it can be understood in basic terms as a prohibition on the use of a person's out-of-court assertions as equivalent to or in place of their in-court testimony.[2]

So defined the rule has a very broad scope, catching all types of assertions – intentional, unintentional, implied, express, oral, documentary and those made by conduct. Herein lies the contentious nature of the rule. Its breadth inevitably creates uncertainty and inconsistency in its operation.[3] When coupled with

---

1 JH Wigmore, 'The History of the Hearsay Rule' (1904) 17 *Harvard Law Review* 437, 458.

2 For this definitional approach, see ibid 437.

3 See detailed discussion and examples in ALRC, *Evidence (Interim)* (Report No 26, 1985) Vol 1, [130]-[131].

an inflexible approach to its application the result may be exclusion of cogent evidence in contradiction of the rule's rationales[4] – evidence, moreover, that might lie at the very outer edge of the rule's reach.[5] In Australia, judicial approaches potentially unlocking the rigidity of the rule[6] have failed to win universal judicial support.[7] In the end, the task of hearsay reform has fallen to the legislature. In the mid-1980s and 2000s the Australian Law Reform Commission (ALRC) undertook comprehensive evaluations of the hearsay rule, which resulted in the implementation of an entirely new hearsay regime in those jurisdictions that have enacted the uniform evidence legislation. Section 59 of the *UEA* seeks to narrow and clarify the reach of the hearsay rule.[8] The critical feature that narrows the definition of hearsay in s 59 and distinguishes it from the common law is that it captures only *intentional* assertions of fact. A more minor, though nevertheless still significant, distinguishing feature of s 59 is that it catches only assertions made by people, whereas at common law assertions from other sources, most notably machines, may also constitute hearsay. Section 59 provides:

> **59. Hearsay rule – exclusion of hearsay evidence**
>
> (1) Evidence of a previous representation made by a person is not admissible to prove the existence of a fact that it can reasonably be supposed that the person intended to assert by the representation.
>
> (2) Such a fact is in this Part referred to as an **asserted fact**.

This chapter will return to this definition later, so that each of the separate (but related) elements that are contained within it can be distinguished and explained. Before embarking on that task, however, this chapter briefly considers the history of the rule in order to locate its rationales and purpose, and to open the door on discussion about its future. The exceptions to the rule, of which there are many, are examined in Chapter 9.

History and Rationales of Hearsay Rule

There is some dispute about the origins of the hearsay rule. However, the general view is that its genesis was institutional, that its existence can be ascribed to the development of the modern jury trial. It is thought that the transformation of the jury, at the end of the Middle Ages, from a self-informing, investigative body to a passive panel instructed in the facts by witnesses, was accompanied by a growing sense of disquiet about hearsay evidence. Nevertheless, what lay at the heart of this disquiet and supplied the engendering cause for its solidification into a generally accepted exclusionary rule is a matter of disagreement. Wigmore attributes its acceptance as settled doctrine[9] to juries' need for reliable evidence,

4 See, eg, *Myers v DPP* [1965] AC 1001; *Re Van Beelen* (1974) 9 SASR 163; *Jones v Metcalf* [1967] 3 All ER 205; *Re Gardner* (1967) 13 FLR 345; *O'Meally* [1952] VLR 499; *Szach* (1980) 23 SASR 504; *Baker* [2012] HCA 27; 245 CLR 632; *Bannon* [1995] HCA 27; 185 CLR 1; *Errigo* [2005] SASC 62; 91 SASR 80.

5 See, eg, *Walton* [1989] HCA 9; 166 CLR 283 (unintended implied statement identifying telephone caller) (Wilson, Deane, Dawson and Toohey JJ).

6 See, eg, *Walton* [1989] HCA 9; 166 CLR 283, 306 (Mason CJ); *Benz* [1989] HCA 64; 168 CLR 110, 117-18, 121, 143-4; and *Pollitt* [1992] HCA 35; 174 CLR 558, 565-6, 610.

7 See *Bannon* [1995] HCA 27; 185 CLR 1, 94 (Brennan CJ); *Pollitt* [1992] HCA 35; 174 CLR 558, 571-83 (Brennan CJ); *Baker* [2012] HCA 27; 245 CLR 632, [83]-[87] (Heydon J).

8 The central components of s 59 are extracted below.

9 Wigmore, above n 1, 458.

but more specifically to the view that a desirable level of reliability could not be achieved for hearsay evidence because its trustworthiness could not be probed by cross-examination.[10] The crux of the problem with hearsay for Wigmore then was the deficiency of cross-examination, cross-examination being, in his view, the greatest engine for exposing the fallibility of evidence.

Like Wigmore, Langbein argues for an institutional explanation of the hearsay rule. However, he pinpoints it more specifically in the rise of the adversarial criminal trial and the affiliated emergence of counsels' dominant role in that process in assisting the truth-determining role of the jury. These inter-dependent developments, Langbein suggests, were in turn the product of the view that cross-examination constituted the best vehicle for ensuring and exposing veracity. This view, of course, told against the reception of hearsay evidence.

Wigmore traced the hearsay rule to the beginning of the 17th century on the basis that it was a creature of the emergent modern jury trial. Because Langbein attributed the hearsay rule to the adversarial *process* rather than the jury trial per se, he dated its acceptance from, at the earliest, the late 18th century and possibly as late as the 19th century. Nevertheless, for both Wigmore and Langbein, the deficit of cross-examination was the central component in the development of the hearsay rule, though each ascribed the influence of that factor to a slightly different source and time.

Early jurists justified the hearsay rule on other grounds of its institutional logic. For example, Lord Mansfield CJ's explanation of the necessity for the rule was based on distrust of juries' capacity to evaluate hearsay evidence and a fear that they would accord it undue weight:

> [W]here the jury are the sole judges of the fact, hearsay evidence is properly excluded, because no man can tell what effect it might have upon their minds.[11]

Other early commentators relied on the fact that hearsay statements are not made on oath. For example, Gilbert stated that, because they are not subject to the admonitory effect or solemnisation of the oath, they could be 'of no value'.[12] Wigmore, however, suggests that, because from an early stage the hearsay rule applied to both sworn and unsworn extra-judicial statements, the absence of the oath was never as strong an influence on the development of the rule as the absence of cross-examination.[13]

More generally, the shift in the role of the jury from an investigative body to a passive receiver of evidence precipitated a preference at trials for oral testimony of witnesses' own observations rather than for their accounts of others' observations.[14] Here we see a concern for the reception of what might be judged as the best evidence, direct evidence that the jury could assess by observing the manner and behaviour of the witness whose observations they were being asked to credit. Again, the impetus was the desire for the best possible evidence judged by the yardstick of reliability.[15]

---

10 Ibid 458.

11 *Berkeley Peerage Case* (1811) 4 Camp 401, 415; 171 Eng Rep 128, 135 (HL, Mansfield, Chief Justice of Common Pleas) (advisory opinion).

12 G Gilbert, *The Law of Evidence* (Dublin, 1754), 107, 108.

13 Wigmore, above n 1, 448-8.

14 As in *Colledge's Trial* (1681) 8 How St Tr 549, 662 and *Gascoigne's Trial* (1680) 7 How St Tr 959, 1019.

15 For discussion of the ability of jurors to assess credibility accurately, see Chapter 6.

The following passage from the judgment of Heydon J in *Baker*[16] provides a full explanation of the principal deficiencies of hearsay evidence. His Honour begins by referring to points made by Brennan CJ in *Bannon*:[17]

> 83. … One of his Honour's points concerned the parties' inability to cross-examine the makers of out-of-court statements who do not give evidence. Another concerned the fact that neither the judge nor the jury would have seen the out-of-court statement being made or seen the declarant giving evidence. To these points may be added the following considerations.
>
> 84. Suppose a witness, Mr W, testifies to a relevant event which he has himself observed. In those circumstances, the jury is invited to accept that Mr W did perceive the event, that he has remembered correctly what he perceived, that there is no ambiguity in his narration of the event to the court, and that he is sincere in his testimony. Sincerity may be promoted by the making of an oath or affirmation. Mr W's fear of criticism for false evidence, inside the court or outside it, and the prospect of prosecution for perjury may also promote truthfulness. But the principal guarantee and test of the witness's honesty and the accuracy of his perception, memory and narration lie in his capacity to be cross-examined. At the end of the day, the jury must be satisfied both that the witness believes that the event took place, and that his belief is justified.
>
> 85. It is obvious that any danger that the jury wrongly reaches, or fails to reach, that state of satisfaction is accentuated when what is offered to the court is not Mr W's account of what he saw, but his account of what another person, who does not testify – Mr Jones – saw. In that instance, the jury must be satisfied that Mr W believed he heard Mr Jones say that the event happened. It must be satisfied that Mr W's belief is justified. It must be satisfied that Mr Jones believed that the event happened. And it must be satisfied that Mr Jones's belief was justified. The jury must decide whether it is so satisfied without the safeguards which the ordinary conditions of testimony would have provided in relation to Mr Jones had he been called as a witness. It must decide without testing of Mr Jones's account in cross-examination. And it must decide despite the diminished value of these safeguards so far as Mr W is concerned. There is no direct link between Mr W's testimony and the conclusion that the jury is invited to reach as a result of it. The direct witness, who asserts that the event occurred, can be cross-examined much more fruitfully about his perception and memory of that event than the hearsay witness can be cross-examined. The direct witness claims personal experience of the event and can be cross-examined on that experience. The hearsay witness, who merely testifies that he heard the direct witness say "the event took place", can only be cross-examined about what he claims he heard the direct witness say. The direct witness is giving the "best" evidence. The hearsay witness is not.

While the desire for reliable evidence lies at the foundation of the hearsay rule, it is reliability as tested by cross-examination that came to occupy and that continues to occupy its epistemological, instrumental and institutional heartland. As Langbein says of the historical prominence accorded to cross-examination:

> [T]here was both a naïve faith in the truth-serving efficacy of cross-examination and a growing deference to that lawyer's dominance of trial that the system of partisan examination and cross-examination of witnesses would require.[18]

A similar faith in cross-examination is evident in the passage quoted above from Heydon J's judgment in *Baker*.[19]

---

16 [2012] HCA 27; 245 CLR 632 (references omitted). For a shorter summation of these points, see *Teper* [1952] AC 480, 486 (PC) (Lord Norman).

17 [1995] HCA 27; 185 CLR 1, 7-8.

18 JH Langbein, 'Historical Foundations of the Law of Evidence: A View from the Ryder Sources' (1996) 96 *Columbia Law Review* 1168, 1199.

19 [2012] HCA 27; 245 CLR 632, [84]-[85].

In recent years, curial justifications for hearsay exclusion, particularly in overseas jurisdictions, have given prominence and flesh to the right to confrontation. This approach appears to have resulted from recognition that reliability rationales for hearsay exclusion do not withstand rigorous theoretical scrutiny or hold up in practice.

The 'Confrontation Clause' in the US Sixth Amendment has had a marked impact on a number of areas of criminal procedure, including the admission of hearsay evidence. The judgment of Scalia J in *Coy v Iowa*,[20] though not a case concerning hearsay evidence, gives us a full explanation of the nature of the right to confrontation:

> The Sixth Amendment's guarantee of face-to-face encounter between witness and accused serves ends related both to appearances and to reality. This opinion is embellished with references to and quotations from antiquity in part to convey that there is something deep in human nature that regards face-to-face confrontation between accused and accuser as "essential to a fair trial in a criminal prosecution." *Pointer v Texas*, 380 US 400, 404 (1965). What was true of old is no less true in modern times. President Eisenhower once described face-to-face confrontation as part of the code of his hometown of Abilene, Kansas. In Abilene, he said, it was necessary to "[m]eet anyone face to face with whom you disagree. You could not sneak up on him from behind, or do any damage to him, without suffering the penalty of an outraged citizenry. … In this country, if someone dislikes you, or accuses you, he must come up in front. He cannot hide behind the shadow." (Press release of remarks given to the B'nai B'rith Anti-Defamation League, November 23, 1953, quoted in Pollitt, supra, at 381). The phrase still persists, "Look me in the eye and say that." Given these human feelings of what is necessary for fairness, the right of confrontation "contributes to the establishment of a system of criminal justice in which the perception as well as the reality of fairness prevails." *Lee v Illinois*, 476 US 530, 540 (1986).
>
> The perception that confrontation is essential to fairness has persisted over the centuries because there is much truth to it. A witness "may feel quite differently when he has to repeat his story looking at the man whom he will harm greatly by distorting or mistaking the facts. He can now understand what sort of human being that man is." (Z Chafee, The Blessings of Liberty 35 (1956), quoted in *Jay v Boyd*, 351 US 345, 375-376 (1956), (Douglas, J, dissenting)). It is always more difficult to tell a lie about a person "to his face" than "behind his back." In the former context, even if the lie is told, it will often be told less convincingly. The Confrontation Clause does not, of course, compel the witness to fix his eyes upon the defendant; he may studiously look elsewhere, but the trier of fact will draw its own conclusions. Thus the right to face-to-face confrontation serves much the same purpose as a less explicit component of the Confrontation Clause that we have had more frequent occasion to discuss – the right to cross-examine the accuser; both "ensur[e] the integrity of the factfinding process." *Kentucky v Stincer*, 482 US, at 736.

In the hearsay context, the right to confrontation is more usually linked to the benefits of cross-examination. However, this link may then be couched principally in terms of achieving procedural fairness rather than being directed exclusively to ensuring the reliability of evidence and hence accurate fact-finding. For example, in *Crawford v Washington*,[21] the US Supreme Court held that the Sixth Amendment Confrontation Clause confers a right on criminal defendants to cross-examine State witnesses that applies notwithstanding common law or State legislated hearsay rules. This aspect of the right, the court held, derives from principles

20 487 US 1012, 1018-20 (1988).

21 541 US 36 (2004).

of natural justice[22] and is directed principally at eliminating aspects of the civil law mode of criminal procedure, specifically its use of extra curial statements as evidence against an accused.[23] Accordingly, the court further held that, while the ultimate aim of the right to confrontation is to secure reliable evidence, it is a 'procedural rather than a substantive guarantee'[24] and that '[i]t commands, not that evidence be reliable, but that reliability be assessed in a particular manner: by testing in the crucible of cross-examination'.[25]

Similarly, European Court of Human Rights jurisprudence on the implications for hearsay of the right to confrontation, guaranteed by Article 6 § 3(d) of the *European Convention for the Protection of Human Rights and Fundamental Freedoms*, tells us that the opportunity to confront witnesses is an aspect of the right to a fair hearing. It constitutes an independent principle against which the legitimacy of exceptions to hearsay exclusion must be judged. In *Al Khawaja and Tahery v United Kingdom*[26] the Grand Chamber held:

> Article 6 § 3(d) enshrines the principle that, before an accused can be convicted, all evidence against him must normally be produced in his presence at a public hearing with a view to adversarial argument. Exceptions to this principle are possible but must not infringe the rights of the defence, which, as a rule, require that the accused should be given an adequate and proper opportunity to challenge and question a witness against him, either when that witness makes his statement or at a later stage of proceedings ...

In the High Court decision in *Baker*, we see a union of fairness and reliability considerations in the majority judges' assessment of the desirability of admitting, in exculpation of the appellant, evidence of a third party confession.[27] Their Honours' reasoning is not without complexity. Nevertheless, their refusal to admit the evidence is plainly based on a coalition of procedural fairness and reliability concerns. Their Honours noted at the outset that one very important reason for the hearsay rule is the unfairness of depriving the party against whom the hearsay is tendered of the opportunity of cross-examining the maker. They conceptualised fairness as the accused's right to a fair trial and acknowledged that a fair trial might be compromised were reliable exculpatory, even though untested, evidence to be excluded. Nevertheless, their Honours concluded that, because the exculpatory implications of the third party confession in question could not be guaranteed and because it did not unambiguously support the appellant's case, there had been no unfairness in excluding it in the appellant's trial.

The inherent weaknesses of hearsay evidence were summarised by the ALRC[28] when it recommended reform rather than abandonment of the rule:

- Hearsay statements are usually made out of court in circumstances where the maker is free from the pressures that the court environment may exert in favour of truth telling, including the making of an oath or affirmation and the prospect of prosecution for perjury.
- The makers of hearsay statements may not be available for cross-examination. This means that the accuracy of their perceptions and memory will

22 Ibid 49.

23 Ibid 50.

24 Ibid 61.

25 Ibid 61.

26 [2011] ECHR 2127 (GC), [118].

27 [2012] HCA 27; 245 CLR 632, [51]-[52] (French CJ, Gummow, Hayne, Crennan, Kiefel and Bell JJ).

28 ALRC, *Evidence (Interim)*, above n 3, [661]-675].

not be tested, and their motivations or other influences on them when they made the statements may not be revealed and may remain unexplored.

- Hearsay statements are usually not made in circumstances when triers of fact have the benefit of observing the declarants' demeanour while making the statements.
- Reporters of hearsay statements may have no first hand knowledge of the events in question, which means that their evidence may not be the best evidence about the facts in issue.
- Reporters of hearsay evidence may have misunderstood what they were told. They may misremember or even misrepresent it. Repetition of another's statements can inflate inaccuracies, delete important details and materially alter what was said.
- Hearsay evidence may be fabricated.
- The admission of hearsay evidence may add to the time and cost of litigation.

None of these justifications is unassailable. The primary problem with hearsay evidence identified in both historical and modern sources – the absence of cross-examination – cannot justify hearsay exclusion where the maker of the statement testifies. Yet the hearsay rule extends to out-of-court statements made by witnesses called to testify.[29] Moreover, as already noted and detailed in Chapter 6, cross-examination is not necessarily the truth revealing 'engine' that it is claimed to be. Very often it distorts testimony and makes reliable evidence unreliable. This is particularly the case where vulnerable witnesses, children and those with cognitive impairments, are concerned (see Chapters 5 and 6). It can produce this effect even for robust witnesses. The same is true of the pressures of the court process itself. It can render witnesses mute, erase or alter their memories, confuse them and play merry hell with their ability to testify accurately or with even a modicum of reliability. Further, as the ALRC notes, some hearsay evidence would not be affected by cross-examination.[30] For example, documents prepared for the purpose of, and in the course of, business operations are unlikely to suffer from the inadequacies conventionally associated with hearsay evidence that might be revealed by cross-examination. A classic example is provided by the business records excluded in *Myers v DPP*.[31] The reliability and accuracy of the records were not disputed. Nevertheless, they were excluded on a formal and rigid application of the common law hearsay rule.

As for the accuracy generating impact of the oath or affirmation, modern western secular societies probably have only modest faith in their abilities in this regard.[32]

The argument that, because hearsay evidence may not be based on personal knowledge, it may not be the best evidence does not hold up where it clearly *is* the best evidence. Records of events made close in time to events in question, in circumstances where there is little danger of fabrication, will often supply vastly superior evidence to that provided at trial by someone with first hand knowledge, but called to testify perhaps years after the events occurred. The justification that hearsay evidence deprives triers of fact of the ability to assess the credibility of

---

29 Ibid [663].

30 Ibid [663].

31 [1965] AC 1001 (HL). Statutory reforms in all Australian jurisdictions now provide for the admission of business records, see *UEA*, s 69.

32 See Chapter 5, pp 157-161, for discussion of oaths.

the evidence by viewing the demeanour of declarants, places too much faith in people's ability to judge creditworthiness on this basis.[33]

With regard to a witness misreporting, misremembering or fabricating hearsay evidence, these are matters that might, in fact, be tested by cross-examination and, in any event, speak to the weight of the evidence rather than the desirability of excluding it altogether.[34] They are not of real concern with some forms of hearsay evidence, such as business[35] or official records or electronically recorded representations.

The rationale that juries may misuse or assign too much weight to hearsay evidence can be countered by the expedient mechanism of judicial warnings in relation to its frailties.[36]

Finally, the argument that the admission of hearsay evidence might add to the length or cost of litigation, while attractive to those ruled by fiscal concerns, weighs negligibly in the balance against the need to place as much relevant information before the court as possible, particularly where the fairness of the proceedings or, indeed, their efficiency would be compromised by the exclusion of cogent evidence. In relation to efficiency concerns consider, for example, the absurdity of requiring strict proof of a person's date of birth or age.

What is Hearsay?

Not all representations made out of court are caught by the hearsay rule. Determining when they will be can be one of the most difficult tasks facing counsel and courts.

Under the Australian uniform evidence regimes, the exclusionary rule and the definition of hearsay are set down together in s 59(1) of the *UEA*.[37] Each element of the definition must be satisfied before the exclusion will apply. In summary there must be:

- a previous representation;
- made by a person;
- containing what can reasonably be supposed to be an intended assertion of fact; *and*
- adduced to prove the actual existence of that fact.

The critical aspect of the definition resides in dot point four – the purpose for which the evidence is tendered in the proceeding. Previous representations may satisfy dot points one, two and three, but will not be considered hearsay within s 59 if they are not adduced for the hearsay purpose of proving the *truth of the contents* of the representation. These first three elements will be considered briefly before we embark on a detailed analysis of that hearsay purpose.

The four components of s 59 can be articulated as two different sets of limiting characteristics. The 'previous representation' and 'made by a person' components define the form of evidence caught by the hearsay rule. They constitute essentially mechanical elements of the definition though, on occasion, they may throw up

---

33 See, in particular, *State Rail Authority of New South Wales v Earthline Constructions Pty Ltd (in liq)* [1999] HCA 3; 160 ALR 588 (Kirby J); *Whisprun v Dixon* [2003] HCA 48; 200 ALR 447.

34 See, eg, discussion of the 'taken at its highest' standard in Chapter 4.

35 For discussion of s 69, see Chapter 9.

36 See Chapter 14.

37 Reproduced above, p 334.

knotty issues. The 'intended assertion of fact' and 'evidentiary function' components of s 59 define hearsay according to characteristics relating to purpose. The former relates to the declarant's purpose, the latter to the forensic purpose for adducing the representation. Together they constitute the most intellectually demanding components of the hearsay rule. Any inquiry into whether evidence is hearsay is likely to focus primarily on:

- whether the declarant *intended to assert a fact* and what precisely the intended assertion of fact is; and
- whether the forensic purpose in adducing the previous representation is *to prove the actual existence of that intentionally asserted fact.*

Representation

The definition of 'representation' in the Dictionary of the uniform legislation (s 3(1) of the Tasmanian *Evidence Act 2001*) is all encompassing:

> ***representation*** includes –
> (a) an express or implied representation (whether oral or in writing), or
> (b) a representation to be inferred from conduct, or
> (c) a representation not intended by its maker to be communicated to or seen by another person, or
> (d) a representation that for any reason is not communicated.

In the High Court decision in *Lee*,[38] Gleeson CJ, Gummow, Kirby, Hayne and Callinan JJ explained the use of the term 'representation' rather than statement in the definition of hearsay:

> 21. "Representation" is often used in the law to refer to words that are intended to induce action or inaction by the person who hears or reads them. It may, therefore, seem to be an unusual word to use in this context. But it is clear from the Interim Report of the Law Reform Commission on evidence that, in the proposals that were later formulated in the Act, the term "representation" was used to apply to statements and to conduct and was used to encompass all that those statements or that conduct would convey to the observer.

The breadth of the term was revealed in *Rose*[39] where the NSW Court of Criminal Appeal held that the failure of 300 students to respond to a police officer's request for information about the deceased in a murder case was an implied representation that the students had no information of the kind requested. The court held:

> 261. There is no reason why the word "representation" as used in the *Evidence Act* should not encompass a communication made by silence or a failure to respond. As the judgment in *Lee* points out, …, the [Australian Law Reform] Commission intended that the word be given a wide application …
>
> 262. Whether a representation does arise from the silence or non-action of a person on any particular occasion will depend upon the circumstances and, in particular, whether an inference can be drawn that the person by silence or non-action made a representation of fact, regardless of whether or not the person intended to convey the representation.

Nevertheless, the court held that the evidence was irrelevant because its significance was a matter of speculation and should have been excluded or not admitted.[40]

38 [1998] HCA 60; 195 CLR 594.
39 (2002) 55 NSWLR 701 (Wood CJ and Howie J, with Smart AJ agreeing).
40 Ibid [267].

The potential scope of the hearsay rule that the breadth of the definition of 'representation' might produce is confined by the requirements that the assertions in the representation be intended and that the representation be adduced to prove the actual existence of the asserted facts.

Previous representation

The Dictionary to the *UEA* (s 3(1) of the Tasmanian Act) defines 'previous representations' as representations that are made other than in the proceedings in which the evidence is sought to be adduced. This term has been given a broad construction to cover all representations made on other occasions except the proceedings before the judge in which the evidence is sought to be adduced.[41] This means that representations made in related proceedings such as interlocutory hearings may fall within the definition of 'previous representation' should a party seek to adduce them at the later trial.

Made by a person

The hearsay rule does not apply to representations produced by machines without human in-put. Nor does it apply to communications made by other animals. Accordingly, it would not apply to evidence in an abduction case of the distressed barking of a dog[42] where that evidence is adduced to prove the time of the crime, its location or that something untoward was happening. The question of whether a representation was made by a person is most likely to arise in relation to information whose production has involved the use of a machine. In such cases, the question of whether the representation will be 'made by a person' for purposes of the hearsay rule will be answered by reference to whether its creation required human contribution and exactly what the nature of that contribution was.

Middleton J explained this aspect of the hearsay definition in *Hansen Beverage Co v Bickfords (Australia) Pty Ltd*.[43] Hansen argued that television ratings data (OzTAM data), collected by a system that operated as an automatic recording of the information displayed on a television and available to a user who 'logged on' to the system by pressing an assigned button to register their presence in a room, was not hearsay. Middleton J rejected this argument:

> 121. Hansen relied on *Rook v Maynard* (1993) 126 ALR 150, a case dealing with the common law rules of evidence, where Wright J considered the admissibility of data obtained from a computer program which traced the user's identification number, stating at 157 that:
>
> > "once the trace was applied to the respondent's log-on identification, the process then undertaken by the trace was entirely mechanical in that the peregrinations through the data base by that computer user were automatically traced throughout the system and were recorded and stored for retrieval in report form as soon as the trace print-out was called for."
>
> 122. His Honour found that the computer output from this process was not hearsay as it did not contain a human element.
>
> 123. In *R v Wood* (1982) 76 Cr App Rep 23, the Lord Chief Justice rejected an argument that where a computer is used in the course of the production of final figures, those figures were hearsay, finding at 27 that:

41 *Moy Mobile Pty Ltd v Allphones Retail Pty Ltd* [2008] FCA 369; 167 FCR 314, [27].
42 This was part of the circumstantial evidence adduced in *Pfennig* [1995] HCA 7; 182 CLR 461.
43 [2008] FCA 406; 75 IPR 505.

"This computer was rightly described as a tool. It did not contribute its own knowledge. It merely did a sophisticated calculation which could have been done manually by the chemist and was in fact done by the chemists using the computer programmed by Mr Kellie whom the Crown called as a witness."

124. The evidence which was being considered in these cases was data which had meaning only by virtue of its analysis or recording by a computer; that is, the computer was performing a function which produced data helpful to the court. Although, in *Rook*, the user had to log on before the computer would begin its tracing function, it was not this logging on which was the fact sought to be proved in that case. Rather, it was that the computer had undertaken certain functions, which were able to be proved by data resulting from the computer program itself.

125. In the present case what Hansen is ultimately seeking to prove by the tender is the audience reach, but derived from some data that a certain number of people in the sample homes pressed the button when near the television, thereby representing that they were "in the room where the television was on". I do not accept that Hansen can avoid this conclusion by asserting that it does not rely on the OzTAM data for the purpose of showing certain people were in the room at the relevant time. Undoubtedly, Hansen seeks to prove the estimated audience sizes for a particular program derived by statistical methods from the data, but such data is not automatically recorded by the meters without the human intervention of deliberately pressing the button to show a person or persons are in the room where the television is on. When the people are in the room they intend to, and do, make the representation to assert the existence of this fact, the existence of which needs to be proved to form the basis of the statistical analysis. It seems to me that the necessary reliance by Hansen on the data derived from the sample homes must involve the representation (as defined broadly in s 3 and the dictionary in the Schedule to the Evidence Act) by a person that the person was in the room on the relevant occasion, namely when the television is operating.

126. This is the previous representation (as broadly defined) which, under s 59 of the Evidence Act, makes the source data hearsay which is then used to calculate the audience reach. It is not because the OzTAM computer processes the information that the data is hearsay, it is because the original makers of the representation (the people pressing the buttons) are not giving the evidence themselves. The fact that the source data which is fed into the OzTAM system by the users is then processed using a computer program is not germane to the question of whether the underlying evidence which has been put to the Court in this instance is hearsay or not.

In concluding that the representation was made by a person, Middleton J focused on the fact of human intervention in the data collection process and the intention to make a particular representation that lay behind that intervention.

In *O'Meara v Dominican Fathers*[44] Gyles and Weinberg JJ provided a slightly different take on this issue. Their Honours stressed that for s 59 to apply the source of the asserted fact must be tied back to a person who had or might reasonably be supposed to have had personal knowledge of it. If the asserted fact was machine-generated it will not be hearsay; if it was recorded or interpreted by a person, then it may be.

Intended assertions of fact

At common law the definition of hearsay is wide enough to catch previous representations that make unintended assertions of fact. This creates the possibility for almost all statements and conduct whether intentionally assertive

44 Unreported, FCAFC, BC200307403, [87].

or non-assertive to be constructed as implied assertions of fact and potentially caught by the hearsay rule. Not only does this make the limits of the hearsay rule at common law virtually boundless but it also renders the common law rule very complex. For example, the fact that a motor mechanic examined his car carefully and then drove away in it might be read as an unintended implied assertion by him that the vehicle was roadworthy.[45] If adduced to prove that fact, his conduct would be caught by the common law hearsay rule. Similarly, the fact that people wrote to an elderly testator addressing him as a rational person may be construed as an unintended implied assertion as to the testator's soundness of mind, and thus excluded if adduced to prove that fact.[46] Clearly, as these examples show, at common law almost anything can be fashioned into hearsay evidence. In contrast, the *UEA* (in accordance with the ALRC's recommendation[47]) has limited the exclusionary rule in s 59 to apply only to *intended* assertions of fact.

Nevertheless, exactly what is encompassed in an intentional assertion of fact has remained uncertain and was the subject of further review by the ALRC in 2006.[48] This review was prompted partly by obiter statements of judges in the NSW Court of Criminal Appeal decision in *Hannes*.[49] For example, Spigelman CJ noted that, if the word 'intended' in s 59 was given a narrow reading so as to require 'some form of specific conscious advertence' by the maker of the previous representation, many implied assertions considered at common law to fall within the hearsay rule would no longer be included.[50] Of course, a legislative goal of s 59 was, in fact, to exclude most implied assertions from the purview of the hearsay rule – all implied assertions, in fact, that do not comprise intentional assertions. Nevertheless, Spigelman CJ suggested that s 59 might exclude, not only the specific facts subjectively adverted to by makers of previous representations, but also any facts that are necessary assumptions underlying the facts subjectively adverted to.[51] This approach adds a significant degree of complexity and uncertainty to decisions about the application of s 59. Further, as noted by the ALRC, it potentially opens the way for unintended assertions to be excluded by s 59, despite its wording and legislative intent.[52] The Commission argued that because Spigelman CJ 'appears to have meant that where an implied assertion is necessarily assumed within an express assertion, *intention to make* the implied assertion is "contained" within the *intention to make* the express assertion. Accordingly, s 59 would necessarily apply to express and to intended and unintended implied assertions'.[53]

In response the Commission recommended some minor adjustment of s 59 to apply an objective test to the assessment of whether an assertion is intended. Intended assertions under s 59 are now assertions of fact that the maker of the representation can reasonably be supposed to have intended, having regard to the circumstances in which they were made. While this amendment clearly obviates the need to establish the subjective intentions of the asserter, it is not clear how

45 This example is derived from and to identical effect as the example given by Baron Parke in *Wright v Doe d Tatham* (1837) 7 Adolph & E 313, 388; 112 Eng Rep 488, 516.

46 Ibid.

47 ALRC, *Evidence (Interim)*, above n 3, [684].

48 ALRC, *Uniform Evidence Law* (Report No 102, 2006).

49 [2000] NSWCCA 503; 158 FLR 359.

50 Ibid [359].

51 Ibid [359].

52 ALRC, *Uniform Evidence Law*, above n 48, [7.45].

53 Ibid [7.45].

it displaces the decision in *Hannes*. Indeed, it has been argued that the revised test will actually result in more evidence being classified as hearsay and that it makes the task for a party arguing for the non-application of the hearsay rule more onerous than the subjective test. For example, Odgers contends that:

> Under the current formulation, the party arguing for admission of the evidence will have to satisfy the court that it could not reasonably be supposed that the person who made the previous representation intended to assert the particular fact. If a consideration of all the circumstances in which the representation was made could lead a hypothetical reasonable person to infer that the fact was intended to be asserted, then the hearsay rule applies to it. Clearly enough, the amended test imposes a heavier burden on the party contending that the evidence is not caught by the hearsay rule. The current test will result in more evidence being classified as hearsay and subject to this exclusionary rule. Although the hearsay rule established by this provision does not apply to all "implied assertions", if the person who made the representation "can reasonably be supposed" to have intended to assert a fact implied in the representation, it will be caught by the rule.[54]

This is not the outcome that the ALRC intended. Rather the Commission sought to 'foreclose'[55] the approach in *Hannes* and the expansion of the exclusionary rule to unintended assertions. Accordingly, the approach to s 59 that the Commission appears to have envisioned is not the extension of the hearsay exclusion to all and any implied assertions of fact that might reasonably be supposed to have been intended in the circumstances. Rather, it is to shape the question as: *having regard to the circumstances in which it was made, what can it reasonably be supposed that the maker of the representation* ***actually*** *intended to assert?* This is a subtle but significant difference. It accords with the High Court explanation in *Lee*[56] of the approach to be adopted to unintended assertions under s 59:

> 22. ... The rule's operation requires consideration first of why it is sought to lead evidence of something said or done out of Court (a previous representation). What is it that that 'previous representation' is led to prove? In particular, is it sought to lead it to prove the existence of a fact that the person who made the representation intended to assert by it? The fact that the statement or the conduct concerned might unintendedly convey some assertion is not to the point. The inquiry is about what the person who made the representation intended to assert by it.

Section 59 of course applies to intended, implied assertions of fact. These do not make a frequent appearance in the case law, but the NSW case of *O'Grady*[57] supplies one instance. The accused was charged with murder by shooting. He claimed that his act was involuntary. In support of his defence he sought to lead evidence of a conversation that he had had with his sister about a month after the event. Over objection from the Crown Hulme J ruled the evidence to be admissible:

> 5. ... During the examination in chief of the accused's sister, she gave evidence of a conversation with the accused about a month after the shooting. When Mr Conditsis appearing for the accused asked her "Q. What did he say to you?", the Crown objected.
>
> 6. At page 714 of the transcript I allowed the question, indicating that I would give my reasons later. These are they. The answer given was: "Kate, tell me what happened. You know that I couldn't do something like that", an answer which was something to the effect of that Mr Conditsis had anticipated.

54 S Odgers, *Uniform Evidence Law* (Thomson Reuters, 15th ed, 2020), [EA.59.210].
55 ALRC, *Uniform Evidence Law*, above n 48.
56 [1998] HCA 60; 195 CLR 594.
57 [2000] NSWSC 1256.

7. My reasons for allowing the question and the answer are these. I regard the evidence as admissible as falling within the exception contained in s 66(2) of the Evidence Act and also as falling within s 72.[58] The answer, in my view, contained implied representations to the effect that the accused's shooting of the deceased was not the ultimate result of a voluntary act, or was done in the circumstances of some abnormality of mind.

The purpose test

The purpose for which the previous representation is adduced is the critical component of the hearsay definition. A previous representation will be hearsay only if it is utilised to prove the existence of a fact that it can reasonably be supposed the maker of the representation intended to assert. If a previous representation is relevant in some other way and relied on according to that relevance, it will not be hearsay. Non-hearsay previous representations are usually called 'original evidence'. Accordingly, in determining whether evidence of a previous representation is caught by the hearsay rule it is crucial to identify:

(1) how it is relevant to the facts in issue,
(2) what precisely it is being adduced to prove; and
(3) how it will be used to prove that matter.

A simple way of encapsulating the essence of hearsay evidence is to think of the previous representation as being deployed in the same manner as a witness's testimony at trial about the events in question.[59] The case law is replete with explanations of this aspect of the hearsay definition. In *Wing Cheong Li*[60] Howie and Hall JJ (with Macfarlane JA agreeing) summarised some of the primary authorities:

> 50. Evidence of a previous representation made by a person is not admissible to prove the existence of a fact that the person intended to assert by the representation: s 59(1) of the *Evidence Act*. However, if evidence of a previous representation made by a person is not adduced to prove the existence of a fact asserted by the representation, it is not classified as hearsay. Evidence of that kind is sometimes referred to as "original evidence" to distinguish it from hearsay evidence: *Walton* at 289 per Mason CJ; *Pollitt v The Queen* [1992] HCA 35; 174 CLR 558 at 571 per Brennan J.
>
> 51. In *R v Lee* [1998] HCA 60; 195 CLR 594 at [22], the operation of the hearsay rule in terms of s 59 was explained by the High Court (Gleeson CJ, Gummow, Kirby, Hayne and Callinan JJ) in the following terms:
>
> > "Section 59 must be understood in this light. The rule's operation requires consideration first of why it is sought to lead evidence of something said or done out of Court (a previous representation). What is it that that 'previous representation' is led to prove? In particular, is it sought to lead it to prove the existence of a fact that the person who made the representation intended to assert by it? The fact that the statement or the conduct concerned might unintendedly convey some assertion is not to the point. The inquiry is about what the person who made the representation intended to assert by it." (per Gleeson CJ, Gummow, Kirby, Hayne and Callinan JJ).
>
> 52. Again in *Papakosmas*, the High Court held that the operation of the exclusion to s 59 depends upon the use that is sought to be made of the evidence in question (at [24] per Gleeson CJ and Hayne J).

58 The then s 72 exception is now contained in s 66A. At the time of judgment in *O'Grady*, the exception in s 72 encompassed both first hand and more remote hearsay. In contrast, the s 66A exception covers only first hand hearsay.

59 This analogy is implicit in Dawson J's description of hearsay evidence as 'testimonial' in *Benz* [1989] HCA 64; 168 CLR 110, 134.

60 [2010] NSWCCA 40; 265 ALR 445, [50]-[52].

Often the greatest difficulty with this aspect of the hearsay definition lies in understanding the non-hearsay relevance of previous representations rather than the use of previous representations for a hearsay purpose. We will look more closely at non-hearsay uses of previous representations below. At this point we put some flesh on the bones of the purpose test by providing some relatively straightforward explanatory examples:

- In a criminal case, evidence of a third party confession is hearsay if adduced to prove that the person who made the confession committed the crime rather than the accused: *Baker*;[61] *Blastland*;[62] *Re Van Beelen*;[63] *Bannon*.[64]
- In a murder case evidence of statements made by the deceased about who had injured her, and how, is hearsay if adduced to prove the source of the deceased's injuries and how they came to be inflicted: *Abel*;[65] *Harris*;[66] *Conway*.[67]
- Evidence of previous representations made by the complainant in a sexual offences case to her friends about what had happened to her, and who had done it, is hearsay if adduced to prove the details of the offence and the identity of the perpetrator: *Papakosmas*.[68]
- In a criminal case where the accused is charged with aggravated assault, evidence that he told an acquaintance shortly after the offence was committed that he 'had just done a job and fired two shots', is hearsay if tendered by the prosecution to prove the identity of the person who committed the offence: *Lee*.[69]
- In a criminal case involving the theft of motor vehicles, records from the factory where the cars were manufactured listing identification numbers placed on the cars at the time of their manufacture is hearsay if adduced to prove that the accused had falsified the registration details of cars he was offering for sale: *Myers v DPP*.[70]
- In a case where the accused is charged with making a false declaration to customs officials about the country of origin of goods he had imported, evidence of labels on the goods' packaging, identifying them as the produce of a country different from that declared by the accused, is hearsay if adduced to prove that the country of origin is that on the labels: *Patel v Comptroller of Customs*.[71]
- In a murder case where the accused raised the defence of diminished responsibility at trial, evidence from the accused's psychiatrist that the accused told her in the weeks before the offence was committed that he was hearing voices in his head instructing him to attack the deceased is hearsay if adduced to prove that the accused was suffering from auditory hallucinations that prompted him to commit murder: *Welsh*.[72]

61 [2012] HCA 27; 245 CLR 632.
62 [1986] AC 41.
63 (1974) 9 SASR 163.
64 [1995] HCA 27; 185 CLR 1.
65 2011 NLTD 173 (Supreme Court of Newfoundland and Labrador, Trial Division (General)).
66 [2005] NSWCCA 432; 158 A Crim R 454.
67 [2000] FCA 461; 172 ALR 185.
68 [1999] HCA 37; 196 CLR 297.
69 [1998] HCA 60; 195 CLR 594.
70 [1965] AC 1001 (HL).
71 [1965] AC 356 (PC).
72 (1996) 90 A Crim R 364 (NSWCCA).

It is vitally important in all examples such as these in which representations may be considered hearsay to identify the representation that is being made. In the first example above, the third-party confession, it is likely easy to reconstruct that the representation would be along the lines of 'I committed the offence [and the accused did not]'. The import of the representation becomes trickier in the second-last example of the customs declaration, in which the representation at issue would be something like 'I am certifying that these goods come from Thailand', which would be hearsay if adduced to prove that the goods did come from Thailand. Once the representations are identified in each of the examples, it should become clear why in all the cases described the evidence may be excluded under s 59. These representations would only then be admissible if either an exception to the hearsay rule can be found or the representation can be constructed as non-hearsay – that is, as having a non-hearsay relevance for which it is admissible.

Non-hearsay previous representations

Previous representations can serve a number of evidentiary functions as original evidence. It is important to remember that when previous representations are used as original evidence they are not admitted as exceptions to the hearsay rule. Rather they fall outside the rule altogether because they are not offered for a hearsay purpose (that is, to prove the truth of their contents) and therefore do not comprise hearsay evidence within s 59. When admitted as original evidence, previous representations are often relied on simply to show that the representation was made. This notion was simply expressed by the Canadian Supreme Court in *Evans*:[73]

> An out-of-court statement which is admitted for the truth of its contents is hearsay. An out-of-court statement offered simply as proof that the statement was made is not hearsay, and is admissible as long as it has some probative value.

In this sense the making of the representation is treated as conduct or a verbal act from which inferences may be drawn. A cautionary point should be made at this juncture: representations adduced to show that they were made will only be admissible on this basis if the making of the representation is itself relevant and provided that the proposed inferences to be drawn from the making of the representation are also relevant and available on the evidence. An obvious example would be where it is necessary to prove that someone was conscious at a particular time or to make a comparison of signatures regarding authenticity.[74] The content of answers given to questions asked at the time where the fact of consciousness is disputed might be offered to prove the person was conscious. In this scenario, the content of the answers given does not matter. The words themselves are essentially irrelevant. It is the fact that the person was capable of responding when questioned that is relevant. However, previous representations may constitute original evidence even where their use requires reference to be made to or reliance to be placed on what was asserted. In such situations it may be difficult to distinguish them from hearsay evidence. The point of distinction is how precisely the evidence is relevant and how it will be used to prove the matter in respect of which it is tendered. A number of examples of how previous representations can be relevant as original

73 [1993] SCR 653, 661-2 (Sopinka J).

74 *Singh v De Castro* [2017] NSWCA 241, [61], citing *Hannes* [2000] NSWCCA 503; 158 FLR 359, [323]-[325] (Spigelman CJ, with Studdert J agreeing).

evidence were usefully listed in *Re Van Beelen*,[75] which, though not a uniform evidence legislation case, remains helpful in this regard:

> It is, of course, fundamental to accepted notions of proof in our courts that due proof that a statement was made by A to B is capable of being used in many different ways, depending on the circumstances. Irrespective of whether A, or B, or both, are or are not parties to the case in which the proof is offered, certain propositions would not, we apprehend, be open to dispute.
>
> 1. It may be established simply that A said something to B. From this it may be inferred, depending on other testimony, and apart altogether from what was said, that, for example, A had the opportunity of imparting some intelligence to B; that, if A spoke when he was near B, B was aware of A's presence; that, if the occasion was one of several, A and B were acquainted; that, if the tone of the voice was detectable, A was cold and distant to B, was quarrelling with B, or was amused by something which he mentioned to B. In those, and other like cases, the suggested inferences can be drawn without resorting to the wording of the statement.
>
> 2. It may be proved that A said something to B and what that something was. By this it may be disclosed that the remarks were, or formed part of, a relevant fact: for example, that A was selling something to B; that A was showing the way to B; that A was ordering B to carry out a certain task; that A was carrying on a certain sort of business; that A was acting toward B as one would act who was occupier of the premises where the statement was made, or as one would act towards another when both were in a gaming house or a brothel. In such cases as these, the words spoken form an integral part of a complex fact.
>
> 3. It may be proved that A said something to B and what that something was in circumstances from which it is possible to infer, in all the circumstances, that A was of unsound mind; that A and B were likely to be husband and wife, or lovers, or deadly enemies or close business associates; that A's or B's state of mind, or of knowledge, or of feeling, was thus and thus depending on what could be inferred from what was said. See, for example, *Subramaniam v Public Prosecutor*. In the circumstances referred to, and in comparable circumstances, what is said is proved, not to establish the truth of what was averred, but as material from which another fact may be inferred. It is the nature and quality of what was said that invites attention, not the purported testimonial operation of it: see, for example, *Lloyd v Powell Duffryn Steam Coal Company Limited*, especially at pages 751-752, and the *Aylesford Peerage Case*.
>
> The above examples, which rest on well-accepted principles, do not, of course, purport to be exhaustive, but it will sufficiently appear from them that it is essential to understand how a party seeking to tender proof of a statement hopes to use it if a court is to reach a satisfactory decision as to its relevance and admissibility.

Other instances of original evidence are:

Transactional words and words having operative legal effect

Representations that create contracts, trusts, deeds or wills are not hearsay. Essentially, such representations have no evidentiary value as assertions of fact. Their relevance lies in the fact that they were made: see, for example, *Macraild*[76] (telephone conversations of the making of an agreement for the sale of cannabis). Similarly, representations that themselves constitute a criminal offence or an actionable tort are not hearsay: see, for example, *Suteski (No 4)*[77] (evidence of words spoken by the accused tendered as 'verbal acts' constituting a conspiracy

---

75 (1974) 9 SASR 163, 200-1 (Walters, Wells and Jacobs JJ) (FC).

76 Unreported, NSWCCA, 18 December 1997.

77 [2002] NSWSC 218; 128 A Crim R 275.

to commit a crime) and *GH*[78] (the words spoken constituted the actus reus of the offence of conspiring to pervert the course of justice).

Representations whose making is relevant to their makers' credibility

Prior representations that are inconsistent with a witness's in-court testimony might be adduced to show simply that the witness has given different accounts of events on different occasions and might therefore be considered to be an unreliable witness: see, for example, *Adam*.[79] The underlying assumption here is that trustworthy witnesses are those whose accounts of their observations remain constant. Consequently, prior representations made by witnesses that are consistent with their in-court testimony might be adduced to demonstrate their constancy over time and, hence, their reliability. Additionally, in some cases the making of particular types of prior representations is something that is generally expected of people as a normal response to particular events. Consequently, evidence that a witness in such a case has acted in accordance with this expectation may be adduced to encourage acceptance of their testimony as trustworthy. For example, there is an assumption that genuine victims of sexual offences will complain about the offence as soon as possible after the offence has been perpetrated on them. The concomitant assumption is that, where no complaint is made or where the making of a complaint is delayed, the allegations of the offence are likely to have been fabricated. Accordingly, evidence that a complainant in a sexual offences case made a proximate complaint about the offence may be adduced to reinforce the complainant's credibility at trial: see the explanation of this phenomenon in *Papakosmas*.[80] In all these cases it is the fact of the making of the previous representations that is being relied on either to reinforce or undermine the witnesses' credibility. Of course, the actual assertions made may also be relevant on a hearsay basis to establish the existence of the facts asserted. Accordingly, many previous representations that are relevant to witnesses' credibility can have a dual relevance as original (that is, credibility) *and* hearsay evidence, as was the case in both *Adam* and *Papakosmas*.[81] In such a case, if the evidence is sought to be used for a hearsay purpose, it will be necessary to consider the availability of an exception to the hearsay rule, such as s 66 or s 60 of the *UEA*.

Evidence of previous representations to show the basis for an expert's opinion

Where experts testify they will almost always need to explain the foundation of their opinions. Very often this will consist of matters that they have been told by other people. For example, medical experts may recount what their patients have told them about their symptoms, how they became ill and the progress of their condition in explaining why they made particular diagnoses or have given particular prognoses. When adduced to show the basis of expert opinions, the previous representations are not being relied on as hearsay, but rather as original evidence. Of course, such representations may also be relevant as hearsay evidence where they are relied on to prove that the matters recounted by

78 [2000] FCA 1618; 105 FCR 419, [23]-[26] (Spender J) and [56] (Miles J).
79 *Adam* [2001] HCA 57; 207 CLR 96, [21]-[23].
80 [1999] HCA 37; 196 CLR 297, [74]-[78] (McHugh J).
81 See Chapter 6 for discussion of credibility evidence, the credibility rule and its exceptions.

patients to their medical practitioners actually occurred. *Welsh*[82] demonstrates the potential dual relevance of previous representations adduced to prove the basis of experts' opinions and how s 60 of the *UEA* may operate to make them available for use on a hearsay basis.

Evidence of representations to establish a person's state of mind

As *Re Van Beelen* shows this is a long-accepted category of original evidence. It covers representations made to a person that might produce an effect on their state of mind and also statements made by a person from whose making their state of mind and feelings might be inferred. So, for example, evidence that an accused had been threatened with physical harm if he or she did not participate in a criminal enterprise might be adduced to show that he or she was acting under duress in committing the offence: see, for example, *Subramaniam v Public Prosecutor*.[83]

Prior representations adduced to show the speaker's own state of mind, knowledge or intentions can comprise one of the trickiest instances of original evidence. However, a relatively straightforward example in this category is provided in *Matthews*.[84] The accused was charged with the rape and murder of his estranged wife. He denied the rape charge on the basis that sexual intercourse had been consensual. Evidence that the deceased had made statements to friends in the days before her death about her fear of the accused and her desire not to see him was held to be relevant to show that she had not consented to sexual intercourse with him: *Matthews*.[85] The same case provides another uncontroversial example in this category: the use of a previous representation to show the maker's esoteric knowledge of an event and so link them to it. In this case the accused had written in his diary on the day of his wife's death, 'Liz dead, 27 years five months nine days'. This was adduced to show that the accused knew of his wife's death before it became public knowledge. In these circumstances it might be inferred that his knowledge derived from his involvement in her death.

The principal Australian authority on the non-hearsay use of prior representations to establish their makers' state of mind is *Walton*.[86] The judgment of Wilson, Dawson and Toohey JJ explains the reasoning behind this construction of original evidence:

> When a person's state of mind is relevant, evidence tending to prove that fact is admissible. That evidence may, of course, take the form of conduct on the part of the person whose state of mind is in question from which the state of mind might be inferred. But it might also take the form of statements made by the person or by another from which a similar inference might be made.[87]

---

82 (1996) 90 A Crim R 364, 367-72.

83 [1956] 1 WLR 965 (PC) where evidence that Subramaniam felt threatened was held to be relevant and admissible to supporting his claim that he was fearful and acted under duress. Evidence of the representation that caused Subramaniam to feel threatened was not excluded by the hearsay rule because it was not adduced to prove that the person speaking to Subramaniam was telling the truth (that is, the statement 'I am a Communist' was not being used to prove that the speaker was actually a Communist), but to show that the statement caused Subramaniam to be fearful.

84 (1990) 58 SASR 19.

85 Similar use of previous representations made by a complainant in a sexual offences case occurred in *Bull* [2000] HCA 24; 201 CLR 443.

86 [1989] HCA 9; 166 CLR 283.

87 Ibid 300.

In *Walton*, the accused had been charged with murder. Evidence was adduced that, on the day before she died, the deceased told others that she was going to meet the accused the next day. This evidence was admitted as evidence of conduct to show the deceased's intention to meet the accused. The jury could then infer from that evidence, when coupled with other evidence, that the deceased had acted in accordance with those intentions, which would explain why her body came to be found where it was.

It is cases like *Walton* where the construction of prior representations as original evidence is particularly problematic. The reasoning involved has the guise of dissimulating verbal acrobatics and the distinction between hearsay and original evidence becomes markedly attenuated. In fact, this category of original evidence comes so close to being hearsay evidence that it might well fit the categorisation of what Birch has termed a 'hearsay fiddle'.[88] In *Kamleh*,[89] Kirby, Hayne and Heydon JJ noted the problems with the *Walton* approach. Kirby J held:

> 27. ... Dissecting [out of court statements] into (1) a fact that a conversation occurred and (2) a fact that emerged from the conversation, and distinguishing that fact from (3) the inculpating content of the conversation as to intention, requires a feat of mental gymnastics that should be avoided in the highly practical context of a criminal trial.

To the same effect, Hayne J held:

> 33. ... Where an out of court statement is tendered to demonstrate that the person making the assertion then had a particular intention, the line between proof of the fact asserted and proof of the fact that the assertion was made is difficult to draw. No less importantly, the fact that the person then had a particular intention must often find its relevance to the facts in issue in a chain of reasoning which begins by accepting that the expressed intention not only was truly held but would probably be acted upon.

As demonstrated in *Walton*, the 'making of a previous representation as evidence of intention' construction can only be used to circumvent the hearsay rule where the maker's state of mind is relevant to a fact in issue or is itself a fact in issue.[90] The uniform evidence legislation has avoided the problems inherent in the *Walton* construction by treating evidence of a person's contemporaneous representations about their state of mind, knowledge, feelings, intentions, sensations and health as hearsay but then creating an exception to the exclusionary rule for them in s 66A of the *UEA*. Nevertheless, the construction of words as verbal conduct adopted in *Walton* remains useful and valid. It may be useful where s 66A cannot apply as, for example, where the evidence, constructed as hearsay, would constitute second hand hearsay, rendering s 66A inapplicable. Additionally, adoption of the approach in *Walton* is uncontroversial where the relevance of utterances genuinely rests in treating them as behaviour or verbal conduct. For example, in a murder case where the intention of the accused is in issue, evidence of the accused's conduct, including verbal conduct, towards the deceased that shows that the accused had a hostile attitude towards the deceased will be relevant to the issue of intent. So, if there is evidence that the accused verbally abused, swore at, threatened and quarrelled violently with the deceased, it is the fact that such conduct occurred that is relevant in establishing the accused's state of mind. Such

---

88 DJ Birch, 'Hearsay-logic and Hearsay-fiddles: Blastland Revisited' in P Smith (ed), *Criminal Law: Essays in Honour of JC Smith* (Butterworths, 1987), 25. See also R Pattenden, 'Conceptual Versus Pragmatic Approaches to Hearsay' (1993) 56 *Modern Law Review* 138, 155-6.

89 [2005] HCA 2; 213 ALR 97.

90 And see in particular in this regard, *Pollitt* [1992] HCA 35; 174 CLR 558.

evidence is adduced as original evidence. The hearsay rule does not prevent the declarant's mental state from being inferred from that conduct simply because it is verbal.[91]

Conclusion

Walton and the line of cases that have adopted its reasoning have been significant in exposing the often-problematic nature of the hearsay rule and accepted common law exceptions to it. At common law the rule is capable of catching too much uncontroversially reliable evidence – evidence, what is more, that it may be unfair to one or other of the parties to exclude. At common law as well, the exceptions to the rule do not cope satisfactorily with modern forms of information or take adequate account of modern mechanisms for ensuring the reliability of previous representations. As noted above, in Australia the rigidity of the common law approach led the High Court to consider adopting a flexible approach to hearsay evidence depending on its level of demonstrable reliability.[92] However, this approach has not gained universal judicial support and conceptually different approaches have been adopted by the individual High Court judges who favoured it. In any event, this development has largely been superseded in uniform *Evidence Act* jurisdictions by the enactment of that legislation, which has attempted to achieve a definition of hearsay that narrows its scope and brings clarity and certainty to its application. It has also sought to provide a comprehensive set of exceptions to the rule that is based on a sound conceptual framework, ensuring that the rule applies rationally, does not exclude inherently reliable evidence and yet protects against the admission of untested, suspect evidence.[93] The *UEA* exceptions to the hearsay rule are considered in the next chapter. Their conceptual underpinnings will be discussed and comparisons with reforms in the United Kingdom and Canada considered.

The approach advocated for reform of the hearsay rule by the ALRC, and subsequently given statutory imprimatur in the *UEA*, was for retention but also for reform of the rule and exceptions to it. The Commission accepted that the rationales long identified and accepted for the rule continue to have merit and justify a moderate approach to reform. Elsewhere, more radical reform has been suggested. The rule's failure to fulfil its own rationales, its capacity to work in some cases against the interests of justice, have been cited as reasons justifying its abolition.[94] The better approach, it has been argued, is to leave the admission of hearsay evidence to trial judges' discretion, that discretion to be exercised by reference to the criteria of the necessity to receive the evidence

---

91 See, eg, *Hissey* (1973) 6 SASR 280, 288-9, where Bray CJ, Hogarth and Mitchell JJ held admissible evidence that the accused, who was charged with the murder of a woman with whom he had been living, had used and threatened physical violence towards her. In *Garner* (1963) 81 WN (Pt 1) (NSW) 120, 128-9, Maguire J held that evidence that the accused had been heard to express great hostility to, or contempt for, the complainant would have been admissible on the question of whether the accused assaulted the complainant as charged.

92 *Walton* [1989] HCA 9; 166 CLR 283 (Mason CJ and Deane J); *Benz* [1989] HCA 64; 168 CLR 110, 118, 143-4 (Mason CJ, McHugh and Gaudron JJ); *Pollitt* [1992] HCA 35; 174 CLR 558 (Mason CJ, Dean, Toohey and McHugh JJ).

93 ALRC, *Evidence (Interim)*, above n 3, [682].

94 See, eg, JD Jackson, 'Hearsay: the Sacred Cow that Won't Be Slaughtered?' (1998) 2 *International Journal of Evidence and Proof* 166.

and its reliability.[95] In the next chapter we attempt to assess whether the new evidence law is achieving its objectives of simplifying the law of hearsay and rendering its operation more certain and rational. In doing this we also evaluate the Australian approach against the generally flexible approach developed by the Canadian Supreme Court.

95 This approach has been adopted by the Canadian Supreme Court: *Khan* (1990) 59 CCC (3d) 92; *Smith* (1992) 94 DLR (4th) 590; *Starr* [2000] 2 SCR 144; *B(KG)* [1991] 1 SCR 740; *Khelawon* [2006] 2 SCR 787.

Chapter 9

Hearsay – The Exceptions to the Rule

Introduction

In this chapter we consider the major exceptions to the hearsay rule created by the uniform evidence legislation for criminal cases. The chapter concentrates on the general exceptions created for first hand hearsay. Consideration is also given to the major second hand hearsay exceptions for business records (*UEA*, s 69), for Aboriginal and Torres Strait Islander traditional laws and customs (s 72), and to the permission created by s 60 for the hearsay use of previous representations admitted originally for a non-hearsay purpose. This chapter does not deal with the admissions exception to the hearsay rule, which is covered in Chapter 7. The exceptions for second hand hearsay in ss 70, 71, 73, 74 and 75 (which cover such things as tags, labels, electronic communications and representations relating to reputation concerning relationships, age and public rights) are noted but not discussed in detail.

As in the previous chapter, we begin with a brief discussion of the rationales and theoretical basis for the exceptions to s 59(1). This gives us insight into their legislative intent and provides a yardstick against which to evaluate their operation. Significantly, it also furnishes us with the grounds for operationalising the exceptions, for arguing for and against suggestions for their interpretation and application. We then turn to an analysis of the exceptions themselves in a 'black letter law' sense. We begin with the exceptions for first hand hearsay. Here, our first task is to summarise *the process* involved in identifying which particular provision of the uniform legislation may supply an exception to s 59(1) for first hand hearsay in any given case. The next logical move is to discuss the definition of first hand hearsay itself and thereafter to detail the exceptions created for first hand hearsay in criminal cases. The exceptions for second hand and more remote hearsay are then discussed. The chapter ends by reviewing the operation of the important mechanism provided by s 60 for *waiving* the hearsay rule in defined circumstances. Examples and problems are provided throughout the chapter to illustrate the exceptions covered.

Rationales for Exceptions to Section 59 of the *UEA*

Wigmore, being an admirer of the common law hearsay rule, maintained that underlying unifying principles can be discerned in the common law exceptions to it. He argued that the key to their rationales could be located in the primary rationales for the hearsay rule itself – the inherent unreliability of hearsay evidence and the inability to expose its untrustworthiness by cross-examination. Accordingly, he reasoned that, in cases where there was no reason to doubt the reliability of the evidence and/or where its unreliability would not in any event be exposed by cross-examination, the interests of 'efficient investigation' justified and might, in fact, necessitate the admission of hearsay evidence and courts' creation of exceptions to the exclusionary rule.

For Wigmore the unifying logic of the common law exceptions to the hearsay rule was their common adherence to essential criteria of necessity and/or circumstantially established indicia of reliability. Yet, while these factors may be discerned as fortifying the existence of common law exceptions to hearsay exclusion, they never operated in or of themselves to achieve admission for hearsay evidence, not, at least, until the Canadian Supreme Court created the 'principled approach' to hearsay admission.[1] Further, the common law inclusionary exceptions were not developed in a unified or systematic manner with reference to any over-arching principles. Rather, they came into existence in an ad hoc and piecemeal way, prompted by the demands of individual cases. As Lord Reid suggested in *Myers v DPP*:[2]

> One might hazard a surmise that when the rule proved highly inconvenient in a particular kind of case it was relaxed just sufficiently far to meet that case, and without regard to any question of principle.

So, in contrast to the admirable unity perceived by Wigmore, other commentators have characterised the common law inclusionary exceptions as chaotic, overly complex, inconsistent, replete with anomalies, illogical and haphazard.[3] This too was the view of the Australian Law Reform Commission (ALRC)[4] and generated its approach to reform:

> *Universal criticism:* The common law rule and its exceptions have been the object of repeated criticism for many years. Criticisms range from 'absurdly technical', through 'a conglomeration of inconsistencies', to the famous Morgan and Maguire comment that the rules 'resemble an old-fashioned crazy-quilt made of patches cut for a group of paintings by cubists, futurists and surrealists'. The difficulties created by the common law are reflected in the vast body of differing legislation which has attempted to address problems as they have emerged. These have added to the 'crazy-quilt' effect. … The fundamental problem has been that the courts ceased to develop the law after 1880 and legislation has been enacted from time to time, usually on an ad hoc basis addressing a specific problem

---

1 *Khan* (1990) 59 CCC (3d) 92; *Smith* (1992) 94 DLR (4th ed) 590; *Starr* [2000] 2 SCR 144; *B(KG)* [1991] 1 SCR 740; *Khelawon* [2006] 2 SCR 787 (all decisions of the Canadian Supreme Court); and see further below, p 366.

2 [1965] AC 1001, 1020.

3 See, eg, Law Reform Commission (Ireland), *Hearsay in Civil and Criminal Cases* (Consultation Paper, LRC CP 60, 2010), [1.30], [3.05]-3.06]; Law Commission (UK), *Evidence in Criminal Proceedings: Hearsay and Related Topics* (No 245, TSO, 1997), particularly at [2.6]-[2.7]; Federal/Provincial taskforce on the Law of Evidence (Canada), *Report of the Federal/Provincial Taskforce on Uniform Rules of Evidence*, prepared for the Uniform Evidence Law Conference of Canada (Carswell, 1982); Law Reform Commission of Canada, *Report on Evidence* (Information Canada, 1975); New Zealand Law Commission, *Hearsay Evidence: An Options Paper* (No PP10, 1989), vi.

4 ALRC, *Evidence (Interim)* (Report No 26, 1985) Vol 1, [329] (references omitted).

> that has arisen. They, however, are additional to the common law exceptions. Both have tended to follow a case by case approach, with the result that the law lacks an appropriate and coherent policy framework.

Clearly what was needed and what the ALRC's proposals sought to construct was a framework for inclusionary exceptions that genuinely and coherently attached them to the notions of reliability and necessity that Wigmore detected in the common law exceptions. By simplifying and unifying the categories of exceptions and by grounding them in an inherently logical set of reliability and necessity indicia and precautions,[5] the Commission aimed to bring rationality to the application of the rule and its exceptions.

The schema proposed by the ALRC for the exceptions to s 59(1) has been adopted in the *UEA*.[6] This means that the exceptions distinguish between first hand and more remote hearsay, between civil and criminal cases, and between cases where the makers of previous representations are available to testify and those where they are not. A restrictive approach is taken to second hand and more remote hearsay so that, for this category of hearsay evidence, specific exceptions to the exclusionary rule exist only for narrowly circumscribed classes of evidence whose reliability is generally established and, in some cases, where circumstantial guarantors of reliability are present. The ALRC took the view that 'secondhand hearsay is generally so unreliable that it should be inadmissible except where some guarantees of reliability can be shown together with a need for admissibility'.[7] This view, the Commission noted, is bolstered by psychological research. Additionally, the distinction between first hand and second hand hearsay was justified on the grounds that second hand hearsay would usually be of little value, that it would be impossible to judge its weight and that its admission would add to the cost and time of proceedings.[8]

For first hand hearsay, the uniform legislation creates separate general exceptions for civil and criminal cases based on relatively broad considerations of necessity and reliability. A less restrictive approach is taken to first hand hearsay because it does not suffer the infirmities generally associated with hearsay evidence to the same degree as second hand hearsay. In particular, research has shown that omissions and changes occur to a much lesser degree in the case of first hand hearsay than with second hand hearsay.[9]

The distinction between cases where the maker of the previous representation is available and called to testify, and those where he or she is not available, is justified because in the former case cross-examination of the maker of the representation can occur, although, of course, it does not happen at the time when the representation was made. Nevertheless, those aspects of trial fairness perceived to be upheld by the right to confrontation and cross-examination will be maintained at the very least notionally and often to positive effect in such cases. The distinction is also made because, where the maker of the previous representation is not available to testify, we are justified in requiring that the evidence meet additional circumstantial guarantees of reliability. This is particularly the case in criminal cases for prosecution evidence.[10] The need to minimise wrongful convictions and to take

5 Ibid [682].
6 See further below, pp 358-401.
7 ALRC, *Evidence (Interim)*, above n 4, [678].
8 Ibid [678].
9 Ibid [667]-[678].
10 Ibid [679].

account of fair trial considerations warrants a conservative approach to the admission of hearsay evidence against an accused where the defence does not have the opportunity to test its trustworthiness by cross-examination. The same concerns warrant the lifting of limitations on the admission of first hand hearsay tendered by an accused. Accordingly, the uniform legislation follows the ALRC's recommendation of imposing stricter restrictions on the admission of Crown evidence than on defence evidence where the maker of the previous representation does not testify. For the accused, the hearsay rule largely does not apply where first hand hearsay is concerned and the maker of the previous representation is unavailable.

The distinction between civil and criminal cases and the dramatically laissez-faire approach to hearsay evidence in civil cases adopted in the *UEA* is best understood as a manifestation of the view that civil proceedings are essentially a form of dispute resolution between usually (or least theoretically) equally armed combatants who should be able to adduce as much relevant evidence as possible in support of their cases. Accordingly, the hearsay rule is effectively abolished in civil cases for first hand hearsay. In contrast, the nature of criminal trials, the often substantial difference in the armoury and resources of the defence and prosecution, and the serious consequences for an accused of any finding against them, warrant a differential and restrictive approach to hearsay evidence tendered by the Crown in criminal cases.

The inclusionary exceptions are divided between two Divisions in Part 3.2 (Chapter 3.2 in Tasmania) of the Acts. Division 2 deals with the first hand hearsay exceptions and Div 3 with the exceptions for more remote hearsay.

Exceptions for First Hand Hearsay

Identifying a potentially applicable exception

Where first hand hearsay is concerned, while the legislative scheme may seem complex at first glance, its application is actually quite straightforward. As explained in the immediately preceding section, the legislation differentiates between civil and criminal cases and between those where the maker of the previous representation is available to testify and those where they are not. Separate inclusionary exceptions are provided for each category. The first question to ask in identifying an applicable provision is whether the previous representation is first hand hearsay. If it is, then two further questions will determine which specific statutory exception to the hearsay rule may be available – first, is the case criminal or civil; second, is the maker of the previous representation available to testify? In criminal cases where the maker of the previous representation is not available to testify, the applicable provision is s 65. Where the maker of the previous representation is available to testify, the relevant provision is s 66.[11]

If the previous representation is second hand hearsay, it will be admissible only if it falls within one of the specific, clearly defined, exceptions covering second hand hearsay located in ss 69-75 of the *UEA*. Section 60 is also relevant in some situations. However, s 60 is not a provision that enables the *admission* of hearsay evidence. Its effect is to waive the hearsay rule in relation to prior representations that have been admitted initially for a non-hearsay purpose and that waiver may, in some circumstances, extend to second hand or more remote hearsay.[12]

11 In civil cases the relevant provisions are s 63 (maker of the previous representation unavailable) and s 64 (maker of the previous representation available).

12 See discussion at pp 400-406.

First hand hearsay – the definition

Section 62 of the *UEA* contains the definition of first hand hearsay:

> **62. Restriction to "first-hand" hearsay**
>
> (1) A reference in this Division (other than in subsection (2)) to a previous representation is a reference to a previous representation that was made by a person who had personal knowledge of an asserted fact.
>
> (2) A person has personal knowledge of the asserted fact if his or her knowledge of the fact was, or might reasonably be supposed to have been, based on something that the person saw, heard or otherwise perceived, other than a previous representation made by another person about the fact.
>
> (3) For the purposes of section 66A, a person has personal knowledge of the asserted fact if it is a fact about the person's health, feelings, sensations, intention, knowledge or state of mind at the time the representation referred to in that section was made.

This definition appears to belie the fact that the concept of first hand hearsay is actually quite straightforward. So, the definition in s 62 is an example of a feature that bedevils so much about the hearsay rule – the inadequacy of language to convey meaning simply and clearly.

A previous representation will only constitute first hand hearsay if the person who made it had personal knowledge of the facts asserted *and* the representation is being used to prove those facts. As sub-s (2) of s 62 makes clear, personal knowledge can only come from what a person has (or can reasonably be supposed to have) seen, heard or otherwise perceived. However, if the previous representation contains another embedded representation made by someone else and it is the asserted facts in that embedded representation that are being proved by the tender of the representation at issue, then the evidence will not be first hand hearsay. Imagine, for example, that a witness to a robbery sees the accused flee the scene in a blue sedan. That witness has personal knowledge of an asserted fact – the robber fled in a blue sedan. Now, imagine that the witness tells a friend about the blue sedan getaway and the friend mentions the witness's representation to the police in the course of the investigation. If the friend gives evidence of the witness's previous representation to him, the evidence will first hand hearsay,[13] because the witness, the maker of the previous representation, had or might reasonably be supposed to have had, personal knowledge of the blue sedan driving off. However, if for some reason the friend cannot or will not testify, police evidence of the friend's previous representation to them that the witness told him (that is, the friend) about having seen the sedan drive off would be second hand hearsay – and far less likely to be admissible. This is because the friend cannot gain knowledge about what the witness *saw*. The friend's knowledge is based solely on what the witness *told* him.

If we create a diagram of the situation, we have the Witness (A) seeing the sedan drive off and telling the friend (B). We are assuming for purposes of this example that A is not going to give evidence in the proceeding. Tracing the representation ('The robber drove off in a blue sedan') back to the maker, *if the friend testifies*, the representation would travel from A → B. This is first hand hearsay. However, if the friend also does not give evidence and the police officer (C) who received B's statement is asked to give evidence of the blue sedan, now we have the representation traveling A → B → C. This is second hand hearsay. To put that into words, it is a case of C giving evidence of what B told her/him that A (the only

13 And therefore the admissibility exceptions for first hand hearsay (discussed below) will apply.

one with personal knowledge of the facts) had said, in a circumstance where we are trying to use C's evidence of B's previous representation to prove the existence of the facts asserted by A. That situation arose in the High Court decision in *Lee*,[14] with the additional complication of the involvement of the accused as the person with personal knowledge.

In that case, a particular Crown witness, in the position of B in the above hypothetical scenario, failed to testify at trial that the accused had made admissions to him. The witness had made a statement to the police detailing what the accused had told him. The Crown attempted to adduce evidence of the witness's previous representations through the police officer to whom they were made in order to establish the accused's involvement in the crime. That evidence was second hand hearsay and inadmissible to prove the facts asserted by the accused. In their joint judgment Gleeson CJ, Gummow, Kirby, Hayne and Callinan JJ observed that the situation would have been different if the witness himself had given evidence of the accused's admissions.[15]

Section 62(2) makes it clear that in establishing that the evidence is first hand hearsay it is not necessary to prove that the declarant actually *had* knowledge of the facts asserted. It is enough to establish that the declarant might reasonably be supposed to have had such knowledge. *Vincent*[16] provides an example of a case where the requirements of s 62 were met on this basis. The appellant was charged with robbery. He objected to the admission of evidence from the complainant of a conversation he had had with a young woman at the front of his shop shortly after the robbery occurred when she said, 'I've got the car number, rego it's RRB 373', and then, 'It's a red car'. The young woman left and was not thereafter able to be identified or located. The appellant submitted that this evidence should have been rejected unless the trial judge was satisfied on the balance of probabilities that the young woman did have personal knowledge about the car. Hodgson JA (with whom Simpson J and Smart AJ agreed) rejected this argument and held:

> 20. The question is whether the trial judge was justified in finding that the facts asserted to [the complainant] by the woman were, or might reasonably be supposed to be, based on something she herself saw. In my opinion, the very short lapse of time from the robbery to the conversation, the circumstances of the conversation, and the words actually used do make it more probable than not that the woman was asserting something that she herself had observed. It is of course possible that she was merely reporting something told to her by someone else, but the categorical assertions 'I've got the car number' and 'It's a red car' are to my mind more suggestive of her own observation of the matter.
>
> 21. In any event, the same considerations to my mind are plainly sufficient to satisfy the requirement that the matters asserted 'might reasonably be supposed to be' based on her own observations.

However, there is some authority that, where it cannot be ascertained one way or the other whether the previous representation was based on personal knowledge, the previous representation will not satisfy the test in s 62.[17]

14 [1998] HCA 60; 195 CLR 594.

15 Ibid [29]. In *Kaddour* [2019] NSWCCA 90. A parallel to *Lee* arose in *Kaddour* [2019] NSWCCA 90, a case raising issues within *UEA*, ss 38, 59 and 60. Bathurst CJ, Harrison and Davies JJ noted that the witness's acknowledgement of the truth of his statement to police, even though he did not give direct evidence of it, converted the statement into first hand hearsay, admissible via s 81 (at [55], [89]-[90]).

16 [2002] NSWCCA 369; 133 A Crim R 206.

17 *Citibank Ltd v Liu* [2003] NSWSC 69, [4] (Hamilton J).

Section 65 – criminal proceedings, maker of the representation unavailable

The most significant constraints on the admission of first hand hearsay in criminal proceedings are those imposed on prosecution evidence where the maker of the previous representation is unavailable to testify. As is discussed further below in relation to s 65(8), there appear to be far fewer obstacles for the defence to admit first hand hearsay representations than for the prosecution. In s 65, sub-ss (2), (3) and (9) contain the relevant inclusionary exceptions for prosecution evidence, with the inclusionary exception for the defence contained in sub-s (8).

65. Exception: criminal proceedings if maker not available

(1) This section applies in a criminal proceeding if a person who made a previous representation is not available to give evidence about an asserted fact.

(2) The hearsay rule does not apply to evidence of a previous representation given by a person who saw, heard or otherwise perceived the representation being made, if the representation:

- (a) was made under a duty to make that representation or to make representations of that kind, or
- (b) was made when or shortly after the asserted fact occurred and in circumstances that make it unlikely that the representation is a fabrication, or
- (c) was made in circumstances that make it highly probable that the representation is reliable, or
- (d) was:
  - (i) against the interests of the person who made it at the time it was made, and
  - (ii) made in circumstances that make it likely that the representation is reliable.

(3) The hearsay rule does not apply to evidence of a previous representation made in the course of giving evidence in an Australian or overseas proceeding if, in that proceeding, the defendant in the proceeding to which this section is being applied:

- (a) cross-examined the person who made the representation about it, or
- (b) had a reasonable opportunity to cross-examine the person who made the representation about it.

(4) If there is more than one defendant in the criminal proceeding, evidence of a previous representation that:

- (a) is given in an Australian or overseas proceeding, and
- (b) is admitted into evidence in the criminal proceeding because of subsection (3),

cannot be used against a defendant who did not cross-examine, and did not have a reasonable opportunity to cross-examine, the person about the representation.

(5) For the purposes of subsections (3) and (4), a defendant is taken to have had a reasonable opportunity to cross-examine a person if the defendant was not present at a time when the cross-examination of a person might have been conducted but:

- (a) could reasonably have been present at that time, and
- (b) if present could have cross-examined the person.

(6) Evidence of the making of a representation to which subsection (3) applies may be adduced by producing a transcript, or a recording, of the representation that is authenticated by:

- (a) the person to whom, or the court or other body to which, the representation was made, or
- (b) if applicable, the registrar or other proper officer of the court or other body to which the representation was made, or
- (c) the person or body responsible for producing the transcript or recording.

(7) Without limiting subsection (2)(d), a representation is taken, for the purpose of that subsection, to be against the interests of the person who made it if it tends:

(a) to damage the person's reputation, or
(b) to show that the person committed an offence for which the person has not been convicted, or
(c) to show that the person is liable in an action for damages.

(8) The hearsay rule does not apply to:
(a) evidence of a previous representation adduced by a defendant if the evidence is given by a person who saw, heard or otherwise perceived the representation being made, or
(b) a document tendered as evidence by a defendant so far as it contains a previous representation, or another representation to which it is reasonably necessary to refer in order to understand the representation.

(9) If evidence of a previous representation about a matter has been adduced by a defendant and has been admitted, the hearsay rule does not apply to evidence of another representation about the matter that:
(a) is adduced by another party, and
(b) is given by a person who saw, heard or otherwise perceived the other representation being made.

'Unavailability' is defined relatively broadly in the *UEA*:[18]

4. Unavailability of persons

(1) For the purposes of this Act, a person is taken not to be available to give evidence about a fact if:
(a) the person is dead, or
(b) the person is, for any reason other than the application of section 16 (Competence and compellability: judges and jurors), not competent to give the evidence, or
(c) the person is mentally or physically unable to give the evidence and it is not reasonably practicable to overcome that inability, or
(d) it would be unlawful for the person to give the evidence, or
(e) a provision of this Act prohibits the evidence being given, or
(f) all reasonable steps have been taken, by the party seeking to prove the person is not available, to find the person or secure his or her attendance, but without success, or
(g) all reasonable steps have been taken, by the party seeking to prove the person is not available, to compel the person to give the evidence, but without success.

(2) In all other cases the person is taken to be available to give evidence about the fact.

Clause 4(1)(c) was enacted[19] to give effect to the ALRC's recommendation[20] that the definition be expanded to incorporate this category of unavailability. However, no iterations of the uniform legislation nominate unwillingness to testify or fear of testifying as a specific basis of unavailability. In contrast, in the United Kingdom, this category is included in the definition of witness unavailability.[21] Such a provision is particularly valuable where vulnerable witnesses are concerned, specifically, children and victims of violent crimes, particularly those involving domestic violence or sexual offences. For a variety of well-documented reasons, such witnesses are frequently very afraid of testifying and so decline to do so.[22]

18 *UEA*, Dictionary, Pt 2 (except for Tasmania, for which see *Evidence Act 2001*, s 3B).

19 *UEA*, Dictionary, Pt 2, cl 4(1)(c) (Cth, NSW, Vic and NT) (except for Tasmania, for which see *Evidence Act 2001*, s 3B(1)(c)).

20 ALRC, *Uniform Evidence Law* (Report No 102, 2006), [8.33]-[8.37].

21 *Criminal Justice Act 2003* (UK), s 116(2)(e).

22 For more detailed discussion, see T Henning and J Hunter, 'Finessing the Fair Trial for Complainants and the Accused: Mansions of Justice or Castles in the Air?' in P Roberts and J Hunter (eds), *Criminal Evidence and Human Rights: Reimagining Common Law and Procedural Traditions* (Hart Publishing, 2013), 357-60.

In Australian *UEA* jurisdictions, in the absence of explicit provision for fear-based unavailability, paras (c) and (g) of cl 4(1) provide the means to cater for the fearful witness. The generous interpretation given in *Suteski (No 4)*[23] to 'unavailability' and specifically to the grounds set down in cl 4(1)(g), confirms this to be the case. This case involved a contract killing. A principal Crown witness who had been involved in the killing (Witness B) refused to testify even after being told that he could be found in contempt of court if he persisted in his refusal. A recording of a statement he had previously made to the police about how the crime came to be perpetrated and Suteski's incitement of its commission was admitted under s 65. Witness B was judged 'unavailable' on the basis that all reasonable steps had been taken to compel him to give evidence but without success.[24] It has been suggested that, in fact, Witness B 'looked more like an unwilling than an unavailable witness'.[25] In contrast, in *Aujla and Singh*[26] strenuous efforts were made by the prosecution to locate a roaming witness, including tracing his whereabouts overseas and attempting to make arrangements for him to testify from that location via videolink. All these efforts came to nought. Forrest J held that the witness was unavailable under both cl 4(1)(f) and (g) and stated that the legislation 'does not impose a requirement of perfection, but merely that the conduct be reasonable'.[27] In this case, his Honour held that the attempts to secure the witness's attendance had, in fact, been more than that.

The approach in *Suteski (No 4)* has been adopted in a number of subsequent cases,[28] including *DPP v Nicholls*[29] where Beach J held that the concept of unavailability in cl 4(1)(g) encompasses both 'a refusal to give evidence that is without legal foundation and a refusal to give evidence that is authorised by an order of the Court'.[30] In this case, it meant that a domestic violence complainant, who was exempted under s 18[31] of the Victorian *Evidence Act 2008* from testifying against the accused, her de facto partner, was held to be 'unavailable' even though she was sitting in court during the hearing of the case against the accused. The ruling that she was 'unavailable' made evidence of her initial complaint to the police potentially admissible under s 65. Beach J noted that, in *Mindshare Communications Limited Taiwan Branch v Orleans Investments Pty Ltd*,[32] Hamilton J accepted the possibility that cl 4(1)(g) had operation where a witness declined to give evidence on the ground of privilege. Beach J held that that situation was analogous to the case at hand, that what Hamilton J had said, albeit obiter, was correct and should be followed.[33]

---

23 [2002] NSWSC 218; 128 A Crim R 275.

24 At the time of this decision, this basis of unavailability was found in cl 4(1)(f) of the definition (in Tasmania, *Evidence Act 2001*, s 3B(1)(f)). Since reform of the definition, it is now contained in cl 4(1)(g) (in Tasmania, s 3B(1)(g)).

25 Henning and Hunter, above n 22, 355.

26 [2012] VSC 602, [8]-[20].

27 Ibid [18].

28 *Alchin* [2006] ACTSC 53; 200 FLR 204; *Darmody* [2010] VSCA 41; 25 VR 209, [24]-[26]; and *DPP v BB* [2010] VSCA 211; 29 VR 110.

29 [2010] VSC 397; 204 A Crim R 306. In this case the court upheld an objection to being compelled to testify made under s 18(2). See more detailed discussion of this section in Chapter 5, 166-168.

30 [2010] VSC 397; 204 A Crim R 306, [22].

31 Spousal non-compellability provision.

32 [2007] NSWSC 976.

33 [2010] VSC 397; 204 A Crim R 306, [22].

The more typically relied-on categories of unavailability are those for deceased, seriously ill or untraceable witnesses. Deceased[34] and untraceable[35] declarants are, of course, unproblematically unavailable. But cases like *Suteski (No 4)*, *Mindshare Communications Limited Taiwan Branch v Orleans Investments Pty Ltd* and *DPP v Nicholls* suggest that courts may adopt a degree of liberality in their interpretation of unavailability. In one case, for example, it is not clear from the case report why the declarant was unavailable, but 'it was accepted'[36] that this was the case. He had made a statement to the police (partially admissible under s 65) providing an eyewitness account of a violent nightclub incident.[37]

This liberality and the decision in *DPP v Nicholls* should provide food for thought for prosecutorial agencies in cases involving fearful and unwilling witnesses. For example, the high rates of witness reluctance and refusals to testify in domestic violence and sexual assault cases are well documented.[38] Prosecutors may be willing to proceed even in the face of complainant reluctance – both in the public interest on grounds of deterrence and in the interests of complainants. In Lievore's study some prosecutors expressed the view that there are times when the public interest overrides the individual's wishes. Otherwise, the prosecution risks the possibility of repeat offences or escalating violence.[39]

Conversely, prosecutors concern for victims' welfare may work as a disincentive to proceed. When coupled with the pragmatic view that a reluctant, possibly hostile, witness will undermine the prospects of conviction, we have prominent reasons for the high drop-out rates in sexual offences and domestic violence cases.[40] However, these are all good reasons for exploring the possibilities of avoiding discontinuance offered by the liberal decisional interpretation of 'unavailability' and the consequent potential applicability of s 65 in cases where reluctant witnesses have made adequately detailed previous representations about offences committed against them.

Hearsay notice

In addition to meeting the preconditions for admissibility imposed by s 65, parties wishing to adduce previous representations of absent witnesses must comply with the stipulation in s 67 that written notice of the intention to adduce the hearsay evidence be given to each other party to the proceedings within a reasonable time. The notice given must comply with rules of court (s 67(2)) and supply the information specified in s 67(3) including the hearsay exception relied on. However,

34 The types of cases and statements admitted for these categories of witness are documented in Henning and Hunter, above n 22, 356-7; and see the cases cited there: *DPP v BB* [2010] VSCA 211; 29 VR 110; *Conway* [2000] FCA 461; 172 ALR 185; *Mankotia* [1998] NSWSC 295; *Polkinghorne* [1999] NSWSC 704; 108 A Crim R 189; *Kuzmanovic* [2005] NSWSC 771; *Dean* (unreported, NSWSC, Dunford J, 12 March 1997); *Jang* [1999] NSWSC 1040; *Toki* [2000] NSWSC 999; 116 A Crim R 536; *Lubik (No 1)* [2010] VSC 465; *Gover* [2000] NSWCCA 303; 118 A Crim R 8; *Harris* [2005] NSWCCA 432; 158 A Crim R 454.

35 *Kazzi* [2003] NSWCCA 241; 140 A Crim R 545; *Morton* [2008] NSWCCA 196; 191 A Crim R 333; *Puchalski* [2007] NSWCCA 220, also documented in Henning and Hunter, above n 22, 356-7.

36 *Vickers* [2006] NSWCCA 60; 160 A Crim R 195, [25].

37 *Vickers* [2006] NSWCCA 60; 160 A Crim R 195.

38 See discussion of the relevant research in Henning and Hunter, above n 22, 357-60.

39 D Lievore, *Prosecutorial Decisions in Adult Sexual Assault Cases: An Australian Study* (AIC for the Office of the Status of Women, 2004), 40.

40 Ibid 30, 40.

a party may apply to the court for a direction that the notice requirement be dispensed with (s 67(4)) on such conditions as the court thinks fit (s 67(5)(a)).

Evidence Regulations prescribe further information to that specified in s 67(3) that must be provided in the notice, including that the substance of the evidence in the representations sought to be adduced and any other relevant representations be set down in the notice; and that particulars of the date, time, place and circumstances of the making of the representations and that the names of the declarants be provided. If the previous representation is in writing, a copy of the document containing the representation must be attached to the notice. Where the declarant will not be available to testify, the notice must specify why.[41]

In *Azizi*,[42] Bongiorno JA (with whom Buchanan JA and Hollingworth AJA agreed) characterised the hearsay notice as:

> the statutorily required foundation for the admission of hearsay to prove facts asserted by it. It must contain the matters required by the [then] Evidence Regulations 2009 [(Vic)]. Relevantly, it must state 'the substance of evidence of a previous representation' that is to say, it must set out the representation relied upon as asserting facts which the party giving the notice seeks to have admitted as proof of those facts. In most cases, the representation will be what a person said, so that the hearsay notice will contain at least the substance of what the person said so that the court and the party's opponent can determine what asserted facts the hearsay is being sought to be adduced to prove. A hearsay notice is no empty formality. Its existence and form are necessary conditions precedent, subject to judicial dispensation, to the non-application of the hearsay rule.

Even though the notice requirement is considered to be 'foundational' and not an 'empty formality', sub-ss (4) and (5) of s 67 empower courts to dispense with it subject to such directions as the court thinks fit to make. In determining whether to waive the notice requirement and what directions, if any, to give, courts must take into account the matters set down in s 192(2).[43]

The statement set out above from Bongiorno JA's judgment strongly suggests that parties cannot assume that courts will readily exercise their discretion under s 67(4). This view is supported by what occurred in *DPP v Azizi (Ruling No 2)*.[44] Here Kaye J refused to waive the notice requirement when the Crown sought to adduce evidence under s 65(2) without notifying the defence before the trial of their intention to do so. Their intention was not in fact conveyed until day three of the trial. Kaye J applied Bongiorno JA's dictum and, even though his tentative view was that the evidence would otherwise have been admissible under s 65(2)(b), he declined to admit it. To do so his Honour said would, 'firstly, result in incurable unfairness and injustice to the accused and secondly, ... disrupt the conduct of the trial and compromise the proper conduct of this trial'.[45] The fairness of the trial was clearly the foremost consideration in his Honour's decision. He noted that the prosecution had provided no explanation for failing to give notice, that they had had ample opportunity to do so, that the evidence was not collateral or incidental, but in fact important, and that had notice been given the accused may have taken a different approach in opening his case to the jury and

41 *Evidence Regulations 2018* (Cth), reg 6; *Evidence Regulation 2020* (NSW), cl 4; *Evidence Regulations 2012* (Tas), reg 4; *Evidence Regulations 2019* (Vic), reg 6; *Evidence (National Uniform Legislation) Regulations 2012* (NT), reg 4.

42 [2012] VSCA 205; 224 A Crim R 325, [32].

43 See the discussion of s 192 and *Stanoevski* [2001] HCA 4; 202 CLR 115 in Chapter 10.

44 [2012] VSC 600.

45 Ibid [14].

in cross-examining witnesses whose evidence had been completed by the time notice was actually given.[46]

Prosecution evidence under section 65

As noted earlier, the most restrictive inclusionary exceptions in s 65 are those that apply to prosecution evidence. The relevant provisions are s 65(2), (3) and (9).

The approach adopted in these exceptions is akin to that identified by Charron J in *Khelawon*[47] for traditional exceptions to the exclusionary rule:

> [T]raditional exceptions to the exclusionary rule were largely crafted around those circumstances where the dangers of receiving the evidence were sufficiently alleviated ... When it may be necessary to resort to evidence in this form, a hearsay statement may be admitted if, because of the way in which it came about, its contents are trustworthy, or if circumstances permit the ultimate trier of fact to sufficiently assess its worth. If the proponent of the evidence cannot meet the twin criteria of necessity and reliability, the general exclusionary rule prevails.

The element of necessity for s 65 is supplied by the fact that the maker of the representation is unavailable. Reliability is then demonstrated by reference to at least one of the specified indicia of circumstantial reliability described in the section, which must be present if the evidence is to be admissible. In this regard a number of the inclusionary exceptions in s 65 reflect longstanding criteria for admissibility of common law hearsay exceptions including res gestae type statements,[48] statements against interest,[49] statements made pursuant to a duty to make them[50] and testimony given in other proceedings.[51] However, their s 65 manifestations are broader and simpler than those at common law. As the court in *Sio*[52] observed:

> 57. It can be seen that the application of s 65(2) proceeds upon the assumption that a party is seeking to prove a particular fact relevant to an issue in the case. It then requires the identification of the particular representation to be adduced in evidence as proof of that fact. The circumstances in which that representation was made may then be considered in order to determine whether the conditions of admissibility are met. This process must be observed in relation to each relevant fact sought to be proved by tendering evidence under s 65.

Section 65(2)(c) reflects Australian common law approaches to hearsay admission based on circumstantial reliability per se.[53] It vacates the application of the hearsay rule for previous representations 'made in circumstances that make it highly probable that the representation is reliable'.

---

46 For a similar outcome, see *Singh v Newridge Property Group Pty Ltd* [2010] NSWSC 411 and *Darlaston v Parker* [2010] FCA 771; 189 FCR 1; but cf an earlier ruling by Kaye J in *DPP v Azizi* [2012] VSC 568 and with the decision in *Puchalski* [2007] NSWCCA 220.

47 [2006] 2 SCR 787, [2].

48 Section 65(2)(b).

49 Section 65(2)(d).

50 Section 65(2)(a).

51 Section 65(3).

52 [2016] HCA 32; 259 CLR 47, 64.

53 These authorities are helpfully collected and analysed by the Full Court in *Bristow* [2020] SASCFC 91. See Chapter 8, pp 351-353, for further details of the brief attempt by some High Court judges to introduce a common law inclusionary exception to the hearsay rule based on reliability in *Walton* [1989] HCA 9; 166 CLR 283, *Benz* [1989] HCA 64; 168 CLR 110 and *Pollitt* [1992] HCA 35; 174 CLR 558 and its subsequent abandonment in *Bannon* and *Baker*.

Section 65 also imposes a quasi-procedural limitation on the admission of previous representations, which has the operational effect of a precondition of admissibility. With the exception of previous representations adduced under s 65(3) (court transcripts), the previous representation must be adduced through someone who saw, heard or otherwise perceived the representation being made. This requirement has particularly restrictive implications for the admission of documentary hearsay evidence tendered by the prosecution, the result of which is that documentary evidence will only be admissible if the witness giving evidence was physically watching the maker of the representation write the words on the paper as they were being written. The force of this restriction was revealed in *Conway*.[54] The ALRC justified the limiting effect of this requirement for written representations because it ensures that there will be a witness who can be cross-examined about the making of the statement, which will assist in assessing the weight of the evidence.[55] By virtue of s 65(8)(b) this particular restriction does not apply to first hand documentary evidence adduced by the defence.

In *Conway* the accused was charged with the murder of his estranged wife. Approximately a week before her death the deceased recorded in her diary her suspicions that the accused had attempted to drug her by lacing coffee she was drinking. The trial judge admitted the diary entry. However, on appeal Miles, von Doussa and Weinberg JJ held:

> 150. … The evidence concerning that entry was not given by a person who 'saw, heard or otherwise perceived' the representation being made. A fundamental condition of admissibility was not met. Although [two of the deceased's neighbours] had been shown the diary by the deceased prior to her murder on 3 May 1997, neither had seen her make the entry for 25 April 1997. It was not sufficient, in our view, for [the neighbours] to have read that entry, whether in the presence of the deceased, or otherwise. …
>
> 153. Section 65(2) has never distinguished between oral evidence of a previous representation, and a document containing such a representation. … such a representation could only fall within the scope of the provision if it was 'seen', or 'otherwise perceived' being made. …
>
> 154. … [Section 65] certainly cannot render admissible an entry in a document where that entry was neither seen nor otherwise perceived being made.

Accordingly the diary entry was found to be inadmissible.

Decisional law in relation to the admission of prosecution evidence under s 65 has accrued predominantly around paras (2)(b) and (c). This is probably because these subsections not only offer the greatest opportunity for the Crown to adduce previous representations of unavailable witnesses but also because they consequently constitute the most contestable terrain in s 65. The discussion in the succeeding sections concentrates on these provisions. Nevertheless, it also traverses the other grounds for the admission of prosecution evidence in s 65. It does so in the order in which they are set down in that section.

Representations made under a duty: UEA, s 65(2)(a)

The exception in s 65(2)(a) is derived from a similar common law exception, which, however, has a much narrower operation. There is a dearth of decisional law on this provision. The common law exception typically applied to representations made in the course of declarants' employment duties, the rationale for the

54 [2000] FCA 461; 98 FCR 204.

55 ALRC, *Evidence (Interim)*, above n 4, [691].

exception being that the prospect of dismissal for making inaccurate or false statements would operate as a guarantor against error and misrepresentation. However, the limiting requirement that evidence of the making of the statement be given by someone who saw, heard or otherwise perceived the representation being made is likely to preclude the admission of most written records, which one would have thought would be the type of previous representation to which this exception would otherwise be most likely to apply. It is therefore difficult to see what advantage this exception offers over and above the business records exception in s 69.

Representations made in circumstances that make it unlikely they are fabrications: UEA, s 65(2)(b)

This exception has its genesis in the common law res gestae doctrine. For a previous representation to be admissible under this paragraph it must satisfy two criteria of circumstantial reliability. First, the previous representation must have been made 'when or shortly after' the asserted fact occurred. Second, it must have been made in circumstances that make it unlikely that the representation was fabricated. Both criteria have been the subject of frequent judicial consideration and their interpretation is now thought to be reasonably settled.[56] However, as noted by T Forrest J in *Bond (Ruling No 4)*,[57] 'subtly different approaches have been taken'. In relation to the meaning of 'when or shortly after' his Honour summarised those approaches as follows:

> 8. … In *R v Mankotia*[58] Sperling J considered that a 'normative judgment' was to be made depending on the circumstances of the case, the predominant factor being the actual time that has elapsed between the asserted fact and the representation. This approach has been followed in *Conway v R*[59] where the Full Federal Court held that matters conveyed ought be 'contemporaneous or, if narrative of a past event, still fresh in the mind of the person recounting that narrative.'[60] In *Williams v R*[61] a differently constituted Full Federal Court cautioned against an overemphasis on the 'freshness' of the memory of the statement-maker and said that the rationale for the exception was also predicated upon the requirement that the evidence was unlikely to be a fabrication. The court applied a test that involved a requirement that the statement be made 'spontaneously during (when) or under the proximate pressure of (shortly after) the occurrence of the asserted fact.'[62]
>
> 9. In *Williams v R* a lapse of five days between the asserted fact and representation was held to be outside the ambit of s 65(2)(b):
>
> > 'Indeed, it would seem to be an unusual case in which a representation made five days after the occurrence of the asserted fact might be regarded as having been made 'soon after' it.[63]

The notion that the declarant should still be experiencing the proximate stress of the situation was rejected by the ALRC as a precondition for admissibility under this provision. The Commission's view was that stress is not a guarantor against fabrication and that it may actually adversely affect perceptions and

56 *DPP v Azizi* [2012] VSC 568, [9] (Kaye J).
57 [2011] VSC 536, [8].
58 [[1998] NSWSC 295.]
59 [[2000] FCA 461; 98 FCR 204.]
60 [Ibid [133].]
61 [[2000] FCA 1868; 119 A Crim R 490.]
62 [Ibid [48].]
63 [Ibid [49].]

performance.[64] In this regard the approach in *Williams*[65] in relation to statements made under the proximate pressure of the asserted facts, arguably more closely reflects the common law position formulated in cases like *Ratten*[66] than the ALRC's approach. In *Ratten* the Privy Council held that 'hearsay evidence may be admitted if the statement providing it is made in such conditions (always being those of approximate but not exact contemporaneity) of involvement or pressure as to exclude the possibility of concoction or distortion'.[67]

The use of the term 'shortly after' in s 65(2)(b) clearly marks a departure from the most restrictive manifestations of the common law res gestae doctrine which had demanded that there be strict contemporaneity between the making of the previous representation and the occurrence of the asserted fact.[68] However, just how far 'shortly after' moves from 'contemporaneity' is uncertain, particularly in light of the judicial disagreement noted by T Forrest J in *Bond (Ruling No 4)*. The interpretive stance in *Mankotia* and *Conway*[69] no doubt tolerates longer lapses of time between the occurrence of the relevant event and the making of the previous representation than does *Williams*.

The view of the Full Federal Court in *Williams*,[70] that 'shortly after' should be interpreted to give effect to the principal concern of s 65(2)(b) to exclude *concocted* evidence, accords with notions of intra and inter section consistency. The concept of 'freshness of memory' that informed the approach in *Mankotia*[71] and *Conway* is not one that is referenced in s 65(2)(b). It is, however, a condition for admissibility under s 66 where reliability can more readily be tested than under s 65 because the maker of the previous representation is available, called to testify and able to be cross-examined. The insurances of reliability prescribed for the two sections must therefore be conceptually and instrumentally different. On the *Williams* construction, 'shortly after' is to be judged according to whether it precludes time for reflection and therefore fabrication, which is clearly the operational target of s 65(2)(b).[72] In contrast, 'freshness of memory' is primarily concerned with excluding *mistakes of memory*. This is the target of s 66, not s 65(2)(b). So, while the interpretation in *Williams* is more restrictive than that in *Mankotia* and *Conway*, it probably accords more closely with the legislative intent of s 65(2)(b).

The requirement that the previous representation be made 'in circumstances that make it unlikely that the representation is a fabrication' has also occasioned differing interpretations. The issues causing difficulty here have been the meaning of 'fabrication' and what scope is to be given to the term, 'circumstances'. 'Fabrication' has been interpreted, on the one hand as extending beyond concocted

64 ALRC, *Evidence (Interim)*, above n 4, [692].

65 [2000] FCA 1868; 119 A Crim R 490.

66 [1972] AC 378.

67 Ibid 391.

68 See discussion of English, US and Australian common law and statutory res gestae authorities and their relationship to *UEA*, ss 65(2)(b), (c), 66 and 66A, by the Full Court in *Bristow* [2020] SASCFC 91, [83]-[196] where (at [89]) the term 'integral narrative' instead of res gestae is adopted to reflect the basis upon which a representation gains its relevance. See, in particular, *Bedingfield* (1879) 14 Cox CC 341.

69 [2000] FCA 461; 98 FCR 204.

70 [2000] FCA 1868; 119 A Crim R 490. See also *Ambrosoli* [2002] NSWCCA 386; 55 NSWLR 603.

71 The same interpretive approach was taken in *Polkinghorne* [1999] NSWSC 704; 108 A Crim R 189; *Kuzmanovic* [2005] NSWSC 771, [16]; and followed in *Conway* [2000] FCA 461; 98 FCR 204.

72 See *DPP v Cooling (Ruling No 1)* [2019] VSC 603.

or mendacious statements to include reconstructions or distortions falling short of untruthfulness,[73] and on the other as being limited to untruths.[74]

In relation to the scope of the term, 'circumstances', there was initially a view that only the precise circumstances in which the previous representation was made, 'its factual setting',[75] are relevant to the question of the likelihood of fabrication. For example in *Mankotia*[76] Sperling J held:

> The second condition prescribed by s 65(2)(b) is that the representation was made in circumstances that make it unlikely that the representation is a fabrication. The test is not one of reliability at large. It is a narrower test. First, it is the unlikelihood of concoction to which the paragraph is directed. Whether the representor might have been honestly mistaken is immaterial. Secondly, it is not unlikelihood at large which is in question, but unlikelihood arising from the circumstances.
>
> I would construe 'circumstances' to mean the circumstances in which the representation was made, its factual setting at the time it was made. That construction has the effect of excluding from consideration, for the purposes of s 65(2)(b), events subsequent to the representation being made and other representations made by the same person on other occasions, notwithstanding that such considerations might logically fortify the unlikelihood of concoction or (in the case of inconsistent representations) have the opposite effect. The same point arises in relation to s 65(2)(c).

The preferred view now appears to be that previous circumstances and representations made on other occasions may be taken into account, but only in so far as they throw light on whether the 'circumstances' of the making of the previous representation make it unlikely that it was fabricated. Adopting this approach in *Ambrosoli*,[77] the NSW Court of Criminal Appeal held:

> 34. It would therefore appear that *R v Mankotia*, *Conway* and *R v Williams* are at one in:
>
> - focussing upon the circumstances of the *making* of the previous representation to determine whether it is unlikely that the representation was a fabrication or highly probable that the representation was reliable; and
> - excluding evidence tending only to prove the asserted fact.
>
> 35. In my view this is a correct approach to s 65(2). To the extent that *R v Dean* and *R v Lock* decide otherwise they should not be followed.
>
> 36. The point of disagreement between *R v Mankotia* on the one hand and *Conway* and *R v Williams* on the other is the legitimacy of resort to inconsistent or consistent statements of the maker of the previous representation or other circumstances (whenever occurring) directly touching the credibility of the maker of the representation at the time of making the representation (cf the victim in *R v Bedingfield*). Sperling J (at 10) indicated obiter that he would disregard these matters (see his reference to excluding from consideration 'other representations made by the same person on other occasions, notwithstanding that such considerations might logically fortify the unlikelihood of concoction or (in the case of inconsistent representations) have the opposite effect'. On this I prefer the view of the Federal Court, a fortiori because it is presumptively binding having regard to the principle in *Australian Securities Commission v Marlborough Gold Mines Ltd*. I would, however, emphasise that prior or later statements or conduct of the person making the previous representation are only to be considered to the extent that they touch the reliability of the circumstances of the making of that previous representation. If they do no more than tend to address the asserted fact or ultimate issue they have no bearing on the issues presented by s 65(2).

73 *Kuzmanovic* [2005] NSWSC 771.

74 *Polkinghorne* [1999] NSWSC 704; 108 A Crim R 189; *DPP v Tran (No 2)* [2019] VSC 824, [25].

75 See, eg, *Polkinghorne*, ibid, [33]; and *Mankotia* [1998] NSWSC 295, p 10.

76 [1998] NSWSC 295, p 10.

77 [2002] NSWCCA 386; 55 NSWLR 603 (Mason P, with Hulme and Simpson JJ agreeing).

> 37. Accordingly, I would not exclude reference to events outside the time and place of the making of the previous representation itself from the range of 'circumstances' capable of reflecting on the unlikelihood of it being a fabrication when made or the high probability of it being reliable when made.

In *Ambrosoli* Mason P in the NSW Court of Criminal Appeal stressed another important matter in relation to the issue to be determined under s 65(2)(b): 'Unrestricted consideration of the unlikelihood of fabrication ... cannot have been intended by the legislature'.[78] This means that the court is not concerned with whether the previous representation was likely or not to have been fabricated or whether or not it is likely to be true. The focus for the court is on the *circumstances* in which the previous representation was made and whether those circumstances were such as to make it unlikely that the representation was fabricated. As Mason P noted:

> The legislature has restricted consideration to unlikelihood arising from the circumstances for a reason. If the legislature had intended unlikelihood to be determined at large, there would have been no mention of circumstances.[79]

The court held that the same approach applies to the interpretation of 'circumstances' and to the focus of the determination to be made under s 65(2)(c).

Representations made in circumstances that make it highly probable they are reliable: UEA, s 65(2)(c)

The ALRC did not recommend an exception to the hearsay rule based on the reliability of the evidence per se. Further, as noted above and in the previous chapter, Australian courts have been wary of unlocking the common law hearsay rule on grounds of reliability alone. This conservatism is mirrored in their interpretation of s 65(2)(c). Of the inclusionary hearsay exceptions in the uniform legislation, s 65(2)(c) has been held to contain the most onerous test. The following frequently referenced extract from *Conway*[80] makes this point:

> 146. The requirement in s 65(2)(c) of the Act that it be 'highly probable' that a representation be 'reliable' in order to be admissible is an onerous one. It is easy to see why that should be so. Section 65(2)(c) has the potential to operate unfairly against an accused person. This particular exception to the hearsay rule was not recommended by either the Australian Law Reform Commission or the New South Wales Law Reform Commission. Treating reliability alone as the basis for admissibility, represents a radical departure from the principle that hearsay evidence, no matter how reliable it may appear to be, is inadmissible unless it falls within a recognised exception to the hearsay rule.

As with s 65(2)(b) the focus of the admissibility inquiry for this section is the circumstances in which the previous representation was made and their implications for the reliability of the representation. The focus is not the representation's actual reliability or truth.[81] The latter is a question for determination by the jury. This distinction is not easy to maintain and even courts sometimes elide the two foci when applying s 65(2)(b) and (c).[82]

78 Ibid [18].
79 Ibid [18], citing Sperling J in *Mankotia*. To similar effect, see *Prasad* [2020] NSWCCA 349.
80 [2000] FCA 461; 98 FCR 204.
81 *Azizi* [2012] VSCA 205; 224 A Crim R 325, [50] (Bongiorno JA), applying *Ambrosoli* [2002] NSWCCA 386; 55 NSWLR 603, [18] (Mason P).
82 See, eg, T Forrest J's application of s 65(2)(c) in *Bond (Ruling No 4)* [2011] VSC 536, [12]-[16].

Clearly, the focus legislated in s 65(2)(b) and (c) aims to maintain the distinction between the trial judge's role in determining the admissibility of evidence and that of the jury in deciding whether to rely on it. Nevertheless, this focus is not one that has been adhered to elsewhere in relation to reliability-based hearsay exceptions. For example, the principled exception for reliable hearsay created by the Canadian Supreme Court no longer strictly ascribes to this distinction, but nevertheless maintains the traditional roles of the judge and jury. In this regard, in *Khelawon*,[83] the Canadian Supreme Court made it clear that in applying the principled exception the trial judge may take into account not only matters relating to the circumstances in which the representation was made to assess their effect on the representation's likely reliability but also matters germane to its reliability generally, including evidence corroborative of its reliability.

Despite differences between the Canadian principled approach and that in s 65(2)(c), the relatively expansive view taken in *Conway* and *Williams* of the circumstances that a court may take into account in applying the test in s 65(2)(c) means that Canadian case law on the principled approach may provide a useful reference point in some respects for Australian courts applying s 65(2)(c). Nevertheless, caution would need to be exercised in this regard. Given the focus mandated by s 65(2)(c), an Australian court is unlikely to be able to have regard to other circumstances outside those in which the representation in question was made or to other representations to the same extent as Canadian courts are able to do in giving effect to the principled exception to the hearsay rule. To do so could result in the directed focus of the section being ignored and the obliteration of the distinction[84] dot pointed in *Ambrosoli*[85] (see the extract from Mason P's judgment quoted above). This problem is highlighted by the decision in *Ambrosoli* itself. Despite the interpretation adopted of 'circumstances' in this case, the Court of Criminal Appeal's determination of the application of s 65(2)(c) shows how difficult it can be to maintain the distinction between matters relating to the reliability of the evidence per se and matters that cast light on the circumstances in which the previous representation was made that might affect its reliability.

The sole ground of appeal in that case was that the trial judge had erred in admitting a statement made to the police by one Shane Cornish and the transcript of his committal evidence. The appellant referred to the committal evidence in arguing that the statement to the police could not satisfy s 65(2)(c). In upholding this submission the Court of Criminal Appeal identified the following statements made by Cornish during committal cross-examination about his police statement as indicating that that statement did not satisfy the test in s 65(2)(c):

(1) 'It seemed to be typed out a little incorrect' (p 44)
(2) he just presumed that the police officer would type up his statement the way he told him (p 48)
(3) he '*pretty much*' never read the statement before he signed it (p 48)
(4) he wouldn't say that the part of his statement dealing with the punching of the victim on the ground was entirely accurate (p 49)
(5) he was generally unhappy that the statement contains a number of things which were probably incorrect (pp 50-51)

---

83 [2006] 2 SCR 787.

84 Witness T Forrest J's application of s 65(2)(c) in *Bond (Ruling No 4)* [2011] VSC 536, [12]-[16], which appears to head in that direction.

85 [2002] NSWCCA 386; 55 NSWLR 603, [34] (Mason P, with Hulme and Simpson JJ agreeing).

(6) there were a considerable number of matters in the statement which were wrong (p 53).[86]

Arguably most of these matters are more germane to an assessment of the general reliability of the police statement than illuminative of the circumstances of its making. Only items (2) and (3) genuinely address the latter.

Representations made against interest: UEA, s 65(2)(d)

This inclusionary exception derives from the common law exception for statements made by deceased persons against their own pecuniary interest. Section 65(2)(d) is more expansive than the common law exception in that it does not apply solely to previous representations made by people who have since died and it is not confined to statements against pecuniary interest. Section 65(7) tells us that it includes, but is not limited to, statements damaging to the representor's reputation, that indicate their commission of a crime and their liability in an action for damages. Such statements are regarded as inherently reliable because of the improbability that people will concoct stories against their own interests. Nevertheless, following its inquiry into the uniform legislation,[87] the ALRC recommended that s 65(2)(d) additionally require that the representations against interest be 'made in circumstances that make it likely that the representation is reliable'. This recommendation was made in view of the fact that certain types of declarant, specifically accomplices and co-accused, may make statements that are against their own interest yet downplay their own culpability and emphasise that of other parties.[88] It was made following concerns generated in this regard by the decision of the NSW Court of Criminal Appeal in *Suteski*,[89] upholding the trial judge's decision to admit an accomplice's ERISP against the appellant.

Despite the reform to s 65(2)(d) consequent on the decision in *Suteski*, that case remains authoritative on a number of points. Specifically, the court held that the context in which a representation is made is relevant to the question whether it is against interest and that the motives of the representor are not relevant in determining whether the statement is against their interests.

The following extract taken from the judgment of Wood CJ at CL (with whom Howie and Sully JJ agreed) deals with these points:

> 93. An argument was also advanced that each question and answer should be considered separately, and that, unless standing alone, it amounted to a representation against interest, it did not qualify for admission. In my view this involved altogether too narrow a proposition. I see no reason why the representations should not be considered in context, that is, in association with the other answers which, when read together, constitute an admission or answer against interest, that is, so far as they tended to prove that Sakisi had committed a crime.
>
> 94. It was also submitted that, in view of Sakisi's position as an accomplice, and the arrest of his girlfriend, such statements as he had made in the ERISP may have been self-serving, or intended to serve *her* interests. Upon that basis, it was argued that the representations could not be held with any certainty to be *against his* interests. His Honour rejected this argument, holding that despite any mixed motives which he may have held, any answer which tended to be incriminatory of him was one made against interest.

86 Ibid [39].
87 ALRC, *Uniform Evidence Law*, above n 20.
88 Ibid [8.45]-[8.48].
89 [2002] NSWCCA 509; 56 NSWLR 182.

> Again, I am of the view that this aspect of his Honour's reasoning was correct, and that the argument to the contrary, repeated on appeal, has no basis. It similarly follows from the commonly accepted meaning of a statement against interest.

Although *Suteski* may still stand for general principles associated with statements against interest, the High Court's judgment in *Sio*, extracted below, may make it more difficult for representations made by accomplices to be admitted through s 65(2)(d). At a minimum, *Sio* requires additional scrutiny of the individual representations at issue prior to admission.

Sio

[2016] HCA 32; 259 CLR 47
(some footnotes omitted)

Sio had been convicted of armed robbery and wounding after serving as the getaway driver for Filihia, who had committed a robbery and stabbing at a brothel. During the investigation, Filihia had given an ERISP in which he stated that Sio had the knife in the car prior to Filihia getting in, such that Sio had supplied the knife that Filihia later used in the course of the robbery. The following day, Filihia gave another ERISP in which he stated that Sio had put him up to committing the robbery and had given Filihia the knife and drove him to the brothel. Filihia refused to give evidence at Sio's trial and the ERISPs were admitted within s 65(2)(d). Prior to *Sio* reaching the High Court, the NSW Court of Criminal Appeal endorsed the approach in *Suteski* and gave detailed consideration to the operation of s 65(2)(d), its legislative history and its relationship to other exceptions in s 65(2), as well as to other provisions in the Act.[90] The analysis focused particularly on the meaning and effect of the requirement in s 65(2)(d) that the representations against interest be made in 'circumstances that make it likely that the representation is reliable'.

> **French CJ, Bell, Gageler, Keane and Gordon JJ:** 45. Mr Sio … submitted that, if s 65(2)(d)(ii) of the Evidence Act had been properly applied in the courts below, Mr Filihia's statements that Mr Sio had given him the knife would not have been in evidence against him. On that basis, it was said that this Court cannot conclude, in conformity with s 7(2) [of the *Criminal Appeal Act 1912* (NSW)], that the jury "must have been satisfied" that Mr Sio gave Mr Filihia the knife, or was otherwise aware that Mr Filihia was in possession of the knife when he entered the brothel. …
>
> 49. Mr Sio submitted that the Court of Criminal Appeal misapplied s 65(2)(d)(ii) of the Evidence Act by viewing all the statements made by Mr Filihia together, and concluding from his demeanour and the freshness of his recollection that these were circumstances which made it likely that Mr Filihia's representations were reliable.
>
> 50. The Crown submitted that the Court of Criminal Appeal was correct to regard Mr Filihia's account as a whole. The Crown submitted that the lies told by Mr Filihia in an otherwise correct account were no basis to exclude Mr Filihia's representation about the source of the knife. The Crown reiterated the circumstances identified by the trial judge and the Court of Criminal Appeal that were said to make it likely that Mr Filihia's account was reliable.
>
> 51. The Crown submitted that there was no difference in the circumstances in which all of Mr Filihia's statements were made, aside from the fact that the statements were made successively within a 24 hour period. But to say this is to take a compendious approach to the admissibility of those statements without focusing upon the representation of the particular fact sought to be proved. That approach is not permitted by s 65(2)(d).

90 *Sio* [2015] NSWCCA 42.

A compendious approach to s 65(2)(d)

52. The Court of Criminal Appeal did not focus upon the particular representation by Mr Filihia which was material to the issue as to Mr Sio's foresight of the possibility of the use of the knife by Mr Filihia. Rather, as noted above, Leeming JA considered the question of likely reliability by reference to the overall impression to be gained from a consideration of the totality of Mr Filihia's statements. …

58. It is apparent in the present case that neither the trial judge nor the Court of Criminal Appeal considered any particular representation upon which the Crown sought to rely in this way; rather, the application of the provision was approached on a compendious basis whereby an overall impression was formed of the general reliability of the statements made by Mr Filihia and then all his statements were held to be admissible against Mr Sio. That compendious approach does not conform to the requirements of the Act.

59. The Court of Criminal Appeal seems to have regarded earlier authority, including the observations in *R v Suteski* by Wood CJ at CL, with whom Sully and Howie JJ agreed, as allowing or requiring a compendious inquiry as to the overall reliability of the hearsay statements made by Mr Filihia over the course of 24 and 25 October 2012. In Suteski, Wood CJ at CL considered, rightly, that representations relied upon should be considered in context so as to determine whether, when read together, they "constitute an admission or answer against interest". But these observations do not support a compendious approach to the reliability of the whole of a hearsay statement inculpatory of the accused, nor do the other authorities referred to by the Court of Criminal Appeal in this context.

60. It is no light thing to admit a hearsay statement inculpating an accused. Where s 65 is successfully invoked by the prosecution, the accused will have no opportunity to cross-examine the maker of the statement with a view to undermining the inculpatory assertion. Further in this regard, the present case is a case in which, had Mr Filihia pleaded not guilty, and he and Mr Sio been tried together, Mr Filihia's hearsay statements would not have been admissible in that trial against Mr Sio. That is because s 83 of the Evidence Act preserves the exclusionary operation of the hearsay rule in respect of evidence of an admission by a co-accused.

61. The serious consequences of the successful invocation of s 65(2)(d) emphasise the need for compliance with the conditions of admissibility prescribed by the section. The focus demanded by the language of s 65 is inconsistent with the impressionistic evaluation involved in the compendious approach adopted by the Court of Criminal Appeal. The language of the statute assumes the identification of each material fact to be proved by a hearsay statement tendered in reliance on s 65 and the application of the section to that statement, whereas the compendious approach applied by the trial judge and the Court of Criminal Appeal is not focused in this way. In addition, the approach which is focused upon the particular representation tendered to prove a particular fact in issue has the associated benefit of being conducive to the preservation of clarity, good order and fairness in the conduct of criminal trials.

Circumstances that make reliability likely

62. The compendious approach taken by the Court of Criminal Appeal contributed to a further error. When one focuses squarely upon each of Mr Filihia's assertions that it was Mr Sio who gave him the knife, one brings greater clarity to the identification of the circumstances which bear upon the likely reliability of those particular assertions. The evaluation of the likely reliability of each of those assertions must be made having regard to the circumstance that Mr Filihia's representations were those of an accomplice in the commission of the crimes in question.

63. Section 65 gives effect to the view that the circumstances of the making of an out of court statement conveying an assertion of a relevant fact may be such as to indicate that the representation is likely to be reliable – and the asserted fact likely to be true – notwithstanding the hearsay character of the evidence. The section operates on the footing that the circumstances in which the representation was made may be seen to be such

that "the dangers which the rule seeks to prevent are not present or are negligible in the circumstances".[91] In such a case, "there is no basis for a strict application of the rule."[92]

64. Section 65(2)(d)(ii) requires a trial judge to be positively satisfied that the representation which is tendered was made in circumstances that make it likely to be reliable notwithstanding its hearsay character. One category of circumstances that has been recognised as warranting a relaxation of the exclusionary effect of the hearsay rule was identified in *Wigmore on Evidence* as those circumstances that "are such that a sincere and accurate statement would naturally be uttered, and no plan of falsification be formed"; in other words, circumstances that of themselves tend to negative motive and opportunity of the declarant to lie.

65. Evidence by an accomplice against his or her co-offender has long been recognised as less than inherently reliable precisely because of the perceived risk of falsification. Statements by an accomplice afford a classic example of a case where a "plan of falsification" may be expected to be formed, given the obvious interest of one co-offender to shift blame onto his or her accomplice, especially where the circumstances also include the opportunity to seek to curry favour with the authorities. That the evidence of accomplices is evidence apt to be unreliable by reason of a motive to shift blame to the co-offender is recognised by s 165(1)(d) of the Evidence Act, which expressly treats, as "evidence of a kind that may be unreliable", evidence:

> "given in a criminal proceeding by a witness, being a witness who might reasonably be supposed to have been criminally concerned in the events giving rise to the proceeding".

66. One must look to the circumstances in which Mr Filihia asserted that Mr Sio "gave [him] the knife" and "put [him] up to robbing the brothel" for reasons to reach the positive state of satisfaction as to the likely reliability of the assertion. In this regard, the best that can be said is that near contemporaneity of the statement with the commission of the crimes in question meant that the risk of an honestly mistaken recollection was slight. But the question mark over the reliability of the assertion by reason of the fact that it was made by an accomplice is not answered by pointing to the unlikelihood that Mr Filihia's memory of events had faded. As Lord MacDermott said in *Tumahole Bereng v The King*:

> "[F]alse evidence given by an accomplice is commonly regarded as more likely to take the form of incriminating the wrong person than of imagining the crime charged."

67. In the Court of Criminal Appeal, Leeming JA identified two circumstances which he said "enhance reliability" of Mr Filihia's statements. These were "contemporaneity (or near contemporaneity) and against interest." While the circumstances which satisfy the condition in s 65(2)(d)(i) may in some circumstances also tend to satisfy the requirement of likely reliability in s 65(2)(d)(ii), that will not necessarily be so. So much is readily apparent from the statutory requirement that both conditions in s 65(2)(d) be satisfied. More importantly for present purposes, the requirement that a representation be against interest in order to satisfy s 65(2)(d)(i) directs attention squarely to the particular representation upon which the party tendering the representation seeks to rely to prove the asserted fact.

68. While it is true to say that, generally speaking, the totality of Mr Filihia's statements were against his own interest, his statement that Mr Sio gave him the knife and put him up to the robbery was, given the circumstances in which that statement was made, plainly apt to minimise his culpability by maximising that of Mr Sio. While it may be accepted that s 65(2)(d)(i) was satisfied in respect of that statement, it did not follow that the circumstances in which it was made were such that the statement was likely to be reliable as evidence against Mr Sio. …

---

91 [*Walton* [1989] HCA 9; 166 CLR 283, 293.]

92 [Ibid.]

70. … The focus of attention of a trial judge tasked with ruling upon the admissibility of a representation is directed by s 65(2)(d)(ii), not to the apparent truthfulness of the person making it, but to the objective circumstances in which it was made. The issue is whether the trial judge is affirmatively satisfied that, notwithstanding the hearsay character of the evidence, it is likely to be reliable evidence of the fact asserted.

71. When one focuses upon the particular representation which conveys the asserted relevant fact, it can be seen that the circumstances in which that representation was made may include other representations which form part of the context in which the relevant representation was made. A representation may be demonstrably unreliable because it is followed by a specific retraction of the assertion of the relevant fact. Statements made by the representor that are demonstrably or inherently incredible, fanciful or preposterous may be circumstances forming part of the context in which a relevant representation is made which tend against a positive evaluation of the likely reliability of that representation. But it is unnecessary to gloss further the statutory language. In particular, it is not profitable to seek to multiply examples of other circumstances which assist the trial judge to conclude that a representation is unlikely to be reliable. It is to risk being distracted from the task set by s 65(2)(d)(ii) to be overly concerned with what circumstances may properly be taken into account to determine the unreliability of a representation. The true concern of the provision is with the identification of circumstances which of themselves warrant the conclusion that the representation is reliable notwithstanding its hearsay character.

72. Section 65(2)(d)(ii) requires the making of an evaluation by the trial judge which positively satisfies the trial judge that the representation is likely to be reliable by reason of the circumstances in which it was made. As was noted in *IMM v The Queen*, s 65(2)(c) and (d) and s 85 provide "[t]he only occasion for a trial judge to consider the reliability of evidence, in connection with the admissibility of evidence". It is desirable to emphasise, however, that the whole point of s 65(2)(d)(ii) is that, where the circumstances in which the statement is made are likely to ensure, as a practical matter, that the asserted fact truly occurred, the fairness of the trial does not require a positive judgment by the tribunal of fact about the reliability of the maker of the statement. Attention is directed by the language of s 65(2)(d) to an assessment of the circumstances in which the statement was made to establish its likely reliability, rather than to a general assessment of whether or not it is likely that the representor is a reliable witness. This is precisely because the representor will not be a witness at the trial.

73. It is sufficient for present purposes to say that a question mark necessarily arose over Mr Filihia's assertion that Mr Sio gave him the knife and put him up to the robbery, by reason of the circumstance that Mr Filihia was Mr Sio's accomplice. Nothing else in the objective circumstances in which the statement was made was apt to shift the balance in favour of a positive finding of likely reliability in respect of this asserted fact. It was not open to the trial judge to be satisfied positively of the likely reliability of Mr Filihia's assertion that Mr Sio gave him the knife by reference to the circumstances in which that assertion was made; and the Court of Criminal Appeal erred in failing to conclude that the trial judge had erred in this respect. The evidence should not have been admitted.

[Special leave to appeal granted; appeal allowed; new trial ordered.]

One example of accomplice testimony held to be admissible subsequent to Sio can be found in the Victorian Court of Appeal's judgment in *Vitale*.[93] Craig Vitale had been convicted of armed robbery and intentionally causing serious injury in connection with a robbery at a bottle shop, in which his brother Wayne Vitale had also been a participant. As a result of a police investigation that included surveillance recordings of Craig and Wayne discussing the events of the robbery, both

93 [2020] VSCA 237. And for a discussion distinguishing and applying *Sio* to a representation made by a complainant with a cognitive impairment, see *Prasad* [2020] NSWCCA 349.

brothers were arrested. When confronted with his participation in the robbery, Wayne initially denied any involvement, but after hearing the surveillance recordings he consulted with a lawyer and subsequently gave a full statement in which, amongst other things, he stated that his brother had planned and executed the robbery, that he had no prior knowledge that Craig had a gun and that Craig was the only one who ever held or fired the gun. Wayne pleaded guilty to armed robbery and handling stolen goods and was called as a witness to testify in Craig's trial, but refused to give evidence. Both the prosecution and defence agreed that Wayne should be considered unavailable to give evidence based on his refusal to testify and the trial judge admitted his statement within s 65(2)(d).

The Court of Appeal found that the statement had been properly admitted. First, and following *Sio*, the trial judge identified specific representations made by Wayne and gave specific consideration to each of them, avoiding the compendious approach precluded by *Sio*. Second, the trial judge gave proper consideration to each of the requirements in s 65(2)(d). The representations were correctly held to be against Wayne's interests because they implicated him in his participation in the robbery, notwithstanding that the statements also tended to be against the interests of his brother. The representation were also correctly held to be made in circumstances that make it likely that the representation is reliable for several interconnected reasons. One was that Wayne gave his statement, abandoning his earlier denials of any participation, after hearing the surveillance recordings in which he discussed his participation. This impacted on the circumstances of reliability by removing his reasons to lie about the events. Another reason was that Wayne had consulted with a lawyer and received advice, prior to giving a sworn statement which could result in a perjury conviction if he was untruthful. The final circumstance considered was that Wayne was testifying against his own brother, which in the court's assessment meant that 'Wayne Vitale would have had to have overcome an instinctive disinclination to implicate his brother'.[94] The judgment in *Vitale* at least suggests that there are ways to admit accomplice testimony, even applying the scrutiny required by *Sio*.

Evidence in an Australian or overseas proceeding: UEA, s 65(3)-(6)

This inclusionary exception has, as was explained by Bongiorno JA in *DPP v BB*,[95] a long pedigree at common law and in previous statutory provisions. Its rationales are that a number of the infirmities associated with hearsay evidence are not present where the previous representation is made in prior proceedings: it was then subject to the pressures against fabrication arising from the taking of an oath or affirmation and from the prospect of being prosecuted for perjury. Most importantly, concerns about reliability and trial fairness are met because the evidence will only be admissible if the defendant either cross-examined the witness or had the opportunity to do so at the time the representation was made. It is not a requirement of s 65(3) that the cross-examination that occurred be of a standard or canvassed all the issues that might, at a subsequent trial, be thought to have been desirable.[96] In fact s 65(3) contemplates a situation where no cross-examination occurs. Its requirements are fulfilled if the opposing party had a reasonable opportunity to cross-examine the witness. Accordingly, absence of

94 [2020] VSCA 237, [86].
95 [2010] VSCA 211; 29 VR 110, [17]-[20].
96 *Puchalski* [2007] NSWCCA 220, [95] (Smart JA, with McClellan CJ at CL and Hislop J agreeing).

cross-examination or as complete a cross-examination as might subsequently be judged desirable is unlikely to be accepted as grounds for excluding the evidence.[97]

Because s 65(3) specifically contemplates the fact that the trier of fact may not be able to observe the witness testifying, it has been held that any procedural unfairness that might arise from it should usually be dealt with by way of judicial direction rather than by the exercise of an exclusionary discretion.[98]

This inclusionary exception applies to both prosecution and defence evidence.[99] Unlike the exception in s 65(2), it does not require that evidence of the previous representation be given by a person who saw, heard or otherwise perceived the representation being made. Section 65(6) provides for the representation to be adduced by the production of an authenticated transcript or recording of the representation.

Section 65(3) is not restrictive as to the type of proceedings in which the representation is made. Accordingly, it covers representations made in committal proceedings (preliminary proceedings in Tasmania),[100] representations made in earlier criminal proceedings for the same offences where a retrial has been ordered,[101] representations made in earlier civil proceedings arising from the same events as those subsequently subject to criminal proceedings, representations made in depositions or taken in special hearings from terminally ill or seriously injured witnesses, and pre-recorded representations made in special hearings by vulnerable witnesses.[102]

Defence evidence under section 65: *UEA*, s 65(8)

The legislative intent of s 65(8) is to permit the accused to adduce exculpatory previous representations that the common law would not countenance. In this regard it seeks to advance the fair trial prospects of the accused in ways precluded by the common law. The ALRC noted that it would 'enable the exonerating statements of the alleged victim to be received, the confessions of third parties and statements of deceased persons who could have given evidence'.[103] We saw in *Nguyen*[104] that the prosecution bears an ethical obligation to adduce representations that are a mix of inculpatory and exculpatory statements). Section 65(8) provides an inclusionary exception for exculpatory statements. It is the most generous of the s 65 exceptions. It equates to the relaxed provision for the admission of hearsay in civil cases[105] and admits hearsay evidence with a lower hurdle than that applied to situations where the declarant is actually called to testify.[106] Where the previous representation is contained in a document, s 65(8)(b) removes the barrier applying to prosecution evidence which requires that evidence of the previous representation be given by a person who saw, heard or otherwise perceived the representation being made (that is, a defence witness *does not* have to have seen the words being written on the paper for the representation

97 *DPP v BB* [2010] VSCA 211; 29 VR 110; *Puchalski* [2007] NSWCCA 220.

98 *DPP v BB*, ibid, [29]-[31] (Bongiorno JA).

99 *Taber* [2007] NSWCCA 116; 170 A Crim R 427.

100 *Puchalski* [2007] NSWCCA 220; *Darmody* [2010] VSCA 41; 213 A Crim R 79; *DPP v BB* [2010] VSCA 211; 29 VR 110; *Ambrosoli* [2002] NSWCCA 386; 55 NSWLR 603.

101 *Taber* [2007] NSWCCA 116; 170 A Crim R 427.

102 See, eg, *Evidence (Children and Special Witnesses) Act 2001* (Tas), ss 6 and 6A.

103 ALRC, *Evidence (Interim)*, above n 4, [692].

104 *Nguyen* [2020] HCA 23 (see Chapters 2 and 7).

105 *UEA*, ss 63 and 64.

106 *UEA*, s 66.

in the document to be admissible). The low threshold of admissibility for defence evidence accords with the conceptual framework for the hearsay exceptions proposed by the ALRC, whose purpose, where the accused is concerned, is to minimise the conviction of the innocent.[107]

Nevertheless s 65(8) does not appear to have provided a bonanza of opportunities for the accused to adduce out-of-court representations made by absent witnesses. Rather, as concluded by Henning and Hunter in their detailed discussion of relevant case law,[108] courts have been wary of admitting exculpatory previous representations under this provision and, instead, have largely adhered to the hostile attitude of the common law courts towards such evidence,[109] and particularly towards exculpatory out-of-court statements made by accused persons themselves.

For example, in *Parkes*,[110] where the admissibility of a previous exculpatory representation made by the accused was in issue, s 65(8) was simply ignored. In this case, the accused was considered by the majority judges (Ipp and Bell JJA) to be 'notionally available' to testify in his own defence, which meant that s 65 could not apply but that s 66 could – provided, of course, the accused forwent his right to silence and testified. In contrast, Hulme J held that s 66 could not apply unless, at the time the question of the admissibility of the previous representation arose, the accused had either already testified or it was established that they would do so. This approach, it is argued, accords most closely with the accused's fair trial rights and right to silence, and with the legislative intent of s 65(8), as explained by the ALRC, to minimise wrongful convictions.

In *Rymer*,[111] while the NSW Court of Criminal Appeal was prepared to countenance the admission of out-of-court exculpatory statements made by the accused, s 65(8) was not identified as the relevant mechanism to support their admission. Instead, the court suggested that the accused's pre-trial denials could have been admitted as prior consistent statements to support the credibility of his not guilty plea and, thereafter, s 60 might be applied to enable the denials to be used as evidence of the facts asserted. While this approach preserves the accused's right to silence and enables the exculpatory evidence to be adduced, it is quite unsatisfactorily and unnecessarily complex. Henning and Hunter dub it 'a contorted technical fix'.[112]

In *O'Connor*[113] the NSW Court of Criminal Appeal did consider the application of s 65(8) to statements made by a co-accused, asserting that O'Connor had not been involved in the offence charged. The co-accused was not available to testify to O'Connor's innocence at her trial. Nevertheless, the court rejected the evidence, holding that while it was prima facie admissible under s 65(8) it was unfairly prejudicial to the Crown to permit it to be adduced.[114]

In another case, *Hemmelstein*,[115] the NSW Court of Criminal Appeal rejected previous representations that impliedly exculpated the accused of knowingly

107 ALRC, *Evidence (Interim)*, above n 4, [692].
108 Henning and Hunter, above n 22, 360-4.
109 See, eg, *Re Van Beelen* (1974) 9 SASR 163; *Baker* [2012] HCA 27; 245 CLR 632; and *Blastland* [1986] AC 41.
110 [2003] NSWCCA 12; 147 A Crim R 450.
111 [2005] NSWCCA 310; 156 A Crim R 84.
112 Henning and Hunter, above n 22, 363.
113 [2003] NSWCCA 335.
114 Cf *Mrish* (unreported, NSWSC, 4 October 1996).
115 [2001] NSWCCA 220.

importing cocaine. The sole issue for determination at trial was whether the accused knew that there was cocaine in his luggage when he entered Australia. He wished to adduce evidence of two previous representations. The first was made in a conversation between Hemmelstein's solicitor, Mr Murphy, and a person called Jim Simonds who had paid $1800 towards Hemmelstein's legal costs. Simonds told Murphy that it was impossible for Hemmelstein's fingerprints to be on the cocaine package. The second previous representation was made to Hemmelstein's brother by someone with the initials JS. JS said that Hemmelstein was not guilty. The implied intentional assertions in both representations were that JS/Simonds and not Hemmelstein had placed the cocaine in his luggage.

Meagher JA (with Hulme J agreeing) held that these representations had no relevance to the facts in issue. In fact, Meagher JA characterised the proposition that they were relevant as verging on 'the ludicrous'. He further stated that '[t]his submission only has to be stated to reveal its absurdity'.[116] In contrast, Smart JA (in dissent on this issue) held that the representations were capable of bolstering the accused's case that he had no knowledge of the cocaine in his luggage. In relation to s 65(8) his Honour held:

> 41. This important provision remedied a defect in the existing law as administered by the courts in this State. Hitherto, it had been difficult to adduce statements by a person other than the defendant to another that the speaker had committed the crime with which the defendant was charged, or had or had not done certain acts, which meant that the defendant had not committed the crime or that it was unlikely that he had done so. Sometimes these statements pointed to a third party having committed the crime. The person making the previous representation may not have been available for a variety of reasons including refusing to come to court or refusing to give evidence. In England, as a matter of practice objection was not usually taken to a defendant leading hearsay evidence which was capable of being believed when it tended to show that a defendant was not guilty. A stricter approach was taken by the prosecution in this State. Section 65(8) brings New South Wales into line with the English practice.
>
> 42. Section 65(8) involves a recognition of the fact that a defendant may not have the resources to obtain evidence and procure the attendance of witnesses. If the witness who is able to give the primary evidence is overseas and declines to come to Australia, the problem is magnified. It is not uncommon for a person, who informally concedes that it was he not the defendant who committed the crime or who informally makes concessions having that effect, to be unwilling to come to Court to give evidence to that effect. There are the further cases of the speaker dying or 'going underground' for a period.
>
> 43. I think that the evidence of Mr Murphy as to statements made to him by Mr Simonds is admissible pursuant to s 65(8). That material bolsters the defence case and makes it seem not so improbable. As the evidence is hearsay the judge would have to give the jury a warning pursuant to s 165(1)(a) and explain the reasons why the hearsay evidence may be unreliable.

Smart JA also considered that the previous representations made to the accused's brother were admissible for the same reasons.

The worrying thing about these cases is that they arguably subvert the clear legislative intent of s 65(8) and retain the common law suspicion of, and approach to, exculpatory hearsay evidence. This means that the 'defect in the law' identified by Smart JA in *Hemmelstein* that s 65(8) was instituted to remedy may instead be preserved by courts' reluctance to give adequate effect to the potential offered by that section.

116 Ibid [11].

'Retaliatory hearsay': UEA, s 65(9)[117]

This provision enables 'retaliatory' evidence to be adduced by another party, including the prosecution, where a defendant has adduced a previous representation about a matter. In *Eastman*,[118] it was stated that s 65(9) applies not only when hearsay evidence is adduced by the defendant under s 65(8) but also when it is admitted under another exception to the hearsay rule such as s 60:

> [I]f evidence of a previous representation by someone who is not available to give evidence about a matter has been adduced by the defendant in a criminal proceeding and has been admitted, the hearsay rule does not apply to evidence of another representation about the matter that is adduced by another party and is given by a person who saw, heard or otherwise perceived the other representation being made. The reference to 'another party' plainly includes the Crown, and the right of the Crown to respond under s 65(9) is not limited by the preconditions that would govern the leading of first-hand hearsay evidence as part of the Crown case in chief under s 65(2): *R v Mrish* (SC(NSW), Hidden J, 4 October 1996, unreported) at 5. Had an application been made by the appellant during the course of evidence to rely on s 60, or if the [previous] representation had been admitted under s 65, s 65(9) would have permitted the Crown to adduce into evidence the other previous representations ...
>
> If s 60 had been considered there would have been a question whether the retaliatory provisions of s 65(9) applied where evidence of a previous representation was admitted under s 60. The language of s 65(9) would appear to be wide enough to encompass that situation.

It is uncertain whether the term 'matter' in s 65(9) would be given a narrow or broad interpretation. The ALRC in its 2006 report on the uniform evidence legislation considered that it should not be necessary to construe the term but that, should it be necessary to do so, then a broad construction is to be preferred:

> [T]he approach should be to identify the content of the representation to be adduced by the defendant and to consider whether the other representations can be said to be relevant to it. As a result, it should not be necessary to construe the term 'about a matter' and it may, in fact, be preferable to avoid defining it. If it is necessary to construe the term, a broad construction should be adopted and, where that may cause unfair prejudice, the mandatory and discretionary exclusions in Part 3.11 should be used. Narrowing the interpretation of any of the hearsay exceptions carries the danger of introducing technicalities, something the uniform Evidence Acts are intended to remove and avoid.[119]

Criminal proceedings, maker of representation available: *UEA*, s 66

This inclusionary exception applies to both prosecution and defence evidence. It provides:

> **66. Exception: criminal proceedings if maker available**
>
> (1) This section applies in a criminal proceeding if a person who made a previous representation is available to give evidence about an asserted fact.
>
> (2) If that person has been or is to be called to give evidence, the hearsay rule does not apply to evidence of the previous representation that is given by:
>
> (a) that person, or

117 This term was used by von Doussa, O'Loughlin and Cooper JJ in *Eastman* (1997) 158 ALR 107, 173, quoting MJ Beazley, 'Hearsay and Related Evidence – A New Era' (1995) 18 *UNSW Law Journal* 39.

118 (1997) 158 ALR 107, 173 (von Doussa, O'Loughlin and Cooper JJ).

119 ALRC, *Uniform Evidence Law*, above n 20, [8.65].

(b) a person who saw, heard or otherwise perceived the representation being made, if, when the representation was made, the occurrence of the asserted fact was fresh in the memory of the person who made the representation.

(2A) In determining whether the occurrence of the asserted fact was fresh in the memory of a person, the court may take into account all matters that it considers are relevant to the question, including:

(a) the nature of the event concerned, and

(b) the age and health of the person, and

(c) the period of time between the occurrence of the asserted fact and the making of the representation.

(3) If a representation was made for the purpose of indicating the evidence that the person who made it would be able to give in an Australian or overseas proceeding, subsection (2) does not apply to evidence adduced by the prosecutor of the representation unless the representation concerns the identity of a person, place or thing.

(4) A document containing a representation to which subsection (2) applies must not be tendered before the conclusion of the examination in chief of the person who made the representation, unless the court gives leave.

Unlike the equivalent inclusionary exception for civil cases (s 64), s 66(2) requires the maker of the previous representation to be not only available to testify but also actually called to testify. The previous representation may then be adduced *either* through the person who made it or through someone who saw, heard or otherwise perceived it being made. It does not matter that the person who made the representation did not give evidence of the representation during their own testimony, or that the person who made the representation even remember having made it.[120]

The rationale for the exception in s 66 lies in the guarantors of reliability it prescribes. This was explained by Gleeson CJ and Hayne J in the High Court decision in *Papakosmas*:[121]

> 34. It is to be noted that, if the exception to the hearsay rule created by s 66 is to apply, certain conditions need to be fulfilled. The person who made the representation, (in a case such as the present, the complainant), of which evidence is to be given must be available to give evidence about the asserted fact. … If the complainant had, for some reason, been unavailable as a witness, and the defence had not been able to cross-examine her, then the evidence of her out-of-court representations would not have been admissible under s 66. … Secondly, by reason of s 62, the operation of Division 2 of Part 3.2 of the Act is restricted to first-hand hearsay, a condition that was satisfied in the present case. Thirdly, by reason of s 66(2), it is necessary that the occurrence of the asserted fact was fresh in the memory of the complainant.
>
> 35. These are important safeguards against two of the dangers which led the common law to exclude hearsay: unreliability; and unfairness to an accused person who may not have an opportunity to test an unsworn assertion made out of court.

McHugh J similarly stated:

> 84. … Whatever the true rationale for the hearsay rule may have been at common law, the Act assumes that the rationales for excluding hearsay evidence are its potential unreliability and the threat that hearsay evidence poses to procedural fairness. Unreliability is seen as a problem in s 66 itself because the section makes it a condition of admissibility that 'the occurrence of the asserted fact was fresh in the memory' of the person who made the statement. The threat to procedural fairness is also seen as a problem in s 66(1) because that sub-section states that s 66 'applies in a criminal proceeding if a person who

120 See, eg, *Brooks (No 3)* [2017] NSWSC 261, [11]-[15].

121 [1999] HCA 37; 196 CLR 297.

> made a previous representation is available to give evidence about an asserted fact.' The purpose of this statement and other conditions in the section is to ensure that the defendant has an opportunity to cross-examine on the representation.

These statements emphasise the importance of the requirement as a condition of reliability that the previous representation be made at a time when the asserted facts were fresh in the memory of the person who made it. This is not a condition for admissibility under s 64. The meaning of this phrase initially occasioned some controversy as a result of the narrow interpretation given to it by the High Court in *Graham*.[122] There the phrase was read as primarily constituting a temporal test so that, while the quality of the memory might be a relevant consideration, it did not connote its core meaning. The result of this reasoning was that the six years between the events in question and the making of the previous representation were considered to be too great a delay for the previous representation to satisfy the requirement of 'freshness'.

This interpretation is problematic primarily because it gives insufficient weight to the nature of the recounted event. Psychological research indicates that for events that have a significant emotional impact, there *may* be little deterioration in memories of them over time.[123] The research results vary, but this variation indicates that a 'one size fits all' approach to memory retention is inappropriate. Further, this interpretation appears to preserve elements of the common law stereotype that only proximate complaints in sexual offences cases can have any real evidentiary value.[124] The rationales given for the temporal interpretation also invoke aspects of common law precepts relating to legal relevance, including the degree of usefulness of the evidence, the possibility that it might distract attention from the quality of the evidence given by the witness in court and the desirability of achieving certainty in the construction of the phrase with consequent cost efficiencies in the use of court time. These considerations are more appropriately allocated to the discretions to exclude evidence provided in ss 135 and 137.

The *Graham* interpretation of 'freshness of memory' also arguably replicates the test of admissibility in s 65(2)(b) (when or shortly after) even though quite different terminology is used. This begs the question why the two tests would be worded differently if they were intended to have the same meaning. Finally, there is a degree of incongruity in the majority judges' reasoning that a temporally proximate statement has value because it may provide the best evidence of what the witness knows of the events because it was made closer in time to them than testimony given at trial. Any account that is given some time before trial may have this quality, not just one given close in time to the events in question.

In response to the narrow reading given in *Graham*, and in view of the most recent psychological research on memory, the ALRC recommended in its 2006 report on the uniform evidence legislation, that interpretive guidance be provided in s 66 to ensure a more flexible approach is taken to the 'freshness of memory' requirement.[125] This recommendation was implemented by the enactment of sub-s (2A) of s 66. The degree of change that this amendment has wrought to the application of s 66 is evident from the decision of the NSW Court of Criminal

122 [1998] HCA 61; 195 CLR 606.

123 See details of relevant research in ALRC, *Uniform Evidence Law*, above n 20, [8.86]-[8.112].

124 See comments to this effect in ALRC, ibid [8.79].

125 Ibid [8.119]-[8.124].

Appeal in *XY*.[126] This case involved an appeal from the trial judge's decision to exclude previous representations made by the complainant in a child sexual offences case on the basis that they were not made when the events were 'fresh' in the complainant's memory. The previous representations had been made approximately four and six years after the commission of the offences. Whealy J (with whom Campbell JA and Simpson J agreed) concluded that the trial judge should not have declined to admit the previous representations and that the decision to do so resulted from a misinterpretation of s 66(2) and (2A). His Honour provided the following analysis of the interpretive approach mandated by sub-s (2A):

> 78. Secondly, s 66(2A) is an interpretative section. It tells the reader how the section is to be interpreted. It makes clear that, in determining whether the occurrence of the asserted fact was 'fresh in the memory' of the person, the court may take into account 'all matters that it considers are relevant to the question'. Thus it will be seen that the three matters mentioned in (a), (b) and (c), although clearly very important, are not the only matters that may be considered.
>
> 79. For present purposes, however, it may be seen that the present legislation makes it clear that the context of the phrase 'fresh in the memory' no longer is to be taken as an indication that it means 'recent' or 'immediate'. The expression 'fresh in the memory' is now to be interpreted more widely than did the High Court in *Graham's* case. No longer is the 'core meaning' of the phrase to be interpreted as 'essentially confined to an examination of the temporal relationship between the occurrence of the asserted fact, and the time of making of the representation'. That temporal relationship remains a relevant consideration but it is by no means determinative of the question. Importantly, the court now must take into account 'the nature of the event concerned'. In Graham's case, that was not seen as a particularly important matter. It now takes its place as an important consideration in the factors to be considered.

In relation to the particular representations in question, his Honour concluded:

> 92. Given the repeated nature of the sexual incidents, their unusual features, and the youth and naivety in sexual terms of the complainant at the time they were said to have occurred, it is likely, indeed highly likely, that the memory of those events would remain with him for many years to come. No doubt, the representations he made to CD at the Aquatic Centre in 2007 would have reinforced their presence in his mind. In the circumstances, there is no reason to suppose that between 2007 and the time he spoke to his parents, approximately a year and three quarters later, his recollection of the essence those matters would have diminished. Regrettably, the trial judge has made no analysis of matters of this kind at all.
>
> 93. For these reasons, I am satisfied that the trial judge fell into error. The ruling substantially weakened the prosecution's case simply because all three complaints were ruled inadmissible.

Despite the significance of the reform wrought by s 66(2A), as Whealy J notes, the temporal relationship between the representation and the events in question remains a relevant consideration. It also appears that, if the time in question is considered to be particularly long, it may be decisive.[127] This is despite Whealy J's statement that the temporal factor 'is by no means determinative'. For example,

126 [2010] NSWCCA 181; 79 NSWLR 629; see also *Kassab (a Pseudonym)* [2021] NSWCCA 46 (complaints made 30-40 years after occurrence of the alleged offences admissible, with finding that ongoing disclosure over that period was relevant to freshness); and *LMD* [2012] VSCA 164 (complaints made between seven and 10 years after the occurrence of the alleged offences).

127 See obiter statements by Priest JA in *Pate (a Pseudonym)* [2015] VSCA 110, [143] to the effect that there will be cases where the effluxion of time will be decisive.

in *Clay*,[128] where the period in question, in the case of at least two of three complainants, exceeded 20 years, the Victorian Court of Appeal held:

> 50. While it is true that the 'nature of the event' concerned is a relevant factor in determining whether to permit evidence of previous complaint to be led, so too, in terms, is 'the period of time between the occurrence of the asserted fact and the making of the representation'. Wherever the line is to be drawn, a period that, in the case of at least two of the complainants, exceeded 20 years seems to us to have been so far beyond what the legislature could ever have contemplated when it enacted s 66(2A) as to make it impossible to say that the requirements of the section were met. In this case, absent any evidence to suggest that these matters were relevantly 'fresh in the memory' of the individual complainant concerned, the hearsay rule was applicable. Evidence of each of the complaints should, accordingly, have been excluded.

Similarly in *Pate (a Pseudonym)*[129] where the alleged offence occurred 12 years before the making of the complaint, Weinberg JA held:

> 65. ... There is no single bright line figure beyond which a representation made long after an event cannot be 'fresh in the memory'. Plainly, however, the greater the period that has passed, the greater the need for there to be some reason why the event would be 'fresh' in the memory.

In the same case Priest JA stated:

> 143. Upon the assumption that consideration of whether a memory is 'fresh' is no longer to be confined to the time that has elapsed between the occurrence of the asserted fact and the representation, nonetheless the effluxion of time will remain relevant (and, in some cases, decisive). Given that s 66(2A) invites a more flexible approach, however, to the concept of 'freshness' – and invites consideration of factors beyond time – it may be that greater attention will need to be given to the subjective features of the person making the representation than was hitherto the case.
>
> 144. The precursor to the enactment of s 66(2A) was the joint report of the Australian Law Reform Commission, NSW Law Reform Commission and Victorian Law Reform Commission, *Uniform Evidence Law*, published in late 2005 ('ALRC 102'). When discussing the 'fresh in the memory' test in s 66, the report made extensive reference to psychological research on memory. In light of that research, it was concluded that the assessment of 'freshness' should not be confined to the time which elapses between the occurrence of the relevant event and the making of a representation about the event.
>
> 145. Whether a memory is 'fresh' ought not, however, be permitted to become an abstruse concept. The experience of the Courts is, I think, reflected in the following passage from *Longman*, where McHugh J remarked:
>
>> The fallibility of human recollection and the effect of imagination, emotion, prejudice and suggestion on the capacity to 'remember' is well documented. The longer the period between an 'event' and its recall, the greater the margin for error. Interference with a person's ability to 'remember' may also arise from talking or reading about or experiencing other events of a similar nature or from the person's own thinking or recalling. Recollection of events which occurred in childhood is particularly susceptible to error and is also subject to the possibility that it may not even be genuine.
>
> 146. Hence, given that determination of 'freshness' of memory is not confined simply to temporal proximity, when assessing whether an asserted fact is 'fresh in the memory', consideration might also be given to whether the particular memory can be said to be free of factors which potentially might taint or influence it (such as – to use a non-exhaustive example – psychological counselling or therapy).

128 [2014] VSCA 269.

129 [2015] VSCA 110.

> 147. As I have said, the asserted fact in this case could not properly have been characterised as fresh in the complainant's memory. Had objection been taken, the evidence of the relevant representation could not properly have been admitted in reliance on s 66. (footnotes omitted)

There are indications in these cases that the Victorian Court of Appeal may be persuaded to depart from the approach of the NSW Court of Criminal Appeal in *XY*,[130] and its own earlier decision in *LMD*,[131] with regard to the significance to be accorded the length of time between the making of the representation and the events in question in determining 'freshness of memory'. For example, in *Pate* Priest JA stated (obiter) that he 'would not hasten to embrace the reasoning in either case'.[132] In an earlier case (*ISJ*[133]) the Victorian Court of Appeal reserved for consideration 'on an appropriate occasion whether *XY* gives sufficient emphasis to the temporal factor that remains within the concept of "fresh in the mind".'

Such statements and the apparent primacy accorded to the effluxion of time in *Pate* and *Clay* in determining whether evidence satisfies the 'freshness of memory' test in s 66(2A) raise the spectre of a revival of the impugned reasoning in *Graham*, perhaps in a modified but nevertheless recognisable form. The indications from cases like *Pate* and *Clay* are that the Victorian Court of Appeal is seeking, in cases involving delayed complaint, evidence of a kind considered sufficient 'to overcome the time barrier in the notion of something being fresh'.[134] Here we see the emphasis placed firmly on the temporal component of the test in s 66(2A) and an apparent sidelining of the significance to be attached to the nature of the events. In *Clay* and *Pate* the type of evidence sought by the Court of Appeal to 'overcome the time barrier' was in the nature of intervening events (including statements made by the witness) that might be viewed as maintaining or renewing the witness's memory of the original events constituting the offence. Unfortunately, this type of evidence can cut both ways. It might equally be regarded as contaminating evidence if one accepts the views expressed by McHugh J in *Longman* (quoted by Priest JA in *Pate*).[135] But considered in a positive light, the attraction of such events for the Victorian Court of Appeal seems to be that they may be treated as resetting the clock on the witness's memory and so effectively reducing the length of time between the making of the relevant representations and the occurrence of the events in issue. The point is, however, that the focus is on time. There is little or no attention given to the nature of the events.

The quality of the previous representation was also nominated in *Pate* as a potential basis for judging the freshness of the witness's memory. The level of detail it contains and the vividness of the picture it paints were suggested to render it more likely that the 'events were "well and truly implanted" in the [witness's] memory'.[136] The concern raised by this approach is that, as the ALRC notes, absence of detail is not necessarily indicative of the extent to which incidents, particularly emotionally arousing and stressful incidents, are remembered. The general nature of the incident may be well remembered, but details may not be.[137]

---

130 [2010] NSWCCA 181; 79 NSWLR 629.
131 [2012] VSCA 164.
132 [2015] VSCA 110, [141].
133 [2012] VSCA 321, [49] (Nettle, Redlich and Osborn JJA).
134 *Pate (a Pseudonym)* [2015] VSCA 110, [65] (Weinberg JA).
135 See above, p 386.
136 *Pate (a Pseudonym)* [2015] VSCA 110, [62] (Weinberg JA).
137 ALRC, *Uniform Evidence Law*, above n 20, [8.95]-[8.98], [8.100]-[8.104], [8.109]-[8.111].

So where does this leave us in relation to s 66(2A)? There are indications that some judges of the Victorian Court of Appeal may be reluctant to embrace fully the legislative intent of s 66(2A) as interpreted by the NSW Court of Criminal Appeal in *XY* and the Victorian Court of Appeal in *LMD*. Their preference appears to be to give primacy to the temporal component of the test in the section. Unfortunately this tends to lend the views of McHugh J in *Longman* and the perspective of the High Court in *Graham* (though perhaps not their precise formulation of the freshness in the memory test) a tenacity that the reform sought to dislodge. The hope, therefore, is that a more holistic approach to s 66(2A) is generally accepted, one that gives weight to the nature of the events in question and their capacity to generate memory retention, and that an approach that privileges temporal considerations is abandoned in accordance with the ALRC recommendations and the legislative aspirations underpinning s 66(2A).

A significant fetter on the availability of s 66 for prosecution evidence is the restriction contained in s 66(3), which proscribes the admission of statements made with the intention of disclosing the evidence that the declarant might be able to give in a proceeding. This exception to the s 66 inclusionary exception contains a further exception to itself for representations concerning the identity of a person, place or thing. The difficulty with this restriction is that it can be difficult to discern what a declarant's precise purpose was in making the previous representation. Some assistance in this regard was provided by the Tasmanian Court of Criminal Appeal in *Saunders*:[138]

> 60. The reference in subs (3) to the purpose of the making of a representation is clearly a reference to the purpose of the maker and not the purpose of whoever may have heard the representation. That was the view of Wood CJ at CL in *Esposito* (1998) 105 A Crim R 27 at 34. If a person makes a detailed statement to a police officer or legal practitioner that is recorded in the form of a proof of evidence, the statement will almost invariably be one made by the person for the purpose of indicating the evidence that the person will be able to give in any subsequent court proceedings. However, the case may not be so clear if immediately or shortly after an incident, a person at the scene makes a representation to a police officer who has just arrived at the scene and is trying to find out what has happened. In such a case, the purpose of the representation may only be to make a complaint or allegation or to provide information to the officer to assist the investigation of what took place. Giving evidence at prospective court proceedings might not form part of the representor's purpose.

Section 66(4) provides a final restriction on the admissibility of previous representations under s 66. Where the representation is contained in a document, this may only be tendered at the end of the examination-in-chief of the maker of the previous representation. This limitation preserves the orality of the trial.

A significant departure from the common law instituted by s 66 is that it lifts the common law restrictions on the use that may be made of prior inconsistent and consistent statements made by witnesses or the accused.[139] Importantly, in doing so it abolishes the common law restrictions imposed on the use of a particular species of prior consistent statement – proximate complaints made by complainants in sexual offences cases. At common law all these categories of previous representation may only be used by triers of fact in assessing the credibility of those who made them, as either undermining or bolstering their makers' creditworthiness.

---

138 [2004] TASSC 95; 149 A Crim R 174 (Crawford J (as he then was), with Evans and Slicer JJ agreeing).

139 See, eg, *Crisologo* (1997) 99 A Crim R 178 and *O'Grady* [2000] NSWSC 1256.

In *Papakosmas*,[140] the appellant argued that conformity with the common law limitations should be retained for recent complaint evidence in sexual offences cases and that s 136 of the uniform legislation should be deployed for this purpose. This section empowers trial judges to limit the use that may be made of evidence in prescribed circumstances and to direct juries accordingly. This proposition was rejected firmly by the High Court. Gleeson CJ and Hayne J held:

> 37. In brief, the appellant contends that this was a case in which s 136 should have been applied to limit the use that could be made of the evidence of complaint to the use which could have been made of such evidence at common law, as explained in cases such as *Lillyman* and *Kilby*. The jury, it is argued, should have been given the standard common law direction in relation to the use of evidence of recent complaint in sexual assault cases.
>
> 38. Counsel went so far as to argue that, as a general rule, a court which receives evidence of complaint in any criminal case should limit its use under s 136 so that it is not used for a hearsay purpose.
>
> 39. The submissions must be rejected. They amount to an unacceptable attempt to constrain the legislative policy underlying the statute by reference to common law rules, and distinctions, which the legislature has discarded.
>
> 40. There may well arise circumstances in which a court, in the exercise of a discretion enlivened by the requirements of justice in the facts and circumstances of the particular case, will see fit to limit the use of complaint evidence, and, in some instances, it may be appropriate to effect that limitation in a manner which corresponds to the previous common law. To assert a general principle of the kind for which the appellant contends, however, would be to subvert the policy of the legislation.

Similarly, McHugh J stated:

> 90. The appellant submitted that the trial judge erred in not exercising the power conferred by s 136 and directing the jury that the recent complaint evidence could only be used on the issue of the complainant's credibility. Section 136 authorises the judge to limit the use of evidence if a particular use of that evidence might be unfairly prejudicial to a party or be misleading or confusing. The appellant submitted that the self-serving nature of recent complaint evidence and the possibility of concoction raise the possibility that the jury would not be able to fairly assess the evidence. He submitted that a warning under s 165 is insufficient to provide adequate protection to an accused because a warning provides no basis by which the jury could 'expose' the concoction. He contended that the judge erred in not limiting the use of the complaint evidence whether it was admitted pursuant to s 108(3)(b) as an exception to the credibility rule or pursuant to s 66(2) as an exception to the hearsay rule. The appellant conceded that the case for a discretionary limitation was much stronger if the evidence was admitted by way of s 108(3)(b) than by way of s 66(2). That was because admissibility under s 66(2) meant that the evidence was relevant to the facts in issue. He contended that the need for the limitation applied not only in the present trial but in all sexual assault trials. …
>
> 94. As Hunt CJ at CL and Bruce J pointed out in *R v BD* it is artificial and wrong to admit evidence pursuant to s 66(2) and then limit the use of the evidence to credibility issues by exercising the power conferred by s 136. In the ordinary case, a warning under s 165 should be sufficient to alert the jury to the dangers of hearsay evidence. For that reason, s 136 should only be invoked in cases where the danger could not be cured by such a warning. …
>
> 97. Sections 135, s 136 and s 137 contain powers which are to be applied on a case by case basis because of considerations peculiar to the evidence in the particular case. It may be proper for appellate courts to develop guidelines for exercising the powers conferred by these sections so that certain classes of evidence are usually excluded or limited. But

140 [1999] HCA 37; 196 CLR 297.

> those sections confer no authority to emasculate provisions in the Act to make them conform with common law notions of relevance or admissibility.

As we will see below where the hearsay rule is waived under s 60 in relation to evidence initially admitted for a non-hearsay purpose, the evidence may be more vulnerable to an application of s 136 than where it is admitted under one of the fully fledged exceptions to the hearsay rule in Div 2 of Part 3.2.

Contemporaneous representations about a person's health, feelings, etc: *UEA*, s 66A

Section 66A provides:

> **66A. Exception: contemporaneous statements about a person's health, &c**
> The hearsay rule does not apply to evidence of a previous representation made by a person if the representation was a contemporaneous representation about the person's health, feelings, sensations, intention, knowledge or state of mind.

This section creates a separate inclusionary exception for previous representations of the type that were constructed as original evidence in order to avoid the hearsay rule (the so-called 'hearsay fiddle')[141] in common law cases like *Walton*.[142] Accordingly, where it is sought to establish a person's state of mind or intention relying on their utterances, this section avoids the linguistic contortions frequently inherent in *Walton's* original evidence construction and commented on by Kirby, Hayne and Heydon JJ in *Kamleh*.[143] In any event, previous representations will only be admissible under s 66A, where the feelings etc of the representor are relevant to a fact in issue or are themselves a fact in issue. Accordingly, in *Hillier*,[144] Gray J held that s 72 (the forerunner of s 66A) might admit evidence of a person's state of mind 'when the state of mind evidenced by the statement is either itself directly in issue at trial or of direct and immediate relevance to an issue that arises at the trial'.

Illustrative examples of the application of s 66A are found in *Edwards (No 2)*[145] where at issue was whether Edwards had killed his wife or whether she had voluntarily gone 'missing'. Evidence of electronic messages (including by Facebook) posted by her showing her happy in her new relationship and looking forward to her son's wedding, to travel and to her school reunion were relevant to prove her state of mind and relevant to supporting the inference that she had not voluntarily disappeared, but had been killed by the accused.[146]

Other common law cases that admitted previous representations as original evidence to establish the declarants' state of mind and where s 66A might now apply include *Ratten*,[147] where the Privy Council held that evidence given by a telephonist of statements made on the telephone by the deceased shortly before

---

141 See Chapter 8, p 352.

142 [1989] HCA 9; 166 CLR 283. See discussion of this case in Chapter 8, p 352.

143 [2005] HCA 2; 213 ALR 97.

144 [2004] ACTSC 81; 154 ACTR 46, [25], quoting *Blastland* [1986] 1 AC 41, 54.

145 [2019] NSWSC 1820.

146 Note it is also suggested that these messages would be admissible under s 65(2)(b), but it is unclear from the report whether the *making* of the representations by Ms Edwards were seen by others. For an example of a representation revealing knowledge, see *Mitolo Wines Aust Pty Ltd v Vito Mitolo & Son Pty Ltd* [2019] FCA 902.

147 [1972] AC 378.

she was shot were admissible on the trial of her husband for murder to show that she was in a state of fear or emotion at the time.

To like effect, consider the scenario in *Bristow*[148] where the appellant was charged with kidnapping DA, a Belgian backpacker, raping and binding her with cable ties and chains. The defence case was that DA was not held against her will. DA was able to loosen the bindings and sent emails and Facebook messages to friends and to police. The court held that the emails were part of the res gestae (or within the common law integral narrative exception as the preferred label). They were calls for help, similar to the call in *Ratten*'s case (so that s 66A would facilitate admission). If DA had not testified, s 65(2)(b), (c) would have offered relevant contexts but for the fact that there would be no one who 'saw, heard or otherwise perceived the representation being made').

What are the requirements and scope of s 66A? The insurances of reliability built into this section are that the exception applies only to first hand hearsay and the previous representation must be made contemporaneously with the experience by the maker of the representation of the feelings, state of mind etc. The contemporaneity requirement accords with thinking underpinning the common law res gestae doctrine that spontaneity, lack of reflection and synchronicity with events enhance the reliability of utterances. However, given that feelings, states of mind, sensations, knowledge etc can endure for a considerable length of time, the contemporaneity requirement is unlikely to offer a significant impediment to exaggeration or fabrication.

Courts have been hostile to the suggestion that 'knowledge' and 'state of mind' might be interpreted to include 'memory' or 'belief'. This is because such an interpretation would effectively obliterate the hearsay rule and all other inclusionary exceptions to it where contemporaneous representations are concerned. As Levine J stated in *Polkinghorne*[149] when speaking of the predecessor to s 66A (s 72):

> 25. … I must say I have great difficulty with s 72 notwithstanding the 'contemporaneity' component in the sense that on one reading of it arguably in respect to contemporaneous statements it renders the whole of the hearsay exclusionary rules irrelevant in the *Evidence Act*. The section makes sense, in my view, up to the point where it deals with 'health, feelings and sensations'. It is the inclusion of the words 'intention, knowledge, or state of mind' that give rise to problems.

While the ALRC recognised this problem, it was of the view that the 'potential absurdity' of interpreting the section so broadly would prevent its occurrence. Accordingly, and in view of the fact that the section appeared to be operating satisfactorily in this regard, the Commission declined to recommend its amendment.[150] Courts have taken different approaches regarding whether s 66A additionally permits the previous representation to be used to prove the reasons for those feelings etc where the previous representation refers to them. In *Xypolitos*,[151] Curtain J admitted a previous representation under s 66A to prove not only the representor's intention but also to establish the reasons for that intention. This approach accords with that of the ALRC, which stated in its discussion of the forerunner to s 66A (s 72) that, provided the relevance requirement is satisfied, evidence admitted under that section 'will be admissible as evidence of any fact

148 [2020] SASCFC 91, [190]-[193].
149 [1999] NSWSC 704; 108 A Crim R 189.
150 ALRC, *Uniform Evidence Law*, above n 20, [8.163]-[8.164].
151 [2013] VSC 514, [9].

in issue'.[152] In contrast, in *Wentworth v Wentworth*,[153] Santow J held that previous representations admitted pursuant to this section were limited to proof of the declarant's state of mind etc and could not be used to prove any other fact to which the representor might refer.

It is argued that Santow J's approach conforms more closely to the framework of the inclusionary exceptions than that of Curtain J and the ALRC in its 2006 Report. This is because, if representations concerning the reasons for the declarants' states of mind etc or the events that precipitated them are admissible pursuant to s 66A, then the safeguards erected by ss 65 and 66 can effectively be evaded by attaching statements about causative events to contemporaneous representations about health etc.

Second Hand and More Remote Hearsay

The exceptions for remote hearsay are contained in Div 3 of Part 3.2 of the *UEA*. As noted above, where second hand and more remote hearsay are concerned, the uniform evidence legislation adopts an individualised approach to the recognition of inclusionary exceptions for specific types of previous representation. These exceptions have been justified either on the basis of the perceived inherent reliability of the particular type of representation (for example, business records) or on the basis of expedience, to facilitate proof of potentially uncontroversial matters (for example, tags, labels).

Here we consider the exception created for business records, which is possibly the most widely used exception in this Division and the exception for representations about Aboriginal and Torres Strait Islander traditional laws and customs. The other exceptions for second hand and more remote hearsay in ss 70, 71, 73, 74 and 75 are noted without detailed discussion.

Business records: *UEA*, s 69

69. Exception: business records

(1) This section applies to a document that:

(a) either:

(i) is or forms part of the records belonging to or kept by a person, body or organisation in the course of, or for the purposes of, a business, or

(ii) at any time was or formed part of such a record, and

(b) contains a previous representation made or recorded in the document in the course of, or for the purposes of, the business.

(2) The hearsay rule does not apply to the document, so far as it contains the representation, if the representation was made:

(a) by a person who had or might reasonably be supposed to have had personal knowledge of the asserted fact, or

(b) on the basis of information directly or indirectly supplied by a person who had or might reasonably be supposed to have had personal knowledge of the asserted fact.

(3) Subsection (2) does not apply if the representation:

(a) was prepared or obtained for the purpose of conducting, or for or in contemplation of or in connection with, an Australian or overseas proceeding, or

(b) was made in connection with an investigation relating or leading to a criminal proceeding.

152 ALRC, *Uniform Evidence Law*, above n 20, [8.166].

153 Unreported, NSWSC, Santow J, 4 September 1997.

(4) If:
(a) the occurrence of an event of a particular kind is in question, and
(b) in the course of a business, a system has been followed of making and keeping a record of the occurrence of all events of that kind,

the hearsay rule does not apply to evidence that tends to prove that there is no record kept, in accordance with that system, of the occurrence of the event.

(5) For the purpose of this section, a person is taken to have had personal knowledge of a fact if the person's knowledge of the fact was or might reasonably be supposed to have been based on what the person saw, heard or otherwise perceived, other than a previous representation made by a person about the fact.

Business records are exempt from the hearsay rule and the restrictions of the first hand hearsay exceptions because they are considered to be particularly stable. They are far less likely than run of the mill second hand hearsay to be affected by multiple repetition, memory loss, mistake, misrepresentation or mendacity. Their very nature and purpose are thought to protect against such defects. As noted by the ALRC, quoting the NSW Law Reform Commission, 'the fact that the statements were to be used by the business provided a strong incentive for accuracy'.[154] For these reasons, s 69 adopts a liberal approach to the admission of business records and its interpretation has largely accorded with the liberality of its legislative intent.[155] In *Lin v Tasmania*,[156] Tennent and Porter JJ stressed this attribute of s 69 and indicated how such liberality directs the interpretation of key components of the section:

85. There is ample authority as to the scope of the operation of s 69 and its equivalents. It is remedial legislation of wide import and should be construed liberally: *Atra v Farmers & Graziers Co-op Co Ltd* (1986) 5 NSWLR 281 at 286 and the cases there cited, *Lewis v Nortex Pty Ltd (In liq)* [2002] NSWSC 1083 at [4] and *Ringrow v BP Australia Ltd* [2003] FCA 933; 130 FCR 569 at 572 [17]. In both s 69(1)(a) and s 69(1)(b), the requirements fashioned by the phrase 'in the course of, or for the purposes of, the business' are ones which are to be liberally approached. The phrase as used in s 69(1)(a) encompasses documents which go beyond documents by which activities of the business are recorded, and include those relevant to the conduct of the business: *Southern Cross Airports v Chief Commissioner of Crown Revenue* [2000] NSWSC 349 at [41]-[44].

86. The factual matters which would inform the fact-finding exercise under s 69(1)(a) would also be relevant in relation to the exercise under s 69(1)(b). The nature of the document and the circumstances of it being kept, would assist in determining whether a representation made in the document was made or recorded in the course of, or for the purposes of, the business. In particular, the fact that the representation was made by a person other than an agent or employee, or by someone associated with the business, is not at all determinative of the factual question. It is sufficient of course if the representation is made for the purposes of the business.

87. In relation to s 69(2), the Court is able to draw inferences from the form of the document and the nature of the information contained in the representation: *Rickard Constructions v Rickard Hails Moretti* [2004] NSWSC 984 at [19]. In any event, s 183 of the *Evidence Act* enables a court, if a question arises about the application of a provision of the Act in relation to a document, to examine the document and draw any reasonable inferences from it. Further, for the purposes of the determination under s 69(2), it is not

---

154 ALRC, *Uniform Evidence Law*, above n 20, [703].

155 The requirements of s 69 may be established by affidavit evidence under ss 170 and 171. Authentication of business records may be facilitated by ss 58 and 183. Section 183 permits courts to examine documents and draw inferences in relation to matters to be established under s 69. Section 58 permits a court to examine a document and draw inferences from it as to its relevance.

156 [2012] TASCCA 9.

necessary that the person who made the representation, or the person who supplied the information on the basis of which the representation was made, be identified.[157]

88. In *Guest v Federal Commissioner of Taxation* [2007] FCA 193 Heerey J said:

'25. The terms of s 69(2)(a) do not suggest that it is an essential precondition of admissibility that the 'person' in question be identified. The ordinary meaning of the language is that it is sufficient that the person who made the representation, whoever he or she is, had or might reasonably be supposed to have had, personal knowledge of the asserted fact. The policy behind the provision is clear enough. Routine business records, made before any legal proceeding arises or is contemplated (cf the exception in s 69(3)), have an inherent likelihood of reliability which outweighs the common law's aversion to hearsay evidence where the maker of a statement cannot be tested by cross-examination. The utility of s 69 would be greatly diminished if it were necessary to locate among large organisations, perhaps over a long period of time, persons who made representations, often in circumstances where the practical needs of the organisation did not require any identification at the time the representations were made.'

26. Prior to the *Evidence Act*, all Australian jurisdictions had legislation based on provisions of the *Evidence Act 1938* (Imp) which rendered admissible statements made in documents outside court where, inter alia, the document formed part of a continuous record. Examples were the *Evidence Act 1898* (NSW) ss 14B-14C and the *Evidence Act 1958* (Vic) s 5. Such legislation required the maker of the statement to be called as a witness, although that requirement could be dispensed with in certain circumstances, such as death or absence 'beyond the seas'. The present s 69, however, says nothing about calling the maker of the statement as a witness. It is therefore hard to see why one should read into the section an obligation to identify the 'person' where there is no need for that person to be called.'

89. In support of the proposition, his Honour referred to *Lee v Minister for Immigration and Multicultural Affairs* [2002] FCA 303; *Duke Group Ltd (in liq) v Arthur Young* (1990) 55 SASR 11 and *Australian Securities and Investments Commission v Rich* [2005] NSWSC 417; 216 ALR 320 at [197]. See also *Forbes Engineering (Asia) Pty Ltd v Forbes (No 4)* [2009] FCA 675 at [104]-[105] where Collier J, after referring to Guest at [25], noted that the absence of the author of a document, or anyone who could explain it, as a witness in the proceedings, was however an issue which went to the weight to be attributed to it. Additionally, for s 69(2) as for s 69(1)(b), there is no requirement for the person who had, or might reasonably be supposed to have had, the requisite knowledge to have had any particular relationship with the enterprise whose business is involved: *Vitali v Stachnik* [2001] NSWSC 308 at [8].[158]

Section 69 applies only to documentary evidence, but of course 'document' is very broadly defined in the *UEA*.[159] The term 'business' is also widely defined. It includes commercial enterprises, government departments and agencies in all their forms:[160] hospitals, educational institutions, the police,[161] parliaments and courts, and not for profit organisations.

Some constraint is intruded on this generosity by the related requirements that:

- the previous representation be in a document that forms part of the records kept in the course of or for the purposes of a business; and

157 But to contrary effect, see *Duncan* [2015] NSWCCA 84, [32] (Simpson J) but without reference to contrary authority on the point.

158 See also on this last point *Duncan*, ibid, [208] (Campbell J).

159 *UEA*, Dictionary, Pt 2, cl 1 (except for Tasmania, for which see *Evidence Act 2001*, s 3(1)).

160 *Seeley International Pty Ltd v Newtronics Pty Ltd* [2001] FCA 1862; *Valoutin Pty Ltd v Furs* (1998) 154 ALR 119.

161 See, eg, *Wormleaton v Thomas and Coffee Ltd (No 3)* [2013] NSWSC 1817, [7].

- the representations have been made or recorded in the course of or for the purposes of the business.

In *Roach v Page (No 15)*,[162] Sperling J explained the meaning of the phrase, 'records of a business', as follows:

> 5. The records of a business are the documents (or other means of holding information) by which activities of the business are recorded. Business activities so recorded will typically include business operations so recorded, internal communications, and communications between the business and third parties.

His Honour drew a distinction between 'records of a business' within the meaning of s 69 and documents that are the products of a business:

> 6. … [W]here it is a function of a business to publish books, newspapers, magazines, journals (including specialised professional, trade or industry journals), such publications are not records of the business. They are the product of the business, not a record of its business activities. Similarly, publications kept by a business such as journals or manuals (say, for reference purposes) are not records of the business.

Sperling J suggested that this approach was dictated by common sense because it could not 'have been intended that newspapers, magazines and journals (publication of any kind produced and/or received in the course of a business undertaking) would be evidence of whatever was stated in them'.[163]

Likewise, in *Hansen Beverage Company v Bickfords (Australia) Pty Ltd*,[164] Middleton J held:

> 131. In my view, s 69(1) was drafted deliberately broadly, with the rationale being to allow as an exception to the hearsay rule the tender of documents which, by virtue of the fact they are kept as records of the business, should be assumed to be accurate. However, a document created to be sold as part of a business should not be considered to be a record kept *in the course of or for the purposes of* the business, just because there is reason to believe that the document is to be regarded as reliable and accurate. One has to determine whether the document is in truth a record of the type described in s 69(1). …
>
> 133. The records referred to in s 69(1) of the *Evidence Act* are the documents a business generates in the course of, or for the purpose of the business, not documents which it may have or keep as the product of that business. The concept of a business record is an internal record, kept in an organised form accessible in the usual course of business, actually recording the business activities themselves and does not include the product of the business itself: see Sperling J in *Roach v Page* [2003] NSWSC 939; *ASIC v Rich* (2005) 216 ALR 320 at [180]-[182] per Austin J.

While s 69 makes admissible representations derived from a number of sources including second hand and more remote hearsay (s 69(2)), it still requires that the representation ultimately be based on information that can be traced to someone who had personal knowledge of the facts asserted. The consideration given to this requirement in *Lin v Tasmania* (quoted above and referencing relevant authorities) indicates that the courts have adopted a flexible approach to it in keeping with the overall liberality of the provision.[165] Nevertheless, in *Daniels v*

162 [2003] NSWSC 939.

163 Ibid [8].

164 [2008] FCA 406.

165 For a narrow interpretation of s 69(2), see *Duncan* [2015] NSWCCA 84, [128]-[131] (Hall J), where his Honour appears to have imposed a personal knowledge requirement akin to first hand hearsay on s 69.

Western Australia[166] Nicholson J held that this condition could not be satisfied in the circumstances of that case. The previous representations in question were the contents of notices on display at a heritage building in a national park in the Pilbara region. They stated that the area continued to be one of the most important to Aborigines in the Pilbara and that Yindjibarndi and Aboriginal park rangers continued to have a close association with the area. Because there was no evidence about who had made the representations or the source of their knowledge, it could not reasonably be supposed that whoever had made the signs had personal knowledge of the facts asserted or had relied on information supplied by someone who did have such knowledge.

A more significant limitation on the application of s 69 is that imposed by s 69(3) which creates an exception to the exception for business records produced in contemplation of or in connection with Australian or overseas proceedings. It can sometimes be difficult to untangle the purpose(s) for which a previous representation in a document was produced and, therefore, to determine whether s 69(3) precludes its admission.[167] Some assistance in this regard may be obtained by bearing in mind the purpose of the s 69(3) restriction. This was considered by Finn J in *Australian Medic-Care Company Ltd v Hamilton Pharmaceutical Pty Limited*:[168]

> 8. … There is now a considerable body of authority dealing with this provision although its proper application is not altogether free from difficulty. The first matter to emphasise about the exception in subs (3) is that it applies not to a document as such but to a representation or representations contained in a document. It is well accepted that the hearsay rule contained in s 69(2) is founded on the 'rationale of reliability' of business records generally. The exception to that subsection is founded on a 'rationale of unreliability' of representations made in the circumstances envisaged by subs (3): see generally *Australian Competition and Consumer Commission v Advanced Medical Institute Pty Ltd* (2005) 147 FCR 235 at [27]. As Barrett J put the matter in *Vitali v Stachnik* [2001] NSWSC 303 at [12]:
>
> > 'The purpose of the exclusion is … to prevent the introduction through this exception to the hearsay rule of hearsay material which is prepared in an atmosphere or context which may cause it to be self-serving in the sense of possibly being prepared to assist the proof of something known or at least apprehended to be relevant to the outcome of identifiable legal proceedings.'
>
> 9. His Honour went on to note that the contemplation or existence of any proceedings might lead even persons of good intent to make purely self-serving statements which would otherwise be admissible through the scheme of s 69 and that it was the tendency for such self serving statements to be made which led to their exclusion from the ambit of s 69(2).
>
> 10. The focus of the contemplation referred to in subs (3)(a) is, as Lindgren J indicated in the *Advanced Medical Institute* case, upon the contemplation of the person who 'prepared' or 'obtained' the relevant representation. As his Honour said at [25]-[27]:
>
> > … In order for s 69(3)(a) to apply, a person must have 'prepared' or 'obtained' the representation (not the document) in contemplation of a proceeding. It is an unusual use of language to refer to the 'preparing' of a representation, but I think that the intention is clear enough; the reference is to the person who prepared, formulated, shaped or framed the terms in which the representation is made. This will typically, perhaps always, be or include the maker of the representation.

166 [2000] FCA 413; 173 ALR 51.

167 See, eg, *Kaplan* [2005] VSCA 316; 14 VR 673; *Edmund-Jones Pty Ltd v Australian Women's Hockey Association Inc* [1999] NSWSC 285.

168 [2008] FCA 1038; 70 FCR 9.

> The person who 'obtains' a representation is a person who seeks the representation or procures it to be made. This person is not the maker of the representation, but may be a person who 'prepared' it.
>
> By referring to persons who prepared or obtained the representation, the legislature was attempting to encompass all those who might cause a representation to be made in the form which it takes.
>
> 11. It is well established that before it can be said that a representation was prepared or obtained in contemplation of a proceeding, it must be established that a proceeding was 'likely' or 'reasonably probable': see *Nikolaidis v Legal Services Commissioner* [2007] NSWCA 130 at [61] and the cases there mentioned. …
>
> 13. In *Kang v Kwan* [2002] NSWSC 1187 Santow J, in a very brief passage in his judgment, held that the relevant misrepresentation must have been prepared or obtained in contemplation of the very proceedings in which the document is sought to be used. No reference was made by his Honour to authorities dealing with this question under either the Evidence Act or earlier similar provisions.
>
> 14. For my own part, I am satisfied that the decision of Santow J places an undue limitation upon the clear wording of s 69(3) and is inconsistent with the underlying purpose of the provision itself. Section 69(3) refers only to a proceeding without any limitation as to parties: see the observations of Hamilton J in *Lewis v Nortex Pty Ltd (in liq)* [2002] NSWSC 1083 at [4](4).
>
> 15. The unreliability of evidence of representations made or prepared in a context which might cause the representation to be self serving is, in my view, as likely to exist whether or not the proceedings in contemplation was the one in which the representation was sought to be tendered. It is, in my view, unsurprising that the decision of Santow J has in this respect attracted criticism: see Odgers, *Uniform Evidence Law* (7th ed) at [1.3.2880]. For my own part I am not prepared to follow the *Kang v Kwan* decision. I am satisfied that the legal proceedings in contemplation referred to in s 69(3) relate to any legal proceedings in which the representation might become admissible and is not confined to the proceedings in which the statement is sought to be tendered: cf *Feltafield Pty Ltd v Heidelberg Graphic Equipment* (1995) 56 FCR 481 at [487A].

A good illustration of the business records exception can be found in the NSW Court of Criminal Appeal judgment in *Adams*.[169] There, one of the grounds for appeal was that the Supreme Court had misapplied the business records exception in admitting a police intelligence document that, over several years, recorded the appearance of the appellant and various cars that had belonged to the appellant with registration information. The representation contained in the document was that the appellant owned a particular car with associated number plate at the time of the rape for which he had been convicted. The representation supported the victim's evidence of the car and number plate belonging to her assailant.

In dismissing this ground of appeal, the Court of Criminal Appeal first found that there was an 'overwhelming inference' from a perusal of the document that it was created by the NSW Police Service for its own intelligence gathering purposes.[170] The court then endorsed the reasoning of the Supreme Court in finding that, following from the inference about the source of the document, an inference could also be drawn that the representation about the car's ownership and number plate was made by a person with personal knowledge of the asserted fact. As the court explained: 'Once one accepts that the document containing the representation came from the Police Service, an inference is available that a police officer made

169 [2017] NSWCCA 215.
170 Ibid [337].

an inquiry or the relevant registry and observed a card or some other document which provided the information contained in the representation'.[171]

Finally, the court rejected the appellant's argument that the document fell within the exception to the exception in s 69(3). The court recognised that the onus was on the Crown to establish on balance of probabilities that the document was not created in connection with an investigation relating to a criminal proceeding, but found that there was no persuasive basis for finding such a connection. The Court of Criminal Appeal again endorsed the reasoning of the trial judge that, rather than being a specific document created in connection with a specific investigation leading to a specific charge, the document at issue was an intelligence report created for the general information of the Police Service.[172] This meant that, even though the document became useful in the investigation of this particular offence, it was not made in connection with the investigation of this particular offence.

The breadth of the exception created by s 69 is nowhere more evident than in sub-s (4), which enables evidence of the absence of a business record, where such a record would normally be produced if particular events occurred, to be adduced as evidence that such an event did not occur. For example, where a business always issues receipts for retail sales, evidence that no receipt was issued for a particular purchase may be admissible under s 69(4) to establish that no such purchase was made. Where a business has a system for recording clients' appointments, the nature of the matters dealt with during appointments and any advice given, s 69(4) may enable the absence of such a record in a particular case to be adduced to show that there was no appointment, that particular matters had not been dealt with or that particular advice had not been given.[173]

Aboriginal and Torres Strait Islander traditional laws and customs: *UEA*, s 72

The current s 72 was inserted into the uniform legislation on the recommendation of the ALRC to remedy a previous deficiency in the hearsay rule and its exceptions that had inhibited the admission of evidence of the traditional laws and customs of traditional Aboriginal and Torres Strait Islander (ATSI) peoples. Section 72 now creates a broad and flexible exception to the hearsay rule that enables evidence of oral traditions about ASTI people's laws and customs to be adduced. Section 72 provides:

> The hearsay rule does not apply to evidence of a representation about the existence or non-existence, or the content, of the traditional laws and customs of an Aboriginal or Torres Strait Islander group.

In recommending the enactment of s 72 the ALRC observed:

> [W]hile courts sometimes apply the hearsay rule flexibly with respect to evidence of traditional laws and customs, it has been observed that 'the ghost of hearsay – the preference of the written over the spoken word – still impacts negatively on the assessment of Aboriginal oral historical evidence'. In the Commissions' view, these problems should be addressed by amending the uniform Evidence Acts. This is consistent with the conclusions of a background paper prepared for the Law Reform Commission of Western Australia,

171 Ibid [340].

172 Ibid [343].

173 See, eg, *Albrighton v Royal Prince Alfred Hospital* [1980] 2 NSWLR 542, 557 where an equivalent provision (*Evidence Act 1898* (NSW), s 14CH) was applied to similar effect.

> which suggested the need for a 'general statutory relaxation of the complex common law requirements for proof of Aboriginal customary law'. It is also consistent with the preponderance of views expressed in consultations and submissions on this issue.
>
> Amending the uniform Evidence Acts to provide an exception to the hearsay rule for evidence relevant to ATSI traditional laws and customs would make the rules of evidence more responsive to the ATSI oral tradition. Currently, a large proportion of evidence of ATSI traditional laws and customs could be objected to on hearsay grounds. The amendment proposed by the Commissions would shift the focus from whether there is a technical breach of the hearsay rule, to whether the particular evidence is reliable.[174]

Clearly s 72 has particular relevance in native title cases. In the civil law context it is also relevant in family law cases involving the placement of children, and also in succession cases.[175] Lindsay J in *Re Estate Jerrard, deceased*[176] provides a flavour of the application of ss 72 and 78A.

> **Assessment of the Evidence of "Traditional Customary Lore"**
>
> 95. The Court is not bound to accept the declarations of "traditional customary lore" to which the plaintiff and her witnesses depose. Nor is it bound to accept evidence merely because it is able to be characterised as evidence of an expert. In each case, the Court is obliged, in all the circumstances, to exercise an independent judgement upon its assessment of the materiality and probative value of the evidence available on questions to be determined by the Court. If the Court is not satisfied about the existence, or content, of "the laws, customs, traditions and practices of the Indigenous community or group to which [an] intestate belonged" the only course ultimately open to it may be to order that an application for a distribution order be dismissed.
>
> 96. In the absence of any challenge to the *bona fides* of the evidence of the plaintiff, and her corroborative witnesses, about "the traditional customary lore" of the Nucoorilma Clan of the Gomeroi People, and having regard to the purpose for which sections 72 and 78A of the *Evidence Act* were enacted, I am persuaded that I should find, as a fact, that the plaintiff's articulation of that "lore" accurately states "the laws, customs, traditions and practices of the Indigenous community or group to which [the deceased] belonged" within the meaning of Part 4.4 of the *Succession Act*.
>
> 97. In a numerically small Indigenous community there is significant probative value in the fact that Elders, other members and official representatives of the community agree upon a formulation of "traditional customary lore" (which has no competing formulation of traditional customary law or practice advanced against it), in circumstances in which substantial notice of these proceedings has been given to the community as a whole. In making a finding about "the laws, customs, traditions and practices" of an Indigenous community the Court should generally endeavour to listen to the voices of the community – not uncritically, but empathetically. …
>
> 98. The fact that declarations of the "traditional customary lore" relied upon are not articulated by reference to an accumulation of factual illustrations of the lore in operation is not, of itself, a reason for rejecting it in light of the *Evidence Act* provisions which authorise its reception by the Court and Parliament's encouragement of courts to accept such evidence. Parliament has endorsed the Law Reform Commissions' recommendation that a liberal, consultative approach be taken to an assessment of Indigenous traditional laws and customs.
>
> 99. Having cast a critical eye over the form and substance of the evidence bearing upon the existence, and content, of the "traditional customary lore" for which the plaintiff contends, I am not satisfied that there is anything untoward in her presentation of evidence about such "lore" in declaration form.

---

174 ALRC, *Uniform Evidence Law*, above n 20, [19.73]-[19.74]. Footnotes omitted.

175 *Re Estate Jerrard, deceased* [2018] NSWSC 781.

176 Ibid.

> 100. Nor am I satisfied that there is reason for characterisation of the plaintiff's marshalling of community voices against the defendant as oppressive. Although he may live on the margins of his community, he has had the benefit of legal representation and substantial opportunities to advance a case contrary to that of the plaintiff. The primary emphasis of his case has been upon the dictates of justice and equity imported by section 134(4) of the *Succession Act*. He has put the plaintiff to proof on the existence, and content, of "traditional customary lore". He has more actively advanced his case on section 134(4).

In the criminal justice arena it may enable traditional laws and customs to inform the sentencing process and to supply defences to criminal offences.[177] *Talbot v Malogorski*,[178] although not a case involving s 72, provides an example of the type of case where traditional customs may provide a defence. Here, the appellant had been charged with fishing offences in contravention of the *Fisheries Act 1988* (NT). Section 53(1) of that Act stated that nothing in the Act would 'limit the right' of Aboriginals who had traditionally used the resources of an area of land or water in a traditional manner from continuing to use those resources in that area in that manner.

Other exceptions for second hand and more remote hearsay

Other exceptions for second hand and more remote hearsay of potential value in criminal trials and hearings include:

- Section 70 (contents of tags labels and writings) allows tags, labels and writing placed on objects in the course of a business to be adduced as evidence of the matter that tag, label or writing describes, for example, the origin, destination or contents of the object.
- Section 71 (electronic communications) enables representations in electronic communications to be adduced where the representation relates to the identities of the sender and recipient or the destination of the communication and the date the communication was sent.
- Section 73 (reputation as to relationships and age) operates slightly differently in civil and criminal cases, but its general intent is to eliminate the application of the hearsay rule in relation to personal matters that technically people actually have no personal knowledge of, in most cases, to their great surprise.[179] These matters include their age and their relationship to others, particularly family members. People's knowledge of these matters is generally passed onto them by others, usually by word of mouth, sometimes through a line of communicants. Accordingly, without this exception, their evidence about these matters would be inadmissible hearsay.
- Section 74 (reputation of public or general right) disposes of the hearsay rule for representations made about the existence, nature or extent of public or general rights. By virtue of s 74(2), in criminal cases the prosecution cannot rely on this exception except to contradict evidence adduced by the defence under s 74(1).
- Section 75 (interlocutory proceedings) permits the reception of hearsay evidence in interlocutory proceedings. It appears that this exemption

177 See detailed discussion in ALRC, ibid, particularly [19.16]-[19.32].

178 [2014] NTSC 54; 290 FLR 216.

179 See comments in this vein by Levine J in *Marsden v Amalgamated Television Services Pty Ltd* [2000] NSWSC 55, [9].

applies to both first and second hand hearsay.[180] Interlocutory proceedings are proceedings that are not final. They generally deal with procedural matters that arise pre-trial. They also include proceedings for restraining orders like interlocutory injunctions to apply pending the outcome of the trial.[181] In *DPP (ACT) v Hiep*[182] Miles, Mathews and Madgwick JJ identified the purpose of s 75, holding that in the absence of provisions like s 75 'the rigidities of the merely procedural laws of evidence, especially the hearsay rule, may in urgent cases (or what ought to be subsidiary and inexpensive proceedings) stultify the doing of justice according to the substantive law'. The proceedings in this case concerned an application by the DPP for a restraining order against the property of certain persons under the *Proceeds of Crime Act 1991* (ACT).

Representations with Dual Relevance – Non-Hearsay and Hearsay Relevance

Section 60 of the uniform evidence legislation provides:

> **60. Exception: evidence relevant for non-hearsay purpose**
> (1) The hearsay rule does not apply to evidence of a previous representation that is admitted because it is relevant for a purpose other than proof of an asserted fact.
> (2) This section applies whether or not the person who made the representation had personal knowledge of the asserted fact (within the meaning of section 62(2)).
> (3) However, this section does not apply in a criminal proceeding to evidence of an admission.

The effect of s 60 is to waive the hearsay rule in respect of previous representations that have both non-hearsay and hearsay relevance; however, this exception will operate only *after* the representations have been admitted for their non-hearsay purpose. We saw in the previous chapter that previous representations can be widely relevant as original evidence – they may be used to bolster or undermine the credibility of declarants, to establish the basis of expert opinions, to establish the state of mind of their representors or of someone to whom they were made, and they may have operative legal effect as transactional words or as the actus reus of an offence. If the previous representations are additionally relevant for a hearsay purpose, s 60 allows the hearsay rule to be waived in respect of them once they have been admitted for their non-hearsay purpose and subject to the application of s 136. Because s 60 does not provide the means for initially gaining admission of previous representations for a hearsay purpose, it is more vulnerable to the application of the discretion in s 136 than the inclusionary exceptions that admit the evidence as hearsay in the first place.[183]

The ALRC gives a number of justifications for s 60:

---

180 *Bray v F Hoffman-La Roche Ltd* [2002] FCA 243; 118 FCR 1, [117] (Merkel J); *Remess v Rabe* [2006] TASSC 105 (Tennent J).

181 The ALRC considered this to be the meaning of 'interlocutory proceedings' in ALRC, *Evidence* (Report No 38, 1987), [143] n 33; and see also *International Finance Trust Company Ltd v NSW Crime Commission* [2008] NSWCA 291; 251 ALR 479, [4] (Allsop J, with Beazley J agreeing at [56]).

182 (1998) 86 FCR 33; 156 ALR 110, 124.

183 *Papakosmas* [1999] HCA 37; 196 CLR 297, [94] (McHugh J); *Roach v Page (No 11)* [2003] NSWSC 907, [66] and [74] (Sperling J).

At common law, a prior statement of a witness can be used in prescribed circumstances for the purpose of deciding whether to believe the witness, but cannot be used for the purpose of deciding the truth of the facts asserted in the statement. Extensive criticism of this situation was identified in ALRC 26. Criticism focused on the following:

- the exclusion of probative evidence;
- the extreme difficulty, if not impossibility, of making the required distinction between use of the evidence for the hearsay purpose and for the non-hearsay purpose;
- the undesirability of proceeding on the assumption that such a distinction can be made easily or at all; and
- the questionable reasoning involved in the distinction.

As to the questionable reasoning involved in the distinction, the following comments of Roden J were quoted in ALRC 26. In relation to prior inconsistent statements, he gave the following illustration:

> Illustration:
>
> > Evidence in Court: 'I was there; I saw it happen'
> >
> > Cross-examination: 'Did you not say on a prior occasion, 'I was not there; I didn't see it happen'?'
>
> Force of Rule: If the prior statement is admitted, or is denied but independently proved, then, subject to considering any explanation given by the witness:
>
> (a) that statement may be taken as making it less likely that the witness was there and saw it happen (ie may be used to lessen the weight to be given to his testimony), but
>
> (b) it may not be used as rendering it more likely that he was not there and did not see it happen (ie may not be used as evidence of the truth of the prior statement).

In relation to prior consistent statements, Roden J commented:

> The prior consistent statement is only admissible in special circumstances, and then again not as evidence of the truth of its contents. When it is introduced, eg in answer to a suggestion of recent invention, it can so back-date any 'invention' to make invention at any time unlikely. The effect must be, it seems to me, to make it more likely that the evidence was truthful, and if the evidence and prior statement was to the same effect (as the term 'consistent' seems to require), then the statement is being used as evidence of the truth of its content. …

The operation of s 60 must be seen in the context of the conduct of trials. First, it only operates where evidence is already before the court – typically, either from the person alleged to have made a prior consistent or inconsistent statement or from the expert who has given evidence of the factual basis of his or her expert testimony. Other points should be noted.

- *Prior statements*. On occasion there will be disputes as to whether the statements were made and whether they were accurate. However, often the statements will be more reliable than the evidence given by the witness. In any event, the person who made the statement will often be a witness and can be cross-examined. Under s 60, it is then for the tribunal of fact to determine what weight it will give that evidence in the context of all the evidence. This is a more realistic approach than expecting the tribunal of fact to draw the artificial and difficult distinction, required by the common law, of using the evidence for one purpose but not for another.
- *Evidence of the factual basis of expert opinion*. In the majority of cases, the person supplying the factual material will be called to testify – for example, the injured plaintiff in a tort action. Through the use of s 60, the tribunal of fact can adopt a more realistic approach. It can assess the weight that the evidence should be given. Under the common law, the tribunal of fact is required to use the evidence for the non-hearsay purpose but not for the hearsay purpose. Further,

> while the statements made to the expert by a party might be self-serving, often the factual basis is reliable and not disputed. In those cases where it is disputed, the dispute will usually be confined to few facts.
>
> For those reasons, it may be said that s 60 enhances the appearance and reality of the fact-finding exercise. It also enhances the fairness of the trial process by allowing evidence admitted for one purpose to be used for other relevant purposes. The focus will be on the weight to be accorded to the evidence, not on admissibility.[184]

The case of *Adam*[185] demonstrates how a prior inconsistent statement, admitted in order to undermine the credibility of its maker, may thereafter be used in proof of the facts asserted. In this case Adam was charged with the murder of a police officer. The deceased was stabbed to death during an altercation in a hotel car park in the early hours of the morning. A witness and alleged participant in the incident made a statement to the police some weeks later about what had happened. When testifying for the prosecution at Adam's trial, the witness resiled from his statement to the police. The Crown then sought and was granted leave to treat him as an unfavourable witness under s 38 of the *UEA* and to cross-examine him about his statement to the police. That statement was then admitted to undermine his credibility (within s 103). Thereafter, s 60 was applied to enable it to be used to establish what had occurred during the events resulting in the victim's death. While this case remains good authority on the application of s 60 to prior inconsistent statements that have been tendered to undermine the credibility of witnesses who made them, it is no longer authority on the operation of the credibility rule in s 102. This rule was amended in response to the decision in this case and specifically in order to abrogate its approach to that rule.[186]

In *Welsh*,[187] we see the operation of s 60 in relation to previous representations admitted to establish the basis of an expert's opinion. Here the appellant raised the partial defence of diminished responsibility at his trial for murder. A psychiatrist testified that, at the time he attacked the victim, the appellant was suffering from an abnormality of the mind that impaired his mental responsibility for his actions. That opinion was based on a history taken from the appellant and on statements made by the appellant's mother. In particular, the psychiatrist relied on the appellant's assertion that he had experienced an auditory hallucination of his father's killer threatening to kill him as well. The appellant's mother corroborated his account by telling the psychiatrist of similar reports of auditory hallucinations the appellant had made to her over the years. The trial judge had instructed the jury that the psychiatrist's opinion would have no 'substance' unless the appellant proved the truth of the history on which that opinion was based. The NSW Court of Criminal Appeal held that this direction was erroneous in view of the operation of s 60. Such a direction would have been correct before the enactment of the *UEA*. However, once a previous representation was admitted to establish the foundation of the psychiatrist's opinion (the non-hearsay purpose) thereafter, pursuant to s 60, it became evidence of the facts asserted (the hearsay purpose).

It is notable that in this case the previous representations forming the basis of the psychiatrist's opinion comprised both first hand and second hand hearsay, the statements of the appellant being first hand hearsay and those of the mother

---

184 ALRC, *Uniform Evidence Law*, above n 20, [7.60]-[7.71], [7.80]-[7.81].

185 [2001] HCA 57; 207 CLR 96.

186 See Chapter 6.

187 (1996) 90 A Crim R 364 (NSWCCA).

being second hand hearsay. Section 60 was applied to both forms of hearsay. This aspect of the decision in *Welsh* was subsequently thrown into doubt by the High Court decision in *Lee*,[188] which did not refer to *Welsh*. In *Lee* the High Court interpreted s 60 in a way that appeared to restrict its application to first hand hearsay. The apparent anomaly in the law created by these two cases was resolved by the insertion of sub-s (2) into s 60 in accordance with recommendations of the ALRC.[189] This makes it clear that s 60 may apply to second hand and more remote hearsay. This is consistent with the Commission's view that s 60 was never intended to be limited to first hand hearsay and that to do so subverts its purpose.[190] However, as a result of the inclusion of sub-s (3) in s 60, it cannot apply to evidence of admissions, whether that evidence constitutes first hand or second hand hearsay. This prevents the deployment of s 60 to evade the legislated hurdles to the admissibility of admissions erected by provisions in Part 3.4 of the *UEA*. It also preserves the decision in *Lee* to the extent that it precluded the application of s 60 to evidence of admissions.[191]

As acknowledged by the ALRC, for many the change wrought to the common law by s 60 may seem quite radical.[192] Additionally, s 60 may on occasion allow evidence of questionable reliability to be adduced. This will be particularly problematic if that evidence cannot be adequately tested by cross-examination. In such a situation the court may rely on the discretions in Part 3.11 of the *UEA* to limit the use of the evidence or to exclude it altogether.[193] In *Roach v Page (No 11)*,[194] Sperling J considered the relationship between s 60 and the discretions to control and exclude evidence in ss 135, 136 and 137 and noted the types of cases that might call for limitations to be placed on the use of evidence to which s 60 applies:

> 34. … [There is] a body of judicial opinion that the inability of the opposite party to test a representation by cross-examination of the person who made the representation may legitimately be held to constitute 'unfair prejudice' notwithstanding that the evidence would otherwise be admissible to prove the truth of the representation under an exception to the hearsay rule.
>
> 35. Where s 60 is involved, a further consideration is introduced. The following observations were made, albeit in obiter, in *Quick v Stoland Pty Ltd* (1998) 87 FCR 371. Branson J said at 377-8:
>
>> It is not necessary in the context of this case to give detailed consideration to the circumstances in which, and the extent to which, evidence of the factual basis of an expert opinion will amount to evidence of the truth of that factual basis: cf *Eastman v R* (1997) 76 FCR 9 at 78-79. It may be that a different result will follow depending upon the form in which the expert gives evidence of the factual basis of his or her opinion; that is, whether such evidence is given in the form of a representation or, alternatively, in the form of an identification of a hypothetical assumption. If s 60 of the Act does operate to give mere form significance in this way, the result cannot be regarded as entirely satisfactory. In cases where there is a genuine dispute as to the relevant facts, it might be expected that a court would ordinarily limit the operation of s 60 of the Act by exercising the power vested in it by s 136 of the Act.

---

188 [1998] HCA 60; 195 CLR 594.

189 ALRC, *Uniform Evidence Law*, above n 20, [7.106].

190 Ibid [7.87]-[7.100] and [7.104].

191 On the operation of s 60(3) and the various permutations of admissions to which it applies and the relationship of s 60(3) to Part 3.4, see *Tasmania v B (No 2)* [2012] TASSC 39 (Blow J, as he then was).

192 ALRC, *Uniform Evidence Law*, above n 20, [7.85].

193 Ibid [7.82].

194 [2003] NSWSC 907.

36. Finkelstein J said at 382:

> In many cases the extraordinary effect of s 60 would be unfair to the party against whom the evidence is tendered. For example, where the hearsay involves 'facts' that are in conflict or 'facts' that are unreliable it is quite unsatisfactory for those 'facts' to be proved by the operation of s 60. One way in which this problem can be overcome is by an order under s 136 limiting the use to be made of that evidence. In the case of evidence given by an expert, he or she can be required to express his opinion in answer to a hypothetical question leaving it to the party calling the expert to prove the facts upon which the opinion is based.

37. According to these opinions, where hearsay representations of fact are included in a document as the basis for an expert opinion stated in the document and the facts so represented are contentious, there is a strong case for limiting the use of such representations to their role as assumptions on which the opinion is based. That the representations in the document have become evidence of the facts stated by the fortuitous circumstance that they provide the basis for an expert opinion is seen as an imposition on the opposite party amounting to unfair prejudice.

38. By parity of reasoning, the same circumspection should apply where a document admitted into evidence as part of a relevant course of events is relied upon as evidence and opinions of the facts stated in it pursuant to ss 60 and 77. That is particularly so where the opposite party cannot test the truth of the representations by cross-examination, or where the basis of the opinion is not adequately disclosed.

39. This situation is to be contrasted with what might be regarded as the paradigm case for the application of s 60, where evidence of complaint in sexual assault prosecutions is made evidence of the fact. There, the complainant is ordinarily called as a witness so that the truth of the representation in the complaint may be tested by cross-examination of the complainant. Section 60, in such a case, avoids the need for nice distinctions to be made unnecessarily.

Subsequently, in this case Sperling J held:

74. … (h) Sections 60 and 77 give rise to special considerations. Unlike other exceptions to the hearsay rule and the opinion rule, it is not the objective of those sections to facilitate proof. They are there to avoid a distinction having to be made about evidence being used for one purpose and not for another. Where a document goes into evidence because the existence of the document is a relevant fact, the operation of these sections without a limiting order under s 136 may have a consequence which the legislature cannot have intended. Any representation in the document which is probative of some other element in the tendering party's case becomes evidence of the content of the representation. Representations of fact become evidence of the truth of the representation, irrespective of whether they are first-hand or remote hearsay and irrespective of whether the source of the information is disclosed. Representations of expert opinion in the document are probative of whatever is the subject of the opinion expressed, irrespective of whether the author of the document is qualified to express the opinion and irrespective of whether the assumptions made for the purpose of expressing the opinion are specified. Such consequences cannot have been intended where the opposite party is disadvantaged by such consequences. Section 136 serves to avoid such unfairness.

(i) Where ss 60 or 77 operate and the author of the document is not called, the truth of facts stated or the efficacy of the opinion expressed cannot be tested by cross-examination. The consequence of the operation of ss 60 or 77 is then potentially the more unfair on that account.

(j) The operation of s 60 on assumption evidence which is given as the basis for an expert opinion is also a special case. Where such evidence is in the form of a bare statement of facts or where facts are stated as having been provided by some other person or persons, s 60 operates to make the account evidence of the truth of the facts so stated. That is not so if the expert says that certain facts are assumed for the purpose of providing the

> opinion. A disadvantage should not be incurred in legal proceedings by happenstance. If the facts stated are contentious, it will ordinarily be unfair that the opposite party is fixed with assumption evidence as evidence of the truth of the facts stated by reason of those facts having been stated in one form rather than the other.

Nevertheless, courts have counselled against using the discretions in Part 3.11 to restore the position at common law when the clear legislative intent in the *UEA* is to reform it.[195]

Reliability warning[196]

In all cases where hearsay evidence is admitted, if requested, a judge should warn the jury that the evidence may be unreliable and explain why this is so: s 165(1)(a). This approach to dealing with admissible hearsay should be preferred to excluding it or limiting its use in the exercise of a discretion under Part 3.11, where a warning will be sufficient to alert the jury to the frailties of the evidence.[197]

Conclusion

While the exceptions to the hearsay rule created by the *UEA* offer a more coherent, principled, flexible and structured approach than the common law, they are not without interpretive difficulties and rigidities. The extensive case law applying these exceptions reveals that the legal profession and courts no longer strain for common law guidance but rather have developed a strong facility with the terms of the provisions and the intention of the legislature to permit the admission of a broad array of hearsay representations.

195 *Papakosmas* [1999] HCA 37; 196 CLR 297, [39] (Gleeson CJ and Hayne J) and [94]-[98] (McHugh J). See also *Prasad* [2020] NSWCCA 349, [105]-[116].

196 See, in greater detail, Chapter 14 regarding judicial warnings.

197 *Papakosmas* [1999] HCA 37; 196 CLR 297, [39] (Gleeson CJ and Hayne J) and [94] (McHugh J).

Chapter 10

Character Evidence

I knew a man who used to say,
Not once but twenty times a day,
That in the turmoil and the strife
(His very words) of Public Life
The thing of ultimate effect
Was Character – not Intellect.[1]

Introduction

It can be tempting to pre-judge a person on the basis of mere allegations and a small amount of ill-informed harmful comment. We witnessed the reality of this tendency in Chapter 1 with the derogatory comments on Facebook about FEW.[2] Psychological profilers also pre-judge in the sense that they draw on assumptions to reason the likelihood of guilt. Profilers are common in crime fiction. Consider this exchange from the movie, *Silence of the Lambs*:[3]

> *Jack Crawford*: Look at him Starling. Tell me what you see?
> *Clarice Starling*: Oh he's a white male; serial killers tend to hunt within their own ethnic groups. …
> *Clarice Starling*: He's not a drifter, he's got his own house somewhere, an apartment, he's in his 30s or 40s, he's got real physical strength combined with an older man's self-control, he's cautious, precise and he's never impulsive, he'll never stop.
> *Jack Crawford*: Why not?
> *Clarice*: He's got a real taste for it now, he's getting better at his work.

But how does such profiling reconcile the fact that there are lots of 30-40 year old white males with a home, self-control, caution and precision, and who are not serial killers? Is it reasonable for one to become 'reasonably suspected' merely for having these qualities? As we saw in *FEW (No 2)*, discussed at the end of Chapter 2, first impressions and assumptions can be quite inaccurate in assessing criminal culpability. The social media about FEW and the above (fictional) example of faux

1 Hilaire Belloc, *The Statesman*, quoted by Kirby J in *Melbourne* [1999] HCA 32; 198 CLR 1.
2 *FEW (No 2)* [2013] NSWSC 1771.
3 ABC Radio National, <http://www.abc.net.au/radionational/programs/allinthemind/profiling-the-criminal-profilers---the-inside-story/2935850#transcript>.

profiling raise questions regarding both the dangers and the potential probative value of placing before the jury information about an accused person's character – such as their criminal past, their drug use or their reputation. Consider instances where an accused's background comes through the media, such as in the murder trial of South African athlete Oscar Pistorius, first finding fame in overcoming physical adversity to achieve Olympic sporting success.[4] His second basis for media attention was when he stood trial for murder. He claimed he accidentally killed his girlfriend, Reeva Steenkamp, when in the early morning of St Valentine's Day 2013 he fired shots through a closed bathroom door, killing her. The shooting took place in South Africa, where homicide and break-ins are not uncommon. The defence case was that Pistorius believed an intruder was in the bathroom. Pistorius was portrayed through defence witnesses (and by Pistorius's own testimony) as a committed athlete, religious and, because of his reliance on prosthetic legs, prone to the danger of vulnerability to home invasion. As the *Washington Times* described:

> Two contrasting images of the double-amputee runner have emerged in court: the defense-led image of Pistorius as a contrite man who had been worried about crime and made a terrible mistake on the night he killed Steenkamp, and the prosecution's depiction of him as an overbearing egotist who was obsessed with firearms.
>
> [Prosecutor Gerrie] Nel referred to a shooting incident at Tasha's restaurant in Johannesburg in which a shot went off after a friend of the runner passed him a loaded gun under the table. Pistorius, who faces a separate charge of firing a gun in a public place because of that episode as well as two other firearms charges, said he didn't have his finger on the trigger when the gun fired. This happened about a month before Pistorius killed Steenkamp.
>
> The prosecutor noted that a police expert had testified that the gun could not be fired without pulling the trigger, and sarcastically described the discharge as a "miracle."
>
> "We have you in possession of the gun, a shot went off, but you didn't discharge the gun," Nel said incredulously of the athlete's account.[5]

The prosecution also showed in court an electronic recording of Pistorius target shooting watermelons, likening watermelons to being 'softer than brains',[6] of lying about the restaurant incident to cover up what had occurred, and also of firing a gun through an open car sunroof. What is the relevance of this evidence – evidence of Pistorius' good sides and bad sides to his character to each parties' cases?

This chapter looks at such matters. Consideration of the law begins with a focus on two important Australian cases, the 1894 Privy Council decision in *Makin v Attorney-General (NSW)* and the High Court case of *Melbourne*[7] from over 100 years later.[8] *Makin* is a prominent example of powerful circumstantial prosecution evidence of criminal conduct. On the other hand, the evidence led by the accused in *Melbourne*[9] reveals the courts' traditional lenient application of relevance requirements (the 'rational affect') threshold to an accused adducing evidence of good character. Beyond matters of relevance are issues relating to

---

4 In the 2012 London Olympics Pistorius became the first double amputee to run in the Olympics, where he reached the 400 metres semi-finals. Pistorius was ultimately convicted of murder and received a lengthy prison sentence.

5 See <http://www.washingtontimes.com/news/2014/apr/10/oscar-pistorius-untruthful-and-egotist-prosecutor-/>.

6 See <https://www.youtube.com/watch?v=Y9E_vlza3YA>.

7 [1999] HCA 32; 198 CLR 1.

8 [1894] AC 57.

9 [1999] HCA 32; 198 CLR 1.

the manner in which the *UEA* regulates character evidence. The relevant *UEA* provisions stem from the common law where the default position is, generally speaking, a person's character is not admissible in a criminal trial because it is inappropriate to judge criminal culpability by the *kind* of person the accused might be. Dixon J in the 1961 case of *Dawson*:[10]

> It is the thesis of English law that the ingredients of a crime are to be proved by direct or circumstantial evidence of the events, that is to say, the parts and details of the transaction amounting to the crime, and are not to be inferred from the character and tendencies of the accused. ... [Once in the witness box, the accused's position] ... is protected accordingly against the disclosure of a discreditable past, unless in exceptional conditions.

The exceptions and their boundaries are an important part of this and the next chapter. The *UEA* contains no definition of evidence of character or reputation and arguably it would have been a tall order, potentially a 'fool's errand',[11] for the *UEA* to have comprehensively defined an elusive concept like character evidence. Traditionally, stemming back to at least the 18th century the common law required good character evidence to be proved by evidence of reputation[12] (that is, gossip and rumour). Witnesses not only could speak to an accused's good character, but having no character witnesses weighed heavily against an accused as well.[13] According to Cockburn CJ in the 1865 case of a *Rowton*,[14] still regularly referred to in modern cases, 'general reputation in the neighbourhood' is the optimal way to establish character.[15] In the time of *Rowton* the accused still did not have the right to testify and it seems permitting the admission of good character evidence acted as a sop to the imbalance created by this testimonial incapacity.[16]

10 [1961] HCA 74; 106 CLR 1, [14].

11 JD Kurland, 'Psychological Research on Character as a Process in Judgment and Decision-making and its Potential Implications for the Character Evidence Prohibition in Anglo-American Law' (2014) 38 *Law and Psychology Review* 135. See also BJ Anderson, 'Recognizing Character: A New Perspective on Character Evidence' (2012) 121 *Yale Law Journal* 1912.

12 Evidence of reputation used to be the sole vehicle for bad character evidence as well. This was on the basis that it was improper to lead evidence of specific acts or events, requiring the defence to meet a particular allegation that was not formally charged: JH Langbein, *The Origins of the Adversary Criminal Trial* (Oxford University Press, 2003), 196, 196-9.

13 See Langbein, ibid, quoting a trial judge in 1784 saying, 'Have you anybody to speak for you, to give you the character of an honest woman? ... If you were an honest woman, there are people that know you, you might have a character'.

14 (1865) Le & Ca 520; [1865] All ER Rep 549. The longevity of the case probably explains the lingering usage of 'reputation' in the creation of the tendency rule – that is, 'evidence of the character, reputation or conduct of a person ... is not admissible to prove that a person has or had a tendency': *UEA*, s 97(1). Character in the form of reputation may in certain proceedings be relevant to the fact in issue – or such evidence may *be* the fact in issue (for example, in defamation proceedings).

15 Note that *Rowton* merely reflected already entrenched principle, see Langbein, above n 12, 196. Note also regarding the 'inherent absurdity' of the rule in *Rowton*'s case, observed by Redlich JA in *Bishop* [2013] VSCA 273, [3] quoting from *Stephen's Digest of the Law of Evidence* (McMillan, 12th ed, 1936), 201: 'A witness may with perfect truth swear that a man who, to his knowledge, has been a receiver of stolen goods for years, has an excellent character for honesty if he has the good luck to conceal his crimes from his neighbours'. His Honour also cited *Donaldson v Western Australia* [2007] WASCA 216; 176 A Crim R 488, 510 [65] (Buss JA). See also A Howard, 'Evidence of Good Character and Bad Character in Criminal Cases' (Leo Cussen Institute, October 1995), 4 [6].

16 The limitation to proving good character by evidence to reputation was replaced in New South Wales in 1876. From 1900 until 1994 good character could be proved by 'the witness's own knowledge, of his habits, disposition and conduct' under *Crimes Act 1900* (NSW), s 413, but the *Rowton* limitation lingered in Australian jurisdictions where there was no statutory intervention (such as in Victoria). It was described as 'not observed in practice' by 1960: *Attwood* (1960)

But, like now (but without the ss 110, 112 and 192 controls or the contemporary judicial inclination to exercise discretionary latitude to protect defendants from rebuttal evidence of marginal relevance), evidence of an accused's character was double-edged, permitting so-called rebuttal prosecution evidence. It could be led by the prosecution with very few limitations.

Character Evidence under the *UEA*

There are four categories of circumstances where evidence of the character of an accused may be admissible. Determining which avenue is open to a party depends on the purpose for which the evidence is adduced, and that it is relevant for that purpose. Then there are options depending on the role of ss 97, 98, 101, 110, 112 (and of course ss 135-137, 192, 192A – and also s 95). The options in relation to character evidence are:

1. *UEA*, **sections 110 and 112:** Section 110(1) provides for an accused to adduce *evidence of good character* in support of their defence. Notably, it is facilitative of the raising of character by the accused. It requires satisfaction of logical relevance under s 55, but this bar for good character evidence is set very low.[17] Further, s 110(1) removes a number of admissibility obstacles. Evidence of the accused's good character can be potentially powerful. One view is that its power may be in inverse proportion to the strength of the prosecution case.[18] Or, as we see in *Melbourne*'s case below, it can have a modest impact in a powerful prosecution case. Where it is not impactful the accused might regret 'raising' character by adducing good character evidence because where character is raised as an issue through good character evidence the prosecution or a co-accused may be able to adduce rebuttal character evidence that would be otherwise inadmissible: s 110(2) and (3).[19]
2. *UEA*, **sections 97, 98, 110, 111, 112:** *An accused jointly prosecuted with another* may seek to support their own claim of innocence (or reduced complicity) by leading evidence of another accused's character – that is, they may (as we saw in Chapter 2),[20] run a cut-throat defence. The co-accused

102 CLR 353, 359 and *SAM v Western Australia (No 2)* [2016] WASCA 64; cf *Bishop* [2013] VSCA 273 (discussed later in the chapter) where the trial judge limited the accused's good character evidence that was otherwise to be given in terms of the witness's personal opinion to evidence of reputation.

17 *UEA*, s 55; *Allen (a Pseudonym)* [2016] VSCA 59, [60]; *Steve* [2008] NSWCCA 231; 189 A Crim R 68, [60]. 'Good character evidence is not subject to the stringent evaluation of its probative force that is applied to evidence of bad character': *Melbourne* [1999] HCA 32; 198 CLR 1, [47] (McHugh J).

18 *Xu* [2019] NSWCCA 178 where counsel's failure to adduce good character evidence formed one of the successful grounds for allowing the appeal. *Miles* [2014] NSWCCA 72, [175] (Button J): '[I]t may be that in a trial in which sexual offences are alleged … [evidence of good character assists the accused] does so with particular force'. Thus, where there is other inculpatory evidence, the power of the character evidence diminishes: *Giallombardo* [2014] NSWCCA 25; *D* (1996) 86 A Crim R 41. See also *Smith* [2015] VSCA 256. On the strategic choice that might be made, see *Parsons (a Pseudonym)* [2016] VSCA 17, [83]: 'In the hands of a skilled prosecutor, such matters [by character witnesses] might have been strong – if not devastating – fodder for cross-examination'.

19 For cross-examination of the defendant on character evidence in this context, see ss 112 and 192. See also, *Evidence Act 2001* (Tas), s 104(4), with respect to cross-examining an accused on credibility evidence where they have raised character.

20 Page 35.

evidence may be tendency or coincidence evidence[21] (or relationship or context evidence), but it will not need to satisfy the same high standards of probative value because s 137 will not apply (though potentially s 135 will be relevant).[22]

3. *UEA*, **sections 97, 98, 101:** In the *prosecution case in chief*, an accused's character may be admissible as tendency or coincidence evidence. In this instance it is likely the prosecution's evidence of the accused's character will be established through evidence of criminal, unsavoury or disreputable behaviour, either by way of proving criminal convictions or calling witnesses to prove allegations. To be sufficiently probative of facts in issue this evidence will typically reveal a pattern of behaviour that supports the guilt of the accused. It will need to satisfy *UEA* requirements that are specific to tendency or coincidence evidence.
4. In the alternative, evidence may be admissible to prove:
   - a particular (and relevant) relationship,[23] or
   - to give context to other evidence (typically evidence from a sexual assault complainant).[24]

   In these cases, as relationship or context evidence, it will need to be relevant (satisfy *UEA*, ss 55) and not be excluded by 135 or 137,[25] and not the stricter requirements for tendency or coincidence evidence[26] about an accused.

In relation to tendency and coincidence evidence, addressed in the next chapter, the classic illustration of this type of evidence is the 19th century case of *Makin v Attorney-General (NSW)*.[27] Being a common law case, it relied on the terminology of 'similar fact evidence'.[28] It illustrates the admission of evidence of bad character in the prosecution case. The grizzly events concerned husband and wife, John and Sarah Makin, and took place in Sydney's inner city suburbs of Redfern and Macdonaldtown. It was the prosecution case that the Makins had killed a baby boy after they had promised his mother to care for him in exchange for a small payment. The mother became suspicious, as did neighbours, and by the time police had finished their investigations not only was a baby boy's body found buried in the Makin back yard, but other children's bodies were also found. The defence claimed that the child had died of natural causes but when the prosecution was permitted to lead evidence that the Makins had received other children on similar terms to the deceased, that these children had disappeared and that 12 infants'

21 This terminology is defined and discussed in detail below, and see Chapter 11.

22 The role of s 111 is to permit a co-accused to call expert evidence about another accused even if the evidence is hearsay evidence or tendency evidence.

23 Requiring close consideration of the purpose or use of the evidence in question, see for example, *MM* [2012] ACTCA 44, [11] (Penfold J) ('The need for critical analysis of evidence sought to be tendered, and any objections made to that tender, is vital where a trial court is dealing with a significant volume of evidence relating to multiple different aspects of the background circumstances or other matters'), and [97]-[98] (Jagot J).

24 There is also the situation catered for in *O'Leary* [1946] HCA 44; 73 CLR 566, discussed in Chapter 11.

25 A s 95 direction will be required.

26 Prosecution evidence: ss 97, 98 and 101. With all these sorts of evidence, once ruled admissible, an accused who testifies can be generally cross-examined on the same matters.

27 [1894] AC 57.

28 Similar fact evidence incorporates tendency (or disposition) evidence and coincidence (or improbability) evidence.

bodies were found buried in yards at the back of various houses where the Makins had lived, the case took on the appearance of 'baby farming' (as the practice was known). The prosecution case offered a compelling inference that the Makins had been in the business of taking in young babies from unmarried mothers for money and then murdering the children to ensure the transaction was profitable. The relevance of the evidence of the bodies buried in back yards was to dispel death by coincidence or accident. The evidence of the bodies, namely, evidence of 'uncharged acts', was admissible because they supported a strong inference that other murders had occurred[29] and that the Makins were the perpetrators, even though their guilt was not proven by convictions. In other words, the evidence revealed a pattern that showed a lack of coincidence with respect to the death of the baby boy. Without a defence of coincidence, the only inference remaining was that the Makins had a tendency (or propensity) to kill infants for financial gain using a very specific *modus operandi*.[30] In the *Makin* case there was only one charge (murder).

Makin is an iconic case graphically illustrating why exceptions to the weighty exclusionary principle are justified. But it is worth appreciating that if the facts are altered a little (for example, if John and Sarah Makin had claimed that the babies died from bubonic plague due to an outbreak of the disease in Sydney at the relevant time)[31] then there would have been a reasonable hypothesis consistent with innocence and the evidence would have been inadmissible as adding little (beyond prejudice) to the prosecution case.

What is Character Evidence?

Section 110 relies on a typology dividing character evidence into 'good' or 'not good' (generally shortened to 'bad'). Evidence of *bad character* – evidence that makes one think less of a person – is for obvious reasons most likely to be adduced by a prosecutor or a co-accused. Evidence of *good character* enhances one's perceptions of a person. However, common experience tells us that people are not one-dimensional. They are not always 'good' or always 'evil'.[32] Nevertheless, the law's characterisation reflects the dichotomy of the trial battle, where good and bad character denote a role in the trial relative to assisting proof of guilt (or not).

The boundaries of what constitutes character, compared to transient or less embedded qualities of our make-up, are not always easy to define. In *Melbourne*, Gummow J indicated that the law does not insist on a rigid definition, describing 'character' as potentially identifying '(i) a trait which serves as an index to the essential or intrinsic nature of an individual, (ii) the sum of such traits, or (iii) the estimate put upon an individual as a matter of repute'.[33] It is clear that the concept of character broadly describes a person's moral and social qualities. Gilbert Harman suggests that character should be given some limitations.

29 Notably, a term to be avoided in judicial directions to the jury, see *HML* [2008] HCA 16; 235 CLR 334, [1], [129], [251], [399], [492]; *KSC* [2012] NSWCCA 179, [64].

30 See also A Cossins, *The Baby-Farmers* (Allen & Unwin, 2013); A Palmer, 'Digging up the dirt on *Makin*' [1993] *Law Institute Journal* 1171.

31 The disease was prevalent in Sydney a few years later. Tom Dudley, of *Dudley and Stephens* (1884) 14 QBD 273, is recorded as its first victim: see AW Brian Simpson, *Cannibalism and the Common Law* (Penguin, 1986).

32 *Melbourne* [1999] HCA 32; 198 CLR 1, [34] (McHugh J), cited by McCallum J in *Gittany (No 5)* [2014] NSWSC 49.

33 [1999] HCA 32; 198 CLR 1, [63].

'Character traits include virtues and vices like courage, cowardice, honesty, dishonesty, benevolence, malevolence, friendliness, unfriendliness, as well as certain other traits like friendliness or talkativeness'.[34] These are all examples of character in a particular respect: see s 110(2) and (3). In court, character evidence typically involves evidence of a person's conduct. Where conduct is repeated, or where it has unique features, it is said to speak strongly to a person's make-up, that is, to their disposition to a particular way of acting and/or thinking. However, psychological research suggests situational variables are highly significant in predicting behaviour, especially in a manner relevant to the trial context.[35] This means that two people who regularly act differently from each other do not necessarily possess different character traits. Their different conduct may be most accurately understood by their actions occurring in different situations. For example, evidence that someone is always happy and relaxed at home with family and another person is anxious when sitting for an evidence law exam does not enable a useful comparison of the two people.[36] Harman adds another illustrative dimension with the following scenarios:

> If fifteen year old Herbert is disposed to refuse to ride any roller coaster, but is not cowardly or fearful in other ways, his particular disposition is not an instance of cowardice or fear and indeed may fail to be an instance of any character trait at all. If Herbert also acquires a disposition to refrain from speaking up in history class (but not in other subjects) and the explanation of this latter reluctance is quite different from the explanation of his avoidance of roller coaster rides, then these two dispositions are not special cases of a single character trait. Nor can cowardice or fearfulness be constructed out of a collection of quite separable dispositions of this sort, if there is no common explanation of the resulting behaviors.[37]

An Accused's Character – Guilt and Credibility

The 'good' accused

The common law's attitude to admitting evidence of good character lies in the notion that 'good people don't commit crimes', and that therefore this is a sufficient foundation for admitting good character on behalf of an accused person.[38] *Melbourne*[39] indicates that leading a relatively blemish-free life is sufficient for Australian law to consider a person to be of good character. Melbourne was on trial for murder. Witnesses described him as '"quiet man", a man who was "always gentle", and who, apart from this occasion, had "never" been "aggressive"'; as 'very quiet'; as 'a very amiable sort of person' and as 'a very quiet, well-behaved gentleman'[40] and

34 Distinguished from psychological orders (such as schizophrenia) or from a person's innate temperate (such as shyness). G Harman, 'Moral Philosophy Meets Social Psychology: Virtue Ethics and Fundamental Attribution Error' (1999) 99 *Proceedings of the Aristotelian Society* 315, <http://www.princeton.edu/~harman/Papers/Virtue.html>.

35 MJ Saks and WC Thompson, 'Assessing evidence: Proving facts' in D Carson and R Bull (eds), *Handbook of Psychology in Legal Contexts* (Wiley, 2nd ed, 2003); R Kamtekar, 'Situationism and Virtue Ethics on the Content of Our Character' (2004) 114 *Ethics* 458, relying on J Doris, *Lack of Character: Personality and Moral Behavior* (Cambridge, 2002).

36 Harman, above n 34.

37 Ibid.

38 *Stalder* [1981] 2 NSWLR 9, 17 (Street CJ), quoted also by the Court of Criminal Appeal in *Murphy* (1985) 4 NSWLR 42.

39 [1999] HCA 32; 198 CLR 1.

40 Ibid [53] (McHugh J).

the High Court accepted that a drink-driving conviction over 20 years before the trial did not disentitle Melbourne from receiving the stamp of good character.

Under the *UEA*, relevance has not to date been a pressure point.[41] The actual relevance of the evidence in this respect depends on the logical connection the evidence has to the facts in issue and to credibility.[42] No case law has to date applied *UEA*, s 55, with rigour to evidence of good character.[43] Instead, by virtue of the law's traditional 'generosity', character evidence is treated as satisfying s 55, the test of relevance,[44] even in its typical form of an absence of criminal convictions and general assertions that the prosecution allegations are 'out of character'. Such evidence is considered to 'rationally affect (directly or indirectly) the assessment of the probability of the existence of a fact in issue in the proceeding' (that is, non-guilt), and to be likewise relevant to the accused's credibility (that is, that an accused's denials and/or alibis are more likely to be true).

The evidence may be relevant to guilt/non-guilt and/or to the accused's credibility (that is, informing on his or her likelihood to lie to police, and when testifying). Good character evidence gains its relevance through tendency reasoning.[45] It is relevant because in the ordinary course of events an absence of misconduct may support the probability of continuing behaviour that does not involve breaches of the law. This thus permits the conclusion of non-guilt to the subject charges and supports any denials as being truthful ones.[46] The Australian courts' satisfaction of the test of relevance by liberal assumption rather than hard-headed rationality creates challenges, particularly as we see in the judges' direction to the jury guiding its task of weighing the worth of character evidence.

The deference shown by the law to evidence of good character is evidenced by courts treating as significant an inexplicable failure of defence counsel to adduce evidence of good character where it is available and is of potential utility.[47] Support for a successful appeal in this context was described in *TKWJ*[48] by Gaudron J as arising where, had the evidence been led 'when viewed in combination with the evidence given at trial ... the jury would have been likely to entertain a reasonable doubt about the guilt of the accused', that is whether the failure of defence counsel to adduce the good character evidence resulted in a substantial miscarriage of justice.

41 Probably because the law has focused on the damaging consequences of raising character as an issue: see, eg, *Stalder* [1981] 2 NSWLR 9, 17 (cited in *Clegg* [2017] NSWCCA 125).

42 The common law recognised that good character evidence bears on the credibility of the accused at the least 'with reference to credibility of the accused in his denial of the charge, and hence the unlikelihood of his guilt': *Murphy* (1985) 4 NSWLR 42, 54. The common law also strictly limited rebuttal evidence (that the accused is not of good character) to the credibility of the accused. That is, it did not extend to likelihood of guilt: *Shrimpton* [1851] ER 521, 523; 2 Den 319, 324 (Lord Campbell CJ).

43 See, eg, *DPP v Newman (a Pseudonym)* [2015] VSCA 25 where the court held the trial judge had erred in considering the absence of convictions not to constitute evidence of good character in light of pending charges.

44 *TKWJ* [2002] HCA 46; 212 CLR 124, [35] (Gaudron J).

45 With s 110(1) removing the application of the tendency rule.

46 Arguably, this light regulation given to evidence of good character defies logic, see *Kant* [2008] NZCA 269, [36]-[41] (Randerson and Winkelmann JJ) to the provisions of the *Evidence Act 2006* (NZ). Section 7(3) of that Act provides: 'Evidence is relevant in a proceeding if it has a tendency to prove or disprove anything that is of consequence to the determination of the proceeding'.

47 *Xu* [2019] NSWCCA 178 where counsel's failure to adduce good character evidence formed one of the successful grounds for allowing the appeal. See *De Silva* [2013] VSCA 339; *GZ* [2015] ACTCA 11; *Smith* [2015] VSCA 256.

48 [2002] HCA 46; 212 CLR 124, [33] (Gaudron J).

A leading common law example of good character evidence is the High Court case of *Melbourne*[49] where 61-year-old Roy Melbourne had stabbed his next-door neighbour, Mrs Chambers. Apparently he believed she was banging on the wall of his apartment throughout the night. In fact, the banging was a water hammer set off by the sprinkler system. It was activated at half-hour intervals during the early morning. Unlike the case of *Murphy*,[50] where the credibility of the accused, Lionel Murphy, was central (because the issue was whether he had said certain things to the Chief Stipendiary Magistrate),[51] here, apart from Melbourne's denials to police, his credibility was not an issue. The judge indicated to the jury that:

> [W]hen you consider that evidence as to good character ... *you are entitled to consider the improbability of Roy Melbourne committing the instant offence*, having a history of good character of some 61 years, and that this is of considerable significance. (emphasis added)

At issue on appeal was whether the judge should have directed the jury specifically that the accused's good character enhanced his credibility (in addition to his improbability of guilt). Melbourne's appeal was dismissed. The majority concluded that a judicial direction to the jury must address the strength and qualities of the good character evidence and, in the case at hand, where the character evidence was weak, no specific direction on credibility was necessary. Kirby and Callinan JJ dissented. Kirby J stated (at [120]): 'Unless in the particular circumstances of the case doing so is unnecessary, or would be unwarranted for reasons which the judge gives, the directions on good character must relate both to (a) the way in which that evidence may be considered by the jury to make it less likely that the accused committed the offence charged (non-guilt) and (b) the reliance which the jury may place upon any evidence which the accused may have given in the trial and any other statements made by the accused out of court ... (credibility)'.[52] His Honour also raised provocative questions regarding the role of both good character and the nature of any judicial directions:

- would they operate like a judicial warning (such as with identification evidence) where the law's experience indicates that judges, to ensure a fair trial, should warn the jury of particular matters that they may otherwise not appreciate? Or, is a direction really a comment on facts that are a jury matter and a matter of common sense?
- Or, 'as a matter of policy, do inconsistent rulings by trial judges, the proliferation of appeals on this point, and the practicalities of framing standard judicial directions for inclusion in Judicial Bench Books require that directions about "good character" be given in every case so as to avoid a justifiable sense of grievance at their omission and unnecessary appeals and retrials as a consequence'?[53]

---

49 [1999] HCA 32; 198 CLR 1.

50 (1985) 4 NSWLR 42.

51 Also, unlike in *Murphy*'s case the judge had not expressly limited good character to the question of guilt (or non-guilt). That limitation in *Murphy* justified a new trial.

52 Quoted approvingly in *SAM v Western Australia (No 2)* [2016] WASCA 64. For a recent repeat of the *Melbourne* scenario, see *Masri* [2020] NSWCCA 24. See also Gummow J in *Melbourne* [1999] HCA 32; 198 CLR 1, [72]: 'The issues in the particular case and the nature of the evidence of "good character" which is proffered will guide the process of reasoning of the tribunal of fact on the path to providing an answer to the ultimate question of whether the accused is guilty beyond reasonable doubt' (citations omitted).

53 *Melbourne* [1999] HCA 32; 198 CLR 1, [90] (citations omitted).

Ultimately his Honour concluded (with the majority) that there should be a judicial discretion on whether and how a jury should be guided on the use of good character evidence, tailored to the particular circumstances of the case.[54]

Adducing evidence of good character and the consequences

At common law raising character as an issue (that is, adducing evidence of good character) involved stepping into a minefield of potentially catastrophic consequences, with an accused person's character treated as 'indivisible'[55] and so *all* prior offences could become known to the jury upon the accused making even a relatively inept self-serving statement as long as it was perceived as an attempt to assert good character.[56] Under the *UEA*:

- There are no *special* rules of relevance applying solely to character evidence. It is a matter of applying *UEA*, s 55.
- Good character can be proved without the restrictions of the hearsay, opinion, tendency and credibility rules.[57] Thus, an inexpert opinion, based on hearsay, of weak probative value to the accused's propensity[58] or their credibility will not be excluded because it fails to meet these requirements elsewhere required by the Act.
- The prosecution and the co-accused, possess equal rights to prove character evidence led in rebuttal under s 110(2) or (3).
- By s 110, character evidence is categorised in two ways – either character 'generally' or in a 'particular respect'. Rebuttal evidence must match good character evidence either 'in that respect' or 'generally'. This means that the Act has jettisoned the common law view of the indivisibility of character (or the 'all or nothing' attitude).[59]
- This means at trial that:
  - evidence of good character is potentially relevant to the unlikelihood of guilt and potentially to support the accused's credibility (when testifying or out of court);[60]
  - rebuttal evidence led under s 110(2) or (3) is relevant to rebut the good character evidence pointing to unlikelihood of guilt and, to the extent that the rebuttal evidence reveals a false claim of good character, to discredit the accused.

Section 112 recognises that cross-examination of the accused requires special consideration, by way of applying the considerations in s 192 over and above that

---

54 Though note the refusal to permit a corporation defending criminal charges to lead evidence of good character: *DPP v JCS Fabrications & JMAL Group (Ruling No 1)* [2018] VCC 1003, [30] (Trapnell J).

55 Ibid.

56 *Stalder* [1981] 2 NSWLR 9, 11 (Street CJ).

57 Note that the coincidence rule still applies, and also that, for *UEA*, s 111, character evidence must satisfy the expert opinion requirements. In rebuttal it need not satisfy these requirements.

58 *Clegg* [2017] NSWCCA 125, [81]-[85], and at [96]: 'Evidence excluded by the Court or by decision the Crown as tendency evidence is capable of being adduced to rebut evidence of good character, unless a relevant rule of exclusion or a discretion under the *Evidence Act* applies' (Payne JA, with Schmidt and Fagan JJ agreeing).

59 *Zurita* [2002] NSWCCA 22, [14] (Howie J, with Hodgson JA and Levine J agreeing), and cited by *Parsons (a Pseudonym)* [2016] VSCA 17, [63] (Maxwell P, Redlich JA, Priest JA).

60 Note that the *UEA* Dictionary (or *Evidence Act 2001* (Tas), s 3) defines credibility in terms of a witness and also of a 'person who has made a representation that has been admitted in evidence'.

required by s 110. This means that the court must first assess the importance of the evidence, fairness to the accused and the other considerations in *UEA*, s 192(2): see *UEA*, s 112. In addition, ss 135, 136 and 137 may apply.

> **110. Evidence about character of accused persons**
> (1) The hearsay rule, the opinion rule, the tendency rule and the credibility rule do not apply to evidence adduced by a defendant to prove (directly or by implication) that the defendant is, either generally or in a particular respect, a person of good character.
> (2) If evidence adduced to prove (directly or by implication) that a defendant is generally a person of good character has been admitted, the hearsay rule, the opinion rule, the tendency rule and the credibility rule do not apply to evidence adduced to prove (directly or by implication) that the defendant is not generally a person of good character.
> (3) If evidence adduced to prove (directly or by implication) that a defendant is a person of good character in a particular respect has been admitted, the hearsay rule, the opinion rule, the tendency rule and the credibility rule do not apply to evidence adduced to prove (directly or by implication) that the defendant is not a person of good character in that respect.
> **Note:** The Commonwealth Act includes an additional subsection relating to unsworn statements. …
>
> **112. Leave required to cross-examine about character of accused or co-accused**
> A defendant must not be cross-examined about matters arising out of evidence of a kind referred to in this Part unless the court gives leave.

Procedurally, an advance ruling before seeking to apply s 110[61] enables parties to plan and commence their case fully armed with a map of the minefield of possible consequences of putting good character in issue under s 110(1). Typically, the defence will check with the prosecution 'whether there is anything known … to rebut the good character evidence'. If there is, 'a forensic decision then needs to be made as to whether to call the good character evidence (regardless), not call the good character evidence because of the risk of the rebuttal evidence being before the jury, or to seek an advance ruling'[62] as to the calling of rebuttal evidence. Note also that, on occasion, the prosecution may adduce in its own case that the accused has no prior convictions (and to that extent is a person of good character).[63]

'Adduced to prove' – conscious intent or emphatic denial?

Determining whether the defence has raised good character is not about the *consequence* of a witness's answer to a question, it is whether the defence intended to introduce evidence of good character. This is clear under the *UEA* by virtue of the language 'adduced to prove' in s 110(2) and (3) which requires the defence to have a conscious intention to put the accused's character in issue.[64] This is an important change from the common law because there are occasions where it will not be in the accused's best interest to raise his or her character. This is chiefly where the rebuttal evidence is more powerful than the defence. Two cases illustrate this danger. Both arise where the accused responded to questions while

---

61 Under s 192A (added in response to the High Court decision of *TKWJ* [2002] HCA 46; 212 CLR 124, [35]); and see *Huges (a Pseudonym)* [2013] VSCA 338, [52] (Lasry AJA).

62 *FB* [2020] NSWCCA 137, [363] (N Adams J), referring to *Clegg* [2017] NSWCCA 125 as such an example where defence counsel decided not to call proposed character evidence following a s 192A process.

63 See, eg, *Giallombardo* [2014] NSWCCA 25, [79].

64 *Gabriel* (1997) 76 FCR 279; *PGM* [2006] NSWCCA 310; 164 A Crim R 426, 434 [35]; *Huges (a Pseudonym)* [2013] VSCA 338.

testifying. Not surprisingly, both were seeking to place themselves in a good light. For example, in *Gabriel*,[65] the accused responded to the prosecutor's questions saying 'I don't go around attacking people'. Gabriel was facing a charge relating to stabbing and the prosecutor had asked the accused, 'Do you need a reason to attack people, do you?', eliciting the response above. Leave to cross-examine Gabriel under s 112[66] on his prior criminal history was held to have been wrongly granted because Gabriel's response was merely an emphatic denial of the offence charged and an accused does not raise character merely by emphatically denying the allegations put to them by the question. As Higgins J observed, Gabriel was faced with limited choices once the question was put. His options were:

(1) to accept the implicit imputation, thereby admitting to bad character and a propensity to act as alleged by the Crown by denying he needed a reason to attack people;
(2) to assert that he would attack people only if given good reason, thereby leaving it open to be inferred that he did have the propensity to 'attack' people, albeit for what he took to be a reason justifying that conduct – he would then open up cross-examination as to the adequacy of his 'reason' or reasons; or
(3) to deny the underlying premise that he 'attacked' people.

Gabriel chose the last option, but this did not justify granting leave to cross-examine him on his prior convictions.[67] In *Gabriel*, the accused was cross-examined in ways that ultimately drew out assertions of good character by him. Similarly, the Victorian Court of Appeal in *Huges (a Pseudonym)*[68] held that Huges's replies in *examination-in-chief* of, '*No, I've never hit my daughter*' and '*I didn't have pornographic [sic], I'm just not into pornographic movies. Not my, not my thing at all*', were no more than occasions for the denial of the allegations. Huges, like Gabriel, did not intend to raise character as an issue because neither his counsel's questions nor Huges's answers 'evince a conscious decision to intentionally and deliberately adduce positive character'.

Directions: good character

As an obvious baseline, any direction must accord with the evidence that is before the court.[69] Given the low threshold for admitting evidence of good character, the exhortation that a trial judge need not give 'a meaningless or absurd direction' or 'go through the charade of giving directions'[70] may require deft consideration. Essentially, a judicial direction should instruct the jury on the potential significance of accepting that the accused is of good character, including where credibility is in issue that he or she is 'less likely to lie or give a false account'[71] and that character is a factor in determining guilt beyond reasonable doubt. The

65 (1997) 76 FCR 279, confirmed in *Zurita* [2002] NSWCCA 22, [14] (Howie J, with Hodgson JA and Levine J agreeing). Sections 112 and 192 are discussed below.
66 Attracting also s 192, and also relating to the evidence admitted through s 110.
67 *Bartle* (2003) 181 FLR 1.
68 [2013] VSCA 338, [23].
69 *DPP v Newman (a Pseudonym)* [2015] VSCA 25; *PKS* (unreported, NSWCCA, 1 October 1998), quoted in *Bishop* [2013] VSCA 273.
70 *Aziz* [1996] 1 AC 41 (Lord Steyn).
71 See Judicial Commission of New South Wales, *Criminal Trial Courts Bench Book*, [2-370]. See also *FB* [2020] NSWCCA 137, [35].

conventional view of the judicial direction as to good character is that it reflects the trial judge's obligation to put the principal points of the defence case to the jury in a fair and balanced way.[72] However, even if a good character direction is given 'the judge may qualify it in order to put it in perspective having regard to the circumstances of the case'.[73] The conception of fairness does not negate the inclusion of 'balancing directions' – namely, a reminder to the jury that people can be first offenders and that jurors should keep in mind that good character evidence cannot prevail against what they may view as convincing evidence of guilt. According to Weinberg JA in *Saw Wah*,[74] balancing directions are usually innocuous and 'merely remind the jury of what is, in any event, perfectly obvious. They do not, in any way, prejudice the accused. Nor do they detract significantly from the very real benefit that can accrue from the giving of a good character direction'. Mr Wahi may see it differently. In his trial[75] on charges of rape, attempted rape and indecent assault, the trial judge's good character direction to the jury included:

> [Y]ou should keep in mind that a fact that a person who has previously been of good character can, of course, commit a crime for the first time. *It is often said by prosecutors, even Jack the Ripper had no prior convictions at some stage.* But it is a factor you take into account in favour of the accused man in assessing whether or not the crime has been committed.[76] (emphasis added)

In *Wahi*, the judge's direction additionally provided to the effect that the accused's lack of prior convictions was relevant 'when determining the likelihood that he would commit the offences for which he is charged'. Osborn JA (with Redlich and Weinberg JJA agreeing) concluded that he did 'not accept that his Honour's comment would convey the imputation to any sensible jury that the accused was to be directly compared to Jack the Ripper. It bore all the hallmarks of attempted judicial levity and such a direct comparison was self-evidently ridiculous'.[77] The appeal was dismissed. The court noted that a preferable course of action would have been for the judge to 're-give' the full good character direction without the reference to categories of offenders whose good character may have been utilised to access vulnerable victims.

The case of *Bishop*[78] provides a striking contrast. Bishop faced charges of incest and indecency. The defence had led evidence of good character (both generally and with respect to children) as relevant to both the unlikelihood of guilt and bearing on Bishop's credibility. The trial judge incorrectly[79] limited evidence of the accused's good character to evidence of general reputation, effectively preventing evidence of the witness's personal opinion. The witnesses had indicated that to their knowledge there had been no prior allegations of improper conduct, whether

72 *Aziz* [1996] 1 AC 41 (Lord Steyn).

73 *Melbourne* [1999] HCA 32; 198 CLR 1, 29 [79] (Gummow J); *Habib* [2015] NSWCCA 261, [23] (Hoeben CJ at CL).

74 [2014] VSCA 7, [72].

75 [2015] VSCA 132, [13].

76 To similar effect, see where the trial judge 'balanced' the direction with 'you should keep in mind that a person who has previously been of good character can commit a crime for the first time. *We have an assortment of scout masters, priests and others who can attest to the good sense of that particular direction*': *Mathis* [2014] VSCA 118, [10] (emphasis added by Court of Appeal).

77 [2015] VSCA 132, [24] (Osborn JA, with Redlich and Weinberg JJA agreeing).

78 [2013] VSCA 273.

79 Section 110(1) providing an exception to the opinion rule, and presumably applying *Rowton* [1865] EngR 53; (1865) Le & Ca 520, 541; 169 ER 1497.

in private or public against his or any other children. However, the trial judge's direction interrogated the character evidence, pointing out that it was limited to Bishop's public life, noting that '[t]here is no allegation that he has offended against children outside of the home'. The judge noted that the offences against Bishop's stepdaughter were alleged to have been at home and in private '[s]o, you bear that in mind as being the essential allegation against him in the context of the good character evidence that has been given in his favour'.[80] This comment was held to have created a substantial miscarriage of justice, leading to the quashing of convictions and the ordering of a new trial. The Court of Appeal held that this was comment 'clothed as directions of law' and inappropriately undermined the value and relevance of the evidence of good character and that 'that the jury would have understood that the evidence of good character could only have borne on the way in which the appellant dealt with children in public'.[81] The court concluded that where character is raised in a particular respect a direction commensurate with the value of the evidence is justified – that is, not one that is hedged with negative comment regarding its limitations.

To give some perspective to this ruling consider the observations by N Adams J in *FB*, where her Honour, considering the prosecutors' actions, distinguished *Bishop*, stating:

> There is nothing improper in [a prosecutor] suggesting to a character witness that an accused person might have acted in a certain way when the character witness was not present. Nor is it improper to point out to the jury in a closing address that those witnesses did not see the accused give his evidence. It is to be inferred from the transcript and the closing address of defence counsel that, consistent with the evidence of the son, the daughter and the mother, and contrary to the evidence of the character witnesses, the applicant was quick to anger in his cross-examination. It was permissible for the Crown Prosecutor to point this out.[82]

Matters such as these, put in cross-examination, could then be appropriate topics for the closing address to the jury.

Rebutting good character

Accused who wish to rely on character are given a choice – to adduce evidence that they are generally of good character, or that they are in a particular respect of good character: s 110(1). As mentioned earlier, under s 110(2) and (3) rebuttal evidence (that is 'evidence of bad character') must respond to the evidence of good character in the same respect (or be general character evidence rebutting general good character evidence). Finally, the admission of rebuttal evidence will need to be considered in light of ss 135, 136 and 137.[83]

---

80 [2013] VSCA 273, [24] (Priest JA, with Redlich and Coghlan JJA agreeing). See also *Hogg* [2019] NSWCCA 323 (prosecutor 'undermined' the good character evidence); *FB* [2020] NSWCCA 137, [365] (N Adams J). Note also the scope in some jurisdictions to reject evidence of good character as a mitigating factor in sentencing an offender who has harnessed their good standing to help commit child sexual offences (for example, using their position to create trust enabling them access to children who are then groomed and sexually assaulted): *Crimes (Sentencing Procedure) Act 1999* (NSW), s 21A(5A); *Criminal Law (Sentencing) Act 1988* (SA), s 10(3)(ba).

81 [2013] VSCA 273, [29].

82 *FB* [2020] NSWCCA 137, [376].

83 In *IW* [2019] NSWCCA 311 the appellant successfully appealed two counts of child sexual assault arising in a foster care context. The defence adduced extensive good character evidence from the foster care agency program manager, including an unsolicited highly supportive email

At common law, the role of rebuttal evidence is to facilitate the rebuttal of the accused's claim of good character. It is the same under the *UEA*. Rebuttal evidence counteracts, negates or sheds relevant light on such defence evidence. In doing so it logically relies on tendency reasoning[84] because for the particular purpose of *rebutting* the defence evidence it invites the trier of fact to draw inferences from particular incidents extraneous to the crime charged. Rebuttal evidence may be potentially relevant to discredit[85] the accused to the extent that the rebuttal evidence casts doubt on the accused's veracity in claiming to be of good character.

Prosecution evidence revealing that the accused has a criminal past can be powerful evidence in the trial. Psychological research[86] vindicates law's traditional circumspection towards tendency evidence. As Gleeson CJ said in *HML*, '[t]he reason for the exclusion is not the irrelevance of propensity, but its prejudicial effect ... It is the risk that evidence of propensity will be taken by a jury to prove too much that the law seeks to guard against'.[87] Deane J in *Phillips*[88] described this principle as recognising 'that such evidence in a jury trial is liable to besmirch justice with the ugly stain of prejudice or prejudgment'. Law's default position of excluding bad character evidence lies in 'reasons of policy and humanity'. Bad character evidence may be logically relevant. '[A]dmitting it you might arrive at justice in one case out of a hundred, you would probably do injustice in the other ninety-nine.'[89] Hayne J in *BBH*[90] expressed the issues bluntly:

> 71. The common law recognised, long ago, the force of the proverb "*give a dog an ill name, and hang him*". Hence the basic rule relating to similar fact evidence that evidence of other discreditable conduct is not admissible if it shows *only* that the accused has a propensity or a disposition to commit crime or a crime of the kind charged. But, as has been said, evidence of other discreditable conduct by an accused may have particular probative value or cogency. (citations omitted)

---

thanking IW and his wife within the period of the alleged offending (where monthly reviews and three monthly home visits formed the basis for her evidence), a longstanding family friend (he was 'very gentle, kind, quiet and just a regular normal dad'). The so-called rebuttal evidence related to IW admitting in cross-examination he had once smacked a child in his care, which the Court of Criminal Appeal held to be irrelevant. No leave had been sought pursuant to s 112. In *Allen (a Pseudonym)* [2016] VSCA 59, [55]-[60], although discussed in a s 110 and s 137 context (rather than s 104(4), combined with s 192), a defence attempt to discredit a prosecution evidence was wrongly converted by the trial judge into loss of character shield: '[H]is Honour seems to have regarded cross-examination to the effect that the challenge that "the mother has put the child up to this" as being on all fours with a "character assassination". We repeat that we do not understand why the judge thought – as the passages above insinuate – that a suggestion of collusion put to BNK might open the floodgates, permitting the defence to be inundated by a torrent of highly prejudicial and otherwise irrelevant material' (at [37]). See also *AKB (No 7)* [2018] NSWSC 1120.

84 Section 110 expressly requires the evidence be adduced to prove that the accused is *not a person of good character* (either generally, or in a particular respect): *UEA*, s 110(2) and (3). Section 101(3) indicates that it is unlikely that the additional requirements of s 101(2) apply in this rebuttal context and see *Clegg* [2017] NSWCCA 125, [83]-[84] (Payne JA).

85 The credibility rule (s 102) is expressly inapplicable to s 110(2) and (3). This raises an issue about the role of s 104.

86 In the next chapter in the context of *UEA*, s 101, there is a summary of the psychological research on the impact of negative information.

87 [2008] HCA 16; 235 CLR 334, [12].

88 [1985] HCA 79; 159 CLR 45, [1] (Deane J), drawing on the observations of Fullagar J and Dixon CJ in *Hall v Braybrook* [1956] HCA 30; 95 CLR 620, 628.

89 Deane J in *Phillips* [1985] HCA 79; 159 CLR 45, [1], quoting from Willes CJ in *Rowton* [1865] EngR 53; (1865) Le & Ca 520, 541; 169 ER 1497, 1506 (and quoted by Dixon CJ in *Hall v Braybrook* [1956] HCA 30; 95 CLR 620, 628).

90 [2012] HCA 9; 245 CLR 499.

A useful illustration of the importance of focusing on the basis upon which evidence is relevant in a character context is found in the 2014 murder trial, *DPP v Bracken*.[91] In *Bracken* the relationship of the accused and the deceased was in issue. The defence sought an advance ruling under s 192A regarding whether the prosecution would be permitted under s 110(3) to adduce in rebuttal evidence of the accused's 25-year-old prior convictions if the defence adduced evidence that the accused possessed 'placid, mild, gentle, kind, quiet, reclusive, introverted and reserved characteristics and/or personality' and that he 'was submissive towards Helen Curtis, would do anything for Ms Curtis and to make her happy, would not question or challenge Ms Curtis, would not behave aggressively towards Ms Curtis and would not react angrily towards Ms Curtis'. Maxwell P ruled that s 110 was not engaged because this defence evidence was adduced to prove the relationship, not to prove that Bracken was of good character (in a particular respect).

> [A]dducing of evidence from prosecution witnesses to that effect, about the identified characteristics of the accused, would not constitute the putting in issue of his character in the accepted sense, provided that the evidence can be seen to be relevant to an understanding of the relationship between the accused and the deceased and/or of their respective temperaments and/or of the interactions between them.[92]

As the Oscar Pistorius trial shows, rebuttal may be in the form of evidence of uncharged conduct, but it is important to note that where evidence of such acts is disputed the prosecution should probably seek a ruling to determine if the evidence can be adduced to rebut evidence of good character.[93] This arose for consideration in *Huges (a Pseudonym)*,[94] a case that also illustrates the ethical duties of prosecutors. The rebuttal evidence was held to be wrongly adduced on two grounds. First, as discussed above, Huges did not put his character in issue. He merely denied the allegations under oath. Second, the rebuttal evidence was in the form of disputed allegations:

> (a) … that the applicant assaulted and raped the complainant when the family lived in the USA;
> (b) … that the applicant had assaulted KJ [one of the two complainant daughters] during an argument immediately before he and his wife separated;
> (c) … that KJ had been constantly in fear of assault by the applicant;
> (d) … of pornographic material having been downloaded to the applicant's computer.[95]

The appeal resulted in the quashing of convictions on 17 counts of incest, indecent assault and gross indecency against Huges's two daughters and the ordering of a retrial. Coghlan JA and Lasry AJA rejected the use of a complainant's allegations

91 [2014] VSC 94.

92 Ibid [43] (Maxwell P).

93 This is not to suggest leave is required under s 110 – as it is not. See *Huges (a Pseudonym)* [2013] VSCA 338 and see also *DPP v Newman (a Pseudonym)* [2015] VSCA 25; cf *ES (No 1)* [2010] NSWCCA 197, [56] where Hodgson AJA observed: 'I do note that the appellant raised good character in a particular respect, relevantly the absence of convictions for sexual assault. In those circumstances, it may well have been open to the Crown to lead the evidence of K [of uncharged criminal conduct] to rebut this evidence of good character'. The matter was further raised in *ES (No 2)* [2010] NSWCCA 198. By way of example, see *AKB (No 7)* [2018] NSWSC 1120 (where evidence is led that the accused has no criminal record, rebuttal evidence of uncharged acts not permitted. Nor was leave granted to cross-examine): ss 110(3), 112 and 192 applied.

94 [2013] VSCA 338.

95 Ibid [4] from Priest JA's judgment.

as rebuttal evidence and commented adversely on the approach taken by the prosecutor in waiting until the defence had committed to a particular course before seeking leave. Lasry AJA described the ethical concerns as follows:

> 51. In this case, the prosecutor left making his application to the trial judge until after counsel for the appellant had opened the evidence he was about to lead and the evidence-in-chief of the appellant was completed. I do not understand that counsel for the appellant had any notice of the consequences of his opening and questioning until the application was made. … The significance of that occurring at that time of the trial and the dangers of it must have been obvious. Assuming the appellant denied the allegation in cross-examination, then evidence would be led in rebuttal after the defence case had closed with the jury understanding that something both unusual and dramatic had happened. That is what occurred and the evidence from the complainant about this inadmissible and dramatic event was the last thing the jury heard from the witness box. It is very likely that the jury were significantly influenced by what had occurred.
>
> 52. The prosecutor could have raised his concerns with counsel for the appellant after the brief opening address or at the first stage of the evidence in chief when the appellant's style of answering led the prosecutor to the view that he was putting his good character in issue. Such a course might have avoided this consequence. Resort might even have been had to s 192A of the Evidence Act 2008 for an advance ruling or finding. In its reports on the Uniform Evidence Law, the Australian Law Reform Commission identified just this situation as being one where such a procedure would be useful.
>
> 53. In my opinion, in such circumstances prosecutors have a significant stake in ensuring that a trial such as this remained fair and, as far as possible, without risk of prejudice and appealable error. The authorities … referred highlight, among other considerations, the caution which is required to be applied to an application such as was made here.

Priest JA (Coghlan JA and Lasry AJA agreeing) referred to the common law:

> 26. Emphasising that a trial judge must approach any exercise of discretion to permit cross-examination on an accused's bad character with a great deal of circumspection, Mason CJ, Brennan, Wilson and Dawson JJ said in *Phillips* (again in a different statutory context):
>
>> It is right to stress the exceptional character of a case in which the credibility of an accused person is open to be attacked by reference to his bad character or previous convictions and *it is undoubtedly right that the discretion of a trial judge to permit such an attack be sparingly and cautiously exercised.* Although the purpose for which such evidence is admitted is confined to questions touching the credibility of an accused person and is not to be accepted by the jury as persuasive of his guilt of the offence charged and notwithstanding that the trial judge will direct the jury clearly as to the use to which the evidence may be put and the use to which it may not be put (cf *R v Beech* (1978) 20 SASR 10, at pp 420-423) *there will always be a keen appreciation that the admission of the evidence may in the absence of countervailing considerations operate unfairly to his prejudice.*
>
> 27. Guidance as to when permission might be given to the prosecution to lead evidence in rebuttal of good character can be derived from cases decided at common law (paying due heed, of course, to the present statutory context). Such a case was *Perrier*. In *Perrier* it was held that the trial judge had been correct to permit the prosecution to lead evidence in rebuttal of the applicant's good character. The applicant had been charged with importing heroin. His counsel, despite being warned by the prosecutor about the course he was adopting, read a letter to a prosecution witness in the course of cross-examination which contained the opinion that the applicant was honest and reliable, and had a 'repugnance to be associated with anything concerning drugs'. The trial judge held that the applicant had put his character in issue and permitted the prosecution to lead evidence of the applicant's prior convictions. Brooking J (with whom Murphy and McGarvie JJ agreed), in refusing

the application for leave to appeal against conviction, made a number of observations which are apposite to the present case. Thus his Honour remarked:

> The common law rule is often expressed by stating that if the accused elicits evidence of his good character the Crown may rebut that evidence by calling evidence of his bad character. That the principle should be stated in this way is understandable since in practice the question will ordinarily arise because the accused has elicited evidence of his own good character. But the principle is a wider one. …

28. And later, he said:

> In general, the Crown cannot lead evidence of the accused's bad character; the evidence is probative but is excluded for reasons of policy: *Attwood v R* [1960] HCA 15; 102 CLR 353, at pp 359-60. But if the accused attempts to establish his own good character, he puts that character in issue, and evidence of bad character is admissible. Where the Crown, the accused having put his character in issue, seeks to prove bad character not by the cross examination of the accused but in some other way, the requirement of obtaining the permission of the trial judge contained in s 399(6) is inapplicable. It is not a matter of obtaining leave or permission. The conduct of the accused in raising the issue of his character has made evidence of bad character admissible.
>
> *The safeguard provided by the law in this situation is not a statutory requirement of permission or leave but the general principle that the trial judge always has a discretion to exclude admissible evidence tendered by the Crown …*

29. So far as the exercise of discretion was concerned, his Honour observed:

> Where the accused suggests he is of good character and the Crown proposes to tender evidence of previous convictions, *a highly important consideration in exercising the discretion is the relative weight of on the one hand the advantage gained by the accused by the steps which have been taken by him or on his behalf in an endeavour to show his good character, and on the other hand the degree of prejudice which may result to the accused* from proof of the prior convictions. (citations omitted)

While rebuttal evidence engages tendency reasoning, such tendency reasoning is not available for the additional purpose of proving guilt by showing a propensity to act or think as alleged by the prosecution.[96] Principle supports this view as well because it is clearly highly undesirable that tendency evidence that is of inadequate probative value to satisfy Part 3.6 is treated as amenable to reasoning directly to guilt when it is before the court in a quite different role. Such caution is recognised in the *UEA*.[97] It is also the assumption made in the Australian Law Reform Commission (ALRC) *Evidence (Interim)* Report.[98] Returning to the case of *Bracken* discussed above, if, instead of treating the evidence as relevant to the relationship, s 110(1) and (3) had been engaged, s 137 would have provided an

---

96 Unless the rebuttal evidence is in addition adduced for a tendency purpose and satisfies the requirements of ss 97 and 101. See *Clegg* [2017] NSWCCA 125 (Payne JA). See also *ES (No 2)* [2010] NSWCCA 198, [87]-[88] where Hodgson JA (Whealy and Buddin JJ agreeing) said that 'evidence supporting a tendency in the appellant to commit sexual assaults would have been admissible under s 110, provided leave to cross-examine had first been obtained under s 112. I think this evidence would have been sufficiently related to the particular respect as to which the appellant led evidence of good character. However, I accept there is a real question whether leave to cross-examine would have been granted … [and] in the absence of challenge by the Crown to what was said in *OGD (No 2)* and *El-Kheir*, I would proceed on the basis that evidence admitted under s 110 can only be used to rebut the accused's evidence of good character, and not otherwise to support the Crown case for the guilt of the accused'.

97 *UEA*, ss 97 and 101, set a baseline standard for prosecution evidence about an accused adduced for a tendency purpose. Arguably this is also the effect of *UEA*, s 95(2), which states that '[e]vidence that under this Part cannot be used against a party to prove a particular matter must not be used against the party to prove that matter even if it is relevant for another purpose'.

98 ALRC, *Evidence (Interim)* (Report No 26, 1985), [803].

additional barrier to the admissibility of evidence of the 25-year-old conviction due to the danger it might be given 'more weight in the jury's assessment than it warrants' or because it invited the 'jury to draw an inference about some matter which would ordinarily be excluded from evidence'.[99] Arguably 'its probative value is outweighed by the danger of unfair prejudice' from the risk that the jury would impermissibly generalise from the conviction against Bracken's character (rather than relying on the evidence of the conviction as rebuttal of Bracken's character in the particular respects introduced by the defence). Further, this negative generalising would have engaged tendency reasoning beyond the scope of s 110 and could be argued as being so seductive as not to be amenable to correction by judicial direction. As discussed further below, research on juror cognition indicates that it is flawed to assume that jurors will compartmentalise their thoughts to avoid improper reasoning where there is no cross-admissibility of evidence across counts. Instead, 'human cognition is dynamic, fluid and adaptive'. Knowledge is organised in associative networks, with information acquired through the senses in turn activating portions of that stored knowledge in a rapid, effortless, automatic fashion almost entirely beyond conscious control. Information that achieves a certain level of activation may then influence whatever cognitive task is underway regardless of its logical (or legal) relevance.[100]

Directions: bad character

A jury needs to be directed on the limited use of rebuttal evidence. Precedent and principle suggest that this may be on the basis of s 95[101] or s 136.[102] In *OGD (No 2)*[103] the judge's charge to the jury, that it was to use evidence adduced as an admission only 'for the purpose of whether the accused has made an admission in relation to charges which the accused faces', was held by Simpson J (with Mason P and Dowd J agreeing) to be 'in effect, a direction under s 136 and in accordance with s 95, limiting the use the jury could permissibly make of evidence that may otherwise have been interpreted as evidence of tendency'.[104] Section 95 appears to provide the preferred basis[105] for a judicial direction that tendency reasoning is not to be applied to rebuttal evidence to permit jurors to rely on the evidence to support the prosecution case.

The directions challenge

A direction on character evidence will be given during the trial judge's summing up to the jury. The judge's summing up guides the jury on the relevant law

99 *Dickman* [2017] HCA 24; 261 CLR 601, [48].

100 N Steblay et al, 'The Impact of Juror Verdicts of Judicial Instruction to Disregard Inadmissible Evidence: A Meta-analysis' (2006) 30 *Law and Human Behavior* 469; DJ Devine, *Jury Decision Making: The State of the Science* (New York University Press, 2012) 184.

101 'Evidence that under this Part cannot be used against a party to prove a particular matter must not be used against the party to prove that matter even if it is relevant for another purpose': *UEA*, s 95(2), and see *El-Haddad* [2015] NSWCCA 10.

102 'The court may limit the use to be made of evidence if there is a danger that a particular use of the evidence might … be unfairly prejudicial to a party': *UEA*, s 136(a).

103 [2000] NSWCCA 404; 50 NSWLR 433.

104 Ibid [88].

105 This is because s 136 applies to limit the use of evidence that is otherwise admissible for multiple purposes and therefore it is inappropriate here where rebuttal evidence is admitted for a singular purpose.

(including the potential relevance of character evidence to proving or disproving guilt and where the accused has given an account in court or out of court, to his or her credibility), directs on any limitations on the jury's use of character evidence and summarises the evidence before the court.

The Judicial Commission of NSW[106] and the Judicial College of Victoria[107] offer judges guidance in relation to summing up and directing the jury on character evidence. The role of the summing up is

> primarily to give directions as to the law, including such warnings as are necessary and appropriate with respect to particular aspects of the evidence. The extent to which the trial judge seeks to summarise the evidence and the addresses of counsel is very much a matter for the individual judge, in the circumstances of the trial. Some repetition will be necessary to ensure that the jury focus on the relevant issues and understand how particular evidence, obtained from a variety of witnesses, may relate to those issues. Closing addresses of counsel may not achieve the necessary balance and degree of objectivity.[108]

As discussed in Chapter 2, traditionally, trials rely on the effectiveness of judicial instruction. Indeed, it is an assumption of our system of criminal justice that, 'as a general rule, juries understand, and follow, the directions they are given by trial judges'.[109] Psychological research casts doubt on these assumptions, suggesting directions can be an exercise in futility.[110] Judicial statements from United States courts have recognised the significance of this research where judicial direction requires jurors to perform 'a mental gymnastic which is beyond, not only their powers, but anybody's else'.[111] Sklansky[112] quotes compelling metaphors describing the flawed assumption of directing someone to undertake the impossible (particularly to 'forget' what they have heard): 'one cannot unring a bell'; 'if you throw a skunk into the jury box, you can't instruct the jury not to smell it'; '[a] drop of ink cannot be removed from a glass of milk'.[113] Clearly, an instruction for jurors to wipe information from their minds can struggle against unconscious biases.

Mock jury research said to be supportive of the inefficacy of evidentiary directions is analysed by Sklansky.[114] Some studies show that 'jurors' violated judicial direction to use prior convictions only for credibility purposes.[115] In some, the

---

106 See <https://www.judcom.nsw.gov.au/publications/benchbks/criminal/character.html>; see also *Simic* [1980] HCA 25; 144 CLR 319; *Melbourne* [1999] HCA 32; 198 CLR 1 (at least with respect to credibility). See also *FB* [2020] NSWCCA 137; *Huges (a Pseudonym)* [2013] VSCA 338, [35].

107 See <https://www.judicialcollege.vic.edu.au/eManuals/CCB/index.htm#19986.htm>; See <https://www.judicialcollege.vic.edu.au/eManuals/CCB/index.htm#1488.htm>.

108 *FB* [2020] NSWCCA 137, [33]. On the requirement for a fair and balanced summing up, see *Gregg* [2020] NSWCCA 245.

109 *Gilbert* [2000] HCA 15; 201 CLR 414, [13] (Gleeson CJ and Gummow J).

110 RL Wissler and MJ Saks, 'On the Inefficacy of Limiting Instructions: When Jurors Use Prior Conviction Evidence to Decide on Guilt (1985) 9 *Law and Human Behavior* 37.

111 *Nash v United States* 54 F 2d 1006, 1007 (2nd Cir, 1932) (Hand J); or a 'judicial lie': *United States v Grunewald* 233 F 2d 556, 574 (2nd Cir, 1956) (Frank J, dissenting in part), (rev'd, 353 US 391 (1957)).

112 DA Sklansky, 'Evidentiary Instructions and the Jury as Other' (2013) 65 *Stanford Law Review* 407.

113 Quoting from *Dunn v United States*, 307 F 2d 883, 886 (5th Cir, 1962); *Virgin Islands v Toto* 529 F 2d 278, 283 (3rd Cir, 1976).

114 Above n 112, 423-39.

115 Wissler and Saks, above n 110; S Lloyd-Bostock, 'The Effects on Juries of Hearing About the Defendant's Previous Criminal Record: A Simulation Study' [2000] *Criminal Law Review* 734, 753-5. See also, where the instruction had no effect, E Greene and M Dodge, 'The Influence of Prior Record Evidence on Juror Decision Making' (1995) 19 *Law and Human Behavior* 67.

direction operated perversely, drawing attention to the evidence.[116] Some studies suggest the direction worked. For example, Sealy and Cornish[117] concluded that '[c]ontrary to common supposition, juries give real weight to an instruction to disregard relevant previous record [evidence] wrongly admitted'. As well as the results being divergent, they raise other issues. Mock studies do not replicate the authentic decision-making experience. They lack real consequences, they lack the *gravitas* of a judge, an accused in the dock, victims and families, all underscoring the moral and personal issues at stake. Further, jurors tend to be picked from the pool most readily available to researchers (often, students). There is no deliberation and, of even greater concern, as Sklansky[118] indicates, the instructions to jurors are drafted by researchers, leading some studies to rely on inappropriate,[119] incomprehensible or baseless[120] instructions. Sklansky quotes from a meta-analysis of mock jury studies regarding the impact of evidentiary instructions that suggests that jurors respond to specific information that they can follow and that jury deliberation enhances the effect of instructions.[121] Sklansky suggests neither theory nor research findings support a conclusion that well-instructed jurors cannot or will not follow instructions. Sklansky concludes with the following observations.

1. Judicial direction or instruction is not a flawless resolution of all issues linked to disregarding or limiting evidence.
2. Timing, content and phrasing of instructions matter. Jurors will not obey senseless or incoherent instructions, or ones that seek the impossible from jurors (such as forgetting). Instruction needs to provide reasons and if an intelligible explanation is not possible then the rationale for the direction requires review.
3. The consequences of juror disobedience or non-compliance should guide when instructions are relied upon. If a flawed appreciation of evidence is not catastrophic to the fairness of the trial, then instruction may be appropriate. Where it is likely to result in an unfair trial, then it is intolerable to rely on direction and the evidence should be excluded.[122]

These observations are relevant to situations that arise under s 110.[123] For example, rebuttal evidence that clearly exposes the falsity of a claim to be a person of good character will be amenable to instruction that the evidence be assessed for what it says about the accused's claims and, to that extent, is relevant to the accused's credibility. It is rarely likely to be relevant to the accused's credibility beyond this exposure of falsity (unless there are convictions for perjury or similar highly discrediting acts). Of course rebuttal evidence that is remote to the claims made by the accused under s 110(1) may strain to have sufficient relevance to justify admission, particularly given the task for judges to convey instructions in

116 S Tanford and M Cox, 'Decision Processes in Civil Cases: The Impact of Impeachment Evidence on Liability and Credibility Judgments' (1987) 2 *Social Behavior* 165.

117 AP Sealy and WR Cornish, 'LSE Jury Project, Juries and the Rules of Evidence' [1973] *Criminal Law Review* 208, 216-18, 222.

118 Sklansky, above n 112, 434.

119 For example, asking the jurors to report whether they found the accused guilty or innocent: Wissler and Saks, above n 110, 41.

120 Citing Greene and Dodge, above n 115.

121 Sklansky, above n 112, 438, citing Steblay et al, above n 100.

122 Sklansky, above n 112, 456.

123 As well as the contexts discussed in the next chapter involving tendency reasoning and directions with respect to relationship, context and *O'Leary*-style evidence (1946) 73 CLR 566.

a coherent and understandable manner and for jurors to comprehend and obey them.[124] This is particularly the case when intuitively it seems a tendency purpose that supports the prosecution case is the most compelling aspect of the evidence.[125] Thus, the role of the direction is an important element in determining the need to apply s 137 to the rebuttal evidence.

Cross-examining Accused on Character

Not all accused will testify but if they do s 112 requires a court to grant leave before he or she can be cross-examined about matters arising out of ss 110 or 111.[126] As we saw in *Gabriel* above, for such cross-examination, in addition to ss 135-137, there is the additional consideration of s 192(2):

> (2) Without limiting the matters that the court may take into account in deciding whether to give the leave, permission or direction, it is to take into account –
> (a) the extent to which to do so would be likely to add unduly to, or to shorten, the length of the hearing, and
> (b) the extent to which to do so would be unfair to a party or to a witness, and
> (c) the importance of the evidence in relation to which the leave, permission or direction is sought, and
> (d) the nature of the proceeding, and
> (e) the power (if any) of the court to adjourn the hearing or to make another order or to give a direction in relation to the evidence.

In *Stanoevski*[127] the High Court made crystal clear that s 192(2) does not contain a set of soft contemplations to be dismissed by boilerplate sentences. Stanoevski, a solicitor, was charged with insurance fraud. She adduced evidence of her good character under s 110(1) and she also testified. The trial judge ruled admissible rebuttal evidence in the form of a report of a purported investigation by the Law Society into an alleged act of professional misconduct, namely, that Stanoevski had forged a signature and falsely indicated that she had witnessed a signature on a document. It was clear that the poor-quality report (referring only to a single incident) failed to rate as important evidence as per s 192(2)(c). The report was described as 'featherweight' by Gaudron, Kirby and Callinan JJ yet the trial judge permitted extensive cross-examination on the report. He made no reference to s 192 at all. The rebuttal evidence was further enlarged by the trial judge in his summing-up, commenting that '[i]f we all accepted some sort of slap-dash approach then sworn documents would have no effect and the whole purpose of sworn documents would be lost'. This extensive reliance on weak rebuttal evidence created what Gaudron, Kirby and Callinan JJ described as a 'certainty of unfairness' with the extensive rebuttal evidence distracting the jury from the main issues in the trial. Gaudron, Kirby and Callinan JJ added:

> **Failure to advert to a statutory discretion**
> 41. Section 192 applies to this case, and in particular to the exercise by the trial judge of his or her discretion under s 112 of the Act. It should be noted that the leave required

124 For example, see *IW* [2019] NSWCCA 311 discussed earlier.
125 See psychological research findings summarised in the next chapter, pp 475-476, 478.
126 There is some discussion in the case law as to whether s 112 requires leave to be given to cross-examine on all character evidence, that is, not just the evidence adduced through ss 110 and 111: *El-Azzi* [2004] NSWCCA 455, [199] (special leave refused: [2005] HCATrans 781); *W* (2006) 16 Tas R 1. It seems clear that it is limited to evidence adduced under *UEA*, Pt 3.8.
127 [2001] HCA 4; 202 CLR 115.

under s 112 is not leave to adduce evidence, but to cross-examine about the character of a defendant. In addition to matters which may be relevant in a particular case, in all cases the court must take into account the matters prescribed by s 192(2). It is clear here that the trial judge (probably because his attention does not seem to have been drawn to it) did not take into account all of those matters, some of which would inevitably have been relevant to the way in which his discretion ought to be exercised had he adverted to them.

42. Paragraphs (a), (b) and (c) were of importance here. As to par (a) a great deal of time was in fact taken up by the pursuit of a collateral issue, not just in cross-examination, but also in chief, addresses and the judge's summing up. Whether its pursuit added unduly to the length of the hearing was a matter to be taken into account and might well have affected his Honour's decision.

43. The cross-examination on the report raised a very grave possibility of unfairness to the appellant within the meaning of s 192(2)(b). By giving permission for that cross-examination to take place the trial judge was allowing the undertaking of an extensive collateral inquiry by the prosecutor. That inquiry necessarily raised a contest of credibility between the appellant and her co-conspirator, Ms Wailes, on a matter on which the latter had not been cross-examined and upon which evidence neither in chief nor in cross-examination should have been led. The risk, in our opinion, indeed the certainty of unfairness, was compounded by the repeated references to signatures and some of the contents of documents which could not be admitted into evidence, were rightly rejected by the trial judge, and were not seen by the jury. An unfortunate example is a recitation by the prosecutor of the effect of part of the statutory declaration made by Ms Wailes and contained in the report. The repeated invitations to the appellant to speculate about Ms Wailes' actions and motivations in relation to the documents were similarly unfair. They also provide an example of the extent to which an attenuated attempt to rebut evidence of good character can be distracting from the main issues with which the jury should be concerned.

44. Section 192 is not exhaustive as to the matters to be taken into account. Plainly the weight to be accorded to the evidence sought to be adduced, whether in cross-examination or otherwise, is a matter of considerable relevance. The trial judge quoted the expert's opinion in the report but yet does not seem to have taken into account how little, if any value it had, that is to say, its feather weight.

In *Huges (a Pseudonym)*,[128] discussed above, Priest JA concluded that the trial judge neither considered ss 135-137 in permitting the admission of the supposed rebuttal evidence nor in permitting cross-examination of the accused on the evidence.

22. I can detect no indication in the judge's reasons for permitting the cross-examination that he properly considered the criteria spelled out in s 192 of the Act bearing on the grant of leave. Nor – apart from his reference to his earlier ruling, Ruling No 3 – do I detect anything to suggest that, in considering the anticipated cross-examination or rebuttal evidence, his Honour distinctly considered the discretions reposing in him under ss 135 and 136, or his mandatory obligation arising under s 137 to exclude the proposed evidence if its probative value was outweighed the danger of unfair prejudice. …

31. But even if I am wrong about that, and counsel's purpose was to elicit evidence of good character, and the evidence adduced actually went to good character, then I am still firmly of the opinion that the cross-examination should not have been allowed. The judge had a discretion whether to allow the cross-examination, the occasion for its exercise being unusual. When a comparison is made of the relative advantage to the defence case and concomitant damage to the prosecution case from the supposed evidence of good character, and regard is then had to the very great prejudice occasioned to the appellant by the cross-examination, it is plain that the proper exercise of discretion dictated that the cross-examination not be allowed.

128 [2013] VSCA 338.

32. Moreover, there was even less occasion to permit rebuttal evidence to be given. The stage at which the evidence was led, coupled with its nature, led the trial to become seriously unbalanced. For the relatively benign evidence of supposed good character to have been met with the grossly prejudicial evidence of the violent rape of his daughter when an eight year old, would have been devastating to the defence case, and unfairly so. The probative value of the evidence clearly was outweighed by the prejudice it would have engendered.

33. The trial judge's ruling does not appear to reflect consideration of the question of unfairness caused to the appellant. His Honour had earlier acknowledged in Ruling No 3 that the evidence of the violent rape in the US was highly prejudicial. It did not become less so following his consideration of the prosecutor's application to cross-examine and call rebuttal evidence about it. Indeed, its late introduction into the trial made it potentially more so. The trial judge was required to carefully balance any disadvantage to the prosecution case from the evidence of good character against any unfair advantage to the defence case. Even were the appellant's evidence the adduction of good character, it was so insignificant in the overall trial as to make introduction of the evidence touching bad character gravely disproportionate.

Expert Evidence of Character about a Co-accused: *UEA*, s 111

> It is one thing to say that it is unjust or unfair for the Crown to put a person in danger of conviction by leading such evidence against him. It is, however, a very different thing to say that he [the accused] is to be restricted in defending himself by excluding such evidence when it tends to rebut his guilt or to prove his innocence.[129]

The cut-throat defence has been mentioned earlier. It arises in a joint trial where defendants seek to exculpate themselves at the expense of a co-accused.[130] This can involve blaming the co-accused from the witness box, commenting on the co-accused's silence in court,[131] leading evidence under s 110(2) or (3), cross-examining the accused in a like fashion and, less frequently, relying on s 111 to lead character evidence about that co-accused through an expert witness.[132] Like s 110, s 111 removes evidentiary obstacles (the hearsay and the tendency rules) to enable character evidence to be proved. It requires, however, that the evidence meet the requirements of expert opinion: s 111(1). The section also facilitates rebuttal evidence (but without the need to rely on expertise): s 111(2). A cut-throat defence does not permit *any* means be used to convey lack of guilt at the expense of blaming a co-accused, only 'all legitimate and relevant means'.[133] A no-holds

129 *Lowery and King (No 3)* [1972] VR 939, 947, approved *Lowery* [1974] AC 85, 102.

130 See also D Ross, 'One Accused's Evidence of Another's Criminal Disposition' (2006) 11 *Deakin Law Review* 179.

131 See *UEA*, s 104(6); s 20(4). As we see in Chapter 14, a judicial warning to the jury regarding evidence from a co-accused who is also 'witness who might reasonably be supposed to have been criminally concerned in the events giving rise to the proceeding' (s 165(1)(d)) must direct the jury maintaining a balance between co-accused. Where only one has testified the judge must not, through a judicial warning, place his or her testimony in a light that creates disadvantage: *Webb and Hay* [1994] HCA 30; 181 CLR 41.

132 It can include cross-examination of a co-accused on character as well (s 112), unless, as character evidence, it is also credibility evidence within s 101A. Section 104(6) must then be complied with.

133 *Lowery and King (No 3)* [1972] VR 939 (CCA), approved *Lowery* [1974] AC 85 (PC). Quite clearly 'all evidence, including that adduced by an accused in order to raise a doubt as to guilt, must be relevant in the sense that it could rationally affect, directly or indirectly, the assessment of the probability of the existence of a fact in issue in the proceedings': *Jones* [2009] HCA 17; 254 ALR 626 (French CJ, Heydon, Kiefel and Bell JJ), citing *Goldsmith v Sandilands* [2002] HCA 31; 76

barred approach would risk the trial degenerating into a mud-slinging spectacle, causing unfairness, potentially to all. A key preliminary consideration for those jointly tried is whether or not separate trials can be ordered.[134]

Section 111 is most typically linked with the common law case of *Lowery*,[135] an appeal to the Privy Council from the Supreme Court of Victoria. A useful summary of *Lowery* is found in the English case of *Randall*[136] by Steyn LJ:

> 27. … A young girl was sadistically murdered. Lowery and King, the two accused, were present when she was murdered. The crime was committed by one or the other, or by both acting in concert. Each accused adduced evidence of the unlikelihood that he could have committed the murder. Lowery emphasised his good character and said that because of fear of King he had been unable to prevent the murder. King said that he had been under the influence of drugs and had been powerless to prevent Lowery from killing the girl. Despite Lowery's objection, counsel for King was allowed to call the evidence of a psychologist as to their respective personalities and, on that evidence, to invite the jury to conclude that it was less probable that King was the killer. They were both convicted and Lowery unsuccessfully appealed to the Supreme Court of Victoria on the ground, inter alia, that the psychologist's evidence ought not to have been admitted.
>
> 28. The Privy Council held that the evidence of the psychologist was relevant in support of King's case to show that his version of the facts was more probable than that put forward by the appellant. Accordingly the Privy Council dismissed the appeal. The reasons for the Board's judgment were delivered by Lord Morris of Borth-y-Gest.
>
> 29. Those reasons raise difficulties in two respects. The first is in regard to the observation (at 101E) that the evidence of the expert was 'not related to … criminal tendencies'. It is true that the evidence was tied in directly to King defending himself against the Crown's case against him. On the other hand the evidence demonstrated Lowery's potential aggressiveness. It is therefore difficult to accept the statement that the evidence did not relate to criminal tendencies. Secondly, the judgment placed emphasis on the fact that Lowery put his character in issue at 101–102. But there must be cases in which the propensity of one accused may be relied on by the other, irrespective of whether he has put his character in issue: *Blackstone's Criminal Practice*, 2003, F12.20, at 2172. Subject to these minor points, *Lowery* is high authority for the proposition that evidence of a co-accused's propensity may be relevant. This was demonstrated by the following passage in the judgment of the Privy Council, at p 102D–G:
>
> > In reference to this matter the Court of Criminal Appeal said, and in their Lordships' view rightly said:
> >
> > > It is, however, established by the highest authorities that in criminal cases the Crown is precluded from leading evidence that does no more than show that the accused has a disposition or propensity or is the sort of person likely to commit the crime charged; …
> >
> > and further:
> >
> > > It is, we think, one thing to say that such evidence is excluded when tendered by the Crown in proof of guilt, but quite another to say that it is excluded when tendered by the accused in disproof of his own guilt. We see no reason of policy or fairness which justifies or requires the exclusion of evidence relevant to prove the innocence of an accused person.
>
> *Lowery* is therefore precedent for the view that, in the circumstances of the present case, the propensity to violence of a co-accused may be relevant to the issues between the Crown and the accused tendering such evidence.

ALJR 1024, 1029-30; 190 ALR 370, 377 [31] (McHugh J); *Nicholls* [2005] HCA 1; 219 CLR 196, 215 [37] (McHugh J).

134 See Chapter 2, pp 36-37.

135 [1974] AC 85 (PC).

136 [2004] 1 All ER 467; [2004] 1 WLR 56.

Any evidence to be adduced by a co-accused still requires consideration of the s 135 exclusionary discretion (and potentially ss 95 and 136 to limit inadmissible or otherwise admissible evidence, respectively).

Conclusion

There was a time when the character of an accused played a significant role in their trial, often as part of a credibility battle between the accused and prosecution witnesses of dubious character.[137] In keeping with the view that the sufficiency of a prosecution should be based on proof of the accused person's commission of a crime, the 21st century Australian criminal trial under the *UEA* has retreated a long way from this position. While one expects the weaknesses in the prosecution case to be put to proof by forensic probing, evidence of good character, even of the *Melbourne*-type, continues to have a role in criminal trials despite the concerns expressed by Kirby J in that case.

Perhaps it is justified to permit evidence of not-so-bad character as 'a badge of good citizenship',[138] but *if* that is the case, one needs to acknowledge that its admission is not a zero-sum game, nor are the reasons that justified reliance on character evidence in pre-industrial England any longer an essential aspect of the 21st century accusatorial trial in Australia. As we know, opening the 'character' door to rebuttal evidence creates a murky recipe (and sometimes also a trap). Where lies the rationality in leaving the jury to treat the badge of good citizenship as a basis for finding reasonable doubt?

The psychological reality of the application of these rules is particularly important in appreciating the setting of admissibility thresholds. In addition to the impact on jurors of potent negative information about an accused, several decades of psychological research casts doubt on the efficacy of judicial directions in decontaminating jurors' impressions once they are exposed to evidence that is potentially unfairly prejudicial to an accused.[139] These issues are particularly important to the application of Part 3.6 in criminal trials. In *Melbourne*, under the heading 'problems', Kirby J added questions that reveal some of the rippling complexities underlying law's traditional acceptance of evidence of the accused's good character in criminal cases.

> 90. It is a measure of the attention which has been given to the subject of "good character" in the context of criminal trials that numerous questions have been raised in the books. Many of them were debated in this appeal.
>
> - Does "good character" exist at all? Is it an outmoded or antiquated notion of morality and human propensity which has been overtaken by psychological experimentation and understanding, and which should no longer be reflected in the directions which judges give to contemporary juries?
> - Are the considerations of propensity to criminal conduct and creditworthiness in statements made, whether on oath or otherwise, separate notions or different facets of the one idea that some people are prone to commit crimes and tell lies in ways that are predictable from their past conduct whilst others are not?

137 J Hunter, 'Book Review: *Character Evidence in the Criminal Trial*' (2016) *International Journal of Evidence & Proof* 162.

138 *Melbourne* [1999] HCA 32; 198 CLR 1, [90] (Kirby J).

139 Steblay et al, above n 100, cited in J Hunter and RI Kemp, 'Proposed Changes to the Tendency Rule: A Note of Caution' (2017) 41 *Criminal Law Journal* 253, 260.

- Is it necessary, or appropriate, to draw a distinction between particular categories of crimes, such that evidence of good character or the absence of convictions will be treated as relevant to, say, a crime of dishonesty, but not necessarily to an unpremeditated, spontaneous crime of a sexual or other nature? Or is good character a badge of good citizenship which the law acknowledges, for policy reasons, so that it stands the accused in good stead when faced by a criminal accusation which goes to trial?
- Is the absence of prior convictions, without more, a demonstration of "good character" entitling an accused to a direction on that ground? Or does the law require more substantial and affirmative evidence to demonstrate the large and elusive concept of a person's "character" from which inferences about that person's conduct or credibility may safely be drawn by a jury?
- Are "good character" and "reputation", which are sometimes used interchangeably in the cases, the same notion? Or does "good character" refer to inner qualities of the accused which may or may not be reflected in that person's public reputation?[140]

Further food-for-thought comes from the US *We Are All Criminals* project[141] regarding the high percentage of people (they suggest 75%) who have committed crimes but 'have had the luxury of living without an official reminder of a past mistake'. They have been either fortunate enough not to be caught or, if caught, privileged enough (perhaps by dint of their social or economic standing, their race, gender or other qualities) to be without a criminal record. The project records anonymous confessions online. These show 'doctors and lawyers, social workers and students, retailers and retirees ... consider[ing] how very different their lives could have been had they been caught. ... The stories are of youth, boredom, intoxication. ... They are ... humiliating, and humbling ... . They are privately held memories without public stigma; they are criminal histories without criminal records'.

The project suggests law's attitudes to people with criminal records is unduly harsh, in particular because they perpetuate inequities. It exhorts further reflection, stating that '[t]his is about how we view others by how we view ourselves. It's true: we are all criminals. But more importantly ... some of us, perhaps one in four of us, may be in need of a second chance'. These observations are obviously less pertinent to people with criminal records for offences at the very serious end of the criminal calendar. Nevertheless, the *We Are All Criminals* project makes clear that, as well as assuming goodness based on no criminal record, we should be less quick to judge badness based on proof of isolated acts of criminality, particularly in light of psychological research that shows we tend to misinterpret a little bit of bad about someone and we also run the risk of giving such information disproportionate weight.

Query whether there is a strong case for questioning whether character evidence of ambiguous probative value earns its place at the table of the modern criminal trial. Or does good character of weak probative value sit like a bonus point or a cashed in loyalty card? Further, it is notable that the role of rebuttal evidence, essentially to expose an accused who has tried to cheat when collecting their bonus point, is dangerously apt to convey messages of negativity beyond its official s 110 task. It is unsurprising that both good and bad character evidence

140 *Melbourne* [1999] HCA 32; 198 CLR 1 (Kirby J).

141 See <http://www.weareallcriminals.com/>. See also <http://www.abc.net.au/radionational/programs/lawreport/we-are-all-criminals-project/6419066>.

can be challenging topics for trial judges required to give appropriately nuanced directions to the jury (not to mention the 'unringing of the bell' assumptions underlying the Victorian Court of Appeal's judgments in *Wahi*[142] and *Mathis*[143]). Additional costs, invisible ones, may exist in jury deliberation and in the integrity of their verdict. In short, rationally locating the place and weight of s 110 evidence in decision-making is fraught, given the human tendency to give disproportionate weight, relative to probative merit, of one's impressions of a person.

And this immense forensic challenge to the trial adds what? It permits the well-resourced and well-connected accused to gamble at creating a clash of spin that distracts the jury from the evidence supporting the facts in issue. Or perhaps, as arguably occurred in Oscar Pistorius's case, it permits the prosecutor to take the trial hostage, employing the same tactic but with greater flamboyance and still greater effect than the defence could achieve. Few would question the unacceptability of the prosecutors' tactics in *Gabriel*, *Huges* and like cases, but, on examining the vista created by s 110, this conduct suggests that the alchemy of history and inevitability means that at best s 110 invites gamesmanship from advocates and at worst permits for whoever is in the dock a life of privilege to trump one of disadvantage.

Perhaps the good *vs* bad character battle is ready for history's dustbin?

142 [2015] VSCA 132.
143 [2014] VSCA 118.

Chapter 11

Tendency and Coincidence Evidence

Introduction

This chapter examines the admissibility of circumstantial (that is, non-direct) evidence[1] that is often relied on where there is a dearth of direct evidence. It relies for its relevance on reasoning about a person's tendency to act in a particular way as inferred from their past acts. In court this typically arises in the context of prosecution evidence about the defendant. Later in this chapter we will see that the law draws distinctions between whether that evidence is adduced in a civil case (perhaps to make certain representations) or, if adduced in a criminal case, is adduced by the defence or by the prosecution. In addition, we examine another form of reasoning-inference, referred to as coincidence or improbability reasoning. This second form of inference arises when a decision-maker is invited to draw the conclusion from circumstantial evidence that the accused is guilty of the crime because the pattern of similarities in events or circumstances is such that they could not be a matter of coincidence.

Tendency and coincidence evidence is circumstantial evidence. The law only permits the adducing of such evidence in relation to specific situations – and not to prove that an accused has a background of criminal offending. Admitting such general evidence risks jurors viewing the accused as likely to be guilty merely because of his general criminal past. For this reason, tendency and coincidence evidence must possess 'significant probative value' (*UEA*, ss 97, 98). In acknowledgement of the danger of unfair prejudice, prosecution tendency and coincidence evidence about a defendant must meet an additional admissibility requirement as well.[2] Further, the party adducing tendency or coincidence evidence must give notice – a device that seeks to promote adversarial testing. This chapter examines the application of these standards and the consequences of the standards not being met. The reason for this regulation of Part 3.6 evidence is because it is recognised that tendency and coincidence evidence engages reasoning that relies upon a prediction that builds on assumption and stereotype (just like Clarice Starling, the fictional forensic profiler at the beginning of the previous chapter). The *UEA* acknowledges that these assumptions may create error. As the cases extracted in this chapter reveal, prosecution evidence about an accused consumes the limelight of the *UEA* case law.

1 *Elomar* [2014] NSWCCA 303, [358].

2 See *UEA*, s 101.

In the *UEA*, the threshold concern is with the *purpose* for adducing the evidence,[3] that is, is the evidence adduced to prove a tendency, or to disprove coincidence – or for some other reason? This heightened care to the reliance on inference was driven home in the 2013 High Court decision in *Aristocrat Technologies Australia Pty Ltd v Global Gaming Supplies Pty Ltd*.[4] Here, French CJ, Crennan, Kiefel, Gageler and Keane JJ affirmed the Full Federal Court ruling that the trial judge had unwittingly applied tendency reasoning when he relied on certain email communications and had failed to apply the Part 3.6 admissibility requirements. The tendency evidence in question was of conduct like the alleged infringement of copyright but related to other occasions of infringement. As their Honours observed, '[i]t would be difficult to find a clearer indication of the use of the evidence as indicative of a tendency'.[5]

> 35. … While the primary judge did not use the word "tendency" nor refer to s 97 of the Evidence Act his Honour … used the email evidence in such a way as to justify the Full Court's view of his reasoning process. The applicants referred to elements of his Honour's reasoning which, it was said, did not link his findings about the infringing transactions to evidence of a tendency. However, the inferences that his Honour drew, that the Global and Impact respondents "sanctioned, approved or countenanced the infringements of copyright carried out by the Tonita respondents", did not appear to have been based upon conduct related directly to the particularised infringing transactions. Once that much is accepted … it must also be accepted that it was open to the Full Court to characterise his Honour's reasoning as based upon discernment of a tendency on the part of the respondents to act in a particular way which involved dealing with articles, the making of which infringed copyright of the applicants.

The classic illustration of circumstantial evidence amounting to disproof of accident and of coincidence is the 19th century case of *Makin v Attorney-General (NSW)*, introduced in Chapter 10.[6] In the *Makin* case there was no finding that John and Sarah Makin had killed the babies left in their care (or the babies whose bodies were found buried in back gardens). The sheer number of bodies, however, was compelling evidence disproving that the death they were charged with had occurred coincidentally. The logical challenge in establishing a *tendency to act* based on *disputed* conduct compared to acts proved by the presence of a criminal conviction was identified by Murphy J in the common law case of *Perry*[7] and described as the danger of the tribunal of fact applying circular reasoning[8] – that is, accepting disputed allegations on the basis of the presence of other disputed allegations. Mrs Perry had been charged with attempting to murder her husband (Perry). In support, evidence was led seeking to link her to the deaths of her ex-husband (Haag), her brother (Montgomerie) and a former de facto partner (Duncan).

> *Circular reasoning*. There is a danger of admitting and using evidence of collateral circumstances (the death of Haag, or of Montgomerie, or the sickness of Duncan) which not only standing alone, but taken together with the other evidence (including any which independently tends to establish the central issue), is insufficient to exclude a rational explanation of that circumstance consistent with the accused's innocence, and then using

3 That is, not the common law's concerns in relation to similar fact evidence (namely, its adverse *impact*) which under the *UEA* is only addressed in s 101, discussed later in this chapter.

4 [2013] HCA 21; 297 ALR 406.

5 Ibid [16].

6 [1894] AC 57. See also A Cossins, *The Baby-Farmers* (Allen & Unwin, 2013); A Palmer, 'Digging up the dirt on *Makin*' [1993] *Law Institute Journal* 1171.

7 [1982] HCA 75; 150 CLR 580.

8 See, eg, *AE* [2008] NSWCCA 52; *Ibrahim v Pham* [2007] NSWCA 215.

> the supposed guilt in relation to that circumstance as proof of others and the central issue. For example, on the prosecution's theory the supposed poisoning of Duncan depended on acceptance that Haag, Montgomerie and Perry were poisoned by the applicant, but the proof of these poisonings depended on the acceptance that she poisoned Duncan. ... [S]ome practical working rules can be adopted for a criminal case like the present. Evidence of any circumstances such as any of the alleged poisonings of Duncan, Haag or Montgomerie should be discarded when it appears on consideration of the whole of the evidence that there is reasonable doubt about the accused's culpability in relation to that circumstance. Otherwise the stage is being set for a miscarriage of justice.[9]

A Propensity to Act: Profiling and Recidivism

Crime statistics may show that certain crimes have high rates of recidivism.[10] They may allow us to link personal characteristics to the likelihood of offending (like men are more likely to sexually offend than women); however, individual differences are shaped both by intrinsic qualities and also by environment. In other words, habitual behaviour or an inclination to act, speak or think in a particular way arises in many contexts and is the product of many variables.[11] In terms of the danger of inferential error, courts must determine what can (and what should) be drawn from evidence of a person's previous actions? As we saw in relation to *Perry*'s case, there is also the additional twist of whether the prior misconduct is proven or merely alleged. Despite the fact that we are all familiar with the notion of a tendency to describe habitual behaviour, its application in criminal trials is remarkably complex.

Broadly speaking, psychologists seem to agree that the frequency of behaviour in the past can be predictive of subsequent behaviour[12] – but not always. A person might have climbed the same mountain a number of times without this repetition creating a routine or a habit – in other words, a tendency. Such an activity may be indicative of capacity, even expertise. It might show a person's attitude to physical exercise, but it is not necessarily probative of a tendency to act in a particular way, or to have a particular state of mind. As we saw in Chapter 10, unsophisticated psychological profiling relies on simplistic notions to predict likely culpability through drawing inferences about a person's tendency to act based on their age, their demographics and/or their past conduct. As Chifflet has observed:

> Traditional approaches to profiling assume that inferences can be made about the characteristics of an offender based on the behaviour, or crime scene actions, exhibited during the commission of the crime. Typologies or classification systems that associate particular crime scene behaviours with particular offender characteristics have flourished in the

---

9 [1982] HCA 75; 150 CLR 580, 594-5 (Murphy J).

10 Note also that some commentators suggest evidence of past criminality is sufficiently probative to be admissible. See, for example, 'a recent previous conviction for a particular offence is considerably more likely than a person without a previous conviction to commit such an offence: previous convictions therefore have considerable probative value as proof of guilt' (M Redmayne, *Character in the Criminal Trial* (Oxford University Press, 2015), 13 (606)) and '[p]rior conviction evidence is probative, not because it is highly probable that someone with a prior conviction is likely to reoffend, but because such a person is far more likely to commit an offence than someone without a prior conviction' (David Hamer, Submission to the Royal Commission into Institutional Responses to Child Sexual Abuse (RCIRCSA), *Consultation paper: Criminal justice* (2016), 6), both quoted from RCIRCSA, *Criminal Justice Final Report*, 606).

11 I Ajzen, 'Residual Effects of Past on Later Behavior: Habituation and Reasoned Action Perspectives' (2002) 6 *Personality and Social Psychology Review* 107, 119.

12 Ibid 108.

> profiling literature. Theoretically, this translates into three fundamental assumptions: (1) offenders exhibiting similar criminal behaviour will possess similar characteristics (homology assumption); (2) offenders behave in a generally consistent manner each time they offend (behavioural consistency) and (3) the manner in which a particular offender behaves is distinguishable from that of another offender (behavioural differentiation). These theories are very much intertwined.[13]

Chifflet concludes that profiling risks engaging in a tautology trap, namely, relying on inferring personality traits from behaviour (for example, assuming that a crime scene that reveals violence) and then drawing a conclusion that the offender is aggressive, in other word employing circular reasoning.[14] Some of the complexity in predicting behaviour through drawing inferences based on their past reoffending is revealed in feminist research,[15] including longitudinal studies, that highlight particular life circumstances as notably important to women's likelihood of reoffending. These show a constellation of reasons why women and girls offend and reoffend. They suggest that circumstantial changes in women's lives – motherhood or being a carer, or being victimised by trauma, sexual abuse and prostitution – typically explain offending. Employment, education and factors related to mental health and economic independence correlate with reduced and terminated offending[16] but circumstances such as marriage, physical and mental health and alcohol or drug use, apply to offending by both women and men, but in different ways. Some of the complexity is illustrated by

> [r]esearch [that] shows a substantial number of women commence offending in adulthood, even after the age of 45, and that women, unlike men, commit a higher proportion of property offences as they grow older. Gender-based studies also identify connections across offending, victimisation, carer roles and the sequencing of changed circumstances in women's lives (such as, for example, abuse leading to homelessness and then to prostitution) (Block et al, 2010: 97).[17]

Other studies also show that patterns of offending are complex. Kocsis's[18] study of criminal profiling, consistently with similar evaluations, failed to reveal any support for the core profiling assumption that offenders who commit crimes in a similar manner share similar background characteristics, beyond 'small pockets of psychologically meaningful consistency'. Similarly, Almond et al's study of 474 British police investigations of stranger rape leading to convictions explored links between the way the rapes were committed and the offenders' criminal history.

---

13 P Chifflet, 'Questioning the validity of criminal profiling: An evidence-based approach' (2015) 48 *Australian & New Zealand Journal of Criminology* 238, 240 (citations omitted).

14 Ibid 242-3 (citations omitted). '[T]he debate in psychology regarding the impact of situational variables and enduring character traits is considered by many central to appreciating the psychological research exploring character evidence and its relevance to determinations of guilt. This research indicates that situational variables are highly significant in predicting behaviour, especially in a manner relevant to the trial context': J Hunter, 'Book Review: *Character Evidence in the Criminal Trial*' (2016) *International Journal of Evidence & Proof* 162, 167-8, citing GL Wells, 'Murder, extramarital affairs, and the issue of probative value' (2003) 27(6) *Law and Human Behavior* 623; MJ Saks and WC Thompson, 'Assessing evidence: Proving facts' in D Carson and R Bull (eds), *Handbook of Psychology in Legal Contexts* (Wiley, 2nd ed, 2003).

15 CR Block, AAJ Blokland, C van der Werff et al, 'Long-term patterns of offending in women' (2010) 5 *Feminist Criminology* 73; E Rodermond, C Kruttschnitt, A Slotboom et al, 'Female desistance: A review of the literature' (2016) 13 *European Journal of Criminology* 3.

16 Rodermond, Kruttschnitt, Slotboom et al, ibid.

17 Hunter, 'Book Review', above n 14, 168-9 (some references omitted) citing Block, Blokland, van der Werff et al, above n 15; Rodermond, Kruttschnitt, Slotboom et al, above n 15.

18 RN Kocsis, 'The Name of the Rose and Criminal Profiling: The Benefits of ViCAP and ViCLAS' (2015) 15 *Journal of Forensic Psychology Practice* 58, 63.

It also found that in over 80% of the cases the solved rape was a one-off sexual assault, and while over 70% of offenders had a criminal record, rather than sexual offences, they were most commonly theft or burglary. Similarly, the shocking revelations of repetition of sexual violence upon children in various institutional settings[19] showed places that ostensibly care for children, such as children's homes, missions or reformatories, schools and at churches or seminaries, were locations for sexual abuse. Of the vast majority of survivors of child sexual abuse who gave information to the Royal Commission on Institutional Responses to Child Sexual Assault (RCIRCSA), almost one third reported that their abusers were from the church, one fifth reported teachers and lesser proportions reported residential care workers or foster carers.[20] These statistics do not enable us to conclude an individual's criminality as a child abuser through their affiliation or employment by a church or a school. This is not to say these revelations tell us nothing. The findings importantly enable jurors, police and prosecutors to appreciate that it is not impossible (or perhaps even improbable) for a person occupying a caring role to be a child abuser. In response to the RCIRCSA findings, in mid-2020 New South Wales legislated specific admissibility rules for tendency evidence adduced in proceedings involving child sexual offences proceeding in which the commission by the defendant of an act that constitutes, or may constitute, a child sexual offence[21] is a fact in issue. The need for special rules was recommended by RCIRCSA, and is implemented in *UEA* (NSW), s 97A. This provision presumes that tendency evidence about a defendant will have significant probative value, as required by s 97, in criminal proceedings in which the commission by the defendant of an act that constitutes, or may constitute, a child sexual offence is a fact in issue where (pursuant to s 97A(2)):

- it is 'tendency evidence about the sexual interest the defendant has or had in children (even if the defendant has not acted on the interest)'; and
- it is 'tendency evidence about the defendant acting on a sexual interest the defendant has or had in children'.

This presumption applies irrespective of whether the sexual interest or sexual actions relate to the complainant, or to another child or children. This presumption is rebuttable[22] if there are sufficient grounds[23] to establish that rebuttal. However, unless there are exceptional circumstances relating to these matters (individually, or in combination), a court must not consider *differences* between:[24]

- the '*tendency sexual interest or act'* and the sexual interest or act alleged in the proceeding';

19 See, eg, <https://www.childabuseroyalcommission.gov.au/sites/default/files/final_information_update.pdf>.

20 With lesser percentages reporting abuse by custodial staff, a housemaster, a medical practitioner or nurse, a volunteer, a youth group leader and a sporting coach: RCIRCSA, *Final Report, Preface and Executive Summary*, <https://www.childabuseroyalcommission.gov.au/sites/default/files/final_report_-_preface_and_executive_summary.pdf>, 11.

21 This term is broadly defined in s 97A(6). A child means a person under 18 years of age: sub-s (6).

22 *UEA* (NSW), s 97A(4).

23 See *Brookman* [2021] NSWDC 110: Sufficient grounds 'should be considered in light of the objective of this reform to facilitate greater admissibility of tendency evidence and, specifically, the intent of the proposed section 97A to facilitate greater admission of tendency evidence in child sexual offences' (New South Wales Legislative Assembly, *Parliamentary Debates* (*Hansard*), 25 February 2020, Attorney General, Second Reading Speech), quoted by Abadee DCJ at [23].

24 *UEA* (NSW), s 97A(5)(a)-(d).

- *the circumstances in which the tendency sexual interest or act occurred* and the circumstances of the alleged sexual interest or act;
- *the personal characteristics* (for example, age, sex, gender) of the subject of the tendency sexual interest or act and the subject of the alleged sexual interest or act; or
- *the relationship between the defendant and the subject* of the tendency sexual interest or act and that of the subject of the alleged sexual interest or act.

Nor can the court, except if there are exceptional circumstances relating to these matters (individually, or in combination), consider:

- *the time* between the occurrence of the tendency sexual interest or act and that of the alleged sexual interest or act;
- the presence or otherwise of *distinctive or unusual features* in the tendency sexual interest or act compared with that of the alleged sexual interest or act; or
- the *level of generality of the tendency* to which the tendency evidence relates.[25]

The operation of the NSW amendments passed in 2020 (including the 2020 revisions to s 101, discussed below) will be subject to ministerial review in 2022. This includes review of 'the circumstances in which tendency evidence or coincidence evidence about a defendant is admissible in proceedings for sexual offences and *whether those circumstances should be broadened*'.[26] The terms of this review, like the terms of the presumption in s 97A, send an explicit legislative message that the NSW parliament has not focused on the traditional concerns in this sensitive area of evidence law, namely, on shoring up the accused's protections from the danger of unfair prejudice. Instead, the accused's protections are potentially compromised to facilitate sexual assault complainants being able to testify in a single trial, rather than in multiple trials, where their accusations against the accused give rise to multiple counts.[27] Further, it is arguable that on many occasions this package of legislative changes will inevitably add undesirable complexity to trial judges' jury directions. Where s 97A applies, this will be in trials that are typically prone to appellate review. This may (ironically) mean that convictions are liable to be quashed because of the inadequacy of judicial directions – potentially leading to retrials.[28]

The Tendency and Coincidence Rules in Overview

Before we examine case law and the key elements of Part 3.6 of the *UEA*, it is important to appreciate that the Part does not address all evidence relied on for tendency reasoning.

---

25 *UEA* (NSW), s 97A(5)(e)-(g).

26 *UEA* (NSW), Sch 2, cl 30, as inserted by *Evidence Amendment (Tendency and Coincidence) Act 2020* (NSW) (emphasis added).

27 These changes to the tendency and coincidence rules are partnered by a significant restriction on courts ordering offences be heard in separate trials where the prosecution has given notice that it intends to rely on tendency or coincidence evidence that relates to two or more offences: *Criminal Procedure Act 1986* (NSW) (*CPA* NSW), s 29A. In these circumstances, subject to *CPA* (NSW), s 21, the court must hear and determine counts against the same person where the offences are charged in the same indictment or where they are listed for hearing on the same day, and at the same place.

28 Regarding joinder of charges, and the challenge of these directions to juries, see Chapter 2, pp 35-37.

- Part 3.6 does not apply if the evidence is relevant *only* to the credibility of a person (or admissible solely for a credibility purpose). Such evidence will be credibility evidence within the terms of s 101A(a), and thus be regulated through the credibility rule (s 102) and its exceptions.
- Part 3.6 does also not apply 'to evidence of ... the character, reputation or conduct of a person, or ... a tendency that a person has or had ... *if that character, reputation, conduct or tendency is a fact in issue*'. This is because such evidence is not being adduced for the purpose of *proving* a fact in issue – the tendency, character, reputation etc *is* the fact in issue. The inferential reasoning discussed in *Aristocrat Technologies Australia Pty Ltd v Global Gaming Supplies Pty Ltd*[29] and addressed in Part 3.6 is absent.
- Note also that *UEA*, s 95, plays an important role in Part 3.6. It requires that a judge direct the jury as to how the evidence may be used where evidence falls outside ss 97 and 98 but is otherwise admissible because it is adduced for a purpose that does not rely on tendency or coincidence reasoning (and there is a danger jurors may engage in impermissible reasoning). This is particularly relevant to the topics discussed last in this chapter: relationship, context or transaction evidence.[30] Such evidence may exhibit the qualities of tendency or coincidence evidence, but they are forms of evidence considered to be outside Part 3.6. The fact that evidence might quack and walk like tendency or coincidence evidence but is in fact treated as different from these evidentiary ducks (typically because the evidence is adduced for a different purpose) requires that parties and courts possess a sharp appreciation of the relevance and purpose of evidence. Such evidence attracts *UEA*, ss 55, 95 and 135, and, if it is prosecution evidence, s 137.

In summary, the tendency rule and the coincidence rule both permit the admission of tendency and coincidence evidence adduced for the purposes expressed in s 97 ('to prove that a person has or had a tendency') and s 98 ('to prove that a person did a particular act or had a particular state of mind on the basis that ... it is improbable that the events occurred coincidentally') if:

- the evidence possesses significant probative value[31] ('by itself or having regard to other evidence adduced or to be adduced by the party seeking to adduce the evidence');[32] and
- a notice is given (or waived);[33] and

29 [2013] HCA 21; 297 ALR 406.

30 Where evidence is adduced to prove a particular relationship or context or is evidence of a series of connected events or transactions, even if such evidence is relevant for a tendency or lack of coincidence purpose, if it is not adduced for those purposes Part 3.6 does not apply.

31 A test that is higher than mere relevance (s 55) but less than the standard set by s 103 for cross-examining on credibility evidence: *Lockyer* (1996) 89 A Crim R 457, 459.

32 Unless the evidence is adduced to explain or contradict tendency evidence adduced by another party. Note, as discussed below, from July 2020 tendency evidence about the sexual interest the defendant has or had in children or tendency evidence about the defendant acting on a sexual interest the defendant has or had in children will have a rebuttable presumption of possessing significant probative value for the purposes of ss 97(1)(b) and 101(2).

33 Sections 99 and 100 (and the *Evidence Regulations*) address notice requirements, and the power of the court to dispense with the notice requirements.

- it 'is adduced by the prosecution' and 'the probative value of the evidence outweighs the danger of prejudicial effect it may have on the defendant' (s 101(2));[34] or
- it is within either s 110 or 112 (permitting in certain circumstances admission of both coincidence and tendency evidence), or within s 111 (which in limited circumstances permits admission of tendency evidence).

Context and trends

At common law, tendency and coincidence evidence is typically referred to as propensity, disposition or improbability evidence and collectively as similar fact evidence. Australian appellate court treatment of the dangers of tendency and coincidence evidence, regulated through the *UEA*, paints a less robust protective picture than its common law counterpart and, as a result of the findings of the RCIRCSA prosecution evidence about a defendant, the rules of admissibility for tendency evidence in child sexual assault proceedings have been loosened,[35] as have the requirements for admitting all prosecution tendency and coincidence evidence about a defendant.[36] This trend of reduced legal protections for the accused is not necessarily a phenomenon isolated to Part 3.6 of the *UEA*. The Victorian Court of Appeal in the 2014 case of *Velkoski*[37] pegs the trend to the late 20th century, noting it occurred in Victoria as well as in the jurisdictions that adopted the *UEA* early. The court's conclusions suggest that, if one compares Australian criminal trials from the past century with their contemporary equivalents, the prosecution case is now more likely to include evidence revealing the accused's character (meaning that the trial judge is likely to be obliged to give more extensive and more complex judicial directions to jurors regarding how they can and/or cannot apply bad character evidence in their deliberations). The *Velkoski*[38] court also suggests that a further modern trend is complex, confused and inconsistent application of the case law on the *UEA* tendency and coincidence provisions. The court locates some of its criticism at the feet of NSW appellate decisions. The judges compare the 80 pages of closely typed, heavily footnoted annotated text in Odgers's *Uniform Evidence Law in Victoria*[39] to the handful of pages needed for an early edition of *Cross on Evidence*[40] to describe a century of similar fact doctrine. The reason for the escalation in detailed coverage, they suggest, may be due to the law predating the status quo setting an 'extraordinarily high threshold for admissibility applicable at common law', making admissibility exceptional and, consequently, in the rare instances where similar evidence was before the jury its 'probative value was self-evident'. In the past, with fewer trials on multiple counts, and therefore fewer cross-admissibility issues, there was only

34 Applicable unless the evidence is used to explain or contradict tendency or coincidence evidence adduced by the defendant.

35 See *Evidence Amendment (Tendency and Coincidence) Act 2020* (NSW).

36 See the amendments to s 101(2) by the *Evidence Amendment (Tendency and Coincidence) Act 2020* (NSW).

37 [2014] VSCA 121, [32] (Redlich, Weinberg and Coghlan JJA). Before the *Evidence Act 2008* (Vic), there was also the *Crimes Act 1958* (Vic), s 398A(2) and (3). See the commentary in *Best* [1998] 4 VR 603, 607 regarding the impact of these provisions and their relationship to the House of Lords' decision in *DPP v P* [1991] 2 AC 447.

38 [2014] VSCA 121, [26]-[27].

39 S Odgers, *Uniform Evidence Law in Victoria* (Lawbook, 2nd ed, 2013), 457-538.

40 JA Gobbo (ed), *Cross on Evidence* (Butterworths, Australian ed, 1970).

rarely the need for direction to the jury on such evidence. As well as making the law simpler, the high benchmark for admissibility of evidence also tended to produce more acquittals. It is, however, clear that common law restrictions do not apply under the *UEA*.[41]

These observations bear reflection in light of the observations of English criminal law theorist Nicola Lacey,[42] regarding a similar trend in England. The result is that now the law enables juries to receive more adverse character evidence about an accused than in the past and effectively, therefore, allows jurors to more readily judge an accused on their character. This, Lacey argues, is not an isolated shift. There is, compared to the past, widespread reliance on strict liability offences and offences that reverse burdens of proof, as well as a proliferation of negotiated pleas with discounted sentences. In 2011 Lacey described the current English law existing under the *Criminal Justice Act 2003* as sitting within a broader movement to penal populism. On Lacey's thesis, the changes noted by the *Velkoski* court might be seen not just as changes within the law of evidence, but as elements of a broad pro-prosecution shift in Parliament's approach to criminal justice law reform. Lacey suggests an historical perspective is informative in understanding the socio-political dynamic. She notes the pivotal role of an accused's character in judging guilt from medieval times[43] to pre-industrialisation when it was the norm for jurors to assess an accused's character because they possessed local knowledge of 'insiders'. Consequently, the approach rationally responded to prevailing small-town social circumstances. However, the growth of an industrialised society meant the centrality in criminal trials of a person's character lost traction. Criminal justice governance shifted to accommodate a society where anonymity was the rule, not the exception. The modern trial format also evolved for other reasons, such as the growth of a robust defence bar where it became the norm to demand of the prosecution that it prove guilt rather than just allowing a court to rely on an accused's lack of social connection. Capacity-based subjective principles of responsibility (*mens rea*)[44] steadily took firm root in criminal courts. It became exceptional for character evidence to be part of the prosecution case. Lacey posits that 'just as the late 19th century classifications reflected prevailing anxieties and contemporary scientific theories and technologies, so today's categories – the anti-social youth, the sex offender, the migrant and, above all, the terrorist – are appropriate symbols of "otherness" relative to contemporary anxieties and technologies'.[45] Undoubtedly the trends described by Professor Lacey and the *Velkoski* court are real, but a note of caution should be sounded. The evidentiary picture is not without complexity, and it is certainly clear that this complexity has not been diminished by the run of High

---

41 *UEA*, s 94(4).

42 N Lacey, 'The Resurgence of Character: Criminal Responsibility in the Context of Criminalisation' in A Duff and S Green (eds), *Philosophical Foundations of Criminal Law* (Oxford University Press, 2011), 151-78, 158.

43 For example, using 'oath-takers' to support one's plea, see J Hunter and K Cronin, *Evidence, Advocacy and Ethical Practice: A Criminal Trial Commentary* (Butterworths, 1995), ch 1. Lacey also cites G Harriss, *Shaping the Nation: England 1360-1461* (Clarendon Press, 2005), 244; N Lacey, C Wells and D Meure, *Reconstructing Criminal Law* (1st ed, 1990), ch 2.1. Lacey uses the description of 14th century English law where local parishes excluded '"sturdy beggars" and vagabonds, refusing them alms and requiring them to return to their own villages': Lacey, above n 42, 158. See also D Hay in D Hay, P Linebaugh and EP Thompson (eds), *Albion's Fatal Tree: Crime and Society in Eighteenth-century England* (Allen Lane, 1975), 42-4 (granting pardons).

44 Lacey, above n 42, 164.

45 Ibid 169.

Court decisions on the topic. Since 2016 there have been four highly significant decisions from that court, namely the cases of *IMM* (2016),[46] *Hughes* (2017),[47] *McPhillamy*[48] and *Bauer*[49] (both 2018). The intense examination of cases in this area by the High Court is not new. Tendency and disposition evidence has been the subject of over 40 appeals to the High Court, with the highly influential 1894 Privy Council appeal from New South Wales, *Makin v Attorney-General (NSW)*, predating the creation of the court.

The *UEA* approach to tendency and coincidence evidence

Unlike the common law similar fact doctrine's pre-eminent concern with the danger of unfair prejudice, the *UEA* regulates *all*[50] circumstantial evidence adduced for the purpose of proving a tendency to act or think in a particular way or to prove the improbability of innocence, irrespective of whether the evidence is adduced in a civil[51] or criminal case, or by the defence or by the prosecution. Thus, Part 3.6 applies even to evidence, such as defence tendency evidence that raises no concerns regarding unfair prejudice. Close attention to statutory terminology is a must.

> ***coincidence evidence*** means evidence of a kind referred to in section 98(1) that a party seeks to have adduced for the *purpose* referred to in that subsection.
>
> ***coincidence rule*** means section 98(1).
>
> ***probative value*** of evidence means the extent to which the evidence could rationally affect the assessment of the probability of the existence of a fact in issue.
>
> ***tendency evidence*** means evidence of a kind referred to in section 97(1) that a party seeks to have adduced for the *purpose* referred to in that subsection.
>
> ***tendency rule*** means section 97(1).[52]
>
> **95. Use of evidence for other purposes**
>
> (1) Evidence that under this Part is not admissible to prove a particular matter must not be used to prove that matter even if it is relevant for another *purpose*.
>
> (2) Evidence that under this Part cannot be used against a party to prove a particular matter must not be used against the party to prove that matter even if it is relevant for another *purpose*. (emphasis added)
>
> **97. The tendency rule**[53]
>
> (1) Evidence of the *character, reputation or conduct of a person*, or a tendency that a person has or had, is not admissible to prove that a person has or had a tendency (whether because of the person's character or otherwise) to act[54] in a particular way, or to have a particular state of mind unless:

---

46 [2016] HCA 14; 257 CLR 300.

47 [2017] HCA 20; 263 CLR 338.

48 [2018] HCA 52; 361 ALR 13.

49 [2018] HCA 40; 266 CLR 56.

50 That is, putting to one side bail or sentencing proceedings, credibility evidence, and evidence where character is the fact in issue: *UEA*, s 94(1).

51 See, eg, *Jacara Pty Ltd v Perpetual Trustees WA Ltd* [2000] FCA 1886; 106 FCR 51; *Australian Competition and Consumer Commission v ACN 117 372 915 Pty Limited (in liq) (formerly Advanced Medical Institute Pty Limited)* [2015] FCA 368.

52 *UEA*, Dictionary (except for Tasmania, for which see *Evidence Act 2001*, s 3).

53 See also sub-s (2).

54 Note that under *UEA*, s 96, 'A reference in this Part to doing an act includes a reference to failing to do that act'.

(a) the party seeking to adduce the evidence gave reasonable notice in writing to each other party of the party's intention to adduce the evidence, and

(b) the court thinks that the evidence will, either by itself or having regard to other evidence adduced or to be adduced by the party seeking to adduce the evidence, have significant *probative value*. (emphasis added)

98. The coincidence rule[55]

(1) *Evidence that 2 or more events* occurred is not admissible to prove that a person did a particular act or had a particular state of mind on the basis that, having regard to any similarities in the events or the circumstances in which they occurred, or any similarities in both the events and the circumstances in which they occurred, it is improbable that the events occurred coincidentally unless:

(a) the party seeking to adduce the evidence gave reasonable notice in writing to each other party of the party's intention to adduce the evidence, and

(b) the court thinks that the evidence will, either by itself or having regard to other evidence adduced or to be adduced by the party seeking to adduce the evidence, have significant probative value. (emphasis added)

(1A) To avoid doubt, subsection (1) includes the use of evidence from 2 or more witnesses claiming they are victims of offences committed by a person who is a defendant in a criminal proceeding to prove, on the basis of similarities in the claimed acts or the circumstances in which they occurred, that the defendant did an act in issue in the proceeding.[56]

Finally, as discussed later in this chapter, as well as satisfying ss 97, 97A and/or 98, tendency and coincidence evidence about a defendant adduced by the prosecution 'cannot be used against the defendant unless the probative value of the evidence outweighs the danger of unfair prejudice to the defendant': *UEA*, s 101(2).[57] As a procedural matter, it should be noted that 'reasonable notice' in ss 97(1)(a) and 98(1)(a) refers to giving notice under s 99 – that is, there must be a formal tendency or coincidence notice. The importance of this notice cannot be understated. In *Hughes*, Gageler J described its role:

> The tendency notice provides the court, at the critical time of assessing the admissibility of tendency evidence, with a statement of the particular tendency which the party seeking to adduce the tendency evidence seeks to prove by it. The importance of explicitly identifying in the notice the particular tendency that is asserted, as Howie AJ put it in *Bryant v R*, 'should be obvious: how else is the court going to be able to make a rational decision about the probative value of the evidence'. By identifying the particular tendency that the evidence is asserted to prove, the notice allows the court to evaluate the strength of the connection between the evidence and the tendency and the strength of the connection between the tendency and the fact in issue.[58]

Trial judges engage in a predictive evaluation: '[I]t is a prediction of the potential value of the evidence when the mosaic of evidence is complete'.[59] The predictive

55 See also sub-s (2) and the statutory notes to the provision.

56 *Evidence Amendment (Tendency and Coincidence) Act 2020* (NSW).

57 Subject to *UEA*, s 101(3) and (4). This replaces the standard before July 2020 that 'the probative value of the evidence substantially outweighs any prejudicial effect it may have on the defendant'.

58 [2017] HCA 20; 263 CLR 338, [105] (Gageler J, dissenting on the appeal outcome), citing *Bryant* [2011] NSWCCA 26, [50] (Howie AJ). See also *Gardiner* [2006] NSWCCA 190; 162 A Crim R 233, [128]-[131].

59 *Burton* [2013] NSWCCA 335, [161] (Simpson J, referring to her observations in *Zhang* [2005] NSWCCA 437; 158 A Crim R 504). And see the discussion in *DSJ and NS* [2012] NSWCCA 9; 84 NSWLR 758, [61]-[76] (Whealy J).

element is in evaluating the *capacity* of the evidence. It is not a prediction of what the jury will make of that item of evidence on completion of the evidence in the trial.[60] Hence the substance and detail of the evidence provided through the notice seeks to address the practical challenges of assessing the capacity of the evidence that witnesses are expected to give. Kiefel CJ, Bell, Keane and Edelman JJ in *Hughes* referred to the consequences of this challenging process for establishing whether 'the court thinks' the evidence possesses 'significant probative value':

> In this case, the evidence given by the witnesses did not differ materially from their anticipated evidence. But in cases where the admissibility of tendency evidence is borderline, there may be risks if the actual evidence does not accord with the evidence as anticipated. Again, this could have consequences for any conviction. …In any event, the open-textured, evaluative task remains one for the court to undertake by application of the same well-known principles of logic and human experience as are used in an assessment of whether evidence is relevant.[61]

Noting that the trial judge's 'open-textured evaluative task' means that it is inevitable that reasonable minds may differ such that appeal courts may ultimately draw a different conclusion to the trial judge's predictive evaluation, Kiefel CJ, Bell, Keane and Edelman JJ reflected that to avoid the risk of a quashed conviction it would be wise for the prosecution to assess conservatively any borderline evidence it might seek to rely on.[62]

The requirements for these notices are established by regulations. For example, in New South Wales, *Evidence Regulation 2020* (NSW), cl 5(2),[63] provides:

> (2) A notice of tendency evidence must state –
> (a) the substance of the evidence to which the notice relates, and
> (b) if that evidence consists of, or includes, evidence of the conduct of a person, particulars of –
> (i) the date, time, place and circumstances at or in which the conduct occurred, and
> (ii) the name of each person who saw, heard or otherwise perceived the conduct, and
> (iii) in a civil proceeding – the address of each person so named, so far as they are known to the notifying party.

Clause 6(2) provides:

> (2) A notice of coincidence evidence must state –
> (a) the substance of the evidence of the occurrence of 2 or more events that the party giving the notice intends to adduce, and
> (b) particulars of –
> (i) the date, time, place and circumstances at or in which each of those events occurred, and
> (ii) the name of each person who saw, heard or otherwise perceived each of those events, and
> (iii) in a civil proceeding – the address of each person so named, so far as they are known to the notifying party.[64]

60 *Zhang* [2005] NSWCCA 437; 158 A Crim R 504; *Burton* [2013] NSWCCA 335, [161] (Simpson J).
61 *Hughes* [2017] HCA 20; 263 CLR 338, [42].
62 Citing *DKA v Western Australia* [2017] WASCA 44, [69].
63 The Commonwealth, Tasmanian, Victorian, ACT regulations are cast in similar terms.
64 Under both notices '[o]n the application of a party in a criminal proceeding, the court may make an order directing a notifying party to disclose the address of any person named by that party

Specificity of allegations

Clauses 5(2)(b) and 6(2)(b) underscore the importance of specificity to meet the higher probative value required than mere relevance. As Kiefel CJ, Bell, Keane and Edelman JJ noted in *Hughes*, '[a] tendency expressed at a high level of generality might mean that all the tendency evidence provides significant support for that tendency. But it will also mean that the tendency cannot establish anything more than relevance. In contrast, a tendency expressed at a level of particularity will be more likely to be significant'.[65] In addition to particularising the events that support the claimed tendency or coincidence, as Kiefel CJ, Bell, Keane and Edelman JJ observed of the arguments in *Hughes*,[66] the articulation of the tendency that the evidence seeks to support is also critical. In *Hughes* the relevant evidence was (at [3])

> The evidence of each complainant and a number of other witnesses was to be adduced in the trial of each count to prove tendencies identified as "having a sexual interest in female children under 16 years of age" and using "his social and familial relationships … to obtain access to female children under 16 years of age so that he could engage in sexual activities with them". The notice particularised differing forms of sexual conduct with underage girls. One particular of that conduct was its occurrence within the vicinity of another adult.

The alleged tendency was (at [56])

> to engage in sexually predatory conduct with underage girls as and when an opportunity presented itself in order to obtain fleeting gratification, notwithstanding the high risk of detection.

The tendency was not, as was argued, to engage in specific acts of indecency to the exclusion of other acts of indecency. The case of *McPhillamy*, extracted below,[67] illustrates prosecution tendency evidence that was expressed at such a high level of generality as to fail the requirements of s 97(1)(b).

Notice can also be dispensed with under s 100. This section confers on courts the power to 'direct' that s 97(1)(a) or 98(1)(a) does not apply,[68] raising the application of s 192. It is crucial that the criteria in s 192(2) be applied. Notably, '[w]hen the power to dispense is engaged, the task of the Court is to weigh the interests of justice, in the circumstances of the particular case, taking account of the purposes for the notice requirement, other ways in which those purposes might be achieved, and any reason for dispensing with the requirement notwithstanding that those purposes might not be achieved'.[69] These include that a direction to hear all counts in a single trial may substantially shorten the totality of proceedings and the probative value of the evidence may be an important consideration. However, there are the countervailing concerns of the extent to which a direction to dispense with notice would be unfair to the accused (in terms of forensic disadvantage in not being on notice, and also with respect to the danger of unfair prejudice

---

in a notice of coincidence evidence who saw, heard or otherwise perceived conduct or events referred to in the notice', and the direction may be given on such terms as the court thinks fit.

65 *Hughes* [2017] HCA 20; 263 CLR 338, [64].

66 Ibid [56].

67 At pp 466-468.

68 There is some inelegant drafting in s 100(1) and (2). It seems clear that the dispensing power in s 100 applies only to the notice requirement in s 97 and not the inapplicability of the tendency rule: *AC* [2018] NSWCCA 130, [22] (Meagher JA, Bellew and Fagan JJ).

69 *AC* [2018] NSWCCA 130, [26].

that cannot be adequately overcome by judicial directions). Section 192 does not explicitly include (or exclude) consideration of the 'persistent non-compliance' of the prosecution, without good excuse to provide tendency notices in a timely manner.[70] In this respect consider the sentiments expressed by Howie J in 2004 in *Harker*[71] of

> another instance of this Court being called upon to intervene at the behest of the Crown at the eleventh hour with a trial about to commence or underway in circumstances where the Crown has to a very large part been the author of the problem that it seeks to redress. It is unfair to the trial judge, the accused and other litigants before this Court that the Crown should appeal against a ruling in circumstances of urgency because of its own failure to properly prepare the matter for trial well before the hearing date.

Tendency Evidence

What is tendency evidence?

Tendency evidence is:

> a means of proving, *by a process of deduction*, that a person acted in a particular way, or had a particular state of mind, on a relevant occasion, when there is no, or inadequate, direct evidence of that conduct or that state of mind on that occasion.[72]

In other words, tendency evidence, which is intrinsically circumstantial evidence (and so to be viewed holistically),[73] is 'a building block or stepping stone to provide the foundation for an inference that, on an occasion relevant to the proceedings, a person behaved in a particular way or had a particular state of mind'.[74]

In other words, the fact that a person said or did something on one (or more) occasions, typically pre-dating the event in question, may be significantly relevant to proving that that person said or did something on the occasion in question (or on a related occasion). This person might be an accused, a victim of crime or someone else connected with the crime, or a participant in a civil action.

State of mind

Section 97(1) sets admissibility hurdles for evidence

> of the character, reputation or conduct of a person, or a tendency that a person has or had, … to prove that a person has or had a tendency … to act in a particular way, or to have a particular state of mind.

The essence of tendency evidence is that it relies on actions or words from one occasion to prove the same or relevantly linked actions or words on another occasion. A person's state of mind is established by evidence of what a person says or

---

70 Ibid [22]. See also *Stanoevski* [2001] HCA 4; 202 CLR 115.

71 [2004] NSWCCA 427, [62].

72 *Elomar* [2014] NSWCCA 303, [360] (Bathurst CJ, Hoeben CJ at CL, Simpson J) (emphasis added).

73 *Vagg* [2020] NSWCCA 134, [92].

74 *DAO* [2011] NSWCCA 63, [179] (Simpson J), citing *Gardiner* [2006] NSWCCA 190; 162 A Crim R 233; *Cittadini* [2008] NSWCCA 256; 189 A Crim R 492. This arose as an appeal under *Criminal Appeal Act 1912* (NSW), s 5F, from the trial judge's refusal to order separate trials relating to counts involving three complainants – that is, whether counts in the indictment should be 'severed'. Three other complaints were ordered to be the subject of separate trials. Ultimately, the court dismissed the appeal on the basis that s 5F involves 'a high degree of restraint'.

by their conduct. From that evidence '[t]he trier of fact reasons from satisfaction that a person has a tendency to have a particular state of mind, or to act in a particular way, to the likelihood that the person had the particular state of mind, or acted in the particular way, on the occasion in issue ... The starting point ... requires identifying the tendency and the fact or facts in issue which it is adduced to prove'.[75] It is this tendency reasoning that attracts the application of ss 97 and 97A, and potentially s 95.

The NSW Court of Criminal Appeal in 2014 in the case of *Elomar* made important observations regarding the concept of tendency in relation to evidence of a person's state of mind, stating that:

> A state of mind, unlike conduct, is not necessarily a series of intermittent events, feelings or ideas. Commonly, a state of mind is continuous. Belief in a deity, opposition to capital punishment, support for a political philosophy are all states of mind. It would not be in accord with ordinary human experience or language to describe a person who held such beliefs as having a "tendency" to have the relevant state of mind. Rather, the person is said to have that state of mind. Proof of a state of mind may be direct, not indirect. In appropriate circumstances, it does not depend upon tendency reasoning.[76]

This prompts reflection of the fact that evidence of a person's state of mind can be relevant in many different contexts.[77] For example, that the accused told others on various occasions that he believed that black dogs embodied the Devil may be relevant in a prosecution for cruelty to animals to prove that the accused intended to harm black dogs. The statement may be evidence relevant to the accused's fitness to stand trial. That, as the *Elomar* court observes, a person's state of mind may be continuous – such as love or anger may be important. But it may not necessarily be so, and continuity cannot be assumed from a single act. Love can end so can anger. Also, a state of mind may be the product of beliefs, knowledge, emotions or attitudes. One might *believe* in the existence of the Devil, UFOs or Santa Claus. A person may believe with wavering conviction or she may have a fervent belief with no doubts, but this may not mean that she has *a tendency* to believe (though evidence of these beliefs might prove that she has a tendency to be easily persuaded to believe in fictional matters).

Like the belief claimed in *Elomar* one does not necessarily possess a tendency to fear (though it may be loosely expressed in those terms). It may be proved by a series of acts to support a claim that it is a continuing fear (or belief). Emotion and knowledge are the same. If I know a body is lying in a park before this is public knowledge,[78] that knowledge, like fear or love, is not in itself tendency. They are all features of who we are. They may reflect character traits or tendencies, but they are not, per se, tendencies.

A commonly discussed area in the context of state of mind issues is evidence that the accused possessed sexual desire towards children. This emotion or attitude is proven typically by words or conduct: see, for example, *McPhillamy*,[79] *Bauer*[80] and *Hughes*[81] below. These cases show that evidence of certain conduct may be adduced to prove a tendency to act in a particular way, with the accused's

75 *Hughes* [2017] HCA 20; 263 CLR 338, [16].
76 *Elomar* [2014] NSWCCA 303, [366] (Bathurst CJ, Hoeben CJ at CL and Simpson J).
77 See, eg, *Subramaniam v Public Prosecutor* [1956] 1 WLR 965.
78 See, eg, *Blastland* [1986] 1 AC 41.
79 [2018] HCA 52; 361 ALR 13.
80 [2018] HCA 40; 266 CLR 56.
81 [2017] HCA 20; 263 CLR 338.

actions explicable (or gaining an underlying unity) by this particular sexual desire. As we see below, this evidence, if it satisfies s 55, subject to exceptional circumstances, will be presumed to have significant probative value: *UEA*, s 97A.

The steps to be taken in relation to the admission of tendency evidence require establishing:

> (i) was reasonable notice of the intention to adduce the evidence given?;
> (ii) did the court think that the evidence, either by itself or in conjunction with other evidence in the Crown case, have significant probative value?; and if (i) and (ii) were satisfied:
> (iii) did the probative value of the evidence [outweigh the danger of unfair prejudice to the defendant]?[82]

Significant probative value: the approach

> [A]n assessment of whether the evidence sought to be led as tendency evidence has significant probative value involves a "consideration of two interrelated but separate matters", namely, the "extent to which the evidence supports the [alleged] tendency" and the "extent to which the tendency makes more likely the facts making up the charged offence" (*Hughes* (2017) 263 CLR 338; [2017] HCA 20 at [41]). A conclusion that such evidence has a high degree of probative value is likely "where (i) the evidence, by itself or together with other evidence, strongly supports proof of a tendency, and (ii) the tendency strongly supports the proof of a fact that makes up the offence charged."[83]

Further, matters suggesting the evidence may be unreliable, are not to be considered in determining whether tendency or coincidence evidence meets the standard of significant probative value.[84] These matters are for the jury. The High Court in 2018 in *Bauer*[85] confirmed that with matters of unreliability clearly outside admissibility determinations, under the *UEA*, courts no longer could apply the *Hoch*[86] principle (that is, that defence claims, based on some factual foundation, that there was a reasonable possibility that multiple sexual complaints had combined to concoct false allegations, justified excluding evidence under the similar fact rule). Cases had continued to apply this common law principle under the *UEA*. The rejection of the *Hoch* principle now has statutory foundation in NSW.[87]

---

82 *Vagg* [2020] NSWCCA 134, [40] (Simpson AJA), noting that *Vagg* applied the pre-2020 amendment to s 101 (requiring the probative value of the evidence to 'substantially outweigh its potential prejudicial effect on the applicant'. Note that this stage requires also taking into account the directions to be given: Rothman J at [96].

83 *Taylor* [2020] NSWCCA 355, [141] (Beech-Jones J). This acknowledges that *UEA*, s 97(1)(b), states that 'evidence will, either by itself *or having regard to other evidence adduced or to be adduced by the party* seeking to adduce the evidence, have significant probative value' (emphasis added). See also s 97A(2).

84 *IMM* [2016] HCA 14; 257 CLR 300, [49]-[55].

85 [2018] HCA 40; 266 CLR 56, [69].

86 [1988] HCA 50; 165 CLR 292, that is applying the principles expressed in *Pfennig*, a common law similar fact case, that the 'no reasonable explanation consistent with innocence' test applied where the defence claimed that sexual assault complainants concocted their allegations.

87 See *UEA* (NSW), s 94(5), implicitly recognising courts' persistence in applying the *UEA* in sexual assault cases tenaciously hanging on to the *Hoch* notion, see, for example, *Velkoski* [2014] VSCA 121, [173]. The rejection of the *Hoch* principle also recognises that a factual foundation for claiming concoction or collusion is not difficult where predatory conduct by paedophiles was identified by RCIRCSA as rife in churches, schools and out of home care, creating a ready base for a factual foundation that complainants had talked to each other (and hence, as the *Hoch* principle stated, a reasonable possibility of concoction).

'having regard to other evidence adduced or to be adduced'

The case of *Hughes* provides a classic illustration of the strength of the tendency evidence when aligned with other evidence. Kiefel CJ, Bell, Keane and Edelman JJ in *Hughes* noted that in this case with evidence from five complainants, 'evidence of a tendency might be weak by itself, but its probative value can be assessed together with other evidence'.[88]

> 62. This point can be illustrated by reference to an example given by the appellant in oral submissions, which was that there was a "world of difference" between the evidence concerning EE (count 10), who was 15 years old and whom the appellant encouraged to commit indecent acts in a park and in a driveway, and the evidence concerning SH (counts 3 to 6), which involved intrusive acts "in a darkened bedroom, in her bed, when she was only six, seven or eight". One problem with this comparison is that it ignores the fact that in relation to, for example, count 4, involving SH, the evidence of EE needed to be considered together with the evidence involving (i) counts 1 to 3 and counts 5 to 11, (ii) uncharged acts relating to the complainants SH, JP, AK and SM, and (iii) uncharged acts relating to the tendency witnesses VOD, AA and BB. Indeed, one of the appellant's concessions on this appeal was that the tendency evidence from counts 1 to 2 (JP) and 3 to 6 (SH) was cross-admissible. This evidence, which was conceded to be admissible, reinforced the other tendency evidence. When considered together, all the tendency evidence provided strong support to show the appellant's tendency to engage opportunistically in sexual activity with underage girls despite a high risk of detection.
>
> 63. The probative value of the evidence of each complainant and of AA, BB and VOD lay in proof of the tendency to act on the sexual attraction to underage girls, notwithstanding the evident risks. The fact that the appellant expressed his sexual interest in underage girls in a variety of ways did not deprive proof of the tendency of its significant probative value.

Are child sexual assault prosecutions different?

The introduction of *UEA* (NSW), s 97A, in 2020, specifically for tendency evidence of child sexual assault in child sexual assault proceedings, suggests that child sexual assault, and the prosecution of such offences, differ from other crimes where tendency evidence may be utilised. The NSW Attorney General in his Second Reading Speech described the seven categories of s 97A(5) listed on pp 439-40 as responding to 'myths and misconceptions that have historically prevented evidence about a defendant's tendency to have a sexual interest in a specific child, or in children generally … from being seen to have probative value in criminal proceedings for child sexual offences, and have therefore excluded such evidence and prevented it from being considered by the trier of fact'.[89] However, the Law Commission (UK) in its 1996 Consultation Paper, *Evidence in Criminal Proceedings: Previous Misconduct of a Defendant*, rejected a separate set of rules for sexual offences. It noted that sexual misconduct is prone to inflame emotions and thus be more prejudicial than other conduct.[90] In 2007 the New Zealand Law Commission (NZLC) expressed doubt over the merits of a special rule removing the tendency rule for sexual offences on the basis that it could lead to the development

---

88 [2017] HCA 20; 263 CLR 338, [61].

89 Quoted in *Brookman* [2021] NSWDC 110, [24] by Abadee DCJ.

90 Tasmanian Law Reform Institute, *Evidence Act 2001 Sections 97, 98 & 101 and Hoch's case: Admissibility of 'Tendency' and 'Coincidence' Evidence in Sexual Assault Cases with Multiple Complainants* (Final Report 16, 2012) (TLRI, Report 16), [5.4.11], quoting from Law Commission (UK), *Evidence of Bad Character in Criminal Proceedings* (Law Com 273, 2001), [6.61].

of *ad hoc* exceptions and the creation of a 'slippery slope'.[91] These views carry some persuasive value. No one wants innocent people wrongly convicted. However, in recent years the repeat and worldwide revelations of sexual assaults by men in positions of trust and/or authority in churches, in institutions and elsewhere suggest large numbers of sexual assault victims have not been well protected by the criminal justice system to date. Clearly the faults in criminal justice lie in many locations and they will not be remediated by quick-fix, isolated or reactive solutions. Nor will they correct themselves. Mechanisms that educate courts and jurors that sexual assault can be perpetrated by otherwise highly regarded men, are highly desirable and long overdue. However, creating a parallel set of permissive rules to admit tendency evidence just in child sexual assault proceedings appears to be no more than a quick and blunt fix, rather than one supported by research.

While the NSW Parliament has created separate rules for the admissibility of tendency evidence in child sexual assault prosecutions, courts continue to operate in terms of broad principle. Hence while all four High Court cases between 2016-2018 respond to applications of the tendency rule under the *UEA* in child sexual assault prosecutions, the court's judgments speak to all offences.

The capacity of evidence to possess significant probative value

The High Court in *Hughes* (and also in *Bauer*) makes clear that the common law is not the source of admissibility standards for tendency and coincidence evidence and that the terms of s 97 indicate that there is not 'a restrictive approach to whether probative value is significant'.[92] The capacity of the evidence adduced for a tendency purpose to support an element of the offence depends in part on the nature of what is sought to be proved. As s 97 explicitly states, tendency evidence is not to be looked at in isolation. Further, it is for the trial judge to establish the extent to which the evidence *could* rationally affect the assessment of the probability of a fact in issue to a significant extent. In *IMM*[93] French CJ, Kiefel, Bell and Keane JJ summarised the s 97(1)(b) standard.

> 45. The use of the term "probative value" and the word "extent" in its definition rest upon the premise that relevant evidence can rationally affect the assessment of the probability of the existence of a fact in issue to different degrees. Taken by itself, the evidence may, if accepted, support an inference to a high degree of probability that the fact in issue exists. On the other hand, it may only, as in the case of circumstantial evidence, strengthen that inference, when considered in conjunction with other evidence. The evidence, if accepted, may establish a sufficient condition for the existence of the fact in issue or only a necessary condition. The ways in which evidence, if accepted, could affect the assessment of the probability of the existence of a fact in issue are various. Within the framework imposed by the statute and, in particular, the assumption that the evidence is accepted, the determination of probative value is a matter for the judge.
>
> 46. *Cross on Evidence* suggests that a "significant" probative value is a probative value which is "important" or "of consequence". The significance of the probative value of the tendency evidence under s 97(1)(b) must depend on the nature of the facts in issue to which the evidence is relevant and the significance or importance which that evidence

91 See NZLC, *Disclosure of Previous Convictions* (No IP4, 2007), [6.67], discussed at TLRI, Report 16, ibid, [5.4.12].

92 *Hughes* [2017] HCA 20; 263 CLR 338, [42] (Kiefel CJ, Bell, Keane and Edelman JJ).

93 [2016] HCA 14; 257 CLR 300.

> may have in establishing those facts. So understood, the evidence must be influential in the context of fact-finding.

The language of these two provisions makes it clear that a court must weigh evidence to assess its heightened probative value in a broad evidentiary context. This requires an evaluative role that is more extensive than in other provisions where 'probative value' sets an admissibility benchmark. In *IMM* the High Court held that, where the principal issue was the complainant's credibility, evidence from the complainant of an uncharged act was unlikely to be rationally capable of adding significantly to the probability of the complainant telling the truth about the charged acts unless there were some special features linked to the uncharged act. The uncharged act in *IMM* was alleged to have occurred sometime after the charged acts and, relative to the charges, was potentially ambiguous as evidence of sexualised conduct.

The plurality judgment generated significant criticism for its lack of clarity and for its narrow approach to a complainant's account of an uncharged act. *IMM* was determined approximately 15 months before *Hughes*, and *Bauer* followed approximately 15 months later. Each of these cases involves child sexual assault (and well before the introduction of the *UEA* (NSW), s 97A). The *Bauer* court responded to this criticism of *IMM*, acknowledging that its 'previous decisions[94] had left unclear 'the rationale of admissibility of tendency evidence in single complainant sexual offences cases', adding:

> 48. Henceforth, it should be understood that a complainant's evidence of an accused's uncharged acts in relation to him or her (including acts which, although not themselves necessarily criminal offences, are probative of the existence of the accused having had a sexual interest in the complainant on which the accused has acted) may be admissible as tendency evidence in proof of sexual offences which the accused is alleged to have committed against that complainant *whether or not the uncharged acts have about them some special feature of the kind* mentioned in *IMM* or exhibit a *special, particular or unusual feature* of the kind described in *Hughes*. …
>
> 55. … [S]trictly speaking the reasoning of the plurality in *IMM* was limited to the case there under consideration: one which involved an uncharged act relevantly remote in time and of a significantly different order of gravity from the charged offending. *IMM* may be distinguished from a case like the present, where what is in issue is a course of offending comprised of a succession of uncharged sexual acts, of generally a similar kind to the charged acts, interspersed between the charged acts throughout the alleged period of offending. Thus, despite the apparent generality of the dicta in *IMM*, henceforth it should not be regarded as implying any departure from the majority opinions expressed in *HML* or, therefore, as contrary to the reasoning in *JLS*, *MR*, *PCR*, *Velkoski* or *Gentry* as to the high probative value which is ordinarily to be attributed to a complainant's evidence of uncharged sexual acts. *IMM* should be understood as confined to the particular, relatively exceptional circumstances of that case.[95]

---

94 *Bauer* [2018] HCA 40; 266 CLR 56, [47], citing the differences of opinion in *HML* [2008] HCA 16; 235 CLR 334; and also *IMM* [2016] HCA 14; 257 CLR 300. Of *HML*, a case not engaging the *UEA*, the court in *Bauer* stated at [52] that under s 97 of the *Evidence Act*, the common law test of admissibility has been superseded by the less demanding criterion of significant probative value. Nevertheless, the court indicated *HML* remains relevant because six Justices on the *HML* court – (2008) 235 CLR 334, 359 [27] per Gleeson CJ; 386 [118], 399 [171]-[173], 414 [234] per Hayne J (Gummow J and Kirby J agreeing at 362 [41]-[42], 370 [59]); 430-2 [287], [289], 451-2 [336], 460-1 [364], 467 [387] per Heydon J; 501-2 [510]-[511] per Kiefel J – held 'that a complainant's evidence of uncharged acts is usually of sufficient probative value to pass even the *Hoch* test of admissibility'.

95 *Bauer* [2018] HCA 40; 266 CLR 56, [55].

The role of similarity

By way of backdrop, the common law similar fact rule focused on features of similarity. This approach was also a hallmark of appellate cases from Victoria. For example, the Court of Appeal in *Velkoski*[96] noted that cases such as *Reeves*[97] supported applying the law regarding tendency evidence under s 97, using 'terms such as '*remarkable*', '*unusual*', '*improbable*' and '*peculiar*' that characterise the subject of tendency evidence. As noted in *Velkoski*, in *Reeves*, Maxwell ACJ reaffirmed that it is the '*degree of peculiarity*', or '*features of commonality*' or the extent to which the conduct can be said to be '*remarkable*', which will guide the assessment of probative value', with Priest JA in dissent noting:

> 94. In my view, the tendency evidence in this case did not possess a high degree of cogency. To adopt the language of the Court in *PNJ*[98] (although uttered in the context of an examination of coincidence evidence), '[t]he allegation that such acts were committed is, sadly, unremarkable'; and 'is a commonplace in sexual offending of this kind, and cannot be said to distinguish the applicant's offending from that of any other such offender'.[99] It must be acknowledged that both complainants were young girls and family members, but, when considering offending of this generic kind, there is nothing particularly unusual about those factors. Nor, it must be said, is there anything particularly unusual about the offending occurring when the complainants were under the appellant's care, or when others were in the premises where the events occurred.[100] …

The Act does not require tendency evidence to be similar.[101] Thus in *Hughes,* the diverse ways in which the sexual assaults were alleged to have occurred did not mean that the evidence failed to meet the required standard of significant probative value (s 97).

> Commonly, evidence of a person's conduct adduced to prove a tendency to act in a particular way will bear similarity to the conduct in issue. Section 97(1) does not, however, condition the admission of tendency evidence on the court's assessment of operative features of similarity with the conduct in issue. The probative value of tendency evidence will vary depending upon the issue that it is adduced to prove. In criminal proceedings where it is adduced to prove the identity of the offender for a known offence, the probative value of tendency evidence will almost certainly depend upon close similarity between the conduct evidencing the tendency and the offence. Different considerations may inform the probative value of tendency evidence where the fact in issue is the occurrence of the offence.[102]

Clearly the common law is not relevant in this field. Nevertheless, the case of *Thompson*[103] illustrates how dissimilarity of situations does not necessarily reduce the probative value of tendency evidence. In this case the High Court considered murder prosecution where Thompson's burnt-out car was positioned as if there had been an apparent collision with a tree. There were the burnt bodies of two young women inside. It was the prosecution case that the accident scene was

96 [2014] VSCA 121, [133].
97 [2013] VSCA 311, and particularly [53], [56] (Maxwell ACJ and Coghlan JA).
98 [[2010] VSCA 88; 27 VR 146.]
99 [Ibid 151 [22].]
100 Citing *CEG* [2012] VSCA 55, [9]-[13].
101 See *Hughes* [2017] HCA 20; 263 CLR 338 [20]-[23], [42], discussing the Australian Law Reform Commission (ALRC), *Evidence* (Report No 38, 1987), Draft Evidence Bill, cl 87(b) and the ALRC, *Evidence (Interim)* (Report No 26, 1985) vol 1.
102 *Hughes* [2017] HCA 20; 263 CLR 338, [39].
103 [1989] HCA 30; 169 CLR 1. The case (a pre-*UEA* one) was treated as a coincidence case by the court.

contrived to hide that the women were murdered (by gunshots to the head). This evidence became relevant some years later the women's sister and three members of her family were shot in their home and an attempt was made to set fire to the house. Thompson admitted to these later murders. There were connections in the events – the family connection, the fire, the shooting. However, only the family connection was indisputable. The other connections were only established on an assumption of guilt for the subject offence. The Court held that it was the underlying unity of the family connection, rather than similarity, that heightened the probative force of the evidence of the four murders. It showed a state of mind (animosity) that supported the conclusion that Thompson possessed a tendency to inflict serious harm to members of the family. This in turn supported the prosecution case that Thompson had murdered the two young women whose bodies were found in the burnt-out car.

Hughes

[2017] HCA 20; 263 CLR 338

A feature of the sexual acts alleged by the complainants was that they claimed the offences were committed in various, different ways (penetration, masturbation, touching, rubbing, exposure). There were also six additional witnesses who described Hughes exposing himself or inappropriately touching them. Three of these women described such conduct occurring in the costume department of *Hey Dad ...!*[104] where they worked with Hughes (the 'workplace tendency evidence'). The others referred to the conduct taking place at Hughes's home.

The defence applied to sever the counts, with a view to enabling a separate trial in relation to each complainant's allegations. The application to sever turned on the cross-admissibility of the tendency evidence to the counts in the indictment. Ultimately, Zahra DCJ ruled inadmissible the so-called workplace tendency evidence in relation to counts 1-10, and gave oral and written directions to the jury that they were not to rely on the three witnesses who gave evidence of the alleged workplace incidents for those counts but could do so for count 11. Hughes was found guilty in a jury trial on 10 of the 11 counts. Kiefel CJ, Bell, Keane and Edelman JJ in *Hughes* described the significance of the tendency evidence, by reference to the evidence of JP, one of the complainants:

> 59. Considered in isolation, JP's evidence might have seemed inherently unlikely: the appellant, a family friend, at dinner in JP's home, absented himself from the party and came into her bedroom, and without making any attempt to ensure her silence, commenced to invasively sexually assault her while his daughter lay sleeping in the same bed. The jury might well be disinclined to accept JP's evidence as satisfying it, beyond a reasonable doubt, that the appellant had, in fact, engaged in conduct which was so much at odds with the jury's experience of the probabilities of ordinary human behaviour. Proof of the appellant's tendency to engage in sexual activity with underage girls opportunistically, notwithstanding the evident risk, was capable of removing a doubt which the brazenness of the appellant's conduct might otherwise have raised.
>
> 60. The force of the tendency evidence as significantly probative of the appellant's guilt was not that it gave rise to a likelihood that the appellant, having offended once, was likely to offend again. Rather, its force was that, in the case of this individual accused, the complaint of misconduct on his part should not be rejected as unworthy of belief because it appeared improbable having regard to ordinary human experience.

---

104 Referencing Hughes's acting role in the TV show by the same name.

The following extract from *Hughes* explains why the High Court rejected the high bar for satisfying s 97 previously established by the Victorian Court of Appeal.[105]

> **Kiefel CJ, Bell, Keane and Edelman JJ: Ground two – a requirement of similarity**
>
> 19. … This ground contends that the Court of Criminal Appeal erred by holding that an "underlying unity" or "pattern of conduct" need not be established before tendency evidence is held to have significant probative value and by declining to follow *Velkoski*.
>
> 20. The appellant's argument acknowledges that s 97(1) does not refer to similarity, unlike s 98(1). Nonetheless, he submits that the inferential process of reasoning from proof of tendency inherently invokes consideration of the similarity between the tendency and the fact or facts in issue: tendency evidence depends for its probative value on how persuasively it can be reasoned that the person will behave in a way that is consistent with the tendency. The legislative choice to condition the admission of tendency evidence on the evidence having significant probative value, and to preclude tendency reasoning if the evidence is not admissible under Pt 3.6 even if it is relevant for another purpose, is said to reflect long-standing scepticism of tendency reasoning and appreciation of the dangers of the unfair prejudice to which it may give rise. The appellant refers to the interim report of the Australian Law Reform Commission ("the ALRC") for the proposition that the dangers of tendency reasoning are greater in cases in which the tendency does not share features of similarity with the conduct in issue.
>
> 21. At the time the ALRC published its reports in its landmark reference on the law of evidence, the preponderance of English and Australian authority was against the admission of evidence of propensity altogether. …
>
> 23. The legislative history of Pt 3.6 of the Evidence Act as enacted is traced in Spigelman CJ's judgment in *R v Ellis*. It suffices to observe that among the differences between the ALRC's draft and s 97, as enacted, is the omission of any requirement of similarity. The legislature's choice to reject the ALRC's recommendation in this respect is unexplained, but, as Spigelman CJ observed, it is a choice which makes the ALRC's reports less useful on this subject than on other subjects. …
>
> 24. The Court of Appeal in *Velkoski* undertook a comprehensive review of the authorities touching on the admission of tendency evidence. Their Honours identified an approach in New South Wales in recent years that is less restrictive than the approach taken in Victoria, or by the Court of Criminal Appeal in earlier years. The Court of Appeal concluded that the more recent New South Wales approach sets the threshold for the admission of tendency evidence too low. The recent New South Wales approach was said to be exemplified by the decisions in *R v Ford* and *R v PWD*. *Ford* and *PWD* were each successful prosecution appeals against a ruling excluding tendency evidence on the trial of sexual offences.

[The High Court summarised *Velkoski*, noting that in its ruling it relied on the purpose of s 97(1)(b) being to protect against the risk of an unfair trial.]

> 31. … Requiring significant probative value to be assessed by the criterion of similarity of operative features was said to protect against this risk. Their Honours were critical of cases in which the prosecution adduces tendency evidence to establish "the offender's interest in particular victims and his willingness to act upon that interest" because such evidence discloses only "rank propensity". … Their Honours said that once the jury is

105 The following extract cites *Velkoski* [2014] VSCA 121; 45 VR 680; Tapper, *Cross and Tapper on Evidence* (Oxford University Press, 11th ed, 2007), 403-16; *DPP v P* [1991] 2 AC 447; *H* [1995] 2 AC 596; *Z* [2000] UKHL 68; [2000] 2 AC 483; Law Commission (UK), above n 90; New Zealand Law Commission, *Disclosure to Court of Defendants' Previous Convictions, Similar Offending and Bad Character* (Report 103, 2008); ALRC, *Evidence (Interim)*, above n 101; *Pfennig* [1995] HCA 7; 182 CLR 461; ALRC, *Evidence*, above n 101; Draft *Evidence Bill*, cl 87(b); *Ellis* [2003] NSWCCA 319; 58 NSWLR 700; *Jacara Pty Ltd v Perpetual Trustees WA Ltd* [2000] FCA 1886; 106 FCR 51; *Ford* [2009] NSWCCA 306; 201 A Crim R 451; *PWD* [2010] NSWCCA 209; 205 A Crim R 75.

satisfied that the acts relied upon as tendency have been committed, any resort to proof of the offender's state of mind to support tendency reasoning is impermissible and highly prejudicial.

32. These statements, couched in the language of the common law, do not stand with the scheme of Pt 3.6. They are apt to overlook that s 97 applies to civil and criminal proceedings. In criminal proceedings, the risk that the admission of tendency evidence may work unfairness to the accused is addressed by s 101(2). Moreover, s 97(1) in terms provides for the admission of evidence of a person's tendency to have a particular state of mind. An adult's sexual interest in young children is a particular state of mind. On the trial of a sexual offence against a young child, proof of that particular state of mind may have the capacity to have significant probative value.

33. The Court of Appeal went on to state that:

> "To remove any requirement of similarity or commonality of features does not … give effect to what is inherent in the notion of 'significant probative value.' If the evidence does no more than prove a disposition to commit crimes of the kind in question, it will not have sufficient probative force to make it admissible."

34. This reasoning glosses the language of s 97(1)(b) of the Evidence Act; it does not explain its "inherent" meaning. The circumstance that the text of s 97(1)(b) does not include reference to similarity or to the concepts of "underlying unity", "pattern of conduct" or "modus operandi" is a clear indication that s 97(1)(b) is not to be applied as if it had been expressed in those terms. The omission of these familiar common law concepts is eloquent of the intention that evidence which may be significantly probative for the purposes of s 97(1)(b) should not be limited to evidence exhibiting the features so described. …

37. The *Velkoski* analysis proceeds upon the assumption that, regardless of the fact in issue, the probative value of tendency evidence lies in the degree of similarity of "operative features" of the acts that prove the tendency. It is an analysis that treats tendency evidence as if it were confined to a tendency to perform a particular act. Depending upon the issues in the trial, however, a tendency to act in a particular way may be identified with sufficient particularity to have significant probative value notwithstanding the absence of similarity in the acts which evidence it. *Velkoski* is illustrative.

38. The expression of the accused's sexual interest in young children was not confined to soliciting them to touch his penis: he repeatedly touched one complainant's penis and he touched other complainants on their vaginas and bottoms. Confining the tendency evidence to counts charging an occasion on which he solicited one of the complainants to touch his penis did not give the tendency evidence its relative strength. There was no reason to find that the accused was more likely to act on his sexual interest in young children by soliciting one of the complainants to touch his penis than he was to sexually molest the complainant at the day-care centre in another way. Given that the issue in each case was the occurrence of the offence, proof of the tendencies which the prosecution identified had significant probative value.

39. Commonly, evidence of a person's conduct adduced to prove a tendency to act in a particular way will bear similarity to the conduct in issue. Section 97(1) does not, however, condition the admission of tendency evidence on the court's assessment of operative features of similarity with the conduct in issue. The probative value of tendency evidence will vary depending upon the issue that it is adduced to prove. In criminal proceedings where it is adduced to prove the identity of the offender for a known offence, the probative value of tendency evidence will almost certainly depend upon close similarity between the conduct evidencing the tendency and the offence. Different considerations may inform the probative value of tendency evidence where the fact in issue is the occurrence of the offence.

40. In the trial of child sexual offences, it is common for the complainant's account to be challenged on the basis that it has been fabricated or that anodyne conduct has been misinterpreted. Logic and human experience suggest proof that the accused is a person

who is sexually interested in children and who has a tendency to act on that interest is likely to be influential to the determination of whether the reasonable possibility that the complainant has misconstrued innocent conduct or fabricated his or her account has been excluded. The particularity of the tendency and the capacity of its demonstration to be important to the rational assessment of whether the prosecution has discharged its onus of proof will depend upon a consideration of the circumstances of the case. The test posed by s 97(1)(b) is as stated in *Ford*: "the disputed evidence should make more likely, to a significant extent, the facts that make up the elements of the offence charged". The only qualification to this is that it is not necessary that the disputed evidence has this effect *by itself*. It is sufficient if the disputed evidence together with other evidence makes significantly more likely any facts making up the elements of the offence charged. Of course, where there are multiple counts on an indictment, it is necessary to consider each count separately to assess whether the tendency evidence which is sought to be adduced in relation to that count is admissible. …

Conclusion …

57. An inclination on the part of a mature adult to engage in sexual conduct with underage girls and a willingness to act upon that inclination are unusual as a matter of ordinary human experience. Often, evidence of such an inclination will include evidence of grooming of potential victims so as to reveal a "pattern of conduct" or a "modus operandi" which would qualify the evidence as admissible at common law. But significant probative value may be demonstrated in other ways. In this case the tendency evidence showed that the unusual interactions which the appellant was alleged to have pursued involved courting a substantial risk of discovery by friends, family members, workmates or even casual passers-by. This level of disinhibited disregard of the risk of discovery by other adults is even more unusual as a matter of ordinary human experience. The evidence might not be described as involving a pattern of conduct or modus operandi – for the reason that each alleged offence involved a high degree of opportunism; but to accept that that is so is not to accept that the evidence does no more than prove a disposition to commit crimes of the kind in question.

58. Given the complainants' ages, consent was not an issue in any of the counts. It was the defence case on each count that the complainant had fabricated her account. That the tendency evidence did more than prove a disposition to commit crimes of the kind in question, and was actually of significant value as proof of his guilt of the offences charged, can be illustrated by hypothesising separate trials in respect of each complainant with the only evidence against the appellant being the evidence of the complainant. In each such case, the jury would be presented with a prosecution case inviting it to conclude beyond reasonable doubt that the appellant had engaged in behaviour towards the complainant which involved predatory sexual activity pursued by taking opportunistic advantage of a social or family or work occasion in circumstances in which the appellant courted a real risk of discovery by other adults …

64. The assessment of the significant probative value of the proposed evidence does not conclude by assessing its strength in establishing a tendency. The second matter to consider is that the probative value of the evidence will also depend on the extent to which the tendency makes more likely the elements of the offence charged. This will necessarily involve a comparison between the tendency and the facts in issue. A tendency expressed at a high level of generality might mean that all the tendency evidence provides significant support for that tendency. But it will also mean that the tendency cannot establish anything more than relevance. In contrast, a tendency expressed at a level of particularity will be more likely to be significant. The Court of Criminal Appeal did not err in finding that the tendency evidence of each of the complainants and AA, BB and VOD met the condition imposed by s 97(1)(b) in relation to each count in the indictment.

Tendency evidence to prove identity

It has been often observed that, while there is no requirement for similarity between the events in the tendency evidence and the offence charged, where tendency evidence is adduced to prove the identity of the offender (rather than proof of an offence occurred) 'close similarity between the conduct evidencing the tendency and the offence'[106] may be crucial. Certainly, where the tendency evidence stands alone in pointing to the accused as the offender it will need features that link strongly to the accused.[107] For example, there may be additional evidence that places the accused at the scene of the crime. This was the case in *Thompson* where in 1981 Thompson's car, carrying two sisters as passengers, ran off the road, hit a tree and burst into flames killing the two women. The prosecution claimed Thompson had staged the car accident and set fire to the car to hide the fact that he had shot and killed the women. The tendency (similar fact) evidence was that three years later Thompson was convicted of the shooting murder of four members of the sisters' family where he had attempted to also set fire to their house. The High Court acknowledged that there was not similarity between the two events but there was an underlying unity that linked Thompson to the sisters' murder.

The role of tendency evidence in proving identity has arisen in a number of cases. For example, in the 2020 NSW Court of Criminal Appeal case of *TL*,[108] the applicant appealed his conviction for the murder of his two-and-a-half-year-old stepdaughter, TM, in 2014. At issue in the trial was whether TL had inflicted blunt force trauma to TM's abdomen, fatally injuring her. The tendency evidence comprised of transcripts of interview with lay witnesses, expert evidence and photographs of first-degree burns or scalds and one third-degree burn or scald occurring while TM was in the sole care of TL. The expert evidence indicated that the burns were consistent with TM being forced into a bath of excessively hot water, linking to an event occurring 10 days before TM's death. TL's version of this incident was that TM had jumped into the bath of her own volition. During the evening when TM sustained her fatal injuries TM's mother and TL's 14-year-old nephew were absent for 15 minutes. This absence did not remove them from being potential alternative suspects with the tendency evidence pointing towards TL's greater likelihood of guilt. At issue was whether this tendency evidence was admissible to support the charge of murder. The factual scenario showed that TL was one of only three persons who had the opportunity to commit the offence, giving the tendency evidence its significant probative value despite the fact that there was no close similarity between the incident in the bath and the manner in which TM was killed. Hoeben CJ at CL noted that a single previous incident[109] is potentially sufficient to form the basis of tendency evidence and that there was no unfair prejudice outweighing the probative value of the evidence, observing that, while evidence of '[h]arm to a child will always engender strong feelings',[110] this was addressed by the trial judge's directions.

106 *Hughes* [2017] HCA 20; 263 CLR 388, [39].
107 *O'Keefe* [2009] NSWCCA 121, [59].
108 [2020] NSWCCA 265.
109 Citing *Aravena* [2015] NSWCCA 288; 91 NSWLR 258, [86], though in *TL* there was in fact an additional incident.
110 *TL* [2020] NSWCCA 265, [226] (Hoeben CJ at CL, with Adamson and Bellew J agreeing). The tendency evidence was ruled admissible.

The case of *O'Keefe*[111] presents a prosecution use of tendency evidence for the purpose of identifying the offender without the context arising in *TL* limiting the potential suspects. The tendency evidence arose in relation to cross-admissibility claims in response to defence submissions that the 11 sexual assault offences against four complainants should be heard in four separate trials. The tendency notice identified that all offences occurred in secluded bushland locations where women jogging or walking alone mid-morning on a weekday were vulnerable to attack due to the isolation; with the offender riding a bicycle, with similar initial greetings and where verbal and/or physical threats were made to the women, all showing a fixation with their breasts (demanding with one that she lift her top (counts 7-11), and with the other three complainants coarsely demanding, 'show me your tits' (counts 1-6)). The four sets of alleged incidents were geographically and temporally separated – the first two incidents were said to have occurred in outer western Sydney (one month apart). Ten months later, the second two incidents were said to have taken place on Sydney's north shore (also one month apart). Howie AJ (McColl JA and Grove J concurring) found that for the tendency evidence to stand alone in identifying the accused as the offender, it would have to be 'sufficiently peculiar or singular to amount to what has been described (at [59]) as a "hallmark" or "signature" of the [accused] such that it would offend common sense to exclude it', adding (at [65] that '[it] would be more peculiar and, therefore, of significantly greater probative value, if the offender had a tendency to sexually assault females in the presence of members of the public'.

> 63. Stripped to its fundamental elements, the Crown was alleging a tendency to sexual assault females in secluded locations with a particular interest in their breasts. The Crown was driven to generalise the tendency because of the difficulty of finding a specific tendency from the evidence in counts 1 to 6 that could be applied in counts 7 to 11. The evidence to prove the appellant committed the offences in counts 1 to 6 was coincidence evidence. The facts giving rise to the coincidence were: a man of 20 to 30 with athletic build and tanned skin dressed in cycling clothing with helmet and dark glasses and a bike accosted lone women on isolated bush tracks and asked them, "Show me your tits" before attempting to sexually assault them by the use of threats or force.
>
> 64. However, the Crown could not rely upon coincidence evidence arising from counts 1 to 6 to prove counts 7 to 11 because there was none: the facts of the attacks upon JG were insufficiently similar to those surrounding the attacks upon the other three complaints. For example, the Crown could not rely upon the offender being dressed in cycling attire including helmet and sunglasses, and with a bike. Nor could it rely upon the type of the sexual assaults committed or the nature of the threats made or the words used. But in generalising a tendency derived from counts 1 to 6 to try to make it apply to counts 7 to 11 the probative value of the evidence was very significantly reduced. …
>
> 67. I might have been prepared to accept that the use of the words, "Show us your tits" as the opening gambit by the offender in each of the four assaults would have given rise to a tendency with sufficient specificity or peculiarity that it could survive the application of s 101(2). But the Crown was in a difficult position because the interest in breasts had to be generalised as there was no significant similarity in how that interest was demonstrated between counts 1 to 6, on the one hand, and counts 7 to 11, on the other.
>
> 68. In my opinion the tendency relied upon by the Crown, when stripped to its essence, could not meet the test in s 97. But, in any event, if that were the only evidence upon which the Crown could rely to prove that the appellant was the offender in the JG assaults, it would fail the application of s 101(2). The major difficulty for the Crown was that there

111 *O'Keefe* [2009] NSWCCA 121, followed in *TL* [2020] NSWCCA 265, [201] (Hoeben CJ at CL); *Bryant* [2011] NSWCCA 26, [79] (Howie AJ); *Donohoe* [2012] NSWCCA 176, [50] (Garling J).

> was little to connect the JG offences with those committed against the other complainants. The singular fact of the offender in the earlier matters being dressed in cycling apparel and accompanied by a bike was absent, a matter which obviously concerned the trial judge.

Howie JA added that the tendency evidence was highly prejudicial and (at [69]-[70])

> it was consistent with a characteristic displayed by the offender in the attacks upon the four complainants in a vague, general sense. There was a very real risk that a jury would give the evidence of such a tendency more weight than it deserved by finding that the kind of person who committed one or more of counts 1 to 6 was also the kind of person who committed counts 7 to 11 and for that reason convict the appellant.
>
> ... I do not believe that the evidence had any more probative value than evidence of an offender's criminal record that showed he had committed similar offences in the past. However, the tendency evidence, such as it was, should be considered against other evidence that the appellant committed the JG offences.

This other evidence was very general and ambiguous admissions, referencing his girlfriend issues 'led to these attacks' and 'I can tell you time, dates and places'.

Multiple complainants *vs* a single complainant

In *Bauer*[112] the High Court distinguished *IMM* and *Bauer*, where multiple offending was alleged by single complainants, from *Hughes*,[113] where the appellant faced 11 counts relating to sexual offences alleged by five complainants. The High Court said in *Bauer*:

> 57. The conclusion of the majority in *Hughes* that particular features of the offending imbued the subject tendency evidence with significant probative value reflected the process of probability reasoning that applies to cases where an accused is charged with a number of sexual offences committed against a multiplicity of complainants. As has been explained, the reference in *IMM* to "special features" of a complainant's account of an uncharged act should be understood as limited to a process of reasoning which sometimes applies in cases where an accused is charged with multiple sexual offences against a single complainant and it is sought to adduce evidence from the complainant of a single relatively remote and innocuous uncharged act as support for his or her evidence of the charged acts. Those two processes of reasoning are essentially different.
>
> 58. In a multiple complainant sexual offences case, where a question arises as to whether evidence that the accused has committed a sexual offence against one complainant is significantly probative of the accused having committed a sexual offence against another complainant, the logic of probability reasoning dictates that, for evidence of the offending against one complainant to be significantly probative of the offending against the other, there must ordinarily be some feature of or about the offending which links the two together. More specifically, absent such a feature of or about the offending, evidence that an accused has committed a sexual offence against the first complainant proves no more about the alleged offence against the second complainant than that the accused has committed a sexual offence against the first complainant. And the mere fact that an accused has committed an offence against one complainant is ordinarily not significantly probative of the accused having committed an offence against another complainant.[114] If, however, there is some common feature of or about the offending, it may demonstrate a tendency to act in a particular way proof of which increases the likelihood that the account of the offence under consideration is true.

---

112 [2018] HCA 40; 266 CLR 56 (emphasis added).

113 [2017] HCA 20; 263 CLR 338.

114 [See *HML* (2008) 235 CLR 334, 354 [11]-[12] (Gleeson CJ), 382-383 [105] (Hayne J, with Gummow J and Kirby J agreeing, 362 [41], 370 [59]); *GBF* [2010] VSCA 135, [26]; *BBH* [2012] HCA 9; 245 CLR 499, 525 [70]-[71] (Hayne J, with Gummow J agreeing at 522 [61]).]

> 59. *Hughes* illustrates the point. The case involved multiple complainants each alleging that the accused had committed one or more sexual offences against her, where the offences that were alleged to have been committed against some groups of complainants were in significant respects different in kind and circumstance from the sexual offences alleged to have been committed against each other group of complainants. It was not disputed that evidence of each sexual offence alleged to have been committed against a complainant was admissible as tendency evidence in proof of other sexual offences alleged to have been committed against that complainant, even though, in some cases, the nature of the offending differed significantly from one charge to another. The issue was how much if any of each complainant's evidence of the sexual offences and uncharged acts alleged to have been committed against her was admissible as tendency evidence in proof of the sexual offences alleged to have been committed against the other complainants. *And the case was ultimately decided by majority on the basis that, taken as a whole, the evidence of each alleged sexual offence and uncharged act demonstrated a common feature that a man of mature years had a sexual interest in female children under 16 years of age and a tendency to act upon it by committing sexual offences against them opportunistically in circumstances which entailed a high risk of detection. In the view of the majority, such was the significance of that common feature that evidence of each alleged sexual offence and uncharged act had significant probative value in proof of each other charged offence.*
>
> 60. By contrast, in a single complainant sexual offences case, where a question arises as to whether evidence that the accused has committed one sexual offence against the complainant is significantly probative of the accused having committed another sexual offence against that complainant, there is ordinarily no need of a particular feature of the offending to render evidence of one offence significantly probative of the other. As was established in *HML* and has since been applied in Victoria under s 97 of the *Evidence Act* in *JLS*, *MR*, *PCR* and *Gentry*, and was recognised, too, in *Velkoski*, evidence that an accused has committed one sexual offence against a complainant taken in conjunction with evidence of another sexual offence against the complainant suggests that the accused has a sexual interest in or sexual attraction to the complainant and a tendency to act upon it as occasion presents. And as has been seen, that is so because, where one person is sexually attracted to another and has sought to fulfil that attraction by committing a sexual act with him or her, it is the more likely that the person will continue to seek to fulfil the attraction by committing further sexual acts with the other person as the occasion presents.

In both *Bauer* and *IMM* the prosecution's tendency evidence arose solely from a single complainant's account. In *IMM* the footprint of tendency evidence was small. It consisted of the complainant's account of one 'uncharged act' to support four counts. In *Bauer* evidence of 18 separate offences and of uncharged acts were admitted as cross-admissible in relation to all counts.

Bauer (a Pseudonym)

[2018] HCA 40; 266 CLR 56 (some citations included)

The prosecution's case was that in approximately 1986 the Department of Human Services placed RC, aged two years, and her younger half-sister, TB, with foster parents, Bauer and his then wife. Eighteen charges were laid against Bauer in relation to sexual offences committed against RC over 11 years, from 1988-98. He was convicted in the Victorian County Court. His appeal to the Court of Appeal was successful, the convictions were quashed and a new trial ordered. The High Court set aside the Court of Appeal's quashing of the convictions and ordered that the appeal to the Court of Appeal be dismissed. The allegations were that:

- when RC was about 5 years old, Bauer had placed RC's hand on his penis, showed her pornography and penetrated her digitally (charge 1);
- when RC was about 7 years of age Bauer had placed RC's hand on his penis while he was in the bath (charge 2),[115] and repeated this action while travelling in the family van (charges 3 and 4);
- when RC was about 8 years old Bauer took her to his bedroom and committed further indecent assaults, including also sexual penetration (charges 14 and 15) and, on another occasion, also in his bedroom made her masturbate him (charge 7);
- when RC was 8-9 years of age, sleeping in TB's bed, Bauer repeated variations of the allegations constituting charges 14 and 15 (charges 5 and 6);
- when RC was 9 years old, Bauer committed another indecent act while she lay in bed, ill (charge 8); and
- in the years following, when RC was 9-11 years of age, acts involving oral and digital penetration were repeated on Bauer's tractor (charge 9), in his work truck or van (charges 10, 11, 12, 13 and 16).

At the age of 12, RC's foster mother told the Department of Human Services that she could not manage RC's 'behavioural problems'. RC was removed from the respondent's care. Between 16 January 1996 and 15 January 1997, when RC was 13 years old, she returned to the family home to visit TB (who had remained in the respondent's care). Charge 17 arose from Bauer allegedly digitally penetrated RC while she lay in the spare room. Events leading to an additional charge of indecent act with a child under 16 arose when RC visited the family home again before Christmas 1998 (charge 18).

Within the *Bauer* judgment is guidance on the two earlier tendency cases, *Hughes* and *IMM*. Note in particular the distinction drawn between multiple complainant cases and sole complainant cases.

> **Kiefel CJ, Bell, Gageler, Keane, Nettle, Gordon and Edelman JJ:** 49. … Taken in combination with other evidence, [a complainant's evidence] … may establish the existence of a sexual attraction of the accused to the complainant and a willingness to act on it which assists to eliminate doubts that might otherwise attend the complainant's evidence of the charged acts.[116]
>
> 50. Since proof of an accused's commission of a sexual offence against a complainant on one occasion makes it more likely that the accused may have committed another, generally similar sexual offence against the complainant on another occasion, at least where the two are not too far separated in point of time, where an accused is charged with a number of counts of generally similar sexual offences against a single complainant the several counts may ordinarily be joined in a single indictment and so tried together.[117] In such cases, evidence of each charged act is admissible as circumstantial evidence in proof of each other charged act and, for the same reason, evidence of each uncharged act is admissible in proof of each charged act.[118]
>
> 51. The juridical basis of cross-admissibility of evidence of charged acts and of the admissibility of evidence of uncharged acts in such cases rests on the "very high probative value" of that kind of evidence which results from ordinary human experience that, where a person is sexually attracted to another and has acted on that sexual attraction and the opportunity presents itself to do so again, he or she will seek to gratify his or her

115 In relation to this charge (only) TB was the only prosecution witness to the offence. For all other charges, RC was the only prosecution witness.

116 Citing various English and Australian common law authorities.

117 [See *Criminal Procedure Act 2009* (Vic), s 194.]

118 [*HML* (2008) 235 CLR 334, 397-8 [168], 401-2 [181] (Hayne J).]

sexual attraction to that other person by engaging in sexual acts of various kinds with that person.[119] …

And the fact of itself that evidence of uncharged acts is given by a complainant does not mean that it lacks significant probative value. Although there is a lack of independence in the sense that the evidence of uncharged acts depends on the complainant's account, once the evidence is admitted, and assuming it is accepted, it adds a further element to the process of reasoning to guilt[120] and so, therefore, may be seen as significantly probative of the accused's guilt of the charged offences. …

53. In *IMM*, a majority of this Court held that a complainant's evidence of a sole uncharged sexual act did not have significant probative value. Their Honours reasoned that, because the principal issue in that case was the complainant's credibility, the complainant's evidence of the uncharged act was rationally incapable of adding significantly to the probability that the complainant was telling the truth about the charged acts. The issue arose in a context in which the uncharged act was alleged to have occurred sometime after the charged acts, and was relatively innocuous by comparison. But the plurality also observed, more generally, that a complainant's evidence of an uncharged act can generally have only limited capacity rationally to affect the probability of the complainant's account of the charged acts being true, unless there are some special features of the complainant's account of the uncharged act.[121]

The direction to the jury on the standard of proof for accepting uncharged acts is the subject of some debate. As we see below, the court continues, noting that in single complainant sexual offences cases a jury should not ordinarily be directed that the standard of proof of uncharged acts is beyond reasonable doubt.

86. ***(vii) Jury directions in single complainant sexual offences cases***

... it is appropriate to say something further of the directions ordinarily to be given to a jury in a single complainant sexual offences case where the Crown is permitted to adduce evidence of uncharged acts as evidence of the accused having a sexual interest in the complainant and a tendency to act upon it. Where evidence is admitted on that basis, the trial judge should direct the jury that the Crown argues that the evidence establishes that the accused had a sexual interest in the complainant and a tendency to act upon it which the Crown contends makes it more likely that the accused committed the charged offence or offences. If the Crown also relies on the evidence as putting the charged

---

119 [Ibid 423 [272] (Heydon J).]

120 [Ibid 427 [280] (Heydon J). See also at 402 [182]-[184] (Hayne J, with Gummow J agreeing at 362 [41]). And necessarily implicit in reasons of Gleeson CJ, Kirby J and Kiefel J.]

121 Regarding the rational incapacity of the *IMM* complainant's evidence of the uncharged act to be 'rationally incapable of adding significantly to the probability that the complainant was telling the truth about the charged acts', as indicated above on p 453 the *Bauer* court (at [55]) ultimately concluded that 'strictly speaking the reasoning of the plurality in *IMM* was limited to the case there under consideration'. *IMM* was distinguishable from the evidence in *Bauer* where there is 'a course of offending comprised of a succession of uncharged sexual acts'. On this point, consider *Gul* [2021] SCC 14, not that dissimilar to this feature of *IMM's* case. Here the Canadian Supreme Court applied the common law similar fact rule to allegations founding a charge of break and enter with intent to commit an indictable offence. The complainant testified in relation to the count against Gul that she awoke around midnight to discover her neighbour in her bedroom, close to her lips. He touched her thigh through the blankets and asked if he could lie next to her. She refused. He left. The similar fact evidence was that two months earlier, one evening, Gul entered the apartment through the patio door without notice or permission. He sat near the complainant while she watched TV and left 10 minutes later without touching her. She made no complaint. Gul denied that he had ever entered the complainant's apartment uninvited. On appeal, the Supreme Court, by majority, accepted the view of the Quebec Court of Appeal, that a '[p]ropensity to visit a neighbour, with or without an invitation, does not imply that the accused assaulted the neighbour during such occasion'. While the 'TV evidence' should have been excluded, the proviso was applied, and appeal dismissed (see above Chapter 4, p 132, fn 79).

offence or offences in context in some other identified fashion or respects, the trial judge should further direct the jury that the Crown contends that the evidence serves also to put the charged offence or offences in context and identify the manner or respects in which the Crown contends that it does so. The trial judge should stress that the evidence of uncharged acts has been admitted for those purposes and, if the jury are persuaded by it, that it is open to the jury to use the evidence in those ways, although no other. The trial judge should further stress that it is not enough, however, to convict the accused that the jury may be satisfied of the commission of the uncharged acts or that they establish that the accused had a sexual interest in the complainant on which the accused had acted in the past; it remains that the jury cannot find the accused guilty of any charged offence unless upon their consideration of all of the evidence relevant to the charge they are satisfied of the accused's guilt of that offence beyond reasonable doubt. *Contrary to the practice which has operated for some time in New South Wales, trial judges in that State should not ordinarily direct a jury that, before they may act on evidence of uncharged acts, they must be satisfied of the proof of the uncharged acts beyond reasonable doubt. Such a direction should not be necessary or desirable unless it is apprehended that, in the particular circumstances of the case, there is a significant possibility of the jury treating the uncharged acts as an indispensable link in their chain of reasoning to guilt.* And, as explained earlier in these reasons, a trial judge is precluded from giving such a direction in Victoria. (Emphasis added, some citations omitted)[122]

The High Court decision in *McPhillamy*, extracted and discussed below, illustrates the application of the tendency rule where additional evidence is adduced from witnesses other than the complainant. In *McPhillamy*, the High Court allowed the appeal from the NSW Court of Criminal Appeal regarding an historical child sexual assault against 'A'. At issue was whether evidence of 'B' and 'C' regarding uncharged acts of sexual misconduct with them a decade earlier was admissible as tendency evidence in relation to the charges McPhillamy faced with respect to A. The court accepted that the evidence established that the basis for McPhillamy to have a tendency to have a particular state of mind or to act in a particular way was because:

A mature man's sexual interest in young teenage boys is a tendency to have a particular state of mind. The evidence of "B" and "C" was capable of establishing that the appellant had such an interest. In this Court, it was not disputed that it is an interest of a kind that is likely to be enduring.[123]

However, for Kiefel CJ, Bell, Keane and Nettle JJ, while proof of sexual interest in young teenage boys may be relevant (s 55), it did not have the capacity to meet the s 97 standard of probative value. Their Honours pointed to 'the tendency *to act* on the sexual interest' as founding the probative value of the tendency evidence. The tendency *to act* on his sexual interest related to two complainants' accounts of events a decade earlier with no evidence of the tendency manifesting during that decade. In addition, there was no feature that served to link the different acts of aggravated sexual indecency to the charges McPhillamy faced in relation to A. According to Edelman J (in concurring with the majority), '[t]he weakness of the support in the evidence for the alleged tendency, combined with the weakness of the support that the tendency had for the alleged offences, had the effect that the evidence of "B" and "C" was not of significant probative value'.[124]

122 Also quoted in *Jackson* [2020] NSWCCA 5, [66] (Price J, with Hoeben CJ at CL and Walton J agreeing).

123 [2018] HCA 52; 361 ALR 13, [26].

124 Ibid [39].

McPhillamy

[2018] HCA 52; 361 ALR 13 (citations omitted)

McPhillamy was charged with six counts of sexual offences against A, an 11-year-old altar boy at the time. The offences were alleged to have occurred on two separate occasions between 1 November 1995 and 31 March 1996 in the public toilets of two churches in Bathurst when A was under McPhillamy's supervision. A testified to the two occasions, both occurring on a Saturday night before mass, and both occasions raised charges of aggravated acts of indecency and aggravated indecent assault. The second occasion also included two charges of aggravated sexual intercourse. The charges related to allegations of masturbation and oral sex after McPhillamy had followed A into the toilets. A did not report the assaults until 2010 when he approached the Professional Standards Office of the Catholic Church seeking compensation. A testified that the appellant said that he, A, was gay and warned he needed to be careful 'everybody would turn against me'. The issue before the court was whether the trial judge had erred in permitting testimony from B and C, 13-year-old boarders supervised by McPhillamy at St Stanislaus' College, also in Bathurst. Their evidence was that, in 1985, they too had been sexually assaulted by McPhillamy. The assaults had occurred in the school boarding house when McPhillamy, an assistant house master, purported to comfort them when they were homesick. B testified that McPhillamy 'cuddled him and this progressed to him rubbing B's genitals'. On a second occasion, the appellant approached B after showering and groped him. C testified to a similar incident to the incident first-described above relating to B. About a week later, the appellant apologised. The appellant denied A's allegations, claiming that they were fabricated to support a fraudulent claim for compensation. In 2015 McPhillamy was found guilty on each of the counts.

Kiefel CJ, Bell, Keane and Nettle JJ (Gageler J agreeing): The probative value of "B"'s and "C"'s evidence

26. As explained in *Hughes*, assessment of the probative value of tendency evidence requires the court to determine the extent to which the evidence is capable of proving the tendency. Assuming the evidence has the capacity to do so, the court must then assess the extent to which proof of the tendency increases the likelihood of the commission of the offence. …

27. Proof of the appellant's sexual interest in young teenage boys may meet the basal test of relevance, but it is not capable of meeting the requirement of significant probative value for admission as tendency evidence. Generally, it is the tendency to *act* on the sexual interest that gives tendency evidence in sexual cases its probative value. The tendency on which the prosecution relied was to act on the appellant's sexual interest in male children in their early teenage years who were under his supervision. The evidence demonstrating that tendency was confined to "B"'s and "C"'s evidence of events that occurred in 1985. As Meagher JA noted, there was no evidence that the asserted tendency had manifested itself in the decade prior to the commission of the alleged offending against "A". …

30. … . It may be accepted that the evidence that the appellant had acted on his sexual interest in young teenage boys on the occasions with "B" and "C" is relevant to proof that he committed the offences alleged by "A", but it is not admissible as tendency evidence unless it is capable of significantly bearing on proof of that fact. In the absence of evidence that the appellant had acted on his sexual interest in young teenage boys under his supervision in the decade following the incidents at the College, the inference that at the dates of the offences he possessed the tendency is weak.

31. Moreover, where, as here, the tendency evidence relates to sexual misconduct with a person or persons other than the complainant, it will usually be necessary to identify some feature of the other sexual misconduct and the alleged offending which serves to link the two together. The suggested link in this case is the appellant's tendency to act on his sexual interest in young teenage boys who were under his supervision. The supervision exercised by the appellant as assistant housemaster in 1985 over vulnerable, homesick boys in his care has little in common with the supervision exercised in his role as acolyte over "A", an altar boy, when the two were at the Cathedral for services in 1995-1996. The evidence does not suggest that "A" was vulnerable in the way that "B" and "C" were vulnerable. The tendency to take advantage of young teenage boys who sought out the appellant in the privacy of his bedroom is to be contrasted with "A"'s account that the appellant followed him into a public toilet and molested him.

32. "B"'s and "C"'s evidence established no more than that a decade before the subject events the appellant had sexually offended against each of them. Proof of that offending was not capable of affecting the assessment of the likelihood that the appellant committed the offences against "A" to a significant extent. It rose no higher in effect than to insinuate that, because the appellant had sexually offended against "B" and "C" ten years before, in different circumstances, and without any evidence other than "A"'s allegations that he had offended again, he was the kind of person who was more likely to have committed the offences that "A" alleged. The tendency evidence did not meet the threshold requirement of s 97(1)(b) of the *Evidence Act*. This conclusion makes it unnecessary to address the submissions respecting s 101(2) of that Act.

Edelman J. 33. I agree with the reasons of Kiefel CJ, Bell, Keane and Nettle JJ for joining in the orders allowing the appeal at the conclusion of oral argument. The following are brief additional reasons why I joined in the orders. These reasons concern why the features of the appellant's alleged tendency conduct with other persons, "B" and "C", were not sufficiently "linked" to the alleged offending with the complainant, "A", for the tendency conduct to have significant probative value within s 97(1) of the *Evidence Act 1995* (NSW).

34. In *Hughes v The Queen*, in the same context as this appeal, involving tendency evidence being led to establish the commission of the offence rather than the identity of the offender, the majority said:

> "The assessment of whether evidence has significant probative value in relation to each count involves consideration of two interrelated but separate matters. The first matter is the extent to which the evidence supports the tendency. The second matter is the extent to which the tendency makes more likely the facts making up the charged offence."

35. As to the first matter – the extent to which the evidence supports the tendency – the jury were directed that the alleged tendency of the appellant was to act in a particular way that demonstrated "a sexual interest in male children in their early teenage years who were under his supervision". The evidence of "B" and "C" provided some support for the appellant having that tendency at the time of trial. It assisted to establish that the appellant had a state of mind involving a sexual interest in early teenage male children under his supervision and a willingness to act upon that state of mind. But that support was not strong. Unlike in *Hughes*, where the tendency evidence was also expressed in reasonably general terms, the evidence in this case was given only by two witnesses. Their evidence involved two incidents that occurred a decade before the date of the alleged offences against "A".

36. As to the second matter – the extent to which the tendency makes more likely the facts making up the charged offence – the tendency was expressed at a high level of generality. The reference to supervision was as a matter of context: it was not alleged that the appellant had a tendency to abuse his authority over children in any particular way, such as taking advantage of the homesickness of "B" and "C", in order to facilitate acts of the nature of the alleged offending. Nor was it alleged that the appellant had a tendency to act

> impulsively with a risk of detection. Nor was it alleged that the acts, or their circumstances, bore any similarity to the alleged offences, other than as demonstrating a sexual interest in early teenage boys. The tendency was described no more specifically than "acting" upon the appellant's sexual interest in early teenage male children under his supervision. ...
>
> 38. It is unnecessary to consider whether this more specific tendency arising from the appellant's alleged acts against "B" and "C", if proved, could have significant probative value for proof of the alleged offences against "A", a decade later. The appellant was not confronted with an alleged tendency with this degree of specificity.

Consider the application of the tendency rule to NSW cases after the commencement of *UEA* (NSW), s 97A, in situations where the evidence before the court is the same as in *IMM*, *Bauer* and *McPhillamy*.

In the 2020 NSW Court of Criminal Appeal case of *Taylor* the majority judgment brought some additional light on *McPhillamy*. In *Taylor*[125] the appellant faced 12 counts of domestic violence, domestic violence related offences and one of resisting arrest. Counts 1-10 related to violence to his partner (Walters); Count 11 related to a charge of intimidation of Walters' friend Ms Lawrence. All counts arise from events in early 2018. Taylor was found guilty on six of these (some being alternative charges). Counts 1-10 related to assaults, threats or attempts to assault or threaten Walters. The prosecution evidence sought to prove a 'tendency to threaten and be physically violent towards women with whom he has an intimate relationship'. The tendency evidence was of Taylor's conduct in 2008 contained in a 2010 statement of agreed facts used in the applicant's sentencing hearing following a guilty plea. The statement described events where Taylor and his former wife had a disagreement and Taylor 'became really angry', told Mrs Taylor 'Just get your gear and shut your mouth' and expelled her from the car, saying 'Get out and fuck off'. Mrs Taylor walked 4-5 kilometres until a friend whom she had phoned picked her up, and took her home where she began packing clothes. Taylor then arrived. The statement continued:

> The offender screamed to [the friend] ... 'Fuck off and stay out of me and my wife's business'. He looked very angry. Mrs Taylor sat down on the lounge putting her hands to the side of her head. Mrs Taylor knew what was coming and she was really scared. She tried to get herself in a foetal position to make herself small. ... The offender started punching Mrs Taylor to the back of her head. Mrs Taylor remembers about 3 good blows with the last one knocking her off the lounge to the floor.

Further threats by Taylor and the subsequent diagnosis that Mrs Taylor had a number of fractured ribs were detailed in the statement.

The majority (Walton and Beech-Jones JJ) held that this tendency evidence in the sentencing statement of events in 2008, tendered in proceedings in 2010, supported a tendency by Taylor to threaten and be physically violent towards women with whom he had an intimate relationship. The 2010 statement was 'capable of significantly bearing on proof of that fact'.[126] There was no evidence of other intimate relationships in the intervening period. While the 10-year lapse of time between the two sets of incidents was significant, it needed to be considered in light of the actual tendency – that is, it was not a tendency to be violent to women generally, but to women with whom he had an intimate relationship, manifesting 'if, and when, the applicant forms a relationship that breaks down' (at [145]). In applying *McPhillamy* to the evidence in *Taylor*, Beech-Jones J observed (at [148]):

---

125 [2020] NSWCCA 355.

126 The majority at [147] quoted from *McPhillamy*, [30] (extracted above).

> [T]he significance of the gap between the alleged offending [by McPhillamy] against "B" and "C" on the one hand, and A" on the other, fell to be assessed against the undisputed evidence that, in the intervening period, the appellant had supervised (many) other boys of similar ages. This stands in strong contrast to the evidence and type of tendency alleged by the Crown in this case which concerned threats and violence directed to a woman at the point of a breakdown of a relationship when there was no evidence that the applicant had been in a relationship between the two relevant sets of events.

In *Taylor*'s case, the defence raised a number of points of distinction challenging whether the evidence supported the alleged tendency to a significant extent – that the tendency evidence related to the ending of a 30-year marriage (not a relationship involving 5-6 months of cohabitation); that Mrs Taylor ended the marriage by leaving, whereas Walters had forced Taylor to leave; and that the 2010 statement described sustained and brutal violence, drinking and the appearance of a male friend (manifesting 'an element of jealousy'), as well as a history of domestic violence throughout the marriage. These features were not considered material by the majority who ruled that the tendency evidence had significant probative value. Bell P dissented, finding the evidence was not of significant probative value,[127] 'it was only evidence of violence towards one other woman'. His Honour concluded that, even if the evidence was significant, (the pre-2020 version of) s 101 would have justified exclusion:

> 129. Particular danger of prejudice lay in the likely emotional (and understandable) response by the jury to the degree of violence inflicted by the applicant on his former wife, his callous indifference to her pain and the cruelty (including emotional cruelty to his former wife) entailed in the threat to break the neck of his wife's dog.

Coincidence Evidence

Mention was made earlier in this chapter of the classic illustration of circumstantial evidence amounting to disproof of accident and of coincidence is the 19th century case of *Makin v Attorney-General (NSW)*[128] and the 'circular reasoning' concern expressed by Murphy J in the common law case of *Perry*.[129]

A novel example of coincidence evidence arose in *Xie*,[130] with Xie facing five counts of murder caused by blunt force injuries to the head. All victims were members of Xie's extended family. Xie denied the charges, and raised alibi evidence. No murder weapon was found, nor could the size of the weapon be discerned from the injuries. Police retrieved from the murder scene a bloodied cloth[131] with DNA

---

127 Relying on the '*very different circumstances* to the conduct the subject of the charges' (essentially agreeing with the appellant's arguments on this point); the lack of physical violence in counts 4, 6, 8 and 9; and the passage of 10 years coupled with 'the lack of any evidence of violence towards women in the intervening years or an admission by the applicant of a continuing tendency to threaten and exhibit violence towards women with whom he was in a relationship'.

128 [1894] AC 57.

129 [1982] HCA 75; 150 CLR 580.

130 [2021] NSWCCA 1 (Bathurst CJ, RA Hulme and Beech-Jones JJ).

131 The retrieved bloodied 'fabric had been folded twice. Circular depressions were evident in each quadrant, variously concave and convex, measuring approximately 1.5cm x 2cm. These depressions were suggestive of the cloth having been tightly secured over something hard' (at [762]). The court noted that both the massage device and the bloodied cloth had been 'placed over a hard, cylindrical object, so as to create circular depressions in the cloth. The prosecution relied

consistent with that of two of the victims. The cloth was folded and it was bound by a red rubber band. It was the prosecution case that this cloth had covered a hammer-like object, to form an improvised murder weapon. At Xie's house, police recovered a 'massage device' constructed by Xie that 'included a long steel bolt to which a folded piece of cloth had been attached with a red rubber band'. It had circular depressions of a similar size to those found on the bloodied cloth. However, the two fabrics differed – one was rayon, the other terry towelling. Also, Xie's DNA was not on the red rubber bands used to bind the folded cloth at crime scene. The court concluded that these dissimilarities did not undercut the improbability of coincidence and that the massage device was coincidence evidence that satisfied *UEA*, ss 98 and 101.[132]

In addition to the considerations raised above regarding establishing significant probative value, s 98(1) (the coincidence rule) requires evidence of 'two or more events' (one of which may be the occurrence which is the fact in issue in the proceedings) adduced 'to prove that a person did a particular act or had a particular state of mind on the basis that, having regard to any similarities in the events or the circumstances in which they occurred, or any similarities in both the events and the circumstances in which they occurred, it is improbable that the events occurred coincidentally'. As with s 97, the evidence will be admissible where the party gives reasonable notice and where 'the court thinks that the evidence will, either by itself or having regard to other evidence adduced or to be adduced by the party seeking to adduce the evidence, have significant probative value'. The judge must establish the capability of 'related events' to affect the probability that the offences were committed by the same person. If that is open to the jury, '[t]he second stage of the analysis is to combine the "related events" with the other evidence ... and pose the question, having regard to all of the evidence, is the jury likely to assign the evidence of the "related events" significant probative value'.[133] With respect to the improbability of certain acts occurring (coincidence reasoning), Murphy J in *Perry*[134] cautioned against the danger of assuming the improbable cannot occur innocently. To make that assumption can have repercussions on the presumption of innocence. His Honour observed:

> 10. … One danger is that the presumption of innocence tends to be brushed aside. In the criminal justice system, every person is taken to be innocent unless the contrary is legally proved. No one should be found guilty on appearances, suspicions, conjecture or anything but evidence establishing guilt beyond a reasonable doubt.

---

on the similarity between these two devices and the pieces of cloth affixed to them by means of red rubber bands' (at [55]).

132 At [781], relying on *Selby* [2017] NSWCCA 40, [23]-[24], the court held that locating dissimilarities 'is not critical to a determination of probative value under s 98'. At [806] the court rejected as insufficiently deferential to 'the intelligence and commonsense of jurors' defence arguments that the jury would be unable to properly evaluate the question of coincidence regarding how common it is for fabric to be attached to an object, the different ways in which fabric can be attached, and how commonplace it is to use an ordinary rubber band to attach one object to another. Note that *Xie* was decided when *UEA* (NSW), s 101, required the probative value of the prosecution coincidence evidence to *substantially* outweigh any prejudicial effect it may have on the defendant.

133 *Ceissman* [2010] NSWCCA 50, [16] (Latham J), referred to approvingly in *Ceissman* [2015] NSWCCA 74, [34].

134 [1982] HCA 75; 150 CLR 580, 594. The facts of the *Perry* case are discussed above.

> 11. In Mrs Perry's case there is a very great temptation in weighing the evidence and more particularly in deciding admissibility, to ignore the presumption of innocence and to replace it with a presumption of guilt. The allegation that a number of the accused's relatives died or suffered from arsenic poisoning immediately conjures up a highly suspicious prejudicial atmosphere in which the presumption of innocence tends to be replaced with a presumption of guilt. The presumption of innocence and the strict standard of proof required in criminal cases tend to be indirectly and subtly undermined from the outset by reference to a sequence of events which according to common human experience would not occur unless the accused were guilty. By a backdoor this tends to reintroduce the standard rejected in *Thomas* [1960] HCA 2; 102 CLR 584 that guilt should be judged "in an ordinary common sense manner and in the way you would consider the more serious matters which come up for consideration and decision in your lives". It is very easy to assume that in common experience a person is hardly ever associated with poisonings of four close relatives, and that if such an association occurs it is so remarkable that it is unlikely to be innocent. Common assumptions about improbability of sequences are often wrong. A suggested sequence, series or pattern of events is often incorrectly regarded as so extremely improbable as to be incredible. However highly improbable, as well as merely improbable, sequences and combinations are constantly occurring. In random tossing the occurrence of a run of ten consecutive heads or tails is generally regarded as highly improbable. But this will occur on the average once in every 512 tosses, and the lesser sequences more frequently (2 runs of 9; 4 runs of 8; 8 runs of 7). If one randomly tosses a coin 257 times, more likely than not there will be a sequence of ten heads or tails. Although it is extremely improbable that any particular ticket will win a large lottery, it is certain that one will.

In *El-Haddad*[135] at issue was whether evidence relevant to each of five counts, already admitted in the prosecution case, was cross-admissible to other counts. The particular concern was whether the evidence in the most serious count was sufficiently lacking in points of connection to satisfy the coincidence rule. The evidence showed activities said to relate to drug importation transactions where similar (but not the same) email addresses, dates of birth and names connected the counts. Leeming JA concluded that the evidence satisfied ss 98 and 101. His Honour added:

> 77. After all, the point of s 98 is to preclude a particular mode of inferential reasoning, as was said by Beech-Jones J, with the agreement of Hoeben CJ at CL, in *R v MR* [2013] NSWCCA 236 at [79]:
>
> > "[G]iven that s 98 is addressing evidence that is put forward to invite the trier of fact to engage in a particular form of probabilistic reasoning, it necessarily follows that the assessment of whether the evidence of the relevant events has either probative or significant probative value requires a consideration of the combined effect of all the relevant similarities. Unless they are all considered then the 'basis' upon which the evidence is put forward, namely that it is 'improbable that the events occurred coincidentally' and that instead the events are explicable by reason of the particular act or state of mind sought to be proved, such as the involvement of the same offender or offenders in all the events, cannot be properly addressed."
>
> 78. The third member of the Court, Schmidt J, reasoned to the same effect at [10]. Likewise, attention was drawn to the inferential nature of these provisions by Simpson J in *R v Gale; R v Duckworth* [2012] NSWCCA 174; 217 A Crim R 487 at [25]:
>
> > "At its heart, s 98 is a provision concerning the drawing of inferences. The purpose sought to be achieved by the tender of coincidence evidence is to provide the foundation upon which the tribunal of fact could draw an inference. The inference is that a person did a particular act or had a particular state of mind."

135 [2015] NSWCCA 10.

A potentially problematic conclusion was reached by the NSW Court of Criminal Appeal in *A2, Magennis and Vaziri*[136] in a case involving two cases of genital mutilation of young girls, known as C1 and C2, where the court responded to an appeal that the trial judge had framed the question to the jury as a logical fallacy when he posed to the jury (at [952]): 'Is it improbable that the two events [that is, those related by C1 and C2] occurred coincidentally?' It was submitted that this was 'asking whether it was improbable that the two events occurred coincidentally assumes that the events did in fact occur (which is what the evidence is being used to prove) and invites circular reasoning'.[137] The court observed:

> 1033. Specifically with respect to coincidence evidence, in *DSJ v The Queen*, a five-judge Bench of this Court held that s 98(1)(b) requires a trial judge to determine whether the evidence is capable, to a significant degree, of rationally affecting the assessment (ultimately by a jury) of the probability of the existence of a fact in issue (per Bathurst CJ at [8], Whealy JA at [55]; Allsop P (as his Honour then was), McClellan CJ at CL, and McCallum J agreeing). Their Honours emphasised that the trial judge makes no evaluation of the actual weight of the evidence, Bathurst CJ observing, for example (at [8]), that:
>
> > [W]hat the court is required to assess is the possibility of the evidence affecting the assessment of the probability of the existence of a fact in issue. It is not required to assess whether the evidence would have this effect, that is, engage in a fact-finding exercise involving an assessment of the reliability and credibility of the evidence.
>
> (This reasoning, albeit not referred to by the plurality in *IMM v The Queen*, accords with the view there adopted.)
>
> 1034. Turning to the present case, it is not in dispute that the evidence of each of C1 and C2 was relevant; the question is whether it rose to the level of "significant" probative value for the purposes of s 98(1)(b). On the assumption (required by *IMM v The Queen*) that C1 and C2's evidence were to be accepted by the jury, it would clearly be influential and important in the context of fact-finding.
>
> 1035. Even accepting the appellants' argument that the relevant similarities in C1 and C2's accounts (given the limited scope of the facts in issue) were effectively reduced to the assertion that there was a cut and that there was hurting, nonetheless those similarities were in our view capable, to a significant degree, of rationally affecting the assessment (ultimately by a jury) of the probability of the existence of a fact in issue in the context of the other evidence led at the trial. Section 98(1)(b) required the trial judge to consider whether the evidence would "either by itself or having regard to other evidence adduced ... by the [Crown] have significant probative value". As we have stated above at [629], a different conclusion might have been reached in the absence of some of the evidence of Dr X and given the fresh medical evidence.
>
> 1036. The appellants pointed to matters which were said to strongly suggest that any similarities in C1 and C2's accounts were not an improbable coincidence but, rather, a result of the form of questioning – referring in particular to the fact that the relevant answers given by C1 and C2 in their interviews were not voluntarily disclosed, in the sense that the idea that there had been a cut to each complainant's private parts was introduced by the interviewer. However, we accept the Crown submission that C1 and C2's answers about the pain they felt during the procedure were in response to non-leading questions, and that C1, especially, provided significant details in response to non-leading questions. The form of questioning which elicited C1 and C2's evidence could be taken into account

136 [2018] NSWCCA 174.

137 See also *Gale and Duckworth* [2012] NSWCCA 174; 217 A Crim R 487. Note that the 2020 amendment to s 98 makes clear it can include 'evidence from 2 or more witnesses claiming they are victims of offences committed by a person who is a defendant in a criminal proceeding to prove, on the basis of similarities in the claimed acts or the circumstances in which they occurred, that the defendant did an act in issue in the proceeding'.

by the jury in assessing the weight (and reliability) of the evidence; this factor does not rob the evidence, taken at its highest, of a significant *capacity* (including in light of other evidence adduced or to be adduced) to rationally affect the assessment of the probability of the existence of a fact in issue.

1037. The appellants relied under this ground on the difficulties arising from C2's interview raised under ground 4, submitting that the probative value of C2's evidence needed to be assessed in the context of C2's lack of understanding of the difference between the truth and a lie. Earlier in these reasons, we have accepted (see above at [877]; [881]) that C2 was not competent to give sworn evidence. However, as stated above at [627], this factor goes to the weight of C2's evidence, not its probative value as defined in accordance with the authorities outlined above.

1038. Under ground 7(c), the appellants maintain that his Honour erred in his directions to the jury on the subject of coincidence evidence. Again, complaint is made that the trial judge focussed on conduct or events, rather than C1 and C2's accounts or allegations. However, reading the directions as a whole, we are satisfied that in referring to "what allegedly occurred" to C1 and C2, his Honour did not direct the jury incorrectly. It is well-established that the trial judge's summing up must be read as a whole, and when addressing a complaint as to a jury direction, it is insufficient to point to sentences or parts of sentence in isolation (see, for example, *Selby v R* [2017] NSWCCA 40 at [41]). His Honour expressly directed the jury that the critical issues in dispute were "whether there was any cutting or nicking so as to constitute female genital mutilation" (SU 60) and reminded the jury that the defence "says that they were not coincidental, but neither involved cutting or nicking, they were a symbolic 'skin sniffing the steel' procedure not involving any cutting or nicking" (SU 61).

Gilham's case, below, illustrates this concern. Jeffrey Gilham claimed he had killed his brother (Christopher) after catching him trying to cover up the murder of his parents, whom, Jeffrey claimed, Christopher had stabbed to death. Jeffrey Gilham admitted stabbing and killing Christopher in these circumstances and was found guilty of his manslaughter. A number of years later he stood trial and was convicted for the stabbing murder of his parents. In *Gilham*[138] he appealed his conviction on several grounds, including the inadmissibility of prosecution expert evidence that concluded that all three members of the family were stabbed in similar ways. Gilham, on appeal, argued that this was coincidence evidence (and so should have been at least considered under the requirements of ss 98 and 101).

McClellan CJ at CL, Fullerton and Garling JJ:

The evidence the Crown relied upon to prove relevant similarity

251. The evidence from Dr Lawrence, Dr Culliford and Dr Cala concerning the issue of similarity was referable to the number of stab wounds on the body of each of the deceased, the grouping of the wounds on the chest and back areas, the configuration of the wounds, and the alignment of the wound tracks relative to [each body].

252. … In cross-examination, dissimilarities in the alignment of some of the wounds suffered by Mr Gilham and Mrs Gilham on the one hand and Christopher on the other were emphasised. Defence counsel also sought to neutralise the significance of the evidence of similarity by inviting each of the expert witnesses to concede that since it was common ground that the same knife had been used to inflict the wounds on each of the deceased, the shape of each wound would necessarily take the shape and dimensions of the blade and that the wound depths were also likely to be comparable for that reason.

253. Defence counsel also sought and obtained the concession, at least from Dr Culliford and Dr Lawrence that the grouping of the wounds to the chest of each of the

138 [2012] NSWCCA 131 (and see also Chapter 2); *Gale and Duckworth* [2012] NSWCCA 174; 217 A Crim R 487 (distinguished in *DSJ and NS* [2014] NSWCCA 77, [102]-[104] (Gleeson JA, with Hidden and Rothman JJ agreeing)).

deceased was unremarkable given that the chest would be expected to be targeted by a person wielding a knife with an intention to kill. …

327. However, the Crown submission that a single stabber inflicted the wounds was an invitation to the jury to engage in coincidence reasoning. … The Crown effectively asked the jury to find that it was improbable that stabbings which exhibited such similarities were coincidentally, or "just so happened", to be inflicted by more than one person. The coincidence reasoning involved was manifest in the Crown Prosecutor's closing address. The issue of coincidence reasoning was not raised at the trial, nor was it argued on the appeal. Nevertheless, … the Crown Prosecutor's use of the evidence of similarity ought to have complied with the coincidence rule set out in s 98 …

328. The identification of the proposed use of the similarity evidence as falling within the coincidence rule is not purely academic. The coincidence rule requires that the court admitting the coincidence evidence be satisfied that the evidence has, either by itself or in conjunction with other evidence, "significant probative value". The coincidence evidence had probative value in the sense that it could have affected the jury's assessment of whether one person stabbed each of the deceased. Proof of that fact would have strongly supported the Crown case. But the question whether the evidence had *significant* probative value was never explored at the trial. Relevant to that question is the varying number of stab wounds; the fact that most stabbings are to the chest area; and the consideration that some of the similarities in the pattern of wounding may be accounted for by the use of the same knife, as distinct from their infliction by the same attacker. For the purposes of this appeal, it is not necessary to decide whether the evidence had significant probative value. We note, however, that that question may fall to be determined at a subsequent trial.

Prosecution Tendency or Coincidence Evidence about Accused

The reception of tendency evidence in a criminal trial may occasion prejudice in a number of ways. The jury may fail to allow that a person who has a tendency to have a particular state of mind, or to act in a particular way, may not have had that state of mind, or may not have acted in that way, on the occasion in issue. Or the jury may underestimate the number of persons who share the tendency to have that state of mind or to act in that way. In either case the tendency evidence may be given disproportionate weight. In addition to the risks arising from tendency reasoning, there is the risk that the assessment of whether the prosecution has discharged its onus may be clouded by the jury's emotional response to the tendency evidence. And prejudice may be occasioned by requiring an accused to answer a raft of uncharged conduct stretching back, perhaps, over many years.[139]

Section 101 of the *UEA* applies a balancing test to set the bar for admitting prosecution tendency or coincidence evidence about an accused. It requires a judgment to be made, not the exercise of a discretion. It applies in addition to ss 97 and 98 and, unless the evidence is led to explain or contradict evidence adduced by the accused, the prosecution cannot lead tendency or coincidence evidence about an accused 'unless the probative value of the evidence outweighs the danger of unfair prejudice to the defendant'. There are a number of factors that come to bear in applying this test. First, not all evidence of events constituting coincidence evidence or adduced to show a tendency to act in a particular way, or have a particular state of mind, necessarily shows criminal conduct or conjures up highly negative connotations. In these circumstances, the danger of

139 *Hughes* [2017] HCA 20; 263 CLR 338, [17].

unfair prejudice is likely to be less severe than with evidence revealing criminal or odious conduct. For example, in *Milat*,[140] there was evidence that Milat had a habit, or a tendency, to pick up hitchhikers, a tendency that on its own is not likely to be unfairly prejudicial. Similar principles apply to assessing prejudicial effect under s 101 as those considered within the context of s 137.[141] The trial judge must consider whether directions to the jury may reduce any unfairly prejudicial effect.[142] Evidence that merely establishes the prosecution case is not *unfairly* prejudicial.

> Rather, the prejudice must be the risk of harm to the interests of the accused in a way that is unfair because there is a real risk that the evidence will be misused by the jury in some unfair way, such as provoking some irrational, emotional or illogical response, or giving the evidence more weight than it truly deserves.[143]

Section 101 provides:

> **101. Further restrictions on tendency evidence and coincidence evidence adduced by prosecution**[144]
>
> (1) This section only applies in a criminal proceeding and so applies in addition to sections 97 and 98.
>
> (2) Tendency evidence about a defendant, or coincidence evidence about a defendant, that is adduced by the prosecution cannot be used against the defendant unless the probative value of the evidence outweighs the danger of unfair prejudice to the defendant.
>
> (3) This section does not apply to tendency evidence that the prosecution adduces to explain or contradict tendency evidence adduced by the defendant.
>
> (4) This section does not apply to coincidence evidence that the prosecution adduces to explain or contradict coincidence evidence adduced by the defendant.

Typically, a major concern with tendency evidence is its role in the prosecution case and particularly the danger of unfair prejudice, because it often exposes the jury to past criminal, immoral or negative information about the accused and hence exposes the accused to the danger of being judged on the basis of unfair prejudice. The UK Law Commission relied on the taxonomy of 'moral prejudice' and 'reasoning prejudice' suggested by Andrew Palmer and concluded that, even allowing for its limitations, psychological research supported a cautious approach to the evidence. Some of the considerations explained by psychological research are summarised as follows.

> This is because it (Pennycook and Thompson, 2012) shows that people tend to exaggerate the significance of a small amount of such knowledge about a person and uninformed probability structures replace robust evidence-based determinations. As a consequence, people will be inclined to conclude someone is a thief if they are told that he or she has stolen previously, irrespective of whether they make the decision with inadequate contextual information. Further, research indicates that we create conjunctions in this way due to deeply entrenched tendencies to build mental models to enable us to understand our surroundings, navigate life (such as establishing who to trust or believe) and

140 Unreported, NSWSC, 5 September 1996.

141 *MM* [2014] NSWCCA 144; *Blick* [2000] NSWCCA 61; 111 A Crim R 326; *Ellis* [2003] NSWCCA 319; 58 NSWLR 700; *PWD* [2010] NSWCCA 209.

142 *DAO* [2011] NSWCCA 63; 81 NSWLR 568, [104].

143 *MM* [2014] NSWCCA 144, [43], citing *Ford* [2009] NSWCCA 306; 201 A Crim R 451, [56]; *Suteski* [2002] NSWCCA 509; 56 NSWLR 182, [116].

144 Until 1 July 2020, *UEA*, s 101(2), required the probative value of prosecution tendency or coincidence evidence about a defendant to '*substantially*' outweigh 'any prejudicial effect it may have on the defendant'.

to reach judgments of a more considered kind. We are tempted to rely on stereotypes when faced with demanding challenges. Particularly challenging for the efficacy of the criminal trial is psychological research showing that as a general rule, human beings do not readily integrate conflicting sources of information, preferring to prioritise one source over others. Further, research has isolated specific dynamics that potentially distort an individual's perceptions of others. Expressed broadly, these are the halo effect (that is, that a general impression colours a broad set of qualities about an individual), the impact of attribution theory (where an individual example of behaviour is treated as indicative of long-standing and stable personality traits) and a decision-maker's diminished regret matrix (that is, a reduced regret that a negative decision about a person may be wrong where a person leaves a negative impression). Cognitive overload – plentiful for jurors in a criminal trial – makes heuristic shortcuts particularly tempting (Kahnemann and Frederick, 2002: 49, 54; Callen, 2012: 312). …

If there are circumstances where evidence of a defendant's bad character can speak logically to a disposition to act in a particular manner without eroding the presumption of innocence, then this dynamic needs to be properly understood, evaluated and incorporated into law reform initiatives. If humans are prone to rely on assumptions, stereotypes and apply cognition shortcuts in a manner that undermines the presumption of innocence and the integrity of the verdict, these tendencies too are worthy of careful consideration and integration into law reform. Further, it is undoubtedly important to appreciate that deep social and political forces can join with psychological ones to make less visible base punitive motivation.[145]

Bell P (with explicit agreement from Walton and Beech-Jones JJ in relation to s 101) in *Taylor* summarised the principles that can be drawn from authorities to date with respect to s 101:[146]

(xix) the assessment required under s 101(2) involves the trial judge making an evaluative judgment; it is not a discretionary exercise: see, for example, *R v Cook* [2004] NSWCCA 52 at [38]; and *Ford* at [63]

(xx) the nature of tendency evidence is inherently prejudicial (see *SK* at [34]; and *RH* at [169]), and may have a powerful subconscious effect on a jury: see *Hughes* at [71]-[74];

(xxi) there is an inevitability that prior illegal acts, especially perhaps where the illegal acts relate to alleged sexual acts or acts of domestic violence, will be prejudicial in terms of their impact: see, for example, *Qualtieri v R* (2006) 171 A Crim R 463; [2006] NSWCCA 95 at [80];

(xxii) "unfair prejudice" in s 101(2) as amended refers to harm to the interests of the accused that is unfair, because there is a real risk that the evidence will be misused by the jury in some unfair way, for example, by providing some irrational, emotional or illogical response or by giving the evidence more weight than it truly deserves;[147]

(xxiii) unfair prejudice might arise from:

145 Hunter, 'Book Review', above n 14, 169-70, citing A Palmer, 'The Scope of the Similar Fact Rule' (1994) 16 *Adelaide Law Review* 161. See generally NZLC, *Evidence Law: Character and Credibility* (Discussion Paper, PP 27, 1997). See also A Tversky and D Kahnemann, 'Extensional versus intuitive reasoning: The conjunction fallacy in probability judgment' (1983) 90(4) *Psychological Review* 293. See also JP Forgas and SM Laham, 'Halo Effects' in (ed), RF Pohl, *Cognitive Illusions: Intriguing Phenomena in Judgement, Thinking and Memory* (Routledge, 2nd ed, 2017).

146 *Taylor* [2020] NSWCCA 355, [122]. Bell P dissented in relation to the application of s 97(1)(b). This case applied s 101 as drafted before the 2020 amendment (though the points remain apt under the amended version as well).

147 See *Ford* [2009] NSWCCA 306; 201 A Crim R 451, [56]; *BD* (1997) 94 A Crim R 131, 139; *Papakosmas* [1999] HCA 37; 196 CLR 297, 325, [91]; *Suteski* [2002] NSWCCA 509; 56 NSWLR 182, 199 [116]; *SSN* [2012] NSWCCA 163, [37]; and *MM* [2014] NSWCCA 144, [43].

(a) the nature or quality of the conduct the subject of the tendency evidence;
(b) whether or not it has been established or the subject of admissions;
(c) where it involves a plethora of factors that might give rise to a confusion or distraction;
(d) whether it is corroborated;
(e) an underestimation by the jury of the number of persons who share the tendency: see *Hughes* at [17];
(f) where there has been no past conviction or admission as to the past conduct, the need for an accused to answer uncharged conduct potentially stretching back over many years: see *Hughes* at [17]; and
(g) a jury's emotional or irrational response to particular tendency evidence; or
(h) any combination of the above (non-exhaustive) factors;

(xxiv) when considering whether the probative value of tendency evidence outweighs its prejudicial effect, the Court is entitled to take into account that juries are to be properly directed as to the use to which such evidence is to be put: see *PWD* at [90]; *RH* at [176]; and *Armstrong* at [24];

(xxv) acceptance of the proposition that juries generally follow directions given to them by trial judges, and that that obedience will often solve problems of prejudice against an accused person, has its limits, and judicial directions to juries are not to be thought of as an unfailing panacea for all forms of prejudice: see, for example, *R v Allen*;[148]

(xxvi) there will be cases (of which *McPhillamy* is an illustration) where directions to a jury, even coupled with an assumption that they will be conscientiously followed, will be incapable of overcoming or ameliorating prejudice: see, for example, *Patel*;[149] *GAC*;[150] and *Sokolowskyj*;[151]

(xxvii) "[a]n assumption that a judicial direction to the jury designed to minimise the risk of unfair prejudice will be completely effective would effectively prevent s 101(2) operating as a safeguard against the potential risk of miscarriages of justice arising from the admission of tendency evidence": see *Sokolowskyj* at [56]; see also *Allen* at [154]. This may, for example, be because of the nature or extent of the prejudice which the evidence carries or the subconscious effect on the jury, notwithstanding directions;

(xxviii) the corollary of the proposition confirmed in *IMM*, namely that the probative value of the tendency evidence is to be assessed on the basis that the jury will accept it at its highest, is that, to the extent that that evidence carried prejudice to an accused, that prejudice is to be assessed on the same basis, namely that the jury will accept the evidence at its highest. In other words, the impact of any prejudice is not to be reduced by reason of the fact that the jury might not accept the evidence as credible or reliable.

Consider also that this evidence is typically brought to bear where there is a paucity of evidence (or evidence that is considered compelling). These are cases that rely substantially only circumstantial evidence. However, as McHugh J in *Pfennig*[152] observed:

> One of the dangers of circumstantial evidence is that the logical coherence of a theory that fits the known circumstances pulls the mind to conclusions that would never be reached if more circumstances were known. The natural tendency of a tribunal of fact in

148 [2020] NSWCCA 173, [111], [115] and [152]-[160].
149 *Patel* [2012] HCA 29; 247 CLR 531, [113], [128] and [129].
150 *GAC* [2007] NSWCCA 315; 178 A Crim R 408, [83].
151 *Sokolowskyj* [2014] NSWCCA 55, [48].
152 [1995] HCA 7; 182 CLR 461, [59].

> a circumstantial evidence case is to dismiss as fanciful or speculative alternative theories that require the existence of circumstances in addition to those that are known. In *res ipsa loquitur* cases, for example, defendants rarely persuade judges or juries that they are not negligent when the cause of the accident is not established. In criminal trials, the tendency to dismiss exculpatory theories as fanciful or speculative is often likely to be present because there would be no case to go to the jury unless there was a theory of the known circumstances that pointed to the accused. For that reason, many counsel, experienced in the conduct of criminal trials, would much prefer to defend a case based on eye-witness evidence than one based on circumstantial evidence.

Cossins explains this advocates' 'know how' through psychological research, beginning by identifying that:

(i) 'jurors' decisions involve a complex and nuanced set of cognitive processes that transform difficult choices into easier ones by amplifying one alternative perspective on the evidence and deflating competing perspectives';[153]
(ii) individuals, generally, hold particular beliefs and attitudes that affect their reasoning processes and 'bias reasoning performance'; and
(iii) when jurors are 'faced with complicated cognitive tasks' and lack the motivation or ability to understand and interpret the evidence, they will rely on heuristic cues to determine guilt.[154]

As Cossins explains, research indicates that when jurors' comprehension difficulties trigger heuristic reasoning, this is associated with poorer evidence recall.[155] Cossins applied this analysis to the *Makin* case where the lack of detail explaining so many babies bodies (other than by applying the prosecutor's explanation) made the assumption of murder compelling, and so made relevant to the evidence of the babies' bodies, yet '"[t]his *kind* of propensity reasoning is of no probative value *unless*"[156] there is evidence to support the heuristic cue. This assumption diverts individuals from more effortful systematic processing and evaluation of the evidence'.[157] The only evidence of foul play was the evidence, that was only relevant if there was foul play. This replicates the issues Murphy J raised with respect to Emily Perry's case. Cossins suggests that tendency and coincidence evidence be treated with caution in murder trials, requiring such evidence be admitted where there is a cause of death and some proof of the commission of the *actus reus* by the defendant. She explains:

> In order to test whether circular reasoning is involved in the relevance inquiry, it is necessary to ask: (i) what actual act or conduct by the defendant does the similar fact evidence reveal? If no conduct is revealed, then (ii) does the evidence invite, via heuristic cues, the assumption that all the people with whom the defendant is associated and who died in a

153 [RJ Winter and E Greene, 'Juror Decision-Making' in F Durso et al (eds), *Handbook of Applied Cognition* (Wiley, 2nd ed, 2007), 731, 741, citing D Simon, 'A Third View of the Black Box: Cognitive Coherence in Legal Decision-Making' (2004) 71 *University of Chicago Law Review* 511.]

154 A Cossins, 'The Legacy of the Makin Case 120 Years on: Legal Fictions, Circular Reasoning and Some Solutions' (2013) 35 *Sydney Law Review* 731, 755, citing S Chaiken, 'Heuristic Versus Systematic Information Processing and the Use of Source Versus Message Cues in Persuasion' (1980) 39 *Journal of Personality & Social Psychology* 752; Winter and Greene, above n 153, 741, citing Simon, above n 153.

155 Citing EA Charman, TM Honess and M Levi, 'Juror Competence and Processing Style in Making Sense of Complex Trial Information' in R Roesch, RR Corrado and RJ Dempster (eds), *Psychology in the Courts: International Advances in Knowledge* (Routledge, 2001).

156 AE Acorn, 'Similar Fact Evidence and the Principle of Inductive Reasoning: Makin Sense' (1991) 11 *Oxford Journal of Legal Studies* 63, 64 (emphasis in original).

157 Cossins, above n 154, 740.

particular way were murdered by the defendant? If the defendant is merely associated with similar, apparently criminal events and no particular type of conduct by the defendant is revealed, then heuristic assumptions and circular reasoning are likely to fill in the gaps.[158]

Returning to consideration of the extent to which child sexual assault proceedings justify special consideration, as the *Hughes* case illustrated, an important dimension of the tendency rule is its capacity to enable charges to be heard in a single jury trial. The RCIRCSA's findings revealed that perpetrators of child sexual assault, unrestrained by institutional culture, were immune from criminal sanction for decades. Multiple acts of child sexual abuse within and across institutions were rife. There are some well-established principles that apply to the joining of counts in a single trial. In *DR*[159] the court found that there was no unacceptable risk of prejudice to DR from evidence admitted against a co-accused (PV) in a joint trial. In reading this conclusion Brereton JA discussed the findings of the Jury Reasoning Study (discussed below) and added the following summary of the law:

> 18. It is well-established that, as a general rule, persons charged with committing an offence jointly should be tried together. This is so, notwithstanding that some prejudice to one or other accused is almost inevitable, because the prejudice may be obviated by appropriate directions to the jury, and it is assumed that juries obey directions. Separate trials should be ordered only where a joint trial would produce a real risk (as opposed to a remote possibility) of positive injustice, in the sense of prejudice that cannot be cured by direction, sufficient to outweigh the public interest in the efficient dispatch of trials, the conserving of costs and the avoidance of inconvenience to witnesses by having to attend multiple trials.
>
> 19. Unfair prejudice may arise, where evidence admissible against one accused is inadmissible against the other, in two ways: first, that evidence may create unacceptable collateral prejudice, by establishing bad character or other prejudicial connotations; and secondly, it may impermissibly bolster an otherwise relatively weak case against an accused against whom it is inadmissible; but in either case that will be so only if the risk of prejudice cannot be cured by judicial direction. A separate trial will usually be ordered in relation to the charges against an accused who applies for severance where (1) the evidence against the applicant is significantly weaker than and different to that admissible against the other accused; (2) the evidence against the other accused contains material highly prejudicial to, but not admissible against, the applicant; and (3) there is a real risk that the weaker Crown case against the applicant will be made immeasurably stronger by the prejudicial material. However these guidelines are not exhaustive, and each case must depend upon its own facts. …
>
> 26. Recently, in [2019] NSWCCA 276, this court has, on an interlocutory appeal, overturned a trial judge's refusal to sever an indictment; the essential reason was that in a joint trial, there would be evidence of admissions made by a co-accused which were not admissible against the applicant, but which would support evidence given by other witnesses who were to give evidence in the case against him. The Court was of the view that there was a significant risk that, despite careful directions, the inadmissible evidence, consistent as it was with the Crown case against the applicant, would be used to reason that the evidence of other Crown witnesses was reliable – in a way which could not sensibly be distinguished from the case against the applicant – so that there was a real risk of positive prejudice to the applicant, as there was significant potential for even a properly instructed jury in a joint trial to be influenced by evidence that they would be told that, as against the applicant, they must disregard.[160]

158 Ibid 755.

159 [2019] NSWCCA 320 (Brereton JA, with Hoeben CJ at CL and Cavanagh J agreeing).

160 Citing *Middis* (unreported, NSWSC, Hunt J, 27 March 1991); *Darby* [1982] HCA 32; 148 CLR 668, 677-8; *Webb* [1994] HCA 30; 181 CLR 41, 88-9; *Patsalis and Spathis* [1999] NSWSC 649;

The 2020 amendment to s 101 requiring the probative value of evidence to merely outweigh the danger of unfair prejudice arose from recommendations from the RCIRCSA to liberalise the admissibility of tendency evidence. This change applies to all offences (and not just to child sexual assault proceedings) and reflects the move also seen in in England and Wales to less restrictive admissibility requirements for tendency and coincidence evidence. A particular feature of the RCIRCSA recommendations is their focus on facilitating more cross-admissibility of evidence and more joint trials in child sexual abuse matters.[161] This potentially saves complainants needing to give evidence in multiple trials and, as we saw in *Hughes*, protected juries from receiving a narrow and distorted impression of the prosecution case. Such insight might help to prevent finding a single complainant's account improbable. This concern was recognised by the RCIRCSA.

> Particularly where abuse is alleged in an institutional context by a number of complainants, the jury does not get a true picture of what is alleged and the trial can be quite misleading if each complainant's allegations are heard by a separate jury rather than in a joint trial.
>
> Excluding tendency and coincidence evidence also unfairly risks undermining the credibility and reliability of the evidence given by some complainants in the eyes of the jury. If tendency or coincidence evidence is excluded, or a joint trial is not allowed, complainants may be restricted in the evidence they can give because their evidence would reveal that the accused has prior convictions or is facing other allegations. This may make the process of giving evidence more difficult for them and they may look uncertain or even dishonest in front of the jury.[162]

The Commission supported the Jury Reasoning Study (JRS)[163] to consider the extent to which multiple allegations by different complainants could be heard by one jury without jurors giving disproportionate weight to the allegations (such as by applying the circular reasoning described at the beginning of this chapter) or other ways in which unfair prejudice might manifest. Such concerns were summed up by Hayne J in *BBH* bluntly through the saying of 'give a dog an ill name, and hang him'.[164] The JRS is a large-scale study with over 1000 participants recruited to watch an electronically recorded enactment of a version of 10 mini-trials. This reliance on evidence-based examination is rare in Australia (and internationally) and is an aspect of the ground-breaking nature of the Royal Commission. JRS participants deliberated as a 'jury', considering scripts that reflected the standards applicable under the pre-2020 tendency rule for prosecution evidence. It created 10 trial types, each with differing judicial instructions according to the situation. The trials included either one or three complainants and between two and six charges. There were scenarios with

---

107 A Crim R 432, [15]-[20]; *Alexander and McKenzie* [2002] VSCA 183; 6 VR 53, [31]; *Gilbert* [2000] HCA 15; 201 CLR 414, [13], [31]; *Decision restricted* [2019] NSWCCA 276, [61]; *Ross* [2012] NSWCCA 207, [24]-[26]; *Henry, Gravett and Swansson* [2008] NSWCCA 248, [12]-[13]; *DPP (Cth) v Burrows* [2017] NSWCCA 105, [47]-[53]; *Demirok* [1976] VicRp 19; [1976] VR 244; *Jones and Waghorn* (1991) 55 A Crim R 159, 164; *Iaria and Young* [2015] VSCA 265, [37]; *Guldur* (1986) 8 NSWLR 12, 16-17; 25 A Crim R 271; *Alexander and McKenzie* [2002] VSCA 183; 6 VR 53, [31].

161 RCIRCSA, *Criminal Justice Executive Summary* (2017), 69.

162 See <https://www.childabuseroyalcommission.gov.au/sites/default/files/file-list/factsheet_-_criminal_justice_report_-_tendency_and_coincidence_evidence_and_joint_trials.pdf>.

163 J Goodman-Delahunty, A Cossins and N Martchuk, *Jury Reasoning in Joint and Separate Trials of Institutional Child Sexual Abuse: An Empirical Study* (2016).

164 [2012] HCA 9; 245 CLR 499, [71].

(1) separate trials (with single complainants of varying credibility);
(2) a trial with a single complainant plus relationship evidence (showing acts of grooming);
(3) a trial with a single complainant plus tendency evidence from two witnesses; and
(4) a joint trial with six counts relating to three complainants.

The Study evaluated juror confusion and the risk of unfair prejudice to the defendant in joint trials, comparing them with the less complex trials. The JRS found no evidence of a 'joinder effect' (that is, an increase in jury (or juror) conviction rates between certain trial types) and concluded that joining trials do not carry unfair prejudice, observing that 'there were no significant differences between conviction rates in the tendency evidence trial compared to the joint trial'.[165] However, these results are not the last word. Apart from the fact that they evaluated joinder under a legislative regime that was more demanding in its application of the tendency rule to prosecution evidence than the post-RCIRCSA situation, its reliance on mock jury rather than real jury circumstances needs to be taken into consideration.

Joinder effect may arise from 'impermissible reasoning' (as described at the beginning of the chapter), or through jurors misremembering some details, leading to deliberations being contaminated with error, potentially giving rise to unfair prejudice. At issue was whether a more complex trial created more complex deliberations, triggering this kind of error. While a statistically significant joinder effect was not identified between *juries*, it was identified between *jurors*.[166] However, this is where 'self-correction' can be important. It is, after all, an intrinsic part of the deliberation process that jurors speak out where they disagree, and also where they consider a fellow juror is in error. Self-correction relies on juror errors being verbalised, and also on a juror standing corrected.[167] It would be useful if this study could be replicated with the current formulations of the tendency rule.

Older studies, also mostly mock jury ones, are not as sophisticated as this RCIRCSA Jury Reasoning Study. The 1995 English *Oxford Study*, a mock jury study conducted by Sally Lloyd-Bostock, involved jury-eligible people watching a 30-minute video of 24 different versions of 'trials' varying jurors' exposure to

165 Goodman-Delahunty, Cossins and Martchuk, above n 163, 24.

166 58.8% (10/17) of juries convicted the defendant on count 1 compared to 87.5% (14/16) of juries hearing the joint trial. This is not a significant variation. The data for individual juror conviction rates show that 73.7% of jurors in the tendency evidence trial reported a willingness to convict after deliberation compared to 90.8% in the joint trial. This is a significant result. See J Hunter and RI Kemp, 'Proposed Changes to the Tendency Rule: A Note of Caution' (2017) 41 *Criminal Law Journal* 253, 258.

167 The JRS found only 7.7% of juries made more than two factual errors. However, overall, most juries (63.3%) made at least one factual error during deliberation, which was in fact higher for joint trials (78.9%) than the tendency evidence trial (47.1%) or the basic separate trial (44.4%). Some errors also went unnoticed, especially in joint trials. Further, reliance on self-correction to heal the damage of the original error is potentially subject to criticism. A juror's factual or reasoning error might persist even after the correction. Indeed, several decades of psychological research show that judicial instruction (correction) to a jury to disregard inadmissible evidence is likely to be ineffective or even counterproductive – the inadmissible evidence still impacts jury decision-making, see N Steblay et al, 'The Impact on Juror Verdicts of Judicial Instruction to Disregard Inadmissible Evidence: A Meta-analysis' (2006) 30 *Law and Human Behavior* 469 and Hunter and Kemp, above n 166, 259.

evidence of the accused's criminal history,[168] and found that mock jurors treated a *similar* previous conviction as significantly increasing the likelihood of a guilty verdict, a finding largely confirmed by other studies. For example, a 2008 study of actual jurors reported by the US National Center for State Courts found a marked increase where juries discovered the accused had a prior criminal record.[169] An older English mock jury study (from 1973), the LSE Jury Project,[170] also found that a co-accused suffered a similar disadvantage to the other accused, if that other accused had similar previous convictions. Mock jury studies suffer the disadvantage of remoteness from reality, but they nevertheless offer valuable insight into the premises relied on by evidence law, and also what it actually achieves.

Additionally, research also suggests that people are prone to under-appreciate the cultural impact of behaviour and how it is interpreted. Cross-cultural 'factors such as reputation or demeanour may have an influence on the fact-finder out of all proportion to their actual evidential value'.[171] In New Zealand cultural distortions were apparent with respect to witnesses and accused people of Mäori or Pacific Island origin. In Australia, the ATSI community and the broad cultural mix of our society make this a particularly pertinent issue.

For a trial judge, in admitting evidence as having satisfied s 101, the balancing task requires identifying the types of unfair prejudice the evidence may give rise to and, in light of the potential for directions to ameliorate this impact, indicate why the probative value outweighs any unfair prejudice that the evidence may have on the accused.[172] As Spigelman CJ observed in the important case of *Ellis*,[173] the section 'calls for a balancing exercise which can only be conducted on the facts of each case'. It is useful to note that the *Ellis* court, a five-judge NSW Court of Criminal Appeal bench, stated that the dissenting opinion of McHugh J in *Pfennig*[174] summarised the logic and application of the express requirements in s 101. After discussing the fact that evidence based on propensity reasoning needs more than just strong probative value, McHugh J observed:

> 38. … The risk of an unfair trial through the use of propensity reasoning is too great to allow such a low threshold of admissibility. Consequently, this Court has insisted that as a matter of law and not discretion the probative value of the evidence must outweigh or transcend its prejudicial effect[175] …
>
> 39. Nevertheless, the proposition that the probative value of the evidence must outweigh its prejudicial effect is one that can be easily misunderstood. The use of the term 'outweigh' suggests an almost arithmetical computation. But prejudicial effect and

168 The Oxford Study, see Law Commission (UK), *Evidence in Criminal Proceedings: Previous Misconduct of a Defendant* (Consultation Paper No 141, 1996), Appendix D; see also S Lloyd-Bostock, 'The Effects on Juries of Hearing About the Defendant's Previous Criminal Record: A Simulation Study' [2000] *Criminal Law Review* 734; and see S Lloyd-Bostock, *Research 2000: Magistrates Study* (Lord Chancellor's Department).

169 DJ Givelber and AS Farrell, 'Judge and Juries: The Defense case and Differences in Acquittal Rates' [2008] *Law of Social Inquiry* 33, cited in DJ Devine, *Jury Decision Making: The State of the Science* (NYU Press, 2012), 98-9.

170 AP Sealy and WR Cornish, 'LSE Jury Project, Juries and the Rules of Evidence' [1973] *Criminal Law Review* 208.

171 NZLC, above n 145, [49].

172 *Ford* [2009] NSWCCA 306; 201 A Crim R 451 (Campbell JA); *PWD* [2010] NSWCCA 209.

173 (2003) 58 NSWLR 700, [95]. The High Court granted, then revoked, special leave: [2004] HCATrans 311; 488.

174 [1995] HCA 7; 182 CLR 461.

175 Citing numerous High Court precedents from the 1980s.

probative value are incommensurables. They have no standard of comparison. The probative value of the evidence goes to proof of an issue, the prejudicial effect to the fairness of the trial. In criminal trials, the prejudicial effect of evidence is not concerned with the cogency of its proof but with the risk that the jury will use the evidence or be affected by it in a way that the law does not permit. In no sense does the probative value of evidence disclosing propensity, when admitted, outweigh its prejudicial effect. On the contrary, in many cases the probative value either creates or reinforces the prejudicial effect of the evidence. In my view, evidence that discloses the criminal or discreditable propensity of the accused is admitted not because its probative value outweighs its prejudicial effect but because the interests of justice require its admission despite the risk, or in some cases the inevitability, that the fair trial of the charge will be prejudiced.

40. If there is a real risk that the admission of such evidence may prejudice the fair trial of the criminal charge before the court, the interests of justice require the trial judge to make a value judgment, not a mathematical calculation. The judge must compare the probative strength of the evidence with the degree of risk of an unfair trial if the evidence is admitted. Admitting the evidence will serve the interests of justice only if the judge concludes that the probative force of the evidence compared to the degree of risk of an unfair trial is such that fair minded people would think that the public interest in adducing all relevant evidence of guilt must have priority over the risk of an unfair trial.

41. If the evidence does no more than prove a mere propensity to commit crimes of the kind in question, it will never have sufficient probative force to make it admissible. If it does have the required degree of probative force, it will be because it is relevant for a reason other than proof of propensity or because it colours one's perception of the other evidence to such an extent that it can be confidently inferred that the accused gave effect to the propensity on the occasion in question. Evidence of a striking similarity between the commission of the crime and the method used by the accused will frequently be sufficient to prove that inference. But striking similarity is not the exclusive test. The circumstantial force of the other evidence together with the propensity evidence may prove the inference. *Ball* [1911] AC 47 is a good example. Without the propensity evidence, the prosecution had proved no more than an opportunity to commit incest. Moreover, the propensity evidence had no intrinsic mark that connected it with the other evidence. However, the combination of the propensity evidence and the other evidence pointed irresistibly to incest having occurred. Proof of the offence depended on probability reasoning not similar facts. For propensity evidence to be admissible, however, it will need to have 'specific probative value *in relation to the crime charged*'.[176] Even then, propensity evidence will not be admitted if the prejudicial value of the evidence makes it contrary to the interests of justice to admit it.[177]

Ellis

[2003] NSWCCA 319; 58 NSWLR 700

Ellis achieved in 2003 what had defied courts up to that date – it insisted that the express words of s 101 be applied to the facts of a case rather than the common law standard of admissibility, the 'no rational explanation consistent with innocence' test, which had been reiterated by the majority in the High Court case of *Pfennig* in 1995.

Ultimately, it is the *application* of s 101 that sheds light on its impact on the admissibility of prosecution tendency and coincidence evidence about an accused. In *Ellis* the defence sought separate hearings regarding 13 counts of break, enter

176 [DK Piragoff, *Similar fact evidence: Probative value and prejudice* (Carswell's Criminal Law Series, 1981), 109.]

177 Citations omitted.

and steal of shops in regional towns in New South Wales. All offences occurred in the early hours of the morning in the first four months of 1999. Cash, cigarettes and similar small items were taken. The 'signature' element of the offences was the removal of a whole pane of glass to enable entry and no fingerprints disclosing identity. Two of the 13 counts were severed. These involved the same modus operandi but were distinguishable because they related to events in 1996. In addition, the judge excluded evidence that Ellis had on four prior occasions in 1994 admitted to break enter and steal matters, or of a break enter and steal at Wodonga (Victoria) in late April 1999.

Summary of Prosecution Case: *Ellis* (2003) 58 NSWLR 700

<table>
<tr><th>Count 1</th><th>Count 2</th><th>Counts 3 & 4</th><th>Count 5</th></tr>
<tr><td>Bathurst</td><td>Mudgee</td><td>Cowra</td><td>Young</td></tr>
<tr><td>Café

12/13 January 1999</td><td>Chicken shop

12/13 January 1999</td><td>2 x Milk bars

15/16 January 1999</td><td>Chicken shop

15/16 January 1999</td></tr>
<tr><td>Cigarettes valued at $7000 + small items</td><td>Nil taken</td><td>Ct 3, $5600 + cigarettes etc
Ct 4, nil taken</td><td>$2000 cigarettes</td></tr>
<tr><td colspan="4">Pane of glass removed/process of removal (when disturbed); no fingerprints left, expertise required; all occurred late night/early morning.</td></tr>
<tr><td colspan="2">Ellis's stepfather hired rental car from western Sydney location for 24 hours & mileage was consistent with prosecution case that car used.</td><td colspan="2"></td></tr>
<tr><td colspan="2"></td><td colspan="2">Telephone records link Ellis to locations early in the morning.</td></tr>
<tr><td></td><td>Glazier testified that task required special glazier skills, at least 2 people and highly likely that two 'jobs' involved the same people.</td><td colspan="2"></td></tr>
</table>

As the tables (above and opposite) show, the connections between the offences relied on by the prosecution were:

- The signature form of break in, requiring expertise. Evidence was given that it was a rare form of break in.
- The offences were all of small businesses in New South Wales regional towns in late evening/early hours of the morning.
- Some multiple thefts occurring on the same evening.
- A narrow repertoire of target businesses: cafés, chicken shops, newsagencies or service stations.
- Links across six counts through the use of rental cars through Ellis's stepfather as well as another two counts linked to de facto partner's car. An employee at the rental car company testified that Ellis was present with his stepfather two of the four times the car was collected. She identified him driving a VK or VL series Commodore car. Ellis's de facto at the time had such a car. Further, a Commodore car matching the registration details of Ellis's de facto partner's car was identified in Yass (counts 10 and 11).

- Links across four counts through telephone records indicating Ellis's phone was near the location of one of the offences at a time consistent with the prosecution case.
- A search warrant executed on 17 March on the father-in-law's home found batteries with Yass Newsagency price stickers as well as a number of items that were consistent with those stolen from the newsagency on 15 March.
- A search warrant executed on 28 March at Ellis's home identified the car belonging to Ellis's de facto partner.

<table>
<tr><th>Counts 6 & 7</th><th>Count 8</th><th>Count 9</th><th>Counts 10 & 11</th></tr>
<tr><td colspan="2">Wagga Wagga</td><td colspan="2">Yass</td></tr>
<tr><td>Cts 6 & 7, Café

19/20 February 1999</td><td>Newsagency

8 March 1999</td><td>Newsagency

15 March 1999</td><td>Service Station

Ct 10, 14 April
Ct 11, 27 April 1999</td></tr>
<tr><td>Ct 6, cash/ cigarettes valued at $1120

Ct 7, cigarettes valued at $1357</td><td>Cigarettes, valued at $2200</td><td>Cigarettes, cash, other items, total value, <$10,000</td><td>Cash, cigarettes, valued at over $3,000</td></tr>
<tr><td colspan="4">Pane of glass removed/process of removal (when disturbed); no fingerprints left; expertise required; all occurred late night/early morning.</td></tr>
<tr><td colspan="2">Ellis's stepfather hired rental car from western Sydney location for 24 hours & mileage was consistent with prosecution case that car used.

In relation to counts 6 & 7, D Ellis signed out car.</td><td>Ellis's stepfather hired rental car from western Sydney location for 24 hours + car returned by man matching Ellis's description (incl tattoos on legs).</td><td></td></tr>
<tr><td></td><td>Telephone records link Ellis to locations early in the morning.</td><td colspan="2"></td></tr>
<tr><td>Disturbed at 3.40 am. Witness described offender as fair haired, 5' 7" average build young male, with bag, gloves</td><td>Car registration noted by eyewitness who described fair young man, with bag</td><td>Car registration noted at time and proximate to break in.</td><td>Ellis' partner's car features (Ct 10) and registration (Ct 11) noted in Yass at time and location proximate to break ins.</td></tr>
</table>

Spigelman CJ (with Sully, O'Keefe, Hidden and Buddin JJ agreeing) noted that the *UEA* has created a comprehensive approach to 'similar fact' evidence. This approach shows a clear intention to 'operate in accordance with its own terms',[178] particularly with innovations such as the notice system, its defining of terms such as 'tendency' and 'coincidence', and the introduction of s 94. The definition of 'probative value' applying across the Act also showed a desire for interpretative consistency across the whole of the legislation. The language of s 101(2) directly replaces the *Pfennig* 'no rational explanation' formulation with a legislative one. Spigelman CJ noted:

> 84. … In the overall context of the significant changes made to the pre-existing common law to which I have referred above, I find this last consideration determinative …
>
> 88. The continued application of a 'no rational view' test is not, in my opinion, consistent with a statutory test which expressly requires a balancing process and tilts that process

178 (2003) 58 NSWLR 700, [78].

> in the same direction as that which the joint judgment in *Pfennig* suggested, but by the use of different terminology, ie 'substantially'.[179]

His Honour noted that the reasoning of McHugh J (dissenting) in *Pfennig* was compelling and directly apposite to s 101(2):

> If evidence revealing criminal propensity is not admissible unless the evidence is consistent only with the guilt of the accused, the requirement that the probative value 'outweigh' or 'transcend' the prejudicial effect is superfluous. The evidence either meets the no rational explanation test or it does not. There is nothing to be weighed – at all events by the trial judge. The law has already done the weighing. This means that, even in cases where the risk of prejudice is very small, the prosecution cannot use the evidence unless it satisfies the stringent no rational explanation test. It cannot use the evidence even though in a practical sense its probative value outweighs its prejudicial effect.[180]

Spigelman CJ added (emphasis added):

> 95. *Section 101(2) calls for a balancing exercise which can only be conducted on the facts of each case. It requires the Court to make a judgment, rather than to exercise a discretion. The 'no rational explanation' test focuses on one only of the two matters to be balanced – by requiring a high test of probative value – thereby averting any balancing process. I am unable to construe s 101(2) to that effect.*
>
> 96. My conclusion in relation to the construction of s 101(2) should not be understood to suggest that the stringency of the approach, culminating in the *Pfennig* test, is never appropriate when the judgment for which the section calls has to be made.

Notably, his Honour expressly disagreed with Hidden and Buddin JJ's suggestion that the common law's recognition of the potential for propensity evidence to be highly prejudicial (guiding the admission of such evidence only when the 'interests of justice' require) applies to the balancing exercise required by s 101 'so that the test for admissibility under that provision remains one of very considerable stringency'.[181] This approach, it was suggested, would seek to equate the s 101 test to the standard of the common law.

Admittedly, where the danger of unfair prejudice[182] is extremely high, as McHugh J observed in *Pfennig*, the probative value may well have to meet the 'no rational explanation' standard of proof.

Consider also the evidence. Could it be tendered on the basis of tendency reasoning? Why is coincidence reasoning appropriate? What is the significance of Ellis offering innocent explanations for some of the offences – for example, that Ellis merely assisted with the return of the rental car on the occasions where he was identified? After all, whoever had been out all-night driving must have been very tired. For counts 3, 4, 5 and 8, could he have lent his telephone to someone? And, finally, are such questions jury or admissibility (judge) ones?

Folbigg

[2003] NSWCCA 17 and [2005] NSWCCA 23

Consider whether the bar was set too low in *Folbigg*[183] (which applied *Ellis*). In *Folbigg* the accused faced homicide charges relating to her four babies who had

179 That is, applying the pre-July 2020 version of s 101(2). Citations omitted.
180 (2003) 58 NSWLR 700, [91], quoting McHugh J in *Pfennig* [1995] HCA 7; 182 CLR 461, 516.
181 (2003) 58 NSWLR 700, [104] (Hidden and Buddin JJ).
182 Which is how the term 'prejudicial effect' in s 101 has been interpreted.
183 [2003] NSWCCA 17 and [2005] NSWCCA 23.

died in 1989, 1991, 1993 and 1999. The fifth incident related to a charge of assault on Patrick, four months before he died. The case has been regarded by some commentators as a potential miscarriage of justice.[184] However, an inquiry that handed down its findings in mid-2019 found otherwise.[185] This inquiry, established following a petition and held under *Crimes (Appeal and Review) Act 2001* (NSW), s 77, was based on fresh evidence, relying on reports by four experts, a Professor of Forensic Pathology, the Chief Forensic Pathologist for Ontario; the Professor of Mathematics, University of Salford United Kingdom; and one by Sharmila Betts, clinical psychologist. Numerous other medical experts were involved in the inquiry. Kathleen Folbigg's application for separate trials had been rejected on the basis that the coincidence rule was satisfied. The coincidence particularised by the prosecution was said to be incapable of explanation unless Ms Folbigg was responsible for all of the events. The case relied on the rarity of the combination of events.[186] The basis of the (lack of) coincidence was:

> a. all five events occurred suddenly: the events were over in a matter of minutes;
> b. all five events occurred unexpectedly: no child had any health problem that preceded the sudden deaths or ALTE, or gave any sort of warning sign or previous symptom;
> c. all five events occurred at home, in circumstances where the children spent a proportion of their time away from the home;
> d. all five events occurred during the child's sleep period, rather than whilst playing at home, watching television, in the bath, or in the garden for example;
> e. all five events occurred when the child was in a bed, cot or a bassinet, rather than whilst asleep on the floor, or sitting, standing, running, jumping, skipping, eating or watching television;
> f. all five events occurred when the only person effectively at home or awake was Ms Folbigg, noting that Mr Folbigg was a deep sleeper, which gave her the opportunity to have done the children harm;
> g. each child was discovered dead or moribund by Ms Folbigg;
> h. each child was discovered by Ms Folbigg during what she claimed was a normal check on their well-being during the course of their sleep period, including on three occasions when she said she was on her way to the toilet;
> i. each child was discovered dead or moribund at around or shortly after death when they were still warm to the touch, and two of them still had a heartbeat, so they were found literally minutes after the cessation of breathing; and
> j. in relation to four of the five events, Ms Folbigg failed to render any assistance at all to the children after discovering them dead or moribund, to the extent that she did not even lift them up out of their beds.[187]

---

184 E Cunliffe, *Murder, Medicine and Motherhood* (Hart Publishing, 2011); <http://sixtyminutes.ninemsn.com.au/extraminutes/8689052/reasonable-doubt-9news-story>; <http://sixtyminutes.ninemsn.com.au/extraminutes/8689051/reasonable-doubt-extended-interview>; <http://sixtyminutesninemsn.com.au/article.aspx?id=8688422>. See also the reference to the lodging of a petition for review of Kathleen Folbigg's conviction made to NSW Governor-General David Hurley: <http://www.abc.net.au/news/2015-07-04/convicted-child-killer-kathleen-folbigg-judicial-review/6594926>.

185 Inquiry into the convictions of Kathleen Megan Folbigg (NSW) (Commissioner Reg Blanch AM QC), <https://www.folbigginquiry.justice.nsw.gov.au/Pages/report.aspx>. See also <https://www.abc.net.au/radionational/programs/lawreport/christian-porter-cab-reshuffle-kathleen-folbigg-loses-appeal/13253178>.

186 Ibid 73.

187 Ibid [135], 72. Prosecution, closing address (13 May 2003), quoted in the Folbigg Inquiry Report, 49-50. '[T]he prosecution and defence agreed that the jury should be directed that they could only use tendency reasoning if they had already come to the conclusion that they were satisfied beyond a reasonable doubt that one of the children was killed by deliberate suffocation by the accused': [13], 50.

As the Inquiry summarised, the prosecutor

> submitted that he could not disprove that Caleb may have died from a floppy larynx or SIDS, that Patrick's ALTE was a first epileptic attack or encephalitis, that Patrick's death may have been caused by an epileptic attack or seizure, that Sarah may have had a displaced uvula or SIDS and that Laura may have died of myocarditis.
>
> I can't disprove any of that, but one day some piglets might be born from a sow, and the piglets might come out of the sow with wings on their back, and the next morning Farmer Joe might look out the kitchen window and see these piglets flying out of his farm. I can't disprove that either. I can't disprove that one day some piglets might be born with wings and that they might fly. Is that a reasonable doubt? No. Is the hypothesis that the defence advances a reasonable doubt? No. Why not? Because if you look at what they are suggesting, not in isolation, but in totality: There has never ever been before in the history of medicine that our experts have been able to find any case like this. It is preposterous. It is not a reasonable doubt. It is a fantasy, and of course the Crown does not have to disprove a fanciful idea.[188]

Before Kathleen Folbigg's trial the Court of Criminal Appeal (Hodgson JA, with Sully and Buddin JJ agreeing) held that the evidence of each infant's death was admissible across counts and thus separate trials were unnecessary. In other words, the prosecution was permitted to apply the evidence of the four infants' deaths (and Patrick's apparent life-threatening event (referred to as an ALTE)) as disproving coincidence and thus also as revealing Folbigg's tendency to mood swings and violent thoughts with respect to her children when they cried and failed to settle. Kathleen's diary entries fanned the tendency reasoning.

There is no doubt that it is factually similar to English cases that were held to be miscarriages of justice. However, a common link with the English cases was the impact of Sir Roy Meadow, a paediatrician, who allowed his now discredited evidence to stray into the field of statistical analysis, for which he had no expertise. As a result of the revelations of his mistakes and of the uncertainties of medical science, the English Court of Appeal in *Clark*[189] expressed the view that, where two or more sudden unexplained infant deaths in the same family occur, criminal proceedings should be considered unsafe where they depend *solely on* 'a serious disagreement between distinguished and reputable experts'. In *Cannings*[190] Judge LJ observed that an 'overwhelming and abiding impression' from studying the expert evidence

> is that a great deal about death in infancy, and its causes, remains as yet unknown and undiscovered. That impression is confirmed by counsel on both sides. Much work by dedicated men and women is devoted to this problem. No doubt one urgent objective is to reduce to an irreducible minimum the tragic waste of life and consequent life-scarring grief suffered by parents. … We cannot avoid the thought that some of the honest views expressed with reasonable confidence in the present case (on both sides of the argument) will have to be revised in years to come, when the fruits of continuing medical research, both here and internationally, become available. What may be unexplained today may be perfectly well understood tomorrow. Until then, any tendency to dogmatise should be met with an answering challenge.

188 Ibid [149], 74. The 'defence counsel submitted that the case was not assisted by statements that pigs might fly or that lightning doesn't strike four times in one place,' additionally pointing out that there was only 'very, very shaky' evidence of motive and 'no positive evidence of suffocation, and that the Crown could not exclude certain natural conditions as the cause of death': [157], [159], 76, [184] 79.

189 [2003] EWCA Crim 1020; [2003] 2 FCR 447. See also [2004] EWCA Crim 1; [2004] 1 All ER 725.

190 [2004] EWCA Crim 1; [2004] 1 All ER 725, [22].

The result of these considerations undertaken in the wake of Meadow's discrediting[191] was the overturning of convictions or acquittal of defendants in English prosecutions. Angela Cannings had had a baby girl who had died of SIDS but in 2002 she was convicted of the murder of her two baby sons. Her convictions were overturned the following year. A BBC investigation reported that her paternal great-grandmother had suffered one sudden infant death and her paternal grandmother two, suggesting (as Professor Michael Patton, a clinical geneticist at St George's Hospital Medical School told the BBC) that genetics was the most likely explanation for the babies' deaths. Trupti Patel was acquitted in 2003 of the murder of three of her babies. In this case, conflicting expert evidence of the likelihood of multiple baby deaths in a family was put before the court, as was the fact that Patel's maternal grandmother had lost five infant children. By the time the Patel case was before the court, Meadow's expertise in this area had been largely discredited. Donna Anthony spent six years in gaol for the murder of her two sons. She was freed in 2005 when her case was sent to the Criminal Cases Review Commission.

So, in 2003 when Kathleen Folbigg faced a jury charged with the murder of her infants (and was subsequently found guilty), the question before the NSW courts was whether this prosecution differed from these English cases. Dr Emma Cunliffe suggests[192] that medical expert evidence in Kathleen Folbigg's trial and appeals misreported the extent of uncertainty within paediatric forensic pathology of the likelihood of unexplained infant deaths from a single family. The misreporting of uncertainty in this area was argued to be a particular problem in Folbigg's case because, as Cunliffe also notes, none of the Folbigg infants had positive signs of smothering.[193] The 2007 Victorian case of *Matthey*[194] lends support to this view. This case, a murder trial, involved consideration of the admissibility of expert evidence relating to the death of Carol Matthey's four infant children. Coldrey J referred to a 2005 study reported in *The Lancet*,[195] which observed that 'not only can SIDS recur in one family, but the risk of a second death increases after one SIDS death has occurred'. Coldrey J cited aspects of the English cases mentioned above and ruled that medical evidence in any trial of Matthey would be limited to opinions of the diagnostic possibility or consistency of asphyxia. As Coldrey J noted, while the prosecutor implied that Matthey was motivated to murder her children to gain the attention of her husband, in fact the evidence did not disclose such a pattern. Instead, Matthey had separated from her husband, rather than the other way around. His Honour concluded:

> 177. … Throughout the process great care must be taken not to allow the rarity of these sad events, standing on their own, to be subsumed into an assumption or virtual assumption that the dead infants were deliberately killed, or consciously or unconsciously to regard the inability of the defendant to provide some convincing explanation for these

---

191 With 'Meadow's law' ('one cot death is a tragedy, two cot deaths is suspicious, and until the contrary is proved, three cot deaths is murder') and testimony in the Clark case with similarly easily absorbed statements such as the chances of two instances of SIDS in one family is 1 in 73 million, criticised by British statisticians, and ultimately discredited. See Blanch Inquiry, above n 185, [140]-141], 138-9.

192 Cunliffe, above n 184, 197.

193 Ibid 198.

194 [2007] VSC 398.

195 RG Carpenter, A Waite A, RR Coombs, C Bamen-Willems, A McKenzie, J Huber J, JL Emery, 'Repeat Sudden Unexpected and Unexplained Deaths: Natural or Unnatural?' (2005) 365 *The Lancet* 29.

deaths as providing a measure of support for the prosecution case. If on examination of all the evidence every possible known cause has been excluded, the cause remains unknown.

As the table below indicates, each of Kathleen's infants died very young. Each was found by Kathleen, in their cot, not breathing. The prosecution claimed that she had smothered them. The defence claimed that they had died of natural causes (SIDS),[196] the original diagnosis in two instances. Expert opinion called at the trial presented diverse and widely differing opinions. Folbigg was ultimately found guilty of the manslaughter of Caleb, maliciously inflicting grievous bodily harm on Patrick, and the murder of Patrick, Sarah and Laura. Post-conviction, a second unsuccessful appeal was heard by the NSW Court of Criminal Appeal regarding the judge's directions, the safety of the verdict, certain expert evidence and sentencing.[197]

	Caleb	**Patrick**	**Sarah**	**Laura**
Date of, Age @ Death	February 1989, 19 days	February 1991 8 months	August 1993 10.5 months	March 1999 19 months
Cause of Death, diagnosed health issues	Transient tach-nypnoea, floppy larynx, SIDS	Asphyxia, airway obstruction. Had ALTE at 4 months, leading to epileptic fits and cortical blindness	SIDS; sleep apnoea	Upper respiratory tract infection; possibly myocarditis, not SIDS
Diary		June 1990		December 1996; Jan, Feb, May, Oct, Nov 1997 Jan, March, April 1998
Other				Letter at 12 months Monitor turned off
Charge/ conviction	manslaughter	GBH + murder	murder	murder

* Sarah's post-mortem noted small abrasions near her mouth and her lungs; petechial haemorrhage, minor congestion and oedema – all are consistent with death by asphyxiation. SIDS was recorded as the cause of death. There was evidence that two days before Sarah's death Folbigg had discontinued the sleep apnoea blanket, saying it generated false alarms. A similar complaint was made about Laura's sleep alarm.

Undoubtedly Folbigg's diary entries are a distinguishing element of her case from the others. These entries showed a loving mother battling stress and anxiety. They also showed a mother who was frustrated, fearful and aggravated when her babies would not stop crying. As Cunliffe notes, the major significant factor in the Folbigg trial was the attention given to Kathleen's diaries, leading to 'an adversarial flattening of a complex field of medical research [that] ultimately and unfairly worked to Folbigg's detriment at trial'.[198] Some of the diary entries selected by Sully J (2005 Court of Criminal Appeal) follow:

> **3 June 1990:** This was the day that Patrick Allan David Folbigg was born. I had mixed feelings this day. wether or not I was going to cope as a mother or wether I was going to get stressed out like I did last time. I often regret Caleb & Patrick, only because your life changes so much, and maybe I'm not a Person that likes change. But we will see?

196 SIDS (sudden infant death syndrome) is the diagnosis given where it is believed to be death by natural causes, but pathology or cause can be isolated.

197 *Folbigg* [2005] NSWCCA 23.

198 Cunliffe, above n 184, 198.

18 June 1996: I'm ready this time. And I know Ill have help & support this time. When I think Im going to loose control like last times Ill just hand baby over to someone else. … I have learnt my lesson this time.

4 December 1996: [found out she was pregnant]. I'm ready this time. But have already decided if I get any feelings of jealousy or anger to much I will leave Craig [Kathleen's husband] & baby, rather than answer being as before. Silly but will be the only way I will cope.

1 January 1997: Another year gone & what a year to come. I have a baby on the way, …This time. I am going to call for help this time & not attempt to do everything myself any more – I know that that was the main Reason for all my stress before & stress made me do terrible things.

4 February 1997: Still can't sleep. Seem to be thinking of Patrick & Sarah & Caleb. Makes me generally wonder whether I am stupid or doing the right thing by having this baby. My guilt of how responsible I feel for them all, haunts me, my fear of it happening again haunts me. … What scares me most will be when Im alone with baby. How do I overcome that? Defeat that?

16 May 1997: … Craig says he will stress & worry but he still seems to sleep okay every night & did with Sarah. I really needed him to wake that morning & take over from me. This time Ive already decided if ever feel that way again I'm going to wake him up. 25 October 1997: … I cherish Laura more, I miss her [Sarah] yes but am not sad that Laura is here & she isn't. Is that a bad way to think, don't know. I think I am more patient with Laura. I take the time to figure what is rong now instead of just snapping my cog. … Wouldn't of handled another like Sarah. She's saved her life by being different.

29 October 1997: felt a little angry towards Laura today. It was because I am & was very tired. … she [Laura] doesn't push my Button any where near the extent she [Sarah] did. Luck is good for her is all I can say.

9 November 1997: … he [Craig] has a morbid fear about Laura. … well I know theres nothing wrong with her. Nothing out of ordinary any way. Because it was me not them. … With Sarah all I wanted was her to shut up. And one day she did.

19 November 1997: Bit nervous tonight. Laura & I are by ourselves tonight.

8 November [sic, December] 1997: Had a bad day today, lost it with Laura a couple of times. She cried most of the day. Why do I do that. … Got to stop placing so much importance on myself. – funny how, now she's [Laura's] here, we can't seem to imagine a life without her dominating every move. Much try to release my stress somehow. I'm starting to take it out on her. Bad move. Bad things & thoughts happen when that happen. I will never happen again.

28 January 1998: I've done it. I lost it with her. I yelled at her so angrily that it scared her, she hasn't stopped crying. Got so bad I nearly purposely dropped her on the floor & left her. I restrained enough to put her on the floor & walk away. Went to my room & left her to cry. Was gone probably only 5 minutes but it seemed like a lifetime. I feel like the worst mother on this earth. Scared that she'll leave me know. Like Sarah did. I know I was short tempered & cruel sometimes to her & she left. With a bit of help. I don't want that to ever happen again. I actually seem to have a bond with Laura. It can't happen again. Im ashamed of myself. I can't tell Craig about it because he'll worry about leaving her with me. Only seems to happen if I'm too tired her moaning, bored, wingy sound, drives me up the wall. I truly can't wait until she's old enough to tell me what she wants.

6 March 1998: Laura not well, really got on my nerves today, snapped & got really angry, but not nearly as bad as I used to get.

13 March 1998: Seem to have a good day. She didn't piss me off more than a couple of times.

1 April 1998: Thought to myself today. Difference with Sarah, Pat, Caleb to Laura, with Laura I'm ready to share my life. I definitely wasn't before.[199]

---

199 [2005] NSWCCA 23, [131].

According to the defence presented at trial 'the diaries exhibited fairly normal reactions not only of grief, but also of shame, guilt and responsibility, though not in the sense contended for by the Crown'.[200] However, Sully J observed about the diary entries:

> 132. These entries make chilling reading in the light of the known history of Caleb, Patrick, Sarah and Laura. The entries were clearly admissible in the Crown case. Assuming that they were authentic, which was not disputed; and that they were serious diary reflections, which was not disputed; then the probative value of the material was, in my opinion, damning. The picture painted by the diaries was one which gave terrible credibility and persuasion to the inference, suggested by the overwhelming weight of the medical evidence, that the five incidents had been anything but extraordinary coincidences unrelated to acts done by the appellant. …
>
> 137. The … point to be made about *Cannings* is that it is a case-specific decision, and that it has features that are quite different from the features of the appellant's case.
>
> 138. **First**, one of the principal Crown experts had given evidence in another trial, and it had been demonstrated, but only after the conclusion of that other trial, that his evidence had been seriously flawed. The Court of Appeal thought that it *"must reflect on the likely impact on the verdict in the present case if ... (defence counsel) ... had been able to cross-examine ... (the particular witness) ... and undermine the weight the jury would invariably attach to his evidence by exposing that, notwithstanding his pre-eminence, at least part of his evidence in ... (the other trial) ... was flawed in an important respect"*. There is no such situation present in the expert evidence given for the Crown at the appellant's trial.
>
> 139. **Secondly**, the Court of Appeal in *Cannings* received at the hearing of the appeal a body of fresh scientific evidence. This fresh evidence is described in paragraph 138 as *"a substantial body of research, not before the jury, and received by us in evidence ... "*. There is no such fresh post-trial evidence before this Court.
>
> 140. **Thirdly**, the Court of Appeal discusses at paragraphs 31-35 inclusive, what it describes as *"The Family Context"*. In that connection the Court of Appeal considers both trial evidence, and post-trial fresh evidence, about the immediate and extended family tree of Mrs Cannings. The Court concludes that: *"That there may well be a genetic cause, as yet unidentified, for the deaths of the Cannings children, manifesting itself in some, but not all of the extended family, through autosomal dominant inheritance with variable penetrance. That would mean that the child in question needed only to inherit the gene from one parent to be liable to develop whatever the genetic mechanism may be"*. There is no comparable situation in the present case.
>
> 141. **Fourthly**, the Court of Appeal emphasises, (paragraph 160), that in the case of Mrs Cannings: *"there is no suggestion of ill-temper, inappropriate behaviour, ill treatment let alone violence, at any time, with any one of the four children"*. In the appellant's case, there is a body of such evidence, and it was not shown to be inherently incredible. That evidence was, rather, bolstered by the diary entries, for which there was no parallel in the *Cannings* case.
>
> 142. The differences between the appellant's case and that of Mrs Cannings entail that it does not follow that the reasoning which led to the quashing of Mrs Cannings' convictions must lead more or less as a matter of course to the quashing of the appellant's convictions.
>
> 143. In the present case there was, in my opinion, ample evidence at trial to justify these findings, reached beyond reasonable doubt:
>
> [1] None of the four deaths, or Patrick's ALTE, was caused by an identified natural cause.
>
> [2] It was possible that each of the five events had been caused by an unidentified natural cause, but only in the sense of a debating point possibility and not in

200 Blanch Inquiry, above n 185, [164] 76.

the sense of a reasonable possibility. The evidence of the appellant's episodes of temper and ill-treatment, coupled with the very powerful evidence provided by the diary entries, was overwhelmingly to the contrary of any reasonable possibility of unidentified natural causes. So were the striking similarities of the four deaths.

[3] There remained reasonably open, therefore, only the conclusion that somebody had killed the children, and that smothering was the obvious method.

[4] In that event, the evidence pointed to nobody other than the appellant as being the person who had killed the children; and who, by reasonable parity of reasoning, had caused Patrick's ALTE by the same method.

144. In my opinion Ground 2 has not been established. [After discussing *Ellis*] …

149. The appellant submits that her case is, indeed, one in which: "… it would not be open to conclude that the probative value of particular evidence substantially[201] outweighs its prejudicial effect, unless the 'no rational explanation' test were satisfied". In that connection the appellant's arguments are encapsulated in the following paragraphs of the appellant's written submissions:

> "94. It is suggested that this is such a case. Indeed, it is submitted that the evidence did not even satisfy the tests posed by sections 97 and 98 of the Evidence Act: the evidence did not, on proper analysis, have significant probative value.
>
> 95. If there were evidence capable of satisfying the Jury in relation to one of the given deaths that, considered alone, the appellant was responsible then the situation would be different. If there were evidence that she had been observed suffocating one of the children or had confessed to such an act then that could be used, given sufficient similarities being established between it and the suspect events, to prove those events. This was not such a case.
>
> 96. This was a matter where, in essence, the Crown case disclosed five events which were, at their highest from the point of view of the Crown, undetermined in their origins. Without such a proven event the approach of the Crown in its endeavours to use the subject evidence had an element of circularity about it. It is suggested that this defect had not been resolved by the close of addresses and the conclusion of his Honour's summing-up. The circularity is that it rested upon an impermissible assumption that each event (considered individually) was relevant in the sense required by the Evidence Act in that it was a non-accidental death."

150. Relevant case law apart, I do not agree with that reasoning.

151. It seems to me that the four deaths and Patrick's ALTE satisfy every relevant part of section 98 of the Evidence Act, the section dealing generally with coincidence evidence. The five events were substantially and relevantly similar. The circumstances in which they occurred were, plainly I should have thought, substantially similar. The five events were, therefore, *"related events"* in the statutory sense established by section 98. The admissibility, when considering any one of those events, of evidence respecting all four other events depended, therefore, upon the section 98(1)(b) test: Does the Court which is asked to admit the coincidence evidence *"think"* that the particular evidence has *"either by itself or having regard to other evidence adduced or to be adduced by the party seeking to adduce the evidence"*, what the section describes as *"significant probative value"*?

152. The concept of *"significant probative value"* is meaningless unless it is related to the fact or facts in issue towards the proof of which the coincidence evidence is being tendered at all. The fact or facts in issue is or are those facts described in section 98(1) itself:

> "…………………….Because of the impossibility of the … (related) … events occurring coincidentally, … (the accused person) … did a particular act or had a particular state of mind."

201 That is applying for pre-2020 formulation of s 101(2).

> 153. Had any one of the five counts charged in the present case been severed and tried separately, there must have been a Crown application to lead as coincidence evidence, evidence that the event central to the severed count was not, in truth, an isolated event at all; but was, rather, but one in a chain of events that were *"related events"* in the section 98 sense; that whole chain of events having occurred in such an overall context, of which the diary entries were a most cogent feature, as to negate any reasonable possibility of mere, albeit somewhat astonishing, coincidence.
>
> 154. I can see no persuasive argument that would have rendered the proposed coincidence evidence inadmissible, except, of course, for the possible operation of section 101, or of section 137 of the *Evidence Act*; – (and perhaps sections 135 and 136, although I would myself have thought that those sections were, as a practical matter, academic in a case of the present kind).
>
> 155. For the foregoing reasons, I would not be persuaded that, absent binding authority to the contrary, there was any miscarriage by reason of the joint trial of all five counts in the indictment. There is, as it happens, authority which seems to me to support the foregoing reasoning.[202]

The Folbigg Inquiry after reviewing the medical literature on SIDS, and medical opinions on the possible alternative causes of death for the four children, and psychological and psychiatric opinions of Kathleen Folbigg, handed down its findings in 2019, concluding:

> 280. … [T]he risk of recurrence [of a SIDS death] is considered small. …
>
> 282. It is accepted that it is clear from the work of the Inquiry that before 2003 there had been reported cases involving the deaths of three or more infants in the same family attributed to unidentified natural causes, or at least not established as attributable to unnatural causes. To the extent that the Crown case as left to the jury asserted or invited otherwise, that was incorrect.
>
> 283. However, the current descriptions in literature and in evidence by experts emphasise the low nature or rarity of recurrence risk, a point which was accurately reflected in the directions of the trial judge. It is also clear that the mere fact of the recurrence of the sudden unexpected death of an infant cannot, by itself, prove beyond a reasonable doubt that the cause was homicide, even in the case of multiple deaths. That is so because our current understanding of the causes of such natural deaths cannot be said to be complete. It is also not helpful to attempt to ascribe a statistical value to the possibility of a recurrence of such an event. …
>
> 285. I note also that the decision of the Court of Criminal Appeal in the present case in 2005 referred to the decision of *Cannings* in the English Court of Appeal in 2004 in which three infant deaths and an ALTE were considered. The Court of Criminal Appeal was thus aware of the existence of such a case when there had been three deaths in the one family but held that the Crown prosecutor's submission that such a case had never been heard of was simply a piece of circumstantial evidence to be added to the other circumstances. I agree with that description. A review of the literature indicates that repeat SIDS deaths are rare.

---

202 Hodgson JA (with Sully and Buddin JJ agreeing) observed in the prior 2003 appeal: '29. … In my opinion, what the primary judge is saying in those paragraphs is that there is little, if any, dispute in the medical evidence, in so far as it indicated that in each case medical considerations alone left a possibility that the cause was asphyxiation, this being a reasonable possibility and not a possibility which was merely remote or fanciful; and that there was no other cause which could be considered as something more than a reasonable possibility. The primary judge having approached the matter in that way, I think it is appropriate for this Court to do likewise, and consider whether, treating the medical evidence in that way, it considers the primary judge erred in holding that the s 101 test was satisfied.'

> 286. In light of the above, I am satisfied that the treatment of the issue of recurrence at trial has not resulted in a miscarriage of justice or irregularity that gives rise to a reasonable doubt as to Ms Folbigg's guilt.[203]

Whether *Ellis* and *Folbigg* reflect the right balance to be applied under s 101, it is important to note that for New South Wales the burden placed on the prosecution is now reduced,

Context, Relationship and Transactional Evidence

In this section we consider three categories of evidence that may *reveal* a relevant tendency or *disprove* coincidence but, because the evidence is adduced for a *purpose* other than for tendency or coincidence reasoning, the evidence need only satisfy *UEA*, ss 55 and 135; and, if it is prosecution evidence, s 137. These categories are evidence:

- of a *relevant relationship* that the prosecution claims exists (typically between the accused and another);
- that explains the broad factual *context* of an incident described by a sexual assault complainant; or
- of a *relevant transaction* inextricably linked to the events in question.

As Priest JA in the Victorian Court of Appeal case of *Murdoch (a Pseudonym)*[204] observed, the firming of these categories as outside the tendency and coincidence rule has contributed immensely to the complexity of the law under the *UEA*. The differential admissibility requirements mean trial judges need to scrutinise carefully each item of disputed evidence for its actual relevance to the criminal charges.[205]

Judges need to consider, in particular, whether any item of evidence invites tendency reasoning. Obviously, evidence that tempts such reasoning, but is not admissible under Part 3.6, has a heightened risk of creating a danger of unfair prejudice to the accused. Judges must also consider whether evidence is necessary for the task of ensuring the criminal charges are placed in their true context. As Jagot J observed in the ACT Court of Appeal case of *MM*:[206]

> 106. ... Consideration of each piece of evidence ... enables assessment of not only the capacity for it to be used permissibly for a non-tendency purpose but also the risk of the probative value of that evidence being outweighed by the danger of unfair prejudice to the defendant. A global assessment of evidence at a high level of generality as falling under the rubric of "relationship evidence" is unlikely to enable either task required by the Evidence Act to be discharged.

Relationship evidence

The High Court case of *Wilson*[207] is generally cited as the definitive exemplar of relationship evidence. In that case the defence claimed that Wilson's wife was shot after the gun discharged accidentally. There were no eyewitnesses. Menzies

203 Blanch Inquiry, above n 185, 163-4.
204 [2013] VSCA 272.
205 *Elomar* [2014] NSWCCA 303, 348.
206 [2012] ACTCA 44.
207 [1970] HCA 17; 123 CLR 334, 344.

J accepted that it was appropriate for the trial judge to have admitted evidence of the relationship between the accused and his wife because:

> To shut the jury off from any event throwing light upon the relationship between this husband and wife would be to require them to decide the issue as if it happened in a vacuum rather than in the setting of a tense and bitter relationship between a man and a woman who were husband and wife. Accordingly ... the evidence in question was properly admitted because it was pertinent to the issues which the jury had to decide.

There remains an argument that tendency reasoning is involved in establishing the relevance of relationship evidence[208] but, as *Aleski* indicates below, courts have separated relationship evidence from s 97. Case law indicates that it is insufficient to rely on evidence merely because it demonstrates 'the nature of the relationship'.[209] There must be an issue which the evidence explains or clarifies through the context of the relationship, and the tendering party should identify with precision what it proposes the evidence establishes.[210] A good illustration of this challenge is found in the case of *Norman*.[211] Norman was convicted of three counts of sexual assault from 2002, 2004 and 2005. The relationship evidence consisted of non-sexual domestic violence between Norman and the complainant that revealed a troubled relationship involving arguments and physical and verbal violence from the accused, including an incident in 1999 where the complainant claimed that Norman slapped and kicked her, as well as a second incident in 2001 when she claimed that he grabbed her by the hair, dragged her into a bedroom and pushed his fingers into her throat. The evidence was not adduced as tendency evidence of sexual assault, or of violence, even though they incidentally revealed a propensity to violence. The NSW Court of Criminal Appeal held that the evidence was irrelevant. It did not explain or explicate the incidents giving rise to the charges. It was just evidence of two isolated incidents of non-sexual domestic violence that were not necessary to contextualise the charges of the sexual assaults within a meaningful context and were without relevance beyond impermissible general propensity reasoning.

Aleski (a Pseudonym)

[2020] VSCA 124

Aleski was convicted of six sexual offences against BC involving a number of acts of digital penetration, indecent touching and kissing, and alleged to have taken place in her home between 2016 and 2018 when BC was between 10 and 12 years

208 See, eg, *HML* [2008] HCA 16; 235 CLR 334, [500] (Kiefel J). This was not an application of the *UEA*.

209 *Qualtieri* [2006] NSWCCA 95; 171 A Crim R 463, [112]; *DJV* [2008] NSWCCA 272; 200 A Crim R 206.

210 See *White v Johnston* [2015] NSWCA 18 (Simpson J). For an example where evidence showing a relationship that consisted of ongoing violence by the accused towards the deceased 'to provide the proper background and context in which the charged offence occurred, and to allow the jury to assess the evidence with knowledge of the relevant facts' and '[i]t could rebut the accused's claim that "it was self-defence", and that his military training "kicked in" unconsciously', see *Merrick (No 2)* [2016] NSWSC 164.

211 [2012] NSWCCA 230. The appeal was dismissed by an application of the proviso under s 6(1) of the *Criminal Appeal Act 1912* (NSW); special leave refused: *Norman* [2013] HCATrans 142. For other discussions of this difficulty, see *MM* [2012] ACTCA 44; *Qualtieri* [2006] NSWCCA 95; 171 A Crim R 463, [112]; *DJV* [2008] NSWCCA 272; 200 A Crim R 206, [28]-[30]; *RG* [2010] NSWCCA 173, [36]-[37]; *SKA* [2012] NSWCCA 205.

of age. Aleski was six years older and the boyfriend of BC's older sister, CC. In summary, the tendency evidence ruled admissible by the trial judge was of Aleski

> pushing the victim, getting on top of her and trying to kiss her on the lips; grabbing the victim's hand and putting it under his pants as she kept pulling it away; kissing her on the back; slapping her on the backside, feeling her vagina over her clothes and trying to kiss her; and kissing her. Evidence of those uncharged acts was admitted as tendency evidence and no complaint is made in that regard.[212]

The judge ruled that evidence by an eyewitness (BD) that Aleski had tried to lift up BC's skirt was not admissible to prove the relevant tendency because it lacked significant probative value in demonstrating an improper sexual interest in BC and a willingness to act on it. However, the judge ruled this evidence was 'relevant as part of the sequence in the narrative as a marker on the time continuum, if you like, that it would be unfair to deprive the prosecution of that step in the process or developing nature of the contact that is alleged between the accused ... and [BC]'. This ruling was challenged on appeal, on the basis that its probative value was outweighed by the danger of unfair prejudice to the accused: *UEA*, s 137. The court observed that, compared to the evidence supporting the charged acts, 'the skirt lifting evidence was relatively benign. Evidently, the strenuous efforts to have that evidence excluded were informed by the fact that, unlike the other evidence, it was supported by a witness, BD. It did not depend solely on the account given by the complainant, BC. That being so, it had some forensic force' (at [64]).

Maxwell P, Niall and Weinberg JJA:

Analysis

55. The first question is whether the evidence is relevant. To be relevant, it must satisfy the threshold erected by s 55 of the *Evidence Act*.

56. Evidence of discreditable conduct, including of a sexual nature, that is not the subject of a charge, may be relevant because it provides evidence of a tendency to act in a particular way or have a particular state of mind. In those cases, such evidence must meet not only the test of relevance in s 55 of the *Evidence Act* but also the much stricter prescriptions contained in ss 97 and 101. To similar effect, such evidence may constitute coincidence evidence admissible under s 98.

57. Such evidence may, however, be relevant and admissible independently of whether it establishes a tendency or coincidence because, for example, it provides relevant evidence of context or relationship that explains the actions of the victim or the conduct of the accused.

58. In *RWC v The Queen*,[213] Simpson J (with whom Price and Garling JJ agreed) identified the distinction between tendency and relationship or context evidence in a way that highlights the potency of tendency reasoning. Its force lies in the fact that it invites a reasoning as to guilt of the charged offence rather than establishing circumstantial facts upon which the prosecution proceeds. Her Honour said:

> Evidence that is called context evidence is not tendered as going directly to the guilt of the accused person. It is tendered to explain the relationship between the complainant and the accused ... or to explain what may otherwise be unexplained, or raise questions in the minds of the jury concerning the behaviour of the complainant in response (or non-response) to the conduct of the accused the subject of the charge or charges. Commonly, evidence of a history of sexual abuse or misconduct is tendered to explain why a complainant passively yields to the abuse, shows no surprise, or makes no complaint.

---

212 [2020] VSCA 124, [23] (Maxwell P, Niall and Weinberg JJA).

213 [[2010] NSWCCA 332.]

> Evidence that is tendered as tendency evidence is tendered as relevant to the guilt of the accused: as showing a tendency on his/her part to act in a particular way, or to have a particular state of mind: from this, the prosecution will seek to have the jury draw an inference that, on the occasion or occasions in question, the accused acted in a particular way or had a particular state of mind. Tendency evidence provides the foundation for an inference of guilt of the conduct alleged on the occasion or occasions the subject of the charge or charges.[214]

59. The admissibility of sexual conduct as evidence of context or relationship is not without controversy or risks. In *Director of Public Prosecutions v Martin (a pseudonym)*, this Court referred to three cases in the High Court where the justices of the High Court expressed different views without establishing a clear statement of principle.[215] Nevertheless, the prevailing view in this Court is that such evidence is admissible.

60. In *Ritchie (a pseudonym) v The Queen*,[216] this Court emphasised the risk that relationship evidence may be used by a jury as though it established a propensity to act in a particular way and thereby infer guilt of the charged offences. In that respect, Kaye, Weinberg JJA and Kidd AJA said:

> In the absence of careful directions by the trial judge, a jury might impermissibly misuse relationship evidence for tendency or propensity purposes. That risk exists, because, generally speaking, most tendency evidence can also fill the role of relationship evidence, and, conversely, nearly all relationship evidence can bespeak a propensity or tendency, without being admissible as tendency evidence.[217]

61. In his submissions, the applicant identified three circumstances in which context or relationship evidence is admitted: to provide essential background information; to explain a victim's failure to complain; and to counter a false impression that the alleged offending was 'out of the blue'. Those examples provide illustrations about how such evidence might be relevant. However, they should not be viewed as exhaustive or approached as if they are statutory tests.

62. In this case, the evidence of the skirt incident was relevant. It was capable of establishing a physical connection between the applicant and BC and an attempt by the applicant to establish a relationship or rapport with her. It was also capable of showing that the applicant had a physical interest in BC. It formed part of an evolving narrative that placed the offending in some context.

63. Once the evidence was relevant, the question becomes whether its admission should have been refused under s 137 of the *Evidence Act*. We note that the judge held that the evidence was not admissible as tendency evidence. Section 137 requires the Court to refuse to admit evidence if its probative value is outweighed by the danger of unfair prejudice to the accused.

64. … [T]he fact that it was supported by another witness did not bear on its admissibility. It did not add to its relevance, nor was it relevant in assessing its probative value or prejudicial effect for the purpose of s 137. Its probative value is to be assessed on the basis that it is accepted by the jury[218] and unfair prejudice is not measured by whether it will be accepted but whether the jury will deploy it in some impermissible way.[219]

65. In our view, the evidence had some, but not any great, probative value. The conduct in question occurred in a different setting to the offending and, given the age

---

214 [Ibid [122]-[123] (citations omitted). See also *Murdoch (a Pseudonym)* [2013] VSCA 272; 40 VR 451, 455-6 [12] (Redlich and Coghlan JJA); *Ritchie (a Pseudonym)* [2019] VSCA 202, [127] (Kaye, Weinberg JJA and Kidd AJA), citing *RWC* [2010] NSWCCA 332; *Henderson (a Pseudonym)* [2017] VSCA 237, [68] (Beach, Ferguson and Coghlan JJA).]

215 [[2016] VSCA 219, [82]-[96] (Redlich, Weinberg and McLeish JJA), citing *HML* [2008] HCA 16; 235 CLR 334.]

216 [[2019] VSCA 202.]

217 [Ibid [128].]

218 [*IMM* [2016] HCA 14; 257 CLR 300, 312 [39] (French CJ, Kiefel, Bell and Keane JJ).]

219 [*Papakosmas* [1999] HCA 37; 196 CLR 297, 325, [91]-[92] (McHugh J).]

of both the applicant and BC at the time, could easily have been seen as immature and unrelated to the charged acts. However, it was relevant to establish a change in the nature of the relationship between the applicant and BC that the jury was entitled to take into account.

66. We are not persuaded that any unfair prejudice attended its admission. The judge gave unexceptionable directions on both tendency evidence and the use to which the jury could put this evidence. In his closing address to the jury, counsel for the applicant identified inconsistencies in the evidence between BC and BD, including as to when the skirt incident occurred, and queried whether they had talked about it before BC went to police. Counsel invited the jury to reject the evidence. Alternatively, he contended that the evidence, at its highest, was a childish, immature act, so far removed from the alleged charges that it was just a distraction in the case. In the circumstances, there was no real risk that the jury would engage in impermissible tendency reasoning or unfairly give the evidence more weight than it was rationally capable of having.

67. Even if the applicant had demonstrated that the evidence should not have been admitted, we are satisfied that its admission could not have given rise to a substantial miscarriage of justice. In making this assessment, we take into account the extent to which the evidence was a focus at the trial.

68. In our view, given the issues at trial, which focused on the reliability of the complainant's account, based on her differing accounts and antipathy towards her sister and the applicant, we are persuaded that this incident was of no real significance, and so even if its admission into evidence was erroneous, it did not result in a substantial miscarriage of justice.

For an example of evidence that was relevant for a tendency purpose as well as to show the relationship between the deceased and the accused, see *Cahill (No 2)*,[220] where Cathrina Cahill claimed that the deceased, Cahill's fiancé, was violent towards her. The case involved a substantial amount of prosecution relationship and tendency evidence, revealing the volatile relationship and Cahill's propensity to violence. This evidence was ruled admissible. Evidence that the defence unsuccessfully sought to adduce for tendency purposes was ruled inadmissible as lacking probative value. Some of this defence evidence was going to be before the jury in any event as relationship evidence adduced by the prosecution but the remainder was significantly remote in time from the events under consideration in the trial, involved the deceased in prior relationships,[221] but lacked detail meaning it had minimal probative value.

Context evidence

As the above extract from *Aleski (a Pseudonym)* shows,[222] relationship evidence is a form of context evidence, though it is generally preferable to distinguish context and relationship evidence, given their different purposes.[223] In *Qualtieri*[224] Howie J (Latham J agreeing) adds a little more to understanding the distinction between context and tendency evidence:

119. Both context evidence and tendency evidence can bolster the credibility of the complainant but they do so in different ways. Context evidence is relevant to the credibility of the complainant only in that his or her version of the particular incident which is

220 [2018] NSWSC 1531.
221 Ibid [90]-[94], [114]-[118].
222 [2020] VSCA 124.
223 *SKA* [2012] NSWCCA 205, [280]-[281].
224 [2006] NSWCCA 95; 171 A Crim R 463 (emphasis added).

> the basis of the charge in the indictment may be more capable of belief when seen in the context of what the complainant says was his or her sexual relationship with the accused. It may explain, on the complainant's version, why the accused and the complainant acted as they did in circumstances where without the context of the relationship those acts might be inexplicable. But other than generally assisting the complainant's credibility in this way, context evidence does not make the complainant's account more reliable than it would be in the absence of that evidence. Context evidence does not make it more likely that the accused committed any of the offences charged in the indictment.
>
> 120. Tendency evidence on the other hand is *direct evidence* relevant to the commission of the offence charged. If accepted by the jury, it makes it more likely that the offence charged was committed by the accused. It bolsters the complainant's credibility because her version is more likely to be true if the accused has a tendency to behave in the way she alleges he did on specific occasions.
>
> 121. It is clear that the trial Judge in the present case confused the relevance of context evidence with tendency evidence when he directed the jury that they could find that the relationship evidence showed that "within the accused there was sexual feeling or passion for the complainant that he was prepared to satisfy". As I have noted, context evidence says nothing about the accused at all. It is not led to prove anything, let alone a propensity or characteristic of the accused. Similarly the Judge was in error in directing the jury that they could draw inferences from the relationship evidence. Context evidence may allow the jury to infer some aspect of the complainant's conduct but it does not give rise to any inference about the accused's conduct.

Typically context evidence is admitted in child sexual assault cases to explain the actions of a sexual assault complainant – for example, to overcome a false impression that might otherwise be conveyed to the jury that the incidents he or she has described 'came out of the blue'[225] or to offer an explanation as to why no reaction or complaint was made at the time.[226] The role of 'context evidence' is to place a specific allegation in the broader context of the complainant's whole account vis-à-vis the accused. Context evidence is admitted commonly to establish 'a pattern of behaviour in which the complainant was relatively unsurprised by the conduct the subject of the charge and made no response, nor any subsequent report'. Thus, the evidence assists to explain the complainant's behaviour 'which may otherwise have appeared surprising and therefore implausible to the jury'.[227] Again, it must have a specific relevance.

Transactional evidence

This designation of admissible evidence originates from the 1946 murder case, *O'Leary*.[228] The events took place in an isolated timber camp where evidence of O'Leary's drunken and violent conduct on the evening proximate to the killing of the deceased was admissible to support the prosecution case that O'Leary was the killer. Dixon J summarised the position:

> In my opinion the evidence objected to was admissible, because, from the time on Saturday 6th July when the prisoner and the party with him came under the influence of drink right up to the conclusion of the scene in the early hours of the following Sunday morning in the presence of the deceased's body lying in front of the huts, *a connected series of events occurred which should be considered as one transaction*. The part which

225 *KTR* [2010] NSWCCA 271, [90].
226 *DJV* (2008) 200 A Crim R 206, [28].
227 *RG* [2010] NSWCCA 173, [38].
228 [1946] HCA 44; 73 CLR 566.

> the prisoner took in the drunken orgy which, as the facts suggest, culminated in the fatal attack upon the deceased man would appear to me to be relevant to the question whether the prisoner was the assailant and, if so, whether he was at the time capable of forming, and did form, the intention which would make his crime murder.
>
> The *evidence disclosed that, under the influence of the beer and wine he had drunk and continued to drink, he engaged in repeated acts of violence which might be regarded as amounting to a connected course of conduct*. Without evidence of what, during that time, was done by those men who took any significant part in the matter and especially evidence of the behaviour of the prisoner, *the transaction of which the alleged murder formed an integral part could not be truly understood and, isolated from it, could only be presented as an unreal and not very intelligible event*. The prisoner's generally violent and hostile conduct might well serve to explain his mind and attitude and, therefore, to implicate him in the resulting homicide. Examples of the admission of evidence of connected incidents of one transaction will be found in *R v Cobden*;[229] *R v Voke*;[230] *R v Rearden*,[231] and as to this case see per *Cussen* J in *R v Herbert*.[232] In my opinion, for the reasons given, evidence of his conduct was admissible for the purpose stated.[233]

Evidence of a series of events forming a transaction linked to the events giving rise to the charge may prove the identity of the offender (as in *O'Leary*),[234] or the accused's state of mind,[235] or a system of work.[236] The case of *Samadi and Djait*[237] provides a good illustration of the interaction of this sort of evidence with tendency and coincidence evidence. The prosecution claimed the two accused were serial offenders, spiking tourists' drinks in bars in Sydney and then accompanying the drugged victims to their apartments and robbing them. In a 16-count indictment, counts 1-3 and 4 alleged drink spiking and robbery on a single night, but at different times and with different complainants. The appellants claimed that the incidents in counts 1-3 were quite different transactions from the one relating to count 4 and so were subject to the exclusionary rules embodied in ss 97, 98 and 101. Their submissions were that:

- *incident 1* (counts 1-3) involved two women at a bar (in fact, it was two women and one man);
- *incident 2* (count 4) involved a gay man (SM) and the drink spiking took place in the victim's home. It was also distinguishable because property was stolen.

The appellants claimed that mere temporal proximity was not a legitimate basis for admission 'simply because two events could be characterised as involving the same two men drugging two sets of victims on the same night, it was not indicative of both events being part of the same transaction'. They were unsuccessful in their submission that the differences in the incidents made them unconnected as a series of events (and so outside the *O'Leary* principle). Beazley JA (Hislop and Price JJ agreeing) described the court's analysis of the events:

---

229 [[1863] EngR 54; (1862) 3 F & F 833; 176 ER 381.]

230 [[1823] EngR 182; (1823) Russ & Ry 531, 533; 168 ER 934, 935.]

231 [[1864] EngR 65; (1864) 4 F & F 76; 176 ER 473.]

232 [[1916] VicLawRp 45; [1916] VLR 343, 349.]

233 [1946] HCA 44; 73 CLR 566, 577-8 (emphasis added). For a modern-day version of the facts of *O'Leary* illustrating the application of the same principle, see *Hothnyang* [2014] VSCA 64.

234 *Samadi and Djait* [2008] NSWCCA 330.

235 Also illustrated by *O'Leary* (1946) 73 CLR 566. See also *Adam* (1999) 106 A Crim R 510; *Player* [2000] NSWCCA 123; *Serratore* [2001] NSWCCA 123; *Mostyn* (2004) 145 A Crim R 304.

236 *Cittadini* (2008) 189 A Crim R 492, [26]-[27].

237 [2008] NSWCCA 330. See also *Toohey* [2020] NSWCCA 166, [155].

> 61. … Three matters were in issue in the counts arising out of each of those incidents: first, the identity of the offenders; secondly, whether the offenders had administered a stupefying drug to the victims; and thirdly, the intention of those offenders when doing so.
>
> 62. The Crown submitted that given the following matters, the evidence was admissible in accordance with the principles in *O'Leary*. First, both incidents involved the same two offenders. Secondly, both incidents were integral parts of a connected chain of events involving the appellants at and about the vicinity of the Pontoon Bar at around midnight on 13-14 October. Incident 2 began almost immediately upon the cessation of incident 1, in the vicinity of the Pontoon Bar, where SM was approached by the appellants. Finally, the Crown contended that incident 1 could only be presented as an "*unreal and not very intelligible event*" without: (1) forensic evidence that the appellants had administered Clonazepam to SM, the victim in incident 2, thereby providing an appropriate evidentiary basis for the inference the appellants had also administered that drug to the victims in incident 1; and (2) the evidence that the appellants had done so to enable the larceny of the property of SM provided an appropriate evidentiary basis for the inference that the appellants had similarly administered the drug to the victims of incident 1 to enable the larceny of their property.
>
> 63. In my opinion, there was no error in the trial judge permitting the evidence in respect of count 4 to be admitted to explain and prove the state of mind of the appellants at the time they were with the complainants in incident 1 and to be used by the jury to draw the inference, both in relation to the intention to steal and the administration of the drug Clonazepam, based upon their symptoms. Had the jury been instructed that the evidence in incident 2 was not part of the same overall circumstances, incident 1 would, in my opinion, be, as was said in *O'Leary*, "*an unreal and not very intelligible event*". It would simply be an event where persons had some wrong purpose.
>
> 64. [Regarding the inference of intention to steal] … In my opinion, the relevant intention for the purposes of [drink spiking] … could be inferred from the circumstances proved in respect of count 4. Nor does it diminish the force of the evidence that that on that night, the appellants were involved in a process of spiking the victims' drinks for the purpose of committing an indictable offence which was to enable them to steal, even if they may also have had some other intention, such as, for example, to commit a sexual offence. Accordingly, this ground of appeal should be dismissed.

Directions to Avoid Improper Use

> The importance of directions in cases where evidence may show propensity should not be underestimated. It is necessary in such a case that a trial judge give a clear and comprehensible warning about the misuse of the evidence for that purpose and explain the purpose for which it is tendered. A trial judge should identify the inferences which may be open from it or the questions which may have occurred to the jury without the evidence. Those inferences and those questions should be identified by the prosecution at an early point in the trial. And it should be explained to the jury that the evidence is to allow the complainant to tell her, or his, story but that they will need to consider whether it is true.[238]

Section 95[239] provides that evidence to be used for purposes outside those regulated by Part 3.6 must not be used to prove 'a particular matter' if it is not admissible for a Part 3.6 purpose. As the court in *Velkoski*[240] observed, at the heart of s 95 are distinctions 'drawn between, on the one hand, tendency and coincidence, and

238 *Roach* [2011] HCA 12; 242 CLR 610, [47] (French CJ, Hayne, Crennan and Kiefel JJ)

239 For Victoria, where the *JDA 2015* now provides a request requirement overriding s 95, discussed below.

240 [2014] VSCA 121, [127].

on the other, relationship and context'. Section 95 requires a judicial direction to the jury on the permissible and impermissible use of evidence (unless a direction is insufficient to serve the requirements of the provision). Such directions must be unequivocal and specific. It is too general for a judge to state that the evidence '*may assist you in determining whether he is guilty or not guilty of any or both of the charges before you*'; or that it could be used '*in your assessment of the background of the relationship between the accused and his stepdaughter*'; or that it is before the jury '*so you can understand the relationship between the accused and his stepdaughter over the relevant period*'.[241]

As Howie J observed in *ATM*:[242]

> 76. Where relationship evidence is admitted only to give context to, or by way of explanation of, the allegation contained in any charge in the indictment, the trial judge should direct the jury against using the evidence as proof that the accused committed any offence on the indictment. This may require the trial judge to direct the jury that they must not use the evidence as proof of any propensity on the part of the accused ...
>
> 77. Further, generally it will be necessary for the judge to give warnings that they should not substitute the evidence of any other sexual activity for the specific activity which is the subject of any charge in the indictment or reason that because the accused may have done something wrong to the complainant on some other occasion that he must have done so on an occasion which is the subject of any charge ...

As the majority indicated in *Roach*[243] the common law also requires clear and comprehensible directions on the use and misuse of evidence that may show propensity but is admissible only for a non-tendency purpose (such as to prove a relevant relationship or context or when adducing *O'Leary*-type transactional evidence). The obligation on the judge to provide directions to the jury on the limited or proper use to be made of certain evidence also arises in other situations.[244] In all these situations a major question is the efficacy of such directions. This is not amenable to a simple response, but the topic is discussed in general terms in Chapter 13.[245]

Victoria

The *Jury Directions Act 2015* (Vic) (*JDA 2015* (Vic)) seeks to reduce the complexity of jury directions in criminal trials and to assist trial judges to give directions that are 'as clear, brief, simple and comprehensible as possible'. The Act aims to simplify and clarify the tasks of juries and judges in their respective roles, and to make clear legal practitioners' duty to assist trial judges with respect to appropriate jury directions in criminal trials. Undoubtedly the provisions discussed below respond to the sentiments expressed in *Velkoski* regarding the undue complexity in the law. A key element in determining how different the *JDA 2015* (Vic) is from *UEA*, s 95 (and the common law), will lie in large part on the extent to which

241 *ATM* [2000] NSWCCA 475, [79], quoted by Adams J (with Hislop J agreeing) in *Norman* [2012] NSWCCA 230, [266] (emphasis added).

242 [2000] NSWCCA 475 (Howie J, with Sully and Whealy JJ agreeing) (citations omitted), quoted by Adams J (with Hislop J agreeing) in *SKA* [2012] NSWCCA 205. See also *Zhang* [2005] NSWCCA 437; 158 A Crim R 504, [135] (italics in original), quoted by Leeming JA in *El-Haddad* [2015] NSWCCA 10, [39].

243 [2011] HCA 12; 242 CLR 610, [47], extracted above, p 502.

244 For example, where admissions are made (*OGD (No 2)* (2000) 50 NSWLR 433) or the circumstances in *Elomar* [2014] NSWCCA 303.

245 See pp 425-428.

appellate courts and trial judges interpret the obligation expressed in s 16 for trial judges to give a direction if they consider there are *substantial and compelling reasons* for doing so.

For the purposes of this chapter, Part 4, Div 2, of the Victorian Act provides directions on the use and the avoidance of inappropriate use of 'other misconduct' evidence. These provisions override *UEA*, s 95.[246] 'Other misconduct' evidence is defined in *JDA 2015* (Vic), s 26. It means:

(a) coincidence evidence; or
(b) tendency evidence; or
(c) evidence of other discreditable acts and omissions of an accused that are not directly relevant to a fact in issue; or
(d) evidence that is adduced to assist the jury to understand the context in which the offence charged or any alternative offence is alleged to have been committed.

Aside from the overriding obligation for a trial judge to give a direction on the basis of '*substantial and compelling reasons* for doing so',[247] the situations below require that a trial judge must not give a direction that is not requested by a party[248] and a trial judge need not give the direction where there are good reasons not to do so.[249]

(1) *Where a party adduces other misconduct evidence that is not tendency evidence* the judge must warn the jury not to use it as tendency evidence. A good reason not to warn is 'if the trial judge considers that there is no substantial risk that the jury might use the evidence as tendency evidence'.[250]

(2) *Where the prosecution adduces other misconduct evidence* the judge must direct the jury:
- on its relevance, indirect or direct, to the existence of a fact in issue;
- not to use the evidence for any other purpose;
- where relevant, regarding the partial role of the other misconduct evidence in the prosecution case; and
- to avoid prejudice-based reasoning.[251]

(3) *For other misconduct evidence adduced by a co-accused* the judge must direct the jury:
- on its relevance, indirect or direct, to the existence of a fact in issue;
- not to use the evidence for any other purpose; and
- to avoid prejudice-based decision-making from what the jury has heard about the co-accused.[252]

---

246 *JDA 2015* (Vic), s 25. The Act also abolishes any common law obligation contrary to its provisions: *JDA 2015* (Vic), s 30.

247 *JDA 2015* (Vic), s 16 (emphasis added).

248 *JDA 2015* (Vic), s 15. And, consequentially, directions require a party to request them: *JDA 2015* (Vic), s 12.

249 *JDA 2015* (Vic), s 14. In determining if 'good reasons' exist, the trial judge must have regard to the evidence in the trial; the manner in which the prosecution and the accused have conducted their cases (including whether the direction concerns a matter not raised or relied on by the accused and whether the direction would involve the jury considering the issues in the trial in a manner that is different from the way in which the accused has presented his or her case).

250 *JDA 2015* (Vic), s 29.

251 *JDA 2015* (Vic), s 27.

252 *JDA 2015* (Vic), s 28(2).

(4) For situations (1) and (2), the judge need not:
- explain further what the jury should consider in deciding whether to use the other misconduct evidence; or
- identify impermissible uses of the other misconduct evidence; or
- refer to any other matter.[253]

Conclusion

Lacey's socio-political explanations for trial courts' increased reliance on evidence of bad character provokes reflection of the law discussed in this chapter. It is arguable that a subtle philosophical shift has created a prosecution-focused process jarring with traditional accusatorial sentiments.

While it is not altogether surprising that appellate guidance on applying admissibility standards for prosecution tendency and coincidence evidence have struggled to find stability, it is unusual that the law should be so trenchantly contested two decades and hundreds of appeal cases after the *UEA* first became law. It is particularly surprising that State appeal courts appear to disagree at the most fundamental level, namely, where the admissibility bar should be set. These are indicators of the tensions intrinsic in the evidence discussed in this chapter. The status quo is that the High Court has categorically rejected the common law and it has consolidated its guidance on the admissibility of tendency and coincidence evidence. The evidentiary categories and requirements for relationship and context evidence have been clarified. Further New South Wales has taken the lead in responding to the RCIRCSA recommendations on child sexual assault trials and reliance on tendency evidence.

All these changes may be a fortuitous benefit for those who advocate a new approach to the trials that dominate these categories – child sexual assault and domestic violence trials where offenders rely on secrecy, vulnerability and opportunism.[254] However, these trials are often fraught in numerous ways, including the danger of the prosecution overloading indictments or relying on an excessive number of uncharged acts. Repeated appeal court exhortations for prosecutors to heed the call of moderation justify close attention if there is to be a reduction in the number of convictions overturned on appeal.

Finally, emphatic reliance on judicial directions is prominent in this area. Psychological research on juror cognition supports the common law's strong stance against the risk of an unfair trial created by low admissibility standards. This research also encourages caution in adopting the view that a judicial direction will cure seductive but improper reasoning by jurors. This is a field where strong appeal points leave hanging the dual dilemma of whether the accused has had a fair trial and whether those vulnerable to such crimes are properly protected by the criminal justice system.

253 *JDA 2015* (Vic), s 28(3).

254 For a comprehensive discussion of the vulnerable populations directly impacted by this violence, see Australian Institute of Health and Welfare, *Family, domestic and sexual violence in Australia: continuing the national story* (AIHW, Canberra, 2019).

Chapter 12

Opinion Evidence

This chapter provides an introduction to opinion evidence, though its primary focus is on issues associated with the admission of expert opinion evidence in criminal proceedings.

Opinion evidence, and particularly expert opinion evidence, has created conceptual and practical difficulties for hundreds of years.[1] More than a century ago the great American jurist Learned Hand expressed concern about comprehension of expert evidence by lay persons:

> The trouble with all this is that it is setting the jury to decide, where doctors disagree. … But how can the jury judge between two statements each founded upon an experience confessedly foreign in kind to their own.[2]

Judges and commentators have also expressed anxieties about expert partisanship. Consider the following statement from Victorian England:

> [T]he mode in which expert evidence is obtained is such as not to give the fair result of scientific opinion to the court. A man may go, and sometimes does, to half-a-dozen experts. I have known it in cases of valuation within my experience at the Bar. He takes their honest opinions, he finds three in his favour and three against him; he says to the three in his favour, 'Will you be kind enough to give evidence?' And he pays the three against him their fee and leaves them alone; the other side does the same. It may not be three out of six, it may be three out of fifty … therefore I always have the greatest possible distrust of scientific evidence of this kind, not only because it is universally contradictory and the mode of its selection makes it necessarily contradictory, but because I know the way in which it is obtained. I am sorry to say that the result is that the court does not get that assistance from the experts which, if they were unbiased and fairly chosen, it would have a right to expect.[3]

---

1 Expert opinion evidence is often described as expert evidence, although experts might also give evidence of fact (and description and explanation) that may not be caught by the exclusionary *opinion rule*: *UEA*, s 76.

2 L Hand, 'Historical and Practical Considerations Regarding Expert Testimony' (1901) 15 *Harvard Law Review* 40.

3 *Thorn v Worthing Skating Rink Co* (1877) 6 Ch D 415n. See also *Abinger v Ashton* (1873) 17 LR Eq 358, 374 (Jessel MR) and I Freckelton, P Reddy and H Selby, *Australian Judicial Perspectives on Expert Evidence: An Empirical Study* (AIJA, 1999). More recent versions include P Huber, *Galileo's Revenge: Junk science in the courtroom* (Basic Books, 1991); K Foster and P Huber, *Judging science: Scientific knowledge and the federal courts* (MIT Press, 1998); M Hagen, *Whores of the Court* (Regan Books, 1997).

As we shall see, judges (and others) have struggled to develop rules that might assist lawyers to identify the kinds of expert opinion evidence that facilitate the rational administration of justice. Whereas Australian judges seem to have been animated by difficulties with expert opinion evidence in civil proceedings, particularly around the issue of costs, delay and partisanship, recent developments suggest that there may be serious and unresolved problems with the reliability of many types of forensic science and medicine evidence routinely relied on by the state in criminal proceedings.[4]

Introduction

Ordinarily, witnesses are required to testify about things they have personally experienced or perceived directly through their senses. Examples might include recounting a conversation, describing a fight in a pub or the nature of the relationship between two persons. Historically, sensory descriptions of these sorts of things have been characterised as facts or factual evidence. Witnesses are expected to describe them by recounting what they saw, heard or otherwise directly perceived – without embellishment or interpretive gloss. Subject to relevance (and exclusionary rules such as hearsay) these kinds of descriptions are generally admissible.

Opinion evidence, in contrast, refers to evidence that involves interpreting facts or drawing inferences from facts.[5] As a general rule, opinion evidence is not admissible. Relevant opinions are only admissible where there is some kind of exception to the exclusionary presumption. For our purposes there are two main exceptions. The first exception pertains to opinions that form part of our everyday experience. These are usually incidental, though occasionally necessary, to enable lay witnesses to describe or convey their experiences. Such *lay opinions* are admissible under the *UEA* where they are based on sensory perceptions (for example, eyewitness observation) *and* are deemed necessary to understand the witness's perceptions: s 78.[6] The other exception is for those with relevant expertise or, as the *UEA* characterises it, for opinions based on specialised knowledge: s 79(1).[7] Most of this chapter is concerned with expert opinion evidence, particularly the admissibility of forensic science and medicine evidence. The chapter touches upon other exceptions, such as where an opinion has evidentiary value unrelated to the existence of a fact about the existence of which it was expressed (s 77),[8] the exception for the opinions of Indigenous Australians concerning their traditional laws and customs (s 78A), and the rules relating to ultimate issues and common knowledge (s 80).[9]

In practice, judges have adopted commonsense (that is, non-philosophical and non-scientific) approaches to opinion evidence and the demarcation between 'fact' and 'opinion'. The following passages, along with some of the case extracts in this chapter (notably from *Smith*[10]), convey the difficulty of maintaining sharp distinctions.

4 See, eg, NSWLRC, *Expert Witnesses* (Report No 109, 2005); Lord Woolf, *Access to Justice: Final Report* (HMSO, 1996).

5 See *Lithgow City Council v Jackson* [2011] HCA 36; 244 CLR 352.

6 Discussed below, pp 510-520.

7 Discussed below, pp 522-531, 539.

8 Discussed below, pp 509-510.

9 Discussed below, pp 520-521, 552-555.

10 *Smith (Mundarra)* [1999] NSWCCA 317; 47 NSWLR 419; *Smith (Mundarra)* [2001] HCA 50; 206 CLR 650.

> The line between opinion evidence and evidence of fact is not always clearly defined. Evidence of physical identification illustrates the point. On the one hand such evidence may be characterised as evidence of fact; but, depending on the circumstances, it may more properly be characterised as evidence of opinion. The ordinary observer would regard evidence given by a man identifying his wife of thirty years as evidence of fact; but a witness who identifies a suspect in a police line-up would be perceived as giving evidence more closely allied to opinion evidence.[11]

And:

> The distinction [between fact and opinion] can serve a useful purpose and is, in the end, unavoidable. Evidence at the extreme of the continuum, which most would be prepared to classify as evidence of opinion, will generally be open to more dispute than material at the opposite end, which most would classify as evidence of fact. For accuracy of fact finding and to minimise confusion and time-wasting, therefore, it is necessary to exercise some control upon material at the opinion end of the continuum.[12]

The difficulty, as these extracts suggest, is that there are few clear or consistent lines between what constitutes fact and what constitutes opinion. In reality, all human perceptions are shaped by assumptions, experiences, expectations and socialisation.[13] Humans cannot transcend such interpretive constraints but they are frequently shared, forming a common background or worldview. Tensions sometimes emerge where, for example, people experience or understand events differently. Such differences may be accentuated by divergent social, educational, demographic, gender or ethnic backgrounds and assumptions, as well as by disability, intoxication and time.

Ever pragmatic, lawyers and judges tend to manage the divide between fact and opinion on a case-by-case basis. Typically, less complex opinions, or those that are widely accepted (or taken for granted), or on subjects not in issue, will rarely be challenged. Indeed, such opinions may be accepted as fact. At trial, many prima facie inadmissible opinions pass without objection. Indeed, the common law recognised a range of interpretations, many of a commonplace nature, that a lay witness might be allowed to express at trial.

> It is a good general rule that a witness is not to give his impressions, but to state the facts from which he received them, and thus leave the jury to draw their own conclusion; and wherever the facts *can* be stated, it is not to be departed from. But every man must judge of external objects according to the impressions they make on his senses; and after all, when we come to speak of the most simple fact which we have witnessed, we are necessarily guided by our impressions. There are cases where a single impression is made by induction from a number of others; as, where we judge whether a man is actuated by passion, we are determined by the expression of his countenance, the tone of his voice, his gestures, and a variety of other matters: yet a witness speaking of such a subject of inquiry, would be permitted directly to say whether the man was angry or not. … I take it, that wherever the facts from which a witness received an impression are too evanescent in their nature to be recollected, or are too complicated to be separated and distinctly narrated, his impressions from these facts become evidence.[14]

---

11 *Leung and Wong* [1999] NSWCCA 287; 47 NSWLR 405, [43].

12 ALRC, *Evidence (Interim)* (Report No 26, 1985) Vol 1, [738].

13 *Nguyen* [2017] NSWCCA 4, [19]. Perception is also limited by cognitive constraints.

14 *Cornell v Green* 10 Seng & Rawle 16, 16 (Pa 1823), quoted in JH Wigmore, *Evidence in Trials at Common Law* (Little, Brown, 1978) and *Lithgow City Council v Jackson* [2011] HCA 36; 244 CLR 352, [46].

So, the basic position is that witnesses should testify about factual matters – that is, things they have directly perceived, usually through their eyes and/or ears.[15] Witnesses are formally prevented from offering interpretations of things they have perceived – that is, the law generally leaves the interpretation of facts and any inferences to be drawn from the facts to the trier of fact.

This chapter begins with the exclusionary *opinion rule*, before moving to consider the limited scope afforded to the opinions of ordinary (or lay) persons under the *UEA*.[16]

The Exclusionary *Opinion Rule*: *UEA*, s 76

Section 76(1) of the *UEA* governs the admission of opinion evidence. It states:

> **76. The opinion rule**
> (1) Evidence of an opinion is not admissible to prove the existence of a fact about the existence of which the opinion was expressed.

Section 76(1) would appear to cover the field when it comes to opinion evidence intended 'to prove the existence of a fact about the existence of which the opinion was expressed'. The vast majority of opinion evidence is admitted 'to prove the existence of a fact about the existence of which the opinion was expressed'.[17] Unless there is an express exception, s 76 deems such opinions inadmissible.

Otherwise Relevant Opinion Evidence: *UEA*, s 77

Among the exceptions for opinions is one that resembles the operation of s 60 in relation to hearsay evidence.

> **77. Exception: evidence relevant otherwise than as opinion evidence**
> The opinion rule does not apply to evidence of an opinion that is admitted because it is relevant for a purpose other than proof of the existence of a fact about the existence of which the opinion was expressed.

Section 77 provides an exception to the general inadmissibility of opinion evidence in circumstances where the opinion is not being relied on for 'proof of the existence of a fact about the existence of which the opinion was expressed'. If the opinion is being used for some reason that has nothing to do with the proof of the fact it is not caught by s 76, and s 77 confirms the admissibility pathway.

An example of such a use might arise where a person is accused of fraudulently practising medicine – that is, practising without qualifications.[18] Let us assume that you had visited this 'Doctor', for an ear ache, assuming her to be appropriately qualified, registered and insured. During the consultation, the 'Doctor' diagnoses

15 There is scope for evidence of smell, touch and taste.

16 Sometimes the word 'expert' is italicised or placed in square quotes. This is because in some cases we do not know if those who are presented and accepted as experts actually possess relevant expertise. In many cases we do not know if they are better than jurors or a jury.

17 We will return to the strength and breadth of s 76 when we consider the curious persistence of *ad hoc expert evidence* below, pp 540-547 and the treatment of some identification and recognition evidence (so-called direct evidence) as fact evidence.

18 According to Harry Collins and Trevor Pinch, *Dr Golem: How to think about medicine* (University of Chicago Press, 2008), ch 2, 'bogus doctors' are much more common than we might think; particularly in the United States. See also Steven Spielberg, *Catch Me If You Can* (Dreamworks LLC, 2002).

you with 'swimmer's ear' and prescribes a regime and a course of antibiotics. Here, for the purpose of the prosecution, we do not care if the opinion about your condition is correct (that is, 'proof of the existence of a fact about the existence of which the opinion was expressed'). The accuracy (or otherwise) of the diagnosis and treatment is not really to the point. Rather, the fact that this person offered an opinion in the capacity of a medical practitioner is not caught by s 76 and so is admissible evidence against her.[19]

Sections 135-137 might limit the admissibility and use of evidence admitted via this section (and all of the other exceptions to s 76 discussed in this chapter).

Lay Opinion Evidence: *UEA*, s 78

As explained in the introduction to this chapter, it is useful to divide opinion evidence into *lay* (or non-expert) opinion and expert opinion. Generally, lay opinions are limited to circumstances where the inferences being drawn are not particularly contentious – that is, the kinds of inferences people routinely draw in their everyday lives. So, for example, the common law allowed lay witnesses to express opinions about whether a person was intoxicated or whether a car was being driven erratically. Such opinions, especially where they enabled the trier of fact to obtain a clearer sense of the general circumstances, could be tolerated, even when closely related to facts in issue; such as in a prosecution relating to dangerous driving.[20]

Lord McDermott LSJ gave examples of various matters that might be reported to the court:

> (1) the identification of handwriting, persons and things; (2) apparent age; (3) the bodily plight or condition of a person, including death and illness; (4) the emotional state of a person – eg whether distressed, angry, aggressive, affectionate or depressed; (5) the condition of things – eg worn, shabby, used or new; (6) certain questions of value; and (7) estimates of speed and distance.[21]

In general, the range of topics is neither clearly nor consistently drawn.

Where lay opinions are deemed inadmissible, the witness is obliged to describe the underlying 'facts' in a manner that enables the trier of fact to draw an appropriate inference (or inferences). In the case of intoxication, for example, if the witness was not permitted to express her opinion that the defendant was drunk she might be required to rehearse the underlying sensory perceptions on which that opinion was based in order for the trier of fact to make an assessment. The witness might, in that case, testify that she observed the defendant: drinking in a public bar for several hours; sitting at a table with five or six empty beer glasses in front of him; making quite a bit of noise and slurring his speech; walking a little awkwardly when he went to the bathroom; and with flushed cheeks and the smell of alcohol on his breath. The trier of fact might be encouraged to draw an inference

---

19 Another example might relate to neo-Nazi and revisionist claims about the Holocaust. Such opinions might reveal something about beliefs and ideology if not historical reality. In some jurisdictions such opinions might be admissible as evidence of hate crimes or holocaust denial. Section 60 might apply to hearsay in these contexts.

20 At common law there were constraints that prevented the witness from expressing opinions about the ultimate issue in proceedings, such as whether some act was negligent. Compare *UEA*, s 80(a), discussed below, pp 552-555.

21 *Sherrard v Jacob* [1965] NI 151, 156. See also *Ex parte Sampson* (1966) 66 SR (NSW) 501, 514; *Wright* [1980] VR 593, 596-7; *Whitby* (1957) 74 WN (NSW) 441, 443.

about the state of intoxication from such *factual* statements. If intoxication or the degree of intoxication was contested, the defence might ask: about the possibility that the empty beer glasses were not associated with the defendant; if the witness was mistaken about the slurring of speech and gait; whether the defendant is normally gregarious; whether the witness herself might have been drinking, or was mistaken about the identity of the defendant, and so on.

Ordinarily, witnesses are encouraged to give evidence of fact. In practice, however, perceptual evidence is interspersed with fact and opinion. This reflects how commonplace and uncontroversial the interpretation of facts tends to be in everyday situations. Usually, it is only when an objection is made at trial that the issue of whether a statement constitutes an opinion arises. On such occasions, the judge will either allow the witness to express an opinion that is part of everyday experience or require the questioner to elicit the underlying facts, as in the example above.

It is to the admissibility of lay opinions under the *UEA* that we now turn.

Section 78

Section 78 provides an exception for lay opinion under the *UEA*. It states:

> **78. Exception: lay opinions**
> The opinion rule does not apply to evidence of an opinion expressed by a person if:
> (a) the opinion is based on what the person saw, heard or otherwise perceived about a matter or event, and
> (b) evidence of the opinion is necessary to obtain an adequate account or understanding of the person's perception of the matter or event.

Section 78 applies to opinions that are based on what the witness perceived, where receiving the opinion is necessary to obtain an adequate understanding of the witness's perception of the matter or event.

Put more simply, s 78 is designed to permit evidence of opinion that would facilitate the understanding of evidence otherwise relevant and admissible. This section assumes that the matter or event as perceived by the witness is relevant to the proceeding. That is the primary evidence. The opinion evidence is admissible as incidental to an understanding of the primary evidence.[22]

According to the High Court:

> The function of the law in relation to [s 78(b)] is to permit reception of an opinion where the primary facts on which it is based are too evanescent to remember or too complicated to be separately narrated … For that reason, s 78 permits the conclusion to be stated: without it the evidence does not convey an adequate account or generate an adequate understanding of the witness's perception of the sobriety, age or emotional state being observed.[23]

As we shall see, courts have been willing to extend the meaning of 'what the person saw, heard or otherwise perceived about a matter or event' beyond direct sensory perception; allowing those who were not present to proffer opinions on the basis of listening to or watching sound and video recordings. On the question of when it is 'necessary' to admit an opinion in order to obtain an adequate account or understanding of the person's perception, the language would seem to require that without the opinion it is not possible to understand the witness's perception.

22 *Leung and Wong* [1999] NSWCCA 287; 47 NSWLR 405, [33].
23 *Lithgow City Council v Jackson* [2011] HCA 36; 244 CLR 352, [48].

In *Lithgow City Council v Jackson*,[24] referring to the meaning of 'necessary' from s 78(b), the High Court explained:

> 54. The word "necessary" is not directed to meeting difficulties that arise where it is impossible or inconvenient to call the person propounding the opinion as a witness. ... Section 78 is not a "best evidence" provision, permitting reception of the evidence if there is no better evidence. The word "necessary" is instead directed to a relationship internal to the evidence of the perceiver – the relationship between the perceiver's perceptions and the perceiver's opinion.

They continued:

> 57. ... It is true, though, that the less the witness or other observer states his or her primary perceptions, the harder will it be for the tendering party to establish the condition of admissibility in s 78(a) (because of the difficulty of establishing that the opinion is "based" on the perceptions) and the condition of admissibility in s 78(b) (because of the difficulty of establishing that the opinion is necessary to obtain an adequate account or understanding of the person's perceptions).[25]

Judges sometimes disagree on whether opinions (that is, interpretations of events) as opposed to more detailed factual descriptions are required.

Whyte

[2006] NSWCCA 75

A young woman working in the family cafe was followed to the toilet by a patron of the cafe. When she attempted to leave the toilet the patron grabbed her and pushed her down. When she resisted he grabbed her by the pony tail and tried to drag her back into the toilet. She screamed, broke free and ran back into the cafe. In an agitated state she said to her mother: 'A man tried to rape me'. The man was subsequently arrested and found to have condoms in his pocket.

Whyte was convicted of detaining a victim, without her consent, with the intention of having sexual intercourse under s 86(2)(b) of the *Crimes Act 1900* (NSW). At trial Whyte objected to the admissibility of the complainant's evidence that: 'A man tried to rape me'. The admissibility of this statement was raised on appeal and the court was split on its admissibility.

> **Spigelman CJ (Barr JA concurring):** 29. On this appeal, the submissions focused on the use of the complaint for a hearsay purpose, ie to prove the truth of the content of the statement made. That such a statement is both relevant and capable of use for a hearsay purpose was established in *Papakosmas v The Queen* [1999] HCA 37; 196 CLR 297 see esp at [20]-[22], [30] on relevance and [33]-[35] on hearsay purpose. The issue in that case was consent. The issue, as argued on this appeal, is the use of the statement for the purpose of proving that the Appellant had a sexual purpose and, more particularly, intended to have penile intercourse. Nevertheless, it is pertinent to point out that detention without consent was an element of the offence in this case and the statement made did negative consent.
>
> 30. The parties make submissions on the basis that the evidence was only an assertion of a belief. Two questions arise. First, is the belief relevant to a fact in issue, most relevantly the intention of the Appellant being of a particular character. Secondly, is it admissible as lay opinion.
>
> 31. The words used – "tried to rape me" – would in their ordinary meaning refer to an attempt to have penile intercourse. In my opinion, the victim of a sexual assault who has a belief as to what is being done is entitled to express that belief.

24 [2011] HCA 36; 244 CLR 352.

25 See also *Wilson (No 2)* [2017] NSWSC 1673.

32. The Appellant's submissions focused on the Appellant's physical acts, eg following the complainant, banging on the toilet door, pulling her hair etc. as if such objective conduct of a physical character constituted the full scope of relevant evidence. That is not so. It is not the case that a description of the objective events was all that was relevant. This is clear from the fact, for example, that the complainant gave evidence that the Appellant "looked angry". Evidence of this character is capable of being given by a victim and is not necessarily able to be identified in terms of physical movements.

33. The same is true of a belief by a woman who has been assaulted that the intention of the attack was sexual gratification. This is not something necessarily capable of full description by describing the movement of parts of the body or other physically observable acts. Such a belief can arise from the impression given at the time by matters which cannot be described in a physical way. Such an impression may only be able to be conveyed to the jury in the form of a statement such as "He tried to rape me", as occurred in this case.

34. In my opinion, the evidence was relevant to a fact in issue. It is sufficient to say that it was relevant to whether the assault had a sexual overtone of any character. I am also of the view that it was relevant to the particularised fact in issue, ie whether the Appellant intended penile intercourse. Whether it was of any weight, especially for the latter issue, was a matter open to be tested in cross-examination.

35. The Crown relies on s 78 of the *Evidence Act* … [s 78 reproduced]

36. I agree that this exception applies. An opinion of this character is obviously based on what the complainant perceived and, in my opinion, it was, in this case, necessary to obtain an adequate account of that perception. Putting aside the issue of whether it supports the particular of an intent to have penile intercourse, the evidence was necessary to give an "account of [the] perception" that the assault had a sexual purpose. That this perception was significant was indicated in the cross-examination directed to supporting the mother's version.

Simpson J (in dissent): 56. … By s 76, evidence of an opinion is not admissible to prove the existence of a fact about the existence of which the opinion was expressed. There are, however, as with the general prohibition on hearsay evidence, a number of exceptions to this general prohibition. By s 78 the opinion rule does not apply to evidence of an opinion expressed by a person if the opinion is based on what the person saw, heard or otherwise perceived about a matter or event, and evidence of the opinion is necessary to obtain an adequate account or understanding of the person's perception of the matter or event.

57. The first condition is, in this case, met; if what the complainant said can be properly characterised as an opinion, then it was plainly an opinion or conclusion based upon what she saw, heard and otherwise perceived about the events in question; however, the second criterion is not met. Evidence of the complainant's opinion is not necessary to obtain (or to give the jury) an adequate account or understanding of her perception of the matters and events in question. S 78 does not operate to render the complainant's statement admissible as opinion evidence.

A useful example of some of the definitional issues around opinion evidence and the operation (or non-operation) of ss 76 and 78 can also be gleaned from the case of Mundarra Smith.

Smith (Mundarra)

[1999] NSWCCA 317; 47 NSWLR 419

Smith was accused of robbing a bank. The robbery was caught by security cameras and the only issue was identity – was Smith one of the robbers? At trial two police officers were allowed to identify Smith as one of the robbers on the basis of their independent reviews of the security images. Each had met Smith on several occasions, ranging from a few minutes to an hour or so during a prior arrest. Is the evidence of the police officers admissible? On what basis?

There are two extracts below, one from the NSW Court of Criminal Appeal and one from the High Court.

Sheller JA (Grove and Hidden JJ concurring): 14. … [C]ousel submitted that, since the evidence was not identification evidence as defined [see *Evidence Act*, Part 3.9], the evidence could only be admitted in accordance with the opinion rule, that is to say s 76. That section provides: "Evidence of an opinion is not admissible to prove the existence of a fact about the existence of which the opinion was expressed."

15. Before coming to consider the application of that section and statutory exceptions to it in ss 77-80, it is helpful to consider what is meant in this Part of the Act by the expression "Evidence of an opinion" or, perhaps, what the expression does not embrace.

16. To characterise as evidence of an opinion a witness's testimony that he recognises a person shown in a photograph as a person he knows presents an obvious problem. Logically, what is the difference between that evidence and that witness's evidence that he recognises somebody he met in the street as a person he knows? If a witness is shown a studio photograph of his spouse, who lives with the witness, and gives evidence that the person shown in the photograph is the witness's spouse, commonsense and common use of language would not treat that as an expression or evidence of opinion but as direct evidence of the fact: "that is a photograph of my wife". Compare *R v Palmer* [1981] 1 NSWLR 209 at 213.

17. In the context of the rule, which has traditionally excluded opinion evidence, any useful definition of "opinion" has proved difficult. In *R W Miller & Co Pty Limited v Krupp (Australia) Pty Limited* (1991) 34 NSWLR 129 at 130 Giles J, as his Honour then was, observed that the distinction between fact and opinion, and what is opinion evidence, are not particularly clear, "but for present purposes I think opinion evidence can be described as evidence of a conclusion, usually judgmental or debatable, reasoned from facts." Typically a person of a particular skill or training, such as a medical practitioner, will give evidence based on history, symptoms and examination about the health of a patient. That is understood as opinion evidence based on factual material or on assumptions consisting of history, symptoms and the results of examination. In *Allstate Life Insurance Co Limited v Australian and New Zealand Banking Group Limited (No 5)* (1996) 64 FCR 73 at 75 Lindgren J, referring to the opinion rule in the *Evidence Act* of the Commonwealth, said:

> "The expression 'opinion' is not defined in the Act. In the context of the general law of evidence, 'opinion' has been defined as 'an inference from observed and communicable data': J D Chadbourn (Ed), *Wigmore on Evidence*, (1978), vol 7, para 1917; and see *Cross on Evidence* (5th Australian Edition, 1996), p 782 para 29010; Australian Law Reform Commission, *Interim Report on Evidence* (ALRC 26, 1985), vol 2, pp 168-169 para 96."

18. … Wigmore … makes the point that no distinction between "opinion" testimony and "fact" testimony is scientifically possible.

> "We may in ordinary conversation roughly group distinct domains for 'opinion' on the one hand and 'fact' or 'knowledge' on the other; but as soon as we come to analyse and define these terms for the purpose of that accuracy which is necessary in legal rulings, we find that the distinction vanishes, that a flux ensues, and that nearly everything which we choose to call 'fact' either is or may be only 'opinion' or inference."

19. If a distinction must be made it can only be one of degree, calling for a decision as to whether, on a continuum which is unmarked and for which there is no exact measure, particular testimony has past the point where it has become evidence of an opinion. In a passage which Wigmore quoted as "the most careful attempt to justify the distinction",

Sir George Cornwall Lewis in *Influence of Authority in Matters of Opinion* 1 (1849) gave the following guide:

> "It is true that even the simplest sensations involve some judgment; when a witness reports that he saw an object of a certain shape and size or at a certain distance, he describes something more than a mere impression on his sense of sight, and his statement implies a theory and explanation of a bare phenomenon. When, however, the judgment is of so simple a kind as to become wholly unconscious, and the interpretation of the appearances as a matter of general agreement, the object of sensation may, for our present purpose, be considered a fact."

20. In *Cross*, 5th Australian edition, at 781 and following the learned editor [Dyson Heydon] emphasises the attractive but deceptive simplicity of the proposition that witnesses must state facts not opinions. At para 29015 it is said:

> "Although the distinction between facts and inference is clear enough, the evidence given by a witness is neither fact nor inference. What the witness utters in each case is a statement about a fact or series of facts. These facts have been processed through the witness' mind via perception, classification, recollection and utterance. … it will be recognised that statements concerning speed, or temperature, or the identity of persons, things and handwriting are indissolubly composed of fact and inference. The law makes allowance for these borderline cases by permitting witnesses to state their opinion with regard to matters not calling for special knowledge whenever it would be virtually impossible for them to separate their inferences from the facts on which those inferences are based."

21. The question posed by s 76 does not require a determination which starts by dividing evidence between evidence of opinion and evidence of fact. The question is whether particular evidence is evidence of an opinion within the meaning of the section. The appellant's submission is that the police officer giving evidence about the photograph was doing no more than infer identity from observed and communicable data.

22. It is not difficult to see that evidence about what a photograph shows may involve using a special knowledge to draw an inference from what can be seen in the photograph. But, to a witness who knows a person well enough to recognise that person on sight, there is no more inference involved in recognising that person as the person whose face is shown in a photograph than there is in recognising the same person when meeting that person in the street. The evidence may be mistaken in either case, for example, if the person recognised is an identical twin. But even so it remains direct evidence of the fact that the person shown in the photograph or met in the street is a particular person.

23. The dangers of reliance on identification evidence are well known; see *Domican v The Queen* [1992] HCA 13; 173 CLR 555 particularly at 560 and following. But evidence of the sort here under consideration proceeds on the basis that the witness had previously known the person identified well enough to recognise that person on sight and then looked at a photograph and given evidence about what the photograph showed. The clarity or otherwise of the photograph and the resemblance of the person depicted to the person recognised is there for the jury to see. That is not to say that there are not dangers but the weaknesses of the recognition are more exposed and to that extent the dangers reduced. It is quite different from the photo identification procedure by which someone who has seen a suspected offender but cannot put a name to him is shown photographs of persons known to others, usually the police, and by recognising one of them as the suspected offender, identifies him; compare *Alexander v The Queen* [1981] HCA 17; 145 CLR 395.

24. The evidence given by the police officers was not evidence of an opinion but was direct evidence that a person shown in the photograph was the accused. As such it was not excluded by s 76 of the Act. Accordingly, there is no need to consider the application of s 78 or other statutory exceptions to the opinion rule.

In the NSW Court of Criminal Appeal, the admissibility of the police officers' opinions was effectively circumvented by characterising them as direct or recognition evidence.[26] The police officers were said to be sufficiently familiar with Smith such that the exclusionary opinion rule (s 76) did not apply to their identifications.[27]

Smith (Mundarra)
[2001] HCA 50; 206 CLR 650

On appeal to the High Court the majority raised the relevance of the police officer's evidence – for the first time in the proceedings. The majority concluded that the opinions of the police officers were not relevant because they were obtained in conditions that were not substantially different from those confronting the jury. Kirby J, on the other hand, found the evidence of the police officers relevant but inadmissible because it was opinion evidence but without an exception.[28]

> **Kirby J**: 58. … [I]t is my view that the evidence of identification (or recognition) of the appellant, offered by the police witnesses, was opinion evidence. Accordingly, by s 76 of the Act, it was not admissible to prove the existence of the fact about the existence of which the opinion was expressed. In these proceedings, the fact to be proved was that the appellant was one of the persons depicted in the security photographs recorded at the time of the robbery and hence a participant in the robbery. Unless the evidence became admissible by virtue of an exception to the opinion rule, reflected in the Act, it should have been excluded.
>
> 59. Two possible bases for exception from the opinion rule were explored in argument. The exception for admitting evidence based on specialised knowledge provided by s 79 of the Act can be disregarded, as no suggestion of such expertise was made in relation to the police officers. Their prior contact with the appellant did not amount to ad hoc expertise based on familiarity,[29] nor did they claim any expertise in, for example, anatomical or photographic comparisons. The exception for lay opinion evidence provided by s 78 of the Act states: "The opinion rule does not apply to evidence of an opinion expressed by a person if: (a) the opinion is based on what the person saw, heard or otherwise perceived about a matter or event, and (b) evidence of the opinion is necessary to obtain an adequate account or understanding of the person's perception of the matter or event."
>
> 60. Neither police officer was present at the "matter or event" in question in the appellant's trial, namely the robbery. Although the security photographs record the robbery taking place, the opinion of the police officers is "based on" the photographs and not, as such, "based on" the robbery itself which they did not see, hear or otherwise perceive. The Australian Law Reform Commission's report makes it clear that this provision of the Act was addressed, essentially, to the opinion of eye-witnesses. It exists to allow such witnesses to recount, as closely as possible, "their original perception [so as] to minimise inaccuracy and encourage honesty". It is important to note that the requirements for the applicability of s 78 of the Act are cumulative ("and"). Neither the language of the Act governing the reception of lay opinion evidence, nor the purposes of those provisions as explained by the Commission, justifies treating the opinions expressed by the two police officers as falling within a permissible exception.
>
> 61. It follows that the evidence, being of an opinion, was not admissible to prove that the appellant was a participant in the robbery. In the result, the opinion, although relevant, could be no more than a step in the process of investigation and detection that led to the

---

26 This is either a species of fact or a type of evidence that at common law, at least, was not subjected to rules regulating opinions.

27 See also *Potts (No 3)* [2016] ACTSC 341.

28 The question of whether the evidence of the police officers is relevant is complex. However, the fact that other people *independently* identified the person of interest as Smith might be considered to be capable of rationally influencing the assessment of the identity of the bank robber.

29 See below, pp 552-555.

> appellant's being charged. Proof of the police officers' evidence should not, in my view, be excluded as irrelevant to the fact in issue. But it should be excluded as nothing more than a lay opinion upon a subject about which the jury were required to form their own opinion.

This example is instructive for several reasons. Not only does it illustrate differences in the way judges might erect the fact/opinion divide, it also demonstrates the implications of characterising something as 'fact' (for example, direct or recognition evidence) rather than 'opinion'. If the evidence of a witness is characterised as fact then, if relevant, it is generally admissible. If, however, it is characterised as opinion then it is generally inadmissible subject to the existence of some kind of explicit exception.

In thinking about policy here, given that identification was the only issue (indeed, the ultimate issue[30]) in *Smith*, simply assuming that identification or recognition was instantaneous or spontaneous (that is, non-interpretive) might be unpersuasive and undesirable. In such circumstances it might be better to assume that this kind of evidence is opinion because we do not know how long it took for the police officers to come to the conclusion that it was Smith. Moreover, it is very difficult to explore such issues months or years later in the context of the trial. Also, we do not know if the police officers who identified Smith were exposed to suggestive information, such as the beliefs of colleagues or forensic science evidence. This last issue has become increasingly important in relation to forensic science evidence – see the discussion of 'Cognitive Bias' below.

From its terms, s 78 would not appear to enable a person watching a video or hearing a recording displaced in time and/or space from the action (for example, via a remote monitor or a recording played back at a later time) to express an admissible opinion about what transpired or the identity of a person of interest.[31] Indeed, in *Lithgow City Council v Jackson*[32] the High Court appears to have endorsed Kirby J's approach to s 78 in *Smith*, placing particular emphasis on the witness's 'personal perception' of a matter or event. Nevertheless, later Australian courts have applied s 78 to enable those listening to voice recordings to opine about the identity of the speakers and even the meaning of words said to be spoken on surveillance recordings.[33]

The Victorian Court of Appeal decision in *Kheir*[34] relied on s 78 to admit the opinion of a police officer, involved in covert surveillance, to identify a voice from a telephone intercept as the appellant. In that case the police officer had listened to the intercepted calls 'over and over again' and compared the voices to an inadmissible 'no comment' interview between Kheir and investigators.[35] The Court of Appeal explained:

> 65. In our view, the evidence of Sergeant Bray was more appropriately viewed as falling within s 78 than s 79 [the exception for opinion based on specialised knowledge]. The 'matter' of which Sergeant Bray had a 'perception' was the audio recordings of the telephone intercepts, the recordings of the applicant's record of interview and a comparison of the two. His perception of that comparison met the test of relevance because he

---

30 See below, pp 552-555.

31 See Kirby J in *Smith (Mundarra)* and Simpson J in *Leung and Wong* [1999] NSWCCA 287; 47 NSWLR 405.

32 [2011] HCA 36; 244 CLR 352, [42]-[46].

33 See also *Nguyen* [2007] NSWCCA 249; *Dodds* [2009] NSWCCA 78.

34 [2014] VSCA 200.

35 Ibid [40]ff, see also [64]. It could have been adduced by the defence; though this was characterised as a tactical decision.

> was in a better position to make that comparison than the jurors were. Whether the voice heard in the intercepts was also that in the record of interview was a fact in issue, and the comparison could rationally affect the assessment of the probability of that fact. Sergeant Bray's opinion was based upon that comparison, and his opinion – that the voices on the two tapes were the same – was necessary to shed light upon the observations he made about the voices' similarities.

Sergeant Bray's opinion was said not to constitute expert evidence.

> The present case was not one in which an expert was asked to give an opinion on facts provided to him for that purpose.[36]

And:

> Sergeant Bray had no special language or interpretation skills. He said nothing as to the content of any conversation. He produced no secondary material to assist the jury in comprehending the tape recorded evidence.[37]

The Court of Appeal characterised Bray's opinion about the identity of the speaker as one that was grounded in familiarity rather than expertise.

> It is difficult to see how a scenario such as this one can be meaningfully distinguished from one of long-held personal familiarity with an individual's voice, such as might arise out of a friendship or a long-term neighbourly acquaintance. It is not, we think, correct to say that repeated exposure to the voice of a friend or neighbour makes a person an 'expert' in that voice.[38]

Repeated listening was said to place the investigator on a similar footing to friends and longstanding familiars (reminiscent of Sheller JA's reasoning in *Smith*).

In addition, the Court of Appeal adverted to the fact that reliance on s 78 overcame the need to attend to the 'difficulties with the *Makita* requirements' for expert opinion – discussed below.

> As recognized in *Lithgow*, s 78 overcomes the difficulties with the *Makita*[39] requirement that an expert witness 'either prove by admissible means the facts on which [their] opinion is based, or state explicitly the assumptions as to fact on which the opinion was based.' ... identity evidence – including voice identification – will not always have a factual basis which is capable of clear explanation. There would be obvious evidentiary difficulties if the requirements of *Makita* were to be fulfilled in the case of recognition identification, as the facts upon which recognition identification rests may be too numerous or nebulous for the witness to enumerate.[40]

Notwithstanding the court's preference for admitting Bray's opinion via s 78, they also considered the opinion to satisfy s 79(1). Such a conclusion might seem curious given the earlier statements about Bray's lack of expertise.

The Victorian interpretation of s 78 represents an extremely broad approach to both what is 'necessary' as well as the 'matter or event'. It was endorsed in *Tran and Chang*[41] where s 78 was described as the preferable admissibility pathway for voice comparison evidence.[42]

---

36 [2014] VSCA 200, [66].

37 Ibid [61].

38 Ibid [66].

39 *Makita (Australia) Pty Ltd v Sprowles* [2001] NSWCA 305; 52 NSWLR 705, below pp 522-523.

40 *Kheir* [2014] VSCA 200, [67].

41 [2016] VSCA 79.

42 H Fraser, 'Covert recordings used as evidence in criminal trials: concerns of Australian linguists' (2018) 30 *Judicial Officers' Bulletin* 1.

Similar evidence has been admitted in New South Wales in a series of decisions; reaching their most expansive form in Basten JA's decision in *Nguyen*.[43] There, responding to an appeal concerned with the admissibility of a police officer's opinion about the identity of a speaker in 32 calls recorded from two telephones, the NSW Court of Criminal Appeal (Hulme and Schmidt JJ, query Basten JA) deemed the evidence admissible via s 79(1) because the officer had transcribed and repeatedly listened to the calls in order to compare the voices with a recording of the defendant's police interview.[44] Section 79(1) has been the preferred admissibility pathway in New South Wales where opinions derived from repeated exposure are treated as *ad hoc expert* evidence – discussed below. For Basten JA, the police officer's opinion about the identity of the caller was admissible in several additional ways. First, it was admissible under the general – that is, common law – approach to voice identification and recognition. It was not caught by s 76, by reason of *UEA* s 9, based on the kind of reasoning advanced by Sheller JA in *Smith*, above. That is, it was either fact (that is, direct or recognition) evidence or common law identification evidence and so not treated as opinion evidence.

Basten JA was also satisfied that the opinion about the identity of the speaker met the requirements for s 78. Following the Victorian Court of Appeal in *Kheir* and *Tran and Chang*, he was not persuaded by Simpson J's approach in *Leung and Wong* where s 78 was said to be incapable of grounding an opinion about the identity of the speaker on the recording.[45] Along with the Victorians, Basten JA considered it preferable to treat the 'matter or event' as the 'suspect's voice on the audio recording'.[46] Consequently, the issue was 'whether the person speaking ... was the accused'.[47] To 'establish that fact, it was necessary to make a comparison between the voice of the accused and the recording of the suspect'.[48]

It might be considered ironic (given that the majority in *Nguyen* treated the evidence as admissible opinion because it was said to be based on 'specialised knowledge' via s 79) that Basten JA insisted that the opinion satisfied s 78(b) because the police officer could offer only a 'tolerably unsophisticated analysis of the reasons for thinking that two recordings were spoken by the same person'.[49] It was '[b]ecause the comparative exercise could not be adequately described' that necessity 'was satisfied'.[50] Indeed, Basten JA accepts that there was no specialised knowledge or expertise.[51] Moreover, notwithstanding the witness being a police officer, and presumably wearing his uniform in court, any dangers of a 'white coat' effect were simply dismissed: '[n]or was [the officer] clothed in any apparent expertise or authority'.[52] The evidence does not seem to have been challenged on the basis of ss 135 and 137 at trial (or on appeal).

Whether s 78 should be used to facilitate the admission of opinions derived from perceptions remote in time and/or space from the original 'matter or event'

43 [2017] NSWCCA 4. Though see also *Narallah* [2015] NSWCCA 188.

44 See below pp 546-547.

45 *Leung and Wong* [1999] NSWCCA 287; 47 NSWLR 405, [34]; *Tran and Chang* [2016] VSCA 79.

46 *Leung and Wong*, ibid, [21], [34] where the Crown conceded at trial that the witness 'did not possess relevant specialised knowledge based on training, study or experience'.

47 *Nguyen* [2017] NSWCCA 4, [39].

48 Ibid [39]. See also *Davey v Tasmania* [2020] TASCCA 12, [59], [68].

49 Ibid [34]. The same inconsistency is a feature of *Kheir*.

50 *Nguyen* [2017] NSWCCA 4, [39].

51 Ibid [39].

52 Ibid [29]. On the 'white coat' effect, see *Honeysett* [2014] HCA 29; 253 CLR 122, [45], where the witness was said to have given 'the unwarranted appearance of science'.

and whether the opinions of investigators (and those working with them) ought to be admissible, let alone whether they are 'necessary' to understand investigators' perceptions, would seem to be matters for further appeals. Should s 78 extend to cover the comparison of voice or image recordings remote from the original matter or event? Should s 78 apply to all types of recordings and evidence – such as CCTV, photographs of fingerprints, or even a cadaver, for example – when characterised as the 'matter of event'? What about the opinion of an experienced detective about whether a witness or the defendant was telling the truth in a recorded interview or even testimony at trial? Would such an approach to s 78 work to circumvent s 79 and other protections (for example, the credibility rule, perhaps) by allowing those who have opinions that are not based on 'specialised knowledge' to express them in court?

Aboriginal and Torres Strait Islander Traditional Laws and Customs: *UEA*, s 78A

> **78A. Exception: Aboriginal and Torres Strait Islander traditional laws and customs**
> The opinion rule does not apply to evidence of an opinion expressed by a member of an Aboriginal or Torres Strait Islander group about the existence or non-existence, or the content, of the traditional laws and customs of the group.

Section 78A avoids the need to rely on anthropologists and other Western experts to provide information about Indigenous cultures and traditions that might be relevant to facts in issue.[53] Such evidence is often relevant in native title, heritage protection and some criminal proceedings.[54] Section 78A makes it easier to receive admissible evidence that might include opinion about 'traditional laws and customs' directly from Indigenous Australians.[55] The language suggests that the exception only applies to opinions about the laws and customs of the 'group' to which the witness belongs.

Previously, at common law, to avoid the constraints of opinion and hearsay rules, it was anthropologists and other experts (such as linguists, historians and archaeologists) who were obliged to provide courts with opinions derived from some kind of analytical synthesis. In the influential case of *Milirrpum v Nabalco*[56] (the *Gove Land Rights* case), Blackburn J described some of the common law rules governing this evidence:

> I do not think it is correct to apply the hearsay rule so as to exclude evidence from an anthropologist in the form of a proposition of anthropology – a conclusion which has significance in that field of discourse. It could not be contended – and was not – that the anthropologists could be allowed to give evidence in the form: Mr Munggurrawuy told me that this was Gumatj land. But, in my opinion, it is permissible for an anthropologist to give evidence in the form: "I have studied the social organization of these Aboriginals. This study includes observing their behavior; talking to them; reading the published

53 *Re Estate Jerrard, deceased* [2018] NSWSC 781.

54 The *Native Title Act 1993* (Cth) briefly repaired some of these problems, but it was revised to make the ordinary rules of evidence applicable in the *Native Title Amendment Act 1998* (Cth).

55 '*Traditional laws and customs*' of an Aboriginal or Torres Strait Islander group (including a kinship group) include any of the traditions, customary laws, customs, observances, practices, knowledge and beliefs of the group. Curiously, the exception to the hearsay rule (*UEA*, s 72) does not appear to be limited to the person's group.

56 (1971) 17 FLR 141, 159-61. Though the boundaries might be blurred: *Western Australia v Willis on behalf of the Pilki People* [2015] FCAFC 186.

> work of other experts; and, applying principles of analysis and verification which are accepted as valid in the general field of anthropology. I express the opinion as an expert that proposition X is true of their organization." In my opinion, such evidence is not rendered inadmissible by the fact that it is based partly on statements made to the expert by the Aboriginals.

Anthropologists, historians, linguists, musicologists and art historians might still proffer relevant opinion evidence, but in order to do so they must satisfy the rules regulating the admission of expert opinion evidence.

Expert Opinion Evidence: Opinion Based on 'Specialised Knowledge': *UEA*, s 79

For a very long time, those with expertise have been allowed to assist with the resolution of legal disputes. In 1554 Saunders J wrote:

> [I]f matters arise in our laws which concern other sciences and faculties we commonly call for the aid of that science or faculty which it concerns, which is an honourable and commendable thing for thereby it appears that we do not despise all other sciences but our own, but we approve of them and encourage them.[57]

In practice, courts have been quite receptive to expert opinion evidence. In ways that are difficult to reconcile with principle, Australian courts seem to have been most critical in their responses to expert opinion evidence adduced in civil proceedings, particularly the expert opinion evidence proffered by plaintiffs. Judges and reform bodies in Australia have expressed anxieties about costs, delay and partisanship (notably adversarial bias), conspicuously among expert witnesses called by plaintiffs and to some degree criminal defendants.[58] They have, in contrast, been accommodating toward forensic science and medicine evidence adduced by the state, and expressed confidence in the effectiveness of admissibility rules and trial safeguards to expose and convey weaknesses and limitations. As a generalisation, Australian trial and appellate judges have been disinterested in the validity and reliability of procedures (or techniques) relied on by forensic scientists in their admissibility decision-making. As we shall see, they have explicitly rejected the need for a reliability standard as part of the Australian admissibility jurisprudence for expert opinion evidence.[59]

At common law, and to some degree under the *UEA*, when asked about the admissibility of expert opinion evidence trial and appellate judges have focused on factors such as: the existence of a 'field'; the qualifications and experience of the witness; whether similar evidence has been admitted in Australia (or elsewhere); perceived need or ability to assist the jury; and the strength of the overall case. These are not, as the following discussion endeavours to explain, especially useful heuristics (or guides) for determining whether there is 'specialised knowledge' or actual expertise. Of immediate interest, these factors do not appear to form part of the exception for 'opinions based on specialised knowledge' in the *UEA*.

---

57 *Buckley v Rice Thomas* (1554) 1 Plowden 118. See also *Folkes v Chadd* (1782) 3 Doug KB 157.

58 See, for example, the challenge to the credibility of Dr McDonald on the basis of his membership of a professional society in *Bropho v Western Australia (No 2)* [2009] WASCA 94.

59 The few references to 'reliability' in the admissibility jurisprudence have not been interpreted such that they require judges to direct their attention to the probative value of expert opinion evidence.

Opinion evidence based on 'specialised knowledge' under *UEA*, s 79(1)

Section 79 of the *UEA* provides the only enumerated exception for expert opinions:

> **79. Exception: opinions based on specialised knowledge**
> (1) If a person has specialised knowledge based on the person's training, study or experience, the opinion rule does not apply to evidence of an opinion of that person that is wholly or substantially based on that knowledge.

Significantly, 'knowledge' appears twice.

Form

Initially, it is useful to direct attention to what appellate courts have said about the requirements of s 79(1). As we shall see, most of the commentary has been focused on questions of form rather than questions of substance. According to the High Court in *Dasreef Pty Ltd v Hawchar*,[60] opinions admitted under s 79(1) 'must satisfy two criteria':

> 32. … The first is that the witness who gives the evidence "has specialised knowledge based on the person's training, study or experience"; the second is that the opinion expressed in evidence by the witness "is wholly or substantially based on that knowledge".

These criteria have been widely rehearsed and the need to satisfy them has led to considerable commentary on the structure and form of expert reports and testimony.[61]

One of the earliest authoritative statements appeared in *HG*.[62] There, Gleeson CJ explained that those proffering opinions based on 'specialised knowledge' must attend to the form of the evidence (usually an expert report) so that it was possible to answer the question of whether the terms of s 79(1) were satisfied.

> 39. … [T]he provisions of s 79 will often have the practical effect of emphasising the need for attention to requirements of form. By directing attention to whether an opinion is wholly or substantially based on specialised knowledge based on training, study or experience, the section requires that the opinion is presented in a form which makes it possible to answer that question.[63]

Perhaps, most famously, in the NSW Court of Appeal in *Makita (Australia) Pty Ltd v Sprowles*,[64] Heydon JA endeavoured to comprehensively capture the admissibility requirements. Based on the *UEA* and the common law, his oft-quoted remarks bear repeating.

> 85. In short, if evidence tendered as expert opinion evidence is to be admissible, it must be agreed or demonstrated that there is a field of "specialised knowledge"; there must be an identified aspect of that field in which the witness demonstrates that by reason of specified training, study or experience, the witness has become an expert; the opinion proffered must be "wholly or substantially based on the witness's expert knowledge"; so far as the opinion is based on facts "observed" by the expert, they must be identified and admissibly

---

60 [2011] HCA 21; 243 CLR 588, endorsed in *Honeysett* [2014] HCA 29; 253 CLR 122. For discussion of *Dasreef*, see M Kumar, 'Admissibility of Expert Evidence: Proving the Basis for an Expert's Opinion' (2011) 33 *Sydney Law Review* 427.

61 See also *Velevski* [2002] HCA 4; 187 ALR 233.

62 [1999] HCA 2; 197 CLR 414.

63 See also *Daniels v Western Australia* [2000] FCA 1334; *Gambro Pty Ltd v Fresenius Medical Care Australia Pty Ltd* [2007] FCA 1828; *Dura (Australia) Constructions Pty Ltd v Hue Boutique Living Pty Ltd* [2012] VSC 99.

64 [2001] NSWCA 305; 52 NSWLR 705.

> proved by the expert, and so far as the opinion is based on "assumed" or "accepted" facts, they must be identified and proved in some other way; it must be established that the facts on which the opinion is based form a proper foundation for it; *and the opinion of an expert requires demonstration or examination of the scientific or other intellectual basis of the conclusions reached: that is, the expert's evidence must explain how the field of "specialised knowledge" in which the witness is expert by reason of "training, study or experience", and on which the opinion is "wholly or substantially based", applies to the facts assumed or observed so as to produce the opinion propounded.* If all these matters are not made explicit, it is not possible to be sure whether the opinion is based wholly or substantially on the expert's specialised knowledge. If the court cannot be sure of that, the evidence is strictly speaking not admissible, and, so far as it is admissible, of diminished weight. And an attempt to make the basis of the opinion explicit may reveal that it is not based on specialised expert knowledge, but, to use Gleeson CJ's characterisation of the evidence in *HG v R* [1999] HCA 2; 197 CLR 414, on "a combination of speculation, inference, personal and second-hand views as to the credibility of the complainant, and a process of reasoning which went well beyond the field of expertise" (at [41]). (emphasis added)

Heydon JA's statement, described by the full Federal Court as a 'counsel of perfection', retains some common law 'baggage'.[65] There is, for example, no reference to a 'field' in the *UEA*.[66] Nevertheless, Heydon JA's attention to legal needs is informative.[67] *Makita* affirms the need to identify the underlying facts and assumptions on which the opinion is based and directs careful attention to the ability to rationally assess the opinion and the reasoning: 'the scientific or other intellectual basis of the conclusions reached'.[68] *Makita* also reinforces the centrality of 'specialised knowledge'. Heydon JA's restatement emphasises the need to attend to 'an identified aspect' of the *specialised knowledge* 'that by reason of specified training, study or experience, the witness has become an expert'. According to *Makita*, we need to know about the procedure and reasoning in order to determine that 'the facts on which the opinion is based form a proper foundation for it'.

In *Dasreef Pty Ltd v Hawchar*,[69] six judges of the High Court (not including Heydon J) insisted that the text of s 79(1), rather than 'any attempt to parse and analyse particular statements in decided cases', should shape its application. Nevertheless, referring to the paragraph from *Makita* extracted above, they explained:

> 37. … Accepting that to be so, it remains useful to record that it is ordinarily the case, as Heydon JA said in *Makita*, that "the expert's evidence must explain how the field of 'specialised knowledge' in which the witness is expert by reason of 'training, study or experience', and on which the opinion is 'wholly or substantially based', applies to the facts assumed or observed so as to produce the opinion propounded". The way in which

---

65 See also *Sydney Wide Distributors Pty Limited v Red Bull Australia Pty Limited* [2002] FCAFC 157, [7].

66 'Field' may, on occasion, be a useful heuristic: see Spigelman CJ in *Tang* [2006] NSWCCA 167; 65 NSWLR 681, [152]. It will, however, rarely take the place of evidence of 'knowledge'. There are many examples of 'fields' where knowledge and abilities are controvertible. Some forms of alternative medicine are conspicuous examples, see, eg, RB Bausell, *Snake Oil Science: The Truth about Complementary and Alternative Medicine* (Oxford University Press, 2007).

67 Notwithstanding *Sydney Wide Distributors Pty Limited v Red Bull Australia Pty Limited* [2002] FCAFC 157, in *Pan Pharmaceuticals Limited (in liq) v Selim* [2008] FCA 416, [29], Emmett J indicated that '[e]ven if the witness is not required to prove by admissible evidence all the facts on which an opinion is based, those facts ought to be stated with sufficient specificity to enable them to be tested by cross-examination'.

68 See also below, pp 531-538. See *Davie v Magistrates of Edinburgh* [1953] SC 34.

69 [2011] HCA 21; 243 CLR 588.

> s 79(1) is drafted necessarily makes the description of these requirements very long. But that is not to say that the requirements cannot be met in many, perhaps most, cases very quickly and easily. That a specialist medical practitioner expressing a diagnostic opinion in his or her relevant field of specialisation is applying "specialised knowledge" based on his or her "training, study or experience", being an opinion "wholly or substantially based" on that "specialised knowledge", will require little explicit articulation or amplification once the witness has described his or her qualifications and experience, and has identified the subject matter about which the opinion is proffered.
>
> 38. But that was not this case.

The High Court insisted on the need to explain the relationship between the opinion, the 'specialised knowledge' and the 'training, study or experience'. This focuses attention, once again, on how the form in which the opinion is expressed provides the ability to determine whether there is 'specialised knowledge' and whether the opinion is based on it. This approach should assist in determining whether the evidence is relevant, satisfies the conditions of s 79(1), and possesses probative value for the mandatory and discretionary exclusions (ss 135 and 137).[70] The court also made it clear that where the 'training, study or experience' is not obviously linked to 'specialised knowledge' the admissibility of the opinion will require careful consideration. Simultaneously, the court provided a 'short-cut' – means of circumventing the rigors of s 79(1) – where the field or procedure can be presented as accepted or unproblematic.[71]

Substance

At this point, having reviewed the commentary on the form of the opinion, we turn to consider what judges have said about the substance of s 79(1) – that is, 'specialised knowledge' and the issue of 'reliability' – in the sense of trustworthiness. Any opinion, according to s 79(1), must be 'wholly or substantially based' on 'specialised knowledge' and the individual proffering the opinion must possess 'specialised knowledge' derived from their 'training, study or experience'. This raises the question of what 'specialised knowledge' means. Limited attention has been directed to the meaning of 'knowledge' or the provision of practical guidance for lawyers and trial judges.

Until fairly recently, the most important and influential decision by a criminal court was *Tang*.[72] Speaking for the NSW Court of Criminal Appeal, Spigelman CJ seemingly endorsed the definition of 'knowledge' adopted by the US Supreme Court in its seminal *Daubert v Merrell Dow Pharmaceuticals Inc* decision.[73] Spigelman CJ explained:

> 138. In the immediate context of "specialised knowledge", picked up by the words "that knowledge" in the second limb of s 79, the word "knowledge" has a different connotation to that which it might have in a different context, eg "common knowledge". The meaning of "knowledge" in s 79 is, in my opinion, the same as that identified in the reasons of the majority judgment in *Daubert v Merrell Dow Pharmaceuticals Inc* 509 US 579 (1993) at 590:

70 See discussion at end of this chapter.

71 See G Edmond and K Martire, 'Knowing experts? Section 79, forensic science evidence and the limits of "training, study or experience"' in A Roberts and J Gans (eds), *Critical Perspectives on the Uniform Evidence Law* (Federation Press, 2017). This 'caveat' was used to avoid taking a closer look at the reliability of fingerprint evidence in *JP v DPP* [2015] NSWSC 1669.

72 [2006] NSWCCA 167; 65 NSWLR 681, extracted below, pp 542-545.

73 *Daubert v Merrell Dow Pharmaceuticals, Inc* 509 US 579 (1993) (emphasis added).

> "[T]he word 'knowledge' connotes more than subjective belief or unsupported speculation. The term applies to any body of known facts or to any body of ideas inferred from such facts or accepted as truths on good grounds."

Notwithstanding the reliance on this definition of 'knowledge', the NSW Court of Criminal Appeal did not follow the US Supreme Court's lead and impose a *reliability* standard. Indeed, in contradistinction, Spigelman CJ insisted that 'the focus of attention must be on the words "specialised knowledge", not on the introduction of an extraneous idea such as "reliability".'[74]

In this context it is enlightening to consider the *Daubert* jurisprudence in a little more detail. Unlike the NSW Court of Criminal Appeal, and the High Court in *Honeysett*[75] (discussed below), the US Supreme Court moved directly from the phrase 'scientific knowledge', in r 702 of the *Federal Rules of Evidence* (FRE), to the need for validity and reliability.[76] Having defined 'knowledge', the US Supreme Court went further, finding that it imposed 'a standard of evidentiary reliability'.

> But, in order to qualify as "scientific knowledge," an inference or assertion must be derived by the scientific method. Proposed testimony *must be supported by appropriate validation* – ie, "good grounds," based on what is known. In short, the requirement that an expert's testimony pertain to "scientific knowledge" *establishes a standard of evidentiary reliability*.[77]

In order to help trial judges assess 'reliability' the Supreme Court provided four criteria – the *Daubert* criteria.[78] They are:

> Ordinarily, a key question to be answered in determining whether a theory or technique is scientific knowledge that will assist the trier of fact will be whether it can be (and has been) tested. …
>
> Another pertinent consideration is whether the theory or technique has been subjected to peer review and publication. …
>
> Additionally, in the case of a particular scientific technique, the court ordinarily should consider the known or potential rate of error. … and the existence and maintenance of standards controlling the technique's operation. …
>
> Finally, "general acceptance" can yet have a bearing on the inquiry. A "reliability assessment does not require, although it does permit, explicit identification of a relevant scientific community and an express determination of a particular degree of acceptance within that community."[79]

The move from 'scientific knowledge' to 'reliability' was not an isolated incident or an interpretive step restricted to scientific evidence. When it came to interpreting

---

74 [2006] NSWCCA 167; 65 NSWLR 681, [137]. The suggestion that the US Supreme Court's construction of 'scientific, technical and other specialized knowledge' from r 702 of the FRE could not inform the interpretation of 'specialised knowledge' from s 79(1) is far from persuasive. See ibid [139].

75 [2014] HCA 29; 253 CLR 122.

76 *Daubert* 509 US 579, 590 (1993). Before amendment in 2000, r 702 stated: 'If scientific, technical, or other specialized knowledge will assist the trier of fact to understand the evidence or to determine a fact in issue, a witness qualified as an expert by knowledge, skill, experience, training, or education, may testify thereto in the form of an opinion or otherwise'. The current version of FRE r 702 states: 'A witness who is qualified as an expert by knowledge, skill, experience, training, or education may testify in the form of an opinion or otherwise if … the testimony is the product of reliable principles and methods …'. The revised formulation endeavours to explicitly encapsulate the *Daubert-Kumho* concern with reliability.

77 *Daubert* 509 US 579, 590 (1993).

78 Some authors consider 'the existence and maintenance of standards controlling the technique's operation' as a fifth criterion.

79 *Daubert* 509 US 579, 596-7 (1993).

'technical and other specialized knowledge', also from r 702 of the FRE, in *Kumho Tire Co v Carmichael*,[80] the US Supreme Court explained that:

> In *Daubert*, the Court specified that it is the [Federal] Rule's word "knowledge," not the words (like "scientific") that modify that word, that "establishes a standard of evidentiary reliability." Hence, as a matter of language, the Rule applies its reliability standard to all "scientific," "technical," or "other specialized" matters within its scope.[81]

In US federal, and most State, courts, the phrase 'scientific, technical and other specialized *knowledge*' required lawyers and judges to direct their attention to the reliability of expert opinion evidence. As gatekeepers, trial judges are obliged to exclude insufficiently reliable *expert* opinions.[82]

Significantly, the United States is not alone in directing attention toward the reliability of expert opinion. Historically, Canadian admissibility jurisprudence has not been concerned with 'knowledge' per se.[83] However, just over a decade ago the Supreme Court of Canada imposed a reliability threshold on expert opinion evidence in response to several high profile wrongful convictions, concerns about the quality of forensic science and medicine evidence, and the effectiveness of criminal trial safeguards.[84] In a series of decisions, culminating in *White Burgess Langille v Abbott and Haliburton Co*, the Supreme Court explicitly endorsed the *Daubert* criteria and now requires trial judges to consider the reliability of expert opinion evidence as part of their 'gatekeeping' responsibility.[85] In *J-LJ*,[86] Binnie J explained that the 'admissibility of expert evidence should be scrutinised at the time it is proffered, and not allowed too easy an entry on the basis that all of the frailties could go at the end of the day to weight rather than admissibility'. Subsequently, in *Trochym*, Deschamps J insisted that '[r]eliability is an essential component of admissibility. Whereas the degree of reliability required by courts may vary depending on the circumstances, evidence that is not sufficiently reliable is likely to undermine the fundamental fairness of the criminal process'.[87] In *White Burgess*, reliability was listed among the factors that a trial judge should take into account when using the exclusionary discretion as part of their 'gatekeeping' responsibility.[88]

Similarly, following extensive consultation the Law Commission of England and Wales recommended a new admissibility standard, requiring expert opinion

80 526 US 137 (1999).

81 Ibid 147.

82 *Kumho* was, in part, a response to lawyers seeking to circumvent the application of the *Daubert* criteria on the basis that the expert evidence was merely 'technical' or 'specialised'. A prominent example from the forensic sciences is *United States v Haavard* 117 F Supp 2d 848 (SD Ind, 2000). That response was decisively rejected. In *Kumho* the Supreme Court explained that it is incumbent on proponents to demonstrate that opinion evidence based on 'scientific, technical, or other specialized knowledge' is reliable. The court accepted that the criteria used to determine reliability need to be applied flexibly; to accommodate the many different types of expertise. See also the discussion in the Canadian case of *Abbey* 2009 ONCA 624 and the revelations in *Abbey* 2017 ONCA 640.

83 See, eg, *Mohan* [1994] 2 SCR 9.

84 See, eg, *Trochym* [2007] 1 SCR 239, [1].

85 *White Burgess Langille v Abbott and Haliburton Co* [2015] SCC 23; *DD* [2000] 2 SCR 275. See also S Goudge, *Report of the Inquiry into Pediatric Forensic Pathology in Ontario* (Queens Printer, 2008).

86 [2000] 2 SCR 600, [28]. See also Justice Binnie, 'Wrongful Convictions and the Magical Aura of Science in the Courtroom' (2011) 10 *Judicial Review* 141.

87 See, eg, *Trochym* [2007] 1 SCR 239, [1] and [27].

88 *White Burgess Langille v Abbott and Haliburton Co* [2015] SCC 23, [54].

evidence to be 'sufficiently reliable' for admission in criminal proceedings.[89] The Law Commission characterised the prevailing approach to the admissibility of expert opinion evidence in English criminal proceedings as 'laissez faire' and questioned widespread beliefs about the effectiveness of trial safeguards at consistently exposing and conveying limitations with expert opinion evidence.[90] The English government was unwilling to adopt the Commission's recommendations on the basis of unsubstantiated concerns about increased costs. Nevertheless, the English *Criminal Procedure Rules* and *Criminal Practice Directions* were subsequently revised to direct attention toward the reliability of *expert* opinion and underlying procedures.[91]

Returning to Australia, in *Honeysett*[92] the High Court was confronted with a challenge to the admissibility of opinion evidence adduced by the prosecutor in criminal proceedings. In response it reproduced several of the definitions associated with *Daubert* (and *Tang*).

> 23. … "Specialised knowledge" is to be distinguished from matters of "common knowledge". Specialised knowledge is knowledge which is outside that of persons who have not by training, study or experience acquired an understanding of the subject matter. It may be of matters that are not of a scientific or technical kind and a person without any formal qualifications may acquire specialised knowledge by experience. However, the person's training, study or experience must result in the acquisition of *knowledge*. The *Macquarie Dictionary* defines "knowledge" as "acquaintance with *facts, truths, or principles*, as from study or in investigation" (emphasis added) and it is in this sense that it is used in s 79(1). The concept is captured in Blackmun J's formulation in *Daubert*: "the word 'knowledge' connotes more than subjective belief or unsupported speculation. … [It] applies to any body of known facts or to any body of ideas inferred from such facts or accepted as truths on good grounds".

The High Court did not take the opportunity to read reliability into s 79(1). Rather, it concluded, following strategic concession by the prosecutor, that 'the appeal does not provide the occasion to consider the appellant's larger challenge respecting the requirement of an independent means of validation before an opinion may be found to be based on "specialised knowledge".'[93] Nevertheless, on the basis of the previous extract, scientific, technical and medical evidence would seem to require 'knowledge' that is independent from the expert (and to represent an improvement on what ordinary persons can do). Scientific and technical witnesses should be able to identify and refer to relevant 'knowledge',

---

89 Law Commission of England and Wales, *Expert Evidence in Criminal Proceedings in England and Wales* (HMSO, 2011). See also G Edmond, 'Is Reliability Sufficient? The Law Commission and Expert Evidence in International and Interdisciplinary Perspective' (2012) 16 *International Journal of Evidence & Proof* 30; P Roberts and M Stockdale (eds), *Forensic Science Evidence and Expert Witness Testimony: Reliability Through Reform?* (Edward Elgar, 2018).

90 Law Commission, above n 89, 1.20 and 3.4: '[C]ross-examination would seem to be an insufficient safeguard against unreliability for expert opinion evidence adduced under a laissez-faire approach to admissibility'. See also G Edmond and M San Roque, 'The Cool Crucible: Forensic Science and the Frailty of the Criminal Trial' (2012) 24 *Current Issues in Criminal Justice* 51.

91 The Rt Hon Sir Brian Leveson's, *Review of the Effectiveness of Criminal Justice* (2015); and the recent reform to the *Criminal Procedure Rules and Criminal Practice Directions*, Part 19. See also Roberts and Stockdale, above n 89. Contrast G Edmond, E Piasecki and S Carr, 'Science Friction: Streamlined Forensic Reporting' (2018) 38 *Oxford Journal of Legal Studies* 764.

92 [2014] HCA 29; 253 CLR 122 (footnotes omitted).

93 Ibid [24]. Prosecutors appear interested in keeping admissibility standards for opinion evidence low.

Photoboard produced by the anatomist in *Tang*

The POI in an armed robbery is juxtaposed to a reference image of Tang. Note the deliberate orientation of the face in '5'.

which should ordinarily take the form of supportive studies (ideally published in reputable biomedical and scientific journals) demonstrating the value of procedures or some enhanced capability.[94]

It is useful to consider the opinions confronting the courts in *Tang* and *Honeysett* to obtain some sense of judicial responses to the contested *expertise*. The actual question in *Tang* was whether an anatomist (Dr Sutisno) could express her opinion about the identity of a person of interest in low quality CCTV images of a robbery – see Figure 1. The identity of the robber was in issue. The anatomist testified that the person of interest and Tang were 'one and the same' based on her comparison of the faces and bodies in the CCTV images and reference images of Tang provided by police. The comparisons were described as face and body mapping.[95] The 'lips, the wide square chin with a dimple and the posture' were said to be particularly influential on the analysis. Writing for the Court of Criminal Appeal – the decision is extracted below – Spigelman CJ questioned the foundations of body mapping. In relation to facial mapping, though without reference to relevant empirical literatures, he was satisfied that there was specialised knowledge, but not 'on the evidence in the trial, … of a character

94 K Martire and G Edmond, 'Rethinking expert opinion evidence' (2017) 41 *Melbourne University Law Review* 967.

95 [2006] NSWCCA 167; 65 NSWLR 681, [25].

Figure 2: Robber alleged to be Honeysett (top left)

which can support an opinion of identity' – that is, categorical identification of a specific individual.[96]

Concerned that the jury would not be able to interpret the low quality images of the robbery, and conscious that the anatomist had spent hours looking at them, he advanced what might be considered a pragmatic compromise. Exposure to the images was said to have made the anatomist an *ad hoc expert* – more below.[97] Her opinion would be admissible via s 79(1) but she would be restricted to describing similarities between the faces and bodies. The significance of those similarities would be for the trier of fact.

In *Honeysett*, a different anatomist (Professor Henneberg) compared CCTV of an armed robbery with reference images of the defendant – see Figure 2. This robber was covered from head to toe with clothing, yet the anatomist purported to identify several features said to be similar, including: somatotype (ectomorphic), height, posture (lumbar lordosis), hair length, skull shape (doliocephalic),

96 *Tang* [2006] NSWCCA 167; 65 NSWLR 681, [146], see also [136] and [144]. Spigelman CJ suggested that there was more support provided for spectrographic voice comparison in the pre-*UEA* case of *Gilmore* [1977] 2 NSWLR 935, 937-8. That technique was subsequently discredited in a report prepared for the US National Academy of Sciences: National Research Council, *On the theory and Practice of voice identification* (National Academies Press, 1979).

97 *Tang* [2006] NSWCCA 167; 65 NSWLR 681, [120]: 'by the experience gained with respect to the videotape itself through the course of multiple viewing, detailed selection, identification and magnification of images. By this process she had become what is sometimes referred to as an "ad hoc expert".'

handedness and skin colour (the appellant was Indigenous, as the reference images suggested).[98] The evidence was deemed admissible in the NSW Court of Criminal Appeal, but the High Court granted special leave. For the High Court, it was 'an error of law to admit the evidence' because the 'opinion was not based wholly or substantially on [the Professor's] specialised knowledge'. The High Court's not entirely helpful explanation of why the comparison and alleged similarities are not admissible is extracted in full below.

> 43. Professor Henneberg's opinion was not based on his undoubted knowledge of anatomy. Professor Henneberg's knowledge as an anatomist, that the human population includes individuals who have oval shaped heads and individuals who have round shaped heads (when viewed from above), did not form the basis of his conclusion that Offender One and the appellant each have oval shaped heads. That conclusion was based on Professor Henneberg's subjective impression of what he saw when he looked at the images. This observation applies to the evidence of each of the characteristics of which Professor Henneberg gave evidence.

This extract exposes a court struggling to explain the exclusion.[99] All human-based image comparison will require 'subjective impressions' of what is seen.[100] While it is true that anatomical training, study and experience, and even anatomical knowledge, may not be of value when engaging in such comparisons, their actual value is uncertain – that is, *unknown*. We are told nothing about any 'knowledge' relating to image comparison, and there is no attention to Henneberg's actual ability at image comparison for the purpose of identification. While, in the absence of appropriate explanation the opinion(s) should be excluded, the High Court offered little practical assistance. We cannot even be confident that the decision extends beyond anatomists (or this anatomist) and whether it is restricted to cases where the defendant is well disguised. Are, for example, opinions about similarities and differences admissible where the person of interest is not disguised (and an anatomist has spent more time looking at the images – as in *Tang*)?

The court's response is, as in *Tang*, declaratory. Without knowing if these anatomists possess expertise in comparing persons in images for the purpose of identifying them, the courts simply declare the opinion is (in *Tang*), or is not (in *Honeysett*), based on 'specialised knowledge'. The courts do not provide meaningful guidelines and tell us nothing about what kind of 'specialised knowledge' might ground an opinion about the identity of a person in images. The reasoning in *Honeysett* does not engage with the propriety of limiting opinions to describing similarities or the relationship between knowledge and reliability (after *Tang*). Legally, it is unclear what future prosecutors, defence counsel and judges should look for when trying to determine if an opinion is based on 'specialised knowledge' (and whether that knowledge is based on 'training, study or experience'), especially where the opinion is not based on images.[101]

98 *Honeysett* [2014] HCA 29; 253 CLR 122, [15]. Similar evidence was excluded by the court in *Morgan* [2011] NSWCCA 257 but a different court – in *Honeysett* [2013] NSWCCA 135 – considered it admissible.

99 See G Edmond, 'A Closer Look at *Honeysett*: Enhancing our Forensic Science and Medicine Jurisprudence' (2015) 17 *Flinders Law Journal* 287.

100 See, eg, National Institute of Standards and Technology, *Latent Print Examination and Human Factors: Improving the Practice through a Systems Approach* (US Department of Commerce, 2012) (NIST Report).

101 Compare J Phillips et al, 'Face recognition accuracy of forensic examiners, super-recognisers, and face recognition algorithms' (2018) 115 *Proceedings of the National Academy of Sciences* 6171.

And, problematically, following on from the approaches in the Victorian Court of Appeal and *Nguyen*, it seems possible that Henneberg's opinion – deemed inadmissible according to s 79(1) – might be admissible via s 78. For, if the identity of the person of interest in the images is treated as the 'matter or event' and it is considered 'necessary' to receive the Professor's opinion to 'obtain an adequate understanding of [his] perception of the matter or event', then s 78 would seem to confer an admissibility pathway by analogy with voice comparison. Some of the practical problems with this interpretation emerge when we observe that opinions about (some) opinions about similarities, inadmissible via s 79(1), seem to be admissible, without qualification, via s 78. Relying on s 78, the Professor might positively identify the person of interest and there would be no apparent need for this highly credentialled anatomist to comply with any of the *Makita* requirements or even the Expert Witness Code of Conduct – discussed below.

New approaches to 'specialised knowledge'?

In the aftermath of *Tang*,[102] the phrase 'specialised knowledge' has played a very limited role in criminal proceedings. Notwithstanding the expanded definition and the exclusion of the opinion evidence in *Honeysett*, s 79(1) has not prevented weak, speculative and unreliable opinions from routinely contaminating criminal proceedings. Australian courts do not typically consider the reliability of expert evidence in their admissibility determinations. Unreliable *expert* opinions, drawing on impressions and untested procedures, and even the speculative opinions of investigating police (discussed earlier in relation to s 78 and voice recordings), have been, and continue to be, admitted – whether characterised as evidence of fact, as lay opinion, as opinion said to be based on 'specialised knowledge', or as *ad hoc expert* opinion based on repeated exposure.[103]

When it comes to forensic science and medicine evidence *Tang's* characterisation of 'reliability' as 'extraneous' is misguided. Unfortunately, the High Court did not take the opportunity to address the issue in *Honeysett*.[104] Without 'reliability' the phrase 'specialised knowledge' is (or risks being) denuded of meaning and practical import. In most cases inattention to reliability leads lawyers and judges to direct their attention elsewhere: to whether the opinion appears to be linked to the witness's 'training, study or experience'; some putative 'field' or body of literature; whether similar opinions have been admitted previously; whether the opinion seems plausible; whether the *expert* is considered likely to be better than the jury; and even the strength of the case. Sections 55, 56, 78, 79(1), 135 and 137 of the *UEA* do not require courts to consider the reliability (or validity and accuracy) of the expert evidence.[105] Indeed, there are no provisions of the *UEA* or other rules and practices that, as currently interpreted, direct attention to reliability or the actual probative value of incriminating expert opinion evidence

---

102 [2006] NSWCCA 167; 65 NSWLR 681.

103 See, eg, *Li* [2003] NSWCCA 290; 139 A Crim R 281 and *Smith (Mundarra)* [1999] NSWCCA 317; 47 NSWLR 419, 422-3.

104 [2014] HCA 29; 253 CLR 122.

105 According to Basten JA, author of the most influential of the judgments in *XY* [2013] NSWCCA 121; 84 NSWLR 363, attention to the reliability of evidence in undertaking the balancing exercise required by s 137 is exceptional. The approach from *Shamouil* (2006) 66 NSWLR 228 and *XY* was adopted by the majority in *IMM* [2016] HCA 14; 257 CLR 300.

as a condition of admission. Consequently, the validity and accuracy of procedures used by forensic scientists and forensic pathologists play little (if any) part in the admission of scientific, technical and other kinds of *expert* opinion evidence adduced by prosecutors.

This approach is not only undesirable, it is difficult to reconcile with the text of the *UEA* and the definitions of 'knowledge' in *Dasreef* and *Honeysett*. Not only are Australian approaches to admissibility inconsistent with the formal interest in reliability in other jurisdictions, but the past decade has witnessed unprecedented scientific interest in the production and evaluation of forensic science evidence. Beginning with the US National Academy of Sciences (NAS) in 2009, a range of independent reviews by committees composed of eminent scientists, engineers, doctors and statisticians have been critical of the forensic sciences. Following its review of the available scientific literature, the NAS was surprised by the dearth of rigorous research supporting many procedures used by investigators and routinely admitted in criminal proceedings. The Committee's assessment of the feature comparison forensics – namely DNA profiling, as well as fingerprint, ballistics, document, hair and fibre, footwear and tyre comparison, and implicitly image and voice comparison – bears repeating:

> With the exception of nuclear DNA analysis, however, no forensic method has been rigorously shown to have the capacity to consistently, and with a high degree of certainty, demonstrate a connection between evidence and a specific individual or source.[106]

This conclusion might be considered disconcerting because the feature comparison forensics had been making these very claims – for example, linking a fingerprint to a person or a bullet casing to a specific gun – for almost a century.

Attentive scientists were also critical of the performance of lawyers and courts.

> In a number of forensic science disciplines, forensic science professionals have yet to establish either the validity of their approach or the accuracy of their conclusions, and the courts have been utterly ineffective in addressing this problem. For a variety of reasons –including the rules governing the admissibility of forensic evidence, the applicable standards governing appellate review of trial court decisions, the limitations of the adversary process, and the common lack of scientific expertise among judges and lawyers who must try to comprehend and evaluate forensic evidence – the legal system is ill-equipped to correct the problems of the forensic science community.[107]

The NAS report identified two issues at the heart of legal reliance on forensic science and medicine evidence:

> (1) the extent to which a forensic science discipline is founded on a reliable scientific methodology, leading to accurate analyses of evidence and proper reports of findings and (2) the extent to which practitioners in those forensic science disciplines that rely on human interpretation adopt procedures and performance standards that guard against bias and error.[108]

The NAS report was followed by inquiries and reports prepared by the US National Institute of Standards and Technology (NIST), the President's Council of Advisers on Science and Technology (PCAST) and the American Association

---

106 NAS, *Strengthening the Forensic Sciences in the United States: A Path Forward* (National Academies Press, 2009) (NAS Report) 7.

107 Ibid 53.

108 Ibid 9, 111.

for the Advancement of Science (AAAS).[109] These independent reports spoke as a chorus. The following subjects are among their most fundamental concerns and recommendations.

Validation. *Foundational* validation involves formal testing to determine whether a procedure (or technique) works, how well and in what conditions.[110] It also provides an indication of the value of the results and the kinds of standards required. *Applied* validation refers to testing to guarantee that the way procedures are used in practice is reliable. As a previous quote from the NAS Report suggests, many forensic science procedures are not validated, or the testing is inadequate and incapable of supporting the way results are reported and explained in courtroom testimony.

According to PCAST:

> valid scientific knowledge can *only* be gained through *empirical* testing of specific propositions.[111]

And:

> methods must be presumed to be unreliable until their foundational validity has been established based on empirical evidence.[112]

All of the scientific reports characterise validation (or validation testing) as a necessary prerequisite to the use of forensic science procedures.

Standards. According to the NAS report:

> Often there are no standard protocols governing forensic [science] practice in a given discipline. And, even when protocols are in place, they often are vague and not enforced in any meaningful way. … These shortcomings obviously pose a continuing and serious threat to the quality and credibility of forensic science practice.[113]

Standards should be informed by the results of validation studies to help to ensure that procedures operate (that is, are *applied*) as intended. In the absence of validation, standards and protocols tend to be consensus-based and it is uncertain if they are appropriate or effective.

Expression of results. The various reports found that the way different forensic science disciplines and practitioners reported results (often the actual opinions) are not consistent and not necessarily based on empirical studies or the rigorous application of statistics. Rather, the expressions used by many practitioners are the result of tradition, the impressions and beliefs of individuals or groups of forensic practitioners, and reliant on untested assumptions, and what courts have historically allowed. The NAS report observed:

---

109 NIST Report, above n 100; President's Council of Advisors on Science and Technology, *Forensic Science in Criminal Courts: Ensuring Scientific Validity of Feature-Comparison Methods* (Washington, 2016) (PCAST Report); William Thompson et al, *Forensic Science Assessments: A Quality and Gap Analysis – Latent Fingerprint Examination* (AAAS, 2017) (AAAS report). See also Anthony Campbell, *The Fingerprint Inquiry Report* (APS Group, 2011).

110 PCAST Report, above n 109, 47: 'For a metrological method to be scientifically valid and reliable, the procedures that comprise it must be shown, based on empirical studies, to be *repeatable*, *reproducible*, and *accurate*, at levels that have been measured and are appropriate to the intended application'.

111 PCAST Report, above n 109, 46.

112 Ibid 32.

113 NAS Report, above n 106, 6.

> [M]any terms are used by forensic examiners in reports and in court testimony ... Such terms include ... "match," "consistent with," "identical," "similar in all respects tested," and "cannot be excluded as the source of." ... the forensic science disciplines have not reached agreement or consensus on the precise meaning of any of these terms. This imprecision in vocabulary stems in part from the paucity of research.[114]

Take a moment to reflect on why DNA evidence is expressed in probabilistic terms or as likelihood ratio, whereas fingerprint and ballistics (and voice comparison) evidence are expressed in categorical terms linking a latent print or a bullet casing (or a sound) to a specific individual or firearm, whereas opinions derived from comparing images (following *Tang*) were limited to describing similarities and differences.

Limitations and error. The NAS, PCAST and AAAS reports all insist on the need to disclose (that is, report) limitations, uncertainties and indicative error rates.

> Few forensic science methods have developed adequate measures of the accuracy of inferences made by forensic scientists. All results for every forensic science method should indicate the uncertainty in the measurements that are made, and studies must be conducted that enable the estimation of those values.[115]

As the fingerprint example, discussed below, reveals, all procedures (and individuals, however expert) are susceptible to error. Performance and accuracy should be studied and reported so that opinions can be appropriately evaluated. We should not be complacent about limitations and error, the first validation studies of latent fingerprint comparison were only undertaken and published in 2011, in response to the NAS Report.

Cognitive bias. Lawyers and judges tend to think they are conversant with bias, but scientists caution about the unconscious risks posed by many contemporary practices; particularly the unnecessary exposure of forensic practitioners to information that is not required for their analyses. The NAS report notes:

> Some initial and striking research has uncovered the effects of some biases in forensic science procedures ... The forensic science disciplines are just beginning to become aware of contextual bias and the dangers it poses. The traps created by such biases can be very subtle, and typically one is not aware that his or her judgment is being affected.

One of the most conspicuous features of the recent reviews and their recommendations concerns human factors, particularly the risks posed by human interpretation. Historically, most forensic scientists did not pay much attention to the risks posed by unconscious biases. However, a series of notorious experiments demonstrated how experienced fingerprint examiners could be induced to change their opinion about whether two prints matched by being given information about the case. That is, the provision of suggestive information that was not relevant to the actual comparison could change the conclusion from a match to a non-match.[116] Similar studies of DNA electropherograms concluded that interpretations were influenced by whether biologists knew (or did not know) the profile of the suspect.[117]

114 Ibid 21, 185.

115 Ibid 184.

116 I Dror et al, 'Contextual Information Renders Experts Vulnerable to Making Erroneous Identifications' (2006) 156 *Forensic Science International* 74.

117 W Thompson, 'Painting the Target around the Matching Profile: The Texas Sharpshooter Fallacy in Forensic DNA Interpretation' (2009) 8 *Law, Probability and Risk* 257.

Cognitive biases are not moral or personal failings. Rather, individuals acting with integrity (including jurors and judges) are vulnerable to these influences. Perhaps surprisingly, scientific training and experience (like legal training and experience), critical thinking and effort are not consistently effective means of avoiding risks and errors. Rather, the appropriate response seems to be to study the risks and their significance and to reform processes to restrict the amount of domain irrelevant (or gratuitous) information provided to those involved in forensic casework. It is no coincidence that highly trained biomedical researchers and many physicists employ blinding (or double blinding) in their experimental work.

Experience, certification, confidence, consensus and so on. The various reviews drew attention to factors that should not be relied upon to ascertain whether an individual is an expert or whether a procedure works and how well.

> We note … that neither experience, nor judgment, nor good professional practices (such as certification programs and accreditation programs, standardized protocols, proficiency testing, and codes of ethics) can substitute for actual evidence of foundational validity and reliability. … Similarly, an expert's expression of *confidence* based on personal professional experience or expressions of *consensus* among practitioners about the accuracy of their field is no substitute for error rates estimated from relevant studies. For forensic feature-comparison methods, establishing foundational validity based on empirical evidence is thus a *sine qua non*. Nothing can substitute for it.[118]

Independence. Finally, several of the reports recommended removing forensic science and medicine from the oversight of law enforcement.[119] There were concerns about institutional bias from shared commitments, orientations and reward structures. Australian forensic science and medicine are mixed in this regard – depending on the State or Territory. Some of the DNA and chemistry processing operates outside of police services (in NSW, SA and WA) for example. Most of the forensic medicine, pathology and toxicology is independent, with the Victorian Institute of Forensic Medicine being a world leader. Almost all of the traditional forensic sciences – such as firearms and toolmarks, fingerprints, document examination, explosives and fire investigation, blood spatter, hair and fibre analysis, accident reconstruction and so on – remain within Australian police forces and under police management; even as the staff are increasingly civilian (that is, not sworn).

Reviewing the progress made across the forensic sciences in the years following the seminal NAS report, President Obama's Council of Advisers on Science and Technology (PCAST) concluded that only two of seven feature comparison procedures it reviewed were foundationally valid. The two foundationally valid procedures are simple DNA profiling and latent fingerprint comparison. The Council relied on just two studies, conducted *after* 2009, to support its assessment of the validity of latent fingerprint comparison but expressed doubts about whether the way fingerprint comparison was performed in practice (as applied) was consistent with foundational studies.

> [L]atent fingerprint analysis is a *foundationally* valid subjective methodology – albeit with a false positive rate that is substantial and is likely to be higher than expected by many jurors based on longstanding claims about the infallibility of fingerprint analysis.

---

118 PCAST Report, above n 109, 6.

119 The National Institute of Forensic Sciences is primarily funded and managed by Australian and New Zealand policing agencies.

> … Although we conclude that the method is foundationally valid, there are a number of important issues related to its validity as applied.[120]

Notwithstanding these findings, PCAST recommended that fingerprint examiners should report an error rate. The way fingerprint examiners in the US and Australia routinely report match decisions – as the categorical identification of a specific individual, without qualification or caveat – was described by the NAS as 'not scientifically plausible' and by the AAAS as 'indefensible'.[121] The PCAST Report explains that:

> [I]t would be appropriate to inform jurors that (1) only two properly designed studies of the accuracy of latent fingerprint analysis have been conducted and (2) these studies found false positive rates [ie, misidentifications] that could be as high as 1 in 306 in one study and 1 in 18 in the other study. This would appropriately inform jurors that errors occur at detectable frequencies, allowing them to weigh the probative value of the evidence.[122]

Significantly, latent fingerprint comparison is better supported by scientific research than many other areas of forensic science and medicine. PCAST concluded, for example, that analysis of complex DNA mixtures as well as bite mark, firearm, footwear and hair comparisons were not foundationally valid. The President's Council recommended that federal prosecutors should not adduce opinions from these later procedures in criminal proceedings.

While forensic scientists, prosecutors and judges might argue that foreign reports and insights have limited application to Australia, and particularly Australian courts, two issues warrant specific consideration.[123] First, if Australian forensic scientists had undertaken (or had access to) validation studies, the NAS, NIST, PCAST and AAAS reports would have cited and relied upon them. Many of the reports and opinions produced by our state employed forensic practitioners – and all of the opinions generated by investigators and ad hoc experts – do not comply with recommendations by the NAS (and other organisations). Secondly, who should bear the risk where techniques have not been formally evaluated, along with the misplaced confidence in our current practices? In a system that purports to cherish liberty and uphold the rights of the innocent, it might be considered curious that unanswered critiques of forensic science and medicine (and by implication traditional legal practices) by some of the world's pre-eminent scientific institutions should be treated with suspicion, or ignored, while legal experience and impressions are privileged. Such an orientation puts non-systematic legal experience above scientific advice, and makes those accused of the most serious crimes bear the risk of incriminating expert evidence being exaggerated or mistaken and the trial safeguards less effective than credible safeguards ought to be.

Practically, our weak admissibility regime shifts burdens from forensic practitioners, prosecutors and judges to under-resourced defendants, trial safeguards and the trier of fact. They put obligations on the defence to expose weaknesses, limitations and errors in individual proceedings rather than require the state to demonstrate that its procedures are valid, its experts proficient and that the opinions of forensic practitioners are reported in ways that are consistent

120 PCAST Report, above n 109, 101-2, 148 (italics added).

121 NAS Report, above n 106, 142; AAAS Report, above n 109, 71.

122 PCAST Report, above n 109, 96, see also 26, 74.

123 E Lander, 'Response to the ANZFSS council statement on the President's Council of Advisors on Science and Technology Report' (2017) 49 *Australian Journal of Forensic Science* 1; G Edmond and K Martire, 'Antipodean Forensics: A Comment on ANZFSS's Response to PCAST' (2017) 49 *Australian Journal of Forensic Sciences* 140.

with empirical evidence and known abilities.[124] In its review of expert evidence in criminal proceedings in England and Wales the Law Commission made the following assessment of conventional trial safeguards.

> Cross-examination, the adduction of contrary expert evidence and judicial guidance at the end of the trial are currently assumed to provide sufficient safeguards in relation to expert evidence ... However, ... it is doubtful whether these are valid assumptions.[125]

Recent empirical studies of forensic science evidence in Australia support these concerns. Cross-examination has not been consistently effective in exposing the lack of testing, limitations, bias or uncertainties.[126] The seminal NAS report, as one prominent example, has been cited in just two Australian judgments – once in the District Court of NSW and once in an appeal concerning the admissibility of complex DNA evidence by the Victorian Court of Appeal in *Tuite*.[127] The later decision, the first Australian attempt to impose a formal reliability standard on expert opinion in criminal proceedings, albeit as part of the balancing act for UEA s 137, was inadvertently de-railed by the High Court in *IMM*.[128] *IMM* was concerned with the meaning of probative value in a case unconcerned with expert evidence.

In the aftermath of the NAS Report and other reviews, Australian courts should draw upon the kinds of criteria advanced in *Daubert* and *Kumho* to guide the interpretation of 'knowledge' (and reliability).[129] On the basis of the advice and recommendations of authoritative, independent reports from peak scientific and technical organisations, it seems that courts responsible for admission and facilitating the rational evaluation of forensic science and medicine evidence should attend to the kinds of criteria listed in Columns 2 and (especially) 3 of Table 1 (*see over page*). As Table 1 makes clear, these indicia of 'knowledge' are not consistent with the kinds of criteria conventionally used by Australian judges in their application of s 79(1) in criminal proceedings.[130]

Most of the conventional legal criteria and considerations (such as those in Column 1) are either misguided or, as with Australian approaches to 'specialised knowledge', interpreted or applied in ways that erode them of practical significance. They shift the focus from the primary epistemic issue (that is, pertaining to 'knowledge'), by substituting misleading legal proxies and secondary considerations such as whether the court (or another) is satisfied there is a 'field', whether courts in other jurisdictions have admitted similar evidence, the length of time courts have been admitting such evidence, the experience of the analyst, and perhaps most curiously (given the text of s 79(1)) whether the jury is perceived

124 See, eg, *Morgan* [2011] NSWCCA 257; *Gilham* [2012] NSWCCA 131; and *Wood* [2012] NSWCCA 21; *Honeysett* [2013] NSWCCA 135.

125 Law Commission, above n 89, 5 [1.20] (citations omitted); see also [1.24]. See also NAS Report, above n 106, 53.

126 G Edmond, E Cunliffe, K Martire and M San Roque, 'Forensic science and the limits of cross-examination' (2019) 42 *Melbourne University Law Review* 858; G Edmond, 'Latent science: A history of Australian Fingerprint evidence' (2019) 38 *University of Queensland Law Journal* 301.

127 *Fittler* [2016] NSWDC 226, [42]; *Tuite* [2015] VSCA 148. These references do not appear to have been party-led.

128 *IMM* [2016] HCA 14; 257 CLR 300.

129 Contrast *HG* [1999] HCA 2; 197 CLR 414: 'It is unnecessary for present purposes to enter into issues of the kind considered in *Daubert v Merrell Dow Pharmaceuticals Inc* [1993] USSC 99; 509 US 579. It is the language of s 79 which has to be applied'. A decade later in *Dasreef* [2011] HCA 21; 243 CLR 588, [59] Heydon J noted: 'Finally, and very importantly, there is increasing concern about the risk of injustice that may flow from unsatisfactory expert evidence'.

130 See G Edmond, 'What Lawyers Should Know about the Forensic "Sciences"' (2015) 35 *Adelaide Law Review* 33; Edmond and Martire, above n 123.

to be able to assess the evidence (for example, CCTV images or voice recordings) without the *expert's* assistance.[131]

Table 1: Criteria for Assessing Admissibility and Evaluating Weight

1. Australian (criminal) jurisprudence	**2. US Supreme Court's *Daubert* reliability criteria (from 'scientific, technical, or other specialized knowledge')**	**3. National Academy of Sciences (US), National Institute of Standards & Technology (US) National Institute of Justice (US), PCAST (US) and AAAS (US)**
'Specialised knowledge' but not 'the introduction of an extraneous idea such as "reliability"'	Testing (ie, validation studies): 'whether a theory or technique … can be (and has been) tested'	Independent (pre-litigation) validation studies
'Training, study or experience' (particularly time spent doing something)		Rigorous proficiency testing and demonstrated proficiency
	Publication and peer review: 'whether the theory or technique has been subjected to peer review and publication'	Supported by peer-reviewed publication
	Error rates: 'the known or potential rate of error'	Error rates and uncertainties disclosed
Previously admitted (though not necessarily in NSW)		
	'the existence and maintenance of standards'	Standards developed and applied
Imputed (or legally recognised) 'field'	General acceptance: 'a relevant scientific community and an express determination of a particular degree of acceptance within that community'	Persuasive to multidisciplinary audiences (beyond parochial forensic science 'fields')
Imputed (or legally recognised) 'expertise'		Probabilistic expression of results
'Adversarial bias' and breach of expert 'Code of Conduct' (though normally only matters for weight and possibly discretionary exclusion)		Processes to remove contextual bias and errors created by human factors (and need to document exposure to domain irrelevant information)
		Independence from law enforcement
		Full disclosure in detailed and transparent reports
		Standardised expressions (preferably probabilistic expressions derived from formal studies)
Assist the jury (and whether the jury will be able to assess the evidence without 'expert' assistance)	Assist the jury	Need for consistent use of terminology and attention to how expressions are actually understood by the trier of fact

131 See, eg, *Tang* [2006] NSWCCA 167; 65 NSWLR 681 and *Honeysett* [2013] NSWCCA 135.

Rational evaluation

The requirement for opinions to be based on 'specialised knowledge' demands not only attention to their form in reports and testimony (following *HG*, *Makita*, *Dasreef* and now *Honeysett*), but also the provision of means of evaluating the evidence. With many, perhaps most, forensic science and medicine procedures this necessitates independent validation studies (published in peer-reviewed journals or made available), indicative error rates, proficiency testing, explanations of uncertainties and limitations, empirically derived standards, attention to cognitive bias and the use of expressions linked to the results of validation studies.[132] Such prerequisites are not merely appropriate but, according to uncontradicted advice from the peak scientific and technical organisations, necessary. The 'knowledge' produced through formal evaluation of procedures enables lawyers, judges and fact-finders to determine whether there is *actual expertise* in the specific domain and its value, regardless of claims about 'training, study or experience'. Validation studies (like independent and rigorous proficiency tests) provide demonstrable evidence of ability and accuracy, thereby providing a framework that enables the trier of fact to determine if an opinion is probative and, if so, to rationally evaluate it.

When determining admissibility, courts should be interested in the form of the opinions in so far as it allows them to identify the 'specialised knowledge' and its basis so that expert opinion is susceptible to rational evaluation. This idea, commonly associated with *Davie v Magistrates of Edinburgh*,[133] is advanced in both *Makita* and *Dasreef*. According to Heydon J in *Makita*,[134] it is:

> a prime duty of experts in giving opinion evidence: to furnish the trier of fact with criteria enabling evaluation of the validity of the expert's conclusions. ... *Davie's* case is not to be read as reflecting only a principle peculiar to Scottish law.

In *HG*,[135] Gleeson CJ insisted that for the opinion to be admissible 'would have required or invited demonstration or examination of the scientific basis of the conclusion'.

Genuine dangers are created by opinions that are not reliable – that is, not based on 'specialised knowledge'.

> Experts who venture "opinions", (sometimes merely their own inferences of fact), outside their field of specialised knowledge may invest those opinions with a spurious appearance of authority, and legitimate processes of fact-finding may be subverted.[136]

Rigorous attention to 'specialised knowledge' allows us to answer questions about the scope of expertise as well as the level of performance (and error). Concern with 'specialised knowledge' should prevent courts from prematurely legitimising speculative procedures or relying on the non-systematic and untested experience of investigators and others with impressive credentials.

---

132 Validation studies tell us whether procedures work (and are therefore potentially relevant), provide indicative error rates, empirically derived standards and expressions, and also delimit the scope of the procedure (and related expertise).

133 [1953] SC 34, 40. *Davie* is cited in *Tang*, although there the approach adopted by the Court of Criminal Appeal does not provide a rational means of assessing the anatomist's opinion and does not direct attention to 'specialised knowledge' or her actual ability.

134 [2001] NSWCA 305; 52 NSWLR 705, [59]-[60]. See also *Hillstead* [2005] WASCA 116.

135 [1999] HCA 2; 197 CLR 414, [41].

136 Ibid [44]. See also *Honeysett* at [45].

Ad Hoc Expert Evidence (and *UEA*, ss 78 and 79)

Criminal trials have, in addition, been subverted by expansion in the use and scope of so-called *ad hoc experts*.[137] The idea of the ad hoc expert emerged (in Australia) in *Butera v DPP (Vic)*,[138] where the prosecutor called on a translator to provide a transcript to assist the jury with the interpretation of a contested voice recording. The transcript was admitted as an interpretive aid. The tape remained, in theory, the primary evidence.[139] Over the past decade, Australian courts have recognised ad hoc expertise as a type of admissible evidence that appears to sit either outside the *UEA* (recall Basten JA in *Nguyen*) or, perhaps less comfortably, within it – via s 78 in Victoria and relying on s 79(1) in New South Wales.[140]

Lamentably, in responding to contested voice recordings and images, NSW courts have allowed investigating police officers and translators to proffer their opinions not merely about what words were allegedly spoken (as in *Butera*)[141] but the identity of the speaker (or person of interest) via s 79(1) as ad hoc experts.[142] These investigators are frequently exposed to a great deal of information about the case (such as the beliefs of investigators, usually highly suggestive of identity) and generally have no relevant training, study or knowledge (and sometimes no experience) in voice or image comparison.[143] They frequently lack familiarity with relevant methods and procedures, they are not necessarily conversant with scientific research and limitations, and they are also likely to be over-confident and error-prone. Furthermore, many do not produce formal reports or comply with Codes of Conduct for Expert Witnesses – more below.[144] Remarkably, many of these issues have not been addressed or are yet to receive judicial consideration.[145]

Sections 76 and 79 would appear to cover the field. This is particularly important in relation to ad hoc *experts*. For, if the witness does not satisfy the terms of s 79(1) they cannot offer an incriminating opinion 'to prove the existence of a fact about the existence of which the opinion was expressed'. We should not encourage investigating police officers (and those in their camp) to express speculative opinions, let alone treat their opinions as 'expert evidence' or ad hoc expertise, in criminal proceedings. Attention must be focused on 'specialised knowledge' (and appropriate indicia of reliability) because attention to the requirements of s 79(1) provides means of enabling expert opinions to be rationally evaluated. Inattention to 'specialised knowledge', and therefore evidence of validity, reliability and

137 For a critical discussion, see G Edmond and M San Roque, 'Quasi-Justice: Ad Hoc Expertise and Identification Evidence' (2009) 33 *Criminal Law Journal* 8.

138 [1987] HCA 58; 164 CLR 180, drawing on *Menzies* [1982] 1 NZLR 41, 49.

139 The issue was partially addressed by s 48 of the *UEA*.

140 There are many problems with such an approach. For a range of criticisms, see G Edmond, K Martire and M San Roque, 'Unsound law: Issues with ("Expert") Voice Comparison Evidence' (2011) 35 *Melbourne University Law Review* 52. See also G Morrison and W Thompson, 'Assessing the admissibility of a new generation of forensic voice comparison testimony' (2017) 18 *Columbia Science & Technology Law Review* 326.

141 Though the transcripts themselves are not without genuine problems, see H Fraser, 'Forensic Transcription: How Confident False Beliefs about Language and Speech Threaten the Right to a Fair Trial in Australia' (2018) 38 *Australian Journal of Linguistics* 586.

142 Though, compare *Sterling and McCook* [2014] NSWDC 199 and *Drollett* [2005] NSWCCA 356.

143 See, eg, *Leung and Wong* [1999] NSWCCA 287; 47 NSWLR 405 and *Li* [2003] NSWCCA 290; 139 A Crim R 281.

144 See below, pp 547-552.

145 See, eg, *Riscuta* [2003] NSWCCA 6; *El-Kheir* [2004] NSWCCA 461. Though compare *Flynn* [2008] EWCA Crim 970, [14] and, more recently, *Nguon and Ream* (unreported, NSWDC, 31 March 2014, Whitford J).

performance, means the evaluation of *expert* opinions depends on impressions of demeanour, credibility, (apparent) impartiality, the effects of cross-examination, and impressions of (frequently untested) experience.[146] Similarly, s 78 should not be used to enable investigators (and others) to express opinions of unknown value. If opinions are not based on what a person perceived about a matter or event that they personally witnessed, then they should only be admissible if there is demonstrable expertise – that is, where the opinion is based on 'specialised knowledge'.

Recourse to ad hoc experts represents an inappropriate relaxation of important rules (and protections) for reasons of convenience and expediency to the state. The opinions of ad hoc experts are likely to be misleading (or exaggerated) and they are prone to over-valuation. Moreover, it is incredibly difficult to contest the incriminating opinions of police officers and others when they can simply acknowledge that they have not studied the procedure, do not know about relevant literatures, have never been tested, but nonetheless sincerely believe the defendant is the person in the voice recording or incriminating images. There is no evidence that the performance of these witnesses is better than the trier of fact (thereby making their incriminating opinions relevant) and their opinions are almost always biased – irreparably contaminated by gratuitous exposure to suggestive information.[147] To compound matters, ad hoc experts are often confident and adamant, yet confidence and persuasiveness are not simply correlated with accuracy.

An argument could be made that ad hoc experts have experience derived through the course of the investigation – usually through repeated listening to voice recordings or viewing images. The real problem emerges when 'specialised knowledge' enters into consideration. Unsurprisingly, the criminal justice jurisprudence has been insufficiently attentive to the issue of 'specialised knowledge' for ad hoc experts. Generally, if there is 'specialised knowledge' about voice and image comparison it does not reside with the ad hoc experts and they rarely seem to be conversant with specialist research literatures or anything that could credibly be equated with 'knowledge' (based on the definitions in *Daubert*, *Tang* or *Honeysett*). Ironically, most of the relevant knowledge in relation to voice and image comparison (in this case the published scientific literature) recommends caution.[148] Published studies confirm how difficult comparison tasks are and

146 On the limits with assessments of credibility and demeanour, see S Bandes, 'Remorse, Demeanour and the Consequences of Misinterpretation: The Limits of Law as a Window into the Soul' in P Roberts et al (eds), *Realising integrity in the criminal process* (Hart Publishing, 2015).

147 See I Dror, D Charlton and A Peron, 'Contextual Information Renders Experts Vulnerable to Making Erroneous Identifications' (2006) 156 *Forensic Science International* 74 and the legal implications discussed in G Edmond, J Tangen, R Searston and I Dror, 'Contextual Bias and Cross-contamination in the Forensic Sciences' (2014) *Law, Probability & Risk* (doi:10.1093/lpr/mgu018).

148 On voice comparison, see M Catanzaro et al, 'Voice Analysis Should Be Used with Caution in Court' (25 January 2017) *Scientific American*; E Gold and P French, 'International practices in forensic speaker comparisons: second survey' (2019) 26 *International Journal of Speech, Language and the Law* 1. On the images, consider A Burton, S Wilson M Cowan and V Bruce, 'Face Recognition in Poor-Quality Video: Evidence From Security Surveillance' (1999) 10 *Psychological Science* 243; Z Henderson, V Bruce and A Burton, 'Matching the Faces of Robbers Captured on Video' (2001) 15 *Applied Cognitive Psychology* 445; J Davis and T Valentine, 'CCTV on Trial: Matching Video Images with the Defendant in the Dock' (2008) 23 *Applied Cognitive Psychology* 482; R Jenkins, D White, X Van Montfort and A Burton, 'Variability in Photos of the Same Face' (2011) 121 *Cognition* 313; R Kemp, N Towell and G Pike, 'When Seeing Should not be Believing: Photographs, Credit Cards and Fraud' (1997) 11 *Applied Cognitive Psychology* 211. These are developed in G Edmond, K Biber, R Kemp and G Porter, 'Law's looking glass: expert identification evidence derived from photographic and video images' (2009) 20 *Current Issues*

how error-prone humans – including experienced investigators and even highly credentialled anatomists and linguists – tend to be.[149]

The following extracts reinforce the frequently superficial explanations attending legal recognition of ad hoc expert opinion.

Li

[2003] NSWCCA 290; 139 A Crim R 281

Detective Watson was involved in a covert surveillance operation for 2-3 months. He purported to identify Li as the person who delivered a package to a hotel room on the basis of his examination of 'poor quality' CCTV images of a person whose features were not resolved. His categorical identification was based on Li's (purportedly) distinctive hairline, manner of walking and posture.

> **Ipp JA (Whealy and Howie JJ concurring)**: 106. Detective Watson had made extensive observations of the appellant during surveillance operations between March and May 1998. From the knowledge so gained he was able to testify as to the appellant's posture and manner of walking, which were distinctive. This involved the swinging of his left arm, the holding of his head to the right and the manner of his walking generally. The jury were not able to see the appellant walking in court. Hence Detective Watson's evidence was not irrelevant and was properly admissible. …
>
> 111. While detective Watson indeed identified "a named person and suspect", he was doing so by reference to characteristics that were of an extraordinary quality. These characteristics involved a singular way of walking. These characteristics were described by Detective Watson and were for the jury to see on the video tape. It was of course open to the appellant to contradict Detective Watson but he did not. … Detective Watson testified that the person he saw on the video tape had the peculiar walking characteristics of the appellant. There was no way in which this evidence could have been made more reliable by some form of identification parade.

Tang

[2006] NSWCCA 167; 65 NSWLR 681

Tang was charged with robbing a convenience store in Ultimo armed with a handgun. There were CCTV images of the robbery and one of Tang's fingerprints was found on a packet of stolen cigarettes. Tang insisted that the print was placed on the packet when, in the aftermath of the robbery, he was invited by the robbers – whom he knew – to purchase stolen cigarettes and had rummaged around in a bag to locate his preferred brand. The Crown alleged that Tang was one of the robbers. The central issue was identity: Was Tang the robber with the handgun? The police asked an anatomist, Dr Sutisno, to compare the person of interest in the CCTV images of the robbery with police reference photographs of Tang (and the other suspects) – see Figure 1.

---

in Criminal Justice 337; G Edmond et al, 'Facial recognition and image comparison evidence: Identification by investigators, familiars, experts, super-recognisers and algorithms' (2021) 45 *Melbourne University Law Review* (forthcoming).

149 Studies suggest that experience and training may have limited value in improving abilities. For example, White et al report that the ability of passport officers to determine whether two portrait photographs are of the same unfamiliar person is unrelated to the duration of employment, with some passport officers who have been in the post for less than a year outperforming others who have held the position for more than 20 years. See D White, R Kemp, R Jenkins, M Matheson and M Burton, 'Passport Officers' Errors in Face Matching' (2014) 9 PLoS ONE e103510.

The admissibility of Dr Sutisno's face and body mapping (that is, image comparison) evidence was challenged at trial and on appeal. (It was accepted by the court that the images were not of a quality that would enable the jury to undertake comparisons by themselves (cf *Smith (Mundarra)*, above).)

Spigelman CJ (Simpson and Adams JJ concurring): 25. With respect to the Appellant, a photo board containing the two sets of photographs was tendered, along with a Morphological Features Chart. Dr Sutisno outlined her mechanism of adjusting the photographs so that they had the same angle. Her evidence included a comparison between the two sets of material in terms of identifying similarities such as the thickness of the lips, the existence of a dimple on the chin, the fact that each chin was "squarish" and the jaw structure "angular". She also identified, in accordance with her classification that was before the jury, that the two facial forms were "pentagonal", that the facial height was "medium", and there was a "lateral projection" of the cheekbones, meaning a projection to the side. She referred to a wide chin and visible lips seam, a slight projection of the ears and what is described as a "mezzo-cranic head shape", meaning a short, broad and high head with a flattened occipital region, being the back of the head. She also identified a number of the features in both sets of material as characteristics of an Asian person. She referred to similarities in terms of the "upright posture of the upper torso". Dr Sutisno also identified three "unique identifiers": the lips, the wide square chin with a dimple and the posture. …

28. Dr Sutisno concluded:

> "Based wholly and substantially on the above knowledge, it is my opinion that the multiplicity of *common morphological features*, *unique identifiers* and *Asian characteristics* to lend support that the offender and the alleged suspect Hien TANG are one and the same." …

Admissibility of the Opinions …

87. The grounds of appeal focus particular attention on the admissibility of the opinions expressed in the evidence and also on the quality of that evidence. It appears to me that there are three distinct pieces of opinion evidence given by Dr Sutisno with respect to the Appellant. These are:

(i) Dr Sutisno's evidence that the two bodies of photographs depict the same person;
(ii) Dr Sutisno's evidence that, on the six point scale[150] she applied to the photographic evidence, "the similarities" did "lend support" to the conclusion that the offender and the Appellant were one and the same person;
(iii) Dr Sutisno's characterisation of certain matters as "unique identifiers". …

120. As indicated above, in the circumstances of this case, the evidence of particular similarities between the two categories of photographs of the accused and the third offender was admissible. The process of identification and magnification of stills from the videotape was a process that had to be conducted by Dr Sutisno out of court. Furthermore, the quality of the photographs derived from the videotape was such that the comparison of those stills with the photographs of the Appellant could not be left for the jury to undertake for itself. The identification of points of similarity by Dr Sutisno was based on her skill and training, particularly with respect to facial anatomy. It was also based on her experience with conducting such comparisons on a number of other occasions. Indeed, it could be supported by the experience gained with respect to the videotape itself through the course of multiple viewing, detailed selection, identification and magnification of images. By this process she had become what is sometimes referred to as an "ad hoc expert". … In any event, as noted above, no complaint is made of this evidence.

121. However, the three opinions I have identified at [87] above, were not, the Appellant contends, admissible. …

150 Dr Sutisno relied on the following six-point scale: Level 1: lends no support; Level 2: lends limited support; Level 3: lends moderate support; Level 4: lends support; Level 5: lends strong support; Level 6: lends powerful support.

134. Section 79 has two limbs. Under the first limb, it is necessary to identify "specialised knowledge", derived from one of the three matters identified, ie "training, study or experience". Under the second limb, it is necessary that the opinion be "wholly or substantially based on that knowledge". Accordingly, it is a requirement of admissibility that the opinion be demonstrated to be based on the specialised knowledge. The Appellant invokes each limb.

135. With respect to the first limb of s 79, I have set out above the evidence of the nature of the specialised knowledge which Dr Sutisno said she had brought to bear in the formulation of the three opinions she expressed. There does appear to be a body of expertise based on facial identification. The detailed knowledge of anatomy which Dr Sutisno unquestionably had, together with her training, research and experience in the course of facial reconstruction supports her evidence of facial characteristics.

136. Nothing was presented to the Court which indicates, in any way, that Dr Sutisno's extension from facial to body mapping, with respect to matters of posture, has anything like that level of background and support. Specialist knowledge of posture can of course exist. (See eg *R v Li* supra at [106].) But the foundation for admissibility must be lain. It was not lain in the present case. The so-called "unique identifier" of posture was an essential element of Dr Sutisno's evidence of identity in the present case.

137. The focus of attention must be on the words "specialised knowledge", not on the introduction of an extraneous idea such as "reliability". …

138. In the immediate context of "specialised knowledge", picked up by the words "that knowledge" in the second limb of s 79, the word "knowledge" has a different connotation to that which it might have in a different context, eg "common knowledge". The meaning of "knowledge" in s 79 is, in my opinion, the same as that identified in the reasons of the majority judgment in *Daubert v Merrell Dow Pharmaceuticals Inc* [1993] USSC 99; 509 US 579 (1993) at 590:

> "[T]he word 'knowledge' connotes more than subjective belief or unsupported speculation. The term applies to any body of known facts or to any body of ideas inferred from such facts or accepted as truths on good grounds'."

The quoted definition is from an American dictionary.

139. I do not mean to suggest that *Daubert* and its progeny in the United States has anything useful to say about s 79 of the *Evidence Act*. Rule 702 of the *Federal Rules of Evidence* (2004), which fell to be interpreted in *Daubert,* is in quite different terms to s 79. The definition of the word "knowledge" in this cognate context is, however, instructive.

140. In the case of the Appellant the relevant evidence about posture was expressed in terms of "upright posture of the upper torso" or similar words. The only links to any form of "training, study or experience" was the witnesses' study of anatomy and some experience, entirely unspecified in terms of quality or extent, in comparing photographs for the purpose of comparing "posture". The evidence in this trial did not disclose, and did not permit a finding, that Dr Sutisno's evidence was based on a study of anatomy. That evidence barely, if at all, rose above a subjective belief and it did not, in my opinion, manifest anything of a "specialised" character. It was not, in my opinion, shown to be "specialised knowledge" within the meaning of s 79.

141. Furthermore, I am of the opinion that the second limb of s 79 was not satisfied with respect to each of the three opinions expressed by Dr Sutisno.

142. There was nothing in the present case remotely like the evidence before this Court when it accepted voice identification as a field of expert study or knowledge which could support evidence in the form that the two voices were the same. (*R v Gilmore* [1977] 2 NSWLR 935 at 937-938, 95-41; See also the considerable detail explaining the new technique in *R v McHardie and Danielson* [1983] 2 NSWLR 733 at 755-763.)

143. In the absence of any kind of objective standard or data base which is capable of leading to a quantification of probabilities, such as is given in the context of DNA evidence, evidence of similarity may have a cumulative effect, by reason of the number of points of similarity. Directions to the jury of the probability of the various matters coinciding can

> be helpfully put in terms of the ordinary experience of jurors. An exceptionally useful direction to the jury of this character is that employed in relation to fingerprint evidence in its early years in *R v Krausch* (1913) 32 NZLR 1229 at 1230-1231, about which I have expressed the view that it could serve as a model for directions on DNA evidence. (See *R v JCG* [2001] NSWCCA 504; 127 A Crim R 493 at [91]-[93].) …
>
> 146. … Facial mapping, let alone body mapping, was not shown, on the evidence in the trial, to constitute "specialised knowledge" of a character which can support an opinion of identity. …
>
> 153. In *Makita* Heydon JA posed a series of questions about the evidence in that case, including:
>
> > "[87] … Did [the report] furnish the trial judge with the necessary scientific criteria for testing the accuracy of its conclusions? Did it enable him to form his own independent judgment by applying the criteria furnished to the facts proved? Was it intelligible, convincing and tested? Did it go beyond a bare *ipse dixit*?"
>
> 154. The three opinions of Dr Sutisno in the present case do not, in my view, go beyond a "bare *ipse dixit*". Dr Sutisno did not identify the terms of the "strict protocol" that she purported to have applied, nor did she set out the basis on which the "protocol" was developed. Indeed, she said that this information was confidential, because of what she described as a "process of patenting my innovations". Accordingly, she had not published any of these "innovations". The critical matter is that she did not identify her "protocol" or explain its basis.

According to Spigelman CJ, '[f]acial mapping, let alone body mapping, was not shown, on the evidence in the trial, to constitute "specialised knowledge" of a character which can support an opinion of identity'[151] and '[t]he … opinions of [the anatomist] in the present case do not, in my view, go beyond a "bare *ipse dixit*".'[152] However, notwithstanding these apparently critical assessments, the anatomist had spent time looking at the images and had, according to the court, thereby become an *ad hoc expert*. Dr Sutisno's opinions about the identity of the offender were inadmissible, though she (and presumably others) would be allowed to describe *similarities* (and in theory differences) between persons of interest in CCTV recordings and defendants in future trials.[153] Interestingly, in a subsequent trial Tang was convicted without Dr Sutisno's opinion evidence.

There is no doubt that Dr Sutisno is a highly qualified anatomist who had spent time comparing the images in this and previous investigations. We do not know, however, anything about the value or accuracy of the procedure used. We do not know if the procedure works. Was she able to identify features in ways that were superior to the performance of the trier of fact (or chance)? We might in addition, wonder what in a person's anatomical training prepares them to be able to undertake comparisons of face and bodies (and posture or gait) using images that are often of low quality.

Paragraph [137] of the decision represents a particularly unfortunate development. It has discouraged meaningful engagement with 'specialised knowledge' in Australian jurisprudence and remains good law; even in the aftermath of *Honeysett*.[154]

---

151 [2006] NSWCCA 167, [146].

152 Ibid [154].

153 See also *Murdoch* [2007] NTCCA 1.

154 See *Tuite* [2015] VSCA 148, [70]; *Chen* [2018] NSWCCA 106, [62]: 'Section 79 is not concerned with reliability of the expert's opinions'.

Nguyen

[2017] NSWCCA 4

More recently in *Nguyen*, the NSW Court of Criminal Appeal confirmed that s 79(1) could accommodate investigators proffering ad hoc expert opinions about the identity of speakers in voice recordings, even as the Victorian courts indicated – in *Kheir* and *Tran and Chang* – that s 78 was the preferable pathway. The background to the police officer's 'expertise' is set out in the judgment of Hulme J and the most expansive explanation of this ad hoc expert evidence is provided by Schmidt J. Nguyen was accused of organising Huynh and supplying drugs for him to on-sell.

RA Hulme J: 85. … Senior Constable Van Der Hout was one of three officers who were assigned the task of monitoring intercepted telecommunications …

86. In the course of carrying out this monitoring, the officer may have listened to calls a number of times; stopping, starting and restarting to listen again. He did this to ensure the accuracy of summaries he was required to prepare. He listened to the calls again after having heard the recording of the police interview. In summary, he said that "in addition to the two months during which I reviewed the telecommunication intercept material, I also spent a further two weeks reviewing and replying [sic – replaying] certain calls as a part of the investigation. I then spent approximately five days reviewing the transcripts of the calls with the actual intercepted material to ensure their accuracy for court". That was up to the date of his statement of 29 August 2013. He also listened to the calls after that date.

87. In the early phase of the investigation in some calls to/from the phone of Thanh Hao Huynh Senior Constable Van Der Hout detected conversation with a female using a phone with a number ending in 997. There was no dispute that this was the applicant's phone. It appears that there were nine such calls and Senior Constable Van Der Hout claimed to recognise the applicant's voice in seven of them; the other two were either indistinct or too short.

88. On 2 May 2012, Huynh received a call from a female who did not identify herself using a phone with a number ending in 617. When Huynh asked, "Who's this", she replied, "It's my new number". Senior Constable Van Der Hout said that when this call was intercepted he immediately recognised the voice as the same as that of the female who used the 997 phone. From 2 May to 15 May 2012 there were 23 intercepted voice calls between Huynh's phone and the 617 phone.

89. The officer claimed to have recognised the voice in the recording of the police interview immediately he heard it but he had listened to that recording "maybe at least ten" times "just like to make sure of myself".

90. The officer claimed to identify the applicant's voice by reference to a combination of three matters: the way in which the person spoke; voice characteristics; and common references. In relation to voice characteristics he referred to a loud female voice; a very distinct high rising inflection at the end of a sentence; and a habit of speaking in English with a Vietnamese accent but sometimes lapsing into Vietnamese language. By common references he meant the repeated use of the phrase "down west" (eg "Just come down west").

Determination

91. Two of the three bases upon which the officer made his identification of the applicant's voice were readily capable of being drawn to the jury's attention and for them to make their own assessment. But the officer relied upon the overall sound of the voice as well as the attributes he was able to articulate. The amount of time he invested in repeatedly listening to the calls and the applicant's police interview is something that would have been impractical for the jury to replicate. The evidence was relevant for this reason.

Schmidt J: 102. … [A]s to the admissibility of the voice identification evidence of Senior Constable Van der Hout, what was in issue was whether his evidence was relevant and admissible under s 79 of the *Evidence Act*.

103. The concept of an ad hoc expert, who can be called to give opinion evidence such as that sought to be called from the Senior Constable, has long been recognised (see *R v Butera* (1987) 164 CLR 180). In *R v Leung and Wong* (1999) 47 NSWLR 405; [1999] NSWCCA 287 it was held at [40] that s 79 is sufficiently wide to accommodate the idea of such an ad hoc expert.

104. RA Hulme J has explained the experience on which the Crown's case that the Senior Constable had the expertise which rendered his evidence both relevant and admissible under s 79 rested. That section provides that the opinion rule does not apply to opinion evidence which is based on a person's specialised knowledge "based on the person's training, study or experience", where the opinion "is wholly or substantially based on that knowledge".

105. All that the Senior Constable had done, in the performance of his duties, which on the Crown's case resulted in his claimed specialised knowledge and the formation of the opinions about which he gave evidence, was not, as RA Hulme J has explained, able to be replicated by the jury. In the result, I too consider that his evidence was correctly admitted, as it was both relevant to what was in issue at the trial and admissible under s 79, given the experience on which his opinions rested.

As these extracts illustrate, there is no engagement with 'knowledge' or how it is that limited exposure to a small set of voice recordings – as 'experience' – provided the basis for 'specialised knowledge'.

The testimony provides no indication of the value of this opinion, its limitations, the risks of error or the dangers posed by cognitive bias.[155] Rather, the opinion seems to be almost entirely based on the police officer's experience – in the guise of repeated listening. Inattentive to whether the police officer is actually better than the jury, the fact that the jury will not be able to spend as much time listening is offered as the primary justification for receiving this testimony. Any police officer could be transformed into a *legally recognised expert* in this way. Time spent listening, and re-listening, is not the same thing as accurately identifying one or more voices. And, there is also the issue of whether such risky and biased opinions – always obtained in suggestive conditions – is necessary or outweighed by the danger of unfair prejudice where the phone sim cards are found in the possession of the defendant and there is an otherwise strong circumstantial case.

The uncertain relationship around voice and image identification at common law as well as the admission of non-expert opinions of investigators via ss 78 and 79(1) are likely to be the subject of further litigation.[156]

Expert Reports, Codes of Conduct and Procedural Rules

To determine whether expert opinions are admissible, criminal lawyers and judges should be much more attentive to the form of the expert report and testimony insofar as that enables them to determine whether the 'opinion is based on

155 G Edmond, J Tangen, R Searson and I Dror, 'Contextual bias and cross-contamination in the forensic sciences: The implications for investigations, plea bargains, trials and appeals' (2014) 14 *Law, Probability & Risk* 1.

156 G Edmond, 'Regulating forensic science and medicine at trial' (2020) 94 *Australian Law Journal* 427.

specialised knowledge'.[157] Lawyers and judges should pay much closer attention to whether expert reports and performances satisfy the various Codes of Conduct, Practice Directions and procedural rules regulating conduct in various Australian courts.[158] Greater attention to the content of expert reports and certificates (*UEA*, s 177), and compliance with formal rules, would greatly assist in admissibility decision-making and the assessment of *expert* opinion evidence.[159] Attending to existing rules and jurisprudence would substantially redress commonplace deficiencies but there remains an obvious imperative to direct attention to the reliability of forensic science and medicine evidence.

The extract below reproduces some of the formal requirements set out in the Expert Witness Code of Conduct for civil and criminal proceedings taken, perhaps revealingly, from r 31.23 and Sch 7 of the *Uniform Civil Procedure Rules 2005* (NSW) (UCPR).[160] Schedule 7 sets out a range of duties and expectations:

> **2 GENERAL DUTIES TO THE COURT**
>
> An expert witness is not an advocate for a party and has a paramount duty, overriding any duty to the party to the proceedings or other person retaining the expert witness, to assist the court impartially on matters relevant to the area of expertise of the witness.
>
> **3 CONTENT OF REPORT**
>
> Every report prepared by an expert witness for use in court must clearly state the opinion or opinions of the expert and must state, specify or provide –
>
> (a) the name and address of the expert, and
> (b) an acknowledgement that the expert has read this code and agrees to be bound by it, and
> (c) the qualifications of the expert to prepare the report, and
> (d) the assumptions and material facts on which each opinion expressed in the report is based (a letter of instructions may be annexed), and
> (e) the reasons for and any literature or other materials utilised in support of each such opinion, and
> (f) (if applicable) that a particular question, issue or matter falls outside the expert's field of expertise, and
> (g) any examinations, tests or other investigations on which the expert has relied, identifying the person who carried them out and that person's qualifications, and
> (h) the extent to which any opinion which the expert has expressed involves the acceptance of another person's opinion, the identification of that other person and the opinion expressed by that other person, and
> (i) a declaration that the expert has made all the inquiries which the expert believes are desirable and appropriate (save for any matters identified explicitly in the report), and that no matters of significance which the expert regards as relevant have, to the knowledge of the expert, been withheld from the court, and
> (j) any qualification of an opinion expressed in the report without which the report is or may be incomplete or inaccurate, and
> (k) whether any opinion expressed in the report is not a concluded opinion because of insufficient research or insufficient data or for any other reason, and

157 See the discussion and example in G Edmond, K Martire and M San Roque, 'Expert reports in the forensic Sciences' (2017) 40 *UNSW Law Journal* 590.

158 See, eg, the Federal Court of Australia's *Expert Evidence Practice Note* (GPN-EXPT), <https://www.fedcourt.gov.au/law-and-practice/practice-documents/practice-notes/gpn-expt>.

159 See *Chen* [2018] NSWCCA 106 and the discussion in J Chin, M San Roque and R McFadden, 'The new psychology of expert witness procedure' (2020) 42 *Sydney Law Review* 69.

160 UCPR, rr 31.17-31.54 which apply in the courts of NSW by virtue of SCR Pt 39, r 2; DCR Pt 28A, r 2; LCR Pt 38B, r 2. See also *Wood* [2012] NSWCCA 21, [725] and *Gilham* [2012] NSWCCA 131, [405].

(l) where the report is lengthy or complex, a brief summary of the report at the beginning of the report.[161]

In Victoria, the relevant Practice Direction is more recent, designed specifically for criminal proceedings, and a little more onerous. Not only is one of the expressed purposes to 'enhance the quality and reliability of expert evidence relied on by the prosecution and the accused in criminal trials' but expert witnesses are required to disclose the existence of controversies and expert disagreement in their reports. The Practice Direction states:

> 4.2 Where an expert is aware of any significant and recognised disagreement or controversy within the relevant field of specialised knowledge, which is directly relevant to the expert's ability, technique or opinion, the expert must disclose the existence of that disagreement or controversy.[162]

While these developments are generally quite positive, many forensic science reports prepared by state-employed forensic scientists and adduced by prosecutors do not comply with these rules.[163] Many expert reports do not provide the kinds of detail required to address the conditions prescribed by s 79(1). Moreover, they do not enable a scientist – let alone a lawyer, judge or juror – to rationally assess the opinion and its basis.[164] They do not 'furnish the trier of fact with the criteria to enable the evaluation of the expert conclusion'.[165] Those recognised as ad hoc experts, and those testifying via s 78, may not even prepare reports or be conversant with Codes of Conduct and Practice Notes.

Reports and testimony, particularly where adduced by the prosecutor as a model litigant, should comply with formal rules.[166] Reports should be presented in a form that satisfies the formal requirements of s 79(1) as well as the express terms of Codes of Conduct. Reports should identify the facts or assumptions on which the opinions are based: UCPR, Sch 7, cl 3(d). They should also provide reasons (cl 3(e), declare limits of expertise (cl 3(f)), refer to relevant literatures and tests (cl 3(e), (g)), proactively disclose limitations (cl 3(j)), and draw attention to the need for further research or evidence (cl 3(k)). Those preparing reports should also be willing to change their mind (cl 4), and may be directed to confer with other experts (cl 5(a)) and even produce joint reports (cl 5(b)). Where there are controversies or substantial criticisms (such as those advanced by peak scientific organisations such as the NAS, PCAST, NIST and AAAS), these should be disclosed and relevant literatures referenced. Compliance will usually assist with decisions about admissibility, probative value (even 'at its highest') and some of the risks of unfair prejudice that might arise.

The Codes of Conduct are not admissibility rules per se. Judges have suggested that in most cases partisanship (and bias) and other shortcomings will generally not lead to the exclusion of expert opinion evidence, under *UEA*, s 79(1), at least.[167]

---

161 UCPR Sch 7.

162 *Practice Direction: Expert Evidence in Criminal Trials* (Victoria, 2014).

163 Edmond, Martire and San Roque, above n 157.

164 G Edmond, 'Forensic science evidence and the conditions for rational (jury) evaluation' (2016) 39 *Melbourne University Law Review* 75.

165 *Makita (Australia) Pty Ltd v Sprowles* [2001] NSWCA 305; 52 NSWLR 705, [59]-[60].

166 On the obligations of prosecutors, see G Edmond, '(ad)Ministering Justice: Expert Evidence and the Professional Responsibilities of Prosecutors' (2013) 36 *UNSW Law Journal* 921.

167 See *FGT Custodians Pty Ltd v Fagenblat* [2003] VSCA 33. Although, there are recent exceptions: see, eg, *Welker v Rinehart (No 6)* [2012] NSWSC 160. See also *White Burgess Langille v Abbott and Haliburton Co* [2015] SCC 23.

However, judges might use their mandatory and discretionary exclusions (that is, ss 135 and 137) to exclude expert evidence that does not comply with the text of such codes where it raises risks to the defendant.[168] In thinking about compliance with s 79(1) and the Codes of Conduct, prosecutors and judges should consider whether non-compliant reports and testimony actually enable them to answer the questions advanced by the High Court in *HG* and *Dasreef*. What is the 'specialised knowledge', is the opinion based on it, and is the 'specialised knowledge' linked to the individual's 'training, study or experience'? In many cases, the failure to address the criteria listed in Column 3 in Table 1 will make it difficult to answer the very questions that ought to determine admissibility (as well as guide assessments of probative value, weight and unfair prejudice to the defendant).[169]

It is useful to contrast the following appeal from civil proceedings with the accommodating approaches adopted in most of the criminal appeals considered in this chapter.

Ocean Marine Mutual Insurance Association (Europe) OV v Jetopay Pty Ltd

[2000] FCA 1463

In these civil proceedings the Federal Court considered the admissibility of several reports relating to the repair of a ship's engine and resulting loss or damage.

Black CJ, Cooper and Emmett JJ: *Mr Crosby's Opinion*

24. Mr Crosby's report is typed on writing paper with the following heading:

"CROSBY & CO

CONSULTING MARINE SURVEYORS and ENGINEERS"

The report is entitled "*Survey Report*" and Mr Crosby is described at the top of the report as:

> *"D.W. CROSBY J.P.*
> *C.Eng., F.I.Mar.E. F.C.M.S."*

25. There was no evidence as to the signification of the letters appearing after Mr Crosby's name. Nevertheless, Jetopay sought to draw inferences that they signified that Mr Crosby had some relevant training, study or experience. Similar inferences were sought to be drawn from the description of Mr Crosby at the end of the report as "*Surveyor*" and the description of his firm as "*Consulting Marine Surveyors and Engineers*". However, those matters are all equivocal and inconclusive. They do not, of themselves, establish that Mr Crosby had any particular specialised knowledge relating to the repair of marine engines, nor do they establish any particular training, study or experience, upon which such knowledge might be based.

26. The part of Mr Crosby's report to which objection was taken was as follows:

> *"8. Opinion:*
> In the opinion of the writer the damage, as noted in para 2 above are a direct consequence of the negligence of the New Zealand repairers in July 1994, in not cleaning out the lub oil system properly after completion of repairs. (There is still particulate debris left in the engine sump)."

27. The report does not demonstrate how Mr Crosby's opinion concerning the negligence of the New Zealand repairers was based on any particular specialised knowledge that he has. Nor does it demonstrate that any relevant specialised knowledge that Mr

168 *Wood* [2012] NSWCCA 21, [728]-[730].
169 See *JP v DPP* [2015] NSWSC 1669.

Crosby has was based on his training, study or experience. The opinion was therefore inadmissible and we consider that that part of the report should have been rejected.

Mr Parker's Opinion

28. Neither of Mr Parker's reports contains any indication of his qualifications or of his training, study or experience. The report contains at its head a reference to "*Rockliff Marine & Engineering P/L*". However, there is no indication as to the nature of the business of that company other than might be inferred from its name. Nor was there any evidence of Mr Parker's involvement or responsibilities with that company.

29. There was, however, other evidence upon which reliance was placed to support a conclusion that Mr Parker had appropriate qualifications. On 14 August 1997 Sealand sent a facsimile communication to Harbour Pacific. The document contained, *inter alia*, the following:

> "*a) Lee Parker Diesel Engineer – Petunia Fisheries:*
>
> Lee originally pulled the motor down and has been involved with this vessel over a number of years – his opinion is that the motor when rebuilt in NZ in 1994 was of a very dubious nature.
>
> b) The engine has suffered an oil failure either by three causes – contamination and the oil sump not being cleaned properly or heavy weather damage or a faulty part has malfunctioned.
>
> He also comments that the engine would be expected to run for 50,000 hours not 5,000 hours – Lee Parker is a very well repected [sic] Diesel Engineer on these type of engines."

That document was admitted into evidence without objection. However, at the time of its tender, his Honour had already admitted Mr Parker's reports over the objection of Ocean Marine. It is clear that the document was not relied upon at the trial in support of the admissibility of Mr Parker's report. It could not have been relied on for that purpose over the objection of Ocean Marine.

30. It would have been admissible as against Ocean Marine as evidence of the fact that a communication in the terms of the document had occurred, if that fact be relevant. It was not admissible against Ocean Marine, if objected to, as evidence of the truth of statements made in the document, unless its admission could be supported as a business record, to prove a specific fact. But for the presence of Sealand and Harbour Pacific as respondents, it is clear that the document would not have been tendered at all. It cannot be relied upon to fill any deficiency in the evidence as to the qualifications of Mr Parker.

31. Mr Parker's report of 14 August 1997 contained the following material:

> ***"It is my belief that poor performance of previous overhauls caused contamination of lubrication system, which in turn caused a gradual yet premature failure of components outside their normal wear schedule. I can make this claim with some authority as*** *I was involved with repairing the engine after its repair and return from New Zealand."*

The part shown in bold in the above extract was the subject of objection.

32. The report does not demonstrate how Mr Parker's opinion is based on any specialised knowledge that he has. Nor does it demonstrate that any knowledge that Mr Parker had was based on any training, study or experience. The opinion of Mr Parker to which objection was taken was inadmissible and that part of his report should have been rejected.

Mr Hughes' Opinion

33. Mr Hughes' report contained the following paragraph to which objection was taken:

> *"In my opinion it would appear that the abnormal abrasive wear and adhesion damage that has been destructive to many of the engine components was the result of debris generated at the time of previous engine failures and had not been properly cleaned up during the process of repairing the engine. This debris had entered the lubrication system where even more debris had been generated by the oil pump itself then transported in the oil to other parts of the engine."*

> Mr Hughes report is headed "*Component Condition and Failure Analysis Report*". It contains no reference at all to any specialised knowledge that Mr Hughes had at the time. Nor does it refer to any training, study or experience of Mr Hughes. For the reasons indicated above, the opinion to which objection was taken was inadmissible and that part of Mr Hughes' report should have been rejected.

In the absence of explicit evidence of relevant 'specialised knowledge' these expert reports were deemed 'not admissible to prove the existence of a fact about the existence of which the opinion was expressed'. The court was unwilling to constructively redeem inadequate reports and opinions even in conditions where the authors might have appeared qualified and where they claimed to have examined the engine in these civil proceedings.

The court insisted that:

> 22. … [I]t is not permissible to conclude, simply because a person expresses an opinion on a particular subject, referring to particular technology, that that person has any specialised knowledge in relation to that subject. There must be specific evidence as to specialised knowledge of the person in relation to that subject and as to the training, study or experience upon which that specialised knowledge is based.

and continued:

> 23. The further requirement that an opinion be *based on* specialised knowledge would normally be satisfied by the person who expresses the opinion demonstrating the reasoning process by which the opinion was reached. Thus, a report in which an opinion is recorded should expose the reasoning of its author in a way that would demonstrate that the opinion is based on particular specialised knowledge. Similarly, opinion evidence given orally should be shown, by exposure of the reasoning process, to be based on relevant specialised knowledge. (emphasis in original)

The 'Common Knowledge' and 'Ultimate Issue' Rules: *UEA*, s 80

> **80. Ultimate issue and common knowledge rules abolished**
> Evidence of an opinion is not inadmissible only because it is about:
> (a) a fact in issue or an ultimate issue, or
> (b) a matter of common knowledge.

At common law witnesses were generally prevented from expressing opinions about the ultimate issue in proceedings. In tort proceedings, for example, medical specialists were not free to express opinions about whether the particular treatment or surgery was performed negligently. Rather, and somewhat artificially, they were obliged to limit their evidence to issues such as whether they would have performed the same procedure (in the same way), whether they would have required additional tests or precautions, what mainstream medical opinion might be, their own responses to a range of hypotheticals and assumed facts, and so forth. Similarly, witnesses (especially expert witnesses) were prevented from expressing opinions about issues that were perceived (by judges) to be common knowledge or within the experience of the trier of fact. The *UEA* has modified the stark common law position in a way that embodies an evolving receptivity. Section 80 makes it clear that opinions are not inadmissible merely because they venture onto the ultimate issue or address a matter considered to be common knowledge.

Interestingly, the terms of s 80 are not particularly inclusive or welcoming. It seems the section was intended to remove the rigidity of the common law proscription without making all opinions touching on the ultimate issue or common knowledge necessarily admissible. This reticence might be applied to some of the facial mapping cases, for example. Where an *expert's* evidence is directly related to a central issues such as identity, judges might maintain a degree of caution. Such concerns were captured by Mason P in relation to DNA evidence in *GK*:[170]

> 40. In New South Wales opinion evidence is not inadmissible only because it is about a fact in issue or an ultimate issue (Evidence Act, s 80(a)). However, judges should exercise particular scrutiny when experts move close to the ultimate issue, lest they arrogate expertise outside their field or express views unsupported by disclosed and contestable assumptions (see *Steffen v Ruban* [1966] 2 NSWR 622 at 626, *Arnotts v Trade Practices Commission* (1990) 24 FCR 313 at 350-1, *HG v The Queen* [1999] HCA 2; 197 CLR 414 at 427-8, *Makita*).

The legacy of the commitment behind the common knowledge rule continues to prejudice judges against the evidence of experimental psychologists and cognitive scientists. According to the common law decision in *Turner*:[171]

> [An expert's opinion] is admissible to furnish the court with scientific information which is likely to be outside the experience and knowledge of a judge or jury. If on the proven facts a judge or jury can form their own conclusions without help, then the opinion of an expert is unnecessary. In such a case if it is given dressed up on scientific jargon it may make judgment more difficult. The fact that an expert has impressive scientific qualifications does not by that fact alone make his opinion on matters of human nature and behavior within the limits of normality any more helpful than that of the jurors themselves, but there is a danger that they may think it does …

The assumption seems to be that lay persons (such as judges and jurors) have, through their ordinary experiences, a solid grounding in problems of perception and many kinds of interpersonal relations (for example, relational difficulties or the responses of victims of child sexual assault – though see *UEA*, s 79(2), and below, pp 555-556). While the desire to prevent trials bogging down into sideshows between experts around marginal issues is an understandable anxiety, a significant proportion of the beliefs held by lay people seem to be simplistic, misguided or mistaken. They are not consistent with the findings of scientific research.[172] The reluctance to draw upon or admit scientific knowledge that relates to basic perceptions and mundane experience means that those deciding, managing and reviewing cases are not necessarily exposed to mainstream scientific research.[173]

Cadbury Schweppes Pty Ltd v Darrell Lea Chocolate Shops Pty Ltd

[2007] FCAFC 70

Cadbury claimed that the use by Darrell Lea of a shade of purple in connection with its chocolate confectionary business had the consequence that consumers

170 [2001] NSWCCA 413.

171 [1975] QB 834, 841.

172 See, eg, D Simon, *In doubt: The psychology of the criminal justice process* (Harvard University Press, 2012); M Saks and B Spellman, *The psychological foundations of evidence law* (NYU Press, 2016); D Kahneman, *Thinking fast and slow* (Allen Lane, 2011).

173 The decision in *Aytugrul* [2012] HCA 15; 247 CLR 170 suggests that if scientific and technical insights are not adduced at first instance they are unlikely to be considered on appeal. See D Hamer and G Edmond, 'Judicial notice: Beyond adversarialism and into the exogenous zone' (2016) 25 *Griffith Law Review* 291.

might mistakenly conclude that Darrell Lea products were Cadbury products or that there was some connection between the respective chocolate confectionary businesses of Darrell Lea and Cadbury. Cadbury called an expert to support its case and the trial judge deemed the evidence inadmissible. On appeal to the Full Federal Court:

> **Black CJ, Emmett and Middleton JJ**: 49. It is significant that no mention was made of s 80 of the Evidence Act in the course of the oral address by senior counsel for either party. In any event, the course of the interchange between senior counsel for Darrell Lea and the primary judge may serve to explain the conclusion that his Honour reached, and his Honour's reasons for the conclusion, without any reference to s 80 of the Evidence Act.
>
> 50. In the primary judge's ruling on the admissibility of Dr Gibbs' evidence, his Honour said that an expert's opinion is admissible to furnish the Court with scientific information that is likely to be outside the experience and knowledge of a judge or jury. His Honour suggested that the concept of specialised knowledge in s 79 imports knowledge of matters that are outside the knowledge or experience of an ordinary person, being knowledge that is sufficiently organised or recognised to be accepted as a reliable body of knowledge and that approach is very close to the common law approach. Thus, his Honour concluded that, even if a proffered opinion is that of a person suitably qualified within an organised area of knowledge, if that area is not outside the experience of ordinary persons, the opinion will not be admissible.
>
> 51. While his Honour accepted that marketing and behavioural science is an organised and recognised area of specialised knowledge and that Dr Gibbs has training, study and experience within that area, his Honour characterised the issues that arise in the case as not being outside the knowledge or experience of ordinary persons. His Honour concluded, therefore, that Dr Gibbs' evidence was inadmissible in its entirety, because it went only to a matter that is within the knowledge and experience of an ordinary person.
>
> 52. His Honour then referred to observations made by the High Court in the *Transport Publishing Case* at 119 to the effect that "*ordinary human nature, that of people at large, is not a subject of proof by evidence, whether supposedly expert or not*". Those observations, of course, were made before the enactment of s 80 of the Evidence Act. His Honour considered that the whole *raison d'être* of Dr Gibbs' evidence was to persuade the Court what ordinary human nature will lead people to do when making purchasing decisions about Darrell Lea chocolates, given the respective packaging, advertising, etc of that company and Cadbury. His Honour held that, before opinion evidence may be given upon the characteristics, responses or behaviour of any special category of persons, it must be shown that those persons form a subject of special study or knowledge.
>
> 53. The primary judge characterised the proceeding as being concerned with the brand names, colours and get-up of rival manufacturers of chocolate and the likely effect of those features on retail purchasing decisions by consumers. His Honour considered that virtually the whole of the Australian population over the age of about 8 years are purchasers or potential purchasers of chocolate, an inexpensive everyday product sold in hundreds of thousands of retail outlets throughout the country. His Honour did not consider that consumers of chocolates could be considered as a special category of persons that would constitute an exception to the rule under the common law. His Honour characterised the questions thrown up by the proceeding as "*quintessentially questions of fact within the experience and knowledge of a trier of fact*".
>
> 54. Such an approach appears to ignore the language of ss 79 and 80 of the Evidence Act. Certainly, opinion evidence will not be admissible unless the opinion is based on specialised knowledge and that specialised knowledge is in turn based on the opinion holder's training, study or experience. However, the former rule of the common law that excluded opinion evidence as to a matter of common knowledge no longer applies. Under s 80, evidence of an opinion is not inadmissible only because it is a matter of common knowledge.

55. Clearly enough, if the matter about which expert evidence is to be given is patent and known to all, the Court's time would normally be wasted by such evidence. Section 135 may be called in aid in those circumstances. Nevertheless, the evidence may still be strictly admissible. Further, an expert may still be of assistance to the Court, even in an area about which most people know something. So long as s 79 is satisfied, and the opinion evidence is based on specialised knowledge and that specialised knowledge is based on training, study or experience, that opinion evidence will be admissible, whether or not it might then be excluded in the exercise of the discretion conferred by s 135 (see generally the Law Reform Commission, *Interim Report on Evidence*, Canberra 1985, paragraph 743).

One of the major problems confronting legal institutions, conspicuous in the emerging problems with forensic science and medicine, is how courts are to identify and incorporate scientific knowledge as evidence capable of enhancing the results in individual cases and information able to enhance system performance, more generally. The failure to develop means to systematically engage with perspectives from beyond the courtroom poses a serious and continuing threat to legal institutional legitimacy and the accuracy of legal fact-finding.[174]

'Specialised Knowledge' of Child Development and Child Behaviour: *UEA*, ss 79(2), (3) and 108C

In response to the ALRC's *Uniform Evidence Law* report,[175] the *Evidence Act 1995* (NSW) was revised in order to address the apparent reluctance of trial and appellate judges to recognise the potential value of 'specialised knowledge' pertaining to 'child development and behaviour', 'including the effects of sexual abuse on the development of children'.[176] Such opinions must satisfy the terms of s 79(1) and the mandatory and discretionary exclusions (ss 135, 137), if challenged.

79. Exception: opinions based on specialised knowledge ...

(2) To avoid doubt, and without limiting subsection (1):

(a) a reference in that subsection to specialised knowledge includes a reference to specialised knowledge of child development and child behaviour (including specialised knowledge of the impact of sexual abuse on children and their development and behaviour during and following the abuse), and

(b) a reference in that subsection to an opinion of a person includes, if the person has specialised knowledge of the kind referred to in paragraph (a), a reference to an opinion relating to either or both of the following:

(i) the development and behaviour of children generally,

(ii) the development and behaviour of children who have been victims of sexual offences, or offences similar to sexual offences.

In addition, those with relevant specialised knowledge might proffer opinions about the credibility of a witness that are not rendered inadmissible by the *credibility rule* (s 102). Such evidence might be used to discredit or support the credibility of a witness. Examples might include where the witness has an intellectual disability, cognitive impairment, been exposed to violence, or there is a risk that behaviour might be misinterpreted. The evidence must be capable of

---

174 G Edmond, D Hamer and E Cunliffe, 'A little ignorance is a dangerous thing: Engaging with exogenous knowledge not adduced by the parties' (2016) 25 *Griffith Law Review* 383.

175 ALRC, *Uniform Evidence Law* (Report No 102, 2006).

176 Ibid [9.155]-[9.156].

substantially affecting the assessment of credibility and the court must give leave (s 192) to adduce the evidence.

108C. Exception: evidence of persons with specialised knowledge

(1) The credibility rule does not apply to evidence given by a person concerning the credibility of another witness if:

(a) the person has specialised knowledge based on the person's training, study or experience, and

(b) the evidence is evidence of an opinion of the person that:

(i) is wholly or substantially based on that knowledge, and

(ii) could substantially affect the assessment of the credibility of the witness, and

(c) the court gives leave to adduce the evidence.

(2) To avoid doubt, and without limiting subsection (1):

(a) a reference in that subsection to specialised knowledge includes a reference to specialised knowledge of child development and child behaviour (including specialised knowledge of the impact of sexual abuse on children and their behaviour during and following the abuse), and

(b) a reference in that subsection to an opinion of a person includes, if the person has specialised knowledge of that kind, a reference to an opinion relating to either or both of the following:

(i) the development and behaviour of children generally,

(ii) the development and behaviour of children who have been victims of sexual offences, or offences similar to sexual offences.[177]

Expert Evidence of 'Fact'

Where expert witnesses testify (or produce expert reports) about *fact*, that evidence is not caught by the exclusionary *opinion rule*. Expert witnesses can, in general, testify about a range of relevant issues that are not caught by s 76. They might, for example, testify about the meaning of technical words, explain how a part of the body or a machine works, or report on a readout from a machine or instrument. They might even testify about how widely beliefs or practices are accepted in some domain – such as profession. As, however, the subject matter becomes less settled or controversial then it is more likely that the evidence will be understood as opinion rather than fact.

As a general rule, when in doubt it is useful to classify interpretive statements as opinion so that the protections afforded by the *UEA* (and common law) might be brought into play.

Although ss 76 and 79(1) do not apply to evidence of fact, a witness testifying to factual matters relating to specialised knowledge will ordinarily need to be able to demonstrate that they possess 'training, study or experience' and knowledge relevant to the proffered factual evidence.

177 For further information on ss 79(2), (3) and 108C, see A Cossins and J Delahunty, 'Misconceptions of Expert Evidence in Child Sexual Assault Trials: Enhancing Justice and Jurors' Common Sense' (2013) 22 *Journal of Judicial Administration* 171; J Goodman-Delahunty, N Martschuk and A Cossins, 'What Australian Jurors Know and Do Not Know about Evidence of Child Sexual Abuse' (2017) 41 *Criminal Law Journal* 86. See also the research and reports of the Royal Commission into Institutional Responses to Child Sexual Abuse, <https://www.childabuseroyalcommission.gov.au>.

Opinion Based on Specialised Knowledge and Judicial Exclusion: *UEA*, ss 135 and 137

In general, Australian judges have been reluctant to assess the probative value of opinions based on specialised knowledge when applying the mandatory and discretionary exclusions because the probative value of evidence is considered a prerogative of the trier of fact. *IMM* confirmed that, when undertaking the balancing exercise, trial judges are not to consider the reliability of the evidence or the credibility of the witness, but rather to treat the evidence as though the jury would *accept* it – to take the evidence 'at its highest'.[178] In practice, inattention to validity studies, proficiency tests, error rates and so forth makes it difficult, in many cases, to meaningfully assess probative value (including 'at its highest') or to gauge the magnitude of risks of unfair prejudice to the defendant (as well as the waste of time and resources, and the risk of confusion). Judicial reluctance to attend to the reliability of expert opinion evidence, along with real dangers of unfair prejudice to defendants, created by the admission of weak, speculative and unreliable opinions, along with inattention to cognitive bias, has practically eviscerated ss 135 and 137 as criminal trial safeguards.

A handful of very recent decisions suggest that some courts are endeavouring to address reliability concerns within the constraints of the existing rules and jurisprudence. Courts in Victoria (and Queensland) addressed reliability issues when considering the probative value and danger of unfair prejudice in s 137 (and under *Christie*, its common law equivalent).[179]

---

178 *IMM* [2016] HCA 14; 257 CLR 300. See also G Edmond, 'Icarus and the *Evidence Act*: Section 137, probative value and taking forensic science evidence "at its highest"' (2017) 41 *Melbourne University Law Review* 106.

179 See, eg, *Volpe* [2020] VSCA 628 and *Crupi (Ruling No 1)* [2020] VSC 654. Compare the common law in Queensland: *Pentland* [2020] QSCPR 10.

Chapter 13

Identification Evidence

Introduction

Identification evidence, broadly defined, links an accused or suspect (or in some cases another person) to a location or activity that is relevant in some way to the facts in issue. Generally, in criminal cases, what is of most interest is an identification that places the accused at the scene of the crime or at a location associated with the charged crime.[1] This could extend to the identification of a vehicle or other item associated with the accused. Expanding the field out from the accused, relevant evidence might also include an eyewitness identifying the victim at a relevant location, or at a particular time.[2] For example, in *Simmons*, the disputed identification was of the deceased, purportedly seen at a time that undermined the Crown case as to the alleged time of the murder.[3] Similarly, in *Milat*,[4] the defence introduced evidence that one of the victims had been sighted after the time that, according to the Crown case, she had been killed by Milat. Supplementing, or in some cases replacing, evidence from an eyewitness it is now becoming more common for an accused (or other relevant person or object) to be identified from surveillance footage, or from public and private recordings,[5] or from images posted on social media sites such as Facebook.[6] These identifications may be made by a police officer, or a member of the public, or a witness who was present at the scene, or indeed by a 'super-recogniser'.[7] We have also seen a rise in the use and promotion of automated facial recognition systems, potentially

1 See, eg, the discussion in *Allan* [2017] NSWCCA 6, [81].

2 *Milat* (unreported, NSWSC, 23 April 1996, Hunt CJ at CL). See also *Wood* [2012] NSWCCA 21, [391]-[434] where a number of witnesses gave evidence that they had seen a girl resembling the deceased, Caroline Byrne, in the vicinity of where her body was later found in the company of two men (one of whom, the Crown argued, was the accused, Gordon Wood) – evidence that was reviewed again in *Wood v New South Wales* [2018] NSWSC 1247.

3 *Simmons (No 7)* [2015] NSWSC 574.

4 Above n 2.

5 A new source of recorded images may also be mobile recordings made by members of the public, or by police themselves. See discussion in C McKay and M Lee, 'Body-worn images: Point-of-view and the new aesthetics of policing' [2019] *Crime Media Culture* 1.

6 P McGorrery, 'The limited impact of Facebook and the displacement effect on the admissibility of identification evidence' (2015) 39 *Crim Law Journal* 208. McGorrery argues that the risks of displacement and the effect of the suggestive context in which many Facebook images appear was not adequately recognised in the cases examined.

7 M Ramon, AK Bobak and D White, 'Super-recognisers: from the lab to the world and back again' (2019) 110 *British Journal of Psychology* 461.

able to offer real time or rapid identifications.[8] With the rise of surveillance, voice identification and voice comparisons, drawing on covert recordings, are also becoming a more frequent feature of criminal trials. Finally, it is important to remember that the accused may be linked to the relevant location by way of trace evidence, such as DNA evidence, GPS or phone location data, or other forensic comparison evidence such as fingerprints or shoe prints.

However, despite the proliferation of these different types and techniques of identification, including the increasing reliance on CCTV and other surveillance images for identification, and the concomitant increasing reliance on the testimony of experts to mediate the introduction of evidence of identification, *eye*witness identification evidence continues to be considered the paradigmatic, and most problematic, form of identification evidence.[9] This is reflected in the structure and provisions of Part 3.9 of the *UEA*.[10] This Part applies solely to criminal trials and focuses almost exclusively on eyewitness identification. For while the Act's definition of 'identification evidence' includes identification of the accused by voice, smell or touch, only eyewitness identification of the accused is subject to a specific and detailed regime – encompassing visual identification parades and certain, limited, photo identification procedures – regulating its *admissibility*. The admissibility of other forms of identification evidence (broadly defined) is governed by general evidentiary provisions, namely, ss 55, 135 and 137. Some identification-related evidence, such as forensic trace evidence (for example, DNA evidence), will be regulated by other exclusionary rules (such as s 79).[11] In addition, the collection of trace evidence, including forensic samples, is regulated separately.

This chapter provides an overview and critical analysis of the way in which the *UEA* regulates the admission of identification evidence in criminal trials. Additionally, it provides an overview of research on the frailties intrinsic to visual and voice identification. This includes examining positive and negative identification evidence, eye and ear witness identification, and identification that is not from a witness at the scene of the crime but is 'displaced' in that the witness gives evidence about a surveillance recording or some other form of identification. We begin with the well-recognised frailties of eyewitness identification. These

---

8 See C Garvie, A Bedoya and J Frankle, *The Perpetual Line-Up: Unregulated Police Facial Recognition in America* (Center on Privacy and Technology, Georgetown Law, October 18, 2016), <https://www.perpetuallineup.org/>. In Australia, see Senate Standing Committee for the Scrutiny of Bills, Scrutiny digest, 2, 2018, The Senate, 14 February 2018, pp 14-15 (Passports Bill), 20-8 (IMS Bill) and <https://www.aph.gov.au/Parliamentary_Business/Bills_Legislation/bd/bd1920a/20bd021>. See also PJ Phillips et al, 'Face recognition accuracy of forensic examiners, super-recognizers, and face recognition algorithms' (2018) 115 *PNAS* 6171, that considers the accuracy of hybrid systems.

9 It is notable, for example, that a recent major report from the National Academy of Sciences in the United States *Identifying the Culprit, Assessing Eyewitness Identification* (National Academies Press, 2015) devotes only one paragraph to the risks posed to traditional eyewitness identifications by the increased circulation of images of suspects via social media and other platforms. This report makes no mention at all of identifications made directly from images, or any other forms of identification, such as voice identification.

10 See *UEA*, ss 114-116.

11 The Australian Law Reform Commission in its final report ALRC 102 considered the question of whether the definition of 'identification evidence' in the UEA included DNA evidence, but concluded that arguments that the definition might be interpreted this broadly were fanciful. In *Simmons*, the defence argued, unsuccessfully, that swabs taken in the course of a forensic procedure, came within the definition of 'identification evidence' within the Act. See *Simmons (No 7)* [2015] NSWSC 574, [74].

weaknesses have caused or contributed to a significant number of wrongful convictions.[12] This preliminary section sets the scene for understanding the initial responses of the Australian courts, via the development of a requirement that judges issue strong warnings to juries, as well as how these expectations were incorporated into the *UEA*. It also provides a basis to reflect on the need to broaden and develop these provisions, particularly in relation to the definition of 'identification evidence' in the *UEA*, which confines the scope of Part 3.9. One might also consider why voice identification, which is increasingly being shown to be as prone to error as visual identification, is not subject to a process equivalent to a line-up. The limited scope of Part 3.9, combined with its outmoded emphasis on the benefits of live identification parades within the *UEA* is blunting the exclusionary force of Part 3.9 and of the Act more broadly as a means of regulating evidence that is prone to error. Further, the limited examples of exclusion of identification evidence obtained in flawed circumstances under s 137, the faith in the efficacy of conventional trial safeguards such as cross-examination, and the clear preference to rely on warnings over exclusion, raises questions about the extent to which courts have truly embraced the history of miscarriages of justice linked to misidentification.

Eyewitness Evidence and the Problem of Assessing Reliability

Misidentification, wrongful convictions and research on eyewitness memory

> The mendacious consequence of these forces is the mis-application of the criminal label. *The Innocents* collects a group of men who look sufficiently like rapists of white women that the corresponding label has been appended to them. The criminal justice system, through its crude methods of evaluating identification evidence, permits the smooth shift from resemblance to recognition, in the process also implicating crime's victims in law's violence. Mostly young, mostly not-white, the men in these photographs – but for the incremental differentiations disclosed through DNA technology – are legally indistinguishable from men who are sexual predators and violent killers.[13]

Awareness of the frailties of eyewitness identification is longstanding, dating back over a century. Significantly, the recognition of the potential contribution of psychological science to understanding and evaluating witness testimony has a similarly long history.[14] One of the earliest English cases that highlighted the difficulties and risks was that of Adolf Beck.

---

12 The most well-known documentation of cases where mistaken identification has contributed to wrongful convictions comes from the US based, Innocence Project. See further below at pp 565-567, 656. In Australia, cases such as *Bromley* [2018] SASCFC 41 continue to raise troubling questions about the safety of convictions relying on dubious eyewitness identification.

13 K Biber, 'Photographs and Labels: Against a Criminology of Innocence' (2006) 10 *Law Text Culture* 20, 25, discussing Taryn Simon's photographic series, *The Innocents*. In the series, Simon photographs men (and one woman) who were convicted on the basis of identification evidence, but who have been exonerated through the work of the Innocence Project and subsequent DNA testing of trace evidence from the scene. Most of the subjects are photographed at the scene of their putative crime and some alongside the witness who originally identified them: <http://www.tarynsimon.com/works_innocents.php>.

14 See, eg, H Münsterberg, *On the Witness Stand: Essays on Psychology and Crime* (Doubleday, 1908).

J Hunter and K Cronin, *Evidence, Advocacy and Ethical Practice: A Criminal Trial Commentary*

(Butterworths, 1995) 394-5 (footnotes omitted)

> One notable English case concerned Adolf Beck who in 1895 was identified by a dozen women as the man who had inveigled each of them into an intimate relationship and then persuaded them to hand over various valuables before disappearing. In the late 1870s, when Beck was in South America, a John Smith had been convicted and imprisoned in England for a series of similar frauds. At Beck's trial the prosecution case was founded on the assumption that Beck and Smith were one and the same. Two police officers from Smith's 1877 case testified that Beck was Smith. As a result of the identification evidence of the women and the police officers, Beck was convicted of the frauds. Beck's prison records assumed that he was the John Smith convicted and imprisoned in the 1870s. The Crown case against Beck also included circumstantial evidence. Beck was unable to prove any alibis, and he had in his possession pawn tickets for women's jewellery, although none of the pawned jewellery belonged to the women victims. The Crown case against Beck also contained certain inconsistencies. The witnesses described the culprit as well-dressed, as speaking with a foreign accent and as writing fluently. Beck wore shabby clothes and was not a fluent writer. One of the victims had been certain that Beck was not the culprit. Despite these inconsistencies, the cumulative strength of the circumstantial evidence, when combined with the identification evidence, convinced the jury. Beck was convicted and imprisoned for seven years. He petitioned the Home Office on the ground that he had been wrongly identified, arguing that as he had been in South America when the frauds first occurred in the 1870s, the Crown case was defective. A Home Office minute described this argument as a 'clever ruse' because it presented an alibi that the Crown could not answer: see ER Watson (ed), *Adolf Beck* (1877–1904), William Hodge & Co Ltd, London, 1924.
>
> After Beck's release from gaol similar frauds were reported. In 1904 Beck was again charged and convicted. This time four women identified him as the person who had tricked them into intimacy and into parting with their possessions. Whilst Beck was in custody awaiting sentencing John Smith was caught red-handed. Smith fitted the descriptions given by his various victims, including their information that the fraudster was circumcised. This information accorded with Smith's prison records relating to the 1877 conviction. Beck was not circumcised. Beck received a pardon and £5,000 compensation. The case led to the introduction of the practice of trial judges warning juries of the dangers of relying on identification evidence whenever a prosecution case was wholly or substantially based on such evidence.

The Beck case highlighted the limits of appeal mechanisms for the wrongly convicted, and it served as the impetus for the establishment of a Court of Criminal Appeal in the United Kingdom. It exemplifies the powerful effect of eyewitness identification since it appears that in this case the identification evidence was able to overpower exculpatory evidence. A contemporary equivalent would be the case of Farah Jama, where strong exculpatory evidence was ignored in the face of what appeared to be convincing DNA evidence.[15] It also demonstrates that misidentifications can arise even in circumstances where the witnesses were, presumably, relatively familiar with the 'real' John Smith, and, further, that mistakes can be made by multiple witnesses. Contemporaneous accounts of the Beck case pointed out that the mistakes made demonstrated the difficulties of distinguishing between people who closely resemble one another. However, those

---

15 See J Gans, 'Ozymandias on Trial: Wrongs and Rights in DNA Cases' in P Roberts and J Hunter (eds), *Criminal Evidence and Human Rights: Reimagining Common Law Procedural Traditions* (Hart Publishing, 2012).

Figure 1: Adolf Beck (top) and John Smith

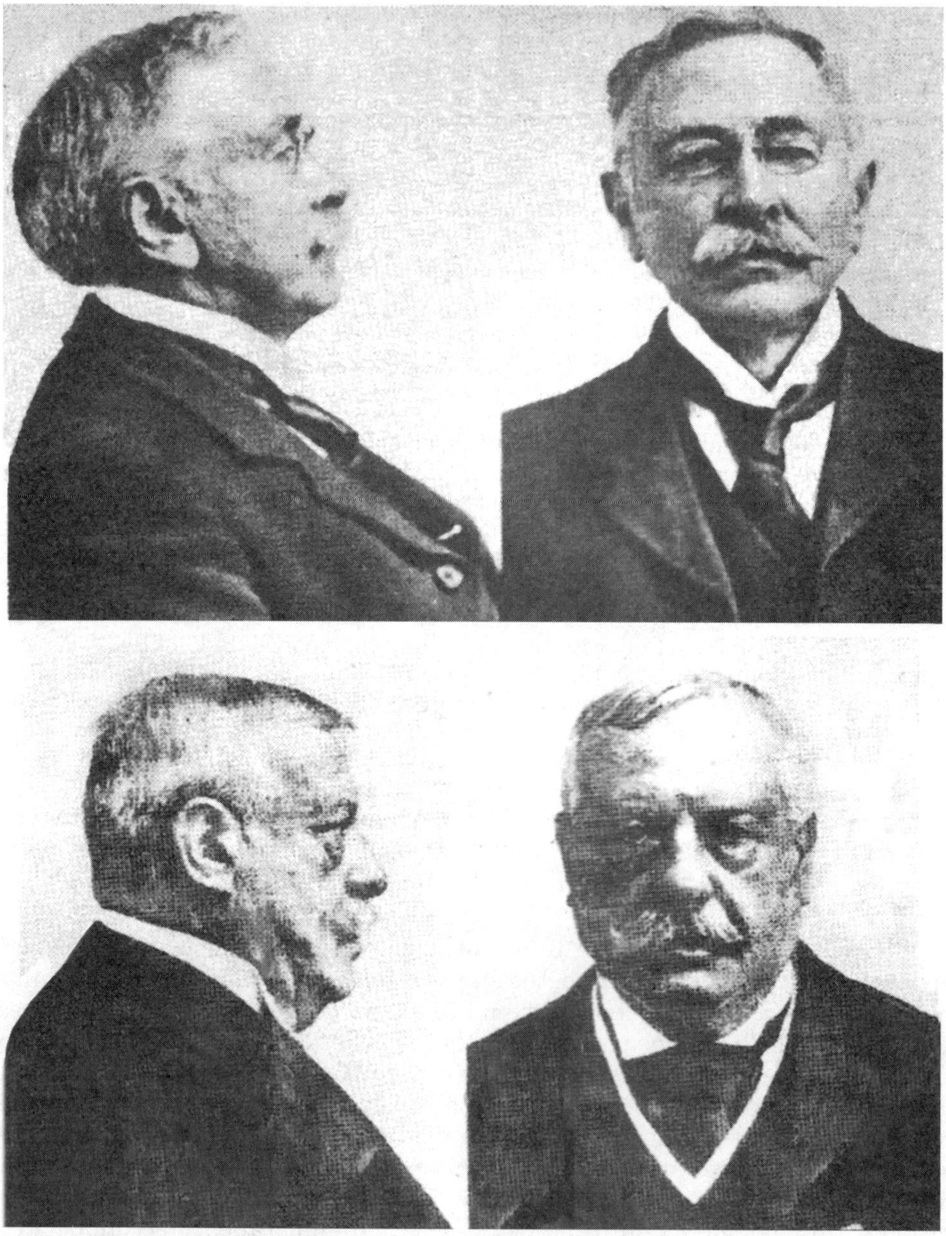

Public Domain via Wiki Media;
Commons: <http://commons.wikimedia.org/wiki/File%3AAdolfBeckMugshot.jpg>

accounts were not yet able to engage with the contextual prejudices and cognitive processes that can facilitate misidentifications and enhance the confidence of eyewitnesses discussed further below. Similarly, early awareness of the risks of misidentification did not generally engage with the suggestive evidence-gathering practices that have been of particular concern in the US jurisprudence, and remain a part of its criminal justice landscape.[16] In the Australian context, examples of suggestive evidence-gathering practices are revealed in cases such as *Mallard*,[17] where poorly conducted identification procedures compounded the effect of police and prosecutorial misconduct.

The resources available to the legal system to inform a cautionary approach to eyewitness evidence have expanded rapidly since the 1970s. At this time, experimental psychologists came to realise that basic research on vision and memory could be applied to address the specific forensic conditions and procedures related to eyewitness identification. Similarly, general research on face recognition and processing can also be applied to eyewitness and other identification tasks.[18] The development of a distinct field of *applied* eyewitness research owes much to the pioneering work of Elizabeth Loftus and it is now characterised by an extensive and diverse literature.[19] This literature is now being developed in the areas of image comparison and image based recognition tasks, including a burgeoning field of research into individual differences.[20] Basic research into memory has established that the processes by, and through, which memories are encoded, stored and retrieved are complex, but it is critical to understand that a memory is non-veridical – that is to say, it is not the case that a memory of an event, once laid down, will remain intact and unchanged throughout subsequent interactions or events:

> Like vision, memory is also beset by noise. Encoding, storage, and remembering are not passive, static processes that record, retain, and divulge their contents in an informational vacuum, unaffected by outside influences. The contents cannot be treated as a veridical permanent record, like photographs stored in a safe. On the contrary, the fidelity of our memories for real events may be compromised by many factors at all stages of processing, from encoding through storage, to the final stages of retrieval.[21]

---

16 See, eg, cases discussed in BL Garrett, 'Eyewitnesses and Exclusion' (2012) 65 *Vanderbilt Law Review* 451, especially at 473-4, as well as a number of cases dealt with by the Innocence Project, discussed below. Significantly, the national admissibility jurisprudence in the US has been apparently concerned with suggestive procedures, but, as pointed out by Wells and others, the tests developed by the courts to ameliorate the risks associated with suggestion may have proved to be counterproductive. See GL Wells and DS Quinlivan, 'Suggestive Eyewitness Identification Procedures and the Supreme Court's Reliability Test in Light of Eyewitness Science: 30 Years Later' (2009) 33 *Law and Human Behavior* 1, discussing the shortcomings of the US Supreme Court's decision in *Manson v Braithwaite* 432 US 98 (1977).

17 [2005] HCA 68; 224 CLR 125. See Chapters 2 and 7.

18 For example, D White, RI Kemp, R Jenkins, M Matheson and AM Burton, 'Passport Officers' Errors in Face Matching' (2014) 9(8) *Public Library of Science [PLoS ONE]* e103510.

19 See, eg, R Wilcock, R Bull and R Milne, *Witness identification in criminal cases: psychology and practice* (Oxford University Press, 2008), ch 1; E Loftus and JC Palmer, 'Reconstruction of Automobile Destruction: An example of the interaction between language and memory' (1974) 13 *Journal of Verbal Learning and Verbal Behaviour* 585.

20 R Jenkins et al, 'Are Super-face-recognisers Also Super-voice-recognisers? Evidence from Cross-modal Identification Tasks' (2020) PsyArXiv, 3 January (doi:10.31234/osf.io/7xdp3); A Towler, RI Kemp, V Bruce, AM Burton, JD Dunn and D White, 'Are face recognition abilities in humans and sheep really 'comparable'? (2019) R Soc open sci.6: 180772, <http://dx.doi.org/10.1098/rsos.180772>.

21 *Identifying the Culprit*, above n 9, 60.

In this 2015 report, the US National Academy of Sciences outlines the extensive basic research that is applicable to eyewitness memory before turning to the specific context of eyewitness identification. Building on the influential classification developed initially by Gary Wells, the report outlines the two types of variables that will affect the quality of identification evidence – estimator and system variables. *Estimator variables* can be investigated, and their effects in respect of individual witnesses can be 'estimated', but critically they are the variables that are outside of the control of the criminal justice system:

> The accuracy and reliability of eyewitness identification are critically modulated by variables that include a witness' extant cognition and memory and related psychological and situational factors at the time of the event, over the ensuing intervals, and at all stages of recall. ... Estimator variables affect the accuracy of eyewitness identification, but they are beyond the control of the criminal justice system. Estimator variables tend to be associated with characteristics of the witness or factors that are operating either at the time of the criminal event (perhaps relating to memory encoding) or the retention interval (the time between witnessing an event and the identification process). Specific examples include the eyewitness' level of stress or trauma at the time of the incident, the light level and nature of the visual conditions that affect visibility and the clarity of a perpetrator's features, and the physical distance between the witness and the perpetrator.[22]

It is now also well established that cross-race identification is especially problematic and that a witness's capacity to recognise an unfamiliar face or person may be affected by an 'own race bias' – that is, we are more likely to make errors when attempting to identify people who are of a different race or ethnicity.[23] Similarly, research indicates that accuracy may also be affected by equivalent 'same gender' and 'own age' biases.[24] This is further complicated if a witness's perception of events is also moderated by expectations and stereotypes in which racial or other biases are implicated.[25] Further, recognition of the suspect may be compromised by displacement, by which the features of an (innocent) bystander are displaced and become the remembered features of the offender.[26]

---

22 Ibid 16. See also GL Wells, 'Applied eyewitness-testimony research: System variables and estimator variables' (1978) 36 *Journal of Personality and Social Psychology* 1546, <https://doi.org/10.1037/0022-3514.36.12.1546>.

23 See, eg, N Brewer and GL Wells, 'Eyewitness Identification' (2011) 201 *Current Directions in Psychological Science* 24, 24; *Identifying the Culprit*, above n 9, 96; and GL Wells and LE Hasel, 'Eyewitness Identification: Issues in Common Knowledge and Generalization' in E Borgida and ST Fiske (eds), *Beyond Common Sense: Psychological Science in the Courtroom* (Blackwell Publishing, 2008), 161. See *Afu and Caleo (No 11)* [2018] NSWSC 190.

24 For work that indicates that 'same gender bias' (as well as 'age bias') which can give rise to equivalent effects to 'same race' bias, see, eg, MA Palmer, N Brewer and R Horry, 'Understanding Gender Bias in Face Recognition: Effects of Divided Attention at Encoding' (2013) 142 *Acta Psychologica* 362 and V Proiettia and S Laurence et al, 'Attending to identity cues reduces the own-age but not the own-race recognition advantage' (2019) 157 *Vision Research* 184.

25 See, eg, Wilcock, Bull and Milne, above n 19, ch 4. See also <http://www.innocenceproject.org/news-events-exonerations/race-and-wrongful-convictions>.

26 Most often discussed in the context of photographs (see below) this effect can also occur during live events. It is important to note, however, that displacement effects can fall into both the category of 'estimator' and 'system' variables. Displacement (or the risk of displacement) can occur prior to the witness's engagement with any formal identification process, but it can also arise if formal procedures are inattentive to the risks of allowing a witness to make multiple attempts to identify an offender using the same or similar images of the suspect. One of the more well known cases where the identification procedure gave rise to a form of displacement was that involving Ronald Cotton: see, eg, the discussion in KM Polimeni, 'New York on Eyewitness Identifications: Progressive or Regressive?' (2018) 68 *Syracuse Law Review* 635, 642. It can also occur where a witness is shown CCTV footage of an event, and then asked to formally identify

By contrast, system variables are more amenable to control by law enforcement and investigative procedures, and to being regulated by courts:

> System variables describe the characteristics of specific procedures and practices (eg, the content and nature of instructions given to witnesses who are asked if they are able to make an identification). The criminal justice system can exert some control over system variables by following standardized procedures that are based on scientific knowledge and strengthened through education and training. One important category of system variables concerns the conditions and protocols for lineup identification. Under current law enforcement practice, eyewitness identification procedures involve having a witness view individuals or images of individuals. Research indicates that accuracy and reliability of eyewitness identifications may be influenced by the type of presentation (eg, lineup) used, the likeness of non-suspect lineup participants (fillers) to the suspect, the number of fillers, and the suspect's physical location in the presentation. Eyewitness performance may be affected by how the lineup images are presented – simultaneously (as a group) or sequentially (one at a time). System variables, such as the nature of the instructions and feedback provided before and after the identification procedure, may also affect the eyewitness' identification.[27]

While the proportion of cases involving mistaken eyewitness identification has fallen slightly over time, it remains the most prevalent factor contributing to the wrongful convictions uncovered by the Innocence Project. Approximately 69% of the cases where the Project has established factual innocence involved at least one mistaken eyewitness.[28] A number of reforms have been recommended by the Innocence Project[29] and the US National Research Council's report[30] to improve the way in which eyewitness evidence is collected and managed. As has been pointed out by a number of commentators, eyewitness testimony (and memory evidence more generally) needs to be treated in the same way as other trace evidence, such that active steps need to be taken to ensure that it is collected, and then preserved, in ways that will enhance its reliability.[31] While it is not possible to control for the estimator variables that may affect the quality of the evidence, it is possible to put in place procedures to address system variables. The reforms that have received most support in the literature include:

Follow a 'double-blind' procedure: A 'double-blind' line-up is one in which neither the person administering the line-up nor the eyewitness knows who the

---

an offender via, for example, a photoboard procedure. See *Dickman* [2017] HCA 24; 261 CLR 601, discussed further below.

27 *Identifying the Culprit*, above n 9, 17.

28 The figure was 77% across the first 225 exonerations. See <http://www.innocenceproject.org/understand/Eyewitness-Misidentification.php>. Some of those who were exonerated were mistakenly identified by multiples witnesses. In many of the cases additional factors, such as invalidated or improper forensics procedures also played a role. The National Register of Exonerations reports that some type of misidentification was implicated in 75% of the first 1365 cases logged in their database. This database differentiates between deliberate falsehoods, tainted (or suggestively elicited) misidentifications and mistaken identifications, with the latter associated with approximately 30% of the 2578 cases listed as at April 2020. See K Jackson and S Gross, *Tainted Identifications* (September 2016), <http://www.law.umich.edu/special/exonseration/Pages/taintedids.aspx>.

29 See <http://www.innocenceproject.org/free-innocent/improve-the-law/fact-sheets/eyewitness-identification-reform>.

30 See *Identifying the Culprit*, above n 9. See also T Valentine and R Fitzgerald, 'Identifying the Culprit: An international perspective on the National Academy of Sciences Report on Eyewitness Identification Evidence' (2016) *Applied Cognitive Psychology* 135.

31 See, eg, Foreword by Brian Clifford to Wilcock, Bull and Milne, above n 19, v.

suspect is. This is an important aspect of avoiding inadvertent influence before or during selection, including providing confirmatory feedback.[32]

Give instructions to the witness to avoid, as far as possible, the eyewitness feeling compelled to make a selection. The most significant of these will be an instruction that informs the witness that the person they saw may or may not be present in the line-up (or among the photographs).[33]

Composing the line-up: A suspect photograph should be selected that does not draw attention to the suspect. Obvious distortions that will affect the functional size of the line-up will occur if a line-up is composed such that the suspect is the only person matching a key element of the witness's description. Less obvious is the recommendation that the foils or fillers (that is, non-suspect photographs and/or live line-up members) should be selected based on their *resemblance to the description provided by the witness* – as opposed to their resemblance to the police suspect.[34]

Confidence statements: Immediately following the line-up procedure, *and before they have received any feedback from the administrator*, the eyewitness should provide a statement, in their own words, describing their level of confidence in the identification they have just made. This takes into account that confirmatory feedback can significantly affect witnesses not only through enhancing their confidence at a later stage, but also their recall of their level of confidence at the time the identification was made.[35] 'Confirmation' bias can arise in situations where there is explicit confirmatory feedback, but also from more subtle cues and prompts.[36]

The line-up procedure should be documented: Ideally, the line-up procedure should be electronically recorded. If this is impracticable, an audio or written record should be made.[37]

There are conflicting studies on the benefits of sequential[38] (one-by-one) presentation of line-ups instead of simultaneous (all at once) line-ups. The Innocence Project endorsed the use of sequential line-up procedures but does not currently include it in its list of recommendations in order to 'ensure that critical eyewitness reforms ... are not blocked because of concerns about sequential presentation'. Sequential line-ups are associated with a lower false positive rate, but also a lower rate of correct identifications, and a more significant concern is

---

32 Recommendation 2, *Identifying the Culprit*, above n 9, 106.

33 See, eg, N Brewer and MA Palmer, 'Eyewitness Identification Tests' (2010) 15 *Legal and Criminological Psychology* 77, 83; and Recommendation 3, *Identifying the Culprit*, above n 9, 107.

34 See, eg, Brewer and Palmer, ibid, 80. Filler characteristics include gender, race, hair length and colour, facial hair, height, skin tone.

35 See, eg, discussion in Wells and Hasel, above n 23, 164, of a UK study on actual eyewitnesses which confirmed that answers to questions such as, 'How good a view did you have of the suspect' either after making their identifications or after they were told they had picked a suspect or an innocent filler. The results indicated that witnesses' recollections changed depending on the feedback. See DB Wright and EM Skagerberg, 'Post Identification Feedback Affects Real Eyewitnesses' (2007) 18 *Psychological Science* 172.

36 See also G Edmond, K Martire and M San Roque, 'Unsound Law: Issues with ("Expert") Voice Comparison Evidence' (2011) 35 *Melbourne University Law Review* 52.

37 See, eg, Recommendations 4 and 5 from *Identifying the Culprit*, above n 9, 108.

38 <http://innocenceproject.org/news-events-exonerations/sequential-presentation-of-lineups?searchterm=sequential+lin>.

that some of the research indicates that a sequential line-up is *more* susceptible to investigator interference.[39] The National Academy of Sciences did not endorse or recommend the use of sequential line-ups, concluding that 'the question as to whether a simultaneous or sequential line-up is preferred is a specific case of the more general question of what conditions might improve the performance of an eyewitness'.[40] Nonetheless, aside from the divergence on sequential versus simultaneous line-ups, there is significant correspondence between the Innocence Project recommendations and the recommendations of the National Academy of Sciences report.[41] In the following section, we review legal responses in Australia to growing awareness of the risks associated with the admission of eyewitness testimony, starting with the development of specific warnings (to jurors) and then turning to the restructuring of the admissibility of identification evidence under the *UEA*.

Recognising the special need for caution in Australia: admissibility, weight and warnings

One of the key difficulties in relation to eyewitness testimony is that identification witnesses will often appear highly confident and have an *honest* belief in the accuracy of their evidence, in circumstances where there may be little or no correlation between these levels of confidence and actual accuracy. This was noted 40 years ago in the influential report from the UK Devlin Inquiry.[42] A useful summary of its findings is captured by the 2006 Australian Law Reform Commission (ALRC) Report:

> The danger of identification is that anyone in this country may be wrongly convicted on the evidence of a witness who is perfectly sincere, perfectly convinced that the accused is the man they saw, and whose sincerity communicates itself to the members of the jury who therefore accept the evidence.[43]

The Devlin Report relied extensively on psychological research and was extensively cited in the ALRC reports published in the 1980s. As the Devlin Report observed, eyewitness evidence is dangerous because of its deceptive and beguiling strength, features that are often impervious to exposure through cross-examination. The impact of this research can be clearly seen as common law cases in Australia and elsewhere instituted an obligation to warn the fact-finder highlighting a special need for caution in determining the weight to be accorded to the evidence of an eyewitness. And, as discussed further below, it has clearly shaped the statutory regime implemented in the *UEA*.[44] However, while

---

39 For an overview of the controversy concerning the use of sequential over simultaneous line-ups, see R Kemp and D White, 'Face Identification' in D Groome and MW Wysenck et al (eds), *An Introduction to Applied Cognitive Psychology* (Routledge, 2nd ed, 2016).

40 *Identifying the Culprit*, above n 9, 80. See also the substantial archive at <http://wells.socialpsychology.org/>.

41 Noting also concerns as to the generalisability or applicability of experimental laboratory studies to the 'real world' of the investigation and trial, the National Academy of Sciences also recommended further applied research.

42 Departmental Committee on Evidence of Identification in Criminal Cases, *Report to the Secretary of State for the Home Department of the Departmental Committee on Evidence of Identification in Criminal Cases* (1976) (Devlin Report).

43 See ALRC, *Uniform Evidence Law* (Report No 102, 2006), [13.5].

44 See, in particular, ALRC, *Evidence (Interim)* (Report No 26, 1985) Vol 1, ch 18.

awareness of the dangers and risks associated with eyewitness identification is longstanding, systematic responses, in the form of developed and restrictive law enforcement procedures and a robust *exclusionary* jurisprudence, have been surprisingly slow to develop. And, in some jurisdictions, even the routine use of warnings is not uncontroversial.[45]

And, while excluding evidence from a key witness can in some case be difficult in the context of the conduct of a particular trial,[46] it is nonetheless worth noting that it was accepted by the ALRC in 1985 that judicial warnings were, by themselves, inadequate to avoid the dangers associated with an identification of low probative value:

> A reading of reported Australian cases leaves the impression of a reluctance on the part of trial judges to exclude eyewitness identification evidence, however unreliable or weak it may seem. Instead reliance is placed on the warning to the jury and appellate courts give lengthy statements about the appropriate detail of such warnings. So, even evidence of identification which is so liable to being mistaken that it would be 'extremely dangerous for a jury to assign any probative value to it' may be properly admitted so long as a warning is given to the jury in such terms.[47]

However, despite this, and the apparently exclusionary orientation that informed the development of the *UEA* provisions in Part 3.9, directions and warnings remain an important, and it seems courts' default, response to the risks associated with unreliable identification evidence.[48] Important to this approach is the influential case of *Domican*, in which the High Court outlined the need for the judge to address in detailed and specific terms the weaknesses in incriminating identification evidence.[49] The *UEA*, through ss 116 and 165(5) (and in Victoria, the *Jury Directions Act 2015* (Vic) (*JDA 2015* (Vic))), built on the case of *Domican* and its English predecessors. As can be seen in this extract, consistent with the common law's longstanding concern about the reliability of eyewitness identification, many of the factors identified in the social science literature have found their way into the case law. But, despite the significant weaknesses associated with identification evidence, the focus of law reform has been on addressing concerns regarding the evidence by adequate warnings, not on the case for exclusion.

45 The US jurisprudence has only recently started to incorporate more stringent principles in relation to, for example, requiring warnings or regulating the procedures relating to the conduct of parades, and these trends are not uniform. See, eg, discussion in KM Polimeni, 'New York on eyewitness identifications: progressive or regressive?' (2018) 68(3) *Syracuse Law Review* 660.

46 See discussion of *Dickman* [2017] HCA 24; 261 CLR 601 below.

47 ALRC, *Evidence (Interim)*, above n 44, [424].

48 As discussed in Chapter 14 and also further below in relation to *Dickman* [2017] HCA 24; 261 CLR 601. In particular, the High Court case of *IMM* [2016] HCA 14; 257 CLR 300 has also had a significant impact in so far as it makes it more difficult for a trial judge to exclude evidence where the probative value is low.

49 The corresponding case from England is *Turnbull* [1977] QB 224, which also informs the approach in Canada, see *Hay* [2013] 3 SCR 694, though the Canadian courts have also indicated that a case that relies solely on eyewitness identification cannot be left to the jury. The risks of witness suggestion (and related due process concerns) were considered by the US Supreme Court in *Perry v New Hampshire* 132 S Ct 716 (2012). Noting that the judicial instructions sometimes given to address evidence that may be affected by suggestion are inadequate, the National Academy of Sciences has recommended that a uniform set of model jury instructions be developed. See Recommendation 9, *Identifying the Culprit*, above n 9, 112. See also *State v Henderson* 27 A 3d 872 (NJ, 2011) and related discussion in ch 3 of *Identifying the Culprit*.

Domican

[1992] HCA 13; 173 CLR 555 (citations omitted)

Mason CJ, Deane, Dawson, Toohey, Gaudron and McHugh JJ:

The circumstances of the case

2. At about 5.50 pm on 27 January 1985, a gunman suddenly fired about 30 shots from an Armalite rifle in the direction of Mr Flannery as he and his wife were walking in the driveway of their home. The gunman was sitting in a green car parked at the front of the driveway. The Flannerys took cover behind the front of their car. A bullet went through Mr Flannery's hand as he pushed Mrs Flannery's head down. When the shooting stopped, she looked up and saw a man in the driver's seat of the car attempting to disconnect "a long square part of the gun". She said that she "just kept on watching him and he just kept on pulling at it and then when he couldn't get it out, after – I don't know how long it was – he just drove off". At the trial of the appellant, Mrs Flannery claimed that the gunman appeared to be wearing a wig and false moustache although, when first interviewed and in subsequent statements, she had not suggested that he was disguised. She also said that some weeks after the shooting she saw the gunman, without the wig or moustache, driving a milk truck near her home. Some time later she and her mother saw the appellant sitting in an orange Ford Falcon sedan at the end of her street. He ducked as they approached. The letters of the number plate were "HHI". A police officer gave evidence that in March 1985 he had seen an orange Ford Falcon sedan "HHI 627" parked outside the appellant's home. Mrs Flannery said that in April 1985 she recognised the appellant as the gunman after seeing him interviewed on four television programmes. But it was not until some months later that she informed the police that the appellant was the gunman. Indeed, in May 1985 she said she could not identify the gunman.

3. The Crown relied on confessional and circumstantial evidence as well as Mrs Flannery's evidence to support the charge against the appellant. …

5. Other witnesses gave evidence that, on the evening in question and after hearing loud noises in the street, they saw a green car driving past. One of the witnesses thought that there were three men in the car; another witness thought that there was one man in the front seat and one in the back seat. Another witness identified the car as a Mazda 121.

6. The son of Mr and Mrs Flannery testified that two days before the shooting he saw a person sitting in a dark green Mazda car parked in the street in which the Flannerys lived. He identified the appellant as the person sitting in the green Mazda after seeing him on one of the television programmes to which we have referred. …

The directions on identification

8. The learned trial judge gave the jury a very full direction on the dangers of acting on identification evidence. In particular, he instructed them that there were four important matters to be considered: whether the witness had previously known the person identified; how good an opportunity the witness had to get a clear picture of the person identified; how long had elapsed between the event and the first identification; and what were the circumstances and nature of that first identification. The appellant makes no complaint about the adequacy of these general warnings and instructions. But he contends that his Honour's directions on identification were inadequate because he failed to draw the jury's attention to a number of alleged weaknesses in the evidence of Mrs Flannery. In the Court of Criminal Appeal, Kirby ACJ, who gave the leading judgment, recorded ten matters in respect of which the appellant claimed that his Honour should have given "specific warnings" in relation to "particular dangers" "desirable" for the trial judge to have drawn these matters to the attention of the jury. It is unnecessary to set them out.

The adequacy of the directions on identification

9. In a criminal trial, the distinction between directions on matters of law and directions on matters of fact or argument is fundamental. A trial judge is bound to direct the

jury as to any principle of law or rule of practice applicable to the case, and a misdirection or non-direction on such a matter will usually mean that the trial has miscarried. But matters of fact and the arguments in relation to them are in a different category. A trial judge is not bound to discuss all the evidence or to analyse all the conflicts in the evidence and, by itself, the failure of a trial judge to do so does not mean that there has been any miscarriage of justice. … Consequently, the conduct of the case necessarily bears on the extent to which the judge is bound to comment on or discuss the evidence. Discussion or comment which is justified or required in one case may be neither required nor justified when a similar case is conducted in a different way.

10. The foregoing statements are applicable to all criminal cases including those where the prosecution relies on identification evidence as the whole or part of the proof of guilt of an offence. Nevertheless, the seductive effect of identification evidence has so frequently led to proven miscarriages of justice that courts of criminal appeal and ultimate appellate courts have felt obliged to lay down special rules in relation to the directions which judges must give in criminal trials where identification is a significant issue.

11. Whatever the defence and however the case is conducted, where evidence as to identification represents any significant part of the proof of guilt of an offence, the judge must warn the jury as to the dangers of convicting on such evidence where its reliability is disputed. The terms of the warning need not follow any particular formula. It must be appropriate to the circumstances of the case. Consequently, the jury must be instructed "as to the factors which may affect the consideration of (the identification) evidence in the circumstances of the particular case. A warning in general terms is insufficient. The attention of the jury "should be drawn to any weaknesses in the identification evidence". Reference to counsel's arguments is insufficient. The jury must have the benefit of a direction which has the authority of the judge's office behind it. It follows that the trial judge should isolate and identify for the benefit of the jury any matter of significance which may reasonably be regarded as undermining the reliability of the identification evidence.

12. In the present case, there were a number of significant weaknesses in the identification evidence. At the time of the shooting, Mrs Flannery did not know the appellant. Nearly nine months elapsed before she formally identified him from photographs which had been altered to show the appellant wearing a wig and a false moustache. By that time the appellant was a definite suspect, and Mrs Flannery had seen him on television on a number of occasions and allegedly in the vicinity of her home. When she saw the gunman, he was some distance away. She was hiding behind another vehicle. He was leaning across the passenger's seat. She alleged that the gunman was disguised. Her opportunity to observe him was fleeting. She said in evidence that things "happened so quick". Moreover, her first observation of the gunman took place after about 30 shots had been fired in her direction, after she had seen her husband shot through the hand, and after her husband had physically pushed her head down. As a result of the shooting, she suffered shock.

13. In addition, in early statements to the police Mrs Flannery did not claim that the gunman appeared to be wearing a wig and false moustache, although at the trial of the appellant she claimed that the gunman was so disguised. There was also a delay in the making of the identification. The incident occurred on 27 January 1985, yet Mrs Flannery did not make a formal statement to the police identifying the appellant as the gunman until 7 October 1985. Mrs Flannery also said to the police in May 1985 that she could not identify the gunman. At the trial she claimed that she was then too scared to do so. She also claimed to be distrustful of the police.

14. It is apparent, therefore, that the circumstances in which Mrs Flannery saw and came to identify the gunman raise serious doubts as to the reliability of her identification. Moreover, parts of her evidence were proved to be unreliable. She appears to have seen only one person in the car, yet the witnesses who saw the green car leave the scene shortly after the shooting said that there was more than one person in the car. Furthermore, she described the car as a green Jaguar, a make of car with which she was familiar. She also

claimed to have seen the appellant jogging near her home at a time when it was proved that his leg was in plaster.

15. Unfortunately, the learned trial judge's directions were not likely to impress upon the jury that the evidence of identification by Mrs Flannery had a number of weaknesses. His Honour told the jury that "(s)udden and unexpected acts of violence such as Mrs Flannery described in this case, can affect people caught up in the events in different ways." He said that the terror of the occasion "can serve to impress indelibly on the minds of some people the features of anyone they see involved in it. With other people the effect may be to obscure their judgment and their later recollection." He also raised the possibility of honest mistakes being made in identification and the need for caution when dealing with this type of evidence. But apart from these statements, his Honour's directions did not refer to any matters concerning Mrs Flannery's evidence which would bring the attention of the jury to the many weaknesses in her evidence. To the contrary, some parts of his Honour's directions were capable of conveying the impression that her evidence of identification was reliable. After pointing out to the jury that "(w)hat it is important to know is whether the identification was aided by any suggestion made to the witness or any expectation on the part of the witness at the time when it was made", his Honour recited the evidence of Mrs Flannery concerning the steps by which she came to identify the appellant. His Honour then said:

> "This is a case you might think where it was a recognition and realisation by the witness that 'that is the man' when it wasn't a circumstance in which there was any particular reason for her to believe that it was. It was a chance occurrence that she saw this man."

16. This passage may have been understood by the jury, as it was probably intended to be understood, as meaning that Mrs Flannery's identification was more reliable than usual because she had no expectation that the person in the milk truck, in the orange Ford Falcon sedan and on television was the person who had shot her husband …

18. However, as we have already pointed out, mere repetition of counsel's arguments is an insufficient discharge of the trial judge's duty to draw the jury's attention to any weaknesses in the identification evidence. If the matters to which counsel has referred may reasonably be regarded as undermining the reliability of the identification evidence, the trial judge must direct the jury that they are bound to take those matters into consideration in determining whether they will rely on that evidence. Consequently, the learned trial judge's directions on the issue of identification were not adequate and constituted a misdirection. …

20. … [T]he adequacy of a warning in an identification case must be evaluated in the context of the evidence in the case. But its adequacy is evaluated by reference to the identification evidence and not the other evidence in the case. The adequacy of the warning has to be evaluated by reference to the nature of the relationship between the witness and the person identified, the opportunity to observe the person subsequently identified, the length of time between the incident and the identification, and the nature and circumstances of the first identification – not by reference to other evidence which implicates the accused. A trial judge is not absolved from his or her duty to give general and specific warnings concerning the danger of convicting on identification evidence because there is other evidence, which, if accepted, is sufficient to convict the accused. The judge must direct the jury on the assumption that they may decide to convict solely on the basis of the identification evidence. If a trial judge has failed to give an adequate warning concerning identification, a new trial will ordinarily be ordered even when other evidence makes a very strong case against the accused. Of course, the other evidence in the case may be so compelling that a court of criminal appeal will conclude that the jury must have convicted on that evidence independently of the identification evidence. In such a case, the inadequacy of or lack of a warning concerning the identification evidence, although amounting to legal error, will not constitute a miscarriage of justice. But unless the Court of Criminal Appeal concludes that the jury must inevitably have convicted

the accused independently of the identification evidence, the inadequacy of or lack of a warning concerning that evidence constitutes a miscarriage of justice even though the other evidence made a strong case against the accused. …

Appeal Allowed. New trial ordered.

Regulating the Admissibility of Identification Evidence

The cautionary approach emphasised in *Domican* was an important step towards regularising the treatment of eyewitness identification evidence. But, as noted, it was limited to a consideration of the nature and scope of the warnings that needed to be given to a jury.[50] The introduction of the *UEA* established a new regime to govern the *admissibility* of evidence of identifications made from photographs and identification parades.[51] In addition to the established awareness of the risks associated with the honest, confident, but mistaken eyewitness, these changes drew also on the implications of existing social science and scientific research that had revealed the corrosive effects of suggestive procedures as well as a more comprehensive understanding of the frailties of memory, and the risks associated with the admission of mistaken (eyewitness) identifications. The sections in Part 3.9 only apply to criminal proceedings (s 113) and only to identification of the defendant in those proceedings. And reflecting the preoccupations of both the scientific and legal literature of the time, as discussed the regime applies only to a limited class of identifications – those performed by an (eye)witness, who was present at the scene or relevant location.

Overview of *UEA*, Part 3.9

The scope of the operation of the specific sections in Part 3.9 rely on three interrelated definitions, 'identification evidence' (defined in the *UEA* Dictionary), 'visual identification evidence' (defined in s 114), and 'picture identification evidence' (defined in s 115). Once again it is important to note that the regime only applies to identifications of the defendant and is structured so as to encourage the use of live parades. In the 1980s and 1990s, when the Act was drafted, it was assumed that live identification parades provided the best conditions for obtaining an identification, and that encouraging their use offers optimal protection against the dangers of unreliable identification evidence.[52] Live line-ups are thus promoted through a cascading structure of interrelated statutory conditions. Section 114 contains some of the threshold conditions that must be met for the admission of

---

50 The significance of implementing an obligation to warn a jury of the need to approach eyewitness identification with (special) caution should not be underestimated. As noted, what would now be regarded as an uncontroversial requirement in jurisdictions such as Australia and the UK, remains contentious in others. As noted in *Identifying the Culprit*, above n 9, this obligation has been resisted in a number of US jurisdictions, and consequently the report recommended the implementation of a set of national model jury instructions.

51 Except in Tasmania, where because the *Evidence Act 2001* does not contain specific provision for these forms of identification (ss 114 and 115 are not included in the Tasmanian Act) the legislated emphasis remains on the giving of comprehensive warnings.

52 See, eg, the discussion in ALRC, *Uniform Evidence Law*, above n 43, 13.47ff. This preference is replicated across jurisdictions. A review of procedures from 54 countries indicated that 46% expressed a preference for live parades or implicitly supported the 'live superiority hypothesis'. See RJ Fitzgerald, E Rubínová and S Juncu, 'Eyewitness Identification Around the World' in AM Smith, MP Toglia and JM Lampinen (eds), *Methods, Measures, and Theories in Eyewitness Identification Tasks* (Taylor and Francis, 2021).

an identification that has occurred *outside* of a formal parade, as well as some conditions for the conduct of an identification parade. Under this provision, 'visual identification evidence' obtained outside of a formal parade will only be admissible if the accused has refused to participate in a parade, or it would not have been reasonable to hold a parade, or it would have been unfair to the accused to hold a parade. Section 115 is concerned with the regulation of identification based on photographs, which includes photographs presented digitally (for example, by way of a computer monitor or other screen device). Investigators can only turn to the use of picture-based identification procedures if it is not possible to hold a parade (for the same reasons indicated in s 114). Thus, the overall effect of the combined operation of ss 114 and 115 is to channel investigators (and thus courts) towards the formal, live parade as the preferred form of 'visual identification evidence'.

Regardless of whether the identification evidence has been elicited in the context of a formal procedure or has arisen informally or spontaneously, it should, at least in theory, be subject to a judicial warning to the jury: s 116.[53] The s 116 warning requirements apply also to 'ear witnesses', or others who may have a direct perception of the events, and are purporting to identify the accused.

New South Wales, the Australian Capital Territory, the Northern Territory and the Commonwealth rely on all three regulatory strands of the *UEA* dedicated to identification evidence in criminal trials, namely a prioritisation of visual identification parades (or line-ups), restricted use of photographs (or pictures) to identify suspects and mandatory judicial warnings for disputed identification evidence. The Victorian *UEA* contains the provisions that apply to identification parades and to picture identification, but their warning requirement is now located in the *JDA 2015* (Vic) replacing and modifying s 116.[54] Tasmania has implemented a reverse regime to Victoria. It has not incorporated the provisions that apply to identification parades and to picture identification but does include the warning obligation in ss 116 and 165(5), tied to the same (limited) definition of 'identification evidence'.

The strength of Part 3.9 of the *UEA* is that it built on the ALRC's appraisal of research studies from the 1970s and 1980s.[55] The Act provided the first legislated rules regarding identification evidence in Australia. Compared to both the common law approach and to the regulation of eyewitness identification in comparative jurisdictions such as Canada and the United States, the Australian approach has adopted as uncontroversial a number of recommendations from researchers that

---

53 Identification made outside the definition of 'identification evidence' may still be subject to a judicial warning through s 165(1), and s 165(5) also retains the *Domican* requirements. However, the regulatory or limiting effect of the provisions has been blunted by a number of developments since the introduction of the *UEA*, over and above the consequences of the narrow definition of 'identification evidence' in the *UEA*. By way of example, s 116 creates an apparently mandatory requirement that a strong warning be given in respect of identification evidence (as defined in the *UEA*) that has been admitted but, as we shall see, the jurisprudence in this area has read down that requirement in a number of cases.

54 *JDA 2015* (Vic), ss 35 and 56.

55 Such as R Hastie, R Landsman and EF Loftus, 'Eyewitness Testimony: The Dangers of Guessing' (1978) 19 *Jurimetrics Journal* 1; EF Loftus, 'The Eyewitness on Trial' (1980) 16 *Trial* 30; EF Loftus, 'Reconstructing Memory: The Incredible Eyewitness' (1974) 8 *Psychology Today* 117; EF Loftus, *Eye Witness Testimony* (Harvard University Press, 1979); EF Loftus, 'Eyewitness Testimony' (1980) 93 *American Journal of Psychology* 746; EF Loftus, *Memory* (Addison-Wesley, 1980; Loftus and Palmer, above n 19; EF Loftus, 'Leading Questions and the Eye Witness' (1975) 7 *Cognitive Psychology* 560; L Re, 'Eyewitness Identification: Why So Many Mistakes' (1984) 58 *Australian Law Journal* 509; DM Thomson, 'The Realities of Eyewitness Identification' (1982) 14 *Australian Journal of Forensic Sciences* 150.

are still contentious in other jurisdictions, and has also developed a more open approach to informing a jury about factors affecting reliability.[56] Further, many of the more specific recommendations associated with the presentation of images (including those recommended by the Innocence Project) have, despite the lack of detailed exposition in the *UEA*, been incorporated into day-to-day practice.[57] However, as an admissibility regime, Part 3.9 is now dated and has been for a number of years. In light of both the rapid expansion of alternative modes of identification, changes in day-to-day investigative practices, and current scientific knowledge, the Part 3.9 provisions represent a partial response to the recognised weaknesses of identification and comparison evidence in criminal trials. Similarly, neither the Act nor its Regulations detail obligations or principles regarding the conduct of parades or, more importantly, the composition of photographic arrays.[58]

What is identification evidence?

The UEA definition of 'identification evidence'

The regulation of 'identification evidence' under the *UEA* depends on the definition, found in the Dictionary in the *UEA*.[59] There are minor differences in the *UEA* jurisdictions:[60]

> ***identification evidence*** means evidence that is:
>
> (a) an assertion by a person to the effect that a defendant/accused was, or resembles (visually, aurally or otherwise) a person who was, present at or near a place where:
>
> (i) the offence for which the defendant is being prosecuted was committed, or
>
> (ii) an act connected to that offence was done, at or about the time at which the offence was committed or the act was done, being an assertion that is based wholly or partly on what the person making the assertion saw, heard or otherwise perceived at that place and time, or
>
> (b) a report (whether oral or in writing) of such an assertion.

As can be seen, the definition captures 'assertions' made by witnesses about an accused based on the observations (or perceptions) of the witness at the scene of the offence (or at a related location). This use of 'assertions' in the definition indicates that the definition catches both assertions made in court, and those made out of court (in whatever context), as well as assertions contained in formal witness statements or other documents.[61] Important points regarding the definition are that it does not capture:

---

56 For example, via allowing experts to provide assistance under s 108C.

57 For example, many picture identification procedures in NSW and the ACT are now conducted sequentially. See, eg, *Carpenter* [2011] ACTSC 71. VIPER video line-ups (discussed below) also, necessarily, adopt a sequential approach.

58 These exist in some jurisdictions. See, in particular, *Crimes Act 1914* (Cth), s 3ZM(3), (4); *Crimes Act 1900* (ACT), s 233(6)(a); Code D of the *Police and Criminal Evidence Act 1984* (UK) (PACE). Police guidelines are discussed further below.

59 In Tasmania, see *Evidence Act 2001* (Tas), s 3.

60 In Victoria the definition of identification evidence in s 35 of the *JDA 2015* (Vic) is broader, encompassing people other than the defendant, negative identification evidence, and explicitly including the identification of objects associated with the person.

61 It is worth noting that in relation to out-of-court assertions the evidence would also be governed by the rules regulating the admissibility of hearsay. See discussion in ALRC, *Uniform Evidence Law*, above n 43, [8.80]-[8.85]; and *Barbaro* [2000] NSWCCA 192; 112 A Crim R 551; and *Gee*

- non-visual resemblance;
- displaced voice or visual identifications (that is, identifications made by those not present at the scene) such as those made by police officers from CCTV footage, as in *Smith (Mundarra)*,[62] or image/voice comparisons (such as those made in *Leung*,[63] *Tang*,[64] *Morgan*[65] and *Honeysett*);[66]
- negative or exculpatory identification evidence;[67]
- evidence relating to the identification of people other than the accused;[68]
- identification of objects associated with the accused;[69]
- 'circumstantial' evidence that contributes to the identification of the offender.[70]

In addition, the *UEA* definition contemplates, subject to circumstances, the application of s 114, 115 or 116 to representations that a witness has *recognised* the offender. In the case of recognition, a witness's assertion identifying the accused is not one of a 'match' between the offender and the person in the line-up, but rather one of a match between their memory or knowledge of the person and the person seen at the relevant scene. Thus, the definition captures representations made by a witness either to police, or to others, that the offence was committed by a person already known to them.[71]

It is important to note that evidence that falls outside the 'identification evidence' definition is not subject to the detailed admissibility requirements of Part 3.9, but may be regulated by other provisions in the *UEA*. So, for example, image or voice comparison evidence, if relevant, may be caught by the opinion rule (s 76), and admitted by way of an exception to that rule, that is via s 79 if characterised as expert opinion, s 78 if characterised as lay opinion, or as 'ad hoc expert' evidence.[72] Alternatively, evidence falling outside the definition will be governed (only) by the general principles of relevance, and discretionary and mandatory exclusions. For example, voice identification evidence from an 'ear witness' is subject to the warning provision in s 116, but the *admissibility* of voice identification evidence is managed (solely) by way of ss 55, 135 and 137.

[2000] NSWCCA 198; 113 A Crim R 376. See also s 66(3). Compare the approach in *Aouad and El-Zeyat* [2011] NSWCCA 61 where assertions that a com-fit image resembling the offender was characterised as original evidence of the witness's state of mind and akin to a witness giving evidence of their own selection of a photograph by a witness.

62 [2001] HCA 50; 206 CLR 650.

63 [1999] NSWCCA 287.

64 [2006] NSWCCA 167.

65 [2011] NSWCCA 257.

66 [2014] HCA 29.

67 See ALRC, *Uniform Evidence Law*, above n 43, [13.3]ff and *Kanaan* [2006] NSWCCA 109.

68 See, eg, *Simmons (No 7)* [2015] NSWSC 574 and *Rose* [2002] NSWCCA 455.

69 Though see the discussion in *Allan* [2017] NSWCCA 6, incorporating a discussion of *Clout* (1995) 41 NSWLR 312. *Allan* does seem to indicate that, in some circumstances, an assertion that related to an object or item associated with an offender could fall within the definition.

70 Including information as to the name used by an offender at the time of the offence. See *Trudgett* [2008] NSWCCA 62; 70 NSWLR 696, endorsed in *DPP (Vic) v Bass* [2016] VSCA 110, [40].

71 See, for example, the evidence discussed in *Speelman* [2016] NSWDC 322. See also *D* [2008] ACTSC 82 and *Taufua* [1996] NSWSC 538, as well as *Trudgett* [2008] NSWCA 62; 70 NSWLR 696 which confirmed that, even though the evidence in the case at hand did not fall within the definition, in principle recognition evidence did within the definition. However, since it is unlikely that it would be fair to an accused to hold an identification parade, the main consideration that arises in cases of 'recognition' is generally the terms of the warning that should be given in relation to such evidence under s 116.

72 See discussion in Chapter 12.

Positive identification, recognition, and 'circumstantial' identification evidence

Clearly the *UEA* regime captures the most readily imagined scenario of an identification – that is, one made during a police investigation, where a witness sees an unknown or unfamiliar suspect in the context of a formal identification procedure and makes an 'assertion' that a person in the line-up (or in one of the photographs) 'is, or resembles', the person they saw at or near where the crime was committed.[73] In such a scenario, the witness is connecting their memory of the appearance of the offender with the appearance of one of the participants in the line-up (who then becomes the 'defendant' referred to in the definition). The witness is making an assertion of a type of 'match' or correspondence between the person they saw at the scene of the crime and the person in front of them. It is this type of scenario, where an accused has been identified by someone with no prior familiarity with that accused, that has given rise to most concern in the cases and commentary. It is also the scenario that has been the subject of the most detailed empirical investigation. An assertion made by witnesses in such a scenario is obviously caught by the definition, and can be analysed in the same way, regardless of whether it is made confidently – 'That is him' – or, more equivocally – 'I think that's the man I saw'. This type of scenario also fits most readily McHugh J's definition of 'positive identification' in *Festa*.[74]

In *Festa* McHugh J articulates the distinction often drawn in case law between positive identification evidence and circumstantial identification evidence (that is, evidence that the general appearance or characteristic of the accused is similar to the person who committed the crime). This distinction is significant in terms of the reach of Part 3.9. Typically, the admission of 'expert' comparison evidence, including in facial and body mapping cases,[75] is characterised as falling into the class of 'circumstantial evidence of identification'. This evidence is outside Part 3.9's purview and so is less likely to be subject to a judicial warning than conventional identification evidence, even where the evidence may have the effect of a positive assertion of identity or correspondence between the appearance of the offender and the appearance of the accused. In *Festa*,[76] an appeal from Queensland's Court of Appeal, the facts concerned the conviction of two accused for armed robbery. Witnesses had given a description of a woman they had seen engaged in acts connected with the robbery (such as sitting in the getaway car). The descriptions included noting that she appeared to be wearing a wig.[77] Items found in the possession of the accused after the robbery included a can of hair spray, wig stands, a set of instructions on the use of disguises and a bottle of spirit gum remover (with the defendant's finger prints on it). These witnesses

73 *DPP (Vic) v Bass* [2016] VSCA 110.

74 [2001] HCA 72; 208 CLR 593. See also *Cope* [2018] VSCA 261.

75 See, eg, *Honeysett* [2013] NSWCCA 135. On appeal in the High Court the Crown argued that the evidence had been led at trial merely to show that the accused could not be excluded as one of the co-offenders. The High Court rejected this mischaracterisation, noting that the evidence had been admitted, and relied on, as circumstantial evidence going to prove identity: *Honeysett* [2014] HCA 29; 253 CLR 122, [40] (French CJ, Kiefel, Bell, Gageler and Keane JJ).

76 [2001] HCA 72; 208 CLR 593.

77 There was evidence of an association between Festa and her co-accused, Renton. Items, such as guns and ammunition, were found in the units occupied by the defendants along with other items not considered to be (according to the Court of Appeal in *Festa* [2000] QCA 73, [8]), '[the] common concomitant of suburban life among law-abiding members of the community'. There was also a mocked-up poster, showing a picture of Renton, with a caption reading, *Armed robber eludes police again*.

had also identified Festa in an informal identification procedure. The identification evidence had been characterised by the judge as 'more circumstantial than direct' and on appeal the defence raised the argument that this had prevented a full exploration of the probative value and prejudicial impact of the evidence. McHugh J addressed this argument by discussing the different ways that the terms 'positive identification' and 'circumstantial evidence of identification' have been deployed:

> 54. Most cases concerned with identification evidence are cases of positive identification. That is to say, cases where a witness claims to recognise the accused as the person seen on an occasion that is relevant to the charge. Positive-identification evidence may be used as direct or circumstantial proof of the charge. A positive identification of the accused is direct evidence of the crime when it identifies the accused as the person who committed one or more of the acts that constitute the crime in question. A positive identification is circumstantial evidence when its acceptance provides the ground for an inference, alone or with other evidence, that the accused committed the crime in question. A witness gives direct evidence of the charge when she testifies that the accused ordered her to hand over the takings. A witness gives circumstantial evidence of the charge when she testifies that the accused was the person who ran out of the bank immediately after other evidence proves it was robbed.
>
> 55. Positive-identification evidence has often proved to be unreliable. This Court has insisted that where identification evidence, direct or circumstantial, represents a significant part of the proof of guilt of an offence, trial judges must warn juries not only of the potential unreliability of that evidence but also of any particular weaknesses in the evidence, in the case being tried.
>
> 56. Unfortunately, another class of evidence is sometimes called "circumstantial identification evidence". It is evidence that asserts that the general appearance or some characteristic or propensity of the accused is similar to that of the person who committed the crime. It may be evidence of age, race, stature, colour or voice or of a distinctive mark or gait. It differs from positive-identification evidence in that the witness does not claim to recognise the accused as the person who committed the crime or was present in circumstances from which it can be inferred that the accused committed the crime. Although such evidence does not directly implicate the accused in the crime or as being present in incriminating circumstances, it is admissible evidence. It is proof of a circumstance – usually, but not always, weak – that with other evidence may point to the accused as the person who committed the crime. It will be weak evidence, for example, when it merely proves that the perpetrator and the accused are persons of the same ethnic background. It may be nearly conclusive evidence of identity when it proves that the accused and the perpetrator have used a unique modus operandi which is admissible in accordance with the principles concerning the admission of similar fact evidence.
>
> 57. When circumstantial identification evidence has no element of positive identification, it usually does not have the potential unreliability of positive-identification evidence. A judge is not automatically required to warn the jury concerning the dangers of circumstantial identification evidence. But the circumstances of a particular case may require a warning. When a witness claims that the facial features of the accused are similar to those of the perpetrator, it would usually be appropriate to give the standard warnings given in cases of positive-identification evidence. But the warnings that must be given to juries concerning positive-identification evidence do not apply to most forms of circumstantial identification evidence.

The *UEA* definition is sufficiently broad to catch some of what is folded into the definition of circumstantial identification evidence in *Festa* – both the evidence relating to acts connected to the offence and evidence of resemblance. This evidence may be in the form of representations by a witness that the defendant resembles the person they saw or heard at the relevant location, representations including, for example, 'he looks like the man I saw', or even 'his hair and face shape look the same'.

However, picking up on McHugh J's discussion of the general characteristics or appearance of the person who committed the crime, the *UEA* definition does not catch the description of an isolated feature of the offender, such as a tattoo or an item of clothing, or other information about their appearance that may identify them, or help to link them to the offence in some way.[78] Nor does the terminology in the definition capture representations made by a witness describing the offender for the purpose of building a composite image, such as via a 'com-fit' procedure where the witness's description is not 'an assertion ... to the effect that a defendant was ... a person who was ... present at or near a place where ... the offence ... [or an act connected to that offence] was committed'. For example, in *Dawiche*,[79] the challenged evidence was the computer-generated image and associated documentation derived from a com-fit procedure, in which the witness had described the offender, and confirmed that the image produced resembled the offender whom they had seen engaged in the offence. This evidence did not fall within the definition because at that point the witness was not making an assertion *comparing* the appearance of the offender whom they had seen with the accused. In *Walford v DPP (NSW)*,[80] Basten JA observed:

> 17. One aspect of the definition which has not always received full recognition is the object of the identification evidence, namely the "defendant". ... Importantly for present purposes, what must be identified is a connection (identity or resemblance) between the person the subject of the criminal proceeding (the defendant) and a person present at or near the place where the offence was committed at the time it was committed. This language encompasses an in-court identification, but less obviously also covers an out-of-court identification. In the latter case, there must be a link between the act of identification and the person on trial. In the case of an identification parade, where there is an affirmative identification, the assertion by the witness will be to the effect, "I identified from the line-up the person whom I recognised as the woman I saw break the shop window". Absent an in-court identification, the link between the person selected at the identification parade and the person on trial will need to be proved by other evidence, for example by the investigating police officer saying that the person identified at the parade is the person on trial.
>
> 18. Accordingly, the fact that a further link is required between the person identified and the defendant does not exclude the operation of the section. On the other hand, evidence involving a physical description of the offender, or the name by which he was addressed, does not involve an "assertion ... to the effect that [the] defendant was, or resembles ... a person", being the putative offender: *Trudgett v R* [2008] NSWCCA 62; 70 NSWLR 696, at [34]-[36] (Spigelman CJ, Hulme and Latham JJ agreeing). In *Trudgett* the complainant was able to identify her assailant as a person introduced to her

---

78 For example, a witness description that includes a reference to a (distinctive) tattoo, may be used, in combinations with other characteristics, to search police databases either to identify potential inclusions in a photographic line-up, or independently to ground further investigation.

79 *Dawiche* [2006] NSWSC 924. See also *Aouad and El-Zeyat* [2011] NSWCCA 61 (arising out of the same facts). Bell J, in *Dawiche*, considered that the witness's assertion that the com-fit image *resembled* one of the offenders was potentially caught by the definition, but the court in *Aouad and El-Zeyat* rejected this reading, holding that even in these circumstances the assertion was not caught by the definition since it was an assertion of resemblance as between the com-fit image and the shooter, not the shooter and the defendant: at [263]. However, either way, s 115 was not enlivened because the accused was not in the custody of the police officer investigating the relevant offence at the time. See also *McKellar* [2000] NSWCCA 523.

80 [2012] NSWCA 290, [17]-[19] (Basten JA).

as "Adam". Spigelman CJ noted that although another witness gave evidence that he had introduced the defendant to the complainant as Adam, that merely allowed the *jury* to make an identification of the defendant as the assailant.

19. *Trudgett* was concerned with the giving of a warning under s 116, which is not limited to visual identification evidence: a link between two parties based on what the witness had heard (namely the introduction of her assailant by name) could not constitute visual identification evidence for the purposes of s 114. What is less clear from the reasoning in *Trudgett* is the extent to which, in particular circumstances, the need for a further link will mean that the actual connection will be made by the jury and not by the witness.

By way of comparison, consider a description that includes some specific individualising information, such as, 'the boy I saw breaking into the car was someone I've seen before, wearing a year 12 jersey from our local high school with the name James written on the back of the jersey'. Even though the description of a particular characteristic may be highly discriminating, Basten JA's judgment applying *Trudgett* would suggest that in and of itself this type of description may fall outside of the definition because it lacks the requisite link between the 'assertion' and the defendant. By way of comparison, in *R v D*, the witness reported that they had been assaulted by a person they recognised as someone with whom they had been at school. The witness was also able to name the offender (who was then charged), and this assertion of recognition thus came within the definition.[81]

Visual Identification Evidence: *UEA*, s 114

As noted, s 114 imposes threshold conditions on 'visual identification evidence', a subset of 'identification evidence' as defined in the Dictionary. 'Visual identification evidence' is, in effect, an assertion of visual resemblance as between the offender and the suspect (who becomes the defendant), but does not include identifications made from images, including 'picture identification evidence'. 'Visual identification evidence' could thus include assertions of identity made during a formal parade procedure, or an assertion made informally to investigators, or others (for example, at the scene), an assertion made during a 'show up' or single suspect viewing,[82] or even an identification made by the witness looking at the defendant in the dock. All of these will fall within the definition of 'visual identification evidence' and are thus regulated by the conditions contained in s 114:

114. Exclusion of visual identification evidence

(1) In this section: ***visual identification evidence*** means identification evidence relating to an identification based wholly or partly on what a person saw but does not include picture identification evidence.

(2) Visual identification evidence adduced by the prosecutor is not admissible unless:

(a) an identification parade that included the defendant was held before the identification was made, or

(b) it would not have been reasonable to have held such a parade, or

(c) the defendant refused to take part in such a parade,

and the identification was made without the person who made it having been intentionally influenced to identify the defendant.

---

81 *R v D* [2008] ACTSC 82.

82 See, eg, the *NSW Police Procedures for the Evidence Act*, <https://www.police.nsw.gov.au/about_us/policies_procedures_and_legislation/procedures_for_the_evidence_act>, and *Identifying the Culprit*, above n 9.

Therefore, under this provision, an assertion made during a formal parade will be prima-facie admissible, provided that there was no intentional influence exercised over the witness's choice during the parade (s 114(2)(a)). Further, the effect of this section is to make the holding of an identification parade a precondition for the admission of (any other) 'visual identification evidence' *unless* the conditions of s 114(2)(b) or (c) have been met.[83] That is, s 114 provides that 'visual identification evidence' – an assertion by a witness identifying the suspect – that is garnered informally, or outside of a formal line-up, is not admissible if an identification parade could have been held before that assertion was made. The section thus recognises, for example, that procedures that involve the witness being shown only one suspect or a single photograph are problematic in terms of subtle and not so subtle pressures on witnesses to make an identification, despite being uncertain. For example, in *Festa*,[84] a case applying the common law, four eyewitnesses had described features of the two robbers. In addition, they identified them after sitting in the court precinct, under an arrangement made by police, to look out for anyone they may see and recognise from the robbery. This arrangement, akin to a confrontation identification, also enabled the four witnesses to collaborate on their observations. While stopping short of holding that the evidence should have been excluded, McHugh J observed:

> 50. … The identifications were obtained in circumstances marked by an absence of the precautions usually taken in the identification of suspects. They were made in informal circumstances, as Ms Festa was entering a court building unaccompanied by any other women. No police officer kept a record of the identification process. No-one made notes of the process. No-one took photographs of the identifications or recorded them on video camera. By asking the witnesses to look out for the female participant and allowing them to remain together, Detective Holmes also removed the possibility of each witness spontaneously identifying Ms Festa as the woman he or she had seen.[85]

Under s 114 informal procedures such as those in *Festa* would be far less likely to be permitted, since it would be necessary to establish as a precondition, that it was not possible to have held a parade (and, even if that were established, the next best option would probably be a properly conducted photographic procedure). Embedded also, within the *UEA* preference for a live line-up, is the recognition that an in-court identification, a so-called 'dock identification', is generally of low or negligible probative value and is highly, and unfairly, prejudicial.[86] As noted in *Alexander*:

> Traditionally it has been accepted that a witness identifies the accused at the trial as the person whom he observed at the scene of, or in connection with, the crime. This 'in court' identification, sometimes described as primary evidence, is of little probative value when made by a witness who has no prior knowledge of the accused, because at

83 'Picture identification evidence' is defined in s 115. The effect of s 115 is to impose restrictions on the use of the use of identification by way of pictures if a suspect is in custody and it would be reasonable to hold a parade.

84 [2001] HCA 72; 208 CLR 593.

85 Citations omitted. Kirby J was alone in the High Court in holding that the trial judge had wrongly admitted this identification evidence. His Honour would have excluded it under the common law equivalent of *UEA*, s 137.

86 Thus, considerations under *UEA*, s 137, also apply (see Chapter 4) in addition to the requirements of Part 3.9. However, see *Aslett* [2009] NSWCCA 188 which, although indicating an in-court identification justified discharge of the jury, also suggested strong and repeated judicial direction may be sufficient remediation for in-court identification; *Tahere* [1999] NSWCCA 170; *Taufua* [1996] NSWSC 538. This position was confirmed in *Fadel* [2017] NSWCCA 134.

the trial circumstances conspire to compel the witness to identify the accused in the dock.[87]

Where a witness is permitted to offer 'visual identification evidence' because a parade has been held, an account of the holding of the parade, and any evidence regarding an identification made during that parade, will be led at the same time.[88] Further, if a parade has been held and the witness has either identified a known foil, or made no selection, then this should be disclosed and should also affect the evaluation of any subsequent (positive) identification.[89] In a reverse of the ordinary scenario, in *Ceissman*,[90] a ground of appeal raised by the defence was the *failure* of the Crown to ask the witness during the trial whether they could identify the accused in court as the man they had seen committing the offence. In rejecting this argument, the court pointed out that 'such a question could not properly have been asked by the Crown in any event. There would first have needed to be an identification parade conducted pursuant to s 114(2) of the *Evidence Act*'.[91] Further, while notionally s 114 could permit an in-court identification in circumstances where a witness has rejected an identification parade containing the defendant, this would be unlikely to be permitted in practice.[92] In contrast, the Canadian rules relating to the admission of identification evidence do contemplate such a situation, and courts have permitted witnesses to make their first positive identification of the defendant (in the dock) during the trial.[93] However, while notionally s 114 imposes a higher threshold in terms of admissibility when compared to other jurisdictions, it is important to note that, in practice, live parades are no longer the primary identification procedure relied on by investigators.[94] This is important when considering the exceptions to the parade requirement in s 114, since meeting the conditions in these exceptions opens the way to either the admission of informal identification(s) as well as the use of alternative image based procedures.[95]

---

87 [1981] HCA 17; 145 CLR 395, 426-7 [20] (Mason J).

88 As indicated, adducing evidence of the conduct of the parade will also include adducing evidence of assertions or previous representations made by that witness, and, as a matter of logic, these ought to be subject to the operation of the hearsay rule. The exception in s 66(3) for representations relating to identity, confirms this position. See also S Odgers, *Uniform Evidence Law* (Thomson Reuters, 15th ed, 2020), [EA.114.90]. Though see discussion in *Barbaro* [2000] NSWCCA 192 on the view that the hearsay rule does not apply evidence from a witness recounting their own prior assertion of identity.

89 See, eg, *Dickman* [2017] HCA 24; 261 CLR 601, extracted below. See also, on the risks of holding multiple line-ups in terms of declining accuracy in subsequent identifications, L Smalarz et al, 'Identification Performance from Multiple Lineups: Should Eyewitnesses Who Pick Fillers Be Burned?' (2019) 8 *Journal of Applied Research in Memory and Cognition* 221.

90 [2015] NSWCCA 74.

91 Ibid [65], relying on *Aslett* [2009] NSWCCA 188, a case where it was clear that an in-court identification, made for the first time by a witness, was inadmissible. See also *Walford v DPP (NSW)* [2012] NSWCA 290, [14] (Basten JA). However, compare *Fadel* [2017] NSWCCA 134.

92 Such an identification would be of such low probative value that it should be excluded under s 137.

93 See, eg, *Hibbert* [2002] 2 SCR 445.

94 Even when the requirement was proposed it was acknowledged that the Australian Federal Police rarely held live parades (ALRC 1985). See also discussion in M San Roque, 'Updating Beliefs: Rethinking the Regulation of Identification Evidence Under the UEL' in A Roberts and J Gans (eds), *Critical Perspectives on the Uniform Evidence Law* (Federation Press, 2017), 200.

95 It is relevant to note that the empirical grounding for the preference for live parades was never as strong as had been assumed, and has now been more comprehensively challenged. See, eg, Eva Rubínová et al, 'Live presentation for eyewitness identification is not superior to photo or video presentation' *Journal of Applied Research in Memory and Cognition* (forthcoming,

Exceptions

There are two main exceptions to the precondition that for 'visual identification evidence' to be admissible there must be an identification parade. These are contained in s 114(2):

- either if the defendant has refused to take part in a parade (s 114(2)(c)); or
- it would not have been reasonable to hold a parade (s 114(2)(b)).

Determining whether the defendant has refused to take part in a parade will, in most cases, be uncontentious, but there are indications that one of the reasons underlying the shift away from the use of live parades once a suspect is in custody is that informal pressure may be brought to bear on suspects to refuse a live parade. An exchange revealed in *Dickman* between the investigating officers leading up to the decision to proceed with a photoboard or image based procedure is perhaps indicative of this reality:

> A couple of days later, on 18 February 2010, Detective Condon sent an email to Detective Scott Dawe of South Australia police – he was the officer who had executed the search warrant – asking about the applicant's (that is, the accused's) participation in an identification parade. The email, which was tendered on the voir dire, was as follows:
>
>> Scott. Wondering if you could do me a favour when you go to drop Dickman's copy of the interview out to him. Can you ask him if he has spoken to his solicitor about participating in a line-up. I'm hoping he will say no. If this is the case, you take a note of it and let me know. Over the next day or so I will work out who I need to get a statement from re exhibits etc, and send a formal request for them. Thanks, Condo.[96]

Reasonableness and fairness to the accused

More complex than the question of a defendant's refusal to participate in a parade is the question of whether it was reasonable not to have held a parade. There are two main scenarios that the courts have been asked to consider under this exception. The first relates to situations where an identification has been made informally, often before the suspect has been charged or is in custody, and the court is asked to consider whether it would have been reasonable to have held a parade before that identification was made. The second arises where notionally a parade *could* have been held (for example, the police have identified and located a suspect), but a decision has been made not to hold one. The reasons behind such a decision could range from practical and logistical questions to a more nuanced consideration of whether it would be unfair to an accused if an informal identification were to be confirmed by way of a subsequent, formal procedure. Section 114 also contains the requirement that there must not have been any intentional attempt to influence the witness in their selection. This requirement applies most obviously to any formal procedure, but is equally applicable to any identification admitted by way of the exception in s 114(2)(b).

---

available online at <https://doi.org/10.1016/j.jarmac.2020.08.009>). For example, contemporary research comparing the accuracy of live versus image based procedures indicates that the differences with respect to accuracy may turn less on the type of procedure and more on whether the witness is confronted with a target absent or target present line-up. See, eg, discussion in RJ Fitzgerald, HL Price and T Valentine, 'Eyewitness identification: Live, photo, and video lineups' (2018) 24 *Psychology, Public Policy, and Law* 307 and SE Clark, MB Moreland and RA Rush, 'Lineup Composition and Lineup Fairness' in T Valentine and JP Davis (eds*), Forensic Facial Identification: Theory and Practice of Identification from Eyewitnesses, Composites and CCTV* (John Wiley & Sons, 2015), as well as Valentine and Fitzgerald, above n 30.

96 *Dickman* [2015] VSCA 311, [69]. Refusal is discussed further below.

Factors to be considered regarding the reasonableness of holding a parade are listed in s 114(3), including:

- the kind of offence, and the gravity of the offence, concerned;[97]
- the importance of the evidence; and
- the practicality of holding an identification parade having regard, among other things, to whether:
  - the defendant/suspect was willing to cooperate, including whether the defendant stipulated that they would only participate if a lawyer/other third party was present (s 114(3)(c)(i) and (5));
  - the length of time between the commission of the offence and the holding of a parade (s 114(3)(c)(ii));
  - the availability of suitable 'foils' at the time the parade could have been held;[98]
  - whether the appearance of the accused had changed significantly between the time of the offence and the time when the parade could have been held;
  - the relationship between the accused and the person making the identification (s 114(3)(d)).

The court is not to take into account the availability of pictures or photographs that could be used in making identifications: see s 114(6).[99] A growing area for consideration is whether it would be unfair to the accused to hold a parade. Under s 114(4) this will be good grounds for finding that it was not reasonable to have held a parade. In particular, where an argument is made that an informal or spontaneous identification ought to have been confirmed by a subsequent, formal procedure, the courts have considered the question of whether it could have been practical to hold a parade before that spontaneous identification alongside a consideration of the utility and *dangers* of holding a subsequent, formal procedure such as a live parade. The cases of *Ilioski* and *Walford*, discussed below, are indicative of courts' responses to situations where the identification has been made at the scene or shortly after the offence occurred.

Ilioski
[2006] NSWCCA 164

The appellant was convicted of malicious wounding. The victim had received serious stab wounds during a brawl outside a Wollongong club. The brawl can be broken into three confrontations across two main locations. It was the prosecution case that:

- A man, possibly the appellant, had made taunts to the victim (by running his finger across his throat) in the car park of the Steelers Club which led

97 The *NSW Police Code of Practice for CRIME*, for example, noted that there was no need to hold an identification parade where the offence is of a minor nature.

98 See *Ilioski* [2006] NSWCCA 164 below, and the argument raised, but rejected, in *Aslett* [2009] NSWCCA 188 regarding the difficulty finding appropriate foils. In *Smith (Mundarra)* [2001] HCA 50; 206 CLR 650 (see above Chapter 4, p 130) the lack of suitable foils was offered as an explanation for the failure to hold a parade and instead rely on the police officers' viewing of the CCTV footage.

99 See also *Alexander* [1981] HCA 17; 145 CLR 395, [20], discussing English cases that have quashed convictions in situations where photographs were used when a suspect was in custody and an identification parade could have been held.

to a 'minor' altercation between the appellant, the victim and his twin brother and others (the 'first' confrontation).

- The appellant then briefly left the scene and returned with a knife, and had stabbed the victim preceded by statements like 'What are you going to do now I've got a knife!' and 'We'll see who's fucking tough now!' (the 'second' confrontation).
- Thirdly, sometime later, the *appellant* was identified by friends of the victim who started attacking him in the street. The appellant received 'marked facial injuries' as a result of this assault. This confrontation attracted police attention to the appellant.

Ground four of the appeal related to the assertions made by Eid Masri, who was present at the scene of the first and second confrontations, and who indicated to police at the scene that Ilioski was the same person who had attacked the victim. At the time Masri identified Ilioski as the assailant who had threatened the victim and who was responsible for stabbing the victim, Ilioski was injured and with police, but had not yet been arrested. Masri had identified Ilioski to police directly after seeing the events himself. His evidence was that he saw the same man from the first confrontation leave and return with a knife, shouting 'Do you want to keep going?', and swing that knife at another man in the course of the second confrontation. The court held that it would not have been reasonable to hold an identification parade for Masri to make his identification before Ilioski was arrested, and it would have been impractical and unfair to hold it after arrest.

Hunt AJA:

Ground 4 – Identification parade

118. This ground of appeal asserts that "[t]he judge erred in admitting visual identification evidence from Eid Masri". The evidence is said to have been inadmissible as there had not been an identification parade and no use of foils (persons of generally similar appearance to the suspect) before Masri made his identification of the appellant to the police. The appellant says that the absence of an identification parade denied him a proper opportunity to scrutinise the process by which he was identified. This complaint requires a brief examination of the circumstances in which Masri made his identification to the police.

119. Masri gave evidence that he saw what I have described (in par [3] *supra*) as the first confrontation, that he saw one of the two men involved in that confrontation leave and return with a knife, and that he saw that man swing the knife at the throat of a man in the course of what I have described (in par [4] *supra*) as the second confrontation, and striking that man in the arm. Masri then saw the assailant walk towards the Steelers Club car park and return to be beaten up in what I have described (in par [5] *supra*) as the third confrontation. He later gave the police a description of that man. Subsequently, he was told by an unidentified security guard that no witnesses had formally identified the man who was then with the police in the car park and he was asked to assist. Masri went to the car park and identified the appellant as the assailant. There was no objection to that evidence. As a result of what he told the police, the appellant was arrested. The police evidence was that, when they spoke to the appellant, a number of bystanders yelled out "he stabbed him", to which the appellant responded "those guys jumped me".

120. … [Section 114 extracted] Section 114 appears to be the statutory provision on which the appellant relies.

121. I accept that the value of holding an identification parade is not only that, if properly carried out, it provides the most reliable method of identification, but also that (unlike an identification from photographs) it is necessarily held in the presence of the accused, who is thereby able to observe, and later bring to light, any unfairness in the way in which the parade was conducted, or any weakness in the way in which the witness

made the identification. It is, however, not always practicable to arrange an identification parade in the circumstances of the particular case.

122. In the present case, Const May very properly was not prepared to effect an arrest merely on the basis of the calls by those present at the time that the appellant had stabbed somebody. It may be assumed that none of those present at the time was able to make the identification based on having personally seen the stabbing. Masri made that formal identification. The formal identification was, strictly, still part of the detection process, as it was necessary in order to effect the arrest: *Alexander v The Queen* [1981] HCA 17; 145 CLR 395 at 400, 409-410, 429-430, 437; *R v Carusi* at 57-60. This distinction made in the common law is, in my view, of some assistance in determining whether it was unreasonable to hold an identification parade in the circumstances of the particular case.

123. However, it could not rationally be expected that, before arresting the appellant for the very serious offence committed, the police could have arranged an identification parade in the circumstances of the present case. It has not been suggested that the appellant would have declined to participate or to cooperate; what is said is that the necessary logistics of arranging an appropriately held identification parade were extraordinary difficult, if not impossible, to perform in the situation which existed at that time. The test proposed by s 114 is whether it would have been unreasonable, not that it would have been impossible, to arrange an identification parade. First, the appellant himself, as Masri noted, had by then developed a black eye and was "pretty well bruised up". It would not have been practicable to find sufficient men of general similar appearance to the appellant, and any identification parade at that time was very unlikely to have provided a fair array. Because the formal identification was necessary in order to effect the arrest, the identification by Masri could not have been put off to a later date. Secondly, the police were in any event very involved at the time in attempting to bring the general situation outside the Steelers Club under control.

124. When asked what value a subsequent identification parade would have been in this case, counsel for the appellant (who had not appeared at the trial) replied that, although it certainly would not have been "perfect", it would have been [preferable to the evidence that had been allowed]. … [However t]he issue at the trial was whether he [Masri] had mistakenly identified the appellant (who was with the police when he made the identification) as the person he had previously seen with the knife. A subsequent identification at an identification parade would necessarily be suspect, as the picture Masri had of the assailant in his mind would by then have been replaced by the picture he had of the man he saw with the police: *Alexander v The Queen* at 409, 412-422.

125. I am satisfied that it would not have been reasonable to hold an identification parade for Masri to make his identification before the appellant was arrested.

The case of *Walford*, in the NSW Court of Appeal, held that out-of-court statements made by a witness to the effect that she recognised the offender were caught by the *UEA*'s definition of 'identification evidence'. The defendant had been charged with breaching an apprehended violence order (AVO). The defendant and the complainant had not been known to each other before the alleged assault that gave rise to the AVO. However, the evidence indicated that the complainant identified the defendant using his name[100] and that, between the assault and the time the complainant called police, the defendant had been in front of her house 'to egg people on'. The complainant called police as the defendant then approached the house. In reviewing the decision of Davies J (extracted below) the Court of Appeal revisited the question. The arguments raised the question, somewhat surprisingly, of whether the section covered both in-court

100 Albeit by way of an alias, rather than the name under which he was charged in this case. The police witness indicated that she had named him because she made the report and 'there was nothing indicating that she didn't know who it was': *DPP (NSW) v Walford* [2011] NSWSC 759, [14].

and out-of-court representations, and then went on to consider whether the failure to hold a (subsequent) line-up breached the conditions of s 114. In the proceeding related to the breach, the magistrate applied s 114 to the evidence of a witness in court identifying the defendant (and, it appears, excluded that evidence because no identification parade had been held), and this seems to have also resulted in the exclusion of the identification made at the time that the breach was occurring. In the Supreme Court, the defendant argued that the words in s 114(2), 'Visual identification evidence adduced by the prosecutor is not admissible unless ... (a) an identification parade that included the defendant was held before the identification was made', should be read to mean 'before the relevant witness gives visual identification evidence in Court'. The defendant argued that a failure to read those additional words into the Act would mean that an identification parade would never be held to be necessary in cases where witnesses assert that they have recognised the offender.[101] Davies J rejected the defendant's submissions and his review of the authorities and the conclusions drawn from them were (in essence) confirmed by the Court of Appeal:[102]

> 36. In my opinion the scheme of the section is understood by looking to when the "identification" is first made by the witness. In that regard the "identification" is to be contrasted with the "identification evidence". If the witness has made an out-of-court identification it is at that time at which the reasonableness of holding the identification parade is to be considered. If the identification is made at or about the time of the commission of the offence the Court will have to consider whether it was not reasonable to have held a parade. If the identification was made at the time of the commission of the offence (eg a witness telephoning the police and identifying the person), it will clearly not have been reasonable to hold a parade because it will not have been practicable to do so. The words "or about the time of the commission of the offence" are sufficiently elastic that they may embrace more than minutes or even hours, and in some cases a few days where the investigation is lengthy. In such cases it will not have been impossible to hold such a parade and the matters in sub-s (3)(c)(ii) will need to be considered in determining whether it was not reasonable to hold one.

Significantly, in the judgment Davies J reviews the authorities to conclude that conducting a line-up in this case would not have been 'reasonable', in part because of the dangers of contamination and/or displacement. This approach in *Walford* is consistent with research indicating that to hold an identification parade once a witness has made an identification is likely to embed and harden, rather than reveal, errors. Many of the cases handled by the Innocence Project demonstrate this problem.[103] Related problems of displacement or recognition arise also in situations where a witness has *rejected* a line-up containing the suspect, but

101 By implication such a reading would also apply to exclude an identification made directly after the event in question, such as in *Ilioski* [2006] NSWCCA 164, even if it did not involve the type of recognition evidence involved in *Walford*.

102 *DPP (NSW) v Walford* [2011] NSWSC 759. Davies J said that '[i]n all of those circumstances the Complainant had identified the Defendant, and that identification (ie an assertion by her to the effect that the Defendant was present at the place where the offence for which the Defendant was being prosecuted was committed) took place at or about the time of the commission of the offence': Ibid [44]. On appeal in *Walford v DPP (NSW)* [2012] NSWCA 290, Basten JA expressed a view that Davies J had 'misstated' the critical question to be considered under s 114, but nonetheless agreed with the outcome and the decision that it would not have been reasonable for a parade to have been held once the witness had reported to police that they had recognised the defendant outside of their unit.

103 This appears to have been one of the problems in the case of Ronald Cotton, see <http://www.innocenceproject.org/cases-false-imprisonment/ronald-cotton>.

when shown a new array, or new line-up, including the same suspect, then (mis) identifies the accused.[104]

The rise of social media and the circulation of images on sites such as Facebook have created new challenges for conventional rules and procedures. There has been, unsurprisingly, a rise in cases where a witness makes an identification from an image on social media before engaging with investigators.[105] In such cases real questions arise as to whether it would be reasonable to hold a parade, given the strong risks of displacement. And while there are reasons to be sceptical about the probative value of the original identification in this and other cases, the conclusions drawn in cases such as *Peterson* as to whether it would be reasonable to hold a parade following an identification made by a witness would appear to be aligned with current empirical research:

> 47. By the time that the victim came to make his statement to police on 3 August 2012, claiming that it was the applicant who had stabbed him, he had already viewed the applicant's image on Facebook. As we have earlier observed, following CB's nomination of the applicant as the assailant with the knife, police made no attempt to have CB attempt to formally identify his attacker by means of a photoboard or an identification parade. One of the reasons given by the informant was that he was concerned about the possibility of a 'displacement effect'. In other words, any identification from a photoboard or identification parade would be open to the criticism that it was polluted by the antecedent viewing of the photograph on Facebook.
>
> 48. In our opinion, the fact that CB had previously viewed a photograph provided a sound reason for the police not conducting an identification parade. To use the language of s 114(2)(b), 'it would not have been reasonable to have held such a parade'. Any later identification after viewing the photograph on the Facebook page would have been open to the criticism that it was tainted by the displacement effect. As Stephen J said in *Alexander*:
>
>> Lastly, there is the 'displacement' effect. Having been shown a photograph, the memory of it may be more clearly retained than the memory of the original sighting of the offender and may, accordingly, displace that original memory. Any subsequent face-to-face identification, in court or in an identification parade, may, on the identifying witness's part, in truth involve a matching of the man so identified with the remembered photograph, which has displaced in his memory his recollection of the original sighting.
>
> 49. For these reasons, the provisions of s 114(2) were not engaged.[106]

By way of contrast, in *Dickman* it was rather the practical difficulties, combined with the apparent refusal of the accused to participate in a parade, that underpinned the conclusion of the trial judge that it would not have been reasonable to have held a parade including the defendant.[107]

Tasmania

As noted above, Tasmania has only incorporated the warning provision (s 116) into its *Evidence Act 2001*. However, something approaching the regime in *UEA*,

104 See discussion in R Fitzgerald, NK Stebley and JE Dysart, 'Repeated Eyewitness Identification procedures with the Same Suspect' (2016) 5 *Journal of Applied Research in Memory and Cognition* 284.

105 See McGorrery, above n 6.

106 *Peterson (a Pseudonym)* [2014] VSCA 111. Note that commentators such as McGorrery, above n 6, dispute the conclusion that there is little to be gained by holding a formal procedure following an informal or spontaneous identification from social media.

107 This conclusion was upheld on appeal, see *Dickman* [2015] VSCA 311, [90].

ss 114 and 115, is provided by guidance about the holding of identification parades and the use of photo identification in the *Tasmania Police Manual* (2021).[108] In relation to photographic identifications the Manual provides that photographs shall only be shown to a witness:

> (a) if a suspect has been given the opportunity and declined to take part in an identification parade; or
> (b) if the person suspected can not be found; or
> (c) in the initial stages of investigation you need to establish the identity of a suspect or offender based on a verbal description given by the witness ...[109]

Like ss 114 and 115 of the *UEA*, this guidance is intended to promote the use of identification parades and reduce reliance on photo identification. Non-compliance with this guidance might be relied on as a basis to argue for the exclusion of the evidence under ss 137 and 138. This was attempted, albeit unsuccessfully, in *Tasmania v Chatters*.[110] Nevertheless, the application was rejected on the facts and not because the argument was intrinsically flawed or unavailable. The frailties and flaws identified in the evidence included the failure to offer or arrange an identification parade, a prior identification by the complainant of the wrong man, the potential displacement by the complainant identifying the accused from CCTV before the photoboard identification, and the fact that he had seen a separate photo of the accused (and was told at that time that it was a photo he should not have seen) before being shown the full photo array. Porter J applied *XY*[111] and *KMJ v Tasmania*[112] to hold that the assessment of the probative value of the evidence should be made on the assumption that the evidence would be accepted and without speculating whether the jury would accept it or give it any particular weight. On this basis his Honour held that the probative value of the evidence was very high.

In assessing its prejudicial effect, he concentrated on the particular circumstances of the photoboard identification and did not consider the generally recognised sources of unfair prejudice associated with photoboard identifications specifically or with eyewitness identification evidence more broadly. Accordingly, although the 'rogues' gallery' effect of photo identifications had been relied on in argument as a source of unfair prejudice under s 137, it was not a matter to which Porter J devoted attention when assessing the prejudicial effect of the evidence. Similarly, his Honour did not consider what we know to be one of the strongest sources of unfair prejudice in identification evidence – the undue weight that juries attach to it because of its high level of *persuasiveness* even where it may be demonstrably weak and of minimal genuine probative worth. Prejudicial effect of this kind may well not be susceptible to displacement by directions made under s 116 or in accordance with *Domican*. Nevertheless, Porter J held that such warnings would alleviate the risk of unfair prejudice. He also declined to exclude the evidence under s 138, finding that because the photo identification had occurred at the request of the DPP it was not improper and that, in any event, given its high probative value and importance, it was more desirable to admit

---

108 See <https://www.police.tas.gov.au/uploads/Tasmania-Police-Manual-PublicRTI-Version.pdf>.

109 At [4.4.8], quoted in its earlier version in *Tasmania v Chatters* [2013] TASSC 61, [29] (Porter J).

110 [2013] TASSC 61.

111 [2013] NSWCCA 121; 84 NSWLR 363, [66]-[67] (Basten JA, with Hoeben CJ at CL and Simpson J agreeing).

112 (2011) 20 Tas R 425.

than exclude it. Thus, the decision in this case aligns with the broad trends in other *UEA* jurisdictions to prefer a reliance on directions over exclusion. This approach extends to cases involving other forms of identification evidence, such as voice identification and comparison.[113]

In Tasmania in particular, the large body of common law jurisprudence relating to preferred identification processes and the precautions that should accompany those processes might be brought to bear in cases like *Chatters* (although in that case this did not happen). The common law remains relevant in this context in Tasmania via s 9 of the *Evidence Act 2001*.[114] Because the common law is the source of ss 114 and 115 it also remains a point of reference in *UEA* cases as we see in *Ilioski*[115] and *Smith (Mundarra)*.[116] The principal influential common law authority is the High Court decision in *Alexander*, which, because of the valuable discussion by the majority judges of the hierarchy of identification processes and their relative flaws and merits, is extracted here.

Alexander

[1981] HCA 17; 145 CLR 395, 399-401 (Gibbs CJ) and 426-7 (Mason J, with Aickin J agreeing)

Gibbs CJ: The safest and most satisfactory way of ensuring that a witness makes an accurate identification is by arranging for the witness to pick out from a group the person whom he saw on the occasion relevant to the crime. If an identification parade is held for that purpose, it goes without saying that precautions must be taken to ensure that no prompting, suggestion or hint is given to the witness that any particular member of the group is the suspect. For example, it would be unfair and improper to show to a witness, before the identification parade was held, a single photograph of a person who was said to be the suspect, and it would be unsafe to act on evidence of identification given in those circumstances: *R v Russell* [1977] 2 NZLR 20 at 27. Indeed, where a suspect had been arrested, and it was intended to ask a witness to attempt to identify him at an identification parade, it would be unfair to show the witness, before the parade, a number of photographs including that of the suspect: *R v Goss* (1923) 17 Cr App R 196; *R v Haslam* (1925) 19 Cr App R 59. On the other hand it may be necessary for a police officer to show a number of photographs to a witness in an attempt to obtain information as to the identity of an offender; if such witness did identify the offender from a photograph, it would not necessarily be unfair for that witness later to be asked to select the offender from a group at an identification parade, but the fact that the witness had seen the photograph might affect the value of the later identification at the parade: see *R v Dwyer & Ferguson* [1925] 2 KB 799.

The value of holding an identification parade is not only that, if properly carried out, it provides the most reliable method of identification, but also that it is necessarily held in the presence of the accused, who is thereby enabled to observe, and later bring to light, any unfairness in the way in which the parade was conducted, or any weakness in the way in which the witness made the identification. However, as a matter of legal principle, it seems to me impossible to say that the admissibility of evidence of a prior act of identification depends on the fact that an identification parade was held. As a matter of law it would be equally admissible to prove that an identification was made by a witness who was shown a collection of photographs and selected one which he said was the photograph of the person concerned. There are, however, two grounds of objection to

113 *Davey v Tasmania* [2020] TASCCA 12, [68].

114 See also *Davey*, ibid [68].

115 [2006] NSWCCA 164, [122] and [124]. See below, pp 607-609.

116 [2001] HCA 50; 206 CLR 650, [29]-[30].

the proof of identification by means of police photographs. In the first place, the accused will of necessity be absent when the identification is made, and has no means of knowing whether there was any unfairness in the process or whether the witness was convincing in the way in which he made the identification. Secondly, the production in evidence at the trial of photographs coming from the possession of the police is very likely to suggest to the jury that the person photographed had a police record, probably for offences of the kind in question.

For these reasons, it is most undesirable that police officers who have arrested a person on a charge of having committed a crime should arrange for potential witnesses to identify that person except at a properly conducted identification parade. Similarly, speaking generally, an identification parade should, wherever possible, be held when it is desired that a witness should identify a person who is firmly suspected to be the offender. …

Mason J (Aickin J agreeing): The problems which afflict identification evidence have their origin in four principal sources: (a) the variable quality of the evidence much of which is inherently fragile; (b) the use by the police of methods of identification which, though well suited to the investigation and detection of crime are not calculated to yield evidence of high probative value in a criminal trial; (c) the consequential need to balance the interests of the accused in securing a fair trial against the interests of the State in the efficient investigation and detection of crime by the police; and (d) the difficulty of accommodating the reception of certain types of identification testimony to accepted principles of the law of evidence.

Identification is notoriously uncertain. It depends upon so many variables. They include the difficulty one has in recognizing on a subsequent occasion a person observed, perhaps fleetingly, on a former occasion; the extent of the opportunity for observation in a variety of circumstances; the vagaries of human perception and recollection; and the tendency of the mind to respond to suggestions, notably the tendency to substitute a photographic image once seen for a hazy recollection of the person initially observed.

The use of photographs by police, especially photographs of known or suspected criminals, is an essential aid to the detection of persons who have committed crimes. Yet the use of such photographs before a jury may tend to suggest that the accused is known to the police as a criminal who has committed offences of the kind charged. And, as I have said, once a witness has seen a photograph which he links with the person seen, he tends to substitute the photographic image for his recollection.

Recognizing these dangers the English courts have tended to draw a distinction between an identification made in the course of investigating a crime, when the police may request a potential witness to make an identification from photographs, and an identification made after the accused has been taken into custody, when the use of photographs is frowned upon and the arrangement of an identification parade is urged as the course to be preferred. In the second situation the purpose of the identification is purely evidentiary; it is designed to produce evidence for use at the trial.

… Traditionally it has been accepted that a witness identifies the accused at the trial as the person whom he observed at the scene of, or in connection with, the crime. This "in court" identification, sometimes described as primary evidence, is of little probative value when made by a witness who has no prior knowledge of the accused, because at the trial circumstances conspire to compel the witness to identify the accused in the dock. It has been the practice to reinforce this "in court" identification by proving that the witness had earlier identified the accused out of court in a line-up or by selecting his photograph from a collection of photographs (*R v Fannon and Walsh* (1922) 22 SR (NSW) 427; *R v Bouquet* [1962] SR (NSW) 563; *R v Doyle* [1967] VR 698; see also *R v Goode* [1970] SASR 69; *Cross on Evidence*, 2nd Aust ed, p 54).

As the outcome in *Alexander* itself demonstrates, the principles it sets down do not necessarily preclude the admission of non-compliant identification evidence. Nevertheless, they do provide the rationales for courts to adopt a stringently wary approach to its admission. Therefore, where the police flout or overlook those principles, courts would be justified in not hesitating to apply the exclusionary discretions in ss 137 and 138.[117]

Desirable precautions attending identification processes include video recording the identification process and the keeping of clear records of what was said by whom.[118] The importance of such precautions is borne out by what occurred in *Chatters* where the court was required to determine precisely what had occurred during the identification process and whether it was flawed or contaminated in any way relying on witness testimony and without the benefit of any clear record or video recording of the identification. In summary, while ss 114 and 115 are absent from the Tasmanian *Evidence Act 2001*, the tenets underpinning them may still be relevant to a challenge to exclude identification evidence under ss 137 and 138, and by referencing relevant common law principles and the guidelines in the *Tasmania Police Manual*.[119] However, the likely impact of an argument to apply s 137 is now likely to be of limited effect, when considered in the light of more recent cases, including the High Court's decision in *Dickman*.

The 'properly conducted' parade, probative value and unfair prejudice

In most jurisdictions in Australia, detailed requirements such as the composition of the parade, including the number and appearance of 'foils', are primarily left to police codes or equivalent guidelines, or by way of interpretive decisions. In New South Wales guidance in identification procedures was found in the *NSW Police Code of Practice for CRIME (Custody, Rights, Investigation, Management and Evidence)* and currently in the *NSW Police Procedures for the Evidence Act*. Equivalent requirements for federal jurisdictions can be found in the ACT's *AFP Practical Guide on Identification Evidence (ACT Policing)*[120] as well as in the specific sections of the *Crimes Act 1900* (ACT).

In New South Wales, for example, guidelines as to the conduct of the identification parade include that:

- the parade consist of a minimum of six or seven foils, 'of similar age, height and appearance as the suspect' and that these foils should not be police officers;[121]
- it is preferable for the parade to be recorded on video, or photographed in colour;[122]

117 Consider, eg, statements of McInerney J tending to similar effect in the common law case *Burchielli* [1981] VR 611, 621. See the recent judgment of McMurdo P in the Queensland Court of Appeal that, relying in part on *Alexander*, takes a more robust approach to the exclusion: *Corowa* [2015] QCA 121.

118 *Festa* [2001] HCA 72; 208 CLR 593 (McHugh J).

119 See above n 108.

120 These procedures include sections on facial and body mapping, as well as the use of photoanthropometry. Victorian Police rely on the more regularly updated and publicly available Victoria Police Manual.

121 The *NSW Police Procedures for the Evidence Act*, above n 82, stipulates a minimum of six additional participants. The minimum number under the *AFP Practical Guide on Identification Evidence: Guidelines (ACT Policing)* is eight. Section 233(6)(a) of the *Crimes Act 1900* (ACT) requires that the parade must consist of at least nine people (including the suspect). In Tasmania, the minimum number is six additional participants.

122 This requirement is included in s 3ZM(3) and (4) of the *Crimes Act 1914* (Cth).

- the parade should be arranged and run by a police officer who is not involved in the investigation;[123] and
- the suspect is able to choose where they appear in the parade.[124]

Given their supplementary status, a failure to comply with such codes will not necessarily give rise to exclusion of evidence. Similarly, in England and Wales (which in Code D of PACE has gone further in the way of outlining the ideal conditions for standard parades as well as other identification procedures involving groups, images or CCTV footage) breaches of the Code do not mean that the evidence must be excluded.[125] A number of elements in the codes indicate attention to the empirical research in the area though they do not always map directly or completely on to the relevant findings or recommendations arising from research.

In contrast to this approach, the Commonwealth *Crimes Act 1914* and ACT *Crimes Act 1900* provide a legislative framework for the conduct of parades, and thus a stronger regulatory regime in terms of ensuring that parades are conducted fairly.[126] The Commonwealth and ACT regime repeats a number of the same factors in the *UEA* as to when it is reasonable to (not) hold a parade, but also includes detail as to the number of foils, and how they are to be selected, and the requirement in s 3ZM(5) of the *Crimes Act 1914* (Cth) that an 'identification parade must be arranged and conducted in a manner that will not unfairly prejudice the suspect'. The requirements in the Commonwealth and ACT *Crimes Acts* offer guidance in other jurisdictions relevant to assessing whether the composition or conduct of a parade has given rise to the risk of unfair prejudice but, undoubtedly, the *UEA* regime on identification parades would be strengthened by Regulations in all jurisdictions that detail requirements for the conduct of parades.

Central to the ideal of a properly conducted parade is the requirement that those conducting the parade must not intentionally influence the identification decision(s).[127] There is no doubt that this is one of the more important requirements and its explicit inclusion in the *UEA* should not be discounted.[128] Research on the conduct of parades identifies features that can have a significant effect on the accuracy of identification decisions. A particularly important requirement is that the witness is instructed that the person they saw at the relevant scene may or may not be present in the line-up. This instruction has been identified in the literature, and also in case law, as being an important protection against the incorrect selection of an innocent suspect, that is, a protection against 'false positive' decisions.[129] Similarly, it has been well established that the use of blind

123 See also *Crimes Act 1914* (Cth), s 3ZM, and *Crimes Act 1900* (ACT), s 233.

124 One of the suspect's rights under the *Tasmania Police Manual* (2021), above n 108, is the right to select where they appear in the parade.

125 See, eg, the discussion in *Lariba* [2015] EWCA Crim 478, relying in part on *Forbes* [2000] UKHL 66.

126 See *Crimes Act 1914* (Cth), s 3ZM, and *Crimes Act 1900* (ACT), s 233.

127 The recommendation from the Innocence Project that line-up and identification procedures be conducted 'double blind' is designed to ensure that the investigators conducting the parade *cannot* unintentionally (or indeed intentionally) influence the selection – and thus goes further than this legislative requirement.

128 The US Supreme Court jurisprudence has been preoccupied with the question of suggestive practice though, as noted above, their response may have had the effect of entrenching, rather than ameliorating, the negative effects of suggestive practices.

129 See, eg, Wells and Hasel, above n 23, 161: '[T]he failure to warn eyewitnesses prior to viewing a line up that the actual perpetrator might not be present serves to increase the chances of a mistaken identification when the perpetrator is not in the line up, with relatively little effect on accurate identifications when the perpetrator is in the line up'.

(or 'double blind') procedures, which would mean using police officers to conduct the identification parade who are not involved in the investigation, and thus do not know which line-up participant is the suspect, is a significant protection against influence upon witnesses.[130] The selection of foils has been investigated also, with research indicating that the best way to select foils is to match the description given by witnesses, not the appearance of the suspect.[131]

A failure to conduct a parade in accordance with guidelines in police codes or manuals can give rise to consideration of ss 137 and 135. And while a challenge under s 137 raises the question of whether the court can consider factors undermining the reliability of the evidence when determining its probative value, after *IMM* and *Dickman*, such an evaluation is unlikely to enable a court to exclude evidence where the weaknesses can be addressed in cross-examination[132] and a judicial warning. And the differences between New South Wales and Victoria, even before *IMM* (and *Dickman*), may have had little practical impact. For example, the fact that the impugned identification evidence in *Dupas* was admitted indicates that weak identification evidence may have been no more likely to be excluded in Victoria than in other jurisdictions.[133] Cases where a successful challenge to the probative value of the evidence in the context of applying s 137 arising from a live dentification parade are rare, but factors that have been raised include those identified in the empirical literature.[134] In *Fisher*[135] the NSW Court of Criminal Appeal, referring to Code D of PACE, held that identification evidence arising from a parade in which none of the foils matched the description offered by the witnesses, and the suspect was the only man of Aboriginal appearance included in the line-up (in circumstances where witnesses had described the offender as Aboriginal), had low probative value and should have been excluded under s 137:

> 21. … Both sides of the scale were infected by the inherent tendency at the identification parade for [the witness] to select the only person who answered two important elements in the description he had given. In my opinion, pursuant to s 137 this evidence should not have been admitted.

By comparison in *To*[136] a challenge to a line-up where the suspect was Vietnamese and the majority of the foils were Korean was unsuccessful.[137] In this case there was also a challenge raised on the basis that the witnesses were told that there would be a suspect in the line-up. The defence argued that not only did this raise concerns about unfair prejudice, it also ran counter to the requirement in s 114(2) that there should be no attempt to intentionally influence the witness to select the defendant. The court noted that the defence had argued that the police did not

130 The Innocence Project recommends identification procedures be conducted 'double blind'.

131 Brewer and Palmer, above n 33.

132 See Chapter 6.

133 *Dupas* [2012] VSCA 328; 218 A Crim R 507, see below, pp 613-615.

134 A survey of Canadian decisions has also indicated that judges (in judge-only trials) are attentive to some of the factors that can undermine the probative value of an identification. In particular, there was an awareness of how the composition and conduct of a parade could influence the probative value (and reliability) of the identification as well as of other system and estimator variables. However, this awareness did not necessarily translate into applying this knowledge to the case at hand: KC Bruer et al, 'Judicial Discussion of Eyewitness Identification Evidence' (2017) 49 *Canadian Journal of Behavioural Science* 209.

135 [2001] NSWCCA 380.

136 [2002] NSWCCA 247.

137 The evidence was challenged under *UEA*, ss 137 and 138, and the defendant also raised breaches of the (then relatively new) *NSW Police Procedures for the Evidence Act*, above n 82.

follow 'the usual practice of informing proposed identification witnesses that the offender himself was not necessarily a participant in the line-up'. This argument was also rejected.[138] As discussed further below, a number of cases involving picture identification evidence have raised similar arguments under s 137, and more recent cases, such as *Dupas*, have accepted that expert witnesses may offer assistance to the court either at the stage of determining the probative value of the evidence or to offer assistance to the jury.

Finally, it is worth noting that the preference for live parades has been handled differently in comparable jurisdictions. In the UK video line-up procedures (VIPER) are the preferred approach. They have the same status as the live parade.[139] The England and Wales Code D of PACE also covers a range of different, more or less formal, procedures, including video line-ups.[140] Each of these processes is more or less susceptible to influence and carries with them different levels of risk in terms of intentional or indeed unintentional influence or bias.[141] However, it is important to bear in mind the growing body of research, as well as the experience documented by organisations such as the Innocence Project, indicates that even properly conducted parades generate a high rate of errors.[142]

Identification from Pictures: *UEA*, s 115[143]

Despite the preference for live parades expressed in the *UEA*, in practice investigators are far more likely to rely on procedures using images and photographs to identify or confirm their suspect. The most common form is the photoboard, or photo array, sometimes presented simultaneously (that is, as noted above, with the suspect and foil images presented to the witness in one view), and, more commonly now in many Australian jurisdictions, sequentially.[144] In circumstances where it is not reasonably possible to hold a live parade, the *UEA* supports the turn to alternative, image based procedures, and the prosecution, in turn, will be able to rely on identification made by the witness from images. In many situations, this recourse to photo arrays, or other image based procedures, will be uncontentious. If the investigation is in its early stages, or the suspect is not in custody, or the defendant has clearly refused to participate in a parade, then it will be reasonable for investigators to rely on picture identification evidence as an alternative. And, as discussed above, the rise in the circulation of images,

138 [2002] NSWCCA 247, [31] (Barr J): 'Nothing was put before the Court to demonstrate that there is such a practice and no authority was cited requiring such a practice to be followed'. The judgment of McHugh J in *Festa* [2001] HCA 72; 208 CLR 593, [48]-[52] suggests that there may not be such a practice.

139 See <http://www.viper.police.uk> and A Memon, C Harvard, B Clifford, F Gabbert and M Watt, 'A Field Evaluation of the VIPER System: A New Technique for Eliciting Eyewitness Identification Evidence' (2011) 17(8) *Psychology, Crime and Law* 711.

140 These include group identification events, and situations where CCTV footage or other images are circulated to police officers in an attempt to identify a suspect: Memon et al, ibid.

141 See, eg, BW Behrman and SL Davey, 'Eyewitness Identification in Actual Criminal Cases: An Archival Analysis' (2001) 25 *Law and Human Behavior* 475; DB Wright and AT McDaid, 'Comparing System and Estimator Variables using Data from Real Line-ups' (1996) 10 *Applied Cognitive Psychology* 75; RCL Lindsay et al, 'Face Recognition in Eyewitness Memory' in G Rhodes et al (eds), *Oxford Handbook of Face Perception* (Oxford University Press, 2015) (note also comment on the fact that there is less research on system variables, as compared to estimator variables).

142 Ibid. In studies of actual line-ups, eyewitnesses tended to pick the innocent fillers approximately 20% of the time.

143 This section is not included in the *Evidence Act 2001* (Tas).

144 See above, p 574, fn 57.

especially via social media, has introduced new challenges to conventional procedures, as it is becoming more common for witnesses to approach police already having made an initial identification. Just as concerns about displacement have been raised in the context of cases examining whether s 114(2)(b) has been satisfied, similar concerns arise in relation to the use of photographic arrays following a spontaneous or informal identification by a witness.

Further, it is important to note that s 115 regulates 'picture identification evidence', defined in s 115 as 'identification evidence relating to an identification made wholly or partly by the person who made the identification examining pictures *kept for the use of police officers*'.[145] The *UEA* does not provide any direct guidance on admissibility or factors to be considered when dealing with spontaneous identifications made by a witness who has been exposed to an image via the print or broadcast media, Facebook, or other social media platforms. And, as a further example of how the legislation is out of date and operates inconsistently, the narrow scope of s 115 can mean that the conditions that are imposed under s 115 do *not* always apply, even where an identification has been made via a procedure that bears all the hallmarks of a formal photographic array.[146]

Turning, however, to the operation of s 115, the effect of the section is that police can turn to photographic (or video) image based procedures:

- at the investigative stage where the suspect is not yet identified or is not in custody; or
- where the suspect may be in custody, but his or her appearance has changed significantly since the offence was committed (s 115(5)(b)); or
- if the accused has refused to participate in a parade (s 115(5)(a)); or
- it would not be reasonable to hold a parade (s 115(5)(c)); or
- it would be unfair to the accused to hold an identification parade (s 114(4)).

The factors to be taken into account when determining either reasonableness or fairness are the same as those included in s 114 and thus the same case law and considerations would apply.[147]

Where image based identification procedures using 'pictures kept for the use of police officers' are relied on, they must be conducted in line with the requirements of s 115, the most important of which is that the identification is inadmissible if it is based on photographs that suggest that the defendant is in police custody: *UEA*, s 115(2), (3).[148] This is to counteract the so-called 'rogues

145 This has been held to preclude images such as CCTV footage of the crime in question, even though such images may be 'used' by police officers and/or in the course of an investigation. See *Hennessy* [2001] NSWCCA 36. Conversely, the ALRC suggests that there is nothing to preclude the use of surveillance images, as long as they do not suggest that the suspect is under observation in connection with a criminal offence.

146 In *Dickman*, for example, it was common ground that the images used by the police, despite being presented in a standard array, were not 'pictures kept for the use of police officers'. See *Dickman* [2015] VSCA 311, [78], though it is not made clear in the judgment(s) the source or nature of the photographs or why they were characterised in this way. In these circumstances, while the protective provisions in s 115 did not apply, the requirement in s 114(2) that the identification be conducted with intentional influence was revived, throwing into sharp relief the lack of such a protection during formal picture identification procedures conducted under s 115.

147 Under s 115(6), 'Sections 114(3), (4), (5) and (6) apply in determining, for the purposes of subsection (5)(c) of this section, whether it would have been reasonable to have held an identification parade'.

148 The section also preferences the use of images taken after the accused has been taken into custody (s 115(3)) and allows an accused to request that the jury be informed that the pictures were taken after the accused was taken into custody: s 115(7)(a).

gallery' effect,[149] the dominant concern at the time the Act was drafted, whereby conventional 'mug shots' might suggest that the suspect already has a criminal record or propensity, or is otherwise known to police.[150] Early cases challenged the use of photographs of suspects in 'prison greens' (clothing which appears to be a generic green tracksuit, associated with being in gaol) as well as photographs of suspects taken in a location that was identifiable as being associated with (criminal) court proceedings. In *Maklouf*[151] the photographs were taken of the defendant outside the cafe of the Downing Centre, a major court complex in Sydney's CBD. Those familiar with the building would have recognised the location. Despite this, these were held to be acceptable on the assumption that the photographs showed the appellant engaging in 'innocent conversation' at that location and, thus, did not give rise to any unfair prejudice by way of suggestion. In *Pace*[152] the witness was shown a book of over 300 photographs labelled, 'Footscray – Photobook – Dark Skinned and African Males'. The photographs were described as 'passport type' photographs, and each was accompanied by an eight- or nine-digit serial number. A small number of the photographs showed a background that was consistent with a cell, and one appeared to have a height scale in the background. All were photographs taken in custody. The defendant challenged the identification(s) made using the photobook, on the grounds that the photographs used breached the condition in s 115(2). In rejecting this ground of appeal, the court said;

> 23. For picture identification evidence to be inadmissible under s 115(2), the 'pictures examined' must 'suggest' that they are 'pictures of persons in custody'. In ordinary parlance, to 'suggest' is to insinuate, create or evoke an impression, or to call up or bring something to mind. Thus, in our view, there must be something in the nature of the photographs themselves which might create the impression in the mind that they are of persons in police custody.
>
> 24. In our opinion, the trial judge was correct to observe that – save for the nine photographs referred to – all of the pictures are 'consistent with the photographs taken for driving, boating and shooter's licences', or 'identification photographs required by many employees who work in all manner of working environments'. Moreover, we agree with his Honour's view that it is 'mere speculation' as to what the eight or nine digit numbers at the bottom of each photograph refer to, or what their function is. The words, 'Footscray – Photobook – Dark Skinned and African Males', and 'Footscray – Confidential', do nothing to add to any impression beyond what the photographs themselves suggest. The Victoria Police logo on the front of the booklet does not, in our opinion, detract from that view (and, in any event, any sensitivity about the jury viewing the logo might be eliminated by the simple expedient of exhibiting a copy of the photobook with the front page removed).
>
> 25. As to the nine photographs which, it is submitted, might independently suggest that they are of persons in police custody, we agree with the trial judge's observations. There is nothing in the background of those photographs – the suggested height scale, presence of

149 See, eg, *Alexander* [1981] HCA 17; 145 CLR 395, 409. In *Buchanan* [2004] NSWSC 816 the witness, himself an inmate, was shown a video of 194 inmates from a wing in prison in which a murder had occurred. All were wearing 'prison greens'. It was common ground that in such a case s 115 had no application, but the court nonetheless had to consider whether it would have been reasonable to hold an identification parade for the purposes of admitting the identification evidence of the witness elicited in part via this procedure (under s 114).

150 See *Maklouf* [1999] NSWCCA 94. Note that contextual information, sometimes referred to as domain irrelevant information, can be present in other identification procedures. For example, fingerprint examiners are routinely exposed to the criminal records associated with the fingerprints that are generated for analysis by algorithmic selection.

151 [1999] NSWCCA 94.

152 *Pace and Collins (a Pseudonym)* [2014] VSCA 317.

> security mesh, the appearance of a secure door with substantial hinges, or the like – which suggests objectively that the males depicted in the photos are in police custody.[153]

It is also necessary as a condition of admissibility, if identification from pictures is permitted (because, for example, the defendant refused to take part in a parade), for the photographs used to be ones that have been taken after the defendant has been taken into custody (s 115(3)), unless their appearance has changed (s 115(4)(a)) or it would not have been 'reasonably practicable' to take a photograph (s 115(4)(b)).[154] So, for example, in a case where there was a substantial delay between the commission of the offence and the trial, a photographic array will utilise image(s) of the suspect taken contemporaneously with the time of the offence, and these will need to be matched with foils of an equivalent aged appearance and style. In this type of case it will not be possible to use a picture taken after the defendant was taken into custody, since it is clear that their appearance will have changed significantly in the intervening period.[155] If picture identification evidence is admitted, and the defence requests it, the jury should be informed either that the picture was made after the defendant was taken into custody (if that was the case, see s 115(7)(a)), or otherwise warned that 'that they must not assume that the defendant has a criminal record or has previously been charged with an offence': s 115(7)(b).

Curiously perhaps, s 115 does not include the same explicit stipulation contained in s 114 that there be no intentional influence on the part of investigators. But this would nonetheless be a factor in considering either exclusion under s 137 (and, potentially, s 138). If the evidence is held to be admissible, it may be raised in the judicial warning: see, for example, *Nelson*[156] where the police officer implied that the accused's photograph was among those about to be shown to the witness, and *Yassar Bakir*,[157] a case concerned with a prosecutor's misconduct in disclosing to the witness that she had incorrectly selected a foil.[158] And, as indicated by *Dickman*, the provision in s 114(2) may become relevant, even where the identification is based on images or pictures, if such pictures are not 'kept for the use of police officers'.

The obligation that those conducting the process should guard against doing anything that might influence the selection is included in police procedures such as the *NSW Police Procedures for the Evidence Act*:

> When using photographs to enable a witness to identify a suspect:
> - use as many as possible. A minimum of 20 photographs is preferable. If the offence is a Commonwealth offence, you must show photographs of at least nine different people

153 See also *DPP (Vic) v Byrne (No 2)* [2016] VSC 345.

154 This is an objective test, and so even in a situation where a decision not to take and use a contemporaneous photograph was apparently made in good faith – based on concerns that such a photograph might stand out in the array – a strict application of s 115(4)(b) led to the exclusion of an identification made using a photograph of the defendant taken 11 months before the relevant offence: *Dargan* [2015] NSWDC 121.

155 In some cases, prosecutions have been initiated up to five decades after the alleged offences occurred.

156 [1999] NSWCCA 221.

157 [2009] NSWDC 12.

158 See also *Cope* [2018] VSCA 261 where an argument was raised about intentional influence and lack of compliance with the Victorian Police procedures. *Afu and Caleo (No 11)* [2018] NSWSC 190 also raised the issue of compliance with *NSW Police Procedures for the Evidence Act*, above n 82.

- use ones of people who resemble the suspect in age and general appearance and which do not have features visibly different from those described by the witness before viewing the photographs
- ensure they do not suggest the people are in police custody
- do not say or do anything which might lead the witness to infer they were taken when the people depicted were in police custody
- do not say or do anything which might cause or influence a witness to select a particular one
- if more than one witness will be asked to identify a suspect from photographs, do not allow any witness to be present when any other witness is called upon to make the identification
- tell the witness the suspect might not be among the photographs being viewed.[159]

If the accused is in custody, investigators can only rely on 'picture' identifications if the accused has refused to take part in an identification parade, or it would not have been reasonable to hold a parade, or the accused's appearance has changed significantly since the time of the offence or observation. In *Carpenter*,[160] the court considered both the detailed requirements governing picture identification procedures in the Australian Capital Territory and the use of digitally modified photographs. It also addressed whether a suspect must have had the opportunity to seek or receive legal advice for their refusal to trigger s 115.[161]

Image based identifications, probative value and prejudicial effect

Just as failure to conduct an identification parade properly can give rise to an argument that the visual identification evidence ought to be excluded under s 137, likewise, there have been a number of attempts to exclude picture identification evidence where there has been a poor choice of foils or the array is considered unfair for other reasons,[162] or there has been some other breach of codes or guidelines. As with the cases involving identification parades, cases where the evidence has been excluded are rare. In *Pace and Collins (a Pseudonym)*,[163] in addition to the arguments based on s 115(2), the defence raised breaches of ordinary procedures as part of an (unsuccessful) argument based on s 138 and also challenged, unsuccessfully, the use of a photobook drawing within s 137:

> 48. … It was submitted that the picture identification is "very likely to suggest to the jury that the persons photographed have a police record, probably for offences of the kind in question". The unfair prejudice to the applicant by virtue of his image appearing in the photobook three times is, it was submitted, incapable of being remedied by direction under s 115(7). That prejudice is "amplified" by the repetition of one of the photographs, and the allocation of two separate numbers, appearing at the bottom of each photograph.

---

159 *NSW Police Procedures for the Evidence Act*, above n 82, 35.

160 [2011] ACTSC 71. The police investigators describe the procedure as a 'photoboard' one, but in fact the process described by the judge was a sequential digital line-up. It is thus consistent with the position held by the Innocence Project, above n 29.

161 See s 114(5). On this point, compare also *Massey* [2009] ACTCA 12, which suggests that the suspect must at least know that an identification parade is contemplated. A general refusal to speak to or see an investigating police officer is insufficient.

162 Some cases, including *Smith (Mundarra)* [2001] HCA 50; 206 CLR 650, have included discussion of the particular dangers and difficulties attendant on identifying people from photographs as opposed to line-ups. Broadly speaking, the research on photo matching and unfamiliar face recognition would indicate that our capacity to recognise unfamiliar faces in images is very poor. See, eg, Wilcock, Bull and Milne, above n 19, ch 2.

163 [2014] VSCA 317. See also *Tasmania v Chatters* [2013] TASSC 61, discussed above, pp 588, 591.

> It was submitted that the probative value of the evidence is reduced by virtue of the images appearing in the book of photographs three times. In particular, so it was argued, the second and third identifications "add nothing". The probative value of the evidence is outweighed by the danger of unfair prejudice, in that the jury will give the evidence undue weight, and misuse the evidence by reasoning that the applicant is someone who has come into contact with the police (on multiple occasions).

Some earlier cases had emphasised the importance of a fair array as critical to ensuring the probative value of the evidence did not outweigh the danger of unfair prejudice to the defendant,[164] and there are cases where the deployment of a distinctive feature in the composition of the array has led to the exclusion of an identification. For example, in *Doidge*,[165] the witness description of the offender included substantial detail about the hair style, including a prominent 'rat's tail'. In rejecting the witness's subsequent identification of the defendant, the judge said:

> 2. Evidence was admitted on the voir dire as to this matter including the printout of the line-up identification comprising 20 people who appeared to be young males, all of whom appeared to be around their mid-20s with some form of tattoo on their face. The accused was in his mid-20s and had a small tattoo below his left eye. The photographic line-up, which is Exhibit VD-A, also contained the charge image in relation to the accused person which showed rat's tail coming from the back of his hair across his left shoulder. There was no other person in the other 19 photographs who has apparent any rat's tail. In fact, the accused's rat's tail seemed placed across his shoulder so as to make it readily identifiable.
>
> 3. It was submitted on behalf of the Crown that others may have had rat's tails but they were not apparent. In my view, that does not ameliorate the risk of unfair prejudice to the accused. …
>
> 14. In any event, the evidence raised serious questions as to prejudice and I have formed the view that the evidence comprising the photograph identification parade is prejudicial. Of course any evidence which implicates an accused person is generally prejudicial. The Court is required to undertake an exercise under s 137 of weighing the probative value of the evidence against the danger of unfair prejudice to the defendant. The assessment of probative value requires the court to have regard to the extent to which the evidence may rationally affect, directly or indirectly, the probative value of the evidence. …
>
> 19. In the present matter, for the reasons which I have given, most particularly the presence of the rat's tail in only one of the twenty photographs shown to the complainant, in circumstances where the complainant has consistently referred to the rat's tail as an identifying feature, inevitably this would cause unfair prejudice to the accused. In my opinion, the unfair prejudice to the defendant substantially outweighs the probative value of the identification evidence in those circumstances.

Overall, however, the courts in New South Wales have generally adopted a less exclusionary orientation. The case of *Shamouil*,[166] establishing the NSW narrower approach to s 137, was concerned with the probative value of photographic identification procedure. Similarly, *Mundine*[167] confirmed that the judge in assessing the probative value of identification evidence was not to consider the potential unreliability of picture identification evidence. This approach has of course been confirmed by the High Court in *IMM*,[168] a decision that underpinned the High Court's decision in *Dickman*.

---

164 See, eg, *Nguyen* [2003] NSWSC 1068.
165 [2018] NSWDC 330 (Wilson SC, DCJ).
166 [2006] NSWCCA 112; 66 NSWLR 228.
167 [2008] NSWCCA 55.
168 *IMM* [2016] HCA 14; 257 CLR 300.

Dickman

[2017] HCA 24; 261 CLR 601 (citations omitted)

Dickman had been convicted in in a 2014 jury trial in the County Court of Victoria of intentionally causing serious injury and making a threat to kill. The facts giving rise to the conviction were complex and multiple modes of identification were at play during the trial, including 'recognition' evidence based on CCTV footage and visual and voice comparisons undertaken by the jury. The key issue on appeal, however, was the admission of identification evidence from the primary witness, Faisal Aakbari (FA), a German national on holiday in Melbourne. Around 3am on the morning of 27 September 2009, FA (who was then 18 years old) sought to gain entry to the Dallas Showgirls Nightclub (the 'Dallas Club') by claiming, falsely, to be a member of the German chapter of the 'Hells Angels Motorcycle Club' at the entrance. He made this claim to Ali Chaouk, who was a prospective member of the Hells Angels, with this claim being passed on to others, including Dickman (who was a full member). Unbeknownst to Chaouk, his phone was being monitored and recorded (in connection with another investigation). These recordings included 'background conversations' between FA and others during the evening in question at the Dallas Club. It was the Crown contention that the voice of the defendant, Dickman, could also be heard in the background. Later the same evening, FA was taken from the Dallas Club to premises used as a Hell's Angels clubhouse and severely assaulted. It was the Crown case that Dickman was the instigator and main assailant during the assault on FA. In his description of the evening, FA described meeting an 'old man' at the Dallas Club (a man who appeared in CCTV footage from the club entrance shown to FA), and it was the Crown case that this 'old man' then went on to lead the assault on FA later in the evening. Police initially suspected that the 'old man' in the footage was a man called Michael Cooper, and in 2009 FA was shown a photo array that included Cooper. FA selected Cooper from this array. Cooper was subsequently eliminated as a suspect, and two years later FA was shown a new array that included an image of the new suspect, Dickman. FA selected the image of Dickman from this array. Overall, the procedures leading up to this identification were described by one judge during the High Court hearing in the following terms: 'One hopes that there are not too many identifications done by photo board like that in Victoria. It broke all the rules that one can conceive of'.[169] In a decision handed down before *IMM*, the Victorian Court of Appeal had rejected the 2011 identification of Dickman from the photoboard on the basis that its probative value was outweighed by the danger of unfair prejudice, taking into account that Aakbari was an unreliable identification witness. On appeal, the High Court restored the trial judge's original decision to allow the evidence to be given.

Kiefel CJ, Bell, Keane, Nettle and Edelman JJ:

The probative value of the August 2011 identification

41. The majority and minority analyses in the Court of Appeal proceeded upon acceptance of the prosecutor's stance at the trial, which was that evidence of Aakbari's initial identification of Cooper would only be adduced in the prosecution case if the August 2011 identification was also admitted. In the event the latter identification was rejected, the prosecutor flagged the likelihood that cross-examination would make it admissible "in rebuttal". In this Court, the respondent contests this analysis, submitting

169 *Dickman* [2017] HCA Trans 71 (Nettle J).

that the prosecutor was obliged to lead evidence of Aakbari's identification of Cooper. In circumstances in which Aakbari had not resiled from the Cooper identification, he submits that its admission did not require that the August 2011 identification, made subsequently, also be received.

42. In this Court, the appellant accepts that discharge of its duty of fairness required that it adduce evidence that within days of the assault Aakbari identified Cooper as his assailant, and that the admission of this evidence did not necessitate that the August 2011 identification also be admitted. While cross-examination of Aakbari may have enabled the prosecution to adduce the August 2011 identification, the appellant's concession should be accepted. The determination of whether s 137 required the exclusion of the August 2011 identification, as the trial judge appreciated, did not turn on whether Aakbari's identification of Cooper was, or was likely, to be received in evidence.

43. In written submissions, the appellant complains that the Court of Appeal majority wrongly took into account their Honours' assessment that Aakbari was an unreliable witness of identification. As the appellant acknowledged on the hearing of the appeal, the complaint is not to the point in circumstances in which there is no dispute that the probative value of the evidence was rightly assessed by the trial judge as low. This was an estimate that did not depend upon his Honour's assessment of Aakbari's truthfulness or reliability as a witness. Assuming that the jury would accept the August 2011 identification at its highest, it was identification with limited capacity to rationally affect the assessment of the probability that the respondent was the "old man". This is to recognise not only the limitations of photographic identification, but also that the August 2011 identification was evidence of Aakbari's opinion that of the 11 men whose photographs were included in the array, the respondent's photograph bore the closest resemblance to his recollection of the appearance of the man who had assaulted him two years earlier.

44. Aakbari's opinion that the photograph of the respondent resembled his assailant was nonetheless a relevant circumstance. The fact that standing alone its probative value was low did not require its exclusion unless that value was outweighed by the danger of unfair prejudice. Yet each of the reasons that the Court of Appeal majority gave for the conclusion that the evidence required exclusion was concerned with its low probative value. The only unfair prejudice to which the Court of Appeal majority referred was the "seductive quality" of identification evidence, which, their Honours said with reference to a passage in the joint reasons in *Domican v The Queen*, is difficult to ameliorate by directions.

45. Recognition of the seductive effect of identification evidence led their Honours in *Domican* to state a requirement of the common law of evidence that where evidence of identification represents a significant part of the prosecution case, the judge must warn the jury of the dangers of convicting on it in a case in which its reliability is disputed. Their Honours did not suggest that the seductive effect of identification evidence cannot be addressed by judicial direction. The point made in *Domican* was the need for cogent and effective directions tailored to the circumstances of the case.

46. Section 116 of the Evidence Act, as at the date of trial, reflected the concerns voiced in *Domican* respecting identification evidence. It required the judge to warn the jury of the special need for caution before accepting identification evidence and of the reasons for that need for caution both generally and in the circumstances of the case.

47. Aakbari's evidence of the August 2011 identification was unlikely to have the seductive effect of an identifying witness who is adamant that the accused is the offender. The Court of Appeal majority did not explain the error in the trial judge's conclusion that directions drawing attention to the readily apparent limitations of the August 2011 identification would minimise any risk that the jury might give the evidence disproportionate weight.

48. Unfair prejudice may be occasioned because evidence has some quality which is thought to give it more weight in the jury's assessment than it warrants or because it is apt to invite the jury to draw an inference about some matter which would ordinarily be

excluded from evidence. The "rogues' gallery" effect of picture identification evidence creates a risk of the latter kind because the appearance of some photographs kept by the police may invite the jury to infer that the accused has a criminal record. On the appeal in this Court, the respondent's argument concentrates on the danger of unfair prejudice of this latter kind, which is said to arise from unsatisfactory features of the August 2011 identification.

49. The respondent points out that Aakbari did not volunteer that he had any doubts concerning his identification of Cooper. The police told Aakbari that he was mistaken and that they had identified the persons who were in fact responsible for the assault on him. This was the context in which Aakbari was told that arrangements would be made for him to look at further photographs. This background made it necessary for defence counsel to cross-examine Aakbari to elicit his agreement that he understood at the time of the August 2011 identification that the array would contain a photograph of the man whom the police suspected of being the "old man". The cross-examination was necessary in order to expose a weakness in the identification but it inevitably served to highlight that the police suspected the respondent of being the offender.

50. Before addressing this aspect of the prejudice on which the respondent's argument relies, the question of the propriety of the police advising Aakbari that his identification of Cooper was mistaken should be addressed. It would have been wrong to tell Aakbari that his identification was a mistake if the police did not have cogent evidence that Cooper was not the "old man". …

[In order to evaluate whether it was appropriate to inform Aakbari that he had made a mistake, the High Court discussed whether the defence strategy at the trial included suggesting that, notwithstanding the alibi evidence that had been accepted by the police, there was nonetheless a possibility that Cooper was the real offender. They concluded that the defence had ultimately made a forensic decision not to make that argument explicitly, and thus had also decided not to directly test the alibi evidence.]

54. … The admissibility of the August 2011 identification is to be determined upon acceptance that the police were in possession of evidence that excluded Cooper as the offender. In these circumstances it was not improper for the police to tell Aakbari that he appeared to have been mistaken and to ask him to participate in a further attempt to identify his assailant.

55. It was wrong, however, to convey to Aakbari that the suspect's photograph would be included in the photoboard presentation. It appears that the photoboards that were shown to Aakbari in August 2011 contained a printed "preamble", stating that the viewer should not assume that the presentation included a photograph of any person suspected of being the offender. The value of this instruction was effectively undermined by Detective Sergeant Condon's earlier advice to Aakbari that the police had spoken to the men whom the police believed to be responsible for the assault and that they would arrange for him to be shown further photographs. Nonetheless, criticism of the police for the conduct of the identification should not have resulted in the exclusion of relevant evidence unless such probative value as it possessed was outweighed by the danger of unfair prejudice.

56. The unfair prejudice occasioned by the disclosure of Detective Sergeant Condon's suspicion that the respondent was the offender was the risk that the jury would infer that his suspicion was based on matters about the respondent known to Detective Sergeant Condon which were not in evidence. That risk, however, does not appear to have been a real one in the context of this trial. The evidence shows that police attended the Thomastown clubroom at about 6.40 am on Sunday 27 September 2009 and took details of the registration numbers of four cars parked outside it. One of these was a car bearing a South Australian plate which was associated with Gerrie. The text message transmitted from the respondent's mobile telephone to Gerrie's mobile telephone on the morning of 26 September 2009 linked the respondent to Gerrie. Telephone records placed the

> respondent in the vicinity of the Thomastown clubroom around the time of the assault. The reasons that the investigation came to focus on the respondent were explained in the evidence. Whether the evidence proved the respondent's guilt was the issue for the jury but there is no reason to conclude that the suspicion that the police entertained as to his guilt was based on information apart from the material that was before the jury.
>
> 57. The appellant is right to contend that the jury was not required to grapple with "abstract notions as to the dangers of identification evidence", as the limitations of the August 2011 identification were apparent. The trial judge's conclusion that the danger of unfair prejudice was minimal and could be adequately addressed by direction was justified. It follows that the admission of the August 2011 identification did not involve error.

As an obiter point, the High Court considered the Victorian Court of Appeal was not justified in quashing the conviction and ordering a new trial on the basis of a miscarriage of justice due to the admission of evidence of the 2011 identification. The High Court concluded that there was ample other unchallenged evidence that Dickman was present at the Dallas Club on the night in question. They also viewed for themselves the CCTV footage from the Dallas Club, indicating that an 'old man', as described by the complainant, can be seen clearly in the (grainy) footage. However, it could be argued that, while there was evidence from Gerrie that Dickman had subsequently travelled to the Clubhouse, overall this could not be said to be as strong as evidence that placed him at the Dallas Club. The numerous errors made by the complainant identifying others at the Thomastown Clubhouse, and the potential contamination of the August 2011 identification process due to the complainant viewing CCTV footage from the Dallas Club, as well as the suggestive environment of the final positive identification of Dickman, raised questions about how the High Court subsumed the issue of guilt into the question of who was present at the Dallas Club.[170] In contrast, the VSCA decision, while inattentive to the questionable quality of all of the other evidence of identification that was put before the jury, did at least identify the very real risk of the displacement effect on the 2011 identification following the complainant viewing the CCTV footage.[171] Like the law reform focus mentioned above, the approach of the High Court in this case reinforces a strong preference to focus on warnings despite the identification evidence in *Dickman* being elicited via highly suggestive or compromised procedures, long recognised by research as heightening the danger of misidentification.[172]

In the s 137 context, identification made spontaneously or where it may have been contaminated by a displacement effect can be persuasive in circumstances that raise concerns about unfair prejudice. For example, consider the Victorian

170 Cf *Dhanhoa* [2003] HCA 40; 217 CLR 1. This elision may be justified in so far as the defence case seems to have been that there were significant differences between the description of the 'old man' and the appearance of Dickman, implying that there had been a misidentification of Dickman as the 'old man' at the Dallas Club (as well as a misidentification of the assailant at Thomastown as that same 'old man').

171 This, however, does not excuse the lack of attention to the invitation to the jury to engage in their own comparisons, a process that has been shown to be susceptible to high rates of error, even under optimal conditions. See JP Davis and T Valentine, 'CCTV on Trial: Matching Video Images with the Defendant in the Dock' (2009) 23 *Applied Cognitive Psychology* 482.

172 See, eg, A Skalon and J Beaudry, 'The effectiveness of judicial instructions on eyewitness evidence in sensitizing jurors to suggestive identification procedures captured on video' (2020) 16 *Journal of Experimental Criminology* 565. See also *DPP v Hague* [2018] VSCA 39 and *Hague* [2019] VSCA 218. In *Hague* it was confirmed that a trial judge cannot take into account inconsistent identifications when assessing the probative value of the evidence. See also *Selby* [2017] NSWCCA 40 on the relevance of 'corroboration'.

case of *Bayley*[173] where evidence of a photoboard identification of the accused was excluded because the witness had earlier identified him from a photograph circulating on Facebook. This case arose after the highly publicised conviction of Adrian Bayley for the murder of Jill Meagher when a number of women came forward alleging that Bayley had sexually assaulted them some years previously. The Victorian Court of Appeal found, applying *IMM*, that the photoboard identification made by one of the witnesses, even 'taken at its highest', was of such low probative value to be, 'not merely weak, but simply unconvincing'.[174] However, the High Court's later approach in *Dickman* indicates that, to the extent that issues of reliability can be considered at all, they may be limited to outlier cases such as *Bayley*, or the rare cases where lack of reliability impacts the reasonableness of the conviction at large.[175]

Obligation on the Judge to Warn the Jury

Scope and content of identification warnings under the *UEA*

Warnings about identification evidence, as defined by the *UEA*, are dealt with under s 116 (or in Victoria, under the *JDA 2015*). Other evidence of identification that falls outside of the definition is governed by s 165[176] and, except in Victoria, the common law obligations are preserved in s 165(5). In Victoria identification evidence warnings, and warnings about evidence that may be unreliable, are now included in a separate Act, discussed below. Section 116 of the *UEA* creates a mandatory obligation on a trial judge to warn the jury of a 'special need for caution' when assessing identification evidence within the definition (that is, incriminating identification evidence about the defendant). It is clear from the definition of 'identification evidence' that *UEA*, Part 3.9, provisions do not apply to 'negative' identification evidence that exculpates the defendant. Nonetheless, it has been recognised that the court may need to address separately the risks associated with such evidence.[177] Negative identification evidence was considered by the NSW Court of Criminal Appeal in *Kanaan*.[178]

Kanaan was one of three men who had carried out a 'contract' shooting. The exculpatory evidence came from a witness who was familiar with Kanaan (and the two other co-accused). There was evidence that they were friends of her husband and that she had met them reasonably frequently over the previous two years.

173 [2016] VSCA 160. The outcome in Bayley may not be representative of the trend, however, when considering the admission of identification evidence obtained in similar circumstances. Compare, for example, the comment in *Dia* [2014] NSWCCA 9, [68], confirming the admissibility of an informal identification made by the witness from Facebook, 'The process of identification undertaken by Ms McCann was analogous with her attending a police station and examining a photographic array or going to a police station to view a line-up'. Compare also *JH* [2017] NSWCCA 22. See generally McGorrery, above n 6.

174 *Bayley* [2016] VSCA 160, [55]; see *IMM* [2016] HCA 14; 257 CLR 300, [50]. See A Skalon and JL Beaudry, 'The science behind *Bayley v The Queen* (2016)' (2018) 26 *Psychiatry, Psychology and Law* 219.

175 See, eg, *Penfold* [2016] NSWCCA 101. In this case the court found that the verdict was unreasonable without recourse to a consideration of s 137.

176 See Chapter 14.

177 *JDA 2015* (Vic), s 35.

178 [2006] NSWCCA 109. See also *Mulholland* [2019] NSWCCA 257 in relation to both exculpatory evidence and descriptive evidence of the kind dealt with in *Trudgett* [2008] NSWCCA 62; 70 NSWLR 696.

Mrs Zahabe had witnessed the lead up to and the actual shooting (under lighting conditions that she described as 'pretty lit up', and for a period of five to ten minutes), and she provided a description (shortly after the event) that did not match the descriptions of the three accused. She had also made a statement to police, 11 days later and, after having been shown an identification video containing images of the three accused, that while she recognised Kanaan and a second co-accused in that video neither of them was one of the three men who had carried out the shooting. There was other positive identification evidence that could be regarded as inculpatory (though none of it was especially compelling). The trial judge had delivered a warning in relation to the identification evidence at the trial, in line with the requirements of s 116. The appellants argued on appeal that the trial judge ought to have dealt with the exculpatory evidence differently – in essence, their argument was that exculpatory identification evidence ought not to be subject to the same type of cautionary treatment. While confirming that the evidence did not fall within the scope of s 116 obligations, the NSW Court of Criminal Appeal rejected the argument that exculpatory identification evidence ought not to be subject of a warning. The court relied instead on the general warning provision, s 165:

> 126. Accordingly, we are satisfied that negative (or exculpatory) identification evidence is "evidence of a kind that may be unreliable", and thus falls within the meaning of s 165(1).
>
> 127. The appellants put forward a further alternative submission, that there existed good reasons for not giving the warning required by s 165(2), thereby relieving the judge of the need to comply with that requirement. Section 165(3) provides:
>
> > The judge need not comply with subsection (2) if there are good reasons for not doing so.
>
> The appellants assert that no warning should be given in relation to evidence which favours the accused. In our opinion, it is not possible to determine in relation to any particular category of evidence that there are good reasons for not complying with the requirement to give a warning where *any* evidence within that category has been given. Section 165(3) is directed to the circumstances of the particular case, not to specific categories of evidence in every case.
>
> 128. In any event, we do not accept that a warning should not be given in relation to negative identification evidence simply because it favours the accused. Whilst there may be good reasons in a particular case not to give the warning in relation to *some* evidence within this category which may be unreliable – for example, because it was led by the Crown and its source is the accused himself and thus self-serving: see *R v Salama* [1999] NSWCCA 105 at [87] – the dangers inherent in any kind of *identification* evidence are such that it would be wrong to exclude warnings in relation to that category of evidence, whatever the nature of the circumstances of the case, as is now submitted by the appellants. Each case must depend on its own circumstances.

It is worth noting that the principles outlined in *Kanaan* apply not only where there has been 'negative' identification evidence such as that given by Mrs Zahabe, but also where, as had been the case in *Rose*,[179] the negative evidence is led by the defence about someone other than the defendant. In *Rose*, the evidence in question had come from a witness who had identified a woman matching the description of the victim at a time and place that was inconsistent with the Crown theory.[180]

---

179 (2002) 55 NSWLR 701. See also *Mulholland*, ibid, discussing *Rose* [2002] NSWCCA 455, [55]ff.

180 This was also the case in *Milat* (unreported, NSWSC, 23 April 1996, Hunt CJ at CL). See also *Williams* [2019] NSWCCA 53, raising the question of whether warnings were sufficient in a case of 'recognition'.

In terms of limiting or defining the circumstances in which a warning under s 116 is required, Gleeson CJ and Hayne J indicated in *Dhanhoa*[181] that a literal interpretation of s 116 would fail to appreciate be 'the adversarial context in which the legislation operates' and instead the section should be 'read down' to apply only where identification is disputed.

Trudgett[182] applied this reasoning from *Dhanhoa*. The court found that no warning under s 116 was required since the 'identification' of the appellant did not fall within the definition, and was not in reality disputed in so far as his *presence* at the party at which the assault was said to have occurred was concerned. Thus, s 116 did not mandate a warning and, in the absence of a request under s 165, there was no obligation on the trial judge to warn the jury about the potential unreliability of the evidence that placed him at the scene. On the other hand, courts have reaffirmed that distinctions as between 'recognition' and 'identification' tend to be unhelpful when determining the need for a cautionary or comprehensive identification warning:

> The suggested distinction between 'recognition cases' and 'identification cases' is of limited utility. In *R v Lovett*, Ormiston JA (with whom Buchanan and Ashley JJA agreed) said that:
>
> > Difficulties of observation at the time a crime is committed frequently are just as great and the possibility of jumping to conclusions as to the identity of the miscreant with a person already known may likewise be just as great, albeit that there will ordinarily be no need for any subsequent formal identification process. What is required in every case will vary, the object in each being to avoid a miscarriage of justice which may flow from the failure to warn a jury of the danger arising from possible confusion or mistake. Even as long ago as *Davies and Cody* the undesirability of placing cases relating to the identity of an offender in separate categories was reflected in the Court's observation:
> >
> > > 'It is almost unnecessary to say that the amount of care and the nature of the precautions which should be taken when a potential witness is brought to identify an accused or suspected person must vary according to the familiarity of the witness with that person'.
>
> The above passage emphasises that cases cannot be determined by reference to labels such as 'recognition case' or 'identification case'. As has long been recognised, the extent of a witness's prior familiarity with the person identified is a question of degree and is but one factor in the mix. The nature of the warning required will depend on all the circumstances of the case, and even where a witness is very familiar with the person identified, the circumstances surrounding the identification may nonetheless be such that a comprehensive warning is required. The judge's overriding duty is to give such directions and warnings as are necessary in the circumstances of the particular case to enable the jury to properly carry out its task as the judge of the facts and thereby avoid the risk of a miscarriage of justice.
>
> In the present case, it is plain that Allahverdi had some familiarity with the applicant from his being a passenger in the taxi for some twenty minutes. Yet, this was not a case of a witness recognising someone with whom he was familiar due to a long acquaintance, in conditions where there was no real possibility of error. On the contrary, as counsel for the applicant demonstrated, there were numerous factors which had the potential to affect the jury's assessment of the reliability of the evidence. Many of the matters referred to by counsel would have been well apparent to the jury. Others perhaps less so. In any event, as *Domican* makes clear, the judge was obliged to 'isolate and identify for the benefit of

181 [2003] HCA 40; 217 CLR 1, [22].
182 [2008] NSWCCA 62; 70 NSWLR 696.

the jury any matter of significance which may reasonably be regarded as undermining the reliability of the identification evidence'.[183]

In *Ilioski*, the appellate court considered not only the obligation to give a warning in relation to both positive and negative (exculpatory) identification evidence, but also the question of whether the warnings given were adequate to identify for the jury both the general and specific reasons that gave rise to concerns about the reliability of the evidence.[184] The court also considered whether the warnings were consistent with the principles outlined in *Kanaan*, which had post-dated Ilioski's trial. Turning to the need to provide detailed warnings to the jury, the court considered not only the need to emphasise the need for 'special' caution, but also the need to highlight for the jury the specific factors that raised doubts about the reliability of the identification evidence. In finding that the warnings were adequate, the court emphasised that s 116 was concerned with the reliability of identification evidence, and not the general honesty of the witness proffering the evidence. The events of the night that had led to the death of the victim were such that it was very difficult to obtain either an accurate account of events or an accurate identification:

> (1) There were approximately twenty-five males involved in the brawl outside the Steeler's Club where the appellant was stabbed.
> (2) Most of those present were wearing dark coloured clothing, including the appellant.
> (3) Three men other than the appellant had expressed a desire to seriously harm either the victim or his identical twin brother in the minutes or hours leading up to the stabbing.
> (4) There were lapses of time between the various distinct phases in the events prior to and following the stabbing.[185]

The exculpatory identification evidence consisted of conflicting descriptions of the main offender (in terms of references to his hair and shape) that were inconsistent with the appearance of the accused. The court considered the evidence to be less significant than the evidence in *Kanaan*. It also considered that the directions were adequate to convey to the jury the importance of considering the prosecution's burden of proof in negating the evidence. In addition to the specific matters discussed below, the trial judge had directed the jury on familiarity of witnesses with the appellant and disparities between the appellant's appearance and descriptions of the assailant. The warnings given by the trial judge in *Ilioski*, included drawing the jurors' attention to the general need for 'special caution':

> Special caution is necessary before accepting identification evidence because of the possibility that even completely honest witnesses may have been mistaken in their identification. I am not suggesting that the evidence of such a witness must be regarded as unreliable. My task is no more than to draw to your attention the possibility that the evidence of such witnesses may be unreliable and to explain why that is so, so as to enable you to exercise the special caution which is required in determining whether you accept that evidence as reliable and what weight you give to it.
>
> The common experience of the criminal courts over the years, both here in Australia and overseas, has demonstrated that identification evidence, however honestly given, may turn out to be unreliable. There have been some notorious cases over the years in which

183 *Sindoni* [2011] VSCA 195, [63]-[65]. See also *Williams* [2019] NSWCCA 53.
184 Compare *Sindoni* [2011] VSCA 195.
185 [2006] NSWCCA 164, [71].

completely honest evidence of identification has been demonstrated to be wrong, after innocent people have been convicted.

The reliability of an identification of a person depends on the circumstances in which the witness observed the person who [sic] he or she has identified as the accused, and any one of those circumstances may possibly lead to error. For example, how long was the period of observation? In what light was it made? And from what distance was it made? Was there anything about the person observed which would have impressed itself upon the witness? Was there any special reason for remembering the person observed? How long afterwards was the witness asked about the person seen? How did the description then given compare to the appearance of the accused? Each of those matters must be considered in every identification case and I will shortly be drawing your attention to some particular matters raised in this present case.

The fact that, in this trial, more than one witness has identified the accused is a matter you may take into account when determining the weight which you place on their evidence. But you must clearly understand that such a fact does not mean that there is necessarily less chance that a mistake has been made. Two or more honest witnesses can be just as mistaken as one. This warning of the need for special caution before accepting the evidence of identification is one which is given in every case in which such evidence is disputed by the accused. It is not given because of any particular view which I may have formed concerning the reliability of the identification evidence in the present case. The weight to be given to that evidence is a matter for your decision and not mine and I have, as I have already said, I have nothing to do with that decision which you have to make.

You should not interpret these directions as indicating any particular view which I may have formed one way or the other. As I have said, you must approach all identification evidence with special caution. There are however, a number of matters in this case, to which I now propose to draw your attention, which are relevant to the reliability of the evidence of identification that's been given and my direction is that you are bound to consider those matters in determining whether you accept the evidence as reliable.[186]

The appeal court then turned to the question of whether, in line with s 116, the trial judge had included a sufficient level of detail about the specific weaknesses in this case. These included the risks of confusion on the night given the chaotic scene, the short duration of some of the observations, the poor lighting, the level of alcohol consumption, the effects of stress, as well as risks of displacement and suggestion, all of which were dealt with at length by the trial judge. Finally, the defendant raised the risk of bias relating to the interests of some of the Crown witnesses. In responding to this challenge, the court in *Ilioski* dealt with the scope of s 116 as compared to the more general warnings regime under s 165:

Bias

97. It was submitted by the appellant that the judge was obliged by ss 116 and 165 of the *Evidence Act* to direct the jury specifically in relation to the bias of the Crown witnesses against him. He says that some of the identification witnesses may have had a motive to lie. The reasons for this are said to be twofold: first, a desire to see the person they believed to be responsible for the stabbing of the victim punished; and, secondly, a desire to ensure that those who set upon and beat up the appellant after the stabbing, especially the victim's cousin Jason Hrstovski, were not punished for their behaviour. The judge did not give such a direction, nor was she asked to do so.

98. The requirements of s 116 are described in pars [62]-[63] *supra*. They are concerned with the *reliability* of the identification evidence given in favour of the Crown, not with its *honesty*. Section 165 is expressly concerned with the *reliability* of certain types of evidence, including identification evidence. The whole point of the need for

186 Ibid [66].

such warnings in relation to identification evidence is to ensure that the jury is made aware of the seductive effect of *honest* evidence, and of the fact that such evidence has led to proven miscarriages of justice when it has subsequently been shown to have been mistaken. The requirements of *Domican v The Queen* have been interpreted in that way: *R v Heuston* (1995) 81 A Crim R 387 at 399; *R v Carusi* (1997) 92 A Crim R 52 at 73-74; *R v Tran* [2000] Qd R 430 at [4]. The same interpretation has been applied to ss 116 and 165 of the *Evidence Act*: *R v Clarke* (1997) 97 A Crim R 414 at 422-427, 433; *R v Coe* [2002] NSWCCA 385 at [67]; *Hajje v R* [2006] NSWCCA 23 at [82].

99. Evidence of a motive to lie – that is, a conscious decision to lie – relates to the *honesty* of the evidence given, not its *reliability* in the sense to which s 116 is directed and to which s 165 refers. The judge gave no specific directions in relation to bias. She did, however, give directions relating to the credibility of witnesses. The judge explained in her summing-up that it was the role of the jury to ascertain the facts. She also explained that, as part of that process, the jury would need to make assessments as to the credibility of the evidence given by each witness and whether there were any matters which might impact on that credibility. No complaint was made as to the way this issue had been dealt with, and no other directions were sought. …

101. It has not been suggested that there was anything else in the way the appellant's case was conducted at the trial which required the judge to go any further than she did. The issue as to the truthfulness of the Crown's identification witnesses was adequately dealt with.

102. I would reject the complaint that the judge did not refer specifically to bias when dealing with the reliability of the identification evidence.

Judicial warnings in Victoria

As mentioned in earlier chapters, the *JDA 2015* (Vic) regulates all directions and warnings to juries in criminal trials. These provisions seek to reduce the complexity of jury directions. The Act provides an overriding obligation for a trial judge to give a direction on the basis of '*substantial and compelling reasons* for doing so'[187] but otherwise requires that a trial judge must not give a direction that is not requested by a party[188] and a trial judge need not give the requested direction where there are good reasons not to do so.[189] Section 36 of the Act specifically addresses identification evidence. It requires counsel request a direction. Despite this, it is likely that '*substantial and compelling reasons* for' providing a warning under s 16 will follow the contours of the *UEA* obligations. The *JDA 2015* improves upon the *UEA* by providing an explicitly broad definition of identification evidence in s 35 that caters for a witness who 'recognises, or does not recognise, a person or object as the person or object that he or she saw, heard or perceived on the relevant occasion; or … the general appearance or characteristics of a person or object are similar, or are not similar, to the general appearance or characteristics of the person or object that he or she saw, heard or perceived on the relevant occasion'. Section 36 places greater responsibility on the party seeking the warning to specify the matters to be addressed, but also indicates that the warning needs to refer specifically to the risk of wrongful conviction based on mistaken eyewitness identification. Section 36(1) provides for counsel to make the request for a direction and sub-s (2) provides that counsel 'must specify the significant matters that may make the evidence unreliable'. Under s 36(3) the trial judge, in giving a requested direction, must:

187 *JDA 2015* (Vic), s 16 (emphasis added).

188 *JDA 2015* (Vic), s 15. And, consequentially, directions require a party to request them: s 12.

189 *JDA 2015* (Vic), s 14.

(a) warn the jury of the need for caution in determining whether to accept the evidence and the weight to be given to it; and
(b) inform the jury of the significant matters that the trial judge considers may make the evidence unreliable; and
(c) inform the jury that –
    (i) a witness may honestly believe that his or her evidence is accurate when the witness is, in fact, mistaken; and
    (ii) the mistaken evidence of a witness may be convincing; and
(d) if relevant, inform the jury that a number of witnesses may all be mistaken; and
(e) if relevant, inform the jury that mistaken identification evidence has resulted in innocent people being convicted.

The Act retains the directions that must be given under s 115(7) of the *UEA*. Section 37 abolishes any residual obligation under the common law to provide a warning in respect of identification evidence.[190]

Voice Identification Evidence

Voice identification evidence – where the witness is identifying the voice of the defendant – comes within the *UEA* definition of 'identification evidence' as 'an assertion by a person to the effect that a defendant was, or resembles (visually, *aurally* or otherwise) a person who was, present at or near a place where ... the offence for which the defendant is being prosecuted was committed; or ... an act connected to that offence was done' (emphasis added). Thus, the warning provisions (whether s 116 of the *UEA*, or s 36 of the *JDA* (Vic)) apply if voice identification evidence about the accused is admitted. However, despite research that indicates that voice identification is just as likely to be unreliable as eyewitness identification, the *admissibility* of voice identification evidence is unregulated beyond the general provisions, that is ss 55, 135 and 137.[191] As Edmond, Martire and San Roque observe:

> Prior to the introduction of the UEA, courts in New South Wales began to consider voice identification evidence – usually where a sensory (or direct) witness positively identified a voice associated with a criminal act – by noting that risks associated with visual identification might apply to voice identification, but in a manner that highlighted some of their occasionally archaic and sometimes superficial concerns. While purporting to develop an admissibility jurisprudence, most courts stopped short of strictly imposing mandatory conditions for the admissibility of voice identification by sensory witnesses. The judges hearing the common law appeals in *R v Smith*, *R v Brownlowe*, *R v Corke* and *R v Brotherton* – and even appeals under the nascent UEA in *R v Colebrook* and *R v Watson* – focused attention on the quantity and quality of material available to the witness, the distinctiveness of the voice in question, the level of the listener's familiarity, and whether voices were compared under similar conditions (eg yelling in anger). In practice, however, such considerations infrequently led to the exclusion of positive identifications by strangers. Rather, appellate judges required that limitations and problems with voice identification evidence should be brought to the attention of the jury through specific directions and warnings from the trial judge. ...

190 See *Davies* [2019] VSCA 66.

191 This reliance on general principles, as opposed to specific admissibility rules, is not uncommon and the result, as in Australia, is that voice identification evidence is rarely excluded. See, eg, the review of US cases in CL Laub, LE Wylie and BH Bornstein, 'Can the Courts Tell an Ear from an Eye? Legal Approaches to Voice Identification Evidence' (2013) 37 *Law and Psychology Review* 119.

> [Under the *UEA*] [v]oice identification evidence is treated as admissible if it is relevant: that is, it will be admissible where, if accepted, it could rationally affect the assessment of the probability of facts in issue. Directions and warnings, and to a lesser extent mandatory and discretionary exclusions, appear to be the preferred way to manage the problematic dimensions of evidence derived from voices and comparisons of voices. Where recorded evidence is available the tribunal of fact is frequently encouraged to undertake its own comparison. Now, voice identification and comparison evidence is routinely admitted and questions about probative value and reliability are left for weight and the tribunal of fact. In consequence, all Australian jurisdictions have either abandoned or elected not to follow the restrictive approach associated with *EJ Smith* and the courts of New South Wales pre-1995 (but which operated until 2000).[192]

While the literature relating to 'ear-witnesses', and voice comparison evidence is not yet as developed or substantial as that relating to eyewitness or image comparisons, the overwhelming conclusion that can be drawn from the current research is that voice identification evidence is subject to all of the same frailties and weaknesses as visual identification evidence.[193] Consequently, the relegation of voice identification to the 'general' law is highly problematic.[194] The reception and assessment of such evidence should be informed by research on the intrinsic challenges in establishing accurate identification. Relevant background to these concerns includes the dangers intrinsic in investigative bias, equally applicable to visual identification, and courts' over-reliance on the use of judicial directions.[195]

Particularly complex situations arise where the voice is not clearly heard, and/or where there are cross-linguistic issues, or where the jury themselves are invited to engage in their own comparison as between suspect recordings and the voice of the accused.[196] The role of familiarity, and how that familiarity is acquired, introduces additional complexity. As we see below in *Dupas* (and as revealed through *UEA*, ss 108C and 106(d)), compared to the common law position it is now possible for parties to inform juries through calling experts who can offer a methodological critique, though the danger of inadequate testing of (incriminating) expert evidence remains a significant concern in relation to voice identification and comparison evidence in particular. One suggestion is that courts should be looking to alternative mechanisms to control the admission of voice identification and voice comparison evidence – perhaps using voice identification parades and/or validated forensic voice comparison methods or a more rigorous approach to assessing the reliability of the evidence or the proficiency of the witness.[197] Just as the rise of

---

192 Edmond, Martire and San Roque, above n 36, 55-6 (citations and footnotes omitted).

193 For example, while face comparison tests are now well developed, including specialised tests to identify 'super-recognisers', there are fewer equivalents for voice comparisons. See, eg, discussion in V Aglieri, R Watson, C Pernet et al, 'The Glasgow Voice Memory Test: Assessing the ability to memorize and recognize unfamiliar voices' (2017) 49 *Behavior Research Methods* 97.

194 Problematic cases such as *Nguyen* [2017] NSWCCA 4 (discussed above in Chapter 12) reinforce this trend. See also *Miller* [2015] NSWCCA 206, *Miller (No 2)* [2016] NSWCCA 158 and *Nasrallah* [2015] NSWCCA 188. See also *Davey* [2020] TASCCA 12.

195 The New South Wales Criminal Trials Bench Book does now include a section on a suggested warning for voice identification evidence: [3-120].

196 See, for example, in *Dickman* [2017] HCA 24; 261 CLR 601, above pp 600-604, where the jury was invited to compare the voice of the defendant in a recorded interview and search with a voice that appeared in the background of a covertly recorded telephone call, or *Korgbara* [2007] NSWCCA 84, where the jury was invited to compare the voice of the accused speaking English briefly from the dock, with a voice in a covert recording speaking Igbo, a Nigerian tonal language. See also *Haddara* (2014) 43 VR 53.

197 The assumption seems to be that holding a 'voice parade' is impractical in most cases. And it is true that the attempt to construct a 'voice parade' in *Miller* [2015] NSWCCA 206 was

CCTV and the proliferation and circulation of images expose the limited scope of the existing rules relating to visual and picture identification, the increased availability of covert and other audio/visual recordings exposes a gap in relation to the regulation of the admission of voice identification evidence.[198]

Calling in the Experts

The *UEA* scheme contained in Part 3.9 acknowledges eyewitness identification evidence as a special class of potentially unreliable evidence and one that needs to be approached with particular caution. Warnings remain the central mechanism for responding to (potentially) unreliable evidence. However, expert evidence is another way in which courts and fact-finders can be informed with respect to identification evidence. Expertise on the frailties of identification evidence has been admitted in a number of cases, including *Bayley*,[199] *Dupas*,[200] *Smith*[201] and *Forbes*.[202] This role for experts is relatively novel, replacing an historical wariness of allowing experts to proffer opinions for the purposes of guiding the jury in their decision-making, in part because of a perception that the evidence did not rise above 'common sense' or 'common knowledge', and in part because of a concern that such evidence trespassed on the province of the jury. However, in line with research that continues to expose the limits of such 'common knowledge',[203] there has been a shift in recent years to accept that expert evidence can offer assistance in some circumstances.[204] This has been facilitated by the inclusion of ss 106(d) and 108C in the *UEA*,[205] though as illustrated in the *Dupas* ruling below it is not unconstrained in terms of the scope and specificity of expert evidence. Other jurisdictions have addressed the same question in different ways. Expert assistance has been widely accepted in a number of US courts, but in the United Kingdom and Canada the traditional caution prevails.[206] In *Dupas*, the Victorian Court of Appeal considered the admissibly of defence evidence that raised concerns

problematic, since it appears that the sample of the suspect's voice was qualitatively distinct as compared to the assembled foils. However, it has been argued that, notwithstanding logistical or practical difficulties, a failure to hold a parade ought to be taken into account when considering the admission of voice identification evidence. See J Robson, 'A Fair Hearing? The Use of Voice Identification Parades in Criminal Investigations in England and Wales' (2017) 1 *Criminal Law Review* 36.

198 By way of comparison, see *Evidence Act 2006* (NZ), s 46.

199 *Bayley* [2016] VSCA 160.

200 [2012] VSCA 328; 218 A Crim R 507.

201 [2000] NSWCCA 388; 116 A Crim R 1.

202 [2009] ACTSC 1.

203 See, eg, the collection of essays in Borgida and Fiske (eds), above n 23.

204 This is consistent with a growing acceptance of the need for 'evidence based' evidence. See, eg, Chapter 1 of the 'Weinberg Report' (*Simplification of Jury Directions Project: A Report to the Jury Directions Advisory Group*, Supreme Court of Victoria, August 2012). Note, however, that there is empirical research that raises questions of the effectiveness of expert testimony on eyewitness identification evidence, vis-à-vis, judicial directions and warnings: K Martire and R Kemp, 'Can Experts Help Jurors to Evaluate Eyewitness Evidence? A Review of Eyewitness Expert Effects' (2011) 16 *Legal and Criminological Psychology* 24; and KA Martire and RI Kemp, 'The Impact of Eyewitness Expert Evidence and Judicial Instruction on Juror Ability to Evaluate Eyewitness Testimony' (2009) 33(3) *Law and Human Behavior* 225.

205 This section is also discussed in Chapter 12, but primarily in the context of the admission of expert evidence about the behaviour of child witnesses.

206 See I Freckelton, 'Admissibility of Expert Opinions on Eyewitness Evidence: International Perspectives' (2014) 21 *Psychiatry, Psychology and Law* 821 and A Skalon, M San Roque and J Beaudry, 'An Interdisciplinary and Cross-national Analysis of Legal Safeguards for Eyewitness

about, inter alia, the risks that identification of Dupas by the eyewitnesses had been contaminated by their exposure to post-event media and reporting. The articulation of the need to distinguish between an expert offering general information versus an application of the research to the specific facts of the case remains the position under the *UEA*.

Dupas

[2012] VSCA 328; 218 A Crim R 507 (citations omitted)

Dupas was charged with the murder of Mersina Halvagis on 1 November 1997 at Fawkner Cemetery in Melbourne. Three witnesses gave evidence in two trials of having seen Dupas at the cemetery on 1 November around the time of the murder. Two of these witnesses had seen images of Dupas on television in relation to *other* murders for which he had been convicted, and had subsequently made a positive identification. The third witness had made a statement six months after the Halvagis murder, describing the appearance of a man she had seen in the cemetery on 1 November 1997 and a year later she had participated in a photoboard procedure in which she had picked out a photograph of Dupas as being 'most likely' the man she had seen that day. Later, in 2000, the same witness made an unequivocal identification, but only after seeing a photograph of Dupas in the *Herald Sun* newspaper alongside a story speculating as to his involvement in the death of Halvagis. Thus, in all cases the positive identification had come several years after 1997 and only one witness had participated in an identification procedure before significant media exposure.

The defence called then Associate Professor Richard Kemp (UNSW) in both trials to support an application to exclude the identification evidence – made under the '*Christie*' discretion in the first trial, and under s 137 in the retrial. The Court of Appeal held that the potential lack of reliability of the witnesses' evidence could be a factor in establishing the probative value of the evidence for the purpose of exclusion of the identification evidence under s 137,[207] but nonetheless confirmed the trial judge's decision to admit the identification evidence. The court also considered the scope of s 108C, the exception to the credibility rule in s 102, that allows for the admission of expert opinion where the evidence has the capacity to substantially affect the credibility of the witness. The court held that 'credibility' in this context includes questions on the reliability (as opposed to merely the truthfulness) of the witness. It also noted that s 108C required a party to obtain leave from the court (applying *UEA*, s 192). There was no dispute over Associate Professor Kemp's expertise in relation to providing general information as to the research on eyewitness identification and the factors that may have affected the identifications in this case to assist the *jury* to assess the reliability of the evidence.[208] But the defence had also challenged the evidence on the basis

---

Evidence' in MK Miller and BH Bornstein (eds), *Advances in Psychology and Law* (Vol 5, Springer, 2020), 137-78.

207 See Chapter 4. See also G Edmond, D Hamer, A Ligertwood, M San Roque, '*Christie*, Section 137 and Forensic Science Evidence after *Dupas v The Queen* and *R v XY*' (2014) 40 *Monash University Law Review* 389.

208 The court held that to allow Kemp to give evidence about the specific witnesses would not satisfy the requirements of s 79, which are equally relevant in the context of s 108C, as laid down in cases such as *Dasreef Pty Ltd v Hawchar* [2011] HCA 21; 243 CLR 588. See the discussion of s 79 in *Dasreef* and *Makita (Australia) Pty Ltd v Sprowles* [2001] NSWCA 305; 52 NSWLR 705, Chapter 12.

of the 'media misinformation effect' – that is, post-event information affecting the accuracy of witnesses' recall without them being aware that their memory has been so compromised – and evidence on the displacement effect as it applied to the specific witness(es).

> **Warren CJ, Maxwell P, Nettle, Redlich and Bongiorno JJA**: 247. The applicant sought to lead general evidence from Dr Kemp about the weaknesses of identification evidence, the displacement effect and the media misinformation effect. As part of his general evidence, he explained by means of general examples how each of these factors could affect reliability. The applicant also sought to lead specific evidence relating to the identification witnesses Burman, Weller and Melnik. Initially, the applicant sought leave to adduce both the general and the specific evidence under s 108C of the *Evidence Act* but, in oral submissions, abandoned reliance on s 108C and sought to adduce the evidence under s 79. …
>
> 249. In the course of ruling that Dr Kemp was only to give the more general evidence, the trial judge referred to the following evidence which he had given on the voir dire:
>
> > Dr Kemp said that there are a large number of factors that influence how any particular individual may respond to post-event information. They include a person's age and the delay between the original event and encountering the post-event information. The duration of the witness's observation of the subject is not as important as the circumstances of the observation. However, even taking such factors into account, the scientific research does not enable Dr Kemp to opine as to whether any particular witness has definitely (or even probably) succumbed to post-event information.
>
> 250. … Her Honour ruled that Dr Kemp could give general evidence about the fact that memory is not static and may be unreliable, and that memory may be affected by subsequent events. The trial judge said:
>
> > The identification evidence of Melnik, Weller and Burman was an important part of the Crown case. The accused had been the subject of an enormous amount of pre-trial publicity over many years, some of which had undoubtedly been seen by the three witnesses. There had also been long delays in the identification processes. A strong Domican warning would clearly be required. After considering the matter further, I accepted the defence submission that Dr Kemp's evidence would support, rather than undermine, the force of the judicial directions as to the dangers and problems with the identification evidence. I concluded that any potential confusion could be prevented or satisfactorily minimised by discussing the relevant parts of the charge with counsel, prior to charging the jury on the identification evidence.
> >
> > I determined to allow Dr Kemp to give general evidence about exposure to post-event information and its effect on memory. This evidence would go no further than what was contained in the second report or had been the subject of evidence given on the second voir dire.
>
> 251. In the course of his evidence on the second voir dire, Dr Kemp was asked to state, in the case of each witness, whether the circumstances in which the witness came to identify the applicant exemplified one or more of the dangers he had referred to in his general evidence – displacement, the intrusion of post-event information before identification, unconscious transference, and increased susceptibility to post-event information with delay in identification. Dr Kemp stated repeatedly, however, that he was unable to express any opinion as to whether the identification made by any of the witnesses was unreliable. He also stated that he was unable to express an opinion as to the degree of likelihood that their identification was unreliable. The applicant eschewed any suggestion that Dr Kemp could, or should, do either of those things.
>
> 252. In the course of the argument, her Honour emphasised that it was not in doubt that an expert could be asked to express an opinion about hypothetical situations and could explain the assumptions on which an opinion rested. With these considerations in mind, counsel for the applicant submitted to her Honour that he wished to have Dr

Kemp repeat that specific evidence before the jury, and relied upon *R v Smith* [2000] as authority. The argument thus focused on whether Dr Kemp should be permitted to comment upon the exact circumstances pertaining to each identifying witness, by saying they were examples of the general evidence he would give about factors that affected the reliability of identification. The trial judge indicated that for him to do so would amount to him stating indirectly that the identifications were unreliable, something Dr Kemp had made plain he could not state directly. Counsel for the applicant then said that, if it would confuse the jury to put the precise circumstances of each identification to Dr Kemp in order to ask him whether they were examples of his general evidence, the defence were content to refrain from doing so. …

279. The trial judge made clear to the applicant's counsel, both during the lengthy submissions on the point and in her ruling, that the applicant was entitled to put hypothetical situations to the expert to amplify each of the dangers developed in the expert's general evidence. The risk factors of displacement, post-event information, subconscious transference and the increased susceptibility of error with delay were all matters that could be cogently illustrated without the expert commenting upon the precise circumstances of each witness's identification.

280. In the event, defence counsel was able in final address to the jury to draw upon that evidence, amplified by hypothetical examples, to support the contention that such circumstances were also to be found in the identifications by the witnesses. And it was acknowledged in argument on the appeal that defence counsel had pointed out to the jury how the factors affecting identification, which Dr Kemp had discussed in his general evidence, were present in the case of each identifying witness.

281. The judge excluded Dr Kemp's specific evidence because he could not express an opinion as to the reliability of the individual identifications. He had not been provided with all of the detail of how those identifications occurred, nor had he interviewed or observed any of the witnesses. As he acknowledged in the case of each witness, he could not express an opinion about the reliability of that witness's identification, nor could he assess the likelihood of the identification being unreliable.

282. The judge therefore concluded – correctly, in our view – that for Dr Kemp to have commented upon the precise circumstances pertaining to each identification, or to have expressed a view as to whether those circumstances gave rise to the risk of unreliability, would have been tantamount to him expressing the opinion that the individual identifications were unreliable. As we have said, the necessary foundation did not exist for him to extrapolate from the research to the circumstances of each identification (about which he was not fully informed) or to the individual witnesses (about whom he knew very little).

283. An opinion about the circumstances would have gone outside the scope of his specialised knowledge. An opinion about the reliability of the identifications would necessarily have rested on a combination of speculation, inference and personal views. At the same time, such an opinion would have been invested with a spurious appearance of authority, and would have subverted the legitimate processes of fact-finding.

Conclusion

The best guidance for legal regulation of eyewitness identification evidence comes not from [judicial] rulings, but from the careful use and understanding of scientific evidence to guide fact-finders and decision makers.[209]

Mistaken identification has played a significant role in documented wrongful convictions. The dangers of unreliable identification being relied on in court arise from the effect of unconscious biases and distortions. These are difficult to recognise, evaluate and control. The reception and management of evidence of

---

209 *Identifying the Culprit*, above n 9, 109.

identification pose unique challenges for the regulation and conduct of criminal trials. The particular potency of eyewitness identification and the difficulties of successfully testing the account of an eyewitness through cross-examination are well established. It is also well established that a judicial warning to the jury is only a partial remediation of the dangers intrinsic in this evidence.[210] Nevertheless, it has become increasingly difficult to exclude identification evidence obtained under flawed circumstances, in part due to the narrow scope of the existing rules under the *UEA*, and in part as a consequence of constraints placed on trial judges, confronted with evidence of low probative value, to exercise their role under s 137 to exclude the evidence.

Importantly, the concerns and risks that accompany eyewitness identification, particularly with respect to unfamiliar people, apply equally to other forms of identification, including voice identification, displaced listener and watcher identification (identification through CCTV, electronic audio recordings, facial mapping and the like). In some instances, these later-generation forms of identification can even magnify the danger of mistake. Psychological research shows that neither Part 3.9 (and the *UEA* more generally), nor conventional trial practice, effectively accommodate the proliferation of audio and visual surveillance materials that may be deployed as part of either the Crown or defence case. In particular, there is a need to reconsider the implications of expecting jurors to perform their own comparisons of images or audio recordings[211] because it is clear that people believe, with entirely misplaced confidence, that they can make accurate identifications even where, because the quality of the recording is poor or language differences apply, they cannot. Consider, for example, *Smith (Mundarra)*,[212] where the evidence of the police officers who claimed to recognise Smith in the CCTV was excluded. This meant that the jury would be left in the subsequent retrial to perform the comparison of a grainy CCTV image with Smith, in the dock, themselves.[213] Similarly, assumptions made in relation to the capacity of jurors and fact-finders to effectively evaluate images, are exacerbated in the case of voice identification and comparisons.[214] As Chapter 12 indicates caution needs to be applied to reliance on forensic comparison based on images or other audio-visual artefacts but, in cases such as *Dickman*, we see that even courts that approach conventional eyewitness testimony cautiously do not extend that caution to comparisons made by the fact-finder between surveillance recordings and the appearance or voice of the accused.

The need for courts to respond to the proliferation of images has been noted in recent reports. It has also given rise to guidelines and a number of additional

---

210 The empirical literature on the effectiveness of warnings, in terms of their capacity to sensitise a decision-maker to the frailties of the evidence has identified, problematically, that directions are particularly *ineffective* when confronted with suggestive procedures. See, eg, Skalon and Beaudry, above n 172.

211 See, eg, discussion in G Edmond and M San Roque, 'Justicia's Gaze: Surveillance, Evidence and the Criminal Trial' (2013) 11 *Surveillance & Society* 252.

212 [2001] HCA 50; 206 CLR 650. See above, Chapter 4.

213 With all of the attendant problems of suggestibility, as well as the known frailties of cross-racial comparisons, see discussion in K Biber, 'The Hooded Bandit: Aboriginality, Photography and Criminality in *Smith v The Queen*' (2002) 13 *Current Issues in Criminal Justice* 286, 288. Though it should be noted that the second jury acquitted Smith.

214 See above n 196 in relation to *Dickman* [2017] HCA 24; 261 CLR 601; *Korgbara* [2007] NSWCCA 84 and *Haddara* [2014] VSCA 100; G Edmond, K Martire and M San Roque, '"Mere Guesswork": Cross-Lingual Voice Comparisons and the Jury' (2011) 33 *Sydney Law Review* 395.

recommendations to assist courts in managing this evidence.[215] Yet, unlike the exclusion of *graphic* images from the jury, evidence that is beyond human ability to accurately assess is rarely excluded, even though the presence of this complex evidence in the prosecution case is itself likely to have a priming impact, and research shows that 'priming' can be a significant additionally distorting factor.[216] If the law recognises that eye and ear witnesses can be confident but wrong (as it has since Adolf Beck's time), it is time that these same dangers are also recognised in displaced visual and voice identification. However, courts and the legislature have been slow to embrace the sobering findings of psychological research and, despite a review of the Act a decade ago, Part 3.9 provides only limited control of identification evidence and offers no regulation of the gathering and admissibility of the extensive array of new forms of identification evidence put forward in criminal trials including the informal identifications made by witnesses from uncontrolled images circulating on social media. These should be the priority of law reformers.

Australian appellate courts (with some exceptions) have shown themselves to be unwilling to countenance the exclusion of flawed identification evidence of low or minimal probative value and have re-expressed their reliance on warnings as the preferred response to managing the known risks of admitting such evidence. So 'evidence of identification, which is so liable to being mistaken that it would be "extremely dangerous for a jury to assign any probative value to it",'[217] gains admission because the judicial warning will follow. How to inform jurors of the dangers intrinsic in all forms of identification remains a key concern. While on the one hand, the increasing openness of courts to allow testimony from experts to offer advice to fact-finders is welcome, the evidence as to the nature and effectiveness of such advice remains limited. And there is a risk that, as with the over-reliance on warnings, allowing in such evidence from witnesses such as Professor Kemp, testifying in *Dupas* (and *Bayley*) of the dangers inherent in identification processes serves merely to justify the inclusion of compromised identifications.

---

215 See, eg, NSW Law Reform Commission, *Jury Directions in Criminal Trials* (Report No 136, 2013); Judicial College of Victoria, *Victorian Criminal Charge Book*; Judicial Commission of New South Wales, *Criminal Trial Courts Bench Book*.

216 See discussion in J Chin, M San Roque and R McFadden, 'The New Psychology of Expert Witness Procedure' (2020) 42 *Sydney Law Review* 69 and H Fraser and D Loakes, 'Acoustic injustice: The experience of listening to indistinct covert recordings presented as evidence in court' (2020) 24 *Law Text Culture* (forthcoming). See also *Nwagbo* [2021] VSCA 93 (also a case involving Igbo) on jury assessment of the accuracy of cross-lingual voice comparisons and the role of interpreters assisting expert witnesses to identify features for comparison.

217 ALRC, *Evidence (Interim)*, above n 44, [424].

Chapter 14

The Rise and Rise of Judicial Instructions, Directions & Warnings

Introduction

> The fundamental task of a trial judge is, of course, to ensure a fair trial of the accused. That will require the judge to instruct the jury about so much of the law as they need to know in order to dispose of the issues in the case. No doubt that will require instructions about the elements of the offence, the burden and standard of proof and the respective functions of judge and jury. Subject to any applicable statutory provisions it will require the judge to identify the issues in the case and to relate the law to those issues. It will require the judge to put fairly before the jury the case which the accused makes. In some cases it will require the judge to warn the jury about how they should not reason or about particular care that must be shown before accepting certain kinds of evidence.[1]

We saw in Chapter 10 that the summing up is typically the occasion for instructing jurors on any restrictions or warnings that apply to evidence, and Chapter 13 illustrates the importance of a particular direction, namely in relation to evidence of identification. Judicial instruction, directions and warnings are, like the rules of evidence, fundamentally directed at insulating a robust jury verdict from certain frailties of lay decision-making. As this chapter shows, the common law tradition is strongly committed to utilising directions and warnings and to having faith – possibly sometimes blind faith – in their powers.[2] The European Court of Human Rights has observed[3] that judicial instruction also functions to frame jury verdicts and to create a public presence of the chain of reasoning shaping jury deliberations. In this way these instructions and directions also provide a formal mechanism of accountability for juries' decisions. One of the most striking features of this area of law is its constant evolution. As we saw in Chapter 2 in the judge-alone case of *Mumbulla*, even where there is no jury trial judges are generally required to explicitly acknowledge their adherence to

1 *RPS* [2000] HCA 3; 199 CLR 620, 637 [41] (Gaudron ACJ, Gummow, Kirby and Hayne JJ) (footnotes omitted).

2 *Gilbert* [2000] HCA 15; 201 CLR 414, [13] (Gleeson CJ and Gummow J), quoted in Chapter 2, p 50.

3 See *Taxquet v Belgium* [2010] ECHR 1806 and *Judge v United Kingdom* (Application No 35863/10, Admissibility, 8 February 2011). See also P Roberts, 'Does Article 6 of the European Convention on Human Rights Require Reasoned Verdicts in Criminal Trials?' (2011) 11 *Human Rights Law Review* 213.

the foundational principles that would be expressed in a direction or a warning to the jury.[4]

Directions and warnings to a jury may be misunderstood or rejected by jurors. For this reason, they are a compromise solution to addressing the danger that the jury will misjudge:

- potentially unreliable testimony, for example, from someone who might reasonably be supposed to have been criminally concerned in the events,
- the nature of the evidence, for example, identification or hearsay evidence;
- a particular witness's intrinsic human frailties, for example, due to their age or their ill health;
- evidence obtained in notoriously unreliable contexts, such as an unsigned or unacknowledged record of questioning by an investigating officer; or
- evidence in circumstances where a party is forensically disadvantaged, that is, unfairly compromised in adequately exposing evidential flaws.[5]

Taking bold steps – such as excluding evidence or staying a trial[6] – removes the danger of jurors misreading the weight of evidence, thereby distorting jury decision-making through a flawed evaluation of weaknesses in evidence. However, exclusion reduces the quantum of information before the jury, which may lead to speculation to fill the information gap, and may prevent the wheels of justice from turning at all. For this reason, the alternative of judicial direction, instruction and warning is attractive, but there is no doubt that it is an imperfect option. This chapter examines judicial directions and warnings relevant to evidence of a kind that may be unreliable.[7] In addition, it briefly explores the law's shift over the past quarter of a century to eliminate many of the out-moded, historically based judicial warnings to juries,[8] reframing law's attitude to sexual assault complainants' and children's evidence from the archaic perception that the witnesses giving that evidence were unreliable. Basten JA in *Ewen*[9] neatly summed up the tension that is intrinsic to having adjudication by amateurs (that is, jurors) within the highly technical domain of law and its processes.

> 11. ... Juries are supposed to bring with them the collective wisdom and experience of the wider community (but also, no doubt, the prejudices and a range of possible misconceptions). Their functioning has long been subject to general law principles imposing checks and balances. ... For example, traditionally jurors were thought to be peculiarly susceptible to accepting false complaints of sexual attacks. The somewhat unedifying,

---

4 For example, the *Criminal Procedure Act 1986* (NSW) (*CPA* (NSW)), s 133(2), provides that 'a judgment by a Judge in any such case must include the principles of law applied by the Judge and the findings of fact on which the Judge relied' and s 133(3) provides that in any legal obligation to warn the jury, 'the Judge is to take the warning into account in dealing with the matter'. See also *Criminal Code* (Qld), s 615B; *Criminal Procedure Act 2004* (WA), s 119; *Supreme Court Act 1933* (ACT), s 68C. See also *Fleming* [1998] HCA 68; 197 CLR 250; *Markou* [2012] NSWCCA 64.

5 As well as s 165B addressing forensic disadvantage arising from delay, see *Bandao & Bruce* [2018] NSWCCA 181 where the trial judge relied on a s 165 warning to explain to the jury the significance of the prosecutor potentially undermining defence cross-examination of the complainant by giving her access to a recorded conversation the subject of the cross-examination.

6 For example, on the basis that there is a danger of an unfair trial due to the forensic disadvantage to the accused created by delay.

7 Chiefly through *UEA*, s 165.

8 See, eg, *UEA*, s 165A.

9 [2015] NSWCCA 117.

> if not misogynist, views accepted in times past are carefully recorded in *Crofts v The Queen*;[10] the attitudes of judges from 1968, as expressed by Salmon LJ in *R v Henry; R v Manning*,[11] are set out in *Longman v The Queen*.[12] In Australia the gender stereotyping was formally abandoned in *Kelleher v The Queen*.[13] The effect, however, was still to cast women (being the majority of complainants of such conduct) into what remained a suspect class,[14] on whose uncorroborated testimony it would be "dangerous to convict".[15] In 1981 the New South Wales legislature attempted to ameliorate the general law by enacting ss 405B and 405C of the *Crimes Act 1900* (NSW),[16] in terms similar to the current s 294 of the *Criminal Procedure Act*.
>
> 12. The effect of those provisions was to permit judges to give such warnings based on "experience derived from other cases" which was, as McHugh J pointed out in *Longman*, logically incoherent once the existence of a class treated as suspect on the basis of experience, had been removed.[17] The warning was now to be justified by some "intrinsic lack of reliability going beyond the mere credibility of witnesses"[18] and somehow obscure to a jury who had heard and seen the witness cross-examined. Fear of an "unfair trial" allowed warnings not dissimilar to the conventional warning to be continued and even required.[19] Further, just as statutory reforms were circumspect and incremental, as the reforms strengthened, they have been treated by judges with circumspection.

We begin with a brief consideration of judicial instruction to juries generally before examining directions available where the defence claims that they are impeded by forensic disadvantage due to a delayed trial. In Australia, the delayed trial scenario is dominated by delayed sexual assault complaints, typically due to the complainant being a child at the time of the alleged assault.

This chapter will also consider the difficulty of evaluating the effectiveness of jury instructions and warnings. This is a difficult task as jury deliberations are secret and mock jury studies are not ideal in seeking to evaluate what happens in a real juryroom where the human dimensions of deliberations, and the real consequences of a verdict are uppermost in jurors' actions. Jurors need to be willing and able to heed instructions. Real jurors, ones who have sat through weeks of trial, may feel overwhelmed during a judge's summing up; they may feel they have a concluded view and that further cognitive engagement is unnecessary. Further, as Baguley et al observe, measuring comprehension and application is complex and differs from measuring recollection.[20] Sklansky[21] notes that timing, content and phrasing of instruction all make a difference to attending to instructions, comprehending them and obeying them. The giving of reasons to jurors to apply instructions is also important. In Australia, the past 20 years has seen a huge growth in what US lawyers have taken for granted for many decades,

---

10 [[1996] HCA 22; 186 CLR 427, 447-8.]

11 [(1968) 53 Cr App R 150, 153.]

12 [[1989] HCA 60; 168 CLR 79, 85, 92 (Deane J) and 104-7 (McHugh J).]

13 [[1974] HCA 48; 131 CLR 534, 553 (Gibbs J).]

14 [As explained by McHugh J in *Longman* at 105].

15 [*Kelleher* at 553 (Gibbs J).]

16 [Inserted by the *Crimes (Sexual Assault) Amendment Act 1981* (NSW).]

17 [*Longman* at 106.]

18 [Ibid, quoting *Carr* [1988] HCA 47; 165 CLR 314, 319 (Wilson and Dawson JJ).]

19 [See *Crofts* [1996] HCA 22; 186 CLR 427, 449, referring to *Omarjee* (1995) 79 A Crim R 355, 368.]

20 CM Baguley, BM McKimmie and BM Masser, 'Reevaluating how to measure jurors' comprehension and application of jury instructions' (2020) 26 *Psychology, Crime & Law* 53.

21 DA Sklansky, 'Evidentiary Instructions and the Jury as Other' (2013) 65 *Stanford Law Review* 407, 456, and discussed in greater detail in Chapter 10.

namely pattern directions, or bench books, chiefly in Victoria and in New South Wales.[22] Their support is important, though as Hayne J noted in *Tully*[23] bench books contain dangers.

> 93. … But there is a risk that the prescription of common forms of instruction, which must necessarily be framed without reference to specific facts, and thus in abstract terms, will be used without relating them to the issues that the jury has to decide.

An illuminating 2019 Australian Institute of Judicial Administration (AIJA) report on a survey of Australian and New Zealand judges found that many Australian judges rely on bench books for model directions. However, the NSW judges surveyed showed their desire to be able to speak to a jury with the emphasis on natural, simple communications, referring to the language used in the bench books as 'far too verbose', 'unduly complex', 'unnatural', 'old fashioned' 'legalistic' and 'clunky'. It is possibly a measure of the need for directions to satisfy appellate court directives that they also criticised the NSW directions as 'overly lengthy', 'repetitive', 'pedantic', 'condescending' and 'patronising' to jurors'.[24] It is not surprising that trial judges at the 'coalface' recognise that supporting jury decision-making requires ensuring judges use language that jurors can understand (and not just the language of appeal court judges). The AIJA 2019 study compared its survey findings with an earlier (2009) survey and found a growth in early judges' instructions on 'the basics' to jurors – the presumption of innocence, the burdens and standards of proof, and the need to focus on the elements of offences in reaching a verdict – which are not matters jurors are likely to appreciate intuitively. While this increase in judges' instructions to jurors on legal basics is undoubtedly significant, it is striking, particularly in light of the High Court's sentiments regarding the fundamental nature of accusatorial justice principles quoted in Chapter 1, that these trial basics are not stated on 100% of occasions during a judge's opening remarks to the jury. Instead:

> Almost all judges always provide information to the jury during their opening remarks about the burden (93.5%, 115/123) and standard (93.4%, 114/122) of proof. … [O]ver 90% of Australian and New Zealand judges always covering these issues. In the present survey there was some difference in discussion of the presumption of innocence. Overall, 93.3% (112/120) of judges always raised this issue in their opening remarks, but this was slightly less common in New Zealand (89.7%, 26/29) than Australia (94.5%, 86/91). Overall, only 3.3% of judges would never discuss the burden (4/123) and standard of proof (4/122) during their opening remarks, while only 2.5% (3/120) would never discuss the presumption of innocence. For the remainder, it would depend on the nature of the trial.[25]

What is also more recently recognised than even a decade ago is that jurors need a framework early on in the trial to enable them to apply appropriate legal principles.

---

22 For New South Wales, see <https://www.judcom.nsw.gov.au/publications/benchbks/criminal/; for Victoria, see https://www.judicialcollege.vic.edu.au/eManuals/CCB/index.htm#19193.htm>.

23 [2006] HCA 56; 231 ALR 712.

24 J Clough et al, *The Jury Project 10 Years On – Practices of Australian and New Zealand Judges* (AIJA, 2019), 38.

25 Ibid 7-8. Notably, the earlier study by AIJA had found '65 and 66% of Australian judges discussed the burden and standard of proof respectively, while 74% of New Zealand judges discussed the burden and standard of proof in their opening remarks' and '[a]gain, on the previous survey findings only 63% of Australian and 61% of New Zealand judges would discuss the presumption of innocence during their opening remarks', comparing JRP Ogloff et al, *The Jury Project: Stage 1 – A Survey of Australian and New Zealand Judges* (AIJA, 2006).

The AIJA study found a significant point of difference between Australian and New Zealand judges on the use of question trails.[26] In New Zealand:

> [A]lmost 90% (27/30) of the judges indicating they always provide one. Only one judge never provides a checklist (3.3%, 1/30). In Australia, far fewer judges (26.9%, 18/67) 'always' provide a checklist, with a further 41.8% (28/67) doing so 'sometimes'. A substantial proportion, almost one-third, (31.3%; 21/67) indicated that they never provide such checklists.[27]

In *Budrodeen*[28] RA Hulme J observed of question trails that 'particular care is needed when prescribing a sequential process of reasoning. It is trite to observe as well that care is required in the identification of the elements of the offence'. If, as Australian appellate cases suggest, trial judges – aided by counsel – find constructing appropriate question trails challenging, these challenges suggest that without checklists and question trails, the law asks a lot of the average juror.

The judicial instructions surveyed by AIJA also reflect the gulf between the legal world and the jury box, a gulf that has grown since the late 18th century when judges played an active, virtually inquisitorial role in criminal trials.[29] The change reflected the 'lawyerisation' of the criminal trial which reduced the judge's role to one that rarely descended into the arena[30] of the trial so that nowadays the trial judge's main speaking part, directing and instructing the jury, involves aiding the jury to digest the parties' cases in the context of the relevant law. It is therefore not surprising that judicial instruction plays a big role in the common law world of jury trials. As Dufraimont has observed, whatever concerns we may have about amateur adjudication, '[t]he issue is the jury's ability to deal with particular forms of evidence rather than its general ability to find facts: it is a question of specific jury competencies, not general jury competence'.[31]

Fair trial by direction?

Strangely enough, the focus of appellate case law is not on ensuring jurors understand the 'basics', such as the issues canvassed by the 2019 AIJA survey, discussed above. Instead, the law focuses on the appropriate application of judicial warnings or directions to the jury urging caution in contexts where the law perceives that jurors may not appreciate potential unreliability. This was historically seen as key to ensuring a trial is fair.

26 Question trails are 'a series of questions that cover the elements of the offence for which proof is required, specific to each charge being determined. The question trails also remind juries about the onus and standard of proof for each element. ... [Question trails] ... help to keep the jury focused on the technical task at hand and to ensure that they do not get distracted into prejudicial, sympathetic or other impermissible reasoning processes' (*Rawle* [2019] NZCA 249): <https://www.courtsofnz.govt.nz/for-lawyers/question-trails/>. An example of a question trail in a sexual assault context can be found in *Star* [2020] VSCA 331; and, in a homicide context, see *Carbone* [2020] NSWCCA 318, [27]-[28] (unfortunately containing an error) and *Kempson* [2020] NZCA 656.

27 Clough et al, above n 24, 41.

28 [2014] NSWCCA 332, [23], [24], quoted by quoted by Bathurst CJ in *Gregg* [2020] NSWCCA 245, [504].

29 JM Beattie, 'Scales of Justice: Defense Counsel and the English Criminal Trial in the Eighteenth and Nineteenth Centuries' (1991) 9 *Law and History Review* 22.

30 To use the language of Lord Greene in *Yuill v Yuill* [1945] P 15, 20.

31 L Dufraimont, 'Evidence Law and the Jury: A Reassessment' (2008) 53 *McGill Law Journal* 200, 232.

In the distant (and not so distant) past competency rules restricted the capacity of categories of *witnesses* to give sworn evidence. Nowadays, competency rules are not as restrictive and of course no category of witness is explicitly excluded in modern trials as long as they are competent to testify.[32] However, some witnesses (such as accomplices or identification witnesses) are recognised as highly likely to give flawed testimony, with tangible risks associated with the integrity of their evidence. As mentioned at the beginning of the chapter, statute can also require that judges act to protect against jurors wrongly *rejecting* a child's or a sexual assault complainant's testimony. These warnings seek to dispel myths that may infiltrate the jury room (as they infiltrated the bench for many centuries).[33]

In the next section we examine the main area where forensic disadvantage in testing evidence typically arises, namely, where a significantly delayed trial might forensically disadvantage a party.

Delay and Forensic Disadvantage

This section explores delay issues in some depth and, as well as looking at the role and danger of relying on judicial warnings, examines an alternative remedy, namely staying proceedings. However, delay is not a category of unreliability. It is a *source* of potential unreliability due to flawed or reconstructed memories, and a situation that creates potential disadvantage, particularly for the defence, because of the difficulty of gathering evidence and testing prosecution witnesses' accounts. Classically, the sort of delay addressed in this section arises from criminal allegations referring to events that are decades old before they end up in court. Delayed proceedings give rise to 'fair trial' concerns. Human rights jurisprudence is also relevant here. For example, the Australian Capital Territory, Victoria and Queensland have legislated fair trial requirements that draw in the international jurisprudence on the right to a trial 'without *unreasonable* delay'.[34] In addition, the *International Covenant on Civil and Political Rights* (the *ICCPR*)[35] provides that 'in the determination of any criminal charge against him, everyone shall be entitled to the following minimum guarantees, in full equality: ... [t]o be tried without undue delay'.[36]

While most crimes in this category involve sexual assault, and typically child sexual assault, there are many reasons why there is delay, or delayed complaint. For example, allegations of criminal atrocity from wars from many years ago are classic instances exemplifying the dilemmas[37] posed by the need to protect a

32 *UEA*, Pt 2, Div 1.

33 For example, *CPA* (NSW), s 294: a warning must be given that an absent or delayed complaint does not indicate that an allegation is necessarily false. In addition, the judge must explain to the jury that there may be good reasons why a victim of sexual assault may hesitate or refrain from making a complaint.

34 See *Human Rights Act 2004* (ACT), s 22(2)(c), *Charter of Human Rights and Responsibilities Act 2006* (Vic) (the Victorian Charter), s 25(2)(c); *Human Rights Act 2019* (Qld), s 32(2)(c).

35 Article 14(3)(c) of the *ICCPR*. Ratified and entered into force for Australia in 1980.

36 See also the 6th Amendment of the United States *Bill of Rights*: 'the accused shall enjoy the right to a speedy and public trial ...'; and Article 6(1) of the *European Convention on Human Rights*: 'In the determination ... of any criminal charge against him, everyone is entitled to a fair and public hearing within a reasonable time'.

37 See *War Crimes Amendment Act 1988* (Cth); *Polyukhovich v Commonwealth* [1991] HCA 32; 172 CLR 501; *Wagner (No 2)* (1993) 68 A Crim R 81; see also *Inspector-General of the Australian Defence Force Report of Inquiry* (the Brereton Report, 2020), <https://afghanistaninquiry.defence.gov.au/>, regarding crimes said to have taken place between 2007 and 2013. These allegations

community's right to expect the administration of justice, as well as an accused person's right to a fair trial. These instances can be hidden due to the context in which they occur and for this reason often get drawn into the criminal justice system many years – decades – after the (alleged) event. Further, they are typically particularly fraught because, as is often the case, the central contest tends to focus on whether a crime actually occurred and, if it did, who did it. The defence is usually a blanket denial, but the defence may also raise the fact that, if the allegation had been made in a timely fashion, they would have been able to produce witnesses to support their alibi or to rebut prosecution witnesses' claims. Their inability to offer an affirmative defence is compounded by the challenges of properly testing prosecution eyewitnesses who are commonly traumatised and sometimes (such as in the case of World War II war crimes) very elderly. Delay can also occur through:

- protracted or stalled[38] investigation, perhaps to be reignited when serendipity strikes, such as a cold case DNA hit, or a witness comes forward many years after the criminal event; or
- through inadequate institutional resourcing for courts or prosecution offices.

It can be difficult to distinguish resourcing challenges from the time it takes for a case to be prepared. The Australian Bureau of Statistics provides figures on the length of time it takes for a criminal trial to be finalised from charge. The mean and median length of time from initiation to finalisation in higher courts was 45.6 and 35.3 weeks respectively.[39] In the higher courts, of those *acquitted* during 2018-19, 49% of defendants' cases took a year (52 weeks) or longer to finalise. Of course, for 2020 and 2021, COVID-19 has brought an extreme challenge to courts with an increased backlog of cases, raising significant human rights challenges and also mental health challenges. Increased domestic violence during the COVID-19 pandemic has exposed more women and children to harm, requiring identifying and prioritising matters related to such violence, as has offenders being held on remand awaiting sentencing and young people in detention. When the pandemic was having its most intense impact, some marginalised and vulnerable groups were disproportionally affected, for example, when the pandemic prompted the suspension of bush courts in the Northern Territory.[40]

Delayed trials caused by courts, process, investigation

'Just as the firetruck must get to the fire, so must a case be prepared'

Morin (Sopinka J)[41]

As Sopinka J in the 1992 Canadian decision in *Morin* noted, there is no Utopian solution based on unlimited resources and systems so 'administratively perfect

---

will be before the court at least a decade, though some credible allegations will not proceed to trial due to the difficulties of proof (Annex C, ch 1, 68).

38 *Johannsen and Chambers v DPP* (1996) 87 A Crim R 126.

39 See Australian Bureau of Statistics, *Criminal Courts, Australia, 2018-19* (Cat No 45130DO001_201819, February 2020). For those who were ultimately acquitted, the mean and median times for finalisation were 63.5 and 51.1 weeks respectively. By way of comparison, in the period 2001-02 the median duration of all finalised defendants in the Higher Criminal Courts in 2001-02 was 20 weeks from initiation to finalisation.

40 See Law Council of Australia, 'A successful recovery: addressing the backlog of cases in the Federal Courts as a result of the COVID 19 pandemic' (2020). For a global perspective, see LA Abraham, TC Brown and SA Thomas, 'How COVID-19's Disruption of the US Correctional System Provides an Opportunity for Decarceration' (2020) 45(4) *American Journal of Criminal Justice* 780.

41 [1992] 1 SCR 771 (Sopinka J).

... that there would be no shortage of judges or courtrooms and essential court staff would always be available'. An ideal world would ensure 'fully adequate funding, personnel and facilities for the administration of criminal justice. As we do not live in such a world, some allowance must be made for limited institutional resources'.[42] While avoiding drifting is important, undue haste expediting cases[43] can also be a danger as, like the firetruck analogy above, cases need time to arrive in court properly prepared. The above statistics reveal that parties need time too. The prosecution must complete its assessment of evidence, prepare its case and engage in the disclosure process.[44] These processes can cause delay – either because the case is complex and time-consuming to prepare, or because there is incompetence or inaction by an officer of the state that directly creates delay.[45] In addition, the defence needs the opportunity to evaluate evidence, meet its disclosure obligations and also prepare its own case. Court administration must be flexible enough to attend to fair trial requirements that permit adjournment due to amended pleadings and orders of disclosure, and accommodate crises relating to any of the essential participants in a trial. It must do so in a manner that keeps a check on unwarranted slippage in cases coming to trial but with recognition that the trials that do proceed do so fairly.

In England and Wales, Sir Brian Leveson P in *Boardman*[46] signalled that in light of the consequences of delay courts should resist developing a 'culture of failure'. Leveson noted that the *Review of Efficiency in Criminal Proceedings* in 2015[47] (chaired by Leveson) emphasised judges' obligations with respect to avoiding unnecessary wastage of court resources:

> [W]e must encourage a reduced tolerance for failure to comply with court directions along with a recognition of the role and responsibilities of the Judge in matters of case management. It cannot be right that a 'culture of failure' has developed in the courts, fed by an expectation that deadlines will not be met. If a deadline (eg for service of a document(s) or an application) is not met, there must be good reason for it and there must be an expectation that the party which failed to comply can provide that reason. A failure to tackle this culture leads to a general indifference to rule compliance. Whichever party has failed to comply or failed to meet the deadline, the opponent perceives objection as a waste of time because it will be largely pointless: there is no sanction that can be applied. Perhaps most significantly, it allows cases to 'drift', and for further hearings to take place unnecessarily.

Delayed complaint

Undoubtedly, the most prominent no-fault cause of delay discussed in Australian case law is the delayed reporting of child sexual abuse.[48] Child sexual assault that is prosecuted many years after the abuse is common in institutional settings

42 *Mills* [1986] 1 SCR 863 (Lamer J), quoted by Sopinka J in *Morin* [1992] 1 SCR 771.

43 RG Fox, 'Criminal Delay as Abuse of Process' (1990) 16 *Monash University Law Review* 64, 64.

44 See, eg, *Boardman* [2015] EWCA Crim 175; [2015] WLR(D) 92.

45 *Edwards* [2009] HCA 20; 255 ALR 399. See also *Johannsen and Chambers v DPP* (1996) 87 A Crim R 126 (20-year delay, murder charge); *Godin* (2009) 309 DLR (4th) 149; 245 CCC (3d) 271; *Williams* [2009] NZSC 41; [2009] 2 NZLR 750.

46 [2015] EWCA Crim 175; [2015] WLR(D) 92, [1], [2].

47 Rt Hon Sir Brian Leveson, *Review of Efficiency in Criminal Proceedings* (Judiciary of England and Wales, 2015), [22], [99].

48 For a discussion of the typicality of delayed complaint among children, see A Cossins, 'Time Out for *Longman*: Myths, Science and the Common Law' (2009) 34 *Melbourne University Law Review* 69, 71-83.

(churches, schools, care homes) or can involve family members, neighbours and family friends.

Australian case law no longer dwells on the reasons for delayed complaint in these situations. It has been accepted that the power imbalance and the immaturity of the complainant make the reasons for delay intrinsic to the context in which abuse can occur.[49] As Cossins reports, studies indicate that sexual predators rely on building a trusting relationship to 'engage in a complex process of grooming their victims in order to initiate and maintain sexual contact and to prevent disclosure'.[50] Cossins summarises the literature on offenders' *modus operandi* – initially grooming victims, then sexualising the relationship, and finally justifying sexual contact and working to maintain the child's cooperation.[51] As Cossins indicates, the studies show that:

> (i) a *majority* of sexually abused children do not report the abuse at the time it occurs;
> (ii) a majority of children either only disclose the abuse some years after it occurred or never disclose at all;
> (iii) the younger the child, the less likely she or he will report the abuse;
> (iv) embarrassment, shame, fear of punishment and feeling responsible for the abuse are key factors that prevent children from reporting;
> (v) a significant minority of children will experience repeated abuse over an extended period of time;
> (vi) repeated abuse appears to be more likely to occur if the abuser is a relative and the intra-familial relationship means a child is less likely to disclose.
>
> Failure to disclose, thus, appears to be compounded by factors such as the closeness of the relationship between offender and victim, the victim's age at time of abuse (with most reported abuse occurring to pre-pubescent children) and repeated abuse.[52]

In short, delay is a *typical* feature of child sexual abuse.[53]

The impact of delay

Delay is never cost-neutral. For victims of crime, a delayed process means that their lives may remain captive to an event that cannot be completely relegated to their past. That event may have caused psychological trauma and, if an accused is prosecuted, it must be relived at some indeterminate, possibly far off, time in the future. As Cory J observed:

> It can never be forgotten that the victims may be devastated by criminal acts. They have a special interest and good reason to expect that criminal trials take place within a reasonable time. From a wider point of view, it is fair to say that all crime disturbs the community and that serious crime alarms the community. All members of the community are thus entitled to see that the justice system works fairly, efficiently and with reasonable dispatch. The very reasonable concern and alarm of the community which naturally arises from acts of crime cannot be assuaged until the trial has taken place. The trial not

49 Cf *Ireland* where in the case of *SH v DPP* [2006] 3 IR 575 Murray CJ proclaimed that courts should only concern themselves with issues of prejudice to an accused, not the causes of delay, see Y Murphy, 'The Effect of Delay on Historical Child Sex Abuse Cases: Commentary on the Irish Experience' (2014) 26 *Current Issues in Criminal Justice* 105, 115-16.

50 A Cossins, 'The Hearsay Rule and Delayed Complaints of Child Sexual Abuse: The Law and the Evidence' (2002) 9 *Psychiatry Psychology and Law* 163, 169.

51 Ibid 170.

52 Ibid 169 (citations omitted).

53 Cossins, above n 48, 82.

> only resolves the guilt or innocence of the individual, but acts as a reassurance to the community that serious crimes are investigated and that those implicated are brought to trial and dealt with according to the law.[54]

To quote from Judge LJ in the English case of *Jisl*:[55]

> 114. ... Resources are limited. ... Time itself is a resource. Every day unnecessarily used, while the trial meanders sluggishly to its eventual conclusion, represents another day's stressful waiting for the remaining witnesses and the jurors in that particular trial, and no less important, continuing and increasing tension and worry for another defendant or defendants, some of whom are remanded in custody.

Human rights jurisprudence expressly accepts that prejudice to an accused spreads beyond just *forensic* disadvantage.[56] It can cause 'stigmatization of the accused, loss of privacy, stress and anxiety resulting from a multitude of factors, including possible disruption of family, social life and work, legal costs, uncertainty as to the outcome and sanction'.[57] For the accused on remand, as well as loss of liberty, there are the collateral damage possibilities – loss of job, home and family. If ultimately acquitted, but having been refused bail, an accused's loss is particularly poignant.[58] Their presumption of innocence may be regained but they are likely to have suffered financially through lost earnings and through incurring legal costs. Salvaging their personal, social and domestic situation will not be automatic. This was the situation for 155 people charged and finalised in 2019-20 who were refused bail and ultimately acquitted of all charges.[59] The cost of post-charge delay for these accused has been immense. It may well have been considerably less physically, emotionally, reputationally and financially damaging if they had entered an early guilty plea[60] in return for a substantial sentence discount. It would also have been quicker but obviously this form of diversion from the trial court means that (with the benefit of hindsight) these people would have sacrificed their presumption of innocence and stood convicted of offences that failed to meet the prosecution standard of proof.

Of course, where no complaint is made until years after the alleged criminal event accused persons are unaware that they will face criminal charges and so do not have the prolonged stress or reputational damage while they are ignorant of impending charges. For them there is no loss of liberty or ancillary damage to employment, family or friends flowing from criminal accusations during this time of ignorance. Life goes on, until a charge is laid. Then an accused must prepare for trial. It is only then that the disadvantage, including the forensic disadvantage in testing the prosecution case and asserting an affirmative defence, crystallises. Notably, it is undoubtedly difficult to expose deceit in a witness account where

---

54 *Askov* [1990] 2 SCR 1199 (Cory J).

55 [2004] EWCA Crim 696; and see also *Boardman* [2015] EWCA Crim 175; [2015] WLR(D) 92.

56 For example, see *Godin* (2009) 309 DLR (4th) 149; 245 CCC (3d) 271, [40]. This has also been recognised by the Australian High Court, but has not been a focal point of its later judgments, see *Jago v District Court (NSW)* [1989] HCA 46; 168 CLR 23, [9] and [20] (Mason CJ), cf at [16] (Brennan J).

57 *Mills* [1986] 1 SCR 863, 920, quoted by Latimer J (dissenting) in *Morin* [1992] 1 SCR 771.

58 See, eg, <http://www.nytimes.com/2015/06/09/nyregion/kalief-browder-held-at-rikers-island-for-3-years-without-trial-commits-suicide.html?_r=0>.

59 *New South Wales Criminal Courts Statistics 2020*, Table 4 (all courts). Note that these figures do not permit ascertaining the period from the date of the alleged offence to charge (which would be when bail consideration would first arise).

60 See Chapter 2 and *Sentencing Act 1991* (Vic), s 6AAA; and *Crimes (Sentencing Procedure) Act 1999* (NSW), s 22; *Sentencing Act 1995* (WA), s 8.

their deficits in recollection or their inconsistent accounts of events long past can be readily interpreted by jurors as honest error rather than malevolent fabrication. As Cory J in the Canadian Supreme Court observed:

> There can be no doubt that memories fade with time. Witnesses are likely to be more reliable testifying to events in the immediate past as opposed to events that transpired many months or even years before the trial. Not only is there an erosion of the witnesses' memory with the passage of time, but there is bound to be an erosion of the witnesses themselves. Witnesses are people; they are moved out of the country by their employer; or for reasons related to family or work they move from the east coast to the west coast; they become sick and unable to testify in court; they are involved in debilitating accidents; they die and their testimony is forever lost.[61]

Both common law and human rights traditions acknowledge that, if a threat to the fairness of a fair trial cannot be corrected or avoided, the trial cannot proceed. Further, both common law and human rights jurisprudence accept that a substantial delay in proceedings inevitably creates below-the-radar forensic disadvantage that an accused may not be able to prove or even identify, encapsulated in pithy observations such as that by Powell J in the US Supreme Court case of *Barker v Wingo*,[62] that 'what has been forgotten can rarely be shown' and by Hardiman J in the Irish case, *P O'C v DPP*,[63] that '[a]bsence of evidence (of prejudice) is not evidence of its absence'.

Remedying delay

No remedy can roll back time or make good lost evidence. Despite the two delay cases (*Jago* and *Longman*) being decided in the same year by overlapping High Court benches,[64] they went in different directions. *Longman*, decided in the context of Western Australia's abolition of corroboration warnings for sexual assault complainants' evidence, followed the 'suspect' witness path of *Bromley*. In *Jago*, with no 'class' of suspect witness identified by the court, the bench focused on delay as a threat to a fair trial proceeding, potentially justifying a permanent stay of proceedings. While *Longman* cemented the importance of the *Bromley*-style warnings, its contrast to *Jago*'s reliance on staying proceedings set Australian 'delay' jurisprudence into two parallel universes, effectively depending on whether the delay occurred in a sexual assault context[65] or not.[66] In the next section we consider the stay remedy and, after that, the judicial warning option. As Lord Bingham of Cornhill in *Attorney-General's Reference (No 2 of 2001)*[67]

61 *Askov* [1990] 2 SCR 1199 (Cory J).

62 407 US 514, 532 (1972).

63 [2000] 3 IR 87, 119, quoted by Murphy, above n 49, 114.

64 Brennan, Deane and Toohey JJ sat on both the *Jago* and *Longman* cases; Brennan and Dawson JJ sat on the cases of *Bromley* and *Longman*.

65 *Longman* [1989] HCA 60; 168 CLR 79 (19-year delay); *Crampton* [2000] HCA 60; 206 CLR 161; *Doggett* [2001] HCA 46; 208 CLR 343 (12 and 19 years delay); *Tully* [2006] HCA 56; 230 CLR 234.

66 In *Edwards* [2009] HCA 20; 255 ALR 399 the alleged breach of law, reckless operation of an aircraft, occurred in October 2001. Prosecutions against the pilot and first officer were commenced in March 2004, with no apparent investigative complexity raised. Procedural delays continued, with the committal conducted in November 2005 and the case was not listed for trial under March 2007. By the time of the committal proceedings, the electronic flight and airport lighting records were missing, leaving the prosecution case dependent on eye-witness accounts. Neither Jago nor Edwards was successful in obtaining stays.

67 [2003] UKHL 68; [2004] 2 AC 72.

observed the issue of delay in the context of rights under Article 6 of the *European Convention on Human Rights*:

> 24. ... The appropriate remedy will depend on the nature of the breach and all the circumstances, including particularly the stage of the proceedings at which the breach is established. If the breach is established before the hearing, *the appropriate remedy may be a public acknowledgement of the breach, action to expedite the hearing to the greatest extent practicable and perhaps, if the defendant is in custody, his release on bail.* (emphasis added)

These alternatives obviously presume that the accused may still be able to have a fair trial, despite delay.

Staying proceedings[68]

A stay of proceedings is a remedy of last resort, 'a "drastic remedy" to be confined to a case that is "exceptional" or "extreme".'[69] As Kiefel, CJ, Bell and Nettle JJ observed in *Strickland*:[70]

> Fundamental amongst the considerations to be weighed in determining whether criminal proceedings should be permanently stayed as an abuse of process is "the legitimate public interest in the disposition of charges of serious offences and in the conviction of those guilty of crime". That is because a permanent stay order has the practical effect of providing immunity from prosecution to a criminal defendant, leaving that criminal defendant under an "irremovable cloud of suspicion" and leaving the potential if not the likelihood of engendering within the community "a festering sense of injustice", if not cynicism.

A stay can apply in numerous contexts and the decided cases should not 'be read as attempting to chart the boundaries of abuse of process'.[71] Permanently staying proceedings can be seen as potentially 'another wound inflicted' on a victim.[72] It is not only a victim issue. As La Forest J observed in the Canadian case of *Rahey*,[73] '[f]ew judges relish the prospect of unleashing dangerous criminals on the public'. Similarly, Brennan J in *Jago*[74] denounced the stay mechanism as overlooking 'the interests of the community and of the victims of crime in the enforcement of the criminal law'. In the five-judge bench New Zealand Supreme Court consideration of the issue in *CT*,[75] allowing a stay, the majority judgment noted that 'a judge should always bear in mind that the burden and standard of proof provide substantial protection for a defendant as does the obligation of a trial judge to take all appropriate measures to mitigate the risk of prejudice'.[76] The majority summed up the principles applied in New Zealand, described as broadly

---

68 Note that a stay can be permanent or conditional.

69 *Strickland v DPP (Cth)* [2018] HCA 53; 266 CLR 325, [166] (Kiefel CJ, Bell and Nettle JJ), citing as examples, *Dupas* [2010] HCA 20; 241 CLR 237 and *Glennon* [1992] HCA 16; 173 CLR 592.

70 *Strickland v DPP (Cth)* [2018] HCA 53; 266 CLR 325, [167] (Kiefel CJ, Bell and Nettle JJ), citing *Walton v Gardiner* (1993) 177 CLR 378; *Rogers* [1994] HCA 42; 181 CLR 251; *Williams v Spautz* [1992] HCA 34; 174 CLR 509; *Jago v District Court (NSW)* [1989] HCA 46; 168 CLR 23.

71 *Truong* [2011] HCA 50; 245 CLR 456, [60] (Kirby J) and referred to approvingly in *Strickland v DPP (Cth)* [2018] HCA 53; 266 CLR 325, [99] (Kiefel CJ, Bell and Nettle JJ).

72 *McBride* (2012) ONCJ 121, [55] (Stephen Brown J).

73 [1987] 1 SCR 588.

74 [1989] HCA 46; 168 CLR 23, [34].

75 [2014] NZSC 155, [32] (Elias CJ, McGrath and William Young JJ), and applied in *P (CA470/2017)* [2020] NZCA 304 (47-year delay did not justify a stay).

76 [2014] NZSC 155, [27] (Elias CJ, McGrath and William Young JJ).

consistent across England and Wales,[77] Australia and Canada,[78] emphasising that delay 'does not erase criminal liability and the adoption of limitation periods is for Parliament and not the courts'.

Historical child sexual assault prosecutions

Australia has seen a dramatic surge in historical child sexual assault prosecutions in recent years, and particularly following the Royal Commission on Institutional Responses to Child Sexual Assault. This has led to renewed consideration of applications for permanent stays on the grounds of forensic disadvantage arising from very lengthy delays in commencing prosecutions.[79] In relation to historical sexual abuse cases, the New Zealand case of *MacGillivray* quoted from *CT*, observing that such

> cases will almost always carry some risk of prejudice, because of the effect of delay on the defendant's ability to "check and challenge the evidence of a complainant." A trial judge should take steps to mitigate the risk of delay-related prejudice. Nevertheless, the decades-long delay between the alleged offending and X complaining to the police is not unprecedented and does not by itself mean the trial would be unfair. There is no issue with the reliability of memory caused by age-related decline in cognitive function. The appellant was 54 years old at the time of trial and said that he did not have "memory fade" or anything like that. X was 49 years old at the time of trial and also did not consider that his memory was affected by the passage of time, depression or drug use.[80]

In the Victorian Court of Appeal case of *McGee*[81] the trial judge had refused a stay application, reversed on appeal. His application was based on charges alleged to have been committed on WP over 50 years earlier, arising from WP, BB and LW, residents of boys' home run by the Christian Brothers, being assigned to McGee's farm. The events were said to have occurred in 1966 and 1967. WP's first statement to police was in 2013. He outlined an extensive history of brutality and persistent sexual abuse on the part of the Brothers at the home as well as making allegations against McGee. Four years of unexplained delay followed. In a second statement in 2017 WP elaborated on the allegations against McGee. During this

77 Citing *Attorney-General's Reference (No 1 of 1990)* [1992] QB 630 (CA). See also *Hewitt* [2020] EWCA Crim 1247 (37-year delay did not justify stay). In *Darmalingum v The State* [2000] UKPC 30; [2000] 1 WLR 2303 (PC) where Darmalingum faced multiple counts of embezzlement and forgery with 'the shadow of the proceedings', trial and appeal hanging over him for 15 years. There were seven years from arrest to conviction. The appeal delays were even lengthier. The cause was institutional delay. The Privy Council considered the option of a non-custodial sentence to replace the four-year gaol sentence but concluded that 'the only disposal which will properly vindicate the constitutional rights of the appellant in the present case would be the quashing of the convictions': at [22]. See also *SP* [2004] ACTCA 16, [63]; *Law* (1995) 84 A Crim R 142, citing *Duncan* (1983) 9 A Crim R 354 regarding instances of reduction of sentence because of delay.

78 Citing *L(WK)* [1991] 1 SCR 1091. However, *Jordan* 2016 SCC 27, [2016] 1 SCR 631; *KJM* 2019 SCC 55; *KGK* 2020 SCC 7 reflect a shift in focus in Canada.

79 As well as the cases discussed below, see also *Higgins* [2020] NSWCCA 149 (appeal allowed, forensic disadvantage in delay established but no warning given); *Cattell* [2019] NSWCCA 297; *Rao* [2019] NSWCCA 290; *SW* [2019] NSWCCA 194; *Porter* [2019] NSWCCA 117; *Lever* [2018] NSWCCA 107; *GD* [2018] NSWCCA 18 (acquittal entered on appeal); *MC* [2017] NSWCCA 316; *Binns* [2017] NSWCCA 280; *Harris* [2017] NSWCCA 254; *WAP* [2017] NSWCCA 212; *Hornhardt* [2017] NSWCCA 186; *TS* [2014] NSWCCA 174 (stay granted); *Webb* [2012] NSWCCA 216; *RM* [2012] NSWCCA 35.

80 *MacGillivray* [2019] NZCA 522, [9] (37-year delay did not justify a stay). On the issue of memory, delay and expert evidence, see *M (CA68/2015)* [2017] NZCA 333; *P (Ca470/2017)* [2020] NZCA 304.

81 *McGee (a Pseudonym)* [2020] VSCA 146 (Maxwell P, T Forrest and Weinberg JJA).

four-year period BB and LW came forward to police with sexual abuse complaints against McGee – however, they died before the 2020 appeal. In response to the applicant's account to police, WP had adjusted his accounts relating to the location of a hayshed where assaults allegedly occurred. KK, McGee's brother, who on WP's version of events witnessed some of the assaults, denied WP's account (at [39]) 'effectively branding WP a liar or, at least, a fantasiser'. KK testified in committal proceedings maintaining (at [45]) 'that he never had any inkling that the applicant may have been behaving inappropriately'. All relevant people were elderly. By the time of a 2021 trial, McGee would be 76 years old, his brother, KK, 82 years old, and his sister, MM, 79 years old. It was anticipated that KK would be called by the prosecution, and that *UEA*, *s* 38, leave would be sought by the prosecution. For guidance, the Court of Appeal drew upon *FJL*[82] and *Morton*,[83] both cases of historical child sexual abuse leading to stays in proceedings. In doing so, their Honours (at [106]) quoted from the judgment of McHugh J in *Brisbane South Regional Health Authority v Taylor*:

> Sometimes the deterioration in quality [arising from delay] is palpable, as in the case where a crucial witness is dead or an important document has been destroyed. But sometimes, perhaps more often than we realise, the deterioration in quality is not recognisable even by the parties. Prejudice may exist without the parties or anybody else realising that it exists. As the United States Supreme Court pointed out in *Barker v Wingo*, 'what has been forgotten can rarely be shown'. So, it must often happen that important, perhaps decisive, evidence has disappeared without anybody now 'knowing' that it ever existed. Similarly, it must often happen that time will diminish the significance of a known fact or circumstance because its relationship to the cause of action is no longer as apparent as it was when the cause of action arose.[84]

Further, in *McGee* they expressed the legal principles before applying them to the facts at hand (emphasis added):

> 137. *The test for the grant of a permanent stay is, rightly, exceptionally stringent. A court should only grant such a stay, in cases involving delay, in rare or exceptional circumstances. It must be shown that the continuation of the proceedings would involve unacceptable injustice or unfairness. Such unacceptable injustice, or unfairness, can result from 'a probable forensic disadvantage which is incurable'.*
>
> 138. In order to justify the extreme step of staying a prosecution, there must be a fundamental defect which goes to the root of the trial of such a nature that nothing that a trial judge can do in the conduct of the trial can relieve against its unfair consequences. The accused must demonstrate that the delay is such that any trial would necessarily be unfair. Accordingly, any conviction would bring the administration of justice into disrepute.
>
> 139. Among the matters that a court should consider in determining an application for a stay are the length of the delay, the explanation provided by the prosecution for the delay, any role played by the accused in bringing about that delay, and the public interest in the disposition of charges involving serious offences. Only in rare and exceptional cases would a court be justified in refusing to exercise its jurisdiction. …
>
> 141. Of course, a trial judge may avoid some of the obstacles to a fair trial by evidentiary rulings and by appropriate directions to the jury which are designed to counteract any prejudice that the accused might otherwise suffer.

In overturning the trial judge's ruling, the Victorian Court of Appeal noted that the applicant's memory from the 1960s showed confusion about some dates and he

82 [2014] VSCA 57; 41 VR 572.

83 [2020] VSCA 49.

84 [1996] HCA 25; 186 CLR 541, 551.

lacked any recall of WP or his brothers. The court also recognised that the applicant's parents, now deceased, would have been able to have given 'important contextual information', a matter of real significance to the defence and observed that:

> 140. *Where*, as in this case, *the main argument in support of the grant of a permanent stay is the unavailability, by reason of the delay that has occurred, of important witnesses, it must be shown that their evidence, had it been available, would probably have materially assisted the defence case*. This flows from the requirement that the accused seeking such a stay *demonstrate the probability, and not mere possibility, that the refusal to grant a stay would result in an unacceptably unfair trial*. (emphasis added)

Their Honours noted[85] the strong public interest in criminal charges being brought to trial particularly in cases involving sexual offences against children, who often do not report allegations until they reach adulthood. They quoted the majority in *Morton* (at [145]):

> [T]he death of a large number of witnesses, some of whom would have been in a position to give highly probative evidence that was capable of supporting the applicant, has deprived him of important means of defending himself. Coupled with the other sources of prejudice in the present case, the death of these witnesses renders it probable that a trial of the charges against the applicant would be unacceptably unfair.

In addition, the court referred to the 55-year delay as 'surely ... at the outer end of what could credibly be regarded as acceptable in any criminal trial'. In permitting the stay, the court noted that the offences were not 'at the upper end of the scale of offending' (at [149]) and referred to a number of significant forensic disadvantages. First, no longer could it be established where the hayshed had been located; and, second, KK would be disadvantaged testifying such that (at [151]):

> the prosecutor will be able to attack KK's reliability on the basis that his memory of the events of more than 50 years ago will have diminished. Inevitably, the potency of his exculpatory evidence will be weakened. Realistically, no significant forensic disadvantage direction can ameliorate the very real damage that will be done to the defence case merely by reason of the effluxion of time.[86]

The statutory delay/forensic disadvantage warning

Beavis[87] illustrates an application of the forensic disadvantage warning given by the judge to the jury under *UEA*, s 165B, regarding the effect of delay, particularly in terms of leaving the defendant only able to make a general denial due to his:

- inability to test the evidence of a witness who was uncertain of the dates of alleged incidents and of precise details which, if known, could potentially be contradicted; and
- the unavailability of employment records and of witnesses who might otherwise have been able to give relevant evidence as to the date when the conduct occurred.

85 Citing *Morton* [2020] VSCA 49.

86 Citing *FJL* [2014] VSCA 57; 41 VR 572 (32-year delay); *Morton* [2020] VSCA 49 (53-56 year delay); *Jago v District Court (NSW)* [1989] HCA 46; 168 CLR 23 (seven-year delay); *Hermanus* [2015] VSCA 2; 44 VR 335 (39-year delay). Note that the *JDA 2015* (Vic), s 39 (rather than *UEA*, s 165B), would have applied in a trial of McGee.

87 [2018] NSWCCA 248, where the trial took place in 2017 and the alleged offending occurred in 2004.

Before s 165B was enacted (and as is discussed in some detail in the next two sections) the *Longman* High Court bench had created a common law warning adapted from the abolished corroboration warnings,[88] with Brennan, Dawson and Toohey JJ in *Longman* indicating that it was 'imperative that a warning be given to the jury' that a 20-year delay meant that the evidence of the complainant could not be adequately tested. The language of corroboration law the Justices drew on suggested that the jury be told '*it would be dangerous to convict on that evidence alone* unless the jury [scrutinised] ... the evidence with great care'.[89] This was an unfortunate recycling of corroboration law's signature tag, '*dangerous to convict*', particularly because it would be typically applied in the context of evidence from a sexual assault complainant.[90] As we see below, the *Longman* direction began with the hallmark of proud flexibility over corroboration law's rigidity, but by the 21st century *Longman* was being called out (quite justifiably) for inferring that delayed complaint requires greater scrutiny of a complainant's evidence (rather than as a warning of the forensic costs to the defence arising from delay). Successive High Court cases, and particularly *Crampton*[91] and *Doggett*,[92] firmed a view that a substantial delay created in effect an 'irrebuttable presumption'[93] of forensic disadvantage and a trial judge's error in failing to warn became fatal to a conviction.[94] These cases were met with amendments in 2007 to the *UEA* creating the current s 165B,[95] placing limitations on trial judges' powers to warn a jury about delay-based forensic disadvantage. Now s 165B(2) requires that where a court (subject to good reasons not to do so (sub-s 3)):

> on application by a party, is satisfied that the defendant has suffered a *significant forensic disadvantage because of the consequences of delay*, ... [must] inform the jury of the nature of that disadvantage and the need to take that disadvantage into account when considering the evidence. (emphasis added).

The factors that may be regarded as establishing a *significant forensic disadvantage* under sub-s (7) include, but are not limited to,

(a) the fact that any potential witnesses have died or are not able to be located,
(b) the fact that any potential evidence has been lost or is otherwise unavailable.

However, s 165B:

- *prohibits* a judge:
  - directing the jury 'about any forensic disadvantage the defendant may have suffered because of delay', otherwise than in accordance with the section ('but this section does not affect any other power of the judge to give any warning to, or to inform, the jury') (sub-s (5));
  - suggesting that it would be *dangerous or unsafe to convict* 'solely because of the delay or the disadvantage (sub-s (4));

88 *Longman* [1989] HCA 60; 168 CLR 79, [11] (Deane J).
89 Ibid [30] (Brennan, Dawson and Toohey JJ) (emphasis added).
90 Discussed further below.
91 [2000] HCA 60; 206 CLR 161 (19-year delay).
92 [2001] HCA 46; 208 CLR 343 (12 and 19 year delays).
93 See ALRC, *Uniform Evidence Law* (Report No 102, 2006), [18.121].
94 *BWT* [2002] NSWCCA 60; 54 NSWLR 241, [15] (Wood CJ at CL describing the High Court cases as elevating the presumption of innocence 'to an assumption that the accused was in fact innocent'), [95] (Sully J).
95 *UEA*, s 165B is repealed in Victoria. See now Part 4 of the *JDA 2015* (Vic), also discussed below. See also *Evidence Act 1929* (SA), s 34CB.

- creates a *duty* to warn that applies only where the judge is satisfied that the defendant has 'suffered a *significant forensic disadvantage* because of the consequences of delay' (sub-s (2));
- provides that *no particular form of words* need be used (sub-s (4)); and
- holds that the obligation to warn will not apply if there are '*good reasons*' not to do so (sub-s (3)).[96]

The section does not by its express terms apply only to historical sexual assault prosecutions, but the cases are the dominant ones considered in practice. A useful summary of the obligations under s 165B is given by Basten JA in *Jarrett*[97] where he observed that:

> [T]he judge must identify the significant forensic disadvantage and must inform the jury of the nature of that disadvantage; the direction will therefore need to be case specific. In directing the jury of the "need" to take that disadvantage into account, it will usually be expected that a direction would identify, so far as it is not obvious, how the disadvantage may affect the jury's consideration of the evidence. *This aspect of any direction will not be straightforward: the usual consequence of delay is the loss of evidence or the loss of opportunity to test evidence; each involves a counterfactual assumption.*

His Honour also noted that 'the proper focus of the section is on the disadvantage to the accused' *and* (at [61]) that:

> Where both complainant and law enforcement authorities have acted with all reasonable expedition, it is not usually apt to describe any lapse of time as involving "delay". Delay is suggestive of hesitation or indecision of the complainant or inefficiency on the part of authorities. That is not to say it involves blameworthy conduct: quite significant lapses of time may be reasonable in the context of a child who is the victim of sexual assault. Whether that which is not unreasonable constitutes "delay" for the purposes of s 165B will depend upon particular circumstances.

The NSW Law Reform Commission, in its dissenting observations in the joint Law Reform Commissions' uniform Evidence Act Report of 2006, raised concerns about the removal of the ready recourse to a judicial warning regarding forensic disadvantage, emphasising the *Longman* warnings 'are dictated by the requirements of a fair trial'[98] and the danger of failing to give due weight to the risk of forensic disadvantage. While not referring to the concern of 'what has been forgotten can rarely be shown' dimension in *Barker v Wingo*, it is implicit in the dissent.[99]

Victoria repealed s 165B on the passing of the *Jury Directions Act 2015* (Vic) (*JDA 2015* (Vic)) and introduced through ss 12, 14, 39 and 40 replacement requirements that are, in broad terms, the same as s 165B,[100] namely:

- a party make a request to the judge;
- that the defence satisfy the court that it has experienced significant forensic disadvantage;

96 Basten JA in *Jarrett* [2014] NSWCCA 140, [54] (emphasis added). His Honour described a situation where there was evidence indicating that the appellant had threatened to suicide if the complainant told anyone of 'our little secret'. If the trial judge was satisfied such a threat had been made, this provided a good reason not to require the forensic disadvantage direction (or for not exercising a discretion to give the direction).

97 [2014] NSWCCA 140, [54].

98 ALRC, *Uniform Evidence Law*, above n 93, [18.131].

99 *Barker v Wingo* 407 US 514, 532 (1972).

100 That is, the provisions equate, subject to the role of s 16 of the *JDA 2015* (Vic). It requires the trial judge to give a direction 'if the trial judge considers that there are substantial and compelling reasons for doing so'.

- that, subject to the court determining that there are good reasons not to direct the jury, the judge must inform the jury of:
  - the nature of the disadvantage experienced by the accused; and
  - the need to take the disadvantage into account when considering the evidence; and
- the judge must not say or suggest to the jury that:
  - it would be dangerous or unsafe to convict the accused; or
  - that the complainant's evidence should be scrutinised with great care.

Finally, consider the concerns expressed by psychologists Coyle and Field that not only are jurors ill-equipped by life's experiences to understand the complexity of delay and recall of traumatic events but that '[i]t requires a suspension of disbelief that instructions given to a jury can cure this deficiency especially since judges cannot be expected to have knowledge of such science. It is our view that judicial warnings in such cases are likely to be of minimal, if any, value in limiting the prejudicial effect of such evidence'.[101] Coyle and Field refer to the lack of

> codified judicial warnings to juries as to the danger of witnesses discussing events that they observed, either among themselves, family, and acquaintances or with investigating officers. And the myriad facts that each case presents precludes the prospect of comprehensive judicial warnings of sufficient clarity and specificity to cover every eventuality of post-event contamination of memory.[102]

They add that 'it is hard to see how a defence could be adequately marshalled without reference to expert psychological evidence as to matters affecting recall'.[103]

Corroboration Law and First-Generation Judicial Warnings

In the late 18th and early 19th centuries, as judges reduced their active role in criminal trials and the opportunity to 'chat' to jurors declined, their formal directions to juries grew. Sometimes the direction required juries not to convict unless, with certain kinds of evidence deemed potentially unreliable, the jurors had applied caution to their assessment of the relevant evidence and examined it in the context of any corroborating evidence. There were many categories of evidence that were seen to require this special caution, including accomplices, sexual assault complainants and children. These early directions were based on corroboration law, a law that had grown from Roman law notions of proof based on a 'reliability' formula grading prosecution evidence according to complex categorisation. Under Roman law full proof was necessary for judgment. One witness was a half-proof. Two witnesses created full proof,[104] which was sufficient for conviction. Other ways to get to full proof included evidence of a confession made under torture, also a half-proof, and evidence of an entry into tradesmen's books or evidence of rumour or reputation that confirmed another half-proof. It was also possible to rely on quarter or one-eighth proofs to create a full proof. This was a system that offered simplicity, but at the price of integrity. Stone offers a succinct description of the fractional proof system:

101 IR Coyle and D Field, 'Psychology from the Bench' (2013) 20 *Psychiatry, Psychology and Law* 91, 101.

102 Ibid 102.

103 Ibid 101.

104 J Stone (ed WAN Wells), *Evidence: Its History and Policies* (Butterworths, 1991), 13-14.

> These situations … might be classified in several ways. … [I]n a few instances, such as treason, at least two witnesses are necessary; in the others, such as perjury, one will suffice, but his story must be confirmed in some material particular. … [I]n some instances the essential consideration is the unreliability of a particular kind of witness; in the rest, the character of a particular kind of witness may be present, as with child witnesses, in any kind of trial …
>
> The most developed branch of this subject, and the one which introduces most of the inherent difficulties is that relating to accomplices.[105]

The common law of corroboration evolved classified categories of witnesses and evidence. Over time, corroboration law was supplemented by statute (and then repealed by statute). It provided, among other things, that for prosecution evidence to sustain a conviction:

- where an accomplice witness testified, the testimony must be accompanied by a corroboration warning – that is, a warning to the jury of the danger of convicting without corroborative evidence;[106]
- for sexual offences, similarly, a corroboration warning must accompany the complainant's account. Stone[107] describes the common law as setting a more exacting corroborative requirement for sexual assault compared to accomplice cases; and
- unsworn evidence from a child complainant witness evidence required actual corroboration as well as a judicial warning.

The last two special requirements for sexual assault offences appear to reach back far in time. For example, Stone refers to a 1905 English King's Bench case[108] where the court noted that rape remained the only instance where it was for the prosecution to show that the injured party/victim had raised a 'hue and cry' – originally the victim's call to those around to detain the offender, and now just known as 'the complaint'. Indeed, the 'hue and cry' evolved from an obligatory verification of *any* crime in medieval times to a strict requirement only for sexual assault complainants. Its absence or delay could be used by the defence to discredit the complainant. Stone, writing in the 1940s, stated:

> This strict rule is now rationalised on the ground of the ease with which false accusations of this kind are concocted, and the difficulty even for an innocent man to disprove them. This aspect of the law of complaints pertains to the sufficiency of evidence, being in effect a very special rule as to corroboration …[109]

Under the *UEA* corroboration requirements, except with respect to the offence of perjury or a similar or a related offence, are abolished: *UEA*, s 164.[110] The back story

---

105 Ibid 711.

106 Corroborative evidence was required to possess particular qualities: independence, implication of the accused on a material point, etc. See *Baskerville* (1916) 12 Cr App Rep 81.

107 Stone, above n 104, 727.

108 *Osborne* [1905] 1 KB 551, 559.

109 Stone, above n 104, 732.

110 See also Victoria, *JDA 2015* (Vic), ss 32(3), 74. The (non-uniform) banning of corroboration requirements for sexual assault complainants and child witnesses took place from the 1980s. In England and Ireland the same steps were also taken: in England, *Criminal Justice and Public Order Act 1994*, s 32(1), and in Ireland, *Criminal Law (Rape) Act 1990*, s 7, abolished mandatory corroboration requirements. In *Makanjuola* [1995] 3 All ER 730, s 32(1) was interpreted as allowing for a continuing judicial discretion to give corroboration warnings, but only where 'necessary' (Lord Taylor CJ); and see *People (DPP) v JEM* [2001] 4 IR 385. Necessity might include the judge urging caution where the witness has been shown to be unreliable, or to have lied, or made previous false complaints, or to bear a grudge against the accused – then a

to s 164 is that by the 1980s corroboration's goals were no longer synchronous with how appeal courts wished jurors to be guided or, as one might infer from Stone's summation, with an evidence-based understanding of sexual assault dynamics. Judicial revisionism and statutory change moved hand-in-hand to announce that the lustre had worn off corroboration law. Corroboration law and its required warnings had generated unmeritorious appeals as the warnings became 'ritualistic formularies'[111] and corroboration requirements were often convoluted, technical and unhelpful. They were no longer practical aids to juries. Beyond the evidence of alleged accomplices, its categories were indefensible and its patently unfair attachment to the evidence of sexual assault complainants had brushed up against the feminist critique that the '*dangerous to convict*' mantra of the corroboration warning was required for victim-witnesses alleging sexual assault, but for no other victims. Its impact was overwhelmingly discounting women's testimony. The Canadian Supreme Court case of *Vetrovec*[112] was the first case to reveal cracks in corroboration law. When describing corroboration warnings with respect to accomplices as 'ritualistic incantations' Dickson J focused not only on the problem with the capture of corroboration law, but also on its 'blind and empty formalism', due, his Honour suggested, to its reliance on a universal rule:[113]

> To construct a universal rule singling out accomplices, then, is to fasten upon this branch of the law of evidence a blind and empty formalism. Rather than attempting to pigeon-hole a witness into a category and then recite a ritualistic incantation, *the trial judge might better direct his mind to the facts of the case, and thoroughly examine all the factors which might impair the worth of a particular witness*. If, in his judgment, the credit of the witness is such that the jury should be cautioned, then he may instruct accordingly. If, on the other hand, he believes the witness to be trustworthy, then, regardless of whether the witness is technically an 'accomplice' no warning is necessary.[114]

By the mid-1990s the Australian High Court took heed of these sentiments and entrenched a new generation of common law warnings based on the cases of *Bromley*[115] and *Longman*.[116] These are discussed in the next section, though it should be noted that the role of these common law warnings varies from jurisdiction to jurisdiction. For example, in Victoria, the *JDA 2015*, s 54, has abolished them,[117] and in New South Wales, *Criminal Procedure Act 1986* (NSW) (*CPA* (NSW)), s 294AA, has made the so-called *Murray* direction all but defunct.[118]

---

stronger warning may be appropriate, with the judge suggesting to the jury that it would be wise to look for some supporting material before acting on the witness's evidence. Suggestion by cross-examining counsel would not suffice: S Leahy, 'The Corroboration Warning in Sexual Offence Trials: Final Vestige of the Historic Suspicion of Sexual Offence Complainants or a Necessary Protection for Defendants?' (2014) 18 *International Journal of Evidence and Proof* 41, 43-5. Leahy shows that the *Makanjuola* guidelines have not prevented the old corroboration attachment to sexual assault complainants continuing to insinuate itself into trials.

111 *Doggett* [2001] HCA 46; 208 CLR 343 (Gleeson CJ).

112 (1982) 136 DLR (3d) 89.

113 Referred to approvingly by Toohey J in *Webb and Hay* [1994] HCA 30; 181 CLR 41. See also *Spencer* [1987] UKHL 2; [1987] AC 128, 141.

114 (1982) 136 DLR (3d) 89 (emphasis added).

115 [1986] HCA 49; 161 CLR 315.

116 [1989] HCA 60; 168 CLR 79.

117 *Evidence Act 2008 (Vic)*, s 164(4), also prohibits a judge from warning the jury that it is dangerous to act on uncorroborated evidence 'or give a warning to the same or similar effect [or] ... direct the jury regarding the absence of corroboration'. This removes the applicability of the *Crofts* direction, see below.

118 *Murray* (1987) 11 NSWLR 12 (Lee J), discussed below.

Subject to statutory provisions restricting the common law approach to warnings and directions, s 165(5) of the *UEA* preserves all of them.[119] The *JDA 2015* (Vic), s 16, provides an overriding and general obligation on a trial judge to direct the jury wherever he or she considers that there are substantial and compelling reasons for doing so (even if no direction is requested by counsel under s 12). Keeping in mind that this Victorian legislation is designed to remove common law excrescences, time will tell the extent to which the pre-existing common law will exert influence in guiding trial judges on what constitutes a 'substantial and compelling' reason for directing a jury in a particular case.[120]

Post-corroboration and Second-Generation Judicial Warnings

> The requirement of the common law explained in *Bromley*, *Crofts* and *Longman* is to warn the jury whenever *a warning is necessary in order to avoid a perceptible risk of a miscarriage of justice. A perceptible risk of that kind arises when there is a feature of the evidence which may adversely affect its reliability and which may not be evident to a lay jury. The risk is perceptible to the court because judicial experience has shown that evidence of this description may be unreliable.* Subject to any statutory prohibition, where there is a feature of that kind the fair trial of the accused requires the judge to draw it to the jury's attention, explain how it may affect the reliability of the evidence and warn the jury of the need for caution in deciding whether to accept it and the weight to be given to it.[121]
>
> Directions are not ritualistic formularies. Their purpose is to assist the jury in the practical task of resolving fairly the issues which have been presented to them by the parties.[122]

In developing the second-generation warnings, the High Court of Australia was drawn towards judicial directions that were sought to be avowedly practical, rather than formulaic. The first significant move was in 1986[123] when the apex courts in both the United Kingdom and Australia shifted their ground. In 1986, the House of Lords' case of *Spencer*[124] delivered a new approach regarding the danger to fair trial process where the defence face forensic challenges exposing the dangers to jurors in relying on suspect prosecution witness testimony. A few months later, in the 1986 case of *Bromley*,[125] the High Court followed suit. In both cases mental illness affected the reliability of the witnesses' testimony and (in

---

119 *UEA*, s 165(5): 'This section does not affect any other power of the judge to give a warning to, or to inform, the jury'. Note, however, the observation by Basten JA in *Ewen* [2015] NSWCCA 117, [18]: 'Because of the imprecision of the description of evidence which "may be unreliable" it is not entirely clear what "other power[s]" may be preserved, unaffected by the section. Indeed, one implication to be drawn from the savings provision is that the section does otherwise affect the powers to which it applies'.

120 *Gul* [2017] VSCA 153, [48]: 'A decision whether to give a direction must be taken paying due regard to the issues raised by the case and to the forensic decisions of counsel; and a direction not requested by the parties can only be given if the reasons for doing so are substantial and compelling. ... [That is] reasons ... [that] are of considerable importance and strongly persuasive in the context of the issues in the trial'.

121 *GW* [2016] HCA 6; 258 CLR 108, [50] (French CJ, Bell, Gageler, Keane and Nettle JJ) (emphasis added), citing *Bromley* [1986] HCA 49; 161 CLR 315, 319 (Gibbs CJ (Mason and Wilson JJ agreeing at 322, Dawson J agreeing at 326), 323-5 (Brennan J); *Crofts* [1996] HCA 22; 186 CLR 427, 435 (Dawson J), 446 (Toohey, Gaudron, Gummow and Kirby JJ); *Longman* [1989] HCA 60; 168 CLR 79, 86 (Brennan, Dawson and Toohey JJ).

122 *Doggett* [2001] HCA 46; 208 CLR 343, [2]-[3] (Gleeson CJ).

123 Note, however, that warnings with respect to identification were recognised earlier, largely as a result of the 1976 Devlin Committee Report, see Chapter 13 and *Turnbull* [1977] QB 224.

124 [1987] UKHL 2; [1986] 3 WLR 348, building on *Beck* [1982] 1 WLR 461.

125 [1986] HCA 49; 161 CLR 315.

Spencer) there were substantial criminal histories to cast even further doubt on the witnesses' reliability. These cases were confirmed by subsequent case law in England[126] and Australia[127] and established the desirability of a new genre of judicial warnings that would, in due course, provide protection for the accused from the increased danger of wrongful conviction arising from unappreciated dangers lurking in certain unreliable prosecution evidence. Unlike corroboration law, the new warnings apply to all manner of suspect testimony and focus on educating the jury regarding the elements of potential unreliability that may not be obvious to jurors. Brennan J in *Bromley* added that 'the sole raison d'être ... requiring a warning to be given "is to ensure that the jury is alive to the danger of convicting on the uncorroborated evidence of a class of witnesses whose testimony may, for reasons already indicated, be untruthful"' (quoting from Mason J in *Kelleher*[128]).

Bromley is the pioneer case in the development of the second generation of warnings. Here the High Court considered a conviction based in part on the prosecution witness, Carter, who had schizophrenia-induced delusions on the evening of the incident. These included that he thought he had seen the devil. According to Gibbs CJ:

> What is required, in a case where the evidence of a witness may be potentially unreliable, but which does not fall within one of the established categories in relation to which the full warning as to the necessity of corroboration must be given, is that the jury must be made aware, in words which meet the justice of the particular case, of the dangers of convicting on such evidence. ...
>
> [T]he jury should be given a warning, appropriate to the circumstances of the case, of the possible danger of basing a conviction on the testimony of that witness unless it is confirmed by other evidence. The warning should be clear and, in a case in which a lay juror might not understand why the evidence of the witness was potentially unreliable, it should be explained to the jury why that is so. There is no particular formula that must be used; the words used must depend on the circumstances of the case.[129]

Ultimately, the *Bromley* court held that the cross-examination of Carter had sufficiently alerted the jury to the dangers in his testimony. Although an unsuccessful High Court appeal, *Bromley* was extremely important because it set the Australian foundation for the new style warnings that blossomed over the following five years. Three years later, in 1989, another two cases were decided by the High Court: *Jago v District Court (NSW)*[130] and *Longman.*[131]

Longman built on the initiatives begun in *Bromley*. As discussed earlier in this chapter, the case involved a sexual assault prosecution where the complainant's accusations were made 21 and 25 years after two alleged acts of sexual indecency on Longman's step-daughter. *Jago* involved charges relating to white collar crime where the applicant sought, unsuccessfully, a stay of proceedings because of the 7-10 years' institutional delay in bringing the charges to trial.

---

126 See *Makanjuola* [1995] 3 All ER 730 (prison informant testimony); *Pringle* [2003] UKPC 9; *Benedetto and Labrador* [2003] 1 WLR 64 (PC); and see *Cundell* [2009] EWCA Crim 2072. See, in relation to delay, *Attorney-General's Reference (No 1 of 1990)* [1992] QB 630; 95 Crim App R 296; and for a useful summary of authorities, see *MacKreth* [2009] EWCA Crim 1849.

127 The important follow-up cases are discussed below: *Longman* [1989] HCA 60; 168 CLR 79. For the progeny, see *Pollitt* [1992] HCA 35; 174 CLR 558 (prison informants); *McKinney* [1991] HCA 6; 171 CLR 468 (confessions made in police custody not electronically recorded); *Domican* [1992] HCA 13; 173 CLR 555 (identification evidence).

128 [1974] HCA 48; 131 CLR 534.

129 [1986] HCA 49; 161 CLR 315, 319.

130 [1989] HCA 46; 168 CLR 23.

131 [1989] HCA 60; 168 CLR 79.

The facts in *Spencer*, *Bromley* and *Longman* lent themselves to the wider rebellion taking place against corroboration law in the 1980s. By the late 1980s and 1990s the surge in historical child sexual assault prosecutions had begun, and these 'new' warnings developed with a focus (in practice, if not in expression) on treating sexual assault complainant evidence differently from that of other witnesses or victims of crime.[132] Two directions of this ilk that are typically[133] applied to sexual assault complainants are the *Murray* ('*where there is only one vital prosecution witness, her evidence should be scrutinised with great care*') direction (1987)[134] and the *Crofts* (delay-related) direction (1996).[135] The case of *GW*, an appeal from the ACT, examined in Chapter 5, is illustrative of this tendency. GW's trial involved six charges relating to acts of indecency in presence of his five-year-old daughter. However, in New South Wales, s 294AA of the *CPA* (NSW) cautions that the judge must not suggest to a jury that 'complainants as a class are unreliable witnesses'; nor can the judge warn of 'the danger of convicting on the uncorroborated evidence of any complainant'. In 2015 in *Ewen*,[136] the NSW Court of Criminal Appeal concluded that there was no role for the *Murray* direction that is based only on the absence of corroboration and that inviting close scrutiny of the complainant's evidence contravenes s 294AA. For Simpson J, this would be 'tantamount to a direction that it would be dangerous to convict on the uncorroborated evidence of the complainant'[137] (and thus transgress the statutory prohibition on warning a jury of the danger of convicting on the uncorroborated evidence

---

132 See *BWT* [2002] NSWCCA 60; 54 NSWLR 241, [32] (Wood CJ at CL).

133 For an example of the *Murray* direction being justified in a case not involving sexual assault, see *Laughton* [2019] NSWCCA 74, [82] (Schmidt J), Meagher JA at [41] applying r 4; Button J at [100] expressly leaving open the appropriateness of the *Murray* direction.

134 That is, 'a direction that in any case in which the sole evidence of the commission of a crime is that of a single witness, the evidence of that witness must be scrutinised with great care' from *Murray* (1987) 11 NSWLR 12 (Lee J). Note, however, that in NSW s 294AA of the *CPA* (NSW) cautions that the judge must not suggest to a jury that 'complainants as a class are unreliable witnesses'; nor can the judge warn of 'the danger of convicting on the uncorroborated evidence of any complainant'.

135 *Crofts* [1996] HCA 22; 186 CLR 427, applying where a jury is informed (for example, in accordance with s 107 of the *CPA* (NSW)) that a delay in complaint does not necessarily indicate that the allegation is false, and good reasons may explain why a victim of sexual assault might hesitate in making a complaint then the jury 'should also be informed that the absence of a complaint or a *delay* in the making of it *may be taken into account in evaluating the evidence of the complainant, and in determining whether to believe him or her (but not in terms reviving the stereotyped view that complainants in sexual assault cases are unreliable or that delay is invariably a sign of the falsity of the complaint*': *BWT* [2002] NSWCCA 60; 54 NSWLR 241, [32] (Wood CJ at CL) (emphasis added). See also the *Markuleski* direction (2001): where cross-admissibility of evidence relating to one count charging sexual assault with other counts alleging sexual assault on a separate occasion 'by a reminder that if the jury has a reasonable doubt concerning the credibility of the complainant's evidence on one or more counts, they can take that into account when assessing his or her reliability on the other counts': *Markuleski* [2001] NSWCCA 290, [259]-[263].

136 [2015] NSWCCA 117.

137 Ibid [136] (Simpson J). In this context it is worth noting that a multi-jury, multi-jurisdictional study by Horan and Goodman-Delahunty of 55 Australian criminal jury trials, including interviews with legal professionals and jurors regarding their perceptions of expert evidence, found support for the view that jurors appear to seek out corroboration: 'In the absence of the corroborating forensic evidence or a viable explanation as to why this evidence was not available, these jurors did not perceive that the high standard of proof was met by the prosecution. With the exception of Juror 4, the jurors did not suggest that the complainant made a false report': J Horan and J Goodman-Delahunty, 'Expert Evidence to Counteract Jury Misconceptions about Consent in Sexual Assault Cases: Failures and Lessons Learned' (2020) 43 *UNSW Law Journal* 707.

of any complainant). Basten JA agreed and noted[138] that the *Murray* direction had two potential problems: it 'comes close to transgressing the long established principle that judges should not seek to paraphrase, explain or embellish what is meant by "satisfaction beyond reasonable doubt"';[139] and/or its general terms disguise a warning suggesting that 'complainants as a class are unreliable'.[140] His Honour observed that 'care must be taken that directions not continue past practices under a neutral guise'[141] and that the *Murray* direction needed to be reformulated to comply with the statutory prohibition on treating complainants as suspect witnesses.[142] As identified in *Ewen*, and discussed in relation to s 165B, it has become increasingly clear that for sexual assault complainants the impact of the *Longman* warning was to send the law backwards not forwards.[143]

However, the *Longman* warning was also the template to cater for newly recognised categories of *unreliable* evidence unrelated to sexual assault prosecutions. In these respects, the warnings focused on educating the jury and attempted to avoid becoming hidebound (like corroboration warnings). One of these warnings we saw in the previous chapter, the *Domican*[144] warning relating to identification evidence. The *Longman* template was also developed by the High Court to apply to confessions obtained in circumstances analogous to *McKinney*,[145] that is, where a suspect was unable to muster independent verification of the circumstances surrounding their stay in police custody and subsequently disputed admissions were allegedly made. Mason CJ, Deane, Gaudron and McHugh JJ explained the rationale for the direction.

> 19. … A heavy practical burden is involved in raising a reasonable doubt as to the truthfulness of police evidence of confessional statements, for, in the circumstances which invariably attend that evidence, a reasonable doubt entails that there be a reasonable possibility that police witnesses perjured themselves and conspired to that end. … Thus, the jury should be informed that it is comparatively more difficult for an accused person held in police custody without access to legal advice or other means of corroboration to have evidence available to support a challenge to police evidence of confessional statements than it is for such police evidence to be fabricated, and, accordingly, it is necessary that [jurors] be instructed … that they should give careful consideration as to the dangers involved in convicting an accused person in circumstances where the only (or substantially the only) basis for finding that guilt has been established beyond reasonable doubt is a confessional statement allegedly made whilst in police custody, the making of which is not reliably corroborated. Within the context of this warning it will ordinarily be necessary to emphasise the need for careful scrutiny of the evidence and to direct attention to the fact that police witnesses are often practised witnesses and it is not an easy matter to determine whether a practised witness is telling the truth.

---

138 Ibid [22].

139 See *Green* [1971] HCA 55; 126 CLR 28, 31-2 (Barwick CJ, McTiernan and Owen JJ), reiterating statements from earlier authorities.

140 [2015] NSWCCA 117, [27].

141 Ibid [35].

142 Ibid [26]. Basten JA quoted (at [28]) from the 2006 NSW Criminal Justice Sexual Offence Taskforce report (at 103) that, despite the removal of the obligation to give a corroboration warning by *UEA*, s 164(3), 'it appears that a *Murray warning* is frequently given in sexual assault trials in NSW' (emphasis added). The sentiments expressed by Simpson J and Basten JA in *Ewen* were repeated in *Hogan (a Pseudonym)* [2019] NSWCCA 125 and endorsed in *Neto* [2020] NSWCCA 128 (Hidden AJ, Basten JA, with Fagan J agreeing).

143 An observation made also by Basten JA in *Ewen* [2015] NSWCCA 117, [12].

144 [1992] HCA 13; 173 CLR 555.

145 [1991] HCA 6; 171 CLR 468 (Mason CJ, Deane, Gaudron and McHugh JJ).

Similarly, prison informant evidence led in the prosecution case requires a warning to the jury concerning the danger of relying on prisoners whose incentives to lie are great, matched only by their talents at presenting a believable tale in the witness box: 'the 'prison-informer witness is often a skilful liar, with ... quick intelligence well suited to the giving of evidence and withstanding cross-examination': see *Pollitt*.[146] All these cases reflect circumstances where the fair trial is compromised because:

- courts do not believe that cross-examination is sufficient to alert the jury to the weaknesses in the evidence; and
- jurors are unlikely to be alert to the dangers that reside in certain testimony unless they are aided by the trial judge's direction.

Third-Generation Judicial Warnings

Unreliable evidence

This final section of this chapter concerns evidence deemed by the law to be potentially unreliable.[147] The origins of *UEA*, s 165, are found in cl 134 of the draft evidence law legislation produced in 1985 by the ALRC.[148] In the decade between this draft and the enactment of the first wave of the uniform evidence legislation, the major cases discussed above took place. Consequently, cl 134 was modified for the enactment of the uniform Evidence Acts. The final form is extracted. It caters for civil and criminal proceedings (except in Victoria where the *Evidence Act 2008* (Vic), s 165, is limited to civil proceedings and the *JDA 2015* (Vic) caters for criminal trials).

165. Unreliable evidence

(1) This section applies to evidence of a kind that may be unreliable, including the following kinds of evidence:

(a) evidence in relation to which Part 3.2 (hearsay evidence) or 3.4 (admissions) applies,
(b) identification evidence,
(c) evidence the reliability of which may be affected by age, ill health (whether physical or mental), injury or the like,
(d) evidence given in a criminal proceeding by a witness, being a witness who might reasonably be supposed to have been criminally concerned in the events giving rise to the proceeding,
(e) evidence given in a criminal proceeding by a witness who is a prison informer,
(f) oral evidence of questioning by an investigating official of a defendant that is questioning recorded in writing that has not been signed, or otherwise acknowledged in writing, by the defendant,
(g) in a proceeding against the estate of a deceased person – evidence adduced by or on behalf of a person seeking relief in the proceeding that is evidence about a matter about which the deceased person could have given evidence if he or she were alive.

(2) If there is a jury and a party so requests, the judge is to:

(a) warn the jury that the evidence may be unreliable, and

146 [1992] HCA 35; 174 CLR 558, 615 (McHugh J).
147 Identification evidence is dealt with separately, see Chapter 13.
148 ALRC, *Evidence (Interim)* (Report No 26, 1985) Appendix A. Relevant to the preceding discussion, cl 134(1) provided: '(e) in the case of a prosecution for an offence of asexual nature – evidence given by a victim of the alleged offence' in the list of kinds of unreliable evidence.

(b) inform the jury of matters that may cause it to be unreliable, and
(c) warn the jury of the need for caution in determining whether to accept the evidence and the weight to be given to it.

(3) The judge need not comply with subsection (2) if there are good reasons for not doing so.

(4) It is not necessary that a particular form of words be used in giving the warning or information.

(5) This section does not affect any other power of the judge to give a warning to, or to inform, the jury.

(6) Subsection (2) does not permit a judge to warn or inform a jury in proceedings before it in which a child gives evidence that the reliability of the child's evidence may be affected by the age of the child. Any such warning or information may be given only in accordance with section 165A(2) and (3).

Note also that to ensure that children are not singled out as unreliable (as corroboration law previously did), *UEA*, ss 165(6) and 165A, prohibit a judge warning juries 'that children as a class are unreliable witnesses' or that their evidence may be affected by their age.[149] Basten JA in *GBB*[150] noted that 'age will usually be a significant factor and thus affect reliability' making it difficult to determine when a warning does not fall within the prohibition in s 165(6). That said, as Basten JA also noted, the preservation in s 165(5) of the obligation to warn of inherent dangers in evidence that may not be obvious to jurors.

'Evidence of a kind that may be unreliable'

In *Ewen*[151] Basten JA considered views on the scope of s 165's 'evidence of a kind that may be unreliable' and quoted Spigelman CJ in *Stewart*,[152] suggesting that:

> 16. The word 'kind' is a word of a breadth and generality which it may be appropriate to read down. *Any* reason that could be advanced for questioning the reliability of evidence in the specific circumstances of a case can be stated at different levels of generality. Once stated at a level of generality higher than the specific facts of a particular case, such a reason could satisfy the description of "a kind" of evidence. That would have the result that in *every case* in which an assertion of lack of reliability is made, the compulsory provisions for a warning on request in s 165(2) would apply, subject only to the exception in s 165(3). The acknowledgment, in s 165(5), that there will be other circumstances in which a judge will be required to warn or inform the jury with respect to these matters, suggests that *the word 'kind' must be read down in some way*.

149 *UEA*, s 165A (like s 165(6) and s 165B), was inserted in 2007. See also *JDA 2015* (Vic), s 33, which specifically details the prohibition on trial judges, the prosecution and defence counsel indicating that child witnesses are of a class unreliable, or a specific child witness is unreliable due to their age. For children and vulnerable adults, see *Crimes Act 1914* (Cth), s 15YQ; for complainant and child witnesses in a sexual offence proceeding, see *Evidence (Miscellaneous Provisions) Act 1991* (ACT), ss 69, 70; for complainants, *CPA* (NSW), s 294AA: 'A judge in any proceedings to which this Division applies must not warn a jury, or make any suggestion to a jury, that complainants as a class are unreliable witnesses' (originally *Crimes Act 1900* (NSW), s 405C); against all witnesses with respect to the *Criminal Code* (Tas), s 136, regarding an alleged victim of crimes contained in Part XIV and XX of the Code (child sexual assault, rape, stalking and related and like offences); (children) *Evidence Act 1906* (WA), s 106D, and 'the judge shall not give a corroboration warning to the jury unless the judge is satisfied that such a warning is justified in the circumstance': s 50; *Criminal Code* (Qld), s 632: 'but the judge must not warn or suggest in any way to the jury that the law regards any class of complainants as unreliable witnesses'.

150 [2019] NSWCCA 296.

151 [2015] NSWCCA 117, [18].

152 [2001] NSWCCA 260; 52 NSWLR 301 (emphasis added).

As Basten JA noted in *Ewen*,[153] Howie J in *Stewart*[154] (with Hulme J agreeing) dealt differently with the scope of s 165(1), preferring to maintain common law loyalties.

> 98. Where a matter which might adversely affect the reliability of evidence in the trial *would readily be understood and appreciated by a jury because it falls within their general experience and understanding and where the court has no special knowledge about the matter or no reason to doubt that the jury will appropriately assess its weight*, then the evidence is not 'of a kind that may be unreliable' and the section does not apply.

Basten JA preferred the Chief Justice's reasoning, noting that sub-s (3) accommodates the fact no warning is needed 'if there are good reasons for not doing so'. His Honour observed that this gives weight to the clear intent to move from the common law's conception of the obligation to warn to a more flexible and practical approach.

With respect to s 165, there is extensive case law on each category of evidence listed in sub-s (1). The key features of the section are:

- The judicial warning in sub-s (2) applies only to a specific type of evidence, namely, 'evidence *of a kind* that may be unreliable'. It does not apply to *any* potentially unreliable evidence. For example, delay is not a matter for *UEA*, s 165,[155] nor is evidence that is merely disputed,[156] or conflicting evidence,[157] or evidence indicating a witness is biased or has a motive to lie.[158]
- Where it is sought to bring evidence within sub-s (1)(a)-(g), the evidence must support the potential unreliability.[159]
- The list of kinds of unreliable evidence in sub-s (1)(a)-(g) is not exhaustive. Other kinds of evidence that may be unreliable include:
  - disputed police informer[160] and police non-confessional[161] evidence;
  - interpreting photographic evidence;[162]
  - tracker dog behaviour;[163]
  - negative identification and non-resemblance evidence;[164]
  - hypnosis-affected evidence.[165]

153 [2015] NSWCCA 117, [19] (emphasis added).

154 [2001] NSWCCA 260; 52 NSWLR 301.

155 *RRS* [2013] NSWCCA 94.

156 *Serratore* (1999) 48 NSWLR 101.

157 *Nguyen* (1998) 102 A Crim R 577.

158 *Stewart* [2001] NSWCCA 260; 52 NSWLR 301, [99] (Howie J).

159 *Allen* [2013] VSCA 263 (sexual assault complainant with intellectual disability and schizophrenia, where psychiatric evidence indicated that under medication her memory and recall 'was fine').

160 *Grey* [2001] HCA 65; 184 ALR 593; 75 ALJR 1708; *Reardon* [2002] NSWCCA 203; 186 FLR 1.

161 For example, that the accused was found with incriminating items on his possession: *Richards* (unreported, NSWCCA, 3 April 1998, Simpson J).

162 *Amante* [2020] NSWCCA 34, [6] (Beech-Jones J) relying on *UEA*, s 9(1) (limiting the application of the Act only to the extent provided by 'a principle or rule of common law or equity', and only in so far as the *UEA* does not provide 'otherwise expressly or by necessary intendment'. His Honour cautioning the prescriptive approach to photographic evidence in *Goode v Angland* [2017] NSWCA 311, noting that s 165 provides for evidence of a kind that may be unreliable. This was a dissenting view as Payne JA agreed with N Adams's application of *Goode* in *Amante*.

163 *Stewart* [2001] NSWCCA 260; 52 NSWLR 301, [103] (Howie J).

164 That is, identification evidence that is exculpatory of the accused: *Rose* [2002] NSWCCA 455; 55 NSWLR 701; *Ilioski* [2006] NSWCCA 164; *Kanaan* [2006] NSWCCA 109. Note the High Court refused special leave in *Kanaan*: [2007] HCATrans 402; *Mulholland* [2019] NSWCCA 257 (where it is described as 'descriptive evidence that was exculpatory for the defence').

165 *JG* [2011] NSWCCA 198.

The central issue in applying s 165, outside its defined categories is

> whether, by reason of a particular circumstance, or combination of circumstances, the evidence in question might be potentially unreliable in a respect, or to an extent, which might not be properly appreciated by the jury, in the absence of an appropriate direction by the trial judge.[166]

- The defence must request a warning. 'The conditions necessary to satisfy the word "requests" in s 165(2) in relation to a warning about "evidence of a kind that may be unreliable" would involve counsel making the request identifying what the "kind" of evidence was, why it was unreliable, and what the terms of the warning requested were.'[167]

  > [Without a request] there was no obligation imposed on the trial judge by s 165 to give a further warning. Nor is the requirement for a request a mere technicality. The obligation to give a warning is contingent in the sense that the judge has a broad discretion not to give a warning for "good reasons": subs (3). *A request would properly focus on the terms of the proposed additional warning and, if the judge were minded not to comply with the request, the reasons for not so doing would no doubt be articulated and debated with counsel.* Where the request is not made, none of that occurs, as it should, in the context of the trial between those involved in conducting the trial. As with a failure to comply with r 4 of the *Criminal Appeal Rules* (NSW), it will be difficult to establish a miscarriage of justice unless both the requirements of fairness to the accused and the absence of any reasons not to comply with the obligation were manifest.[168]

- A judge need not comply with such a request if 'there are good reasons for not doing so': sub-s (3). This reflects the discretionary nature of the trial judge's assessment of whether to give a s 165 warning, and what its content should be. The trial judge is required to make a discretionary judgment in all the circumstances of the case whether to give a warning and what the content of the warning should be. Subsection (3) applies to each matter set out in sub-s (2) (why the evidence is unreliable, the terms of the warning, whether caution is necessary in accepting the evidence, and or giving it weight).

  > [W]here the evidence favours the accused, there would be good reason for the trial judge to temper the warning and information given to the jury in respect of that evidence. Clearly there would be no basis for the trial judge to warn the jury that mistaken identification has led to erroneous convictions. Generally speaking it would not be necessary for the trial judge to caution the jury in terms of s 165(2)(c) although we would not hold that such a caution could never be given. ...[169]

- No special form of warning need be used: sub-s (4).
  - 'To borrow an analogy from Lord Devlin's report on identification evidence, the warning is like a road sign that reads, "caution, slippery road, slow down". ... [A]part from requiring the jury to be made aware of the need for caution in assessing the evidence, s 165(2)(c)

166 *Danny* [2020] VSCA 8. See also *Greenhalgh* [2017] NSWCCA 94, [21] where Basten JA stated that 'in cases where no direction was sought [at trial], it will usually be a pre-condition to a grant of leave under r 4 that the omitted direction should be expressly formulated'.

167 *Evans* [2007] HCA 59, [232] (Heydon J).

168 *McGavin* [2014] NSWCCA 171, [26].

169 *Rose* [2002] NSWCCA 455; 55 NSWLR 701, [297] (Wood CJ at CL and Howie J), quoted approvingly by Ierace J (Simpson AJA, Wilson J agreeing) in *Mulholland* [2019] NSWCCA 257.

does not require that the judge tell them how to apply the warning. It seems to me that a warning to be given under the section is like a road sign that reads, "Caution, slippery road, be careful". The warning does not tell the driver what specific action to take to meet the danger warned against.'[170]

- For a case that pre-dates the Act, but shows the power of simple language, see *Chidiac*[171] where the trial judge referred to the witnesses in his caution to the jury as 'two self-confessed liars ... down and out villains ... self-confessed perjurers and liars ... I have never heard two witnesses so readily admit that they have lied on oath ... [L]ook very carefully at what they said before you would hang a dog on their evidence'.

- Post-corroboration warnings flowing from the cases of *Bromley* and *Longman* are expressly retained: sub-s (5).

Victoria

Section 165 of the *Evidence Act 2008* (Vic) applies only to civil proceedings. The passing of *JDA 2015* (Vic), ss 12, 14, 31, 32 and 34, is the product of a major review in Victoria of judicial instruction and directions to the jury.[172] As we have seen in earlier chapters, this review has replaced numerous common law directions to the jury with modified codified direction requirements. In Victoria under the *JDA 2015*, for criminal trials where a party wishes a trial judge to warn the jury with respect to 'evidence of a kind that may be unreliable':[173]

- the party must request under s 12 a warning (s 32(1) ('counsel may request')):
  - specifying the significant matters that may make the evidence unreliable (or, if the request concerns evidence given by a child, the significant matters, other than solely the age of the child, that may make the evidence of the child unreliable);
- that, subject to the court determining that there are good reasons not to direct the jury, the judge must:
  - warn the jury that the evidence may be unreliable; and
  - inform the jury of:
    - the significant matters that the trial judge considers may cause the evidence to be unreliable; or
    - if the direction concerns evidence given by a child, the significant matters, other than solely the age of the child, that the trial judge considers may make the evidence of the child unreliable); and
  - warn the jury of the need for caution in determining whether to accept the evidence and the weight to be given to it.

---

170 *Stewart* [2001] NSWCCA 260; 52 NSWLR 301, [165]-[166] (Howie J).

171 [1991] HCA 4; 171 CLR 432, 438. Despite this direct and robust warning, it may have been inadequate. In *Chidiac – Application pursuant to s 78 Crimes (Appeal and Review) Act 2001 (NSW)* [2015] NSWSC 157, Beech-Jones J referred Mr Chidiac's case for review of his conviction to the Court of Criminal Appeal.

172 And subject to the role of s 16 of the *JDA 2015* (Vic). This section requires the trial judge to give a direction 'if the trial judge considers that there are substantial and compelling reasons for doing so'.

173 Defined by *JDA 2015* (Vic), s 31, in terms replicating *UEA*, s 165(1)(a), (c)-(f).

In the Victorian Court of Appeal case of *Wade*[174] the s 32 request was based on 'the passage of time, the complainant's age when the events were said to have occurred, the complainant's intervening decade-long intermittent psychotic illness and the complainant's own evidence of his tortuous reconstructive thought processes, the recollections of the complainant – even if honest – may be unreliable'. The court in *Wade*[175] noted that a 'concatenation of circumstances to which we have adverted had a real potential to adversely affect the reliability of the complainant's memory' and adds to a case for giving a warning when one is requested. The court added (at [38]) that '[t]he prospect of confabulation is well understood by those who regularly practise criminal law, but in our view, may not have been fully appreciated by this jury, in the absence of a carefully tailored s 32 direction along the lines of the model direction at 4.8.7 of the Criminal Charge Book'.

Those criminally concerned/accomplice evidence: UEA, s 165(1)(d) [176]

One of the most common categories of s 165 evidence is 'evidence given in a criminal proceeding by a witness, being a witness who might reasonably be supposed to have been criminally concerned in the events giving rise to the proceeding'. This subsection recognises that 'evidence of accomplices is evidence apt to be unreliable by reason of a motive to shift blame to the co-offender'.[177] It can encompass a witness whose advantage has included a sentence discount in return for assisting police and/or prosecutors. The case of *Grey* below emphasises the importance of the judge's position of authority with respect to judicial warnings.

Grey

[2001] HCA 65; 184 ALR 593; 75 ALJR 1708 (citations omitted)

Grey was charged with offences linked to the rebirthing of stolen cars. The trial had proceeded without the prosecution disclosing that a key prosecution witness, Reynolds, had received a letter of comfort from police. This letter outlined Reynolds's assistance in police investigations. It revealed a close relationship between Reynolds and a detective. The defence ignorance of the letter (and of this relationship) removed a potentially fertile line of cross-examination regarding Reynolds's incentive to blame Grey and distance himself from criminal responsibility. Grey's appeal to the High Court was upheld by Gleeson CJ, Gummow, Callinan and Kirby JJ. Kirby J made the following comments.

> **Kirby J**:
>
> *Deprivation of a foundation for a judicial warning*
>
> 73. There is a further consideration that reinforces this conclusion. In Pt 4.5 of the *Evidence Act*, dealing with 'Warnings', s 165(2) provides expressly for a judicial duty

---

174 [2019] VSCA 168.

175 Ibid [38], citing *Hudson* [2017] VSCA 122. See also *Danny* [2020] VSCA 8 which distinguished *Wade* where the request was based on the fact that the complainant had spoken with her parents and stepsister before participating in a recorded interview, giving rise to the risk of contamination of her evidence. The court held this was quintessentially for the jury and a direction would have constituted an intrusion by the judge into the jury's role.

176 On navigating complexities in applying the 'criminally concerned' limb, see *Kaddour* [2019] NSWCCA 90. See also *JDA 2015* (Vic), ss 31(c), 32.

177 *Sio* [2016] HCA 32; 259 CLR 47, [65] (French CJ, Bell, Gageler, Keane and Gordon JJ.

to warn a jury, where the judge is so requested by a party, that certain evidence may be unreliable; to inform the jury of the matters that may cause such evidence to be unreliable; and to warn the jury of the need for caution in determining whether to accept the evidence and the weight to be given to it.

74. In the appellant's trial, an application was made for a warning along these lines in relation to the evidence of Mr Reynolds. The trial judge declined to give such a warning. However, as recorded by the trial judge, no application was made, in support of the request for such a warning, upon the basis of the examples set out in s 165(1). Those examples may enliven such warnings. One such example is that contained in par (d) of s 165(1) which reads:

> *(d) evidence given in a criminal proceeding by a witness, being a witness who might reasonably be supposed to have been criminally concerned in the events giving rise to the proceeding.*

75. At the appellant's trial, instead of relying on this consideration, the application for a warning was based on the footing that the evidence of Mr Reynolds was unreliable because 'he has a bad memory and … has tried to expunge this period of his life from his mind'. Reference was also made to the fact that the events went back to a time six years before the trial. On these propounded bases, the trial judge was unconvinced that any special warning from him was required. By s 165(3), the judge need not comply with the duty to give a warning 'if there are good reasons for not doing so'. Having regard to the bases argued before the trial judge, there would indeed have been no foundation for disturbing the ruling that his Honour made.

76. If, however, the appellant had known of the bargain that had been struck between the police and Mr Reynolds, evidenced in Ex G, significantly different considerations would have arisen for the exercise of the judicial duty to give a warning as s 165 of the *Evidence Act* contemplates. The Act specifically includes in the examples of instances of 'unreliable evidence' the 'evidence given in a criminal proceeding by a witness who is a prison informer'. In this respect, s 165 reflects the common law as stated by this Court in *Pollitt v R*. But some of the considerations relevant to the unreliability of prison informants (particularly that they may be of bad character and may be motivated to fabricate evidence by a perception of a likely benefit for themselves) could, in certain cases, apply to a police informer. At least, it could do so, where that informer stands to gain a personal benefit from the provision of such information to the police and to a court or may be viewed as having been an accomplice.

77. If the appellant's advisers had enjoyed access to Ex G, or its contents, they would have had a much stronger basis for persuading the trial judge to give the jury a warning. *Such a warning would have contributed the weight of judicial authority* to assist the appellant's arguments, admonishing the jury to be extremely cautious about the evidence of Mr Reynolds. This additional element in the judicial instructions could have assisted the appellant's case. That is enough. Certainly, it is impossible to say that it would not have been of assistance. As it was, Mr Reynolds appeared before the jury as a person who had owned up to his own wrongdoings, suffered his punishment, had turned over a new leaf and was anxious to forget the errors of his past which were, in any case, on his testimony, wholly unconnected with the appellant's crimes. The letter, Ex G, or its substance might, if it had been provided to the defence, not only have placed a different complexion on Mr Reynolds' evidence for the consideration of the jury. It could also have encouraged the judge, when asked, to give a s 165 direction. (emphasis added)

The disclosure obligations on the prosecutor extend to revealing to the defence the witness's status and circumstances relevant to their being called as a witness, including any discount in sentencing, and any scope for that discount to be reviewed should the witness fail to comply with undertakings given with respect to their evidence. As Buddin J (with Smart J agreeing) observed in *Sullivan*:[178]

178 [2003] NSWCCA 100.

> 95. … [I]n further discharge of its obligations, [the prosecution] ought to lead in evidence all material of that kind which is relevant in order that the jury is fully informed of those matters which would enable it to make a proper assessment of the witness' credibility. I respectfully agree with what was said by this Court in *Chen*[179] that the evidence should be led by the Crown without having to be "dragged out in cross-examination". I would only add this. Material of the kind to which I have made reference is far too significant for it to emerge, as it did in this case, for the first time only in re-examination. All that the jury was told in evidence in chief in the present case was that the witness was serving a term of imprisonment by reason of his having pleaded guilty to various offences about which he then proceeded to give evidence.
>
> 96. … The fact that a person has received a benefit in the form of a discount on sentence is, as I have observed, clearly capable of bearing on that person's credibility because it provides them with an incentive or motive to give false evidence. In the same way the extent of that discount is similarly relevant and important evidence because it is capable of affecting the degree to which the witness has an incentive or motive to give false evidence. The Crown should also in my view have led evidence of the undertaking given by the witness as well as evidence, in clear and explicit terms, as to the consequences of a failure on the part of the witness, to fulfil that undertaking. … As I have already said, this evidence should have been led by the Crown.
>
> 97. Had the evidence to which I have referred been led then a warning in appropriate terms, pursuant to s 165 of the *Evidence Act*, could have been fashioned by the trial judge to accord with that evidence. It was not.

The lessons offered to prosecutors by *Grey* appear to have gone unheeded in *Council of the Law Society of New South Wales v DWO*[180] where the prosecution failed to disclose the status of a prosecution witness, A107 (a person 'reasonably suspected of being criminally involved'), who was also a registered police informer. It had been conceded that the police did not disclose to the Office of the DPP or to the defence that an affidavit of assistance had been provided to the Local Court in relation to the sentencing of A107. This affidavit referred to A107's assistance in relation to the charge of murder faced by JB. Further, A107's record of interview had been 'edited' to remove reference to A107's informer status. See also *Bradley v Chilby*,[181] in which the interaction of prosecutors' disclosure duties and the limits of courts' powers fits with the remedy of staying proceedings until the prosecutor meets its disclosure obligations.

McGavin's case is a useful illustration of the application of s 165 to evidence from a 'witness who might reasonably be supposed to have been criminally concerned in the events giving rise to the proceeding': s 165(1)(d). Steven Welland, if he had not pleaded guilty and been sentenced before testifying, may have been a co-accused jointly charged in the same trial as his father, the appellant (McGavin), Shane Welland (his brother) and Hanson (his cousin). Instead, he was a prosecution witness at their trial.

McGavin

[2014] NSWCCA 171

Anthony McGavin, aged 56, appealed his convictions on five counts of break, enter and steal, in company. The offences were committed over a one-month

---

179 [2002] NSWCCA 174.

180 [2020] NSWCATOD 123.

181 [2020] NSWSC 145. The appeals arising from the Victoria Police reliance on Nicola Gobbo also raise disclosure issues. See Chapters 1 and 15.

period in early 2011. Each involved breaking into a club or hotel south of Sydney early in the morning and stealing cigarettes and money. For four of the five crimes McGavin was said to be with his two sons, Shane and Steven Welland, and his nephew, Trevor Hanson. Steven testified implicating the others. Telephone records linked the group to each other and to the crimes in various respects. Basten JA noted that the judge had summed up to the jury, referring to counsel's arguments regarding Steven Welland's evidence and the suggestion by defence counsel that the jury would have 'some real doubts about the accuracy and reliability of his evidence'. He quoted the trial judge's direction to the jury at [22]:

> You also heard evidence that in respect of that interview in May 2012 he indicated that he would be prepared to give evidence in respect of what he had told the police in that interview. You have also been told that he ultimately pleaded guilty to a whole range of matters and that he has been dealt with in this Court in relation to those matters. In the course of being sentenced an assessment was made of the assistance that he provided to the authorities and he was given a 25 percent discount on his sentence for that assistance.
>
> A direction that the Courts must give to jurors in respect of witnesses who have received discounts for sentences is as follows and it is in effect a warning to you that you need to exercise considerable caution when making an assessment of the evidence of that witness. The need arises for these directions because the Courts over the years have experienced in respect of the reliability of evidence given by persons who had been involved in crimes, have been concerned in those crimes and that experience might not be readily known to members of the public. That experience has shown that on some occasions that evidence can be unreliable. Now I do not intend to suggest, however, that such evidence is always unreliable. My purpose in giving you these directions is only to warn you that the evidence of such a witness may be unreliable and for that reason alone you must approach that evidence with considerable caution in the way in which I will outline to you shortly.
>
> There are no doubt a number of reasons why the evidence of such a person may be unreliable. Possible reasons are that it is only natural you may think that a witness who might have been involved in a particular crime giving rise to these proceedings may want to shift the blame from himself or herself onto others and to justify his conduct. In the process the witness may construct untruthful stories which tend to play down his part in a crime and play up the part of others of the crime even going so far as to blame quite innocent people. Persons reasonably supposed to have been involved in the commission of an offence may make false claims as the involvement of others motives of revenge or a feeling of dislike or hostility. Such a person may be motivated to give false evidence in order to qualify for a reduction in his or her own sentence. There may be reasons why false evidence has been given by such a witness and it is not for the accused to establish the reason or reasons why that witness was lying.

At issue was whether:

- the judge failed to warn the jury adequately of the need for caution in determining whether to accept Steven Welland's evidence and the weight to be given to it, relying on s 165(1)(d), (2)(a) and (c);
- the content of the warning should have included the actual reduction in gaol time to be served by Steven as a result of his plea and assistance to the prosecution (and not merely the percentage discount (25%)); and
- the warning should have included an explanation of the liability to be resentenced if Welland reneged on his undertaking to testify in accordance with his police statement.

Irrespective of the request issue (discussed below) the court rejected the argument that the actual reduction in time to be served was a required element of the warning (though noting some limited support for this proposition from *Sullivan*[182]).

In *McGavin* Basten JA (with Price and Fullerton JJ agreeing) concluded that '[i]t may well be a significant error for the jury not to be warned of the possibility of resentencing for failure to comply with an undertaking, in circumstances *where such a direction is sought, the matter having been raised in evidence with the witness*: but that is not this case'.[183] In addition to a request for a warning (not present in this case), a significant consideration in this case, pointed out by Basten JA, was the absence of evidence on the possibility of Welland being resentenced should his evidence fall short of the arrangement made with authorities.

> **Basten JA:** 13. There can be little doubt that, if the jury believed Mr Steven Welland's evidence, conviction of the applicant on all counts was almost inevitable. The attack on Mr Welland's credibility was twofold: first, there were inconsistencies between his evidence and previous exculpatory statements he had made to the police. He had clearly told lies to the police; the question for the jury was whether he had lied on earlier occasions or was lying in the witness box. The second challenge was based upon the fact that he himself had been charged and pleaded guilty to four of the five offences. The jury were invited to disbelieve his evidence on the basis that he had agreed to implicate his father in return for a significant discount on the sentence he was required to serve. The grounds of appeal were squarely directed at the alleged failure by the trial judge adequately to direct the jury with respect to the incentives for Steven Welland to give false evidence against his father.
>
> 14. … [I]t is convenient to note how the evidence of Mr Welland was dealt with in the course of the trial. His evidence was referred to by the prosecutor in relation to each offence when he opened the case to the jury. Counsel for the applicant also addressed the jury by way of an opening statement. He noted that the prosecutor had made much of the anticipated evidence of Mr Steven Welland and said that '[o]ne of the most significant issues in this case is going to be your assessment as to the honesty and the reliability of Mr Steven Welland' … . He then said that Mr Welland had in fact been sentenced for his involvement in a number of the offences and continued …:
>
>> In that regard then you might consider, well what was the deal that Mr Steven Welland struck in relation to his sentence? There might be some evidence I [anticipate] in relation to that, I'll be clear, I anticipate the evidence to be that he was afforded about a 25% reduction in his sentence for agreeing to give evidence against his father. He, you might consider the evidence will establish, received a very considerable benefit for merely saying 'Yeah, Dad was involved as well, I'll give evidence against him'.
>>
>> He told the jury that they would hear of the "very poor state of the relationship" between the applicant and Mr Welland and suggested they would ask whether he, Mr Welland, had an axe to grind with the applicant. …
>
> 27. Beyond those general considerations, whether a further warning was required in the present case depends on the alleged deficiencies in the content of the warning actually given. The relevant legal obligation is founded upon the duty of the judge to ensure that the accused gets a fair trial, of which s 165 is a part but not a comprehensive statement: sub-s (5). It is convenient to start with the contention that the statement that a 25% discount had been allowed was not of itself sufficient to demonstrate the benefit obtained by the witness. Before turning to the authorities, it may be noted that the logic of that contention is by no means self-evident. The underlying assumption appears to be that, if the sentence were 20 years, the actual discount (namely five years) is so significant that it needs to be spelled out. Whether the same reasoning applies to a two year sentence is less clear. …

182 [2003] NSWCCA 100.
183 [2014] NSWCCA 171, [47] (emphasis added).

Warning as to possibility of resentencing

35. The statutory basis for resentencing an offender whose sentence was reduced because he or she undertook to assist law enforcement authorities, but wholly or partly failed to fulfil the undertaking, is to be found in s 5DA of the *Criminal Appeal Act*. One of the early cases discussing the obligation to include such information in a warning under s 165 was a judgment of the Full Court of the Federal Court, *Conway* [2000] FCA 461; 98 FCR 204 (Miles, von Doussa and Weinberg JJ). After noting that the jury had been informed of the dangers of acting on the "uncorroborated evidence" of two accomplices (albeit without reference to s 165 of the *Evidence Act*), the Court continued …:

> "In addition to what his Honour told the jury in the passages set out above, he had, earlier in the trial, used the expression 'Sword of Damocles' when referring to the threat of a Crown appeal against the sentences imposed upon [the accomplices] if they did not adhere to their statements implicating [the accused]. The concept of the 'Sword of Damocles' was canvassed thoroughly in cross-examination of the accomplices. It was dealt with also in counsel's addresses. The jury could hardly have failed to understand the danger that an accomplice might adhere to a story implicating others because of the threat of a Crown appeal against sentence."

36. The next important case was *R v Stewart* [2001] NSWCCA 260; 52 NSWLR 301, where this Court dealt with a similar issue, although not speaking with one voice. In *Stewart* a warning had been given under s 165 which was described by Spigelman CJ as "a comprehensive warning which, save in one specific respect, was all that was required": at [23]. The matter omitted was any reference to s 5DA, being the mechanism by which the witness could lose the benefit obtained by the assistance to law enforcement authorities: at [24]. Spigelman CJ would have upheld the appeal, despite the absence of complaint at trial that the warning given was defective: at [28]. The majority, RS Hulme and Howie JJ, refused leave to raise the issue. …

38. Howie J addressed in some detail the requirements of the common law with respect to accomplice evidence, the terms of s 165 and the related but separate issue of obtaining a contingent benefit on sentence for undertaking to give assistance in a forthcoming prosecution. Noting the importance of determining the adequacy of directions and warnings in the context of a specific case, as explained in *Domican* [1992] HCA 13; 173 CLR 555 at 561 – see *Stewart* at [116] – Howie J considered the course of the trial and reached the following conclusions in terms of principle:

> "[158] Provided that the consequences for the witness in failing to give evidence in accordance with his undertaking has been sufficiently placed before the jury so that they would understand the significance of the fact that a witness is still at risk of further punishment when giving evidence in the trial, I do not believe that the trial judge is always required to raise this matter with the jury and inform them of its relevance in order to ensure that a miscarriage of justice did not arise. Whether or not the failure to refer to the matter in the summing up gives rise to the possibility of a miscarriage of justice will depend upon the circumstances of the particular trial. In this case the summing up followed immediately after defence counsel's address and there was a single issue before the jury: Braddick's reliability when implicating the appellant in the offence.
>
> [159] I acknowledge that it is important that the jury understands that a witness, who has been given a sentence discount or some other benefit for giving evidence implicating an accused, has at the time of giving evidence before the jury an obligation to give such evidence on pain of further punishment. The jury should not be left to assume that the witness has no reason to give false evidence implicating the accused at the time of the trial. They should be made aware that the fact that the witness has been sentenced for his part in the offence did not necessarily diminish the likelihood that his evidence might be unreliable: *Conway* at [207]."

Basten JA concluded:

> 42. … If the judge had told the jury that Mr Welland had a strong incentive not to depart from the account he had given to police, for he might otherwise be resentenced and lose some or all of his discount, thus increasing the time he would serve in gaol, should he also have said that how he would have responded to such a suggestion could not be known because he was never asked the question? Counsel for the accused could not have invited the jury to assume that he would have recanted in the face of cross-examination which did not take place; nor that, if he dismissed the suggestion as unfounded, the jury would necessarily find his response implausible. Of course, counsel did not ask the jury to take that step, because he lacked the evidential basis to make the submission. At the very least, there would have been an anxious discussion between counsel and the judge as to what direction could properly have been given. The absence of a testimonial basis for the direction would have provided a good reason, within the terms of s 165(3), for the judge to decline to give a direction of the kind now mooted.
>
> 43. In these circumstances, it should not be concluded that there was a breach of s 165: further, if there were a breach, it was not one which gave rise to a miscarriage based on the unfairness of the trial. Accordingly, the third limb in the attack on the conviction must be rejected.

Conclusion

Over the past century, case law has resisted excluding evidence outside traditional exclusionary categories. It has instead relied heavily on judicial direction and warnings to ensure trials are fair. As the justifiably maligned corroboration warnings show, paradoxically these mechanisms for fairness often became instruments of unfairness for sexual assault complainants. Even after corroboration warnings were replaced, the legislature has had to work hard to ensure new warnings were not merely veiled attempts to reintroduce the flaws of the old warnings. Signs suggest the tide has turned in this respect with appellate courts (such as *Ewen*) showing that they are alert to these concerns. Nevertheless, the growth in reliance on judicial instruction, warning and direction to juries remains a potentially fruitful location for appeal points. Victoria's quest to implement statutory reform of judicial directions has much merit. Its 2015 Act seeks to simplify and clarify the law on directions in criminal trials and to increase responsibility on parties to guide trial judges. Time will tell if this initiative marks a significant break from the problems besetting judicial warnings.

Chapter 15

Epilogue

> [H]uman nature is represented in the witnesses, the counsel, and the jurors. All three, in their weaknesses, have been kept in mind by the law of evidence. The multifold untrustworthinesses of witnesses; the constant partisan zeal, the lurking chicanery, the needless unpreparedness of counsel; the crude reasoning, the strong irrational emotions, the testimonial inexperience of jurors – all these elements have been considered.[1]

Wigmore's portrayal of mistrust driving the rules of evidence and procedure, perhaps fitting in his day, sits uncomfortably with the contemporary Australian trial. That said, his concern for the dangers in human nature explains the driving forces shaping the law of evidence and, if one softens his strident language, is revealing of where weaknesses in the law and practice of the trial may lie.

The goal of the Australian trial can be conceived of in many ways. Because the perfect investigation is impossible,[2] the trial serves to monitor the investigatory phase of the criminal justice process, at least in the context of ensuring its own processes are protected, as best it can. The trial is also the vehicle of proof for the party bearing the burden of persuasion, and it is the setting for the prosecution to present its case in the full gaze of the public, amenable to testing and to evaluation by an impartial and properly informed tribunal of fact. Notably, the trial is not as singularly truth-seeking as its inquisitorial cousins.[3] The adversarial and the inquisitorial traditions are philosophically driven by different norms, albeit to achieve the same end.

As we know, a prosecution case does not arrive in court fully formed. It is founded on pleadings that are in turn based on the fruits of investigation. The pleadings give the trial its forensic boundaries; they set its terms of reference. Prosecutorial success, in the form of a verdict that is the product of establishing guilt beyond reasonable doubt, requires the case to withstand the prosecution being put to proof by the defence. Appellate courts (as this book shows) set the jurisprudential guideposts for those administering justice in the future. Procedural success is ultimately the 'right' verdict achieved in a fair and effective manner. Its goals are aspirational because, as yet, law reformers have not created a 'retrospectoscope' to ensure perfect judgment by all and on all occasions.

---

1 JH Wigmore, *Evidence in Trials at Common Law*, rev ed by Peter Tillers (Little, Brown, 1983) Vol 1, 632-3, quoted by L Dufraimont in 'Evidence Law and the Jury: A Reassessment' (2008) 53 *McGill Law Journal* 200, 241.

2 *Dietrich* [1992] HCA 57; 177 CLR 292, [25].

3 See, for the civilian tradition perspective of the common law trial, Dufraimont, above n 1.

This chapter acknowledges that an intrinsic element of the trial – its reliance on human judgment – means that inevitably errors infiltrate processes. Below, we consider the lessons beyond the appeal courts' guideposts, focusing on how the innocent accused, despite exhausting the appeal processes, remains wrongly convicted. Across Australia, a defendant's appeal against conviction relies on three broad grounds:

- that the verdict is unreasonable or cannot be supported by the evidence (that is, the evidence fails to support the verdict);[4]
- an error of law (for example, on the admissibility of evidence, on judicial directions to the jury or on a procedural matter); or
- on any ground there has been a miscarriage of justice.

The 'proviso' overrides these grounds to the extent that it permits the court to dismiss an appeal, even where a ground of appeal is established, if it is satisfied that there has been no *substantial* miscarriage of justice.[5] The proviso acknowledges that errors occur in trials, but not all errors defeat the essential goals of criminal trial adjudication, and so, despite a wrong decision, given the strength of the evidence in the case if the error had not occurred the jury would still have convicted – or put another way, no reasonable doubt remains. As we see below, an appeal court will make its own evaluation of whether an accused would inevitably have been convicted without the inadmissible evidence or other form of error.

Of the Trial Misfiring

> When a person has by a final decision been convicted of a criminal offence and when subsequently his conviction has been reversed or he has been pardoned on the ground that a new or newly discovered fact shows conclusively that there has been a miscarriage of justice, the person who has suffered punishment as a result of such conviction shall be compensated according to law, unless it is proved that the non-disclosure of the unknown fact in time is wholly or partly attributable to him.
>
> *International Covenant on Civil and Political Rights*, Article 14(6)

As Gans notes, this is a provision that 'bristles with caveats',[6] demanding little from the state beyond paying up. Even then, in Australia compensation tends to be delivered in an *ex gratia* formulation. A trial must safeguard rights and it must create the optimal environment for the decisions, including the ultimate decision, the verdict, to be accurate. Accusatorial justice is built on ensuring fairness to the accused. Alexander Volokh in his essay, 'n Guilty Men', observed:[7]

---

4 See, eg, *Pell* [2020] HCA 12; 376 ALR 478; *Baden-Clay* [2016] HCA 35; 258 CLR 308.

5 See generally A Ligertwood and G Edmond, *Australian Evidence: A Principled Approach to the Common Law and the Uniform Acts* (LexisNexis, 5th ed, 2010), 72-7 and see *Criminal Appeal Act 1912* (NSW), s 6; *Supreme Court Act 1933* (ACT), s 37O; *Criminal Code* (NT), s 411; *Criminal Code* (Qld), s 668E; *Criminal Law Consolidation Act 1935* (SA) s 353; *Criminal Code* (Tas), s 404(1); *Criminal Procedure Act 2009* (Vic) s 276; *Criminal Code* (WA), s 689.

6 J Gans, 'Ozymandias on Trial: Wrongs and Rights in DNA Cases' in P Roberts and J Hunter (eds), *Criminal Evidence and Human Rights: Reimagining Common Law and Procedural Traditions* (Hart Publishing, 2013), ch 8, 199.

7 A Volokh, 'n Guilty Men' (1997) 146 *University of Pennsylvania Law Review* 173.

> 'Better that ten guilty persons escape than that one innocent suffer,'[8] says English jurist William Blackstone. The ratio 10:1 has become known as the 'Blackstone ratio.'[9] Lawyers 'are indoctrinated' with it 'early in law school.'[10] 'Schoolboys are taught' it.[11]...
>
> The maxim has been 'so long in use as to be deemed a mere sound, signifying nothing.'[12] Thus, in the 1940s, two Alabama defendants (unsuccessfully) tried to have their juries given simultaneous instructions that n = *infinity* and n = *"many,"* that is, "that no innocent person should be convicted and that it is better that many guilty go unpunished than one innocent person be convicted."[13] Nonetheless, all innocent readers who have never been convicted may now take a moment to thank Blackstone's maxim for having inspired Western criminal law. All guilty readers who have been acquitted may do so too.
>
> The story is told of a Chinese law professor, who was listening to a British lawyer explain that Britons were so enlightened, they believed it was better that ninety-nine guilty men go free than that one innocent man be executed. The Chinese professor thought for a second and asked, 'Better for whom?'[14]

But the trial serves more than a single master, not just the accused. There are others who have a stake in a fair process. The community and victims of crime need a justice system that serves their needs. How are these met? Working out the value of *n* engages important philosophical dimensions. But more critically in the context of the material in this book, determining how *n* is calculated sets a procedural challenge in which the law of evidence and procedure play a vital role.

Justice Served Cold

The *Innocence Project*, first started in the United States, and is now a global movement. Its statistics on its website[15] graphically reveal the risks and dangers within, and challenges for, the law of evidence with respect to:

- eyewitness misidentification (69% of exonerations);
- unvalidated or improper forensic evidence (43% of exonerations);[16]
- false confessions (29% of exonerations); and
- informants (17% of exonerations).

---

8 [William Blackstone, *Commentaries on the Laws of England*, Vol 4, 358.]

9 [WS Laufer, 'The Rhetoric of Innocence', 70 *Washington Law Review* 329, 421 n 17 (1995).]

10 [GT Aynesworth, 'An illogical truism', *Austin Am-Statesman*, 18 April 1996, A14. Specifically, it is 'drilled into [first year law students'] head[s] over and over again', H Green, Sr, 'Shifting Scenes', *Chi Independent Bull*, 2 January 1997, 4. 'I think it was attributed to a Supreme Court judge.']

11 [DD Ellis, 'A Comment on the Testimonial Privilege of the Fifth Amendment' 55 *Iowa Law Review* 829, 845, n 87 (1970).]

12 [*Silver v State* 17 Ohio 365, 369, 1848 WL 117, 3 (1848).]

13 [*Robinson v State* 243 Ala 684, 11 So 2d 732 (1943); *Daniels v State* 243 Ala 675, 11 So 2d 756 (1943).]

14 [D Lawson, 'Notebook: The voters want cash, Mr Clarke', *Daily Telegraph*, 8 April 1995, 17.]

15 See <https://innocenceproject.org/dna-exonerations-in-the-united-states/>. The Innocence Project was founded in 1992 by Barry C Scheck and Peter J Neufeld at the Benjamin N Cardozo School of Law at Yeshiva University.

16 See D Hamer and G Edmond, 'Forensic Science Evidence, Wrongful Convictions and Adversarial Process' (2019) 38 *University of Queensland Law Journal* 186 for an argument that adversarial process and current assumptions fail to offer adequate protection where flawed scientific evidence is before the court; G Edmond, 'What Lawyers Should Know About the Forensic "Sciences"' (2015) 36 *Adelaide Law Review* 33 and a response in A Ligertwood, 'What Lawyers Should and Can do now that They Know About the Forensic "Sciences"' (2015) 36 *Adelaide Law Review* 153.

These categories dominate the causes of miscarriages of justice. As at the end of 2020, 375 people have been exonerated through the US Innocence Project, with an average of 14 years of imprisonment. Forty four defendants pleaded guilty to crimes that they did not commit.

This is not just a problem for the United States. Catering for England, Wales and Northern Ireland, the Criminal Cases Review Commission (CCRC) is a state-funded investigative body established under statute to investigate alleged miscarriages of justice. It has been functioning since 1997 and, up to November 2020, it had referred 751 cases to the Court of Appeal giving rise to 456 successful appeals. The impetus for establishing the CCRC was a series of trials (linked by their description as being 'IRA terrorism trials') that were found to have led to miscarriages of justice: the *Guilford Four* (1974); The *Birmingham Six* (1975); the *Maguire Seven* (1976) and *Judith Ward* (1974). It was established on the recommendation of the Royal Commission on Criminal Justice (the Runciman Commission) in 1991 by the Home Secretary to examine and recommend law reform to the English system of criminal justice. It continued the work of an earlier inquiry by Sir John May into another miscarriage of justice for the group known as the *Maguire Seven*. All the trials were linked by systemic flaws in the justice processes that virtually repeat the US experience: 'These cases featured a mixture of false confessions, police misconduct, non-disclosure and issues about the reliability of expert forensic testimony'.[17] This excellent institution has been exported to Scotland and, in 2020, also to New Zealand.

Since the Commission commenced, it has carried a massive case load with tens of thousands of applications and over 26,000 completed cases.[18] It has the power to refer a case back to an appeal court if it considers that there is a real possibility of the court quashing the conviction or reducing the sentence. Before the CCRC was established those who had exhausted their appeal rights could only make a claim for review to the Home Secretary (or the Secretary of State for Northern Ireland). According to the CCRC website, under this arrangement only 4-5 cases were referred annually from approximately 700 applications. This process, which remains the norm in Australia, included no thorough review and post-conviction investigation process.[19]

Australia has no shortages of its own home-grown miscarriages of justice. Sangha, Roach and Moles, in *Forensic Investigations and Miscarriages of Justice: The Rhetoric Meets the Reality*,[20] detail others: Rupert Maxwell Stuart, John Button, Edward Splatt, the Mickelberg brothers, Tim Anderson, Andrew Mallard. These reveal police and prosecutorial misconduct, false confessions and vulnerable accused. Henry Keogh's wrongful conviction[21] for the murder of his fiancé arose from flawed pathology evidence. The pathologist, Colin Manock, had given this faulty evidence at Keogh's trial and he had also testified at the trial of Fritz Van Beelen many years earlier. In this earlier trial, Dr Manock's

17 See <http://www.ccrc.gov.uk/about-us/our-history/>. See also the Scottish Criminal Cases Review Commission. For an online searchable registry including interactive graphs and interdisciplinary research on identifying causes, consequences of miscarriages of justice in the UK over the past 50 years, see <https://evidencebasedjustice.exeter.ac.uk/>.

18 As of November 2020, the CCRC had referred 753 cases to the Court of Appeal, and 457 appeals have been allowed.

19 See also D Hamer, 'Wrongful Convictions, Appeals, and the Finality Principle: The Need for a Criminal Cases Review Commission' (2014) 37 *UNSW Journal* 270.

20 B Sangha, K Roach and R Moles, *Forensic Investigations and Miscarriages of Justice: The Rhetoric Meets the Reality* (Irwin Law, 2010).

21 *Keogh (No 2)* [2014] SASCFC 136.

evidence was described in Van Beelen's second High Court appeal as 'unequivocally highly erroneous', but whilst the High Court accepted Manock's evidence was incorrect, it maintained Van Beelen's conviction, holding that the prosecution case remained sufficiently strong to sustain it.[22] This approach essentially followed that taken by the High Court[23] in Lindy Chamberlain's appeal. Her 1982 conviction for the murder of her baby relied on prosecution evidence that a scientific test had confirmed traces of foetal blood found under the dashboard of the family car. This implicated Chamberlain and exonerated the dingo. This test was subsequently found to be flawed. Although Murphy J (in dissent) described this flawed evidence as 'the hinge of the Crown's theory that the baby was murdered in the family car' (at [26]), the majority held otherwise, navigating around the significant obstacles in the prosecution case to dismiss Chamberlain's appeal. It was only two years later that the baby's matinee jacket was found in circumstances that ultimately exonerated Lindy and placed the blame back on the dingo.[24] In another instance of justice long-delayed, Harold Eastman was found to have been wrongfully convicted of the murder of senior AFP officer Colin Winchester in 1995. A judicial inquiry found:

> 1831. The applicant did not receive a fair trial according to law. He was denied a fair chance of acquittal. As a consequence, a substantial miscarriage of justice has occurred.
>
> 1832. The issue of guilt was determined on the basis of deeply flawed forensic evidence in circumstances where the applicant was denied procedural fairness in respect of a fundamental feature of the trial process concerned with disclosure by the prosecution of all relevant material. In addition, evidence of inadequacies and flaws in the case file and case work of the key forensic scientists were unknown to everyone involved in the investigation and trial.
>
> 1833. A substantial miscarriage of justice occurred in 1995, as a consequence of which the applicant has been in custody for almost 19 years. For numerous reasons, a retrial is not feasible. Notwithstanding that the question of a retrial could arise for consideration of the Full Court, the DPP did not undertake any investigations in that regard and declined to make submissions concerning this issue. In my view, the passing of so many years, coupled with the death of numerous witnesses and publicity prejudicial to the applicant, mean that a further trial would be unfair both to the prosecution and to the applicant. A retrial would not be in the best interests of the community. …
>
> 1835. I am unable to agree with the submission that the case is 'overwhelming'. While a strong circumstantial case remains, based on the admissible and properly tested evidence the case for the prosecution is not overwhelming. There is also material pointing to an alternative hypothesis consistent with innocence, the strength of which is unknown.
>
> 1836. I am fairly certain that the applicant is guilty of the murder of the deceased, but a nagging doubt remains. Regardless of my opinion as to the applicant's guilt, in my view the substantial miscarriage of justice suffered by the applicant should not be allowed to stand uncorrected. To allow such a miscarriage of justice to stand uncorrected

22 *Van Beelen* [2017] HCA 48; 262 CLR 565, [15]. The appeal arose from a conviction (following what was Van Beelen's second trial – the first also ended in a conviction, which was quashed on appeal). Van Beelen's second conviction was unsuccessfully appealed in *Van Beelen (No 3)* (1973) 7 SASR 125. Under *Criminal Law Consolidation Act 1935* (SA), s 353A(1), a second appeal became available, leading to *Van Beelen* (2016) 125 SASR 253, and then the High Court appeal. All were unsuccessful.

23 *Chamberlain (No 2)* (1984) 153 CLR 521.

24 It took until 2012 for a coronial finding to finalise the public record that Azaria died at Uluru on 17 August 1980 as a result of a dingo attack. See Royal Commission of Inquiry into Chamberlain Convictions, Report, Commonwealth Parliamentary Papers (1987).

> would be contrary to the fundamental principles that guide the administration of justice in Australia and would bring the administration of justice into disrepute.[25]

Despite this view, Eastman's appeals against the order for a retrial were unsuccessful.[26] He was retried and in late 2018 was found not guilty in a jury trial in the ACT Supreme Court. The list of miscarriages regularly lengthens yet the standard post-appeal mechanism for correcting unsafe convictions that applies in Australia has immense limitations. Like the predecessor arrangements to the CCRC, Australian miscarriages of justice cases involving McDermott, Chamberlain, Eastman[27] and Jama reveal that the Australian process beyond the appeal courts relies on a petition to the Minister (or Governor) seeking discretionary action.[28] The potential to recognise the shortcomings of Australia's review processes is not recent. It is not even as recent as 1986 when the full vista of Lindy Chamberlain's miscarriage became clear. Arguably, 1951, and the inquiry into the conviction of Frederick McDermott sets a significant marker for reflection that appeal courts do not resolve all mistaken convictions and state-based structures like the CCRC are needed.

McDermott, a mid-20th century instance of justice served cold, was convicted in 1947 for the murder, in 1936, of Lavers. McDermott's death sentence was commuted to life imprisonment. Two appeals to the NSW Court of Criminal Appeal were unsuccessful and the High Court refused leave to appeal.[29] In 1951 a Royal Commission was established to inquire into the conviction and a year later it found that there was a strong probability the conviction was unsafe (due to incorrect evidence). Mr McDermott was released in early 1952 and died 25 years later. In 2004 Lavers's remains were discovered at a location entirely inconsistent with the prosecution case. A coronial inquiry led to a recommendation that McDermott be pardoned. In 2010 this recommendation was pursued by McDermott's second cousin, who wrote to the Attorney General. Later that year the case was referred to the Court of Criminal Appeal to be dealt with as an appeal. This was heard in late 2012 and the court ordered the quashing of McDermott's conviction. It was crystal clear that the trial was utterly flawed. There was no evidence that provided any reliable basis to connect McDermott with the murder – not his confession, not the car he was supposed to be driving, not the identification evidence. Lavers was vulnerable to police misconduct – an

---

25 *Eastman v DPP (No 2)* [2014] ACTSCFC 2, [11] (Rares and Wigney JJ, Cowdroy AJ), quoting from Martin AJ, *Inquiry into the Conviction of David Harold Eastman for the Murder of Colin Stanley Winchester* (Report of the Board of Inquiry, 29 May 2014).

26 These were in the form of seeking a permanent stay of proceedings: *Eastman v DPP (No 13)* [2016] ACTCA 65 and *Eastman v DPP* [2017] HCASL 70 (holding the 'application for special leave to appeal does not raise a question of general importance').

27 A judicial inquiry recommended that Eastman's 1995 conviction for the murder of AFP Assistant Commissioner Colin Winchester be quashed and Eastman be given a pardon.

28 See, eg, *A reference by the Attorney General (NSW) under s 77(1)(b) of the Crimes (Appeal and Review) Act 2001 re conviction of McDermott* [2013] NSWCCA 102; *Reference under s 433A of Criminal Code by Attorney-General (NT) of Convictions of Chamberlain and Chamberlain; Chamberlain* (1988) 93 FLR 239; *Inquiry into the Conviction of Eastman for Murder of Winchester*, above n 25; *Inquiry into the Circumstances that Led to Conviction of Mr Farah Abdulkadir Jama* (6 May 2010, the Hon Frank Vincent QC); Gans, above n 6, ch 8.

29 *McDermott (No 1)* [1947] NSWStRp 16; 47 SR (NSW) 379; *McDermott (No 2)* [1947] NSWStRp 21; 47 SR (NSW) 407; *McDermott* [1948] HCA 23; 76 CLR 501. For two accounts of the McDermott miscarriage of justice, see C Dobraszczyk, 'The conviction of Frederick Lincoln McDermott' (2013) *Bar News* (Journal of the NSW Bar Association) 66; and C Porter, 'The conviction of Frederick Lincoln McDermott' (2013-2014) *Bar News*, Summer 74.

itinerant worker and an alcoholic, described by Porter[30] as 'the ideal suspect to solve an old [ie cold case] murder'. While the police notebook shorthand verbal 'confession' by Lavers would not have been admissible today, this vista tells us that trials deserve to have prominently displayed 'handle with care', 'fragile packaging' labels. The pervasiveness of the global spread of miscarriages of justice shows that the pressure points for error are in system failures identified by the *Innocence Project*, the CCRC and by Australian miscarriages of justice: zealotry of police and prosecutors, misidentification, flawed forensics and confessions. The Australian scandal of the 21st century in this respect must surely be the police reliance on 'Lawyer X', Melbourne lawyer Nicola Gobbo as a registered informer. Obviously, as a practising barrister, her betrayal of those who had retained her, like the police misconduct, was deeply improper. Gobbo's conduct and that of Victoria police officers had been investigated in 2014 by the Independent Broad-based Anti-corruption Commission with Victoria Police resisting disclosure of the ensuing report on the ground of public interest immunity, later joined by Ms Gobbo relying on the equitable obligation of confidence. Resisting disclosure was based on the virtual certainty that revelations would endanger the life of Ms Gobbo. All avenues of appeal finally resolved the matter in favour of disclosure in *AB (a Pseudonym) v CD (a Pseudonym)*,[31] stating that Ms Gobbo's actions of covertly informing on clients and others

> were fundamental and appalling breaches of [Ms Gobbo's] obligations as counsel to her clients and of [Ms Gobbo's] duties to the court. Likewise, Victoria Police were guilty of reprehensible conduct in knowingly encouraging [Ms Gobbo] to do as she did and were involved in sanctioning atrocious breaches of the sworn duty of every police officer to discharge all duties imposed on them faithfully and according to law without favour or affection, malice or ill-will. As a result, the prosecution of each Convicted Person was corrupted in a manner which debased fundamental premises of the criminal justice system.[32]

It remains to be seen how the fallout of the Lawyer X affair plays out. Clearly many convictions, unfairly obtained, have been and will be quashed.[33] There are suggestions this affair will place renewed pressure on traditional obligations, including those relating to disclosure where the prosecution does not make adequate attempts to determine the provenance of information relied upon by investigators. In *Visser* the court indicated (at [85]) that 'in the circumstances of a joint operation of the type here in issue, we consider the better view to be that the information known to Victoria Police concerning the manner in which [certain evidence] ... is to be regarded as having been constructively known by the AFP and, in turn, by the CDPP'.[34] Further, the Royal Commission has recommended a suite of reforms to increase accountability and transparency in Victoria Police's use and management of 'human sources'.[35]

---

30 Porter, ibid, 75. See also Dobraszczyk, ibid.

31 [2018] HCA 58; 93 ALJR 59.

32 *AB (a Pseudonym) v CD (a Pseudonym)* [2018] HCA 58; 93 ALJR 59, 62 [10] (citations omitted).

33 Particularly prominently, *Mokbel v DPP (Cth)* [2020] VSCA 325 where the Commonwealth DPP determined that there would be no retrial. See, however, *Mokbel v DPP (Cth)* [2021] VSCA 94 (Beach and Osborne JJ, with a strong dissent by Maxwell P), formally ordering a retrial.

34 *Visser v DPP (Cth)* [2020] VSCA 327 (McLeish, Emerton and Osborn JJA).

35 Royal Commission into the Management of Police Informants: An inquiry into Victoria Police's use of Nicola Gobbo as a human source, Summary and Recommendations, An inquiry into Victoria Police's use of Nicola Gobbo as a human source, <https://www.rcmpi.vic.gov.au/summary/final-report-summary>.

However, the most compelling lesson to be learnt from this vista is that the human cost (not to mention the financial cost) of cleaning up after unsafe convictions is immense and is borne by just a few. Inevitably, in a century's time, those who reflect on the delivery of criminal justice in the early decades of the 21st century will have a clear view of how it might have been improved. We do not yet have the benefit of hindsight, but hindsight is not the only tool to hand. There are things we know now.

Of Courts and Accusatorial Justice

> Often it is the judges alone who will safeguard those basic rights. Elected officials, journalists and community groups sometimes prove to be no more than fair weather friends to basic legal principles and the rule of law. But it is in defending them that courts like this are put to the test.[36]

The Supreme Court of Canada has observed:

> Experience in Canada and elsewhere teaches that wrongful convictions are often traceable to evidence that is either unreliable or prejudicial. When the two combine, they make for a potent mix – and the risk of a wrongful conviction increases accordingly. Wrongful convictions are a blight on our justice system and we must take reasonable steps to prevent them before they occur.[37]

We know that the people who most commonly enter the criminal justice system accused of crime often fit the category of the kind of special vulnerability that goes with justice misfiring. For these people, disadvantage permeates their lives and creates obstacles for testing the prosecution case optimally. For them support and legal advice is a premium requirement for protecting the rights of suspects and the accused because law is 'a complex and complicated discipline'.[38] We know that confessions can be persuasive but flawed evidence of guilt. We know that the quality of the circumstances in which confessions are obtained is highly indicative of their safety. We know that those who are vulnerable because of their upbringing, their poverty, their cognitive impairment, their mental ill-health, their mistrust or their lack of linguistic skills need to be well supported when being questioned by investigators. Further, cultural distortions[39] can work harshly on our perceptions of people. The overwhelming overrepresentation of ATSI people in the criminal justice system demands that special attention be paid to addressing the pervasive disadvantage suffered by ATSI people during the conduct of investigations and at trial.

We also know that the accused person is the only participant in the trial who is 'brought up through a hole in the floor; ... surrounded by a barrier, ... guarded by a keeper of thieves; ... made to stand up alone ... [with their] latest address ... the gaol' while they are judged[40] and that, according to psychological research, information about an individual's propensity runs the risk of being misleading or creating 'an invalid inference of guilt'.

36 *Tofilau* [2007] HCA 39; 231 CLR 396, [210] (Kirby J in dissent).
37 *Hart* [2014] SCC 52; [2014] 2 SCR 544.
38 *Grant v Downs* [1976] HCA 63; 135 CLR 674, 685 (Stephen, Mason, Murphy JJ).
39 New Zealand Law Commission, *Evidence Law: Character and Credibility* (Discussion Paper, PP 27, 1997).
40 Darling, *Scintillae Juris* (6th ed, 1914), 33-4, quoted in *AK v Western Australia* [2008] HCA 8; 232 CLR 438, [101], fn 100 (Heydon J).

Guilty or innocent, how does the accused view the experience? Few scripts reveal how an accused feels about the process, but the famous English Marxist political theorist and activist, Harold Laski, wrote of his own experience in *civil* proceedings in 1945 seeking damages for defamation. He lost. His observations of the process provide food-for-thought regarding the trial process for all individuals who are parties (or victim/witnesses) in a trial:

> In the proceedings themselves you are almost bound to feel like a marionette. The speeches on both sides seem remote from the events you knew; they are like blood in a test tube compared with blood in a living person. You know, of course, that it is about you the lawyers are talking, but all that they say seems to have lost its colour, its vividness, its sense of life, and to be reduced to a shadowlike skeleton which will never be clothed once more in flesh and blood. … And, all the time, there sits above you the brooding and impassive judge, to whom this operation is no more than another day in an endless routine of similar days; while facing you are the seven impassive men and women to whom it is a kind of play in which they are half actors, half spectators.[41]

On the one hand it is crystal clear that the presumption of innocence and the accusatorial structure of criminal justice are to be fiercely guarded by courts, but on the other it is clear that it is not uncommon for an accused's presumption of innocence to brush up against a number of pragmatic variables. It is one thing to have a presumption in favour of innocence. It is another to operationalise it when there are indicators that the accusatorial fundamentals are not necessarily well-embedded in the community or in the jury room.[42] In the context of commemorating 800 years of the *Magna Carta* and contemplating its significance, and what those who gave it life may have anticipated would flow from it, Lord Neuberger suggested that 'we can and should maintain and develop the rule of law by reference to current fundamental principles without worrying about the fact that standards and perceptions change. We must do what we believe is right today. And that, one hopes, is what at least some of those who congregated at Runnymede eight centuries ago believed and tried to put into effect'.[43]

The Canadian Supreme Court in *Hart*[44] offers examples that illustrate that sometimes courts need to innovate in order to put into practice what we have learnt from miscarriages of justice; that, to attain the aspirations of justice, they need to act with greater courage and urgency[45] than the common law method often achieves. First, with respect to open justice and the accused being denied his wish to testify away from the full gaze of the public in the courtroom, the court weighed what was at stake:

> 53. … [T]he respondent's testimony was critically important in the circumstances of this case. If he was to be acquitted, the jury would have to believe, or at least have a reasonable doubt, that the confessions he made during the Mr Big operation were false. Testifying in order to disavow them was a near tactical necessity for the respondent. …

41 H Laski, 'My Day in Court' in L Blom-Cooper (ed), *The Law As Literature; An Anthology of Great Writing In and About the Law* (Bodley Head, 1961), 119, 120, 121-2.

42 J Hunter, *UNSW Jury Study: Jurors' Notions of Justice, An Empirical Study of Motivations to Investigate and Obedience to Judicial Directions* (2014), 24-5; and see the Facebook comments with respect to Mr Few from *FEW (No 2)* [2013] NSWSC 1771 in Chapter 2 above.

43 Lord Neuberger, 'Fairness in the Courts: The Best We Can do Address to the Criminal Justice Alliance' (10 April 2015), <https://www. supremecourt.uk/ news/speeches.html>.

44 [2014] SCC 52; [2014] 2 SCR 544. See also *Bradshaw* [2017] SCC 35; [2017] 1 SCR 865; and for New Zealand, see *Reddy* [2020] NZCA 16.

45 Urgency was not a hallmark of the *Hart* decision. It notes that, from the 1990s to 2008, the Mr Big scenario investigative approach had been used by Canadian police more than 350 times.

> [H]e was concerned that the stress of testifying in front of a full courtroom would cause him to have a seizure. It was incumbent on the trial judge, in the unique circumstances of this case, to take reasonable steps to accommodate the respondent's disability and to facilitate his testimony.

The court noted that Hart was not asking for a non-public trial. Broadcasting his testimony into another courtroom on closed circuit television would have maintained the open court principle.

In the second aspect of the *Hart* ruling the court acknowledged that human rights protections could not achieve what could be done by their own common law innovation. The Canadian Supreme Court established new admissibility hurdles for confessions made by a person pressured by a Mr Big scenario in circumstances that, in Australia, and until *Hart* in Canada, had avoided exclusion under conventional confessions law:

> 72. … And although it will be easier for a jury to understand why an accused would falsely confess to Mr Big than to the police during a conventional interrogation (because of the more obvious nature of the inducements and the accused's belief that it is in his self-interest to confess), this does not provide a complete answer to the reliability concerns raised by these confessions. Under the confessions rule, we do not abandon our concern for reliability in cases where a confession is the product of clear threats or inducements, on the assumption that the jury will have an easier time understanding why it is unreliable.

If we look at other aspects of the law of evidence and procedure, and the lessons to be learnt, it is clear that trial by ambush causes trials to take a wrong turn. The prosecution must not only lay 'its cards on the table' to avoid the danger of a miscarriage of justice but it must also be accountable where it fails to maintain the standards of a minister of justice. Professional ethics are not unimportant because they are, in effect, the soft management of justice. They are intrinsic to just outcomes, and prosecutorial duties are a crucial antidote to the vortex of battle that can envelop the trial process. Courts and those who have oversight of prosecutorial conduct cannot be forgiving of breach. Further, whereas the High Court and State appellate courts nowadays lead by example, this is a case where the vigilance of trial judges is a premium requirement. Accusatorial justice is not met if an accused must seek appeal court resolution for mistreatment at trial. This is particularly the case because the miscarriage of justice message shows that it is the prosecution case – built on confessions, identification evidence or informant testimony – that is often at the root of wrongful conviction. Prosecutors too must be alert to danger and not complicit in its creation. For example, they, courts and law reformers recognise that many established and emerging forensic techniques are fallible and that relying on such evidence, cloaked in the trappings of science to address the dangers in identification evidence or to help resolve ambiguous evidence, may add rather than remove frailties. Much could be strengthened in each of these quarters to safeguard the trial from miscarrying.

Of Witnesses and Adversarialism

> And you are then handed over to that same counsel whose life has so largely been passed in pricking men until they bleed. He performs his war dance about you like a dervish intoxicated by the sheer ecstasy of his skill in his own performance, ardent in his knowledge that, if you trip for one second, his knife is at your throat. He makes a pattern from bits and pieces picked with care from a pattern of life you have been steadily weaving for

> a quarter of a century to prove either that you never meant what you intended, or that you lacked every element of skill to give the world the sense of your intent. He moves between the lines of sarcasm and insult. It is an effort to tear off, piece by piece, the skin which he declares no more than a mask behind which any man of understanding could have grasped the foulness of your purpose. He treats you, not as a human being, but as a surgeon might treat some specimen he is demonstrating to students in a dissecting room. …
>
> Then you must watch the effort of your enemies to break in pieces the confidence of the witnesses who have come to support your fate. … Counsel … is mainly concerned to throw them off their balance, to confuse them, to shrug them with a lift of his shoulders into people about whom he and the jury share a common and private contempt.[46]

We know that the criminal justice system has not met the needs of vulnerable people who have been victims of sexual and domestic violence. We also know that historically the law has got it wrong in treating these people as prone to make false accusations. The adversarial mode of testing evidence has strengths, but in many contexts it functions weakly and distorts accounts. It is not that cross-examination is the evil. It is a crucial element of the maintenance of a fair trial. The problem is how it is performed. Once cross-examination has moved beyond ensuring jurors do not complacently accept flawed testimony[47] and begins to cut down the witness through personal attack, trickery, misuse of power, inappropriate questioning or gamesmanship, it becomes dysfunctional. This makes 'soft targets' most vulnerable. Admiration for the prowess of the skilful advocate is deeply embedded in the common law justice system. Psychological research suggests that this admiration, combined with the traditional tentativeness for trial judges to intercede, may have distracted appreciation of the pernicious tendency for cross-examination to include confusing questions for those who are easily confused.[48] Further (and as part of this issue), it is time to heed psychological research which suggests that the law has inflated the importance of inconsistency in a witness's account.[49] Examined holistically, it is apparent that the courtroom is often not conducive to obtaining the best account of events from those who are intimidated and inarticulate. The discourse of the trial, the function of the cross-examiner and the spatial layout and architecture of the courtroom are outside most witnesses' comfort zone for explaining what they saw, heard or perceived, particularly when these are topics of sensitivity, rawness and emotion.

In much the same way that modern understanding of the dynamics of policing and confessions throws light on the dangers of confessional evidence, so too do modern insights support contemporaneous accounts of events as being often superior to testimonial accounts. Indeed, given the challenges that can exist for sexual assault complainants in court, even non-contemporaneous accounts are likely to offer the jury a useful understanding of events. Yet, whether it is because a historical fear of the unreliability of hearsay evidence has cast a long shadow or, perhaps, because traditional suspicion of the sexual assault complainant lingers, the application of the exceptions to the hearsay rule often fails to extend to vulnerable witnesses and, with respect to exculpatory statements, to the accused. These

---

46 Laski, above n 41, 121, 122.

47 C Callen, 'Human Deliberation in Fact-Finding' in Roberts and Hunter (eds), above n 6, ch 13, 321-3.

48 P Bowden, T Henning and D Plater, 'Balancing Fairness to Victims, Society and Defendants in the Cross-Examination of Vulnerable Witnesses: An Impossible Triangulation?' (2014) 37 *Melbourne University Law Review* 539.

49 *Douglass* [2012] HCA 34; 290 ALR 699.

two people for whom the trial means so much are, ironically, often also least likely to have their out-of-court statements admitted into evidence.[50]

What is the take-away message? The administration of justice is too complex to have a single message. One lesson from the discreditable Lawyer X scenarios is that lawyers' considerable power and authority when representing clients must be deployed consistently with principles underpinning the integrity of the criminal justice system. As well as respecting defendants' rights, witnesses' rights are not to be trampled on. Indeed, the temptation for law reformers to leap to expedience, such as to think that much will be improved if police have more power or that injustice will be met if juries are directed differently (or more often) on legal complexity, risks missing the obvious lessons from miscarriages of justice. Many of these remain unheeded. Further, justice-gone-wrong rarely shows that the right offender would have been convicted if the police had had more power. Nor does it often show that the jury is blameworthy for failing to appreciate a nuance in the trial.[51] Ultimately jurors can only work with what is in front of them and, if that is wrong or is distorted, all the reviews on efficiency in the criminal trial[52] count for little weighed up against the judge-hours of appellate review, retrials and the jury convicting the wrong person.

No single element of the trial and the pre-trial process is immune from contributing to justice misfiring – impacting on the accused, the victim of crime or the community more broadly. There is no need to pit the needs of these three groups against each other.

> You may be beaten in a game and enjoy, nevertheless, the pleasure of combat. You may be 'plucked' in an examination and yet know that it is a temporary setback you will overcome in a month. You may even be routed in a skirmish and rest confident in the knowledge that it is only part of a larger campaign. But when you are beaten in the Courts of Law there is a kind of dumb finality about it which I can only compare with the ultimate emphasis of death.
>
> Every element in a … trial goes to deepen this sense of finality.[53]

A good trial, like a good death, depends on the process being optimal for everyone.

50 T Henning and J Hunter, 'Finessing the Fair Trial for Complainants and the Accused: Mansions of Justice or Castles in the Air?' in Roberts and Hunter (eds), above n 6, 347.

51 Notably, if the jury question posed in Farah Jama's trial had been a question raised earlier in the process, or even taken seriously when posed, the flawed DNA evidence (and Jama's innocence) would have come to light earlier. Instead, as Gans notes, the jury received the 'non-answer do-not-speculate' direction instead: Gans, above n 6, 208.

52 Albeit that they may provide solutions to important issues, see Chair, Rt Hon Sir Brian Leveson (Judiciary of England and Wales, January 2015).

53 Laski, above n 41, 120.

Appendix

Flowchart of Key Provisions: Uniform Evidence Acts
Cth, ACT, NSW, NT, Tas, Vic

Appendix I: Uniform Evidence Acts — Key Provisions*

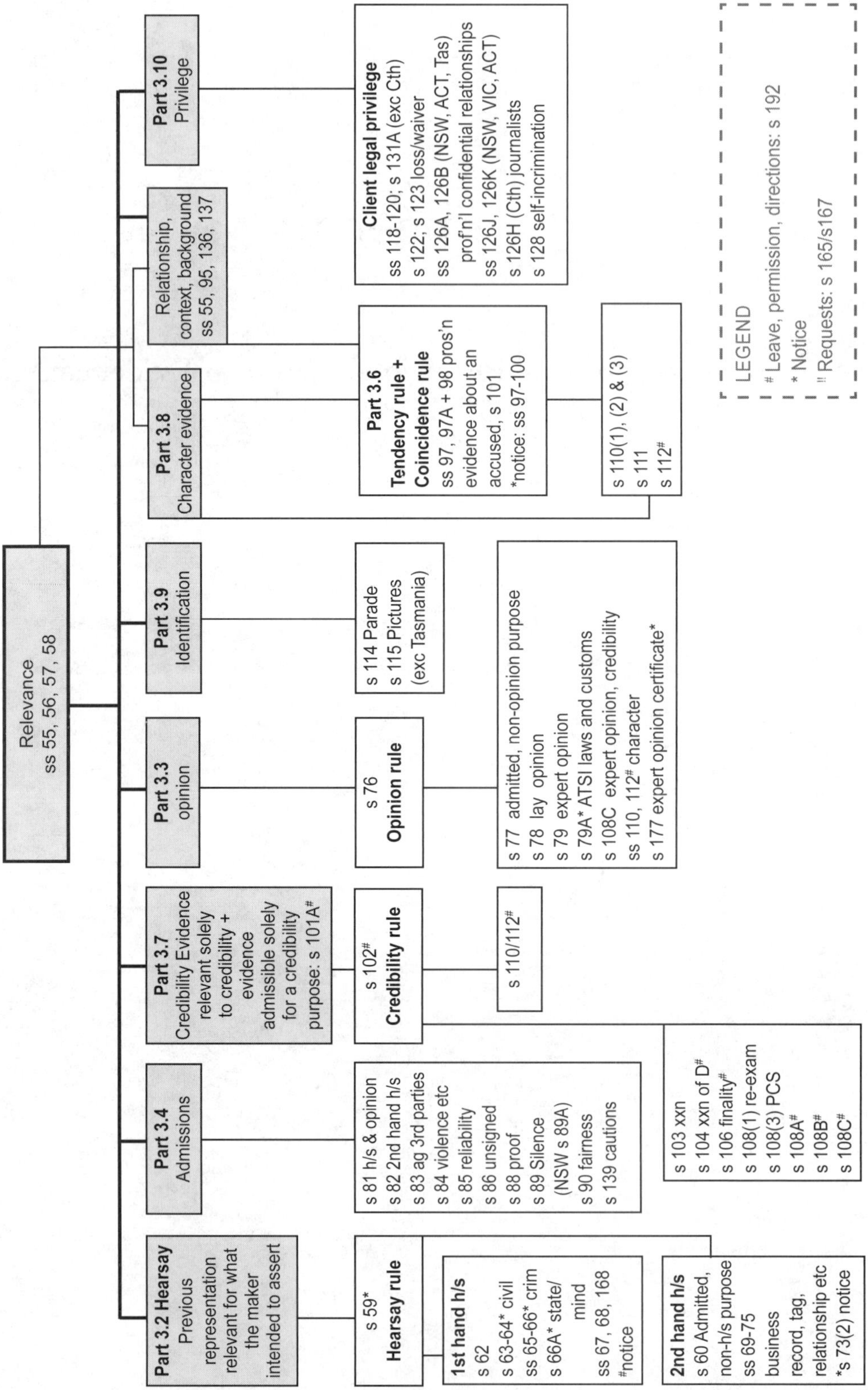

Does s 135, s 137 or s 138 apply?

Witnesses
Competence ss 12, 13, 16
Compellability ss 14-16, 18-19
The accused etc: s 17
[Comment/silence]: s 20
Oaths/affirmations: ss 21-24

Witness questioning
EiC: ss 32[#], 33, 34, 37[#], 38[#]
Xxn: ss 41, 42[#], 44-45[#], 103, 104, 106(1)
R-Ex: s 39[#]
Browne v Dunn: s 46[#]

Non-testimonial evidence + proof
Proof/parties: ss 140-142
Judicial notice: ss 143-144
Documents etc: ss 29(4), 48, 50[#], 57, 69, 146-163, 167-68,[‼] 177, 183
Voir dire: s 189

Does the judge need to direct/limit/warn re evidence: ss 95, 116, 136[#] or 165[‼], (165A)?
(& in Victoria, warn[‼] under the Jury Directions Act 2015)

Does the judge need to inform re s 165B?

LEGEND
[#] Leave, permission, directions: s 192
* Notice
[‼] Requests: s 165/s167

* See also the useful charts and resources at <https://www.judicialcollege.vic.edu.au/resources/uniform-evidence-resources>.

Index